MID/HEAVY-DUTY TRUCK
ELECTRICAL AND ELECTRONIC
SYSTEMS

Reston Diesel Mechanics Series

ROBERT N. BRADY
Series Editor

MID/HEAVY-DUTY TRUCK ELECTRICAL AND ELECTRONIC SYSTEMS

ROBERT N. BRADY

*Vancouver Community College
and
HiTech Consulting Ltd.*

Prentice
Hall

A RESTON BOOK

PRENTICE HALL, Upper Saddle River, NJ 07458

Library of Congress Cataloging-in-Publication Data

Brady, Robert N.
    Mid heavy-duty truck electrical and electronic systems / Robert N.
Brady.
       p.   cm.—(Reston diesel mechanics series)
    "A Reston book."
    Includes index.
    ISBN 0-13-385659-3
    1. Trucks—Electric equipment. 2. Trucks—Electronic equipment.
I. Title. II. Series.
TL230.B67 1991
629.25'4—dc20
                                   90-19752
                                       CIP

Acquisition editors: Rick Williamson and Rob Koehler
Editorial/production supervision and
   interior design: Ed Jones
Cover photo: D. Luria, FPG International
Manufacturing buyers: Mary McCartney and Ed O'Dougherty

© 1991 by Prentice-Hall, Inc.
Upper Saddle River, NJ 07458

Printed in the United States of America

10 9 8 7

ISBN 0-13-385659-3

Prentice-Hall International (UK) Limited, *London*
Prentice-Hall of Australia Pty. Limited, *Sydney*
Prentice-Hall of Canada, Inc., *Toronto*
Prentice-Hall Hispanoamericana, S. A., *Mexico*
Prentice-Hall of India Private Limited, *New Delhi*
Prentice-Hall of Japan, Inc., *Tokyo*
Prentice-Hall Asia Pte. Ltd., *Singapore*
Editora Prentice-Hall do Brasil, Ltda., *Rio de Janeiro*

Contents

11

ENGINE/VEHICLE SENSORS AND COMPUTERS   441

Preface

Although the midrange and heavy-duty truck industry has been slower than the passenger car market to respond to the need for various electronic controls, the industry is now well into a process whereby adoption of the electronics technology that has been so successful on cars is now being engineered into trucks. In view of this, the fundamentals of electricity, together with a sound knowledge of the operating characteristics of basic electronics, are essential for any truck mechanic/technician if he or she is to analyze, troubleshoot, and repair electrical problems on heavy-duty trucks and semitrailers. The evolution of electronics technology to the heavy-duty truck market has been initiated not only by the original equipment manufacturers' desire to lengthen the life of their components, but more important, by the U.S. Environmental Protection Agency's mandated exhaust emissions limits. It is here, in the diesel engine powerplant of both midrange and heavy-duty trucks that the electronics explosion has taken hold. Consider that today, Detroit Diesel Corporation, Caterpillar, Cummins Engine Company, Mack Trucks, DAF Trucks, Saab-Scania, Volvo, Robert Bosch, Mercedes-Benz, Diesel Kiki, Allison Division of GMC, Voith, ZF, and Eaton, just to name some of the major players, have committed many millions of dollars to adopting electronics technology to heavy-duty trucks.

The result of this research and development is reflected in the various heavy-duty truck components in which electronics is now used. In addition, satellite-based tracking (navigation) of heavy trucks and trailers is now a reality in North America. Such a system permits the shipper/dispatcher or fleet maintenance manager to pinpoint the actual location of a vehicle at any time of the day or night. Many of these electronics components require the use of special diagnostic equipment to locate an operating problem quickly and accurately. The early days of the proverbial sealed black box have a new meaning to fleet mechanic/technicians who now have to contend with the problems that occur in truck electrical and electronics systems. Electronics is here to stay, and the teething problems that accompanied their introduction have now been ironed out fairly successfully. In a harsh environment such as heavy-duty trucking, it did not take long to uncover areas requiring improvement and redesign. However, it is a testimony to the determination of the manufacturers that most of the electronics components now in use on trucks can be said to be at least as reliable as those of their earlier electrical counterparts.

In a recent study by the U.S. Federal Bureau of Motor Vehicle Safety, lighting and electrical problems were still found to rank very high on the list of failures that occur regularly on heavy-duty trucks and trailers. Figure 3–23 illustrates the leading causes of battery failure on a heavy-duty truck/tractor/trailer and the failure rates during the operation of the vehicle. The braking system leads the list, with problems associated with either the lighting or the electrical system next, accounting for one-third of all roadside violations. The electrical system includes any electronics components used on the truck/trailer combination.

Because of the expanding role and importance of electrical and electronics systems in the successful operation of any truck, it is of paramount importance that you, as an up-to-date commercial vehicle mechanic/technician, have a solid grounding in both systems. In this book we present information that deals systematically with knowledge that is essential to the development of a broad-based foundation in the fundamentals of electricity and electronics as they apply to diesel-powered midrange and heavy-duty trucks and semitrailers. Although the book is designed to fill a need for a reference book related strictly to truck electrics/electronics, information is also provided on a wide variety of electrical and electronics accessories. In addition, the more commonly used batteries, starters, and alternators are described in such detail that you will be able to analyze, troubleshoot, and repair these important units. Information related to the cab and chassis wiring systems, lighting systems, and instruments and gauges is all given in simple terms to broaden your existing knowledge of truck electrical systems. The knowledge and information that you glean from the chapters dealing with the fundamentals of electricity and electronics will serve as a base while you expand your understanding of truck engine sensors and diesel engine electronic control modules, now used to control the diesel fuel injection and governing systems on Caterpillar, Cummins, and Detroit Diesel Corporation engines.

Questions similar to Automotive Service Excellence (ASE) questions are provided at the end of each chapter to allow you to test your recall ability and understanding of the new information that you have been exposed to in each chapter. The questions have been designed to facilitate not only your understanding of various system concepts, but also to allow you to build on the knowledge that you gain from the hands-on experience that you accumulate daily in the shop environment. To become a competent and effective truck mechanic/technician with the ability to analyze, troubleshoot, and repair the various electrical and electronics problems that you will be faced with in your daily service operations, you will need the following ten characteristics:

1. A solid foundation and understanding of the basic fundamentals of electrical and electronics systems.

2. An in-depth understanding of the function and operation of the various electrical components used on trucks and trailers.

3. A knowledge of what test instruments and diagnostic tools should be used, and how to safely hook them up to test or prove where a problem may lie in a given system.

4. The ability to trace a truck wiring diagram and interpret the possible reasons for an open, a short, or a ground in a system or component.

5. The amount of hands-on-experience that you accumulate, which allows you to put into practice the theoretical information that you possess.

6. An awareness of the need for systematic and proven methods of repair.

7. A commitment to standards of excellence to ensure that the same problem will not recur after a repair has been made.

8. A concerted effort on your part to upgrade your knowledge on a continuing basis by means of manufacturers' update service bulletins, training programs, and new developments.

9. An exchange of troubleshooting and service tips with other truck mechanics/technicians. Don't keep new information to yourself!

10. A willingness always to learn new ways and methods, for without an inquiring mind, you will quickly be left behind in the fast-paced and continually changing technological adoptions taking place in your chosen career path.

With my many years of experience in the design, service, troubleshooting, and repair of heavy-duty trucks, accompanied by both factory and college training, I have found one of the weak links in the chain of multiple skills required by today's successful and highly valued service technician to be the ability to diagnose problems in electrical and electronics systems quickly and accurately. I am confident that the material presented in this book will provide you with the confidence to tackle any problem that you may encounter when servicing an electrical/electronics problem on a truck or trailer. I wish you success in your studies and in the daily application of your newfound knowledge.

R. N. (Bob) Brady

Acknowledgments

In order to produce an up-to-date and comprehensive text, approximately thirty major truck manufacturers and major truck equipment component suppliers were contacted for assistance with their latest product offerings. A text such as this could never have been written without the strong support and assistance that I received during my research from a number of companies and individuals who went out of their way to ensure that I received the necessary sales and technical service information required to present their products to you, the reader.

To those companies and individuals who offered their assistance, encouragement, and support during this process, I hope that the finished product before you is equal to your expectations.

The following companies and individuals therefore deserve special mention for taking the time and effort, and most of all for allowing me to present their product views so that you the reader can be exposed to the latest technology and to the standards of excellence that these companies strive to maintain in their product offerings.

To each company and individual listed below, I offer my sincere thanks and appreciation for their assistance.

R. N. (Bob) Brady

Caterpillar, Inc., Service Publications, Marketing Support G.O., 100 N.E. Adams, East Peoria, IL 61630. Mr. R. J. Wilson, Editor, and Mr. Tim J. Harris, Publications Consultant, Publications Division, Marketing Support Department. (309) 675-7349.

Cummins Engine Company, Inc., P.O. Box 3005, Columbus, IN 47201. Mr. L. F. (Lloyd) Morley, Tech/Spec/Training Manager, Service Training Department. (812) 377-6835.

DAF Trucks, Van Doorne's Bedrijfswagenfabriek, DAF B.V., Geldropseweg 303, 5645 TK, Eindhoven, The Netherlands. Mr. William J. M. Quik, Director, Product Development Powertrain. 040-149111.

Delco Electronics Corporation, Subsidiary of GM Hughes Electronics, 700 E. Firmin Street, One Corporate Center, Kokomo, IN 46904-9005. Ms. Marilyn Y. Grant, Manager of Public Affairs.

Delco Remy, Division of General Motors Corporation, 2401 Columbus Avenue, P.O. Box 2439, Anderson, IN 46018-9986. Mr. Milton Beach, Public Relations.

Detroit Diesel Corporation, 13400 Outer Drive West, Detroit, MI 48239-4001. Mr. Charles Yount, Manager, Advertising and Publications. (313) 592-5000.

Dominion Automotive Industries, Inc., 2155 Drew Road, Mississauga, Ontario, Canada L5S 1S7. Mr. Clewell W. Smith, President. (416) 672-5267.

Eaton Corporation, Axle and Brake Division, P.O. Box 4008, Kalamazoo, MI 49003. Mr. Leo J. Wenstrup, Technical Service Manager. (616) 342-3018.

Electrodyne, Division of the Gauss Corporation, P.O. Box 660, One Gibson Road, Scarborough, ME 04074-0660. Mr. Robert D. Sampson. (207) 883-4121.

Ford Motor Company, 3000 Schaefer Road, P.O. Box 1902, Dearborn, MI 48121. Mr. Souren Keoleian, Publications Manager.

GMC Truck Division, General Motors Corporation, 31 Judson Street, Pontiac, MI 48058-8990. Mr. G.A. Fishwild, Supervisor, Service Publications.

GNB Inc., Automotive Battery Division, 13210 Hunters Spring, San Antonio, TX 78230. Mr. James E. Bald, Fleet Consultant. (512) 493-8756.

Grote Manufacturing Company, 2600 Lanier Drive, Madison, IN 47250. Mr. Dan McCann, Senior Product Manager. (812) 273-1296.

Horton Industries, Inc., P.O. Box 9455, Minneapolis, MN 55440. Mr. Thomas J. Kleich, Product Specialist. (612) 331-5931.

Jacobs Manufacturing Company, Vehicle Equipment Division, Chicago Pneumatic Tool Company, 22 East Dudley Town Road, Bloomfield, CT 06002. Mr. Robert S. Perkins, Marketing Manager.

John Fluke Manufacturing Company, Inc., P.O. Box C9090, Everett, WA 98206. Mr. George T. Noe, Chief Patent Counsel. (206) 347-6100.

Kent Moore Heavy Duty Division, SPX Corporation, 28635 Mound Road, Warren, MI 48092-3499. Ms. Andrea W. Kolton, Advertising Manager. (313) 574-2332.

Lite-Check, Inc., N10220 Nevada, Suite 5, Spokane, WA, 99218. Mr. Bob Blair, President. (509) 466-2927.

Mack Trucks, Inc., World Headquarters, 2100 Mack Boulevard, Box 1791, Allentown, PA 18105-1801. Mr. R.E. Davis, Manager, Publications and Technical Support. (215) 439-3011.

Motorola Automotive and Industrial Electronics Group, Corporate Offices, 1303 E. Algonquin Rd., Schaumburg, IL 60196. Mr. Phillip H. Melamed, Attorney, Intellectual Property Department. (708) 576-5218.

Peterbilt Motors Company, Division of PACCAR, 38801 Cherry Street, Newark, CA 94560. Mr. Virgil E. Pound, Assistant General Manager. (415) 790-4000.

Prestolite Electric, Inc., Heavy Duty Products Division, 5109 Hamilton Avenue, Cleveland, OH 44114. Mr. Donald C. Wilson, Manager, Technical Service Department. (216) 431-0740.

Robert Bosch Sales Corporation, 2800 S. 25th Avenue, Broadview, IL 60153. Mr. Thomas A. Buesch, Service Project Manager, Automotive and Diesel Products. (708) 865-6430.

Rockwell International Corporation, Automotive Operations, 2135 West Maple Road, Troy, MI 48084. Ms. Diane Weidman, Technical Publications. (313) 435-1816.

SAE (Society of Automotive Engineers), Inc., 400 Commonwealth Drive, Warrendale, PA 15096-0001. Mr. Antenor R. Willems, Publication Director; Ms. Ginger Joa, Administrative Assistant. (412) 776-4841, FAX (412) 776-5760.

Square Wheel Inc., P.O. Box 26, Temple, PA 19560. Mr. Joseph R. Butchko, President. (215) 921-8561.

Sun Electric Corporation, One Sun Parkway, Crystal Lake, IL 60014. Mr. Joseph D. McGrath, Director of Legal Affairs. (815) 459-7700.

Sure Power Industries, Inc., 10189 S.W. Avery, Tualatin, OR 97062. Mr. Steve Scheidler, President. (503) 692-5360.

About the Author

Robert N. Brady has been involved in the automotive and heavy-duty truck and equipment field for 32 years, having served a recognized five-year apprenticeship, and having worked as a shop foreman, service manager, and fleet maintenance superintendent. In addition, his experiences have included positions as National Service Trainer (Canada) for Detroit Diesel Allison Division of GMC, as well as a Field Service Representative and Sales Application Engineer.

He has taught for 20 years at Vancouver Community College, ten of those as a Department Head of the Diesel Mechanic/Technician Program, in Commercial Transport Mechanics, Heavy-Duty Mechanics, and Diesel Engine Mechanics.

He has developed technical training programs for a number of major companies in both the automotive and heavy-duty truck and equipment fields, and acts as a technical consultant through his own company, HiTech Consulting Ltd.

This is his ninth book for Reston/Prentice-Hall. His others include *Automotive and Small Truck Fuel Injection Systems: Gas and Diesel; Automotive Computers and Digital Instrumentation; Diesel Fuel Systems; Electric and Electronic Systems for Automobiles and Trucks; Heavy Duty Truck Fuel Systems: Operation, Service, Maintenance; Heavy-Duty Truck Power Trains: Transmissions, Drive Lines, and Axles; Heavy-Duty Truck Suspension, Steering, and Braking Systems;* and *On-Highway Trucks: Power Trains and Suspension Systems.*

He is a certified automotive mechanic/technician as well as a heavy-duty truck and equipment mechanic/technician.

He is a member of the Society of Automotive Engineers, Inc., and currently he sits on the governing board of the British Columbia chapter (past chairman of the B. C. Section 1989–1990). Beginning in February, 1991, he will serve as a member of the SAE Sections Board for a three-year term. He is also a member of the Association of Diesel Specialists, NACAT (National Association of College Automotive Teachers), the Canadian Vocational Association, the Vocational Instructors' Association of Vancouver Community College (Past President), and TMC/ATA—The Maintenance Council, American Trucking Associations.

MID/HEAVY-DUTY TRUCK ELECTRICAL AND ELECTRONIC SYSTEMS

CHAPTER

1

Fundamentals of Electricity

OBJECTIVES

In this chapter we discuss and describe the fundamentals that you must know in order to understand the basic operation of all electrical components. Upon completion of this chapter you will be able to understand and recall the information necessary to identify, trace, and troubleshoot a basic electrical circuit. Specifically, you will acquire or review the skills needed to:

1. Describe the meaning of volts (electrical pressure), amperes (electrical quantity/current), and resistance.
2. Use Ohm's law to determine the relationship between volts, amperes, and resistance in any electrical circuit.
3. Describe the basic makeup of a conductor, a resistor, and an insulator.
4. Describe and understand open and closed systems or circuits.
5. Describe the relationship between magnetism and

electricity to produce electron flow in a copper wire.
6. Identify and describe series, parallel, and series-parallel circuits.
7. Understand why some systems are positive ground, while others are negative ground.
8. Determine voltage drop in an electrical circuit.
9. Be aware of and identify AWG (American Wire Gauge) sizes and color codes.

INTRODUCTION

No discussion of computers or solid-state devices can be considered prior to understanding the basic concept of magnetism and the flow of electrons within a wire. In this chapter, we review the principles of electricity to assist you in understanding the close links between conventional electrical flow and circuitry, before moving onto a discussion of electronic devices.

The modern electrical system used on passenger cars, commercial, and heavy-duty equipment is an intricate system that supplies the necessary electrical energy to operate lights, horns, radios, stereo tape decks, heaters,

windshield wipers, defrosters, air-conditioning systems, powerseats, and the vehicle ignition system on gasoline engines. In addition, the electric starter would not be possible without the use of a battery, which itself requires a generator or alternator to keep it in a state of charge. All of the other fancy factory options, or aftermarket add-ons, would be of little use without the electrical system.

Considering the little attention that it often receives, the electrical system does a remarkable job in maintaining trouble-free operation throughout its life. When electrical problems occur, they can usually be traced to a lack of maintenance or to improper service procedures.

Although the reader may have a limited knowledge of electricity, most people do understand the typical freshwater system that is found in the normal family home and office. Everyone has probably used a garden hose at some time and has found that with no nozzle on the end of the hose outlet and the hose tap turned on, a large volume or quantity of water flowed from the hose, but with little pressure. In the water system we commonly refer to this quantity or volume as gallons per minute, or liters per minute. This can be likened to quantity or volume in an electrical system, but it is commonly called amperes or amps when discussing electricity.

When you place your thumb over the end of the garden hose or screw an adjustable nozzle onto the hose end, you are able to control the quantity or volume flowing from the end of the hose by manipulation of the adjustable nozzle. In either instance, what is actually achieved is a reduction in quantity or volume but a definite increase in the force of water leaving the hose. This is *pressure,* which in an electrical system is known as *voltage* or *volts.*

We can still have pressure in water flow without placing a thumb or the nozzle over the hose end. However, this pressure remains reasonably constant and is developed at a municipality's pumping station by the use of mechanically driven water pumps. It is not variable as with the adjustable nozzle on the hose end.

City water pressure will force water through the street pipes until it meets resistance, such as a closed water tap or faucet. This water flow (volume) is the same as the current pushed through an electrical circuit, which will also meet resistance, in the form of lights or other electrical accessories in the system. Water pipes and electrical wires both offer resistance to flow. The size and length of the pipes and wires will vary the amount of resistance present in a given circuit. In an electrical circuit this resistance is measured in ohms.

The main properties that we are concerned with at this time are:

- Quantity or volume, expressed as amperes
- Pressure, expressed as volts
- Resistance, expressed as ohms

When considering any electric system, remember these three properties.

The water pump at the pumping station supplies the pressure and, in effect, becomes the battery in the electrical system. The battery stores electrical energy in the form of both amperes and volts, in quantities determined by the actual physical size and design of the battery. We discuss this later in the chapter when studying batteries.

An understanding of the actual relationship between the three properties listed so far—current (amperes), pressure (volts), and resistance (ohms)—will assist you in future discussions related to any electrical system.

Common electrical terms include:

- *Volts:* Unit of measure for electrical pressure or force, commonly measured by the use of a voltmeter
- *Amperes:* Unit of measure for current flow, measured by an ammeter
- *Ohm:* Unit of electrical resistance that opposes current flow and causes heat to be created by this resistance (friction) to flow; measured by the use of an ohmmeter

CONDUCTORS

In the typical water system, pipes are used to carry the flow throughout the system; in an electrical system, wires are used for the same purpose. These wires are usually made of copper, since it is reasonably plentiful and inexpensive. Aluminum wiring has also been used, especially in house wiring and commercial buildings. However, in automotive and heavy equipment, copper is used extensively for wiring, since it has proven to be less troublesome than aluminum and stands up better under the types of operation encountered by these electrical systems.

Most metals, in fact, are good conductors of electricity, with silver, copper, and aluminum being the most widely used. When flexibility is desired in a wire, copper wiring may be composed of a large number of very small strands of wire wound together and covered with an insulating sheathing.

The size of the wire used can have an adverse effect on the resistance created when electricity flows through the wire. This can best be explained by considering Fig. 1-1. Here water is seen to be directed through pipes of two different diameters, called pipe 1 and pipe 2. Since pipe 2 is larger than pipe 1, the tank immediately under pipe 2 will fill up much faster than the tank under pipe 1. Obviously, we can direct a greater volume or quantity of water through pipe 2 than through pipe 1 in the same amount of time because of the larger diameter of pipe 2. Both pipes will create resistance to water flow. However, since pipe 1 has the smaller diameter, it will have a higher resistance to the flow of water through it.

The flow of electricity is caused by the movement of electrons within a wire. The greater the electron flow

FIGURE 1-1 Pipe size versus flow rate and resistance.

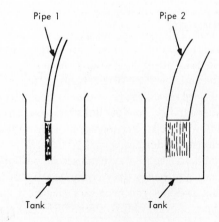

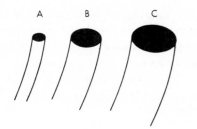

FIGURE 1–2 Wire size versus flow rate (current, in amperes).

within the wire, the greater the quantity or volume flow will be in a given period, much like the gallons or liters per minute flowing through the water pipe. The electrical flow, you will remember, is measured in amperes.

Now consider Fig. 1–2: Which of the three wires shown would have the greatest resistance to current or ampere flow? If you said wire A, you are correct. Which wire in Fig. 1–2 would allow the greatest current or amperage flow? If you said wire C, you are correct.

USE OF ELECTRICAL ENERGY

To systematically evaluate how electrical energy can be used in a system or circuit, let's compare a simple water wheel system to an electrical system through the use of basic line diagrams. One of the easiest ways in which water power can be used to provide electricity is through a dammed reservoir, where water from a river or stream is used to drop over an embankment and drive a large water wheel or paddle wheel. A shaft running from the center of the wheel is connected to a generator, which is continually rotated by the water wheel.

If work is required from a water wheel, however, with no river or stream close by, the only way to achieve this is to use a pump driven by some means to direct water to and against an impeller, which is then continually rotated by the water pressure produced in the pump. An example is shown in Fig. 1–3. Although the figure shows a sealed system, it is only because this system requires less water than that needed by an open system, which would require a continual supply of water, such as in a hydroelectric waterdam system. In the illustration, the

pump creates a flow within the system to drive the shaft. As the pump rotates, it will create not only flow (quantity or volume) but also pressure, because of the sealed system, and resistance is created through the effort required to drive the shaft and by the size of the piping.

If we now substitute a similar arrangement, but use electrical components, we would have the view shown in Fig. 1–4. Here, we have substituted wires for the water pipes, a storage battery for the pump, and a light bulb for the shaft connected to the load. In Fig. 1–3, the water flow and pressure rotated the shaft, whereas in Fig. 1–4, the current being pushed through the wires by the voltage causes the light bulb to glow. Remember that the battery contains both quantity (amperes) and pressure (volts); therefore, the battery has "replaced" the water pump. The system shown in Fig. 1–4 is a sealed system, similar to Fig. 1–3, with no means of recharging the battery at this time. Current flows out of the battery to the light bulb and then returns to the battery.

In Figs. 1–3 and 1–4 we called each system a sealed system; however, in an electrical system, the more common term used is a *closed circuit,* because there can be direct loss of electrical energy other than that which is used to light the bulb. If we were to break a water pipe, or cut a wire, there would be a loss of energy. In this condition, the shaft in Fig. 1–3 would no longer rotate, and in Fig. 1–4, the light bulb would no longer glow. Such a condition in an electrical circuit is commonly called an *open circuit,* meaning that there is a loss of electrical energy. The word *circuit* is derived from the simple word *circle.* In other words, to complete the circuit, the current must be capable of flowing around the circle from the point of origin and back again to that same point.

In Fig. 1–4, the light bulb is an energy-absorbing device, since it requires current to keep it lighted. In turn, the current or amperes are forced through the circuit by the electrical pressure or voltage. Anything wired into an electrical circuit that uses current is therefore part of the electrical load placed on that circuit. The greater the number of accessories wired into the circuit, the greater will be the current requirements or amperage needed to operate them all. In addition, as we add accessories to

FIGURE 1–4 Basic electrical system concept.

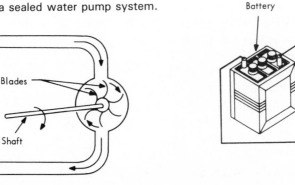

FIGURE 1–3 Example of a sealed water pump system.

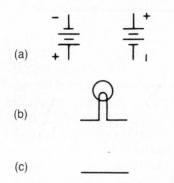

(a)

(b)

(c)

FIGURE 1–5 Electrical symbols: (a) battery; (b) light bulb; (c) wire.

TABLE 1–1 Examples of commonly used electrical symbols

A.	⏚	ground AC source
B.	—Ⓥ—	voltmeter
C.		connected wires
H.		
D.		unconnected wires
F.		
G.	(AC GEN)	generator
I.		electromagnet → *needs current to be magnet*
	coil only with no current	
E.		variable resistor
P.		
J.	⊹||⊢	battery
K.		SPST switch
O.		
L.	—ᴡᴡ—	fixed resistor
M.	(MOT)	motor
N.	(A)	ammeter

a circuit, these current-carrying devices will offer greater resistance to the flow of electricity, and will, in many instances, require additional voltage to overcome this added resistance.

BASIC ELECTRICAL SYMBOLS

In Fig. 1–4 we showed a battery, wires, and a light bulb. This was done for clarity and for ease of instruction. However, this is not the way that such a circuit would be shown in normal electrical terminology and layout. An easier and less involved method is shown in Fig. 1–5. Note that the battery terminals are shown by two different symbols. These are used to differentiate between the positive and negative terminals. The positive battery terminal can be a large T or a plus sign (+). The negative terminal is shown as either a short ⊥ or a minus sign (−). Other commonly accepted and used electrical symbols are shown in Table 1–1.

RESISTORS

All conductors will offer some form of resistance to the flow of electrons (current/amperes) through the wire. This resistance is caused by the resistance of both the wire and the circuit. A resistor is therefore an electrical component that can be used to add or alter a fixed amount of resistance to any electrical circuit.

By adding a resistor to a circuit we thus decrease the current flow. For example, Fig. 1–6(a) shows a simple circuit with no resistance other than that offered by the wiring and a single light bulb. This arrangement allows 4 amperes (A) to flow through the closed circuit. However, in Fig. 1–6(b), we have installed a fixed resistor to the closed circuit, which will therefore decrease the current flow from the 4 A shown in Fig. 1–6(a) to only 2 A, as shown in Fig. 1–6(b).

Resistors that have more or less resistance can be used to suit the situation as desired in the circuit. Therefore, in Fig. 1–6(b), the light bulb will not glow as brightly as it did in Fig. 1–6(a) because of the lower current (amperage) flow. As the value or amount of resistance is increased, the current flowing through the circuit must

FIGURE 1–6 Resistance versus current flow.

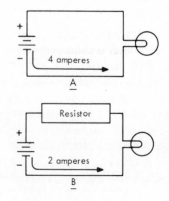

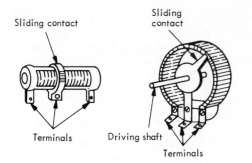

FIGURE 1-7 Variable resistance concept.

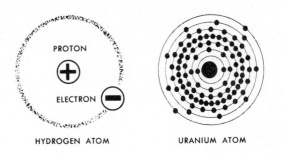

FIGURE 1-8 Hydrogen and uranium elements.

decrease. Thus, by employing different resistors in a circuit, we can change the value of a fixed resistor, change the voltage source, and control the amount of current (amps) flowing in that circuit. The symbols for resistors are shown in Table 1-1.

A fixed (nonvariable) resistor is used in most automotive and heavy equipment circuits to limit the current flowing at any given point. However, there are resistors available that can be adjusted in position by use of a sliding contact that provides variable resistance to suit a variety of conditions. To change the resistance of a variable resistor, a sliding contact connected to an insulated hand- or foot-controlled (e.g., throttle pedal) potentiometer sliding contact makes it possible to dial in the resistance to suit almost any condition within the circuit. A simple variable resistance is shown in Fig. 1-7.

INSULATORS

When it is necessary to prevent a loss of electrical energy by a bare wire (e.g., one touching a metal object), the wire must be covered by a material that will not allow any external flow of current. Materials such as rubber, plastic, glass, and wood are examples of good insulators, since all of these materials have a very high resistance to the flow of current.

Without this insulation in an electrical circuit, you would get a severe shock when you touched or handled wiring. By preventing other components from coming into contact with one another, the insulator also protects them from short-circuiting or creating an open circuit.

GENERAL THEORY OF ELECTRICITY

In its simplest statement, *electricity* can be said to be the flow of electrons from one atom to another atom within a conductor. All matter is composed of atoms, and these atoms are so small that they are invisible to the naked eye and even to powerful microscopes. The *atom* is the smallest particle into which one of the elements can be divided while retaining its properties. The elements combine in many different combinations to form the various kinds of matter found on earth. The elements hydrogen and oxygen, for example, combine to produce water; and combined, sodium and chlorine produce salt. All atoms

have a center or core made up of particles known as *protons,* around which other particles called *electrons* rotate. Both of these types of particles become extremely important in our more detailed study of electricity.

Let's start with what is known as the simplest of all elements, hydrogen. The hydrogen atom consists of two particles: a proton, which is a positive charge at the center of the core, and an electron, which has a negative charge, circling the proton. We will compare this hydrogen element with the very complex one of uranium. Figure 1-8 shows the typical arrangement of protons and electrons in both these elements.

The uranium element contains 92 protons (+) in its core and 92 electrons (−) in an orbit about its core. Between these two are the remaining elements, each having an atomic structure that differs from its two neighbors by one proton (+) and one electron (−). Other well-known elements are nickel with an atomic number of 28, copper with an atomic number of 29, and zinc with an atomic number of 30.

Since we deal frequently with copper in electrical systems (wiring, connectors, etc.), let's look a little more closely at this element. Within the copper atom are 29 protons (+) and 29 electrons (−). The protons are concentrated at the core, while the electrons are distributed in four separate shells or rings, with each shell or ring located a different distance from the core of the atom.

Figure 1-9 shows the basic core of the copper atom, with the 29 electrons clustered around it. You will notice that the two electrons in the ring closest to the core remain equally spaced from each other, the eight electrons

FIGURE 1-9 Copper atom arrangement.

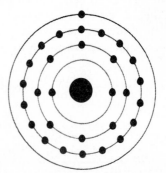

in the second ring from the core are equally spaced, and the 18 electrons in the third ring are also equally spaced from each other. Also note that the outer ring contains only one electron.

Any element that has fewer than four electrons contained within its outer ring is a good *conductor* of electricity, while elements with more than four electrons in this outer ring are known to be poor conductors of electricity. From our earlier discussions, you will recollect that any element that is a poor conductor of electricity is called an *insulator*. Those elements that contain four electrons exactly in the outer ring are classified as *semiconductors*, which we deal with later in the book. Any conductor with fewer than four electrons in its outer ring makes it rather easy to dislodge these electrons from their orbits by use of a low voltage. This action will therefore create a flow of current (electron flow) from atom to atom.

In summation, remember that the proton is positively charged, while the electron is negatively charged. Opposite charged particles are attracted to one another. Therefore, opposing electric charges will always attract. The negatively charged electron (−) will be pulled toward the positively (+) charged proton.

Because of the electron movement that exists around the core of the atom, it is not at all uncommon for an atom to lose some of its electrons. These electrons that leave the atom's outer rings are generally called *free electrons,* and they tend to gather in the same place, creating what is known as a *charge* of electricity. When these free electrons begin to move, say along a copper wire, a certain number of these electrons pass a given point on the wire in a set time period; in other words, we have a certain quantity or volume flowing or moving within the wire. The electrical term for quantity or volume is current, which is measured in amperes. Electricity is flowing in the wire at this time. The free electrons moving along the copper wire will always move away from areas of many electrons into areas where there are fewer.

ELECTRON FLOW IN A COPPER WIRE

If a negative (−) charge were placed at one end of a copper wire, while a positive (+) charge were located at the other end, the condition shown in Fig. 1–10 would result. As we already know, when electrons (−) flow through a wire, a current is created which is measured in amperes. The number of electrons required to produce 1 ampere is 6.28 billion billion passing a given point in 1 second.

Figure 1–10 illustrates the flow of these electrons within a typical copper wire. For simplicity, we show only

FIGURE 1–10 Electron flow in a copper wire.

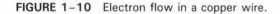
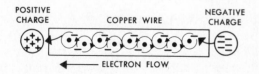

the single electron contained within the outer ring of the atom. The positive charge at the left side of the wire attracts the electron, thereby causing it to leave its atom. The loss of the electron now makes the atom positively charged, and the atom exerts an attractive force on the outer ring electron of its neighboring atom. This reaction causes a chain reaction to occur along the length of the copper wire, with each succeeding atom giving up its electron to another atom. Because of the great number of electrons flowing, electricity is created.

The negative charge at the right-hand side of the wire shown in Fig. 1–10 provides a repelling force equal to the attractive force created by the positive charge at the other end. Electron flow will continue within the wire as long as the positive and negative charges are maintained at each end of the wire.

VOLTAGE

In earlier discussions we described voltage as being similar to water pressure. It is this electrical pressure that pushes the current or amperes (electron flow) through the wire. In Fig. 1–10 we saw how electron flow was initiated in a wire; the unlike charges at each end of the wire have potential energy due to their capability to move electrons through the wire because of the forces of attraction and repulsion.

The potential energy between the wire ends is called voltage or *electromotive force* (EMF). We can produce voltage by various means. In cars, trucks, or heavy equipment, we generate this voltage by chemical means within a battery. Voltage can also be produced through friction and mechanical energy, as in a generator or alternator.

A typical vehicle battery of 12 volts (V) has a potential voltage of 12 V between the positive and negative terminals (posts). With no current absorbing devices connected to the battery posts, there is still a potential energy of 12 V. Voltage can exist on its own without the presence of current (amperes), but current cannot exist if there is no voltage present to push it along through the wiring.

In a battery, the voltage is limited by the strength of the charges between the positive and negative terminals or posts. Therefore, the greater the lack of electrons (−) existing at the positive (+) end or post, and the greater the excess of electrons at the negative post, the higher the voltage will be.

In Fig. 1–4 we showed a battery supplying power to a light bulb. If we were to substitute a generator for the battery, the generator when driven would supply a continuous flow of current (amperes) through the light bulb. In effect, the battery or generator pumps electrons through the wiring to the light bulb and back to the source of supply, which can be either a battery or a generator.

RESISTANCE

Earlier we discussed that if water is forced through a pipe, some resistance to flow exists because of the friction created between the surface of the pipe and the water. When electrons are forced through a conductor such as a copper wire, resistance will also be created, because of two conditions. First, each atom resists the removal of an electron, due to the attraction exerted on the electron by the protons (+) in the core of the atom. Second, collisions are always taking place between electrons and atoms as the electrons (−) are moving through the wire. Such collisions create resistances that build up heat within the conductor when the current is flowing.

We mentioned earlier that resistance is measured in ohms. An ohm can be defined as the resistance that will allow 1 ampere to flow under the force or pressure of 1 volt. The electrical symbol for the ohm is Ω, the Greek capital letter omega, which is similar in shape to a horseshoe. The number preceding the horseshoe indicates the total number of ohms; therefore, 10 Ω indicates a total resistance of 10 ohms. The mathematical symbol for resistance is the Greek lowercase letter omega (ω).

TYPES OF ELECTRICAL CIRCUITS

The basic types of electrical circuits that we are concerned with in cars, trucks, and heavy equipment are either series or parallel circuits. Certain applications, however, sometimes employ a combination of these, and are therefore known as *series–parallel circuits.* One example of the series–parallel circuit is the use of batteries for both starting and charging; through the use of a series–parallel switch, two 12-V batteries can be tied together in series to produce 24 V of cranking power to the starter. Once the engine starts, the automatic operation of the series-parallel switch allows the generator to charge the batteries at a rate of 12 V. (See Chapter 8.)

Prior to looking at several examples of series and parallel circuits, Fig. 1–11 depicts the simplest form of basic electrical circuit. A battery supplies the energy for the system (volts and amperes), and a resistor (load) offers a fixed resistance in the circuit.

Also shown in Fig. 1–11 are an ammeter and a voltmeter, used to measure the current (amperes) and voltage in the circuit, respectively. Take careful note that the ammeter is placed into the circuit, not across the battery. If the ammeter were placed across the battery, damage to the ammeter would result. The voltmeter, however, can be placed across the circuit at any two points to obtain a voltage reading.

FIGURE 1–11 Basic electrical circuit.

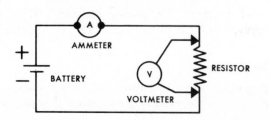

CURRENT FLOW

In the early years of electricity, it was assumed that current in a wire flowed from the positive source of the voltage to the negative terminal of the source after having passed around the circuit. However, in the year 1897, this theory was proven to be totally incorrect. Scientists discovered and proved that, in reality, the current flowed from the negative terminal, through the circuit, and back to the positive source.

Since that time, both theories have been used. For example, some companies in the industry choose to use one theory, others choose to use the other theory. These two theories are known as:

1. The *conventional theory,* in which the current flow is considered to be from positive to negative
2. The *electron theory,* in which the current flow is considered to be from negative to positive

The conventional theory is widely used and accepted within the automotive industry, although some major manufacturers of heavy-duty equipment prefer to use the electron theory. Either theory can be used.

BASIC ELECTRICAL FLOW

There are two theories commonly used to answer the often-asked question: Does electricity flow from the positive battery terminal to the negative battery terminal, or is it the other way around?

1. What is referred to as the conventional theory depicts the electrical flow as from the positive to the negative battery terminals. This theory is most often used in discussion and accepted as standard practice in this book.
2. The electron theory maintains that the flow is from the negative battery terminal to the positive battery terminal.

Since either theory can be used, although the conventional theory is most often followed, most manufacturers state in their manuals which of the two should be used when studying their electrical systems. History records that 2500 years ago the ancient Greeks knew that amber rubbed on cloth would attract feathers, cloth fibers, and so on. Since the Greek name for amber is *elektron,* the term *electron* was coined in our language, meaning basically the property of attraction. Electrons are negatively charged. However, many manufacturers of heavy-duty equipment prefer to use positive ground systems rather than negative ground systems, for reasons given in the following sections.

POSITIVE- VERSUS NEGATIVE-GROUND ELECTRICAL SYSTEMS

A discussion of electrical systems invariably involves the question of why one system is a negative-ground system and another is a positive-ground system. Most cars built in North America are negatively grounded, while some imported vehicles are positively grounded. Similarly, many trucks and heavy equipment are positively grounded.

The main reason that positive-ground electrical systems are used on some heavy-duty trucks is that in the electroplating of the vehicle during manufacturing, the plating material is attracted from the positive anode to the item to be plated, which is the negative cathode. If, for example, during manufacture of a heavy-duty truck you could dip a negative-ground vehicle into the electrolyte in a plating tank, the positive electrical system, consisting mostly of copper (wiring, etc.), would immediately start to plate itself over to the negative structural and steel portion of the vehicle. You would end up with a copper-plated chassis, but no electrical system! However, if you were to dip a positive-ground vehicle into the same plating tank, the material flow would be from positive to negative, but you would not end up with steel-plated copper. When you removed the positive-ground vehicle from the tank, it would certainy be nice and clean, but otherwise undamaged.

The situation just described can be compared with the conditions that the average heavy-duty highway truck is exposed to in wet and winter weather. Salt placed on the highways to melt snow and ice becomes a very efficient electrolyte. During high-speed winter driving, this spray envelopes the vehicle in a manner similar to the tank situation described herein. Severe corrosion will result to the electrical accessories if the negative pole of the battery is grounded.

Heavy-duty truck manufacturers have found that the positive-ground electrical system practically eliminates the worst type of corrosion or electrolysis affecting the electrical system. To explain further the disadvantages of the negative-ground system, consider that all of the steel structural parts of the truck are negative or cathodic. The energized electrical system, copper wires, terminals and switches, solenoids, motors, and so on, are positive or anodic. The voltage differential between the steel parts and the copper electrical system is approximately 14 V.

When the negative-ground vehicle is exposed to moisture (in particular to salt-laden moisture through salt deicing), the condition that exists is similar to that of an electroplating bath in which steel items are being copper-plated. The positive copper anode in the electrolyte bath is ionized and attracted to the negative steel. The same situation exists on the negative-ground vehicle, with the result that the electrical system deteriorates.

On a positive-ground vehicle, the action is reversed. However, due to the large mass of steel in comparison to the small amount of energized copper in the electrical system, the effect is insignificant. The advantage of the negative-ground system is that if you can totally seal out any entrance of moisture to the electrical system and accessories, the system will function extremely well. However, the configuration of heavy-duty, on- and off-highway trucks is such that this approach becomes rather impractical, due to the operating environments. Many generators and alternators on such trucks are open to allow the passage of cooling air through them. The salt fog, drawn through the radiator by the vehicle movement or the engine fan, circulates through these devices, causing electrolytic corrosion of all energized surfaces with which it comes into contact.

When two dissimilar metals meet at a junction in the presence of salt-laden moisture or liquid, the resulting galvanic action generates a voltage that will electrolytically cause ionic material transfer. The voltage generated is dependent on the electrode potential between the two metals. In the case of a typical truck, copper has a voltage potential of plus 0.347 V, and steel has a voltage potential of minus 0.340 V. Therefore, the voltage generated at the junction point becomes, in effect, 0.687 V. Electrolytic activity supported by the typical 14 V of the vehicle electrical system is 20 times the galvanic 0.687 V, or 20 times as severe.

The negative-ground electrical system was developed because, years ago, few electrical accessories were in use on vehicles other than the basic ignition system and some running lights. However, with the advent of the transistor, research was increased to apply it to automotive use. The car radio was an ideal place in which to use this device. The first transistors were of the germanium PNP type and were more easily applied to a negative-ground system than to a positive-ground system, because of their makeup. This development generated a swing away from positive-ground systems on both cars and trucks. Little information was available about the problems that could develop with a negative-ground system. Since the PNP germanium transistor was developed, major advances have been made, and the silicon transistors are now widely used.

The negative-ground system on passenger cars and low-mileage vehicles presents no major problem, and it may be economically impractical to change over to positive ground. However, on high-mileage trucks that are in operation 24 hours a day, seven days a week, where high maintenance-free mileage is expected, and where road failures caused by electrical system problems must be kept to a minimum, some heavy-duty truck manufacturers favor the positive-ground electrical system.

OHM'S LAW

There are a variety of calculations and formulas that are needed and used when designing electrical circuits and components; however, it is not necessary for the automotive or heavy-duty mechanic to be familiar with these. It is extremely helpful, though, to know the relationship among current, voltage, and resistance within an electrical circuit, because if any two of these are known, one can calculate the value of the third. When adding components to an existing circuit or when wiring a new circuit, the application of this principle ensures that each component within the circuit will receive the current necessary to operate at peak efficiency.

For example, if the resistance within a circuit is too high, certain components will not operate properly, or will operate at reduced efficiency. In addition, one must know the total current draw (load) in the circuit in order to calculate what size battery is required, and also what capacity of generator is required to ensure that the battery will maintain its full state of charge under varying conditions of load. The wrong-size wiring can also produce a high resistance to current flow. If we know how to calculate the necessary current, voltage, and resistance demands of the circuit, we can establish all the demands to be placed on the circuit. We can accurately establish this through the application of Ohm's law.

Ohm's law is an expression of the relationship between the current, voltage, and resistance in any circuit. The formula for Ohm's law is arrived at by substituting the letter I for amperes, the letter E for voltage, and the letter R for resistance. Sometimes the letter V is used in place of the letter E for voltage, but we will use the more common E designation. From these letters, we establish the following formulas:

$$\text{amperes} = \frac{\text{volts}}{\text{ohms}} \quad \text{or} \quad I = \frac{E}{R}$$

(current)

$$\text{volts} = \text{amperes} \times \text{ohms} \quad \text{or} \quad E = I \times R$$

$$\text{ohms} = \frac{\text{volts}}{\text{amperes}} \quad \text{or} \quad R = \frac{E}{I}$$

To demonstrate how effective the application of this formula is, let's look at some examples of simple circuits, both series and parallel.

SERIES CIRCUITS

In a *series circuit,* all current leaving the source of supply, such as a 12-V battery, must flow through each component of the circuit in sequential order. A simple example of this are three light bulbs connected in a series circuit, as shown in Fig. 1–12. Here the current leaves the positive battery terminal and returns to the negative battery terminal by one direct path through the circuit, having, of course, first passed through each light bulb in series.

FIGURE 1–12   Basic series circuit flow path.

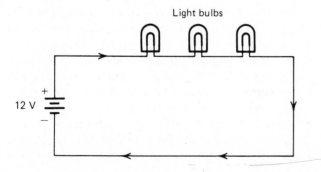

Light bulbs

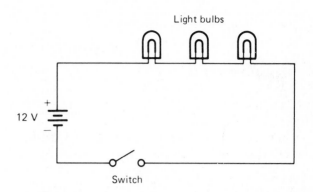

Light bulbs

Switch

FIGURE 1–13   Series circuit with switch control.

In the arrangement in Fig. 1–12, no switches are shown; therefore, the light bulbs would glow constantly. In order to be able to switch them on and off at will, it is necessary to insert a switch somewhere in the circuit. Figure 1–13 shows how this could be done. To reemphasize the difference between an open and a closed circuit, Fig. 1–12 is a closed circuit, because current can continually flow to and through the light bulbs and back to the battery.

In Fig. 1–13, the control switch is shown in the open position, which will prevent current from flowing to and through the light bulbs; however, the battery still has a potential voltage (electromotive force, or EMF) of 12 V, although no current is flowing.

As mentioned earlier, each accessory or electrical component in a circuit uses current, but it also creates a resistance to current flow. This resistance will vary between accessories, and Ohm's law allows us to calculate just what this resistance is. The following examples show the Ohm's law formula at work.

EXAMPLE 1–1 (SERIES CIRCUIT)

Calculate the amount of current flowing in the circuit shown in Fig. 1–14.

The Ohm's law formula for finding current is: amperes = volts/ohms, or $I = E/R$. Therefore, $I = 12/3$, or 4 A of current.

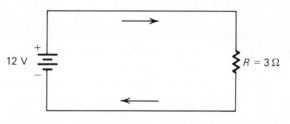

FIGURE 1–14   Example 1–1: Series circuit current flow.

EXAMPLE 1–2 (SERIES CIRCUIT)

Calculate the total resistance in the circuit shown in Fig. 1–15.

The Ohm's law formula for finding resistance is: ohms = volts/amperes, or more simply, $R = E/I$ ($R = 12/4$) equals 3 Ω.

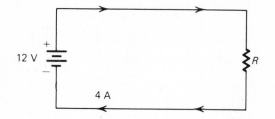

FIGURE 1–15 Example 1–2: Series circuit resistance.

EXAMPLE 1-3 (SERIES CIRCUIT)

Calculate the total voltage in the circuit shown in Fig. 1–16.

The Ohm's law formula for finding voltage is: volts = amperes × ohms; therefore, volts = 3 × 4, which is 12 V.

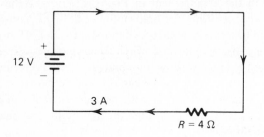

FIGURE 1–16 Example 1–3: Series circuit voltage.

When more than one resistance is present in a series circuit, the total resistance is simply the total of all the resistors. If three light bulbs were wired into a series circuit, and they all had 4 Ω of resistance to current flow, the total resistance would be 12 Ω. If one light bulb had a resistance of 3 Ω, the other a resistance of 4 Ω, and the last one a resistance of 5 Ω, the total resistance to current flow would be 12 Ω.

In a series circuit, regardless of the number of accessories wired into the flow path, the current flowing is the same at all points of the circuit. If two light bulbs of 4 Ω resistance each were wired into a series circuit, then with a voltage source of 12 V, $1\frac{1}{2}$ A would flow through each light bulb: $I = E/R$, or $I = 12/8 = 1.5$ A. If we were to double the voltage, yet use the same two light bulbs, the current flowing would be 3 A. In each of these situations, the same amperage that flows through the light bulbs will also flow through the battery.

When more than one accessory is used or wired into a series circuit, the voltage (electrical pressure) must give up some of its potential energy to force the current through the resistance of the accessory. Therefore, a percentage of the source voltage is used up as it passes through each accessory (load). An example of this is given in Fig. 1–17.

The source voltage or potential energy of the battery is 12 V, with 2 V being used to force the 2 A current through the accessory with 1Ω of resistance, and the remaining 10 V being required to force the 2 A current through the accessory resistance of 5Ω.

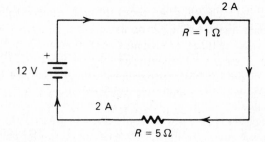

FIGURE 1–17 Voltage, current, and resistance relationship in a series circuit.

The previous examples characterized the value of using Ohm's law; however, in addition to calculating what an unknown quantity is in a series circuit, we can also use:

- An ammeter to measure current
- A voltmeter to measure voltage
- An ohmmeter to measure resistance

These gauges can be used independently or can be bought in what is known as an AVR (amps/volts/resistance) *meter,* commonly called a *multimeter.* By use of a selector switch on the face of the meter, either current, voltage, or resistance can be measured.

Figure 1–18 shows a simple series circuit, with the placement of both an ammeter and a voltmeter in the circuit; the ohmmeter can be placed across any two points in the circuit to establish a given resistance at any point.

Figure 1–19 shows a series circuit with four resistors (accessories) wired into the system. Total circuit resistance is established by adding all of the resistance together; the current flowing is $I = E/R$, or 12/12, a current flow of

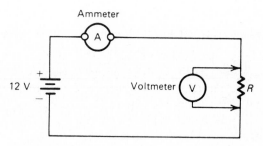

FIGURE 1–18 Voltmeter and ammeter placement in a series circuit.

FIGURE 1–19 Series circuit with four resistors.

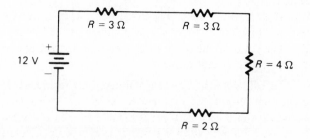

1 A. An increase in resistance through an accessory will cause a higher voltage drop to occur in the circuit, while a lower resistance through an accessory results in a smaller loss or drop in voltage through the respective accessory.

From the basic information we have learned so far about a series circuit, we can state three known facts related to this type of electrical circuit:

1. The current that flows through each resistor (accessory load demand) will remain the same.

2. The amount of voltage required to force the current through each resistor will be proportional to the actual resistance within that resistor (accessory); therefore, the voltage drop across each resistor or accessory will be different if the resistance through each accessory is different.

3. The amount of voltage loss or drop through the circuit will always equal the source voltage; for example, if a 12-V battery is the source voltage, the voltage drop in the circuit will be 12 V.

In addition to the three facts listed above, we can list several other known specifics about the series circuit that we have learned about so far. These will allow you to recall quickly some major aspects of the earlier discussions.

1. Total circuit resistance is the total of all resistors in the system.

2. Total series resistance must be more than the largest individual resistance.

3. If an open exists at any one component, the entire circuit will be open and no current can flow.

4. A short across part of the circuit will cause increased current in the wire between the short circuit and the voltage source.

PARALLEL CIRCUITS

In the series circuits that we just looked at, the current flowing in the circuit followed one path only from the battery post, through the accessories, and back to the opposite polarity battery post. In a *parallel circuit* the current leaving the battery can flow through more than one path before returning back to the opposite polarity battery post or terminal. Figure 1–20 shows the layout for a simple parallel circuit.

The three main facts related to a parallel circuit that distinguish it from the series circuit are:

1. The voltage across each resistor (accessory) is the same.

2. The current (amps) through each accessory or resistor will be different if the resistance values are different.

3. The total of the separate currents (amperes) equals the complete circuit current.

To calculate the current, voltage, and resistance in a parallel circuit, we can always refer to Ohm's law. However, let's look at some typical examples of calculating various unknown quantities in a parallel circuit.

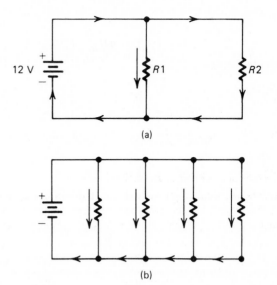

FIGURE 1–20 (a) Simplified parallel circuit; (b) parallel circuit with four resistors.

EXAMPLE 1–4 (PARALLEL CIRCUIT)

In a parallel circuit with two resistors, you find the total resistance by using the following formula:

$$R = \frac{R_1 \times R_2}{R_1 + R_2}$$

where R represents resistance. What is the total resistance of Fig. 1–21?

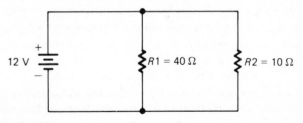

FIGURE 1–21 Calculation of total resistance in a two-resistor parallel circuit.

By application of the formula shown above, we simply replace the R_1 and R_2 portion of the formula with the values of each resistor. We therefore have resistance

$$R = \frac{40\ \Omega \times 10\ \Omega}{40\ \Omega + 10\ \Omega}$$

The result is now 400/50 = 8 Ω. Therefore, what we have proven is that the total resistance in a parallel circuit is less than that of any individual resistor.

EXAMPLE 1–5 (PARALLEL CIRCUIT)

What is the total resistance of Fig. 1–22?

Figure 1–22 shows four resistors (accessories) in parallel. These accessories will each require a given current to operate them, so we can refer to these as *branch currents* since they are

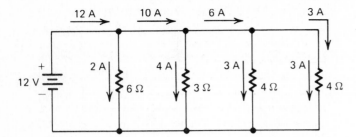

FIGURE 1–22 Calculation of parallel circuit resistance with four resistors.

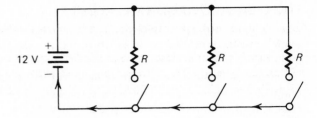

FIGURE 1–23 Parallel circuit resistance with three switches controlling resistors.

all attached to the main supply as branches are attached to a tree trunk. Ohm's law for finding current is

$$\text{current} = \frac{\text{voltage}}{\text{resistance}} \quad \text{or} \quad I = \frac{E}{R}$$

Therefore, in Fig. 1–22, with four branch currents, we would, in effect, have $I = E/R$ four times, or 12/6 = 2 A, 12/3 = 4 A, 12/4 = 3 A, and 12/4 = 3 A, to give us a total battery current of 2 + 4 + 3 + 3, or 12 A. The circuit resistance together, however, would only be equivalent to 1 Ω because Ohm's law for resistance is $R = E/I$, or 12 V/12 A = 1 Ω. We can calculate this actual circuit resistance by the following method:

$$\frac{R_1 \times R_2}{R_1 + R_2}$$

for the first two resistors, and repeat this formula for the next two resistors. We therefore have

$$R = \frac{6 \times 3}{6 + 3} = \frac{18}{9} = 2 \text{ Ω}$$

for the first two resistors. In the next two resistors, we have

$$R = \frac{4 \times 4}{4 + 4} = \frac{16}{8} = 2 \text{ Ω}$$

Remember that the total circuit resistance in a parallel circuit is always less than that of any individual resistor. Therefore, the two-ohm equivalent resistor in parallel with the other two-ohm equivalent resistor will be equal to

$$R = \frac{R_1 \times R_2}{R_1 + R_2} = \frac{2 \times 2}{2 + 2} = \frac{4}{4} = 1 \text{ Ω}$$

The total circuit resistance in Fig. 1–22 is thus 1 Ω.

As we have seen so far, parallel circuits provide more than one path for the current to flow. Therefore, a break in one path (open circuit) will not prevent current from flowing through other parts of the circuit, unless the break existed in the wire before the current reached the individual branch wires. If, however, each branch circuit were to be fitted with a switch as shown in Fig. 1–23, each circuit or branch could be opened or closed when desired.

Remember that in a series circuit, since the current has only one path of flow, a break in the wire (or the installation of a switch) would result in all accessories losing current flow because of the wire break (or if the switch were to be placed in the off or open position).

Because it is desirable in automotive and heavy equipment installations to have independent control of each accessory to suit conditions, the parallel circuit is usually used. The series circuit is used for certain circuitry to provide, for example, greater starting voltage by wiring two 12-V batteries together. Parallel circuit wiring is also commonly used in house wiring.

VOLTAGE DROP

The total *voltage drop* in a series circuit must equal the source voltage. In a parallel circuit, the voltage drop across any component is the same as the source voltage. To ensure that you understand this concept, look at Fig. 1–24 and establish the source voltage for both the series and parallel circuits shown.

In Fig. 1–24(a), we see a series circuit with two resistors or accessories. What is the source voltage?

Figure 1–24(b) shows a parallel circuit. What is the source voltage?

The correct answer to Fig. 1–24(a) is 12 V. The answer for Fig. 1–24(b) is 6 V.

FIGURE 1–24 Calculation review: (a) series circuit resistance; (b) parallel circuit resistance.

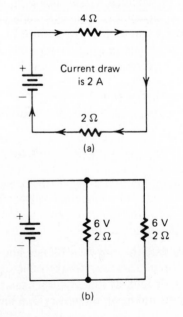

EXAMPLE 1-6 (PARALLEL CIRCUIT)

From Fig. 1–25, establish the total resistance in the circuit; also find the current flowing.

Remember that total resistance in a parallel circuit is less than the resistance of either of the resistors; therefore, to solve Fig. 1–25, we simply use the formula for resistance calculation in a parallel circuit:

$$R = \frac{R_1 \times R_2}{R_1 + R_2}$$

$$= \frac{12 \times 12}{12 + 12} = \frac{144}{24} = 6 \ \Omega$$

To find the battery current we refer to Ohm's law, which states that current = volts/resistance, or $I = E/R$; therefore, $I = 24/6 = 4$ A.

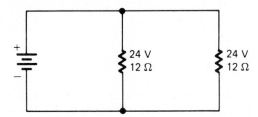

FIGURE 1–25 Establishing resistance and current flow in a parallel circuit.

SERIES–PARALLEL CIRCUITS

As mentioned earlier, series–parallel circuits are used in certain instances rather than a straight series or single parallel circuit. Figure 1–26 shows a typical series–parallel circuit. Note that the figure shows current flowing from the battery through a series (one path) accessory first, where it then flows to two other accessories in parallel.

The total current flowing in the circuit is equal to the total voltage divided by the total resistance. To find the total resistance of Fig. 1–26, follow the same sequence as you would in finding the resistance in a parallel circuit first, in addition the sequence required to find the resistance in a series circuit. We therefore have

$$R = \frac{R_1 \times R_2}{R_1 + R_2}$$

$$= \frac{6 \times 3}{6 + 3} = \frac{18}{9} = 2 \ \Omega$$

for the parallel part of the circuit. The resistance for the series part of the circuit is shown as 2 Ω. Therefore, if we add these two resistances together, we have a total circuit resistance of 4 Ω.

From Ohm's law we can now find the current flowing in this series/parallel circuit; current = voltage/resistance is $I = E/R$, or $I = 12/4 = 3$ A. The circuit is arranged as follows. The voltage drop across the series resistor is voltage = current × resistance, or $E = I \times R$, which is $E = 3 \times 2 = 6$ V. The source voltage remaining after passing through the series resistor or accessory is 6 V, which will pass through both branches of the parallel part of the circuit.

The current flow through both of these branches is arrived at simply by Ohm's law, where current = voltage/resistance or $I = E/R$, to give $I = 6/6 = 1$ A. Current flow in the second branch is also shown and is arrived at in the same fashion: $I = E/R$, or $I = 6/3 = 2$ A. Total current flow through the parallel branches is therefore the sum of the two, which is $1 + 2 = 3$ A.

COMPARISON OF CIRCUITS

Having now looked at and studied the series, parallel, and series–parallel circuits, we can conclude from the examples and calculations that each system would offer a different resistance to current flow because of individual design. In summation, we can say that the resistance to current flow in similarly designed circuits of the three types discussed would be as follows:

1. Series circuits offer the highest resistance to flow.
2. Parallel circuits offer the lowest resistance to flow.
3. Series–parallel circuits offer medium resistance to flow.

CONDUCTOR PROPERTIES

Earlier in the chapter we discussed the basic makeup of what is classified as a conductor of electricity. Because some degree of flexibility is required in the conductor (wire) used in cars, trucks, and heavy-duty equipment applications, we mentioned that instead of using a solid strand of wire, we most often find a large number of very small strands of wire.

Small-strand wire is generally used because current flows on the surface of the conductor; therefore, more

FIGURE 1–26 Typical series–parallel circuit.

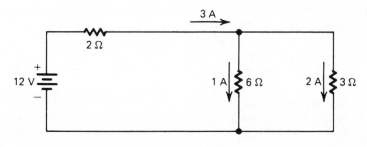

surface area is exposed than with that of a one-piece solid wire, with the net result that there is lower resistance with stranded wire than with solid wire. Based on the earlier discussion of how resistance is created, it makes sense to select a conductor that will offer a minimum amount of resistance to the flow of current in the electrical circuit. Selection of a wire with too high a resistance can dramatically affect the current flow to the accessories and can cause heat buildup within the wiring and lead to potential fire damage. Because of its plentiful supply and relative low cost, copper is widely used for wiring in electrical systems.

The amount of resistance in any wire is caused by the following:

1. Wire length
2. Wire diameter
3. Wire temperature

Using a length of wire that is unusually long is not only a waste of wire and money, but increases the circuit resistance to current flow. Doubling the length of a wire will double its resistance. Also, using a wire that is too small in diameter will similarly create added resistance to current flow. Again, if the cross-sectional area of a wire is doubled by using a wire twice as large, the resistance will be cut in half for the same length of wire. Therefore, select a wire of the smallest size that will not cause excessive voltage drop throughout the circuit.

Let's consider a typical example of a circuit with a given wire size. Figure 1–27 shows a simple electrical circuit with a parallel wire arrangement to two headlights. The wires shown have a known resistance of 0.25 Ω each; each headlight has a known resistance of 2 Ω. What is the effective circuit resistance?

To calculate the circuit resistance, we substitute the formula given earlier in parallel circuits:

$$R = \frac{R_1 \times R_2}{R_1 + R_2}$$

Therefore, the effective resistance through the two headlights is

$$R = \frac{2 \times 2}{2 + 2} = \frac{4}{4} = 1 \ \Omega$$

FIGURE 1–27 Establishing circuit resistance in a parallel light circuit.

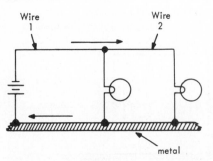

The total resistance of this circuit, however, is the 1 Ω through the headlights plus the resistance of each piece or length of copper wire. Each wire has a resistance of 0.25 Ω, for a total circuit resistance of 0.25 + 0.25 + 1 Ω + 1.5 Ω. The current flow is $I = E/R$, or $I = 12/1.5 = 8$ A.

We mentioned that voltage drop is a factor in an electrical circuit because of resistance, which can cause problems. Let's calculate what the voltage drop would be in this circuit. Ohm's law for voltage is: voltage = current × resistance. Therefore, we have $E = I \times R$, or $E = 8 \times 0.25 = 2$ V, or a total of 4 V for both wires. This is a poorly designed circuit, because having started with a 12-V source at the battery, we have only 8 V left to operate the headlights. Since the sum of the voltage drops must equal the source voltage, we have 8 + 2 + 2, for a source voltage of 12 V.

Eight volts would provide a very dim headlight indeed. The answer to our problem is to select a wire having resistance values to allow adequate voltage across the load (accessory) for proper operation: in this case, a high enough voltage for proper illumination of the headlights. The size and resistance of wire can again be likened to the size or diameter of a water pipe and to water pressure.

Although you may not yet be thoroughly familiar with wire sizes, consider that the wires used from the vehicle battery to the starter motor and vehicle frame (ground or earth) are much larger than the wiring used for the accessories. This explanation is easy to understand when we consider that the starter motor requires very high amounts of current or amperes to crank the engine for starting. Remember that current or amperes in electricity is the equivalent of gallons or liters per minute in a water system. Therefore, the smaller the wire, the smaller the flow rate at the other end for a given pressure (voltage). We would not be able to supply the high-amperage requirements to the starter motor with small-gauge wiring, and moreover we would burn out the smaller wire through overheating (electron bombardment and heat buildup).

Temperature Effect on Wire

An increase in temperature creates a similar increase in resistance. Consider a length of wire 10 ft long having a total known resistance of 0.4 Ω at 70 °F (21 °C). At a temperature of 170 °F (76.6 °C), the resistance increases from 0.04 Ω to 0.05 Ω per foot.

Wire Gauge Sizes

Copper wiring used in both automotive and heavy-duty equipment is classified by a wire gauge number, which denotes its size, resistance, and so on. This is shown in Table 1–2.

WIRING RECOMMENDATIONS

The copper wiring used in automobiles, trucks, and heavy-duty equipment is basically broken into two cate-

TABLE 1-2 Recommended conductor construction (AWG strands)

SAE Wire Size	Class I No. Strands/ AWG Size (in.)	Class II No. Strands/AWG Size (in.)
6	37/21 (.0285)	7 × 19/27 (.0142)
4	61/22 (.0253)	7 × 19/25 (.0179)
2	127/33 (.0226)	7 × 19/23 (.0226)
1	127/22 (.0253)	7 × 37/25 (.0179)
0	127/21 (.0285)	7 × 37/24 (.0201)
2/0	127/20 (.0320)	7 × 37/23 (.0226)
3/0	—	7 × 37/22 (.0253)
4/0	—	19 × 22/23 (.0226)

Note that the lower the wire number, the larger its size.

TABLE 1-3 Metric wire strand size

SAE Wire Size	Metric Size, mm²	Class I No. Strands/mm Size	Class II Size
6	13.0	37/.66	—
4	19.0	61/.63	—
2	32.0	127/.57	7 × 19/.57
1	40.0	127/.63	7 × 19/.63
0	50.0	127/.71	7 × 19/.71
2/0	62.0	127/.79	7 × 19/.79
3/0	81.0	—	7 × 37/.63
4/0	103.0	—	7 × 37/.71

gories: wire used to carry current for lighting and accessories, and wire required to carry larger currents such as that required for starting motors from the battery. Tables 1-2 and 1-3 show the recommended SAE (Society of Automotive Engineers) and AWG (American Wire Gauge) stranded wire specifications. Note that the lower the wire number, the larger its size. Wire gauge sizes from 4/0 up to 6 are generally used on vehicles and equipment that require large current-carrying capacities, although size 4 is generally the minimum size that would be used for battery cables.

Tables 1-4 and 1-5 show the accepted wire size recommendations required for vehicle lighting and acces-

TABLE 1-4 Recommended construction

SAE Wire Size	Class III No. Strands/ AWG Size (in.)	Class IV No. Strands/AWG Size (in.)
20	7/28 (.0126)	—
18	16/30 (.0100)	65/36 (.0050)
16	19/29 (.0113)	—
14	19/27 (.0142)	—
12	19/25 (.0179)	—
10	19/23 (.0226)	—
8	19/21 (.0285)	—
6	37/21 (.0285)	7 × 19/27 (.0142)
4	61/22 (.0253)	7 × 19/25 (.0179)

TABLE 1-5 Metric sizes

SAE Wire Size	Metric Wire Size mm²	Class III No. Strands/mm Size
20	0.5	7/.31
18	0.8	19/.23
16	1.0	19/.28
14	2.0	19/.36
12	3.0	19/.45
10	5.0	19/.57
8	8.0	19/.71
6	13.0	37/.66
4	19.0	61/.63

sories. Wire gauge size 14 is widely used on automotive applications for lighting and accessories.

WIRE COLOR CODE

The recommended colors of wire cable should match as closely as possible the colors set forth by *The Color Association of the U.S. Inc.,* ninth edition (Table 1-6). Stripes can be used where additional color combinations are required. The stripes shall be applied longitudinally along the cable. Black or white stripes are recommended, but other colors may be specified.

In addition to the wire sizes and color codes, wires are further identified as to their specification types by the following abbreviations:

Type GPT general purpose, thermoplastic insulated
Type HDT heavy duty, thermoplastic insulated
Type GPB general purpose, thermoplastic insulated, braided
Type HDB heavy duty, thermoplastic insulated, braided
Type STS standard duty, synthetic rubber insulated
Type HTS heavy duty, synthetic rubber insulated
Type SXL standard duty, cross-linked polyethylene insulated

TABLE 1-6 TECA Colors

Color	Nom.	Dark	Light
White	70003	70004	
Red	70180	70082	70189
Pink	70098	70099	70097
Orange	70072	70041	70071
Yellow	70205	70068	70067
Lt. Green	70062	70063	70061
Dk. Green	70065	70066	70064
Lt. Blue	70143	70144	70142
Dk. Blue	70086	70087	70085
Purple	70135	70164	70134
Tan	70093	70094	70092
Brown	70107	70108	70106
Gray	70152	70153	70185
Black	None	—	

ELECTRICITY AND MAGNETISM

In a truck or piece of heavy-duty equipment, the battery or batteries can supply the reservoir of electrical energy required to operate all the electrical loads (accessories), including supplying adequate power to the starter motor to crank the engine. The battery alone, however, can supply this source of energy only as long as it retains a sufficient state of charge to overcome the circuit resistance. If some means is not used to recharge the battery as it is supplying this electrical load on the circuit, eventually the battery will lose this source of energy. We all know what happens then—the battery goes dead!

Batteries today are constantly kept in a state of charge by the action of either a dc generator or, more commonly, an alternator that develops ac current. (The letters *dc* mean *direct current,* and the letters *ac* mean *alternating current.* The generator and the alternator both rely heavily on the principles of magnetism to produce the necessary electrical energy required to keep the battery or batteries in a constant full-charge condition. Because the theory of magnetism is so important to these two units, let's study how magnetism and electricity are related to the needs of an electrical system.

Magnetism

For well over a thousand years, sailors have used the compass as a means of knowing their approximate location. The basic use of the compass was derived from the fact that fragments of iron ore called lodestone were found to attract other pieces of ferrous metals, such as other pieces of iron ore. Furthermore, if a long piece of iron ore or an iron bar were to be suspended in the air, one end would always point toward the earth's North Pole. Naturally, this end was therefore called the *north pole,* while the opposite end was referred to as the *south pole.* In a compass, the needle will always swing into a north/south pole position, because the earth itself is basically a giant magnet.

An iron bar that exhibits magnetic properties is commonly called a bar magnet. You may recall from basic science tests conducted at school with bar- and horseshoe-shaped magnets that they are both capable of attracting other metal objects to them without having to come into actual physical contact with those objects. A good demonstration of this fact may be given by sprinkling iron filings onto a tabletop, then placing the magnet in the vicinity of the filings. The result is that the filings are pulled against the magnet as by some unseen force. This attraction occurs because a magnetic field of force exists around all magnets.

A simple method of establishing what these unseen lines of force look like can be done with the use of a magnet placed underneath a sheet of paper, then sprinkling iron filings onto the paper. By lightly tapping the paper, the iron filings will arrange themselves into a clear pattern around the bar magnet as shown in Fig. 1–28.

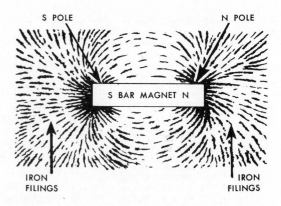

FIGURE 1–28 Magnetic attraction of iron filings. (*Courtesy of Delco Remy, Division of General Motors Corporation.*)

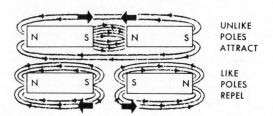

FIGURE 1–29 Like and unlike magnetic poles. (*Courtesy of Delco Remy, Division of General Motors Corporation.*)

The area around the bar magnet that attracts the iron filings is called the *field of force* or *magnetic field.* The strongest field of force is created next to the two poles of the magnet, with the lines of force leaving the north pole and entering the south pole. When two bar magnets are placed opposite one another as shown in Fig. 1–29, unlike poles will attract one another, while like poles will tend to repel one another.

Magnetic Theory

Magnetism can be simplified further by the use of two commonly known theoretical models:

1. Any magnet consists of a very large number of minute magnetic particles, which will align themselves with one another to form the magnet. This concept is shown in Fig. 1–30(b). If these particles have no particular arrangement, however, the bar will be nonmagnetic, and the minute particles will be as shown in Fig. 1–30(a), not aligned.

2. The second theory of magnetism deals with the electron, which we discussed in some depth earlier in the chapter. You may recall that the electron has a circle of force around it; therefore, any time that the electron orbits align themselves in a bar of iron so that these circles of force are added together, the bar of iron will also become magnetized.

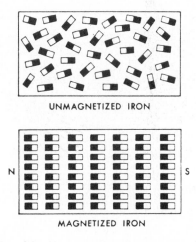

FIGURE 1–30 Unmagnetized and magnetized iron. *(Courtesy of Delco Remy, Division of General Motors Corporation.)*

Creating a Magnet

Not all iron bars are magnetic, and, of course, we would not want them to be. How can we create a magnetic bar from one that is not magnetic? One simple method is to stroke the nonmagnetic iron bar with one that is magnetic, to induce the necessary realignment of the particles within the nonmagnetic iron bar.

Another method is to place an iron bar into a strong magnetic field so that the lines of magnetic force within the field will pass through the iron bar and will induce the particles to realign themselves so that the bar will become magnetized. Figure 1–31 shows this process of magnetic induction.

Here the north and south poles of the magnet can be readily identified by placing the large magnet in suspension on a piece of string and allowing the magnet to rotate of its own free will to the north and south poles of the earth.

Although we can magnetize an iron bar by these two methods, the specific composition of the iron bar will determine just how much of the induced magnetism will remain after it is removed from the force field of the original magnet. If the iron bar retains this magnetic force with no loss over time, it will be known as a *permanent magnet*. Uses of permanent magnets are very common,

FIGURE 1–31 Magnetic induction. *(Courtesy of Delco Remy, Division of General Motors Corporation.)*

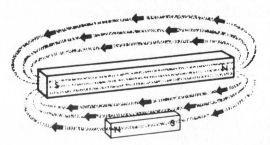

one example being in a generator. Other uses of such magnets are in starter motors, and in meters such as voltmeters and ammeters.

Electromagnetism

Although magnetism has been used for well over a thousand years, it was not until the year 1820 that some relationship was found to exist between both magnetism and electricity. A small experiment showed that when electricity flowed through a wire and a compass was placed over the wire, the needle of the compass automatically swung around to place itself perpendicular or crosswise to the wire. From such an experiment it was concluded that as the only force that could cause the compass needle to move would be magnetism, the current flowing in the wire obviously created a magnetic field around the wire.

To obtain a more positive understanding of how these lines of magnetic force emanated from a current-carrying wire, a further simple test was conducted, in which the wire was placed through a hole in a piece of cardboard, as shown in Fig. 1–32. With iron filings sprinkled onto the cardboard, current was then induced through the wire; the result was that the iron filings arranged themselves into concentric circles around the wire.

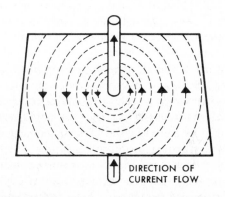

FIGURE 1–32 Field strength (magnetic) versus distance. *(Courtesy of Delco Remy, Division of General Motors Corporation.)*

The concentric circles of iron filings are very heavy near the wire, but become less heavy the farther away from the wire they are. This allows us to conclude that the force of the magnetic field decreases as we move away from its center or core. Magnetism produced by passing a current through a wire is known as electromagnetism. This electromagnetic field will exist along the total length of the wire.

If we were to wind a length of wire into a coil, then pass a flow of current through the wire, we would create a magnetic field around the coil of wire with both a north and a south pole, similar to a bar magnet. Figure 1–33 shows such an arrangement. The strength of the magnetic field around the coil will depend on the number of turns in the coil and the amount of current flowing in the wire.

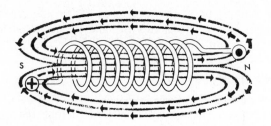

FIGURE 1–33 Current flow of magnetisim in a coiled wire. *(Courtesy of Delco Remy, Division of General Motors Corporation.)*

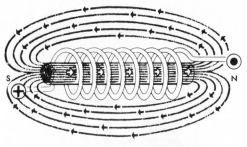

IRON CORE INCREASES FIELD STRENGTH

FIGURE 1–35 Iron core increases magnetic field strength. *(Courtesy of Delco Remy, Division of General Motors Corporation.)*

Therefore, the strength of the magnetic field depends on the ampere-turns of the coil. In order to establish the polarity of the coil ends, we can use what is known as the right-hand rule for coils. This is done by holding your hand as shown in Fig. 1–34, with the thumb extended in the normal direction of current flow, which will also be the north pole of the coil. Should the current flow through the coil be reversed, the polarity of the coil ends will be reversed.

One additional method that is often used to increase the magnetic field of a coil of wire is simply to insert an iron core into the middle of the coil windings, as shown in Fig. 1–35. The use of iron in a magnetic path can increase the magnetic strength by as much as 2500 times over that of a coil that simply has air in the center. Because iron is a much better conductor of magnetic lines than is air, the addition of the iron core to the coil shown in Fig. 1–35 creates a considerable increase in the magnetic field when current flows through the wire. In effect, the coil with the iron core has now been transformed into an electromagnet. Such an arrangement is typical of the system used in a generator to create the strong magnetic fields required to produce a steady output of electricity. (A coil without an iron core is usually referred to as a *solenoid*.)

The resistance that a magnetic circuit offers to lines of force, or flux, is commonly called *reluctance*. The effect of an air gap on the total reluctance of a circuit is very important. As we mentioned earlier, air has poor conductibility compared to iron. Therefore, air will also have a higher reluctance than iron. Doubling the size of the air gap in a magnetic circuit will also double the reluctance of the circuit, and the field strength will be reduced by half.

One common application of an electromagnet is the use of the large steel circular weight used on the end of a crane for picking up scrap steel. When current is directed through the coils within the weight, the steel weight becomes magnetized and allows steel to be picked up. When the current through the coils is cut off, the reduced magnetic field allows the scrap steel to be deposited or dropped from the end of the weight.

Creating Electricity from Magnetism

With a good understanding of magnetism, we can now look at how electricity can be produced in a wire through the use of magnetic lines of force. If we move a conductor, such as a piece of copper wire through a magnetic field, a voltage is induced in the wire. Such a condition is called *electromagnetic induction*, and is commonly defined as the induction of voltage in a conductor that moves across any magnetic field. (This induced voltage is also known as electromotive force, as mentioned in the early part of our discussion on basic electricity.)

Figure 1–36 shows a simple horseshoe magnet with magnetic lines of force passing between the ends of the north and south poles. If a length of copper wire were placed at the right-hand end of the magnet and moved parallel to the magnet in order that the wire would be forced through the magnetic field, a small voltage would be induced in the wire. This voltage could be measured by placing the ends of a voltmeter across the ends of the wire. The wire must be moved so as to cut the magnetic lines of force. If the wire is moved up and down or parallel to the magnetic lines of force, these lines of force would not be cut, and no voltage would be induced in the wire.

In previous discussions we indicated that the magnetic lines of force always originate from the north pole to the south pole of the magnet. For this reason, when

FIGURE 1–34 Establishing polarity by the right-hand rule method. *(Courtesy of Delco Remy, Division of General Motors Corporation.)*

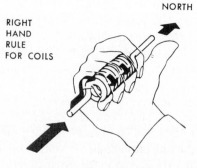

RIGHT HAND RULE FOR COILS

NORTH

DIRECTIONS OF CURRENT FLOW

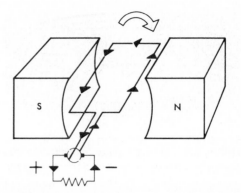

FIGURE 1–37 Basic generator principle. *(Courtesy of Delco Remy, Division of General Motors Corporation.)*

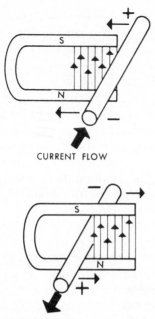

FIGURE 1–36 Inducing voltage flow in a wire. *(Courtesy of Delco Remy, Division of General Motors Corporation.)*

the wire is moved from the right to the left in Fig. 1–36, the end of the wire closest to the north pole will be the negative end, while the end of the wire closer to the south pole will become the positive end. The positive and negative ends of the wire are reversed once we move the wire from the left-hand side of the magnet to the right-hand side. Although we have shown the conductor (wire) as the moving object, there are times when it may be easier to move the magnetic field rather than the wire, such as the spinning rotor design of an automotive alternator.

In summation, the factors that determine the magnitude or amount of induced voltage are:

- How strong the magnetic field is
- How quickly the magnetic lines of force are cutting across the conductor (wire)
- The total number of conductors (wires) that are cutting across the magnetic lines of force

One other important point to consider is that when a straight wire is wound into a coil and moved across a magnetic field, all the loops of wire are in a series circuit arrangement, so that the induced voltage of all the loops will be added together to produce a higher voltage.

Inducing Voltage by Electromagnetic Induction

Since the induction of voltage in a wire is necessary in any electrical circuit to produce current flow, how can we actually do this successfully? Three methods are commonly employed to induce voltage flow in a wire conductor. One of the most widely used methods is that of

using the magnetic field in a generator to produce current to keep the vehicle's battery in a permanent state of charge. This method results in *generated voltage*. Figure 1–37 shows a simple line diagram of the basic components required to produce this voltage flow in the wire. This generator produces direct current (dc) by moving a wire through a stationary magnetic field.

There is only one single loop of wire shown rotating through the magnetic field. In reality, a generator uses many loops of wire; however, the principle remains the same. These wires are wrapped around an iron core called an *armature,* with the ends of the wires attached to individual segments of the armature. These segments are known as a *commutator*. As the loop of wire in Fig. 1–37 rotates (driven by a belt or gear drive from the engine to the armature pulley), the current flow in the wire loop is from the negative to the positive terminals. The voltage induced in the wire loop produces a coil voltage at the two commutator segments attached to the wire ends. Spring-loaded brushes in contact with the rotating commutator/armature pick up the current generated and feed this to the external circuit. The current flowing through the wire loop is established by applying the right-hand rule for induced voltage, as shown in Fig. 1–34. This method establishes the direction of current flow.

A second method used to create generated voltage is that used in the alternator or alternating-current (ac) generator. The main difference between this unit and the dc generator is that in the alternator the magnetic field is rotated, whereas in the dc generator the magnetic field was stationary. The principle of voltage generation within a simplified alternator is shown in Fig. 1–38. Here the magnetic field is rotated by a shaft connected to a pulley or gear drive on the engine. The wire or windings of wire are attached to the stationary alternator body or frame. Applying the right-hand rule, current will flow through the wire loop. We have demonstrated in Figs. 1–37 and 1–38 that voltage can be induced in a wire loop either by moving the wire through the stationary magnetic field, or by rotating the magnetic field past a stationary wire loop.

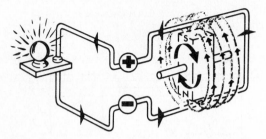

FIGURE 1–38 Basic alternator principle. *(Courtesy of Delco Remy, Division of General Motors Corporation.)*

Self-Induced Voltage

Another way in which we can induce voltage in a conductor is by *self-induction,* in which no separate magnetic field is used. Instead, by changing the current flowing through a wire that is wrapped around an iron core, the magnetic lines of force around the wire are caused to increase or decrease. The changing current through the wire will induce a voltage in the wire; therefore, the voltage is self-induced.

A good example of self-induced voltage is the standard ignition system coil that produces the high-voltage surge to fire the spark plugs. Basically, the coil consists of an iron core with two sets of wire coils wrapped tightly around the iron core. One set of these coils is of larger, heavy wire, while the other coil is made up from much smaller, finer wire. The large coil is known as the *primary coil* and the smaller coil is known as the *secondary coil.* An increase in current flow through one loop will cause an increase in the strength of the magnetic field around the wire of the coil. This magnetic field will cut across the neighboring loops of wire, thereby inducing a voltage in these loops.

Current flowing from the battery of the vehicle through the primary coil winding will set up a magnetic field which is absorbed by the secondary windings in the coil. When the distributor points, or the transistor functions, open, the current will drop to zero, since the energy from the battery flowing through the primary winding of the coil can no longer return to the battery circuit.

Since the secondary winding of the coil has not only a smaller diameter of wire than the primary but contains a much greater number of turns, the making and breaking of the ignition primary circuit transfers, by mutual induction of the magnetic field within the coil, an increase in voltage through the secondary winding. This voltage increase induced in the secondary winding of the coil will be proportional to the ratio of the number of turns between the primary and secondary coil windings. For example, if the primary winding has 20 turns, and the secondary winding has 2,000 turns, the voltage induced in the secondary windings will be 100 times greater than that developed in the primary windings. The battery voltage of 12 V flowing through the primary coil windings creates a magnetic field that induces a voltage of approximately 250 V. This 250 V of energy in this example will be boosted to 25,000 V in the secondary winding, forming the arc at the spark plug to fire the mixture in the cylinder. Voltages as high as 40,000 volts can be achieved in solid-state ignition systems.

Mutual Induction

Another method of inducing voltage in a wire is *mutual induction,* whereby a voltage is induced in one coil due to the changing current in another coil. The changing magnetic flux created by the current flow in one coil links or cuts across the windings of the second coil, thereby inducing voltage in proportion to the number of turns in both coils. Mutual induction follows the same pattern as that of self-induction.

QUESTIONS

1-1. Every substance is composed of:
    a. Protons   c. Matter
    b. Atoms   d. Mass
    (see page 5)

1-2. Particles that orbit around the center of an atom are:
    a. Electrons   c. Neutrons
    b. Protons   d. Molecules
    (see page 5)

1-3. When an atom gains or loses one electron, it is generally referred to as being:
    a. A molecule   c. A charged particle or ion
    b. An electron   d. A conductor
    (see page 6)

1-4. When a material has many free electrons, it is called:
    a. A conductor   c. A semiconductor
    b. An insulator   d. A negatively charged ion
    (see page 6)

1-5. When a material has many bound electrons, it is called:
    a. A conductor   c. A semiconductor
    b. An insulator   d. A positively charged ion
    (see page 6)

1-6. A particle that is said to be negatively charged is called:
    a. An atom   c. A protron
    b. A neutron   d. An electron
    (see page 5)

1-7. The term used to express electrical pressure is:
    a. Current   c. Amperage
    b. Resistance   d. Voltage
    (see page 2)

1-8. The term used to express volume, quantity, or current flow in an electrical circuit is:
    a. Amperage   c. Resistance
    b. Voltage   d. Electromotive force
    (see page 6)

current = how much
voltage = push   *Amps = flow*   *Watt = over time*

1-9. The term used to describe resistance in an electrical circuit is:
- a. Voltage
- (b.) Ohms
- c. Amperes
- d. Electromotive force

(see page 2)

1-10. Mechanic A says that the conventional theory of current flow in an electrical circuit is from negative to positive. Mechanic B says that it is from positive to negative. Who is correct? (see page 7) *B*

1-11. Mechanic A says that the resistance in a larger-diameter wire is less than it is in a smaller-diameter wire. Mechanic B disagrees. Who is correct? (see page 3) *A*

1-12. Mechanic A says that the longer the length of wire used in a circuit, the greater will be its resistance. Mechanic B says that length has no bearing on the resistance value. Who is right here? (see page 14) *A*

1-13. Resistance in a wire is not affected by:
- (a.) The direction of current flow
- b. The diameter of the wire
- c. The temperature rise in the wire
- d. The atomic structure of the wire

(see page 14)

1-14. Ohm's Law is used to express the relationship between current or amperes (I), voltage (E), and resistance (R) in an electrical circuit. Which formula would be used to determine the current flowing in a circuit?
- a. $E = \dfrac{R}{I}$
- (b.) $I = \dfrac{E \; volts}{Resistance}$ *Amps*
- c. $I = \dfrac{R}{E}$
- d. $I = E \times R$

(see page 9)

1-15. Which one of the following formulas would be used to determine the voltage flowing in a circuit?
- a. $R = \dfrac{E}{I}$
- b. $I = \dfrac{E}{R}$
- c. $I = E \times R$
- (d.) $E = I \times R$

(see page 9)

1-16. The amount of electrons flowing past a fixed point in a circuit in a given time period is actually a measure of:
- a. Electromotive force
- b. Resistance
- (c.) Current or amperage
- d. Voltage

(see page 6)

1-17. Current can flow only in a(an) __Closed__ circuit. (see page 3)

1-18. Current cannot flow in a(an) __Open__ circuit. (see page 3)

1-19. Mechanic A says that to complete an electrical circuit, current must flow from one battery terminal and return to the other. Mechanic B says that it does not have to return to the opposite battery terminal as long as it returns to a good ground path. Is only one mechanic correct here, or are both right? (see page 3) *A ground to Battery*

1-20. A break in the wiring of an electrical circuit creates:
- a. A high voltage reading
- b. Low current flow
- c. High current flow
- (d.) An infinite resistance caused by an open circuit

(see page 3)

1-21. The word *circuit* is derived from the word:
- (a.) Circle
- b. Circus
- c. Complete
- d. Return trip

(see page 3)

1-22. The electron theory of current flow is:
- a. From the positive to the negative terminal
- (b.) From the negative to the positive terminal

(see page 7)

1-23. An electric current consists of the flow of:
- a. Atoms
- b. Neutrons
- (c.) Electrons
- d. Protons

(see page 6)

1-24. Like charges are said to:
- (a.) Repel
- b. Attract
- c. Cancel or neutralize one another
- d. Create a loss of electrons

(see page 16)

1-25. The loss of one electron causes an atom to become:
- a. Unstable
- b. Negatively charged
- c. Positively charged
- d. Proton heavy

(see page 6)

1-26. The greatest resistance to current flow is created by:
- (a.) A resistor
- b. An insulator
- c. A conductor (wire) diameter that is too small
- d. A conductor (wire) diameter that is too large

(see page 4, 14)

1-27. An increase in circuit resistance will cause a decrease in:
- (a.) Current flow
- b. Voltage
- c. Electron action
- d. Proton movement

(see page 4)

1-28. In a series circuit:
- (a.) All current flows through a common path to complete the circuit
- b. All current branches off to feed separate components on individual wires

(see page 9)

1-29. The amperage in a series circuit is:
- a. The same at certain points
- b. Often the same under some conditions of operation
- c. Never the same value at any point
- (d.) Always the same at any point in the circuit

(see page 11)

1-30. To determine the value of the total resistance in a series circuit, you:
- a. Multiply all resistances
- (b.) Add all resistances
- c. Divide all resistances
- d. Subtract all resistances

(see page 10)

1-31. Total voltage drop in a series circuit is always equal to:
- a. The shunt circuit voltage
- b. The resistance value
- (c.) The source voltage
- d. The amperage draw

(see page 11)

1-32. Technician A says that in a parallel circuit, current can follow only one path. Technician B says that current can flow through two or more paths. Who is correct? (see page 11) *B*

1-33. To determine the branch resistance in a parallel circuit, you would divide the voltage by:
   a. The impedance
   b. The wattage
   c. The conductance
   (d.) The amperage
   (see page 12)

1-34. Electron flow in a wire can be produced by applying voltage or by:
   a. Applying amperage
   b. Decreasing resistance
   (c.) Moving the wire through a magnetic field
   (see page 17–18)

1-35. Magnetic lines of force radiate from both ends of a bar magnet. In a horseshoe magnet, magnetic lines of force flow
   (a.) From the north to the south pole
   b. From the south to the north pole
   (see page 18)

1-36. Mechanic A says that an iron core is used with a coil to concentrate and increase the field strength. Mechanic B says that the iron core is simply used to support the number of windings wrapped around it. Who is correct?
   (see page 18)

A

1-37. The total resistance in a parallel circuit is:
   a. Greater than any individual resistor
   b. The same as that of the weakest resistor
   (c.) Less than that of any individual resistor
   (see page 12)

1-38. The total resistance value of three resistors rated at 2, 2, and 4 Ω in a parallel circuit would result in a combined resistance value of:
   a. 0.2 Ω   c. 2 Ω
   b. 0.8 Ω   d. 8 Ω
   (see page 12)

1-39. The resistance values listed in Question 1–38, if applied to a series circuit, would result in a combined value of:
   a. 0.2 Ω   c. 2 Ω
   b. 0.8 Ω   (d.) 8 Ω
   (see page 11)

1-40. When magnetic lines of equal force and in opposite directions pass between adjacent conductors, they will tend to:
   (a.) Cancel one another out
   b. Attract one another
   c. Reduce the system voltage
   d. Reduce the current flow
   (see page 16–20)

CHAPTER

2

Introduction
to Electronics

OBJECTIVES

In this chapter we build on the basic knowledge that you have gained from Chapter 1. Specifically, you will acquire or review the skills needed to:

1. Be aware of the basic history of electronics as it applies to passenger cars and heavy-duty trucks.
2. Describe the meaning of *integrated circuit*.
3. Describe the meaning, basic function, and operation of a semiconductor, a diode, a transistor, a chip, an LED (light-emitting diode), and various other widely used electronic devices.

4. Describe how a silicon chip is manufactured.
5. Describe the basic difference between an N and a P semiconductor.
6. List the major advantages of an integrated circuit over its electromechanical counterpart.
7. Know how to use an ohmmeter to test various components within an integrated circuit.

VARIOUS ELECTRONIC DEVICES APPLIED TO CARS AND TRUCKS

The word *electronics* is now used in all languages, and it immediately conjures up visions of hundreds of items that owe their success to this field: hand-held computers; computers in automobiles, heavy-duty equipment, medical equipment, home entertainment devices, and business and space research programs; and numerous other devices with which we come into contact in our daily lives.

Vehicle and equipment electrical systems have improved tremendously as a direct result of the electronics explosion, with their use being particularly prominent in the application of gasoline and diesel fuel injection systems, ignition systems, antiskid braking systems, automatic airbag, safety restraints and seat-belt

tighteners, tone sequence control devices, car alarms, cruise control, overvoltage protection, alternator controls, trip computers, transmission controls, power seat positioning systems, automatic in-car heater and climate control systems, driver guidance and data systems, car ride height controls, digital instrumentation systems, and on-board computerized logbooks for heavy-duty on-highway trucks. These are just a few of the better known applications that would not have been possible without the successful adaption of electronics to these systems.

It is generally agreed that the semiconductor industry began with the development of the transistor at Bell Laboratories in 1948, although transistors remained a laboratory curiosity until the early 1950s, when they began to appear in car radios such as those manufactured by Delco Electronics. The use of transistors allowed manufacturers to replace the vacuum tubes then in use and therefore eliminate the unreliable mechanical vibrator that converted the battery dc voltage to ac. The first application of the transistor occurred in 1956 in the Chevrolet Corvette, manufactured by General Motors Corporation. By the latter half of the 1970s, germanium transistors began to be replaced by silicon transistors, the reason being that germanium units had several serious limitations that ultimately doomed its application in automotive electronics. One of these problems was that germanium has a poor high-temperature operating characteristic, and in an underhood environment, germanium transistors were essentially useless. Second, the material does not lend itself to what became known as the *planar process*, which is the condition whereby an insulating oxide is thermally grown on the surface of the semiconductor. This oxide serves the dual purpose of becoming a dielectric insulator and a mask that can be selectively etched to allow subsequent doping of the underlying bulk semiconductor material. Germanium does not form a thermal oxide with these properties. On the other hand, silicon forms an excellent thermal oxide, and silicon transistors have good high-temperature operating characteristics.

In addition to its use in radios, the transistor was commercially applied to automobile voltage regulators, with both Ford Motor Company and Delco Remy introducing these in 1968. This basic design continued until the 1986 model year, when replacement of this concept was phased in with more technologically advanced designs. Early voltage regulators were made using the *chip and wire* technique whereby the input chip was wire-bonded to the hybrid substrate. Later chips employed a small conductive bump in place of wire bond pads.

Other uses for solid-state componentry occurred in 1967 with the early work on an ignition module by Delco Electronics, which ultimately led to an across-the-board application in General Motors cars in 1975. The first integrated circuits (solid state) can be traced back to about 1959, to the pioneering work done by Jack Kilby at Texas Instruments and Robert Noyce at Fairchild. This was followed in 1963 at Delco Electronics, with the first integrated circuit (IC) actually being designed at Delco in 1965. However, it never got into production because Texas Instruments came out with a commercial device that better suited automotive applications. The single product that transformed the IC operation at Delco Electronics and started them on the road to large-scale manufacturing was the seat-belt interlock chip. The U.S. government had mandated that all 1974-model-year cars have a system installed that would prevent starting of the engine unless the seat belts were locked in the proper sequence. (Due to loud complaints regarding this seat-belt/engine starting routine, the government eventually rescinded the law.)

Up to 1975, power transistors manufactured at Delco Electronics were made using bipolar technology; however,

as applications requiring a substantial amount of logic started appearing, PMOS (positive-anode metal oxide semiconductor) technology, devices made on an N-type silicon substrate, where the active carriers are holes flowing between P-type source and drain controls) allowed the design of logic ICs that were smaller and consumed less power than the equivalent function designed in bipolar technology. In 1975 the PMOS device entered car production in the cruise control system.

In 1974 both NMOS (negative-cathode metal oxide semiconductor) and CMOS (complementary metal oxide semiconductor) technology was under development at Delco, and in 1977 Delco signed an agreement with Motorola that became the forerunner of the program that led to the design and development of the GM Custom Microprocessor (GMCM) chip set for engine controls that continues in production today. Full application of the GMCM to General Motors passenger cars and light trucks was initiated in the 1981 model year. In 1982 Delco signed a further agreement with Motorola for the GMP-4 microprocessor, which became the replacement for the venerable GMCM unit. (See p. 32, for more detail on N- and P-type semiconductors.)

In 1985, when Detroit Diesel Allison Division of General Motors was still wholly owned by General Motors, DDC became the first mass producer of high-speed diesel engines to install an electronically controlled diesel fuel injection system on their series 92 heavy-duty highway truck engines. This system, which was known as DDEC 1 (DD Electronic Controls 1), was followed up in 1987 with a much more advanced system known as DDEC 11. The introduction of DD's series 60 four-stroke-cycle engine, which is available only with the DDEC system, is further testimony to Detroit Diesel Corporation's commitment to the use of electronics for their product line through the 1990s. The DDEC system has now been expanded to cover both the series 71 and 149 DDC engine lineup. The ECM (electronic control module) used with these diesel injection systems adopted the technology that had already been widely used on all GMC passenger cars since 1981. Obviously, there were changes required to adapt the car ECM to a diesel truck engine, but the largest part of the necessary research and development had already been tested and proven over billions of miles in the passenger car marketplace.

Caterpillar was the next major high-speed diesel engine manufacturer to adopt electronic fuel injection controls—to their 3406B heavy-duty truck engine in 1987—using a system known as PEEC (Programmable Electronic Engine Control). The PEEC system was enhanced and expanded in 1989 to the 3176 midheavy series highway truck engine. The 3176 engine also adopted the use of electronically controlled unit fuel injectors, which operate similar to those found on Detroit Diesel engines in their DDEC system. Caterpillar had gained electronics experience through the adoption of various electronic components to their line of heavy equipment and crawler tractors, which feature an automatic fire suppression system. Cummins Engine Company has a CELECT (Cummins electronic engine control) available for their line of 14-L (855 in.³) six-cylinder and 10 L engines. Other companies committed to electronic control of their heavy-duty truck diesel engines include Mack Trucks, DAF Trucks, Saab-Scania, Volvo, Mercedes-Benz, and Robert Bosch Corporation and their Japanese counterpart Diesel Kiki, which together supply 60% of the injection pumps used on diesel engines worldwide. In addition, the Allison Transmission Division of GMC with their ATEC (Allison Transmission Electronic Controls) for their lineup of heavy-duty truck automatics, and both Voith and ZF with similar electronic systems for their transmissions, show that electronics is here to stay. Both Eaton Corporation (Fuller Roadranger Twin Countershaft Transmissions) and Scania with their CAGS (Computer-Assisted Gear Shift) have released electronically controlled gear shift systems for their respective lineups of heavy-duty gear-type transmissions. In the heavy-duty truck brake lineup, there are no fewer than seven major companies now offering new-generation ABS (anti-brake-skid) systems for trucks and semitrailers.

If you consider that in 1970, approximately $1.50 per vehicle went into electronic components, and that by the 1985 model year, this amount had leaped to approximately $350 per vehicle, spiralling upward to about $1400 per vehicle by the 1990 models, you can appreciate just how extensive the adoption of electronics components is in the passenger car market. In the midrange truck line, GMC has adopted gasoline fuel injection in its two gasoline engine offerings in 1990 model trucks as well as using electronics throughout the vehicle for control of various other components. In the heavy-duty truck line, all major OEMs (original equipment manufacturers) have adopted electronics technology throughout the vehicle for sensing and control of such items as diesel engine injection and governing, ABS, HVAC (heating, ventilation, and air conditioning), transmission control, cruise control, automatic engine idle shutdown, vehicle recording devices, instrumentation, cellular telephones, satellite navigation systems, suspension systems, tire pressure monitoring devices, and automatic control of trailer refrigeration systems (reefers). Today's truck mechanic/technician must have a solid grounding in the fundamentals of both electricity and electronics.

Typical electronics components now being used in both passenger cars and trucks are illustrated in Fig. 2–1 for a typical heavy-duty tractor and trailer. This illustration is used since there are few mechanics, whether they specialize in cars or truck/trailer repair, who do not own their own car and have an understanding of its operation and repair procedures. In this diagram the various transistors, diodes, ICs (integrated circuits), capacitors, thryristors, and other electronics devices are shown. Figure 2–2 shows examples of where these electronics components might be applied to a heavy-duty class 8

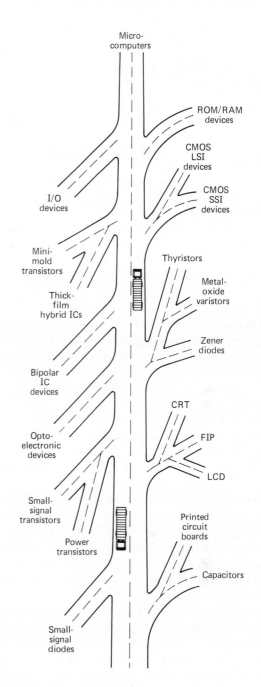

FIGURE 2–1 Typical electronic devices in use in passenger cars and trucks.

truck/tractor. Keep in mind that electronics componentry used on a car and a light (pickup) truck are the same basic design, with much midrange and heavy-duty truck components technology having been adapted from the passenger car and light truck market. Of course, in many cases the heavy truck component may be of heavier-duty design, but this is not true of all items. In addition, car components that have been designed for the 12-V battery-powered system can be applied equally to a car or a truck.

The word *electronics* refers to the design and use of devices and components that are totally dependent on the

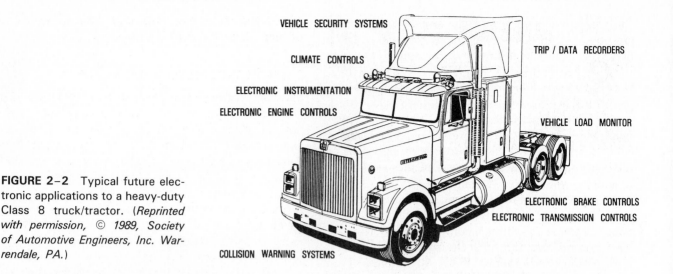

VEHICLE SECURITY SYSTEMS

CLIMATE CONTROLS

TRIP / DATA RECORDERS

ELECTRONIC INSTRUMENTATION

ELECTRONIC ENGINE CONTROLS

VEHICLE LOAD MONITOR

ELECTRONIC BRAKE CONTROLS
ELECTRONIC TRANSMISSION CONTROLS

COLLISION WARNING SYSTEMS

FIGURE 2-2 Typical future electronic applications to a heavy-duty Class 8 truck/tractor. (*Reprinted with permission, © 1989, Society of Automotive Engineers, Inc. Warrendale, PA.*)

conduction of electricity, not through the conventional copper wire as in the typical wiring in a car or truck, but rather through a vacuum, a gas, or what has now become known as a *semiconductor*. These electronic devices consist of solid, nonmoving parts capable of transmitting an electrical signal without the use of bulky devices such as tubes, relays, or mechanical switches. In addition, these solid-state devices can be a fraction of the size and weight of devices used in the past, still perform the same job as well, and do it considerably faster. Electronic devices are also much more compact, efficient, and reliable than their mechanical or semimechanical predecessors, and they have the capability to perform many more jobs within a single electrical/electronic system.

The term *solid-state* element was coined with the introduction of electrical systems that used devices such as transistors, diodes, conductors, and capacitors to form what is commonly called an integrated circuit, rather than the conventional copper-wire designed system. Automotive integrated-circuit use, although prevalent today, is not a recent development. As far back as the late 1950s, germanium transistor radios were being installed in passenger cars, while the mid-1970s saw the introduction of the on-board microprocessor or minicomputer, with the adoption of the early-stage gasoline fuel injection systems manufactured by Robert Bosch Corporation. Today, and on a worldwide basis, almost every manufacturer of gasoline engines in passenger cars employs a derivative fuel injection system produced by this corporation. In addition, the majority of domestic and foreign-built vehicles have microprocessor (computer-based) control systems that contain ICs for their base of operation.

Integrated circuits can contain as few as two or three to as many as several thousand electrical circuits that incorporate diodes, transistors, capacitors, resistors, and so on. These circuits are then assembled or built onto a silicon chip, an example of which is shown in a magnified state in Fig. 2-3. Note in this diagram that the electrodes are generally connected through gold-wire connections.

Each electrode serves a particular component of the chip. The silicon wafers shown being inspected in Fig. 2-3 contain a complete IC, which consists of diodes, transistors, and various logic gates. A transistor built onto such a silicon wafer might have a thickness of ½ mm (0.020 in.). All of the active parts of microelectronic devices are very near the surface of the wafer or chip, usually within the

FIGURE 2-3 Inspecting a silicon chip less than $\frac{1}{4}$ in. (6.35 mm) square through a magnifying glass. The chip contains more than 10,000 elements and is used in GMC passenger car and Detroit Diesel Corporation ECMs. (*Courtesy of Delco Electronics Corporation, Subsidiary of GM Hughes Electronics.*)

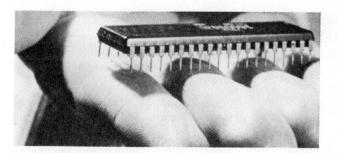

FIGURE 2-4 Assembled IC unit in its enclosed casing. (*Courtesy of Delco Electronics Corporation, Subsidiary of GM Hughes Electronics.*)

top 1 to 5 microns. A micron is a millionth of a meter, or stated as a decimal, 0.00003937 in.

Figure 2-4 illustrates a chip with its ICs assembled and encased in a plastic or ceramic holder assembly. A chip can be as small as a pinhead, with current designs including chips 1 cm (0.3937 in.) square and containing approximately 500,000 transistors. Future designs will provide up to 1 million transistors per chip.

To highlight the physical size of a silicon chip, Fig. 2-5 illustrates dramatically the phrase "as small as a pinhead." In this particular diagram we see a magnified needle and thread being used to show the relative size of a Delco Electronics microprocessor chip in a gasoline or diesel electronic engine control system. The chip, which is $\frac{2}{10}$ in. $\times$ $\frac{2}{10}$ in. or 5 mm square, is the heart of the ECM (electronic control module), which calls the signals for the fuel injection and exhaust emission control system. Delco Electronics engineers designed this chip to contain

FIGURE 2-5 Microprocessor chip shown alongside a needle and thread for size comparison. (*Courtesy of Delco Electronics Corporation, Subsidiary of GM Hughes Electronics.*)

10,000 elements, with the original design covering an area of more than 10 feet (0.929 meters) square.

STEPS IN PRODUCING A MICROCHIP

Since the electronic circuits now in use in passenger cars, heavy-duty trucks, and other types of equipment could not exist without silicon chips, it is interesting and important that you have some basic knowledge of just how these chips are manufactured. The microchip is so named because of its ability to shrink the basic building blocks of electronics—transistors, diodes, resistors, and wiring—to microscopic proportions. In addition, microprocessors (small on-board vehicle computers) require much less energy to perform the same functions carried out by non-solid-state devices.

The foundation of producing an integrated circuit containing transistors, diodes, and resistors begins with a simple grain of sand that has been reduced and purified into the element silicon. Silicon crystals are grown molecularly inside special furnaces through the process of carefully controlled temperature. These silicon crystals are produced in the general shape of a large sausage, similar to one you might see hanging in a local delicatessen. The sausage of silicon crystal can be anywhere from 2 to 6 in. (50.8 to 152.4 mm) in diameter and between 4 and 12 in. in length. It is then cut into thin round slices of nearly pure crystalline material, with the thickness of each slice generally being about 10 mils (0.01 in. or 0.254 mm). Each slice is generally referred to as a *wafer* of silicon.

Each slice is then ground and polished so that one side is as smooth as a mirror, and then the individual circuits are formed on these chip slices through the use of laser technology, which imprints (cuts) a matrix of rows and columns to form literally thousands of circuits on a single slice, as illustrated in Fig. 2-6. All of the components of the IC are formed at the same time by using photolithography (photographic printing) and diffusion, which is the process of modifying one material by combining it with another through the use of technology.

Once the individual circuits have been formed on the slice, the individual chips are cut from the silicon slice with either a diamond scribe or laser. Each chip is then mounted to a metallized frame for support and, more important, to provide a means of connecting the chip with its circuitry to other ICs in a large interconnecting system. To appreciate the intricate manufacturing process involved in producing a silicon wafer chip, consider that only several years ago the connecting lines on most silicon chips averaged 4 to 6 microns in width. By contrast, a human hair is about 50 microns in diameter or approximately 0.002 in. Current CMOS (complementary metal-oxide semiconductor) chips are now in the 1.5-micron (0.00006 in.) range. The smaller these junctions, the denser a chip can be and therefore the greater its operating efficiency. Current chips are made by either the MOS

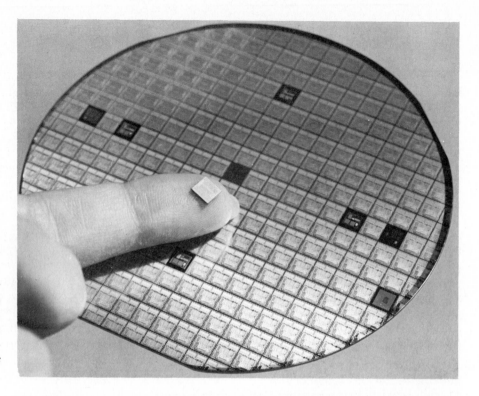

FIGURE 2–6 Microprocessor chip shown on a fingertip. (The chip was produced from a 3-in. (75-mm) wafer of silicon.) (*Courtesy of Delco Electronics Corporation, Subsidiary of GM Hughes Electronics.*)

(metal-oxide semiconductor) or CMOS process, although much research is under way to produce a chip from a gallium arsenide process, since this material is capable of operating at faster speeds than silicon chips.

The easiest way to picture this process is to list the steps required to produce the chip and integrate it into an electronic circuit. The following numerical listing systematically leads you through this manufacturing process.

1. The actual circuit that is desired on the chip must first be drawn by an engineer. Today, this is usually accomplished by creating a composite drawing of what is desired. This is done on a lighted or transparent drafting table, which is also known as a flatbed digitizing device; 35-mm slides are viewed on similar light tables.

2. A horizontal and vertical guide bar, which contains a cursor mechanism on the flatbed, can be slid up, down, and sideways by the person who is electronically tracing the prepared circuit drawing. During what is known as the *digitizing* process, when the cursor is centered over an element in the drawing, such as a transistor or diode, a button is pressed that enters this information and transfers it to the computer storage system.

3. When the complete drawing has been traced electronically, the entire circuit can be called up on the face of a computer screen (CRT or cathode ray tube), where it can be modified, if desired. This is done by use of an electronic light pen touched to the screen, or by typing in new commands to add, remove, or redirect the lines in the electronic circuit.

4. Prior to the actual manufacturing of the chip, the initial digitized circuit drawing is blown up (magnified) to as much as 500 or 600 times its original size on a backlighted transparent screen. Careful analysis is then made of the circuit to check for possible problems or mistakes. This large-scale duplication of the very tiny chip makes the job of designing much easier. This circuit reproduction or image can then be reduced or scaled down in size by a photographic process to the actual finished size of the desired chip. Once prepared, the circuit can then be duplicated several hundred times or more on the silicon wafer slice.

5. The chip is made from an ingot of silicon which is produced in a molten state, the end result being a shape similar to that of a large sausage. Both the diameter and the length of this ingot can vary, depending on the desired number of chips that are to be reproduced from a single slice.

6. Once the ingot has been produced, it is sliced into wafers, just as a delicatessen owner does when you ask for a pound of a certain type of sausage in slice form. One side of the chip is ground and polished to a mirror-like image.

7. The wafers are then immersed in a photoresist bath of liquid-type honey or emulsion that will harden when exposed to ultraviolet light.

8. Chip manufacturing is carried out in extremely sterile rooms, even more sterile than operating rooms in hospitals, because the smallest particles of dust or dirt would cause a malfunction of the chip. Once this emulsion-type liquid has hardened, a stencil-type mask that represents the previously drawn circuit is laid over each wafer slice and ultraviolet light is projected through this stencil. In this way, only the desired circuit receives the light and, because of the photoresist applied in step 7, hardens to form the desired circuitry. Since each wafer can be anywhere from 3 to 6 in. in diameter, the chip design is repeated hundreds of times on the surface area of the wafer during this process, just as sheets of stamps are printed. Each chip must be identical.

9. The areas of the wafer that are not exposed to this ultraviolet light will not harden. Therefore, the chip must be washed/rinsed to remove this nonhardened photoresist material. Since each chip is constructed to represent more than one circuit in a layered fashion, it is necessary to repeat this stencil/mask process from 5 to 20 times.

10. The completed chip is then inspected under a microscope in an inspection room that has subdued lighting (often called a yellow room because of the type of lighting) to ensure that no outside ultraviolet rays can enter the room during the inspection.

11. The individual chips are then cut from the wafer by a diamond-tipped die-cutting machine, although laser technology is sometimes used for this procedure.

12. Robots then connect minute wires between the chip and its metal carrier to allow electrical current to pass into and out of the chip circuitry.

13. One or more chips can be mounted to a circuit board to create the desired operating system, or the chip can be packaged as is for sale in a hermetically sealed and damage-proof package.

Improvements in fabrication techniques and device design now allow hundreds of transistors to be included in areas of a square millimeter. Circuits with more than 100,000 transistors are now conventionally fabricated for

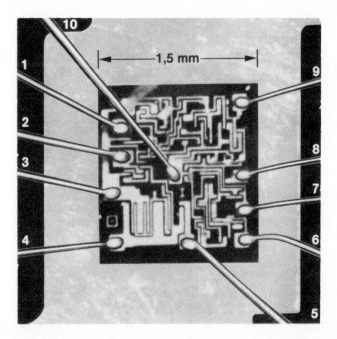

FIGURE 2–7 Magnification of an IC chip to 400 times actual size. (*Courtesy of Robert Bosch Corporation.*)

use in numerous applications. An integrated circuit is basically a silicon wafer or chip that has been doped, insulated, and etched many times so that an entire circuit can be contained within each tiny chip. The chips are then encased in insulated capsules for use in the electrical system of a vehicle or any other solid-state system. Figure 2–7 illustrates an IC for a passenger car hazard-warning

FIGURE 2–8 Schematic of the IC chip circuit for that shown in Fig. 2-7. (*Courtesy of Robert Bosch Corporation.*)

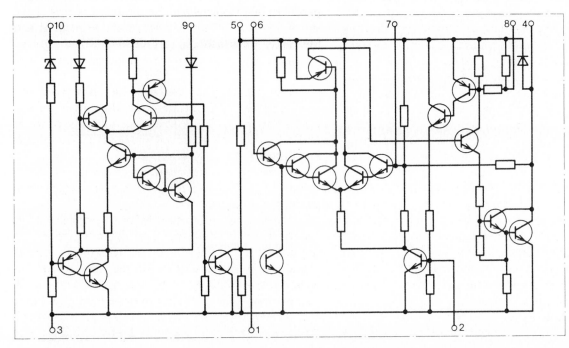

and turn-signal flasher shown 400 times its actual size, with the numbers 1 through 10 simply indicating the number of terminals connected to this IC. Figure 2-8 depicts the schematic for this IC.

The classification of ICs is generally based on the number of parts, elements, or logic gates included on the one chip. The designation is classified as follows:

1. *SSI* (small-scale integration), containing about 100 elements.

2. *MSI* (medium-scale integration), containing between 100 and 1000 elements.

3. *LSI* (large-scale integration), containing between 10,000 and 100,000 elements

4. *VLSI or ELSI* (very-large-scale integration or extra large), containing over 100,000 elements

Chips with 10,000 or more elements or logic gates, as they are known, translate into more than 32,000 bits of memory. Therefore, any LSI, VLSI, or ELSI chip provides the power of a microcomputer on a single chip. Chips presently under test have shown that they take only 210 trillionths of a second to complete a calculation in a central processing unit (CPU). However, current chips operate at speeds of between 16 and 47 billionths of a second. Recent developments at IBM have doubled the speed of silicon-based transistors to a frequency of 75 billion cycles a second.

Integrated circuits are classified as being of either analog or digital type. An *analog* IC is one that handles or processes a wave-like analog electrical signal, such as that produced by the human voice and similar to that shown on an ignition oscilloscope. An analog signal changes continuously and smoothly with time as shown in Fig. 2-9. Its output signal is proportionate to its input signal.

Digital signals, on the other hand, have a wavelength that is more rectangular in shape, as shown in Fig. 2-10. This is because these signals change intermittently with time, which means that they are either on or off. This is quite different from the analog operating mode. The general characteristic of operation of the digital circuit can best be explained by considering that when the input voltage signal rises to a predetermined level, the output signal is then triggered into action. For example, assume that a sensor is feeding a varying 5-V maximum reference

FIGURE 2-9   Analog wave signal shape.

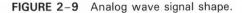

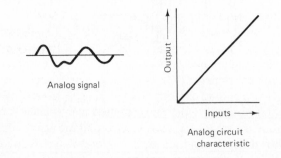

Analog signal

Analog circuit characteristic

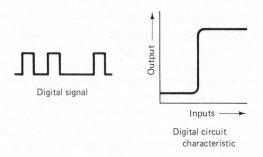

Digital signal

Digital circuit characteristic

FIGURE 2-10   Digital wave signal shape.

signal to a source such as a diode. In this condition, the output signal remains at zero until the actual input signal has climbed to its maximum value of 5 V.

This is why digital signals are classified as being either on or off. *On* means that a signal is being sent, and *off*, that a signal is not being sent. For convenience sake, in electronics technology, when a voltage signal is being sent (on), the numeral 1 is used. When no voltage signal is being set (off), it is indicated by the numeral 0. These numerals are used so that the computer can distinguish between an on and off voltage signal.

Figures 2-11 and 2-12 show how this numerical system operates. Since most sensors in use today in automotive applications are designed to operate on a 5-V reference signal, anything above this level is considered as being in an on or numeral 1 condition, while any voltage below this value is considered as an off or 0 numeral, since the voltage signal is too low to trigger a diode response. Digital systems consist of many numbers of identical logic gates and flip-flops, which are discussed in Chapter 11 in the section ''Logic Circuits.''

There are few home appliances, entertainment devices, children's toys, cars, trucks, and industrial machinery today that do not use solid-state devices to perform one or more functions. When these solid-state devices are combined to operate in a system, they are

FIGURE 2-11   Digital voltage signal in an ON and OFF mode; 5-V reference or trigger value.

FIGURE 2-12   Example of digital wave signal when voltage values are either above or below the standard voltage reference.

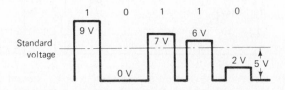

generally referred to as *integrated circuits*, with each doing a specific job in the overall successful performance of the designed unit, whether it be a microwave oven, a car or home stereo system, a wristwatch, an on-board vehicle computer, or a child's fancy toy.

Since 1980, the greatest growth of the solid-state or integrated circuit in vehicles has been in the adoption of electronically controlled gasoline and diesel (truck) fuel injection and distributorless ignition systems for passenger cars. Few car manufacturers today, whether domestic or foreign, do not use some form of solid-state device or minicomputer to achieve superior results from their automotive products. Heavy-duty on-highway trucks are now leaving the factory with minicomputers that perform a similar job for diesel fuel injection systems and engine and road-speed governing as is done for their gasoline counterparts. Perfect examples of this are the DDEC (Detroit Diesel Electronic Controls) system on Detroit Diesel Corporation engines as well as that employed by GMC on their Allison Automatic transmissions, the ATEC (Allison Transmission Electronic Controls) for both on- and off-highway equipment. Both Caterpillar with its 3406B PEEC (Programmable Electronic Engine Control), and 3176 electronic unit injected, and Cummins diesel engines with its Pace and ECI (CELECT) system have joined DDC with similar heavy-duty electronically controlled fuel injection systems.

Many passenger cars and trucks are now leaving the factory with digital instrument clusters rather than the long-used conventional analog system. Many of the electronic circuits in a car interact with one another and provide feedback to engine control functions or to other systems based on signals received from other operating sensors.

BASIC ELECTRONIC CONTROL DEVICES

We begin our discussion of basic electronic devices by considering the semiconductor. The fundamental operating principle of the semiconductor was discovered in 1948, and from this basic discovery sprang the modern world of electronics. *Semiconductors* are devices that have no moving mechanical parts; however, electricity can flow through them. Although capable of conducting electricity, the semiconductor is a material that will not do so as readily as that of copper or iron—two materials that are used extensively in a conventional electrical system. The resistance of the semiconductor, although higher than that of copper (nonferrous metal) and iron (ferrous metal), is lower than that of such insulators as glass or rubber, which are poor conductors of electricity. Typical resistances of various components used in automobile electrical circuits are shown in Fig. 2–13.

From our discussion in Chapter 1 dealing with basic electricity, you will recall that a conductor allows electricity to flow through it with a minimum amount of resistance, while an insulator is designed to prevent the

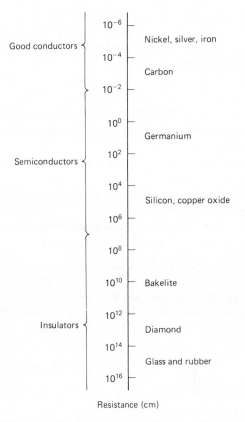

FIGURE 2–13 Typical resistances of various automotive electrical components.

free flow of electrons (electricity) through it. A semiconductor has the following properties:

1. Its electrical resistance will change with an increase in temperature.
2. Its ability to conduct electricity will rise when it is mixed with certain other substances.
3. When struck by light, the semiconductor's resistance changes greatly, and it will give off or emit light when an electrical current is passed through it.

You may remember from Chapter 1 that all matter is composed of atoms. The atom is the smallest particle into which an element can be decomposed. Any element that has fewer than four electrons (negative charge of electricity) contained within its outer valence (ring) is a good conductor of electricity; any element that contains more than four electrons in its outer ring is a poor conductor of electricity. In any element, the number of electrons in the valence ring is never greater than eight.

Two elements that have four valence ring electrons are silicon and germanium. However, since the mid-1970s, silicon has been the most widely used semiconductor material. The electrons in the valence ring of one silicon atom join with the outer ring electrons of other silicon atoms when they are combined in crystalline form, so that the atoms will share electrons in the valence ring. With this combination, we have each atom effectively sharing eight electrons, which causes the material to be an excellent insulator since any element that contains more than four electrons in its outer ring is a poor conductor of electricity.

By adding a mixture of other materials to the silicon crystal, the new material comes to possess different electrical properties. In fact, the material is no longer a good insulator and is commonly said to have been *doped*. The elements that are used most widely to dope the silicon crystal are phosphorus and antimony, which both contain five electrons in their valence ring.

Combining the phosphorus with silicon creates a condition known as *covalent bonding*. The electron left over is commonly referred to as a *free electron*, and it can be triggered into moving through the material quite easily.

NOTE: Any material that contains a free electron or excess of electrons is referred to as a *negative* or N-type material doped with arsenic (As) or antimony (Sb).

Boron and indium can also be used to dope the silicon crystal, since these two additional elements contain only three electrons in their valence ring. The addition of these various materials to the silicon crystal in extremely small quantities can produce a wide variety of results in the finished product. Adding the material boron to the silicon will produce covalent bonding, which simply means that the final material will possess properties that neither of the original materials possessed alone. This is similar to alloying metals to produce stainless steel, high-carbon steel, and so on.

The boron additive to the silicon results in a deficiency of one electron (negative charge), which creates a hole that can be considered to a positive charge of electricity or a P-type of material, doped with gallium (Ga) or indium (In).

Doping material added to the silicon semiconductor can be as little as 1 part doped material to 10 million parts of the silicon crystal. Another interesting feature is that the silicon crystal is refined to a state of purity that contains only a few parts of impure material to over 1 billion parts of pure crystal. Electricity can be made to flow through semiconductors in the same basic way that electricity is made to flow through a copper wire. This action was described in Chapter 1 in the section, "Electron Flow in a Copper Wire."

In summary, a semiconductor such as silicon falls between that of a good conductor and a good insulator. The most widely used materials from which high-speed semiconductors are manufactured today is silicon, to which has been added such other materials as phosphorus, antimony, boron, and indium. When phosphorus is added, the doped material is commonly called an N-type substance; if doped with boron, it is called a P-type substance, with N denoting negative and P denoting positive. Both the N- and P-type substances have a lower resistance than that of the associated pure substances.

CURRENT FLOW AND SEMICONDUCTORS

Applying battery voltage to an N or P semiconductor is commonly known as *biasing*. If the positive battery terminal is connected to the P-side (anode) of the semiconductor and the negative side to the N-type (cathode), this is known as *forward biasing*, with most diodes having a forward resistance of 5 to 10 Ω.

If the positive battery terminal is connected to the N-side (cathode) of the semiconductor and the negative side to the P-type (anode), this is known as *reverse biasing*. Diodes are excellent insulators when reverse biased, having a resistance of 1 million ohms or more. A more detailed description of this action is described in later sections of this chapter.

Because of this feature of the semiconductor, too much forward or reverse voltage and current can completely destroy any diode. This is one of the reasons that diodes in an alternator can be severely damaged if a battery is hooked up backwards (reverse polarity), or if high voltage from a battery charger is applied to a battery without disconnecting it from the vehicle electrical system. Therefore, diodes operate as one-way check valves in an electrical system by allowing flow in one direction but not in the other.

NOTE: Although a solid-state diode is similar to a transistor in general makeup, the diode does not provide any gain (voltage greater than its input). Transistors, on the other hand, are active elements, since they can amplify or transform an input signal level.

DIODES

A diode is a two-terminal electrical device that contains two electrodes; one electrode, known as the *anode* is constructed from a P-type semiconductor material; the other electrode, commonly called the *cathode*, is constructed from an N-type semiconductor. The junction that is formed between the anode and cathode results in the solid-state device known as a *diode*. When conventional current flow (positive to negative) is applied to the diode, the P electrode (anode) is + and the N electrode (cathode) is −.

Figure 2–14 is a simplified example of an N and P semiconductor diode, showing the change in the actual

FIGURE 2–14 Semiconductor diode showing (a) low and (b) high resistance.

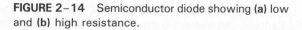
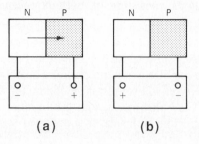

(a)   (b)

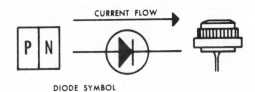

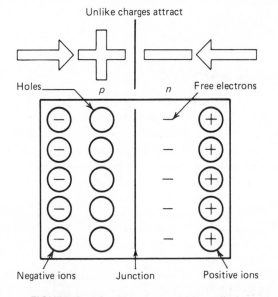

FIGURE 2-15 Typical semiconductor diode symbol. (*Courtesy of Delco-Remy Division, General Motors Corporation.*)

FIGURE 2-16 Electrons within a diode.

junction resistance with respect to the voltage polarity used. On the left-hand side of the diagram (A), the forward-biased NP junction exhibits a low resistance value. The right-hand side of the diagram (B) shows a reverse-biased PN junction that exhibits a high resistance value. If the same current value is made to cross both the left- and right-hand junctions, this results in a voltage gain or current amplification, due to the voltage being equal to the product of the current and resistance.

A diode is similar to a one-way resistor or current check valve in that it is a device that passes electric current in one direction but blocks or restricts current flow in the other direction. The diode is used extensively in many fields of electronics; however, in automobiles, trucks, and heavy-duty equipment, it can be used specifically to change alternating current to direct current. The classic example of the use of the diode is in the battery-charging alternator, in which six diodes (three positive and three negative) are used to handle the alternating current that is developed in the three-phase stator windings, so that current can only flow to the battery in the direction to charge it. Any reversal of battery current is blocked or prevented by the diodes.

The diode allows electrons to flow from its cathode to its anode terminal, as shown in Fig. 2-15. Flow through a diode is always indicated by an arrowhead symbol. The diode is actually made up of two sections of material, with one of the semiconductor materials formed into an N (negative) material, while the other part represents the P (positive) material. These two sections of material form a junction of P- and N-type substance that are structurally integral, as shown in Fig. 2-15.

Diode Operation

If we consider the basic principle that unlike charges attract while like charges repel, the structural components of the diode consisting of both N (negative) and P (positive) materials would be attracted to one another. Figure 2-16 shows what actually happens within the diode.

In Fig. 2-16, an attraction exists between the free electrons (negatively charged) and the holes (positively charged); however, as the electrons drift toward the junction area at the center of the diode, they leave behind charged particles called positive ions, which are atoms

having a deficiency of electrons. Similarly, the holes (positive) leave behind negative ions which exert an attractive force on the remaining holes to prevent them from crossing the junction, because the positive ions exert an attractive force on the remaining free electrons to prevent additional electrons from crossing the junction. The end result is that a stabilized condition with a deficiency of both electrons and holes occurs at the junction area.

The condition that would exist in the diode if a battery were connected to it is shown in Fig. 2-17. In Fig. 2-17(a) the negative battery voltage tends to repel the electrons in the N material, while the positive battery voltage will repel the holes in the P material. This condition will therefore produce current flow from the negative to the positive battery terminal and is known as a *forward-biased connection*. Current is allowed to flow forward when the amount of voltage applied in the forward direction exceeds a given threshold value. This value is commonly referred to as the *diode forward direction voltage drop*, which is approximately 0.7 V for silicon diodes and

FIGURE 2-17(a) Diode condition when forward biased. (*Courtesy of Delco Remy, Division of General Motors Corporation.*)

(a)

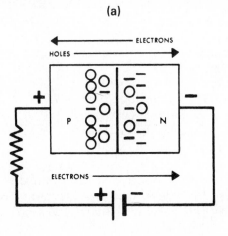

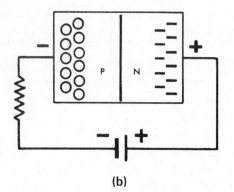

(b)

FIGURE 2-17(b) Diode condition when reverse biased.

about 0.3 V for germanium diodes. A typical voltage-current operating characteristic curve for a diode is illustrated in Fig. 2-18(a).

In Fig. 2-17(b), if the battery connections are reversed, the positive battery terminal will attract the electrons away from the junction area in the N-type material, while the negative battery terminal will attract the holes away from the junction area of the P material. This arrangement produces no current flow, since a very high resistance is created at the junction area. The diode is

FIGURE 2-18 **(a)** Voltage–current characteristics of a diode; **(b)** diode transfer characteristic.

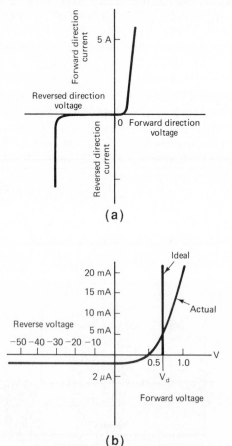

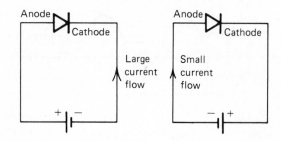

FIGURE 2-19 Battery connected to a diode junction.

therefore blocking current flow, and this configuration is commonly called a *reverse-biased connection*.

To clarify this arrangement, let's look at Fig. 2-19. When a battery is connected across the diode in forward polarity, a large amount of current will flow. Reversing the battery leads to the diode allows a very small or nearly zero amount of current flow. If an ohmmeter is placed across a diode, the measured forward resistance value will be very much smaller than the reverse value. Should this not be the case, the diode is defective. Silicon diodes have a higher forward resistance value than those of germanium diodes.

A good example of the use of a diode is in a circuit that requires some form of rectification, with a very common circuit being called a *half-wave rectification system*, since it is designed to effectively cut the ac (alternating current) waveform in half. Figure 2-20 illustrates a simplified diode rectifier circuit where ac voltage is applied between points *A* and *B*. This action can best be represented by reference to Fig. 2-21, where both ac voltage and current waveforms are shown. The *a–b* and *c–d* waveforms will be added as forward direction voltage with respect to the diode, while the *b–c* waveform will be added as reverse direction voltage, resulting in only one-half cycle of current flow to resistor *R*, which is shown in the system schematic of Fig. 2-20. The half-wave rectifier circuit is therefore used to convert an ac voltage that rises above and below zero volts into a dc (direct current) voltage, which remains either above or below zero volts depending on which way the diode is installed into the circuit. This half-wave rectification circuit shown is typical of the basic operation of ac voltage conversion to dc voltage in an automotive/truck alternator to provide dc current to charge the battery.

FIGURE 2-20 Example of a simplified diode rectifier circuit.

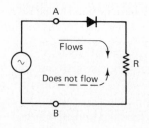

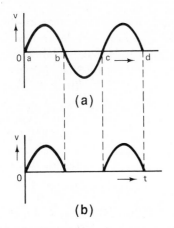

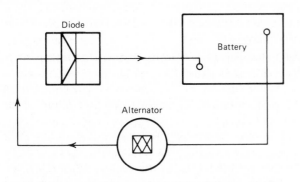

FIGURE 2–21 Ac voltage and current waveforms.

FIGURE 2–22 Diode placement to prevent a reversal of current flow.

Diode Designs

Typical diodes used in automotive applications are listed in Fig. 2–1. Some diodes are designed for higher voltages and currents than are others. Therefore, when replacing a faulty diode, use the correct type. Excessive heat or mechanical stress can damage a diode. An example of diode placement is the diode pressed into the metal end frame of the alternator housing to allow dissipation of heat from the diode. This area is called a *heat sink*.

In any electrical conductor, moisture can create serious problems. Therefore, a desiccant material is used inside a diode housing to absorb moisture. The glass seal around the diode stem prevents the entry of moisture. Diodes can be damaged if reverse-polarity connections are made to them.

A typical example of the placement of a diode in an oversimplified alternator charging system is shown in Fig. 2–22.

Should the battery polarity be reversed, a small current can flow through the diode. However, this reverse current, if high enough, will break down the covalent bond structure of the diode, and a sharp increase in the reverse current will occur, which will overheat the diode and burn it out. Normally, the diodes selected for operation in any given situation are capable of handling an ade-

quate reverse voltage, so that normally this condition will not occur during operation. Attempting to polarize an alternator or reversing the battery leads usually succeeds in burning out the diodes within the alternator.

ZENER DIODES

Another type of special diode that is widely used in electronic ignition systems as well as in many other areas of vehicle electric systems is the *zener diode*. The main function of this type of diode is to provide protection for standard diodes in a circuit when reverse current and voltage exist. Although the zener diode can conduct current in a reverse direction, it will do so only when a predetermined reverse bias voltage is obtained. For example, the zener diode used in a particular electronic circuit may have a threshold as high as 100 V in an electronic ignition system before it will actually allow this reverse-biased voltage to conduct. When the contact breaker points open, the zener diode provides an escape route for the kickback energy that occurs so that the collector junction of the transistor used in the ignition system is not damaged. At any voltage below a given value for the particular zener diode being used, no current can flow when reverse-biased voltage occurs.

Another common use for the zener diode is in the control of the electronic voltage regulator in most heavy-duty alternators. The zener diode activates transistors that shut off current to the field winding of the rotor to effectively reduce the alternator voltage output. As soon as the output voltage falls below the trigger value of the zener diode, it will no longer conduct the reverse current. This allows deactivation of alternator transistors, which will again let battery current flow through a brush to the slip ring and field winding of the rotor, and as a result alternator output again rises. Figure 2–23 shows the symbol and action of a typical zener diode.

Figure 2–23 illustrates that the diode will remain in the off position when the applied voltage is less than the conduction voltage of the diode, in this instance less than 10 V. As the voltage increases to 10 V, a very high resistance builds up until a critical voltage known as the zener, or operating, voltage is reached. When 10 V is present in this particular example, the diode will conduct and act like a very low resistance or closed switch. At approximately 10.2 V, the diode is in full conduction, or turned on.

FIGURE 2–23 Zener diode symbol and operation.

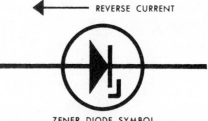

TRANSISTORS

The transistor is probably the most important semiconductor device in the electronic circuit, because current can be amplified and switched on and off through the transistor. The word *transistor* basically is a combination of two words, *transfer* and *resist*. A transistor is used to control current flow in a circuit. It can be used to control a predetermined flow of current in the circuit and can also be used to resist this flow; in so doing, circuit current is controlled.

Transistors are used at junction points in the electrical system and therefore are often referred to as *junction transistors*. The transistor can be made from germanium or silicon material with N and P substances sandwiched together, as shown in Fig. 2–24. In the transistor symbol shown in the figure, *B* represents the base, which is normally indentified by a thick or heavy solid line; *E* is the emitter, which is the line with the arrow; and *C* is the collector, which is always shown simply as a straight line. The arrow (emitter) is shown as pointing in the direction of conventional current flow, which is accepted as being from positive (+) to negative (−) in the external circuitry.

Current flow in a PNP transistor is generally considered to be the movement of holes (positive charge), while in the NPN transistor, the current flow is considered to be a movement of electrons (negative charge). Based on this theory, the electrons move against the emitter arrow in the NPN transistor since it is easier to picture the flow of electrons as being sent out by the emitter into the transistor base and collector. This is explained below in the section "Transistor Operation."

Figure 2–24 shows that two types of transistors are

FIGURE 2–24 (a) PNP transistor structure; (b) NPN transistor structure.

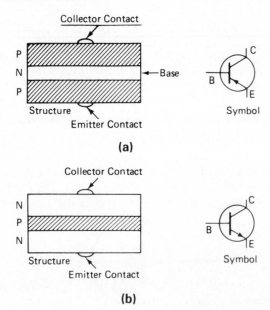

(a)

(b)

readily available for use in electronic systems, PNP or the NPN type. In automotive electronics, the PNP type is more commonly used than the NPN type. It is important that you remember this fact, because a PNP transistor cannot be replaced with an NPN transistor, for example, in an electronic ignition system. As shown, the transition regions between N- and P-type substances are called the *collector–base junction* and the *emitter–base junction,* respectively. When these two transistors are connected into a circuit, either an N- or a P-type will operate as an amplifier or as an electronic switch.

Transistors used in automotive electrical systems are generally classified as either a signal type or a power type. The major difference is that the signal type operates with an input voltage up to 10 mV, whereas the power transistor functions with an input voltage greater than 10 mV.

Transistor Operation

As mentioned earlier in the chapter, the transistor can be operated as either an amplifier or a switch. The actual construction of the transistor accounts for this unusual operating characteristic. By controlling the base current, a much greater collector current can also be controlled. The easiest way to follow what actually occurs within the transistor is to refer to Fig. 2–25.

In an NPN transistor, the emitter (*E*) conducts current flow to the collector (*C*) only when the base (*B*) and collector (*C*) are positive with respect to the emitter. The transistor, however, cannot conduct until the base voltage exceeds the emitter voltage by approximately 0.4 V for germanium transistors, and approximately 0.7 V for silicon transistors.

In the PNP transistor shown in Fig. 2–25(b), the emitter (*E*) current will flow to the collector (*C*) only when the base (*B*) and collector are negative with respect to the emitter. For example, when the transistor is used in a voltage regulator, it functions as a switching device when the collector (*C*) current is allowed to flow. The transistor will then become saturated and its emitter–collector voltage drops to a very low value. In this condition, the transistor is operating similar to a closed switch (transistor is on) or in a low-resistance state. When collector current is cut off, the transistor appears as an open switch (transistor is off) due to the high resistance within it [see Fig. 2–25(b)].

In Fig. 2–26 we have oversimplified a circuit with a transistor placed in it. With battery power connected to a PNP transistor, current will flow through the emitter-base junction of the transistor, because the switch connected to the transistor base is closed. Current will also flow through the collector circuit, where it will meet or join with the current flow leaving the base circuit switch, where the current then returns to the battery to complete the path of flow of circuit path.

For simplicity, let's assume that the transistor in the

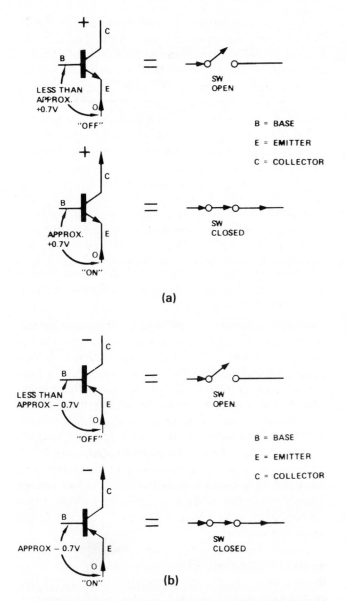

FIGURE 2-25 **(a)** NPN transistor action; **(b)** PNP transistor action. (*Courtesy of Motorola Automotive and Industrial Electronics Group.*)

FIGURE 2-26 Simplified transistor circuit flow. (*Courtesy of Delco Electronics Corporation, Subsidiary of GM Hughes Electronics.*)

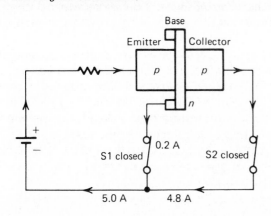

example has an emitter–base current of 3 A. With both switches closed, you might assume, and rightly so, that the current flow through both switches would be the same. It is not! The reason for unequal current flow through both switches is due to the physical arrangement of the component parts of the transistor, which includes the emitter, the base ring, and the collector. The emitter and the collector are closer together than the emitter and the base ring. Because of this placement, the holes (positive charge) injected into the transistor base from the emitter will travel into the collector because of their velocity (speed and direction). This movement is further assisted by the negative potential at the right-hand side of the collector, which will attract the positive holes from the transistor base into the collector. The resultant action might produce a current flow of 2.8 A through the collector switch, with the remaining 0.2 A passing through the base switch. The exact values that will flow through any transistor will vary based on the specific type and size of transistor used as well as the circuit design. The collector current in this example would be 14 times that of the base current. This is one of the unusual operating characteristics of a transistor.

Another condition possible in this same circuit would be caused by opening the switch connected to the collector while leaving the switch to the base closed. The result would be that we would have a current of 3 A through this circuit only. One other phenomenon of the transistor would be to open the switch connected to the base while closing the switch to the collector. Again, you would anticipate that the current flow through the closed switch should be that of the circuit, 3 A. However, no appreciable current will flow under this condition because with the base circuit switch open, there are no holes (positive charged) being injected into the base from the emitter. Subsequently, the negative battery potential cannot attract nonexistent holes in the base into the collector. In addition, the base–collector junction undergoes a very high resistance condition due to the negative battery potential at the collector, attracting the holes (positive charged) in the collector away from the base–collector junction, preventing further current flow.

The operation of an NPN transistor is the same as that for a PNP; however, the current flow consists of electron (negative charge) movement from the emitter to the base and collector. The examples given in Fig. 2-26 showed that the transistor can be operated in the amplifier condition, such as when both switches were closed. We were able to increase the bias current flow in the base–emitter circuit by stepping it up in the collector–emitter circuit. Our example showed a base current of 0.2 A stepped up to 2.8 A in the collector circuit, for a current gain or amplification of 14 times. When the collector switch was closed and the base switch was opened, no flow was apparent in the circuit. The transistor acted as a switch to prevent a flow of current through the circuit.

Application of the Transistor

Let's see if we can put into practice the examples discussed in Fig. 2-26 by applying the same transistor principles to a voltage regulator used with a generator or alternator arrangement, as shown in Fig. 2-27. The purpose of any voltage regulator is exactly what the name implies—to regulate the maximum voltage output of the charging system. It accomplishes this by automatically opening and closing the current flow to the generator field windings so that the output decreases or stops until the battery or accessories require additional charging or electrical energy.

When the generator voltage reaches a preset level (adjustable), magnetism developed in the core of the voltage regulator shunt winding will pull apart the regulator points directly above it against light spring pressure. When the contact points separate (see Fig. 2-26), there will be no current at the transistor base. Therefore, no collector current can flow either. This action causes the transistor to cut off or stop any current flow to the generator field windings and automatically reduces the generator output.

Immediately after this occurs, the magnetic field of the shunt winding decreases and spring pressure pulls the contact points together again. This action is similar to closing a switch, and field current will again flow to the generator field windings, again allowing the generator to produce its maximum value. This action of the points opening and closing can occur 10 times a second or several thousand times a second, depending on conditions. With this type of transistorized regulator, minimal current exists at the contact points, which ensures a much longer point life.

Current model votage regulators do not use vibrating contact points to control the generator output. This type of regulator is similar in action to the one shown in Fig. 2-26. If the switch to the base circuit is opened, although we keep the switch to the collector closed, no current flows in the circuit because of the design of the transistor. Figure 2-28 shows this type of voltage regulator arrangement.

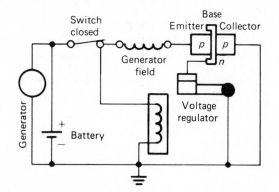

FIGURE 2-27 Basic transistor regulator action. (*Courtesy of Delco Electronics Corporation, Subsidiary of GM Hughes Electronics.*)

Here other diodes can be used to alternately impress both a forward or reverse bias across the emitter–base of the transistor shown (a PNP type). Anytime that a forward bias is present, the transistor will conduct current through the collector to the generator field windings to allow generation of voltage and current flow to the accessories and battery circuit.

When a reverse bias is impressed across the emitter–base of the transistor (similar to opening the switch at the base circuit as was explained in Fig. 2-26), no current flows in the collector to the generator field winding. Therefore, the output of the generator drops off. When a minimum value is reached, the transistor is triggered to a forward-biased condition again, which allows restoration of the field current, and the generator produces current once more.

BIPOLAR TRANSISTORS

Digital ICs (integrated circuits) can be divided into bipolar ICs and MOS (metal-oxide semiconductors) on the basis of the differences in their transistors. The operation of a *bipolar* transistor is dependent on the polarized charge of both its electrons and its holes; the MOS transistor is operated by either the electrons or the holes and can

FIGURE 2-28 Noncontract point transistorized regulator arrangement. (*Courtesy of Delco Electronics Corporation, Subsidiary of GM Hughes Electronics.*)

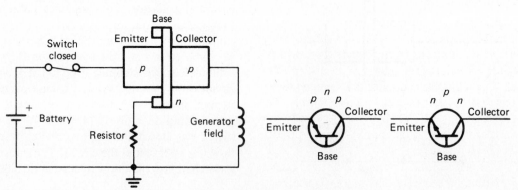

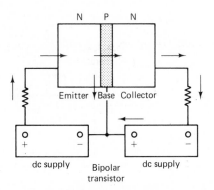

FIGURE 2-29 Bipolar transistor arrangement. (*Reprinted with permission, © 1990 Society of Automotive Engineers, Inc.; Warrendale, PA.*)

be referred to as a *unipolar* transistor to distinguish it from the bipolar unit. Bipolar transistors are controlled by current flow, while MOS transistors can be controlled by voltage; therefore, MOS units are sometimes referred to as FETs (field-effect transistors). Generally, bipolar transistors operate at higher speeds than do MOS ICs, but they tend to consume more power.

Figure 2-29 illustrates an NPN bipolar transistor which appears as though two diodes have been connected back to back. However, the P material forms a very thin surface between the two N materials. In this diagram the NP junction on the left-hand side is forward biased to allow the current that is applied to be associated with a low resistance across the junction interface. However, the right-hand side of the diagram, which shows the PN junction, is reverse-biased and will exhibit a high resistance at the PN junction interface. Due to the fact that the electrons flowing around the left-hand circuit have considerable momentum and energy, most will flow across the high-resistance PN junction. This means that the potential energy at the first junction will be the product of its current and the low resistance value, resulting in a fairly small potential. At the PN junction, however, the potential energy is the product of this current value, but with a much higher resistance, causing its voltage to be much higher. Therefore, the gain in voltage and power is due to amplification.

TRANSISTOR AMPLIFIERS

Electrical and electronic automotive solid-state systems, which now make extensive use of silicon diodes and transistors, require some means of multiplying or amplifying the low current values produced in these devices. The widely used silicon bipolar transistor is a semiconductor device with amplification caused by current gain. The *maximum available gain* (MAG) is theoretically the highest transducer power gain that the transistor can deliver at a given frequency.

Simple frequency can be considered as the number of complete cycles per second of an alternating current,

such as the 60 cycles per second used in all electrical devices in homes in North America. In other countries of the world, the frequency for home electrical devices is often only 50 cycles (design factor only). In a transistor, for example, it is the natural frequency of free oscillations of the sensing element of a fully assembled transducer. The resonant frequency of the element is the measured frequency as a transducer responds with maximum output amplitude. The advantages that silicon bipolar transistors have over other transistor types are mature technology, low cost, and proven reliability.

In solid-state electronic circuits and because of the low-current flow design of the diodes and transistors used in a circuit, it is often necessary to increase the output current signal in order to activate the end accessory (load). This accessory can be any component requiring current to cause it to output its desired characteristic. One such example is an idle air-control valve used on gasoline fuel injected engines, that is incremented while the engine runs at idle speed so that a predetermined air/fuel ratio figure can be maintained.

The transistor or operational amplifier is designed to increase the power level of the input signal to a predetermined output that will successfully handle the necessary load on the circuit. An operational amplifier in a standard analog circuit can have a very high voltage gain, of 10,000 or more. An example of how operational amplifiers are adapted to automotive solid-state circuits can be seen in Fig. 2-30. In Fig. 2-30(a), the operational amplifier is arranged so that it has two inputs and one output. Any signal applied to the inverting input ($-$) is therefore amplified and subsequently inverted at the output. Any signal that is applied to the noninverting input ($+$) is amplified, but it is *not* inverted at the output.

The percentage of actual gain from any operational transistorized amplifier can be adjusted/controlled by the actual ratio of the two resistors. The amplifier is not normally operated at maximum gain, but is tailored for a specific systems circuit. This action can best be described by referring to Fig. 2-30(b), where the percentage of gain can be calculated by the formula

$$A_v = \frac{-R_f}{R_i} = \frac{V_{out}}{V_{in}}$$

By applying the input signal to the ($-$) terminal of the inverting amplifier, the minus sign in the formula indicates that the signal is inverted from the input to the

FIGURE 2-30 Typical arrangement of automotive operational amplifiers: **(a)** schematic symbol.

(a)

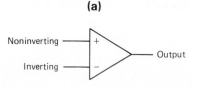

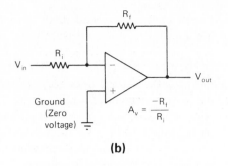

$$A_v = \frac{-R_f}{R_i}$$

(b)

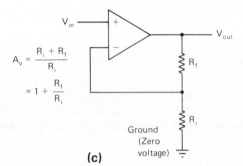

$$A_v = \frac{R_i + R_f}{R_i}$$

$$= 1 + \frac{R_f}{R_i}$$

(c)

FIGURE 2–30 (*cont.*) **(b)** Inverting amplifier; **(c)** noninverting amplifier.

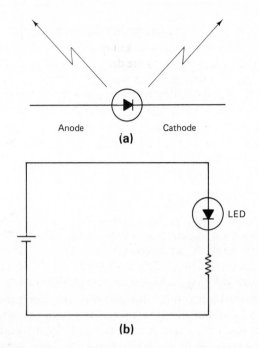

FIGURE 2–31 **(a)** LED (light emitting diode) graphical symbol; **(b)** typical placement of a LED in a basic electronic circuit).

output. In other words, if the input is positive, the output will be negative. Since an operational amplifier increases (gains) the voltage difference between its two inputs, it is possible to select the op amp's capability as either a differential amplifier or a single-value output.

A third option open to us from an op amp is the capability of using it as a noninverting amplifier, as illustrated in Fig. 2–30(c). In this option, the input signal is connected to the noninverting ($+$) terminal, while the output is fed back through a "series" connection of resistors to the inverting ($-$) terminal. This action results in gain A_v through the op amp as shown by the formula

$$A_v = \frac{V_{\text{out}}}{V_{\text{in}}} = 1 + \frac{R_f}{R_i}$$

In addition to adjusting output gain, this negative feedback signal can also assist in correcting the amplifier's tendency for nonlinear operation as well as the distortion of the signal. This distortion occurs as a result of the increased noise from a stronger signal which is added to the desired signal, as well as from the distortion of the input signal. The end result is that the amplified output waveform will appear slightly different than the input waveform. Depending on the desired rate of signal amplification, the frequency of the input signal, and various other conditions, such as heat effects, the output characteristics of the amplifier will change.

LIGHT-EMITTING DIODES

The *light-emitting diode* (LED) is used extensively in vehicle electric systems for a variety of functions. The LED

has a PN-junction diode that radiates both light and heat rays when it is subjected to an electric current in the forward direction. The typical symbol used for an LED is shown in Fig. 2–31.

LEDs have three distinct advantages when used as a light bulb:

1. Low power consumption
2. Operate at lower voltages (about 3 V) than that of a standard light bulb
3. Because of the operating characteristics listed in (1) and (2), operate at a cooler temperature than an ordinary light bulb and therefore exhibit longer overall bulb life

LEDs are available in a variety of colors, the three common colors being high-efficiency red, yellow, and high-performance green. The red and yellow LEDs are

FIGURE 2–32 LED bulb arrangement.

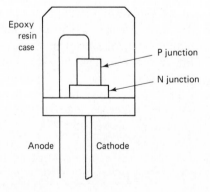

gallium arsenide phosphide on gallium phosphide diodes, while the green device is a gallium phosphide diode. These rugged solid-state lamps are designed for applications requiring a bright, compact source of light with uniform light output, wide viewing angle, and a flat top that makes the lamp ideal for flush mounting on a front panel. Figure 2–31(b) illustrates in simplified form how a simple LED would appear in a circuit, and Fig. 2–32 shows the basic makeup of a LED.

PHOTODIODES

A typical junction *photodiode* is shown in Fig. 2–33. A photodiode functions as a switch when it is actuated by a light beam. If a predetermined reverse-biased voltage is applied to it and a light is shone on the diode, reverse current will flow, with the amperage of the current being inversely proportional to the amount of light directed onto the diode. However, the photodiode will not conduct electric current in the reverse direction while the diode is in the dark. When exposed to light, the diode no longer blocks current flow. Therefore, the light triggers the diode and it operates as a switch. These types of diodes can be used as basic elements in breakerless (solid-state) ignition systems or to control the operation of an automatic air conditioner in direct response to the amount and intensity of the daylight.

PHOTOCONDUCTIVE CELLS

Somewhat similar to the photodiode, when exposed to light, the *photoconductive cell* will exhibit a resistance change. An example of such a device, illustrated in Fig. 2–34, consists of a cadmium sulfide (CdS) photocell designed to act as a variable resistor based on the degree of light to which it is exposed. Because of such a feature, this device is commonly used to turn the vehicle headlights on and off automatically in response to changing light patterns during the day or evening. By allowing light to strike the CdS element, voltage applied to its electrodes will cause the amperage requirement to change in response to the resistance that is controlled by the degree of light.

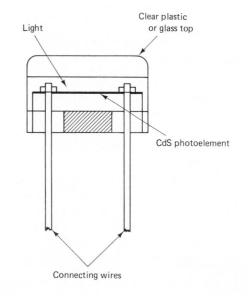

FIGURE 2–34 Photoconductive cell arrangement.

PHOTOTRANSISTORS

A *phototransistor* operates in proportion to the degree of light to which it is exposed, with this light being converted into an electrical current. This device is commonly used to monitor either vehicle or engine speed in conjunction with an LED (light-emitting diode), as shown in Fig. 2–35. When it is employed in this fashion, it is often referred to as a photocoupler, as shown in Fig. 2–34.

In Fig. 2–35, which illustrates the arrangement for an optical crankshaft position sensor, the sensor is capable of sensing static position, and it can have constant output with speed. A disadvantage of these types of optical sensor in automotive applications is that when used in an external environment such as an engine compartment, they are difficult to protect from dirt and possi-

FIGURE 2–35 Arrangement of an optical crankshaft position sensor. (*Reprinted with permission, © 1990 Society of Automotive Engineers, Inc. Warrendale, PA.*)

FIGURE 2–33 Photodiode concept.

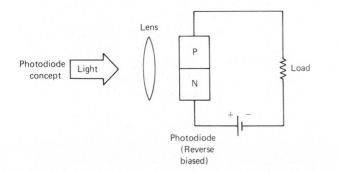

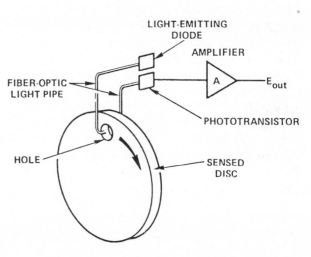

ble engine oil accumulations. To operate they require a light source, a photodetector, and a preamplifier integral to the sensor.

In Fig. 2–35 a fiber optic light tube/pipe is used to reflect the light source to the phototransistor, thereby allowing remote mounting capability. Rotation of the crankshaft continually makes and breaks the beam of light passing between the LED and the phototransistor. The net effect is that the transistor will be alternately turned on and off by this action, with the speed of engine rotation controlling this switching effect. Another location for the use of the optical sensor is in some ignition distributor assemblies, where it senses a number of slots that have been chemically etched onto a thin stainless steel plate. This arrangement allows a pulse signal to be generated for a given number of crankshaft degrees of rotation.

USING AN OHMMETER

Ohmmeters are used in electrical circuits to check resistance values between two points and to check for continuity between two points. For example, by placing one end of the ohmmeter on a wire with the other lead on the opposite end of the wire, we can measure the resistance of the wire.

If, however, a break exists in the wire, no reading signifying a problem will be registered on the ohmmeter faceplate.

CAUTION: An ohmmeter should be used to test circuit continuity (no breaks in the wiring) and resistance only when no power is being applied to the circuit from the battery. Therefore, disconnect the battery, or if the wire or component has been removed from the circuit, the ohmmeter can be used. Failure to disconnect the circuit from the battery can result in damage to the ohmmeter unit.

The selector switch used on the ohmmeter can normally be placed at position R1, R10, R100, R1000, or R10,000, which controls the top range of resistance that can be measured accurately on the ohmmeter. For example, if the ohmmeter reads 8 on the scale with the selector at position R1, 8 Ω is the resistance; similarly, if the scale selector switch were at position R10, 80 Ω would be the measured resistance; at R100 it would be 800 Ω and so on, depending on the selector switch position.

Prior to using the ohmmeter, zero in the scale by plugging in both the red and black contact probes to the meter; touch them together with the range selector switch at the desired position for the test, and with the two contact probes held together at their contact ends, turn the adjustment knob on the meter until the scale needle indicates zero.

When using an ohmmeter, the following conditions may exist:

1. *Infinity.* With the test probes placed across a circuit,

should the needle on the scale swing across and hit the stop peg, you should switch to the next-higher scale; however, if you are already on the highest scale, the reading that you obtained obviously has a much higher resistance than you can measure. Therefore, it is described as infinity; the sign for infinity resembles a figure 8 lying on its side (∞).

2. *Open.* When checking a wire with an ohmmeter, a deflection of the meter needle is an indication that the wire is good. Failure of the needle to register is an indication that the wire is defective or open.

3. *Grounded.* When using an ohmmeter on an insulated circuit, no reading should exist between the insulated terminal and ground. Otherwise, it indicates that there is a short circuit somewhere connecting both the insulated terminal and grounded connection to the same common location, such as the vehicle frame or body. Therefore, a short circuit is generally indicated by a low or zero ohms reading.

Diode Resistances

Obviously, the resistance through various diodes and transistors varies depending on its particular location/circuit. However, a general consideration in a typical situation would indicate a forward resistance through a diode of 3000 Ω and a reverse resistance value of possibly 4 million ohms. This is known as the *front-to-back ratio*; in this instance it is somewhat greater than 1000:1. If a diode measures open-circuited (infinite ohms), it is defective; a zero ohms reading indicates that it is short-circuited. Acceptable industry standards or a rule-of-thumb figure for an operational diode is a front-to-back ratio of at least 100:1.

TESTING DIODES AND TRANSISTORS

If it is necessary to check the operation of either a diode or a transistor, select an ohmmeter having a 1.5-V cell across the diode or transistor. Refer to Fig. 2–36. To check the diode, select the lowest scale on the selector switch of the ohmmeter to start with. If the reading is too low, switch the selector to the next-higher scale.

When checking the diode, both the forward and the reverse resistance values must be checked. If a reading of zero is obtained with the ohmmeter leads placed both ways across the diode, the diode is shorted out and should be replaced. If both readings are high, the diode is open and should be replaced. When checking a diode, it is important that the measured forward-resistance value is much smaller than the reverse-resistance value. If not, the diode is defective. A good diode will give one very low and one very high reading.

To check out the condition of a diode when no ohmmeter is readily available, select a 12-V dc test light. When the leads of the light are connected across the diode both ways, failure to light in both checks indicates that the

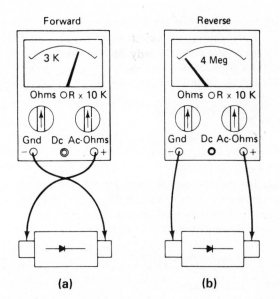

Forward

3 K

Ohms OR x 10 K

Gnd   Dc   Ac-Ohms
─○   ◎   ○+

Reverse

4 Meg

Ohms OR x 10 K

Gnd   Dc   Ac-Ohms
─○   ○   ○+

(a)   (b)

FIGURE 2–36   How to check a diode condition using an analog ohmmeter.

diode is open. If the light glows in both checks, the diode is shorted.

Several steps in using the ohmmeter to check the condition of the transistor are listed below:

1. With the ohmmeter connected, note the reading. Then reverse the leads. The transistor is shorted if both readings register zero.

2. Connect the ohmmeter and if the reading is zero in both directions when the leads are reversed, the transistor is shorted. If both readings are high, the transistor is open.

3. For step 3, basically follow the same procedure as for step 2.

When checking the same diodes or transistors, different ohmmeters can show different readings because of battery condition or internal ohmmeter conditions, such as resistance. Therefore, always use the same ohmmeter when checking the condition of diodes and transistors.

CAUTION: Many shops and service personnel today use a digital type of ohmmeter to check diodes and transistors. This can present a problem because some digital ohmmeters have an output current limitation of 0.001 A, while others may have an output current of as little as 0.000001 microampere. This low current is inadequate to turn a PN junction on, even though it is forward-biased. The problem is that when the ohmmeter is connected to a forward-biased condition, a very high resistance will be registered. This may lead you to believe that the diode or transistor is defective, when in fact it may be perfectly OK. Therefore, these types of digital ohmmeters should not be used for this purpose.

NOTE: Certain models and makes of digital ohmmeters may be used for checking both diodes and transistors. Such ohmmeters are designed to produce sufficient current flow and will therefore provide an accurate test of a diode's or transistor's condition. Always check the particular ohmmeter to be used to be sure that it does use at least one or two 1.5-V cells.

NOTE: In Chapter 4 we illustrate and discuss in greater detail the use of digital-type multimeters for electronic system checking.

QUESTIONS

2-1. In electronic systems, we are dealing with:
   a. How magnets create an electrical field
   b. The movement of electrons
   c. Electromotive force
   d. Electrochemical effects
   (see pages 25–26)

2-2. Elements that have four electrons in their valence rings are known as:
   a. Protons   c. Electrons
   b. Neutrons   d. Semiconductors
   (see pages 6, 31)

2-3. Doping a semiconductor is done to provide it with the characteristics of:
   a. Either a conductor or an insulator
   b. An electron
   c. A proton
   d. A neutron
   (see page 32)

2-4. Which of the following doping materials is not generally used to create a semiconductor?
   a. Silicon   c. Phosphorus
   b. Antimony   d. Arsenic (see page 32)

2-5. Semiconductor material known as an N-type substance usually has had which one of the following doping materials added to it?
   a. Boron   c. Phosphorus
   b. Antimony   d. Arsenic
   (see page 32)

2-6. Technician A says that an N-type semiconductor is a positive conducting unit, while technician B says that it is a negative conducting unit. Who is correct here? (see page 32)

2-7. Semiconductor material known as a P-type substance usually has had which one of the following doping materials added to it?
   a. Boron   c. Phosphorus
   b. Antimony   d. Arsenic
   (see page 32)

2-8. When a semiconductor is doped to create a P material, some atoms will be produced that have the following number of electrons in their valence ring:
   a. Five   c. Seven
   b. Six   d. Eight
   (see pages 31–32)

2-9. The solid-state device that acts as a one-way check valve in an electronic circuit is known as:
a. A diode
c. A zener diode
b. A transistor
d. An LED
(see page 32)

2-10. A diode is actually a device used to join:
a. N material to N material
b. P material to P material
c. P material and N material
d. A diode to a transistor
(see page 32)

2-11. The device that can be used to provide gain in an electronic circuit is known as:
a. A diode
b. A transistor
c. An analog/digital converter
d. A zener diode
(see pages 32, 33, 36, 39)

2-12. Which of the following combinations of materials is not used in a transistor?
a. PPN
c. NPN
b. PNP
(see page 36)

2-13. The basic function of a diode is to:
a. Allow current flow from either direction at once
b. Allow current to flow in alternating directions
c. Stop current flow
d. Allow current to flow in only one direction
(see page 33)

2-14. The only moving component within a transistor is:
a. Protons
c. Electrons and holes
b. Neutrons
d. N and P material
(see page 36)

2-15. The letters CMOS mean:
a. Complementary metal-oxide semiconductor
b. Conductive metallic oxide system
c. Cross-mounted offset system
d. Complete mass offset semiconductor
(see page 24)

2-16. Silicon that is the main base element used to manufacture semiconductor devices is obtained from:
a. Metallic oxides
b. Reduced and purified sand
c. A mixture of alloyed steel
d. Doped copper molecules
(see page 27)

2-17. Silicon crystals are:
a. Grown molecularly inside special furnaces
b. Assembled through chemical processes
c. Fabricated from alloyed elements
d. Produced through bonding/gluing grains of sand
(see page 27)

2-18. The basic function of a capacitor is to:
a. Maintain a steady voltage in the circuit
b. Balance the circuit frequency
c. Convert ac signals to dc signals
d. Accumulate electrostatic charge
(see Glossary of Terms, pages 492–501)

2-19. Current flows into the base and collector of an NPN transistor and out the emitter, whereas in a PNP transistor, current flows into the emitter and out of the base and collector. *True* or *False* (see page 36)

False

2-20. The base–emitter junction of a transistor acts like:
a. A neutron
c. A diode
b. A proton
d. An insulator
(see pages 36–37)

2-21. Transistors are three-terminal circuit elements that act like:
a. Voltage regulators
b. Current valves
c. Predetermined value resistors
d. Static circuit elements
(see pages 36–37)

2-22. The designation LSI regarding the classification of IC means:
a. Large-scale integration
b. Large system input
c. Limited system input
d. Large-scale interference
(see page 30)

2-23. An LSI IC contains:
a. Between 10 and 100 elements
b. Between 100 and 1000 elements
c. Between 10,000 and 100,000 elements
d. More than 100,000 elements
(see page 30)

2-24. An analog wave signal appears as:
a. A wavelike electrical signal
b. A rectangular-wave-shape signal
c. A square-wave-shape signal
d. A combination of a and b
(see page 30)

2-25 A digital signal is usually classified as being ON by the numeral:
a. 0, so that the computer can distinguish between and ON/OFF signal
b. 1
c. 2
d. 3
(see page 30)

2-26. The term *forward bias* in relation to a diode indicates that:
a. A positive or plus voltage is applied to the cathode of the two-terminal diode
b. A positive or plus voltage is applied to the anode of the two-terminal diode
c. A negative voltage is applied to the cathode of the two-terminal diode
d. A negative voltage is applied to the cathode of the two-terminal diode
(see page 32)

2-27. The term *reverse bias* in relation to a diode indicates that:
a. A positive or plus voltage is applied to the cathode of the two-terminal diode
b. A positive or plus voltage is applied to the anode of the two-terminal diode
c. A negative voltage is applied to the cathode of the two-terminal diode
d. A negative voltage is applied to the cathode of the two-terminal diode
(see page 32)

2-28. Using a transistor as a solid-state relay in an integrated circuit would require that:
a. Both the emitter–base junction and the collector–base junction be reverse biased

b. The emitter–base junction be reverse biased and the collector–base junction be forward biased

c. Both the emitter–base junction and the collector–base junction be forward biased

d. The emitter–base junction be forward biased and the collector–base junction be reverse biased

(see page 38)

2–29. A bipolar transistor is normally controlled by:

a. Voltage   c. Resistance values

b. Current flow   d. Capacitors

(see page 38)

2–30. During a forward-biased condition in a diode, the free electrons that move into the P material continue to move toward the positive voltage source. *True* or *False* (see pages 33–34)

TRUE

2–31. Applying reverse bias to a diode will result in:

a. Current flowing across the junction

b. The holes of the P material moving toward the junction

c. The free electrons moving away from the junction

d. All of the above

(see pages 32, 38)

2–32. A photodiode functions as:

a. A switch when actuated by cancellation of a light beam

b. A current transformer

c. A voltage reducer

d. A switch when actuated by a light beam

(see page 41)

2–33. Technician A says that an LED (light-emitting diode) has a junction that radiates both light and heat rays when it is subjected to an electric current. Technician B disagrees, saying that an LED is activated by a light source. Who is correct? (see page 40)

A

CHAPTER

3

Batteries

OBJECTIVES

In this chapter you will gain both the theoretical and practical knowledge required to understand how a lead–acid battery produces electrical energy and how to maintain, test, and troubleshoot it. Specifically, you will acquire or review the skills needed to:

1. Describe the physical construction of a heavy-duty lead–acid battery.
2. Be aware of and understand the chemical makeup/reaction of the battery electrolyte.
3. Be conversant with the many safety precautions necessary when working with lead–acid batteries.
4. Describe a series, a series–parallel and a parallel battery hookup arrangement in a heavy-duty truck application.
5. Identify and describe the difference between a conventional and a maintenance-free battery.
6. Describe the maintenance requirements of both a conventional lead–acid and a maintenance-free battery.
7. Select and/or repair battery cables.
8. Safely load-test a battery.
9. Know how to store batteries properly.
10. Know how to "boost charge" and "slow charge" a battery.
11. Be capable of performing regular preventive maintenance procedures to the battery system.

STORAGE BATTERIES

Few people today involved in the maintenance of cars, trucks, or heavy-duty equipment have not at some time or other used an item that required battery power to make it operate. In this age of electronic wizardry, almost everything from hand-held calculators to toys and portable radios, cassette tape decks, and portable television sets employ batteries in a wide variety of shapes, sizes, and capacities. Since this chapter will be concerned with the storage battery as it applies to cars, trucks, and heavy-duty equipment, we will study several types of batteries: their function, design, ratings, testing, and maintenance.

Every truck must have a source of electrical energy available at all times to supply power to the electrical accessories on the vehicle or equipment. When the engine is running, the battery is kept fully charged by the use of a generator or alternator. When the engine is stopped and electrical accessories are in use, the battery must supply the necessary power. When a gasoline engine is started, the battery must supply high current to the starter motor as well as provide sufficient energy to the ignition coil to create the high-tension energy required to fire the spark plugs. In diesel-engines, the battery is required to preheat the glow plugs for cold weather starting on pre-combustion-chamber engines in addition to cranking.

The lead-acid storage battery is an electro-chemical

device for storing energy and converting chemical energy into electrical energy. It has three major functions:

1. It provides a source of current for starting the engine.
2. It acts as a stabilizer to the voltage in the electrical system.
3. It, can, for a limited time, furnish current when the electrical demands exceed the output of the alternator.

The amount of electrical energy that is contained in the battery is known as its capacity, which in turn is established by the volume of chemicals within the battery casing.

TYPES OF BATTERIES

Batteries used in cars, trucks, industrial, marine, and heavy-duty equipment are either conventional or maintenance-free batteries. Batteries can be constructed of nickel cadmium (Ni-Cad), lead/calcium maintenance-free (M-F), lead/low antimony (low maintenance, L-M), lead/antimony, and "deep cycle" lead/antimony. Each type is constructed to produce particular voltage/current requirements for recharging. Therefore always ensure that if more than one-type of battery is to be used in any system, that you seek the individual battery manufacturers advice if more than one battery type is to be intermixed in any system.

CAUTION: Different battery types should never be mixed when hooked together in a parallel battery hookup system.

Batteries in use in most heavy-duty trucks are lead–acid units (see the sections "Battery Construction" and "Battery Operation"). Lead–acid batteries produce hydrogen and oxygen during charge and discharge. These gases are produced by the disassociation or breaking apart of water molecules in the electrolyte. Therefore, as the gases escape, the quantity of water within the battery cells is reduced. It is the amount of water usage by a battery that determines its type. Standard or conventional lead–acid batteries are designed with either push-in or screw-in individual cell covers that can be accessed to allow water to be added. Some batteries are manufactured under the term *low maintenance*, which implies that they will require less water to be added to the battery during its lifetime. The maintenance-free battery is designed not to require the addition of makeup water during its life cycle and does not have cell access plugs mounted on the top of the battery case.

The conventional type of battery is available in two forms: wet and dry. The conventional battery must be checked regularly to ensure that the electrolyte level is maintained by the addition of distilled water. When a conventional battery is ordered new from a supplier, it can be supplied in either wet or dry form. The wet battery already has the (acid) electrolyte added to it to activate the chemical reaction within the battery so that it is ready for service. The dry battery has no electrolyte, thus can be stored for much longer periods of time without the possibility of becoming discharged. Its shelf time is therefore increased. When desired, the battery is activated by the addition of electrolyte.

The maintenance-free battery is a sealed-top unit that does not require the addition of makeup water over its normal life; therefore no regular maintenance is required. General maintenance required is discussed later in this chapter. The first maintenance-free battery was released in 1971 by the Delco-Remy Division of General Motors Corporation for use in their line of passenger cars. These early types of batteries were known by the tradename Energizer since they stored electrical energy in chemical form.

SAFETY PRECAUTIONS

When batteries are being charged, an explosive gas mixture forms beneath the cover of each cell. Part of this gas escapes through the holes in the vent plugs and may form an explosive atmosphere around the battery itself if ventilation is poor.

CAUTION: Explosive gas may remain in or around the battery for several hours after it has been charged. Sparks or flames can ignite this gas, causing an internal explosion that could shatter the battery. Flying pieces of the battery structure and splash of the electrolyte can cause personal injury. Battery electrolyte is acid. Extreme care should be exercised to avoid skin or eye contact with the electrolyte. If you come in contact with battery electrolyte:

1. Flush your skin with water.
2. Apply baking soda or lime to help neutralize the acid.
3. Flush your eyes with water for 10 to 15 minutes.
4. Get medical attention immediately.

BATTERY CONSTRUCTION

Minor variations exist between types and styles of batteries manufactured by different companies; however, in the final analysis, they are very similar in general construction. Figure 3–1 illustrates a sectional view of a maintenance-free 12-V heavy-duty battery, and Fig. 3–2 shows the basic construction of a conventional 12-V battery. Many conventional batteries employ either a one-piece cell cover over the six cells, or a two-piece (one cover for three cells) design for access to the cells when the addition of water is required. Twelve-volt batteries always have six cells; 6-V batteries have only three cells. In a conventional battery, there would therefore be six plastic screw-in cell covers along the top of the battery cover, and a 6-V battery would contain only three cell cover caps. The battery is manufactured from a number of individual components which together comprise the finished battery. Figure 3–3 illustrates and describes the individual

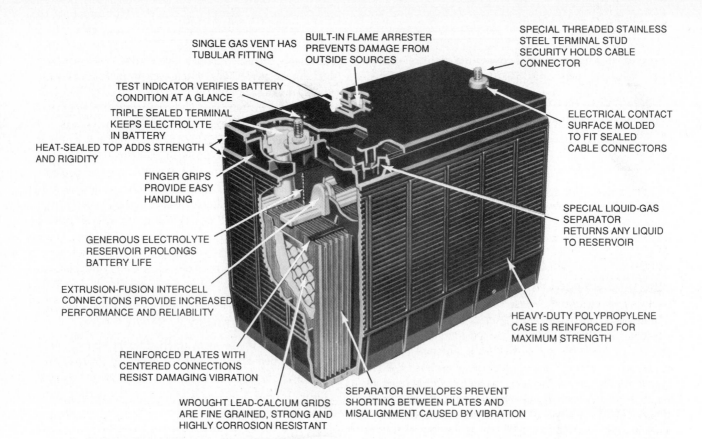

SINGLE GAS VENT HAS TUBULAR FITTING

BUILT-IN FLAME ARRESTER PREVENTS DAMAGE FROM OUTSIDE SOURCES

SPECIAL THREADED STAINLESS STEEL TERMINAL STUD SECURITY HOLDS CABLE CONNECTOR

TEST INDICATOR VERIFIES BATTERY CONDITION AT A GLANCE

TRIPLE SEALED TERMINAL KEEPS ELECTROLYTE IN BATTERY

HEAT-SEALED TOP ADDS STRENGTH AND RIGIDITY

ELECTRICAL CONTACT SURFACE MOLDED TO FIT SEALED CABLE CONNECTORS

FINGER GRIPS PROVIDE EASY HANDLING

GENEROUS ELECTROLYTE RESERVOIR PROLONGS BATTERY LIFE

SPECIAL LIQUID-GAS SEPARATOR RETURNS ANY LIQUID TO RESERVOIR

EXTRUSION-FUSION INTERCELL CONNECTIONS PROVIDE INCREASED PERFORMANCE AND RELIABILITY

HEAVY-DUTY POLYPROPYLENE CASE IS REINFORCED FOR MAXIMUM STRENGTH

REINFORCED PLATES WITH CENTERED CONNECTIONS RESIST DAMAGING VIBRATION

WROUGHT LEAD-CALCIUM GRIDS ARE FINE GRAINED, STRONG AND HIGHLY CORROSION RESISTANT

SEPARATOR ENVELOPES PREVENT SHORTING BETWEEN PLATES AND MISALIGNMENT CAUSED BY VIBRATION

FIGURE 3–1 Cross-sectional view of an 1100 series Delco heavy-duty 12-V maintenance-free truck battery. *(Courtesy of Delco Remy, Division of General Motors Corporation.)*

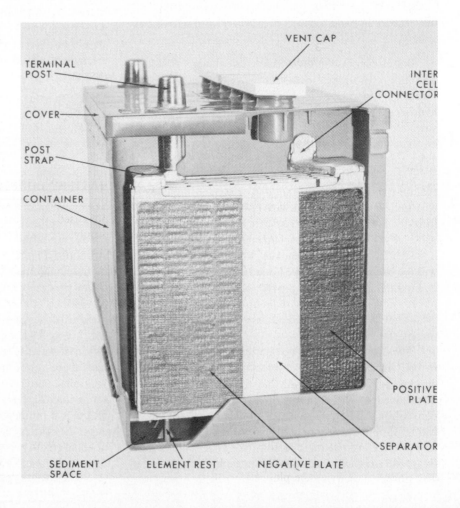

TERMINAL POST

VENT CAP

INTER CELL CONNECTOR

COVER

POST STRAP

CONTAINER

POSITIVE PLATE

SEPARATOR

SEDIMENT SPACE

ELEMENT REST

NEGATIVE PLATE

FIGURE 3–2 Cross-sectional view of a 12-V vent cap type battery showing the individual cell connectors and other major features. *(Courtesy of GNB Incorporated.)*

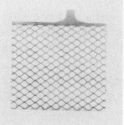

Wrought Lead-Calcium Grids...offer considerable strength while maintaining a very fine and consistent grain structure. Conventional lead-antimony battery grids and competitive lead-calcium cast grids are susceptible to attack by corrosion. Delco wrought grids are substantially resistant to grid corrosion, over-charge, gassing, water usage, self-discharge and thermal runaway.

Polypropylene Case...is a reinforced design, precisely tailored to support the battery elements. The case has beveled corners to reduce handling damage and breakage, while outside case bottom is waffled to prevent puncture. Polypropylene case material is exceptionally strong and durable and easily withstands road shock and vibration.

Envelope Separators Encapsulate Plates...replacing the traditional separator during element assembly. Envelope construction or encapsulation, improves vibration durability. It prevents "treeing" and internal shorting between the plates. The Delco element rests on a flat case bottom, as there is no need for a sediment chamber beneath the plates.

Exclusive Liquid-Gas Separator...has been built into the battery cover to prevent minute electrolyte losses by collecting the liquid and returning it to the main electrolyte reservoir of the battery. Although gassing is virtually eliminated, this vent also allows the battery to "breathe", especially during temperature changes and charging.

Centered Cast-on Plate Straps...used to connect plates. . .are stronger than the thinner gas-burned conventional connections. These straps are located near the center of the plates, which reduces the lever action movement resulting from road shock. In addition, the element is reinforced with thermoplastic anchors to further improve vibration durability.

Heat-Sealed Cover...is installed to the case at the factory after the battery is charged. This prevents future contamination and also adds to the strength and rigidity of the case-cover assembly. Permanent flame arrestor has been built-in to prevent an accidental explosion which could be caused by either sparks or flame from outside the battery.

FIGURE 3–3 Construction details for a heavy-duty 12-V battery. *(Courtesy of Delco Remy, Division of General Motors Corporation.)*

components of the battery. More detailed information on the components follows.

Battery Case

The *case* is normally constructed of an acid-resistant material, which can be either hard rubber, plastic, or polypropylene. Polypropylene has the advantage of lighter weight and improved cold weather durability. The polypropylene case also withstands road shock and vibration better than does the hard rubber style.

Molded externally to some battery cases at the bottom are lugs or mounting ridges to allow the battery hold-down clamps to secure it into position.

Running along the inside of the battery base are molded element rests which support the individual positive and negative plate assemblies. This is necessary because during the life of any battery, chemical discharge causes particles of material to drop from the plates, which can accumulate in a sediment chamber between the element rests and below the bottom of the plates. Without these sediment chambers at the bottom of the battery case, short-circuits would occur, because the particles of material that drop off the plates contain lead, which is electrically conductive. Without the sediment chamber, these particles could lodge between both the positive and negative plates, creating a short circuit.

Each battery case is subdivided into *cells*. The cells consist of a number of positive and negative plates insulated from one another by separators. The number of cells used depends on the battery voltage, with the commonly used 12-V battery containing six of these cells, while the 6-V battery would contain only three cells. The stack-up of positive and negative plates is called a *cell pack*. For instance, a typical group 4 (6-V) battery has 12 negative and 11 positive plates per cell.

Battery Cover

The battery *cover* is a one-piece unit with individual openings for each cell, to allow filling the cell with electrolyte on conventional batteries, or for the addition of water for maintenance purposes. Battery or cell *plugs* are then screwed or pushed into place, each plug having a small hole in it to serve as a vent. On the newer-style batteries, a porous top allows venting of each cell to the atmosphere, due to the chemical reaction within the battery. On maintenance-free batteries a special liquid-gas separator is heat-sealed to the top of the battery case, and a cover is heat-sealed to the top of the liquid–gas separator. The liquid–gas separator on the maintenance-free battery is designed to collect very small particles of electrolyte liquid and return the liquid to the main reservoir of the battery.

Elements

The *elements* or cell packs contain a number of positive and negative plates back to back but insulated from each other by the use of separators between pairs of plates. The capacity or battery rating in ampere-hours is established by the physical size of the positive and negative plates and by how many plates are used per cell.

The plates within the battery are made up of a grid network, as shown in Figs. 3–1 and 3–2. Currently, two types of grids are in use. In the conventional battery the grid is made of lead–antimony; the grid of the maintenance-free battery is made of a wrought lead–calcium alloy. The elimination of the antimony from the maintenance-free battery results in less water usage and gassing throughout the life of the battery. In addition, the lead–calcium grid is very resistant to oxidation or grid corrosion.

As can be seen in Fig. 3–3, the grid looks like a flat, rectangular, lattice-style casting surrounded with a heavy border. The mesh can be either of horizontal and vertical wire, or may be diamond-shaped. Lead peroxide (PbO_2) is pasted or coated onto the grid to the positively charged plates. This is dark brown in color, while the material pasted or coated to the negative grid plate contains pure lead in the form of sponge lead (Pb), which is metallic gray in color. This material is porous and provides a large effective surface area.

Figures 3–1, 3–2, and 3–3 show how each group of positive and negative plates are held together by the use of a plate strap. A plate group is made by lead-burning or welding each stack-up of similar plates together to the plate strap. Each element or plate group usually has one more negative plate than positive plate, so that the outside plates are negative at the exposed positions on both sides of the interlaced group.

Separator Envelope

To pack as much electrical energy as possible into the smallest space, batteries are designed to be as small and lightweight as desired. Because of this design, the positive and negative plates must be kept very close together

FIGURE 3–4 **(a)** Medium- and heavy-duty truck sealed battery (maintenance-free) with tapered post top terminals. *(Courtesy of GMC Truck Division, General Motors Corporation.)* **(b)** Medium- and heavy-duty truck sealed battery with top-mounted screw-on terminal connectors. *(Courtesy of GNB Incorporated.)*

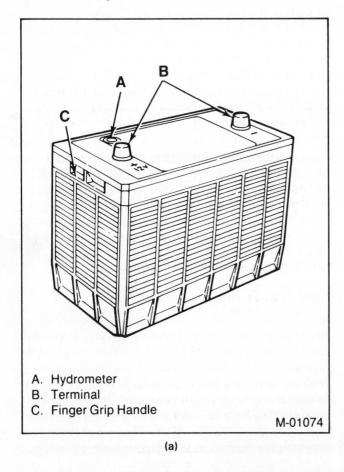

A. Hydrometer
B. Terminal
C. Finger Grip Handle

M-01074

(a)

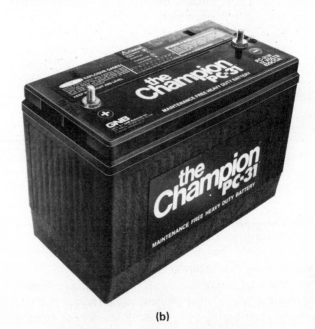

(b)

The new Champion® PC-31™ introduced by GNB Batteries Inc. (formerly Gould) is the first American battery to use a Duratrel™ container and cover. Tests have shown that Duratrel combines the vibration resistance of hard rubber with the impact resistance of thin-wall polypropylene to provide superior protection for a battery's internal components. The Champion PC-31 comes with 3/8″ stainless-steel stud terminals as shown above, or with SAE automotive posts. Starting power capacities of 480 and 625 cold-cranking-amperes (CCA's) are available. The battery can be used in all heavy duty vehicles and applications that accept a Group 31 battery.

within the battery case. To prevent a short circuit between these dissimilar plates, an insulating material called a *separator envelope* must be installed between the individual plates when an element is assembled (see Fig. 3–3).

Separators must present no notable resistance to the flow or movement of ions in the electrolyte (dilute sulfuric acid) and must be able to withstand the chemical reaction of the acid, as well as being microporous and permeable so that the electrolyte can pass through the separator. Without the microporous structure of the separator, it is possible that very fine lead fibers could pass through the separator, resulting in a short circuit between the positive and negative grid plates.

Intercell Connectors

Figure 3–1 shows how the individual cells of the battery are connected by the use of *intercell connectors*. The plate straps of the cells are connected by the shortest and most direct path through the cell partition.

Battery-Terminal Posts

The plate strap of each cell is connected back to both the positive and negative battery *terminal posts*. Figure 3–4(a) illustrates a 12-V heavy-duty maintenance-free model battery with tapered negative and positive post top-mounted terminals, finger-grip handle slots, and a built-in hydrometer eye to determine the condition of the state of charge. Figure 3–4(b) shows a similar battery but with screw-type top terminals. Both of these types of battery post top terminals are widely used on heavy-duty trucks. An alternate arrangement is a side-mounted battery post connection, more commonly used on passenger cars, pickups, and midrange trucks, where a small captive bolt inserted through the positive and negative battery cable leads actually screws into the threaded side-mounted battery connection (see Figure 3–5). Side-mounted battery connections are used to lower the overall height of the

FIGURE 3–5 Features of a bolt-on type side attachment battery connection. *(Courtesy of GNB Incorporated.)*

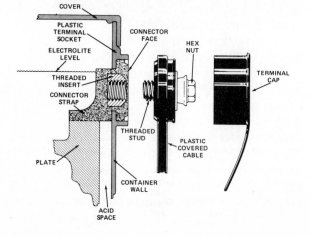

battery assembly, which is desirable in many forward-sloping hood designs. The side-mounted connection generally provides less self-discharge and less resistance, in addition to the design features mentioned.

BATTERY OPERATION

So far we have looked at the main components of the battery and how they go together. Let's now study the battery in detail to establish just how it is capable of producing the electrical energy used to operate all the accessories in an electrical system.

Current within the battery is produced by a chemical reaction between the positive and negative coated plates which are submerged in the electrolyte (dilute sulfuric acid). This chemical reaction that occurs within the battery causes the battery to self-discharge. If the battery is not constantly recharged by the use of a generator or alternator, such as on a car or truck, eventually the battery becomes completely discharged or flat and must be recharged before it will produce any more electrical energy.

Water Usage. All lead-acid batteries produce hydrogen and oxygen during charge and discharge. These gases are produced by the disassociation (or breaking apart) of water molecules in the electrolyte. As the gases escape, the amount of water in the electrolyte is reduced.

To recharge a battery, it must be supplied with a flow of direct current in a direction opposite the normal flow of current from the battery during discharge.

The electrolyte weight or specific gravity in a fully charged battery is made up of a solution of dilute sulfuric acid in water. This specific gravity is approximately 1.260 to 1.270 at 80 °F (26.6 °C), which means that it is heavier than water, which has a specific gravity of 1.000 or 10 lb/gallon (4.536 kg/3.78 liters). In other words, the electrolyte of the battery is 1.270 times heavier than an equivalent volume of water.

The percentage breakdown of the electrolyte consists of approximately 64% water and 36% acid, with the acid having a specific gravity of 1.835. These two percentages combine to give us 1.270 at 80 °F (26.6 °C) for a fully charged battery. The voltage produced in each battery cell depends on the chemical difference between the active materials (positive and negative plates) and also on the strength concentration of the electrolyte.

Temperature Correction of Electrolyte Specific Gravity

The specific gravity readings of battery electrolyte are directly affected by changes in temperature either above or below 80 °F (26.6 °C). To correct for specific gravity readings above this figure, simply add 4 points (0.004) to the reading for every 10 ° above 80 °F, or subtract 4 points (0.004) from 80 °F for every 10 °F (3.7 °C) below this figure. For example, if the electrolyte showed a temperature of 0 °F when a thermometer was placed into it, and read 1.232 with a hydrometer sample, the corrected specific gravity to 80 °F (26.6 °C) would be 1.200.

One precaution that must be exercised with respect to electrolyte is that of low ambient temperatures, because the electrolyte can freeze. Typical temperatures at which electrolyte freezes are shown in Table 3–1.

Chemical Reaction within a Battery

To understand thoroughly the chemical reaction that exists in a battery during discharge (battery supplying electrical energy to a system), consider the following conditions:

1. The positive grid or plate in a battery consists of lead peroxide with chemical formula PbO_2, in color dark or chocolate brown, and the negative grid material consists of pure lead with chemical symbol Pb, metallic gray in color.

2. Two classes of conductors are used in electrical systems. The first class includes copper wiring or any metallic substance in which current flow takes place by means of electron conduction, as explained in Chapter 1. The second class includes chemical compounds dissolved in water which decompose or dissociate into positive and negative components (ions). Current flow in this class of conductor takes place by means of larger charged particles (ion conduction). Such a second-class conductor is the electrolyte used in the lead storage battery, which is dilute sulfuric acid, H_2SO_4; this means that every molecule of sulfuric acid has two atoms of hydrogen, one atom of sulfur, and four atoms of oxygen.

In its normal state, sulfuric acid molecules will tend to split into positively charged hydrogen (H +) ions and negatively charged sulfate (SO_4) ions; the charges will match one another on an overall basis. In its usual concentration, the electrolyte solution has almost all the sulfuric acid molecules in a disassociated state. However, if an electrode of metallic lead is immersed into dilute sulfuric acid such as a battery contains, electrically charged particles or ions are forced from the electrode into the electrolyte due to the pressure of the solution. In other words, positively charged lead ions (lead atoms that have given up two electrons) pass into the electrolyte (dilute sulfuric acid), leaving negative charges (electrons) remaining on the lead electrode with respect to the electrolyte.

If another electrode of different material is immersed in the electrolyte, different potentials develop at the two electrodes with respect to the electrolyte. This action creates what is commonly called *potential* or voltage between the two dissimilar electrodes. In the lead–acid battery, this potential or voltage is equal to 2 V per cell.

Battery Discharge

When the terminals of the battery are connected to each other through an electric load (accessories), electrons will flow from the negative electrode, through the load, and back to the positive electrode because of the difference of potential or cell voltage existing between the terminals. The chemical reaction or change within the battery during discharge (loss of electrical energy) is shown in Fig. 3–6.

During discharge of the battery, oxygen in the positive active material combines with the hydrogen in the electrolyte to form plain water (H_2O). While this is occurring, the lead in the positive active material combines with the sulfate radical, thereby forming lead sulfate ($PbSO_4$).

A similar reaction occurs at the negative plate, where lead (Pb) of the negative active material combines with the sulfate radical to form lead sulfate ($PbSO_4$). We therefore have lead sulfate being formed at both the positive and negative grid plates of the battery during discharge. Both electrodes (positive and negative) have now returned to their initial condition; the chemical energy stored in the cell has been transformed back into electrical energy and has been used up by the electrical load or accessories, and the battery has returned to its discharged state. In a discharged lead–acid battery, the electrolyte is in a diluted state comprising about 17% pure sulfuric acid and about 83% water.

Chemical Reaction When Charging a Battery

To charge the lead–acid battery, the positive and negative battery posts must be connected to a suitable source of direct current (dc). This can be done by use of a generator, alternator, or battery charger. This charging process does not take place naturally, but must be forced by the introduction of electrical energy into the cell so that it has a higher energy level after the charging process than before. The source of charging current draws electrons from the positive electrode and forces them into the negative electrode.

The chemical reactions that take place in battery cells during charging are the reverse of those occurring during the discharge cycle. Figures 3–6 and 3–7 show a schematic of the chemical reaction within the battery cells during both the discharge and charge cycles. During charging, the lead sulfate on both the positive and negative plates is separated into lead (Pb) and sulfate (SO_4). This sulfate leaving both plates combines with hydrogen in the electrolyte to form or recreate sulfuric acid (H_2SO_4). While this is going on, the oxygen (O) in the electrolyte combines with the lead (Pb) at the positive

TABLE 3–1 Electrolyte freezing temperatures

Specific Gravity	Freezing Temperature
1.270	− 83°F
1.160	0°F (− 18°C)
1.100	18°F (− 8.2°C)

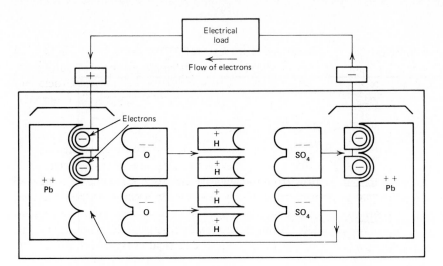

(a)

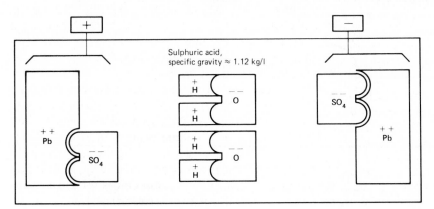

(b)

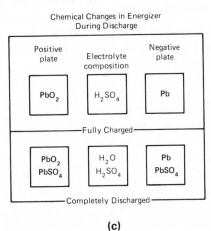

Chemical Changes in Energizer
During Discharge

Positive plate	Electrolyte composition	Negative plate
PbO₂	H₂SO₄	Pb

————Fully Charged————

| PbO₂ PbSO₄ | H₂O H₂SO₄ | Pb PbSO₄ |

————Completely Discharged————

(c)

FIGURE 3–6 Chemical reaction during a battery discharge cycle. **(a)** Discharge of battery or current drain. Electrons flow from the negative electrode through the electrical load to the positive electrode. $PbSO_4$ (lead sufate) forms at both electrodes. **(b)** Cell discharged, $PbSO_4$ (lead sulfate) has formed at both electrodes and H_2O (water) has formed in the electrolyte. **(c)** Sequence of chemical changes during battery discharge.

plate to form lead dioxide (PbO_2), and the negative plate returns to the original form of lead (Pb).

Gassing of the Lead–Acid Battery

Due to the chemical reaction within the cells of the battery, after a certain period of time under charge, a saturation limit will be reached. If the battery is charged continually after this point has been reached, damage to the battery can occur. This gassing starts at a charging voltage of about 2.4 V per cell and will result in a continuing loss of water. The sulfuric acid concentration (specific gravity of the electrolyte) will rise above the value specified for a fully charged battery. Continued overcharging will damage the battery beyond acceptable usage, and in certain cases the battery could explode.

When a battery is being charged, gassing, together with the increase in sulfuric acid specific gravity and the terminal voltage, indicates that the battery cells are fully

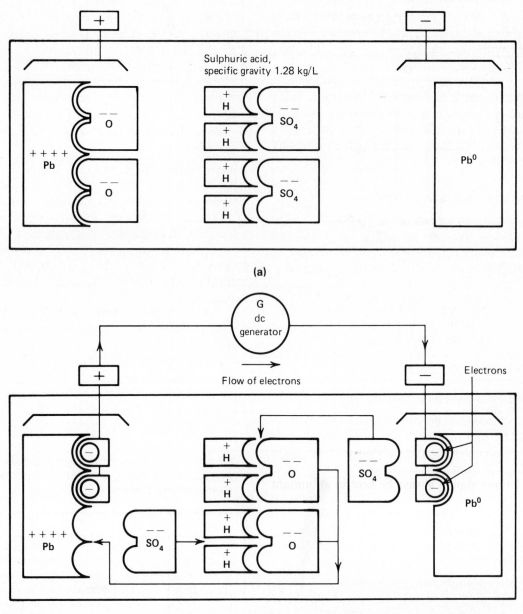

FIGURE 3–7 Chemical reaction during battery charging. **(a)** Cell charged. Positive electrode, PbO_2 (lead peroxide); negative electrode, Pb (metallic lead). **(b)** Charging the cell. During charging, the flow of electrons (forced around by a dc generator) is from the positive to the negative electrode [i.e., in the direction opposite to the flow during discharge (current drain)]. PbO_2 (lead peroxide) forms at the positive electrode, and Pb or metallic lead forms at the negative electrode.

charged. A fully charged battery will continue to gas freely for a fairly long time after the battery charger has been disconnected. This gas mixture, which has been developed during charging, consists of a mixture of both hydrogen and oxygen and is therefore highly explosive. For this reason, battery charging rooms must be well ventilated at all times.

Maintenance of the water level in each battery cell is very important. If this level drops below the tops of the plates, the exposed active material will dry and harden, leading to battery failure. If maintenance-free batteries are overcharged, they can be permanently damaged, just as non-maintenance-free batteries can.

Overcharging in old-style (non-maintenance-free)

batteries forms hydrogen and oxygen gases, which cause oxidation of the positive plate grids. This oxidation causes the grids to crumble and leads to early failure. However, in the maintenance-free battery, the plate grid contains wrought lead–calcium alloy and has no antimony such as is used in the conventional battery. The wrought lead–calcium used in maintenance-free batteries is very resistant to oxidation of the grid and also to overcharge or thermal runaway, because of the removal of antimony from the grid.

MAINTENANCE-FREE BATTERIES

A lead–antimony battery can accept up to 10 times as much overcharge current as can a fully charged maintenance-free battery. The maintenance-free battery offers high resistance to the following undesirable characteristics:

- Water usage
- Corrosion of the grid
- Gassing of the cells
- Self-discharge —*less condensing*
- Overcharging or thermal runaway

Venting of Maintenance-Free Batteries

Some maintenance-free, or freedom, batteries never require the addition of water. There are no filler caps in the battery cover, which is sealed and has vent holes which allow small amounts of gases to escape. Because of these vents, the battery should always be kept in an upright

FIGURE 3–8 Features of the Champion PC-31 battery manifold venting system. *(Courtesy of GNB Incorporated.)*

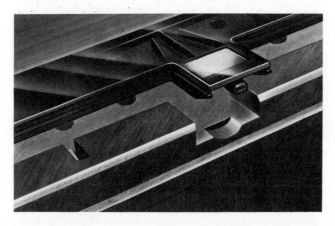

The new Champion® PC-31™ maintenance-free, heavy duty battery has a serviceable manifold venting system that offers quick access to the electrolyte when extreme operating conditions (such as severely hot weather) make addition of water necessary. The manifold also locks tightly back into place.

The one-piece, T-shaped venting system minimizes corrosion accumulation by directing escaping gases through a single exit point at a distance from the terminals. A built-in flame arrestor inside the outlet (highlighted above) minimizes the possibility of an external spark penetrating the battery and causing an exploion.

Baffles inside the manifold trap spewing acid—usually caused by overcharging or vibration—and return it to the cells.

position, or electrolyte can leak out. However, some heavy-duty maintenance-free batteries, such as the Champion PC-31 illustrated in Fig. 3–8 have a serviceable manifold venting system. Generally, do not exceed a 45° angle when carrying or installing a maintenance-free type of battery.

Checking the Condition of Maintenance-Free Batteries

Some companies that manufacture maintenance-free batteries seal them completely; others employ a special temperature-compensated hydrometer which is built into the battery cover. This device readily allows the service technician or mechanic to identify the state of charge of the battery. One example of how this type of hydrometer operates is shown in Fig. 3–9. This is the method employed on all Delco-Remy maintenance-free batteries.

The hydrometer device shown in Fig. 3–9 consists of a small green-colored ball (within a cage fastened to the end of a plastic probe) which can float up or down within one of two small tracks. If the battery electrolyte is at or beyond a specific gravity of 1.220, the ball will float, and the mechanic or observer will see a green dot when he or she looks down on the top of the built-in

FIGURE 3–9 How to interpret a built-in battery hydrometer. *(Courtesy of GMC Truck, Division of General Motors Corporation.)*

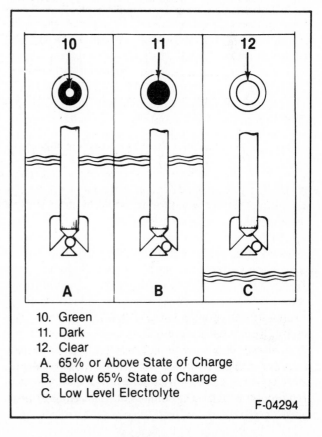

10. Green
11. Dark
12. Clear
A. 65% or Above State of Charge
B. Below 65% State of Charge
C. Low Level Electrolyte

F-04294

hydrometer from the top of the battery case. If the observer sees only a dark surface when viewing the clear top of the hydrometer, it indicates that the specific gravity of the battery is less than 1.220. This is caused by the fact that the ball will sink down one of the two tracks in the cage. If a dark surface appears within the hydrometer, the battery must be charged until the green ball floats.

In the maintenance-free battery, only one indicator or hydrometer is used in one cell, because since the battery is of sealed construction, the specific gravity per cell will be almost identical. If the hydrometer becomes clear or light yellow in color, this is an indication of low electrolyte caused by possible overcharging; tipping the battery beyond 45°, which would allow the electrolyte to spill out; a cracked case; or a worn-out battery.

Advantages of Maintenance-Free Batteries

Maintenance-free batteries have the following major advantages:

1. Require no addition of water
2. No spewing or gassing of cells
3. Lower rate of self-discharge
4. Higher resistance to possible overcharging
5. Greater resistance to grid corrosion
6. Service free
7. No terminal oxidation or corrosion (sealed surfaces)

The disadvantage of a maintenance-free battery is that they should not be used in applications where the current draw cannot be replaced by a steady charge from a generator or alternator. An example would be as boost-start batteries, because should the state of charge be allowed to fall too low, recharging can be impossible. However, various manufacturers do state that an attempt can be made to recharge a maintenance-free battery at a slow rate if the voltage falls within a minimum level. These levels will vary among battery manufacturers; therefore, a close check should be made with the supplier prior to attempting to charge a maintenance-free battery.

Delco-Remy Division of General Motors offers the following basic rules regarding charging of any of their maintenance-free batteries:

1. Do not charge a battery if the hydrometer is clear or light yellow; replace the battery.
2. Charge rates between 3 and 50 A are generally satisfactory as long as spewing of electrolyte does not occur or the battery does not feel excessively hot (over 125°F, 52°C); if spewing occurs or the temperature exceeds 125°F, the charging rate must be reduced or halted temporarily to permit cooling. Touch the battery case to establish the temperature.
3. On rare occasions the indicator (hydrometer) may turn light yellow. Although the battery is capable of further service, if a cranking complaint has been reported, replace the battery. *Do not charge, test, or jump-start.*

Disadvantages of a Conventional Lead-Acid Battery

1. Requires regular addition of make up water
2. Spewing or gassing of cells is not unusual (check the charging rate)
3. Higher self-discharge rate than that of a maintenance-free battery
4. Lower resistance to overcharging than that of a maintenance-free battery
5. Lower resistance to grid corrosion than that of a maintenance-free battery
6. Requires regular maintenance

The main advantage of the conventional lead-acid battery is that it can be recharged at any time. Therefore, in situations where it is being used as a booster battery, it can be placed back on charge and brought back to a service condition.

SPECIFIC GRAVITY VERSUS VOLTAGE

There is a direct correlation between the actual specific gravity of the battery electrolyte and that of an equivalent voltage that would be registered on a voltmeter. Table 3–2 illustrates this relationship. As a battery ages, shedding or loss of active material from the plates will cause the fully charged specific gravity reading to drop. This is further compounded by the normal loss of electrolyte due to gassing of the cells. Operating temperature and rate of charge, in addition to maintenance practices, will determine the battery's life expectancy.

BATTERY SELECTION

The actual life of a battery is based on certain standard practices that must be followed for long life with a minimum of trouble. Selection of the proper battery is one of the most important criteria in establishing long trouble-free life. The total electrical load of the electrical system must be calculated, and then the type of vehicle or equipment operation and application must be analyzed carefully prior to selecting the best battery for the job. Selecting a battery that has a high amperage rating may seem like a good idea; however, if the operating conditions are such that high electrical loads are constantly placed on the battery during periods of low-state-of-charge conditions from the alternator or generator, the battery will continually suffer from a low-state-of-charge condition.

If the engine operates constantly at low rpm, the alternator/generator used must be capable of producing a high charge rate at this slow speed to maintain the battery in a fully charged state, especially if high electrical loads are constantly in use at these low speeds. In addition, increasing the electrical load on the circuit by introducing a variety of add-on accessories may exceed the reserve power capability of the battery as well as the charging system. The system must be designed to ensure

TABLE 3-2 Specific gravity and voltage

Open Circuit Voltage Reading	Corresponding Spec. Gravity	State of Charge	
1.95	1.100	1.100 to 1.130	discharged
1.96	1.110		
1.97	1.120		
1.98	1.130		
1.99	1.140		
2.00	1.150		
2.01	1.160		
2.02	1.170	1.170 to 1.190	25% charged
2.03	1.180		
2.04	1.190		
2.05	1.200	1.200 to 1.220	50% charged
2.06	1.210		
2.07	1.220		
2.08	1.230	1.230 to 1.250	75% charged
2.09	1.240		
2.10	1.250		
2.11	1.260	1.260 to 1.280	100% charged
2.12	1.270		
2.13	1.280		
2.14	1.290		
2.15	1.300		

that the total load placed on it can in fact be handled adequately by both the battery and charging system.

Most electrical systems in use on cars, trucks, and other forms of equipment are designed to handle all types of conditions; however, special situations may require a reevaluation of the design and load-carrying capacity of the existing circuit.(See Tables 8-6 and 8-7.)

The introduction of maintenance-free batteries has done much to reduce the minor service checks required on the battery; however, other regular service checks, inspections, and tests are required. Generally, the battery can be serviced and checked on the vehicle or equipment, but if continued problems are encountered that indicate a possible battery problem, the battery should be removed for further testing and analysis.

BATTERY RATINGS

Earlier in the chapter we mentioned the fact that the battery capacity is dictated by the number of plates per cell and by the total surface area of the active plate material. In addition to these two controlling factors, strength and volume of electrolyte have a bearing on the battery output. The method used to rate batteries is common in most countries of the world. The Society of Automotive Engineers (SAE) and BCI (Battery Council International) provides information that defines a battery's ability to deliver a given amount of usable cranking power.

Reserve Capacity

A *reserve capacity rating* represents the approximate time in minutes that it is possible to travel at night with a minimum electrical load and no generator/alternator output to the battery. The time in minutes is based on a current draw of 25 A while maintaining a minimum battery terminal voltage of 10.2 V at 80°F (26.6°C) or equivalent cell voltage at 1.75 V. This rating replaces the previous 20-hour capacity (ampere-hour) rating, and more accurately represents the electrical load that must be supplied by the battery in the event of a charging system failure. The ampere-hour rating will eventually be dropped.

Cold Cranking Test

The *cold cranking rating* specifies the minimum amperes available at 0°F (-18°C) and at -20°F (-28°C). This rating replaces the old method of relating voltage and time as measures of cranking and starting ability. It is much more accurate because it allows cranking capacity to be related to such significant variables as engine displacement, compression ratio, temperature, cranking time, condition of the engine and electrical system, and lowest practical voltage for cranking and ignition. The old tests did not take these factors into account.

This new test relates a discharge rating in amperes that a fully charged battery will maintain for 30 seconds without the terminal voltage falling below 7.2 V for a

12-V battery, or 3.6 V for a 6-V battery (1.2 V per cell or greater).

To provide enough starting power under severe conditions, a 12-V system normally requires at least 1 A for each cubic inch of engine displacement. For example, a 450-in.³ (7.37-L) engine would require a battery with a cold cranking rating of at least 450 A. Most manufacturers of batteries will provide the ampere-hour ratings. If however, the ampere-hour rating is not available and cannot be determined, divide the cold cranking rating at 0°F (−18°C) by 2. The figure obtained equals the load that should be applied when making a battery capacity test and is about equal to the value of three times the ampere-hour rating of batteries that used the old rating system.

Estimating Battery Capacity

The capacity of the battery is generally shown on a decal stuck onto the side or the top of the battery; others have the rating molded onto the battery case. However, if the battery capacity cannot be determined, it can be approximated by multiplying the total area of the positive plates in square inches in each cell by two-thirds.

For example, if a battery has six positive plates, each measuring 4 × 3 in. (10.16 × 7.62 cm) the total area is 72 in.² (464.51 cm²). Two-thirds of this is 48 (309.64); therefore, the ampere-hour capacity at a 20-hour rate of discharge is 48 A.

Most batteries today are capable of at least a capacity of 1 ampere-hour for each 3 in.² of plate surface. Suppose that the total area of each plate (both sides) is 24 in.²; multiply this area by the number of positive plates,

which we will assume to be six; then we have the product 6 × 24 = 144 in.²

Using the basic standard, that 3 in.² provides 1 ampere-hour capacity, then for 144 in.² it would be 144/3 = 48 ampere-hours.

TABLE 3-3 Typical battery CCA recommendations

Engine Make	Model	Cranking Voltage (volts)	Recommended CCAs (amps)
Caterpillar	3208	12	1600
Caterpillar	3406	12	1800
Caterpillar	3406	24	900
Cummins	14L	12	1800
Detroit Diesel	6V-53	12	900
Detroit Diesel	6V-71/6-71	12	1200
Detroit Diesel	8V-71	12	1800
Detroit Diesel	6V-92	12	1800
Detroit Diesel	8V-92	12	2500
Detroit Diesel	8.2L	12	1250
Detroit Diesel	8V-92	24	900
Detroit Diesel	Series 60	12	950 above 0°C (32°F)
	Series 60	12	1250 below 0°C (32°F)
NAVISTAR	DT-466	12	1600
Mack	6 cyl.	12	1360
Mack	V8	12	1900

FIGURE 3-10 Typical features and ratings of various Delco medium- and heavy-duty truck batteries. *(Courtesy of Delco Remy, Division of General Motors Corporation.)*

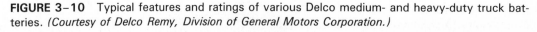

The pioneering **Delco 1200 Series** is now rated at 550 cold cranking amps. A four-battery complement provides 2200 CCA's and 696 minutes RC and is suitable for virtually all popular diesel engines.

The **Delco 1110** is rated at 625 cold cranking amps. A four-battery complement provides 2500 CCA's and 816 minutes RC and is suitable for diesels which operate in cold climates. A three-battery complement provides 1875 CCA's and 583 minutes RC and is suitable for diesels which have limited battery mounting space.

The **Delco 1150 High-Cycle Series** is now rated at 625 cold cranking amps and is the first heavy-duty maintenance-free battery with cycling capability. A four-battery complement is suitable for large diesels in cycling applications, while a three-battery complement is suitable for mid-range diesels.

The **Delco 31-750** is rated at 750 cold cranking amps. A four-battery complement is suitable for diesels which operate in cold climates, and/or where improved cranking is requisite...a three-battery complement is suitable for limited battery mounting area and where extra starting power is required...a two-battery complement is suitable for mid-range diesel trucks with limited cycling and where less starting power is required.

The **Delco 31-900 Dura-Power** is rated at 900 cold cranking amps. A three-battery complement is suitable for diesels which operate in cold climates and/or where extra starting power is required. A two-battery complement is suitable for high mileage or high hours applications where cycling is very limited.

In addition to SAE, TMC/ATA (The Maintenance Council, American Trucking Associations) TMC Recommended Practice RP-109A deals in detail with battery ratings and engine cranking requirements for heavy-duty trucks. The RP manual can be obtained by contacting the TMC/ATA at 2200 Mill Road, Alexandria, Virginia 22314. Current battery ratings are based on a standard established in 1971 by the SAE and BCI (Battery Council International). This rating system, known as SAE standard J537h, is based on CCA (cold cranking amperes) and battery reserve capacity ratings, which can be keyed directly into engine cranking requirements. Each gasoline and diesel engine manufacturer issues minimum cold cranking ampere specifications for each model of engine built. This should always be your guide when selecting a new battery or batteries for a heavy-duty truck. Table 3-3 lists some typical heavy-duty truck diesel engine makes and models along with the starting system voltages and required CCAs at 0°F. Note closely that the correct weight of engine oil *must* be used to ensure that the batteries CCAs will spin the engine fast enough to initiate successful startup at this low ambient temperature.

Typical battery CCA ratings are listed on the battery performance decal. Figure 3-10 illustrates five models of Delco heavy-duty truck maintenance-free batteries, along with information on their CCAs and hookup. For more information on series and parallel battery hookup arrangements, refer to the following section, "Series and Parallel Hookup of Batteries."

SERIES AND PARALLEL HOOKUP OF BATTERIES

On midrange, medium-duty, and heavy-duty trucks, the electrical circuit can be designed to operate on either a 12- or a 24-V system. Most North American vehicles operate on a standardized 12-V electrical system; however, in cases where the vehicle may operate under extreme heavy-duty operation and is exposed to low ambient temperatures, a series–parallel switch is used to allow a 24-V starter system with a 12-V charging system. On the other hand, most European and Australian heavy-duty trucks and buses operate on a 24-V starting, charging, and electrical accessories system.

Whether a 12- or 24-V system is used, due to the cyclical nature of heavy-duty truck operation, the desired system voltage is obtained by connecting two, three, or four individual batteries in either a series or a parallel hookup arrangement. The arrangement of both a series and a parallel battery system hookup is illustrated in Fig. 3-11. When batteries are connected in a series arrangement, all the battery voltages are added together. For example, connecting four 6-V batteries in series would provide 24 V. Similarly, two 12-V batteries in series would provide 24 V. However the amperage would not increase in a series hookup but would remain the same as that of one battery (the cold cranking amperes would remain the

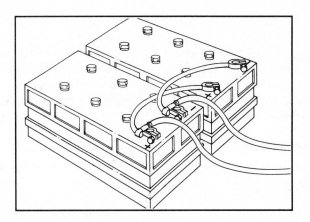

(a)

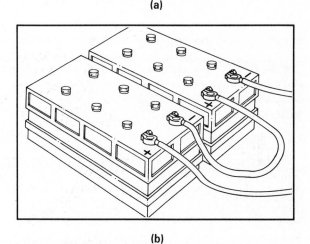

(b)

FIGURE 3-11 **(a)** Example of how batteries are hooked together to form a parallel connection; **(b)** How batteries are hooked together to form a series connection. *(Courtesy of Cummins Engine Company, Inc.)*

same), although it would provide a greater reserve of power since either two or four batteries can be used. Therefore, if each battery is rated at 12 V and 600 CCA, we would have 24 V but still only 600 CCA of power.

Figure 3-12(a) illustrates four 12-V batteries in a parallel hookup arrangement with either an A- or B-rated battery selection. When batteries are connected in a parallel arrangement as shown in Fig. 3-12(a), the result is an increase in amperage while the voltage remains the same as that for one battery. For example, four 6-V batteries connected in parallel would still only provide 6 V; similarly, two, three, or four 12-V batteries in a parallel arrangement still supply only 12 V.

NOTE: Figure 3-12(a) illustrates a 12-V hookup, or parallel connection, where all battery positive posts are interconnected and all negative posts are interconnected. Assuming that four batteries were connected in a parallel hookup and were each rated at 500 CCA (cold cranking amps), then total cranking power would be equal to $4 \times 500 = 2000$ CCA. If four 650 A batteries were used, cranking power would be equal to 2700 CCA. If only three batteries were used, then cranking power would be

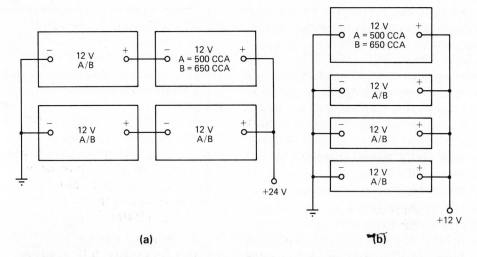

(a)   (b)

FIGURE 3–12 Recommended battery layout for **(a)** typical series–parallel (+ connected to −); **(b)** parallel arrangement (all + connected, all − connected) showing the net effect of the CCA (cold cranking amps) output.

equal to the sum of the batteries individual ratings. Parallel battery hookups provide increased amperage, but the voltage is the same as with one battery. In Fig. 3–12(b) a series battery hookup provides increased voltage. Our example shows a 24-V hookup. The CCA, however, is the sum of only one battery. The arrangement in Fig. 3–12(b) provides 24-V cranking, but 12-V charging. It is commonly referred to as a series/parallel hookup.

Advantages of Series and Parallel Battery Hookup

Earlier, we described briefly the basic arrangement of the series and parallel battery arrangements. Let's look at a specific comparison between the batteries used on a typical diesel highway truck of 325 to 350 brake horsepower (bhp). Manufacturers of diesel engines in this power range recommend that two 8DR205 or equivalent batteries connected in parallel be used, utilizing a 12-V high-output starting motor. However, some truck manufacturers use four 4HR150T or equivalent batteries connected in series–parallel, which connects all of the batteries together for starting. An example of the two systems is shown in Fig. 3–13.

The two 12-V batteries connected in parallel give a system voltage of 12 V, but a capacity of 410 ampere-hours (Ah). The system terminal voltage of this arrangement as per the cold cranking test after a 30-second discharge at 300 A and 0 °F (26.7 °C) equals 9.8 V. However, with the two 12-V battery arrangement, fewer terminals are required to make the connections, and consequently, there is less potential of voltage drops due to loose or corroded terminals. This is particularly important to ensure adequate voltage to the starter motor solenoid.

Figure 3–13(b) shows four batteries connected in a series/parallel arrangement. The system voltage is equal to 12 V with a capacity of 300 Ah, since each 6-V battery

is rated at 150 Ah. These four 6-V batteries are classified as an automotive-rated battery hookup; therefore, unlike the two 12-V 8DR205 diesel rated batteries, the 30-second diesel rating is not applicable. The system terminal voltage of the four 6-V batteries after a 5-second discharge at 300 A and 0 °F (26.7 °C) is equal to 9.4 V.

With the 6-V arrangement, there are more potential voltage drops that can hamper cranking motor operation,

FIGURE 3–13 **(a)** Two 12-V batteries connected in a parallel arrangement; **(b)** four 6-V batteries connected in a series–parallel arrangement.

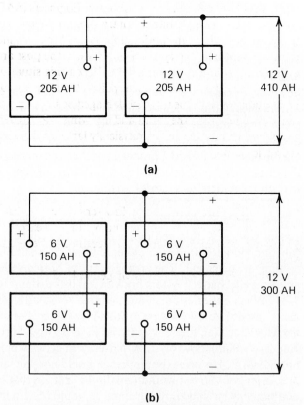

due to the number of connections required in this type of system. One major advantage that the parallel system offers is economy, since it is more economical to replace the smaller batteries than the larger 12-V 205-Ah units. However, the smaller batteries are of lower capacity and will require more frequent replacement due to cycling (discharging and charging). Therefore, while the series–parallel system is adequate for moderately cold weather operation, the recommended system will provide better sustained cranking motor operation in colder climates. In summation, we have the following:

- *Series connection.* The system capacity is equal to that of one battery (amperage), while the voltage is equal to that of all the batteries.
- *Parallel connection.* The system capacity (amperes) is equal to the sum of all the batteries, while the voltage is equal to that of only one battery.

SUMMARY NOTE: A detailed analysis and in-depth test conducted by the TMC/ATA (The Maintenance Council, American Trucking Associations) regarding the use of multiple 6-V versus multiple 12-V batteries in heavy-duty line-haul trucks confirmed that the use of 12-V batteries provides longer life and less overall electrical system problems. A detailed report on this test can be found in the TMC/ATA RP (Recommended Maintenance Practices Manual), RP-106, VMRS (Vehicle Maintenance Reporting Standard) 32-001-001.

BATTERY TERMINAL POST DIMENSIONS

The dimension of the battery posts for all batteries is established by the Society of Automotive Engineers (SAE) and the BCI (Battery Council International). When battery posts wear through continual removal of the terminal clamps, eventually the connection between the post and clamp can no longer be kept tight. When this situation occurs, the battery post can be repaired by using a small mold placed around the worn or damaged post, and pouring melted lead into the mold and allowing it to harden. Note that the positive post is physically larger in diameter than the negative post!

BATTERY CABLES

Battery cables are classified as low-tension cable, since they are seldom required to conduct voltage in excess of 12 to 32 V. Anything under 50 V is accepted as being low tension.

SAE specifies three types of general cable for this purpose:

1. *Type SGT*—starter or ground, thermoplastic insulated
2. *Type SGR*—starter or ground, synthetic rubber insulated
3. *Type SGX*—starter or ground, cross-linked polyethylene insulated

The wire used is either bunched, concentric, or rope stranded, and is manufactured of annealed copper wire. Figure 3–14 illustrates the characteristics of a typical heavy-duty battery cable, and Fig. 3–15 illustrates a number of types of ground cables used on trucks.

Core stranding should be concentric or bunched for gauges 6 through 0, while rope-stranded core is recommended for gauges 00, 000, and 0000. Cable insulation characteristics are important and can be either PVC (polyvinyl chloride) or neoprene rated to 220 °F, or cross-linked polyethylene insulation when heat exceeds 220 °F (104 °C). It is important when selecting and using a battery wire cable that the voltage drop in the circuit not exceed SAE (J541a) accepted values, which are:

1. 6-V light and medium duty: 0.12 V/100 A
2. 12-V heavy duty: 0.12 V/100 A
3. 12-V light and medium duty: 0.20 V/100 A
4. 24- and 32-V heavy duty: 0.20 V/100 A
5. 24-V light and medium duty: 0.40 V/100 A
6. 12-V high-output heavy duty: 0.075 V/100 A
7. 12-V super heavy duty: 0.060 V/100 A

Recommended battery cable gauge size guidelines can be determined by reference to Table 3–4 (see page 64). Note that the minimum recommended wire gauge size for 12-V high-output starter motor systems *must* be size 00, with dual-path circuitry preferred. Should it become necessary at any time to replace the battery-to-starter motor wiring, Table 3–5 (see page 65) lists the equivalent metric versus AWG (American Wire Gauge) wire size.

Battery Cable Terminals

A number of types and styles of battery cable terminal connections are used in the industry. Figure 3–16 illustrates two different types, with the + and − (positive and negative) terminal sizes shown. The terminals shown in Fig. 3–16 can be used only on top-post-mounted batteries such as the one shown in Figure 3–4(a). On batteries such as that shown in Fig. 3–4(b), an eyelet-type cable connection terminal must be used with a retaining nut, although some applications may choose to use a wing-nut style retainer. If a side-mounted battery terminal is used, a special hole-type terminal with a captive bolt is used. See Fig. 3–5.

To avoid damage to the electrical accessories when connecting up the battery cables, the battery terminal posts are identified by either the letters POS or NEG cast or etched into the battery cover immediately adjacent to each post. In addition to this feature, the POS (positive) or NEG (negative) battery posts are manufactured so that the diameter of the positive post is larger than that of the negative post.

Automotive batteries can produce a very high current when the terminals are shorted directly to each other. Never allow a current conductor to contact both terminals at the same time. Even a battery in a low state of charge can produce sparks at the terminals and heat a conduc-

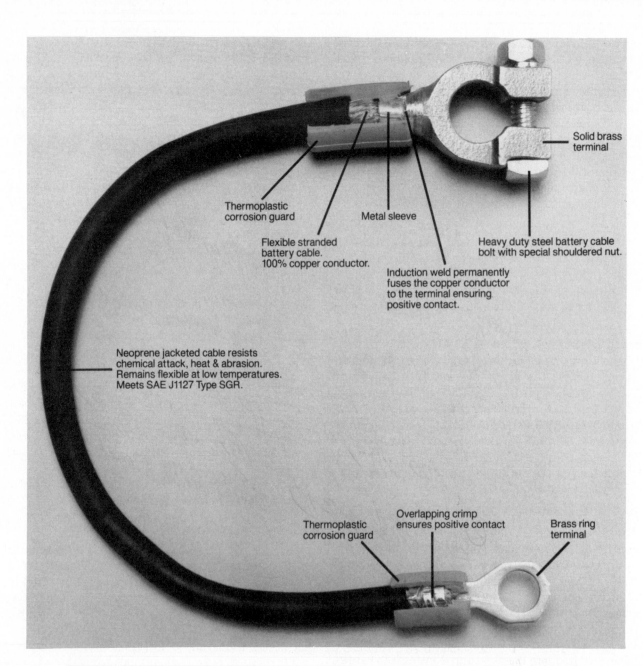

Thermoplastic corrosion guard

Metal sleeve

Solid brass terminal

Flexible stranded battery cable. 100% copper conductor.

Induction weld permanently fuses the copper conductor to the terminal ensuring positive contact.

Heavy duty steel battery cable bolt with special shouldered nut.

Neoprene jacketed cable resists chemical attack, heat & abrasion. Remains flexible at low temperatures. Meets SAE J1127 Type SGR.

Thermoplastic corrosion guard

Overlapping crimp ensures positive contact

Brass ring terminal

FIGURE 3–14 Features of a typical heavy-duty induction welded battery cable. *(Courtesy of Dominion Automotive Industries, Inc.)*

tor to a dangerously hot temperature in a few seconds. If an object such as a wrench does accidentally fall against the terminals, use extreme caution in removing it to avoid burns.

Terminal Connections.

Battery terminal connections must be kept clean and tight. Always wire-brush both the terminal and connector to a tarnish-free condition before assembling cables to the battery. A baking soda solution should be used to wash away any buildup of corrosion that may have occurred.

Corrosion forms on the exposed metal areas of terminal connections from exposure to air, moisture, and traces of electrolyte that come into contact with them. If the terminal connectors are not designed to seal the connection from the atmosphere, periodic disassembly and cleaning of the terminals will be necessary to prevent high-resistance connections from developing. After cleaning and reassembling the cables, application of light

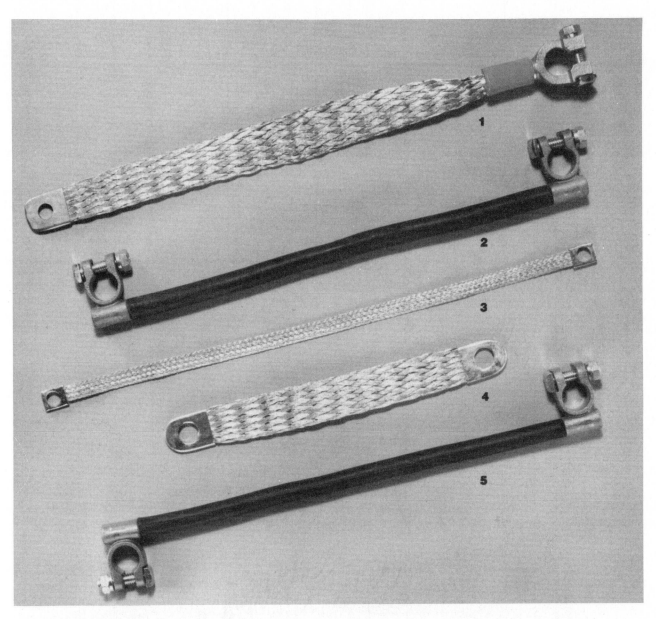

FIGURE 3–15 Commonly used types of battery ground cables. *(Courtesy of Dominion Automotive Industries, Inc.)*

grease or other commercial preparations will retard the formation of new corrosion. The time between cleanings will vary from application to application. A good rule of thumb is to clean them when changing engine oil.

Note that some battery and vehicle manufacturers utilize terminal and connector designs that seal the metal connections from the atmosphere, reducing or eliminating the need for periodic disassembly and cleaning. Refer to the manufacturers' instructions for maintenance of these designs.

SPECIAL NOTE: Refer to Chapter 9 dealing with starter motors, and the section "Making and Installing Starter Motor Cables," as well as Figure 9–54 which il-

lustrates the correct procedure to solder cables and connections properly.

BATTERY-MOUNTING RECOMMENDATIONS FOR HEAVY-DUTY TRUCKS

The physical mounting of the batteries in heavy-duty line-haul trucks is a very important part of ensuring long life from each battery. Extensive studies by TMC/ATA (The Maintenance Council, American Trucking Associations) has shown that the mounting recommendations illustrated in Figure 3–17 should be adhered to at all times. The following procedures should be closely monitored to ensure that the battery mounting system is acceptable.

TABLE 3-4 Determining battery/starter approximate cable gauge size

System Voltage and Type	Maximum Circuit Voltage Drop per 100 Amps (in Volts)	2	4	6	8	10	12	14	16	18	20	22	24	26	28	30	32	34	36	38	40
12-V heavy duty	0.12	6	4	2	1	0	00	000	0000 or 2-00 in parallel		2-00 in parallel		2-000 in parallel			2-0000 in parallel					
12-V light and medium duty 24- and 32-V heavy duty	0.20	6	4		2	1		0	00			000		0000 or 2-0 in parallel			2-00 in parallel				
24-V light and medium duty	0.40		6		4		2				1			0			00				
12-V high output heavy duty with single path to and from starter	0.075	00			000	0000 or 2-0 in parallel	2-00 in parallel		2-000 in parallel		2-0000 in parallel										
12-V high-output heavy duty with dual path to and from starter	0.075 (0.150 per Leg)	00						000			0000 or 2-0 in parallel			2-00 in parallel			2-000 in parallel				
12-V super heavy duty	Single path—0.060	00		000	0000 or 2-0		2-00	2-000		2-0000												
12-V super heavy duty	Dual path—0.120 per Leg	00			000				0000			2-00			2-000			2-0000			

TABLE 3-5 Replacement battery cable wire size selection chart

Metric Size (sq mm)	CMA	American Wire Gauge Replacement
1	1,974	16
2	3,947	14
3	5,921	12
4–5	7,894–9,868	10
6–8	11,841–15,788	8
9–13	17,762–25,655	6
14–21	27,629–41,444	4
22–33	43,417–65,126	2
34–42	67,099–82,887	1
43–53	84,861–104,596	1/0
54–67	106,569–132,225	2/0
68–85	134,198–167,748	3/0
86–107	169,721–211,165	4/0

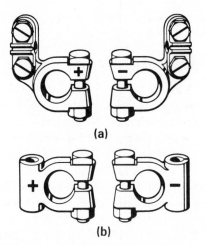

FIGURE 3-16 Identification of positive and negative battery cable terminals showing **(a)** screw and **(b)** solder types. *(Courtesy of Robert Bosch Corporation.)*

Mounting Procedures

1. All battery carriers and hold-down straps and brackets must be designed to accept heavy-duty truck batteries manufactured to the dimensions conforming to SAE J537 standards.

2. All battery carriers, hold-down bracketry, covers, and associated hardware should be manufactured from or be painted/treated with acid-resistant coating.

3. To minimize vibration, rubber sheet padding ¼ or ⅜ in. (6 or 9.5 mm) thick should be located in the bottom of each battery carrier.

4. All cables and terminal fittings should conform to TMC cable insulation, routing, and support practice number 105.

5. The location of any battery carriers that would place the batteries in close proximity to exhaust system heat radiation should have adequate heat shielding installed.

6. To ensure that maintenance personnel inspect the bat-

FIGURE 3-17 Examples of recommended battery mounting in a heavy-duty truck: **(a)** batteries mounted on top of the chassis frame rails; **(b)** batteries mounted on top of the fuel saddle tanks; **(c)** batteries mounted parallel to the chassis side frame rails; **(d)** batteries securely mounted between the chassis frame rails.

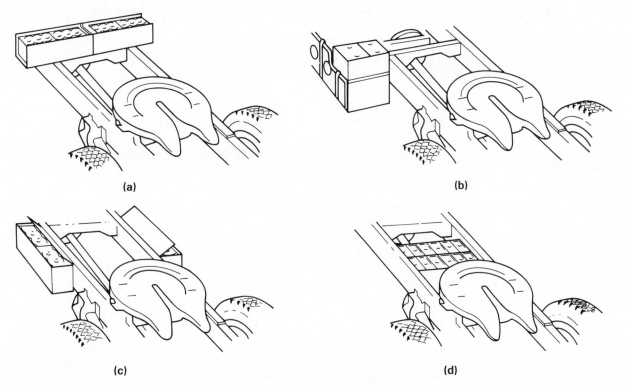

(a)

(b)

(c)

(d)

teries on a regular basis, the battery covers should be easily accessible and removable.

SAFETY PRECAUTIONS PRIOR TO SERVICING

Anytime that maintenance or service is to be carried out on the battery or batteries, it is extremely important that you appreciate the dangers that can occur through neglect and failure to follow certain safety precautions. Batteries can explode; therefore, do not use poor work habits around batteries. The sulfuric acid in batteries is poisonous and can cause severe burns. Explosive gases are also generated from batteries while in normal use and while on charge. Therefore, keep sparks, open flames, burning cigarettes or cigars, and other ignition sources well clear of the battery at all times. To protect yourself, wear safety glasses when working around a battery. Avoid leaning directly over a battery when it is on charge since gassing at each cell will emanate a high concentration of poisonous sulfuric acid fumes. The same precaution should be exercised while testing or jump starting the battery. Do not lay wrenches, screwdrivers, or other tools on the top of the battery at any time, since they can act as perfect conductors between cell connectors on exposed batteries, or can short out the battery between the positive and negative posts. Do not break live circuits at battery terminals, since a spark will normally occur at any point in the circuit when a live circuit is broken.

If the battery is to be charged, be sure that the charger cable clamps or booster cable leads are clean and have a solid connection. Poor electrical connections between clamps and the battery terminal posts can easily create an electrical arc which may cause ignition of the gas mixture from the battery, causing an explosion.

When a battery is on charge, avoid using a voltmeter across either the exposed cell connectors or the positive and negative posts, since any scratching movement by the end of the voltmeter leads to obtain a good connection can also create a spark, causing the battery to explode. Always use a hydrometer to sample the electrolyte and read the specific gravity. If desired, specific gravity can be converted to a voltage reading using Table 3–2.

Handling Battery Acid

Battery acid should never be added to a battery that is or has been in service. The only time that sulfuric acid is added to the battery is when it is new and requires activation prior to placing it into service. Most manufacturers supply the correct quantity of acid for each new battery in plastic containers. However, bulk containers are available and are often used by large fleets where battery turnover is frequent. The acid used in the battery is dilute sulfuric acid, which can burn the skin and eat its way through clothing very quickly. For this reason, protective clothing should be used, including the use of safety glasses or goggles when using acid. If electrolyte (battery acid) is ever splashed into the eyes, quickly force the eye open and flood it with cool clean water for about 10 to 15 minutes, then see a physician immediately.

If for some reason you were to drink out of a container that contained battery acid, drink large quantities of water or milk, follow this up with milk of magnesia or a beaten egg or vegetable oil, and contact a doctor.

Electrolyte spilled on clothing or painted surfaces can be neutralized with a solution of baking soda and water, then rinsed with clean water. Should it be necessary for you to prepare a given volume of electrolyte, always pour the concentrated acid into water slowly, never add the water to the acid, since spattering of the liquid would result because of the high heat generated through the chemical reaction. It is advisable to stir the liquid gently while the acid is being added to the water.

Carrying Batteries

When moving batteries from one spot to another, use a battery cart, or if only one battery is to be moved a short distance, a battery carrier should be used.

HYDROMETERS

Using a Hydrometer

Hydrometers are used in industry for a variety of reasons, but specifically, to check the specific gravity of a liquid. Hydrometers can be used, for example, on automotive applications to check the condition of the coolant in the cooling system or the electrolyte within the battery. However, the same hydrometer is not used for both purposes. Another place that the hydrometer is used is in wine or beer processing, where the brewmaster monitors the specific gravity of the liquid to determine when it is ready for bottling.

The specific gravity of the battery electrolyte is a unit of measurement that allows us quickly to determine the condition of the battery by analyzing the sulfuric acid content of the individual cells. The recommended and accepted specific gravity for 12-V or 6-V batteries is 1.265 corrected to a temperature of 80°F (26.6°C). If the cell electrolyte reads 1.265, it signifies that the battery is fully charged, with the electrolyte containing approximately 36% sulfuric acid by weight or 25% by volume. The remaining 64% (75% by volume) is made up of pure water.

Sulfuric acid in its pure concentrated form has a specific gravity of 1.835 and water has a specific gravity of 1.000. The concentration of the cell electrolyte within the battery is therefore 1.265 times heavier than pure water. Although these specific gravity readings are shown as 1.265, for example, the accepted industry jargon for this reading would be "twelve sixty-five"; similarly, a reading of 1.230, would be called "twelve thirty."

Types of Hydrometers

Several types and styles of hydrometers are readily available and used in the industry for checking the specific gravity of the battery electrolyte. These various types are shown in figures in the text that follows.

Bulb-Type Hydrometer. This is the most commonly used type of hydrometer, and is available in several basic styles. The hydrometer in Fig. 3–18 contains a built-in thermometer encased in the rubber shock-proof mount at its base. This is extremely handy, since the specific gravity of the electrolyte must be correct for variations in temperature by adding or subtracting points from the scale when the temperature is above or below 80°F (26.7°C). This correction factor is 0.004 specific gravity point for each 10°F (5.5°C) above or below 80°F (26.7°C). You add 0.004 point to the specific gravity scale for each 10°F increase beyond 80°F, and you subtract 0.004 point, for every 10°F below 80°F.

When using the hydrometer, care should be exercised when placing the tube end into the battery cell. Do not jam this into the cell, because damage to the tops of the separators can result. Gently squeeze the bulb end prior to inserting the hydrometer into the cell electrolyte, then release the bulb gently. This allows a sample of electrolyte to be drawn up into the glass tube. The float within the glass tube will rise and stay suspended at a given position, depending on the specific gravity of the liquid.

To read the hydrometer properly, wear a pair of safety glasses to prevent possible eye damage from electrolyte splash. Then hold the hydrometer steady, and straight up and down, as shown in Fig. 3–19, place your eye level with the electrolyte within the hydrometer glass and read the specific gravity on the float. Remember to correct for temperature to 80°F (26.7°C).

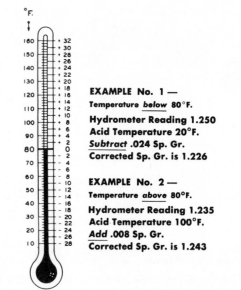

EXAMPLE No. 1 —
Temperature *below* 80°F.

Hydrometer Reading 1.250
Acid Temperature 20°F.
Subtract .024 Sp. Gr.
Corrected Sp. Gr. is 1.226

EXAMPLE No. 2 —
Temperature *above* 80°F.

Hydrometer Reading 1.235
Acid Temperature 100°F.
Add .008 Sp. Gr.
Corrected Sp. Gr. is 1.243

FIGURE 3–19 Reading the battery electrolyte hydrometer. *(Courtesy of GNB Incorporated.)*

Some hydrometers use a series of little balls within the glass tube rather than a float. When a sample of electrolyte is taken, the number of balls that float establishes the percentage state of charge of each cell. Table 3–2 can be referred to in order to establish the state of charge of the battery from the sample readings taken by the hydrometer.

CAUTION: Avoid the possibility of allowing sample electrolyte to drip onto your skin, clothing, the vehicle, or any painted surface.

Refractometer. A relatively new device that can also be used to check the specific gravity of each cell is a refractometer, which employs the basic principle of light refraction or the bending of light rays through a sample of the electrolyte to establish its specific gravity. Figure 3–20 shows this test instrument.

FIGURE 3–20 Refractometer battery electrolyte tester. *(Courtesy of Kent-Moore Heavy Duty Division, SPX Corporation.)*

FIGURE 3–18 Bulb-type hydrometer unit.

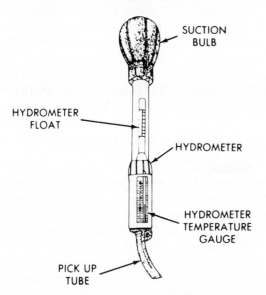

SUCTION BULB

HYDROMETER FLOAT

HYDROMETER

HYDROMETER TEMPERATURE GAUGE

PICK UP TUBE

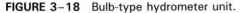

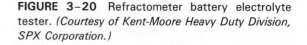

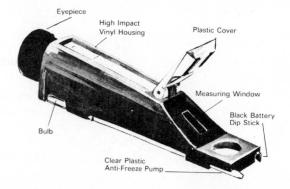

Eyepiece

High Impact Vinyl Housing

Plastic Cover

Measuring Window

Black Battery Dip Stick

Bulb

Clear Plastic Anti-Freeze Pump

The device shown in Fig. 3–20 can be used to test the coolant (anti-freeze) or battery specific gravity readings. For this reason, the instrument is called a Duo-Chek tester by the manufacturer. The tester is designed specifically for rapid and accurate checking of permanent antifreeze protection, and for checking the condition of the battery state of charge by sampling the electrolyte. It requires only several drops of either coolant or battery acid, depending on which specific gravity you wish to test. The Duo-Chek tester automatically compensates for temperature changes.

Prior to using the tester, swing back the plastic cover at the slanted end as shown in Fig. 3–21(a). Wipe clean and dry both the measuring window and the bottom of the plastic cover.

Once the tester has been cleaned with tissue or a clean soft cloth, close the plastic cover. To use the tester, do not remove the clear plastic pump from the tester, but release the tip of the pump from the tester housing if a coolant condition test is required.

To test the specific gravity of the battery electrolyte, use the small black dipstick from the side of the tester to obtain a sample of battery acid. Place a few drops of acid onto the measuring surface through the opening in the cover plate as shown in Fig. 3–21(b).

Reading the Duo-Chek tester: Several precautions must be exercised when attempting to read the Duo-Chek

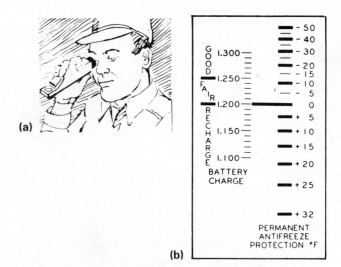

(b)

FIGURE 3–22 **(a)** Reading the tester; **(b)** sample reading. *(Courtesy of Kent-Moore Heavy Duty Division, SPX Corporation.)*

tester. Never open the plastic cover of the tester when taking readings, since evaporation of water from the fluid sample being tested can affect the reading. The precautions given above for battery acid handling hold true here.

Make sure that the eyepiece is completely free of any battery electrolyte before you attempt to look into the measuring window. Rinse the window with clear fresh water and wipe it dry prior to and after testing the sample. Wear both safety glasses and gloves when testing acid or caustic solutions.

Refer to Fig. 3–22(a) and point the tester toward a bright source of light as you look into the eyepiece. The specific gravity reading on the tester measuring surface will be at the point where the dividing line between light and dark (edge of the shadow) crosses the scale, as shown in the sample reading at Fig. 3–22(b). Note that the scale shows the battery specific gravity on the left-hand side, while the right-hand side of the scale relates to permanent antifreeze solution.

If the reading is not accurate because the edge of the shadow was not sharp enough, the surface of the measuring window probably was not clean enough. Wipe the surface clean again, and take another sample. Repeat this procedure for each battery cell.

BATTERY TEMPERATURE VERSUS CRANKING POWER

The battery or surrounding ambient air temperature will cause not only a change in the temperature of the battery electrolyte, but will also increase the frictional drag on rotating engine parts (e.g., while the engine is being cranked) due to oil viscosity changes. Similar slow cranking can be encountered in hot weather if the battery's state of charge is low, or if a replacement battery has been installed that is not of the same rating as the unit replaced.

FIGURE 3–21 **(a)** Preparing Duo-Chek refractometer battery electrolyte tester for a reading; **(b)** placing drops of battery acid onto Duo-Chek tester. *(Courtesy of Kent-Moore Heavy Duty Division, SPX Corporation.)*

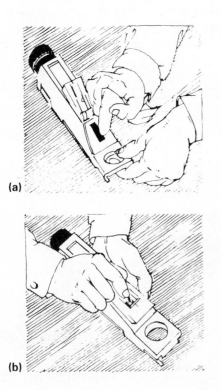

Table 3.6 Temperature and Battery Power

Ambient Temperature	Percentage of Battery Capacity (Fully Charged)
80°F (26.7°C)	100 percent
32°F (0°C)	65 percent
0°F (−17.8°C)	40 percent
−20°F (−28.8°C)	20 percent

Additional electrical loads placed on the system can create additional loads on the battery, or if driving conditions are stop-and-go all day long, the battery may not receive a sufficient rate of charge from the generator/alternator. In summation, battery power, or cranking power, is reduced as the battery temperature is lowered. Table 3–6 shows the typical percentage of output capacity of a fully charged battery at various temperatures. The base for the 100% state of charge is 80°F (26.7°C). Note that a fully charged battery at 0°F (−17.8°C), gives only an equivalent cranking power of 40% of what it can produce at 80°F (26.7°C).

If the battery is at less than a fully charged state, it will provide even less of its output capacity as the temperature drops. Therefore, ensure that the battery can be maintained in a fully charged state in cold weather operation.

BATTERY MAINTENANCE IN THE VEHICLE

Battery maintenance is an ongoing part of fleet service to ensure long life and a minimum of problems while a vehicle is in revenue service. The leading causes of heavy-duty battery failure are shown in Fig. 3–23. Although regular battery maintenance is a normal part of any fleet maintenance program, the degree of maintenance will vary slightly between the normal lead–acid and low-maintenance or maintenance-free batteries. However, the following checks are typical of what is required.

1. Carefully inspect the battery and its mounting pad, hold-down brackets, and cables for signs of loose connections, cracked or broken components, damaged terminal posts or studs, post clamp condition, possible clogged vents or damage to the battery cover, excess dirt buildup, moisture, and corrosion. Any damaged parts should be replaced or repaired immediately.

2. If it is necessary to remove the terminal post clamps for cleaning due to corrosion, always remove the ground cable first. If the terminal clamp is tight, do not beat on it with a hammer or stretch it beyond use with a large screwdriver. Also avoid prying directly against the top or side of the battery case with a large screwdriver or pry bar in order to remove a tight cable clamp. If the cable clamp is tight, use a battery clamp puller similar to that shown in Fig. 3–24(a).

Once the terminal clamps have been removed, they can be cleaned in several ways. If excessive corrosion is evident, hot water can be poured over the terminal clamp to remove the major buildup, followed by wire brushing and emery cloth. Special terminal cleaning brushes are available as shown in Fig. 3–24(b), which can be used effectively for both the battery post and cable clamps.

Battery cable terminal clamps and the top of the battery should be cleaned with a solution of baking soda and water. If excess amounts of corrosion or battery acid exist on the cover of the battery, place all cell caps into place securely, sprinkle baking soda onto the cover, which will neutralize the acid, then flush or wash off with clean water. Do not pile the baking soda up on the cover, since some may enter the individual battery cells and damage the battery.

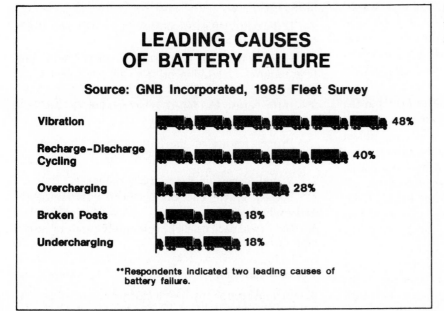

LEADING CAUSES OF BATTERY FAILURE

Source: GNB Incorporated, 1985 Fleet Survey

Vibration	48%
Recharge-Discharge Cycling	40%
Overcharging	28%
Broken Posts	18%
Undercharging	18%

**Respondents indicated two leading causes of battery failure.

FIGURE 3–23 Leading causes of battery failure. *(Courtesy of GNB Incorporated.)*

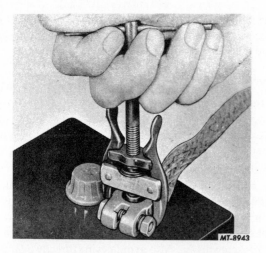

(a)

(b)

FIGURE 3-24 (a) Pulling off a tight battery cable clamp; (b) cleaning brushes for battery terminals and clamps.

If the battery cover only has a dusting of acid or corrosion, a wet cloth, baking soda, and water can be used. Cleaning is done with a solution of baking soda and water at the rate of 1½ cups baking soda per gallon of water. The top of the battery can be dried with a low-pressure air hose and lint-free rag. The battery tray should always be cleaned of corrosion by removing the battery to facilitate the job. Wire-brush the tray and paint it with an acid-resistant paint.

Ensure that no nuts, bolts, or foreign debris at the base of the battery tray can possibly puncture the battery case. Small, hard rocks can also create a problem in this manner by being pounded into the case; remove any dirt or mud that may contain such dangerous objects.

After the battery and tray have been cleaned and serviced, replace the tray. Take care that the battery hold-down strap is not overtightened since this can lead to case cracking, especially in the type of hold-down that runs around the perimeter of the case top. Coat the battery posts and cable terminal clamps with a commercially available terminal grease, and connect the cables to the battery posts. Always connect the grounded cable last; otherwise, severe arcing can occur.

3. On low-maintenance batteries or conventional lead–acid units, the electrolyte level must be checked regularly. Low-maintenance batteries require less attention than the conventional type; however, they require periodic checking. Less antimony is used in the low-maintenance battery than in the conventional battery; maintenance-free models contain no antimony at all in the lead of the grid plate.

Odorless drinking water should be added to those batteries that require topping up of the electrolyte. If a level indicator is not used on the battery, bring the electrolyte level to ½ in. (12.7 mm) above the tops of the separators. On batteries with a split-guide ring inside the cell filler opening, the electrolyte should be brought to the bottom of the ring.

Overfilling of the cell will cause electrolyte to spew from the vent cap when gassing of the battery occurs. Danger of an explosion is increased when this happens, and it causes excessive corrosion to occur on the top of the battery cover and surrounding parts. In addition, short circuits can occur due to this situation.

Maintenance-free batteries do not require the addition of water during their lifetime unless the battery has been mounted or carried at an angle in excess of 45°, which allows the electrolyte to spill from the vent holes under the cover. Check the manufacturer's instructions regarding the electrolyte level for the specific battery.

BATTERY TROUBLESHOOTING

Battery problems are generally a result of poor maintenance practices and neglect. Hard starting can be a direct result of high circuit resistance caused by corrosion of battery terminals or associated wiring, loose wires, and so on. Do not declare the battery to be faulty until you have checked these other causes first.

The purpose of a battery test is to determine the following:

1. If the battery is satisfactorily charged and can therefore remain in service
2. If the battery has a low state of charge, and therefore requires recharging prior to placing it back into service
3. If the battery has failed, is not serviceable, and must therefore be replaced

Proper testing of the battery should include the following:

1. Visual inspection for physical damage
2. Specific gravity check of each cell with the use of a battery hydrometer
3. Battery capacity check, commonly referred to as a load test

Visual Inspection

A visual inspection involves a close check of all areas of the battery case, cover, terminals, hold-down areas, and cell covers (non-maintenance-free type) for possible damage. A check of the electrolyte level must also be done. On maintenance-free batteries, there is no provision for access to check the level of the battery electrolyte. Maintenance-free batteries must have an OCV (open-circuit voltage) check performed with a voltmeter that is accurate to within 0.1-V graduations. This is performed simply by using the voltmeter connections placed between the positive and negative battery posts.

On some low-maintenance and even on some maintenance-free batteries, if the battery fails to perform correctly within a short time of being placed into service, and subsequent tests indicate that the charging system is performing according to specifications, there may be a problem with the battery itself. Under such conditions, the battery OEM dealer should be contacted for possible warranty adjustment. Generally, the battery OEM dealer will perform their own OCV and load tests to confirm the state of the battery. On maintenance-free batteries, closely inspect the built-in hydrometer, such as that shown in Fig. 3–9; if the eye is clear or light in colour, the electrolyte level is low. If it is suspected that there has been a loss of electrolyte caused by the battery having been tipped beyond a 45° angle, it is possible to remove the top cover or a top-cover plaque on some battery models by using a sharp utility knife. In some cases the battery top-cover decal is imprinted with a series of dotted lines that can be cut with the utility knife blade. The ends of the battery vent manifold can then be pried open gently. Close inspection of the individual battery cells and plates can then confirm the reason for failure. This check is not recommended by personnel other than the battery OEM

service personnel. In any case, safety glasses and clothing should always be worn when working around any battery during service.

Specific Gravity Test

If the specific gravity test of the battery after charging, or prior to charging (no additional water added), is 1.225 or higher when corrected to 80 °F (26.7 °C), this indicates that the battery is at least in a 75% charged state, and the load test can now be performed as described in the section "In-Service Battery Capacity or Load Test." If, however, the specific gravity readings are lower than 1.225 but are within 0.050 points between the highest and lowest cells, recharge the battery as recommended in Table 3–7. If the battery state of charge is low, it usually indicates that some problem exists in the vehicle or equipment charging circuit.

Should the specific gravity readings show a variation in excess of 0.050 point between the individual cells, the battery should be replaced because the weak cells will eventually pull the good cells down to their level, as the good cells have to compensate for the weak ones.

Some manufacturers specify that a fully charged battery should have a specific gravity of 1.265, while others state 1.270 corrected in both cases to 80 °F (26.7 °C). Therefore, any reading between 1.265 to 1.270 can be considered acceptable for a fully charged battery. In special environments such as subzero or tropical climates, a fully charged battery may read as high as 1.290 or as low as 1.225, respectively. These readings are, of course, adjusted to suit the particular climate in which the battery will operate.

TABLE 3–7 Battery Charging Guide

| | | (6-Volt and 12-Volt Batteries) | | | | |
| | | Recommended Rate* and Time for Fully Discharged Condition | | | | |
Reserve Capacity Rating	Twenty Hour Rating	5 Amperes	10 Amperes	20 Amperes	30 Amperes	40 Amperes
75 Minutes or less	50 Ampere-Hours or less	10 Hours	5 Hours	2½ Hours	2 Hours	
Above 75 To 115 Minutes	Above 50 To 75 Ampere-Hours	15 Hours	7½ Hours	3¼ Hours	2½ Hours	2 Hours
Above 115 To 160 Minutes	Above 75 To 100 Ampere-Hours	20 Hours	10 Hours	5 Hours	3 Hours	2½ Hours
Above 160 To 245 Minutes	Above 100 To 150 Ampere-Hours	30 Hours	15 Hours	7½ Hours	5 Hours	3½ Hours
Above 245 Minutes	Above 150 Ampere-Hours		20 Hours	10 Hours	6½ Hours	5 Hours

*Initial rate for constant voltage taper rate charger
To avoid damage charging rate must be reduced or temporarily halted if:
    1. Electrolyte temperature exceeds 125°F.
    2. Violent gassing or spewing of electrolyte occurs.
Battery is fully charged when over a two hour period at a low charging rate in amperes all cells are gassing freely and no change in specific gravity occurs. **For the most satisfactory charging, the lower charging rates in amperes are recommended.**
Full charge specific gravity is 1.260-1.280 corrected for temperature with electrolyte level at split ring.

Courtesy of Delco Remy, Division of General Motors.

Battery Testing and Evaluation

When any battery is suspected of being faulty, it is important that you follow the manufacturer's recommended procedures in order to determine whether or not the battery in question can be:

1. Recharged and placed back into service
2. Boost charged and placed back into service
3. Replaced due to being unserviceable
4. Is perfectly satisfactory and requires no service

There are a variety of tests that can be done on the battery; not all of these tests are required since each manufacturer lists what it considers acceptable test procedures for the particular brand of battery. However, many of these tests are considered common to all batteries, and each is listed and explained in the following pages.

Two basic tests are undertaken which will cover all types of batteries in use in both cars and heavy-duty service, such as diesel trucks and equipment. These two basic tests are:

1. The hydrometer (specific gravity) test.
2. The open-circuit voltage test, which can only be used on batteries with exposed cell connectors, or removable vent (filler) caps, because it is important that each cell can be individually monitored. Table 3–2 allows you to correlate specific gravity and voltage readings.

With the use of an expanded scale voltmeter, the actual voltage across the battery terminals can be determined, or on batteries with exposed cell connectors, individual cell voltages can be established.

A serviceable battery with a low specific gravity will have a voltage reading across the positive and negative battery terminals of less than 12 V, whereas a battery in good condition would reflect a reading usually in excess of 12.40 V. These voltmeter readings are always taken with the battery leads disconnected to ensure an accurate reading. Should the voltage read less than 12.40 volts, it should be recharged as shown in Table 3–7.

NOTE: Maintenance-free batteries cannot be checked for specific gravity with a hydrometer, since they have a sealed cover; however, they do include their own built-in hydrometer for evaluating the condition of the battery. A voltmeter can be used across the battery terminals to monitor the actual overall voltage of the battery at any time.

Several battery manufacturers state that prior to testing the battery, the specific gravity of the electrolyte should be at a minimum of 1.225 to 1.230 (2.075 to 2.08 V per cell). However, this is necessary only prior to conducting a high-rate discharge test or a full-load battery test.

One test that can be undertaken on batteries with exposed cell connectors is the monitoring of each cell with a voltmeter. Hard cover batteries require the use of a hydrometer to evaluate cell condition by removing each cell vent plug or filler cap, and the maintenance-free type requires monitoring of the built-in hydrometer, plus the use of a voltmeter.

Several types of battery load-testing equipment are available commercially, and the equipment shown here for illustration may not necessarily be common to your shop or service dealership. However, regardless of the particular brand of testing equipment used, the end results obtained are the same. When special test equipment is unavailable, many service personnel use a simple carbon pile and a bank of headlights, along with a resistor arrangement, in order to apply the necessary load to a battery for testing purposes. When a battery is suspected of being faulty or in a low state of charge, a quick check that is often used is the light-load voltage test, explained below.

Light-Load Voltage Test (Use on New Conventional Batteries). This test is a simple and quick check that allows you to evaluate each individual cell voltage prior to charging the battery. If the battery is charged before the light load test, it is possible for any defective cell to give a false reading and therefore pass the test. Batteries with one-piece covers should be tested by the specific gravity test, not by the voltage method! For the light-load test, use an expanded scale voltmeter with 0.01 scale divisions on its face.

Procedure

1. Check and adjust (top up) the electrolyte in each cell by the addition of distilled water if necessary.
2. To remove the surface charge from the battery, two methods can be used:
   a. By energizing the starter motor for 3 seconds; to prevent the engine from starting, pull the high-tension lead from the coil on a gasoline engine; or on a diesel engine, place the fuel stop lever in the off position.
   b. If the battery is not in the equipment, place a 150-A load across the battery.
3. For a period of 1 minute, place a light load on the battery, such as turning on the headlights, or place a 10-A load across the battery terminals when the battery is not installed in the equipment.
4. Check the voltage of each cell after this 1-minute period by placing the prods of the voltmeter across the individual (+) and (−) cell connectors. At this time it is only necessary to note the highest and the lowest cell voltage readings.
5. Once all cell voltages have been monitored, the battery condition can be evaluated as follows:
   a. The battery is in satisfactory condition if all of the cell voltages read 1.95 V (1.100 specific gravity) or higher, with the difference between cells being less than 0.05 V.
   b. The battery requires changing if the cell voltages

are both above and below 1.95 V (1.100 specific gravity) but the maximum variation between cell readings is less than 0.05 V.

c. Replace the battery if any individual cell reads 1.95 V or more and there is a difference of 0.05 V or greater between cells.

d. Boost charge the battery if all the cells read less than 1.95 V (1.100 SG), and repeat the test.

NOTE: After boost charging should the battery cells still fail to read 1.95 V (1.100 SG), boost charge it once more, and if any cell fails to read a minimum of 1.95 V (1.100 SG), replace the battery. If, however, the battery does come up to at least 1.95 V (1.100 SG) per cell after boost charging, place it on slow charge prior to returning it to service.

Remember that a fully charged battery should read between 1.265 and 1.270 corrected to 80 °F (26.7 °C) prior to returning it to service. A reading of 1.230 SG is equivalent to a 75% charge, while a specific gravity reading of 1.200 is only 50% charged.

In-Service Battery Capacity or Load Test. The use of the light-load test is usually confined to brand new batteries after activation, although it can be used as simply a quick check once the battery is in service. However, a high-rate discharge test or battery load test is more often used to check the ability of the battery to deliver current under load. The instrument used for this purpose is basically a high-capacity or variable resistor. Cell or terminal voltage is used to evaluate the condition of the battery after discharging.

Satisfactory load testing of the battery can be accomplished only if the specific gravity of the electrolyte is 1.225 or higher when corrected to a temperature of 80 °F (26.7 °C). Follow the prechecks and procedure outlined below to conduct a battery load test.

Prechecks

1. If the test is to be done with the battery in the vehicle or equipment, disconnect both battery cables at the terminal posts, and always be sure to disconnect the grounded cable first.

2. Prior to load testing, ensure that the electrolyte level is at the proper level and that the specific gravity is at a minimum of 1.225, although it is advisable to place the battery on charge to bring it to at least 1.260 at 80 °F (26.7 °C). Attempting to load test the battery with a low specific gravity will give false readings. Therefore, either the battery or the charging system may be at fault when low specific gravity readings are obtained prior to load testing.

3. Prior to load testing the maintenance-free battery, look at the cell test indicator, which should appear green in color. If so, the battery is in a sufficient state of charge to be tested. A dark color is a positive indication that the battery is in need of charging prior to testing. A light or yellow color means that the electrolyte level is low and

the battery should be replaced. However, certain low-maintenance and some maintenance-free batteries can have the vent manifold or battery cover removed as discussed earlier to allow access to the cells for purposes of refilling (if, e.g., the electrolyte has been lost through the battery having been tipped over or mounted at an angle in excess of 45 °; either condition allows the electrolyte to spew from the vents of the cover).

However, if the battery does not contain a removable vent manifold, do not attempt charging or testing, but replace the battery. If a maintenance-free battery requires charging, you may have to tip the battery gently slightly from side to side to disperse any gas bubbles from the test indicator.

4. When testing or charging a maintenance-free battery out of the vehicle, special adapter tools are necessary for the side-mounted and top-screw-threaded battery terminals.

a. *Threaded side and top terminal batteries.* After the battery cables have been disconnected from the battery, attach terminal adapter AC-Delco ST-238 or equivalent to the battery terminals as shown in Figs. 3–25 and 3–26. Charge the battery as necessary.

FIGURE 3–25 AC-Delco battery adapter testing tool ST-238 for testing and charging side terminal maintenance-free batteries. *(Courtesy of GMC Truck Division, General Motors Corporation.)*

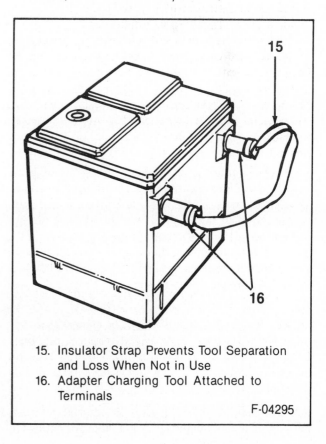

15. Insulator Strap Prevents Tool Separation and Loss When Not in Use
16. Adapter Charging Tool Attached to Terminals

F-04295

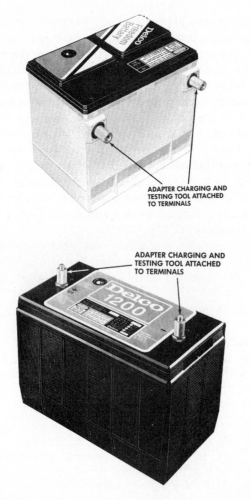

FIGURE 3-26 AC-Delco battery adapter testing tool ST-1201 for testing side or top terminal heavy duty batteries. (*Courtesy of Delco Remy, Division of General Motors Corporation.*)

a particular model of battery and for what period. This load should not be exceeded. Similarly, if insufficient load is placed on the battery, it may appear serviceable when in fact it is not.

If there is more than one battery in the vehicle, check each battery separately after disconnecting them from each other.

Remove battery cables from battery terminals and proceed as follows: When the battery has been brought to a testable state of charge, use the load test to establish whether the battery is performing properly.

Procedure

1. Following the test equipment manufacturer's instructions, assure that the test circuit is off and then connect the battery to the test equipment. Figure 3-28 shows the typical circuit for this test. As noted before, some or all of the instrumentation may be built into the test equipment. Typical test equipment is shown in Fig. 3-29.

2. Connect the battery load tester leads to the respective battery terminals. If the tester leads are red and black, which is usual, the red lead would be connected to the

FIGURE 3-27 Heavy-duty battery load clamps securely attached to battery terminals. (*Courtesy of Delco Remy Division, General Motors Corporation.*)

HEX NUT   ALLIGATOR CLAMPS

LEAD PAD

ALLIGATOR CLAMPS   LEAD PAD   HEX NUT

b. *Threaded top terminal batteries—option.* After the battery cables have been disconnected from the battery, attach terminal hex nuts (AC-Delco 7802) or equivalent required for testing and charging as shown in Fig. 3-27. After the battery cables have been disconnected, it is important that the alligator clamps of the tester or charger be placed between the terminal nuts and the lead pads of the terminal studs as shown in Fig. 3-27. If special adapters are not available, it is very important that the leads from the load-tester machine clamps come into contact with the battery terminal lead pads. Tighten the hex nuts on the threaded battery terminals to hold the load clamps securely, as shown in Fig. 3-27.

NOTE: If the load clamps cannot be clamped securely to the battery lead pads, the suggested load current *must be decreased* according to the manufacturer's recommendations—to 210 A for Delco 1100 and 1200 series batteries.

5. Each manufacturer will list in the test specifications booklet what load (amperage draw) should be applied to

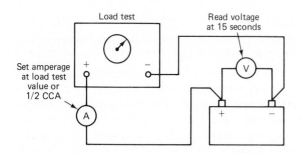

FIGURE 3–28 Simplified schematic of a typical battery load test circuit.

positive battery terminal, while the black lead would be connected to the negative battery terminal.

3. Remove the surface charge from all batteries that have been on charge *if the green hydrometer dot is visible*. This includes batteries in the vehicle having been charged by the vehicle generator. Do not remove surface charge from batteries that have been in storage.

4. Connect a 300-A load across the battery terminals for 15 seconds to remove the surface charge from the battery. With the load turned off, wait at least 15 seconds to allow the battery to recover before proceeding.

5. Turn on and quickly increase the ampere flow to the load test value for the battery being tested (see the example in Table 3–8 for Delco 1100 and 1200 series batteries). As soon as that value is reached, start the timer and hold the current at the load test value for 15 seconds. At the end of 15 seconds and with the current still flowing at the load test value, read the voltage (see Table 3–9 for acceptable 6- and 12-V batteries).

If the battery voltage does not drop below the minimum value shown in Table 3–8 and 3–9, the battery is good and should be returned to service. (The battery

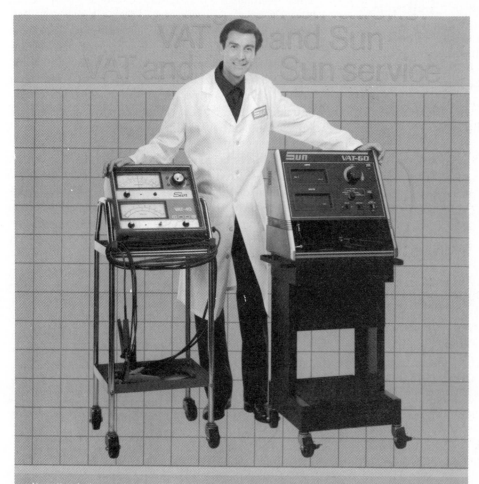

FIGURE 3–29 VAT (volt/ampere tester) model 40 and model 60 load tester mounted on a portable dolly. *(Courtesy of Sun Electric Corporation).*

TABLE 3-8 Battery ampere load chart and voltage readings

PART NUMBER	MODEL NUMBER	AMPERE LOAD
1980337	1200	230
1980474	1110	310
1980514	1150	290

Voltage and Temperature Chart

DEGREES TEMPERATURE	MIMIMUM VOLTAGE
21°C & Above (70°F)	9.6
10°C (50°F)	9.4
–1°C (30°F)	9.1
–10°C (15°F)	8.8
–18°C (0°F)	8.5

temperature must be estimated by feel and by the temperature the battery has been exposed to for the preceding few hours.) If battery voltage drops below the minimum voltage listed, replace the battery.

SUMMARY OF BATTERY TESTS

Detailed instructions have been given in this chapter on how to perform effective checks and tests on both conventional and maintenance-free batteries. It is important that you have a good basic understanding of the minor differences that exist between these two styles of batteries. With an understanding of the previous test procedures, Fig. 3-30 shows in a one-page step format the sequence that can be used to test a heavy-duty truck 12-V battery whether of conventional or maintenance-free design. This test sequence is reproduced courtesy of GNB Batteries, a company known for their Champion PC-31 line of maintenance-free heavy-duty truck batteries, which are capable of 1050 CCA (cold cranking amperes).

COLD WEATHER BATTERY CRANKING POWER

One of the enemies of a lead–acid battery is operation in cold ambient temperature, since a cold battery will not accept a charge as readily as it will when operating in warmer climates. At 0 °F the lead–acid battery loses more than 50% of its ability to crank an engine. A good example of how the battery's energy decreases with a drop of ambient temperature is illustrated in Figure 3–31 for four specific cases, and Fig. 3–32 shows various battery power losses in graph form. One of the main reasons that bus/truck batteries suffer from operation in low ambient temperatures is that they are generally mounted as shown in Fig. 3–17—alongside the chassis frame—where they are exposed to the elements (i.e., both temperature and wind chill factors) as they move along the road.

To counteract the effects of cold weather operation, the battery must be kept in as near a full state of charge as possible by proper selection, hookup, and maintenance of the electrical charging system. This is why the most popular type of battery arrangement for heavy-duty line-haul trucks is the maintenance-free 12-V parallel hookup. This eliminates series–parallel switches, and cable hookups are less complicated. Select a heavy-duty battery that is rated for the engine manufacturer's CCA (cold cranking amperes) with sufficient reserve capacity. Truck batteries are not designed to be totally discharged and recharged several hundred times such as batteries in golf carts. Golf cart batteries are known as *deep cycle* operation units, because of the complete cycling of the battery from a full state of charge to a completely discharged state. Heavy-duty truck group 31 batteries are designed specifically for cranking a diesel engine. Consequently, they will lose 50% of their reserve capacity once they have been totally discharged and recharged 50 to 70 times. This figure is much less on some makes of batteries than on others. Table 3–3 lists some examples of the required CCA requirements for various models of heavy-duty truck engine makes.

Engines that are hard to start due to poor maintenance or a mechanical malfunction will pull down the state of charge of the battery, particularly in cold weather operation. Cold batteries that are allowed to drop to a half-charged condition in winter operation because of excess cranking times will generally accept only a couple of amperes at a charging rate of 14.4 V. This charging rate is insufficient to maintain the battery in a ready state of charge! During the charging and discharging cycles of the battery, both hydrogen and oxygen gases

TABLE 3-9 Ambient temperature versus voltage reading value when load-testing batteries

	21°C (70°F and above)	16°C (60°F)	10°C (50°F)	4°C (40°F)	–1°C (30°F)	–7°C (20°F)	–12°C (10°F)	–18°C (0°F)
12-Volt Battery	9.6	9.5	9.4	9.3	9.1	8.9	8.7	8.5
6-Volt Battery	4.8	4.75	4.7	4.6	4.5	4.4	4.3	4.2

Testing the 12-volt Battery

Equipment
Use a variable load tester having the capacity of loading the
battery at least 600 amps. Tester should have both ammeter
and voltmeter.

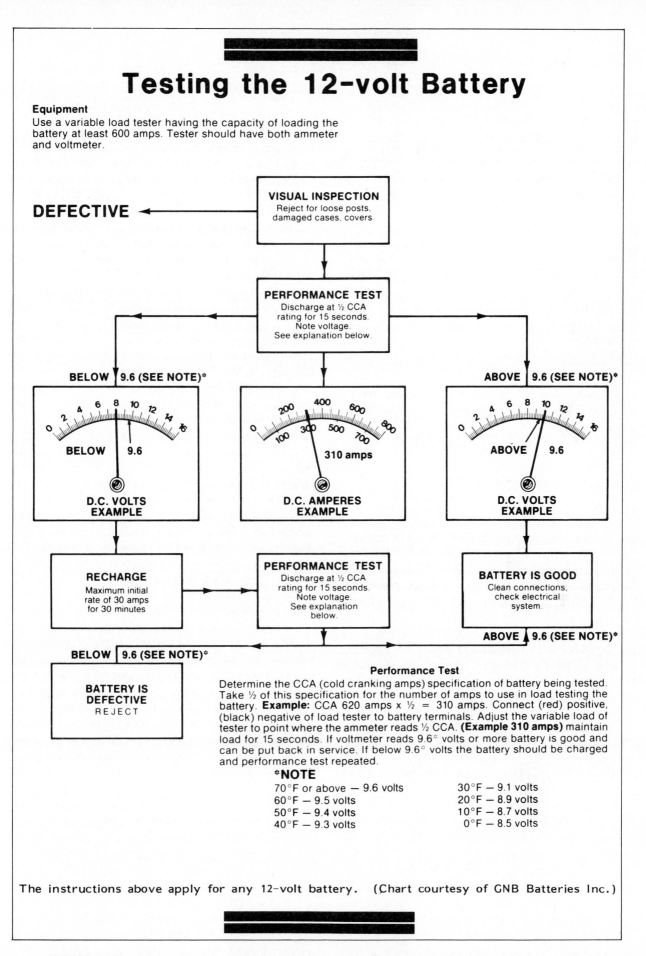

DEFECTIVE ←

VISUAL INSPECTION
Reject for loose posts,
damaged cases, covers.

PERFORMANCE TEST
Discharge at ½ CCA
rating for 15 seconds.
Note voltage.
See explanation below.

BELOW 9.6 (SEE NOTE)*

BELOW 9.6

D.C. VOLTS EXAMPLE

310 amps

D.C. AMPERES EXAMPLE

ABOVE 9.6 (SEE NOTE)*

ABOVE 9.6

D.C. VOLTS EXAMPLE

RECHARGE
Maximum initial
rate of 30 amps
for 30 minutes

PERFORMANCE TEST
Discharge at ½ CCA
rating for 15 seconds.
Note voltage.
See explanation
below.

BATTERY IS GOOD
Clean connections,
check electrical
system.

ABOVE 9.6 (SEE NOTE)*

BELOW 9.6 (SEE NOTE)*

**BATTERY IS
DEFECTIVE**
REJECT

Performance Test

Determine the CCA (cold cranking amps) specification of battery being tested.
Take ½ of this specification for the number of amps to use in load testing the
battery. **Example:** CCA 620 amps x ½ = 310 amps. Connect (red) positive,
(black) negative of load tester to battery terminals. Adjust the variable load of
tester to point where the ammeter reads ½ CCA. **(Example 310 amps)** maintain
load for 15 seconds. If voltmeter reads 9.6* volts or more battery is good and
can be put back in service. If below 9.6* volts the battery should be charged
and performance test repeated.

*NOTE

70°F or above — 9.6 volts	30°F — 9.1 volts
60°F — 9.5 volts	20°F — 8.9 volts
50°F — 9.4 volts	10°F — 8.7 volts
40°F — 9.3 volts	0°F — 8.5 volts

The instructions above apply for any 12–volt battery.   (Chart courtesy of GNB Batteries Inc.)

FIGURE 3–30 Sequential test routine for testing a truck 12-V battery. *(Courtesy of GNB Incorporated.)*

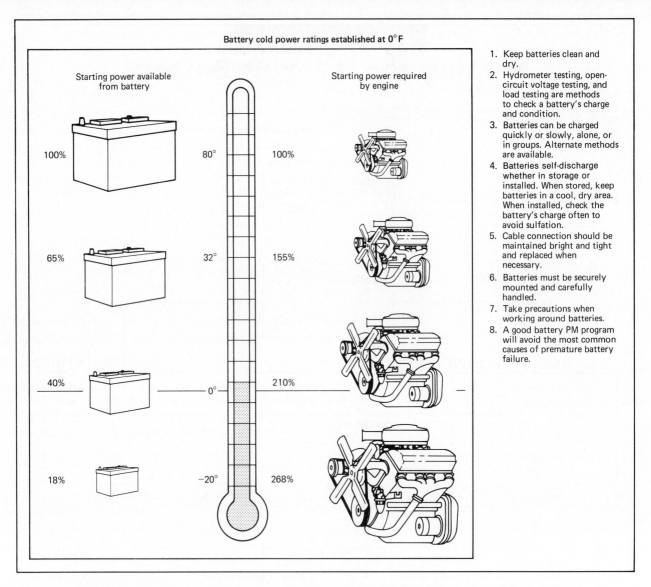

Battery cold power ratings established at 0°F

Starting power available from battery

100%	80°
65%	32°
40%	0°
18%	−20°

Starting power required by engine

100°	
155%	
210%	
268%	

1. Keep batteries clean and dry.
2. Hydrometer testing, open-circuit voltage testing, and load testing are methods to check a battery's charge and condition.
3. Batteries can be charged quickly or slowly, alone, or in groups. Alternate methods are available.
4. Batteries self-discharge whether in storage or installed. When stored, keep batteries in a cool, dry area. When installed, check the battery's charge often to avoid sulfation.
5. Cable connection should be maintained bright and tight and replaced when necessary.
6. Batteries must be securely mounted and carefully handled.
7. Take precautions when working around batteries.
8. A good battery PM program will avoid the most common causes of premature battery failure.

FIGURE 3-31 Battery efficiency and cranking power with respect to ambient temperatures.

are produced, which in turn creates lead sulfate while discharging. When the battery is charged, the process is reversed and the lead sulfate is reconverted into lead dioxide. (This chemical reaction was explained in detail earlier in the chapter.) Batteries that are pulled down to a half-charged condition in winter months will never warm up enough to accept a suitable charge. If a discharged battery is not recharged to an acceptably high enough level, or if it is left in a partially charged state, the lead sulfate formed on the plates will crystallize, becoming extremely hard and brittle. The longer this condition is allowed to exist, the more difficult it becomes to break down when the battery is subjected to a suitable charging rate. Attempting to reactivate the poorly charged battery by a high or even moderate rate will cause extreme temperature levels since the plates will tend to reject a large percentage of the applied charging current. The current not accepted by the plates will cause other chemical reactions that create this heat. For sulfated batteries, recharge should be made at half the normal rate, approximately ½ A per positive plate per cell. To improve battery life

in truck or line-haul operations that are subjected to winter conditions, the battery must be kept warm enough to allow it to readily accept a suitably high charging rate from the engine generator/alternator. Many fleets have a program whereby they check and recharge the batteries inside the maintenance shop each evening. Heat-retaining insulation can also be installed around batteries in winter operating conditions to help the battery accept a higher charging rate.

In cold weather, starting is difficult if the engine cranking speed is too low. For example, on diesel engines used in trucks, heavy equipment, and marine applications, the engine can become hard to start when the cranking speed drops below 150 rpm. Should it drop below 100 rpm, starting may be impossible even with the use of cold weather starting aids.

As far as the electrical system is concerned, where possible use a 24-V system or 12-V high-output system to start the engine. Install slave terminals on the batteries to provide extra power when required. A good electrical system will have a low-resistance cranking motor circuit

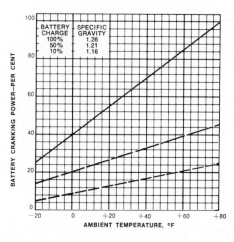

FIGURE 3–32 Effect of ambient temperature on battery cranking power. *(Courtesy of Delco Remy, Division of General Motors Corporation.)*

and will recharge the batteries fully before the engine is stopped at the end of each operating shift.

Freezing of Batteries

Battery electrolyte will freeze at various temperatures, depending on its specific gravity. However, the chances of a battery freezing can be minimized by keeping it in a full state of charge at all times in cold weather operation. Table 3–1 shows the temperatures at which the electrolyte within the battery case will freeze.

CAUTION: Under no circumstances add antifreeze to a battery to prevent freezing of the electrolyte. This will damage the battery and quickly render it unfit for use.

The lower the ambient temperature, the slower will be the chemical reaction within the battery. The effect of low temperature reduces the battery power considerably compared to that which it can produce at 80 °F (26.7 °C). The effect of this reduction in cranking power is shown in the graph of Fig. 3–32.

Battery Heaters

One method that is used by fleet truck operations is that of a battery box with a heater, especially among diesel engine users during cold weather operation. The types of battery heaters used can be classified as follows:

1. Electric strip heater
2. Forced hot air circulated through the battery box
3. Warm coolant circulated through passages in the battery box

With the electric strip type of heater, the energy source can be an electrical wall socket, readily available at service depots or truck stops. Some electric strip type heaters can be operated directly from the vehicle's battery power; however, this tends to lower the reserve power needed to start the engine in cold weather. Some trucks

do carry a separate battery for this purpose, which is then recharged once the engine is running.

When a battery heater is desired, the actual battery box or compartment must be larger than normal to allow ⅝ to ¾ in. (15.87 to 19 mm) of Styrofoam insulation to be placed around all sides of the battery box area. General recommendations are that a 3-in. (7.62-cm) space be designed into the battery box compartment to ensure heating of this area in order to warm the battery.

Figure 3–33 shows the typical arrangement of the electric strip heater which is itself controlled by a temperature-sensing device to maintain a temperature of approximately 80 °F (26.7 °C) inside the battery box compartment. With the electric strip heater, care must be exercised that the hottest spot at any point in the battery does not exceed 125 °F (51.6 °C), since battery damage, plus loss of electrolyte, will occur.

Should the electric strip heater not be considered suitable, and if the engine is in an over-the-road tractor that has occasion to stop at night, then since the engine would be running at a fast idle for cab heat, some of this heat can be directed to the battery box compartment. However, with the engine running all the time, battery freezing would not occur, although it could drop sufficiently in extreme cold ambients to slow the charging process due to the slower chemical reaction.

Many fleets use in-cab and coolant heaters as well as oil pan heaters where legal. Coolant heat or in-cab heat can be directed through circulation passages in the battery box in order to keep it warm. These heaters would be used only at the service depots where the vehicles are parked at night. During warm weather operation, any battery box compartment that has been designed for a battery heater should be opened or the Styrofoam and heater removed or disconnected to ensure that the bat-

FIGURE 3–33 Battery box with an electric strip heater for use in winter operation. *(Courtesy of Detroit Diesel Corporation.)*

Electric strip heater

tery receives adequate ventilation. Improper ventilation of the battery area can cause excess gassing and spewing of electrolyte, leading to premature battery failure.

WINTER PREVENTIVE MAINTENANCE

To ensure that batteries will deliver peak power and therefore quick starting in cold weather, the charging rate must be adjusted for the typical ambient temperatures in which a vehicle is expected to operate. Adjust the rate of charge as recommended by the manufacturer.

In addition to the charging rate, regularly check the following areas:

1. Keep the battery and its connections clean and tight by washing off any acid deposits from the top of the battery with a baking soda and water solution, and rinse with clear water. Take care not to allow any of the solution to enter the cell caps.

Loose or badly corroded connections or terminals will cause high resistance in both the charging and starting circuits, with low charging rates and poor starting the result. Use a battery post cleaning wire brush for this purpose and for the cable clamp ends. As a regular part of the service routine, check the tightness of all connections.

2. Maintain the electrolyte level at all times by the addition of distilled water. Never add acid to the battery since the addition of pure acid to the battery will cause a violent chemical reaction, leading to spatter of the acid. This can cause serious personal injury and battery damage. If, for example, a maintenance-free battery with a removable cover or a regular serviceable battery had been tipped over, producing a loss of electrolyte, a mixture of acid and water could be prepared in the shop for addition to the battery. However, never attempt to add acid to a worn-out battery.

3. Batteries should always be mounted properly to avoid damage from road dirt, water, or flying objects. Vibration can loosen the internal battery plates, wear holes in separator plates, break the seal between the case and cover, and crack the case in several places. The effects of vibration can be minimized on heavy-duty highway trucks by mounting the batteries between the frame members so that the battery plates are mounted at right angles to the direction of normal forward vehicle movement. Although many companies mount the batteries on the outside of the vehicle frame members (outrigger fashion), this should be avoided at all costs, since vibration is greatest in these areas, and the possibility of physical damage from road objects is also greatest. If the batteries are used on a stationary application such as a diesel generator set or irrigation pump, mount the batteries as close to the unit as possible, but not directly to it.

Mount all batteries securely in their hold-down trays. However, avoid overtightening of hold-down brackets since this action can cause cracking of the battery case. Check the degree of resiliency of any cushioning or isolating material, and replace any cushions or shock absorbers that have become hard, brittle, or worn.

4. Damage to a battery is often the direct result of removal or installation procedures. Never attempt to lift a battery by its positive or negative terminal posts, as this can loosen the post and crack the battery case cover. In extreme cases the post could come right out. Do not pry or hammer at terminal post clamps to remove them; loosen all nuts and use a battery cable clamp puller to remove tight ones such as shown in Fig. 3-24(a). Placing a large screwdriver or pry bar under the clamp to force it off the post can puncture the battery cover or crack it, as well as loosening the post.

Do not hammer on a clamp to drive it back onto the battery post when reinstalling it. Use a clamp spreader, as shown in Fig. 3-34. Ensure that the clamp ends have not been pulled together through overtightening on previous occasions, and that you have the correct type of clamp, POS or NEG, for the corresponding battery terminal. Remember that the POS battery post is larger than the NEG one; therefore, do not attempt to use a NEG clamp on a POS post. Similarly, the use of a POS clamp on a NEG post will result in a loose connection. Ensure that when the cable clamp is placed onto its mating battery post, it is installed all the way down, or is flush with the top of the post.

5. Make certain that the engine oil used is of the correct viscosity as recommended by the engine manufacturer. Heavy oil can really play havoc with the cranking speed, lowering the state of charge of the batteries and creating starter motor problems through overheating.

6. Ensure that the alternator drive belts are properly adjusted to avoid slippage, which will cause a low charging rate. Be careful not to overtighten drive belts, particularly in winter operation, since belt breakage can result. Always check the drive belt tension with a drive belt tension gauge.

7. Always avoid unnecessary idling at any time, but more so in the winter months since the alternator output

FIGURE 3-34 Spreading the battery cable clamp with a pair of special pliers. *(Courtesy of Kent-Moore Heavy Duty Division, SPX Corporation.)*

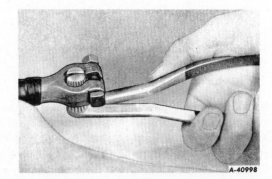

at this low speed will not produce sufficient charging current to charge a cold battery. Wasted fuel and incomplete combustion will result in the cylinders due to idling. This is why a programmable (time) automatic engine idle shutdown is found on the new electronic engine fuel control systems such as those manufactured by Detroit Diesel Corporation, Caterpillar, Cummins, and Mack.

8. Some fleets employ engine block heaters with an optional cable spliced into this cord to allow a battery trickle charger connection so that when the block heater is plugged in to an electrical outlet, the battery charger will also operate.

COLD WEATHER BOOST STARTING PRECAUTIONS

In extremely low temperatures, it is often the practice, albeit not a good one, for service personnel to use booster batteries and/or special generators that develop up to 24 V and apply this voltage to a 12-V system of cars and trucks to provide additional power to crank stalled engines. Severe damage to electrical system components can be caused by applying cranking voltages that exceed the voltage for which the equipment is designed. Although excessive voltage is specifically damaging to the electronic components, it can also be detrimental to the battery, ignition system, charging circuit, cranking circuit, lights, and other electrical accessories. Therefore, voltages higher than those for which the system was designed should *never* be used.

The following damage will result from applying excessive voltage during cranking:

1. *Battery.* When discharged, the battery will accept a high charging current from the slave setup or booster arrangement. This will usually cause the electrolyte to spew out of the vent plugs, resulting in a loss of electrolyte, which lowers the capacity of the battery for future use. Also from a safety standpoint, spewing electrolyte in the presence of a spark may result in an explosion and serious personal injury.

2. *Charging circuit.* Regulator contacts may weld together or diodes and transistors can be burned out, requiring regulator replacement.

3. *Cranking circuit.* The solenoid contacts have a tendency to weld together, which makes it impossible to break the cranking circuit leading to motor winding damage through burning; or the windings may be thrown out of the armature.

4. *Ignition system.* Extremely high currents will pass through either the distributor contact points or semiconductor components in high-energy ignition systems, causing severe point damage or immediate system failure.

CAUTION: Under no circumstances attempt to boost-start any vehicle or piece of equipment rated at 12 V with a 24-V arrangement.

EMERGENCY JUMP STARTING

It is very common for people to jump start one vehicle from another vehicle, especially in cold weather when a boost charger is not readily available. This practice can lead to serious charging system problems if the jump start procedure is not followed very closely. Connecting cables improperly can lead not only to charging system problems, but can also damage both the starting system and battery. Prior to the sequence of events for jump starting, pay special attention to the following safety precautions.

Safety Precautions

1. Wear safety glasses or shield your eyes.

2. Cover the vent caps after ensuring that they are tight on the batteries of both vehicles; place a damp cloth over the vents of both batteries to minimize gassing or spewing of electrolyte during jump starting.

3. Clean the tops of both batteries of any sulfation, dirt, grease, and so on.

4. Ensure that both the discharged battery and the booster battery are of the same voltage.

5. Ensure that vehicles are of the same ground polarity.

6. Do not allow the vehicles to touch one another at any time.

Avoid jump-starting vehicles by bringing bumpers into contact because by this procedure direct electrical connection is made, and serious short circuiting can occur.

7. Ensure that all vehicle electrical loads or accessories are switched off.

8. Make certain that the parking brakes of both vehicles are securely set; place the transmission in neutral or park, as the case may be.

9. Do not lean over the battery when jump starting.

10. On maintenance-free batteries, do not atempt to jump-start a battery if the built-in hydrometer is light yellow in color; replace the battery.

11. Do not allow the clamps from one booster cable to touch the clamps on the other cable.

12. When attaching the jumper cable clamps to the positive terminals of the batteries, make certain that neither clamp contacts any other metal.

13. To lessen the chance of an explosion, never expose the battery to open flames or electric sparks. Do not smoke near the battery. Batteries give off a gas that is flammable and explosive.

14. To lessen the risk of a short circuit, remove rings, metal watch bands, and other metal jewelry. Do not allow metal tools to contact the positive battery terminal (or metal in contact with it) and any other metal on the vehicle.

15. Make certain that no one is standing in front of or behind the vehicles.

16. When connecting booster cables, ensure that you avoid hot or electrical hazards on the vehicle such as moving fans and exhaust manifolds. Avoid causing sparks!

17. The major safety precaution is to make the final connection to ground on the engine at some distance from the battery. This helps reduce the chance of an explosion due to sparks.

Although the foregoing list may seem lengthy, it is precisely these types of safety precautions that most people forget, leading to injury to either vehicle or person during jump starting.

CAUTION: Do not attempt to jump-start vehicles having opposite grounds; serious charging system damage can result.

CAUTION: To prevent the vehicle from moving and the engine from starting while performing these checks, engage the parking brake and place the transmission in neutral or park position.

12-V Systems

Vehicles with diesel engines have more than one battery because of the higher torque required to start a diesel engine. This procedure can be used to start a single-battery vehicle from any of the diesel vehicle batteries. However, in the opposite case, it may not be possible to start a diesel engine from a single battery in another vehicle, at low temperatures.

Procedure

1. Turn off all electric motors and accessories in both vehicles. Turn off all lights except those needed to protect the vehicle or light up the work area. Turn off the ignition, apply the parking brake firmly. If the vehicle(s) has an automatic transmission, shift to "park" (if no "park" position, shift to "neutral"). If the vehicle(s) has a manual transmission, shift to "neutral." Do this in both vehicles. For vehicles with ac wheel lock control, refer to step 13.

2. If the discharged battery has filler caps, check the fluid level. *Do not check with an open flame and do not smoke.* Add clear drinking water to the proper level if low, and replace caps before jump starting.

3. Inspect the vehicle with the discharged battery to establish whether it is a NEG(−) or POS (+) ground. The grounded cable is always the one that is bolted to either the engine block or vehicle frame. The battery cable that is connected to the starter body, relay, or solenoid is the nongrounded connection.

4. On negative-ground systems, connect one end of a jumper or booster cable to the (+) terminal of the battery in the operating vehicle or booster battery, and the other end of the same cable to the positive (+) terminal of the discharged vehicle's battery. If both units are positively grounded, connect the negative terminals first from the charged battery to the discharged battery.

CAUTION: When connecting the ground booster cable to the system, it should first be connected to the charged battery, then the opposite end of the cable/clamp should

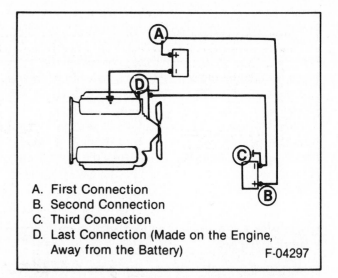

A. First Connection
B. Second Connection
C. Third Connection
D. Last Connection (Made on the Engine, Away from the Battery)

F-04297

FIGURE 3–35 Example of a 12-V single battery starting system jumper cable connections (gas or diesel engine). *(Courtesy of GMC Truck Division, General Motors Corporation.)*

preferably be connected to ground on the truck chassis frame at some distance from the flat batteries. This action will minimize the chance of an explosion due to sparks. On cars, light pickup trucks, and vans, although service personnel often connect the ground cable clamp directly from the negative battery terminal of the charged battery to the negative post on the flat battery, this can cause an explosion. It is better to place the grounded booster cable clamp to the engine block or frame. Failure to do this can result in excessive resistance through the dead battery and failure to crank the engine of the stalled vehicle fast enough for starting purposes. Refer to Fig. 3–35 for typical booster starting cable connections for a single 12-V battery midrange truck arrangement, and to Fig. 3–36 for the connections to a heavy-duty truck with a 12-V parallel battery hookup arrangement using either two, three, or four batteries connected as shown.

5. Connect the first jumper cable from positive "+" (red) terminal on one battery to the positive "+" (red) terminal on the other battery. Never connect "+" (red) to "−" (black), or "−" to "+".

6. Connect one end of the second cable to the grounded negative "−" (black) terminal of the good (charged) battery.

7. Connect the other end of the second jumper cable to a solid, stationary, metallic point on the engine of the vehicle with the discharged battery but at a point *away from the battery,* 450 mm (18 in.) or more from the battery, if possible. Do not connect it to pulleys, fans or other parts that will move when the engine is started.

8. Start the engine on the vehicle with the good (charged) battery and run the engine at a moderate speed, then attempt to start the engine of the stalled vehicle. If the

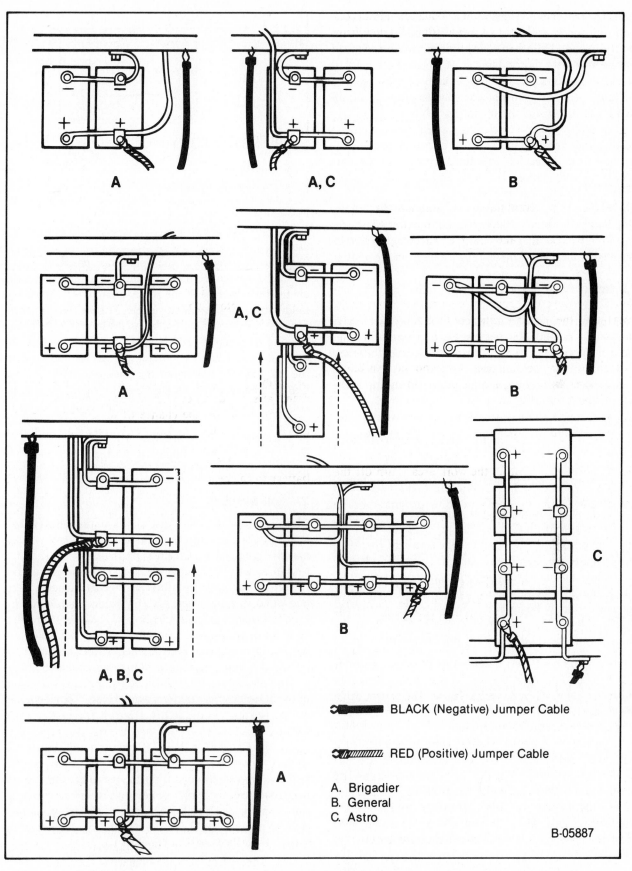

BLACK (Negative) Jumper Cable

RED (Positive) Jumper Cable

A. Brigadier
B. General
C. Astro

B-05887

FIGURE 3–36 Where to place the battery cables when attempting to jump start a truck engine. *(Courtesy of GMC Truck Division, General Motors Corporation.)*

stalled engine does not start within 15 to 20 seconds, pause and wait for 30 seconds to 1 minute to allow the starter motor to cool. Failure to follow this precaution can lead to serious starter motor damage. If repeated attempts to start the stalled engine fail, check further for the reasons of failure to start. Do not continue to crank and pull down the battery of the operating vehicle.

9. Once the stalled vehicle has started, idle the engine of the other vehicle, and remove the ground cable connection from the vehicle with the discharged or low battery condition; remove the other end of the same cable from the booster battery vehicle.

10. Failure to follow the reverse sequence of disconnecting battery booster cables can result in battery damage.

11. Remove the other cable by disconnecting it from the boosted or discharged battery first, then from the booster battery.

12. Remove and discard the damp cloths from the battery vent covers.

13. Jump starting with ac wheel lock controls or ABS (anti-brake skid). If it is necessary to jump-start the vehicle from a booster battery, the circuit boards in the wheel lock control may be damaged. To avoid this condition, the following procedure should be used for jump starting a vehicle equipped with wheel lock control:

   a. Connect the jumper cables between the booster battery and the discharged vehicle battery, according to normal recommended procedures.

   b. Start the vehicle according to normal procedures.

   c. Turn on major electrical accessories, including lights and heater blower.

   d. Disconnect the jumper cables from the vehicle battery according to normal procedures.

The procedure above allows the transient energy to be dissipated through several circuits rather than having it all flow through the wheel lock control system.

14. Remove the battery cables by reversing the preceding sequence exactly. Begin by removing the last clamp first; that is, remove the jumper cable from the engine of the vehicle with the discharged battery as the first step.

12- to 24-V Electrical Systems

Some heavy-duty diesel starting systems operate on the series–parallel principle, where the starting motor operates on 24 V but the charging system is only 12 V. This is accomplished through the use of a series–parallel switch or transformer–rectifier in the electrical circuit (see Figs. 9–36 through 9–46 and 8–71 through 8–74).

Proper precautions must be taken when jump starting vehicles with 24-V cranking/12-V operational electrical systems. Prior to starting, check to make sure that the electrical systems of the stalled vehicle and the operating vehicle are the same. A vehicle with a 24-V cranking and 12-V operational system should be started only with a vehicle containing the same system. Use two sets of jumper cables heavy enough to carry the current.

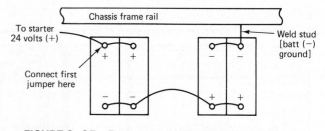

FIGURE 3–37 Battery connections required for jump starting a 24-V system. *(Courtesy of Detroit Diesel Corporation.)*

Procedure

1. Ensure that the electrical accessories of both vehicles are off.

2. Start the engine of the operating vehicle.

3. Take one pair of jumper cables and connect the vehicle load (A) battery of the running engine to the vehicle load battery of the stalled vehicle. Follow the same procedure when attaching cables as given above for jump starting of straight 12-V systems.

4. Take the second set of jumper cables and connect the cranking (B) battery of the operating vehicle to the cranking battery of the stalled engine. Again ensure that correct polarity is observed when connecting this set of cables.

5. Attempt to crank and start the stalled engine.

6. When the stalled engine is started, disconnect the jumper cables in the exact reverse order of attachment.

24 Volt Systems

Many European and Australian market heavy-duty trucks, buses, and tour coaches employ a 24-V starting and charging system. Coaches, particularly, use the 24-V system because of the large electrical accessories that they require for passenger comfort. Such items include TV sets and video tape machines, AM/FM radio headphones for each passenger, cellular telephones, and a host of other comfort features not normally found on heavy-duty trucks. These vehicles are equipped with either two 12-V or four 6-V batteries connected in series as shown in Fig. 3–37. To isolate voltage-sensitive equipment on a coach or truck such as the radio/cassette player, CB, video, and accessories such as the DDEC (Detroit Diesel Electronic Controls), ATEC (Allison Transmission Electronic Controls), the Caterpillar PEEC (Programmable Electronic Engine Controls), or 3176-ECM, all system control switches *must* be turned off during the jump/boost starting procedure. Once the connections have been made as shown in Fig. 3–37, follow the same precautions and procedures as you would for the heavy-duty 12-V starting system described and shown earlier.

ACTIVATING DRY CHARGED BATTERIES

We briefly discussed wet versus dry batteries earlier in the chapter, the major difference being that the wet battery contains electrolyte at its time of manufacture, whereas the dry battery contains no electrolyte at manufacture. When the dry charged battery is required for service, it can be activated by the addition of electrolyte (dilute sulfuric acid), which is readily available from the battery supplier either in bulk form or in quart or liter containers.

The dry charged battery therefore has a longer shelf life than a wet battery, which of course will self-discharge over a period of time due to the internal chemical reaction within the battery cells.

To activate a dry charged battery, follow the manufacturer's instructions supplied with the battery; however, the following sequence is typical of the procedure that can be followed when activating a dry charged battery.

1. Prior to opening the acid container or containers, remember that acid can burn the skin and clothing and damage painted surfaces. Wear a protective apron, gloves, and eye protection.
2. Use a small funnel to assist you in pouring the electrolyte into each battery cell. Fill each cell to the top of the separators, which will allow for expansion of the electrolyte as the battery chemically reacts and also in case it requires boost charging.
3. Rock the battery from side to side very gently to force out any trapped air. This will also assist in saturating the cell plates with electrolyte.

NOTE: Many dry batteries have protective cell cover seals that must be punctured once the vent plugs or screw-in cell caps are removed. These seals hermetically seal each cell to prevent moisture from entering the battery during storage. Before adding electrolyte to the battery, break these cell seals by pushing a blunt instrument down into them, taking care not to damage the tops of the separator plates.

On batteries with temporary built-in cell seals push the vent plug down into each cell very carefully. Do not attempt to fish out these seals, as damage to the separator plates may occur, causing a short circuit. The seals will normally drop into the cells and stay there with no damage to the battery.

4. Boost-charge automotive 12-V batteries at about 15 A and 6- or 12-V heavy-duty diesel batteries at 30 A until the specific gravity of the electrolyte is at 1.250 or higher corrected to 80 °F (26.7 °C); the battery should be at a minimum temperature of 60 °F (15.5 °C) prior to activating it. During charging, if smoke appears from any cell, or a blue haze, switch off the charger because the battery is faulty. If the electrolyte bubbles excessively or spews out, reduce the rate of charge and gradually allow the specific gravity to climb to at least 1.265 at 80 °F (26.7 °C) or 1.250 at 60 °F (15.5 °C).
5. Once the battery has reached the recommended specific gravity, allow it to sit for 15 or 20 minutes, then recheck the level of the electrolyte in each cell. If

necessary, add additional electrolyte, but do not add water at this time.
6. The open-circuit voltage of the battery can also be checked now with a voltmeter placed across the positive and negative battery posts; should the voltmeter read less than 10 V on a 12-V battery, or less than 5 V on a 6-V battery, a reverse cell or an open circuit exists within the battery, and it should be replaced.

BATTERY STORAGE

Storage of batteries is often considered an unimportant item, when in fact it can cause serious problems if not done properly. Although it is possible to stack batteries one on top of another while they are in cartons such as with dry charged units, do not stack them more than four high. If possible, place them on shelving, which removes the weight from each battery. An example of a battery storage rack is shown in Fig. 3–38.

New or out-of-use batteries must be stored properly to assure maximum use and life once they are put into service. A cool, dry area will best preserve the battery. Warm, hot, or humid areas will accelerate self-discharge. Batteries that contain electrolyte should always be brought to a full state of charge prior to storage. Batteries should also be clean to prevent dirt, moisture, and traces of electrolyte from forming a discharge path between the terminals on the battery case. Monitor the battery state of charge on a periodic basis, and if the state of charge goes below 75% or the hydrometer indicates a low state of charge, recharge. Maintaining a good state of charge while in storage is important to prevent the formation of crystalline sulfate in the plates, which reduces the amount of active material available for battery performance.

Dry, unactivated batteries must be stored in a dry atmosphere to prevent humidity in the air from entering the battery and causing the plates to self-discharge. Wet batteries while in storage will of course self-discharge; the rate of self-discharge depends on the ambient temperature in which they are stored. Wet lead–acid batteries will self-

FIGURE 3–38 Typical battery storage rack.

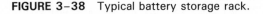

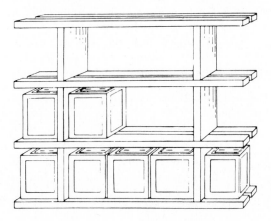

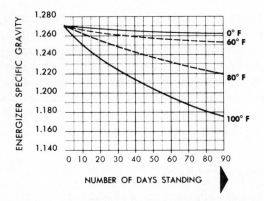

FIGURE 3-39 Self-discharge rate of wet storage batteries. *(Courtesy of Delco Remy, Division of General Motors Corporation.)*

discharge at 0.001 specific gravity per day over a typical 30-day period. To reduce the degree of self-discharge, store wet batteries in a cool, dry place away from heat ducts and shielded from direct sunlight in the summer. A typical example of how storage temperatures will affect the specific gravity of the battery is shown in Fig. 3-39.

When storing wet or dry batteries, rotate them on the basis of first in, first out so that no battery is stored longer than another prior to using. Check the state of charge of wet batteries once a month and recharge them at the rate of approximately 1 A per each positive plate. Dry charged batteries can be stored for up to a year without problems, or even longer. Maintenance-free batteries have already been filled with electrolyte at the time of manufacture; however, since they contain no antimony in their plate structure, they will self-discharge at a lower rate than will a conventional lead–acid battery. The maintenance-free battery can be stored for up to one year.

Batteries are breakable. Cases are made of hard rubber or plastic, and even the toughest may split or crack if dropped or hit with a sharp object. If this happens, hazardous electrolyte can leak out and create a dangerous or damaging situation. Always keep a neutralizing agent such as baking soda in battery-handling areas to neutralize spilled electrolyte. After neutralizing, flush away with plenty of water.

Always dispose of unwanted batteries properly. Used, dead or defective batteries still contain sulfuric acid and lead or lead compounds. These materials can create hazardous conditions unless disposed of properly.

CHARGING OF BATTERIES

A routine maintenance procedure with batteries is the occasional need to either slow or fast charge a battery that has lost some of its potential. The correct charging rate will depend on the type and actual rated capacity of the battery. Battery manufacturers publish charts showing the rate of charge recommended for both slow and fast charging.

Automotive (car) batteries usually have a slow-charging rate of 4 to 5 A, with as much as 7 to 8 A on the heavy-duty type. Commercial or heavy-duty diesel batteries usually average a slow charging rate of 8 to 10 A, but in the larger sizes, initial charging currents up to 20 A are recommended. Generally speaking, normal recharging rates are about 50 to 70% greater than the initial charging rates for new batteries.

Charge rates between 3 and 50 A are satisfactory as long as spewing of electrolyte does not occur or the battery does not feel excessively hot [over 52 °C (125 °F)]. If spewing occurs or temperature exceeds 52 °C (125 °F), the charging rate must be reduced or temporarily halted to permit cooling. Battery temperature can be estimated by touching or feeling the battery case.

Given in this chapter are charts and tables showing the recommended rate of charge, both slow and fast, for maintenance type and maintenance-free batteries. However, if the charging rate of a battery is not known, it may be calculated by dividing the actual capacity by 12; therefore, the charging rate (slow charge) for an 80-Ah battery would be 6.6 A.

CAUTION: Prior to attempting to recharge any battery, you should remember that while under charge, the battery will emanate explosive fumes. Exercise the necessary safety precautions, such as adequate ventilation, safety glasses, and so on, while charging batteries.

Batteries that have been allowed to completely discharge over a long period or allowed to stand in a discharged condition may be very slow in accepting current when placed on charge. In fact, some batteries may even have an open-circuit voltage that is so low that it will not turn on polarity protection circuits built into some chargers. Refer to the charger manufacturer's specific instructions for overriding this protective circuitry when necessary.

Batteries in a very low state of charge may also appear to be unable to accept a charge when the charger is operating properly. These batteries are usually accepting a charging current that is too low to measure on typical charger ammeters. As a general rule of thumb, a 12-V battery with an open-circuit voltage of 10.0 V or less (5 V or less for a 6-V battery) before the battery is placed on charge will be very slow to accept a charge. Some 12 V maintenance-free batteries may be slow to accept a charge if the open-circuit voltage is below 11.0 V.

If the charger is capable of placing a charging voltage of 16 V or more across a badly discharged 12-V battery (8 V across a 6-V battery), it may take as many as four hours for a measurable current to flow. At lower charging voltages, it may take as many as 16 hours for a measurable current to flow. If no measurable current is flowing after these times, it may be assumed that the battery is chemically unable to accept a charge and it should be replaced.

When dealing with maintenance-free batteries, do not

confuse this low initial current at a charging voltage of 16 V as indicating full charge. The open-circuit voltage check prior to placing the battery on charge will verify that the battery is very discharged rather than fully charged. Once the battery is accepting charge, the current will increase and/or the charging voltage will decrease until the battery approaches full charge.

Methods of Battery Charging

A battery or batteries can be recharged by two widely used methods:

1. Slow charging
2. Fast, or boost, charging

The decision whether to use the slow or fast charge method will depend on the time available in which to charge the battery, the actual existing state of charge of the battery in question, and whether the battery has just been activated from storage or is new. Generally, boost or fast charging will provide only a surface charge condition, while the slow-charge method allows a complete recharge of the battery plates.

The degree of charge that a battery receives is equal to the charging rate in amperes multiplied by the time in hours. Therefore applying a 6-A rate to a battery for 6 hours would be equal to a 36-Ah charge to the battery; a 25-A charging rate for 2 hours would be a 50-Ah charge to the battery.

To charge the battery fully, you must replace the ampere-hours or ampere-minutes that have actually been removed from it. Also, when recharging a battery, because of breakdown of the plates (shedding), an extra 20% charge rate is usually required to ensure complete charging.

In most cases maintenance-free batteries whose load test values are less than 200 A will have the green dot visible after at least a 50-Ah charge. Most batteries whose load test values are greater than 200 A will have the green dot visible after at least a 75-Ah charge. In the event that the green dot does not appear after this amount of charging, continue charging for another 50 to 75 Ah. If the green dot still does not appear, replace the battery.

The time required for a charge will vary based on several factors:

1. *Size of battery*. Example: A completely discharged large heavy-duty battery requires more than twice the recharging time as that for a completely discharged small passenger car battery.
2. *Temperature*. Example: A longer time will be needed to charge any battery at −18 °C (0 °F) than at 27 °C (80 °F). When a fast charger is connected to a cold battery, the current accepted by the battery will be very low at first; the battery will accept a higher rate as the battery warms.
3. *State of Charge*. Example: A completely discharged battery requires more than twice as much as a half-charged battery. Because the electrolyte is nearly pure

water and a poor conductor in a completely discharged battery, the current accepted is very low at first. Later, as the charging current causes the electrolyte acid content to increase, the charging current will increase.
4. *Charger Capacity*. Example: A charger that can supply only 5 A will require a much longer period of charging than will a charger that can supply 30 A or more.

The state of charge of the battery can be ascertained in three general ways.

1. *By plate color*. Batteries that use clear transparent cases allow you to monitor the color of both the positive and negative plates. When discharged, the positive plates are darker than the negative ones. When fully charged, the positive plate is a rich chocolate brown, and the negative one is gray.
2. *By the density of the acid* (a widely used method). When the battery is fully charged and corrected for specific gravity to 80 °F (26.7 °C), the density of the battery electrolyte should be 1.265 to 1.270. However, some batteries may show specific gravity readings as high as 1.280 when corrected to 80 °F (26.7 °C).

Any battery that exhibits the 1.265 to 1.270 reading is fully charged and can be placed into service without any problem. Some batteries for special ambient operating conditions can exhibit specific gravity readings of from 1.280 to 1.300. When a battery has been on charge for some time, readings taken a half-hour after the charger has been shut off or the battery disconnected will show minor variations from those taken while the battery is on charge.
3. *By measuring the voltage*. When a battery is fully charged and allowed to stand for more than half an hour, the voltage value per cell will be approximately 2.6; this value will fall to about 2.1 V per cell within a few hours. For example, the voltage of a typical 12-V battery is equal to the number of cells multiplied by 2.6 (when just charged), to give us six cells × 2.6 = 15.6 V, which will drop to six cells × 2.1 = 12.6 V in a few hours.

NOTE: When a battery is being charged by either the slow or fast (boost) method, the temperature of the electrolyte should be monitored to ensure that it does not exceed 51.6 °C (125 °F). If violent gassing or spewing of electrolyte occurs, the charger should be switched off, or its rate reduced; otherwise, severe damage to the internal plates will occur and the battery will have to be replaced. On maintenance-free batteries, overcharging can cause a loss of water from the electrolyte through the battery cover vents.

Slow Charging

Charging batteries requires a source of direct current. Slow charging is generally done in a shop environment in which one or more batteries can be charged at the same time. Maintenance shops or service outlets today employ slow chargers adjusted by a variable rheostat on the control panel, so that the rate of charge is established easily and quickly to suit batteries of various ratings.

Whether one or more batteries are to be charged, it is very important that the charger's positive and negative leads be readily identifiable. Most chargers will clearly indicate leads by the letters POS (+) or NEG (−) at the respective terminals. Some may simply be color coded, with a red lead for the positive and black or blue for the negative lead. If for some reason these leads are not readily identifiable, use a voltmeter, since its leads are always clearly marked. Unless the voltmeter leads are properly connected, it will not read at all and will actually cause

FIGURE 3–40 Typical causes of battery failures: **(a)** plate swelling due to overcharging; **(b)** overcharging caused positive plate to swell and short out against negative plate strap; **(c)** short between positive and negative plates at upper left corner; **(d)** blistered and washed out negative plate; **(e)** washed out positive plate; **(f)** lower growth has shorted out negative and positive plates; **(g)** growth on top of negative plate caused shorting to positive plate strap; **(h)** sulfation growth, both normal and permanent on battery plates.

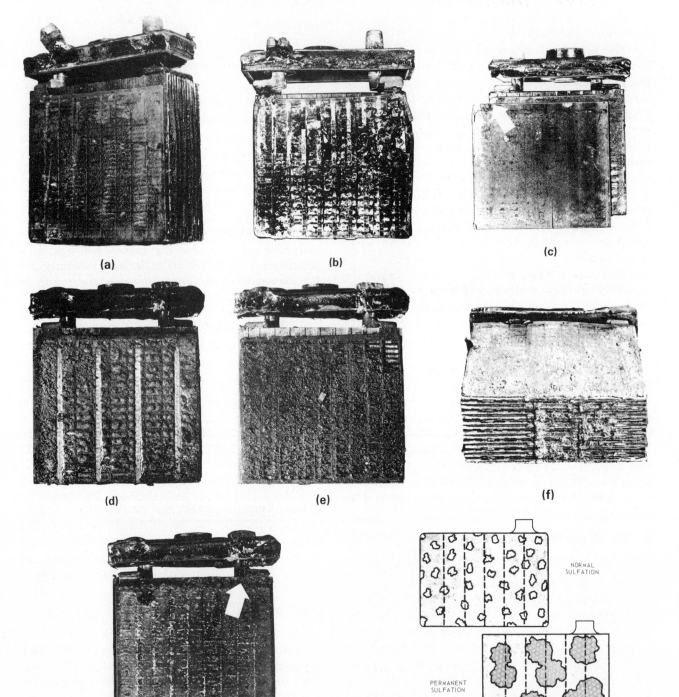

(a)

(b)

(c)

(d)

(e)

(f)

(g)

(h)

the needle on the face dial to kick in the wrong direction if improper polarity is attempted.

Table 3-7 shows the recommended charge rates for both slow and fast charging of batteries. However, a typical charging rate for slow charging would be 1A per positive plate/cell. With nine plates per cell in the average battery, four of the nine will be positive plates; therefore, the slow charge rate would be 4 A. While the battery is on-charge, check the specific gravity once per hour unless the battery is in a very low state of charge, which means that it can be left on charge for several hours before checking the specific gravity.

Once it has been on charge for several hours, check each cell's specific gravity once per hour; maximum specific gravity is reached when no change occurs in the specific gravity over a 3-hour period or when the charging current stabilizes on a constant-voltage charger.

If a maintenance-free battery is to be charged for a period of time that requires overnight charging, a timer or voltage controller charger is definitely recommended, since overcharging of the maintenance-free type battery can cause a loss of water from the battery electrolyte. If the battery charger is not equipped with these special safety controls, ensure that a 3-A rate is not exceeded for batteries rated at 80 minutes or less capacity. On batteries that are rated between 80 and 125 minutes, a maximum of 5 A should be used. Heavy-duty diesel batteries rated in excess of 125 minutes should be charged at the rate recommended in Table 3-7.

Although slow charging will bring most batteries back to a full state of charge, batteries that have been in storage for extended periods, or that have operated with low electrolyte levels, can become sulfated. This condition is caused by rapidly discharging the battery, by allowing the electrolyte level to fall below the tops of the plates, by the use of impure or dirty water, or by allowing the battery to discharge too far and to remain discharged. A defective generator/alternator that only partially charges the battery will eventually cause sulfation of the plates. Sulfation is the chemical effect resulting in the formation of white lead sulfate on the surfaces of the plates, which is a normal result of completely discharging a battery. An example is shown in Fig. 3-40.

Sulfated Batteries

Battery recharging should always be done as soon as possible after the battery has been used, and preferably within several days at the longest. The reason for this is that lead sulfate, which is formed on the battery plates due to the chemical reaction that occurs during discharge, will tend to harden over a short period if the battery is not recharged correctly. This would result in a condition commonly known as a sulfated battery. This sulfation will cause the battery to be unable to absorb a complete charge from either an alternator or a battery charger. The capacity of the sulfated battery is therefore substantially reduced, and if undercharging continues, the battery soon becomes useless. In cold weather conditions, a discharged or undercharged battery can be subject to electrolyte freezing. Also keep in mind that a low water level can also cause a battery to become sulfated.

Types of Battery Chargers

The two basic types of battery chargers that are widely used for charging a group of batteries are:

1. The current-limiting type, also called a constant-current or series charger
2. The voltage-limiting type, sometimes referred to as a constant-voltage or parallel charger

Each of these systems has advantages and disadvantages. The major ones are as follows:

Series Charger (Fig. 3-41)
1. Various sizes and voltages of batteries may be charged in the same circuit at the same time.
2. The same current flows through all batteries in the circuit, and that current is adjustable.
3. Persistent monitoring of each battery in the circuit is necessary to avoid damaging overcharge.
4. Assures that all batteries in the circuit are being charged.

Parallel Charger (Fig. 3-42)
1. All batteries charged at the same time must be of the same nominal voltage (i.e., must have the same number of cells). They will all be charged at the same voltage.
2. Variable current often allows batteries to be charged faster, with individual batteries accepting current according to their internal condition.
3. Monitoring is necessary to prevent overcharge, but this type closely resembles a vehicle charging system. Many chargers of this type have a voltage limit that will prevent overcharge.
4. Certain batteries in the circuit may provide a lower-resistance path for the current, retarding the recharge of

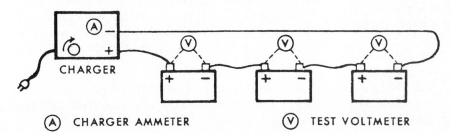

FIGURE 3-41 Batteries connected in series for charging purposes.

CHARGER

(A) CHARGER AMMETER   (V) TEST VOLTMETER

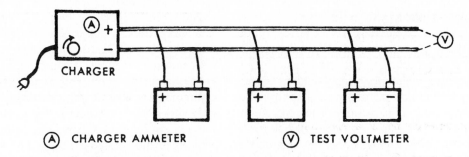

FIGURE 3-42 Batteries connected in parallel for charging purposes.

others. A battery with a shorted cell may prevent good batteries in the circuit from being charged much at all. On the other hand, if all batteries in the circuit are good, usable batteries, they will all reach full charge at about the same time, regardless of their initial state of charge.

When a series charger is used, as shown in Fig. 3-41, all batteries on charge receive the same amount of charging current. When a parallel charger is used, the batteries are connected so that the charging current is divided and each battery receives only the charging current that it can accept at the charger's voltage. Because of these differences, the charging procedures also differ. The following recommendations should be closely followed to ensure correct charging of batteries for both series and parallel hookup.

Series Hookup Charging

The batteries can be connected as shown in Fig. 3-41. However, prior to connecting up all batteries to be charged, conduct the necessary safety and visual checks.

Procedure:

1. If any battery cases or covers are cracked, broken, or otherwise damaged, do not attempt to charge them prior to repairing this damage. If nonrepairable, replace them.

2. On batteries with screw or push-in filler caps, remove them and check them with a hydrometer for specific gravity. If the reading is higher than 1.230, the battery is serviceable and does not require charging, unless a fault was found in the vehicle charging system that had allowed a low charge rate to exist for some time; then the battery could be recharged to 1.265 to 1.270 corrected to 80°F (26.7°C).

3. If the battery electrolyte level is low, add distilled water to bring the cell level above the level of the separators or just to below the level of the split-guide ring prior to charging. After charging, add water to the bottom of the split-guide ring.

4. On maintenance-free or Delco-Remy freedom batteries, always check the color of the magic-eye or built-in hydrometer; if the color is clear or yellow, the battery must be replaced unless it has the removable vent manifold that is found on some maintenance-free units

to allow topping up of the water as described earlier in this chapter. If the hydrometer shows a green color, the battery does not require charging. If the hydrometer is dark, the battery requires charging.

5. With the individual battery terminals clean, connect up the necessary leads as shown in Fig. 3-41. Keep in mind that the battery charger only has a certain load-carrying capability; therefore, make sure that you do not connect up more batteries than the charger is capable of handling. Prior to switching on the battery charger, double check that all leads and connections are tight, since loose connections can result in blowing the fuse of the charger, causing a spark to occur at the loose connection.

6. On the face of the charger is a variable resistor or similar arrangement that allows you to set the charging rate. For most slow-charge conditions, this can be set to within 5 to 10 A, or to whatever is recommended by the particular battery manufacturer.

7. Allow the batteries to remain in this steady state of charge for at least 3 hours prior to checking their condition. On filler-cap batteries, check the specific gravity of each cell with a hydrometer and correct the readings to 80°F (26.7°C). A testable state is reached when the gravity exceeds 1.225. If no change in the specific gravity reading is observed in three consecutive hourly readings, then remove the battery from charge, as it will not take any more charge. The battery is near full charge when the specific gravity reaches 1.265. Also, as mentioned previously, do not allow the temperature of the electrolyte to exceed 125°F (52°C). If any cell gases or spews electrolyte, reduce the charging rate or remove the battery from test.

8. On maintenance-free batteries, when the green dot is clearly visible, gently shake or tilt the battery to ensure that the green dot stays visible. With the use of a voltmeter, check the terminal voltage across the positive and negative battery terminals. Take care when using the voltmeter leads that you do not create a spark by scratching the terminals to make good contact, since you could create an explosion. Switch off the charger while voltage testing.

If a voltage of 16 V or more is noted, remove the battery from charge, then test according to the manufacturer's instructions.

Parallel Hookup Charging

Connect the batteries as shown in Fig. 3–42 for group charging with voltage-limited or parallel battery chargers. Conduct the same basic checks as you would when series charging, namely steps 1 through 5 above. Then, at step 6:

Procedure:

6. With the batteries connected as shown in Fig. 3–42, switch on the battery charger with the voltage setting adjusted to a maximum of 16 V. On initial switch-on, the charger voltmeter may not show 16 V; however, as the batteries accept the charge, less current is required, which will cause the voltage to rise.

The charger's ammeter registers the actual total current flow to the batteries, which divides to each individual battery; however, this current flow showing on the face of the ammeter does not individually measure the current flow to each battery but simply shows the total current flowing to the batteries from the charger.

Steps **7** and **8** are the same as that given for the series hookup charging procedure.

NOTE: When monitoring the specific gravity of each individual battery cell, a difference of more than 0.050 (50) specific gravity point between cells usually is an indication that one or more cells are defective. Conduct a load test on the battery.

Fast or Boost Charging

Fast charging, or what is commonly referred to as boost charging in the industry, is used only when time prevents the slow charging of the battery or batteries. The boost charge method provides a high charging rate for a very short period of time compared to that of slow charging. Charging rates up to 60 A for 12-V batteries are not uncommon, with double the ampere value for 6-V batteries above the 180 reserve capacity rating. Typical examples of boost charging rates are given in Table 3–7.

Boost charging of a completely discharged battery will not bring it to a 100% state of charge, but will only surface charge it for practical service. To charge the battery completely, it must be placed on slow charge for the recommended period as shown in the charging tables.

CAUTION: Do not boost charge any battery with a specific gravity of 1.225 or higher, since severe damage due to overcharge can occur, with the possibility of violent gassing, spewing, and electrolyte temperature increase beyond 125 °F (51.6 °C). Under these conditions, the battery might explode.

A typical portable fast charger is shown in Fig. 3–43. When boost charging a battery in place in the vehicle or equipment, always connect the positive (+) charger lead to the (+) battery terminal, and the negative (−) lead to the (−) battery terminal. Remember that battery terminals are marked with either the letters POS or (+) beside the battery post, and the letters NEG or (−) beside the negative terminal. If no markings are visible, the

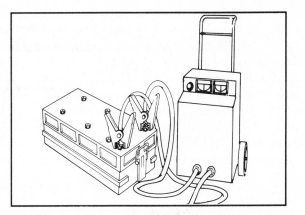

FIGURE 3–43 Boost charger connected to the battery while out of the vehicle. *(Courtesy of Cummins Engine Company, Inc.)*

positive terminal is always physically larger than the negative one.

Charger leads are normally color coded, with red being positive and either black or blue for negative. If you are in doubt regarding battery terminal polarity, use a voltmeter with its probes connected to one terminal post each. If the leads are connected backwards, the voltmeter will not read. The voltmeter leads are color coded also, with red for (+) and black for (−).

Boost charging the battery while still in the vehicle allows you to connect the grounded lead to the engine block for a better connection. Note whether the NEG or POS lead is grounded from the battery to the frame or engine block prior to placing the same charger lead to the block.

Make sure that all connections are clean and tight, then switch on the fast charger at the low charge rate. Slowly increase the rate of charge until the recommended ampere value is attained. Any sign of smoke or haze from any battery cell would indicate a shorted battery; switch off the charger immediately and replace the battery.

If severe gassing or spewing of electrolyte occurs, double check that your rate of charge is not in excess of that recommended. Reduce or halt the rate of charge until the condition has been corrected.

BATTERY GROUND PATHS

The fairly recent introduction of electronic components, particularly to heavy-duty diesel truck fuel injection systems makes it imperative that any battery connections that are made, or any attempt to boost/jump start a vehicle equipped with these ECM systems must be done by closely following the manufacturer's recommendations. Many of these newer-style engines make extensive use of aluminum components to reduce the overall weight of the engine assembly. Consequently, the battery grounding system requires special consideration to ensure both satisfactory vehicle cranking and charging system performance. Engine manufacturers such as Detroit Diesel Corporation with their DDEC (DD Electronic Controls) used on their 71 and 92 two-stroke-cycle and series 60 four-stroke-cycle engines, Caterpillar with their 3406B PEEC (Programmable Electronic Engine Controls) and electronic unit injector on their 3176 engines, Cummins with their Pace and ECI (electronically controlled injector) and CELECT L10 and 14L engines, and Mack with their electronically controlled Robert Bosch in-line fuel injection pump system on their E7 engine employ an ECM to effectively improve engine exhaust emissions and performance. In addition, many trucks are now equipped with satellite navigation location controls as well as electronic on-board reporting devices and instrumentation. By way

of example, consider the 3176 Caterpillar six-cylinder diesel engine model that is equipped with an ECM (electronic control module) to control the electronic unit injectors. Incorrect battery system grounding can lead to electrical system component malfunction or galvanic corrosion problems of the aluminum components. Caterpillar recommends that single-point grounding for both the engine and the vehicle electrical systems is therefore required for satisfactory performance and reliability. Therefore, all electrical sensors and switches on the engine *must* be an externally grounded two-wire design. Under no circumstances should internally grounded or case-grounded sensors or switches be used. Caterpillar recom-

FIGURE 3-44 Caterpillar 3176 engine cylinder head to battery ground path. *(Reprinted courtesy of Caterpillar, Inc.).*

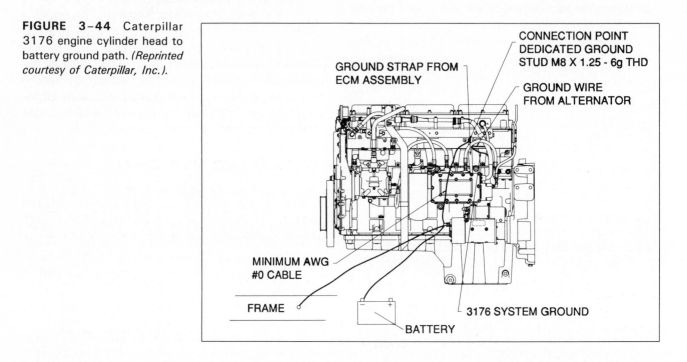

FIGURE 3-45 Alternate cylinder head-to-battery ground path for the Model 3176 engine. *(Reprinted courtesy of Caterpillar, Inc.)*

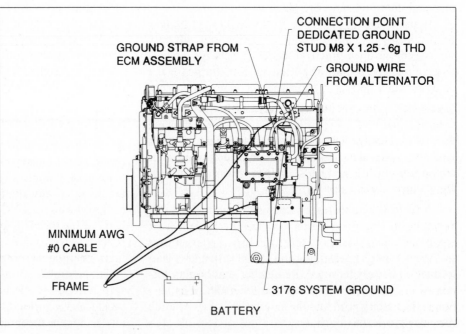

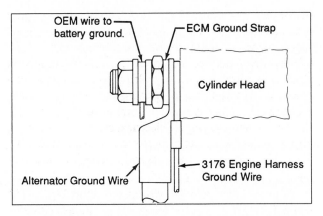

FIGURE 3–46 Close-up of 3176 engine cylinder head ground stud. *(Reprinted courtesy of Caterpillar, Inc.)*

mends that the following components be used as part of the battery ground system on 3176 engine models:

1. Cylinder head ground stud; this unit becomes the central grounding point for all components on the engine. All engine-related ground wires from the OEM (original equipment manufacturer) should be attached to this stud.
2. Alternator ground wire; this wire is installed by Caterpillar to the cylinder head ground stud. The opposite end of this wire should be attached to the alternator!
3. Battery ground paths are illustrated in Figs. 3–44 and 3–45. An AWG (American Wire Gauge) size 0 cable or larger must provide a ground path from the cylinder head stud location to the negative post of the battery. Figure 3–46 illustrates a close-up view of the cylinder head ground stud in detail.

Many European and Japanese import trucks use the term *earth connection* in reference to the battery ground system. On trucks equipped with electronic components, these vehicles often use two ground-return systems referred to as either the switching earth or the signal grounding. The *switching earth* is the usual battery ground circuit that has always been required on all vehicles and is necessary for switching and heavy electrical loads such as the battery, starter, and alternator systems. The newer *signal grounding* circuit is used as a ground for such items as gauges and electronic component systems. The wiring color code for both of these ground systems, although usually white, uses an extra mark on the cable for the signal grounding to allow the technician to differentiate between them. A color other than white may be used by different vehicle manufacturers!

WARNING: Never use the signal-ground return circuit when other components are fitted, since this can cause a malfunction of the electronic systems. When installing an electronic system, its ground must be connected to the central signal grounding point on the vehicle, which can be located in the electrical center control box in the cab area for protection purposes.

Ground Problems

Problems with the ground connection are generally caused by corrosion between the contact surfaces of electrical connections and are often hard to determine by a visual sighting alone. Ground problems are best traced by using a digital AVR (amps/volts/resistance) meter rather than an analog type, the reason being that the digital unit is capable of reading values much lower and reflecting these on its control panel than is a floating-needle analog unit. In addition, when checking a circuit for either a low voltage loss or resistance value, the digital meter flashes this value quickly, and some models can store a number of values for recall later.

One example of how to use a digital voltmeter on the battery circuit is shown in Fig. 3–47, which illustrates a voltmeter connected between the battery negative pole and the ground point requiring checking. The grounded circuit to be checked must be switched on, and if the circuit is correctly grounded, no voltage should be registered on the voltmeter. A voltage reading would confirm a completed circuit (positive to negative) and therefore a short in the system.

ELECTRICAL LOAD DETERMINATION

Although correct test procedures must be followed in order to perform, analyze, and pinpoint electrical system problems successfully, there are often instances, particularly in medium- and heavy-duty truck fleet opera-

FIGURE 3–47 Using a digital voltmeter to check the battery ground circuit. *(Courtesy of DAF Trucks, Eindhoven, The Netherlands.)*

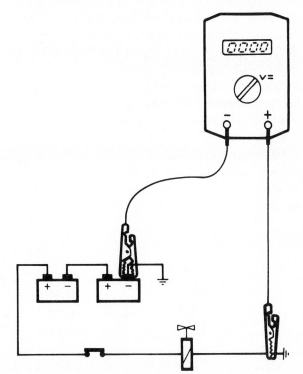

tions, where continued complaints of low battery power, resulting in slow or no cranking, occur. Although electrical tests may confirm that the alternator charging system and batteries are performing correctly, the addition of add-on electrical accesories can often be detrimental to continued successful operation of the truck, tractor, and trailer. Often these complaints of low power are more noticeable in cold winter operating conditions since the batteries will not accept as high a charge rate when ambient temperatures drop. For more information on battery power loss, refer to Table 3–6 and Figs. 3–31 and 3–32.

When a continual electrical complaint is received and all systems appear to be performing satisfactorily, yet low battery power recurs, you should consider measuring the total electrical loads placed on the battery and alternator charging systems. If the worst-case condition loads exceed that produced by the alternator and stored by the batteries, a larger-capacity alternator and batteries may be required. To perform such a check, the TMC/ATA (The Maintenance Council, American Trucking Associations) released an advisory procedure in 1988 in their Recommended Maintenance Practices Manual under guideline AV1-7 that covers suggested procedures for determining the requirements of charging systems on straight trucks or tractor/trailer combinations. Basically this procedural check provides the vehicle user with a checklist of data to establish and determine the best charging system for a given vehicle based on the type of truck operation. To measure the electrical loads, proceed as follows.

Load Measurement

It is imperative that the vehicle batteries be in a full state of charge prior to attempting this test sequence. If necessary, remove and replace the batteries with a fully charged set for the test. Battery testing procedures are described in detail in this Chapter.

NOTE: The following test procedure is performed with the vehicle engine shut off in order to determine the battery amperage and voltage draw.

Procedure

1. Connect a voltmeter across the batteries to record voltage values prior to and during the test procedure.
2. Clamp an inductive pickup type ammeter such as the one shown in Fig. 4–10 or the pickup that is part of a

VAT tester similar to the one shown in Fig. 3–29 around the positive battery cable that feeds the various vehicle system loads.
3. To determine the voltage and current draw of each individual load circuit, the instrument panel control switch for that electrical accessory is switched on and off. The amperage and voltage draw is then noted and recorded. This is repeated for every electrical accessory and duly recorded on a load measurement worksheet.
4. For example, if the headlight control switch is turned on, quickly note and record the test ammeter reading as well as the test voltmeter value and record them. Turn off the control panel switch. Repeat this procedure for all electrical systems. On those control switches that will operate only when the ignition key switch is on, identify these loads on the worksheet.

NOTE: If the headlight control switch is of multiposition design, place it in the various positions, such as side/marker and park positions, individually, and record the amperage and voltage draw. When placed in the headlight position, the total system draw for all of these circuits will be recorded; however, individual circuit power draw can then be determined by subtraction of the various readings.

5. Once all electrical accessory circuits have been recorded, they can be added to determine what the total amperage draw is under worst-case conditions.

An analysis can then be made of the alternator output and the battery reserve capacity to determine whether or not the starting/charging/battery system is adequate for the truck in question and its type of application/operation. An operational profile of the maximum continuous electrical load (amperes) with the engine running versus the maximum anticipated electrical load with the engine off can then be systematically appreciated. You should also try to determine what percentage of the time during vehicle operation electrical loads are on or off, the percentage of idling time versus road time, the average operating hours per day and per week, and the average ambient operating temperature. The alternator, starter motor, and battery manufacturer, type, model number, and ratings can be reached from information in the fleet data files. If unavailable, this information is easily obtained from information stamped on the component or from the OEM (original equipment manufacturer) dealer locally.

QUESTIONS

3-1. Battery cases are usually manufactured from:
    a. Hard rubber   c. Polypropylene
    b. Plastic   d. All of the above
    (see page 49)
3-2. A battery cell pack consists of:
    a. The positive and negative plates
    b. The positive and negative plates, plus their separators

    c. The positive plates only
    d. The negative plates only
    (see pages 49–50)
3-3. A maintenance-free battery contains no:
    a. Antimony in the
       plates   c. Arsenic
    b. Lead–calcium alloy   d. Boron (see page 50)

3-4. Battery electrolyte is a mixture of water and:
   a. Lead sulfate   c. Sulfuric acid
   b. Lead peroxide   d. Hydrogen
   (see page 51)

3-5. When a lead–acid battery becomes discharged, the electrolyte contains a greater percentage of:
   a. Lead peroxide   c. Hydrogen
   b. Water   d. Sulfuric acid
   (see page 51)

3-6. Battery electrolyte is composed of approximately:
   a. 36% water and 64% acid
   b. 36% hydrogen and 64% water
   c. 64% hydrogen and 36% water
   d. 64% water and 36% acid   (see page 51)

3-7. Chemical action within a battery consists of the reaction between the sulfuric acid, the sponge lead in the negative plate, and:
   a. The lead peroxide in the positive plate
   b. The lead zinc in the positive plate
   c. The lead sulfate in the positive plate
   d. The lead acid compound in the positive plate
   (see page 52)

3-8. The chemical reaction within the battery causes:
   a. The negative plate to gain electrons and remain in a negative state of charge
   b. The positive plate to gain electrons and remain in a positive state of charge
   c. The positive plate to lose electrons while the negative plate will gain electrons
   d. The negative plate to gain protons
   (see page 52)

3-9. The electrolyte in a fully charged battery at 80 °F (27 °C) has a specific gravity of approximately:
   a. 1.100 to 1.150   c. 1.240 to 1.260
   b. 1.200 to 1.240   d. 1.265 to 1.280
   (see page 51)

spongey lead peroxide

3-10. Each cell in a 12-V battery is capable of producing approximately:
   a. 2.0 to 2.05 V   c. 2.2 to 2.25 V
   b. 2.1 to 2.2 V   d. 2.5 to 2.3 V
   (see page 52)

3-11. A specific gravity of between 1.205 and 1.235 at 80 °F (27 °C) indicates that the battery state of charge is equivalent to approximately:
   a. 75%   c. 25%
   b. 50%   d. Full discharge
   (see page 57)

3-12. A battery specific gravity reading of 1.150 at 80 °F (27 °C) would correspond to a voltage reading of approximately:
   a. 2.00 V per cell   c. 2.10 V per cell
   b. 2.05 V per cell   d. 2.15 V per cell
   (see page 57)

3-13. The cranking ability of a fully charged battery at 32 °F (0 °C) is equivalent to approximately:
   a. 85%   c. 50%
   b. 65%   d. 35%
   (see pages 69, 78)

cold slows Down   *Engine load is more*

3-14. As battery electrolyte temperature rises:
   a. Its specific gravity increases
   b. Its specific gravity decreases
   c. There is no change in the specific gravity
   (see page 51)

3-15. The major cause of loss of battery water is due to:
   a. Conversion of water to sulfuric acid
   b. Spillage from the vent caps
   c. Evaporation as a result of the heat created from the chemical action due to the charging current
   d. A poor ground condition
   (see page 51)

3-16. The specific gravity of the battery electrolyte must be corrected by adding or subtracting how many points for every 10 °F change from 80 °F (27 °C)?
   a. 0.001 point   c. 0.003 point
   b. 0.002 point   d. 0.004 point
   (see page 51)

3-17. The electrolyte in a fully charged battery will not freeze until the ambient temperature drops to between:
   a. −30 and −40 °F   c. −60 and −70 °F
   b. −50 and −55 °F   d. −80 and −90 °F
   (see page 52)

3-18. In a battery that is in a fully discharged state, the electrolyte consists of approximately:
   a. 17% pure sulfuric acid and 83% water   *never will*
   b. 23% acid and 77% water   *Be pure water*
   c. 30% acid and 70% water
   d. 40% acid and 60% water
   (see page 52)

3-19. When a battery cell gases, the following mixture emanates from the cell cap: *emanates - means leave*
   a. Hydrogen and nitrogen
   b. Hydrogen and oxygen
   c. Oxygen and nitrogen
   d. Hydrogen only
   (see page 51)

3-20. A maintenance-free battery is much more resistant than a conventional lead–acid battery to oxidation from overcharging since its plate grids contain a lead–calcium alloy with no:
   a. Lead peroxide   c. Arsenic
   b. Lead sulfate   d. Antimony
   (see page 50)

3-21. A maintenance-free battery state of charge can be checked with a voltmeter or by viewing the built-in hydrometer, which will confirm a sufficient state of charge when it appears:
   a. Yellow in color   c. Green in color
   b. Dark in color
   (see page 55)

3-22. The addition of cell plate area to a battery will result in an increase in: *increase's capacity*
   a. Voltage
   b. Amperage
   c. Both voltage and amperage
   d. Cell resistance (ohms)
   (see pages 50, 58)

3-23. When batteries are connected in series, you will have:
   a. Greater voltage availability for cranking
   b. Greater amperage (current) availability   *Amps stay same*
   c. Greater voltage/amperage
   d. Less cranking circuit resistance
   (see page 59)

3-24. When batteries are connected in parallel, you will have:
   a. Greater voltage availability for cranking
   b. Greater amperage (current) availability

voltage same

for each 10° on 80° up add, down subtract

c. Greater voltage and amperage
d. Greater cranking circuit resistance
    (see page 59)

3-25. Batteries are generally rated by either the SAE or the BCI. SAE stands for the Society of Automotive Engineers. What does BCI stand for?

a. Battery Corporation Industry *BCI*
b. British Battery Council Industry
c. Battery Council International
d. Battery Corporation International
    (see page 57)

3-26. The battery positive post is usually always larger in diameter than the negative post. *True* or *False* (see page 61)

TRUE

3-27. Batteries are usually rated by:

a. The 20-hour rating
b. The reserve capacity rating and a cold cranking amperes test
c. The physical size and number of cells in its construction
d. The current load rating over a 30-second discharge time
    (see page 57)

3-28. Under an ampere-hour (Ah) rating, a battery that delivers 8 A for 10 hours would be rated as:

a. An 8-Ah battery   c. An 80-Ah battery
b. A 10-Ah battery
    (see page 57)

3-29. A battery should never be boost charged if its specific gravity is higher than:

a. 1.220   c. 1.240
b. 1.230   d. 1.250
    (see page 91)

3-30. When slow charging a battery when not having access to a charging rate chart, you can determine the rate of ap-

plied charge to use by dividing the capacity of the battery by:

a. 2   c. 6
b. 4   d. 12
    (see page 89)

3-31. Boost charging a battery will result in providing:

a. A surface charge condition only
b. The same charge rate as a slow charge in a shorter time period
c. Twice the voltage for quick starting
d. Twice the amperage for quick starting
    (see page 91)

Fast = lots of amps

3-32. The state of charge of a battery can be determined by:

a. A specific gravity test
b. A voltage test
c. The color of the hydrometer eye on maintenance-free batteries
d. All of the above
    (see pages 55, 57, 71–72)

3-33. When disconnecting a battery, always remove:

a. The positive cable clamp first
b. The negative grounded cable clamp first
c. Either one first   (see page 69)

3-34. When connecting a battery, always connect:

a. The grounded cable last
b. The grounded cable first
c. It doesn't matter which one is connected last
    (see page 70)

3-35. To neutralize spilled battery electrolyte, you can use:

a. Distilled water   c. Baking soda
b. A steam cleaner   d. Baking powder
    (see page 70)

3-36. If a battery's specific gravity is low, you can safely add sulfuric acid to each cell to restore the strength of the electrolyte. *True* or *False* (see page 66)

False Asphix will Eats away Plates Better to Charge

Motorcycle Battery at max 1 Amp

Keep Battery Below 125°

more charge = more Resistance

Baking Soda is alkalyne/Base it neutralize's Foams up Don't get in cells

CHAPTER
4
Electrical Troubleshooting

OBJECTIVES

In this chapter you will acquire or review the skills needed to:

1. Recall and understand series, parallel, and series–parallel circuits.
2. To describe how voltage, amperage, and resistance can be measured in a circuit or component.
3. To identify and recommend what special tools and equipment should be used and how to insert them safely and correctly into a system to confirm where a problem might exist.

4. Understand system circuit and component operation.
5. Describe the various protective devices employed to ensure that an electrical circuit will not be damaged during operation.
6. Appreciate the importance of melding your knowledge of theoretical and hands-on information to become an effective troubleshooter.

INTRODUCTION

Having been involved in the automotive/truck/equipment field for more than thirty years in many capacities, and having been involved in automotive and heavy-duty truck/bus and heavy equipment training at both the factory and community college level, I have always searched out new ways in which to present and exchange information with students, apprentices, mechanic/technicians, service management, and engineers. In most textbooks that deal with a given subject, the chapter that deals with troubleshooting is relegated to the back of the book. I have used this technique myself in several books; however, after much thought during the writing of this book, due to the difficulty of the subject matter, troubleshooting tips and recommended procedural checks appear regularly throughout each chapter as relevant to the component/topic under discussion. Consequently, the ability to troubleshoot any electrical or electronic component must be supported with encouragement and recall information on a continuing basis throughout the book.

To apply the knowledge that you gain here and on the shop floor, you should consider the following points, since you alone will determine how effective you want to be in the field of electrical and electronic maintenance and repair. You must possess the following knowledge or abilities:

1. A solid foundation of basic electrical principles that allow you to understand fully exactly how a system or circuit operates.
2. A solid foundation of basic electronic (solid-state) devices, such as the transistors, diodes, and resistors that make up most of the operational components now in use on cars and light-, medium-, and heavy-duty trucks.
3. A good grasp of items 1 and 2, discussed in detail in Chapters 1 and 2, respectively. While this information is still reasonably fresh in your mind is a good time to discuss how to diagnose and troubleshoot series, parallel, and series–parallel circuits.
4. Detailed information on starting systems, alternator charging systems, and other electrical devices contained

in this book and how to diagnose these systems. As you progress through these chapters you will find yourself continually referring back to the basic information contained in Chapters 1 and 2, since no electrical or electronic system and component can be trouble tested effectively without having a full understanding of the types of wiring systems used and the function and purpose of each solid-state component.

5. An understanding of how each one of the various special tools and test equipment operates and how each can be connected into a wiring circuit or component to determine whether an open, a short, or a ground is the cause of the nonoperational complaint. To understand why a circuit or electrical/electronic component exhibits a specific problem, you first have to know how it functions and is supposed to operate.

6. Continual hands-on exposure to circuits and components where you can apply the theoretical knowledge gleaned from these pages and from truck and OEM (original equipment manufacturer) literature. Although hands-on experience cannot be learned by reading a book, the information and thought processes that lodge in your mind will spill forth when you are faced with actually applying a working procedure to circuits and components. Remember that to be an effective mechanic/technician takes patience, motivation, desire, pride in workmanship, and an appreciation of how to merge the theoretical and practical aspects.

With the foregoing comments and thoughts in mind, we discuss what you should consider before tackling any electrical or electronic circuit diagnosis. We review quickly and succinctly some of the important review fundamentals that should be applied to a systematic approach to effective troubleshooting. The fundamental approaches and special tools discussed here will reappear continually throughout other chapters, where you will be able to recognize and recall how a circuit and its switches, relays, fuses, and circuit breakers operate regardless of the electrical component in question.

I believe that placement of this basic electrical troubleshooting chapter fairly early in the book will prove to be very beneficial as you are exposed to more detail in succeeding chapters. I wish you well in your search for more success in understanding and working with truck electrical and electronic systems. *Never forget the fundamentals and they will serve you well.*

HOW TO FIND AN ELECTRICAL PROBLEM

Vehicle electrical and electronic systems often scare people off because they are not familiar enough with the fundamentals of electricity. Many people have at one time or another received a minor shock from an ignition circuit, or may have connected a battery with the polarity reversed, especially when jumpstarting a vehicle. The resultant shock or electrical system damage tends to create a hesitant approach. Others may not have had this type

of experience, but because electricity cannot normally be seen, trained personnel who are excellent mechanics or technicians in other areas of the trade shy away.

Although the electrical system is often compared to a basic water flow system, this analogy is not adequate for the current electronic componentry now in extensive use on both cars and trucks. To gain confidence and become an effective troubleshooter, the mechanic/technician must systematically establish an analytical approach to any problems encountered. Don't short out wires, disconnect wires, install jumper wires, or follow haphazard routines when unsure of the problem, because expensive and time-consuming damage will invariably be the result.

Although the introduction of solid-state electronic components may appear to have made the mechanic/technician's job harder; the availability of special tools and test equipment has removed a tremendous amount of trial and error in troubleshooting techniques. Pinpoint accuracy is now possible with these test machines. However, the test machines and special tools are effective only if you closely follow their directions for operation. You must also follow to the letter the vehicle manufacturer's test sequence; otherwise, you may be misled as to where the problem actually is. In addition, many vehicles today are equipped with onboard diagnostic computers that facilitate the mechanic/technician's approach and effectively pinpoint problems in the electrical or electronic systems.

In this book reference is often made to the use of these special test tools and equipment; use these to advantage when required. Don't hope that you might be lucky enough to stumble on the problem by a trial-and-error method of component parts replacement. This is not only expensive but is time consuming, and with the rate for labor charges continually going up, the end result can be totally unacceptable.

The degree of experience of the person obviously will determine to what degree he/she can tackle a given problem area. However, diligence and patience, a study of this book, and with hands-on shop exposure under the supervision of a mechanic/technician or a vocational, trade school, or college program instructor will bring success in understanding and troubleshooting any part of a vehicle electrical/electronic system.

When an electrical problem occurs, generally there is some sort of telltale warning prior to a failure that can indicate the problem area. However, if no tell-tale sign is evident, you should approach the problem systematically beginning with the simplest possible cause before condemning or replacing a major component.

In many instances, problems can be caused by such simple items as a poor ground connection, or:

1. Loose connections or wire fittings
2. Corroded plug-in wire harnesses or snap-in connectors

3. High circuit resistance caused by corrosion, or a wire with too small a gauge size inserted or spliced into an existing circuit

4. Circuit overload, too many accessories tied into the same circuit breaker or fuse especially true of aftermarket add-on accessories

5. A loose drive belt on an alternator or air-conditioning system which causes slippage and low power output

6. Light bulb burned out

7. A faulty switch mechanism

8. Shorted wire (bared) caused by contact with hot engine parts

9. Fusible link melted

10. Corroded battery terminals

11. Low state of battery charge

In addition, use a voltmeter to find out where the circuit is live and where it is not. In this way you can establish specifically where the problem originates and progress from there.

In particularly tricky situations, it may be necessary to substitute a suspected faulty component with one known to be good, to confirm your suspicions. Care should be exercised here, however, to ensure that you are not simply correcting a problem that will recur shortly. Often the replacement of a component will appear to have corrected the problem initially, but within a short time, the problem reappears.

These are just some of the more common areas that can create problems in the electrical system, although there can certainly be others. The key is to analyze the problem from a simple possible cause, and then to move toward more difficult causes. Degree of experience will obviously prepare you to troubleshoot any electrical system problem effectively; however, even the experienced automotive/truck electrician occasionally requires a reference to pinpoint a problem. Do not hesitate to refer to the vehicle manufacturer's system wiring diagrams in the appropriate service manual, because with improvements and product change, a system that you were once familiar with may have been redesigned.

When an unusual problem exists, it is wise to spend a little time in tracing the print of the wiring circuit to be sure that you are on the right track. When a complaint is received, gather as much information as you can, then check and operate the suspected faulty circuit or component yourself to find out exactly what is not working and if any other symptoms are apparent. Think through the wiring or controls that serve the circuit in question before attempting to repair the problem. Understand the complete problem, then proceed to check it out systematically, and once you have confirmed your suspicions, make the necessary repairs.

All vehicle service manuals list a number of possible complaint areas that should be checked and omitted one by one. In addition, with the great number of electronic items now used on vehicles, ensure that you are familiar with the location of each component.

When you feel that you have located the specific problem area and the repair has been made, double check the repaired circuit and any other circuit that may be tied into this one to confirm that you have corrected every problem that existed and that you don't now have problems that did not exist before.

CIRCUIT REVIEW

Now that you have formed a solid foundation and understanding of basic electricity, you must also be able to determine the most acceptable method to use in locating or pinpointing a system problem. Since electricity is an invisible source of power, it cannot be clearly seen and identified inside a wire or operating component. Therefore, you must be able to determine just what tools and equipment should be employed to monitor and confirm the operation of an electrical circuit or accessory. It is not practical to remove and or disassemble a number of electrical components in attempting to locate a specific cause and whether a component is operating properly.

From Chapter 1, where we discussed various types of electrical circuits, we now know that an electrical circuit conducts a supply of electricity to a load and must return the electricity to the battery power source via a suitable ground connection to complete the circuit. When we want to switch on the component, accessory, or circuit, we use a control device such as a switch to control current (amperage) flow. Closing the switch allows power to flow, while opening the switch stops the flow of power. To protect a circuit or power absorbing accessory from too much current flow due to overload, we protect the system by using either a fuse or a resettable circuit breaker. If the fuse burns out (blows), it must be replaced. A circuit breaker can be reset manually by tripping the switch.

SAFETY NOTE: A fuse or circuit breaker that continually blows or opens the circuit indicates that there is a problem in the system. Closer inspection is required to determine the cause; otherwise, serious electrical system damage can result.

Prior to looking at how to check out a circuit or electrical accessory systematically, let's take a few minutes to review the various types of circuits and protective devices that are commonly used on cars and trucks. The three main types of circuits in use in truck applications are:

1. The series circuit

2. The parallel circuit

3. The series–parallel circuit

Figure 4-1 illustrates both a series and a parallel circuit arrangement. In the series circuit, all electrical devices and accessories are connected together, so that power must flow from one item to the next before returning to the battery source of supply. Remember that in a series circuit the same current flows through all of the electrical

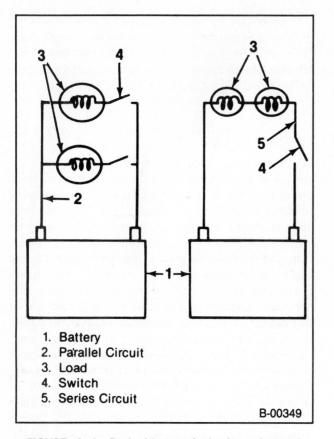

FIGURE 4-1 Basic layout of simple series and parallel electrical circuits. (*Courtesy of GMC Truck Division, General Motors Corporation.*)

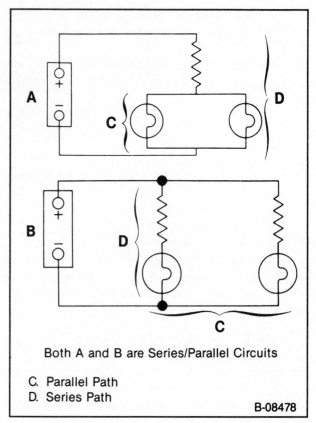

Both A and B are Series/Parallel Circuits

C. Parallel Path
D. Series Path

B-08478

FIGURE 4-2 Basic layout of a simple series-parallel electrical circuit. (*Courtesy of GMC Truck Division, General Motors Corporation.*)

accessories. In a parallel circuit arrangement more than one current power path is used, with each electrical accessory having its own individual wire feed to and from the battery power source. Because of this feature, each electrical accessory can draw a different amount of current (amperes); however, the supply voltage to each will be the same.

Figure 4-2 illustrates a series-parallel circuit, which is a combination of the two circuits just described. A perfect example of where you would find a series-parallel circuit on a heavy-duty truck would be when 24-V starting is desired but 12-V charging is required. This type of a circuit is discussed in detail in both the battery and alternator charging systems chapters. The series-parallel (SP) circuit is arranged so that it consists of a single current path and a circuit segment with more than one current path to and from the voltage (electrical pressure) supply.

Let's place these circuit types into a typical wiring arrangement for a truck. Figure 4-3 illustrates how this may appear. The circuit shown in the diagram consists of all the components that we need to start the engine (item 13, starter motor), the battery for the power supply (item 14), a generator/alternator (item 10) to recharge the battery while the engine is running, a control switch (item 12, ignition key), and finally a protective fuse, fusible link, or circuit breaker (item 11) to guard against too

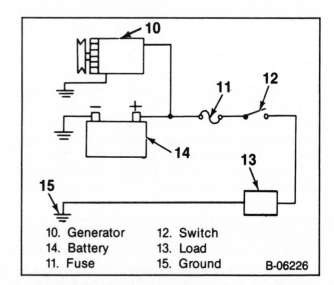

FIGURE 4-3 Simplified electrical system and components parts. (*Courtesy of GMC Truck Division, General Motors Corporation.*)

much current (amperage) flow due to a possible overload condition. All of these components are connected together by suitable wiring. Note that all components in the circuit must be connected to a good ground supply to ensure a completed circuit back to the battery. This ground can be achieved through a wire or through the electrical accessory into its metal body or frame.

CIRCUIT PROTECTIVE DEVICES

In any electrical circuit we must provide some form of protection against too much current flow, which can occur as a result of system overload caused by high circuit resistance. Three types of protective devices are commonly used in cars and trucks:

1. Replaceable fuses of different ratings (amperage)
2. Fusible links inserted into the wiring harness that will melt when too much current flows
3. Circuit breakers, either automatic or manual reset types

NOTE: Detailed information on fuses, fusible links, and circuit breakers is given in Chapter 5.

FIGURE 4–4 Electrical circuit controllers. (*Courtesy of GMC Truck Division, General Motors Corporation.*)

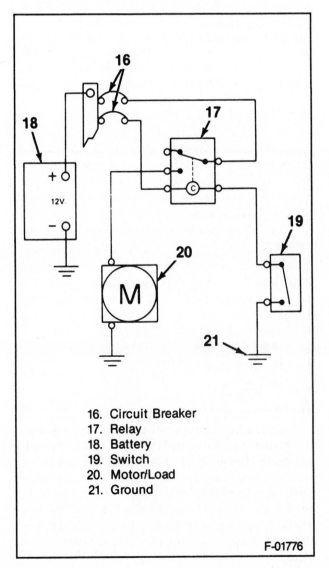

16. Circuit Breaker
17. Relay
18. Battery
19. Switch
20. Motor/Load
21. Ground

F-01776

In addition to the circuit protection devices discussed above, the actual control of current flow through a circuit is normally done by inserting a series of switches and relays, as illustrated in Fig. 4-4. Here we see a switch (item 19), a relay (17), and a circuit breaker (16). In this example the switch is manually operated, as in the case of an ignition key switch. Here the switch is inserted into the system at the beginning however, other control switches, such as that for the truck marker lamps, headlights, fog lights, and interior lights, are controlled from their own individual switches with their own ground return circuit. The relay in this example is controlled remotely by the flow of electricity to it. The relay functions to handle the high current necessary for starter motor operation, since if we were to route the current through the key switch, it would burn out almost instantly. In this case we have used the ignition key switch as a slave to handle the small current necessary to energize the relay electrically. Power from the battery flows through the circuit breaker (16) as a means of protecting the wiring, relay, and starter motor from excessive current flow. The size of wiring used in any circuit depends on the amount of current it has to handle as well as the length of the circuit and the voltage drop allowed. Wire sizes and color codes were discussed in detail in Chapter 1 (see p. 15).

REVIEW: BASIC CIRCUIT DIAGNOSIS

With the knowledge that you now possess about various types of circuits and the purpose of switches, relays, fuses, fusible links, and circuit breakers, we can discuss the three major types of problems that you will be faced with when troubleshooting any electrical circuit.

1. An *open circuit*, the condition that exists when there is a break in the wiring or continuity (no continuation) of electrical flow. Figure 4–5 illustrates a typical simplified open-circuit condition. Causes of an open condition can be traced to high circuit resistance as a result

FIGURE 4–5 An ''open'' in an electrical circuit. (*Courtesy of GMC Truck Division, General Motors Corporation.*)

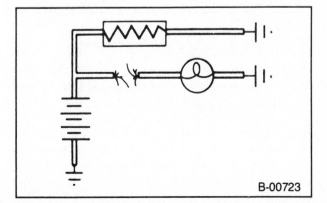

B-00723

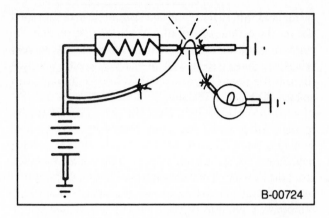

FIGURE 4–6 A "short" in an electrical circuit. (*Courtesy of GMC Truck Division, General Motors Corporation.*)

of severe corrosion at the terminal connectors or a broken wire that can be traced to mechanical damage from any number of reasons. An open circuit can also be caused by a blown fuse, burned fusible link, an open circuit breaker, or internal damage within an electrical switch, relay, or accessory.

2. A *short circuit*, a condition that occurs as a result of current (amperage) bypassing the normal circuit. In multiple-wire harnesses, any break in the wire insulation can allow two or more wires to come into contact, causing an accessory to operate when its switch is off, or damage to the component. Salt spray from roads in winter can play havoc with insulated wires and components since it can act as a bridge between a number of electrical connections. In extreme cases, solder has been known to melt in high-current accessories and then act as a bridge between circuits or components. Figure 4–6 illustrates a typical short-circuit condition.

3. A *grounded circuit*, which is very similar to the short circuit, the major difference being that the current flows directly to a ground circuit that is not part of the original

FIGURE 4–7 Example of a "GROUNDED" electrical circuit. (*Courtesy of GMC Truck Division, General Motors Corporation.*)

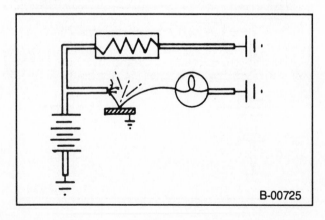

wire flow path. This can usually be traced to broken insulation, allowing the wire to ground itself on the chassis or some other good ground path. Other reasons for a ground circuit can be traced to corrosion, dirt, oil, water, or moisture around terminals or connections. Figure 4–7 illustrates a typical grounded circuit.

BASIC DIAGNOSTIC TOOLS

As you progress through this book and study the function and operation of the major electrical and electronic components that together make a medium- or heavy-duty truck a unique piece of machinery, you will be faced with knowing how to troubleshoot, diagnose, and repair these systems. Throughout this book, particularly within various chapters, a number of special diagnostic tools and instrumentation are shown. Many of these diagnostic tools are quite expensive and are generally not purchased by the mechanic/technician but are part of the fleet garage shop equipment.

There are, however, a number of smaller diagnostic tools that the truck mechanic/technician cannot be without, and these are discussed below. An understanding of the purpose of each of these tools and instruments is mandatory prior to moving on to a study of major electrical components. A solid foundation in the concepts of basic electricity and electronics will always be the base from which any effective troubleshooting procedure will start. An understanding of a basic electrical system arrangement such as that illustrated in Fig. 4–4, with its switches, relays, circuit breaker, power supply, accessory loads, and ground system, can be applied to almost any component and system that you deal with on the truck. With such an understanding, we must now determine what tool/instrument to use to diagnose an electrical circuit problem complaint.

The following general electrical test equipment is required:

1. Analog/digital multimeter with at least a 10-megohm (MΩ; 1 million ohms) impedance value.
2. Fused jumper wire
3. Short finder
4. Unpowered test light
5. Powered test light
6. Fuse tester and remover

Item 1: Multimeter

The tool the mechanic/technician will access most often when conducting an electrical/electronic system check is the multimeter, so named because it can be used to measure resistance in ohms, electrical pressure in volts, and current or quantity in amperage. If you can measure these three items, you will be able to trace a problem in any circuit. Although individual voltmeters, ammeters, and ohmmeters can be purchased, the grouping of all three into a compact hand-held unit is the most popular form.

The multimeter is available in both analog (swinging needle type of gauge) and digital display types, the digital model being recommended for effective testing of many electrical and electronic components, since it can be set on a scale that will read down to as low as 1/1000 of a volt. There are also multimeters that offer analog and digital selection in a single hand-held unit. Still others are referred to as an AVR (amps/volts/resistance) meter or a DVOM (digital volt-ohmmeter) meter. An analog multimeter (swinging needle) can be used, or the digital and combination analog–digital models shown and highlighted in Figs. 4–8 and 4–9.

The common automotive multimeter has been in wide use for many years, but with the advent of various electronic controls such as sensors and on-board computers, the more elaborate multimeters of today have features that can check such things as frequency and temperature as well as make diode tests. Older multimeters do not have the appropriate scales and functions to handle computer-equipped vehicle testing.

Not only is the common analog multimeter inadequate in many instances when checking automotive electrical and electronic circuitry, but it can also damage delicate computer circuitry. Because of their low internal resistance (input impedance), most analog multimeters draw too much power from the component being tested on computer-equipped vehicles. In addition, many analog multimeters employ 9-V battery power for their opera-

FIGURE 4–8 Fluke 20 series analog/digital multimeters. (*Courtesy of John Fluke Manufacturing Company, Inc., Everett, WA.*)

The Fluke 20 Series offers additional safety with fuses on all current inputs and optional high visibility yellow cases. The Fluke 25 and 27 are totally sealed against dirt, dust, and airborne contaminants. They are impervious to water, oil, grease, antifreeze and gasoline, making them ideal for shop use.

John Fluke Mfg. Co., Inc.
P.O. Box C9090, Everett, WA 98206
Tel. 206-347-6100

For more product information—
or where to buy Fluke products call;

800-426-0361 (toll free) in most of U.S.A.
206-356-5400 from AK, HI, WA
and 206-356-5500 from other countries

Fluke (Holland) B.V.
P.O. Box 2269, 5600 CG,
Eindhoven, The Netherlands
Tel (040) 458045, TELEX 51846

Phone or write for the name of your local Representative.

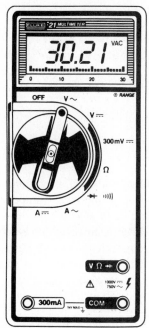

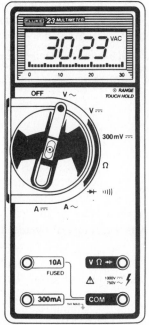

Fluke 21

Safety yellow case
Fluke 75 features and specs, less 10A input

Fluke 23

Safety yellow case
Fluke 77 features and specs, plus fused 10A input

Fluke 25

Charcoal or yellow case
Analog/Digital display
0.1% basic dc accuracy
100 μV to 1000V ac & dc
0.1 μA to 10A, all fused
−15°C to 55°C operation
Touch-Hold™
Two year warranty

Fluke 27

Charcoal or yellow case
Analog/Digital display
0.1% basic dc accuracy
100 μV to 1000V ac & dc
0.1 μA to 10A, all fused
−15°C to 55°C operation
Touch-Hold™
Relative (difference) mode
Min/Max recording mode
Two year warranty

J 34029-A
DIGITAL MULTIMETER

The J 34029-A is designed for years of dependable service under the most rugged shop conditions. The single rotary dial incorporates a patented design eliminating friction wear which reduces the life of typical wafer type switches. Other superior design features include extra overload protection, 100% factory testing of all ranges and functions, a specially designed case which seals out contaminants encountered in the field.

Features:
● In Circuit Diode Test ● 0.50% Basic DCV Accuracy ● Easy to Read LCD 0.5" High Digits ● 2000 Hour Battery Life - Standard 9 Volt ● Audible Continuity Beeper ● 22 Mega Ohm Input Impedance ● In Circuit Measurements ● Spare Fuse ● Test Leads With Alligator Clips ● Patented Long Life ● Rotary Dial ● Built-In Multiposition Tilt Bail ● Plastic Storage/Carrying Case ● Complete Instructions

ACCESSORIES FOR J 34029-A

J 34029-15
EZ MINI-HOOK TEST LEAD SET
Contains a red and black 36" long spring-loaded hook end which can be used to fit over up to .059 diameter components when continuous hook up is required.

J 34029-248
DELUXE TEST LEAD KIT
Includes safety designed test leads with push-on probes plus banana plug extensions insulated alligator clips, extension probe tips, medium size hook type prods, large size hook type prods all in a nylon pouch with velcro closures.

J 34898
HIGH CURRENT SHUNT
J 34898 is an inexpensive calibrated resistance wire which is connected in series with the electrical accessory to be tested and plugged into the J 34029-A Multimeter. The multimeter range switch is set on the 200 MV DC scale. This will provide a direct readout of the accessory current draw in .1 amp increments. From 0 to 99 amps.

J 35590
CURRENT CLAMP

SERVICE PARTS FOR J 34029-A

J 34029-13
Replacement Test Lead Set Consists of:
(Available Separately)
J 34029-14 (2) Alligator Clips
J 34029-18 (2) Probe Tips
J 34029-19 (2) Test Lead Wires
J 34029-20 (2) Banana Plug Extenders
J 34029-21 (1) Storage Pouch
J 34029-2 Molded Storage Case
J 34029-7 Instruction Manual
J 34029-12 Special 2 Amp Fuse (Package of 4)

FIGURE 4–9 Model J34029-A digital multimeter. (*Courtesy of Kent Moore Heavy Duty Division, SPX Corporation.*)

tion, and this voltage is sufficient to destroy sensitive digital components when these multimeters are used to perform a resistance test.

The latest types of digital multimeters (DMMs) are constructed so that they have a much higher input impedance than analog multimeters. This impedance is generally 10 MΩ, to ensure that the multimeter will draw very little power from the component under test. Test voltages for resistance checks are usually well below 5 V, so selecting a multimeter that has a voltage setting below 5 V is desirable.

Various models of Fluke analog–digital multimeters are illustrated in Fig. 4–8. All of these Fluke DMMs have test voltages of 3.5 V, which therefore greatly reduces the chance of damage when testing an electrical/electronic circuit or component.

In the past, the one problem with digital readouts for the mechanic/technician was that the numbers displayed did not give any indication of whether the value was increasing or decreasing. Technicians may have experienced the typical frustration associated with attempting to read ever-changing temperature values when monitoring a digital exhaust gas or an engine analyzer.

Fluke multimeters overcome this problem by providing a combination display that provides the accuracy of a digital readout together with the dynamic measurement capabilities of an analog meter. The Fluke analog–digital multimeters have the following major features which make them ideal for use in automotive troubleshooting techniques:

1. *Analog–digital display.* A combined 31-segment analog bar graph and a 3200-count digital display.

2. *Touch-hold feature.* The meter display "freezes" a reading until you are ready to look at it.
3. *Automatic polarity and range selection.* This feature permits the meter to select the range and polarity automatically for the best possible reading.
4. *Continuity beeper.* An audible-tone beeper provides easy testing for continuity, shorts, and diode tests.
5. *Rugged construction.* A tough plastic case resists the possibility of damage when working in the day-to-day hazards of a shop environment.

Analog–Digital Multimeter. The key to using a multimeter on an electronic system is that it have an impedance of at least 10 MΩ so that the solid-state devices will not be damaged. Many multimeters are available on the market under various brand names; the well-known and widely used Fluke models were illustrated in Fig. 4–8. Another widely used digital multimeter is the Kent-Moore J34029-A or J35500. Figure 4–9 illustrates the J34029-A unit, which has a 22 MΩ input impedance. In addition, a current clamp J35590, shown in Fig. 4–10 can be plugged into either one of these multimeters for up to a 600-A reading in 0.1-A increments. This addition is particularly helpful in identifying problems with low-power accessories.

When measuring resistance with a digital multimeter, either the vehicle battery or the ignition switch or component control switch must be disconnected to prevent a false reading. Digital multimeters apply such a low voltage when measuring resistance that the presence of voltages can give a false resistance reading. The use of diodes and solid-state components in electronic circuits can cause an ohmmeter to register an incorrect value. If you reverse the leads of the multimeter/ohmmeter and the readings on the component you are checking differ, the solid-state device is affecting the measurement. The vehicle manufacturer's service manual procedure should always be your guide when taking voltage or resistance reading checks of any electronic circuit or component.

The multimeters illustrated in this section are capable of measuring current in amperes, voltage (electrical pressure), and resistance in ohms. By manually rotating the multimeter selector dial, the mechanic/technician determines what type of measurement is desired. The ammeter, voltmeter, and ohmmeter each has a particular application for troubleshooting an electrical circuit. The vehicle manufacturer will always indicate in the component test procedure just what type of test/reading is to be accessed. Typically, voltage, current, and resistance are used to confirm the operating condition of an electrical/electronic component. Figure 4–11 illustrates the electrical system component and the types of readings that can be recorded with a multimeter.

Voltmeter. The voltmeter can indicate to the technician more valuable information than the ammeter, the

FIGURE 4–10 Model J35590 current clamp. (*Courtesy of Kent Moore Heavy Duty Division, SPX Corporation.*)

J 35590 is used with a digital multimeter (such as J 34029-A or J 35500) to precisely measure DC current flow (AMPS) in 0.1 AMP increments without breaking into the circuit or affecting the operation of the circuit. During operation the inductive pick-up type jaws of the J 35590 are simply clamped around the vehicle battery cable or a wire leading to the accessory to be tested. A readout of the current draw will be indicated on the multimeter digital display. J 35590 is especially helpful in identifying problems with low power accessories because it will measure 0 to 200 AMPS in 0.1 AMP increments.

FIGURE 4–11 Typical electrical system components and measurement types. (*Courtesy of John Fluke Manufacturing company, Inc., Everett, WA.*)

System/Component	Measurement Type				
	VOLTAGE PRESENCE & LEVEL	VOLTAGE DROP	CURRENT	RESISTANCE	TEMPERATURE
CHARGING SYSTEM					
Alternators	●		●		
Regulators	●				
Diodes		●		●	
Connectors	●	●		●	
STARTING SYSTEM					
Batteries	●	●			
Starters		●	●		
Solenoids	●	●			
Connectors		●		●	
Interlocks	●				
IGNITION SYSTEM					
Coils	●			●	
Connectors	●	●		●	
Condensors				●	
Contact Set (points)	●			●	
Distributor Caps				●	
Plug Wires				●	
Rotors				●	
Magnetic Pick-up	●			●	
LIGHTING & ACCESSORIES					
A/C Condensors					●
A/C Evaporators					●
Compressor Clutches	●		●		
Lighting Circuits	●	●	●	●	
Relays	●	●		●	
Transmissions					●
COOLING SYSTEM					
Connectors	●	●		●	
Fan Motors	●		●		
Relays	●	●			
Temperature Switches	●	●		●	●
Radiators					●

ohmmeter, or a test lamp combined, since voltage readings will always provide you with answers to the following questions:

1. Is there voltage present at the circuit test point? If there is, it is an indication that the wiring, circuitry, and various system components are capable of delivering voltage to the item suspected of being at fault.

2. What voltage reading is recorded? Compare the voltage value to the truck or electrical component manufacturer's specifications to determine whether it is too high or too low.

3. Is there a voltage drop across the component being tested? A voltage drop tells you how much voltage is being consumed by that component.

To use the voltmeter portion of the multimeter, rotate the volt selector scale to a value that you anticipate to measure. If you are not sure, select the highest value and bring it down by gradual rotation of the selector knob to obtain the working range that you need. Figure 4–12 illustrates how to connect a voltmeter into the electrical circuit, which should always be in a parallel hookup. If you connect the voltmeter in series, the nature of the circuit will be changed and no value will be registered on the meter. A series hookup is such that current will try to flow through the voltmeter test leads. Make sure that you observe correct battery polarity by connecting the red voltmeter test lead to the positive side of the circuit and the black test lead to the negative (ground) side of the circuit. An alternate circuit hookup where either a voltmeter or an unpowered 12-V test light can be used to confirm that voltage is present is illustrated in Fig. 4–13. Illumination of the test light will confirm that voltage is present; however, the voltmeter tells you just how much voltage, and this reading can be compared to

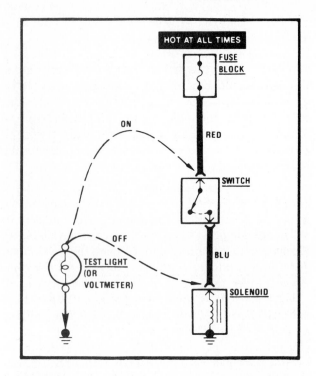

FIGURE 4–13 Typical hookup for a voltage check. (*Courtesy of GMC Truck Division, General Motors Corporation.*)

the manufacturer's specifications. As a general rule of thumb, if the voltage reading is more than 1 V less than battery voltage, there is a problem. Of course, this does not hold true for electronic systems that use 5-V sensors and for components with very low current draw.

A voltmeter can be placed into the circuit similar to the way it is shown in Fig. 4–13. The positive lead (red) is connected to the top of the circuit, which in this case is the lower side of the fuse block. The black (negative lead) is connected to the solenoid at the lower side of the illustrated circuit. Operate the circuit and the voltmeter will indicate the difference in voltage passing through the circuit/switch in relation to battery power.

Throughout the book you will come across many uses for the voltmeter, such as checking for battery voltage drop while the engine is cranking. In addition, while the engine is running, alternator output voltage can be checked. Both of these conditions can be a valuable first step in diagnosing a starting/charging system problem.

Ammeter. When the ammeter is selected, it will record the current (amperes) flowing in a circuit. Always install the ammeter into the circuit as illustrated in the simplified example shown in Fig. 4–14, which is known as a series hookup. To do this, disconnect the circuit from the power supply (battery) first; then, observing correct battery polarity, connect the multimeter red test lead to the positive side of the circuit and the black test lead to the negative (ground) side of the circuit. Make certain that the ammeter is capable of handling the anticipated

FIGURE 4–12 Voltmeter placement in an electrical system to monitor a reading/value. (*Courtesy of GMC Truck Division, General Motors Corporation.*)

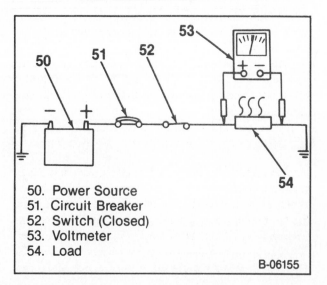

50. Power Source
51. Circuit Breaker
52. Switch (Closed)
53. Voltmeter
54. Load

B-06155

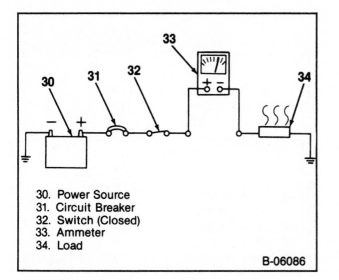

30. Power Source
31. Circuit Breaker
32. Switch (Closed)
33. Ammeter
34. Load

B-06086

FIGURE 4–14 Ammeter placement in an electrical system to monitor a reading/value. (*Courtesy of GMC Truck Division, General Motors Corporation.*)

current flow; otherwise, you will blow the ammeter fuse or cause serious internal damage. Therefore, always select the highest amperage scale on the multimeter first; then, if need be, you can turn it to a lower scale for a more accurate reading. Also keep in mind that the current clamp shown in Fig. 4–10 can be used with the Kent-Moore model J34029-A or J35500 shown in Fig. 4–9. A good example of how to use the ammeter portion of a multimeter is shown in Fig. 4–15 for an alternator current leakage test.

FIGURE 4–15 Digital multimeter hookup for checking alternator current leakage. (*Courtesy of John Fluke Manufacturing Company, Inc., Everett, WA.*)

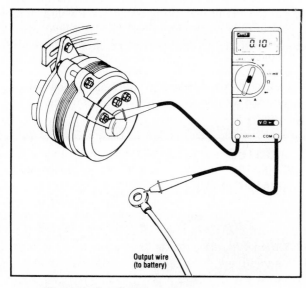

Output wire (to battery)

—Alternator Leakage Current
To check alternator diode leakage, connect the multimeter in series with the alternator output terminal with the truck not running. Leakage current should be on the order of a couple of milliamps at most, and more often will be on the order of 500 microamps or less.

Locating current drains: Current drains cause the battery to be in a continual low-charge condition, so that often there is not enough amperage available to crank the engine over first thing in the morning. Although the condition can be caused by a low charging rate, often it can be traced to an underhood, trunk, or domelight that was left on overnight.

If you are working on a computer-equipped vehicle and if the service procedure requires you to activate the self-diagnostic feature of the system to withdraw trouble codes, keep in mind that a trickle charger should be applied to the battery if the computer code withdrawal period exceeds 30 minutes. Underhood or dome light switches can be isolated by placing a small piece of masking tape over the switch plunger.

NOTE: When using a multimeter, it is wise to select the 10-A rating until you are sure that the current draw is less than 320 mA; otherwise, you could blow the multimeter's protective fuse.

Never crank the engine or operate accessories that draw more than the selected ampere rating on the multimeter; severe damage to the meter could result.

When checking the entire electrical system for current drains, the digital multimeter should always be connected in *series* with the battery. The scale on the digital multimeter can be set to 10 A; once the current draw has been determined to be less than 0.3 A, the selector switch can be placed in the 320-mA range to determine the total current drain across a circuit. Figure 4–15 illustrates the correct hookup for a current leakage check of an alternator, and Fig. 4–16 shows a typical hookup for isolating the circuit that may be causing a continual current drain in the system.

Bad grounds: Often, many problems associated with electrical and electronic systems can be attributed directly to poor connections in the live part of the circuit; very often the circuit cannot be completed because of a bad ground connection. Poor or loose connections create a high circuit resistance since they can produce a wide range of symptoms, particularly with snap-in and Weather-Pack-type connectors. Examples of poor grounds are lights that do not illuminate as brightly as they should, lights that may illuminate when they are not supposed to, gauges that change their value when another switch is turned on, and lights that fail to illuminate. Many manufacturers recommend that conductive grease be applied to various connections before they are reassembled, to minimize the growth of corrosion.

Ohmmeter. When the ohmmeter (resistance) scale on the multimeter is selected, the battery within the test instrument will self-power this phase of measurement. Due to the nature of the resistance values that we can measure in an electrical or electronic circuit, the ohmmeter range selector scale offers a wide choice of values. Most ohmmeters are designed with only one scale, that

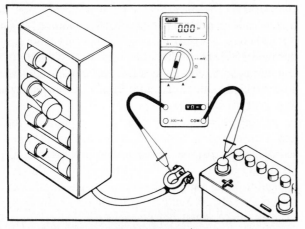

—Isolating the Circuit Causing A Current Drain

CAUTION—*Do not crank the engine or operate accessories that draw more than 10 amps. You could damage the meter, possibly beyond repair. Connect the DMM in series with the battery using the current function. Isolate the circuit causing the current drain by pulling one fuse after another while watching the multimeter.*

The current reading will drop to 0 when the fuse in the offending circuit is pulled. Reinstall the fuse and disconnect the components in that circuit one at a time to find the defective component. Again, keep in mind that on modern cars there are many computer circuits that draw current normally and they may not all be on the same fuse.

FIGURE 4–16 Digital multimeter hookup for isolating a circuit causing a current drain. (*Courtesy of John Fluke Manufacturing Company, Inc., Everett, WA.*)

is used with a multiplier stage selected by the range selector knob. The multipliers are generally scaled as R (resistance) $\times 1$, $\times 10$, $\times 100$, $\times 1000$, and so on. The range switch may show 200 Ω; therefore, you would read the ohms directly; if 2, 20, 200, or 2000 Ω is shown, read the ohms in thousands. If 20 MΩ is selected, read the ohms value in millions.

SERVICE TIP: Never use an ohmmeter to measure resistance in a live circuit (battery power flowing); switch all power off first! In addition, never use an ohmmeter when either a voltage or current value is desired since serious damage can occur to the ohmmeter or multimeter, as the case may be.

On some models of digital ohmmeters the number 1 displayed in all ranges indicates an open circuit, a zero display in all ranges indicates a short circuit, while an intermittent connection in the circuit can be indicated by a digital reading that will not stabilize.

Figure 4–17 illustrates how to connect an ohmmeter into the circuit. However prior to using an ohmmeter, you should always calibrate the instrument by inserting the red and black test leads into the instrument first; then:

1. Touch the two test lead probes together to complete a circuit through the ohmmeter gauge and the analog meter needle will deflect. If it is a digital ohmmeter, the numbers will rotate. If the needle or numbers do not read zero ohms at this time, rotate the CAL (calibrate) or ADJ (adjustment) knob to properly zero the needle or numbers.

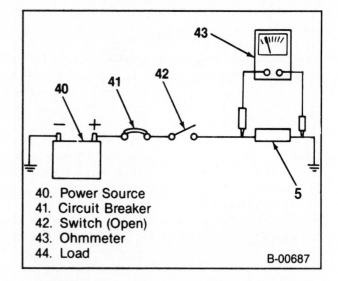

40. Power Source
41. Circuit Breaker
42. Switch (Open)
43. Ohmmeter
44. Load

B-00687

FIGURE 4–17 An ohmmeter placement in an electrical circuit. (*Courtesy of GMC Truck Division, General Motors Corporation.*)

2. Separate the two test lead probes; the needle or numbers should move to the maximum resistance value on the scale (infinite reading).

3. The ohmmeter is now ready for use.

Item 2: Fused Jumper Wire

A jumper wire is simply a length of wire with an alligator clip attached to each end. The length of the wire can be sized to suit various circuit demands. Many mechanics like to use a fused jumper wire since this will prevent damage to the circuit should you inadvertently connect the jumper wire wrong; the fuse will blow and can be replaced. Figure 4–18 illustrates a fused jumper wire which can contain either a 5- or 10-A fuse in the holder to suit the circuit load being tested. You would employ a jumper wire or an unpowered 12-V test light when it is suspected that an open exists in a circuit. *Open* is the

FIGURE 4–18 Model J36199 fused jumper wire. (*Courtesy of Kent-Moore Heavy Duty Division, SPX Corporation.*)

J 36169
FUSED
JUMPER WIRE

- In line fuse holder with test leads.
- Provides an easy means of bypassing open circuits.
- Adapts to most GM connectors with a small clamp.

term used to describe the condition that exists when there is a break in the wiring or a lack of continuity (no continuation of the electrical flow). Figure 4-5 illustrates a typical simplified open-circuit condition. Causes for an open condition can be traced to high circuit resistance as a result of severe corrosion at the terminal connectors, or a broken wire that can be traced to mechanical damage because of any number of reasons, such as a blown fuse, burned fusible link, an open circuit breaker, or internal damage within an electrical switch, relay, or accessory.

To locate an open in an electrical circuit one end of the jumper with its alligator clip can be attached to a power supply (battery of hot wire terminal), with the opposite end attached to the accessory (load) in the circuit that is not functioning. This could be a motor, switch, relay, and so on. If when you use the jumper wire to bypass the existing wiring to the accessory and it now operates, you can then work back up the wiring toward the power supply. When the accessory stops working, you have identified the area where the power loss or open exists. The fused jumper wire can also be used to check a switch in a circuit that is wired in series with the load connections as shown in Fig. 4-19. With the jumper wire placed across the switch terminals as shown, the switch has no bearing on the current flow in the circuit; therefore, if the illustration as shown resulted in the motor operating with the jumper wire in place, the switch can be considered faulty.

Item 3: Short Finder

The short circuit is a condition that occurs as a result of current (amperage) bypassing the normal path of flow. Figure 4-6 illustrates the short condition in a simplified circuit arrangement. In a multiple-wire harness, any break in the wire insulation can allow two or more wires to come into contact, causing an accessory to operate when its switch is off, or damage to the component. Salt spray from roads in winter can play havoc with insulated wires and components since it can act as a bridge between a number of electrical connections. In extreme cases, soldered joints have been known to melt in high-current

accessories, with the solder acting as a bridge between circuits or components. Shorts that blow fuses or trip circuit breakers can generally be found by following the same troubleshooting techniques that are used to find current (amperage) drains discussed in this section, even though the symptoms may be different. An electrical short can be located in three basic ways:

1. By the use of a 12-V nonpowered test light or a voltmeter
2. By the use of a self-powered test light and an ohmmeter
3. By the use of a special short finder gauge

Figure 4-20 illustrates how to test for a short with an unpowered test light or a voltmeter. The voltmeter or multimeter range selector should be rotated to the dc volts function and it should be hooked into the circuit in series with the battery. This method will self-limit the actual current flowing in the system, thereby avoiding an excessive amount of blown fuses. If the circuit being checked has a blown fuse in place, remove the damaged fuse first and disconnect or switch off the load (accessory) prior to beginning the test. Starting at the fuse block, the test light leads are bridged across the removed fuse contacts to determine if power is being fed to one side of the fuse holder. It may be necessary to turn the ignition key switch on to supply power to one side of the fuse contact. Some fuses are hot at all times without the ignition switch being on. If you now disconnect the ground lead and connect it to the load side of the fuse, two things may happen. If the test light does not illuminate, the short

FIGURE 4-20 Testing for a short with a test light or voltmeter. (*Courtesy of GMC Truck Division, General Motors Corporation.*)

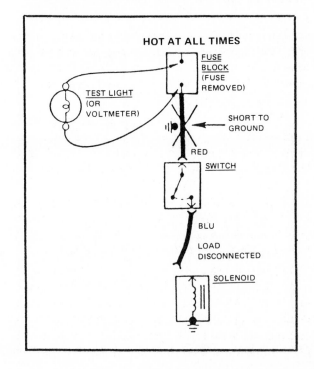

FIGURE 4-19 Using a jumper wire to determine if a switch is faulty. (*Courtesy of GMC Truck Division, General Motors Corporation.*)

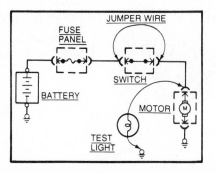

exists in the disconnected equipment; if the test light illuminates, the short is probably in the wiring and can be found by a process of elimination.

Wiggle the wiring harness from side to side and repeat this action about every 6 in. If the test light glows or the voltmeter registers a value, there is a short to ground in the wiring near that point. If a nonpowered test light or voltmeter is unavailable, a test for a short can also be made with either a self-powered test light (see Item 5 later in this section) or by using an ohmmeter. To find the short with these tools, refer to Fig. 4–21, which illustrates the hookup to a basic circuit.

Procedure:

1. Remove the blown fuse and disconnect the battery. Turn the control switch for the accessory to be checked to the OFF position.

2. Connect one lead of the self-powered test light or ohmmeter to the fuse terminal on the load side and the other lead to a good clean metal ground surface. Many new trucks use plastics, fiberglass, rubber, and insulated grounds, therefore ensuring that the test light is well grounded.

3. The remainder of this test follows the procedure described above for the unpowered test light or a voltmeter. Wiggle the wiring harness from side to side and repeat this action about every 6 in. (150 mm). If the test light illuminates or the ohmmeter registers a resistance value, there is a short to ground in the wiring in that general area.

The cause of a battery discharging overnight is often attributed to a short, although the cause is actually related to current (amperes) drainage. Shorts that blow fuses can generally be found by following the same troubleshooting techniques used to find current drains (later in this section), even though the symptoms may be different. When checking the alternator/charging system, keep in mind that the alternator diodes do leak some current. Therefore, disconnect the alternator wiring to remove this possible sensed condition. If there is any current draw for whatever reason, the voltmeter will record battery voltage. More specific detail on alternator charging systems are given in Chapter 8.

SERVICE TIP: On both gasoline- and diesel-powered trucks the adoption of electronic on-board computer systems and digital circuitry similar to that found on passenger cars makes the normal electrical procedure of using a multimeter and setting it to dc volts an unacceptable practice. The reason for this is that some devices/components are always in the ON position, and the voltmeter will reflect battery voltage when the system is normal.

Figure 4–22 illustrates one type of short finder gauge, which if available is ideal for locating shorts to ground, since it creates a pulsing magnetic field in the shorted circuit, thereby indicating to the mechanic/technician the location of the short, through either the vehicle body trim or sheet metal. When using a short finder such as the Kent-Moore J8681, conduct the following procedure:

FIGURE 4–21 Testing for a short with a self-powered test light or ohmmeter. (*Courtesy of GMC Truck Division of General Motors Corporation.*)

FIGURE 4–22 Model J8681 short finder. (*Courtesy of Kent-Moore Heavy Duty Division, SPX Corporation.*)

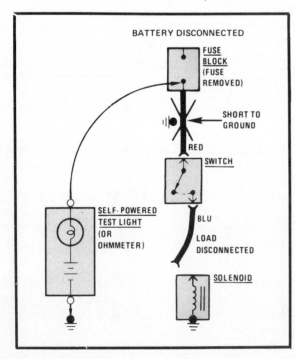

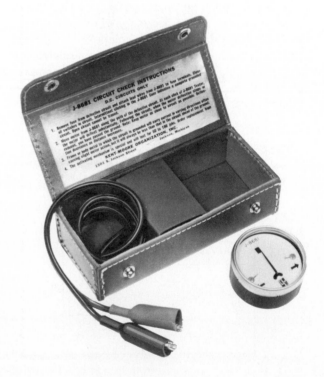

Procedure:

1. With the battery connected, remove the blown fuse from its socket and connect the short finder across the fuse terminals.

2. Close all the switches in the circuit that you are trouble-shooting.

3. Operate the short finder to create a pulsing magnetic current to the short, which will cause a pulsing magnetic field around the circuit wiring between the fuse block and the short (see Fig. 4–23).

4. Moving the short meter slowly along the suspected wiring from the fuse block will cause the needle to pulse

FIGURE 4–23 Finding a short with a short finder. *(Courtesy of GMC Truck Division, General Motors Corporation.)*

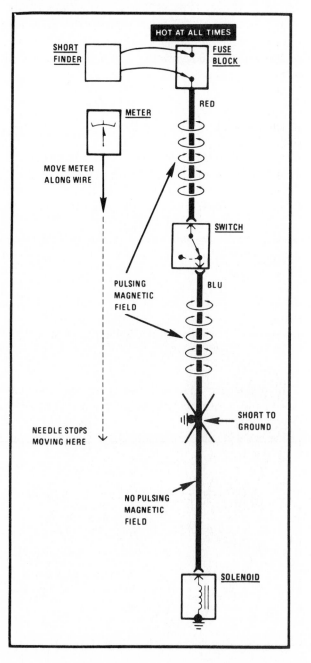

back and forth. When the meter needle stops moving, it indicates there is a break or short in the wire at that point or in that general area.

In addition to the magnetic pulse type of short finder shown in Fig. 4–22, the latest technology now allows the use of a solid-state short tester such as the one shown in Fig. 4–24. The advantage of the short tester illustrated in Fig. 4–24 is that it allows hands-free operation once connected into the circuit. Other major features are described in the figure text.

Having discussed a short circuit, this would be a good time to consider the grounded circuit illustrated in Fig. 4–7 since it is very similar to the short circuit. The major difference is that in the grounded circuit, the current flows directly to a ground that is not part of the original wire flow path. This can usually be traced to broken insulation caused by a wire rubbing against the chassis frame, body, or other good ground path. Other reasons for a ground circuit can be traced to corrosion, dirt, oil, and water, or moisture around terminals or connections.

Item 4: Unpowered Test Light

The unpowered test light is required to perform many of the diagnostic procedures on electrical systems, and can be used to determine if current/voltage is flowing in the wiring. It can also be used to trace an open circuit, discussed above under item 2, using a jumper wire. You can also check for shorts in a circuit with the unpowered test light. There are many different makes of unpowered test lights available. Figure 4–25 illustrates a 12-V model, although 6-V, 12-V, 24-V and 48-V models are available. The most widely used voltage for trucks and buses is 12 or 24 volts. The unpowered test light is used on a live circuit (switch on or closed) to determine if current is flowing. One end of the test light has a sharp needle probe so that it can be scratched to a terminal (live side or positive battery power) for good contact, while the other end, with an insulated wire lead and alligator clip attached, is connected to a good ground source to complete the circuit. Figures 4–13, 4–19, and 4–20 showed how the unpowered test light can be hooked into the circuit.

SERVICE TIP CAUTION: Most medium- and heavy-duty trucks today employ Weather-Pack-type terminal connectors or totally sealed electrical wire harnesses and plug-in connections. Under no circumstances, puncture or penetrate this protective wire insulation/covering with the sharp probe of the test light, since this will allow moisture and dirt to enter the previously sealed system, causing corrosion and system damage/failure.

If an unpowered test light is not available to you, make one up by using a simple 12-V light bulb and socket with two insulated wire leads (14-gauge copper wire) extending from the bulb socket holder. Connect a small alligator clip to the end of each wire.

BT 8034-B
SHORTELL®
Locates shorts in minutes

Technicians are finding Shortell® to be the fastest, most reliable aid in locating shorts and overloads in automotive, truck, marine & aviation electrical circuits.

Not an induction meter, volt meter, test light or sharp-tipped probe, Shortell® is a revolutionary circuit diagnostic tool superior in performance to any method now available. Because Shortell® actually **locates** shorts - and does it fast! End those costly and time consuming trial-and-error searches once and for all!

Shortell® is a one-man tool that frees both hands to work on the problem. Simply connect the three test cables, and it automatically signals the status of the circuit. Its loud tone and lamp don't quit till the fault is repaired. Green lamp signals that the circuit is clear.

Features include solid-state tone generator, 15 amp current limiter, three test cables and clamps, Meter, and complete instructions.

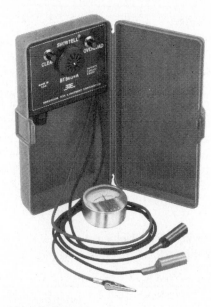

FIGURE 4–24 Optional short-circuit diagnostic solid state tool with an audible tone generator and visual test lamp. (*Courtesy of Kent-Moore Heavy Duty Division, SPX Corporation.*)

Item 5: Powered Test Light

The self-powered test light differs from the unpowered test light in that it contains a light bulb and its own 1.5-V battery, so that it can be used to check circuits that are disconnected from the vehicle battery. The self-powered test lamp is illustrated in Fig. 4–26 with its sharp probe and insulated wiring connected to an alligator clip. This arrangement forms a series connection, so that when the test lead and probe are bridged across an unpowered circuit, the light bulb will illuminate in any continuous circuit.

FIGURE 4–25 Model J34142-A unpowered test light that is micro-pack-compatible. (*Courtesy of Kent-Moore Tool Heavy Duty Division, SPX Corporation.*)

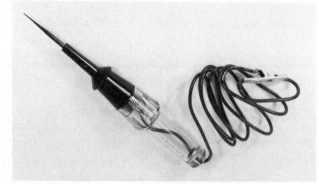

A test light such as J 34142-A is required to perform many of the diagnostic procedures on General Motors electronic control systems. J 34142-A has a unique specially shaped probe tip which will plug directly into female Micro-Pack connectors minimizing danger of over expansion. This durable unit is built of high strength material and includes a 48″ long lead.

SERVICE TIP CAUTION: Never use a self-powered test light when checking a circuit containing solid-state devices such as transistors unless the truck or equipment manufacturer specifically states that it is safe to do so; otherwise, the voltage impressed across these devices may result in severe damage.

The self-powered test light can also be used to establish continuity in a circuit as well as for a ground check. When a lack of continuity is suspected in a circuit, first turn off or disconnect it from any vehicle battery power supply. Connect the self-powered test light or an ohmmeter into the circuit as shown in Fig. 4–27 for example. Any deflection of the ohmmeter needle on an analog model, or reading on a digital model, or test light

FIGURE 4–26 Model J21008-A self-powered test light. (*Courtesy of Kent-Moore Heavy Duty Division, SPX Corporation.*)

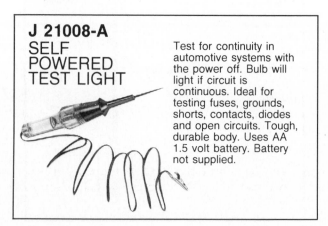

J 21008-A SELF POWERED TEST LIGHT

Test for continuity in automotive systems with the power off. Bulb will light if circuit is continuous. Ideal for testing fuses, grounds, shorts, contacts, diodes and open circuits. Tough, durable body. Uses AA 1.5 volt battery. Battery not supplied.

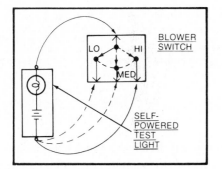

FIGURE 4–27 Circuit continuity check. (*Courtesy of GMC Truck Division, General Motors Corporation.*)

J 34764 AUTO FUSE TESTER & REMOVER/ INSTALLER

This handy tool tests, removes, and installs both blade and glass type automotive fuses. It features adjustable contacts and a red light which glows upon contact with a bad fuse. This slender hand tool makes it easy for the technician to check and service fuses within the tight confines of the fuse block area.

FIGURE 4–28 Model J34764 fuse tester, remover, and installer. (*Courtesy of Kent-Moore Heavy Duty Division, SPX Corporation.*)

illumination confirms that the circuit is closed—in other words, continuity exists between the two test points.

Item 6: Fuse Tester and Remover

The handy tool shown in Fig. 4–28 can be used to remove, install, or test a miniature (blade type) or glass-tube fuse assembly. The tool features adjustable contacts and a red LED (light-emitting diode) which glows on contact with a bad fuse (open). When checking a fuse, the tester is applied directly to the fuse while it is in position in the fuse block seat. Two probes contact the fuse in the slots of a flat miniature fuse, or to the metal ends of the glass-tube type. Figures 5–9 and 5–10 illustrate both good and bad fuses.

QUESTIONS

4-1. Typical wiring used in truck electrical circuits or conductors is composed of:
   a. Solid-state printed circuits
   b. Single-strand copper wire
   c. Multistrand copper wire
   d. All of the above
   (see pages 13–14)

4-2. A common problem area in any electrical system is:
   a. At the ground connection
   b. At the point where two wires have been joined or spliced
   c. At any point where a snap-in connector is used
   d. At any point where the wiring must be bent to route it through the system
   (see pages 98–99)

4-3. Ground wires used in automotive and truck electrical systems are generally identified by insulation that is:
   a. Black   c. Green
   b. White   d. Red
   (see page 119)

4-4. Which of the following items is not used to protect the electrical circuit in a truck?
   a. Copper bus bars   c. Fusible links
   b. Circuit breakers   d. Fuses
   (see pages 99, 101)

4-5. Fuses and circuit breakers are protection rated by the amount of:
   a. Resistance value   c. Current
   b. Voltage   d. Voltage and current
   (see pages 99, 101)

4-6. A fuse or a circuit breaker will blow or trip when subjected to too much:
   a. Resistance   c. Voltage
   b. Amperage   d. Alternating current/voltage
   (see pages 99, 101)

4-7. The advantage of a circuit breaker over a fuse is that they:
   a. Can be automatically or manually reset
   b. Can be reset 10 times prior to replacement
   c. Are cheaper than fuses
   d. Can be used only in the headlight circuit
   (see page 99)

4-8. A voltmeter is used to measure:
   a. Circuit resistance   c. Electron flow
   b. Current flow   d. Electrical pressure
   (see pages 2, 106)

4-9. An ohmmeter is used to measure:
   a. Circuit resistance   c. Voltage
   b. Current flow   d. Electromotive force
   (see pages 2, 107)

4-10. An ammeter is used to measure:
   a. Circuit resistance   c. Current flow
   b. Electromotive force   d. Electron/proton flow
   (see pages 2, 106)

4-11. Ohmmeters should only be used on:
   a. Live (powered) circuits
   b. Dead (nonpowered) circuits
   c. AC circuits
   d. DC circuits
   (see page 108)

4-12. When using an ammeter on a circuit, it should always be connected:

a. In series with the load to be measured
b. In parallel with the load to be measured
c. To a negative ground circuit only
d. To a positive ground circuit
(see page 106)

4-13. When using a voltmeter in a circuit, you should always connect it:
a. In series with the load to be measured
b. In parallel with the load to be measured
c. To a negative ground circuit only
d. To a positive ground circuit only
(see page 106)

4-14. The conventional flow of electricity in a circuit is accepted as being from positive to negative. *True* or *False* (see page 7)

4-15. A series circuit is one whereby the same:
a. Resistance is present in all electrical devices
b. Voltage flows through all electrical devices
c. Current flows through all electrical devices
d. Electromotive force is present in all electrical components
(see pages 9, 99)

4-16. A parallel circuit is one whereby the same:
a. Resistance is present in all electrical devices
b. Voltage flows through all electrical devices
c. Current flows through all electrical devices
d. Electromotive force is present in all electrical components
(see pages 11, 100)

4-17. If one or more batteries are connected in series, there will be an increase in:
a. Available cranking voltage
b. Circuit current
c. Circuit resistance
d. Neutron flow
(see page 59)

4-18. Connecting one or more batteries in a parallel hookup arrangement will provide:
a. Increased voltage
b. Increased current
c. Less circuit resistance
d. More circuit resistance
(see page 59)

4-19. A series–parallel circuit on heavy-duty trucks is usually designed to provide:
a. 12-V cranking and 6-V charging
b. 12-V cranking and 12-V charging
c. 24-V cranking and 6-V charging
d. 24-V cranking and 12-V charging
(see pages 13, 100)

4-20. If a starter motor fails to crank after several attempts, it is more than likely caused by:
a. Starter motor burnout
b. Pinion seizure
c. The temperature-controlled thermostatic switch cutting out to protect the starter windings from overheating
d. Solenoid damage
(see page 352)

4-21. Should you have to solder any wiring in the electrical circuit, always use:

a. Silver solder   c. Acid-core solder
b. Resin-core solder d. Plain solder
(see page 139)

4-22. A fusible link is located in the wire circuit for protection purposes and should therefore be located:
a. As close to the fuse as possible
b. As close to the circuit breaker as possible
c. As close to the electrical accessory being protected as possible
d. Between the ignition switch and the fuse block
(see pages 101, 128)

4-23. To facilitate easy identification of wiring circuits, most truck manufacturers employ:
a. Color-coded wiring
b. Letters on the wire insulation
c. Numbers on the wire insulation
d. All of the above
(see pages 15, 118)

4-24. Corrosion or a bad connection at the battery terminals can lead to:
a. High circuit resistance and a high battery charging rate
b. Low circuit resistance and a low battery charging rate
c. Melting of the fusible link
d. High circuit resistance and a low state of battery charge
(see page 109)

4-25. Prior to performing a systematic check of an electrical system problem, you should always ensure that:
a. The battery is maintaining a correct state of charge
b. The system voltage is at least 10 V
c. The system current is at least 60 A
d. The resistance does not exceed 5 Ω
(see pages 70–72)

4-26. When a fuse or circuit breaker continuously blows or has to be reset repeatedly, you should:
a. Use a higher-rated fuse or circuit breaker
b. Find the cause for the circuit overload condition
c. Replace the fusible link
d. Use heavier wiring in the circuit
(see page 99)

4-27. Corrosion at wiring connectors will create:
a. A need for greater system voltage
b. A need for greater system current
c. Increased circuit resistance
d. Melting of the fusible link
(see pages 99, 101–102)

4-28. High circuit resistance can be created by:
a. Inserting a smaller wire into a circuit
b. Inserting a larger wire into a circuit
c. Too short a wire
d. Using an inline fuse for protection
(see pages 2, 14, 99)

4-29. Circuit overload can be caused by:
a. A loose alternator drive belt
b. Too many electrical accessories on the same circuit
c. Using too high a rated fuse
d. Low circuit resistance
(see page 99)

4-30. A closed electrical circuit generally means that current cannot flow or complete its return path. *True* or *False* (see page 99)

4-31. The main type of circuit used on heavy-duty trucks is:
  a. A series circuit
  b. A parallel circuit
  c. A series–parallel circuit
  d. All of the above
  (see page 99)

4-32. A relay is designed to function as:
  a. A voltage control switch
  b. A high-current-carrying device
  c. A transformer
  d. A resistance-decrease device
  (see page 101)

4-33. The size of wire diameter used in any electrical circuit is dependent on:
  a. The voltage it must carry
  b. The resistance required to balance the circuit
  c. The current-carrying requirements of the circuit
  d. Available space and initial cost
  (see pages 1, 14)

4-34. An open circuit is created by:
  a. Damaged wire insulation that allows the wire to contact a metal component on the vehicle
  b. A broken wire
  c. Current flowing directly to ground
  d. Moisture around a terminal connection
  (see page 101)

4-35. A short circuit is created when:
  a. Current bypasses the normal circuit
  b. A shorter wire than normal is spliced into a circuit
  c. Too small a wire diameter is used in a circuit
  d. Too long a wire is used in a circuit
  (see page 102)

4-36. A grounded circuit is a condition that exists when:
  a. Current returns to the negative side of the battery through an electrical accessory
  b. High circuit resistance is present
  c. Current flows directly to ground through other than the normal flow path
  d. Voltage is grounded to any point in the system
  (see page 102)

4-37. A multimeter can be used to measure:
  a. Voltage
  b. Current
  c. Resistance
  d. All of the above
  (see page 102)

4-38. A voltage drop indicates:
  a. How much current is being used by an electrical accessory
  b. How much voltage is being consumed by a component
  c. The amount of circuit resistance
  d. If the charging rate is correct
  (see page 106)

4-39. Prior to using an ohmmeter to measure circuit resistance, you should always:

  a. Switch all power off
  b. Switch all power accessories on
  c. Check the condition/charge of the vehicle battery
  d. Remove the system circuit fuse
  (see pages 107–108)

4-40. When using a digital ohmmeter, if the number 1 appears on the meter face in all ranges, it usually indicates:
  a. A grounded circuit
  b. A short circuit
  c. An open circuit
  d. High circuit resistance
  (see page 108)

4-41. When using a digital ohmmeter, if a zero display appears in all ranges, it usually indicates:
  a. A grounded circuit
  b. A short circuit
  c. An open circuit
  d. A damaged ohmmeter
  (see page 108)

4-42. Prior to using an ohmmeter, you should always calibrate it by touching the black and red probe leads together and rotating the scale adjustment to provide a zero-ohms reading. *True* or *False* (see page 108)

4-43. A short circuit can be checked with:
  a. A voltmeter
  b. An ammeter
  c. An unpowered test light
  d. Both a and c are correct
  (see page 109)

4-44. An unpowered test light is used on:
  a. A live (closed) circuit to determine if current is flowing
  b. A dead (open) circuit to check for continuity
  c. A live circuit to check for high circuit resistance
  d. A live circuit to determine if voltage is present
  (see page 111)

4-45. A self-powered test light is used to:
  a. Check live circuits to determine if current is flowing
  b. Check circuits that are disconnected from the vehicle battery
  c. Trigger a system relay into operation
  d. Reduce circuit resistance when bad connections are suspected
  (see page 112)

4-46. To prevent damage to solid-state devices, the multimeter should have an impedance value of at least:
  a. 5 MΩ
  b. 10 MΩ
  c. 20 MΩ
  d. 50 MΩ
  (see page 104)

4-47. A fused jumper wire is recommended when bypassing a circuit to:
  a. Protect excessive current flow
  b. Limit the resistance value added to the circuit
  c. Protect the circuit breaker from damage
  d. Determine where the short circuit might be
  (see page 108)

CHAPTER
5
Cab, Chassis, and Trailer Wiring Systems

OBJECTIVES

In this chapter we discuss the cab and chassis wiring harnesses and the subsystems that are controlled by them. Specifically, you will acquire or review the skills needed to:

1. Identify and state the routing of the subsystem wiring harnesses found on heavy-duty trucks.
2. Describe the recommended wiring practices that are considered acceptable industry practice.
3. Identify and state the differences between a circuit diagram and a wiring diagram.
4. Trace a wiring circuit from a diagram and apply/ transfer this knowledge to an actual vehicle cab and chassis wiring.
5. Describe and identify the various wiring circuit protection devices commonly employed on medium- and heavy-duty trucks and buses.
6. Describe how to analyze and repair circuit protection devices to industry standards.
7. Describe how to perform an industry-acceptable wiring system repair.
8. Identify and state the major characteristics of the various types of wire harness connectors used in medium- and heavy-duty trucks.

INTRODUCTION

Throughout specific chapters of this book detailed descriptions of component function, operation, maintenance, and repair of such items as the batteries, the alternator, and the starter motor are given. Other electrical and electronic accessories generally receive their power supply from wiring that originates in the truck cab, taken from a power source or control panel protected by either fuses or circuit breakers. All vehicle running lights, such as parking, marker, signal, tail, and stop lights, plus the trailer lighting supply, receive their power from the cab by means of *chassis wiring*.

Various specific wire harnesses are constructed to handle the necessary power flow to various points on the vehicle. These circuits are often referred to as *subsystems* since they are tied into the main cab power source, which is generally the fused or circuit breaker–protected central power supply. Basically, we can consider these subsystems to include the following:

1. The main cab harness, which supplies all of the power requirement connections for other electrical/electronic systems on the vehicle. The main cab harness receives its power from the vehicle batteries.
2. The truck hood harness on a conventional hooded vehicle; on a COE (cab over engine) truck design, this would be classified as part of the cab harness. This harness would feed cab parking, marker, signal, hazard lamps, and fog/driving and headlights.

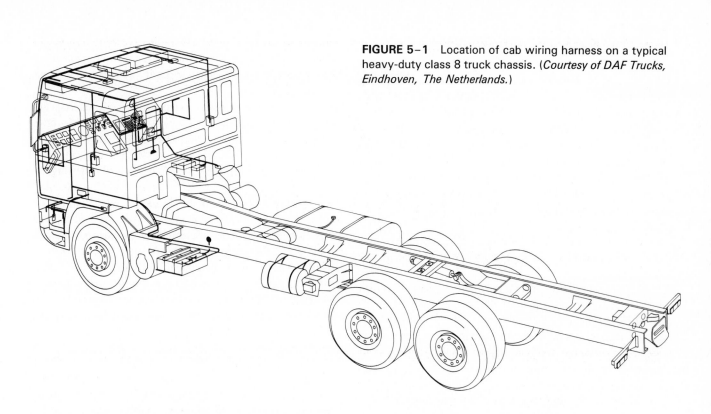

FIGURE 5–1 Location of cab wiring harness on a typical heavy-duty class 8 truck chassis. (*Courtesy of DAF Trucks, Eindhoven, The Netherlands.*)

3. The engine harness, which supplies all of the power requirements necessary to handle the starter motor, the alternator, the Jacobs engine brake, preheating/starting system, fan clutch, shutterstats, and the heater/air conditioner systems.

4. The chassis harness, generally fed from the engine harness. The chassis harness supplies power for all of the frame-mounted electrical and electronic accessories such as lighting, antiskid brakes, fuel tank level gauge, and a feed to the trailer coupling connector.

5. The trailer harness, which is tied into an electrical connector at the rear of the truck chassis to supply all lighting to the trailer (s).

Figure 5–1 illustrates in line schematic form the typical location and general routing of the cab wiring harness, and Fig. 5–2 shows the basic routing of the chassis wiring harness.

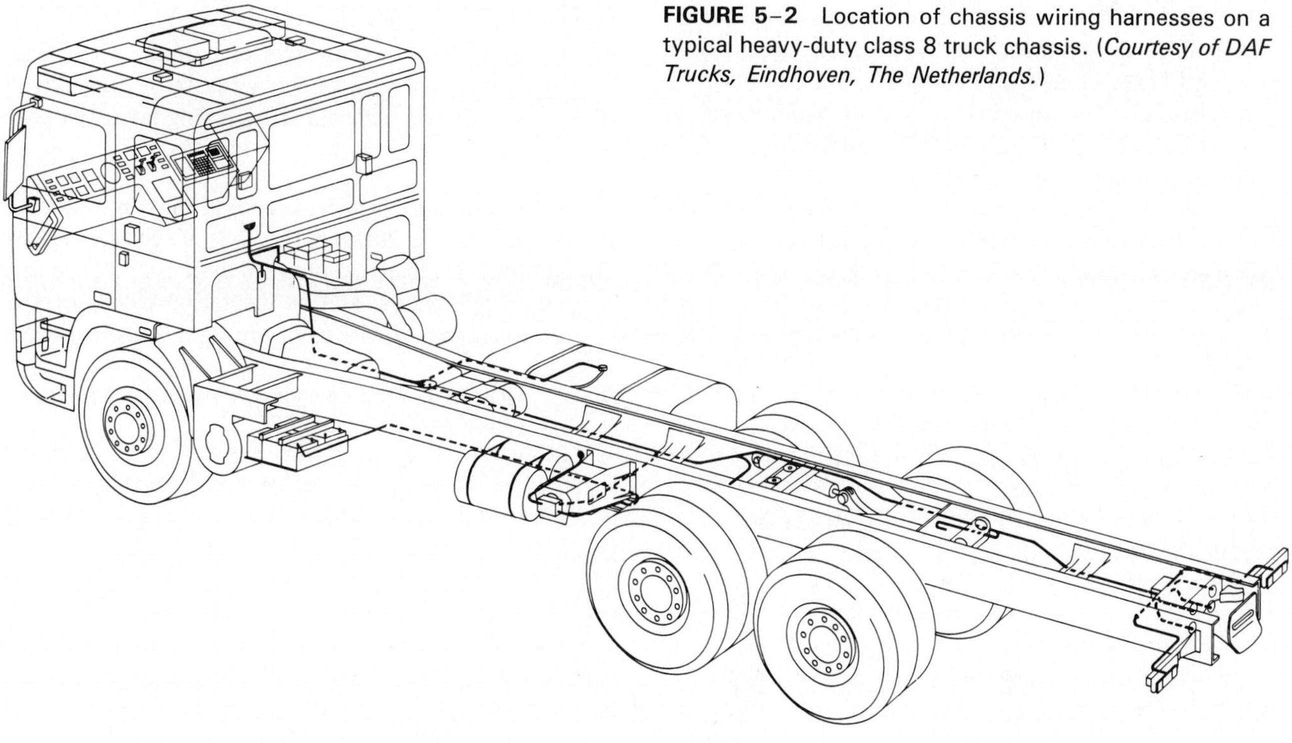

FIGURE 5–2 Location of chassis wiring harnesses on a typical heavy-duty class 8 truck chassis. (*Courtesy of DAF Trucks, Eindhoven, The Netherlands.*)

RECOMMENDED WIRING PRACTICES

All North American (domestic) truck manufacturers closely follow the electrical wiring standards laid down and approved by both the SAE (Society of Automotive Engineers) and the TMC/ATA (The Maintenance Council, American Trucking Associations). Import model truck manufacturers, although not necessarily allied with SAE or TMC/ATA, have similar standards in their own countries that follow closely the SAE standards, since many of the engineering societies in other parts of the world are closely affiliated with SAE. Chapters of SAE exist all over the globe and close liason exists with all major car and truck manufacturers. SAE standards are therefore generally recognized as being an acceptable standard.

It is recommended that a permanent wiring diagram or a wiring diagram pouch or pocket be provided or affixed to every commerical duty vehicle so that the owner/operator, fleet maintenance manager, and/or service technician has ready access to this information for electrical troubleshooting purposes. Generally, the vehicle electrical system is illustrated in two types of diagrams which are invaluable to the mechanic/technician when he or she is attempting to isolate a wire, circuit, or component whose origin and how it fits into the overall electrical circuitry are not clear.

1. A *wiring diagram* makes it possible for the technician to trace every cable from component to component, with most wiring diagrams being laid out so that a grid reference system is used, similar to the design pattern used on maps. This means that you will often see letters illustrated on the vertical axis at the left of the diagram, while figures/numbers are used along the horizontal axis at the top of the wiring diagram. Figures are usually numbered consecutively on the wiring diagram sequence sheets since more than one wiring diagram is required to show all of the circuits and components used on a vehicle. These grid lines used on the wiring diagram key us into coordinates that are usually referenced in a service manual description of operation.

2. A *circuit diagram* illustrates at a glance just how the electrical components are connected to each other without showing the detail of the wiring diagram. The circuit diagram also uses a reference bar that contains figures/numbers placed strategically below each electrical component which are usually referred to as *location numbers*. You will also often see arrows with a number that refers to the location of the electrical wire or cable that serves the accessory item.

With the aid of both a wiring and a circuit diagram, the mechanic/technician is able to trace not only component wiring, but also its location on the vehicle. The wiring diagram allows you to key-in visually on where an electrical problem may originate, as well as letting you see other possible circuit areas that might be causing a specific type of problem. In Chapter 4 we covered basic circuits, the types of problems (shorts, opens, and grounds), and the typical electrical troubleshooting tools that you could use to find an electrical problem. In addition to these tools, always refer to the vehicle wiring diagram when you desire to trace a specific circuit or unusual problem.

Electrical circuit identification is generally identified by a minimum of two methods—color and number, and circuit number and circuit name—although an abbreviation is usually used rather than a name by each vehicle manufacturer. It is possible that you may encounter all three methods of circuit identification. From this information, the mechanic/technician will be able to identify all harness electrical circuit wires. In summation, all wiring systems can be identified by:

1. Circuit numbers assigned by the truck manufacturer or the OEM (original equipment manufacturer) supplier of the wiring harness or electrical component and accessory.
2. Wire colors can be assigned according to accepted SAE standards or by the wire harness manufacturer's standards.
3. A wire printed name identification that uses standard nomenclature or abbreviations.
4. Letters or numbers can be printed on the wire insulation every 4 in. (10 cm), or the wire can be tagged with plastic or dielectric material self-sticking labels on both ends.

An example of how wire coding may appear on a heavy-duty truck is shown in Fig. 5–3, which lists the wire circuit number, the actual physical dimension of the wire in square millimeters, and its insulation color.

Various types of wire color are identified throughout

FIGURE 5–3 Wire coding interpretation. (*Courtesy of Mack Trucks, Inc.*)

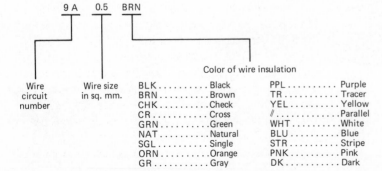

Wire circuit number	Wire size in sq. mm.	Color of wire insulation	
		BLK . . . . Black	PPL . . . . Purple
		BRN . . . . Brown	TR . . . . Tracer
		CHK . . . . Check	YEL . . . . Yellow
		CR . . . . Cross	// . . . . Parallel
		GRN . . . . Green	WHT . . . . White
		NAT . . . . Natural	BLU . . . . Blue
		SGL . . . . Single	STR . . . . Stripe
		ORN . . . . Orange	PNK . . . . Pink
		GR . . . . Gray	DK . . . . Dark

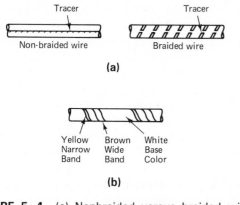

Tracer   Tracer

Non-braided wire   Braided wire

(a)

Yellow   Brown   White
Narrow   Wide   Base
Band   Band   Color

(b)

FIGURE 5–4 (a) Nonbraided versus braided wire color tracer identification, (b) wire band width color ID. (*Courtesy of Mack Trucks, Inc.*)

this section, together with a number of commonly used abbreviations to identify wiring circuits. For example, you might find that the main power supply wiring is red, the lighting is yellow, the warning and indicator circuits are blue, power to the starter motor and other heavy-duty accessories are black, and ground circuit or earth connections are white. These colors are examples and may not hold true on all makes of trucks. Consider also that with so many other circuits in use on a heavy-duty truck, additional colors are used, with multicolored wiring (a main color with a tracer or secondary stripe) being common.

Figure 5–4(a) illustrates typical nonbraided and braided wire with a tracer color through both. Letters indicate wire color, and where two colors are shown for any given wire, the first color is the basic color of the wire and the second color is the tracer. Numbers indicate the size of the wire gauge. Consider, for example, a wire identified as 16 BN-R; this means that it is a 16-gauge wire, brown in color, with a single red tracer throughout its length. A 14 W wire would be a 14-guage wire that uses white color insulation. An additional wire arrangement using the insulation base color and three tracer color bands is shown in Fig. 5–4(b). In Fig. 5–4(b) the base color of the wire insulation is shown as item 1, white; the wide band tracer is identified by what is commonly known

as the first color code designation and is shown as item 2, brown; the narrow tracer color, which is the third color code, is shown as item 3, yellow. The band color widths are usually 2 mm, 1 mm, and 0.5 mm, respectively.

Some manufacturers utilize color-coded sleeves instead of tracer color bands along the length of the wire. All wire insulation color, tracers, and sleeve colors appear on the truck manufacturer's wiring diagram and schematics in abbreviated form, such as those listed in Table 5–1 for typical wire colors. In addition, TECA wire colors are shown in Table 1–6.

All wire conductors used on cars and trucks are produced from annealed copper wire in accordance with ASTM (American Society for Testing and Materials) specification B3, while the cross-sectional area of the wire conductor on all gauge sizes must conform to the specifications shown in SAE J558 data. Wire gauge size is shown in Tables 1–2 through 1–5. Wire insulation for all truck primary wiring cable should be SXL (standard-duty thermosetting cross-linked polyethylene) or equivalent that meets the specified physical properties and testing according to SAE J878 data. The maximum temperature rise in vehicle wiring due to current passing through it will normally not exceed 100°F (38°C), but if the ambient temperature of the electrical system subjects the cable and wiring to 300°F, the cable must be protected by either nylon conduit or metal heat shielding, or a special high-temperature cable should be used. Most vehicle working environments permit the use of a thermoplastic-insulated SAE-type GPT general-purpose cable. On heavy-duty and severe environmental applications, upgraded insulation such as SAE types HDT, GPB, HDB, STS, HTS, and SXL should be used. Specific continuous-duty temperature limitations for each cable type should not exceed the ambient temperature plus the cable temperature rise due to current flow. Recommended maximum temperatures for continuous-duty operation for the various types of insulated cables are:

- Cable type GPT, HDT, GPD, HDB: 194°F (90°C)
- Cable type STS, HTS: 221°F (105°C)
- Cable type SXL: 275°F (135°C)

All wiring should be sized so that the voltage drop through the cable does not exceed 0.5 V, with anything lower being advisable. In addition, due to the physical strength of the cable, no cable should be smaller than 18 gauge.

Wire harnesses should be secured/supported throughout their length by plastic cable ties or rubber-insulated brackets at equal spacings not to exceed 18 in. (450 mm), to prevent chaffing or rubbing that could break through the insulation, causing a number of associated wiring and electrical accessory problems. Wire harness coverings that are commonly used on trucks are electrically insulated friction tape, cotton and kraft paper braid, vinyl/nylon single-layer braid, vinyl plastic tape, plastic sleeving or conduit, nonmetallic loom (woven asphalt, impregnated

TABLE 5–1

Color	Abbreviation	Color	Abbreviation
Black	B	Maroon	M
Orange	O or Or	Brown	BN or Br
Pink	P	Purple	PU or P
Blue	BL or Bl	Green	G
Dark blue	DBL	Light green	LG
Light blue	LBL	Dark green	DG
Red	R	Tan	T
White	W	Grey	GY or Gr
Yellow	Y		

loom, extruded vinyl plastic or elastomer tubing and sheet material), and rigid and flexible conduit. When installing wiring it should always be located so that protection is afforded from heat, road splash, flying rocks, possible abrasion, grease, oil, and fuel leakage. This can usually be achieved by routing the wiring through protective channels along the length of the vehicle chassis frame or similar protective devices.

NOTE: Experience in fleet operation has shown that wiring insulated with PVC (polyvinyl chloride) material should be avoided since a short circuit developing in one circuit in a wire harness can destroy all of the other circuits in the harness. It is best to use thermosetting plastics or cross-linked polyethylene braid insulation.

CAB HARNESS ROUTINGS

The actual wire harness routing through a given truck model cab will, of course, be peculiar to a certain manufacturer. However, for purposes of instruction, we can consider these routings to be reasonably common for our base circuit layout. Figure 5–5 illustrates a top view of the cab harness routing for a conventional cab medium- or heavy-duty truck, with the various major connections

shown and identified. Figure 5–6 illustrates the cab harness routing from the top of the truck cab (view A in the diagram) as well as from a frontal view (view B in the diagram) for a COE (cab over engine) truck model.

CIRCUIT PROTECTION

It is necessary to protect vehicle electrical and electronic circuits from voltage surges, temporary overload conditions, and damage from problems caused by shorts in the wiring or electrical accessory. Failure to provide some form of easily replaceable protective device can lead to overheated wiring that can in severe cases cause complete burnout of the wire harness and a fire in the vehicle. To avoid these conditions, truck manufacturers use either a replaceable fuse in each wire circuit, a circuit breaker, or a fusible wire link. Heavy-duty power circuits (high current draw) such as the battery cables, the starter motor, and the alternator charging circuit are normally wired without any circuit protection, although the starter motor can be equipped with a thermostatic switch for overcrank protection (see Fig. 9–47) and the alternator may employ a fusible link in its wiring. All other power circuits on the vehicle, however, should employ adequate

FIGURE 5–5 Typical cab harness routing on a conventional cab truck. (*Courtesy of GMC Truck Division, General Motors Corporation.*)

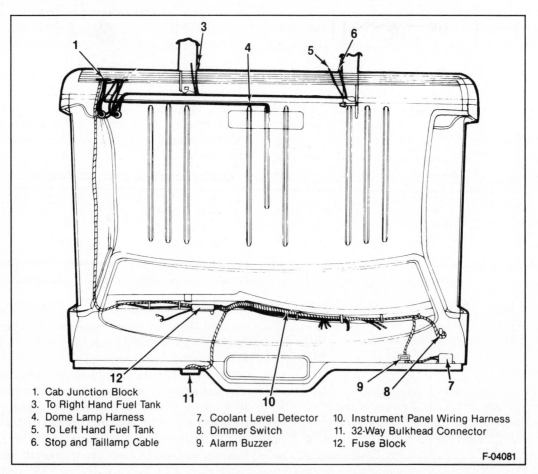

1. Cab Junction Block
3. To Right Hand Fuel Tank
4. Dome Lamp Harness
5. To Left Hand Fuel Tank
6. Stop and Taillamp Cable

7. Coolant Level Detector
8. Dimmer Switch
9. Alarm Buzzer

10. Instrument Panel Wiring Harness
11. 32-Way Bulkhead Connector
12. Fuse Block

F-04081

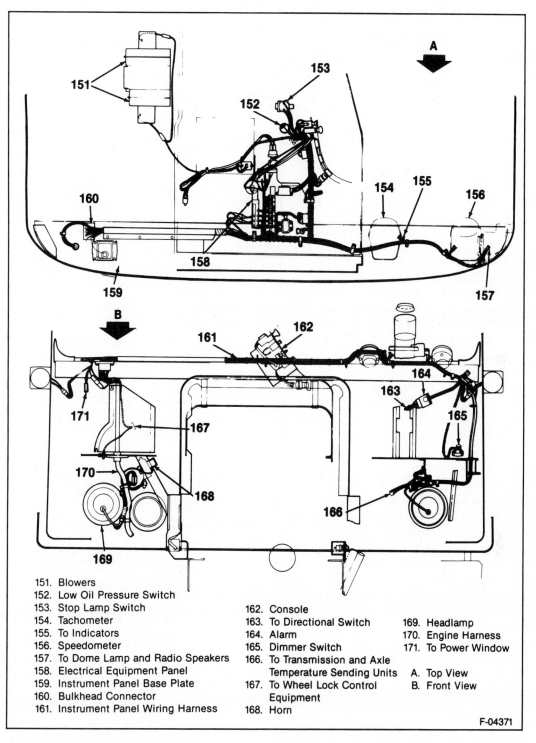

151. Blowers
152. Low Oil Pressure Switch
153. Stop Lamp Switch
154. Tachometer
155. To Indicators
156. Speedometer
157. To Dome Lamp and Radio Speakers
158. Electrical Equipment Panel
159. Instrument Panel Base Plate
160. Bulkhead Connector
161. Instrument Panel Wiring Harness

162. Console
163. To Directional Switch
164. Alarm
165. Dimmer Switch
166. To Transmission and Axle
    Temperature Sending Units
167. To Wheel Lock Control
    Equipment
168. Horn

169. Headlamp
170. Engine Harness
171. To Power Window

A. Top View
B. Front View

F-04371

FIGURE 5–6 COE (cab over engine) example of cab harness routings. (*Courtesy of GMC Truck Division, General Motors Corporation.*)

circuit protection devices that preferably incorporate both a primary and a secondary safety feature. The primary safety device usually takes the form of either a fusible link or an automatic or manual reset circuit breaker. The secondary protection device can take the form of a replaceable fuse or a circuit breaker. The primary device is placed into the circuit to protect the power feed be- tween the battery and the passenger compartment, while the secondary protection device protects the wiring as well as switches, gauges, motors, and any other power con- suming devices in the passenger compartment. Note that the vehicle headlight circuit is normally protected by one fuse or circuit breaker per side, or by the use of four fuses (one fuse per headlight) on a four-headlamp system.

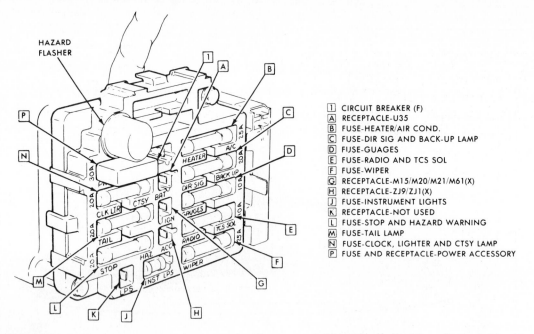

FIGURE 5–7 Typical cartridge fuse panel. (*Courtesy of GMC Truck Division, General Motors Corporation.*)

1. CIRCUIT BREAKER (F)
A. RECEPTACLE-U35
B. FUSE-HEATER/AIR COND.
C. FUSE-DIR SIG AND BACK-UP LAMP
D. FUSE-GUAGES
E. FUSE-RADIO AND TCS SOL
F. FUSE-WIPER
G. RECEPTACLE-M15/M20/M21/M61(X)
H. RECEPTACLE-ZJ9/ZJ1(X)
J. FUSE-INSTRUMENT LIGHTS
K. RECEPTACLE-NOT USED
L. FUSE-STOP AND HAZARD WARNING
M. FUSE-TAIL LAMP
N. FUSE-CLOCK, LIGHTER AND CTSY LAMP
P. FUSE AND RECEPTACLE-POWER ACCESSORY

Fuses

Fuse Panel Location. Although most fuse panels or blocks can be found in various locations on different vehicles, the majority of vehicle manufacturers locate these inside the passenger compartment for both ease of access and, more important, to protect the fuses and wiring from the elements. The usual location for the fuse panel on light-duty trucks is either under the dash or instrument panel or at the left- or right-hand side of the vehicle (kick pad area) inside the passenger compartment. Some vehicles have fuse panels under the hood, but this area is subjected to direct heat radiation and the like. On heavy-duty trucks, fuse panels can be located in a variety of positions. Most are placed in hinged panels somewhere on the instrument/dash panel for ease of access to the maintenance mechanic/technician.

These safety devices are necessary to protect not only the wiring circuitry, but also to ensure that instruments and other gauges are protected. Failure to use proper-size fuses and circuit breakers can lead to excessive loads on the system due to short circuits. Fires through installation of too great a rating fuse can occur, while using a fuse rating too low can lead to constantly blown fuses and failure of one or more circuits on the vehicle. Several types of fuses are used in vehicles. The glass cartridge in-line fuse, used for many years, is shown in Fig. 5–7. This fuse is still used in all types of vehicles and equipment. However, later-model light-, medium-, and heavy-duty trucks employ a fuse panel or fuse block assembly that uses what are known as miniaturized fuses; these blade-type fuses are plug-in type rather than the push-in type used with the cartridge fuse arrangement. Figure 5–8 shows a typical fuse panel with a miniaturized fuse arrangement.

Figure 5–9 shows a miniaturized blade type of fuse, how to identify the load-carrying capacity of each, and the location of the miniaturized fuse test terminals. Also shown is both a good and a blown fuse.

FIGURE 5–8 Fuse panel, L-series truck, city delivery models. (Reprinted with Ford Motor Company's permission)

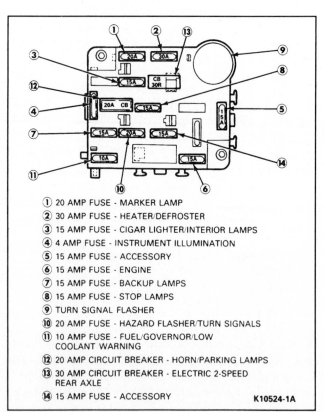

1. 20 AMP FUSE - MARKER LAMP
2. 30 AMP FUSE - HEATER/DEFROSTER
3. 15 AMP FUSE - CIGAR LIGHTER/INTERIOR LAMPS
4. 4 AMP FUSE - INSTRUMENT ILLUMINATION
5. 15 AMP FUSE - ACCESSORY
6. 15 AMP FUSE - ENGINE
7. 15 AMP FUSE - BACKUP LAMPS
8. 15 AMP FUSE - STOP LAMPS
9. TURN SIGNAL FLASHER
10. 20 AMP FUSE - HAZARD FLASHER/TURN SIGNALS
11. 10 AMP FUSE - FUEL/GOVERNOR/LOW COOLANT WARNING
12. 20 AMP CIRCUIT BREAKER - HORN/PARKING LAMPS
13. 30 AMP CIRCUIT BREAKER - ELECTRIC 2-SPEED REAR AXLE
14. 15 AMP FUSE - ACCESSORY

K10524-1A

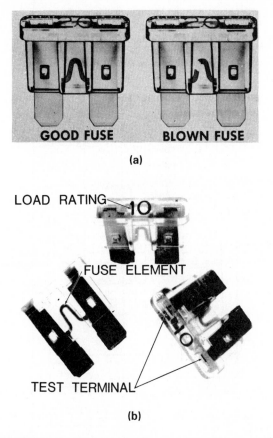

(a)

LOAD RATING

FUSE ELEMENT

TEST TERMINAL

(b)

FIGURE 5-9 Miniaturized fuses: (a) usable or good fuse versus a blown (nonusable) fuse; (b) miniaturized fuse load rating and test terminals. (*Courtesy of GMC Truck Division, General Motors Corporation.*)

Fuse Color Codes. Truck manufacturers identify their fuses by a color code method that conforms to SAE standards (see Table 5-2).

Cartridge Fuse Evaluation. The purpose of a fuse is to protect the wiring circuit and accessories from current surges. Several things can damage a fuse to the point that it is no longer usable. Careful note of the specific type of fuse break can often reveal what actually caused the condition of a blown fuse. It is important to be able

TABLE 5-2 Fuse color codes

Ampere Rating	Color	Ampere Rating	Color
1	Dark Green	9	Orange
2	Gray	10	Red
2.5	Purple	14	Black
3	Violet	15	Light Blue
4	Pink	20	Yellow
5	Tan	25	White
6	Gold	30	Light Green
7.5	Brown		

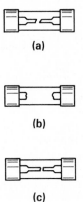

(a)

(b)

(c)

FIGURE 5-10 Cartridge fuse damage caused by (a) normal zinc strip burnout, (b) a short circuit resulting in a vaporized fuse, (c) a high current surge.

to recognize this, because if you simply replace the fuse each time that it blows, eventually you may be faced with a much more serious problem.

The material used in the fuse is made from zinc in strip form, and this strip is bonded between the end caps. Figure 5-10 illustrates common types of fuse damage. Replacement of a fuse with a higher-rated one is a dangerous practice since overheating of the wiring and accessory damage may result. Check the fuse holder for good contact and any other conditions that might prevent a good connection through the particular fuse circuit. Figure 4-28 illustrates a fuse remover/installer/tester tool.

The fuse rating for glass cartridge fuses is marked on the end caps along with the manufacturer's name or trademark, although some fuses have the rating marked on the glass. Still others use a color-coded stripe for identification. Figures 5-11 through 5-18 illustrate some examples of the fuse box and combination circuit breaker locations. Figure 5-11 illustrates one typical fuse block that would be found on GMC/Isuzu W4, W7, and W7 HV steel tilt cab forward models. Note that items 1, 26, and 27 of the wiring diagram are all fusible links; items 1 through 15 in the fuse block are all individual fuses to protect a specific circuit identified as items 5 through 19 listed in the accompanying index.

Figure 5-12 illustrates glass-tube fuses, together with one circuit breaker and the signal/hazard flasher relay, which are all assembled into one single panel on Mack Midliner cab-over model trucks. The index for this diagram lists the individual components, their wire colors, color abbreviations, and fuse and circuit breaker ratings. The basic fuse block circuit for the same truck model is shown in Fig. 5-13 which shows the wiring system schematic. Figure 5-14 illustrates the location of the fuses, circuit breakers, and relays for Mack CS-200, 250, and 300 conventional model trucks. Note the liberal use of symbols to identify the individual components on the panel.

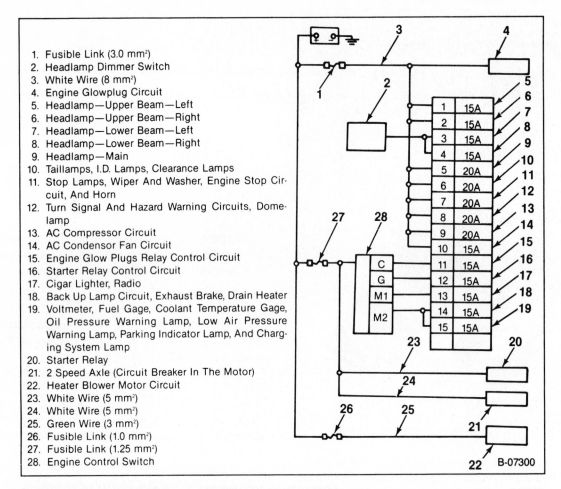

1. Fusible Link (3.0 mm²)
2. Headlamp Dimmer Switch
3. White Wire (8 mm²)
4. Engine Glowplug Circuit
5. Headlamp—Upper Beam—Left
6. Headlamp—Upper Beam—Right
7. Headlamp—Lower Beam—Left
8. Headlamp—Lower Beam—Right
9. Headlamp—Main
10. Taillamps, I.D. Lamps, Clearance Lamps
11. Stop Lamps, Wiper And Washer, Engine Stop Circuit, And Horn
12. Turn Signal And Hazard Warning Circuits, Dome-lamp
13. AC Compressor Circuit
14. AC Condensor Fan Circuit
15. Engine Glow Plugs Relay Control Circuit
16. Starter Relay Control Circuit
17. Cigar Lighter, Radio
18. Back Up Lamp Circuit, Exhaust Brake, Drain Heater
19. Voltmeter, Fuel Gage, Coolant Temperature Gage, Oil Pressure Warning Lamp, Low Air Pressure Warning Lamp, Parking Indicator Lamp, And Charging System Lamp
20. Starter Relay
21. 2 Speed Axle (Circuit Breaker In The Motor)
22. Heater Blower Motor Circuit
23. White Wire (5 mm²)
24. White Wire (5 mm²)
25. Green Wire (3 mm²)
26. Fusible Link (1.0 mm²)
27. Fusible Link (1.25 mm²)
28. Engine Control Switch

FIGURE 5–11 Typical fuse block and identification of the various components. (*Courtesy of GMC Truck Division, General Motors Corporation.*)

Incorporated into the instrument panel wiring harness of many heavy-duty trucks is a combination circuit breaker and fuse block, shown in Fig. 5–15 that provides a number of circuit takeoffs and fuse clips for the circuits. This fuse block is mounted inside the access panel on the instrument panel. This panel uses automatic circuit breaker reset.

Circuit Breakers

Two types of circuit breakers are used on medium- and heavy-duty trucks:

1. The automatic reset type
2. The manual reset type

On some vehicles the automatic reset type can be identified by a long accessory terminal stud and a short battery terminal stud on the circuit breaker. Two stud nuts are used to retain the terminal leads to the circuit breaker. Contained inside the circuit breaker is a bimetallic strip which expands when electricity (current) flows through it. Should an overload pass through the circuit breaker, the bimetallic strip will expand to a point where it will cause the circuit to operate. Figure 5–16 illustrates

the basic operation of a bimetallic strip. Once the bimetallic strip has cooled (between 35 and 45 seconds), it will contract and the circuit breaker will close again, allowing the circuit to operate. Continued cutting out of an automatic circuit breaker is a positive indication that there is a problem in either the circuit itself or in the breaker. Check it out. If you have to replace the circuit breaker, disconnect the batteries, allow the breaker to cool, and proceed to check and replace it.

On manual reset circuit breakers such as the ones illustrated in Fig. 5–17, these can be mounted into the truck instrument panel or behind a protective cover. These circuit breakers will open the protected circuit any time that the electrical load becomes greater than the current-carrying capacity of the breaker. These units function in a similar manner to those found in your house or apartment power control panel. The manual circuit breaker also contains a bimetallic element strip inside its body; when the load is too high, the bimetallic strip will expand and open the circuit, stopping power flow. At the same time, the expansion of the bimetallic strip will force the reset button outward. To reset the manual type, you simply have to push in the red reset button or the actual cir-

(a)

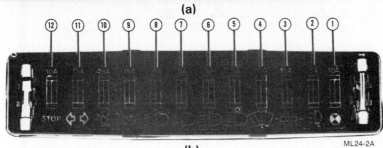

(b)

ML24—2A

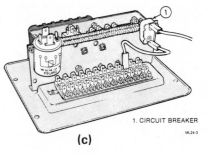

1. CIRCUIT BREAKER

ML24-3

(c)

No.	Fuses	Color of Wires and Sleeving	Abbreviation	Rating
1	Supply of instruments and warning lights; and heater—defroster	yellow with red sleeve; yellow with red-black sleeve	Y(R); Y(R-B)	10A
2	Supply of back-up lamps, and Eaton unit speedometer corrector (if applicable)	yellow with red-blue sleeve	Y(R-Bl)	5A
3	Dome lamps, cigar lighter	red with white sleeve	R(w)	10A
4	Supply windshield wipers and washer	blue with white sleeve	Bl(w)	10A
5	Left headlight—high beam	green with green sleeve	G(G)	5A
6	Right headlight—high beam	green with brown sleeve	G(Br)	5A
7	Left headlight—low beam	grey with green sleeve	Gr(G)	5A
8	Right headlight—low beam	grey with brown sleeve	Gr(Br)	5A
9	Supply marker/clearance lamps	blue with purple sleeve	Bl(P)	15A
10	Horn	purple with white-blue sleeve	P(w-Bl)	15A
11	Supply hazard warning, and turn signal:			15A
	—turn signal and warning flasher	purple with white sleeve	P(w)	
	—hazard warning switch	purple with white-brown sleeve	P(w-Br)	
	—turn signal switch	purple with white-black sleeve	P(w-B)	
12	Supply stop switch for stop lights	red with white sleeve	R(w)	10A

Type	Circuit Breaker	Color of Wires and Sleeving	Abbreviation	Rating
I	Supply headlights, dimmer switch, tail lights and instrument panel lamps	green with purple sleeve	G(P)	15A

(d)

FIGURE 5–12 (a) Fuse box location shown below the instrument panel; (b) close-up of fuse box cover; (c) circuit breaker location in the fuse box; (d) location chart. (*Courtesy of Mack Trucks, Inc.*)

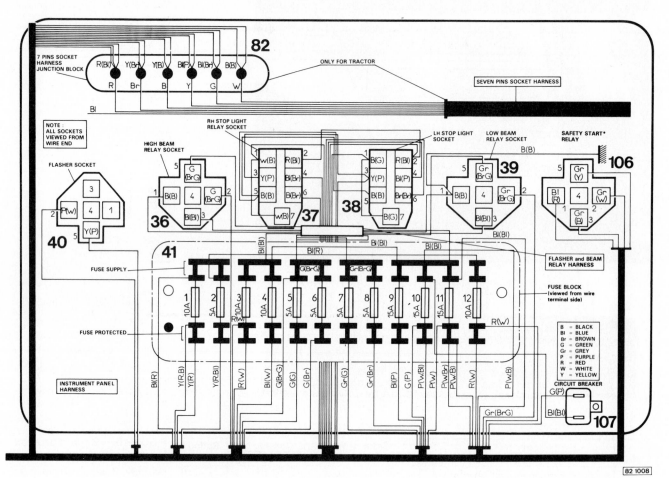

KEY: * With automatic transmission

No.	FUSES	RATING
1	INSTRUMENTS AND WARNING LIGHTS, AND HEATER-DEFROSTER	10A
2	BACK-UP LAMPS, AND EATON UNIT SPEEDOMETER CORRECTOR (IF APPLICABLE)	5A
3	DOME LAMPS, CIGAR LIGHTER	10A
4	WINDSHIELD WIPERS AND WASHER	10A
5	LEFT HEADLIGHT—HIGH BEAM	5A
6	RIGHT HEADLIGHT—HIGH BEAM	5A
7	LEFT HEADLIGHT—LOW BEAM	5A
8	RIGHT HEADLIGHT—LOW BEAM	5A
9	CAB MARKER CLEARANCE LAMPS	15A
10	HORN	15A
11	HAZARD WARNING, TURN SIGNAL	15A
12	STOP SWITCH FOR STOP LIGHTS	10A

TYPE	CIRCUIT BREAKER	RATING
I	HEADLIGHTS, DIMMER SWITCH, TAIL LIGHTS, AND INSTRUMENT PANEL LAMPS	15A

NOTE: If a problem develops in this circuit (i.e., short or overload), the Type I circuit breaker will automatically reset after it breaks and "cools." Nevertheless, it is recommended that the vehicle be taken out of service as soon as practicable, and the problem remedied before continuing vehicle operation.

FIGURE 5–13 Wiring diagram showing the fuse block, circuit breaker, and relay circuits for the Midliner COE truck model. (*Courtesy of Mack Trucks, Inc.*)

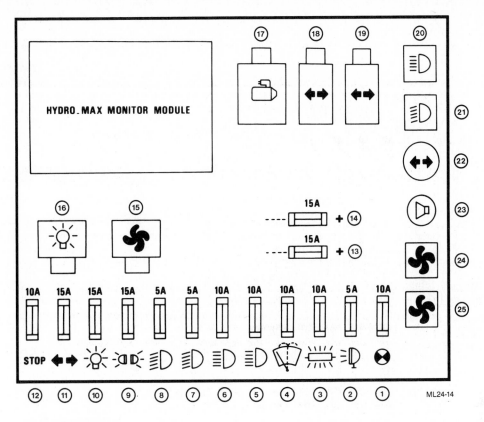

LOCATION CHART

No.	FUSES	WIRE COLORS	COLOR ABBRE.	RATING AMP
1	SUPPLY OF INSTRUMENTS AND WARNING LIGHTS	YELLOW · RED	Y R	10
2	SPEEDOMETER CORRECTOR, BACK-UP LAMPS, AND WEATHER—DEFROSTER	WHITE · RED	W R	5
3	DOME LAMP, CIGAR LIGHTER	RED · WHITE	R W	10
4	WINDSHIELD WIPERS AND WASHER	BLUE · WHITE	Bl W	10
5	LEFT HEADLIGHT—HIGH BEAM	GREEN · GREEN	G G	10
6	RIGHT HEADLIGHT—HIGH BEAM AND INDICATOR LIGHT	GREEN · BROWN	G Br	10
7	LEFT HEADLIGHT—LOW BEAM	GREY · GREEN	Gr G	5
8	RIGHT HEADLIGHT—LOW BEAM	GREY · BROWN	Gr Br	5
9	SUPPLY MARKER/CLEARANCE LAMPS	YELLOW · BLACK	Y B	15
10	HORN	BROWN · GREEN	Br G	15
11	TURN SIGNAL AND HAZARD WARNING	PURPLE · WHITE	P W	15
12	STOP LIGHTS	PURPLE · YELLOW	P Y	10
13	DIRECT FEED LINES—FOR ANY PURPOSE	BLUE · BLUE	Bl Bl	15
14	AFTER STARTER SWITCH FEED LINE—FOR ANY PURPOSE	BLUE · RED	Bl R	15
	CIRCUIT BREAKERS	WIRE COLORS	COLOR ABBRE.	RATING AMP
15	FOR HEATER—DEFROSTER (TYPE III)	YELLOW · BLUE	Y Bl	20
16	FOR HEADLIGHTS, TAIL LIGHTS, AND INSTRUMENT PANEL LAMPS (TYPE I)	GREEN · PURPLE	G P	15
	RELAYS			
17	SAFETY START (WITH AUTOMATIC TRANSMISSION)			
18	LEFT STOP AND SIGNAL LIGHTS			
19	RIGHT STOP AND SIGNAL LIGHTS			
20	HEADLIGHT/HIGH BEAM			
21	HEADLIGHT/LOW BEAM			
22	TURN SIGNAL			
23	BUZZER (WHEN INSTALLED)			
24	HEATER—DEFROSTER HIGH SPEED			
25	HEATER—DEFROSTER LOW SPEED			

FIGURE 5–14 Location of fuses, circuit breakers, and relays for a Mack CS conventional truck model. (*Courtesy of Mack Trucks, Inc.*)

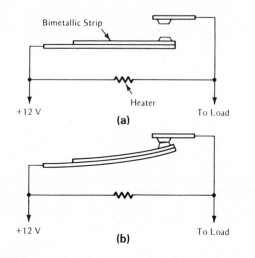

FIGURE 5–15 Circuit breaker and fuse block example for a heavy-duty truck. (*Courtesy of GMC Truck Division, General Motors Corporation.*)

ITEM	AMPERES	
	Breaker	Fuse
71. Hazard and Directional Signal	20	20
72. Stoplamps	30	30
73. Domelamp	10	5
74. Domelamp Socket (Protected by No. 3)		
75. Taillamps	15	15
76. Battery Outlet Socket (Protected by No. 5)		
77. Marker Lamps	20	20
78. Accessory Outlet Socket (Protected by No. 7)		
79. Radio	—	5
80. Accessory Outlet Socket (Protected by No. 9)		
81. Panel Lamps	10	5
82. Accessory Outlet Socket (Protected by No. 11)		
83. Rear Axle	20	20
84. Wiper	15	15
85. Back-Up Lamps	10	10
86. Accessory Outlet Socket (Protected by No. 15)		
87. Wheel Lock Control System	20	20
88. Accessory Outlet Socket (Protected by No. 17)		
89. Heater	30	30
90. Accessory Outlet Socket (Protected by No. 19)		
91. Wheel Lock System	—	3
92. Flasher	—	—
93. Flasher	—	—
94. Engine Control Circuit	20	20

F-04370

FIGURE 5–16 Circuit breaker bimetallic strip operation.

FIGURE 5–17 Circuit breaker installation showing reset button arrangement. (*Courtesy of GMC Truck Division, General Motors Corporation.*)

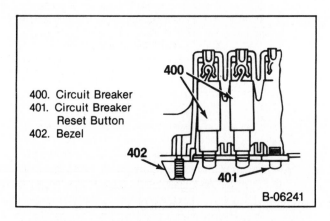

400. Circuit Breaker
401. Circuit Breaker Reset Button
402. Bezel

B-06241

cuit breaker rocker switch, shown in Fig. 5–17. An example of where these circuit breaker reset buttons might appear on the instrument panel of a heavy-duty class 8 truck is shown in Fig. 5–18.

Fusible Links

In addition to the safety features afforded the electrical system by the use of both fuses and circuit breakers, many vehicles now employ fusible links, which are used specifically to protect the actual wiring harness. The fusible link is used where a replaceable fuse is normally not required, such as in the ignition circuit or the alternator-to-starter relay. Figure 5–19 indicates typical locations of fusible links used in some truck applications.

A very important point to note about the fusible link is that because of the heavy insulation wrapped around it, it appears to be of a heavier gauge wire than it actually is. The fusible link is a short length of special Hypalon wire (high-temperature insulated wire) that is integral with the engine compartment wiring harness and is usually

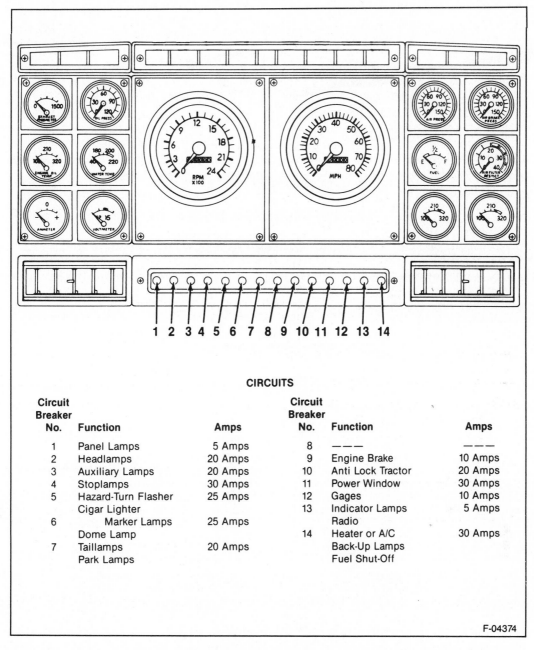

CIRCUITS

Circuit Breaker No.	Function	Amps	Circuit Breaker No.	Function	Amps
1	Panel Lamps	5 Amps	8	— — —	— — —
2	Headlamps	20 Amps	9	Engine Brake	10 Amps
3	Auxiliary Lamps	20 Amps	10	Anti Lock Tractor	20 Amps
4	Stoplamps	30 Amps	11	Power Window	30 Amps
5	Hazard-Turn Flasher	25 Amps	12	Gages	10 Amps
	Cigar Lighter		13	Indicator Lamps	5 Amps
6	Marker Lamps	25 Amps		Radio	
	Dome Lamp		14	Heater or A/C	30 Amps
7	Taillamps	20 Amps		Back-Up Lamps	
	Park Lamps			Fuel Shut-Off	

F-04374

FIGURE 5–18 Circuit breaker identification example for a typical heavy-duty truck. (*Courtesy of GMC Truck Division, General Motors Corporation.*)

FIGURE 5–19 Locations of fusible links in a truck electrical system.

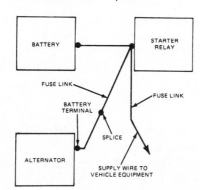

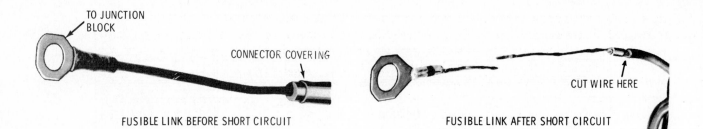

TO JUNCTION BLOCK

CONNECTOR COVERING

FUSIBLE LINK BEFORE SHORT CIRCUIT

CUT WIRE HERE

FUSIBLE LINK AFTER SHORT CIRCUIT

FIGURE 5-20 Fusible link condition before and after a short-circuit condition. (*Reprinted with Ford Motor Company's permission.*)

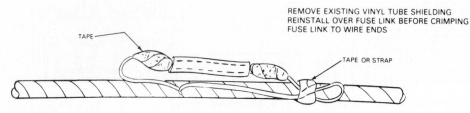

REMOVE EXISTING VINYL TUBE SHIELDING
REINSTALL OVER FUSE LINK BEFORE CRIMPING
FUSE LINK TO WIRE ENDS

TAPE

TAPE OR STRAP

TYPICAL REPAIR USING THE SPECIAL #17 GA. (9.00" LONG-YELLOW) FUSE LINK REQUIRED FOR THE AIR/COND. CIRCUITS (2) #687E AND #261A LOCATED IN THE ENGINE COMPARTMENT

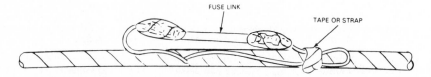

FUSE LINK

TAPE OR STRAP

TYPICAL REPAIR FOR ANY IN-LINE FUSE LINK USING THE SPECIFIED GAUGE FUSE LINK FOR THE SPECIFIC CIRCUIT.

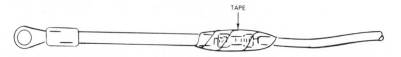

TAPE

TYPICAL REPAIR USING THE EYELET TERMINAL FUSE LINK OF THE SPECIFIED GAUGE FOR ATTACHMENT TO A CIRCUIT WIRE END

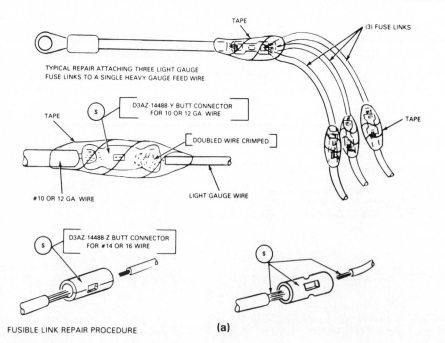

TAPE

(3) FUSE LINKS

TYPICAL REPAIR ATTACHING THREE LIGHT GAUGE
FUSE LINKS TO A SINGLE HEAVY GAUGE FEED WIRE

TAPE

D3AZ-14488-Y BUTT CONNECTOR
FOR 10 OR 12 GA. WIRE

S

DOUBLED WIRE CRIMPED

TAPE

#10 OR 12 GA. WIRE

LIGHT GAUGE WIRE

D3AZ-14488-Z BUTT CONNECTOR
FOR #14 OR 16 WIRE

S

S

FUSIBLE LINK REPAIR PROCEDURE

(a)

FIGURE 5-21 (a) Fusible ink repair procedure; (b) typical fusible link locations; (c)fusible link and butt connector identification; (d) optional fusible link service procedure. (Reprinted with Ford Motor Company's permission.)

three or four wire gauge sizes smaller than the cable it is designed to protect. It is imperative that a fusible link never be replaced with a length of standard-gauge wire cut from bulk stock or another wiring harness. Figure 5–20 shows a typical fusible link both prior to and after a short circuit.

The higher melting temperature of the Hypalon insulation used with the fusible link is designed to allow the smaller fuse wire to actually melt with the Hypalon casing, but not damage the outer wire insulation other than for the possibility of slight heat discoloration or minor bubbling of the surface. The actual fusible link wire size is usually marked on the insulation covering, or a

flag is molded on the wire or the terminal insulator. For example, typical color coding on the flag or connector of the fusible link indicates the following wire gauge sizes:

1. *Blue:* 20-gauge wire
2. *Red:* 18-gauge wire
3. *Yellow:* 17-gauge wire
4. *Orange:* 16-gauge wire
5. *Green:* 14-gauge wire

Fusible Link Continuity Test. If a circuit is inoperative and the fuse or circuit breaker to the main circuit is serviceable, or if there is no fuse or circuit breaker in the particular circuit in question but a fusible link is

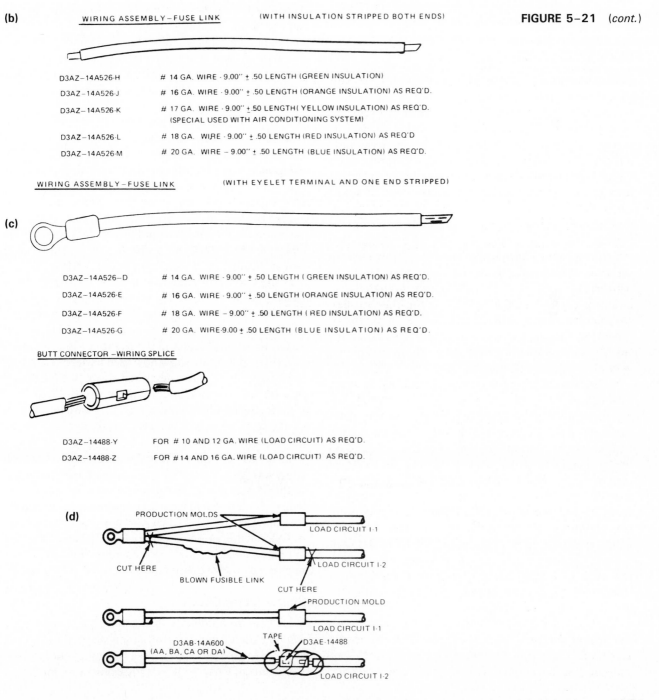

(b) WIRING ASSEMBLY–FUSE LINK   (WITH INSULATION STRIPPED BOTH ENDS)   FIGURE 5–21   (cont.)

D3AZ–14A526-H   # 14 GA. WIRE - 9.00'' ± .50 LENGTH (GREEN INSULATION)

D3AZ–14A526-J   # 16 GA. WIRE - 9.00'' ± .50 LENGTH (ORANGE INSULATION) AS REQ'D.

D3AZ–14A526-K   # 17 GA. WIRE - 9.00'' ± .50 LENGTH(YELLOW INSULATION) AS REQ'D.
(SPECIAL USED WITH AIR CONDITIONING SYSTEM)

D3AZ–14A526-L   # 18 GA. WIRE - 9.00'' ± .50 LENGTH (RED INSULATION) AS REQ'D

D3AZ–14A526-M   # 20 GA. WIRE – 9.00'' ± .50 LENGTH (BLUE INSULATION) AS REQ'D.

WIRING ASSEMBLY–FUSE LINK   (WITH EYELET TERMINAL AND ONE END STRIPPED)

(c)

D3AZ–14A526–D   # 14 GA. WIRE - 9.00'' ± .50 LENGTH (GREEN INSULATION) AS REQ'D.

D3AZ–14A526-E   # 16 GA. WIRE - 9.00'' ± .50 LENGTH (ORANGE INSULATION) AS REQ'D.

D3AZ–14A526-F   # 18 GA. WIRE – 9.00'' ± .50 LENGTH (RED INSULATION) AS REQ'D.

D3AZ–14A526-G   # 20 GA. WIRE-9.00 ± .50 LENGTH (BLUE INSULATION) AS REQ'D.

BUTT CONNECTOR –WIRING SPLICE

D3AZ–14488-Y   FOR # 10 AND 12 GA. WIRE (LOAD CIRCUIT) AS REQ'D.

D3AZ–14488-Z   FOR #14 AND 16 GA. WIRE (LOAD CIRCUIT) AS REQ'D.

(d)   PRODUCTION MOLDS
LOAD CIRCUIT I-1
CUT HERE
BLOWN FUSIBLE LINK
LOAD CIRCUIT I-2
CUT HERE
PRODUCTION MOLD
LOAD CIRCUIT I-1
D3AB-14A600
(AA, BA, CA OR DA)
TAPE
D3AE-14488
LOAD CIRCUIT I-2

used, then prior to attempting to replace the fusible link, check it for continuity with either an ohmmeter or by use of a voltmeter. For example, in Fig. 5–19, which shows some typical locations of the fusible links, turn on the headlamps or other accessory, and if they do not operate, the fusible link is probably burned out. To check the fusible link feeding the alternator circuit, check with a voltmeter or 12-V test light at the BAT terminal of the alternator. No or low voltage, or no light or a dull light, usually indicates that the fusible link is probably burned out, if the battery connections are good.

Fusible Link Replacement. Figure 5–21 shows the accepted procedure for replacement of a fusible link into the wiring circuit of a vehicle, as well as wiring harness repair (see pages 130-131).

READING A WIRING DIAGRAM

The manufacturer's wiring diagram is designed to allow the mechanic/technician to trace a power supply to a specific component, switch, relay, fuse, circuit breaker, or junction block to its ground. All wiring receives its power source from the vehicle battery, but not necessarily directly. Some electrical components, such as the starter motor and alternator systems, are usually not protected by a fuse or circuit breaker, but some alternators may employ a fusible link in their wiring. Both of these major electrical components receive power directly from the battery. The starter motor gets its power by the ignition switch energizing a magnetic relay switch, which acts to carry the heavy current to the starter solenoid. The alternator receives its power from the battery through the ignition switch and a diode to feed the slip-ring brushes. No protective device is used for the starter or alternator other than in some systems that employ a small in-line fuse for the ignition key switch circuit. If this fuse blows, ignition would not be possible.

The type of wiring diagram supplied by the truck manufacturer can take one of several forms. Many wiring diagrams resemble a map in that various coordinates in the form of alphabetical letters are used along the top and bottom horizontal line, while numbers are used on the left-hand side vertical axis. In this way, the electrical section of the service manual is able to direct you to a specific area for a given component, circuit, or system that you need to trace wiring information on. For example, coordinate H9 would direct you to the RH door lamp, while coordinate J9 might lead you to the RH door switch. The term *bus bar* which often appears in a wiring diagram means that the bus carries current to a number of different areas and systems. Therefore, the bus is a main power feeder.

Other wiring diagrams may not use map coordinates, but instead, an electrical components code list which accompanies the wiring diagram. One example of this arrangement is illustrated in Table 5–3; this electrical components code list must be used in conjunction with the wiring schematic shown in Fig. 5–22 and the wiring diagram illustrated in Fig. 5–23. Take careful note that the numbering sequence in the electrical components code does not run consecutively from 1 through 114. Consider, for example, that numbers 77 and 78 appear after the groupings 75–79 and 76–80, since these groupings incorporate components that are closely related to one another. Similarly, numbers 95 and 97 appear out of sync since they are grouped with similar components. Also appearing in Figs. 5–22 and 5–23 are various symbols that are best described by reference to Fig. 5–24. Figure 5–22 is a simplified wiring schematic for Mack Trucks CS conventional cab midrange truck models, specifically the model CS 200 and CS250; the CS300 would be similar. This illustration shows in a line diagram form that the battery power (+ and −) appears at both the top left and right, respectively. Individual components are identified by a large number; refer to the electrical components code for specific information on this number. Located down the right-hand side of Fig. 5–22 are individual component names to show you their ground return circuit. This diagram does not identify the wire number that appears throughout the length of every wire used on the vehicle harnesses, but it does show how these components tie in to the overall electrical system of the vehicle. For information on how all the truck electrical components would appear on the vehicle, refer to Fig. 5–23; this diagram identifies the individual wiring harnesses on the vehicle by a solid heavy black line. For example, in Fig. 5–23(a), the engine harness is clearly identified at the top left of the diagram; the cab front harness is at the lower left-hand side, and the instrument panel harness is shown along the bottom center as well as at the right center. The cab upper harness is shown vertically in the lower center position, and the panel harness appears almost dead center in the diagram. Connections to part (b) of this figure show how each harness is tied back to its respective harness described above [see the broken lines on both parts (a) and (b) of Fig. 5–23]. Figure 5–23 includes the numbers assigned to every wire on the vehicle; these numbers would be affixed to each wire so that the mechanic/technician can trace any wire from its start to its conclusion when troubleshooting an electrical problem. Note also that both Figs. 5–22 and 5–23 include all of the respective wire insulation colors. These are shown with their abbreviated letters. For example, BrW indicates that the wire color is brown with a white tracer through it. Color abbreviations appear in Figs. 5–3 and Table 5–1. We showed earlier how color combinations and tracers appear on the wire insulation.

Starter Motor Circuit

Since you are familiar with the basic starter motor circuit operation from the information supplied in Fig. 4–4, as well as with the battery function and operation from your study of Chapter 3, let's trace the starter motor wir-

TABLE 5–3 Wiring schematics and diagrams electrical components code (*Courtesy of Mack Trucks, Inc.*)

1	R.H. front turn signal lamp	59	Hazard warning switch
2	R.H. Head lamp	60	Dimmer switch junction block
3	Electric horn	61	Dimmer, turn signal, horn switch
4	Windshield wiper motor	62	Alternator
5	Windshield washer motor	63	-110-115 Main ground
6	Heater-defroster motor	64	Fuel level sending unit
7	L.H. Head lamp	65	Eaton 2 speed/speedometer switch
8	L.H. front turn signal lamp	66	Back-up lamp switch
9	Parking brake indicator switch	68	Oil pressure warning light switch
10	R.H. front clearance lamp	69	Oil pressure sending unit
11-12-13	Front identification lamps	70	Cranking motor
14	Dome lamp	71	Electric control valve (Eaton unit)
15	L.H. front clearance lamp	72	Hydraulic pressure warning light switches
16	Air conditioner (spare connection)	73	2 or 3 batteries 12 V, 80A/H
22	Automatic transmission fluid temperature warning light (*) or spare warning indicator light	74	Air pressure warning light switches
		75-79	Back-up lamps
23	Brake system warning light	76-80	Stop, tail, and rear turn signal lamps
24	Parking brake light	77	Rear lamps junction block
25	High beam indicator light	78	Connection for rear body lamps
26	Turn signal indicator light	81	Connector
27	Coolant temperature warning light	83	7 pins socket (tractor)
28	Charging system indicator light	84	Circuit breaker for heater/defroster
29	Low oil pressure warning light	85	Heater/defroster switch
30	Spare warning indicator light	86	Low speed heater/defroster fan relay
31	Stop light switch	87	High speed heater/defroster fan relay
32	Cab upper harness junction block	88	Free fuses for additional customer installation
33	Radio	89	Connection for rear left body lamp
34	Heater control lamps	90	Connection for rear right body lamp
36	High beam relay	91	Engine harness junction block
37	Right stop relay	92	Engine harness junction block
38	Left stop relay	95	Engine harness junction block
39	Low beam relay	93	Windshield washer connection
40	Turn signal and warning flasher	94	Chassis harness junction block
41	Fuses	98	Chassis harness junction block
42	Marker lamps switch	97	Trailer harness junction block
43	Head and tail lamps switch	99	Cab front harness junction box
44	Head lamp switch illumination lamp	101	Gear selector illumination lamp (*)
45	Marker switch illumination lamp	102	Stop light switch for trailer brakes
46	Cigar lighter	105	Resistor for battery/charging system
47	Cigar lighter illumination lamp	106	Safety start relay (*)
48	Windshield wipers and washer switch	107	Circuit breaker for headlights, dimmer switch, tail lights and instrument panel lamps
49	Windshield wipers and washer switch illuminating lamp	108	Automatic transmission fluid temperature warning light switch (*)
50	Key and starter switch	109	Neutral start switch (*)
51	Tachometer	111	Water temperature sending unit
52	Coolant temperature gauge	112	Water temperature warning light switch
53	Oil pressure gauge	113	Engine stop connection
54	Air pressure gauge	114	Minimum hydraulic brake fluid level sending units (on CS200 only)
55	Fuel gauge		
56	Speedometer and odometer		
57-58	Instrument lamps rheostat		

* Vehicles equipped with automatic transmission

ing circuit as one example to assist us in understanding the vehicle wiring diagram. To crank the diesel engine over, we need:

1. Two 12-V batteries connected in parallel (+ to +, − to −) which results in 12 V, with the sum of the amperage of both batteries being added together. The batteries are identified as item 73 in Figs. 5–22 and 5–23.
2. An ignition key switch and starter engagement button, which in this case is the combination key/starter switch identified in Figs. 5–22 and 5–23 as item 50.
3. On vehicles equipped with automatic transmissions such as an Allison, we would employ a safety start relay, shown as item 106, as well as a neutral start switch, shown

as item 109, to ensure that the engine can be started only while the gear selector is in the neutral position.

If you look closely at Fig. 5–23(b), you will see the truck batteries identified as item 73. Power from the positive battery posts (parallel hookup supplying 12 V) flows directly to the starter motor [item 70 in part (a) of the figure] via the heavy insulated battery cable. This battery power from the cable connector is attached to the starter motor solenoid. You will note on closer inspection that there are a number of wires that take power from this positive connection at the solenoid. These are identified as wire numbers 16, 91, 92, 91, 62, 95, and 91, respectively. If you trace these wires they all disappear

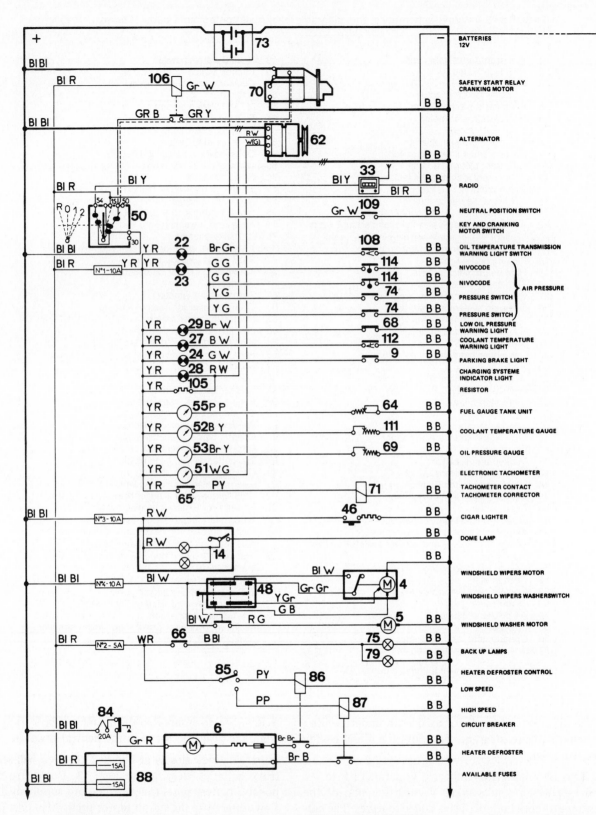

FIGURE 5–22 Wiring schematic for the model CS200/CS250 MidLiner truck. (*Courtesy of Mack Trucks, Inc.*)

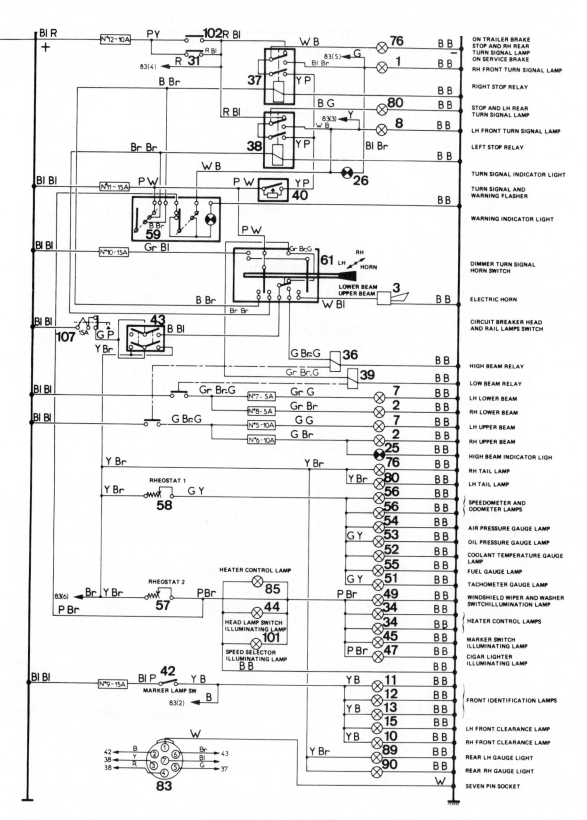

FIGURE 5-22 (Cont'd)

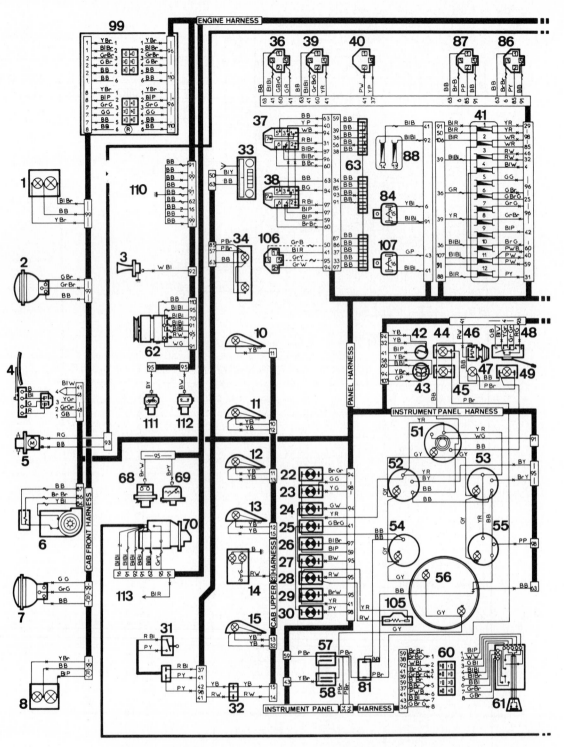

FIGURE 5–23 Wiring diagram for the model CS200/CS250 MidLiner truck. (*Courtesy of Mack Trucks, Inc.*)

into the engine wiring harness, shown as a solid heavy black line. The important wire number here is 95 GR Y (gray with a yellow tracer) at the actual starter solenoid. To activate the solenoid pull-in windings from the ignition key/starter switch, power must flow through this wire. If you identify item 50, the key/starter switch shown in Figs. 5–23(b) and 5–22(a), you will notice that there

is a contact number 30; this contact receives positive battery power through a wire identified as color Bl Bl (Blue/blue). Turning the ignition key to the crank position closes the contacts within the ignition switch to relay power to connection 50 inside the switch; power from connection 50 flows through wire 95 GR Y to the starter solenoid. Energizing the starter solenoid allows the pull-

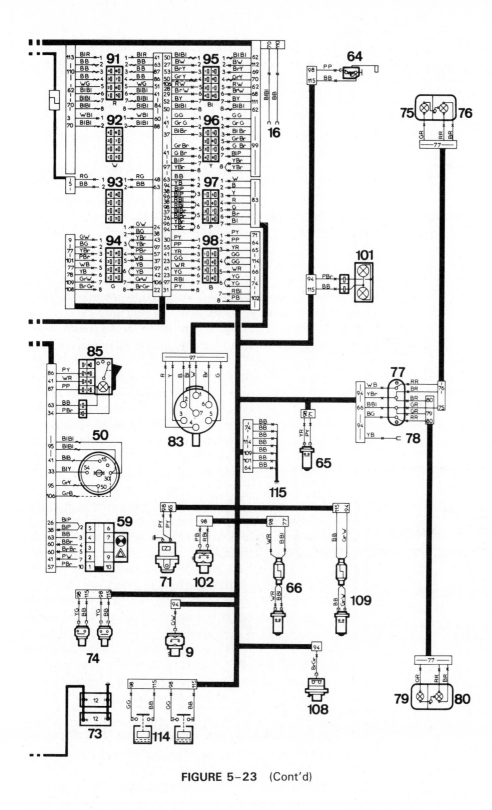

FIGURE 5-23 (Cont'd)

in windings to complete the circuit and the solenoid shift linkage moves at the same time that the starter motor begins to crank. For detailed starter motor operation, refer to Chapter 9.

Once the engine starts, the driver releases the spring-loaded key switch, and power from connection 50 inside the switch no longer flows through wire 95 GR Y. If an automatic transmission is used (items 106 and 109), the safety relay and the neutral start switch ensure that power to the starter solenoid cannot occur unless the gear selector is in the neutral position. These two switches are shown in simplified form in Fig. 5–22(a), where the safety start relay (106) receives power from ignition switch contact 15 through the Bl R (blue wire with a red tracer).

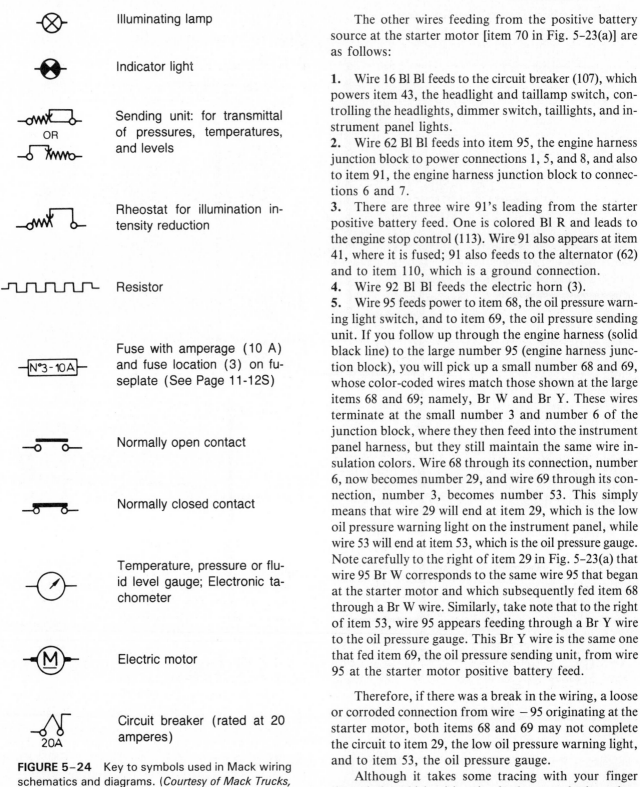

Illuminating lamp

Indicator light

Sending unit: for transmittal of pressures, temperatures, and levels

OR

Rheostat for illumination intensity reduction

Resistor

Fuse with amperage (10 A) and fuse location (3) on fuseplate (See Page 11-12S)

N°3 - 10A

Normally open contact

Normally closed contact

Temperature, pressure or fluid level gauge; Electronic tachometer

Electric motor

Circuit breaker (rated at 20 amperes)

20A

FIGURE 5–24 Key to symbols used in Mack wiring schematics and diagrams. (*Courtesy of Mack Trucks, Inc.*)

For item 106 to complete its circuit to ground, the gear selector that controls the neutral start switch (109) must be in the neutral position. If this is the case, then when the ignition key switch is turned to the crank position, power can flow from connection 50 through wire 106 GR B and wire 95 GR Y to the starter motor solenoid to complete the circuit.

The other wires feeding from the positive battery source at the starter motor [item 70 in Fig. 5–23(a)] are as follows:

1. Wire 16 Bl Bl feeds to the circuit breaker (107), which powers item 43, the headlight and taillamp switch, controlling the headlights, dimmer switch, taillights, and instrument panel lights.

2. Wire 62 Bl Bl feeds into item 95, the engine harness junction block to power connections 1, 5, and 8, and also to item 91, the engine harness junction block to connections 6 and 7.

3. There are three wire 91's leading from the starter positive battery feed. One is colored Bl R and leads to the engine stop control (113). Wire 91 also appears at item 41, where it is fused; 91 also feeds to the alternator (62) and to item 110, which is a ground connection.

4. Wire 92 Bl Bl feeds the electric horn (3).

5. Wire 95 feeds power to item 68, the oil pressure warning light switch, and to item 69, the oil pressure sending unit. If you follow up through the engine harness (solid black line) to the large number 95 (engine harness junction block), you will pick up a small number 68 and 69, whose color-coded wires match those shown at the large items 68 and 69; namely, Br W and Br Y. These wires terminate at the small number 3 and number 6 of the junction block, where they then feed into the instrument panel harness, but they still maintain the same wire insulation colors. Wire 68 through its connection, number 6, now becomes number 29, and wire 69 through its connection, number 3, becomes number 53. This simply means that wire 29 will end at item 29, which is the low oil pressure warning light on the instrument panel, while wire 53 will end at item 53, which is the oil pressure gauge. Note carefully to the right of item 29 in Fig. 5–23(a) that wire 95 Br W corresponds to the same wire 95 that began at the starter motor and which subsequently fed item 68 through a Br W wire. Similarly, take note that to the right of item 53, wire 95 appears feeding through a Br Y wire to the oil pressure gauge. This Br Y wire is the same one that fed item 69, the oil pressure sending unit, from wire 95 at the starter motor positive battery feed.

Therefore, if there was a break in the wiring, a loose or corroded connection from wire −95 originating at the starter motor, both items 68 and 69 may not complete the circuit to item 29, the low oil pressure warning light, and to item 53, the oil pressure gauge.

Although it takes some tracing with your finger through the vehicle wiring circuit, the example above does serve to illustrate and explain just how easy it can be to trace a wire from its source to its ending. By paying attention to the wire color(s), the wire number, and the various wire harness connections, you will be able to determine quickly where a problem in a given electrical wire harness may exist. This type of information can be applied equally to any medium- or heavy-duty truck; therefore, always refer to the vehicle wiring circuit and vehicle wiring diagram when unusual electrical problems seem to exist.

CHASSIS WIRING REPAIR

Wiring connections on trucks and tractor/trailers must be kept clean and tight since corrosion or loose or damaged terminal connections will cause high circuit resistance, dim lamps, and cause failure of many electrical accessories to operate at full capacity. These conditions can also lead to a discharged battery and hard starting, which are discussed in detail in Chapters 3 and 9. Although wiring used on chassis wiring systems is insulated and often protected by being inserted into a loom covering, electrical repairs may be required at some time during the life of the vehicle. It is imperative that a set procedure be followed to ensure that the repaired wiring will not lead to a repeat failure.

We have discussed in this chapter how to check and replace fuses as well as replacement of fusible links in the wiring circuit. Any wire that shows signs of heat discoloration, burning, cracking, or general deterioration must be replaced if the system is to function correctly with a minimum of problems. When splicing into a wire harness, although many mechanic/technicians simply twist the wires together and tape them closed, this procedure is usually only a stop-gap measure and is sure to cause future problems. It is much better, when possible, to use a rosin-flux solder to bond the splice first; never use acid-core solder! You can then use electrical insulating tape or heat-shrink tubing to cover and seal all repaired wiring.

Several other optional methods to repair truck wiring, particularly when single or multiple broken wires are encountered, is also described below. When any wire is found to be severely corroded or damaged, it is best to cut and splice. Although an insulated wire can be bared and stripped with side-cutter or lineman's pliers, or a sharp knife, this job is much easier to do using a pair of wire-stripper pliers, which have been designed specifically to handle all of the various wire gauge sizes encountered on trucks. The two-wire stripping and terminal crimping pliers illustrated in Fig. 5–25 allow wiring to be stripped of the protective insulation quickly and accurately. In addition, a crimping tool is formed on the end of these wire stripper pliers that can be used to crimp the various special wire terminals after a repair has been made.

To use these special wire-stripping pliers, insert the wire into the corresponding correct wire gauge detent of the pliers to the length that you wish to peel off the insulation. Close the pliers over the wire, then manually pull the backside of the wire; alternatively, you can hold onto the length of insulated wire behind the pliers and pull the cutting edge of the pliers away from the wire. Figure 5–26 illustrates one method that can be used when repairing conventional twisted-wire systems, and

J 25563
WIRE CUTTER, STRIPPER & TERMINAL CRIMPER

This heavy-duty service plier is designed to handle wire sizes 10 through 20 gage for wire stripping and crimping insulated terminals. It will also crimp small and large non-insulated terminals.

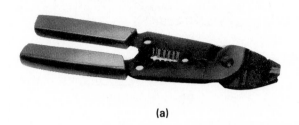

(a)

AUTOMATIC WIRE STRIPPER

J 35615 strips 8 to 22 gauge solid or stranded wire quickly, without crushing, nicking, or damaging the wire. Simply squeeze the handles to strip and remove the insulation.

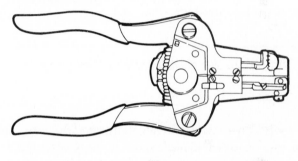

(b)

FIGURE 5–25 (a) Model J25563 wire cutter, stripper, and terminal crimper; (b) model J35615 automatic wire stripper. (*Courtesy of Kent-Moore Heavy Duty Division, SPX Corporation.*)

Fig. 5–27 illustrates a procedure that can be used when repairing twisted/shielded wire systems.

Figure 5–28 illustrates a broken wire that has been cut along with a small length of insulation that has been removed with the pliers. If you have access to heat-shrink tubing, slide a length of tubing over the wire insulation that will be long enough after the repair to cover and seal the bare wiring. The damaged wiring can be soldered as shown in Fig. 5–26 or 5–27, or you can use a splice clip of the correct wire gauge size as shown in Fig. 5–29. Again, although many clips can be crimped closed with the pliers, if you can use rosin-core solder to join the wire and clip together, a much better repair can be achieved. There are many small portable electric soldering irons available that can be used for this purpose. Solder should be applied to the heated wire until it flows freely into the splice clip. Allow several minutes for the solder to set

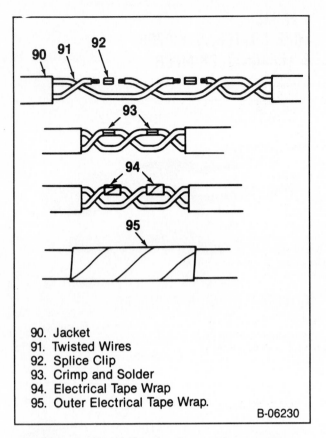

90. Jacket
91. Twisted Wires
92. Splice Clip
93. Crimp and Solder
94. Electrical Tape Wrap
95. Outer Electrical Tape Wrap.

B-06230

FIGURE 5-26 Twisted wire repair procedure. (*Courtesy of GMC Truck Division, General Motors Corporation.*)

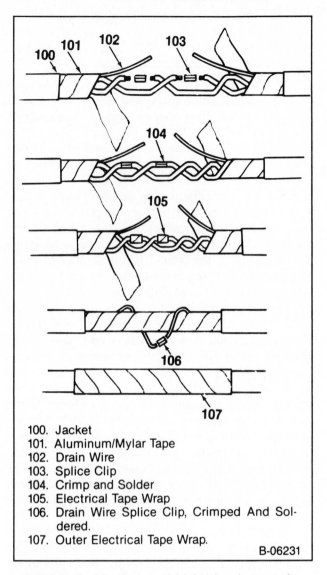

100. Jacket
101. Aluminum/Mylar Tape
102. Drain Wire
103. Splice Clip
104. Crimp and Solder
105. Electrical Tape Wrap
106. Drain Wire Splice Clip, Crimped And Soldered.
107. Outer Electrical Tape Wrap.

B-06231

FIGURE 5-27 Twisted/shielded wire repair. (*Courtesy of GMC Truck Division, General Motors Corporation.*)

(blowing on it can help to cool it faster), then gently pull on the connection to make sure that the repair is secure.

Figure 5–30 illustrates the correct (staggered) versus incorrect repair procedure to employ when faced with repairing a multiple-broken-wire arrangement. Staggering the wire splice will prevent two undesirable conditions:

1. A large bulge in the repaired harness
2. The possibility that the repaired splices will rub or chafe against each other, leading to a future repair being required.

Note that three-way splice connectors are readily available to splice this kind of wire harness damage. Once you have soldered the ends of the wires together in a staggered form, wrap them securely with insulated electrical tape even though you may have used a crimped and insulated splice terminal. Pull the length of heat-shrink tubing over the repaired area and seal it in place following the instructions given in the next section.

WIRE AND CABLE SHRINK TUBING

As a means of sealing out moisture, acting as a strain relief, and minimizing vibration at mechanical connections, a dual-wall polyolefin tubing with a meltable inner wall can be used to encapsulate any electrical connection. In order to apply the shrink tubing, a shrink-tubing heat gun must be used; the heat gun is shown in Fig. 5–31(a), together with examples of how the tubing can be applied to different wiring situations. The shrink tubing is designed so that when it is exposed briefly to temperatures of 135 °C (275 °F), the inner wall will melt and force its way into voids and around the connected parts to hermetically seal the area. The tubing is both chemical and solvent resistant. The shrink tubing can be used in the following basic applications:

1. *Twisted-in-line splice,* shown in Fig. 5–31(b). Insert the tubing over one wire, then twist the stripped wires together and bend the bare wire in-line with the wire as shown. Position the shrink tubing over the wire splice and center the reflector of the minigun on the splice. Switch the gun to the heat position and hold until the tubing shrinks, the wrinkles disappear, and the melted bead appears at each end of the tubing, then switch the blower

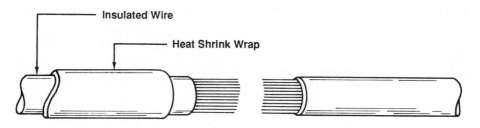

FIGURE 5–28 Heat-shrink tubing applied to an insulated wire. (*Courtesy of Detroit Diesel Corporation.*)

FIGURE 5–29 Placement of a wire splice clip in a damaged wire, covered with heat-shrink tubing. (*Courtesy of Detroit Diesel Corporation.*)

Correct

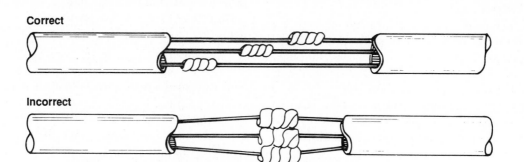

Incorrect

FIGURE 5–30 Correct versus incorrect method for splicing and repairing a multiple bundled wire set. (*Courtesy of Detroit Diesel Corporation.*)

FIGURE 5–31 (a) Shrink-tubing heat gun; (b) twisted in-line splice; (c) twisted pigtail splice; (d) battery cable heat-shrink tubing usage. (*Courtesy of Dominion Automotive Industries, Inc.*)

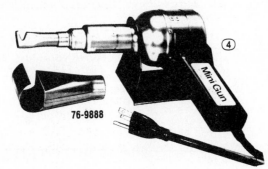

(a)

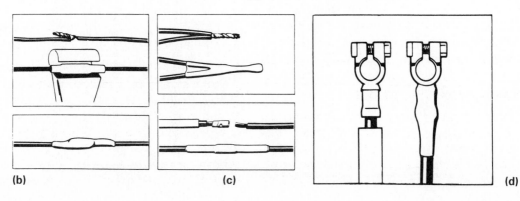

(b) (c) (d)

TABLE 5–4 Shrink tubing size before and after shrinkage

I.D. Before Shrinkage	I.D. After Shrinkage
³/₁₆ in (4.76 mm)	¹/₁₆ in (1.58 mm)
¼ in (6.35 mm)	⁵/₆₄ in (1.98 mm)
⅜ in (9.52 mm)	⁹/₆₄ in (3.57 mm)
½ in (12.7 mm)	¹³/₆₄ in (5.15 mm)
¾ in (19 mm)	⁵/₁₆ in (7.93 mm)
1 in (25.4 mm)	¹³/₃₂ in (10.31 mm)

to the cool position for a short period before removing the gun.

2. *Twisted pigtail splice*, shown in Fig. 5–31(c). Twist the stripped wires together and position the shrink tubing so that it extends ¼ in. beyond the end of the wires. Heat and shrink with the minigun until wrinkles disappear. Squeeze the open end shut with pliers and pinch the crotch with a pair of needle-nose pliers while still hot. Switch the blower to cool for a short period.

3. *Battery cable* usage, shown in Fig. 5–31(d). The battery terminals can be sealed with the use of shrink tubing by sliding the tubing over the cable and applying the heat gun to it.

The shrink tubing is available in a variety of sizes, as shown in Table 5–4.

WIRE SELECTION

Truck manufacturers state in their service manuals and technical literature what size wire gauge should be used for specific circuits on their vehicles. Generally speaking, most heavy-duty truck applications use an 18-gauge wire size unless otherwise specified. When replacing a wire or wires on a heavy-duty truck or trailer, if the manufacturer's specifications are not readily available you have to consider the circuit load and the length of wire that is required. Consider, for example, that a 10% drop in battery voltage caused by wire resistance will result in a 30% loss in candlepower output at a lamp. In other words, voltage drop must be kept at a minimum through proper selection of both wire and cable. To establish the correct wire gauge, you must consider the following three items:

1. Measure the length of the wire/cable required.
2. Add up the total candlepower to be used in the circuit, or find the total ampere load of the circuit. This can be facilitated by referring to Table 5–5 to determine the correct wire gauge size.
3. Determine the proper gauge of wire to minimize voltage drop in the circuit.

TABLE 5–5 Wire cable size chart

Recommended cable sizes for replacement or additional electrical unit installations
Original equipment cable sizes on some vehicles may vary slightly from recommendations due to special electrical system design.
This chart applies to chassis grounded return systems. For two-wire circuits, use total length of both cables, or the double length to most distant electrical unit.

12-VOLT SYSTEM		Total Length of Cable in Circuit from Battery to most Distant Electrical Unit									
AMPERES (APPROX.)	CANDLE POWER	10 Feet	20 Feet	30 Feet	40 Feet	50 Feet	60 Feet	70 Feet	80 Feet	90 Feet	100 Feet
		Gge.	Gge.	Gge.	Gge.	Gge.	Gge.	Gge.	Gge.	Gge.	Gge.
1.0	6	18	18	18	18	18	18	18	18	18	18
1.5	10	18	18	18	18	18	18	18	18	18	18
2	16	18	18	18	18	18	18	18	16	16	16
3	24	18	18	18	18	18	16	16	16	14	14
4	30	18	18	18	16	16	16	14	14	14	12
5	40	18	18	18	16	14	14	14	12	12	12
6	50	18	18	16	16	14	14	12	12	12	12
7	60	18	18	16	16	14	14	12	12	10	10
8	70	18	16	16	14	14	12	12	12	10	10
10	80	18	16	14	12	12	12	10	10	10	10
11	90	18	16	14	12	12	10	10	10	10	8
12	100	18	16	14	12	12	10	10	10	8	8
15	120	18	14	12	12	10	10	10	8	8	8
18	140	16	14	12	10	10	8	8	8	8	8
20	160	16	12	12	10	10	8	8	8	8	6
22	180	16	12	10	10	8	8	8	8	6	6
24	200	16	12	10	10	8	8	8	6	6	6
36	—	14	10	8	8	8	6	6	6	4	4
50	—	12	10	8	6	6	4	4	4	2	2
100	—	10	6	4	4	2	2	1	1	0	0
150	—	8	4	2	2	1	0	0	00	00	00
200	—	6	4	2	1	0	00	000	000	000	0000

(Courtesy of Dominion Automotive Industries, Inc.)

TABLE 5-6

Metric versus AWG
(American Wire
Gauge) wire size
table

Metric Size (mm)²	AWG Size
0.22	24
0.5	20
0.8	18
1.0	16
2.0	14
3.0	12
5.0	10
8.0	8
13.0	6
19.0	4
32.0	2
40.0	1
50.0	0
62.0	00

Many truck manufacturers now use either the AWG (American Wire Gauge) or metric size to identify their wire sizes. A wire size conversion table from metric to AWG is shown in Table 5-6.

All wire sizes have a certain resistance to current flow, with the value of this resistance being relative to the size and type of wire used. However, when current flows through a wire, the smaller the wire, the greater the resistance value will be. As the current (ampere) value increases, the resistance value in ohms will also increase. For example, on a heavy-duty truck, truck/tractor, or semitrailer prior to selecting a new wire size or a replacement wire during a maintenance repair, you have to take into account the following two considerations:

1. The length of the wire in any circuit is the major contributing factor to voltage drop in the system. Figure 5-32(a) illustrates the voltage drop per foot in amperes through AWG sizes 10 through 20.

2. The load in amperes that the wire must carry. Using an undersized wire can increase the temperature of the PVC insulation beyond the safe level of 180°F (82°C). Figure 5-32(b) illustrates the maximum current (ampere) carrying capacity of AWG sizes 10 through 20 for a 12-V system at the anticipated temperatures shown.

Three types of wire insulation are commonly used to protect bare wires:

1. *GPT:* general-purpose thermoplastic insulated

2. *HDT:* heavy-duty thermoplastic insulated

3. *SXL:* standard-duty cross-linked polyethylene insulated

The type of insulation used will cause the wire being used to appear either thicker or thinner than another wire of the same AWG size. An example of the difference in the outside diameter of various wires using the three types of insulation listed above is shown in Fig. 5-32(c).

FIGURE 5-32 (a) Chart showing voltage-current drop per foot of wiring; (b) current-carrying capacity versus cable temperature; (c) wire insulation maximum outside diameter and nominal wall thickness. (*Courtesy of Grote Manufacturing Company, Madison, IN.*)

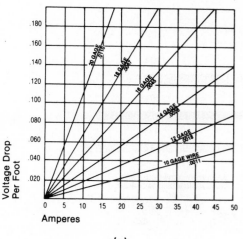

(a)

CABLE SIZE GAGE NO.	MAXIMUM CURRENT CARRYING CAPACITY (AT 12 VOLTS · AT LISTED TEMPERATURE)		
	120°F.	125°F.	150°F.
20 Ga.	15 Amps	13 Amps	9 Amps
18 Ga.	18 Amps	15 Amps	11 Amps
16 Ga.	22 Amps	19 Amps	14 Amps
14 Ga.	27 Amps	23 Amps	17 Amps
12 Ga.	40 Amps	32 Amps	24 Amps
10 Ga.	50 Amps	42 Amps	31 Amps

(b)

Note: *Currents above these listed in the chart may increase the temperatures of the P.V.C. above a safe design level of 180° F.*

GAGE	G.P.T.		H.D.T.		S.X.L.	
	NOM. WALL	MAX. DIA.	NOM. WALL	MAX. DIA.	NOM. WALL	MAX. DIA.
18	.023	.100	.037	.130	.030	.120
16	.023	.115	.040	.145	.032	.135
14	.023	.125	.041	.165	.035	.155
12	.026	.150	.046	.190	.037	.180
10	.031	.185	.046	.215	.041	.210
8	.037	.247	.055	.280	.043	.245

(c)

TYPE	DESCRIPTION
GPT	General Purpose Thermoplastic Insulated
HDT	Heavy Duty Thermoplastic Insulated
SXL	Standard Duty Crosslinked Polyethylene Insulated

EXAMPLE 5-1

Let's assume that you wanted to rewire a 45-ft (13.71-m) semitrailer that was being repaired due to accident damage or updating. What wire gauge size would you require to safely carry the current requirements of the clearance lamps distributed around the trailer, a total of 11 lights, using No. 97 bulbs?

Solution: To determine the wire size, we have to establish the total amperage load for the clearance lamp circuit.

1. In this instance each of the No. 97 bulbs draws 0.69 A; therefore, the total circuit load will be 11 × 0.69 A, or 7.59 A.

2. We now must determine the maximum distance from the power supply to the farthest-mounted clearance light on the trailer. Figure 5–58 illustrates a simplified example of the semitrailer used in this calculation. If we assume that the tractor electrical cord plugs into the front of the trailer 3 ft (91.5 cm) above the floor area. The power must now run the length of the trailer, 45 ft (13.7 m), where it now must branch upward a distance of 8 ft (2.43 m) toward the roofline. At the roofline it splits both left and right to the individual clearance lights; it is 4 ft (1.2 m) to the most distant light. Therefore, the total length of the wiring to the most distant clearance lamp is 3 ft + 45 ft + 8 ft + 4 ft, for a total distance of 60 ft (18.3 m).

3. Determine the wire gauge size from Table 5–5. The closest amperage to 7.59 is 8 A; bisect a line from the 8-A rating underneath the 60-ft distance and we find that we require a 12-gauge wire size for this circuit.

4. To confirm if the 12-gauge wire can safely handle the 8-A load for this circuit at a mean operating temperature of 125 °F (52 °C), refer to Figure 5–32(b) and bisect a line between the 125 °F horizontal line and the 12-gauge wire size in the left-hand column. At the intersecting line we find that at 125 °F the 12-gauge wire is capable of handling a current load of 32 A. Therefore, we have incorporated this circuit into a safety factor of 4:1, which will provide a long, trouble-free life expectancy.

CABLE TIES

When it is necessary to wire a truck or trailer with non-bundled or no-rubber-sheathed preassembled wires, it is customary that these wires be supported at least every 18 in. (45.72 cm). A commonly employed industry practice is to use plastic cable ties, as shown in Fig. 5–33, which illustrates the various lengths and widths commonly available from an automotive/truck electrical supplier.

FIGURE 5–33 Wire cable plastic ties. (*Courtesy of Dominion Automotive Industries, Inc.*)

PART NO.	WIDTH	BUNDLE DIAMETER	LENGTH	MINIMUM LOOP TENSILE STRENGTH
76-2825	.100	0-$^{15}/_{16}$"	4$^{1}/_{16}$"	18 lb.
76-2827	.145	0-1$^1/_4$"	5$^3/_8$"	30 lb.
76-2830	.187	0-1$^3/_4$"	7"	50 lb.
76-2832	.145	0-3"	10$^{15}/_{16}$"	30 lb.
76-2833	.300	0-3$^1/_2$"	13"	120 lb.
76-2818	.187	0-4"	14$^1/_{16}$"	50 lb.
76-2819	.187	0-4"	14$^{17}/_{32}$"	50 lb.
76-2820	.300	0-3$^1/_2$"	13$^5/_8$"	120 lb.
76-2821	.145	0-3"	11$^9/_{16}$"	30 lb.
76-2840	.187	0-1$^3/_4$"	7$^7/_{16}$"	50 lb.
76-2822	.145	0-1$^1/_4$"	5$^3/_4$"	30 lb.
76-2823	.100	0-$^{15}/_{16}$"	4$^3/_8$"	18 lb.

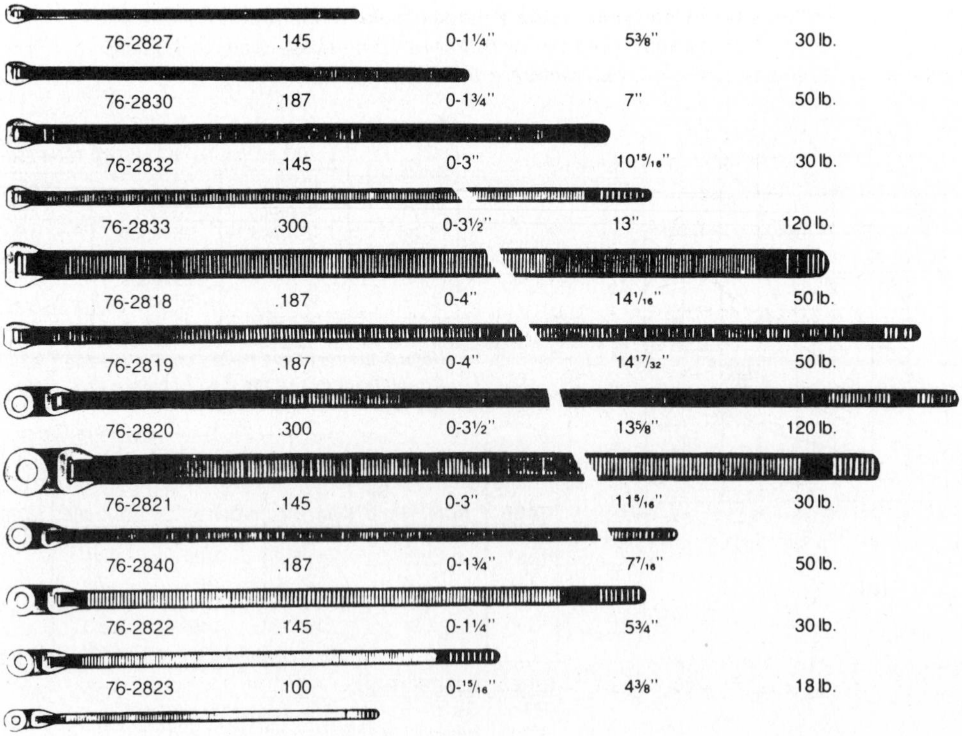

① **Single-unit Mounting head**
Mounting clamp is integral part of tie head for quick attachment to panel or chassis with screw, rivet or bolt.

② **Self-locking Head**
Easy application by tool or by hand. Will not loosen when pulled tight.

③ **Releasable Locating Tip**
Double-bend tip locates around wires. Guides operator's hand for easy 90° insertion, even in confined areas. Second bend prevents snagging. Tip can be inserted in head and later released. Makes for easier positioning of ties on bundle.

④ **76-2824 Tension-control Application Tool**
Available on special order only. Easy, three step installation: 1 – Place tie around wire bundle. Double-bend tip locates toward locking head. Second bend prevents snagging. 2 – Pull tie through head to tighten. Serrations on tip are easy to grip. 3 – Lock into place with tension-control tool. Cuts flush.

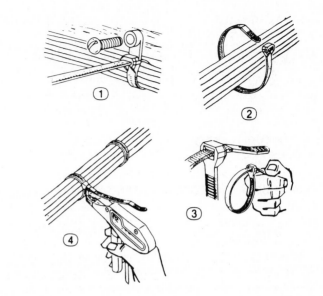

FIGURE 5–34 Four styles of plastic cable ties. (*Courtesy of Dominion Automotive Industries, Inc.*)

Types of Cable Ties

Although Fig. 5–33 shows the widths and lengths of cable ties commonly used, there are four general styles, illustrated in Fig. 5–34.

1. Type 1 is known as a single-unit mounting head style, since its mounting clamp is an integral part of the tie head for quick attachment to the panel or chassis with a screw, rivet, or bolt.

2. Type 2 is a self-locking head for easy application by hand or with a tool. Once tightened, this style will not loosen.

3. Type 3 is a releasable locating tip style; the double bend tip locates around the wires for ease of insertion. The second bend prevents snagging and the tip can be inserted in the head and later released, facilitating easier positioning of the ties on bundled wire groups.

4. Type 4 shows a tension-control application tool, Dominion Auto part 76-2824; this involves a three-step installation procedure:

    a. Place the tie around the wire bundle with the double-bend tip located toward the locking head.

    b. Pull the tie through the head to tighten; the serrations on the tip are easy to grip.

    c. Lock the tie into place with the tension-control tool and cut it flush.

TYPES OF CONNECTORS

There are a variety of shapes and styles of wire terminal connectors used in medium- and heavy-duty truck applications. Due to the severe operating conditions to which trucks are often subjected, it is very important that all wiring harness connectors be capable of withstanding the rigors of the weather and the elements. When service/repair of chassis or cab wiring is required, ensure that you use a good-quality terminal connector. There are a wide variety of connectors for different wire gauge sizes that can be preinsulated with either nylon or PVC. Typical examples of connectors that you can use in the repair of the wiring system are shown in Fig. 5–35.

In some cases a crimped connector will be suitable; however, in some cases, a soldered terminal will be better. The crimped connector offers a simpler and easier way to perform a repair and is usually used in a well-protected environment such as an in-cab repair. Connectors that are exposed to the elements are normally soldered to ensure long, trouble-free service. Connectors that are located inside the cab can be of the snap-together type, such as those shown in Fig. 5–36, which are commonly referred to as being *"in-line"* connectors.

In addition to the in-line snap connectors shown in Fig. 5–36, a *blade-type* or a *twin-lock wiring connector terminal* is used. The blade-type connector illustrated in Figs. 5–37 and 5–36 can be serviced as follows:

1. To remove the terminals from the blade-type connector, refer to Fig. 5–37(a).

2. To reset the blade-type terminal lock tang, refer to Fig. 5–37(b). If a twin-lock terminal connector is used, Kent-Moore J22727 terminal remover is required, as shown in Fig. 5–38, to push the wire terminal (80) from the wiring harness connector.

Wire harness connectors that are subjected to moisture or to the elements or that are used with gasoline or diesel engine electronic ECMs require special terminals

SPADE TERMINALS
HEAVY DUTY .050" STOCK

76-1301–(50 pak)
STUD SIZE 8-10 (M4, M4.2)
16-14 GA.

NYLON INSULATED TERMINALS

RING TERMINAL
HEAVY DUTY–.050" STOCK

76-1518–(50 pak)
STUD SIZE 12-¼" (M5, M6, M6.3)
16-14 GA.

SLIDE CONNECTORS

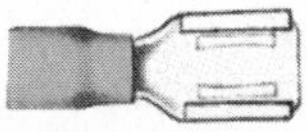

76-1444–(100 pak)
.25 (6.3mm) FEMALE
QUICK DISCONNECT
16-14 GA.

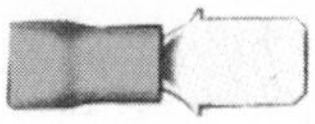

76-1445–(100 pak)
.25 (6.3mm) MALE
QUICK DISCONNECT
16-14 GA.

CLOSED END CONNECTORS

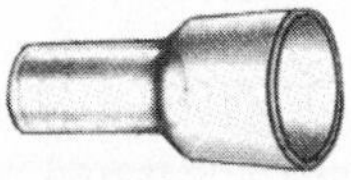

76-1291–(100 pak)
CLOSED END CONNECTOR.
NYLON INSULATION
22-14 GA.

HOOK TERMINALS

76-1200–(100 pak)
STUD SIZE 4-6 (M3.5)
16-14 GA.

BULLET CONNECTORS

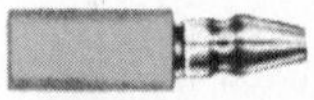

76-1251–(100 pak)
68-1251–(20 pak)
.156 (4.0mm) MALE SNAP PLUG
16-14 GA.

76-1261–(25 pak)
68-1261–(10 pak)
.156 (4.0mm) FEMALE SNAP PLUG
RECEPTACLE (JOINS TWO
76-1251 PLUGS)

68-1288–(5 pak)
T-TAP CONNECTOR
(JOINS ONE 76-1251
BULLET CONNECTOR)
16-14 GA.

INSTANT CONNECTORS

76-1371–(25 pak)
68-1371–(9 pak)
18-14 GA. QUICK SPLICE

3- AND 4-WAY SPLICES

76-1281–(25 pak)
68-1281–(9 pak)
3-WAY SPLICE
16-14 GA.

76-1286–(25 pak)
3-WAY SPLICE
12-10 GA.

BUTT CONNECTORS

76-1231–(100 pak)
68-1231–(23 pak)
22-18 GA.

HEAT SHRINKABLE BUTT CONNECTORS

Provides an easy and highly
effective means of insulating and
protecting terminal connections
and splices against moisture, dirt
and corrosion

76-1244–(25 pak)
18-22 GA

FIGURE 5–35 Typical preinsulated wire terminals and connectors. (*Courtesy of Dominion Automotive Industries, Inc.*)

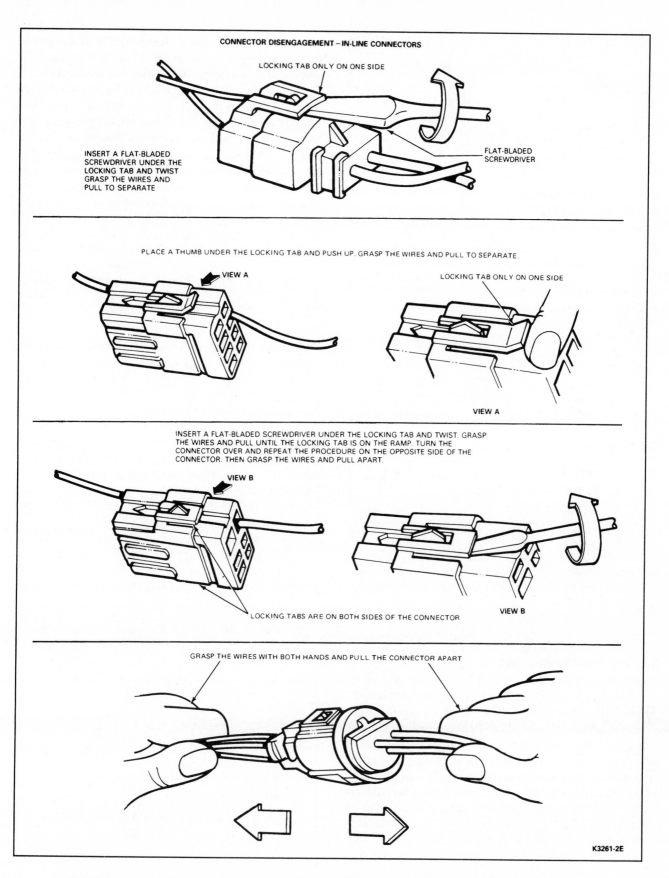

FIGURE 5–36 Disengagement procedure of in-line connectors (*Reprinted with Ford Motor Company's permission.*)

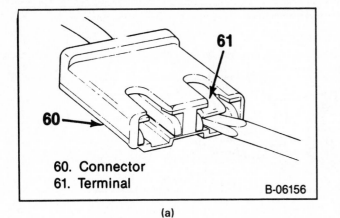

60. Connector
61. Terminal

B-06156

(a)

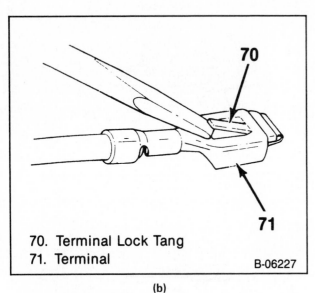

70. Terminal Lock Tang
71. Terminal

B-06227

(b)

FIGURE 5–37 (a) Removing terminals from a blade-type connector; (b) resetting blade type terminal lock tang. (*Courtesy of GMC Truck Division, General Motors Corporation.*)

known as *Weather-Pack, Metri-Pack,* or *Micro-Pack* designs. The Weather-Pack terminals illustrated on the left-hand side of Fig. 5–39 are also referred to as group II connectors. The Metri-Pack terminals shown on the right-hand side of Fig. 5–39 are known as group I connectors, and the smaller Micro-Pack terminals are known as group III connectors. The Micro-Pack connectors (group III) are used on the 7- and 8-pin dash connectors found on such truck electronic systems as the DDC (Detroit Diesel Corporation) DDEC systems described in Chapter 11. The group III connectors are also used on the transmission 6-pin connector of trucks equipped with an Allison automatic transmission that is fitted with ATEC (Allison Transmission Electronic Controls). The group III connectors do not require seals, whereas the group I and II types do. Special tools are required to disassemble/assemble all of these special connectors. Figure 5–40 illustrates these tools, which are all supplied by Kent-Moore.

When servicing any of these terminals, the special tools must be used to avoid terminal or connector damage. For example, on Weather-Pack connectors, if pin and sleeve terminal removal is attempted without using tool J28742-A shown in Fig. 5–40(a), deformation or bending will probably occur, making it almost impossible to straighten the bent and damaged terminal. This terminal is designed as shown in Fig. 5–39, so that the sealing rings are held securely in place by the use of a hinge-type flap to ensure a secondary locking feature for the terminals. The Metri-Pack connectors are designed to use either a pull-to-seat or push-to-seat type of terminal. When disassembling this type of terminal, always use special tool J35689-A shown in Fig. 5–40(b); otherwise, the same type of damage as that mentioned for the Weather-Pack design will occur. Similarly, use the special tool shown in Fig. 5–40(c) when working with Micro-Pack terminal connectors. Various special crimping tools are also required to service and repair Packard, Weather-Pack, and Metri-Pack connectors. These tools are illustrated in Fig. 5–41(a), (b), and (c), respectively.

Due to the low current and voltage levels that pass through all of the Weather Pack, Metri-Pack, and Micro-Pack terminals, all new connections should be soldered in place using rosin-core solder. Caution should be exercised when attempting to probe terminals during troubleshooting since it is possible to short between opposite terminals that are mounted so closely together in the connector housing. To avoid this possibility, you should always use special jumper wires that are available from companies such as Kent-Moore.

Figure 5–42 illustrates a jumper wire kit that can be used with both Metri-Pack and Weather-Pack terminals. *Never* probe through any Weather-Pack or Metri-Pack terminal since seal damage will occur and moisture or dirt

FIGURE 5–38 Twin-lock connector terminal (*Courtesy of GMC Truck Division of General Motors Corporation.*)

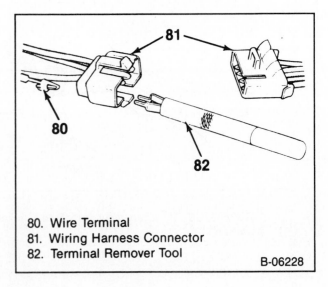

80. Wire Terminal
81. Wiring Harness Connector
82. Terminal Remover Tool

B-06228

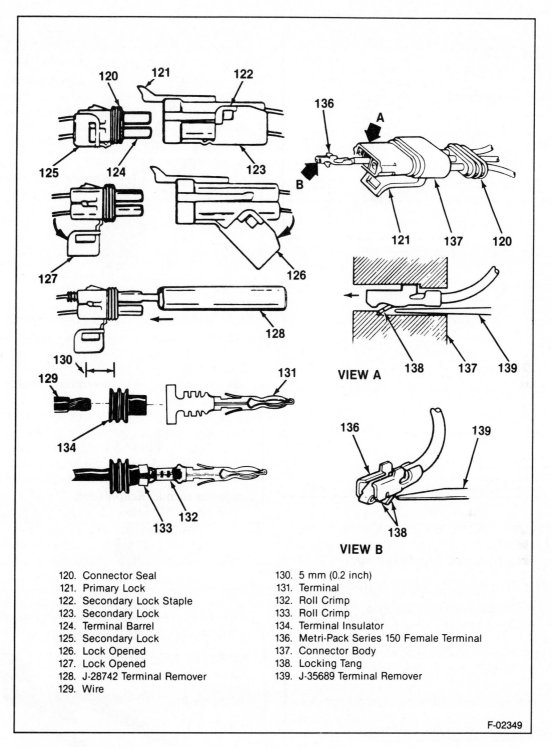

120. Connector Seal
121. Primary Lock
122. Secondary Lock Staple
123. Secondary Lock
124. Terminal Barrel
125. Secondary Lock
126. Lock Opened
127. Lock Opened
128. J-28742 Terminal Remover
129. Wire
130. 5 mm (0.2 inch)
131. Terminal
132. Roll Crimp
133. Roll Crimp
134. Terminal Insulator
136. Metri-Pack Series 150 Female Terminal
137. Connector Body
138. Locking Tang
139. J-35689 Terminal Remover

F-02349

FIGURE 5–39 Weather-Pack and Metri-Pack connectors. (*Courtesy of GMC Truck Division, General Motors Corporation.*)

can enter the connector, causing not only corrosion but also short circuiting between terminals. Because of this unique construction, it is usually a physical impossibility to locate an open circuit, due to possible oxidation or terminal misalignment; this condition can cause an intermittent problem condition that may result in the CEL or ECM troublecode not registering it in computer memory, such as in a DDEC or Caterpillar PEEC system, which are both described in Chapter 11. Simply wiggling a connector on a sensor or in the wiring harness may correct the open-circuit condition.

Another type of heavy-duty truck connector that you are liable to come across, particularly on some models of Mack trucks, is the Deutsch cylindrical multiple-pin

J 28742-A WEATHER PACK II TERMINAL REMOVER

Application: Weather Pack II

This tool is designed to allow easy removal of the Weather Pack II terminals. Included is a protective cap for the precision thin wall tubular end of the tool.

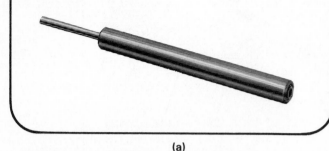

(a)

J 35689-A TERMINAL REMOVER

Application: Metri-Pack

Removal of the extremely small metri-pack locking tang requires this needle like tool with handy holder.

(b)

J 33095

TERMINAL REMOVER MICRO-PACK, COM-PACK III and ECM EDGE BOARD CONNECTORS Application: Micro-Pack

General Motors Vehicles with Electronic engine controls incorporate Micro-Pak, Com-Pak III and ECM Edge Board Connectors on the wiring harnesses. J 33095 is designed to allow easy removal of the terminals when servicing these connectors.

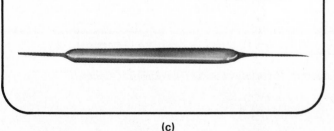

(c)

FIGURE 5–40 (a) Model J28742-A Weather-Pack II terminal remover; (b) model J35689-A terminal remover; (c) model J33095 terminal remover Micro-Pack, Com-Pack III and ECM edge-board connectors. (*Courtesy of Kent-Moore Heavy Duty Division, SPX Corporation.*)

J 35603 TERMINAL CRIMPING TOOL

Application: Packard

This quality crimping tool is designed to crimp many Packard terminals and the new wire splices which are being supplied with some General Motors service connector kits. Its compound leverage design provides a smooth crimping action with a minimum amount of effort.

(a)

J 35606 WEATHER-PACK TERMINAL CRIMPER

Application: Weather-Pack

J 35606 simultneously crimps the wire to terminal and terminal to Weather-Pack Boot; very easy to use. Wire, terminal, and boot are held in alignment by the guide block ensuring accurate and weather-tight crimps. Tool incorporates a self-releasing ratchet for consistent application pressure. Maintains integrity of the Weather-Pack design and function.

(b)

J 35123 TERMINAL CRIMPER

Application: Metri-Pack

Automatically releases to prevent damage after terminal is properly crimped.

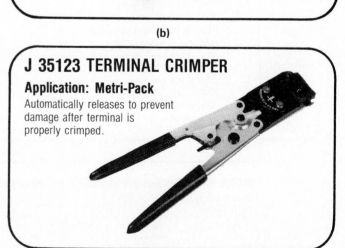

(c)

FIGURE 5–41 (a) Model J35603 terminal crimping tool; (b) model J35606 weather-pack terminal crimper; (c) model J35123 terminal crimper. (*Courtesy of Kent-Moore Heavy Duty Division, SPX Corporation.*)

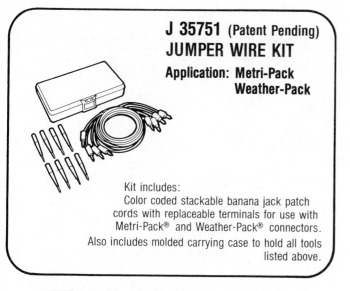

FIGURE 5–42 Model J35751 jumper wire kit.
(*Courtesy of Kent-Moore Heavy Duty Division, SPX Corporation.*)

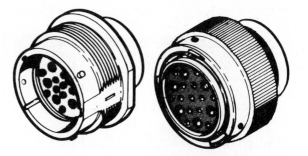

FIGURE 5–44 Deutsch 50 series connector plug and receptacle HD56-24-19SN (plug) and HD54-24-19PN (receptacle). (*Courtesy of Mack Trucks, Inc.*

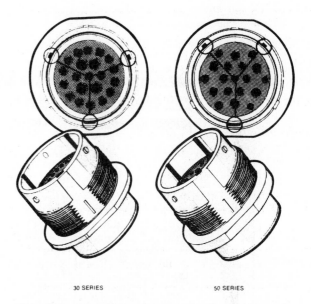

30 SERIES   50 SERIES

FIGURE 5–45 Deutsch connector plug mating slot positions. (*Courtesy of Mack Trucks, Inc.*)

FIGURE 5–46 Identification of Deutsch series 30 and 50 pins. (*Courtesy of Mack Trucks, Inc.*)

electrical connector shown in Fig. 5–43. This connector can be found on Mack models RWL, RWS, WL, WS, MC-MR, and MH. This type of connector offers total sealed protection from moisture or corrosion and is available in what is known as either a 30 or 50 series connector. The difference is that the 30 series connector is used on the RWL, RWS, WL, and WS models as an in-line distribution model for all light connections, while the 50 series unit is used on the MC-MR as a connector plug and receptacle for the main cab-to-engine harness connection. Figure 5–43 illustrates an assembled view of the Deutsch connector and how to mate and unmate the connector plug and receptacle. The two-piece Deutsch connector is shown in Fig. 5–44, and Fig. 5–45 illustrates the mating slot positions for both the 30 and 50 series units. In addition, the 50 series connectors use a split pin/solid socket, while the 30 series uses a solid pin/split socket, as shown in Fig. 5–46.

FIGURE 5–43 Mating and unmating Deutsch plug and receptacle. (*Courtesy of Mack Trucks, Inc.*)

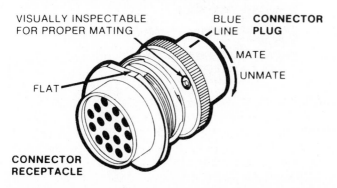

VISUALLY INSPECTABLE
FOR PROPER MATING

BLUE **CONNECTOR**
LINE **PLUG**

MATE

UNMATE

FLAT

CONNECTOR
RECEPTACLE

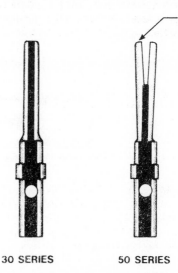

SPLIT
PIN

30 SERIES   50 SERIES

Contact Insertion

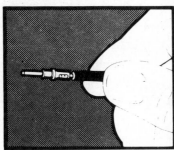 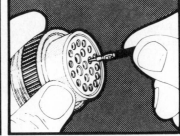 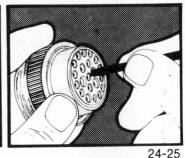

24-25

Grasp contact approximately 1 inch (25.4mm) behind the contact crimp barrel.

Hold connector with rear grommet facing you.

Push contact straight into connector grommet until a positive stop is felt. A slight tug will confirm that it is properly locked in place.

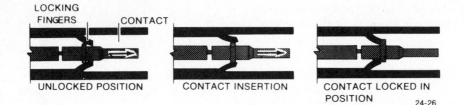

24-26

Contact Removal

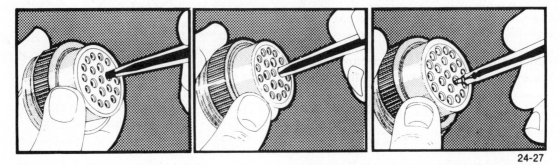

24-27

With rear insert toward you, snap appropriate size extractor tool over the wire of contact to be removed.

Slide tool along wire into the insert cavity until it engages contact and resistance is felt.
NOTE: Do not twist or insert tool at an angle.

Pull contact-wire assembly out of connector.

 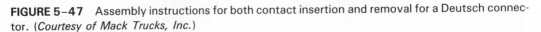

FIGURE 5–47 Assembly instructions for both contact insertion and removal for a Deutsch connector. (*Courtesy of Mack Trucks, Inc.*)

To insert a contact or remove it from a Deutsch connector, refer to Fig. 5–47. A special service kit is available from Mack dealers which contains all of the necessary series 30 and 50 pins and sockets (quote part number 5583-HDT-4802 when ordering). Exercise caution when unscrewing or tightening a Deutsch connector; only hand pressure should be used.

FAULT TRACING

When a problem occurs in any electrical circuit, the cause can usually be traced to short circuits, opens, or grounds due to poor conditions that have become corroded. In Chapter 4 we discussed electrical system troubleshooting in detail and described special tools and instruments required to trace a problem to its source. Basically, you will require a digital multimeter capable of checking for resistance in ohms, voltage, and current in amperes. Additional tools include a nonpowered test lamp, a 12-V powered test lamp, and a jumper wire. These items are all illustrated and described in Chapter 4.

Many problems that exist can often be traced and repaired quickly in simple circuits such as the lighting system where a burned out bulb, blown system fuse, or visible corrosion at the lamp socket can be seen. If a problem is hard to trace, refer back to the vehicle wiring diagram and trace the wire circuit shown on the diagram to determine where it receives its power from and where it completes or grounds the circuit.

CAUTION: If a fuse or circuit breaker blows, do not assume that this is normal. Often when a fuse blows or a circuit breaker opens, it is due to a short circuit caused by a positive cable/wire shorting to ground.

Briefly, if a fuse blows or a circuit breaker opens, it usually indicates that a hot wire (positive wire/cable) is shorting somewhere to ground. Refer first to the vehicle wiring diagram to determine what electrical components are protected on that circuit. Turn off the electrical accessory or accessories that are on the fused circuit. Remove the fuse and use either a nonpowered test lamp of the proper voltage for the vehicle system (6, 12, or 24 V), or an audible test buzzer that can be inserted into the circuit as shown in Fig. 5–48 on the battery positive feed side. Switch on the electrical accessories in that circuit one at a time; if the test light illuminates brightly in the ON position, you can be reasonably sure that the problem lies in the wiring to that particular accessory. Closely inspect the vehicle or system wiring diagram for that circuit to determine what connectors (wire color and number) feed that electrical accessory or block of accessories.

You can then disconnect the wiring connection closest to the fuse; if the test light still glows brightly, the fault lies between the fuse and the wiring connection. If the test light does not illuminate, the fault lies farther along

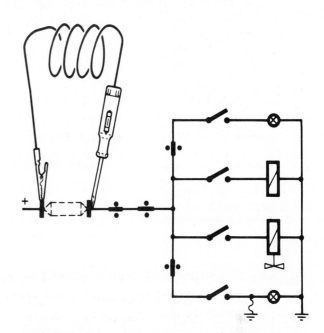

FIGURE 5–48 Using a test light to determine where a ''short'' may exist in a circuit. (*Courtesy of DAF Trucks, Eindhoven, The Netherlands.*)

the wiring. Reconnect the wiring at the previously disconnected point, then disconnect the next connection in the system. If the test light still illuminates, the problem exists between these two wiring connections. Should the test light go out or fail to illuminate, this confirms that the problem lies farther along the wiring. Therefore, by a sequential process of elimination, the problem can be effectively traced.

An open circuit can be suspected when an electrical accessory or piece of equipment fails to function. The problem might be in the accessory itself or in the wiring. Using a nonpowered test lamp or buzzer such as that illustrated in Fig. 5–49, switch on the accessory in question and check for the presence of voltage. Remember that a test light will not tell you how much voltage there is; therefore, if you suspect a voltage loss, use a voltmeter to confirm just what voltage there is in the circuit. If the test lamp fails to illuminate, check the condition of the

FIGURE 5–49 Using a test light to trace an ''open'' in a circuit. (*Courtesy of DAF Trucks, Eindhoven, The Netherlands.*)

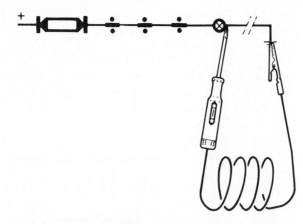

FIGURE 5-50 Using a test light to check a circuit for a poor ground condition. (*Courtesy of DAF Trucks, Eindhoven, The Netherlands.*)

tion exists due to corrosion, a loose connection, or a broken ground wire. To check this condition, refer to Fig. 5–50 and use a self-powered test lamp placed as illustrated in the circuit. Make sure that the electrical switch to the circuit is turned off when using a self-powered test lamp! If the test lamp illuminates brightly, this would confirm that a good ground connection exists. If the lamp fails to illuminate, flickers, or glows dimly, a poor ground condition exists. If both the positive and the negative connections are confirmed to be in good shape, the electrical accessory is at fault. Replace it and recheck for correct system operation.

When problems are traced to or are suspected to exist in the vehicle or individual ground connection, you will invariably discover that the cause can be attributed to terminal corrosion, damaged or broken terminals, severe wire corrosion, or poor contact to the grounding surface. Always use a digital multimeter for the ground check, due to the very low voltage values that may exist. Figure 3–47 illustrates one example of how you could check and confirm a good or bad ground connection. Place the voltmeter between the negative battery post and the suspected poor ground point in question, then switch on the electrical accessory that has the ground problem. If the ground connection is good, no voltage should be measured on the voltmeter since we are connecting negative to negative.

fuse or circuit breaker. If, however, voltage is recorded by a voltmeter or by illumination of the test light, check the wiring between the fuse and the electrical accessory. This may involve a number of test points, depending on how the circuit is wired. If no voltage exists at any of the test connections in the circuit, you have found the problem area. If voltage is recorded at the electrical accessory, the problem may be that a poor ground condi-

FIGURE 5-51 Heavy-duty truck 32-way bulkhead electrical connector. (*Courtesy of GMC Truck Division, General Motors Corporation.*)

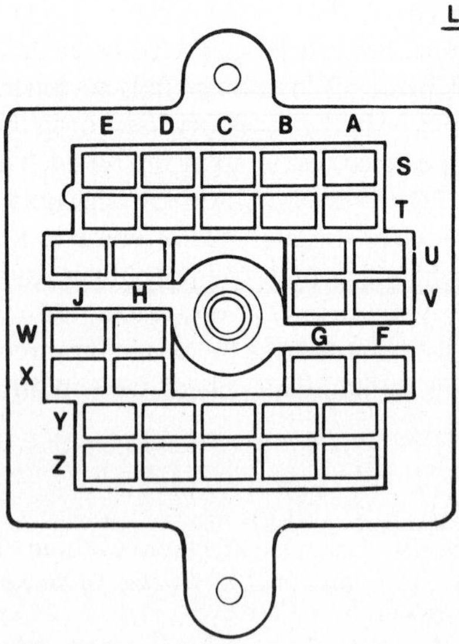

32 WAY BULKHEAD CONNECTOR TABULATION

Circuit Terminal Location	Color Code	Wire Size (mm²)	Wire Gage	Circuit
AS	Pink	1.0	16	Engine Shutdown Solenoid
DS	Black	2.0	14	ICC Marker Lamp Body Builders Reference
ES	Light Green	1.0	16	Back-Up Lamp Switch
AT	Yellow	1.0	16	Low Coolant Probe
ET	Dark Green/White Hash	1.0	16	Engine Oil Temperature Sender
FU	Yellow	1.0	16	Spare 4
GU	Dark Green	1.0	16	Spare 3
HU	Black/White Stripe	2.0	14	Ammeter to Generator
JU	Black	2.0	14	Ammeter to Battery
FV	White	1.0	16	Spare 2
GV	Dark Blue	1.0	16	Spare 1
FX	Light Green	2.0	14	Right Headlamp — High Beam
JX	Dark Green	2.0	14	Horn
BY	Purple	1.0	16	Start Switch — Auxiliary
CY	Tan	2.0	14	Right Headlamp — Low Beam
EY	Dark Green White Stripe	1.0	16	Engine Brake Unit
CZ	Dark Green	1.0	16	Water Temperature Sender
EX	Pink/Black Stripe	1.0	16	Backup Lamp Switch

F-04372

ELECTRICAL BULKHEAD CONNECTORS

The style of instrument display panel will vary considerably between makes and models of heavy-duty trucks. The conventional cab layout will differ from that found on a COE (cab over engine) model, and the actual gauges and instruments used and their location will differ. One example of a COE cab instrumentation system console is shown in Fig. 7–15 as a general guide to where you might find some of these instruments and gauges. The electrical power feed to the various instruments/gauges is generally taken from the cab or engine harness, which we discussed earlier. The necessary connections between the engine compartment and the instrument panel wiring connector are usually made through what is referred to as a *bulkhead connector*. An example of a bulkhead connector is shown in Fig. 5–51, which illustrates the circuit terminal location, the wire color code, wire size (in mm), AWG number, and the electrical circuit served.

The wires that feed off the 32-way bulkhead connector shown in Fig. 5–51 feed such items as the electrical equipment panel, two examples of which are illustrated in Figs. 5–52 and 5–53. The vehicle cab harness usually

FIGURE 5–52 Electrical equipment panel showing various circuit breakers and controls. (*Courtesy of GMC Truck Division, General Motors Corporation.*)

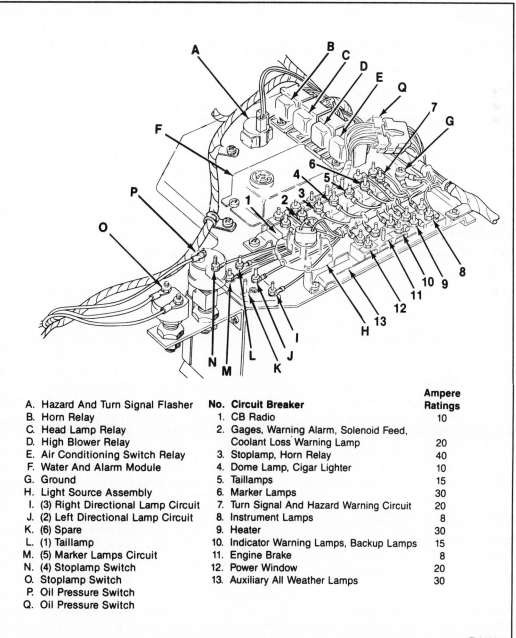

		Ampere Ratings
A. Hazard And Turn Signal Flasher	**No. Circuit Breaker**	
B. Horn Relay	1. CB Radio	10
C. Head Lamp Relay	2. Gages, Warning Alarm, Solenoid Feed, Coolant Loss Warning Lamp	20
D. High Blower Relay	3. Stoplamp, Horn Relay	40
E. Air Conditioning Switch Relay	4. Dome Lamp, Cigar Lighter	10
F. Water And Alarm Module	5. Taillamps	15
G. Ground	6. Marker Lamps	30
H. Light Source Assembly	7. Turn Signal And Hazard Warning Circuit	20
I. (3) Right Directional Lamp Circuit	8. Instrument Lamps	8
J. (2) Left Directional Lamp Circuit	9. Heater	30
K. (6) Spare	10. Indicator Warning Lamps, Backup Lamps	15
L. (1) Taillamp	11. Engine Brake	8
M. (5) Marker Lamps Circuit	12. Power Window	20
N. (4) Stoplamp Switch	13. Auxiliary All Weather Lamps	30
O. Stoplamp Switch		
P. Oil Pressure Switch		
Q. Oil Pressure Switch		

F-01284

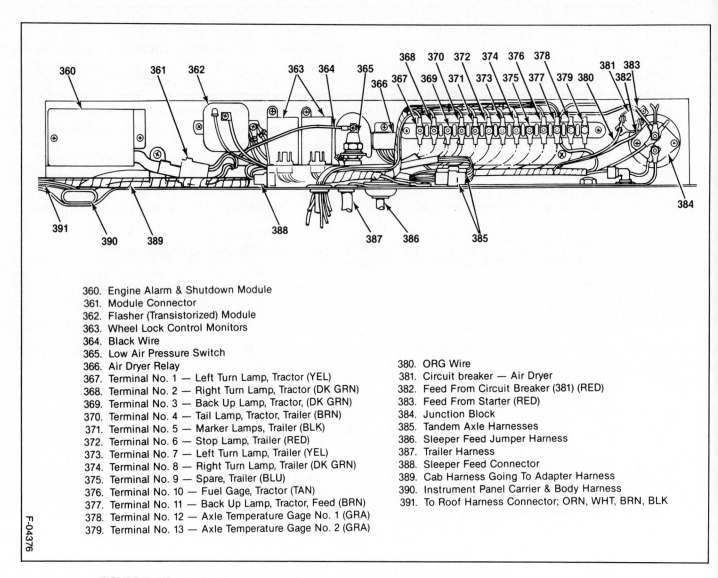

360. Engine Alarm & Shutdown Module
361. Module Connector
362. Flasher (Transistorized) Module
363. Wheel Lock Control Monitors
364. Black Wire
365. Low Air Pressure Switch
366. Air Dryer Relay
367. Terminal No. 1 — Left Turn Lamp, Tractor (YEL)
368. Terminal No. 2 — Right Turn Lamp, Tractor (DK GRN)
369. Terminal No. 3 — Back Up Lamp, Tractor, (DK GRN)
370. Terminal No. 4 — Tail Lamp, Tractor, Trailer (BRN)
371. Terminal No. 5 — Marker Lamps, Trailer (BLK)
372. Terminal No. 6 — Stop Lamp, Trailer (RED)
373. Terminal No. 7 — Left Turn Lamp, Trailer (YEL)
374. Terminal No. 8 — Right Turn Lamp, Trailer (DK GRN)
375. Terminal No. 9 — Spare, Trailer (BLU)
376. Terminal No. 10 — Fuel Gage, Tractor (TAN)
377. Terminal No. 11 — Back Up Lamp, Tractor, Feed (BRN)
378. Terminal No. 12 — Axle Temperature Gage No. 1 (GRA)
379. Terminal No. 13 — Axle Temperature Gage No. 2 (GRA)

380. ORG Wire
381. Circuit breaker — Air Dryer
382. Feed From Circuit Breaker (381) (RED)
383. Feed From Starter (RED)
384. Junction Block
385. Tandem Axle Harnesses
386. Sleeper Feed Jumper Harness
387. Trailer Harness
388. Sleeper Feed Connector
389. Cab Harness Going To Adapter Harness
390. Instrument Panel Carrier & Body Harness
391. To Roof Harness Connector; ORN, WHT, BRN, BLK

F-04376

FIGURE 5-53 Back view of a typical heavy-duty truck electrical equipment panel. (*Courtesy of GMC Truck Division, General Motors Corporation.*)

starts at the dash panel junction blocks, as illustrated in Fig. 5-54, which shows the circuitry and wire colors for each post. The cab harness then goes to the instrument carrier, where it terminates at the various switches, gauges, and circuit breakers. Then from the instrument carrier, another inside cab harness feeds to the steering column, the electrical equipment panel, ground, and roof harness, as shown in Fig. 5-55, and also in Figure 5-1.

SEMITRAILER LIGHTING SYSTEMS

Heavy-duty truck/tractors are connected to a semitrailer by the fifth wheel on the tractor frame. The trailer has three connections to it from the truck/tractor:

1. The air brake service glad hand
2. The air brake emergency glad hand
3. The electrical wiring cable harness to supply all the power to operate all of the trailer's lighting requirements

The actual location of the clearance, marker, and taillights on any trailer depends not only on the actual type of trailer body shape being used, but all lighting must conform to FHWA (Federal Highway Administration) and FHTSA (Federal Highway Traffic Safety Administration), local and state regulations. Consequently all trailer manufacturers must comply with these lighting standards. Refer to the TMC/ATA Recommended Practice RP-702 for dimensional placement of all trailer lighting.

Trailer and dolly lighting and wiring specifications in North America generally use a seven-conductor truck/trailer jumper cable and connector. Recommendations for the wiring circuits for these heavy-duty trailer units conform to TMC/ATA (The Maintenance Council, American Trucking Associations) RP-107 (Recommended Practice 107), SAE (Society of Automotive Engineers) wiring gauge standard J1067, and SAE standard J560 for

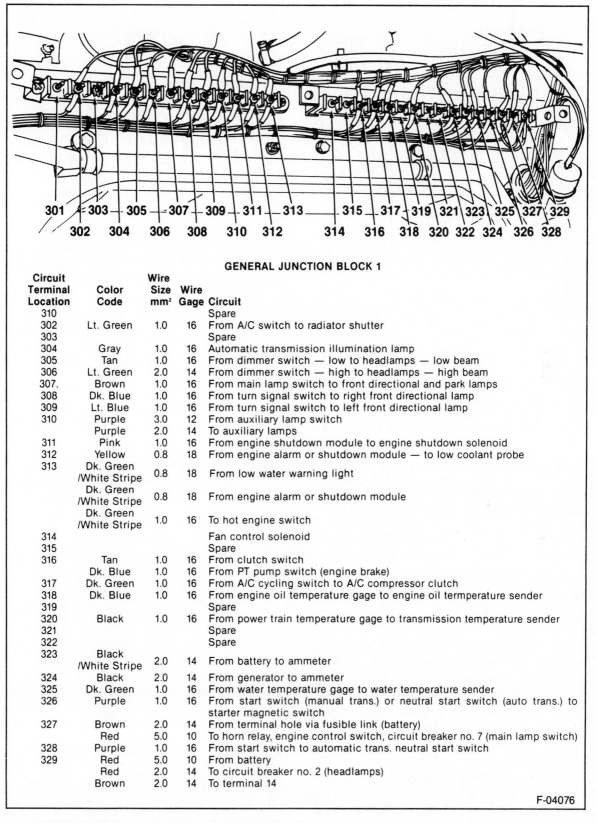

GENERAL JUNCTION BLOCK 1

Circuit Terminal Location	Color Code	Wire Size mm²	Wire Gage	Circuit
310				Spare
302	Lt. Green	1.0	16	From A/C switch to radiator shutter
303				Spare
304	Gray	1.0	16	Automatic transmission illumination lamp
305	Tan	1.0	16	From dimmer switch — low to headlamps — low beam
306	Lt. Green	2.0	14	From dimmer switch — high to headlamps — high beam
307.	Brown	1.0	16	From main lamp switch to front directional and park lamps
308	Dk. Blue	1.0	16	From turn signal switch to right front directional lamp
309	Lt. Blue	1.0	16	From turn signal switch to left front directional lamp
310	Purple	3.0	12	From auxiliary lamp switch
	Purple	2.0	14	To auxiliary lamps
311	Pink	1.0	16	From engine shutdown module to engine shutdown solenoid
312	Yellow	0.8	18	From engine alarm or shutdown module — to low coolant probe
313	Dk. Green /White Stripe	0.8	18	From low water warning light
	Dk. Green /White Stripe	0.8	18	From engine alarm or shutdown module
	Dk. Green /White Stripe	1.0	16	To hot engine switch
314				Fan control solenoid
315				Spare
316	Tan	1.0	16	From clutch switch
	Dk. Blue	1.0	16	From PT pump switch (engine brake)
317	Dk. Green	1.0	16	From A/C cycling switch to A/C compressor clutch
318	Dk. Blue	1.0	16	From engine oil temperature gage to engine oil termperature sender
319				Spare
320	Black	1.0	16	From power train temperature gage to transmission temperature sender
321				Spare
322				Spare
323	Black /White Stripe	2.0	14	From battery to ammeter
324	Black	2.0	14	From generator to ammeter
325	Dk. Green	1.0	16	From water temperature gage to water temperature sender
326	Purple	1.0	16	From start switch (manual trans.) or neutral start switch (auto trans.) to starter magnetic switch
327	Brown	2.0	14	From terminal hole via fusible link (battery)
	Red	5.0	10	To horn relay, engine control switch, circuit breaker no. 7 (main lamp switch)
328	Purple	1.0	16	From start switch to automatic trans. neutral start switch
329	Red	5.0	10	From battery
	Red	2.0	14	To circuit breaker no. 2 (headlamps)
	Brown	2.0	14	To terminal 14

F-04076

FIGURE 5–54 Junction block connections showing wire color, wire gauge size, and circuit terminal location. (*Courtesy of GMC Truck Division, General Motors Corporation.*)

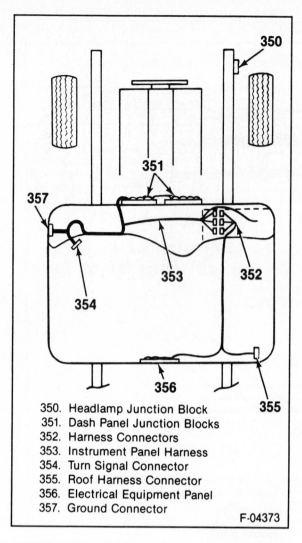

350. Headlamp Junction Block
351. Dash Panel Junction Blocks
352. Harness Connectors
353. Instrument Panel Harness
354. Turn Signal Connector
355. Roof Harness Connector
356. Electrical Equipment Panel
357. Ground Connector

F-04373

FIGURE 5–55 Overhead view of the cab harness routing for a conventional model heavy-duty truck. (*Courtesy of GMC Truck Division, General Motors Corporation.*)

connector receptacles and plugs as well as the specifications agreed to by the TTMA (Truck Trailer Manufacturers Association).

Figure 5–56 illustrates a seven-conductor semitrailer electrical connector and cable plug for interchangeability with electrical connectors of different manufacture. The conductors should be cabled together with a maximum lay of 6 in. (152.4 mm) and the wire configuration shown in Fig. 5–57(a). The conductor wiring should also conform to the specifications shown in the table of Fig. 5–57(b). The force required to connect or disconnect a plug and receptacle when hooking up or unhooking a tractor to a trailer should not exceed 50 lb, and the cable and trailer plug should be capable of withstanding a straight pull of 150 lb.

Selection of the correct wire cable size is a very important consideration that is sometimes overlooked, particularly when a trailer is being rebuilt or repaired. Consider also that a 10% drop in battery power from the truck/tractor to the trailer due to wire resistance can

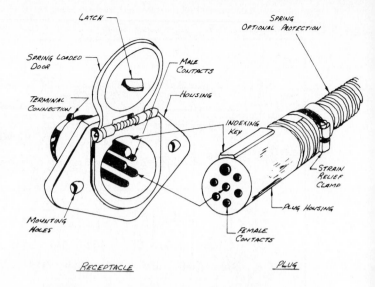

RECEPTACLE   PLUG

FIGURE 5–56 Seven-conductor electrical connector and cable plug. (*Reprinted with permission, © 1989, Society of Automotive Engineers, Inc. Warrendale, PA.*)

result in a 30% loss in illumination brilliance at the trailer lamps. Therefore, the voltage drop from the tractor to the trailer and through the length of the trailer wire can be kept to a minimum by selection of the proper wire gauge size.

Figure 5–58 illustrates a typical trailer wiring guide along with the ATA, SAE, and TTMA wire colors for

FIGURE 5–57 (a) Conductor cable arrangement; (b) conductor dimensions. (*Reprinted with permission, © 1989, Society of Automotive Engineers, Inc. Warrendale, PA.*)

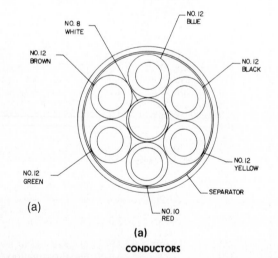

(a)

CONDUCTORS

SAE Wire[a] Size	No. of Wires	Nominal Size of Strand		Lay in.	Conductor Area Cir Mils	Max Dia of Stranded Conductor, in.
		AWG	in.			
12	65	30	.010 (.254 mm)	1.5 (38.1 mm)	6487	.100 (2.54 mm)
10	105	30	.010 (.254 mm)	1.5 (38.1 mm)	10479	.125 (3.18 mm)
8	168 or	30	.010 (.254 mm)	2.0 (50.8 mm)	16414	.175 (4.45 mm)
	427	34	.0063 (.160 mm)	2.0 (50.8 mm)		

[a]SAE wire size numbers indicate that the circular mil area of the stranded conductor approximates the circular mil area of American Wire Gage for equivalent gage size.

(b)

Trailer Wiring Guide

Truck-Lite

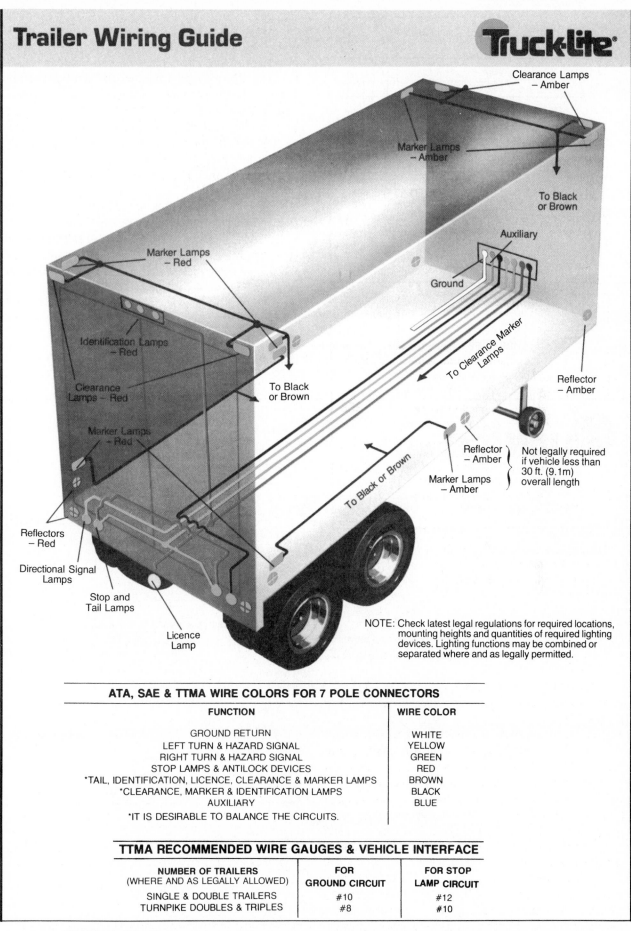

Clearance Lamps – Amber

Marker Lamps – Amber

To Black or Brown

Auxiliary

Ground

Marker Lamps – Red

To Clearance Marker Lamps

Reflector – Amber

Identification Lamps – Red

Clearance Lamps – Red

To Black or Brown

Marker Lamps – Red

Reflector – Amber

Not legally required if vehicle less than 30 ft. (9.1m) overall length

Marker Lamps – Amber

To Black or Brown

Reflectors – Red

Directional Signal Lamps

Stop and Tail Lamps

Licence Lamp

NOTE: Check latest legal regulations for required locations, mounting heights and quantities of required lighting devices. Lighting functions may be combined or separated where and as legally permitted.

ATA, SAE & TTMA WIRE COLORS FOR 7 POLE CONNECTORS

FUNCTION	WIRE COLOR
GROUND RETURN	WHITE
LEFT TURN & HAZARD SIGNAL	YELLOW
RIGHT TURN & HAZARD SIGNAL	GREEN
STOP LAMPS & ANTILOCK DEVICES	RED
*TAIL, IDENTIFICATION, LICENCE, CLEARANCE & MARKER LAMPS	BROWN
*CLEARANCE, MARKER & IDENTIFICATION LAMPS	BLACK
AUXILIARY	BLUE

*IT IS DESIRABLE TO BALANCE THE CIRCUITS.

TTMA RECOMMENDED WIRE GAUGES & VEHICLE INTERFACE

NUMBER OF TRAILERS (WHERE AND AS LEGALLY ALLOWED)	FOR GROUND CIRCUIT	FOR STOP LAMP CIRCUIT
SINGLE & DOUBLE TRAILERS	#10	#12
TURNPIKE DOUBLES & TRIPLES	#8	#10

FIGURE 5–58   Trailer wiring guide example. (*Courtesy of Dominion Automotive Industries, Inc.*)

TABLE 5-7

Conductor Number	Wire Color	Wire Abbrev.	Lamp and Signal Circuit
1	White	W	Ground return to towing vehicle
2	Black	B	Clearance, sidemarker, and identification
3	Yellow	Y	Left-turn signal and hazard signal
4	Red	R	Stoplamps and antilock brake devices
5	Green	G	Right-turn signal and hazard signal
6	Brown	BN/Br	Tail, clearance, sidemarker, license plate
7	Blue	BL	Auxiliary lighting

a seven-pole connector as well as the TTMA recommended wire gauge size. The wire colors listed in Fig. 5–58 are generally assigned a number for identification purposes on the trailer connector/plug receptacle. These wire numbers are as shown in Table 5–7.

The number 1 white circuit in the cable cluster shall be an AWG size 8; the number 4 red wire shall be an AWG size 10; all other circuits shall be at least AWG size 12 according to SAE J1067 recommendations.

For additional information dealing with trailer wiring, refer to TMC/ATA standards in their RP-501 (Recommended Practice) for a seven-conductor trailer arrangement. Problems with trailer wiring fall into the same three categories that we discussed in Chapter 4. These three main categories, which are shown and discussed in detail in Figures 4–5, 4–6, and 4–7, are:

FIGURE 5–59 Exploded view of a semitrailer wire harness junction box and components manufactured from high-impact, chemically resistant plastic. (*Courtesy of Dominion Automotive Industries, Inc.*)

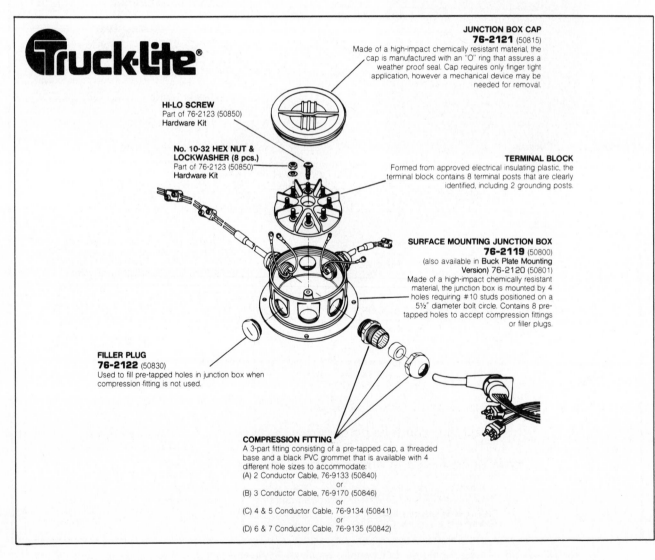

**JUNCTION BOX CAP
76-2121** (50815)
Made of a high-impact chemically resistant material, the cap is manufactured with an "O" ring that assures a weather proof seal. Cap requires only finger tight application, however a mechanical device may be needed for removal.

HI-LO SCREW
Part of 76-2123 (50850)
Hardware Kit

No. 10-32 HEX NUT & LOCKWASHER (8 pcs.)
Part of 76-2123 (50850)
Hardware Kit

TERMINAL BLOCK
Formed from approved electrical insulating plastic, the terminal block contains 8 terminal posts that are clearly identified, including 2 grounding posts.

**SURFACE MOUNTING JUNCTION BOX
76-2119** (50800)
(also available in **Buck Plate Mounting Version**) 76-2120 (50801)
Made of a high-impact chemically resistant material, the junction box is mounted by 4 holes requiring #10 studs positioned on a 5½" diameter bolt circle. Contains 8 pre-tapped holes to accept compression fittings or filler plugs.

**FILLER PLUG
76-2122** (50830)
Used to fill pre-tapped holes in junction box when compression fitting is not used.

COMPRESSION FITTING
A 3-part fitting consisting of a pre-tapped cap, a threaded base and a black PVC grommet that is available with 4 different hole sizes to accommodate:
(A) 2 Conductor Cable, 76-9133 (50840)
or
(B) 3 Conductor Cable, 76-9170 (50846)
or
(C) 4 & 5 Conductor Cable, 76-9134 (50841)
or
(D) 6 & 7 Conductor Cable, 76-9135 (50842)

1. An open circuit
2. A short circuit
3. A grounded circuit

Use the various special tools and test instruments shown in Chapter 4 to troubleshoot and pinpoint a trailer electrical problem systematically and effectively.

Trailer Lighting

The transfer of electrical power from a truck/tractor to a semitrailer is achieved by securely coupling the seven-pin male connector on the truck to the female receptacle on the trailer. This union is illustrated in Fig. 5–56. To minimize possible lighting problems to the trailer, the electrical system should be a durable weathertight plug seal at the front of the main harness to the tractor. The power distribution to the various trailer light assemblies can be through a junction box arrangement such as that shown in Fig. 5–59. This particular junction box is part of the Truck-Lite easy seal harness system, where all components are manufactured from a chemically resistant high-impact plastic. All of the wiring outlets are PVC with extreme temperature characteristics, and the wire terminals are tin-coated brass for excellent conductivity. The mounting plate is steel with a zinc dichromate finish to resist corrosion. This plate can be used as a chassis ground, if required. The plug-in wire harnesses have molded PVC module plugs which create a seal to the cable jacket and are compatible with the module outlets. The junction box can be matched to a four- or eight-outlet distribution module. The four-outlet unit is commonly used on 28-ft (8.5 m) van-type trailers, straight trucks with bodies, and for trailers that require a center module to feed side-turn indicators or auxiliary electrical functions. The eight-outlet unit is used for most trailer applications and can feed power to wire harnesses for stop/taillamps, license plate lamps, marker/clearance lamps, and double trailer hookups.

FIGURE 5–60 (a) Ultra-Blue Seal rear sill master union, Ultra-pin receptacle, and central plug distributor; (b) How all of the above components would appear in the trailer. (*Courtesy of Courtesy of Grote Manufacturing Company, Madison, IN.*)

ULTRA-PIN RECEPTACLE
Final link in UBS sealed trailer electrical system. A durable weathertight plug-seal at front of main harness to tractor. Solid brass pins, top slotted for easy engagement. No-rust die-cast zinc housing. Floating pins for total plug compatibility.

REAR SILL MASTER UNION
Angled to avoid strain on seal, curb-side and road-side. Provides sealed plug-in connections to upper and lower clearance and-marker lamps, identification lamps, license lamps, and stop, turn, tail combination lamps. Fully versatile, adapting to all wiring configurations. May also provide other improved conspicuity devices. Multi-rings in all four female receptacles assure durable weathertight connections. Four dummy plugs provided each side to seal any receptacle not used.

CENTRAL PLUG DISTRIBUTOR REPLACES THE OLD JUNCTION BOX.
No unjacketed lead-ins. No confusing connections. 7-pin traditional SAE-TTMA configuration and color code. Simply snaps together for foolproof, polarity-protected mating. Unique snap-clamp firmly locks connector. Grease fitting permits pressure grease injection if desired. Rear sill terminal available with "Y" cable for double trailer connections.

NO "CAN-OF-WORMS"
Compare with the usual junction box. Time-consuming, error-prone, with extreme corrosion potential.

An alternative system now available to trailer manufacturers that replaces the early metal type of junction box system is illustrated in Fig. 5–60. This central plug distributor not only replaces the metal junction box concept but takes up far less space. At the rear sill of the semitrailer, weather-sealed connections molded of unique Grote Manufacturing Company high-tech Blue-Seal compound ensure that all wiring from trailer nose box to the lamps has the wiring jackets molded into the plugs. The rear sill master connection shown in Fig. 5–60 is angled to avoid strain on the seal as well as to the curbside and roadside connections. An example of where the central plug distributor and rear sill connections would be located on the trailer can be seen in Fig. 5–61. Existing trailers that still use the metal junction box method can be updated to the newer PVC easy-seal system shown in Figure 5–59 or alternatively, to the Blue-Seal weathertight system by purchasing repair kits or components, as required. The physical shape of the various lamps used on semitrailers will vary with the actual legal location of the light being used. Typical heavy-duty trailer light wiring circuits and their connections would normally appear as shown in Figs. 5–62 and 5–63.

A unique clearance/marker lamp model is also available whereby the service technician does not have to cut and splice any wiring in order to hook up a new lamp system. One example of a no-splice lamp system is illustrated in Fig. 5–64, which explains just how the no-splice system operates.

For specific information dealing with the design, construction, and types of heavy-duty truck and trailer lights and signals, as well as lighted and heated mirrors and other electrical accessories, refer to the latest catalog of any major truck lighting manufacturer. Two manufacturers who are major OEM (original equipment manufacturer) suppliers to many major truck and trailer marques are the Grote Manufacturing Company, located in Madison, Indiana, and Toronto, Ontario, Canada, Dominion Automotive Industries, Inc., Mississauga, Ontario, Canada, and Florence, Kentucky.

TRUCK/TRAILER LIGHTING DIAGNOSTIC TEST EQUIPMENT

All truck fleets are inflicted with burned-out light bulbs or corrosion and wiring problems during the life of any vehicle, truck, tractor, or trailer. Considerable time can be spent by a fleet mechanic/technician in pinpointing the cause of a problem when one or more lights fail to operate. In some cases it requires two technicians working together to trace out a particularly unusual wiring/lighting system problem. Often a technician must trace down an electrical system problem on a trailer when it is not connected to a truck/tractor. Power must then be supplied to the trailer seven-pin connector from a fabricated plug-in wire harness that draws its power from a battery mounted in a small wheeled dolly. Numerous

fleet maintenance shops have designed and implemented their own trailer light tester for this purpose.

Several major companies have released up-to-date electronic testing devices that allow one fleet mechanic/technician alone to perform a truck/tractor/trailer or trailer system lighting test. Figure 5–65 illustrates one such model manufactured by Lite-Check. The model 700B is designed to allow one mechanic to inspect, maintain, repair, and troubleshoot truck/trailer and tractor lighting circuits. By using this tester, one mechanic can perform the necessary repairs in as little as one-third of the time that it might require two mechanics working together to complete. The tester allows the fleet mechanic to check and diagnose fault types within 8 to 10 seconds prior to having to walk around the vehicle. Built-in to the 700B tester is a Lokator audio signal, which permits the mechanic to track down and correct electrical faults within minutes. The tester is designed to prevent possible electrical system overload since the test voltage is reduced to 5 V while the current flow is reduced to milliamperes.

In addition to the model 700B tester, the model 900R tester, shown in Fig. 5–66, allows a fleet mechanic to check and adjust the air brake system as well as checking the lighting circuits on trailers, truck tractors, and double or triple tractor/trailer combinations within 5 to 7 minutes, including the setup time. Both the service and emergency air brake system can be checked, adjusted, and

FIGURE 5–61 Ultra-Blue-Seal semitrailer main wiring harness and rear sill connector locations. (*Courtesy of Grote Manufacturing Company.*)

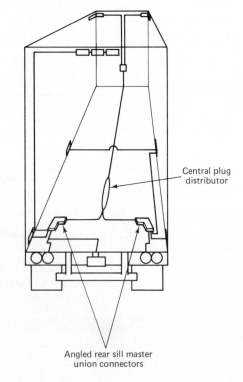

Central plug distributor

Angled rear sill master union connectors

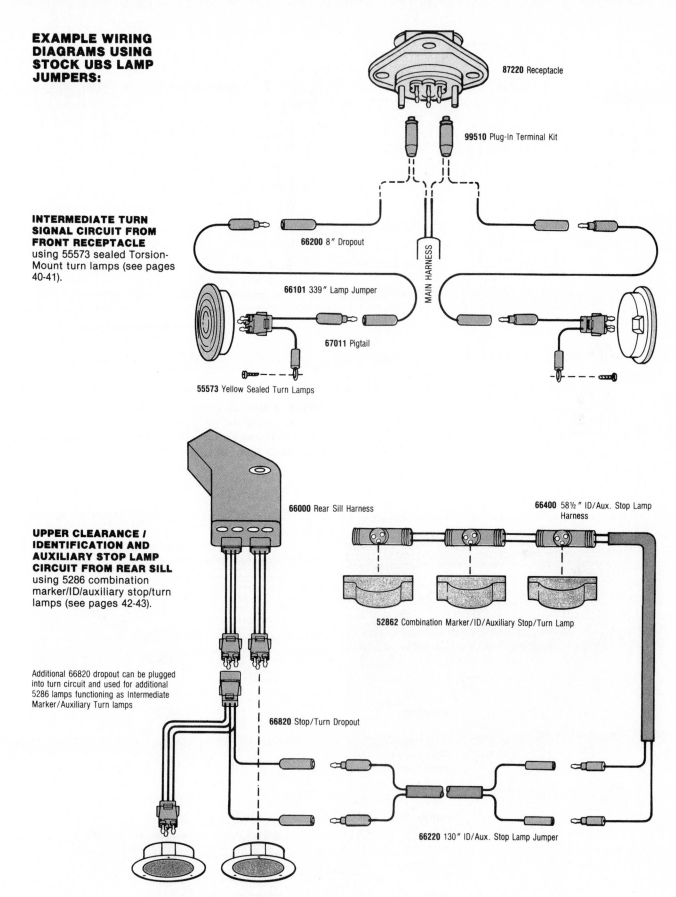

EXAMPLE WIRING DIAGRAMS USING STOCK UBS LAMP JUMPERS:

87220 Receptacle

99510 Plug-In Terminal Kit

INTERMEDIATE TURN SIGNAL CIRCUIT FROM FRONT RECEPTACLE
using 55573 sealed Torsion-Mount turn lamps (see pages 40-41).

66200 8″ Dropout

MAIN HARNESS

66101 339″ Lamp Jumper

67011 Pigtail

55573 Yellow Sealed Turn Lamps

66000 Rear Sill Harness

66400 58½″ ID/Aux. Stop Lamp Harness

UPPER CLEARANCE / IDENTIFICATION AND AUXILIARY STOP LAMP CIRCUIT FROM REAR SILL
using 5286 combination marker/ID/auxiliary stop/turn lamps (see pages 42-43).

52862 Combination Marker/ID/Auxiliary Stop/Turn Lamp

Additional 66820 dropout can be plugged into turn circuit and used for additional 5286 lamps functioning as Intermediate Marker/Auxiliary Turn lamps

66820 Stop/Turn Dropout

66220 130″ ID/Aux. Stop Lamp Jumper

52732 Re-sealable Torsion-Mount Stop/Tail/Turn Lamps

FIGURE 5–62 Intermediate turn signal circuit from front receptacle and upper clearance/identification and auxiliary stop lamp circuit from rear sill. (*Courtesy of Grote Manufacturing Company, Madison, IN.*)

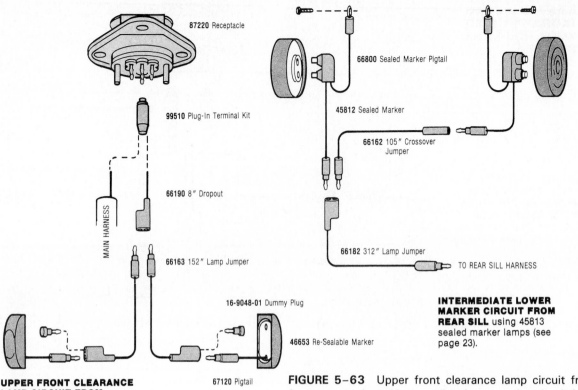

87220 Receptacle

66800 Sealed Marker Pigtail

45812 Sealed Marker

66162 105" Crossover Jumper

99510 Plug-In Terminal Kit

66190 8" Dropout

MAIN HARNESS

66163 152" Lamp Jumper

66182 312" Lamp Jumper

TO REAR SILL HARNESS

16-9048-01 Dummy Plug

46653 Re-Sealable Marker

67120 Pigtail

INTERMEDIATE LOWER MARKER CIRCUIT FROM REAR SILL using 45813 sealed marker lamps (see page 23).

UPPER FRONT CLEARANCE LAMP CIRCUIT FROM FRONT RECEPTACLE using 46653 re-sealable Turtleback marker lamps (see page 21).

FIGURE 5–63 Upper front clearance lamp circuit from front receptacle and intermediate lower marker circuit from the rear sill as well as standard wiring kits for vans trailers. (*Courtesy of Grote Manufacturing Company.*)

FIGURE 5–64 No-splice two-bulb Duramold clearance/marker lamp construction. (*Courtesy of Grote Manufacturing Company, Madison, IN.*)

2-BULB DURAMOLD NO-SPLICE

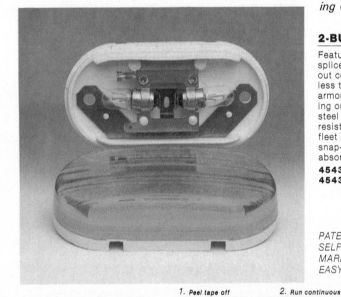

Features Grote exclusive no-splice wiring system to lock out corrosion. Lowest profile, less than one inch. Internal armor shields against shorting on impact. Two stainless steel grounds, corrosion-resistant contacts, lubricated fleet service bulbs. Standard snap-on lens. Oval shock-absorbing DURAMOLD body.

45432 Red
45433 Yellow

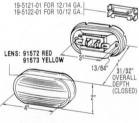

19-5121-01 FOR 12/14 GA.
19-5122-01 FOR 10/12 GA.

LENS: 91572 RED
91573 YELLOW

13/64"

31/32" OVERALL DEPTH (CLOSED)

2"

4"

HEAVY DUTY	
Finish:	White
Material:	DURAMOLD
FMVSS SAE Code:	PC
Voltage/Amps:	12V.—.66 AMP

PATENTED NO-SPLICE SELF-SEAL DURAMOLD MARKER LAMPS INSTALL EASY AS 1, 2, 3.

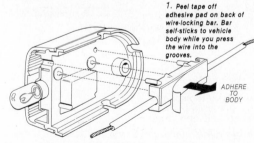

1. Peel tape off adhesive pad on back of wire-locking bar. Bar self-sticks to vehicle body while you press the wire into the grooves.

ADHERE TO BODY

2. Run continuous wiring in and out, any way. Note diagram showing versatility of groove pattern to fit any wiring system. Lamp comes with two wire-locking bars: one for wire .120"-.165" O.D., the second for .165"-.210" O.D.

3. Now you simply press the lamp over the bar and tighten down the two screws that mount the lamp to the vehicle body. As you do, the twin spikes cleanly pierce the insulation, making positive contact into the wire. Heavy resin coating on spikes automatically seals puncture in insulation.

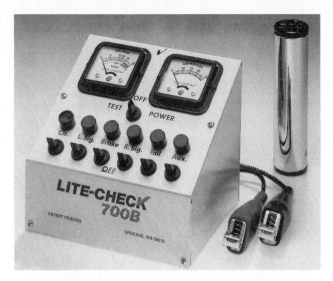

FIGURE 5-65 Model 700B Lite-Check Diagnostic Tester. (*Courtesy of Lite-Check, Spokane, WA.*)

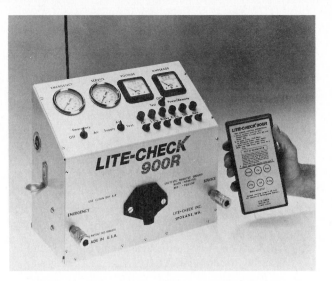

FIGURE 5-66 Model 900R Lite-Check Diagnostic Tester. (*Courtesy of Lite-Check, Spokane, WA.*)

thoroughly inspected to ensure proper operation. A hand-held remote control feature assists the mechanic in locating hard-to-find air leaks, as well as allowing him or her to make brake adjustments more efficiently in less time than would otherwise be required.

The 900R tester shown in Fig. 5–66 features a hand-held remote control unit to permit the mechanic/technician to control the operation of the brakes and lighting circuits from any point around the vehicle. The Lokator audible alarm also enables one mechanic to track down wiring problems in a short time. Various accessory items are available with the 700B and 900R testers:

1. A 330A pedal actuator, employed with the 900R model, can be used inside the vehicle cab since it attaches to the steering wheel and depresses the brake pedal on command from the hand-held remote control unit.
2. A 210H hose and cable kit, contains air hose, electrical cable, and connections required to hook up the 900R.
3. A 202P battery charger, fits on the 200K Lite Cart for ease of maneuverability. The charger allows quick battery recharge without the possibility of overcharging.
4. A 201P 12-V dc battery, a heavy-duty deep-cycle battery that provides a high-quality reliable power source for the 900R or 950E.
5. A 200K Lite Cart, a two-wheeled cart to allow the mechanic/technician to transport the test instrumentation to a yard trailer, or to place in a service truck for a field service call.

SCANNER LIGHT TESTER

An alternate heavy-duty trailer lighting system tester is the Scanner model shown in Figure 5–67. This unit contains its own 12-volt battery encased within the carrier. Therefore there is no need for a service truck or external battery power source in order to check the trailer lighting,

correct wiring, and proper grounding. Designed for one-person operation, the Scanner will perform a systematic check/test of all trailer lights in approximately 60

FIGURE 5-67 Portable trailer light tester. (*Courtesy of Square Wheel, Inc., Temple, PA.*)

seconds, allowing the mechanic/technician to perform a visual check as he or she walks around the trailer. The Scanner, when connected and activated, will automatically operate all lights on the trailer in a sequential order.

QUESTIONS

5-1. There are basically five main wiring harnesses used on a heavy-duty truck/tractor and trailer:
a. _____ harness   d. _____ harness
b. _____ harness   e. _____ harness
c. _____ harness
(see pages 116–117)

5-2. The location of a specific wire circuit can be found by referring to the vehicle _____ diagram.
(see page 118)

5-3. A specific wire circuit can be found on the vehicle by referring to the color-coded wire which also has letters and numbers imprinted on the wire or tagged approximately every:
a. 4 in. (10 cm)   c. 12 in. (30 cm)
b. 6 in. (15 cm)   d. 24 in. (60 cm)
(see page 118)

5-4. When letters are used to indicate wire color, the second letter is used to indicate:
a. The base color   c. The wire size
b. The tracer color   d. Both b and c are correct
(see pages 118–119)

5-5. A wire tag that contains the number and letters 16 BN-R would indicate:
a. A 16-gauge wire; black and neutral tracer with a red secondary tracer
b. A 16-strand copper wire; black with a red tracer
c. A 16-gauge wire; base color is brown with a red tracer
d. A 16-gauge wire; brown color only
(see page 119)

5-6. When three wire insulation tracer color bands are used on a single wire, they are usually of the following widths:
a. 3.0 mm, 2.0 mm, and 1.0 mm
b. 2.5 mm, 1.5 mm, and 0.5 mm
c. 2.0 mm, 1.0 mm, and 0.5 mm
d. 1.5 mm, 1.0 mm, and 0.5 mm
(see page 119)

5-7. All wire conductors used on cars and trucks are produced from annealed copper wire in accordance with ASTM specification B3. *True* or *False* (see page 119)

5-8. The cross-sectional area of the wire conductor on all gauge sizes conforms to SAE specification data. *True* or *False* (see page 119)

5-9. Wire insulation for all truck primary wiring cable is usually made from:
a. SXL (standard-duty thermosetting cross-linked polyethylene)
b. STR (standard thermosetting resin)
c. SPWBC (standard plastic wire braided covering)
d. SPC (standard polyethylene covering)
(see page 119)

5-10. Nylon conduit, metal heat shielding, or special high-temperature cable must be used when truck cable and wiring is subjected to temperatures in excess of:
a. 100 °F (38 °C)   c. 300 °F (149 °C)
b. 200 °F (93 °C)   d. 400 °F (204 °C)
(see page 119)

5-11. Wire harnesses should be supported throughout their length by plastic cable ties or rubber-insulated brackets at equal spacings not to exceed:
a. 12 in. (30 cm)   c. 24 in. (60 cm)
b. 18 in. (45 cm)   d. 36 in. (90 cm)
(see page 119)

5-12. Fleet experience has shown that wiring insulated with PVC (polyvinyl chloride) material is the ideal material to use in wiring harnesses. *True* or *False* (see page 120)

5-13. The most commonly used electrical circuit protection devices used on trucks are:
a. Replaceable fuses   c. Circuit breakers
b. Fusible links   d. All of the above
(see page 120)

5-14. The starter motor circuit is generally protected by:
a. A fuse
b. A circuit breaker
c. A fusible link
d. A thermostat switch for overcrank protection
(see page 120)

5-15. The alternator circuit may be protected by:
a. A replaceable fuse   c. A fusible link
b. A circuit breaker   d. A thermostat switch
(see page 120)

5-16. The vehicle headlight circuit is usually protected by:
a. One circuit breaker per side
b. One fuse per side
c. One fuse per headlight (four headlight system)
d. Any one of the above is possible
(see page 121)

5-17. You should never replace a fuse or circuit breaker with a higher rating than that listed in the vehicle wiring diagram. *True* or *False* (see page 122)

5-18. The rating of a fuse or circuit breaker is:
a. Determined by color coding only
b. Stamped on the fuse or circuit breaker
c. Established by a part number on the unit
d. Checked with an ohmmeter
(see page 123)

5-19. Material used in fuses is usually made from:
a. Solder wire   c. Copper wire
b. Zinc strip   d. Aluminum wire
(see page 123)

5-20. The two types of fuses in common use in trucks are:
a. The glass tube cartridge and blade type
b. The bimetallic strip and minifuse
c. The circuit breaker and cartridge type
d. The bimetallic strip and circuit breaker
(see page 122)

5-21. Automatic resettable-type circuit breakers depend on the rate at which:
   a. A copper wire cools internally
   b. An aluminum wire cools internally
   c. A bimetallic flat strip cools internally
   d. A relay coil cools internally
   (see page 124)

5-22. Continued closing of an automatic circuit breaker is usually an indication of:
   a. A faulty circuit breaker
   b. An overload circuit
   c. High circuit resistance
   d. Both a and b are correct
   (see pages 124, 153)

5-23. Prior to replacing a faulty circuit breaker, you should:
   a. Disconnect the associated wiring
   b. Disconnect the batteries
   c. Use a fused jumper wire to bypass the circuit
   d. Disconnect the electrical accessory from that circuit
   (see page 124)

5-24. A manual reset-type circuit breaker is reset by:
   a. Removal and replacement of the unit after allowing 35 to 45 seconds for cool down
   b. Removing it and then resetting a small internal switch
   c. Pushing a small reset button
   d. Using a fused jumper wire across its terminals
   (see page 124)

5-25. A 14-gauge fusible link is usually color coded:
   a. Blue   c. Yellow
   b. Red   d. Green
   (see page 131)

5-26. A recommended and effective method of sealing a wire splice is to use:
   a. Heat-shrink tubing
   b. Plastic electrical tape
   c. Friction-type electrical tape
   d. C first and then b
   (see page 140)

5-27. Staggering a wire splice has the following advantage:
   a. A large bulge in the repaired harness is avoided
   b. Less insulation tape is required to make the splice waterproof
   c. It allows heat-shrink tubing to fit over the repair
   d. It removes the possibility of splices rubbing/chaffing against one another
   e. Both a and d are correct
   (see page 140)

5-28. A 10% drop in battery voltage caused by wire resistance will result in a candlepower loss output at the light bulb of:
   a. 10%   c. 30%
   b. 20%   d. 40%
   (see page 142)

5-29. List the three main considerations in selecting a wire gauge size for use in a cab or chassis electrical circuit.
   (see page 142)

5-30. The three common types of wire insulation used on trucks to protect bare wires are:
   a. GPT, HDT, and SXL   c. GFT, HDT, and SXT
   b. GPC, HDI, and SXX   d. GPV, HVPV, and STL
   (see pages 119, 143)

5-31. Wire harness connectors that are subjected to moisture or to the elements are generally known as:
   a. Waterproof terminals   c. Heavy-duty blade-type terminals
   b. Weather-pack terminals   d. Snap-connectors
   (see page 145)

5-32. Piercing a wire's insulation to obtain a good contact is acceptable practice when using a multimeter. *True* or *False* (see page 148)

5-33. Due to the low current and voltage levels that pass through the Weather-Pack, Metri-Pack, and Micro-Pack terminals, all new connections should be soldered in place using:
   a. Silver solder   c. Rosin-core solder
   b. Acid-core solder   d. Plain 50/50 solder
   (see page 148)

5-34. Another commonly used sealed connector in heavy-duty trucks is:
   a. The snap-in connector   c. The twist and pull connector
   b. The push/pull connector d. The Deutsch connector
   (see page 149)

5-35. Generally, if a light bulb flickers or glows dimly it is caused by:
   a. Lack of voltage   c. A poor ground connection
   b. Lack of current   d. An open circuit
   (see page 153)

5-36. The ground return to the towing vehicle on a semitrailer uses wire that is normally color-coded:
   a. White   c. Green
   b. Black   d. Blue
   (see page 159)

5-37. The stoplamp wiring circuit on a semitrailer is usually color-coded:
   a. Yellow   c. Red
   b. Brown   d. Blue with a yellow tracer
   (see page 159)

CHAPTER

6

Truck and Trailer Lighting Systems

OBJECTIVES

In this chapter we identify the various types of lamps used in the vehicle lighting system and trace and understand their operation. Specifically, you will acquire or review the skills needed to:

1. Identify and describe the various lighting circuits found on a heavy-duty truck and semitrailer.
2. Describe the basic construction of a light bulb.
3. Identify the different types and styles of vehicle light bulbs, such as single-filament, double-filament, single-contact, double-contact, straight, and offset pin.
4. Identify and describe the different types of light bulb failures commonly found on heavy-duty truck applications.
5. Describe the various shapes and types of headlights (sealed beam versus halogen lamp), describe the cir-

cuits and perform headlamp alignment procedures, and know how to trace the electrical circuit.
6. Identify, trace the circuit, and perform taillight (park, signal, and stoplight) repairs.
7. Identify, trace, and repair the directional signal and hazard flasher light system, and flasher unit and steering column–mounted control lever.
8. Identify, trace, and repair clearance and marker lamp circuits.
9. Maintain and repair heated external mirrors.

INTRODUCTION

In this chapter we identify the various lighting circuits on a truck, discuss their arrangement, and describe how they operate with the aid of schematic wiring diagrams. The lighting circuits are generally the longest circuits on the truck since power has to be carried to the front, top, side, and rear of the vehicle. Generally, the lighting systems covers such circuits as:

1. Taillights
2. Clearance and marker lights
3. Headlights
4. Stoplights

5. Turn signal and hazard lights
6. Instrument and gauge lamps
7. Dome lamp
8. Fog lamps
9. Backup lamps

The placement and number of lights that must be used on commercial vehicles and trailers to comply with FMVSS (U.S. Federal Motor Vehicle Safety Standard) 108, October 1, 1983, and FMVSS 111, January 1, 1982, are listed in Table 6–1. Table 6–1 will allow you to determine, quickly and accurately, just how many lights and reflectors should be used on a specific type of vehicle

TABLE 6-1 Federal motor vehicle safety lighting summary chart

TYPE OF VEHICLE	Multi-purpose Passenger Vehicles, Trucks & Buses other than School Bus (GVW over 10,000 lbs., 80" wide or over)	Full Trailers & Large Semis (80" or wider)	Truck Tractors	Multi-purpose Passenger Vehicles, Trucks & Buses (GVW 10,000 lbs. or less, under 80" wide)	Full Trailers & Small Semis (Under 80" wide)	Pole Trailers (80" or wider)	Driveaway-Towaway (Towing vehicle —80" or wider)	Driveaway-Towaway (Towed vehicle —80" or wider)	
TRAFFIC HAZARD WARNING SWITCH	1		1	1			1		INSIDE CAB
TURN SIGNAL SWITCHES	1		1	1			1		INSIDE CAB
REARVIEW MIRRORS (Unit magnification 19½ sq. in. reflective surface)				2					OUTSIDE CAB
REARVIEW MIRRORS (Unit magnification 50 sq. in. reflective surface)	2		2				2		OUTSIDE CAB
TURN SIGNAL LAMPS	2		2	2			2		FRONT
CLEARANCE LAMPS	2	2	2			2	2	2	FRONT
IDENTIFICATION LAMPS	3		3				3		FRONT
TAIL LAMPS	2	2	2	2	2	2	2	2	REAR
STOP LAMPS	2	2	2	2	2	2	2	2	REAR
TURN SIGNAL LAMPS	2	2	2	2	2	2	2	2	REAR
CLEARANCE LAMPS	2	2				2		2	REAR
IDENTIFICATION LAMPS	3	3				3		3	REAR
REFLECTORS	2	2	2	2	2	2		2	REAR
BACK-UP LAMPS	2		2	2			2		REAR
LICENSE PLATE LAMP	1	1	1	1	1	1	1	1	REAR
MARKER LAMPS	1	1		1	1	1		1	AT REAR EACH SIDE
REFLECTORS	1	1		1	1	1		1	AT REAR EACH SIDE
MARKER LAMPS	1	1		1	1	1		1	AT CENTER EACH SIDE (30' & longer vehicles)
REFLECTORS	1	1		1	1	1			AT CENTER EACH SIDE (30' & longer vehicles)
MARKER LAMPS	1	1	1	1	1	1	1	1	AT FRONT EACH SIDE
REFLECTORS	1	1	1	1	1	1	1	1	AT FRONT EACH SIDE

NOTE: FMVSS 111 applying to new vehicles manufactured after Feb. 26, 1977, requires that outside rearview mirrors have minimum reflective surface areas on certain type vehicles. See pages 36023 through 36206, Federal Register, Vol. 41, No. 167 dated Thursday, August 26, 1976. Accordingly, "Reflective Surface" areas in square inches for separate mirror heads are specified on pages 8–16.

Source: Grote Manufacturing Company, Madison, IN.

and/or trailer unit. The numbers 1, 2, and 3 in the chart refer to the actual quantity of lights that must be installed on a given vehicle type to ensure minimum compliance with the FMVSS code in the United States.

The lamp circuits usually originate at the fuse box or circuit breakers on medium-duty truck models, pass to the control switches on the dash or switch control panel, and then to the lights. However on some models of heavy-duty class 8 trucks, the lamp circuits may originate at a bus bar which receives positive battery power supply, then through a fuse or circuit breaker, and on to a control switch. In either case, power from the control switch flows to the lamp(s) in question, which comprise the circuit load. From the lamp(s) the power returns to the battery negative post via the ground circuit. Early light bulb filaments manufactured by Thomas Edison were made with thread and bamboo. In 1905, William D. Coolidge began experimenting with tungsten, which has a melting temperature of 6170 °F (3410 °C). By 1917, bulb manufacturers were using coiled filaments and gas-filled bulbs. Today's car and truck light bulbs generate their incandescence from a tungsten filament which glows when battery power is passed through it.

During bulb manufacture all air must be kept out of the bulb either by the use of a vacuum or by filling the bulb with an inert gas such as argon. To ensure a sealed bulb, Dumet wire, which has the same coefficient of expansion as the glass, is used. Long-life bulbs tend to draw more power than a standard bulb; therefore, they also generate more heat. The bulb manufacturer designs the lighting device to handle this extra heat, and the cost of the bulb is higher than that of a standard one. Prior to discussing the various individually controlled lighting systems, let's identify the various bulb types and bulb identification numbers found in these lamps.

LIGHT BULB IDENTIFICATION

Due to the many different styles of headlights, taillights, marker, clearance, stop, backup, and signal lense shapes available to the truck market, a variety of bulbs are used for illumination purposes. Of course, keep in mind that a sealed beam headlight does not use a replaceable bulb, but is replaced as a complete unit. Many different types and wattages of light bulbs are used in automotive and heavy equipment electrical systems. The configuration at the base of the bulb can be a straight or staggered pin arrangement for locating the bulb into its holder. On smaller applications, some bulbs are even of the screw-in type similar to a house light bulb. Typical lamp bulbs are described and illustrated below.

Parking Lamps

Parking lamps are generally of the single- or double-contact type at the base of the bulb. If the lamp is strictly for parking purposes, a single-contact, single-filament bulb would be used; however, if the lamp bulb is both

FIGURE 6–1 Double-contact bulb with grounding accomplished through the bulb base housing in contact with its holder. Notice the staggered locating pin arrangement.

for parking and directional signal, it will be a double-contact double-filament bulb, as shown in Fig. 6–1. This bulb is usually numbered 1034, 1157, 1034A, 1157A, 1034NA, or 1157NA. The letter A indicates that the bulb lens is amber coated, while the letters NA signify a natural amber color. The only time that an A or NA bulb would be used is when a lens cover is clear glass or plastic rather than colored. When an amber lens cover is employed, a clear light bulb would be used.

When the parking lights are switched on from the headlight switch, the parking filament of the bulb will light producing about 4 candlepower (4 cp) of illumination, with an amperage draw of 0.5 A at 12 V.

Taillamps

The number of taillamps can vary in different vehicles. Regardless of how many lamps are employed on a vehicle at the rear, one lamp will always be of the dual-filament type, with a number 1034 or 1157 configuration, so that one filament can be used in the turn signal and brake light circuit. When single-filament bulbs are used at the rear of the vehicle, a single-bayonet or double-contact base bulb is used, the bulb numbers of these 4-cp bulbs being 1095, 1155, 1178 or 1232. Figure 6–2 illustrates a typical rear single-contact bayonet-base bulb,

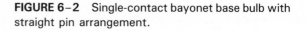

FIGURE 6–2 Single-contact bayonet base bulb with straight pin arrangement.

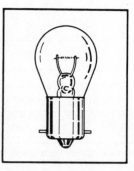

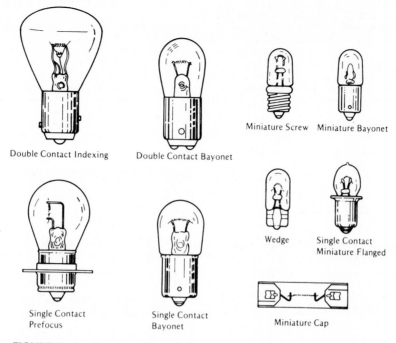

Double Contact Indexing   Double Contact Bayonet   Miniature Screw   Miniature Bayonet

Single Contact
Prefocus

Single Contact
Bayonet

Wedge   Single Contact
Miniature Flanged

Miniature Cap

FIGURE 6-3 Common lamp bulbs used in automotive applications.

while Fig. 6-3 shows other common lamp bulbs used in both automotive and truck applications. License plate lamps are usually single-filament, single-contact bayonet-base type of only 1 or 2 cp. Side-marker lamps located on the side of the vehicle can be single-filament bulbs. If they are tied into the turn signal lights, these will be of the double-contact single-filament type with a bayonet base.

Signal lamps share a common circuit with the tail-lamps and are controlled through a separate set of contacts in the turn signal switch. They can be used to increase driver visibility when cornering and will light on either the left or right of the vehicle and cancel when the turn signal switch is turned off. Clearance lamps are common in pickup trucks, heavy-duty trucks, and off-highway vehicles, with their size and candlepower being similar to parking lights.

Reverse or backup lights are controlled by the transmission shift linkage. This switch can be a part of the neutral safety start switch.

Lamp Bulb Information

In the United States all vehicle lighting must comply with the FMVSS (Federal Motor Vehicle Safety Standard) standard 108, which covers a multitude of SAE Recommended Practices. Lamp bulbs are identified by a standard technical practice such as those laid down by SAE (Society of Automotive Engineers). All of SAE's ground vehicle standards (over 1100) are available in a four-volume set. Volume 1, Materials; Volume 2, Parts and Components; Volume 3, Engines, Fuels and Lubricants, Emissions and Noise; Volume 4, On-Highway Vehicles, Off-Highway Machinery. This information is also available on microfiche from SAE, 400 Commonwealth Drive, Warrendale, PA 15096.

The construction and use of heavy-duty filaments for use in medium/heavy-duty trucks provides longer service life than that of a standard automotive passenger car bulb, due to the more demanding conditions of shock and vibration encountered in truck operation. Figure 6-4 illustrates three typical miniature lamp bulbs and their filament type in wide use on truck applications. Table 6-2 lists typical technical data for widely used fleet service lamps. For more detailed information on vehicle lighting systems and lamps, refer to the *SAE Handbook*, Volume

FIGURE 6-4 Features of miniature lamps.

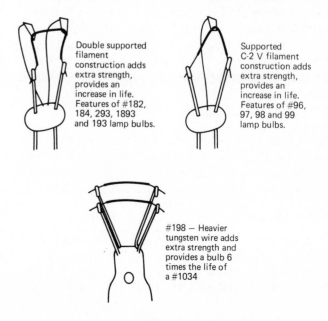

Double supported filament construction adds extra strength, provides an increase in life. Features of #182, 184, 293, 1893 and 193 lamp bulbs.

Supported C-2 V filament construction adds extra strength, provides an increase in life. Features of #96, 97, 98 and 99 lamp bulbs.

#198 — Heavier tungsten wire adds extra strength and provides a bulb 6 times the life of a #1034

TABLE 6-2 Technical data for truck fleet service lamps

Miniature Service	Fleet Service Types Trade No.	Original Equipment Types Trade No.	Design: CP	Design: Volts	Design: Amps	Base Type
Instrument	182		1	14.4	0.18	Min. bay
Indicator		53X	1	14.4	0.12	Min. bay
		53	1	14.4	0.12	Min. bay
	184		1	14.4	0.24	Wedge
		161	1	14.0	0.19	Wedge
Instrument	293		2	14.0	0.33	Min. bay
Indicator		1895	2	14.0	0.27	Min. bay
Identification		57	2	14.0	0.24	Min. bay
Clearance marker	1893		2	14.0	0.33	Min. bay
		1889	2	14.0	0.27	Min. bay
		1891	2	14.0	0.24	Min. bay
	193		2	14.0	0.33	Wedge
		194	2	14.0	0.27	Wedge
		158	2	14.0	0.24	Wedge
Instrument	97		4	13.5	0.69	Single contact bayonet
Parking		1155	4	13.5	0.59	
Clearance marker		67	4	13.5	0.59	
Tail	96		4	13.5	0.69	Double contact bayonet
License plate		68	4	13.5	0.59	
Front turn signal	199*		32	12.8	2.25	Single contact bayonet
		1156*	32	12.8	2.10	
		1073	32	12.8	1.80	
Rear turn signal	1159		21	12.8	1.60	Single contact bayonet
		1141	21	12.8	1.44	
Stop	1093		15	12.8	1.19	Single contact bayonet
		93	15	12.8	1.04	
Front park and turn	198*		32/	12.8/	2.38/	Double contact index bayonet
Tail and turn signal			3	14.0	.68	
Stop and Tail		1157*	32/	12.8/	2.1/	
Stop, tail and			3	14.0	.59	
Turn signal		1034	32/	12.8/	1.8/	
			3	14.0	.51	
	1376		21/6	12.8/	1.6/	Double contact bayonet
				14.0	.64	
		1176	21/6	12.8/	1.31/	
				14.0	.57	
Dome	105		12	12.8	1.0	Single contact bayonet
		1003	15	12.8	.94	
	104		12	12.8	1.0	Double contact bayonet
		1004	15	12.8	.94	
	1093		15	12.8	1.19	Single contact bayonet
		93	15	12.8	1.04	
	98		6	13.0	0.62	Single contact bayonet
		631	6	14.0	0.63	
		89	6	13.0	0.58	

TABLE 6-2 (Continued)

Miniature Service	Fleet Service Types Trade No.	Original Equipment Types Trade No.	Design:			Base Type
			CP	Volts	Amps	
	99		6	13.0	0.62	
		632	6	14.0	0.63	Double contact bayonet
		90	6	13.0	0.58	

Sealed Beam Service	Fleet Service Types Trade No.	To Replace Trade No.	Design:		Max. Amps at Design Volts	Terminals	
			Volts	Watts		No.	Type
Super-beam headlamps	4040		12.8	37.5/60	3.14/4.97	3	Lugs
		4005	12.8	37.5/50	3.14/4.20	3	Lugs
		4002	12.8	37.5/50	3.14/4.20	3	Lugs
	4101		12.8	55	4.60	2	Lugs
		4006	12.8	37.5	3.14	2	Lugs
		4001	12.8	37.5	3.14	2	Lugs
	6016		12.8	60/50	5.04/4.20	3	Lugs
		6015	12.8	60/50	4.97/4.20	3	Lugs
		6013	12.8	50/40	4.20/3.36	3	Lugs
		6012	12.8	50/40	4.20/3.36	3	Lugs

Service	Trade No.	Wattage	Bulb
Spot lite	4416	30	PAR36
Spot lite	4405	30	PAR36
Spot lite	4435	30	PAR46
Fog lamp	4415	35	PAR36
Fog lamp	4415A	35	PAR36
Fog lamp	4412	35	PAR46
Fog lamp	4412A	35	PAR46
Fog lamp	4421	100	PAR46
Fog lamp	7415A	35	Hi-dome PAR36
Auxiliary driving lamp	7701	50	PAR 46
Auxiliary driving lamp	7416A	50	Hi-dome PAR36

2, *Parts and Components*, Section 21. This publication is available from SAE, 400 Commonwealth Drive, Warrendale, PA 15096-0001. Additional truck lamp bulb information is also available in the *Recommended Maintenance Practices Manual*, Section AV1-2-2 which is available from TMC/ATA (The Maintenance Council, American Trucking Associations), 2200 Mill Road, Alexandria, VA 22314.

The repair of lighting systems on trucks costs both time and money and can be a major part of a fleet's operating expenses. The mechanic/technician must be familiar with the various types and bulb ID numbers and ensure that the correct bulb replacement is always used. In addition, problems with lighting systems are most often a result of corrosion, shock failure, or wiring damage. Information on chassis wiring repair was given in Chapter 5. When the mechanic/technician is faced with a lamp illumination problem, he or she may be required to replace either the lamp pigtail assembly or socket, due to severe corrosion or other damage. Figure 6-5 illustrates some typical lamp pigtail assemblies, and Fig. 6-6 shows typical lamp bulb sockets that would be found on truck lighting systems.

Typical failure modes experienced with lamps in truck fleet operation usually include telltale signs such as corrosion in the sockets, water seepage, blackened bulbs, broken lenses, and broken filaments. There are seven major reasons that lamps fail in a truck application, and these are described briefly below.

1. *Physical damage.* Although lamp manufacturers protect lenses with guards as well as by flush-mounting installations, they also manufacture lenses from polycarbonate material for both the lens and housing. Even though this material is exceptionally strong, a direct impact can damage or shatter the lens and damage the bulb and socket.

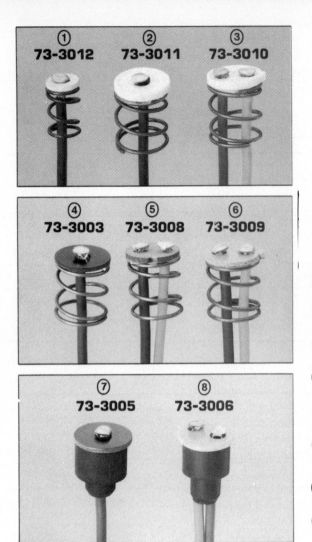

FIGURE 6–5 Various light bulb socket pigtail assemblies.
(*Courtesy of Dominion Automotive Industries, Inc.*)

Pigtail Assemblies

① **MINIATURE CERAMIC DISC PIGTAIL**
73-3012 7″ (178mm) length single contact

② **CERAMIC DISC PIGTAIL**
73-3011 7″ (178mm) length, single contact

③ **CERAMIC DISC PIGTAIL**
73-3010 7″ (178mm) length, double contact

④ **PHENOLIC DISC PIGTAIL**
73-3003 7″ (178mm) length, single contact

⑤ **PHENOLIC DISC PIGTAIL**
73-3008 7″ (178mm) length, double contact

⑥ **PHENOLIC DISC PIGTAIL**
73-3009 7″ (178mm) length, double contact
index — tab style

⑦ **RUBBER PLUG PIGTAIL**
73-3005 7″ (178mm) length, single contact

⑧ **RUBBER PLUG PIGTAIL**
73-3006 7″ (178mm) length, double contact

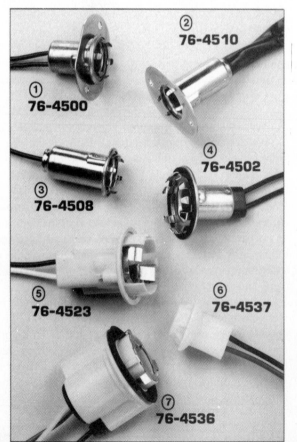

FIGURE 6–6 Examples of typical light bulb socket
assemblies. (*Courtesy of Dominion Automotive Industries, Inc.*)

Sockets

① **UNIVERSAL DOUBLE CONTACT SOCKET**
76-4500 Assembly, offset 'J' slots. Flush mounting
zinc-plated bracket. 7″ (178mm) leads.

② **UNIVERSAL SINGLE CONTACT SOCKET**
76-4510 Assembly, parallel 'J' slots. Neoprene boot.
Flush mounting, zinc-plated bracket.
30″ (762mm) lead.

③ **UNIVERSAL SINGLE CONTACT SOCKET**
76-4508 Assembly, parallel 'J' slots. Snaps into ¾″
(19mm) dia. panel hole. 7″ (178mm) lead.

④ **UNIVERSAL DOUBLE CONTACT SOCKET**
76-4502 Assembly, offset 'J' slots. Large flange has
integral seal. Snaps into 1⅛″ (28mm) dia.
panel hole. 7″ (178mm) leads.

⑤ **DOUBLE CONTACT STOP/TAIL LIGHT SOCKET**
76-4523 Assembly for late model G.M. cars.
Heavy-duty plastic housing.

⑥ **TWIST-IN STYLE**
76-4537 Socket assembly for side marker lights,
Ford and G.M.C.

⑦ **TWIST-LOCK STYLE**
76-4536 Socket assembly for tail and stop lights, G.M.C.

2. *Excessive voltage.* The bulb life can be shortened by up to 50% when voltage has been increased over the design parameters for the lamp. Generally, most lamp bulbs are able to withstand 14 V on a 12-V battery system; however, if the lighting circuit is not protected, even a small voltage surge that lasts only milliseconds can burn out the bulb filament. An overvoltage condition can be identified when the filament and lead wires exhibit a melted-down feature. Often this may appear as a round ball of molten wire.

3. *Shock and vibration.* To protect the lamp bulb filament it is usually mounted in a molded rubber or neoprene base together with a rubber grommet to exclude the entrance of moisture. Some fleets have modified the original mounting to offer added protection.

4. *Loss of bulb contact.* A loss of bulb contact can occur as a result of vibration, impact, or even due to corrosion. Some bulb manufacturers employ a baseless bulb design with a soldered or welded lead wire to the bulb contact as a means of a solid contact. Spring-loaded J sockets that are often used with base bulbs can lose tension and become corroded after being in service for several years.

5. *Corrosion.* When lamp lenses are removed for the purpose of replacing burned-out bulbs, it is very important that the sealing ring/gasket not be damaged or broken, since that would allow the entrance of water and moisture. Many fleets use a nonconductive corrosion-resistant compound to seal areas of lighting that are subject to corrosion. In lights that have open insulation or loose wiring, consider installing heat-shrink tubing such as that illustrated in Fig. 5–31.

6. *Poor grounding.* Some trucks use a separate grounding wire to complete the lighting system return circuit. This ensures that it will be free from corrosion. Regardless of what type of ground return circuit is employed, it must be designed in such a manner that it is suitably protected and will provide a good, clean, trouble-free arrangement.

7. *Filament burnout.* Lighting manufacturers perform a series of tests for proper bulb seal, filament construction, candela ratings, vibration, heat and warpage, plus the entrance of moisture, which can lead to corrosion. Filament burnout can be a result of moisture as well as of high-voltage spikes. Charging systems should be checked for voltage output settings when continued short bulb life is experienced. In addition, check that the lighting circuit is properly protected by a fuse or circuit breaker. When a bulb feature exhibits a smoky condition, such as a yellowish or white color, this is normally caused by air leaking inside the glass bulb envelope through a crack in the glass. A failure that turns the bulb light blue is indicative of a very slow leakage that may be traced to corrosion around the Dumet sealing wire. To allow lamps to breath, both the lenses and the housings must be kept clean, to allow effective heat radiation.

Typical light bulb specification numbers that would be used in a medium-duty truck are listed in Table 6–3 and Tables 6–4 and 6–5 list examples of bulbs that might be used on a heavy-duty class 8 truck. Notice that some of the bulb numbers are common to both the medium- and heavy-duty vehicles. Another interesting feature of the bulb listings for both the medium- and heavy-duty trucks is the use of a fiber optic ribbon, now being used by many truck manufacturers to illuminate instruments and gauges.

TABLE 6–3 Various light bulb ID numbers for assorted truck components

Exterior Lamps	Bulb No.
Headlamp	
Dual (Type 1) Rectangular High-Beam	4651
Dual (Type 2) Rectangular High/Low-Beam	4652
Dual (Type 1) Rectangular High-Beam Halogen	H4651
Dual (Type 2) Rectangular High/Low-Beam Halogen	H4652
Single 7″ Diameter	6014
Single 7″ Diameter Halogen	H6014, H6024
Rear Taillamp/Stoplamp/Directional Signal Lamp	1157
Backup Lamp	1156
Front Parking/Directional/Signal Lamp	1157
Roof Marker Lamp	194
Interior Lamps	
Dome Lamp	211-2
Instrument Panel Lamps (Push-In Type)	168
Instrument Cluster	168
Speedometer	168
Headlamp High-Beam Indicator	1445
Fiber Optic Ribbon	168
Transmission Oil Temperature Gage	57
Air Pressure Gage	53

Source: GMC Truck Division, General Motors Corporation.

TABLE 6-4 Light bulb ID numbers for assorted truck components

LIGHT BULBS	Bulb No.
Headlight, Single 178 mm (7")...............................	6014
Stop and Taillight	1157
Parking Lights	1157
Back-up Lights	1156
Directional Light	
Front	1157
Rear	1157
Dome Light	211
Instrument Cluster	1895
Speedometer	1895
Fiber Optic Ribbon..	168
Side Marker Lights	1157
Headlight Hi Beam Indicator	313
Trans. Oil Temp. Gage	1895
Air Press., Vacuum Gage...................................	1895

Source: GMC Truck Division, General Motors Corporation.

TABLE 6-5 Light bulb ID numbers for assorted truck components

LIGHT BULB	Bulb No.
Headlights	
178 mm (7") Single...........................	6014
Stop Lights, Directional Lights and Taillights......................	1157
Instrument, Warning and Indicator Lights........................	1895
Hi-Beam and Direction Indicator	1895
Dome Light	1141
Back-up Lights	1156
Clearance and Identification Lights.............................	194
Front Directional Light	1156
Parking Light	194
Side Marker Light..	194

Source: GMC Truck Division, General Motors Corporation.

HEAVY-DUTY HEADLAMPS AND CIRCUITS

There are basically two types of headlamp systems now in use: the long-used sealed beam unit, and the more recent halogen light bulb system. It is only recently that the NHTSA (National Highway Traffic Safety Administration) acceded to the request that major passenger car and truck manufacturers use the halogen bulb concept. Up until 1968 the headlight standards were basically the same as those that had been in existence since 1940. Quartz halogen lighting systems have been in use in Europe for many years, since halogen gas is a more efficient medium than the nitrogen used in the conventional sealed beam headlight. Halogen light bulbs provide greater illumination characteristics than does the conventional sealed beam, and they do not darken as sealed beams do after long usage.

Despite the efforts of major car and truck manufacturers, NHTSA turned down all requests for the adoption of halogen bulbs between the years 1968 and 1973 citing the fact that American headlight manufacturers were reluctant to change a system that had been in place for many years, and that NHTSA felt that since a halogen bulb was a separate part of the light reflector and lens, not a one-piece sealed unit similar to the conventional sealed beam headlight, their performance would disintegrate over time. In addition, NHTSA felt that correct lamp alignment would be much more difficult with a separate light bulb rather than with a sealed beam unit. The gridlock was finally broken open in 1973 when Ford Motor Company proposed that a rectangular 4 in. × 6.5 in. flat (100 mm × 165 mm) sealed beam headlight be used that would allow a reduction in the overall hoodline, thereby resulting in better vehicle fuel performance. Since at that time the first Arab oil embargo was in full swing, NHTSA relented and thus we saw the first shift away from the round-type headlamp system in the 1975 model year. However, NHTSA still limited the illumination to 75,000 cd until 1977, when GM was granted a waiver to use a larger rectangular lamp producing 150,000 cd illumination on high beam at 65 W of power draw and 45 W on low beam.

Continuing efforts by the car/truck manufacturers finally persuaded NHTSA to grant the first use in North America, for the 1980-model-year cars, of a halogen bulb in place of the previous nitrogen-filled sealed beams. Currently approved light sources for cars and trucks in North America include the following arrangements:

1. All sealed beams, including halogen, are identified as follows:

Type A: small rectangular

Type B: single 7-in. (178-mm) round high beam

Type C: single 7-in. (178-mm) round low beam

Type D: 5.25-in. (133-mm) single round high beam

Type E: 5.25-in. (133-mm) single round low beam

Type F: 3.62-in. × 5.90-in. (92 mm × 150 mm) rectangular

Types G and H: Chrysler vehicles only; simplified mounting system for type A and E lighting systems (see above)

2. Halogen bulbs for composite lighting systems, which are identified as follows:

HB1: dual-filament bulb for use in both high- low-beam systems

HB2: specific to European imported vehicles only, therefore minor variations in lamp sizing and mounting

HB3: single-filament halogen bulb for high-beam use only

HB4: single-filament halogen bulb for low-beam use only

3. Replacement bulbs, sometimes referred to as halogen capsules, are identified as follows:

Bulb No. 9004 for HB1 lights

Bulb No. 9005 for HB3 high-beam lights

Bulb No. 9006 for HB4 low-beam lights

Bulb No. 9007 for axial filament bulb mounting used for high-beam lighting systems

All lights used in both cars and trucks are fitted with an ID number on the headlight lens to guide in replacement bulb selection. If in doubt, refer to the vehicle service manual for service replacement suitability.

Halogen Principles

The conventional sealed beam headlight using nitrogen gas as a filler was not able to meet the higher demand for greater illumination from increased candela power without adopting heavier vehicle wiring as well as increases to the existing battery power supply system. Consequently, the halogen-filled light bulb has become the lighting system of choice in both Europe and North America.

Just what is halogen? In its simplest form, halogen refers to a basic family of gases that are made up from chlorine, fluorine, iodine, bromine, and astatine, with iodine being the least active of the halogen gases cited. Since iodine is the least active of these gases, it is preferred for use in light bulbs such as those found on cars and trucks since one of the prerequisites for this application is that the bulb last for a long time. The actual filler gas used in a halogen bulb consists of argon, nitrogen, or krypton, with a small quantity of halogen. In most cases you will find that manufacturers add a small amount of oxygen not only to keep the bulb wall clean, but to prevent blackening.

The reason halogen bulbs are much more expensive to produce than their earlier ntirogen-filled sealed beam counterpart is that use of these rare gases and the manufacturing processes they necessitate are much more detailed. To achieve the much brighter illumination of the halogen light, bulb wall temperatures have to be maintained at a minimum of 250 °C (482 °F), with higher temperatures being desirable. These high temperatures are required to ensure that when small particles of tungsten boil off the light bulb filament, they will be circulated by the action of convection currents to other areas of the bulb. This action allows the tungsten–halogen compounds to form in the much cooler regions of the bulb wall; they are then broken down again in the hot region of the filament, where the tungsten is redeposited, thereby avoiding any possibility of bulb blackening, which otherwise would occur as a result of any deposits forming on the bulb wall.

Tests have shown that during long periods of halogen bulb operations, operating temperatures at the bulb wall can reach as high as 500 °C (932 °F). At such elevated temperatures, ordinary bulb glass would soften and melt in some cases. To prevent this from occurring, a material such as quartz must be used with the halogen bulb resulting in additional manufacturing costs. Headlight and bulb technology is ongoing, with current information indicating that Robert Bosch is presently attempting to successfully develop a gas-discharge, low-operating-temperature lamp that would offer almost twice the brilliance/output of twin-filament halogen bulbs at a reduced power draw, approaching 35 W, versus the existing 45 W on low beam and 65 W on high beam.

To provide adequate brilliance for nighttime driving, all vehicles today employ two or more headlamps. Some European vehicles, and many North American units employ what is commonly referred to as a sealed beam because the actual light bulb is hermetically sealed within the glass portion that forms the headlamp or headlight. Present-day sealed beam headlights are improved versions of the first sealed beam units that were invented by Delco-Remy in 1928, but were not introduced until 1939. In 1940 U.S. safety legislation made the use of the sealed beam headlamp mandatory. Up until the year 1958, the two-headlamp system was considered both adequate and acceptable; however, demands for improved lighting systems resulted in the four-headlamp system in 1958. These were round in shape, and in the early 1970s we were introduced to the rectangular headlamp, a fairly standard arrangement these days.

Recent advances have resulted in the introduction of a headlamp system that will project a beam capable of illuminating a road sign at a distance of 530 ft (161.5 m).

Sealed Beam Shapes

Figure 6–7 shows both round and rectangular sealed beam headlight construction. Although the headlight shape may vary from round to rectangular, the reflective surface in-

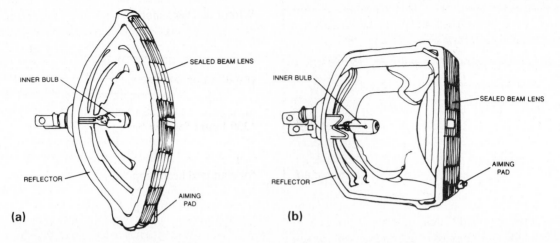

FIGURE 6–7 (a) Round headlight; (b) rectangular headlight. (*Courtesy of GMC Truck Division, General Motors Corporation.*)

side the headlamp is aluminized and is parabolic in shape to obtain maximum light reflection.

The bulb filaments are always placed forward of the center of the reflector to establish optimum focusing of the light assembly. Headlights are rated by their brilliance in units called candlepower, a carryover from early lighting systems. Candlepower will vary between given headlights, however, the rating for a typical headlight is 75,000 cp. Halogen sealed beam headlights, which come fitted as standard equipment on many top-line vehicles, have candlepower ratings as high as 150,000. Halogen lamps differ from the standard tungsten lamps in that the filaments of the halogen lamps consist of a bulb within a bulb, whereas the tungsten lamps have filaments (high and low beam) within the same bulb. Special rally and sport-driving headlights are available with up to 300,000 cp brilliance.

A variety of headlight shapes and configurations are employed on vehicles today: a single round light, a single rectangular light, two round lights, or two rectangular lights per side at the front of the vehicle. Regardless of the shape and number used, the headlight system can employ either a replaceable bulb or the more widely used sealed beam unit, which is replaced as an assembly when it burns out or is damaged. When a single-headlight arrangement is used, a dual-filament bulb is employed in which one filament serves as the low beam, while the other serves as the high beam. When dual headlights are used on each side, one acts on the low-beam circuit, while the other acts as the high-beam circuit.

According to a detailed study conducted by the TMC/ATA (The Maintenance Council, American Trucking Associations), of all the headlamps available, the 7-in. (178-mm) round sealed beam heavy-duty truck headlamp has proven reliability and is also low in cost. Figure 6–8 illustrates a single sealed beam headlamp unit, and Fig. 6–9 shows the arrangement used with a dual sealed beam headlamp system. Many heavy-duty trucks now in use due to their aerodynamic fender and hood styles employ

a four-headlamp rectangular system (dual lamps on each side) such as that illustrated in Fig. 6–10. Although there are many four-headlamp systems in use, it is almost impossible to wire the four-headlamp system so that it can operate in conjunction with either fog or driving lamps and be legally acceptable in all of the lower 48 contiguous U.S. states. Therefore, where possible, TMC/ATA specifies a two-headlamp system as the acceptable standard

FIGURE 6–8 Single round sealed beam headlamp unit. (*Courtesy of GMC Truck Division, General Motors Corporation.*)

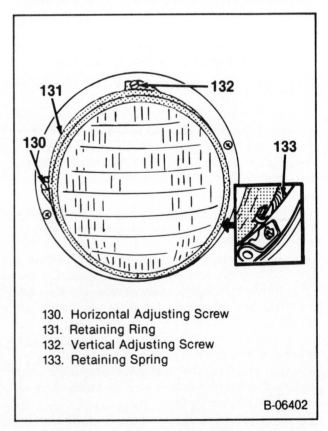

130. Horizontal Adjusting Screw
131. Retaining Ring
132. Vertical Adjusting Screw
133. Retaining Spring

B-06402

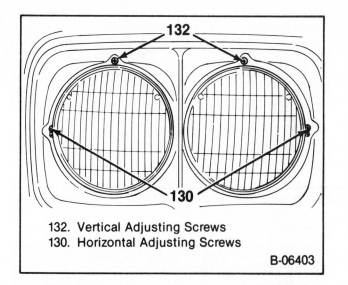

132. Vertical Adjusting Screws
130. Horizontal Adjusting Screws

B-06403

FIGURE 6–9 Dual round sealed beam headlamp arrangement. (*Courtesy of GMC Truck Division, General Motors Corporation.*)

for commercial trucks/tractors. Table 6–6 lists a heavy-duty truck headlamp chart with information on both a two-lamp round and four-lamp round system. Typical acceptable SAE and headlamp manufacturer operating voltages for headlamps are that they not exceed 14 V; therefore, properly designed headlamp wiring circuits are generally designed to include a fuse or circuit breaker arrangement for each side of the vehicle, or even for individual headlamps, to protect them from possible voltage spikes, which may only last for several microseconds.

Within this very short period, however, voltages as high as 150 V have been recorded in tests on heavy-duty trucks, particularly during such operating conditions as engine cranking and during both starting and stopping of air-conditioning compressors.

Typical life expectancy of high-quality headlamps during static laboratory tests should be in the vicinity of 1200 hours for low beams at a test value of 14 V, and approximately 1500 hours for halogen bulb models. The high beam life expectancy is in the region of 500 hours for standard headlamps and up to 900 hours for halogen models. For more specific information on recommended practices for heavy-duty headlamps, refer to TMC/ATA RP-124 in their *Recommended Practices Manual.*

Headlamp Circuits

The headlamp circuit and its specific wiring arrangement will vary between medium- and heavy-duty trucks as well as having control circuits that have unique design features common to a particular make of truck. Some trucks may employ a combination pull-type lamp switch that controls the parking lights, instrument panel, dome light, and headlights, all within this single switch arrangement. Many heavy-duty trucks use toggle switches mounted on the vehicle dash.

The wiring feed to the headlamps can be taken from the engine, the instrument panel, or from the vehicle hood harness where it extends from the cab down through the left or right frame rail forward to the radiator support. The hood harness is routed through the radiator support and then branches left and right behind the bumper sup-

FIGURE 6–10 Dual rectangular headlamps and a directional signal lamp arrangement. (*Courtesy of GMC Truck Division, General Motors Corporation.*)

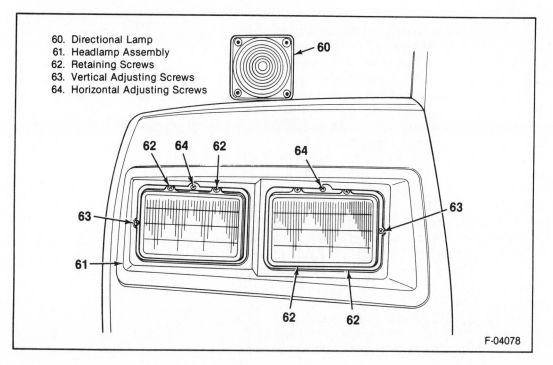

60. Directional Lamp
61. Headlamp Assembly
62. Retaining Screws
63. Vertical Adjusting Screws
64. Horizontal Adjusting Screws

F-04078

TABLE 6–6 Chart showing headlamp system bulb type number, rated life, and wattage

H-L System	Type No.	Rated Life (Hrs)		Wattage		Shock Mount	Manufacturer
		UB	LB	UB	LB		
2 lamp round	6015	300	500	60	50	Yes	1
	6015	300	500	60	50	Yes	2
	6015	300	500	60	60	Yes	3
	6016	900	1500	60	50	?	2
4 lamp round	4040	300	500	37.5	60	?	1
	4040	300	500	37.5	60	?	2
	4040	200	320	37.5	60	?	3

Note: UB = upper beam, LB = lower beam; wattage is watts @ 12.8 V (industry rating); manufacturer 1 = General Electric 2 = Philips-Westinghouse 3 = Wagner

ports on the front hanger, similar to that illustrated in Fig. 6–11. One example of how this wiring harness arrangement might appear on a class 8 heavy-duty truck is shown in Fig. 6–12. Regardless of the specific wiring arrangement used, the connectors for the headlights and fog lights are generally weather-pack sealed connectors. The power feed to the headlights can originate at a junction block located on the forward frame rail, or it might begin at a junction block located on the engine side of the cowl. The protective circuit for the headlamps can be by conventional fuse or circuit breaker. These protective devices are normally located inside the truck cab in the fuse or circuit breaker block.

For example, on class 8 Peterbilt 379 family trucks, the Dill Blox fuse and circuit breaker panel is located inside the cab at the left-hand forward corner, where it is covered with a door in the kick panel. Opening the cab door actuates a light on the Dill Blox assembly, which

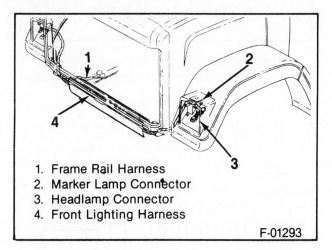

1. Frame Rail Harness
2. Marker Lamp Connector
3. Headlamp Connector
4. Front Lighting Harness

F-01293

FIGURE 6–11 Forward lamp wiring harness routing for a conventional cab heavy-duty truck. (*Courtesy of GMC Truck Division, General Motors Corporation.*)

FIGURE 6–12 Close-up of a forward lamp wiring harness. (*Courtesy of GMC Truck Division, General Motors Corporation.*)

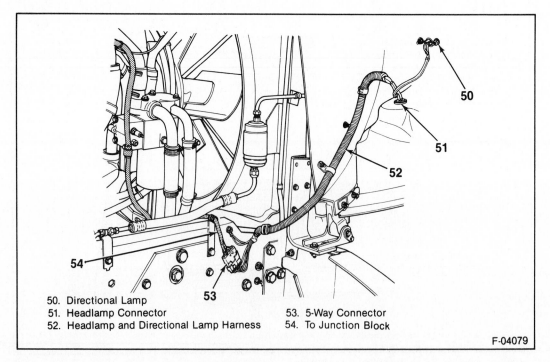

50. Directional Lamp
51. Headlamp Connector
52. Headlamp and Directional Lamp Harness
53. 5-Way Connector
54. To Junction Block

F-04079

illuminates the circuit panel so that the technician can identify the labeled circuits. Within the Dill Blox upper center section there are three relays, to control the horn and the left and right headlights. The center lower section of the Dill Blox contains manual reset circuit breakers that control the ignition, taillights, stoplights, and the left and right headlights. The left and right headlight power feed begins at the vehicle main distribution panel shown in Fig. 6–13 with wire numbers 8, 24, 28, and 298 serving the lights. A simplified wiring diagram of the headlight circuit for the model 379 family of Peterbilt heavy-duty trucks is shown in Fig. 6–14.

Main Lamp Switch. A toggle control switch such as the one illustrated in Fig. 6–14 or a rocker switch to turn the headlights on and off is a very simple design that

FIGURE 6–13 Heavy-duty class 8 truck main wiring distribution panel. (*Courtesy of Peterbilt Motors Company, Division of PACCAR, Newark, CA.*)

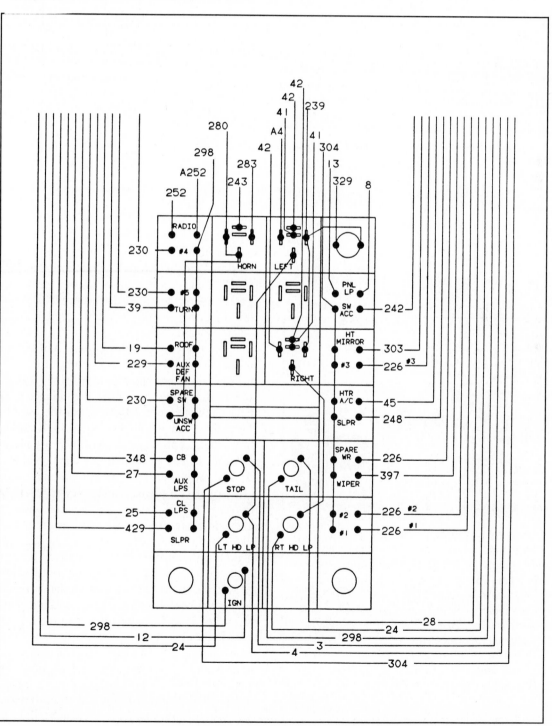

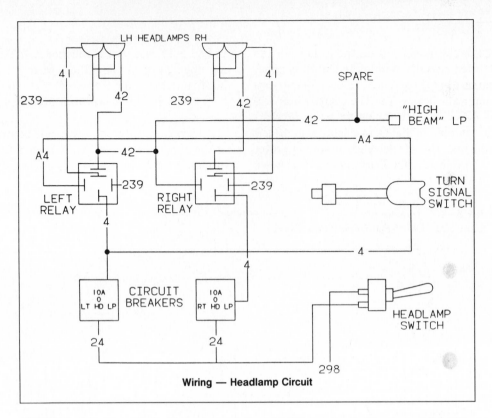

FIGURE 6–14 Simplified wiring schematic for a headlamp circuit. (*Courtesy of Peterbilt Motors Company, Division of PACCAR, Newark, CA.*)

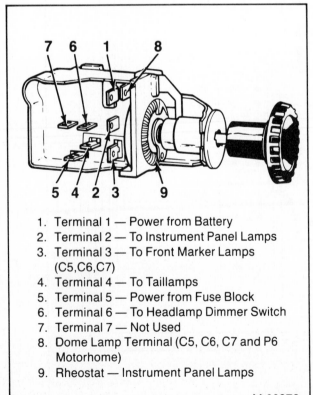

FIGURE 6–15 Major components found in a typical truck main lamp control switch. (*Courtesy of GMC Truck Division, General Motors Corporation.*)

1. Terminal 1 — Power from Battery
2. Terminal 2 — To Instrument Panel Lamps
3. Terminal 3 — To Front Marker Lamps (C5,C6,C7)
4. Terminal 4 — To Taillamps
5. Terminal 5 — Power from Fuse Block
6. Terminal 6 — To Headlamp Dimmer Switch
7. Terminal 7 — Not Used
8. Dome Lamp Terminal (C5, C6, C7 and P6 Motorhome)
9. Rheostat — Instrument Panel Lamps

M-00372

requires no explanation since it is either in the ON or OFF position. A toggle switch is commonly used on midheavy class 7 trucks, baby 8, and full-size class 8 truck/tractors. However, many medium-duty trucks in the class 1 through class 6 category employ a combination three-way switch such as the one illustrated in Fig. 6–15, which functions to control the parking lights and taillamps when pulled out to its first detent position, turns the headlights on when in its second detent position, and can also be rotated to change the degree of brilliance of the instrument panel and gauge lighting via the use of a built-in rheostat, shown as item 9 in Fig. 6–15. Rotating this type of headlight control switch all the way around will usually result in the cab interior dome light coming on.

Although some control switches may contain either a fuse or circuit breaker, most newer trucks have these protective devices located in the circuit wiring where the power originates from either a fuse or circuit breaker box. Figure 6–16 illustrates a wiring schematic for this type of multiple control switch. No battery power can flow from either terminal 1 or 5 to any output circuit when the switch is in the OFF position. In the ON position, when the control knob is pulled out to its first detent position, power can flow from terminal 5 to the taillamp circuit through terminal 4 to the instrument panel lamp dimmer rheostat (9) and to the front marker lamps through terminal 3. Pulling the switch all the way out to its second detent position allows battery positive power to flow through wire terminal 1 and into an automatic reset circuit breaker, shown as item 17, which can be located in-

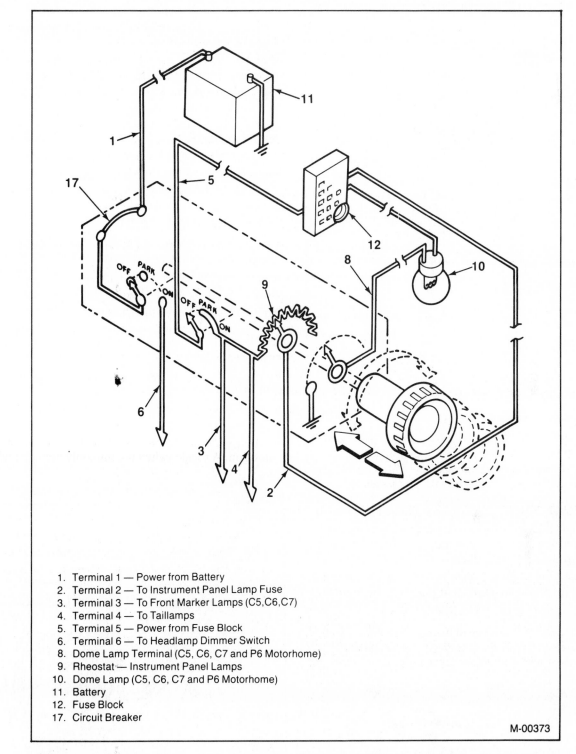

1. Terminal 1 — Power from Battery
2. Terminal 2 — To Instrument Panel Lamp Fuse
3. Terminal 3 — To Front Marker Lamps (C5,C6,C7)
4. Terminal 4 — To Taillamps
5. Terminal 5 — Power from Fuse Block
6. Terminal 6 — To Headlamp Dimmer Switch
8. Dome Lamp Terminal (C5, C6, C7 and P6 Motorhome)
9. Rheostat — Instrument Panel Lamps
10. Dome Lamp (C5, C6, C7 and P6 Motorhome)
11. Battery
12. Fuse Block
17. Circuit Breaker

M-00373

FIGURE 6–16 Main lamp switch schematic. (*Courtesy of GMC Truck Division, General Motors Corporation.*)

side the switch itself or can be separate. The circuit breaker is connected in series with terminal 6. From 17 power flows to and through the switch contacts, exiting at terminal 2. The headlamp circuit is also connected to a dimmer switch for control of the low and high beams through terminal 6. To remove the headlight switch, refer to Fig. 6–17, which illustrates switch removal; Fig. 6–18 shows an alternative arrangement that requires a knob release button on the switch to be depressed in order to free the headlight control knob and shaft from the switch assembly when it is necessary to remove or replace the assembly.

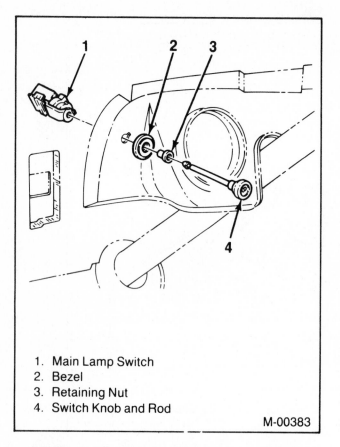

1. Main Lamp Switch
2. Bezel
3. Retaining Nut
4. Switch Knob and Rod

M-00383

FIGURE 6–17 Procedure to remove main lamp switch from dash panel. (*Courtesy of GMC Truck Division, General Motors Corporation.*)

Dimmer Switch. Two types of dimmer switches are employed on trucks: the foot-operated type shown in Fig. 6–19, and the steering column mounted type shown in Fig. 6–20. Basically, the dimmer switch controls a relay, which then turns on the high or low beam as the truck driver steps on the foot switch or pushes in the small but-

FIGURE 6–18 Location of knob release button and rheostat within the main headlight switch assembly. (*Reprinted with Ford Motor Company's permission.*)

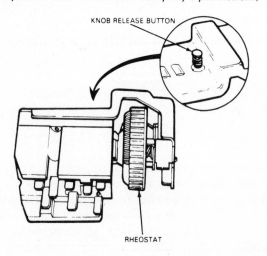

KNOB RELEASE BUTTON

RHEOSTAT

ton on the end of the steering column stalk-mounted lever. Floor-mounted dimmer switches normally use a single-pole double-throw switch, while the steering column mounted type usually employs a two-pole relay to select the upper and lower headlight beams. With the foot-operated dimmer switch there is always a distinct click when the switch is activated. If the dimmer switch is a steering column mounted unit that has to be pulled upward to dim the light, you may also hear a distinct click from the switch assembly. Figure 6–21 illustrates how the dimmer switch operates as well as a procedure to use when checking its operation.

HEADLIGHT ADJUSTMENT

To ensure a maximum illumination of the road surface at night, yet ensure that oncoming vehicle drivers are not blinded by the headlights' brilliance, it is imperative that the headlights be checked and adjusted any time that a new lamp or bulb is installed, when the vehicle has suffered front-end damage to the body, or when alterations have been made to the suspension or tires. To adjust the headlights properly, both a vertical and a horizontal adjusting screw are located at the headlamp retaining circumference. Turning these screws in or out will move the

FIGURE 6–19 Foot-operated headlight dimmer switch location and features. (*Courtesy of GMC Truck Division, General Motors Corporation.*)

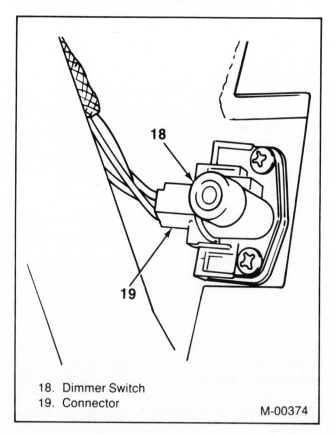

18. Dimmer Switch
19. Connector

M-00374

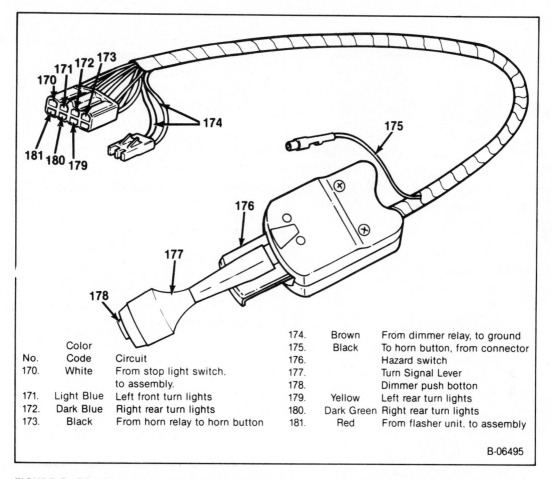

No.	Color Code	Circuit			
			174.	Brown	From dimmer relay, to ground
			175.	Black	To horn button, from connector
170.	White	From stop light switch. to assembly.	176.		Hazard switch
			177.		Turn Signal Lever
			178.		Dimmer push botton
171.	Light Blue	Left front turn lights	179.	Yellow	Left rear turn lights
172.	Dark Blue	Right rear turn lights	180.	Dark Green	Right rear turn lights
173.	Black	From horn relay to horn button	181.	Red	From flasher unit, to assembly

B-06495

FIGURE 6-20 Steering column–mounted dimmer switch features. (*Courtesy of GMC Truck Division, General Motors Corporation.*)

mounting ring in the body against the tension of a small coil spring. It is not necessary to focus a sealed beam headlight, since this is done at the time of manufacture; however, it should be aimed.

Figure's 6-8, 6-9, and 6-10 show the location of head-lamp adjusting screws for three different arrangements of lights.

Prior to attempting to adjust the headlamps for proper aim, ensure that the following conditions have been checked; otherwise, a false setting may be obtained:

1. If the vehicle is heavily coated with compacted snow, ice, or mud under the fenders, this should be knocked off and flushed with a water hose, since this additional weight can alter the riding height.

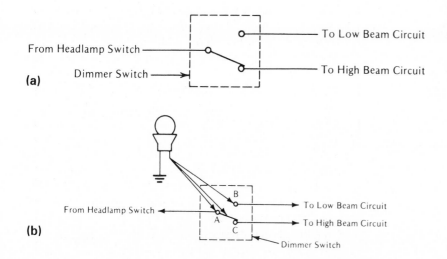

FIGURE 6-21 (a) Dimmer switch wiring circuit; (b) basic test of dimmer switch using either a test lamp or voltmeter.

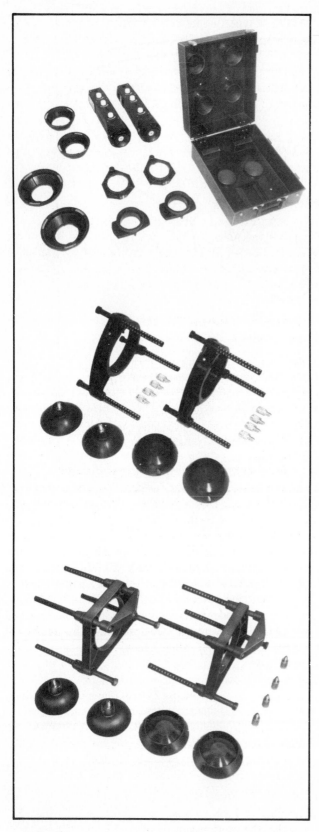

FIGURE 6-22 Headlight aiming tool kit, J25300-A. (*Courtesy of Kent-Moore Heavy Duty Division, SPX Corporation.*)

J 25300-A
Headlight Aimer

APPLICATION: UNIVERSAL

In the J 25300-A, Kent-Moore presents an aimer for all round and dual rectangular sealed beam lamps. Additional flexibility may be introduced by the addition of the new J 25300-10 adapter for 5 x 8 single rectangular sealed beams (Not part of J 25300-A).

The SQUARE PAIR aimers represent a new design, new materials, new concepts with major new advantages for you that include:

- PUSH BUTTON VACUUM RELEASE — For quick and easy removal of the aimer without disturbing adjustment.
- OPTICAL CONTRAST BUBBLE — Improves the bubble visibility at low light levels.
- GRAVITY CAM FOLLOWERS — Completely eliminates backlash and gives more accurate dial readings.
- PLANETARY GEARS — Gives four-to-one vernier type dial movement for accurate checking of headlight aim.
- OFFSET DIAL — Eliminates the need for a screwdriver in floor slope compensation.

2. The only load on the vehicle should be that of a half-full gas tank or fuel tank (diesel).

3. Are the springs or shock absorbers OK? Not weak or broken?

4. Check all tire pressures and inflate to recommended levels. Allow for hot or cold tire conditions.

5. If the vehicle has sustained accident damage, are the wheel alignment and rear-axle tracking path correct?

Next, clean the headlamp lenses and obtain the particular vehicle manufacturer's special headlight aiming kit, such as the one shown in Fig. 6-22, which will speed this adjustment. If these special headlight aiming tools are not readily available, a headlight aiming screen can be used, such as shown in Fig. 6-23. The screen used should have a matte-white surface finish that is well shaded from outside or reflected light sources.

When an aiming screen arrangement is used to adjust the vehicle headlights, the high and low beams should be adjusted until they appear as shown in Fig. 6-23. When adjusting truck headlights without the aid of a special headlight aiming tool, average requirements are that the high-intensity zone of the high beam of inner lamps on dual units be straight ahead and 51 mm (2 in.) below the headlamp horizontal level at a distance of 7.6 m (25 ft). The low beam of outer lamps of dual units and all 178-mm (7-in.)-diameter headlights should be adjusted so that the high-intensity zone of the lamp beam is just off to the right of the headlamp vertical centerline as well as being just below the headlamp level when at a distance of 7.6 m (25 ft). Headlight adjustment should always be performed with a truck loaded since this is more reflective of normal operating conditions.

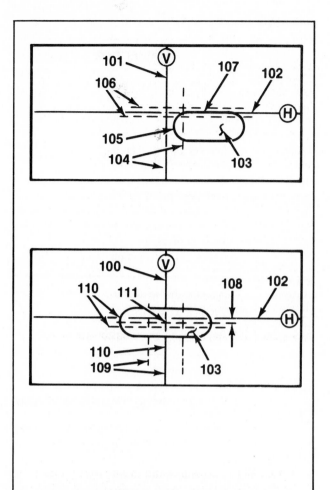

101. Vertical Centerline — Straight ahead of Light Bulb Center.
102. Horizontal Centerline — Located at the level of the Light Bulb Center.
103. High Intensity Zone.
104. Limits: V to 6 inches to the right.
105. Lateral Aim — Left edge of the High Intensity Zone which is located 2 inches to the right of (V). The limits are from (V) to 6 inches to the right of (V).
106. Limits — Horizontal Centerline plus or minus 2 inches.
107. Vertical Aim — Top edge of the High Intensity Zone which is located at the Horizontal Centerline.
108. 2 inches.
109. Limits — Plus or minus 6 inches.
110. Lateral Aim — High Intensity Zone is centered on the Vertical Centerline.
111. Vertical Aim — High Intensity Zone is centered 2 inches below the Horizontal Centerline.

FIGURE 6-23 Visual headlamp beam adjustment sequence. (*Courtesy of GMC Truck Division, General Motors Corporation.*)

NOTE: A type 1 upper beam $5\frac{3}{4}$-in. (146-mm)-diameter headlamp is a single-filament bulb lamp that is used in a four-lamp system to provide the principal portion of the upper beam. A type 2, $5\frac{3}{4}$-in. (146-mm) sealed beam headlight is a unit with two filaments used in a four-lamp system to provide the lower beam and a secondary portion of the upper beam. A type 2, 7-in. (178-mm) is used in a system employing two sealed beam units. When a numeral 2 is molded in the lens, the unit provides an upper and a lower beam. Sealed beam units that can be identified by the absence of the 2 on the lens should be aimed visually on the upper beam.

Numbers commonly found on rectangular headlamps are listed in Tables 6-2 through 6-6. However, these units can also be identified by a code on the lens; 1A identifies the lamp as an inner or high-beam unit, while 2A indicates that the lamp is an outer or low-beam unit.

HEADLIGHT TROUBLESHOOTING AND REPLACEMENT

Problems with headlight malfunction can be traced to such simple things as loose or corroded terminals, especially with plug-in bayonet connector harnesses. Poor grounds can also be a cause of failure. Damaged and corroded wiring or an overheated circuit breaker (contained within the headlight switch on some vehicles) can cause the headlights to fail to operate.

The circuit breaker employed by some vehicle manufacturers ensures that if an overload occurs to the headlight circuit, the circuit breaker will trip open and the headlights will not operate until the breaker cools, after which time it will reclose. However, if the overload condition continues, the lights will blink on and off. To assist you with effective troubleshooting of a headlight system, refer to Table 6-7 which lists typical problems, possible causes, and corrections.

Damaged or burned-out sealed beam headlamps must be replaced as a complete assembly, while headlights using replaceable halogen bulbs can simply have the light bulb removed and replaced. To remove the sealed beam headlight, you have to remove the chrome trim and retaining ring around the headlight. One such example is illustrated in Fig. 6-24 for a single-headlight arrangement. On replaceable bulb models, you can generally access the bulb from the back side of the headlight. On heavy-duty conventional cab or COE (cab over engine) models, you can tilt the hood or complete cab forward to gain easy access to the headlight.

CAUTION: Prior to tilting a COE unit forward, make sure that the transmission gear shift lever inside the cab is in a position that will not interfere with the cab's movement. In addition, secure any item or component that could fall forward from the cab or sleeper compartment that could crack or break the windshield as the cab is tilted forward.

TABLE 6-7 Diagnosis of a headlamp system

PROBLEM	POSSIBLE CAUSE	CORRECTION
Headlamp Broken, Cracked or Discolored Inside	Impact damage or improperly installed or damaged terminals.	Replace the headlamp.
Headlamp Does Not Light or Lights Intermittently	1. Wrong wiring connections to terminals. 2. Wrong voltage at upper and lower beam terminals. 3. Faulty ground connections of headlamp connector to body.	1. Correct the connections. 2. Replace the headlamp. 3. Replace the headlamp.
Headlamp Filament Glows Dimly	1. Open ground connection. 2. Wrong headlamp.	1. Repair the open. 2. Replace the headlamp.
Headlamp Will Not Aim Properly	1. Chipped or broken aiming pad on lens. 2. Improper calibration and floor compensation of mechanical aimers. 3. Faulty unit retaining components.	1. Replace the headlamp. 2. Move to new location. 3. Replace the retaining components.
One Headlamp Out	1. Faulty headlamp. 2. Corroded headlamp and connector terminals. 3. Open circuit.	1. Replace headlamp. 2. Clean headlamp and connector terminals by scraping, emery cloth and spray cleaner. 3. Check connector terminals for voltage and ground. Repair as needed.
Both Headlamps Out	1. Blown fuse. 2. Faulty dimmer switch.	1. Check and replace fuse. 2. Replace dimmer switch.
Both Headlamp Low Beams or High Beams Out	Faulty dimmer switch.	Replace dimmer switch.
Headlamp Too Bright and/or Burns Out Quickly	1. Faulty voltage regulator. 2. Wrong headlamp.	1. Replace voltage regulator. 2. Check the headlamp for a 6 volt unit in a 12 volt system. Install the proper headlamp.
Both Headlamps Dim	1. Faulty generator ground wire. 2. Loose connections from generator to headlamps. 3. Corroded connections. 4. Faulty switches.	1. Repair or connect as needed. 2. Connect or tighten connections. 3. Clean connections. 4. Bypass switches with jumper and replace if necessary.
Headlamp Flickers	1. Loose connections. 2. Faulty dimmer switch. 3. Broken wire(s).	1. Check and tighten connections. 2. Replace dimmer switch. 3. Repair wire or wires as needed.
Headlamp Beams Won't Change When Dimmer Switch Is Cycled	Faulty dimmer switch.	Replace the switch.

Source: GMC Medium Duty Truck Division, General Motors Corporation

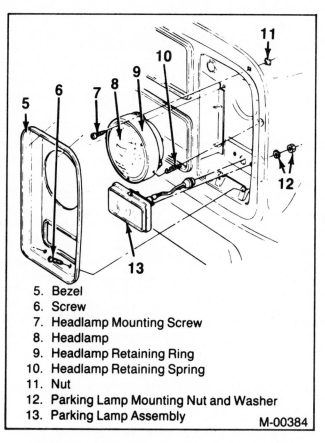

5. Bezel
6. Screw
7. Headlamp Mounting Screw
8. Headlamp
9. Headlamp Retaining Ring
10. Headlamp Retaining Spring
11. Nut
12. Parking Lamp Mounting Nut and Washer
13. Parking Lamp Assembly

M-00384

FIGURE 6-24 Replacing a single round headlamp assembly. (*Courtesy of GMC Truck Division, General Motors Corporation.*)

Removal of the headlight involves the following:
1. Removal of the headlight bezel retaining screws.
2. Bezel (chrome trim) removal.
3. Retaining ring screw removal. Be careful not to alter the position of the headlight adjusting screws, although in some instances where corrosion or rust has affected the ability of the headlight to be removed, you may be forced into loosening the adjusting screws.

SERVICE TIP: Any time that a sealed beam headlight is to be removed, count the actual number of full or partial turns that the adjusting screws have to be loosened to gain adequate clearance. Once the new lamp has been installed, it is much easier if you run the adjustment screws back in to the same position that they were in previously. In this way, headlamp adjustment requires a minimum amount of time to check and reset.

4. Remove the retaining ring spring using a hooked tool that you can fabricate from a piece of oxyacetylene welding wire.
5. Remove the retaining ring from the mounting ring.
6. Remove the actual headlight.
7. Pull off the plug-in electrical connector on the back of the sealed beam unit.
8. Installation of the new unit is basically the reverse of removal.

If dual fog lamps or dual road driving lamps are mounted below the front bumper or inserted in a bumper cutaway, sealed beam units require complete replacement if burned out. If they have replaceable light bulbs, they

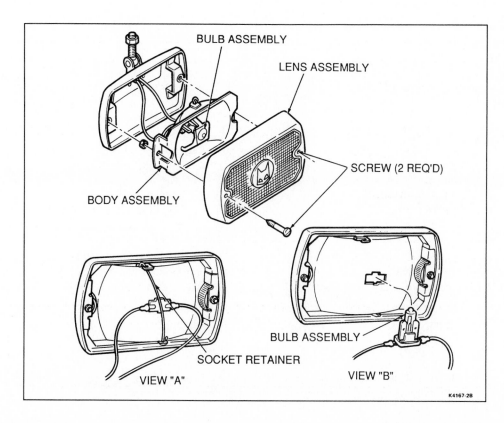

FIGURE 6-25 Fog and road lamp bulb replacement on a model LTL-9000 truck. (*Reprinted with Ford Motor Company's permission.*)

can be replaced as shown in Fig. 6-25 by removing the lens cover assembly.

SERVICE TIP: Any time that you have to replace a halogen bulb in a headlight, fog light, or driving light, exercise care when handling the new bulb. Do *not* touch the bulb or the bulb contact surfaces, since dirt, sweat, or fluid from your hands can shorten the life of a new bulb. Always grasp the new bulb by its circular collar with clean, dry hands and install it into its holder gently but firmly.

TAILLAMP ASSEMBLIES

The physical shape of the taillamp, the number used and the specific location will vary between makes and classifications of trucks; however, most lamp lenses are constructed from a polycarbonate material for toughness and durability. The term *taillamp* indicates that it is located at the rear of the vehicle and it is designed to provide illumination for the stop, tail, direction, backup, and license plate systems. Tables 6-2, 6-3 and 6-4, and 6-5 list typical light bulb numbers used in taillamp assemblies.

Some truck models offer a warning system to indicate to the truck driver when a stoplamp bulb or a taillamp bulb turns out, or when the taillamp circuit has an open circuit. Should an open circuit occur in the taillamp circuit, the taillamp/stoplamp malfunction detector relay located in the left taillamp assembly turns on the warning lamp in the indicator and warning lamp strip located on the instrument panel. This light will remain ON until power is disconnected from the circuit. Figure 6-26 illustrates one example of how the vehicle taillamp harness

is routed along the truck chassis frame. The power supply to the taillamp circuit generally originates at the cab-located fuse/circuit breaker panel, where the wiring runs to the main lamp switch on light- and medium-duty trucks, or to individual toggle switches on the instrument panel on heavy-duty truck models. On medium-duty trucks, the circuit from the control switch splits; one part feeding the front parking lights while the other feeds the rear taillamps. Power usually enters the left taillamp at the terminal block on the lamp, where the wiring then branches off to the right taillamp assembly as shown in the typical wire harness arrangement shown in Fig. 6-26. On heavy-duty class 8 truck/tractors, the taillamp power supply may start, for example, at the cab-located Dill Blox fuse/circuit breaker panel on both Kenworth and Peterbilt trucks. This Dill Blox is located inside the cab at the left-hand forward corner, behind the kick panel. The center lower section of the Dill Blox contains manual reset circuit breakers to control the ignition, taillights, stoplights, and left and right headlights. Other heavy-duty truck models may employ a junction box located as shown in Fig. 6-27 behind item 331. One example of the actual connections behind the taillight lens cover would appear as shown in Fig. 6-28.

In the taillight system shown in Fig. 6-27, there are two bulbs installed in each lamp assembly, with the upper bulb being a single-contact No. 1156, and the lower bulb is a double-contact No. 1157. In both the 1156 and 1157 bulbs the plane of the pins with respect to the filament is $90° \pm 15°$. Both bulb types are classified as type S-8. For specific information on bulbs, refer to Tables 6-1 through 6-4. When two bulbs are used in a lamp

FIGURE 6-26 Taillamp harness wiring. (*Courtesy of GMC Truck Division, General Motors Corporation.*)

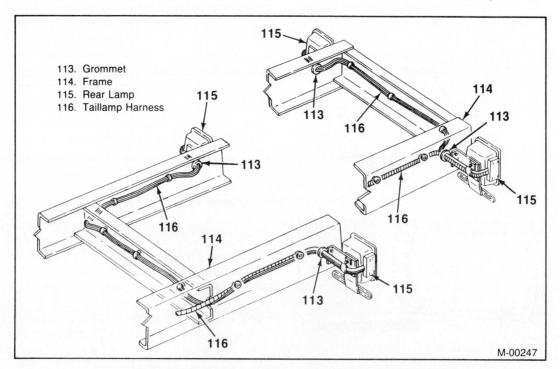

113. Grommet
114. Frame
115. Rear Lamp
116. Taillamp Harness

M-00247

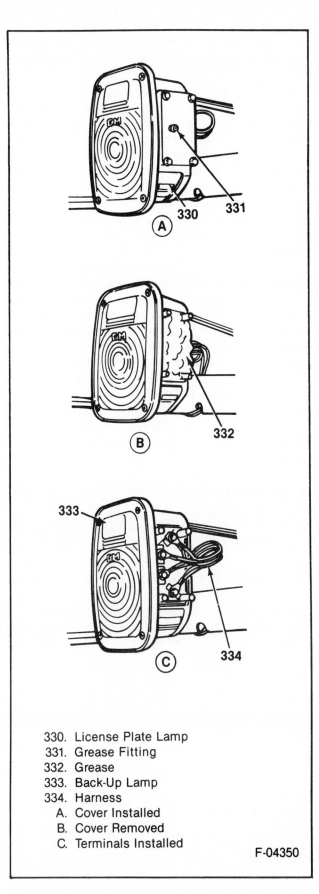

330. License Plate Lamp
331. Grease Fitting
332. Grease
333. Back-Up Lamp
334. Harness
  A. Cover Installed
  B. Cover Removed
  C. Terminals Installed

F-04350

FIGURE 6-27 Taillamp and harness features. (*Courtesy of GMC Truck Division, General Motors Corporation.*)

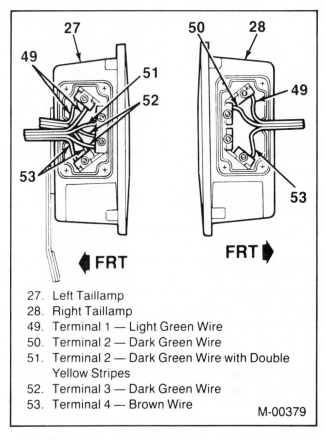

27. Left Taillamp
28. Right Taillamp
49. Terminal 1 — Light Green Wire
50. Terminal 2 — Dark Green Wire
51. Terminal 2 — Dark Green Wire with Double Yellow Stripes
52. Terminal 3 — Dark Green Wire
53. Terminal 4 — Brown Wire

M-00379

FIGURE 6-28 Taillamp terminal blocks ID (*Courtesy of GMC Truck Division, General Motors Corporation.*)

assembly, a shield is generally installed between the upper and lower sections of the lamp housing to prevent cross-illumination between the lamp functions. Often, these types of lamps will employ a clear lens in the bottom-side section to disperse lamp illumination toward the license plate when the taillights are on. Other heavy-duty trucks often employ a junction block located close to the left headlamp, since the wire feed to the taillights taps off the forward harness assembly. One example is shown in Fig. 6-29, which also identifies the typical wire circuits originating from this rear lamp junction block.

SPECIAL NOTE: To prevent corrosion at the junction block terminals, there is usually a cover to enclose the wiring and connections. A chassis lubricant should be injected into the junction block cavity (not a graphite-based grease) through the grease fitting identified as item 331 in Fig. 6-27 and through item 310 in Fig. 6-29.

Stoplamp Circuit

The stoplamp is a part of the taillight unit shown in Fig. 6-27 and usually receives its power supply from the in-cab circuit breaker panel. The circuit breaker will then feed to the stoplight switch and then to a junction block, where it then branches off to the rear of the vehicle via the chassis harness. The location of the stoplamp switch varies between vehicles, but is usually positioned so that

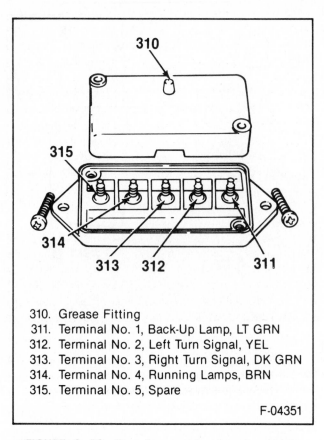

310. Grease Fitting
311. Terminal No. 1, Back-Up Lamp, LT GRN
312. Terminal No. 2, Left Turn Signal, YEL
313. Terminal No. 3, Right Turn Signal, DK GRN
314. Terminal No. 4, Running Lamps, BRN
315. Terminal No. 5, Spare

F-04351

FIGURE 6-29 Rear lamp wiring junction block. (*Courtesy of GMC Truck Division, General Motors Corporation.*)

when the brake pedal linkage is actuated, the switch will be closed to energize the stoplamp bulbs. Vehicles with hydraulic brakes normally employ a plunger switch assembly that is mounted to the brake pedal arm, an example of which is illustrated in Fig. 6-30. Some trucks may employ an actuating lever that is connected to the stoplamp switch. The lever is moved by brake linkage stroking action to open or close the switch contacts. When

the brake pedal is in the OFF or released position, the return spring on the pedal linkage will force the linkage to push the switch plunger into the switch housing, causing it to remain in an open position. Therefore, no current can flow through the stoplight switch at this time. When the brake pedal is depressed, a spring within the stoplight switch plunger will cause the plunger to move out from the housing, thereby closing the switch contacts and completing the electrical circuit, to allow the stoplight bulbs to illuminate. In some instances it may be necessary to adjust the plunger-type stoplamp switch in its retainer bracket by rotation of the retaining nut to ensure that the switch will remain open when the brakes are released.

On heavy-duty trucks that employ air brakes, a plunger switch is usually not used. Normally, two switches are employed, such as those shown in Fig. 6-31. One switch serves the truck brake service supply line during normal service brake application from the pedal, while the other one serves to activate the stoplamps when the emergency line is drained of compressed air. These two stoplamp switches are screwed into suitable brass fittings or elbows as shown in the diagram. When a stoplamp problem exists, check for a blown fuse or an open circuit breaker, a faulty stoplamp switch, a bad ground at the bulb socket through corrosion, or power not reaching the lights.

Directional Signal Lights

The control for the vehicle directional signal lights can be a separate steering column–mounted lever, or it can be a combination stalk lever mounted on the steering column that is also designed to operate the horn, the windshield washers and wipers, the headlight dimmer switch, and the directional signal lights. Figure 6-20 shows a combination-type switch assembly. Generally, when this lever is pulled toward the driver of the truck, a left-hand turn is indicated, and when the lever is moved away from the

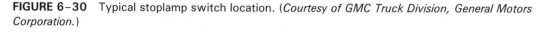

FIGURE 6-30 Typical stoplamp switch location. (*Courtesy of GMC Truck Division, General Motors Corporation.*)

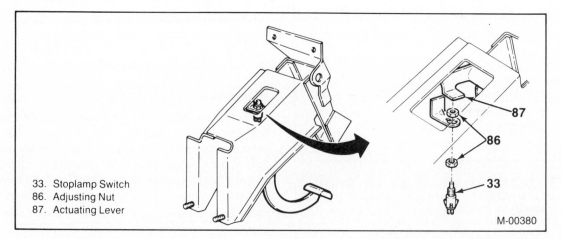

33. Stoplamp Switch
86. Adjusting Nut
87. Actuating Lever

M-00380

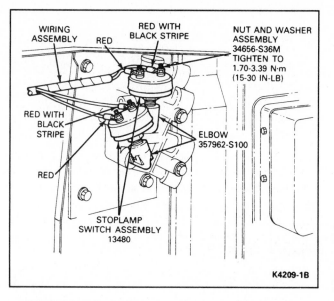

FIGURE 6-31 Stoplamp switch location for an air brake equipped truck. (*Reprinted with Ford Motor Company's permission.*)

driver, a right-hand turn is indicated. This is usually confirmed to the driver by a directional signal light in the form of an illuminated arrow flashing on/off repeatedly. These arrows are located on the instrument panel. In addition, the signal flasher unit located in the vicinity of the fuse/circuit breaker box area will emanate a clicking sound when the signal lights are operating as the switch opens and closes repeatedly. On some trucks the steering column–mounted control lever may self-cancel once the steering wheel is returned to a straight-ahead position, while on others you may have to manually pull the lever back to the center/neutral position after completion of a turn.

The wiring for the directional signal control lever is usually located behind the steering column and may be accessed by removing the trim covering around the steering column assembly. Figure 6-32 illustrates a simplified circuit that could be used to operate the directional signal lighting system. This system is arranged so that power

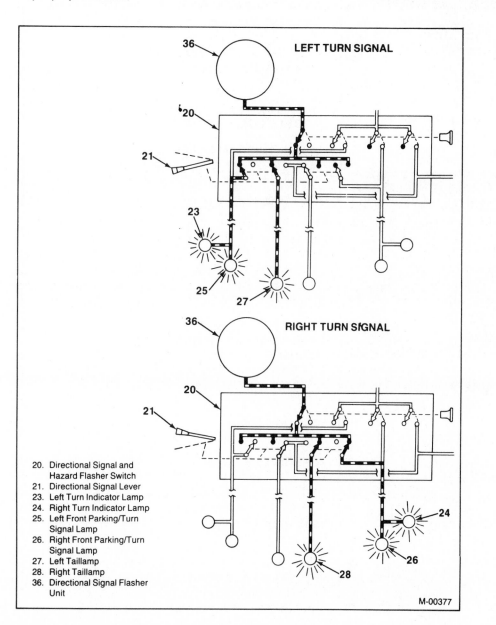

FIGURE 6-32 Directional signal wiring and current flow paths. (*Courtesy of GMC Truck Division, General Motors Corporation.*)

20. Directional Signal and Hazard Flasher Switch
21. Directional Signal Lever
23. Left Turn Indicator Lamp
24. Right Turn Indicator Lamp
25. Left Front Parking/Turn Signal Lamp
26. Right Front Parking/Turn Signal Lamp
27. Left Taillamp
28. Right Taillamp
36. Directional Signal Flasher Unit

from the fuse/circuit breaker panel feeds to the directional signal flasher unit, shown as item 36 in the diagram.

NOTE: Some trucks may employ two flasher units, one for the directional signal lights and one for operating the vehicle hazard lights. Others may only employ one (combined) flasher unit to handle both duties.

If the truck driver moves the directional signal control lever (item 21 in Fig. 6-32) toward him or her (downward), the left-hand turn bulbs would flash as follows. In the upper part of Fig. 6-32, the turn signal switch contacts in item 20 would close to complete the circuit from the signal flasher unit (36) to the left-turn indicator lamp (23) on the instrument panel, and to the left front indica-

FIGURE 6–33 Features of heavy-duty signal lamp flashers. (*Courtesy of Dominion Automotive Industries, Inc.*)

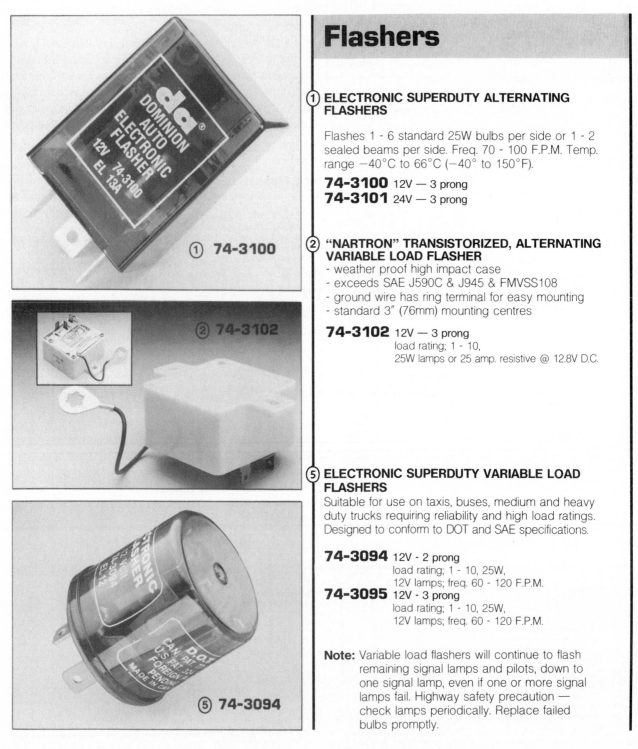

Flashers

① ELECTRONIC SUPERDUTY ALTERNATING FLASHERS

Flashes 1 - 6 standard 25W bulbs per side or 1 - 2 sealed beams per side. Freq. 70 - 100 F.P.M. Temp. range −40°C to 66°C (−40° to 150°F).

74-3100 12V — 3 prong
74-3101 24V — 3 prong

② "NARTRON" TRANSISTORIZED, ALTERNATING VARIABLE LOAD FLASHER
- weather proof high impact case
- exceeds SAE J590C & J945 & FMVSS108
- ground wire has ring terminal for easy mounting
- standard 3" (76mm) mounting centres

74-3102 12V — 3 prong
load rating; 1 - 10,
25W lamps or 25 amp. resistive @ 12.8V D.C.

⑤ ELECTRONIC SUPERDUTY VARIABLE LOAD FLASHERS
Suitable for use on taxis, buses, medium and heavy duty trucks requiring reliability and high load ratings. Designed to conform to DOT and SAE specifications.

74-3094 12V - 2 prong
load rating; 1 - 10, 25W,
12V lamps; freq. 60 - 120 F.P.M.
74-3095 12V - 3 prong
load rating; 1 - 10, 25W,
12V lamps; freq. 60 - 120 F.P.M.

Note: Variable load flashers will continue to flash remaining signal lamps and pilots, down to one signal lamp, even if one or more signal lamps fail. Highway safety precaution — check lamps periodically. Replace failed bulbs promptly.

tor lamp (23) as well as the left rear indicator lamp (27). Within the actual flasher unit (36), current passes through a bimetallic spring (see Fig. 5-16) which has an electrical contact at one end. Any time that current passes through a bimetallic spring contact, heat is generated and the bimetallic spring will expand, thereby breaking the contact and opening the circuit, which prevents further illumination of the light bulbs. Due to the design feature of the bimetallic spring chosen, it will cool fairly quickly and the contacts are closed again, resulting in further illumination of the bulbs. This rapid oscillation from a closed–open–closed–open circuit results in the light bulbs flashing on/off to signal the direction of vehicle movement. Some types of heavy-duty flasher units employ solid-state

transistorized circuitry rather than a bimetallic strip to perform the same function. Figure 6-33 shows some typical flasher units.

Moving the directional signal switch lever (item 21 in Fig. 6-32) results in the same operating procedure as for the left-turn system described above, except for the fact that bulbs 24, 26, and 28 for the right-hand side of the vehicle will flash on/off. This circuitry is shown in the bottom half of Fig. 6-32. If the directional signal control lever (item 21 in Fig. 6-32) is placed in a turn position and the truck driver depresses the brake pedal, only one of the rear stoplight bulbs will illuminate since the same bulb and filament is usually used for both stop and signal conditions.

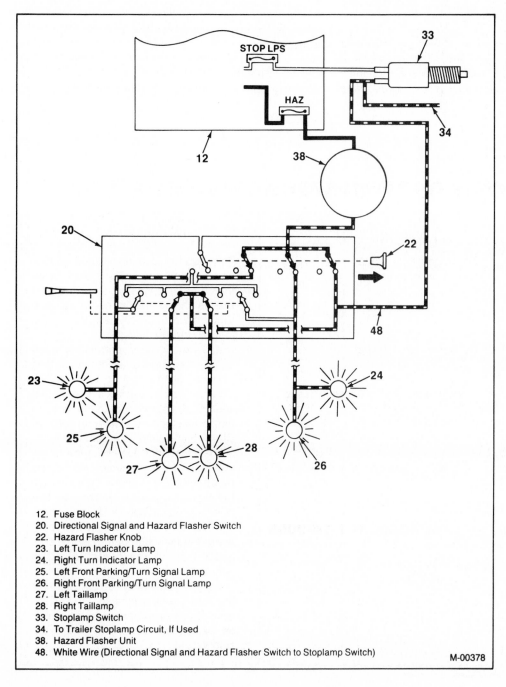

FIGURE 6-34 Hazard light flasher system current flow path. (*Courtesy of GMC Medium Duty Truck Division, General Motors Corporation.*)

12. Fuse Block
20. Directional Signal and Hazard Flasher Switch
22. Hazard Flasher Knob
23. Left Turn Indicator Lamp
24. Right Turn Indicator Lamp
25. Left Front Parking/Turn Signal Lamp
26. Right Front Parking/Turn Signal Lamp
27. Left Taillamp
28. Right Taillamp
33. Stoplamp Switch
34. To Trailer Stoplamp Circuit, If Used
38. Hazard Flasher Unit
48. White Wire (Directional Signal and Hazard Flasher Switch to Stoplamp Switch)

M-00378

The best way to understand this is to refer to Fig. 6-34, which shows a complete system arrangement for a directional signal, hazard, and taillight system. When the driver depresses the brake pedal, the stoplight switch (33) circuit is closed to allow current to flow through wire 48, which supplies power to the directional signal and hazard flasher switch (20). Switch 20 will relay a steady flow of current to both taillamps 27 and 28 via wires 45 and 46 for stoplamp bulb illumination. During the combination stoplight/directional signal action, switch 20 will supply a steady flow of current only to the taillamp bulb that is not already being pulsed on/off to indicate the vehicle direction. Therefore, only the rear bulb not indicating the turn will receive power to its stoplamp to advise following car/truck drivers that the vehicle is in fact being braked as well as negotiating a turning maneuver.

When faced with a troubleshooting problem in the directional turn signal light circuitry, the problem may be due to a faulty bulb, corrosion, an open or short in the circuit or a faulty flasher unit. Table 6-8 lists some typical problems, causes, and suggested corrections. Note in this table that any reference to a specific color of wiring relates only to certain models of GMC trucks.

Hazard Flasher Circuit

The hazard flasher circuit is controlled by either a separate flasher unit or can be combined into a single unit that controls both the directional signal and flasher light systems. Power is fed to the hazard flasher from the fuse/circuit breaker panel on the vehicle. Figure 6-34 illustrates the action of the vehicle hazard flasher system when it is necessary to park the vehicle in a nonparking zone or when the vehicle must be left standing due to mechanical failure or accident.

The hazard flasher control can be in the form of a rocker switch, a pushbutton switch, or a small toggle switch located on the steering column. When pulled out, the control switch (22) in Fig. 6-34 causes three contacts within the directional and hazard switch (20) to change their previous positions. Power flow is disconnected from the directional signal flasher to the directional signal switch contacts; this pulsing current then flows from the

TABLE 6-8 Diagnosis chart for turn signal problems

DIAGNOSIS OF TURN SIGNALS (BOTH SIDES)

PROBLEM	POSSIBLE CAUSE	CORRECTION
Hazard Flasher Indicators Do Not Light	1. Turn signal fuse is open.	1. Turn hazard warning system "OFF" and position turn signal switch for either turn. If lamps work, turn signal fuse is O.K. If fuse is open, find and repair short between the fuse and the lamps. Replace fuse.
	2. Defective signal flasher.	2. Install a known good, correct part number, turn signal flasher. If circuit does not work, go to step 3.
	3. Power not getting from fuse to flasher.	3. Check for power, using a 12-Volt test light, on the purple wire at the turn signal connector on the steering column. Check both sides of the connector. If the test light does not glow on either side of the connector, locate and repair the open in circuit from the fuse block through the flasher to the steering column connector. If the test light glows when connected to feed side of turn signal connector, clean the contacts in the connector. If the test light glows on both sides of the turn signal connector, repair the wiring from the connector to the switch or replace the turn signal switch assembly.

Source: GMC Truck Division, General Motors Corporation.

TABLE 6-8 *(Continued)*

DIAGNOSIS OF TURN SIGNALS (ONE SIDE ONLY)

PROBLEM	POSSIBLE CAUSE	CORRECTION
Turn Signal Lamp Off, Indicator Lamp On, Flasher Cannot Be Heard	1. Burned out bulb. 2. Faulty ground. 3. Open circuit.	1. Check the bulbs and replace the faulty bulb. 2. Check the ground at the bulb socket. 3. Determine wire color at bulb and locate the wire at the turn signal connector. Use a 12-volt test light to test for voltage in wire and connector. (Do not disconnect connector while checking with test light). 　　If the test light glows, locate and repair the open circuit from the connector to the lamp socket. 　　If the test light does not glow at either side of the connector, check for a faulty turn signal switch.
Turn Signal Lamp Off. Flasher Cannot Be Heard. Indicator Lamp Does Not Light.	1. Open circuit breaker or blown fuse. 2. Burned out bulb. 3. Open circuit.	1. Check and reset open circuit breaker or replace blown fuse. If circuit breaker opens or fuse blows, check circuit for a short or ground. 2. Check and replace any burned out bulbs. Also check indicator lamp bulb. 3. Use a 12-volt test light and check at bulb socket connector for voltage in wire to indicator lamp (lt. blue-left, dk. blue-right). If the test light glows, check for a faulty ground. If the test light does not glow, find and repair open circuit between bulb socket and turn signal connector.
Turn Signal Lamp Off. Indicator Lamp Off. Flasher Is Heard.	1. A short or grounded wire at either front or rear lamp circuit.	1. Locate the ground in the front or rear circuit by disconnecting the front lamp circuit at the front body connector. If the flasher can still be heard but no lamps operate, repair the short between the front lamp circuit and the turn signal switch. 　　If the flasher now stops operating and indicator lamp stays on, this is normal. 　　Now, connect the front lamp circuit and disconnect the rear lamps at the connector or junction box on the rear lamp. 　　Now, if the flasher cannot be heard but the indicator and front turn signal lamps stay on, repair the short between the connector and the rear lamp assembly. However, if the flasher can be heard and the indicator lamp and turn signal lamps are off, find and repair the short between the front lamp and connector or junction.

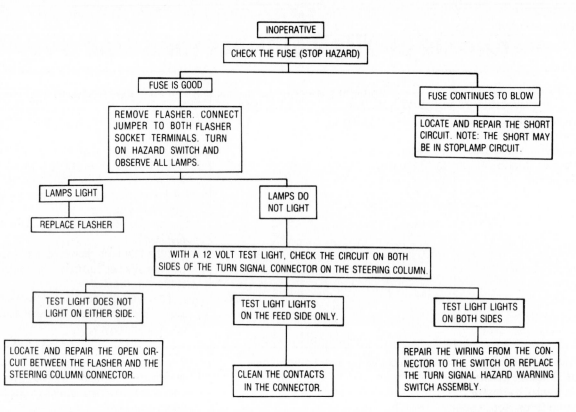

FIGURE 6–35 Diagnosis chart for the hazard warning lamp circuit. (*Courtesy of GMC Truck Division, General Motors Corporation.*)

hazard flasher unit (38) to both turn signal lamps (23 and 24). Power also flows to both front parking and directional signal lamps (25 and 26), as well as to both taillamps (27 and 28). Power would also be directed to any auxiliary stoplamp circuit, such as a trailer connector through wire 48 to the stoplamp switch (33). Upon a brake application, however, a steady nonpulsing current will flow to all six lamps (23, 24, 25, 26, 27, and 28) in the hazard warning circuit.

Many problems with the hazard warning circuit can be considered common to the directional signal circuit, particularly when both systems use a common flasher switch unit. Figure 6-35 shows some typical problems, possible cures, and suggested corrections.

CLEARANCE AND MARKER LAMPS

The clearance and marker lamps are designed to outline the truck/tractor and straight truck body or trailer assembly dimensions. (For more information on semitrailer lamp wiring, refer to Fig. 5-58). Clearance and marker lamps on a truck/tractor are mounted across the front of the cab roof and receive power from the cab wiring harness, as shown in Figs. 5-1 and 5-5. The power circuit originates at the fuse/circuit breaker panel and then feeds to a control switch, which may be a rocker, pull, or toggle switch. Power flow through the cab roof harness illuminates all lamps in a parallel hookup (see Chapter 1 for a description of a parallel system). Figure 6-36(a)

illustrates a round type of marker lamp, and Fig. 6-36(b) shows the design features of what is commonly referred to as a *west coast* marker/clearance lamp. The round marker lamp usually has its bulb and socket grounded by a wire with a clip terminal connected to the outer roof panel underneath the marker lamp assembly mounting pad. West coast lamps are normally grounded by the forward mounting screw through a wire terminal.

BACKUP LAMPS

Backup lamps are illuminated any time the driver selects reverse gear in the transmission, whether it is a gear shift or automatic model. The backup lamp switch is installed so that it will be activated by the transmission shift linkage either externally or internally. Figure 6-37 illustrates some typical examples of backup lamp switch locations on some gear shift and Allison automatic transmissions that would be used with medium-duty and medium-heavy-duty trucks. On class 8 heavy-duty trucks, the switch would also be located as illustrated in Fig. 6-37. Usually, the backup switch is activated through the transmission reverse shift rail in a gear shift mechanical transmission, while on an Allison automatic transmission the switch is powered by the reverse signal oil pressure within the transmission oil gallery. Power to the backup lamp switch usually originates at the fuse block or circuit breaker panel, with a fuse/breaker rating of 10 to 30 A being used, depending on the vehicle. Power flows to the

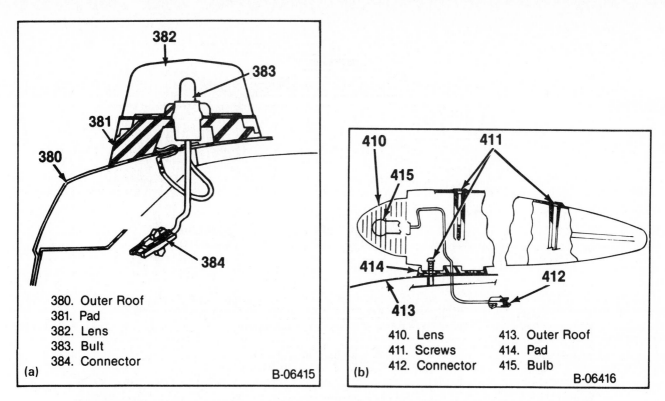

(a)

380. Outer Roof
381. Pad
382. Lens
383. Bult
384. Connector

B-06415

(b)

410. Lens
411. Screws
412. Connector
413. Outer Roof
414. Pad
415. Bulb

B-06416

FIGURE 6–36 Marker and clearance lamp: (a) round type; (b) west coast type. (*Courtesy of GMC Truck Division, General Motors Corporation.*)

FIGURE 6–37 Reversing/backup lamp switch locations on standard gear shift and automatic transmissions. (*Courtesy of GMC Truck Division, General Motors Corporation.*)

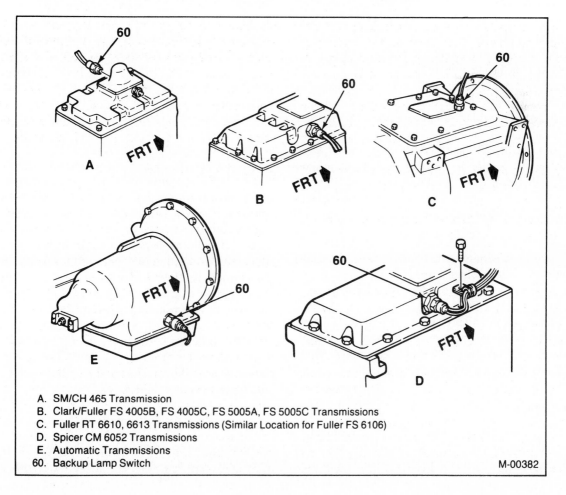

A. SM/CH 465 Transmission
B. Clark/Fuller FS 4005B, FS 4005C, FS 5005A, FS 5005C Transmissions
C. Fuller RT 6610, 6613 Transmissions (Similar Location for Fuller FS 6106)
D. Spicer CM 6052 Transmissions
E. Automatic Transmissions
60. Backup Lamp Switch

M-00382

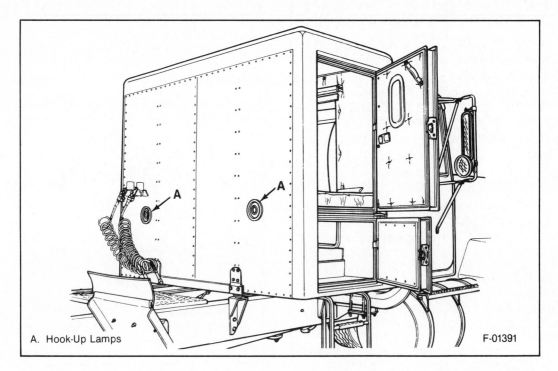

A. Hook-Up Lamps   F-01391

FIGURE 6-38 Location of sleeper cab hookup lamps. (*Courtesy of GMC Truck Division, General Motors Corporation.*)

switch and then passes to the rear lamp junction block, where it energizes the backup lamp bulbs within the taillight assembly or to a separate backup lighting system.

In addition to the backup lamps located within the taillight assemblies, many heavy-duty truck/tractors employ auxiliary spotlamps that are mounted on support brackets at roof level on the outside of the cab. These spotlamps will not be activated from the transmission switch, but are controlled by a separate toggle switch on the instrument or auxiliary lighting console. These reversing spotlamps would be fed from the fuse/circuit breaker panel, and the fuse/breaker would be labeled to allow the technician to locate the circuit. These reversing spotlamps usually have a replaceable bulb assembly.

TRUCK-TRACTOR HOOKUP LAMPS

Both conventional and COE (cab over engine) truck tractors are equipped with hookup lamps to assist the driver when hitching or unhitching a semitrailer at night. Figure 6-38 illustrates one example of where these hookup lamps might be found on a COE (cab over engine) sleeper cab model. These lamps usually use an 1156 bulb that is accessible after removing the lamp lens covers. These lights are usually fed directly from the fuse/circuit breaker panel and an independent toggle switch.

DOME LAMPS

The interior cab lights or dome lamps can be controlled from a separate rocker switch on the instrument panel console, or may be part of the parking and headlamp switch as shown in Fig. 6-16, item 10, where rotation of the switch control knob will result in power being fed to the dome light. Dome lamps can be installed on both sides of the cab above the doors and also at both ends of the sleeper compartment. In some heavy-duty trucks the sleeper compartment lighting is controlled by an independent switch. Some trucks may use a center lamp and two reading lamps, with the center lamp being turned on by switches in the door jams (spring loaded to complete the circuit), while the reading lamps can be turned on either by switches in each end of the dome lamp housing or by console-mounted control switches. The dome lights are protected by a fuse or circuit breaker, with the wire feeding from the protective panel to the instrument panel and then up through the door pillar to the roof harness; alternatively, the harness may begin at the electric panel on the cab rear wall and pass upward and then to the center of the cab where the light is located. Figure 6-39 illustrates a round dome light with a small switch item 214 located on the left-hand side of the assembly, and Fig. 6-40 shows a rectangular dome light arrangement.

To change the light bulb inside the dome lamp, take a small electric screwdriver and insert it between the lens and the bezel at the lug areas, then gently squeeze the lens with your fingers as you pry downward with the screwdriver. Take care during this operation not to crack the lens or break the small lugs off.

HEATED AND LIGHTED MIRRORS

Most heavy-duty truck/tractors have small marker/clearance lights located on the outside of the mirrors on each side of the cab. In addition, many trucks that operate in wet and snowy weather employ heating strips behind the mirror glass. Some heavy-duty truck mirror manufacturers now offer small electric motors in the mirror base to allow mirror adjustment from the driver's seat in the cab. Figure 6-41 illustrates the location of the mirrors for a conventional cab truck, along with the location of the mirror wiring harness. On COE truck models the wiring harness would pass across the truck just below the windshield. The dual mirror heaters are activated by a dash/instrument console–mounted toggle switch which usually indicates ON, OFF, and HIGH or LOW heating positions. The wire harness originates at a circuit breaker, then goes to the toggle control switch and mirror heater condition indicator lamp. From the back side of the instrument panel the wiring exits through the cab and door pillars via a rubber grommet. The wiring is secured to the mirror support brackets by plastic ties or similar

FIGURE 6-39 Cab interior round dome lamp features. (*Courtesy of GMC Truck Division, General Motors Corporation.*)

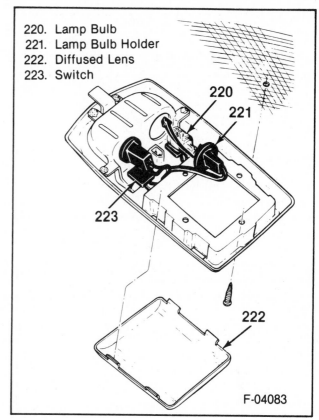

220. Lamp Bulb
221. Lamp Bulb Holder
222. Diffused Lens
223. Switch

F-04083

FIGURE 6-40 Cab interior rectangular dome lamp features. (*Courtesy of GMC Truck Division, General Motors Corporation.*)

FIGURE 6-41 Wiring harness routing for dual heated mirrors on a heavy-duty truck. (*Courtesy of GMC Truck Division, General Motors Corporation.*)

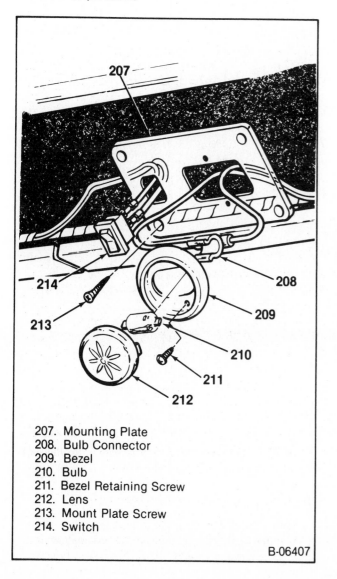

207. Mounting Plate
208. Bulb Connector
209. Bezel
210. Bulb
211. Bezel Retaining Screw
212. Lens
213. Mount Plate Screw
214. Switch

B-06407

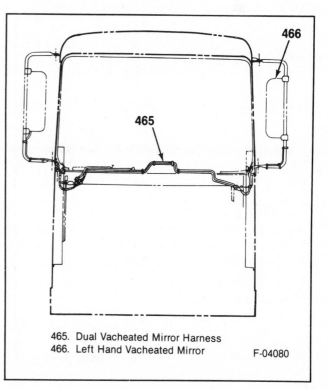

465. Dual Vacheated Mirror Harness
466. Left Hand Vacheated Mirror

F-04080

securing devices. Figure 6-42 illustrates a close-up exploded view of the heated mirror assembly used on a heavy-duty class 8 Peterbilt 379 truck model. The procedure for replacing the heating element in one of these mirrors is given below.

Procedure

1. Locate the manufacturer's ID mark, which is usually found on the lower surface of the mirror housing or lower end cap. This may be a P for Prutsman, or a C for Cham-Cal.
2. Obtain the correct heating element according to the manufacturer's letter brand.
3. Remove the mirror head from the yoke.
4. Remove the two Phillips head screws from each end cap and separate the end cap.
5. Carefully separate the trim channels to free the mirror glass. Exercise caution here so as not to damage the glass.
6. Disconnect the two spade-type wire terminals, then remove the rubber cushion. Inspect the rubber cushion to make sure that it can safely be reused; otherwise, order a new one.
7. The new heating element is a self-adhesive unit that can be attached to the rear of the mirror glass.
8. Reinstall or replace the rubber cushion.
9. Reconnect the mirror to the two wire spade terminal connectors and complete the reassembly procedure.

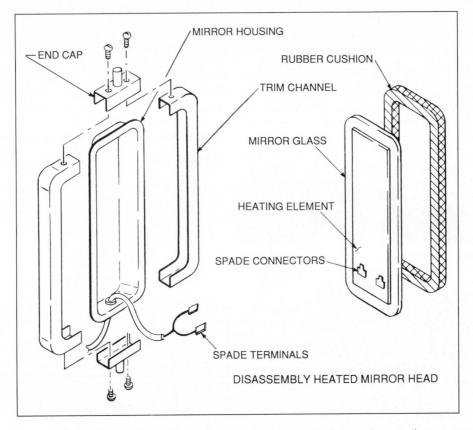

FIGURE 6-42 Component parts arrangement for a heavy-duty truck heated mirror assembly. (*Courtesy of Peterbilt Motors Company, Division of PACCAR, Newark, CA.*)

QUESTIONS

6-1. Lighting circuits generally originate at:
  a. The fuse block or a circuit breaker
  b. The fusible link
  c. The control switch
  d. The relay switch
  (see page 170)

6-2. Most light bulb filaments in use today are made from:
  a. Thread and bamboo
  b. A zinc strip
  c. Tungsten
  d. Stainless steel wire
  (see page 170)

6-3. During light bulb manufacturer all air must be kept out of the bulb through the use of a vacuum or by filling the bulb with an inert gas such as argon. *True* or *False* (see page 170)

6-4. If light bulbs of the same resistance value are wired in series and one bulb burns out:
  a. The other bulbs will fail to illuminate
  b. Only the damaged bulb will fail to illuminate
  c. The remaining bulbs will have increased brightness

d. The circuit resistance will decrease
(see page 9)

6-5. If two bulbs of the same resistance value are placed in a parallel circuit and one bulb filament burns out:
a. The circuit current will double
b. The circuit current will decrease by 50%
c. The other bulb will fail to illuminate
d. The remaining bulb will also burn out, due to high current flow
(see page 11)

6-6. Corrosion at a wire contact terminal will create:
a. High voltage   c. Short bulb life
b. High current   d. High circuit resistance
(see page 99, 175)

6-7. If the headlamp(s) on one side of a truck are less bright than those on the other side, the problem is probably due to:
a. Use of the wrong sealed beam
b. High dimmer switch resistance
c. A poor ground to the headlight circuit on that side
d. High circuit resistance through the control fuse or circuit breaker for that side
(see page 188)

6-8. If one clearance/marker light burns out on a semitrailer, the remaining lights will:
a. Continue to illuminate
b. Become less bright
c. Illuminate with more intensity
d. Fail to illuminate
(see page 198)

6-9. When a semitrailer travels over a bumpy road, the taillights tend to flicker off/on. This problem does not occur when traveling over smooth road surfaces. The most likely cause for this condition is:
a. Corroded light bulb sockets
b. Intermittent ground
c. High circuit resistance
d. Low current flow
(see page 175)

6-10. Failure of one semitrailer clearance/marker lamp to illuminate when all others operate correctly is probably due to:
a. A broken or corroded wire
b. A damaged light bulb filament
c. Severe corrosion at the bulb contact surface
d. All of the above
(see pages 173, 198)

6-11. Both license plate and sidemarker lamps are usually:
a. Single-filament, double-contact offset pin bulbs
b. Double-filament, double-contact straight pin bulbs
c. Single-filament, single-contact bayonet base bulbs
d. Double-filament, single-contact straight pin bulbs
(see page 171)

6-12. Reverse or backup lights are generally controlled by:
a. An instrument panel light switch
b. The transmission shift linkage
c. The clutch linkage
d. Both b and c
(see page 198)

6-13. In the United States all vehicle lighting must comply with standards set by:

a. FMVSS 108   c. ASTM 101
b. SAE J1654   d. API 312
(see page 168)

6-14. Problems associated with truck lighting systems are usually caused by:
a. Corrosion   c. Wiring damage
b. Shock failure   d. All of the above
(see page 173)

6-15. Light bulb life can be shortened by up to 50% due to:
a. Corrosion
b. Shock failure
c. High voltage
d. High ambient temperatures
(see page 175)

6-16. An over voltage bulb failure condition can be identified when:
a. The bulb is darkened
b. The filament and lead wires exhibit melt-down, often in the form of a round ball of molten wire
c. The bulb glass explodes
d. The fuse protecting the circuit fails
(see page 175)

6-17. Technician A states that some trucks use a separate ground wire to complete the lighting system return circuit rather than grounding each component circuit to the vehicle chassis. Technician B says that he has never heard of this and sees no advantage in such a system. Is the statement by technician A correct? (see page 175)

6-18. Bulb failure that turns a bulb light blue in color is indicative of:
a. Overvoltage
b. High circuit resistance
c. Slow leakage due to corrosion around the Dumet sealing wire
d. Short to ground in the wiring
(see page 175)

6-19. A smoky condition in a bulb, such as a yellowish or white color, is normally caused by:
a. Air leaking inside the glass bulb envelope through a crack in the glass
b. Too much voltage
c. Too much current
d. Low circuit resistance (see page 175)

6-20. Bulb filament burnout can be the result of:
a. Moisture, which can lead to corrosion
b. Vibration
c. High voltage spikes
d. Both a and c are correct
(see page 175)

6-21. In a series-wired circuit:
a. The total circuit resistance is always lower than the smallest resistor in the circuit
b. The sum of all the voltage drops is the same as the source voltage
c. There is more than one path for the current to flow
d. System voltage remains the same throughout the circuit
(see page 9)

6-22. In a parallel-wired circuit:
a. The current is the same throughout the circuit
b. There is a voltage drop across each resistance
c. The voltage remains the same throughout the circuit,

but the current is divided

d. All of the statements above are correct

(see page 11)

6-23. When two adjacent wire conductors come into contact, thereby creating a bypass of the circuit, it is commonly referred to as:

a. An open   c. A ground

b. A short   d. Split voltage

(see page 102)

6-24. Four lamps are wired in parallel; if we add another two lamps in parallel:

a. The circuit resistance will increase

b. The circuit resistance will decrease

c. There will be increased voltage drop in the circuit

d. There will be a decrease in current flow

(see page 11)

6-25. Six lamps are wired in parallel; should one of these lamps short out:

a. The other five lamps will remain illuminated

b. The other five lamps will go out

c. Current consumption will decrease

d. Circuit resistance will increase

(see page 11)

6-26. If the low-beam headlamps fail to illuminate, the cause is probably due to:

a. Burned-out low beam filaments

b. The fuse or circuit breaker

c. A bad ground

d. A faulty dimmer switch

(see page 188)

6-27. The right front signal light fails to illuminate on a truck/tractor although the left front, left rear, and right rear signal lights operate properly. The problem is probably due to:

a. Faulty wiring

b. A damaged column-mounted directional switch

c. A burned-out bulb filament

d. A burned-out flasher unit

(see page 197)

6-28. Technician A says that many medium-duty trucks now use fiber optic light ribbons to illuminate instruments and gauges. Technician B says that this is used ony in passenger cars, since it is not durable enough to use on heavy-duty trucks. Who is correct? (see page 218)

6-29. Halogen headlamps are capable of providing brightness levels up to:

a. 50,000 candela   c. 125,000 candela

b. 75,000 candela   d. 150,000 candela

(see page 178)

6-30. The term "watt" is used to express the relationship of:

a. Current × resistance

b. Current × volts

c. Voltage × resistance

d. Current, voltage, and resistance

(see page 501)

6-31. Average power draw of a high-beam headlight can range between:

a. 55 and 65 W   c. 85 to 95 W

b. 75 and 85 W   d. 100 and 105 W

(see page 176)

6-32. The average power draw of a low-beam headlight can range between:

a. 30 and 35 W   c. 50 and 55 W

b. 40 and 45 W   d. 60 and 65 W

(see page 176)

6-33. Dual-filament halogen light bulbs are identified by the following letters stamped on the bulb assembly:

a. HB1   c. HB3

b. HB2   d. HB4

(see page 177)

6-34. The replacement number for a dual-filament halogen light bulb used for both high- and low-beam lighting is identified by the number:

a. 9007   c. 9005

b. 9006   d. 9004

(see page 177)

6-35. Normal halogen bulb wall operating temperatures can become very high during operation. The service technician should therefore avoid touching the bulb, to prevent personal injury. The bulb wall temperatures run between:

a. 100 and 150°C (212 to 302°F)

b. 200 and 250°C (392 to 482°F)

c. 250 and 500°C (482 to 932°F)

d. 350 and 600°C (662 to 1112°F)

(see page 177)

6-36. Typical acceptable SAE and headlamp manufacturer operating voltages should not exceed:

a. 12 V   c. 14 V

b. 13 V   d. 15 V

(see pages 173, 179)

6-37. Normal standard-design high-beam headlamp life expectancy is in the region of:

a. 250 hours   c. 750 hours

b. 500 hours   d. 1000 hours

(see page 179)

6-38. Halogen high-beam headlights have a normal life expectancy of approximately:

a. 300 hours   c. 750 hours

b. 600 hours   d. 900 hours

(see page 179)

6-39. Technician A states that headlight floor-mounted dimmer switches normally use a double-pole single-throw type of switch. Mechanic B disagrees, saying that they use a single-pole, double-throw type of switch. Who is right? (see page 184)

6-40. Technician A says that a steering column–mounted headlight dimmer switch usually uses a two-pole relay to select the upper and lower headlight beams. Technician B says that it would use a single-pole relay only. Who is correct? (see page 184)

6-41. When adjusting truck headlights without the aid of a special headlight aiming tool, average requirements are that the high-intensity zone of the high beam of inner lamps on dual units be straight ahead and:

a. 2 in. (51 mm) below the headlamp horizontal level at a distance of 25 ft (7.6 m)

b. The same distance below as in a above, but at a distance of 20 ft (6 m)

c. 3 in. (76 mm) below the headlamp horizontal level and at a distance of 25 ft (7.6 m)

d. 3 in. below at a distance of 20 ft (6 m)

(see page 186)

6-42. The numeral 1 or 1A molded into a sealed beam headlight indicates that it is:

a. An upper and lower beam combination headlamp

b. An upper (high-beam) unit only

c. A lower-beam unit only

(see page 187)

6-43. When replacing a halogen bulb, you should never touch the new bulb or the bulb contact surfaces; otherwise:

a. You might crush the bulb glass

b. Dirt, sweat, or fluid from your hands could shorten the bulb life

c. You might rub the P/N off of the bulb glass

d. You will cause a dull spot to appear in the light when it is illuminated

(see page 190)

6-44. On a truck using a taillamp warning circuit on the instrument panel, the warning light will normally illuminate any time there is:

a. An open-circuit condition

b. A short-circuit condition

c. A grounded-circuit condition

d. High circuit resistance

(see page 190)

6-45. Technician A says that on many trucks, the circuit from the control switch splits, with one part feeding the front parking lights while the other feeds the rear taillamps. Technician B disagrees, stating that both the front and rear lights have their own individual fuse- or circuit breaker-protected circuits. Who is correct? (see page 190)

6-46. A light bulb with the part number 1156 identifies:

a. A double-contact bulb

b. A single-contact bulb

(see pages 172, 190)

6-47. To prevent corrosion at the junction block power feed on many trucks, a grease fitting is attached that should have the following type of lubricant injected:

a. Graphite-based grease

b. Liquid-silicon sealer

c. Chassis lubricant

d. Caulking

(see page 191)

6-48. The stoplight switch can be activated by:

a. The brake pedal linkage

b. Hydraulic fluid pressure buildup

c. Compressed air from the service line

d. All of the above

(see page 191)

6-49. Technician A says that some trucks may employ two flasher units, one for the directional signal lights and one for the vehicle hazard lights. Technician B disagrees, saying that only one flasher is required and ever used. Who is correct? (see page 194)

6-50. Technician A says that all heavy-duty flasher units use a bimetallic strip to operate. Technician B says that newer-model flasher units employ solid-state transistorized circuitry instead. Who is correct? (see page 195)

6-51. The turn-signal flasher unit operates to supply a rapid on/off/on current flow, similar to:

a. A transistorized regulator

b. A zener diode

c. A circuit breaker

d. A fuse

(see page 195)

CHAPTER

7
Instruments and Gauges

OBJECTIVES

In this chapter we describe operation of the various instruments and gauges used on heavy-duty trucks, as well as tracing their wiring circuits. Specifically, you will acquire or review the skills needed to:

1. Identify a single- versus a two-coil gauge arrangement.
2. Describe the basic operation and function of the various gauges used in truck applications.
3. Describe and understand how a fiber optic light ribbon operates.
4. Remove and replace a faulty ignition switch.

5. Describe the operation of an engine protection system and automatic engine shutdown test procedure.
6. Describe how a low-air-pressure alarm system operates.
7. Describe how an electrohydraulic brake booster pump operates on trucks equipped with hydraulic brakes.

BASIC GAUGE OPERATION

The instrumentation and gauges are the functional link between the driver and the various monitored systems on the truck. Some gauges must be monitored on a regular basis by the truck operator, while other gauges and warning devices can be wired to activate a warning buzzer and flashing light automatically to alert the driver of a possible serious operating condition. Many gauges are straight mechanical gauges such as the air brake reservoir pressure, air inlet restriction gauge, and possibly the engine oil pressure gauge. Speedometers can also be mechanical or electrical in design, as well as the tachometer and tachograph.

Many gauges used on vehicles are electrically operated devices that indicate a particlar operating condition in a given system on the vehicle. Most gauges are either of the thermoelectric or the electromagnetic type. The thermoelectric type operates on a supply voltage less than that of the battery, usually about 5 V, while electromagnetic gauges are powered from the regular 12-V battery system.

Thermoelectric gauges receive their 5 V from a voltage-limiting device whose action is illustrated in Fig. 7–1. Basically, the voltage-limiting device consists of a bimetallic strip with a fine wire coil wrapped around it. Applying 12 V to the coil causes it to heat up and the bimetallic strip bends to open the contact points. With the points open, cooling of the bimetallic strip occurs and the points again close; this action occurs very rapidly, to produce a pulsating current in the region of about 5 V from the voltage-limiting device.

The constant-voltage regulator or limiter input source

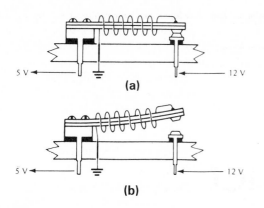

FIGURE 7–1 Thermoelectric gauge bimetallic strip: (a) points closed; (b) points open.

can be dc, intermittent or interrupted dc, or ac as long as the effective input voltage does not drop below 5 V since a voltage lower than this results in a proportionately lower gauge indication. The standard automotive constant-voltage (CV) regulator has input voltages varying from 5.6 to 8 V, or some from 11 to 16 V; however, voltages in excess of 16 V will overload the regulator contacts, causing damage.

Basically, there are two types of electric gauge measurement systems:

1. The single-coil gauge
2. The two-coil gauge

Figure 7–2 illustrates the two types of electric coil gauge operating systems, which use a magnetic field to cause a movement at the gauge indicator needle. The major dif-

ference between the two lies in the fact that the single-coil gauge/meter shown as item 101 in Fig. 7–2 has two electrical terminals, while the two-coil gauge shown as item 100 in Fig. 7–2 has three electrical terminals. Examples of single-coil gauges include the ammeter, the voltmeter, and some fuel level gauges. Two-coil gauges are usually used to measure pressure, temperature, or a liquid level. The two-coil gauge has the advantage that its readings are not affected by rapid fluctuations in the system voltage. You have probably noticed on a truck that there are operating conditions that tend to make the voltmeter and ammeter gauges fluctuate occasionally.

In the single-coil gauge, battery power flows from the engine control switch (16) and enters the gauge (101) at one terminal, where current flows through the coil, and then exits the gauge at the opposite terminal, where power completes the circuit by returning to ground. The actual position of the gauge floating needle is controlled by the strength of the current flowing through the coil. In the two-coil gauge shown in Fig. 7–2, the floating needle is connected to a small magnet that is suspended between the two coils. The greater the flow of electricity through these coils, the stronger will be the magnetic field that is created. During operation, battery power from the engine control switch (16) will flow to the gauge and pass through both coils, which are wired in series. The circuit is completed by the power flowing out of the opposite gauge terminals to ground. Note carefully that there is a potentiometer or variable resistor connected between the two coils of the gauge. Therefore, some current will bleed off from the first coil before it can reach the sec-

FIGURE 7–2 Typical gauge and instrument circuit. (*Courtesy of GMC Truck Division, General Motors Corporation.*)

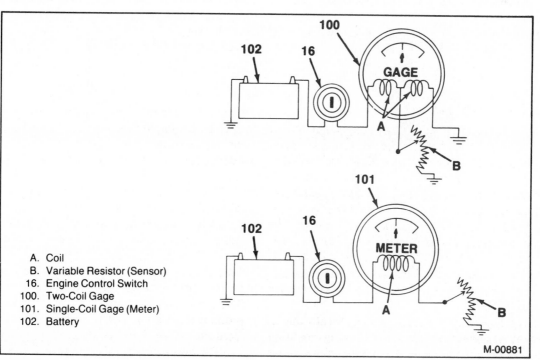

A. Coil
B. Variable Resistor (Sensor)
16. Engine Control Switch
100. Two-Coil Gage
101. Single-Coil Gage (Meter)
102. Battery

M-00881

ond; the resistor current flow completes the circuit through a ground connection. This action means that the first coil will always have a constant magnetic field, while the second coil's magnetic field strength will vary according to how much current is tapped off through the variable resistor. Therefore, during operation, the first coil will exhibit a steady magnetic pull on the floating gauge needle toward the low-value side of the instrument, while the second coil will tend to exhibit a magnetic pull toward the high-value side of the gauge. The action of both coils therefore tends to determine the placement of the floating needle, based on the degree of variable resistance from the sensor/probe caused by the pressure, temperature, or liquid level being sensed.

FIGURE 7–3 Automatic transmission temperature sensor/gauge location example. (*Courtesy of GMC Truck Division, General Motors Corporation.*)

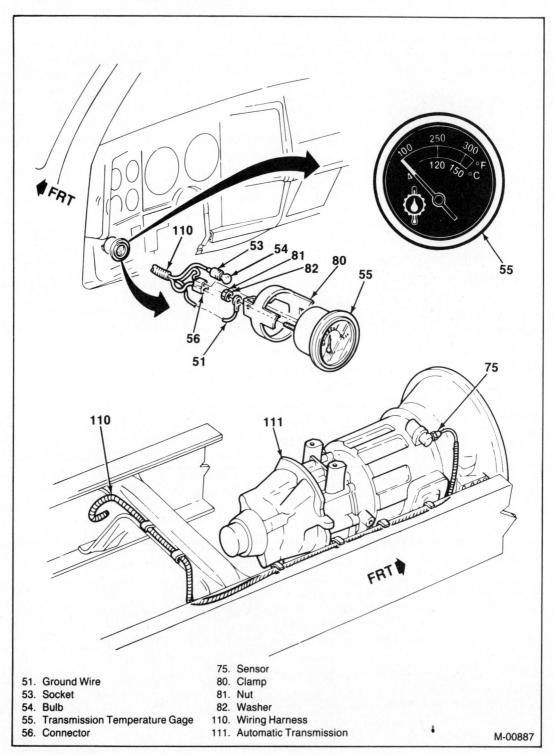

51. Ground Wire	75. Sensor
53. Socket	80. Clamp
54. Bulb	81. Nut
55. Transmission Temperature Gage	82. Washer
56. Connector	110. Wiring Harness
	111. Automatic Transmission

M-00887

WATER AND OIL TEMPERATURE GAUGES

The engine water and oil temperature gauges are usually constructed from a two-coil gauge design, although some vehicles may use a single-coil design. Basically, a temperature gauge, whether it is monitoring water, oil, or exhaust, operates on the thermistor principle. The word *thermistor* is actually derived from a combination of the words *thermal resistance*. In simplified terms, this means that when the sensor probe is cold, the material used in the sensor will exhibit a very high electrical resistance, which is usually in the region of 100,000 Ω when measured with an ohmmeter. As the liquid or air temperature being measured warms up, the probe material will cause the circuit resistance to decrease so that it may only show a value of 70 to 80 Ω when at a temperature of 130°C (266°F). Sensors and probes that operate on this characteristic are commonly known as *negative temperature thermistors*. Sensors or probes that operate on a positive temperature coefficient would exhibit a low circuit resistance when cold and increase the resistance when hot. An example of a negative temperature sensor/probe resistance graph is shown in Fig. 11-70.

The location of the water temperature gauge will vary with the type of engine (gas and diesel) and the make. Generally, the scale value on gasoline engines will register a higher temperature than will that used on a diesel engine, due to the greater thermal efficiency of the diesel engine and its greater flow of air through the engine during normal operation. The sensor or probe is usually located fairly close to the thermostat housing so that it can monitor the engine coolant at the warmest part of the engine. Figure 7-3 illustrates the location of the oil temperature gauge and its attachment hardware to the

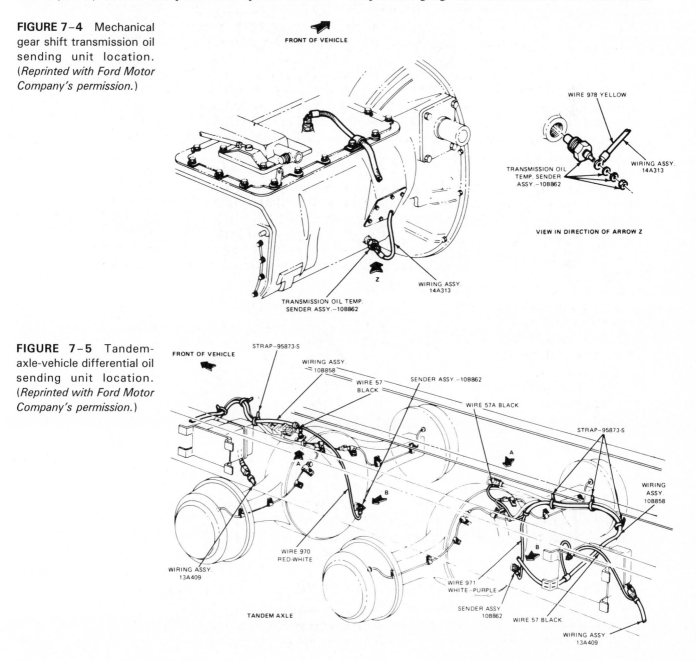

FIGURE 7-4 Mechanical gear shift transmission oil sending unit location. (*Reprinted with Ford Motor Company's permission.*)

FIGURE 7-5 Tandem-axle-vehicle differential oil sending unit location. (*Reprinted with Ford Motor Company's permission.*)

instrument panel for a truck equipped with an Allison automatic model transmission. Figure 7–4 illustrates a typical example of where the oil temperature sending unit would be located on a Fuller Roadranger heavy-duty truck transmission, and Fig. 7–5 shows the location of the oil temperature sending units for a tandem-axle-equipped heavy-duty class 8 truck application.

A good example of how the engine coolant, engine oil, transmission oil, and axle/differential oil temperature switches and gauge wiring circuits would appear is shown in Fig. 7–6. Note also that an engine temperature warning lamp system is shown in the upper part of the figure. When normal temperature limits are exceeded, a

warning buzzer is activated or a warning lamp is illuminated to indicate to the truck operator that there is a system problem. More information on monitoring systems is contained in this chapter in the section "Engine Protection Systems."

OIL PRESSURE GAUGE

The oil pressure gauge is installed in the oil filter housing adapter, the engine block main oil gallery, or can be remote-mounted on a bracket with a high-pressure hose or steel-backed line running to it from a fitting on the engine takeoff point. The dial calibrations may be in

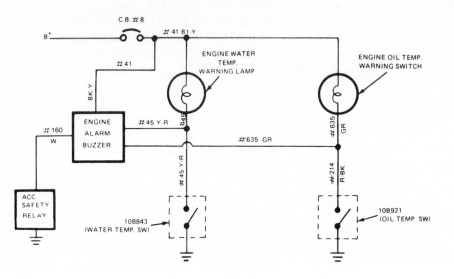

FIGURE 7–6 Typical heavy-duty truck temperature indicator gauge wiring system. (*Reprinted with Ford Motor Company's permission.*)

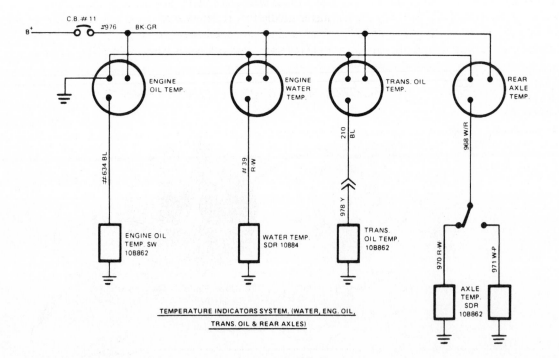

either English/American or metric values. In American values the gauge can run from 0 to 80 or 0 to 100 psi, with the equivalent in metric values being from 0 to 550 or 0 to 700 kPa (kilopascal). As with the coolant temperature gauge, either the single- or two-coil gauge design system can be used. The oil pressure gauge sensor/probe is a pressure-sensing variable resistor that controls the current flow through the gauge coil(s). Many pressure gauges employ a silicon wafer or alumina ceramic capacitor type of electrical sending unit that is deflected by the oil pressure. The degree of deflection of the wafer will alter the resistance value, which in turn will vary the current flow through the gauge to affect the floating needle position.

VOLTMETER GAUGE

Voltmeters usually operate on a single-coil principle, as shown in Fig. 7–2. An example of how the voltmeter is wired into the electrical system is illustrated in Fig. 7–7, where it must be wired in parallel with other electrical circuits on the truck.

CAUTION: Wiring a voltmeter in series with an electrical circuit can result in the gauge being burned out due to the high current that might flow through the instrument.

The range of the voltmeter will of course vary depending on whether the electrical system is a 12- or 24-V design; however, on the conventional 12-V circuit, the voltmeter will register to a low value of 8 V and a high value of 18 V, although on a properly maintained and adjusted electrical charging system, the normal charging voltage will usually run between 13.5 and 14.2 V. Refer to Chapter 8 for more specific information on this.

The gauge facia is often marked by different-colored band widths to show quickly what the charging rate is. Typical colors for a low state of charge may be either amber/yellow or white; normal charge value is green, and a high charging rate is red. Turning the ignition key to the ON or START position with the engine not running will result in the voltmeter gauge showing the state of charge of the vehicle battery (batteries), while with the engine running the voltmeter should register a higher value to indicate that the charging system is performing correctly. The degree of charge will depend on the state of charge of the batteries and the load(s) on the electrical system. Consequently, a voltmeter is an excellent place to start when an electrical system charging system problem is reported.

AMMETER GAUGE

The ammeter registers the amount of current flowing from the alternator to the batteries. When the engine is off, the ammeter can show the discharge rate when the ignition key switch is on and one or more electrical accessories are in use. The ammeter will not provide as accurate an interpretation of the state of the charging system as will the voltmeter, but can serve to indicate to the truck driver the general state of charge of the alternator charging system and the battery condition. The ammeter is usually a single-coil gauge that is connected in series between the alternator charging circuit and the battery.

The ammeter gauge scale may show a simple − or + sign to indicate a discharge or charge rate, respectively, while some gauges may actually show the degree of charge in amperes. Figure 7–8 illustrates a typical ammeter connection into a charging circuit. Generally, when the engine is running, some slight movement of the ammeter needle toward the positive side will occur, meaning that the alternator is supplying some of the power requirements for the various electrical systems in use on the truck. An ammeter needle that registers zero is usually an indication that the alternator and battery voltages are the same. Any time the alternator voltage charging rate is less than that

FIGURE 7–7 Voltmeter circuit arrangement. (*Courtesy of GMC Truck Division, General Motors Corporation.*)

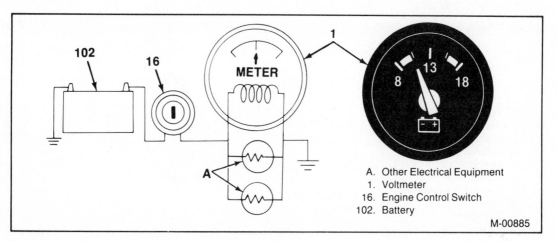

A. Other Electrical Equipment
1. Voltmeter
16. Engine Control Switch
102. Battery

M-00885

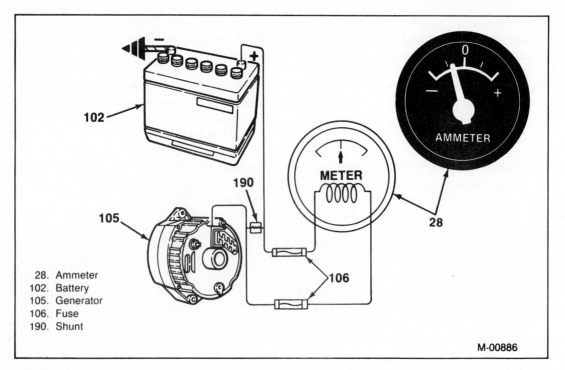

28. Ammeter
102. Battery
105. Generator
106. Fuse
190. Shunt

M-00886

FIGURE 7–8 Ammeter circuit arrangement. (*Courtesy of GMC Truck Division, General Motors Corporation.*)

FIGURE 7–9 Fuel gauge and sending unit arrangement. (*Courtesy of GMC Truck Division, General Motors Corporation.*)

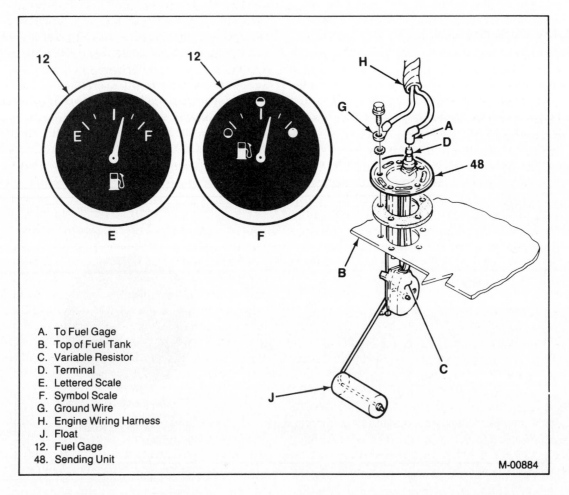

A. To Fuel Gage
B. Top of Fuel Tank
C. Variable Resistor
D. Terminal
E. Lettered Scale
F. Symbol Scale
G. Ground Wire
H. Engine Wiring Harness
J. Float
12. Fuel Gage
48. Sending Unit

M-00884

in the battery system, the gauge needle will show a − value. You may find wired into the ammeter circuit a shunt similar to that shown as item 190 in Fig. 7–8. The shunt acts as a resistor to allow a percentage of the current in the circuit to bypass the ammeter gauge to provide greater gauge needle stability.

FUEL LEVEL GAUGE

The fuel level gauge requires a sensor or sending unit, shown as item 48 in Fig. 7–9. A float assembly ''J'' will rise and fall with the level of liquid in the tank (either gasoline or diesel), causing its float arm to rise and fall. The float arm is connected to a variable resistor unit (item C in the diagram) and therefore affects the resistance value and consequently the current flow to the gauge (12). The sending unit (48) is grounded through a wire in the wiring harness. Various model types are used with the sending unit (48), being combined with the fuel pickup or the fuel return pipe in some cases, while in others a protective shield covers the top of the sending unit. On truck models with dual fuel tanks, the grounding wire from the sending unit (48) in each tank is routed to the fuel tank selector valve. The actual position of this selector valve therefore determines which tank circuit will be completed to ground, allowing only one fuel tank's level to be registered at one time.

ELECTRIC TACHOMETERS

The tachometer continually displays the actual rotative speed of the engine in rpm (revolutions per minute). Generally the tachometer gauge is calibrated so that the numbers indicated by the needle must be multiplied by 100 to determine the engine speed. When the needle points to 25 on the gauge, in fact the engine speed would be 2500 rpm. The range shown on the tachometer will depend upon the make of truck and also whether or not it uses a gasoline or diesel engine for power. Gasoline engines that rev higher than diesels to produce rated horsepower will usually have a top end limit of 5000 to 6000 rpm on the tach, whereas heavy duty diesel engine tachometers are usually limited to no more than 3000 rpm. Most heavy-duty class 8 truck diesels are governed between 1900 and 2100 rpm so some tachs may only go as high as 2500.

The tachometer sensor or magnetic pickup can be located in different positions on the engine. On gasoline engines the pickup can be from the ignition distributor, while the diesel engine tach sensor pickup can be assembled into the engine flywheel housing. In some cases an air gap must be set by how far this sensor is screwed into the housing for the unit to operate correctly. Generally on a diesel engine, the sensor is placed so that the teeth on the flywheel starter motor ring gear continually make and break the magnetic field generated between the end of the sensor and the rotating teeth. The sensor receives battery power, which creates a magnetic field between the end of the sensor and the metal ring gear teeth. When a tooth is opposite the sensor, a strong magnetic field exists; when the tooth passes the sensor, a large air gap is created, thereby weakening the magnetic field. This magnetic flux creates an alternating-current voltage signal that is fed to the tachometer through the engine and tachometer wiring harness to position the needle on the tach face. On gasoline engines, the voltage pulses from the ignition primary circuit are controlled by the making and breaking of the primary circuit by the opening and closing points, or by transistor action in electronic distributors. This pulsing action is taken from the tachometer terminal on the distributor cap and relayed through wiring to the tachometer gauge.

NOTE: Electronic tachometers/speedometers used on many heavy-duty trucks such as Peterbilt and Kenworth models use discrete (separate) signal wires for their electrical signals with the wires running parallel using jumper harnesses. These wires must be kept discrete to avoid possible signal interference between the two systems.

PROGRAMMABLE ELECTRONIC SPEEDOMETERS

Many midrange and heavy-duty trucks and truck/tractors now employ electronic speedometers and tachometers in place of the long used mechanically cable-driven types. These electronic instruments are activated through the use of either a signal generator, or alternatively through the use of a magnetic pickup sensor. It is therefore possible to retrofit an electronic tachometer or speedometer instrument into an existing truck dashboard that was originally designed as a mechanical drive arrangement. Two methods are readily available to perform this conversion, and these are through the adoption of either a small-signal generator and wiring harness, or by adoption of a magnetic pickup sensor and wiring harness that effectively replaces the mechanical drive cable. Such an example can be seen in Fig. 7–10(a) for the signal generator arrangement, while Fig. 7–10(b) illustrates the magnetic pickup sensor arrangement. Both of these types of electrical pickups are mated to a replacement instrument (tachometer or speedometer) that is easily installed into the truck instrument panel in place of the existing mechanical drive unit. One major supplier of these types of instruments to many heavy-duty truck OEMs (original equipment manufacturers) is Trekstar of Prestolite Electric Incorporated, Heavy Duty Products Division. Well-known heavy-duty truck users of these instruments include Autocar, Chevrolet, Ford, Freightliner, GMC, IVECO, Navistar, Kenworth, Mercedes-Benz, Mack, Peterbilt, Volvo/White/GMC, and Western Star.

Trekstar also offers programmable electronic speedometer/odometers so that if an existing mechanical or electronic speedometer is being replaced, the accumulated mileage to date on the vehicle can be programmed into

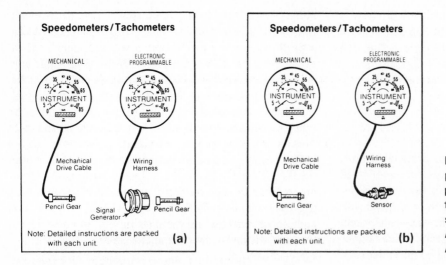

FIGURE 7-10 (a) Signal generator and pencil gear arrangement; (b) magnetic pickup sensor arrangement for an electronic speedometer and tachometer instrumentation. (*Courtesy of Prestolite Electric Incorporated, Heavy Duty Products Division.*)

the new electronic instrument. In some cases a fleet may change transmission or axle ratios, or even tire sizes. In all cases a reprogramming of the electronic instruments is required. This can be done in some models of Trekstar instruments by removing tape exposing the odometer drive gear teeth as shown in Fig. 7-11, then with the use of two wooden picks, the instrument mileage tumblers can be set to the desired accumulated mileage prior to installation. On programmable electronic speedometers or tachometers, a dip switch setting, also illustrated in Fig. 7-11, can be toggled to a specific binary code number to suit the changes that have been incorporated into the truck driveline ratios or tire sizes. A detailed description of a binary code is given in Chapter 11 (see the description starting on p. 457).

As shown in Fig. 7-10, a suitable drive tang driven from the existing mechanical drive on the truck mates with a pencil gear drive to the small electric signal generator, which transfers the equivalent rotational speed of the shaft to the electronic tachometer or speedometer, as desired. If an electronic sensor is used for the engine speed pickup, the ideal location for this is to access a flywheel housing plug that will permit the sensor to be threaded into place. Installation instructions are supplied with the

replacement kit for all electronic tachometers and speedometers. The sensor is threaded into position until a specified air gap exists between its tip and the teeth of a flywheel ring gear. With the proper engine/vehicle identified, a specific sensor is selected that will match the configuration and ensure accurate instrument operation.

Basically, the sensor operates by being supplied with battery power. When a flywheel ring gear tooth is opposite the tip of the sensor, a strong magnetic field is created. As the ring gear tooth rotates away from the sensor tip, the magnetic field collapses (weakens) due to the large air gap that is created between the sensor tip and the space between the ring gear teeth. Consequently, the magnetic field flux is constantly increasing and decreasing in strength. This action causes an analog voltage signal to be impressed through the sensor assembly, which is relayed back to the instrument head (tachometer or speedometer). Since each sensor is designed to have a specific resistance in ohms, the speed at which the magnetic field flux changes results in a voltage signal value that will change in relation to the engine or vehicle transmission output shaft rpm. Consequently, a very accurate signal is created to provide an accurate quick response and a stable reading. For example, Trekstar sen-

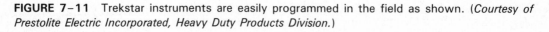

FIGURE 7-11 Trekstar instruments are easily programmed in the field as shown. (*Courtesy of Prestolite Electric Incorporated, Heavy Duty Products Division.*)

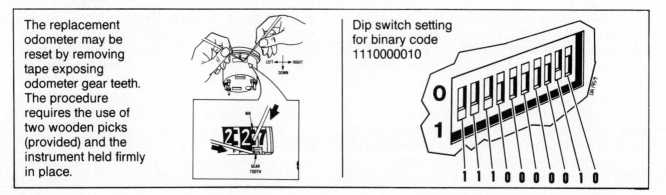

sors supplied for use with Fuller Roadranger and Spicer SST transmissions exhibit a resistance value of 265 Ω of impedance. On the Trekstar 118-mm ($4\frac{5}{8}$-in.)-diameter speedometer or tachometer sizes illustrated in Fig. 7–12, a microprocessor counts the pulses from the sensor or signal generator to assure extremely high odometer accuracy. All instruments employ Weather-Pack-type electrical wiring harnesses for long, trouble-free life. In addition, the accuracy of the speedometer is easily checked by using a Trekstar pulse counter test instrument, which counts the number of pulses over a measured mile course. The resultant pulse count is then used to calibrate the speedometer should minor variations exist due to variations in tire rolling radius caused by tire profiles and inflated air pressures. Figure 7–13 illustrates the Trekstar pulse counter, and the following section describes its features and usage.

Trekstar Pulse Counter

The Prestolite pulse counter illustrated in Fig. 7–13(a) is designed to count the electrical pulses generated by a variety of different magnetic sensors or a signal generator mounted at a pencil gear or to count cable revolutions in a mechanical speedometer. The pulses are counted when the vehicle is driven through a measured distance or course. The resultant pulse count is then used to calibrate the speedometer. Switches enable the pulse counter to record the pulses per mile in terms of either a product number, which is used by Navistar, a pulses per mile reading, or cable revolutions per mile.

Included with the pulse counter is an interconnecting cable with a 6294544 Packard connector. This connector matches Prestolite's 118-mm programmable speedometers and Prestolite's aftermarket speedometer

installations. It includes a harness adapter cable for use with installations that do not have the matching Packard connector. The pulse counter will work with either a positive- or negative-ground 12-V system. Kit 4-905 is available for counting cable revolutions per mile. The display in the pulse counter has a lithium battery which will hold the count on the counter until the display is reset. This display cannot be turned off. The battery in the pulse counter will last up to seven years.

Using the Pulse Counter

1. Attach the pulse counter interconnecting cable to the pulse counter [Fig. 7-13(b)]

2. Set the mode switch to the PULSES PER MILE position. (*Note:* If the OEM service manual uses the product number instead of pulses per mile to calibrate the speedometer, set the mode switch to the PRODUCT NUMBER postion.)

3. Connect the pulse counter cable into the vehicle's wiring harness as illustrated in Fig. 7-13(b) for installations of Prestolite's 118-mm speedometers and 86-mm aftermarket speedometers. In installations where the vehicle's wiring harness does not have a connector that matches the Packard connector on the pulse counter cable, connect the pulse counter into the vehicle's wiring harness as illustrated in Fig. 7-13(c) using the harness adapter cable.

4. Measure exactly and mark off a distance of 1 mile in a straight course. If a 1-mile course cannot be marked off, measure and mark off a distance of $\frac{1}{10}$ of a mile, which is the minimum distance that can be used with this tester. The course should have no curves, stop signs, or stoplights.

5. Drive the vehicle to the start mark of the course.

FIGURE 7–12 Trekstar 110-mm (4⅝-in.) diameter programmable instruments. (*Courtesy of Prestolite Electric Incorporated, Heavy Duty Products Division.*)

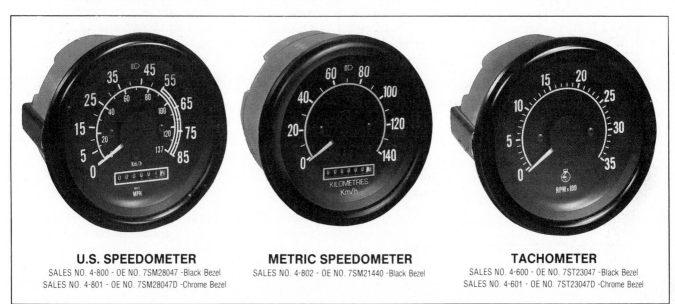

U.S. SPEEDOMETER
SALES NO. 4-800 - OE NO. 7SM28047 -Black Bezel
SALES NO. 4-801 - OE NO. 7SM28047D -Chrome Bezel

METRIC SPEEDOMETER
SALES NO. 4-802 - OE NO. 7SM21440 -Black Bezel

TACHOMETER
SALES NO. 4-600 - OE NO. 7ST23047 -Black Bezel
SALES NO. 4-601 - OE NO. 7ST23047D -Chrome Bezel

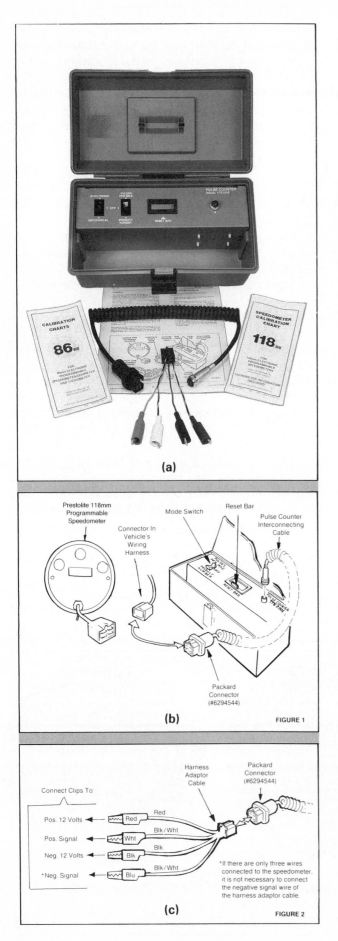

(a)

(b)   FIGURE 1

(c)   FIGURE 2

6. Press RESET BAR on the pulse counter. The pulse counter should now show a zero reading.

7. Drive the vehicle through the marked course, being sure to start and stop exactly at the course markers.

8. When stopped at the end of the course, center the mode switch to the OFF position. The pulse counter will display the pulses per mile or product number until the RESET BAR is pressed.

Electric Speedometer Troubleshooting

Some programmable electric speedometer/odometer gauges feature an analog air-core meter movement for vehicle speed indication, along with a small digital stepper motor to drive the odometer portion of the instrument. Figure 7-10 illustrates the basic system used with an electric speedometer. In the diagram shown, electrical pulses are generated either from a VRM (variable reluctance magnetic) sensor that is mounted in the manual transmission to detect the position of a metal tooth interrupter gear ring, or from a signal generator mounted at the rear of the transmission. The electrical pulses are converted to an analog speedometer/odometer display. The faster the vehicle speed, the quicker will be the electrical pulses generated at the VRM or sensor. For proper operation, the transmission-mounted sensor must have an air gap of between 0.05 in. + 0.030 in. or − 0.040 in. for the VRM sensor. When problems exist with the electric speedometer, always check the fuse or circuit breaker first, then inspect the wiring at the rear of the transmission as well as at the instrument panel. If problems still exist, disconnect the VRM sensor or signal generator connector at the rear of the transmission. Insert a voltmeter into one of the sensor output pins; insert a jumper wire between the sensor ground pin and chassis ground. Either raise the vehicle drive wheels clear of the shop floor, or road test the truck so that you can closely monitor the voltmeter for VRM output. The voltage value generated should usually read between 0.5 V rms (root mean square) to 35.5 V rms over the normal operating range of the truck. You should also verify that the mechanical drive tang on the signal generator is square and not damaged. If the drive tang appears serviceable, replace the signal generator. You can also check the speedometer by removing the instrument and performing both a resistance and a voltage check with a multimeter at the wiring harness connector. Check the black ground wire pin to the chassis ground, which should read 1 Ω or less of resistance. Similarly, the sensor pin resistance to the VRM sensor should have the same value.

FIGURE 7-13 (a) View of a Trekstar instrument pulse counter diagnostic tool; (b) connections from the pulse counter to the programmable electronic speedometer; (c) wiring harness hookup to a Trekstar electronic instrument. (*Courtesy of Prestolite Electric Incorporated, Heavy Duty Products Division.*)

For voltage, turn on the ignition switch and make sure that there is a 12-V reading between the positive pin and the red wire with the green stripe.

INSTRUMENT PANELS

The physical style and arrangement of gauges on any instrument panel will vary depending on the systems that have to be monitored and the actual make of truck. Flat dash, curved dash, and wraparound aircraft styles are widely used in various models of trucks. Figure 7-14 illustrates a typical conventional cab instrument panel showing all of the various gauges and instruments, while Fig. 7-15 shows a wraparound type of instrument panel cluster. Another example of a heavy-duty truck instru-

FIGURE 7-14 Conventional cab instrument panel layout. (*Courtesy of GMC Truck Division, General Motors Corporation.*)

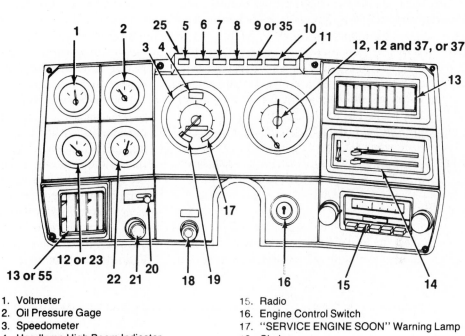

1. Voltmeter
2. Oil Pressure Gage
3. Speedometer
4. Headlamp High Beam Indicator
5. Left Turn Directional Signal Indicator Lamp
6. Oil Pressure Warning Lamp
7. "BRAKE" Warning Lamp
8. "DIFF LOCK" Indicator Lamp
9. "BRAKE ELEC HYD BOOST" Warning Lamp
10. "HOT ENGINE" Warning Lamp
11. Right Turn Directional Signal Indicator Lamp
12. Fuel Gage
13. Air Conditioning Vent
14. Heater or Air Conditioning Controls

15. Radio
16. Engine Control Switch
17. "SERVICE ENGINE SOON" Warning Lamp
18. Choke
19. "OVERSPEED" Warning Lamp
20. Windshield Wiper/Washer Switch
21. Main Lamp Switch
22. Temperature Gage
23. Air Pressure Gage
25. Indicator Lamp Cluster
35. "LOW AIR" Warning Lamp
37. Tachometer
55. Transmission Temperature Gage

M-00873

FIGURE 7-15 Heavy-duty truck cab console layout. (*Courtesy of GMC Truck Division, General Motors Corporation.*)

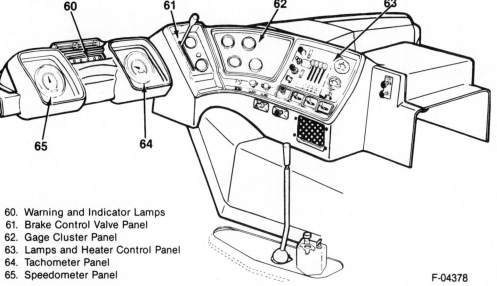

60. Warning and Indicator Lamps
61. Brake Control Valve Panel
62. Gage Cluster Panel
63. Lamps and Heater Control Panel
64. Tachometer Panel
65. Speedometer Panel

F-04378

ment panel is shown in Fig. 7-18. Access to the wiring and gauges in the conventional cab instrument panel shown in Fig. 7-16 is achieved simply by removing a series of retaining screws and bezel retainers.

Many class 8 truck instrument panel clusters are hinged to allow ease of access to the back side of the gauges and instruments as well as to check the wiring connections to all accessories. Figures 7-16 and 7-17 illustrate the rear views of the instrument cluster panels shown in Fig. 7-15. These diagrams show all of the various gauges and wire harness connections that you would be faced with when attempting to trace a gauge problem. Keep in mind that all gauges are protected by fuses or circuit breakers and that they are all fed from a junction block behind or underneath the dash panel on the truck. Examples of fuses and circuit breaker locations were discussed and shown in Chapter 5; see specifically Fig. 5-7 through 5-18. Figure 7-18 illustrates a Ford L-9000 heavy-duty truck RH instrument cluster panel.

Fiber Optics

A fiber optic light source and ribbon is used to illuminate the instrument panel switches and controls on many medium- and heavy-duty truck models. The fiber optic light source consists of a bulb and socket assembly. The light source bulb is illuminated whenever the mainlamp switch is energized. Fiber optic ribbons are actually very small bore tubes that transmit/carry light sources by a process of reflected illumination through the transparent core of the fiber. When the source lamp bulb is turned on, light is passed through the ribbon behind each control and switch nameplate, providing illumination to the nameplate lens. Fiber optic tube/wires will not operate if they are kinked, cut, or broken. Because of their design, all fiber optic wires must be carefully routed through the vehicle from their respective sender lamps to the monitor housing with gradual smooth bends. Sudden twists or right-angle bends must be avoided. Ensure that the end of the fiber optic wire is cut square and is smooth before pushing it fully home into the gauge lamp socket, housing, or lens. Several fiber optic ribbons are used to illuminate the various switch nameplates, and they often all use the same bulb mounted in a special connector shell behind the instrument control panel. Should you experience a condition whereby all nameplates fail to illuminate, it is probable that the single light source (bulb) has burned out. However, if only one or two switch headlights do not illuminate, begin by checking the fiber op-

FIGURE 7–16 Back-side view of a speedometer and tachometer panel assembly. (*Courtesy of GMC Truck Division, General Motors Corporation.*)

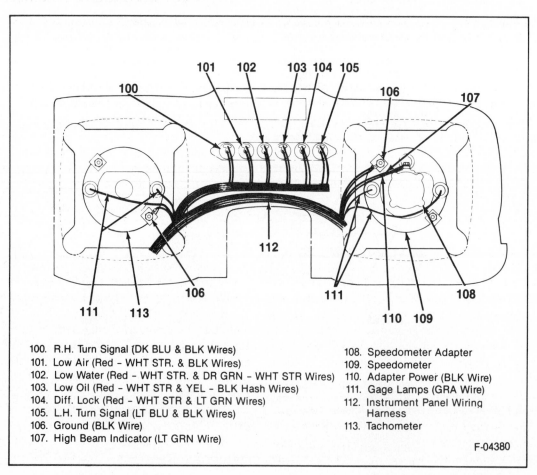

100. R.H. Turn Signal (DK BLU & BLK Wires)
101. Low Air (Red – WHT STR. & BLK Wires)
102. Low Water (Red – WHT STR. & DR GRN – WHT STR Wires)
103. Low Oil (Red – WHT STR & YEL – BLK Hash Wires)
104. Diff. Lock (Red – WHT STR & LT GRN Wires)
105. L.H. Turn Signal (LT BLU & BLK Wires)
106. Ground (BLK Wire)
107. High Beam Indicator (LT GRN Wire)

108. Speedometer Adapter
109. Speedometer
110. Adapter Power (BLK Wire)
111. Gage Lamps (GRA Wire)
112. Instrument Panel Wiring Harness
113. Tachometer

F-04380

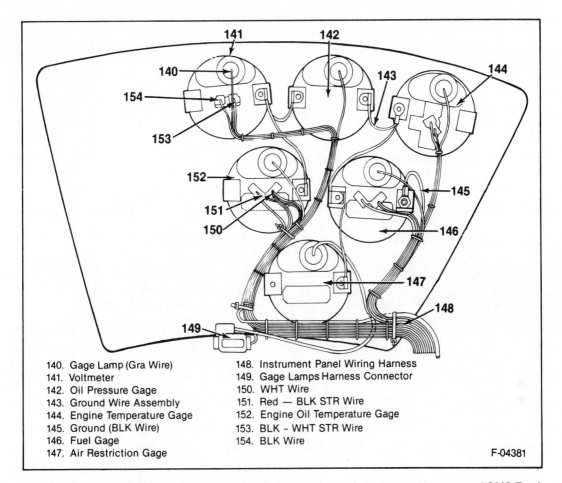

140. Gage Lamp (Gra Wire)	148. Instrument Panel Wiring Harness
141. Voltmeter	149. Gage Lamps Harness Connector
142. Oil Pressure Gage	150. WHT Wire
143. Ground Wire Assembly	151. Red — BLK STR Wire
144. Engine Temperature Gage	152. Engine Oil Temperature Gage
145. Ground (BLK Wire)	153. BLK - WHT STR Wire
146. Fuel Gage	154. BLK Wire
147. Air Restriction Gage	

F-04381

FIGURE 7–17 Back-side view of a multiple-gauge cluster instrument panel. (*Courtesy of GMC Truck Division, General Motors Corporation.*)

tic ribbon to see if it has become disconnected from the light distribution connector shell. If the ribbon is connected, turn the panel light dimmer switch to the full-brightness position, then visually examine the ribbons on the back of the control panel. Bright spots or lines of bright light are usually indicative of problems in the ribbon, which can be damaged by abrasion, cutting, bending, or tight folding.

Ignition Switch

Contained within the instrument panel cluster is an ignition key that can be used to control vehicle accessory power, as well as acting as the trigger switch for the starter motor. Other systems may use the ignition key only for accessory power and to carry the small current required to trigger the magnetic starter switch, instead using a heavy-duty pushbutton switch to relay battery power to and through the magnetic switch. For more information on starter motors, refer to Chapter 9. Figure 7-19 illustrates one example of an ignition key switch used on Ford medium- and heavy-duty trucks and its control positions. When ignition switch removal is necessary, begin by disconnecting the ground cable from the batteries, followed by unplugging the ignition wire harness plug from the back side of the ignition switch. Refer to Fig. 7-20 and with the key in the switch, rotate it to the ACC position; using a small solid wire such as a paper clip or equivalent, firmly depress the release pin, then rotate the key counterclockwise (CCW) and gently pull the key and lock cylinder out of the switch assembly. Figure 7-21 illustrates the use of a small paper clip to release the pin.

NOTE: On some ignition key switches, you may have to place the switch in the OFF position, insert the paper clip, then rotate the switch to the ACC position.

If only a new lock cylinder is to be inserted, install the key in the cylinder and rotate the key to the ACC position. Install both the key and the lock in the ignition switch. Gently depress the release pin; turn the key CCW and push the new lock cylinder into the switch. Rotate the key to ensure that the new lock cylinder is in position and operates correctly. If it is necessary to remove the ignition key switch assembly completely from the instrument panel, refer to Fig. 7-22, which shows how the unit is retained in position by a bezel. You must rotate the bezel CCW to loosen it off.

To check an ignition switch for continuity once the wire harness has been removed from the rear of it, you

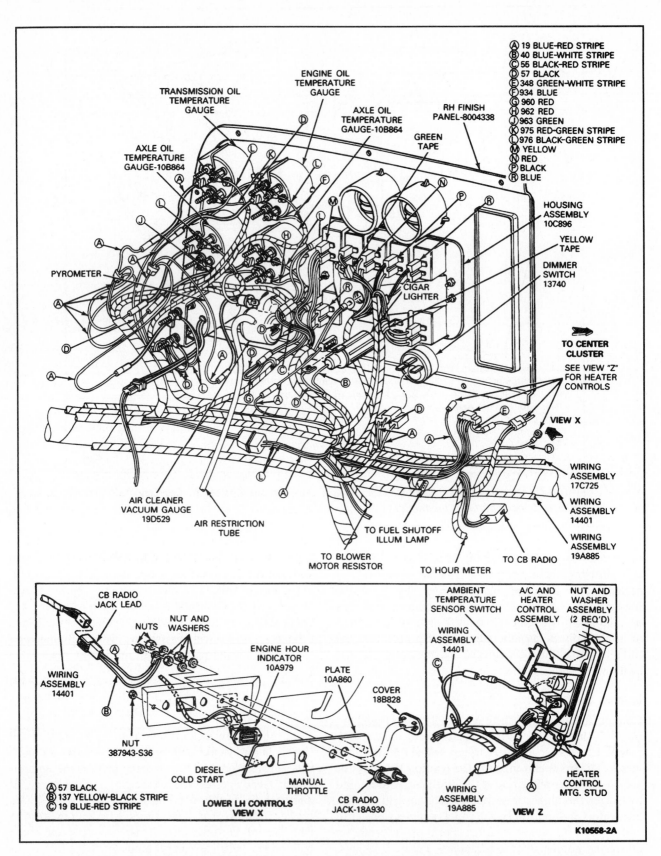

FIGURE 7–18 View of a Model L-9000 truck RH instrument cluster panel. (*Reprinted with Ford Motor Company's permission.*)

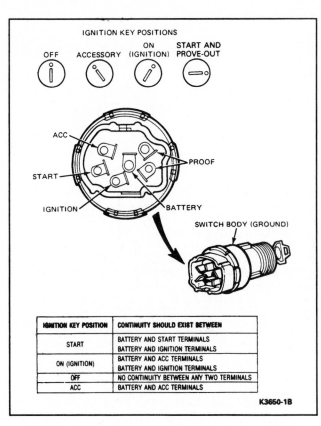

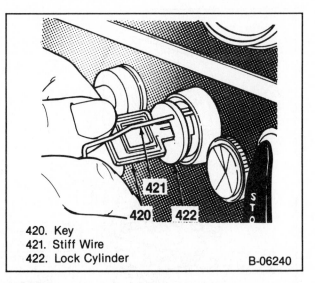

420. Key
421. Stiff Wire
422. Lock Cylinder
B-06240

FIGURE 7-21 Ignition switch lock cylinder replacement procedure. (*Courtesy of GMC Truck Division, General Motors Corporation.*)

FIGURE 7-19 Ignition switch continuity test procedure for an L-series truck model. (*Reprinted with Ford Motor Company's permission.*)

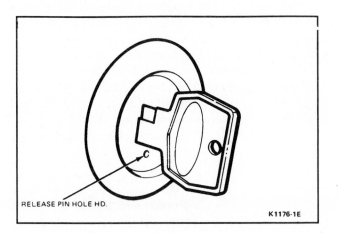

FIGURE 7-20 Location of ignition switch release pin hole for switch removal. (*Reprinted with Ford Motor Company's permission.*)

can employ either an ohmmeter or a self-powered test light (both are shown in Chapter 4). Refer to Fig. 7-19, which lists where continuity should exist in the various switch positions. A lack of continuity in any switch position would render a switch unusable.

ENGINE PROTECTION SYSTEMS

Medium- and heavy-duty trucks, particularly those with diesel engines, employ either a visual/audible alarm system or an engine shutdown system to protect the engine from serious mechanical damage. The alarm system is provided to alert the truck driver that there is a problem in a specific circuit; the operator must then make a conscious decision as to whether to pull the vehicle over and shut the engine down. If the engine is equipped with an automatic shutdown system, the driver will first receive a warning light/buzzer, followed shortly thereafter by an automatic engine shutdown procedure.

A good example of where you will find automatic engine shutdown features is in Detroit Diesel Corporation's DDEC (DD Electronic Controls) system, used in their two- and four-stroke-cycle engines, and also in Caterpillar's PEEC (Programmable Electronic Engine Control), used on both the 3406B and 3176 series truck engines. In both cases the ECM (electronic control module) will initiate an engine power reduction sequence first, followed by an automatic shutdown if the condition being monitored becomes serious enough to cause engine damage. For more detailed information on these two types of heavy-duty truck electronic control systems, refer to Chapter 11. An example of the warning light bars used on a heavy-duty class 8 Peterbilt 379 conventional instrument panel are shown in Fig. 7-23. These warning light bars are the same as those used on the Peterbilt truck model 362. Some circuits use a power signal to actuate the light, while some ground out a power signal to actuate the warning light. Some circuits are wired to activate a specific warning system. The most common type of warning lamp sensor is the grounding switch, which

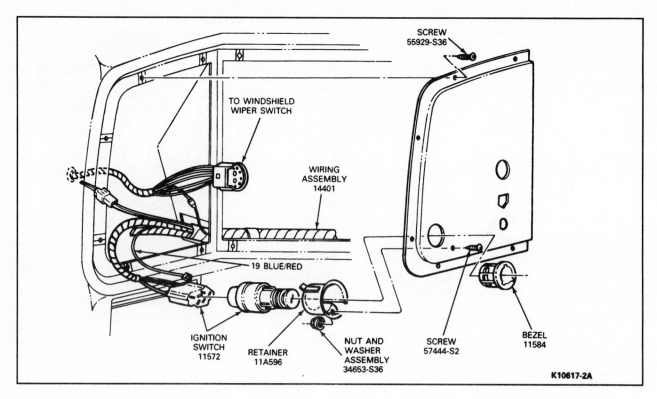

FIGURE 7–22 Ignition switch and wiring harness hookup. (*Reprinted with Ford Motor Company's permission.*)

responds to any undesirable operating condition by grounding the warning lamp circuit to complete it.

SERVICE TIP: A grounding switch sensor should not be installed with thread sealer or any other nonconducting material that might prevent a good metal-to-metal contact between the sensor case and the mounting hole. Typical grounding switch sensors usually include the low engine oil pressure warning lamp switch, the low air pressure warning lamp switch used with air brakes, the brake warning lamp pressure differential switch used with hydraulic brakes, and the engine water coolant level and hot engine warning lamps switches.

The differences in wiring arrangements can be traced in the truck service manual. The numbers appearing above and below the warning light bars in Fig. 7-23 are circuit numbers printed on the wire insulation cover every 4 in. (100 mm) or less to allow the technician to trace a specific circuit. Circuit insulation colors on Peterbilt 359, 362, and 379 truck models are black for circuit 239, red for circuit 242, blue for circuit 253, yellow for circuit 280; all others would be white. However, colors for these circuits may be stripes on white insulation, or colored insulation with a contrasting circuit marking.

The lights used in the warning bar are small wedge-

FIGURE 7–23 Warning light bars located in dash. (*Courtesy of Peterbilt Motors Company, Division of PACCAR, Newark, CA.*)

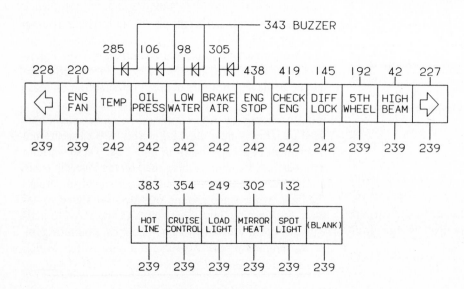
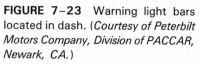

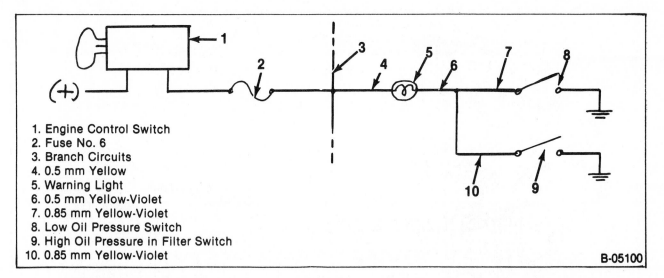

FIGURE 7-24 Engine oil low-pressure warning circuit. (*Courtesy of GMC Truck Division, General Motors Corporation.*)

1. Engine Control Switch
2. Fuse No. 6
3. Branch Circuits
4. 0.5 mm Yellow
5. Warning Light
6. 0.5 mm Yellow-Violet
7. 0.85 mm Yellow-Violet
8. Low Oil Pressure Switch
9. High Oil Pressure in Filter Switch
10. 0.85 mm Yellow-Violet

B-05100

base bulbs pressed into a socket-type base. Two contacts protrude from the socket base to make physical contact with the circuit board in order to energize the bulb. Warning lights used on different makes of trucks may show slight variations; however, all are designed to function in the same general manner. A combination buzzer and warning light is used with the Peterbilt system to warn the driver of a system problem. All buzzer functions for this system are carried out by a single buzzer located on the main cab wiring harness. The upper part of Fig. 7-23 shows the main warning light bar, while the lower half of the figure shows the auxiliary warning light bar.

Engine warning and shutdown systems usually consist of the following items:

1. Low engine oil pressure
2. High engine oil temperature
3. High coolant temperature
4. Low coolant level
5. Water in the fuel

Low Oil Pressure Alarm

An example of one engine low oil pressure alarm warning system circuit is illustrated in Fig. 7-24. Here the system is turned on by either the low oil pressure switch (engine or remote mounted) or the high-pressure switch at the oil filter. In this system the low oil pressure warning switch will close to complete the circuit any time that the oil pressure drops to between 4.3 and 7.1 psi (29.4 and 49 kPa). The reason that this system is set so low is that pressures only slightly higher than this may occur during low-idle operation. Also used in this system is an oil filter high pressure switch that will close when the oil filter becomes plugged or pressure exceeds 18.5 to 24.2 psi (127.5 to 168 kPa) across the filter. Engine shutdown will *not* occur in this system; it is simply a warning device to which the operator must respond.

On heavy-duty diesel engines, the low oil pressure switch location will vary between truck makes; however, Fig. 7-25 is an example of where the switch is located on the side of the engine block. This may be on either the left- or right-hand side of the engine. On some trucks, the low oil pressure switch may even be found behind the lamp and heater dash control panel.

FIGURE 7-25 Low-oil-pressure switch location on the engine. (*Courtesy of GMC Truck Division, General Motors Corporation.*)

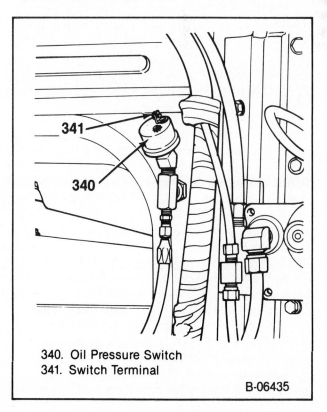

340. Oil Pressure Switch
341. Switch Terminal

B-06435

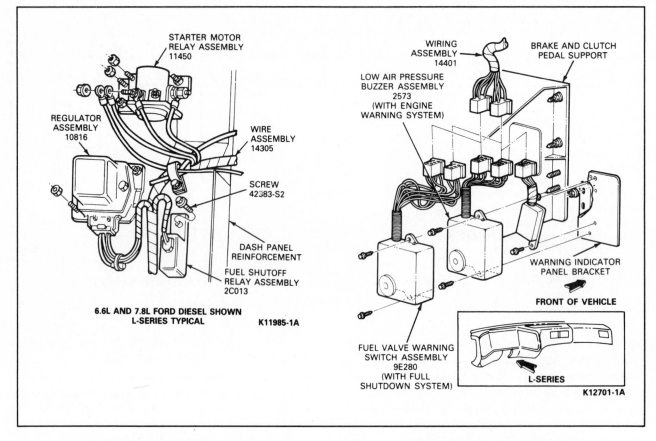

FIGURE 7-26 Automatic engine shutdown system components. (*Reprinted with Ford Motor Company's permission.*)

In the system shown in Fig. 7-26 an automatic engine shutdown feature will occur after a 30- to 40-second warning lamp illumination and an audible warning alarm or buzzer have been activated by low oil pressure, high coolant temperature, or low coolant level. This system is similar to that used on both the DDEC and Cat PEEC systems described in Chapter 11. However on the Ford truck system shown in Fig. 7-26, after the engine has been stopped by the automatic shutdown feature, it can be restarted and run again for between 30 and 40 seconds more only if the ignition key has been turned off first. On the DDEC system, a manual override button must be held in prior to the expiration of the 30-second delay period; otherwise, the engine cannot be restarted again. On the Ford system, there is no limit to how many times the engine can be restarted. However, after any automatic shutdown has occurred, if the engine is restarted without first turning the key off, the engine can be restarted, but it will only run for approximately 2 to 3 seconds before shutting down again.

In the automatic shutdown system shown in Fig. 7-27 the oil pressure switch is NC (normally closed); it requires 15 psi (103 kPa) or higher to cause this switch to open and stay in this position. This means that when the engine is first started, the low oil pressure indicator lamp and

audible buzzer will be on. Once this predetermined oil pressure has been reached, both the light and buzzer go off. During engine operation if the oil pressure should drop to the 15-psi level, the switch will close, completing the circuit to ground and once again both the warning light and buzzer will be activated. Should this condition continue for between 30 and 60 seconds, the engine audible warning control opens the ground circuit for the fuel shutoff system relay, and the engine will be shut down. A shutdown module used on heavy-duty trucks is shown in Fig. 7-28, where it is located in the general vicinity of the electrical equipment panel cover. This solid-state device will cause automatic engine shutdown in the event of sensed systems operating outside predetermined parameters.

High Coolant Temperature/Low Coolant Level Alarm

The coolant system may employ simply a warning light and buzzer, or it may be wired to an automatic shutdown module. On some engines, the coolant alarm system may consist of two separate sensors: one to monitor the engine coolant temperature, and the other to monitor the engine radiator coolant level. Figure 7-29 illustrates the location of the coolant temperature switch for a V71/92 two-

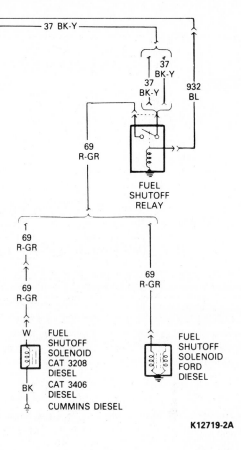

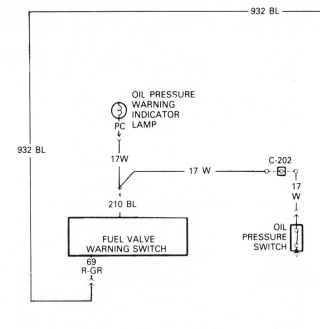

FIGURE 7-27 Automatic engine shutdown schematic showing the NC (normally closed) oil pressure switch. (*Reprinted with Ford Motor Company's permission.*)

K12719-2A

FIGURE 7-28 Automatic engine shutdown module and wiring harness. (*Courtesy of GMC Truck Division, General Motors Corporation.*)

FIGURE 7-29 Location of the engine temperature switch at the thermostat housing on a DDC series V92 engine. (*Courtesy of GMC Truck Division, General Motors Corporation.*)

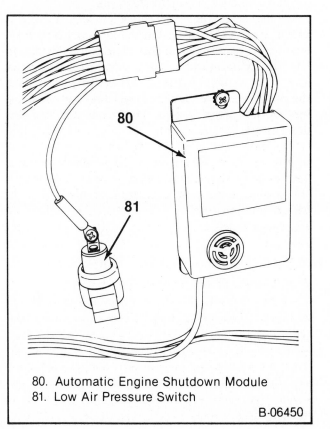

80. Automatic Engine Shutdown Module
81. Low Air Pressure Switch

B-06450

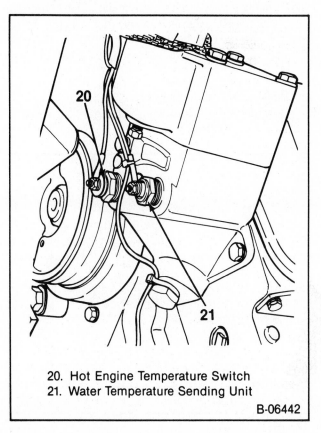

20. Hot Engine Temperature Switch
21. Water Temperature Sending Unit

B-06442

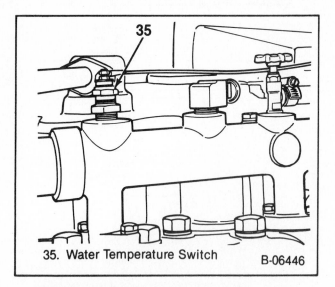

35. Water Temperature Switch

B-06446

FIGURE 7–30 Engine temperature switch location on a 14-L (855-in.³) Cummins NT series engine. (*Courtesy of GMC Truck Division, General Motors Corporation.*)

stroke DDC engine at the front of the engine in the thermostat housing. Figure 7-30 illustrates the sensor switch locations on a Cummins NTC 14L engine on top of the water manifold, and Fig. 7-31 shows the switch location on a 3406B Caterpillar engine near the right center of the cylinder head.

One example of a high coolant temperature system sensor that would cause automatic engine shutdown is shown in Figure 7-32. In this system the coolant temperature switch is NO (normally open); the switch is preset to activate a warning light and audible buzzer followed by automatic engine shutdown any time the coolant tem-

FIGURE 7–31 Hot engine temperature switch on a Caterpillar 3406B engine. (*Courtesy of GMC Truck Division, General Motors Corporation.*)

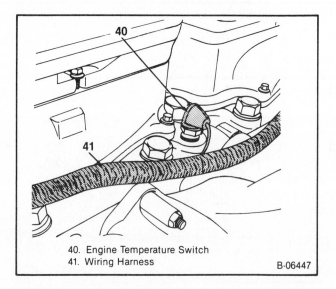

40. Engine Temperature Switch
41. Wiring Harness

B-06447

perature reaches or exceeds a preset level. This range is usually between 205 and 215 °F (96 to 102 °C) on diesel engines; on a gasoline engine it would be slightly higher. At this elevated temperature, the coolant switch would close and complete the circuit to ground, alerting the driver to a problem via the warning buzzer and illuminated warning light. After 30 to 60 seconds the engine audible warning control opens the ground circuit to the fuel shutoff relay and the engine stops.

NOTE: An engine oil temperature sensor will function and operate in the same general manner as described for the coolant temperature sensor.

If the engine is equipped with a low coolant level sensor, as shown in the circuit for Fig. 7–33, a loss of coolant causes the sensor probe to be exposed, and since air has a much higher resistance value than water, the system indicator warning control grounds the circuit to activate both the warning light and an audible buzzer. After 30 to 60 seconds the shutdown module is energized to stop the engine. Coolant-level probes work on the principle of using the coolant in the radiator to provide a constant ground for alternating current (ac); direct current (dc) is changed into ac by the low coolant circuit in the shutdown module. This ac current is required to minimize the buildup of material on the low coolant sensor probe; therefore, when the ground circuit is broken by a low water level, the module reacts by providing a ground for the tone alarm and coolant warning lamp. Generally, a 5-second delay is built in to the system to allow for coolant slosh within the radiator top tank.

If the engine is equipped with a low coolant level sensor, it is normally installed in the radiator reservoir or expansion tank on medium-duty diesel trucks. In this system, the circuit consists of a magnetic float switch so that should the coolant level drop to a predetermined level, the switch will close, thereby completing the circuit and turning on a warning light. The engine does not shut down in this system.

In heavy-duty class 7 and 8 trucks, a low coolant level detector sensor probe is located in the radiator top tank. This sensor is normally installed by the OEM (original equipment manufacturer); therefore, it should be in the correct position.

CAUTION: If the coolant level sensor is not covered with water, it can lead to a no engine start condition on electronically equipped fuel injected diesel engines, such as the DDEC system (see Chapter 11).

If the engine loses coolant due to a slow water leak or to a ruptured radiator water hose, the coolant level sensor will react much faster than a coolant temperature sensor will. The coolant level sensor will immediately activate the warning light and buzzer, and the engine will shut down within 30 to 40 seconds. A no-engine-start condition is typical when the coolant level sensor is uncovered.

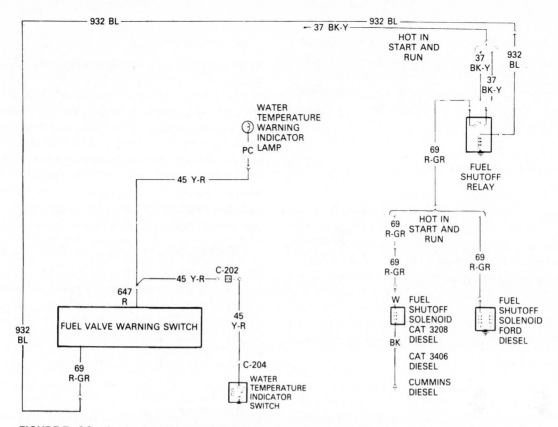

FIGURE 7-32 Automatic engine shutdown system showing the NO (normally open) water cooling temperature switch. (*Reprinted with Ford Motor Company's permission.*)

FIGURE 7-33 Automatic engine shutdown system showing the low-coolant-level sensor circuit. (*Reprinted with Ford Motor Company's permission.*)

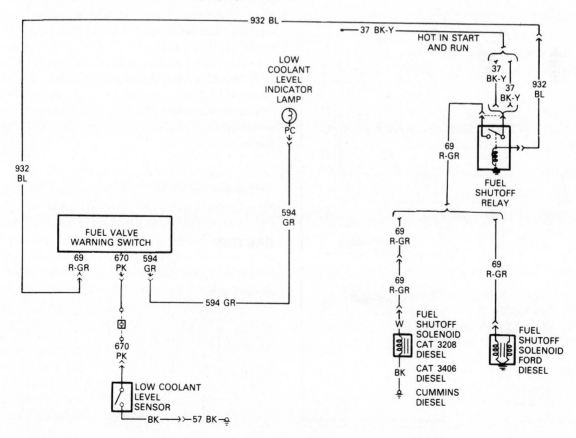

Figure 7–34 illustrates a low coolant level detector test harness arrangement that can be fabricated from an existing good detector wiring harness. Note that this test harness has all the connections necessary as well as a test light bulb. The test harness is used to check a suspected faulty system.

Procedure

1. Connect the test harness module to the system detector module after unhooking the instrument panel wiring harness from the shutdown module.
2. Take the test harness ground lead (56) with black wire insulation and connect it to a good clean ground.
3. Connect the positive terminal lead (54) of the test harness to a 12-V power supply; the test harness light bulb should illuminate immediately. If the bulb fails to light, discard the low coolant level detector and install a new one.
4. Touch the probe lead of the test harness to ground. The harness test light bulb should go out. If it remains on, replace the detector.
5. Remove the 12-V power source to the test bulb check lead. By touching and removing the test harness, the bulb should turn on and off.

FIGURE 7–34 Low-coolant-level detector test harness. (*Courtesy of GMC Truck Division, General Motors Corporation.*)

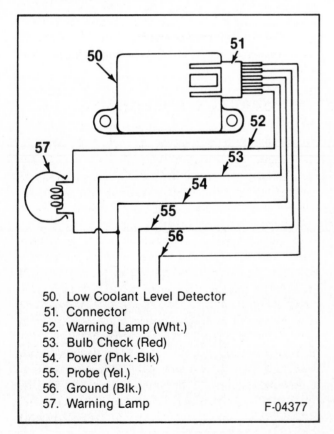

50. Low Coolant Level Detector
51. Connector
52. Warning Lamp (Wht.)
53. Bulb Check (Red)
54. Power (Pnk.-Blk)
55. Probe (Yel.)
56. Ground (Blk.)
57. Warning Lamp

F-04377

Water in Fuel Detector

Although water is a nondesirable property in both gasoline and diesel fuel systems, it is much more dangerous in a diesel fuel injection system, due to the much smaller operating tolerances mandated by the very high injection pressure created in the system. Consequently, most diesel engines are now equipped with a fuel filter/water separator system as well as a fuel heater for trucks that operate in low ambient temperatures. A water-in-fuel sensor is usually located in the base of the fuel filter/water separator bowl. When diesel fuel is present to surround the two tips of the sensor, a high resistance value is present that prevents the electronic relay from activating the system warning light. However, if a substantial amount of water collects in the base of the fuel filter/water separator bowl, water, which has a much lower resistance value than diesel fuel, will cause the electronic relay sensor to complete the circuit to ground, allowing the water-in-fuel warning light to illuminate on the instrument panel. This will not cause engine shutdown, but the operator of the vehicle should, as soon as possible, drain the accumulated water from the fuel filter bowl. On some vehicles the water can be drained simply by pulling a lever inside the vehicle cab; on others the drain cock on the base of the fuel filter/water separator has to be opened manually. Figure 7–35 illustrates a water-in-fuel detection circuit.

Automatic Engine Shutdown Test Procedure

Most automatic engine shutdown systems used on medium- and heavy-duty trucks are equipped with an engine shutdown test switch. This may be located on the dash console, or at the electrical equipment panel cover at the back of the cab behind the driver, as shown in Figure 7–36. With the engine running and the test switch activated, automatic engine shutdown should occur within 20 to 25 seconds to confirm that all systems are operational.

LOW-AIR-PRESSURE WARNING SYSTEM

On trucks equipped with air brakes, the low-air-pressure alarm system consists of a low-air-pressure switch, a tone alarm, and a low-air warning lamp to indicate to the driver that the reservoir pressure is below a safe limit. When the circuit through the low-air warning lamp and the tone alarm is completed to ground through the low-air switch, both the lamp and alarm will turn on. Generally, the low-air-pressure switch is a preset, nonadjustable model from the OEM. It is adjusted and sealed usually between 68 and 74 psi (470 to 510 kPa); therefore, if the switch malfunctions, replace it. The location of this switch will vary between different makes of vehicles, but can be located on the right-hand side of the engine cowl, next to the air compressor, in the cab tunnel plate below

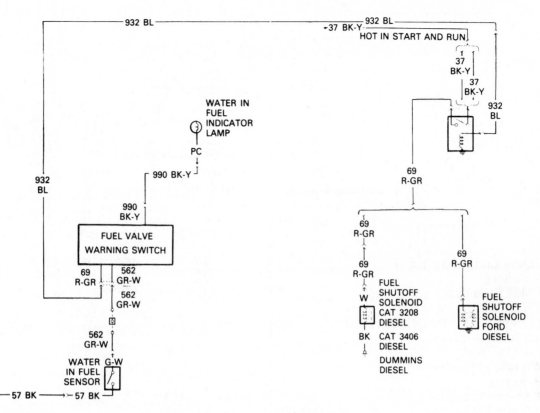

FIGURE 7-35 Water-in-fuel detection circuit. (*Reprinted with Ford Motor Company's permission.*)

the heater control panel, or on the electrical equipment panel at the back of the cab.

SERVICE TIP: Do not use sealing compound on the threads of a switch when installing it since this may insulate the threads from obtaining a good ground.

FIGURE 7-36 Engine shutdown test switch arrangement. (*Courtesy of GMC Truck Division, General Motors Corporation.*)

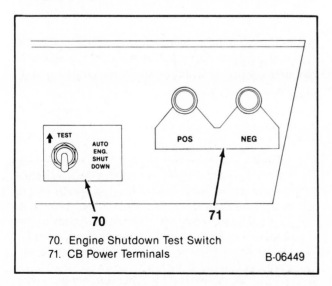

70. Engine Shutdown Test Switch
71. CB Power Terminals

B-06449

Figure 7–37 illustrates one type of low-air-pressure warning system. The circuit is activated by one of three low-air-pressure switches that are located on the air reservoirs. Should any one of the three switches close, the circuit is completed and the warning light and audible buzzer will sound.

ELECTROHYDRAULIC BRAKE BOOSTER PUMP

On certain models of conventional cab GMC medium-duty trucks, an EH (electrohydraulic) pump is used to provide boost pressure equal to about one-half that normally provided by the main power steering hydraulic pump on trucks equipped with hydraulic brakes. Figure 7–38 illustrates such a system. Any time there is a failure of the power steering/brake pump system, the primary system warning lamp and the reserve system warning lamp will illuminate, as well as the tone alarm emitting an audible sound to warn the driver of the condition. EH pump operation is controlled by two electrical switches in series; therefore, both must be on to complete the reserve circuit and supply power to the 12-V dc permanent-magnet electric motor, shown as item 33 in Fig. 7–38. Any time both series switches close, they activate a relay that supplies electric power to the pump (33). The relay is an integral part of the solid-state control module. A flow sensing switch (31) in the hydraulic head return

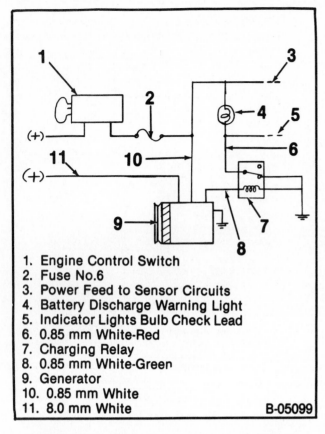

1. Engine Control Switch
2. Fuse No.6
3. Power Feed to Sensor Circuits
4. Battery Discharge Warning Light
5. Indicator Lights Bulb Check Lead
6. 0.85 mm White-Red
7. Charging Relay
8. 0.85 mm White-Green
9. Generator
10. 0.85 mm White
11. 8.0 mm White

B-05099

FIGURE 7–37 Air brake low-pressure warning circuit. (*Courtesy of GMC Truck Division, General Motors Corporation.*)

line senses the fluid flow through the primary hydraulic system, and it will close a series circuit to the pump relay whenever the flow drops below a predetermined minimum. There is also an EH pump switch on both the brake and clutch pedal brace that reacts to complete the series circuit any time that the brakes are applied while the normal primary hydraulic circuit is inoperative. Therefore, with a brake pedal application, the EH pump will provide reserve boost power.

The two dash-mounted lamps warn of failure of the main braking system, while the second warning light will warn of failure of the reserve boost braking system. The solid-state warning system consists of the solid-state module and electronic sensor, which is a polarized plug-

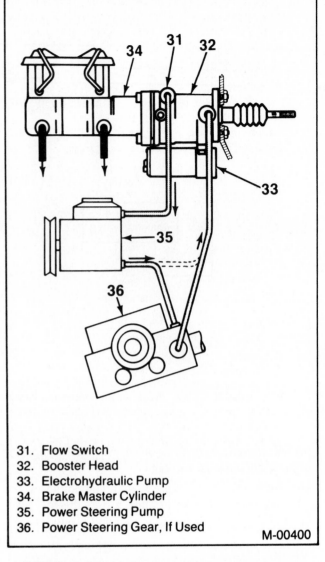

31. Flow Switch
32. Booster Head
33. Electrohydraulic Pump
34. Brake Master Cylinder
35. Power Steering Pump
36. Power Steering Gear, If Used

M-00400

FIGURE 7–38 Hydraulic brake booster system. (*Courtesy of GMC Truck Division, General Motors Corporation.*)

in unit that contains a transistor, two diodes, one zener diode, and two resistors. It is designed to complete the system to the reserve braking system warning lamp if the EH pump should also fail.

QUESTIONS

7–1. A thermoelectric gauge operates on a voltage less than that supplied from the battery. This voltage is generally:
a. 10 V c. 7 V
b. 8 V d. 5 V
(see page 206)

7–2. Technician A states that an electromagnetic gauge operates on the 12-V battery supply voltage, while technician B says that it operates at only half-battery voltage. Who is correct? (see page 206)

7–3. Technician A says that a bimetallic strip functions when 12 V is applied to its coil, causing it to heat up and open a set of contact points, thereby breaking the electrical circuit. Technician B says that when the points open, the bimetallic strip cools off, allowing the points to close again, thereby creating circuit power flow once again. Are both technicians correct in their respective statements, or only one? (see page 206)

7–4. Technician A says that a lower-than-normal voltage

power supply to a thermoelectric type gauge will cause it to be inoperative. Technician B says that this situation will simply cause an inaccurate gauge reading in proportion to the loss of voltage. Who is right? (see page 207)

7-5. Technician A says that there are basically two types of electric gauge measurement systems, the single-coil and two-coil designs. Technician B says that gauges operate on either a two-coil or a four-coil design principle. Who knows gauges better? (see page 207)

7-6. Supply the missing word in the following statement: An ammeter and a voltmeter are examples of _____ coil gauges. (see page 207)

7-7. Supply the missing word in the following statement: Rapid fluctuations in system supply voltage to a _____ coil gauge will generally not affect the gauge reading. (see page 207)

7-8. To ensure accuracy, many truck electrical gauges depend on which one of the following types of voltages:
a. Regulated   c. Alternating
b. Battery   d. Direct
(see page 206)

7-9. Temperature compensation in gauges using a bimetallic strip is achieved by:
a. An external resistor in the circuit
b. Vacuum sealing the assembly
c. The shape of the bimetallic strip
d. Current flow through the heater coil
(see page 206)

7-10. Technician A states that the word *thermistor* in relation to a temperature-sensing gauge is derived from the words *thermometer* and *resistor*. Technician B disagrees, saying that the word *thermistor* originates from the combination of the words *thermal resistance.* Who is correct? (see page 209)

7-11. Technician A says that a negative temperature resistance sensor (thermistor) is one that will exhibit a very high resistance value when the liquid being sensed is cold. Technician B says that the sensor would exhibit a very low resistance value when cold, gradually increasing as the liquid being measured heats up. Which technician is correct? (see page 209)

7-12. When normal engine temperatures are exceeded or low oil pressure occurs on an engine, a warning lamp may be activated by:
a. Grounding of the sensor
b. A voltage drop condition
c. Grounding the switch
d. All of the conditions above
(see page 210)

7-13. A warning buzzer used to alert the vehicle operator to a faulty engine operating condition is usually activated by:
a. A voltage drop condition
b. A current drop condition
c. Grounding of the switch
d. All of the conditions above
(see page 210)

7-14. Many pressure gauges employ a silicon wafer or alumina ceramic capacitor type of electrical sending unit that is deflected by pressurized liquid such as engine oil in order to operate. *True* or *False* (see page 211)

7-15. Technician A says that the degree of deflection of the diaphragm assembly within an oil pressure sending unit will alter the resistance value of the assembly, thereby varying the current flow through the gauge to affect the position of the floating gauge needle. Technician B disagrees, stating that the diaphragm deflection controls the flow rate of the fluid through a restricted orifice which in turn alters the position of an electric solenoid. Who is correct? (see page 211)

7-16. Technician A says that a voltmeter will not provide as accurate an interpretation of the state of the charging system as will an ammeter. Technician B disagrees, saying that the voltmeter is more accurate. Which technician is correct? (see page 211)

7-17. Supply the two missing words from the following statement. An ammeter is usually a _____ coil gauge that is connected in _____ between the alternator charging circuit and the battery. (see page 211)

7-18. A shunt wired into an ammeter circuit is used as:
a. A resistor   c. An insulator
b. A conductor   d. All of the above
(see page 213)

7-19 The purpose of the shunt in an ammeter circuit is to allow a percentage of the current in the circuit to bypass the ammeter gauge in order to provide:
a. Half-circuit voltage to feed an accessory
b. Half-circuit current to feed an accessory
c. Greater gauge needle stability
d. Melting of a fuse when excessive voltage occurs
(see page 213)

7-20. The float arm of a fuel level gauge is connected to:
a. A variable resistor unit
b. A bimetallic strip
c. A voltage regulator
d. All of the above
(see page 213)

7-21. Generally, the pickup for an electric tachometer is located at:
a. The distributor or coil unit on a gasoline engine
b. The engine flywheel or a metallic gear on a diesel engine
c. The crankshaft damper or pulley on both a gasoline and a diesel engine
d. Both a and b are correct
(see page 213)

7-22. Technician A says that an electric speedometer/odometer gauge features an analog air-core meter and small digital stepper motor. Technician B says that it employs a digital air-core meter and an analog stepper motor. Who is correct here? (see page 213)

7-23. Solid-state gauges are usually designed to provide:
a. Analog value readings through the use of LEDs (light-emitting diodes)
b. Digital value readings through the use of LEDs
c. More stability to the gauge pointer during fluctuating engine operating conditions
d. Gauge illumination through the use of fiber optics
(see pages 214–215)

7-24. All gauges on a truck are generally protected by either fuses or a circuit breaker. *True* or *False* (see page 218)

7-25. Fiber optic light sources are designed to transmit/carry light through a process of:
a. Bulb intensity relayed by small mirrors

b. Reflected illumination through the transparent core of the fiber

c. Many small LEDs located throughout the transparent core of the fiber

d. A small LED at each end of the transparent core of the fiber

(see page 218)

7-26. Technician A says that fiber optic tubes will not operate if they are kinked, cut, or broken. Technician B says that this will simply increase the voltage resistance through the wire. Who is correct? (see page 218)

7-27. Prior to pushing a fiber optic wire fully home into a lamp socket, housing, or lens, it should be:

a. Cut at an angle and the ends roughened to ensure a good contact

b. Smooth and cut square

c. Twisted at the ends to ensure good electrical contact

d. Equipped with soldered bullet-type connectors on the cut end of the wire

(see page 218)

7-28. When inspecting a panel-light fiber optic ribbon with the light switch turned to the full-bright position, bright spots or lines of bright light are usually indicative of:

a. Problems in the ribbon due to abrasion, cutting, bending, or tight folding

b. A correctly operating fiber optic ribbon

c. Excessive voltage through the control switch

(see page 218)

7-29. To remove an ignition switch from its panel normally requires that you:

a. Place the switch in the RUN position, depress the body, and turn it CCW to pull the key and lock cylinder out of the switch assembly

b. Place the switch in the RUN position, depress the body, and turn it CW to pull the key and lock cylinder out of the switch assembly

c. Place the switch in the ACC position and use a small solid wire to firmly depress the release pin, then rotate the key CCW to pull the key and lock cylinder out of the switch assembly

d. As in answer c above, but rotate the key CW

(see page 219)

7-30. Technician A says that to remove some ignition switches, you may have to place the switch in the OFF position, insert a solid wire or paper clip into the access hole, depress the pin, then rotate the switch to the RUN position. Technician B agrees with this statement, only he/she believes that the switch should be placed in the ACC rather than the RUN position. Who is correct? (see page 219)

7-31. Technician A says that to check an ignition switch for continuity once the wire harness has been removed, you can employ either an ohmmeter or a nonpowered test light to check the various switch positions. Technician B agrees with this statement, but believes that you should use either an ohmmeter or a self-powered test light for this check. Who knows their test routine better? (see page 219)

7-32. An engine protection system using a warning light uses:

a. A power signal to actuate the warning light

b. Grounding of the power signal to actuate the warning light

c. Both a and b above

(see page 221)

7-33. Technician A says that the most commonly employed type of warning lamp sensor is the grounding switch type. Technician B disagrees, stating that the most common is the use of a power signal to activate the warning lamp. Who is correct? (see page 221)

7-34. Technician A says that it is acceptable to use thread sealer such as Teflon tape when installing a grounding switch sensor to effectively seal the loss of fluid from a low engine oil pressure warning lamp switch or a low brake system air pressure switch. Technician B disagrees, saying that this action could prevent a good metal-to-metal contact between the sensor and the mounting hole. Which technician is correct? (see page 222)

7-35. Lights commonly used in truck dash warning bar panels are usually:

a. Full-size straight pin bulbs

b. Full-size offset pin bulbs

c. Small wedge-shaped bulbs

d. LEDs (light-emitting diodes)

(see pages 222–223)

7-36. On an automatic engine shutdown system, after warning lamp/buzzer activation, the engine will stop after approximately:

a. 2 minutes   c. 30 to 40 seconds

b. 1 minute   d. 10 to 15 seconds

(see page 224)

7-37. The letters NC and NO stamped on a switch indicate:

a. Normally closed or normally open

b. Negative circuit wiring or negative option wiring

c. Negative current or negative ohms resistance

d. Not certified for greater than a 12-V circuit or non-operational for greater than a 12-V circuit

(see pages 224, 226)

7-38. Technician A says that coolant level probes now in use on many heavy-duty truck radiator systems operate on the principle of using the coolant to provide constant grounding for the current flow. A reduction or loss of coolant around the sensor probe results in a loss of the ground circuit path, causing the control module in the circuit to activate a warning lamp/buzzer. Technician B says that the coolant acts as an insulator, and when the level drops, this action causes a grounding of the circuit. Who is correct? (see page 226)

7-39. Technician A says that if a coolant level sensor on an electronically controlled fuel-injected diesel engine is not covered by water, this can lead to a "no-engine-start" condition. Technician B says that the engine will start, but will immediately activate the low coolant warning light/buzzer system. Who is correct? (see page 226)

7-40. Technician A says that diesel fuel has a much lower resistance value than water and that this is what triggers the "water-in-fuel" sensor on a fuel–filter–water separator unit. Technician B says that it is water that has the lower resistance value. Who is correct? (see page 228)

CHAPTER

8

Alternator Charging Systems

OBJECTIVES

Within this chapter you will be able to:

1. Identify and name the major manufacturers of truck alternators.
2. Understand and describe the basic operation of an alternator charging system.
3. Describe the basic differences between various models of commonly used truck alternators.
4. Determine the correct procedures required to isolate a charging system problem using specialized instrumentation.
5. Disassemble, inspect, and repair an alternator assembly.
6. Perform regular preventive maintenance checks and adjustments.

GENERAL INFORMATION

The name *alternator* originates from the fact that this engine-driven component (belt or gear) is designed to produce an alternating current that when rectified will supply the battery or batteries with a direct-current flow to maintain them in a full state of charge. Often referred to as a *generator,* the alternator is part of the charging system on any car or truck. The alternator forms part of the basic heavy-duty electrical system, which consists of the following components, which are illustrated in Fig. 8–1.

Heavy-Duty Electrical System Components

1. Batteries, the number of which can vary, depending on whether the system desired is a 12- or a 24-V design. In addition, a high-output 12-V starter will generally use four batteries connected in parallel, while a standard 12-V starter motor may only use two. If a 24-V system is required, generally four batteries can be used. This may take the form of two, three, or four 12-V units or four 6-V units. The batteries can be connected to a series–parallel switch for 24-V starting and 12-V charging. Refer to Chapter 3 and Chapter 9 for specific information on battery hookup arrangements.

2. The starting motor for engine cranking purposes. This can be a 12- or a 24-V unit.

3. The alternator or generator required to keep the batteries in a full state of charge.

4. A magnetic switch to carry the high current requirements to the starter motor.

5. An ignition switch that is used to open (start) and close (off) the circuit to start the engine through the magnetic switch.

6. All of the necessary wiring to connect all these components together as a working team.

Alternators must be closely matched to the load requirements of the truck electrical system if long, trouble-

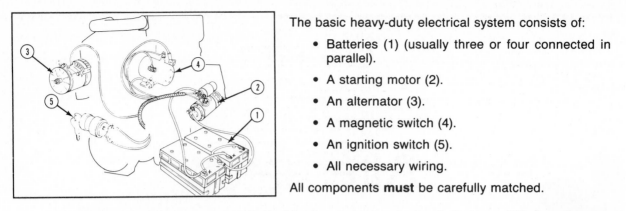

The basic heavy-duty electrical system consists of:

- Batteries (1) (usually three or four connected in parallel).
- A starting motor (2).
- An alternator (3).
- A magnetic switch (4).
- An ignition switch (5).
- All necessary wiring.

All components **must** be carefully matched.

FIGURE 8–1 Basic components required with a heavy-duty truck electrical system. (*Courtesy of Cummins Engine Company, Inc.*)

free operation is to be expected. There are many different sizes and rated outputs of alternators readily available from a number of major OEMs (original equipment manufacturers). The major starter, battery, and alternator suppliers to midrange and heavy-duty truck manufacturers, who are also known as OEMs, include some of the following well-known names:

1. Delco-Remy Division of General Motors Corporation
2. Robert Bosch Corporation
3. Nippondenso
4. Leece-Neville
5. Motorola
6. Motorcraft (Ford)

All of these manufacturers are well known and respected for their wide range of automotive and heavy-duty electrical and electronics products, with all of them having sales organizations located throughout the world. Of these, Delco-Remy is the major supplier and has been an integral part of the automotive/truck industry since 1896. Throughout its history, Delco has introduced numerous industry firsts, such as the first self-starter, battery ignition, and alternators with integral regulators. In addition, Delco is credited with converting the entire U.S. auto industry from 6- to 12-V systems in the mid-1950s. More recent innovations include high-energy electronic ignition, brushless Delcotron charging systems, and maintenance-free batteries. Delco has manufacturing facilities, including joint ventures and licensees, in North and South America, Europe, and Eastern Asia, with sales and service facilities located in the United States and Canada, England, West Germany, France, Italy, Japan, and South Korea, which is testimony to the success of this well-known and respected auto/truck electrical component supplier.

Although there are many similarities in the basic design of the alternators produced by these excellent OEMs, there are unique design features common to one make or model that require clarification so that you, the mechanic/technician, in your daily exposure to charging

system problems will be familiar with these differences and know how to approach them correctly. Consequently, in this chapter you will be exposed to the major makes and models of alternators that you will usually come across in a fleet operation for light-, medium-, and heavy-duty trucks.

In comparison with the dc generator, the ac alternator has the following major advantages:

1. Lighter and more compact
2. Fewer moving parts
3. Produces power even at idle speeds
4. Less maintenance
5. Newer models include build-in solid-state regulators
6. Less wear and therefore longer life
7. Reduction in battery size due to the rapid recharging characteristic of the alternator
8. Longer brush life, since only low current passes through them compared to full generator output on a dc system
9. Alternators can be rotated in any direction (unless a pulley fan with inclined blades is used)
10. Capable of high maximum speeds
11. Easier to troubleshoot and adjust

BASIC ELECTRICAL SYSTEM LOADS

Typical electrical loads placed on the batteries and charging system of a vehicle will vary depending on the classification of truck. A tractor/trailer will have more marker lights, parking lights, and stoplights than those on a straight-body medium-duty truck. The options specified for any given vehicle determine the maximum electrical load that the alternator/battery charging system must handle. In addition, even though medium- and heavy-duty trucks often use the same electrical accessories, the construction of the component is usually more rugged on a diesel powered class 8 high-way tractor than in a gasoline-powered mid-range straight-body truck, which necessitates a heavier current (amperage) draw. Figure 8–2 illustrates typical electrical accessories and their respective fuse or circuit breaker amperage ratings to protect

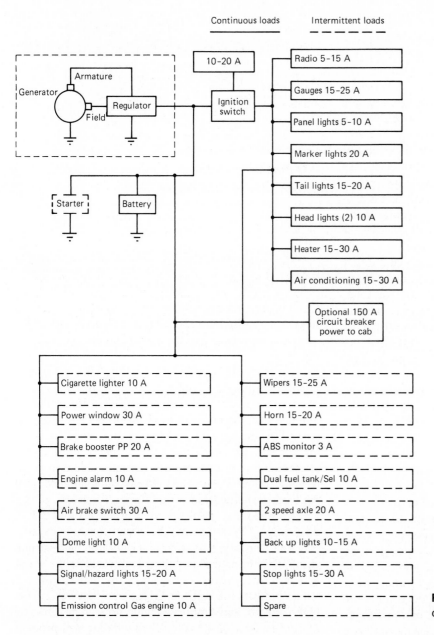

Continuous loads — **Intermittent loads** - - -

10-20 A

Generator / Armature / Regulator / Field

Ignition switch

Radio 5-15 A
Gauges 15-25 A
Panel lights 5-10 A
Marker lights 20 A
Tail lights 15-20 A
Head lights (2) 10 A
Heater 15-30 A
Air conditioning 15-30 A

Starter / Battery

Optional 150 A circuit breaker power to cab

Cigarette lighter 10 A
Power window 30 A
Brake booster PP 20 A
Engine alarm 10 A
Air brake switch 30 A
Dome light 10 A
Signal/hazard lights 15-20 A
Emission control Gas engine 10 A

Wipers 15-25 A
Horn 15-20 A
ABS monitor 3 A
Dual fuel tank/Sel 10 A
2 speed axle 20 A
Back up lights 10-15 A
Stop lights 15-30 A
Spare

FIGURE 8-2 Typical medium- and heavy-duty truck electrical loads.

the circuit. If a fuse blows, it has to be replaced, whereas a circuit breaker can be reset manually. Items depicted in the diagram by solid lines are continuous-duty loads that would normally be on for long periods of time, while accessories that may only be on for short periods are commonly referred to as intermittent-duty loads and are shown by dashed lines.

On many heavy-duty trucks a single feed power supply to the cab is used to supply all of the electrical accessories from a circuit breaker–protected central point. An example would be a 150-A circuit breaker fed from the positive battery terminal. Combination fuse and circuit breaker protection is usually employed on most vehicles.

BASIC ALTERNATOR OPERATION

Prior to studying several types of widely used alternators, it may be helpful to explain the simple construction and basic operation of an alternator. This will give you a base from which to work as you progress into the more detailed models.

Basically, there are two types of alternators in use today. These are the automotive type, which is widely used on cars and light pickup trucks and vans, and the heavy-duty type, which is used in trucks both on- and off-highway, in marine applications, in heavy-duty equipment, and in special applications such as police cruisers, ambulances, emergency vehicles, and firefighting vehicles.

All of these alternators work on the same general principle. The components of the ac, or alternating-current, generator (another term sometimes used to describe an alternator) function to produce both voltage and current. From earlier discussions on electrical fundamentals you will recall that the flow of electricity (the flow of electrons) is called current. This is a measure of the quantity of electron flow, similar to water flow in a water system, although it is measured in gallons per minute or liters per minute. The electrical unit that is used for measuring current is the ampere. Remember, however, that current cannot flow without pressure being present in the system.

The electrical pressure is known as voltage, which is the effort needed to force the current through the wire carrying conductors and electrical accessories. The unit of electrical pressure is the volt. You will also recollect from basic electrical fundamentals that both electricity and magnetism are involved in an electrical system. If we pass current through a wire and an electromagnet is produced. The strength of this magnetic field is proportional to the amount of current flowing in the wire; the greater the current, the stronger the magnetic field.

Under basic fundamentals, we also pointed out that if a piece of straight copper wire is bent into the shape of a coil, we are able to produce a much stronger magnetic field with the same amount of current flowing in the wire, due to the fact that we concentrate the magnetic field in a given area. By placing a soft-iron core within the coil windings as shown in Fig. 8-3, the strength of the magnetic field around the coil is increased further due to the fact that the iron core will conduct these magnetic lines of force much better than air will. This concentration of the magnetic field allows the magnetic lines of force to become stronger.

Using iron in a magnetic path can increase the magnetic strength as much as 2500 times over a coil that simply has air in the center. All magnets, of course, contain a north and a south pole, as shown in Fig. 8-3.

Within the alternator or ac generator, these same basic principles are applied. Figure 8-4 shows a basic alternator rotor assembly, which is the only moving component of the alternator (driven by a belt and pulley, or gear driven). A field winding consisting of many turns of insulated wire wound around an iron spool is contained within the rotor assembly; when current is passed through this field winding, we produce an electromagnet and also a magnetic field just as we did with the simple coiled wire and iron core shown in Fig. 8-3.

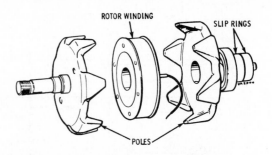

FIGURE 8-4 Alternator rotor assembly. (*Courtesy of Motorola Automotive and Industrial Electronics Group.*)

The structure of the rotor assembly consists of the field winding, two iron segments that contain individual poles or interlacing fingers whose number can vary between makes, a support shaft (which is rotated), and two slip rings on which brushes ride on one end of the rotor shaft and are attached to the leads from the field coil (see Fig. 8-4).

The rotor field winding current flow has a direct bearing on the strength of the pole pieces (north and south) of the rotor assembly. A certain residual magnetism is retained in these pole pieces at all times. However, by controlling the strength of the generator rotor field winding current, we can control the output voltage of the alternator. In this respect, the alternator is said to be externally excited because the field current is supplied from the battery and ignition switch through resistors, diodes and transistors at a voltage of between 1.5 and 2.5 V, on average. Fig. 8-5 shows the circuit for a typical slip-ring and brush-type alternator. Generator field current is supplied through a diode trio connected to the stator windings. A capacitor, or condenser, mounted to the end frame protects the rectifier bridge and diode trio from high voltages, and suppresses radio noise. The direction of current flow in the rotor field winding will produce a north magnetic pole in each finger of one half of the rotor segment, and a south magnetic pole in each finger of the other half of the rotor segment.

In order to use effectively the force of this rotating magnetic field produced by the rotor, we need to mount a series of copper wires within the magnetic field that will absorb the electrical energy from the lines of force; for this purpose we commonly use a *stator*. The basic stator is a simple loop or loops of wire arranged in such a fashion as to allow the magnetic lines of force from the spinning rotor to cut across this wire (see Fig. 8-6).

As this action occurs, electrical pressure or voltage is produced in the loop or loops of wire (the stator, which is stationary); the greater the speed of rotor rotation, the greater will be the voltage induced within the stator windings. Stators currently used in all alternators generally consist of a laminated iron frame and three stator or output windings which are wound into the frame slots. The

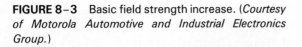

FIGURE 8-3 Basic field strength increase. (*Courtesy of Motorola Automotive and Industrial Electronics Group.*)

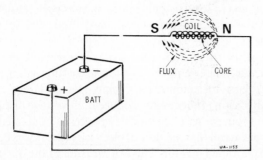

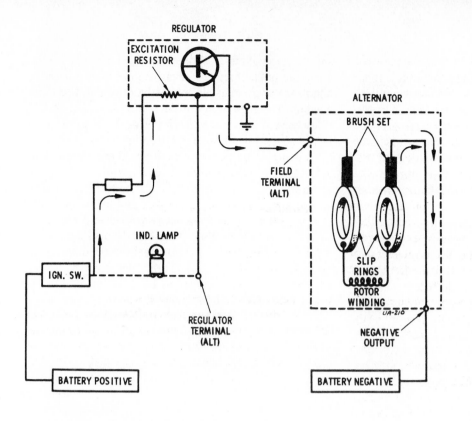

REGULATOR

EXCITATION
RESISTOR

ALTERNATOR

BRUSH SET

FIELD
TERMINAL
(ALT)

SLIP
RINGS

ROTOR
WINDING

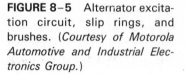

IND. LAMP

IGN. SW.

REGULATOR
TERMINAL
(ALT)

NEGATIVE
OUTPUT

BATTERY POSITIVE

BATTERY NEGATIVE

FIGURE 8–5 Alternator excitation circuit, slip rings, and brushes. (*Courtesy of Motorola Automotive and Industrial Electronics Group.*)

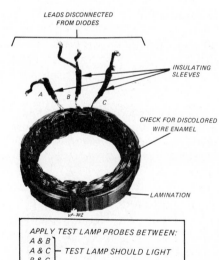

(a)

VA 2013

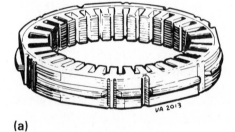

LEADS DISCONNECTED
FROM DIODES

INSULATING
SLEEVES

A   B   C

CHECK FOR DISCOLORED
WIRE ENAMEL

LAMINATION

UP-302

APPLY TEST LAMP PROBES BETWEEN:
A & B
A & C — TEST LAMP SHOULD LIGHT
B & C
(IF LIGHT FAILS TO LIGHT, AN OPEN
WINDING IS INDICATED)

APPLY TEST LAMP PROBES
BETWEEN A, B, OR C & LAMINATION—
LAMP SHOULD NOT LIGHT (LIGHTED
LAMP INDICATES A GROUNDED
WINDING)

(b)

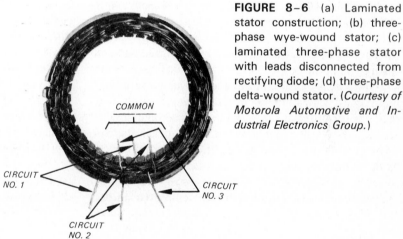

COMMON

CIRCUIT
NO. 1

CIRCUIT
NO. 3

CIRCUIT
NO. 2

(c)

FIGURE 8–6 (a) Laminated stator construction; (b) three-phase wye-wound stator; (c) laminated three-phase stator with leads disconnected from rectifying diode; (d) three-phase delta-wound stator. (*Courtesy of Motorola Automotive and Industrial Electronics Group.*)

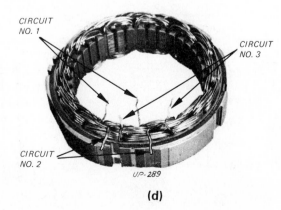

CIRCUIT
NO. 1

CIRCUIT
NO. 3

CIRCUIT
NO. 2

UP-289

(d)

stator laminations are insulated with an epoxy coating prior to installation of the windings. The assembly is then varnish-coated for added insulation and to prevent movement of the windings. The stator assembly is then sandwiched between the opposite ends of the alternator to form part of the generator frame. Battery current that flows through one slip ring into the field windings of the rotor leaves the field coil through the other slipring and brush and returns to the battery through the ground return path (see Fig. 8–5).

When all components are assembled to produce the alternator, the rotor turns freely within the inner diameter of the stator. However, a very small air gap does exist between the rotor poles and the stator laminations to prevent contact between the rotor and stator; otherwise, physical damage could occur.

Movement of the rotor will alternately allow each pole finger (north and south poles) to pass each loop in the stator windings, thereby inducing a voltage and subsequent current flow in the stator windings. The voltage induced within the stator windings will therefore be constantly alternating between these north and south poles. This oscillating or back- and forth-voltage will cause the current (amperes) within the stator windings to flow in one direction, then the other. This type of current, known as alternating current (or ac), is explained in more detail later in the chapter. Since all of the electrical accessories in use today in cars and trucks are designed for direct current, which flows in only one direction, we have to change the ac to dc.

The simplest method available for the purpose is to use a diode, which allows current to pass through it in only one direction; it operates in a manner similar to a one-way check valve. Within the end frame of the alternator, six diodes are located in a rectifier bridge connected to the stator windings to form a heat sink at the end closest to the slip rings, as shown in Fig. 8–7. These six diodes are required because commonly employed stators contain three windings; three diodes are positive in design, while the other three are negative in design in order to handle the alternating current produced within each stator winding. The alternating current is therefore changed into direct current through the diodes. This dc voltage appears at the generator output BAT terminal.

Finally, we require a voltage regulator to control the ac output of the alternator. The ac output is dependent on the quantity of current flow through the rotor field coil windings; therefore, to ensure and maintain a constant-voltage output, alternators commonly employ a solid-state voltage regulator built into the alternator housing itself. This voltage regulator measures the output voltage and automatically adjusts the field current to keep the output voltage constant as the load changes in the vehicle electrical system demand.

Very briefly, then, we can summarize the operation of the alternator by saying that the rotor and stator act as a unit to provide alternating-current flow, which is then converted to direct current by the diodes for charging the battery and to supply power for the electrical accessories.

WHAT IS ALTERNATING CURRENT?

Electrical accessories in use on cars and trucks today require dc, or direct-current, flow in order to operate. This simply means that the current flowing through the conducting wires follows the same path at all times.

The electrical flow (electron flow) within the windings of both a dc, generator and an ac alternator is induced by the strength of the magnetic field. In both, this induced voltage produces alternating-current flow, which is then converted to direct-current flow by the use of a commutator in the dc generator, and by the use of positive and negative diodes in the alternator.

Figure 8–7 shows the basic rectification of the internally generated ac voltage in an alternator to usable dc voltage output.

FIGURE 8–7 Alternator basic rectification circuit. (*Courtesy of Motorola Automotive and Industrial Electronics Group.*)

FIGURE 8–8 Alternator diodes, brushes, slip rings, stator, and field windings arrangement. (*Courtesy of DAF Trucks, Eindhoven, The Netherlands.*)

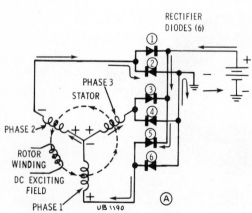

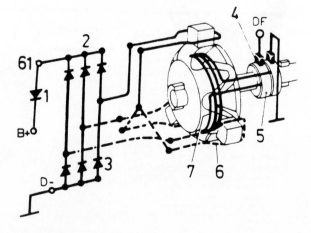

Figure 8–8 shows the main components of a three-phase alternator. The basic difference between a dc generator and alternator is simply that the magnetic field (magnets) is stationary in the dc generator, while in the ac alternator, the magnetic field or rotor is rotating. In the dc generator, the magnets are bolted to the fixed generator housing with a wire-wound armature rotated by a belt-driven pulley. In the ac alternator, the magnets or pole pieces are part of the rotor, which is driven by a belt and pulley or gear driven in heavy-duty applications, while the stator, which is made up of loops of wire, is stationary. In both cases, electrical energy is produced by the fact that voltage is induced into copper wires cutting magnetic lines of force.

From our earlier discussion on the basic operation of the alternator, you will recollect that the rotor is made up of a series of interlacing fingers, some of which are identified as being magnetic north (north poles), while the others were magnetic south (south poles), as shown in Fig. 8–4.

SINGLE-PHASE ALTERNATING CURRENT

The simplest form of alternating current is the single-phase type. If we consider Fig. 8–9, we see one pole of the rotor assembly as it relates to a single stator winding.

The strength of the magnetic lines of force shown in Fig. 8–9 are controlled by the small flow of electricity that leaves the battery when the ignition switch is turned on. This electrical flow (see Fig. 8–5) then passes through one of the small brushes riding on the slip ring and into the field winding wound internally within the rotor, which is surrounded by the rotor poles (interlacing fingers). This type of rotor with interlacing poles or fingers is often referred to as a *claw pole rotor* and is illustrated in Fig. 8–4.

As the rotor turns within the inside diameter of the stator assembly, a voltage is induced in the winding of the stator. This induced electromotive force changes with the field strength and with the speed at which the magnetic lines of force are cut.

Since the magnetic lines of force always flow from north to south, the voltage induced in the stator winding will flow one way and then the other. If a voltmeter were placed across the stator winding as shown in Fig. 8–9, the needle of the gauge would swing first one way and then the other, indicating that an alternating current is being produced within the stator winding. Figure 8–10 shows a typical example of what is commonly referred to as a *sine wave*, or curve of alternating current induced during one complete revolution of the rotor having one north and one south pole. Notice that the greatest amount of induced voltage in the stator winding will occur when the magnet is at 90° and 270°. At these two positions, the relation of the magnet to the stator windings causes the greatest number of magnetic lines of force to be cut.

If we study Fig. 8–10 a little closer, at 0° no voltage is induced in the stator wire (winding) because there are no magnetic lines of force cutting across the conductor. As the rotor turns from 0° toward 90°, the magnetic field at the leading edge of the rotor starts to cut through the wires of the conductor (stator), thereby steadily increasing the induced voltage into the wire until it reaches its maximum at 90°. Continued rotation from 90 to 180° will reduce the magnetic field, cutting the wires of the conductor or stator, thereby reducing the induced voltage.

The current flow from 0 to 180° will be in one direction, the positive direction, which is shown as the area above the centerline of Fig. 8–10. Rotor rotation from 180° toward 270° will cause the magnetic lines of force that are leaving the north pole to continue to enter the south pole. This action means that these magnetic lines of force are now cutting the stator wires from top to bottom rather than from bottom to top as was shown earlier when the rotor poles were at the 90° position. This action will cause a reversal of induced voltage in the stator windings (wires), so that we now have a negative current

FIGURE 8–9 (a) Magnetic flux (magnetic field) in the stator winding. The lines of force flow from the north to the south pole; (b) when the magnetic field is reversed, the polarity of the induced voltage changes. (*Courtesy of Robert Bosch Corporation.*)

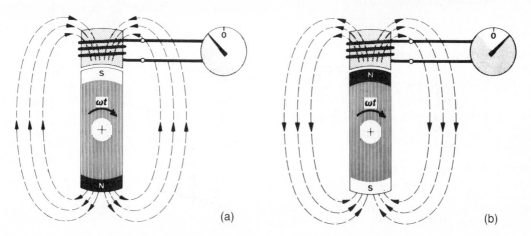

(a)   (b)

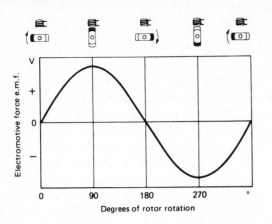

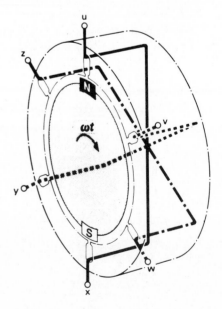

FIGURE 8–10   Sine wave of induced alternating current during one turn of the rotor. (*Courtesy of Robert Bosch Corporation.*)

flow from 180° back to 360°, with the peak voltage being induced at 270° because of the position of the pole, allowing the magnetic field to cut the windings. The voltage will again be zero when the pole piece sits at a horizontal position because once again no magnetic lines of force are cutting the stator windings (wires).

The sine wave shown in Fig. 8–10 represents one complete turn of the rotor with one north and one south pole. This action is more commonly referred to as one cycle. If this one pole rotor were driven at a speed of 3600 rpm, in 1 second it would complete 60 turns or cycles. The number of cycles per second is known as the *frequency* of the alternator. Since engine speed, and hence alternator drive speed, will vary when a vehicle is being driven, the frequency will not remain constant but will fluctuate.

NOTE: The speed at which a given alternator will produce its greatest current output is determined by the manufacturer. Consequently, when any alternator is installed on a truck, the truck OEM must determine what the drive ratio to the alternator must be to ensure that the generator speed will be fast enough to produce a current output that will ensure a full state of battery charge during normal vehicle operation. This speed is calculated by determining where the generator will be driven from on the engine, then selecting a generator pulley diameter that will provide the rotational speed necessary. Examples of various generator current outputs and the speed of rotation are given in Table 8–5 relevant to the model in question.

The induced voltage, and therefore the current flow, that could be taken from the stator winding employing only one coiled wire would not be very steady, and its output (amperage) would be low. To improve both of these conditions, all alternators in use today employ what is known as a three-phase stator winding.

THREE-PHASE STATOR WINDING

In the three-phase alternator, two additional wire windings are added to the single winding that we illustrated in Fig. 8–9 and whose sine wave is shown in Fig. 8–10.

We can refer to these three windings as simply U, V, and W, shown in Fig. 8–11 being 120° apart in phase relationship. In this three-phase arrangement, the opposite end of the winding is simply identified as X, Y, and Z, as shown in Fig. 8–11. Each winding would exhibit a combined sine-wave diagram such as that shown in Fig. 8–12. Note that the maximum voltmeter deflection of each separate winding in a three-phase arrangement will be 120° opposite to the other windings.

Figure 8–13(a) illustrates an oversimplified alternator setup that uses one winding and a six-pole magnet (rotor), meaning it has six north and six south poles. In this example the voltmeter will deflect six times to the positive side and six to the negative side in one complete revolution (360°) of the magnet (rotor). Since one winding would not allow us to produce a steady enough or strong enough current output, the alternator usually uses six windings, as shown in Fig. 8–13(b), where they are connected in series so that their respective axes will intersect at 60° angles rather than at 120° angles. This will produce a cycle for every 60° of rotation. Therefore, to produce the desired three-phase current supply for automotive/truck use, the sine wave, U, V, and W shown in Fig. 8–11, each consisting of six windings, we must connect them in such a manner that each individual group requires 60° to produce one cycle and so that the maximum voltage and current produced will occur at equal intervals. What must exist, then, is that after each 60° of rotation of the rotor divided by the three-phase concept, we will find that for every 20° of rotation the maximum output is obtained from each winding (either, U, V, or W). This concept is best explained by referring to Fig. 8–14. With a multipole (finger) rotor, the voltage generated within the stator windings would now appear as shown in Fig. 8–15.

FIGURE 8–11   Three-phase stator winding simplification. (*Courtesy of Robert Bosch Corporation.*)

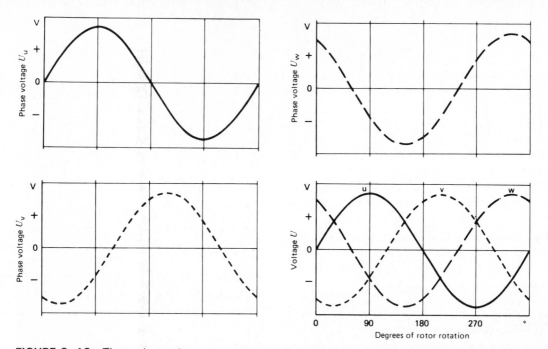

FIGURE 8-12 Three-phase sine-wave relationship. (*Courtesy of Robert Bosch Corporation.*)

FIGURE 8-13 (a) Sine-wave action for a six-pole rotor arrangement; voltmeter will deflect six times to the + side and six times to the − side in 360° of rotor rotation; (b) Six-pole rotor windings producing a cycle every 60°. (*Courtesy of DAF Trucks, Eindhoven, The Netherlands.*)

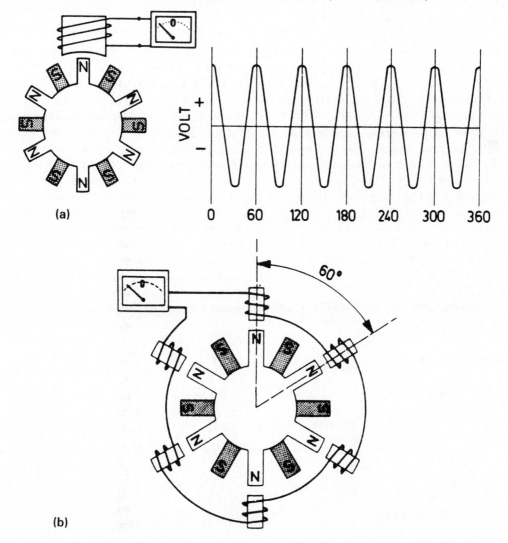

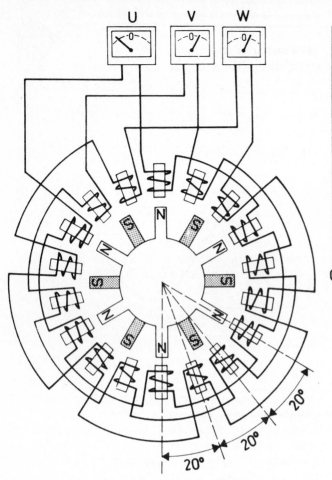

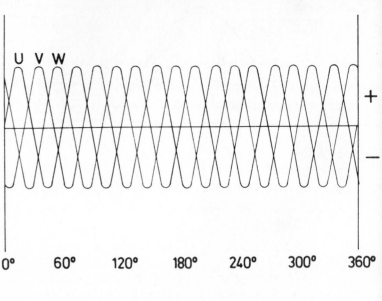

FIGURE 8-14 Maximum output (voltage/current) from each winding of a three-phase alternator occurring every 20° in windings U, V, and W. (*Courtesy of DAF Trucks, Eindhoven, The Netherlands.*)

In Fig. 8–15 the magnetic field produced between the north and south poles jumps the air gap that exists between the rotor and the stator. Magnetic conduction will travel through the iron laminations to the opposite rotor pole piece. Continued rotation of the spinning rotor causes alternate north and south poles to cross each loop in the stator windings, thereby inducing a voltage into

FIGURE 8-15 Generated-voltage concept in a multipole rotor. (*Courtesy of Delco Remy Division, General Motors Corporation.*)

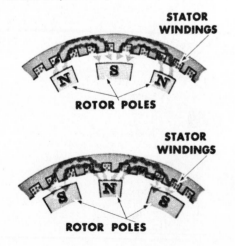

these windings. The speed of the rotor (belt or gear driven, remember) will determine the amount of induced voltage; faster speed, greater voltage. An alternating current is produced in the stator windings as the direction of the rotating magnetic field changes from north to south and back again to north, as discussed for single-phase induced voltage earlier in the chapter.

Electrons always flow from the negative to the positive terminal; in practice, however, the conventional theory discussed in Chapter 1, is normally used. This conventional theory states that the direction of current flow is always away from the positive terminal, and in circuit diagrams this is occasionally indicated by the use of arrows. For this reason, alternating-current flow in a stator winding of an alternator may be shown as reaching its maximum positive value when the south pole of the rotor is at a position corresponding to 90° of its rotation, while other books on electricity may show this maximum value at 90° occurring when the north pole of the rotor is in this position.

For purposes of general explanation of alternating-current flow, it matters little which pole piece is referred to. Delco-Remy, for example, usually places the south pole at the 90° position, while the Robert Bosch Corporation normally places the north pole in this same position when explaining alternating-current flow within the typical alternator.

STATOR WIRING DESIGNS

To enable the generated current within the alternator windings to be coordinated in a useful manner, the individual windings must be connected together to produce a steadier current output as well as allowing the generated alternating current (ac) to be converted or rectified to direct current (dc) for battery-charging purposes. This is achieved by connecting the alternator windings together into either:

1. A star or wye connection (both terms are used and they have the same meaning)
2. A Delta connection

Figure 8–16 illustrates these two types of stator windings.

Three ac voltages are available from a delta-connected stator, which is like having three individual single-phase units wired together. However, in the Y-connected stator, the voltages produced consist of the voltages in two loops of wire added together, which will be approximately 1.7 times as large in magnitude as any one individual loop voltage. Three ac voltages, however, are available from the Y-connected stator spaced 120° apart. The delta-connected stator is common to cars and trucks, with the Y-connected stator being optional, for example, on standby diesel electric generating sets.

FIGURE 8–16 (a) Delta-wound stator winding; (b) wye (Y)-wound stator winding. (*Courtesy of Motorola Automotive and Industrial Electronics Group.*)

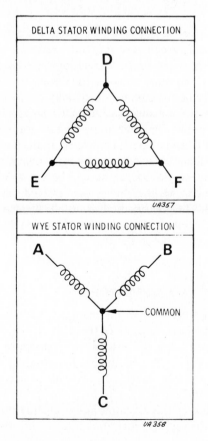

As a matter of interest, and as a way of giving you an appreciation of the differences between these two types of stator winding connections, they can be described by a formula:

- For the star/wye connection, $V = V_f \times \frac{1}{3}$ and $I = I_f$
- For the delta stator connection, $V = V_f$ and $I = I_f \times \frac{1}{3}$

where V = alternator voltage
V_f = phase voltage
I = alternator current
I_f = phase current

The difference in output obtainable from an alternator with the same stator, but with a delta versus a wye winding, is that the delta stator will produce a higher output at the top end of the speed range, while the wye winding will produce current equal to a delta winding at the low speeds at a lower rpm.

RECTIFICATION OF AC VOLTAGE

To convert ac voltage to dc voltage in an alternator, six silicon diodes are used. These diodes function as one-way check valves to allow current flow in only one direction. Three of these diodes are positive (+), while the other three are negative (−), in order to rectify the alternating current voltage produced in each of the windings (three-phase).

Figure 8–17 shows a simple layout of a typical diode, both positive and negative. The positive diodes (cathode

FIGURE 8–17 Positive and negative diodes. (*Courtesy of Motorola Automotive and Industrial Electronics Group.*)

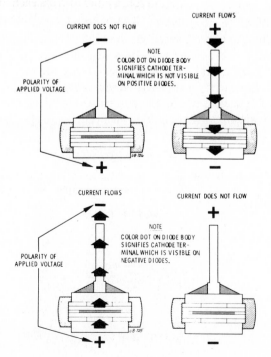

to heat sink), are mounted in a common insulated heat sink so that they cannot contact the alternator body end frame. The three negative diodes (anode to heat sink) are mounted in another heat sink, called the negative diode assembly, which is physically and electrically connected to the alternator body, which is the negative or ground output terminal. The positive rectifier is insulated from the alternator body in a negative-ground system, and connected to the positive output stud of the machine.

The three-phase stator windings are mounted to the stator assembly as shown in Fig. 8–18.

Phase 1 forms the inner winding row, phase 2 the middle winding row, and phase 3 the outer winding row. Each winding set has a coil per rotor pole, or two coils per pole pair (360°) connected in series opposing. All windings are spaced 120 electrical degrees (not mechanical) apart with respect to the rotor poles and are terminated in a delta or wye (Y) arrangement.

A typical 12-pole rotor (six pairs of north and south poles) will produce six output cycles for every revolution of the rotor in each stator winding set. When the rotor is in position to produce maximum positive output from phase 1, the other two phases have opposing outputs. At this point, therefore, the instantaneous voltage polarities and direction of current flow will be as shown in Fig. 8–19(a). This will be known as half-wave rectification of the positive alternation.

As the rotor continues to turn within the stator windings, the voltage in phase 1 will be reversed (180°) along with the current flow, so that the battery receives this charge rate through a different set of diodes as shown in Fig. 8–19(b).

Figure 8–19(a) shows half-wave rectification of phase 1, while Fig. 8–19(b) shows the full-wave rectification of phase 1 since both positive and negative alternations of one cycle were rectified from ac to dc through the positive and negative diodes. With six diodes and the rotor turning at varying speeds as the engine is operating, this rectification action occurs for a very short period of time (waveform peak), with all phases being the same.

If a battery is connected up backwards, such as connecting the positive battery post cable to a vehicle ground, or if any negative connection on an alternator is subjected

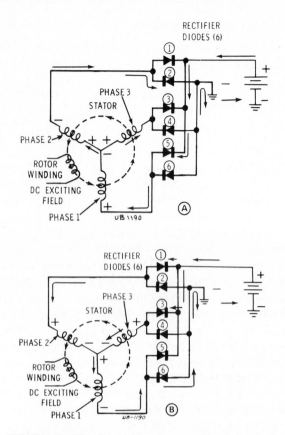

FIGURE 8–19 (a) Half-wave rectification of the positive alternation; (b) reversal of phase 1 voltage (rotor has turned 180° current reversal. (*Courtesy of Motorola Automotive and Industrial Electronics Group.*)

to positive battery flow, the internal diodes within the alternator, which have very little resistance value, would simply have too much current impressed through them. This would immediately destroy the diodes, requiring that the alternator be removed for major repair. To protect the alternator against such damage, some manufacturers install a polarity diode along with a fuse into the circuit so that if the battery is connected up backwards, the polarity diode fuse will blow, thereby protecting the alternator diodes. The battery should be connected up in the right direction, the blown fuse replaced, and the engine started. The polarity diode is usually located between the ground circuit and the alternator isolation diode. The fuse is located between the two.

TYPES OF ALTERNATORS

In the earlier part of this chapter, we discussed the purpose and basic function of the alternator assembly to give us a base from which to work from, prior to studying the various types and makes of alternators that are now in use on cars, trucks, heavy-duty off-highway equipment, and industrial and marine applications.

To keep this as simple as we possibly can, let's break down the types by manufacturer (see list on p. 234), be-

FIGURE 8–18 Stator winding assembly. (*Courtesy of Motorola Automotive and Industrial Electronics Group.*)

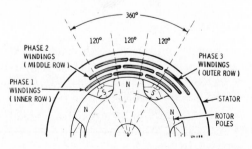

cause specific designs and minor operating changes between different makes can tend to confuse you during an explanation. Your train of thought will be less confused with individual sections dealing with one type and style than with five or six different types being discussed at once. In addition, if each manufacturer's alternator is discussed individually, the chapter section becomes a very handy reference for you at any future date. At the end of the chapter dealing with alternators, a wide variety of questions appear that deal with all the makes. Your ability to answer these questions will provide a quick method of review for you any time that you feel the need to refresh your memory on specific points or topics.

No amount of theoretical training, however, can provide you with the dexterity obtained only by putting into practice what you read. Therefore, once you feel confident about the operation of each alternator, have your instructor or a shop mechanic guide you through all of the maintenance, overhaul, testing, and troubleshooting steps required for each model, style, and type of alternator assembly. Supplement this hands-on training with a review of the theory as you progress from step to step, and by all means use the manufacturers' service information manuals when output specs or troubleshooting tips are required. With the wide variety of alternators in use today, along with the product improvement and updates, it is incumbent on the auto/truck electrician, fleet mechanic, and apprentice to be totally familiar with all current information relating to each and every model that you are dealing with. In this way, your job of maintaining, testing, and troubleshooting the alternator charging system will become a pleasant and rewarding one. Above all, don't second-guess yourself when dealing with electrical charging systems, because serious damage or expensive downtime can be the result. When in doubt, check it out properly and to your complete satisfaction.

Although there are many manufacturers of alternators worldwide, without a doubt the market is dominated by five or six major producers. The current state of the art in alternator design is such that there is not a wide variation in either the design or the components used between different makes, although there are peculiarities specific to particular models and manufacture.

Regardless of the make of alternator used, current truck alternators can generally be classified in one of the following categories:

1. Solid-state bolt-on voltage regulators, usually located at the rear of the alternator housing for ease of access.
2. SI (systems integral) Delco-Remy models, which use a diode trio and rectifier bridge to change stator ac voltage to dc voltage at the alternator output. For protection, all components are located inside the alternator housing end frame, where they are secure from external damage or any tendency for tampering. The SI system is very popular on both cars and trucks.
3. CS (charging system) Delco-Remy models, which appeared in the 1986 model year. These alternators use a

new type of voltage regulator with built-in fault detection but do not require the use of a diode trio. A rectifier bridge is used and on cars or trucks equipped with ECMs (electronic control modules) and BCMs (body computer modules), the BCM monitors the battery voltage. CS models use a digital regulator and passivated chips in place of button diodes in the rectifier bridge.

In addition to the main features listed above, alternators can be of the conventional brush type for standard-duty applications, or of the brushless type, which is more common to heavy-duty truck applications. All of these types are discussed in detail in this chapter.

Alternators are not unlike engines today, in that there are literally hundreds of manufacturers of engines worldwide, but in the final analysis, all engines contain pistons, crankshafts, valves, cylinder heads, and so on. Alternators are no different from engines in this respect; they all contain a rotor, a stator, diodes, a capacitor, in order to operate efficiently.

Therefore, do not feel threatened if faced with troubleshooting an alternator with which you are unfamiliar. Take a few minutes to familiarize yourself with the minor changes incorporated in the alternator in question—the recommended method of testing, troubleshooting and adjusting—and you will very quickly be capable of correcting the problem at hand.

DELCO-REMY ALTERNATORS

As a major producer of electrical equipment for cars, trucks, and heavy-duty equipment, the Delco-Remy Division of General Motors Corporation can be credited with many firsts in the design and development of components for vehicle electric systems. Without a doubt, this division of General Motors is one of the world's leaders in the manufacture and development of electrical and electronic equipment in a wide variety of applications of motive and stationary power.

Basic (Delco) Alternator Models

At the present time Delco-Remy manufactures a complete line of alternators for almost any application and rating. Many of these alternators follow the same general design and maintenance procedures; therefore, we will concern ourselves with the range of alternators that are most widely used on cars, trucks, buses, and heavy-duty equipment.

Basically, two main type of alternators are used in these applications.

- The slip-ring and brush types
- The brushless type

Each model of alternator is easily identified by referring to the small identification plate riveted to the housing on earlier models, or on current models by referring to the part number cast into the housing behind one of the mounting flanges, as shown in Fig. 8–20 for a 25-SI series unit. The letters SI, which stand for "systems inte-

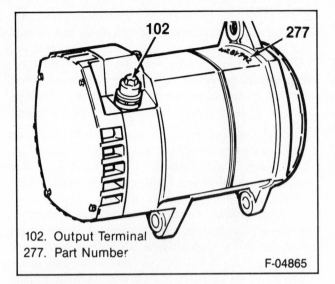

102. Output Terminal
277. Part Number

F-04865

FIGURE 8–20 Model 25-SI series 400 and 450 generator ID. (*Courtesy of GMC Truck Division, General Motors Corporation.*)

TABLE 8–2 Heavy duty brushless-type generator ratings

Series	Available Output (Amps)			
	12 Volts	24 Volts	30 Volts	32 Volts
20-SI	60	35 & 45	—	—
25-SI	85	50 & 75	—	50
30-SI	105	60 & 75	60	60
50-DN	300	240 & 270	—	—

Source: Delco-Remy Division, General Motors Corporation.

gral,'' indicate that the solid-state regulator is located inside the generator slip-ring end frame. Note that the voltage regulator is set for a specific value and is not adjustable. Current models of brush-type alternators produced by Delco-Remy for use in cars, light- and medium-duty trucks, and farm and stationary applications are listed in Table 8–1; Table 8–2 lists the current heavy-duty brushless construction models applicable to heavy-duty trucks, buses, and farm, construction and stationary applications.

In addition to the alternator models listed in Tables 8–1 and 8–2 you will come across a number of other models not shown in these tables that are still in use on cars, and on light, medium-, and heavy-duty trucks. These models include the 5SI (CS-121), 9SI (CS-130), 10SI, 17SI, and 27SI units. The 5SI and 9SI models are better known by their new designation of CS-121 and CS-130, with the CS meaning ''charging system,'' and the number indicating the diameter of the alternator in millimeters (mm). The CS models use passivated chips

in place of the conventional button-type diode used in the SI models, as well as a digital regulator and R and F terminals for on-board computer interface. In addition, many of these alternators require only one wire between them and the battery, plus an adequate ground return circuit to operate, which simplifies the wiring system and minimizes possible problem areas.

Some of these alternators use a Y-connected stator winding, while others employ the delta-wound winding (see Fig. 8–16). This will be discussed in more detail later in the chapter as we look more closely at each model.

The output capacity of the alternator models that we will look at will vary for different applications. Accessory load, battery capacity rating, alternator field current flow, circuit wiring, and minor internal changes to each model alternator within the same series can vary its rated output. Therefore, when the rated output of any alternator is desired, always refer to the latest Delco-Remy Service Test Specifications Bulletin, which is available direct from Delco or your local Delco-Remy dealer. Each model alternator is designed to provide a specified maximum current output. The output rating is generally stamped on the end frame of the alternator.

Delco Brush-Type Generator Models

Brush-type alternators produced by Delco-Remy, regardless of their rated output and model designation, all operate on the same basic principle. In this section we describe the operation of the 10-SI, 15-SI, 17-SI, and 27-SI series type 100 standard-duty generators. We then compare these type 100 models to a 27-SI type 200 and 27-SI type 205 to show the basic difference in the construction and the circuit arrangement. Figure 8–21 illustrates an external view of a 10-SI series 100 generator, with the connections on the 15-SI and 17-SI series 100 models being very similar to that shown for the 10-SI unit. Figure 8–22 shows the external features of a 27-SI series 200 model, which differs from the others in that the BAT terminal (76) is higher up on the generator body.

The basic operation of all alternators was discussed in detail earlier in the chapter, so you should, by now,

TABLE 8–1 Standard-duty brush-type generator ratings

Series	Available Output (Amps)	
	12 Volts	24 Volts
CS-121	61 & 74	—
CS-144	108 & 120	—
12-SI	56, 66, 78 & 94	—
15-SI	85 & 105	—
21-SI	100, 115, 125, 130	50, 60, 70

Source: Delco-Remy Division, General Motors Corporation.

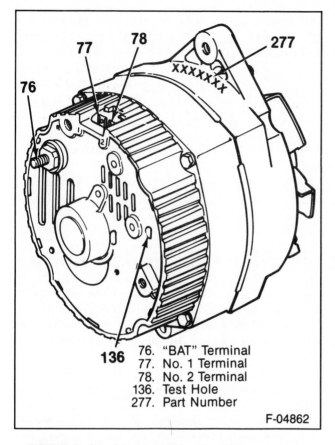

76. "BAT" Terminal
77. No. 1 Terminal
78. No. 2 Terminal
136. Test Hole
277. Part Number

F-04862

FIGURE 8–21 Model 10-SI series 100 generator. (*Courtesy of GMC Truck Division, General Motors Corporation.*)

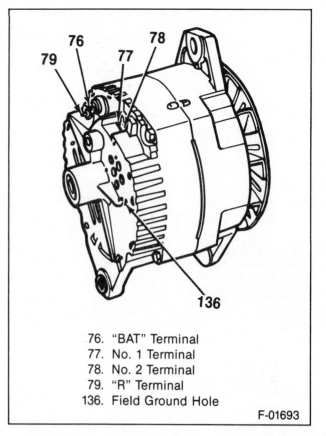

76. "BAT" Terminal
77. No. 1 Terminal
78. No. 2 Terminal
79. "R" Terminal
136. Field Ground Hole

F-01693

FIGURE 8–22 Model 27-SI series 200 generator with two-terminal connector. (*Courtesy of GMC Truck Division, General Motors Corporation.*)

be reasonably familiar with the general concept of operation. However, to take this description one step further and to allow you to trace the exact flow through the various diodes and solid-state devices, we discuss the sequence of events for a 10-SI series, type 100 unit, which we will use as the base unit for all further model descriptions. Refer to Fig. 8–23 and familiarize yourself with the connections between the battery and the alternator. Everything identified with the symbol R is a resistor, while the letters TR indicate a transistor, and the black triangles in the diagram indicate diodes. The function and purpose of these solid-state devices are explained in Chapters 2 and 11. The two small circles and rectangles above the field rotor indicate the two brushes and slip rings. The two brushes that ride on the rotor shaft copper slip rings carry battery current through one of them to supply the rotor field winding, while the other brush acts as a return circuit to the battery. Light springs ensure that the brushes remain in good contact at all times. Keep in mind that the rotor is driven by the generator pulley by a belt or gear drive, and that the stator is held in a fixed position being bolted between the generator frame.

You will also note that the stator is a Y-connected type for both the 10-SI and 12-SI models, while the stator for the 15-SI, 17-SI, and 27-SI models uses a delta-wound

stator. These two stator types are illustrated and discussed in Fig. 8–16. In a wye-wound (Y) stator, the stator windings operate in pairs so that the output voltage is the total voltage between one stator winding lead and another. With a delta-wound stator the windings are not connected in pairs, but act independently, although they are producing voltage and current flow at 120° intervals, as explained earlier for three-phase operation.

The generator field current is supplied through a diode trio and is connected to the stator windings, which are assembled inside the laminated iron core that forms part of the generator frame. A capacitor or condensor C1 mounted in the generator end frame acts to protect both the rectifier bridge and the diode trio from high voltages (surges and spikes created by sudden load changes) as well as acting to suppress vehicle radio noise interference. The rectifier bridge, which is connected to the three-phase stator windings, is constructed to hold six diodes with two diodes per stator lead (phase) to change the ac voltage to dc voltage.

On negative-ground systems, three of these diodes are positive (+) and are mounted into a heat sink which is insulated from the generator end frame. The other three diodes are negative (−) diodes which are also mounted into a heat sink; however, this heat sink is mounted direct-

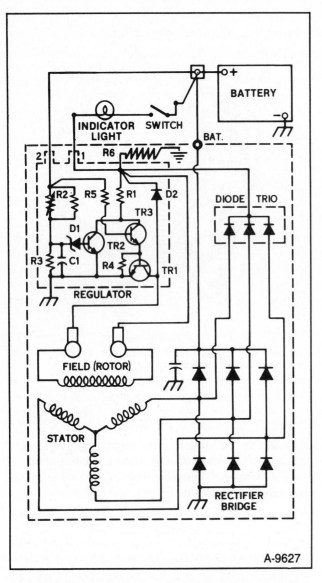

FIGURE 8-23 Model 10-SI series 100 generator wiring schematic. (*Courtesy of GMC Truck Division, General Motors Corporation.*)

ly to the end frame of the generator. Also connected to the stator windings is a diode trio which controls the field current to the generator. To protect the rectifier bridge diodes and diode trio from high-voltage surges, and to suppress radio noise, a capacitor or condensor is mounted in the end frame of the generator. The diode trio works with the three negative diodes in the rectifier bridge to give us a dc voltage of the same magnitude as that at the generator output terminal.

Operational Flow: SI Models (Type 100; 10, 15, 17, and 27 Series). The following description refers to the 10-SI series, type 100 shown in Figs. 8-21 and 8-23. The generator is connected to the battery by a plug-in harness located on the generator housing by two terminals, terminal 1 and 2, identified as items 77 and 78 in Fig. 8-21 for the 10-SI and in Fig. 8-22 for the 27-SI model. Termi-

nals 2 and 1, in that order, appear at the top left of the 10-SI circuit wiring diagram of Fig. 8-23, where terminal 2 is connected to the positive battery post, which supplies voltage through resistor R5 to the base emitter of transistor TR3 to turn it on. TR1 then turns on to allow field current to flow to ground. Due to the combined resistance of R2, R3, R5, TR1, and TR3, although the battery is connected through terminal 2 to resistors R2 and R3, the discharge current from the battery will be very low.

Although having turned on transistors TR3 and TR1, this action prevents any current from flowing through them due to such a low value. As soon as the ignition switch is closed, battery current can flow through the indicator lamp to terminal 1. If no indicator lamp is used, a diode would be inserted in its place to prevent charge current from attempting to return to the battery from the diode trio. Battery current will flow through resistor R1 and transistors TR3 and TR1 to ground and the indicator lamp will illuminate on the vehicle dash. At this time, resistor R6 will absorb some of the battery current passing to the lamp.

Battery power flowing through TR1 to ground (battery negative terminal) and to the right-hand brush in the diagram will flow through the rotor slip ring, the generator field winding inside the rotor, and out the other slip ring and brush on the left-hand side of the diagram through TR1 and to battery ground. This sequence occurs only if the ignition key is on but the engine has not been cranked over. With the ignition key in the START position or the starter pushbutton activated, engine cranking takes place. This action causes the alternator rotor to spin, and ac voltages are generated in the stator windings as the poles of the rotor and the magnetic field cut the stator windings, thereby inducing current flow in all three windings of the stator.

NOTE: Rotor field current supply on a 12-V alternator can vary from as low as 3.6 to 4.3 A on a Delco-Remy 30-SI model to between 5.7 and 7.1 A on a Delco 17-SI model. Table 8-5 lists typical rotor field current ratings for both Delco and Leece-Neville alternators.

The stator ac voltage is converted to dc by the action of the six diodes in the rectifier bridge. This dc voltage appears between the battery ground and the generator battery or BAT terminal. In addition, this dc-generated field current leaving the stator through the diode trio, which works with the three negative diodes in the rectifier bridge to give us a dc voltage of the same magnitude as at the generator output terminal, also flows to the field (through brush and slip ring), TR1, and as mentioned, through the grounded (negative) diodes in the rectifier bridge back to the stator. This combined action will produce voltage and current flow to the battery and system accessories.

With the generator producing voltage, this voltage will, of course, increase with an increase in speed so that this increase is applied through resistors R2 and R3. When the voltage between R2 and R3 is high enough, zener diode D1 is triggered, which conducts voltage to transistor TR2, and it turns on. Placement of transistor TR2 in the circuit will now turn off TR3 and TR1.

Turning off current flow to TR1 automatically reduces both the rotor field current and system voltage; D2 stops conducting and blocks current flow, allowing both TR3 and TR1 to turn back on. Both field current and system voltage increase and the cycle is repeated from 10 times per second, to 7000 times a second to limit the generator voltage to a preset value. The purpose of the capacitor C1 is to smooth out voltage surges across resistor R3 to protect the rectifier bridge and diode trio plus suppress radio noise. Some generators may contain two capacitors in the end frame.

Resistor R4 prevents excessive current leakage through TR1 at high temperatures, and diode D2 prevents high induced voltages in the field windings when TR1 turns off. To provide the ideal or optimum rate of voltage charge to the battery, a thermister (resistor R2) causes the regulated voltage to vary with any change in temperature.

If for any reason an open circuit should occur in the number 2 generator terminal circuit, transistors TR3 and TR1 will automatically turn off, which isolates any current flow from the field, thereby preventing an overcharge condition.

When the ignition key switch is on, battery current flows through the indicator lamp and resistor R6 to ground to illuminate the lamp. An open in the circuit would also cause the lamp to come on. If however, an open occurs in terminal 1, this would cause the lamp to remain off and no current will be able to flow from the generator. Minor variations can occur between SI-type generator circuitry. Some earlier-model generators did not use an indicator lamp but had a diode inserted between the ignition switch and terminal 1.

Figure 8–24 shows a typical simplified external circuit used with these types of generators, with an indicator lamp, which would be used with the wiring diagram shown in Fig. 8–23; if the circuit did not use this warning lamp, it may use an ammeter instead.

Operation: 27-SI Series Type 200 and 205. The type 200 series generators are similar in design to the type 100 described earlier, with the major difference being that the type 200 has large bearings since these models are used in more demanding applications than the type 100 units. Most of the information described earlier for the type 100, 10-SI, 15-SI, 17-SI, and 27-SI generators can be applied to the operation of the 27-SI type 200 and the 27-SI type 205. Both of these models also use slip rings and brushes for their operation and also use solid-state voltage regulators mounted inside the slip-ring end frame. Some of these models are designed to operate with one wire from the generator to the battery along with a ground return and an R terminal to operate auxiliary equipment.

Figure 8–22 illustrates a two-terminal regulator connector model. The voltage regulator used with these models is nonadjustable. The 205 series model shown in Fig. 8–25 differs from the others in that it has a splined shaft that extends from the rear of the housing that can be used to drive a vacuum pump for use on an air-conditioning installation. Often when the type 200 generators are used, you may find that the number 1 and 2 terminal connector and wires are taped back on the wiring harness since these models are self-energizing and therefore do not require connections to these two terminals.

NOTE: The generator wiring, which is part of the engine wiring harness, is connected to some Delco-Remy generators at three terminals: a single connector at the generator BAT terminal and a two-wire connector at the number 1 and 2 terminals. However, the 27SI type 200 generator used with diesel engines does not require the connection at the terminals 1 and 2. The two wires and

FIGURE 8–24 Delco generator basic external wiring circuit. (*Courtesy of Delco Remy Division of General Motors Corporation.*)

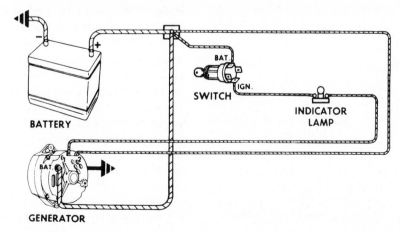

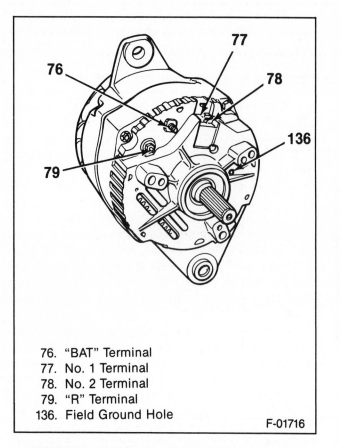

76. "BAT" Terminal
77. No. 1 Terminal
78. No. 2 Terminal
79. "R" Terminal
136. Field Ground Hole

F-01716

FIGURE 8-25 Model 27-SI series, type 205 generator features. (*Courtesy of GMC Truck Division, General Motors Corporation.*)

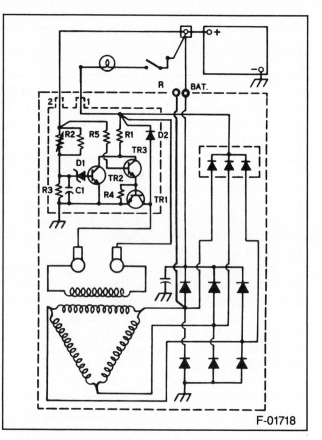

F-01718

FIGURE 8-26 27-SI generator wiring diagram (two-terminal regulator connector). (*Courtesy of GMC Truck Division, General Motors Corporation.*)

the connector are taped back on the harness. If the taped-back wires and connector are connected to the 27SI type 200 generator by mistake, the voltage regulator may be damaged and the batteries may discharge.

The wiring arrangement for the 27-SI two-terminal regulator connector model is shown in Fig. 8-26 and is very similar to that for type 100 units. The difference on type 200 is that it uses a delta-wound stator rather than a wye unit; it does not use the R6 resistor and has an R terminal for operating auxiliary equipment. Note that on some models of Delco generators the R terminal is wired to provide only half circuit voltage. Other than these changes, the descriptive text for the type 100 units shown in Fig. 8-23 can be applied to Fig. 8-26.

Figure 8-27 is a wiring schematic for the 27-SI 205 generator model. Note that at the top left of this schematic there is a small rectangular box. On some earlier models, this box contained a voltage adjustment cube that could be lifted out and turned to different positions so that the voltage output of the generator could be changed. This feature was used on a number of Delco heavy-duty alternator models. Resistors R2 and R3 were connected to the battery through the external voltage adjustment cube. In addition, if this cube ever became open circuited,

TR1 and TR3 were turned off, thereby preventing high system voltage.

Delco CS Type Alternators

Unlike the Delco SI (systems integral) generators, which use a diode trio connected to the stator windings, through which field current is supplied, the Delcotron generators identified as CS (charging system), illustrated in Fig. 8-28, do not use a diode trio. The ac voltage produced within the generator is converted to dc by the use of the rectifier bridge shown in the CS system wiring schematic of Fig. 8-29. The numbers following the CS designation, such as CS-144, indicate that the generator outside diameter is 144 mm (5.66 in.). The Delco CS-144 is rated at either 108 or 120 A output, while the CS-121 is rated at either 61 or 74 A, and the CS-130 model is available at either 85, 100, or 105A. The alternator regulator uses digital techniques to supply the rotor current and to control output system voltage; therefore, the rotor current is proportional to the width of the electrical pulse supplied by the regulator.

Major advantages of the CS generator are as follows:

1. New digital regulator with:
   a. Integral load response control

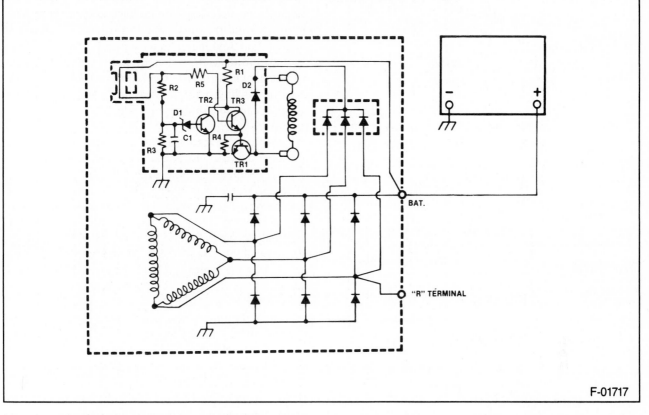

F-01717

FIGURE 8–27 27-SI series and 205 generator wiring diagram. (*Courtesy of GMC Truck Division, General Motors Corporation.*)

FIGURE 8–28 External features of a Delco CS model generator. (*Courtesy of Delco Remy Division, General Motors Corporation.*)

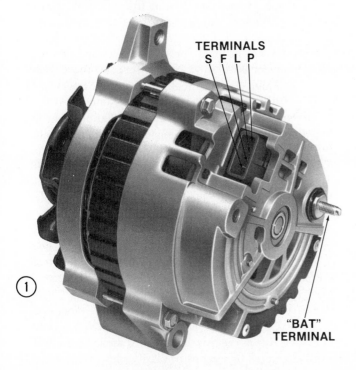

**TERMINALS
S F L P**

"BAT" TERMINAL

①

b. Positive turn-on

c. Overvoltage and undervoltage indications

d. Internal voltage sense option

e. Reduced radio noise potential

f. R and F terminals for on-board computer interface

g. Reduced V_f (power FET output device)

2. New rectifier bridge with:

a. Centralized load dump/voltage transient protection

b. Passivated chips in place of button diodes in some models

c. Integral capacitor

In addition, the CS models are smaller and lighter weight than comparable SI models, to produce a higher output/weight ratio.

CS System Operation. When the ignition key switch is turned to the engine ON position prior to engaging the starter motor, battery voltage is supplied to terminals F and L shown in Figs. 8–28 and 8–29. Note that this power is generally fed from the on-board computer or ECM (electronic control module) on the latest gasoline-powered and fuel-injected midrange trucks (GMC) as well as on diesel engines using electronic fuel

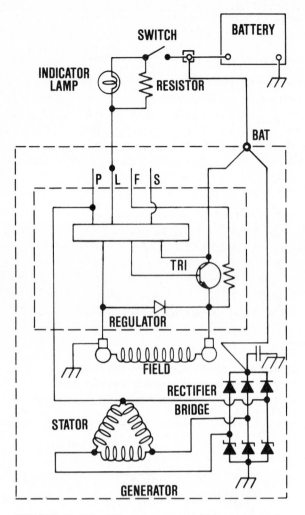

FIGURE 8-29 CS generator wiring schematic. (*Courtesy of Delco Remy Division, General Motors Corporation.*)

the alternator output voltage automatically. The ECM monitors the regulator from the field terminal of the generator. Should the duty cycle fall below 7%, the ECM senses a fault and indicates a problem. The digital regulator also controls the "charge" indicator lamp through a solid-state lamp driver which turns on the lamp whenever low or high voltage exists, or when the engine is stopped and no power is flowing from the alternator system.

The CS alternator can only be used with two connections. One of these is battery positive, and the other is an L terminal to the charge indicator light and the ECM/BCM, which sources 12 V to the L terminal to excite the field (stator coils). The L terminal is connected internally to the voltage regulator ignition terminal, and externally to the ECM and from the ECM to the battery no-charge light. Use of the P, F, and S terminals is optional, with the P terminal being connected internally to the stator; it may also be connected externally to a tachometer or other device.

The F terminal is connected internally to field positive and goes to the ECM externally. Input from the F terminal is used by the ECM to turn on the service diagnostics (service electrical system telltale). For the telltale light to come on, the battery voltage has to be less than 11 V or greater than 15.5 V. The S terminal may be connected externally to the starter solenoid, where it monitors battery voltage. The S terminal is connected to the regulator inside the generator.

The regulator voltage setting varies with temperature and limits system voltage by controlling rotor field current. The regulator actually switches field current on and off at a fixed frequency of about 400 cycles per second. By varying the actual on/off time (pulse width), a correct average field current for proper system voltage control is maintained. For example, at high engine speeds, the ON time may account for 10%, while the OFF time will account for 90% of the cycling time. At low engine speeds with high electrical loads, the ON time may be as high as 90%, while the OFF time would only be 10%.

In the CS system the ECM monitors battery voltage at all times; therefore, with the engine running and system voltage either too high or too low, or alternatively, if the 12-V source to the L terminal becomes grounded or lost, a trouble code would be logged into the computer memory for retrieval by the technician when he or she connects up a diagnostic test tool/instrument. For example, a Code 53 on a GMC vehicle is an indication of system overvoltage that signifies a basic generator problem. Code 53 will set if the voltage at the ECM (engine control module) terminal B2 is greater than 17.1 V for 10 seconds.

CS Generator Operation. The power generated within the CS Delcotron generator is achieved basically in the same way as that for the earlier SI models described in this chapter. For reasons of clarity, however, and to ensure that you have a good understanding of the major

controls, such as those manufacturered by Detroit Diesel, Cummins, and Caterpillar. On vehicles that use both an ECM and a BCM (body computer module), the power flows from the BCM. This voltage that flows to terminals F and L acts to turn on the regulator assembly within the generator end frame.

The digital regulator controls the field directly with a PWM (pulse-width-modulated) signal that is valued in duty cycles. The regulator, which is in a field strobe function, applies a small percentage of its duty cycle to the field windings to produce a weak magnetic field. During the cranking stage, lower battery voltage is available, due to the high current draw of the starter motor; therefore, narrow pulse widths (weaker magnetic field) are supplied to the alternator rotor assembly. Once the engine fires and runs, the belt-driven alternator pulley will rotate at a faster speed (the field strobe function is disabled) and the regulator will sense this rotation by detecting the ac voltage at the stator through internal wiring. When the engine is running, the regulator functions to vary the field current by controlling the pulse-width signal to regulate differences between these two types of generator/alternators, the following descriptive text will allow you to follow closely the actual power control features of the CS type model. Figure 8–29 illustrates a wiring diagram of a CS Delcotron generator assembly. In the introductory comments for the CS model, we described briefly the function of each terminal. If you refer to Figs. 8–28 and 8–29, you see that each generator terminal—P, L, F, and S—is clearly shown. Let's deal individually with each of these terminals and see how they relate to overall control of the system.

Terminal L: When the ignition switch is turned to the RUN position, the instrument panel indicator light will glow and a voltage signal is applied to the regulator at the L terminal that causes transistor TR1 to turn on and off very rapidly. In effect, this transistor will oscillate between an ON and an OFF condition, with 30% of its time in the ON position and 70% in the OFF position.

During this time, battery power automatically supplies generator field current which flows into the generator output or BAT terminal. This power then flows through transistor TR1 and the field coil to ground, thereby completing the circuit. Note, however, that no field current will flow through the indicator lamp at this time. Field current is great enough to cause the generator to turn on (magnetic field created) once the engine fires and runs at its idle rpm. The voltage induced in the delta-wound stator causes the stator to supply field current as well as output voltage and current at the BAT terminal to charge the battery and supply power to the vehicle electrical system.

To ensure that the generator will receive battery power and actually turn on if the indicator lamp bulb were to burn out, a small resistor is used in parallel with the lamp circuit. In addition, to protect the system against high voltages in the stator, a number of zener diodes are used within the rectifier bridge.

Terminal S: The S or sensing terminal is normally connected to some point in the charging circuit by a wire lead, the usual place being as close to the positive battery terminal as possible. The reason for this is that the voltage to be controlled is measured directly across the battery and therefore will ensure better control of battery charging current. On most CS generator regulators, should the S terminal lead become an open circuit, the generator operates to sense the voltage internally. In this way the charging system will continue to operate in the normal condition. When the regulator is operating to limit the system voltage, the voltage regulator setting appears at the S terminal on the regulator.

Terminal F: The F terminal or field monitor terminal is internally connected through a resistor to the positive side of the generator field coil. Because of this design feature, any change in the monitored voltage signal at the F terminal caused by a generator problem would be noted and displayed to the vehicle operator as a system defect. Therefore, most vehicle manufacturers connect a specially designed electronic systm to this F terminal so that it can function as a fault monitoring system. An optional system to that shown in Fig. 8–29 for the CS charging system is illustrated in Fig. 8–30, where the regulator F terminal is identified as an I terminal for dual turn-on by connecting the I terminal directly or alternately through a suitable resistor to the load side of the ignition switch. With this system either the L or I terminal or a combination of the two can be used to provide the turn-on feature described earlier. The switch is connected to the I terminal either directly or through a resistor, but not through both.

Terminal P: The P terminal can be used by the vehicle manufacturer as a speed or engine tachometer signal since it supplied only half system voltage. In this way it can be compared to the R terminal found on other Delcotron charging systems in that the terminal is connected internally to a single stator phase.

FIGURE 8–30   Optional wiring arrangement for a CS model generator where the F terminal is designated by the letter I. (*Courtesy of Delco Remy Division, General Motors Corporation.*)

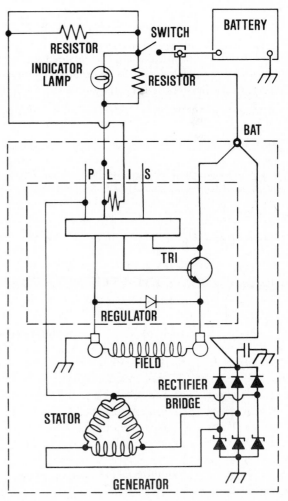

CS System Voltage Control. CS generators use a 12-pole rotor containing six north pole and six south pole magnets to produce six complete cycles of ac voltage for each revolution of the rotor, which is reflected as three-phase ac voltage. The basic operation of the CS generator is very similar to that for the SI (system integral) described earlier in the chapter, the major difference between the two being that the CS model does not use a diode trio. This difference is readily apparent if you compare wiring diagrams for the SI and CS models. The rectifier bridge, which is clearly visible in Figs. 8–29 and 8–30, contains six small button-type diodes assembled between two heat sinks, with the stator being connected to three studs on the bridge to form a complete electrical circuit. The delta-connected stator used with the CS generator provides smooth voltage and current output when connected to the six-diode rectifier. You may recall from Chapter 2 that when a diode is connected to an ac voltage source with its ends marked A and B, current will flow through the diode when A is (+) and B is (−), a condition commonly known as being *forward-biased* that allows the diode to conduct current. However, when the voltage at A is (−) while at B it is (+), the diode is now in a reverse-biased condition and will no longer conduct current. This condition means that current would flow only half of the time and therefore produces half-wave rectification.

With six diodes used in a 12-pole generator the three-phase ac voltage output takes place within 360° of the generator rotor rotation and can best be described by dividing the three positive and three negative voltage impulses into six distinct reactions. Figures 8–12, 8–13, and 8–14 will refresh your memory on this concept; these diagrams represent a sine wave, with everything above the horizontal line being positive and everything below the line being negative. These sine waves, along with the delta-wound stator and the six diodes, are shown in Fig. 8–31 for a CS model Delcotron generator.

The six periods of rectification are best described by breaking them down into individual sequences.

Period 1: Step 1 in Fig. 8–32 produces maximum voltage in the stator in phase BA. We can determine the current flow direction by considering the instant that the voltage is at a maximum. This voltage is usually in the range of 16 V, and since the curve is above the horizontal line, the voltage potential at point A is + 16, while at point B it is zero. The voltage of phase CB would provide 8 V at C and zero volts at B since the curve is below the horizontal line. In phase AC, which is also below the horizontal line, A is 8 V positive with respect to C.

Period 2: In period 2 the maximum voltage developed is in phase AC with the voltage potentials shown in Fig. 8–33 at the instant of maximum value. The other phase voltages and current conduction are also illustrated.

Periods 3 to 6: Figure 8–34 illustrates periods 3 and 4, and Fig. 8–35 shows periods 5 and 6, with all current flow directions indicated by arrows.

The voltage obtained from this six-diode stator–rectifier to the battery is not a straight-line output, but the three-phase design ensures that the dc output has very little variation.

FIGURE 8–31 CS generator wiring schematic showing the six rectification diodes and the accompanying sine-wave action. (*Courtesy of Delco Remy Division of General Motors Corporation.*)

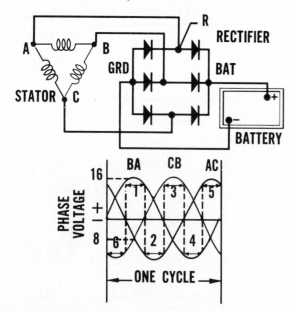

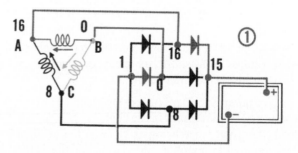

FIGURE 8–32 Period 1 (phase BA) action in a CS generator. (*Courtesy of Delco Remy Division, General Motors Corporation.*)

FIGURE 8–33 Period 2 (phase AC) action in a CS generator. (*Courtesy of Delco Remy Division, General Motors Corporation.*)

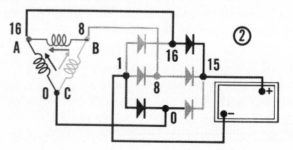

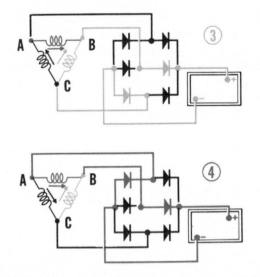

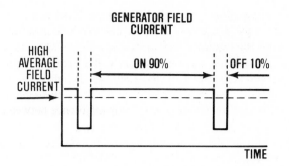

FIGURE 8–36 CS generator field current switched on/off at a fixed frequency of 400 cycles per second (field ON for 90%) to provide a high average field current. (*Courtesy of Delco Remy Division, General Motors Corporation.*)

FIGURE 8–34 Periods 3 and 4 reaction in a CS model generator. (*Courtesy of Delco Remy Division, General Motors Corporation.*)

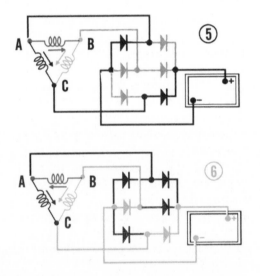

FIGURE 8–35 Periods 5 and 6 (current flow indicated by arrows) in a CS generator. (*Courtesy of Delco Remy Division, General Motors Corporation.*)

the remaining 10% of the power-producing cycle. Remember that with a 12-pole rotor, six complete cycles of ac voltage are produced for each complete rotation of the rotor. This action will ensure that a relatively high average field current at a low generator rotor speed will produce the desired system voltage. Figure 8–36 illustrates this concept. When the engine speed is increased during normal driving, less field current is required to generate the system voltage because of the faster rate at which a cycle is completed. Therefore, we require the opposite situation to that described for an idle or low engine speed. During a high-engine-speed condition, the regulator may only be in the ON phase for 10% of the cycle time and be in the OFF mode for the remaining 90% of the time. Figure 8–37 illustrates the condition that exists when a low-average field current is present. Compare this to that for a high-average field current condition. Therefore, at any given engine speed and load condition, the regulator is capable of turning the field current on or off to suit changing requirements.

Another feature of the regulators used in today's generators is that they are temperature compensated to provide optimum (ideal) voltage requirements for battery

Regulator Action. The regulator, which is assembled inside the generator and visible in Fig. 8–29, is a completely sealed unit and contains integrated circuits consisting of hundreds of resistors, capacitors, diodes, transistors, and other semiconductor devices. The main function of the regulator is to switch the field current voltage on and off at a fixed frequency of about 400 cycles per second. Compare this to the normal electrical frequency of your house or apartment power, which operates on a frequency of 60 cycles per second. In the Delcotron CS generator, the voltage control is regulated by varying the actual on–off time of the rotor field current. Therefore, at low engine speeds, the field might be turned on for as much as 90% of the time, and off for

FIGURE 8–37 CS generator field current switched on/off at a fixed frequency of 400 cycles per second (field ON for 10%) to provide a low average field current. (*Courtesy of Delco Remy Division, General Motors Corporation.*)

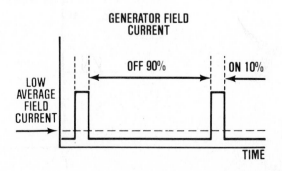

charging. Therefore, when the temperature increases, the voltage will decrease, and during cold operating conditions, the regulator will operate at a higher voltage setting to provide the necessary higher voltage to the battery to maintain a suitable state of charge. In addition to the temperature-compensated system, the regulator circuitry is designed to perform what is commonly known as *load response control* (LRC). Consider an engine sitting idling at a stoplight with a heavy electrical load being added, such as increasing the HVAC blower fan speed. The LRC will act to increase the field current gradually so that the generator output current will also increase gradually. This prevents any noticeable change in engine speed. Through this action, the generator can handle an additional load over a time span of a few seconds rather than instantly. In the interim period the battery is capable of supplying the demands of this additional electrical load, which is then transferred to the generator.

Delco Brushless Generators

In addition to the brush-type SI (system integral) and CS (charging system) ac generators, Delco-Remy also offers brushless generators for use on heavy-duty truck applications. Although not commonly found on passenger cars and light-duty pickup trucks, you should have some concept of just how these models operate.

The brushless generator derives its name from the fact that it contains no brushes to carry electricity to and from the slip rings as is the case in an SI or CS model. The brushless type employs a rotor with permanent magnetism; therefore, when the rotor is driven by the generator pulley/belt, the rotor induces a voltage in the stator windings. This current then flows through diodes and resistors back to the stator winding. A built-in voltage regulator is commonly used with brushless generators, with some earlier heavy-duty models employing an external voltage adjustment cap in the shape of a cube. This cap can be removed and repositioned to change the generator voltage setting. Other models require that the generator end cover be removed to expose a voltage adjustment potentiometer, and some models that are similar to the SI and CS brush models in that the voltage output is preset at the factory and cannot be altered.

Current brushless types of generators are listed in Table 8-2 along with their available current output at both 12- and 24-V ratings. The 50-DN generator listed is commonly used on buses/coaches and can be either belt or gear driven, although gear drive is preferable since the 50-DN is rated at 300 A on a 12-V circuit, and 240 or 270 A on a 24-V system. Also note in Table 8-2 that the 25-SI model can be obtained in a 32-V configuration, and that the 30-SI model is available in either 12-, 24-, 30-, or 32-V circuitry. You may also come across earlier Delco generator models such as the 29-SI, which is similar in construction and features to the existing 20-SI models. In addition to the 30-SI model, there is a 30-SI/TR (transformer rectifier) type that can provide a separate voltage to charge a cranking battery on trucks that use a series–parallel hookup (24 V cranking and 12 V charging). The 31-SI and 32-SI are two other models that you may encounter which are oil-cooled high-output generators that operate similar to the 30-SI unit. In this section we discuss the operational flow of the 20-SI, 25-SI, and 30-SI models with the aid of a wiring schematic for each.

Brushless Generator Flow Paths

20 and 29 SI Series: Figure 8–38 shows that the wiring circuit for the 20 and 29 SI is very similar to that used with the brush-type generators—the 10, 15, 17, and 27 SI—which was shown in Fig. 8–23 along with a detailed explanation of the flow path.

The only difference between this circuit and that shown in Fig. 8–23 is that resistors R2 and R3 in the brushless circuit are connected to the battery through the

FIGURE 8–38 Model 20-SI generator wiring diagram. 29-SI is the same, but the stator is delta wound rather than wye wound. (*Courtesy of Delco Remy Division, General Motors Corporation.*)

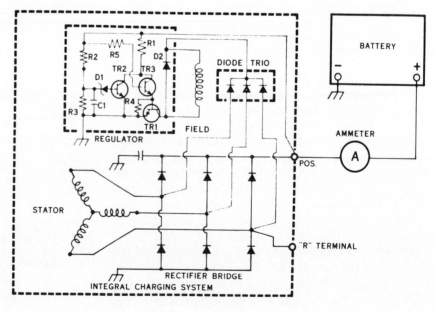

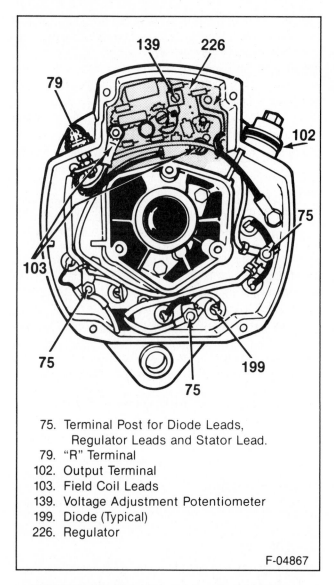

75. Terminal Post for Diode Leads,
    Regulator Leads and Stator Lead.
79. "R" Terminal
102. Output Terminal
103. Field Coil Leads
139. Voltage Adjustment Potentiometer
199. Diode (Typical)
226. Regulator

F-04867

FIGURE 8–39 Rectifier end frame with cover removed. (*Courtesy of GMC Truck Division, General Motors Corporation.*)

a voltmeter prod placed against this hex-head bolt (see Fig. 8–20, item 102).

NOTE: On negative (–)-ground models, a red output terminal is used, which should only be connected to the battery positive (+) circuit or terminal. On positive (+)-ground models, a black output terminal is used, which should only be connected to the battery negative (–) circuit or terminal.

This generator is equipped with an R terminal on some models to provide a feed to operate auxiliary equipment. On some models a plug beside the R terminal can be removed to allow access to a voltage adjustment screw inside the regulator of the generator (see Fig. 8–39) for later models where the generator end plate has to be removed for access to this voltage adjustment.

The flow path for the 25 SI series generator shown in Fig. 8–40 is slightly different from that for the 29 SI. Rotor movement through its permanent magnetism induces voltage flow in the stator windings, which causes current flow through diodes D1, D2, D3, R1, R3, and the generator diodes back to the stator winding, which is Y wound. "Y wound" means that the output voltage is the total voltage between one stator winding lead and another. See Fig. 8–16.

Transistors TRI and TR2 are turned on, and the battery can supply current through R5, the field coil and TR1, and R2 and R4. With a speed increase and therefore a voltage increase, the voltage generated across R4 is impressed through diodes D5 and D6, due to the current flow through R5, R2, and R4.

When the preset (adjustable) voltage is reached, both D5 and D6 conduct and TR3 turns on, which turns off TR1 and TR2, subsequently decreasing generator voltage because of a reduction in current flowing to the rotor field coil windings. This reduction of generated voltage causes D5, D6, and TR3 to again turn off and TR1 and TR2 to turn back on. This switching from off to on can occur as few as 10 times per second or as many as 7000 times per second to limit the generator's preset voltage.

FIGURE 8–40 Model 25-SI brushless generator, negative-ground circuit. (*Courtesy of Delco Remy Division, General Motors Corporation.*)

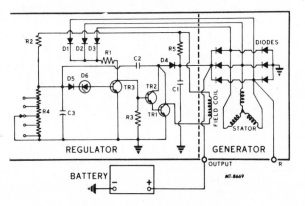

voltage adjustment rather than through terminals 2 as on the brush type.

In addition, the dc voltage from the rectifier bridge in the 20/29 SI series appears between ground and the POS generator terminal rather than at the generator BAT terminal as on the 10/15/27 SI series. If the connection between POS and R2 on the 20/29 SI should become open-circuit, transistors TR3 and TR1 will turn off, preventing high system voltage.

25 SI Series: With the 25 SI Delcotron generator, types 400 and 450, only one wire is needed to connect the battery and integral charging system, along with an adequate ground return to complete the circuit. The one output terminal on the generator body is specially designed so that it is electrically insulated from the housing; therefore, no voltage reading can be registered with

Capacitor C1 functions as it did in other circuits, protecting the generator diodes from high transient voltages with this rapid switching, and also suppressing radio interference.

On 24-V systems, an additional capacitor C2 causes TR1 and TR2 to turn on and off quickly. Diode D4 works along with TR1 and TR2 to prevent high field-coil induced voltages when these two transistors turn off. To smooth out voltage across R4, capacitor C3 is used. To compensate for line voltage drop, R5 raises the generator voltage slightly to maintain a more constant voltage across the battery as the generator output increases.

The wiring circuit used with the 25 SI series 400 and 450 types varies slightly, and an alternate circuit may be found on some of these models. This circuit is shown in Fig. 8-41. This circuit shown in the figure can be either positive or negative ground.

Flow in Fig. 8-40 is similar to that in Fig. 8-41, the difference being that current from the stator flows through the three diodes to R6 to turn on TR1 and TR2. Current can also flow from the stator windings through the diode trio D1, D2, and D3 to the rotor field coil windings and TR1, returning to the stator windings through the other three diodes. When current flows through R1, R2, and R3, a voltage high enough will conduct through zenor diode D4 and the base–emitter of TR3 to turn it on, which turns off TR1 and TR2. This action reduces flow to the rotor field winding, reducing the system voltage and both D4 and TR3 turnoff; TR1 and TR2 turn back on to provide current flow to the rotor field winding once more, and generator output again increases. This switching from off to on occurs rapidly, as explained for other generators. Potentiometer (adjustable) R2 and R3 controls the generator's output voltage limit.

Capacitor C1 functions the same as in the other circuit; D5 prevents high transient voltages in the rotor field coil windings when the field current is decreasing, while

R5 prevents current leakage through TR3 at elevated temperatures. R7, C3, and R4 operate together to turn TR1 and TR2 rapidly on and off.

30 SI and 30 SI/TR Series: Figure 8–42 illustrates an external view of a 30-SI type 400 Delco generator that uses one wire with a ground return to charge the vehicle battery. Figure 8–43 depicts a wiring schematic for the 30-SI type 400 generator. If you study this diagram closely, you will notice that the system arrangement follows the same layout as that of other Delco models shown and discussed in this chapter. The wiring diagram and circuit used with the 30 SI models uses a delta-wound stator rather than a wye (Y) as has been shown in the last several circuits. The stator windings of a delta unit are not connected in pairs.

Although the 30-SI operates similar to previous units, the following information will clarify its operating principles. When the engine is cranked over and starts, ac voltages in the stator winding are produced by residual magnetism in the spinning rotor. Current (amperes) will then flow through the diode trio, resistor R1, and transistors TR3 and TR1 to ground. Dc field current from the stator passes through the diode trio, the field, TR1, and then through the grounded diodes in the rectifier

FIGURE 8–41 Alternate wiring diagram for a model 25-SI generator model. (*Courtesy of Delco Remy Division, General Motors Corporation.*)

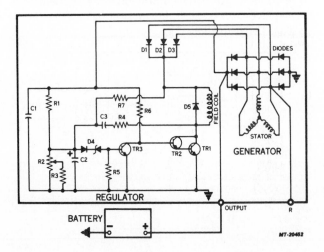

FIGURE 8–42 30-SI series 400 generator external features. (*Courtesy of GMC Truck Division, General Motors Corporation.*)

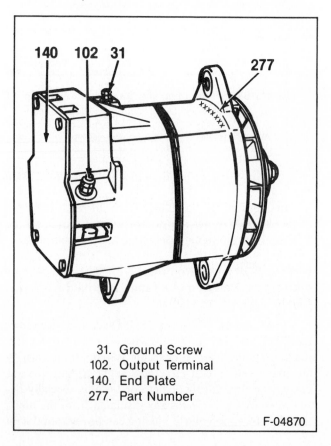

31. Ground Screw
102. Output Terminal
140. End Plate
277. Part Number

F-04870

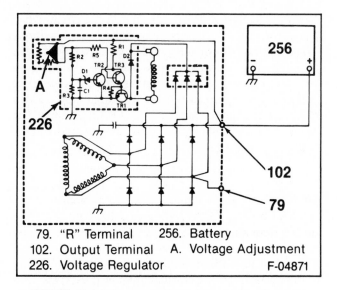

FIGURE 8–43 30-SI series 400 wiring diagram. (*Courtesy of Delco-Remy Division, General Motors Corporation.*)

79. "R" Terminal	256. Battery
102. Output Terminal	A. Voltage Adjustment
226. Voltage Regulator	F-04871

decrease, allowing DI to block current flow and subsequently let TR3 and TR1 turn back on. Both field current and system voltage increase and the cycle is repeated to limit the voltage to the preadjusted value. This action occurs from as few as 10 times per second to as many as several thousand, depending on the state of battery charge and the system load demands. As with the other Delco systems shown in this chapter, capacitor C1 is designed to smooth out the voltage level across R3, while resistor R4 is there to prevent excessive current through TR1 at high operating temperatures. Diode D2, on the other hand, is provided to prevent high induced voltages in the field windings when TR1 turns off.

Another model of 30-SI generator is the 30-SI/TR unit (the TR standing for "transformer rectifier"), which is used for heavy-duty truck applications requiring 24-V starting and 12-V charging. Additional information on TR systems is given in Chapters 3 and 9. The use of a TR generator eliminates the need for a separate series–parallel switch arrangement.

The circuit for the 30 SI/TR is basically the same as the 30-SI, with the exception that the upper half of the wiring diagram shown in Fig. 8–44 includes the transformer rectifier circuit with two delta-wound stators, a TR bridge with six more diodes, and a C or cranking battery, plus the regular system battery. The 30 SI does not have the additional battery for cranking, or the two delta stators and transformer wiring.

The flow path for the lower portion of the 30 SI/TR and 30 SI generators is the same as that for the 10, 15,

bridges back to the stator. The rectifier bridge diodes actually change the stator ac voltage to a dc voltage which is reflected between ground and the battery terminal. With any increase in engine speed, the voltage between R2 and R3 increases to a value that triggers the zener diode D1, and it conducts, turning on transistor TR2. This action then causes both TR3 and TR1 to turn off. With TR1 off, the field current and system voltage will

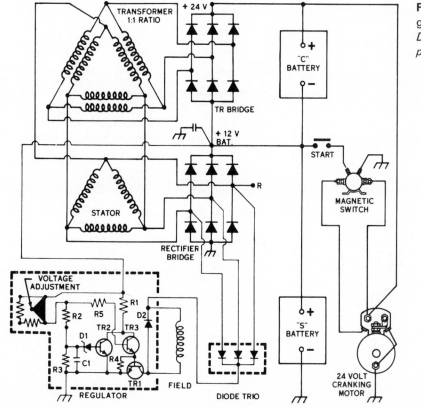

FIGURE 8–44 Model 30-SI/TR negative-ground circuit wiring diagram. (*Courtesy of Delco Remy Division, General Motors Corporation.*)

17, and 27 SI type explained earlier in the chapter and shown in Figs. 8-23 and 8-27.

In Fig. 8-44 a TR (transformer–rectifier) unit is mounted to the rectifier end frame and connected to the C or cranking battery as shown in the diagram. Both batteries are automatically connected into a series hookup arrangement to provide 24 V for cranking or starting purposes only.

Within the transformer windings, we have a dual delta-wound stator. The inner stator is wired to the delta stator in the lower half of the diagram; therefore, induced ac voltages in the stator while the generator is operating will also be sensed at the upper stator (inner) windings.

An ac current will therefore flow in the primary (inner) delta stator in the upper half of the diagram. Basic electricity taught us that if we pass a current through a wire, we create a magnetic field. This changing ac current, creating a magnetic field, will induce voltages in the transformer secondary winding similar to the action in an ignition coil or transformer. The difference here is that we do not require an increase in voltage such as we obtain in a coil with fewer windings in the primary than in the secondary. Here, the windings in the secondary are similar to those in the primary. The induced current and voltage flow in the secondary winding is rectified through the rectifier bridge to charge the C or charging battery.

This transformer rectified circuit eliminates the need for a series–parallel switch and the associated wiring, which is shown in Chapter 9.

NOTE: The basic difference in the wiring circuit when a positive rather than a negative system is used is simply that everything shown in Fig. 8-44 that has a positive sign should be changed to a negative sign; also, the diodes in both rectifier bridges would conduct current flow in the opposite direction, and resistor R1 would be grounded rather than running up to the +12-V BAT terminal. The negative battery posts in the wiring circuit would also become positive (+).

With the 30 SI/TR circuit, the cranking battery is charged at a low rate to maintain its full state of charge while the engine is running. With the exception of the cranking motor, the vehicle electrical system is 12 V.

This completes the wiring circuits for both slip-ring and brush generators as well as for the brushless type. You will have noticed quite a similarity between many of the wiring circuits discussed in this chapter. This similarity makes it a relatively easy task to assimilate fairly quickly the flow paths and differences between all of the generator models produced by Delco-Remy. This should help you to remember many of these flow paths with a short review of each circuit any time that you contemplate testing or troubleshooting one of these systems.

ALTERNATOR PRECAUTIONS

Before an attempt is made to service or troubleshoot a suspected alternator problem, there are a number of precautions that you should be aware of to avoid possible

TABLE 8-3 Do's and Don'ts alternator precautions

Some of the more important "Do's" and "Don'ts" that should be observed during charging system operations and test procedures are listed below.

Do Not	Short Field terminal of alternator to ground while charging system is in operation. Indiscriminate grounding of alternator or regulator terminals can result in damage to the charging or electrical system of the vehicle.		**Do**	Make sure all charging system connections are clean and tight (especially regulator ground lead output terminal and battery connections).
Do Not	Disconnect voltage regulator while alternator is in operation. Also, don't remove regulator ground lead while system is functioning or regulator damage may occur.		**Do**	Observe proper system ground polarity when installing battery or alternator.
Do Not	Disconnect load (alternator output lead) while alternator is operating.		**Do**	Make sure battery is in good condition and fully charged before performing in-vehicle and troubleshooting tests.
Do Not	Disconnect battery while charging system is in operation.		**Do**	Use accurate test equipment since system malfunction can sometimes be indicated by very small differences in voltage and current.
Do Not	Remove alternator from vehicle without first disconnecting the ground cable (the negative (−) battery cable in most cases).		**Do**	Disconnect battery ground cable to avoid possible system damage when charging battery or welding on the vehicle.
Do Not	Remove battery from vehicle without disconnecting the ground cable first (negative (−) side of battery is most cases), then disconnect the insulated cable (positive (+) side of battery in most cases).		**Do**	Check harness wire size to prevent excessive loss, especially when replacing the alternator with a higher capacity unit.
Do Not	Allow charging system voltage to exceed approximately 16 volts during in-vehicle tests, or system damage may result.		**Do**	Check alternator drive belt for proper tension and condition before proceeding with system tests.
Do Not	Attempt to polarize an alternator.			

Source: Motorola Automotive and Industrial Electronics Group.

charging system damage. If a charging system test is to be performed but the batteries are flat, never use a fast charger with the batteries connected or as a booster for battery output. If a booster battery is to be used, the batteries must be connected correctly regarding polarity. Always connect negative to negative and positive to positive. Accidental polarity reversal can severely damage the diodes in the alternator end frame.

Never disconnect the battery (batteries) while the engine and alternator are operating since this can lead to diode damage caused by a momentary high voltage and current surge that is created by the rapid collapse of the magnetic field surrounding the field windings. If an insulated starting motor is used on an engine, it is imperative that a ground strap be used and correctly installed; otherwise, faulty alternator operation can occur.

Never ground or short the alternator output wire(s) or the field wires between the alternator and the voltage regulator, and never operate an alternator on an open circuit. Although some alternator voltage regulators are designed to prevent reverse polarity damage, never ground the alternator output wire or terminals since they are always hot, regardless of whether or not the engine is running. Grounding of the field current can also result in diode burnout. The alternator diodes are sensitive to heat and are mounted in a heat sink within the alternator end frame so that the airflow produced from the alternator pulley fan will force air through the assembly for cooling purposes. Any restriction to this airflow can result in diode damage. In addition, take care not to route hot exhaust pipes in close proximity to the alternator. Do not weld or solder around the alternator either. If welding is to be conducted on a vehicle, always disconnect the batteries and isolate the alternator.

Although polarizing of an alternator is not normally required, there are occasions whereby the rotor residual magnetism can be weakened or lost, particularly when a generator has been disassembled for repair or has been nonoperational for some time. On Delco-Remy models this is usually accomplished by connecting the generator to the battery in the normal manner (ensure correct polarity), then momentarily connecting a jumper lead from the battery positive post to the generator R (relay) terminal. On Leece-Neville alternators, momentarily connect a jumper wire between the diode trio terminal and the generator positive output terminal. Table 8-3 lists typical do's and don'ts for alternator service; take special note of the polarizing information described above when you read the last "do not" in the table.

ALTERNATOR TEST EQUIPMENT

To check/test any alternator system, many major generator manufacturers offer special test equipment designed to be used specifically with their products. More often, however, these special test tools and instrumentation are manufactured and distributed by a number of major well-known tool suppliers, such as the Kent-Moore Heavy Duty Division and OTC Tool & Equipment Division, both of SPX Corporation, Sun Equipment Corporation, Allen Test Equipment, and Snap-On Tools. There are many other tool suppliers that also manufacture excellent test products. When testing alternator charging systems, you must keep in mind that although several special tools are required, you can perform most checks with the aid of a good-quality multimeter capable of checking amperage, voltage, and resistance. In addition, tools such as a carbon pile load tester that are required to perform a generator full-rated output test are also required to check the condition of a battery or batteries that form part of the charging system.

A simple self-powered test light that can be used for continuity testing, although desirable, can also be substituted by the use of an ohmmeter. Various test wire/leads with alligator clips at each end, preferably with an insulated cover over them to prevent short circuiting, are of great help in connecting instruments into the system.

Multimeters are readily available in both analog (swinging needle gauge), and digital form. The digital models are very popular now since they are designed to operate safely with electronic components in the various circuits now so prevalent in both cars and trucks. In addition, many specifications relating to alternator system components are so low that effective interpretation with an analog gauge becomes almost impossible making the digital unit a necessity for successful testing purposes. Various charging system analyzer instruments are available that make suspected charging system problems quick and easy. Pocket-sized models allow the mechanic/technician to rapidly check the battery and charging system regulator, as well as locate an open or shorted rectifier, rotor field, stator, or diode trio.

Various special tools and equipment that can be used to check the battery and alternator charging system are shown in this section. Also, located throughout Chapters 3 and 9 are descriptions of a number of other special tools and equipment that can be considered when attempting to troubleshoot a system. Many of these special tools can be applied to more than one system on the vehicle to trace a problem or to confirm that the system is operational. Figure 8-45 illustrates one type of charging system analyzer and its function.

NOTE: Refer also to the section "Basic Diagnostic Tools" in Chapter 4 for more information on the correct procedural use of the various tools and test instrumentation applicable to effective electrical system service. Typical test tools that can be used on alternators are shown in Figs. 4-8, 4-9, 4-10, and 4-15.

VAT Tester

One of the most important and helpful test instruments that the mechanic technician can access and which all

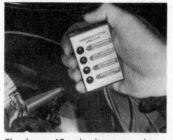

Check any 12 volt alternator charging system in seconds with this hand-held electronic analyzer.

7200

Charging System Analyzer

Now you can diagnose suspected charging system problems quickly and easily with this pocket-sized analyzer. It's designed for use on any vehicle with a 12 volt, positive or negative grounded alternator charging system. In seconds you can discover if the battery and regulator are working properly and single out an open or shorted rectifier, rotor field, stator or diode trio. Solid state design provides instant read-out; no meters or scopes to decipher. To use, simply attach the clip-on connectors to the alternator and start the engine—it's like a charging system test stand in your pocket!

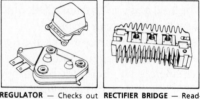

REGULATOR — Checks out internal or conventional regulators.

RECTIFIER BRIDGE — Readout displays open or shorted heat sink.

STATOR/FIELD — Open/shorted field or stator winding shown.

DIODE TRIO — Check possible diode trio malfunction.

BATTERY — Determine low voltage or possible bad cell quickly.

FIGURE 8–45 Model J26290-A or OTC Model 7200 charging system analyzer. (*Courtesy of Kent-Moore Heavy Duty Division, SPX Corporation.*)

well-equipped truck service shops have is what is commonly called a VAT tester. The letters VAT simply stand for "volt/amp tester." Two types are readily available, and these are illustrated in Fig. 3–29. One is the well-known and long-used analog (swinging needle gauge) model, while the later VAT model employs digital readout gauges. The Sun Electric Corporation is a major producer of VAT testers for the automotive and heavy-duty truck industries.

With passenger car and heavy truck electronic content expanding every year, the condition of the starting and charging system remains one of the most important systems from a service/maintenance standpoint. The analog and digital readout testers are both designed to allow easy hookup to the starting and charging systems. The analog model VAT-40 shown in Fig. 3–29 contains large-scale ammeter and voltmeter gauges, while the VAT-60 digital unit shown in Fig. 8–46 contains two large vacuum-tube fluorescent display panels showing both amperage and voltage. Both testers are equipped with a built-

in carbon pile tester for load testing the battery and alternator systems. A convenient load light is illuminated any time that the carbon pile is drawing current from the battery or alternator. In the VAT-60 the internal and external voltage and carbon pile heat conditions are constantly monitored. In the event that safe limits are exceeded, an audio alarm sounds and the display panels will flash. All voltage measurements are accurate to 1 one-hundredth of a volt, with the voltage range of the VAT-60 being 0 to 39.99 V dc, while the current range is 0 to 1000 A, making it ideal for use on truck applications. The VAT-60 model is a highly precise, microprocessor-based volt/amp tester with built-in limits as well as its own diagnostic capability. When the automatic mode test sequence is selected, the tester will perform a fast but comprehensive programmed test sequence, at the end of which the VAT-60 automatically delivers good/bad determinations on battery, starting system, charging system, and diode stator condition. A manual mode is of course available at the flick of a switch. Data from each test seg-

FIGURE 8-46 Close-up of the features of the VAT-60 unit. (*Courtesy of Sun Electric Corporation, Crystal Lake, IL.*)

ment can be recalled at the completion of a test program so that the technician can examine the results more closely.

DELCO GENERATOR OUTPUT TESTS

The operation and general design of all Delco generators discussed in this chapter should give you an appreciation of just how similar the various models are. Because of these similarities, the actual testing procedures for all units are also very similar. Differences occur only in the location and type of voltage regulator used; therefore, the information contained in this section will allow you to quickly assimilate and remember these basic test procedures. Two basic types of output tests can be performed on the generator assembly:

1. An on-vehicle charging system check
2. An off-vehicle bench check on a test stand

Figure 8–47 shows a sequential troubleshooting chart that can be used when a problem exists in any Delco-Remy generator. Whether the generator is tested on or off the vehicle, you need to know the rated output of the generator in amperes; Table 8–4 lists typical Delco and Leece-Neville test specifications for medium- and heavy-duty trucks. Basically, there are two test hookups and two test procedures for all Delco generators discussed in this chapter. The 10-SI, 15-SI, 17-SI, 27-SI type 100, and the 27-SI type 200 models use the same test procedure. The second test hookup and procedure is specific to the Delco 25-SI and 30-SI models, which can be tested in the

same manner. In this section we begin with a subheading dealing with an on-vehicle generator output test for a heavy-duty truck. This basic description can be applied to any make and model of alternator. Following the on-vehicle output test, the recommended procedure for bench checking (off vehicle) a generator is given in two parts. The first subheading deals with the Delco brush type 10, 15, 17, and 27-SI Delco models, and the second deals with the heavy-duty brushless 25-SI and 30-SI models as well as the 30-SI/TR (transformer-rectified) type used on series–parallel systems requiring 24-V starting and 12-V charging.

Heavy-Duty Alternator Test: On Vehicle

When a problem is reflected in the starting/charging system through complaints of hard starting or low power to operate accessories, there are a couple of checks that can be performed fairly quickly to confirm whether the problem is actually in the batteries, starter motor, alternator, or associated wiring. Simple causes such as high circuit resistance in a number of wiring connections can lead the mechanic/technician to suspect either battery or starter problems, with some suspicion that the problem might also be in the alternator or voltage regulator. High circuit resistance will cause a voltage loss to the batteries, and this can be caused by corrosion, loose or dirty terminals, or damaged wiring or connections.

The first step in pinpointing any starting/charging system problem is to note whether the lack of power occurs only during a cranking/starting attempt. If it does, you can refer to Chapter 3 for batteries or to Chapter

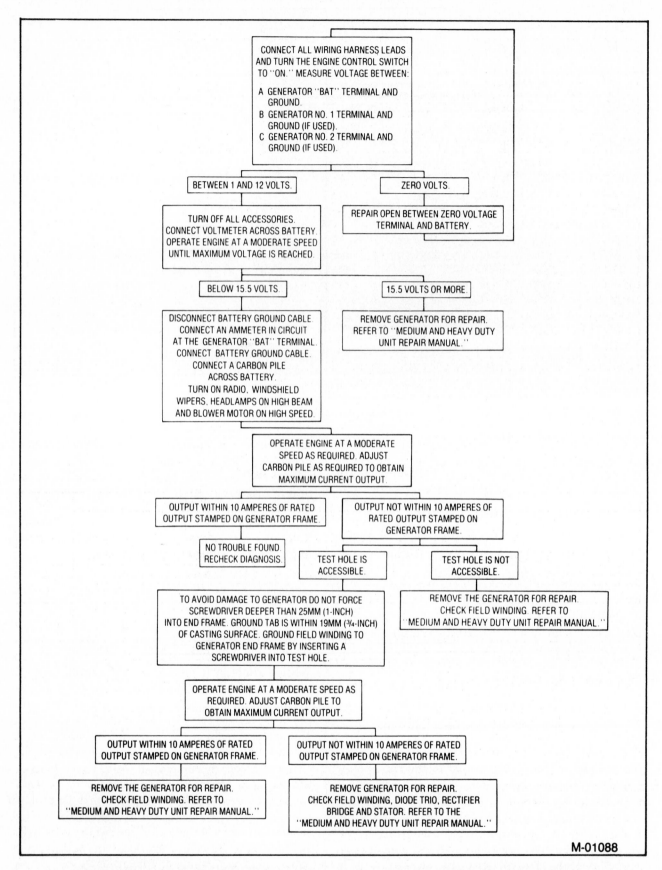

FIGURE 8–47 Diagnostic troubleshooting chart for Delco Remy generators. (*Courtesy of GMC Truck Division, General Motors Corporation.*)

MEDIUM DUTY TRUCKS

Part No.	Series	Rotation Viewing Dr. End	Field Ohms 27°C, 80°F	Field Current @ 14 Volts (27°C, 80°F) AMPS	Cold Output			Hot Output AMPS
					AMPS @ 2000 RPM	AMPS	RPM	
711925	JB2600	Either	—	2.8	81	105	7000	105
1100094	27SI205	Either	2.4-2.7	4.4-4.9	55	68	7000	65
1100095	27SI205	Either	2.4-2.7	4.4-4.9	52	72	5000	80
1100096	27SI205	Either	2.4-2.7	4.4-4.9	63	97	5000	100
1105332	15SI100	CW	2.6-3.0	4.0-4.6	55	70	5000	70
1105351	10SI100	Either	2.4-3.0	4.0-5.0	25	38	5000	42
1105366	17SI100	CW	2.4-2.8	4.2-5.0*	45**	108	6500	****
2009386	JB2700	Either	—	5.0-6.0*	85	130	6000	130
2009669	JB2800	Either	—	5.0-6.0*	90	160	5000	160
1105460	27SI200	Either	2.4-2.7	4.4-4.9	46	58	5000	65
1105465	27SI200	CW	2.4-2.7	4.4-4.9	52	72	5000	80
1105472	27SI200	CW	2.2-2.7	4.5-5.5	73***	83	7000	100
1101252	17SI100	CW	1.7-2.1	5.7-7.1	50**	120	6500	****
1101058	27SI100	CW	2.4-2.7	4.4-4.9	55	76	5000	80

*   @ 12 Volts
**   @ 1600 rpm
*** @ 2850 rpm
**** Same as cold output

HEAVY DUTY TRUCKS

Model No.	Series	Type	Rotation Viewing Dr.	Field Current 27°C (80°F) Amps	Volts	Specified Volts	Amps	Approx. RMP	Amps	Approx. RPM	Hot Rated Output
							Cold Output				
1105465	27SI	200	Either	4.4-4.9	12	(A)	52	2000	72	5000	80
1117241	25SI	400	Either	4.1-4.5	12	(A)	—	—	77	5000	75
1117242	25SI	450	Either	4.1-4.5	12	(A)	—	—	70	5000	75
1117732	30SI	400	Either	3.6-4.3	12	13	72	2500	90	6500	90
—	3425	JC	Either	—	—	14	15	600	75	6000	75

(A) Voltmeter not needed for cold output check. Load battery with carbon pile to obtain maximum output. Refer to application service bulletin for test procedure.

Source: GMC Truck Division, General Motors Corporation.

9 for starting motors. Visually check and feel the battery connections and all other wire terminals and connections between the battery, starter, and alternator. If nothing unusual is noted, perform a load test on the batteries according to the instructions on page 74 and Fig. 3–28. Replace any faulty batteries and clean and tighten all battery connections. What we want to do now is to perform a charging circuit voltage drop and alternator output test.

For purposes of discussion, we select a heavy-duty truck equipped with four 12-V batteries in parallel using a Delco 42MT starter motor and a Delco 25-SI brushless generator. Refer to Fig. 8–48, which illustrates the starter, alternator, and battery arrangement for a heavy-duty diesel engine using a Delco 42MT starter and a Delco 25-SI brushless generator.

Procedure

1. With the engine stopped, connect a carbon pile load tester (make sure that the carbon pile control knob is in the OFF position) between the alternator output terminal and the ground of the alternator housing. The alternator output terminal is at battery voltage.

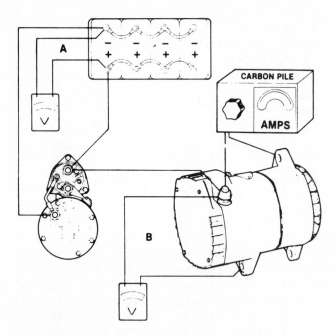

FIGURE 8-48 Step 1: electrical test hookup to check the charging circuit voltage drop condition with a voltmeter connected in position A, then in position B. (*Courtesy of Detroit Diesel Corporation.*)

CAUTION: Care must be exercised when connecting the carbon pile to the alternator output terminal to ensure that the pile clamp does not touch a ground circuit such as the alternator body or other metal bracket that may be in close proximity.

2. Battery voltage can be monitored simply by connecting the red voltmeter lead to the + battery post and the black lead to the − battery post, as shown in Fig. 8-48 at position A.

NOTE: Determine the alternator part number from the information shown in Fig. 8-42, then refer to Table 8-4 and pick out the rated output in amperes from the chart for the alternator model in question. Some alternators have the rated output stamped on the alternator housing or on a name tag attached to the housing.

3. Slowly rotate the control knob on the carbon pile until the built-in ammeter registers the alternator rated output in amperes. If the carbon pile does not have an ammeter, connect a separate ammeter into the system so that amperage draw can be monitored.

4. Quickly note and record the battery voltage on the voltmeter while the carbon pile is drawing the recommended amperage, then turn the carbon pile control knob OFF.

5. Disconnect the voltmeter from position A in Fig. 8-48 and reconnect it to position B. This requires that the red voltmeter lead (+) be attached to the alternator (BAT) output terminal and that the black lead (−) be attached to the alternator housing for ground purposes.

CAUTION: Do not connect the voltmeter leads to the carbon pile leads; otherwise, when the carbon pile is

turned on, the high amperage will damage the voltmeter and its leads.

6. Slowly rotate the carbon pile control knob once again until the ammeter registers rated alternator output according to the note between steps 2 and 3 above.

7. Quickly note and record the voltage at the alternator (BAT) output terminal, then turn off the carbon pile by rotating the control knob OFF or to the MIN position.

8. The system voltage drop can now be determined simply by subtracting the voltage reading that was obtained at the alternator BAT terminal in step 7 from that recorded previously in step 4.

9. If the reading determined in step 8 is greater than 0.5 V for a 12-V system, or 1.0 V for a 24-V system, proceed to step 10. If, however, the voltage drop is within specifications, proceed directly to the alternator output test described after step 16.

10. With the carbon pile still connected but in the OFF position, connect a digital scale voltmeter, since we want to read precisely what the voltage drop is on either the + or − side of the charging circuit.

11. Refer to Fig. 8-49 step 1, and connect the digital voltmeter red (+) lead to a battery positive terminal. Connect the black (−) lead of the voltmeter to the alternator (BAT) output terminal. If the batteries are too far away from the alternator, hook up a jumper wire to extend the voltmeter leads.

12. Slowly rotate the carbon pile load control knob until the ammeter registers rated alternator output once again.

13. Quickly note and record the voltmeter value, then turn the carbon pile load control knob OFF.

14. Refer to Fig. 8-49 step 2, and connect the voltmeter leads to the negative side of the charging circuit, which

FIGURE 8-49 Step 2: electrical test hookup to check the charging circuit voltage drop condition. (*Courtesy of Detroit Diesel Corporation.*)

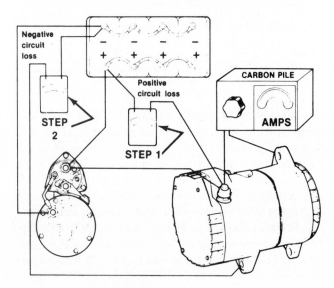

involves placing the red (+) lead to the alternator housing and the black (−) lead to the battery negative terminal.

15. Rotate the carbon pile load control knob slowly until the ammeter registers the alternator rated output in amperes, then quickly read and record the voltmeter reading. Turn off the carbon pile by rotating the control knob.

16. Add the positive circuit voltage loss to that for the negative circuit loss. This combined value should not exceed 0.5 V for a 12-V system, or 1.0 V for a 24-V system.

Once you have determined where the voltage loss is, correct by removing the necessary connections and cleaning and tightening them again. Recheck the system voltage drop again, then proceed to the alternator output test.

On-Vehicle Alternator Output Test

This check will quickly confirm if the problem is in either the alternator or voltage regulator.

Procedure

1. Make sure that the engine is at shop ambient temperature prior to conducting this test.

2. Refer to Fig. 8–50 and select a starting/charging system analyzer, such as a Sun Electric VAT tester model, that contains both an ammeter and a voltmeter and usually, a built-in carbon pile. Such a tester is illustrated in Fig. 8–46.

3. Connect the voltmeter leads to one of the 12-V batteries, making sure that the red lead goes to a + connection and that the black lead goes to a − connection.

4. Place the tester inductive pickup plastic clamp around the alternator output wire as shown in Fig. 8–50.

5. Connect the carbon pile leads or a separate carbon pile if the tester is not equipped with one so that it spans

FIGURE 8–50 Using a VAT tester inductive pickup to monitor the alternator rated output value. (*Courtesy of Detroit Diesel Corporation.*)

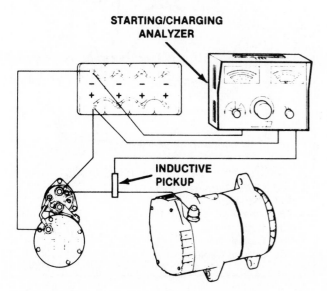

STARTING/CHARGING ANALYZER

INDUCTIVE PICKUP

one battery on a 12-V parallel-connected system. If the system is a 24-V arrangement, connect the carbon pile leads across one 12-V battery and the voltmeter across the normal 24-V battery connection.

6. Make sure that all vehicle electrical accessory load switches are off.

7. Make sure that the carbon pile load control knob is off.

8. Start the engine and accelerate it to a fast idle, between 1000 and 1200 rpm maximum.

9. Turn the carbon pile on and slowly rotate the control knob to cause the alternator to produce its rated amperage output. Read and record the voltage value.

10. The voltage value should not exceed 15 V on a 12-V system, or 30 V on a 24-V system, although 28 V is usually stated and accepted as maximum. If the voltage exceeds these limits by more than 1 V, and the alternator output is not within 10 A, a voltage adjustment can be attempted on a Delco 25-SI alternator, which is described in the section "Generator Output Test: Bench Check."

11. Failure of the alternator to function to rated amperage and voltage after any voltage adjustment on a Delco 25-SI model would require that the voltage regulator be replaced.

12. Voltage that exceeds the limit by more than 1 V and that cannot be lowered by adjustment would require that the generator be removed for inspection and repair as described in the section "Alternator Disassembly and Repair."

Generator Output Test: Bench Check

10- 15- 17- 27-SI Series

The test hookup for the 10-SI, 15-SI, 17-SI, and 27-SI type 100 brush generators, as well as for the 27-SI type 200 model with a two-terminal connector is illustrated in Fig. 8–51. A minor change in the hookup for the 27-SI type 200 one-wire terminal model is shown in Fig. 8–52. Although there is a slight change in the connections between these two types, the test sequence is the same for both.

Procedure

1. Install the generator and clamp it into position in a suitable test stand designed for this purpose.

CAUTION: To prevent any damage to the generator, ensure that the ground polarity of the battery and the generator is the same. To ensure a true reflection of the generator output, a fully charged battery must be used for the output test.

2. Make the necessary wire connections as shown in either Fig. 8–51 or 8–52, but be sure to leave the carbon pile disconnected.

3. Make sure that you install a 10-Ω resistor rated at 6 W or more between generator terminal 1 and the battery for all models except the 27-SI type 200 with the one-wire terminal connector.

SPECIAL NOTE: If the generator is being tested after having been disassembled, you may have to reestablish

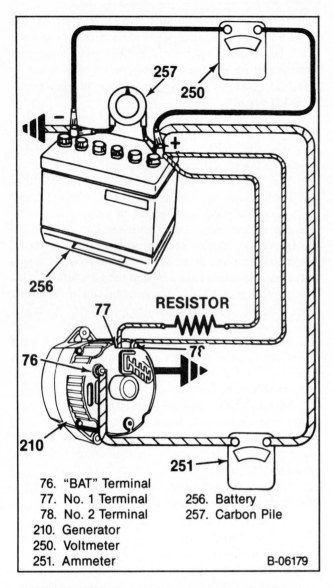

76. "BAT" Terminal
77. No. 1 Terminal
78. No. 2 Terminal   256. Battery
210. Generator   257. Carbon Pile
250. Voltmeter
251. Ammeter

B-06179

FIGURE 8–51 Test hookup requirements for a bench check of a generator. (*Courtesy of GMC Truck Division, General Motors Corporation.*)

trol feature. If this occurs, it is also advisable to check the field winding.

7. However, if the voltage output remains lower than 15.5 V on a 12-V system, connect the carbon pile load tester as illustrated in Figs. 8–51 and 8–52.

8. Increase the test stand drive speed according to the test stand specifications shown in Table 8–4 and adjust the carbon pile as necessary to apply enough load to cause the ammeter to show maximum current output.

9. A current output within 10 A of that listed in the test tables, or as stamped on the generator frame, indicates that the unit is operating correctly.

10. If the generator output is not within 10 A of the rated output value, then with the test stand at the same speed and the carbon pile still loading the system, ground the generator field ground tab by inserting a screwdriver into the test hole. This test hole is generally within 25 mm (1 in.) of the rear casting surface of the generator end frame as shown in Fig. 8–21; in Fig. 8–22 it is shown as the field ground hole.

CAUTION: Be very careful when inserting the screwdriver into this hole. Push it gently into position (about 25 mm or 1 in.) until it touches a small tab, then apply light pressure to the screwdriver and hold it in this posi-

FIGURE 8–52 27-SI series 200 bench check connections for a one-wire model generator. (*Courtesy of GMC Truck Division, General Motors Corporation.*)

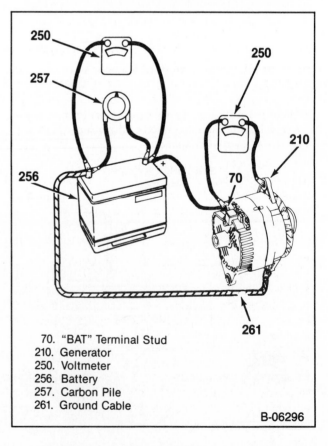

70. "BAT" Terminal Stud
210. Generator
250. Voltmeter
256. Battery
257. Carbon Pile
261. Ground Cable

B-06296

the correct magnetism in the rotor to ensure that charging will occur. This can be done by connecting the battery to the generator in the normal hookup. Momentarily connect (flash) a jumper lead from the positive battery post to the generator R terminal.

4. With the generator securely clamped in the test stand machine and the drive belt properly adjusted, double check that all connections are as shown in Fig. 8–51 or 8–52.

5. Start the test stand drive motor by the on/off switch and slowly increase the drive speed to the generator pulley while noting the voltage increase on the voltmeter.

6. The voltage regulator in the generator requires replacement if the voltage output rises quickly above 15.5 V on all 12-V-rated systems without showing any sign of change through manipulation of the test stand speed con-

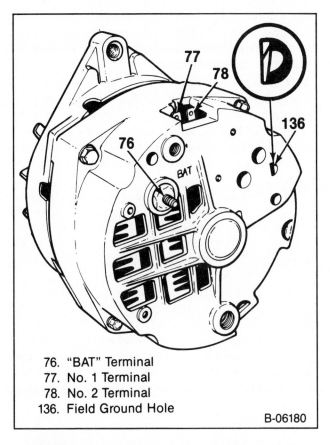

76. "BAT" Terminal
77. No. 1 Terminal
78. No. 2 Terminal
136. Field Ground Hole

B-06180

FIGURE 8–53 Location of generator field ground tab. (*Courtesy of GMC Truck Division, General Motors Corporation.*)

tion. Figure 8–53 illustrates the field ground tab for a model 17-SI type 100 generator.

11. Operate the test stand/generator at moderate speed and adjust the carbon pile as required to try to obtain maximum output of the generator according to the test specs or to the number stamped on the generator frame.

12. If the output is still not within 10 A of the listed value, then replace the regulator and check out the field winding, the diode trio on units so equipped, the rectifier bridge, and the stator as shown in the section "Alternator Disassembly and Repair" in this chapter.

25-SI and 30-SI Series. The generator output test procedure for the 25-SI series, types 400 and 450, and the 30-SI series, type 400 models, follows the same routine. For best results the generator should be bolted to a suitable shop test stand. Figures 8–20 and 8–42 illustrated the external features of both the 25-SI and 30-SI models.

Procedure

1. Install the generator and clamp it into position in a suitable test stand designed for this purpose. Adjust the test stand drive belt to the generator pulley for correct tension.

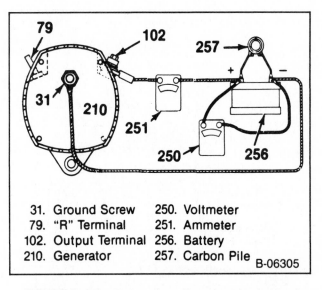

31. Ground Screw	250. Voltmeter
79. "R" Terminal	251. Ammeter
102. Output Terminal	256. Battery
210. Generator	257. Carbon Pile

B-06305

FIGURE 8–54 Connections for a bench check of models 25-SI and 30-SI. (*Courtesy of GMC Truck Division, General Motors Corporation.*)

2. Refer to Fig. 8–54 and make the necessary test connections as shown, but make sure that the carbon pile is in the OFF position at this time.

CAUTION: To prevent any damage to the generator, ensure that the ground polarity of the battery and that of the generator are the same. In addition, to ensure a true reflection of the generator output, a fully charged battery must be used for the output test.

3. If the generator has been disassembled prior to the output test, it may be necessary to reestablish generator magnetic polarity in the rotor. This can be done by:

a. Connecting the generator to the battery in the normal manner according to the wire terminal connections shown in Fig. 8–20 for the 25-SI model, and in Fig. 8–42 for the 30-SI model.

b. Momentarily connecting (flashing) a jumper lead from the battery positive post to the generator R (relay) terminal, which is located on the opposite side from the large BAT output terminal on the generator end frame. The R terminal for the 25-SI can be identified as item 79 in Fig. 8–39; the R terminal for the 30-SI model can be seen as item 79 in Fig. 8–55, which shows the component parts of the rectifier end frame with the cover removed.

4. Double check that all connections are secure and that the battery carbon pile is in fact turned off.

5. Start the test stand drive motor and gradually increase test stand speed until the maximum voltage reading is registered on the machine voltmeter. Typical operating voltages for the 25-SI and 30-SI would be as follows for a 12-V system and a 24-V system:

a. System voltage	12 V	24 V
b. Rated voltage	14 V	28 V
c. Operating range	13.0 to 15.0 V	26-30V

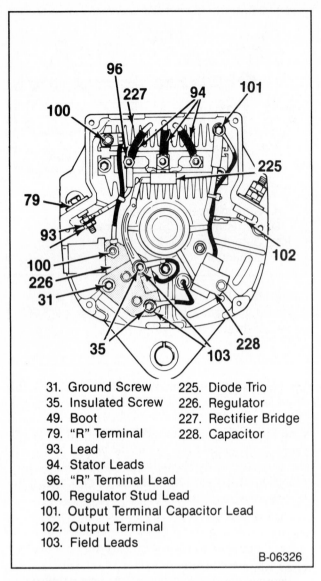

31. Ground Screw
35. Insulated Screw
49. Boot
79. "R" Terminal
93. Lead
94. Stator Leads
96. "R" Terminal Lead
100. Regulator Stud Lead
101. Output Terminal Capacitor Lead
102. Output Terminal
103. Field Leads

225. Diode Trio
226. Regulator
227. Rectifier Bridge
228. Capacitor

B-06326

FIGURE 8-55 30-SI series 400 with end plate removed. (*Courtesy of GMC Truck Division, General Motors Corporation.*)

6. Adjust the test stand controls to establish a drive speed of approximately 4000 rpm, then turn the carbon pile on and adjust it to obtain maximum current output. The test specs in Table 8-4 list the ampere values for each model of generator. It may be necessary to increase the drive speed to the generator to pull the maximum rated current value from the generator.

7. If the rated output of the generator according to the test specs or as stamped on the generator frame or nameplate is within 10 A, the generator is acceptable.

8. If the rated output is not within 10 A of the spec, a voltage adjustment can be attempted on the 25-SI series types 400 and 450. This adjustment procedure is described in Steps 9 through 13.

CAUTION: There is no voltage adjustment for the 30-SI generator model; therefore, if the rated output is not

within 10 A of the spec, the generator should be disassembled from the rectifier end in order to test or replace the voltage regulator components. The regulator is shown as item 226 in Fig. 8-55.

9. The voltage adjustment on the 25-SI generator can be accessed by removing the end cover from the generator to expose the voltage adjustment potentiometer screw (item 139 in Fig. 8-39).

10. Prior to performing any voltage adjustment, connect a voltmeter across the battery so that you can determine the setting.

11. If you want to increase the voltage output, use a small screwdriver to rotate the screw clockwise. To lower the voltage setting, rotate the adjustment screw counterclockwise. Be very careful when turning the adjustment screw since the smallest movement will affect the voltmeter reading across the battery.

12. When the adjustment is complete, install the generator end cover and tighten the retaining screws securely.

13. If this adjustment is performed while the generator is in place on a truck, closely monitor the battery charge condition over a period of several days or longer, and if the setting does not correct the battery charge problem, remove the generator for repair.

SPECIAL TIP: The voltage regulator adjustment should never be attempted prior to determining whether the battery or batteries are in a serviceable state, since batteries in a low state of charge or that have cell damage can cause any adjustment to be misleading. Consider, for example, that when the battery state of charge condition is low, the voltage regulator was probably not limiting the voltage.

On any alternator charging system, the battery supplies a small amount of current to the field circuit to create magnetism. If the state of charge of the vehicle battery is low, it is possible that the voltage regulator will not limit the generator voltage produced. This can be misleading, because you may adjust the regulator adjusting screw clockwise to increase the rate of charge, with no change occurring on the voltmeter scale. An increase in the voltage regulator setting has actually been accomplished. However, this increase will not show up on the voltmeter until the state of charge of the battery increases. This is why it is imperative that prior to checking and adjusting the voltage regulator assembly, the state of charge of the battery is first checked to ensure that it is at least 75% charged; otherwise, false interpretations can result.

Troubleshooting the 30-SI/TR Series Delcotron Integral Charging System

We have discussed the general procedures required to troubleshoot both the slip-ring and brush-type Delco alternators, and the brushless type. The sequence for both follows the same general pattern; however, the procedure for the 30-SI/TR unit does present some changes in the normal routine as described so far. The reasons for these changes result from the fact that the 30-SI/TR unit is a standard 30-SI alternator assembly with the addition of a transformer rectifier (TR) unit mounted on the end frame. The purpose of the TR unit is to provide a separate voltage to charge a cranking battery, which is connected in series with a 12-V system battery to provide 24-V cranking power.

When the engine is running, the cranking battery receives a low rate of charge. Since it does not supply any power to the vehicle accessories at any time, it does not require as high a state of charge as does the S or system battery. The accessories in the vehicle electrical system all operate on 12 V, other than the starter motor, which is, of course, 24 V. The main purpose, then, of the 30-SI/TR unit is to eliminate the use of the older-style series–parallel switch.

In the earlier section that dealt with the operating principles for Delco generators (alternators), a typical wiring circuit for the 30-SI and 30-SI/TR units was discussed. Figure 8–56 shows the typical external wiring circuit that would be used with the 30-SI/TR series unit.

The layout of the external wiring circuit in Fig. 8–56 shows both the C and S batteries, with the C battery being used only during cranking along with the S or system battery to provide 24-V starting. The transformer rectifier (TR) is simply an add-on item to the basic 30-SI unit in order to charge the cranking battery at a low state of charge when the engine is running.

When a problem exists in the 30-SI/TR charging system, such as the cranking or system battery being under- or overcharged, check out the system as follows:

Procedure

1. Take care not to allow any leads or terminals to touch ground.

2. Disconnect the batteries to isolate the generator and TR unit.

3. Completely remove the TR unit from the generator by removing the necessary screws and wires, which will now leave us with a 30-SI 12-V charging system connected to only the S or system battery once the battery leads are reconnected.

4. Check out the operation of the 30-SI generator in the

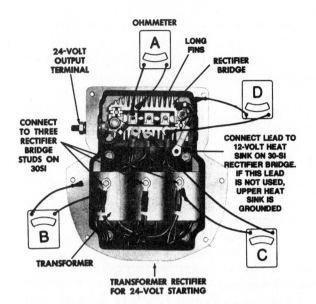

FIGURE 8–57 Model 30-SI/TR transformer and rectifier bridge diodes check with an ohmmeter. (*Courtesy of Delco-Remy Division, General Motors Corporation.*)

same manner as discussed earlier. If the 30-SI unit checks out OK, proceed to check the rectifier bridge of the TR unit, as follows.

5. Disconnect the transformer leads from the rectifier bridge as shown in Fig. 8–57 and connect an ohmmeter with a 1.5-V test cell to the heat sink, with the other lead to one of the three terminals. This is actually step A in Fig. 8–57. From earlier discussions of solid-state devices, you may remember that when checking a diode, the ohmmeter should register one high and one low reading when the ohmmeter leads are connected one way, and then reversed, which would indicate a good diode. If the readings are the same, the diode is faulty. The ohmmeter check should be done between the same heat sink and the other two terminals, and then between the other heat sink and each of the three terminals, for a total of six checks with two readings taken for each check.

To ensure an accurate reading on the ohmmeter, it is necessary to press the ohmmeter lead very firmly against the flat metal clips of the rectifier bridge studs. If this is not done, and the ohmmeter lead is connected to the threaded stud of the rectifier bridge only, a poor or false reading may be obtained.

CAUTION: The rectifier bridge assembly can be used on both positive and negative ground systems. Therefore, when installing a new rectifier bridge on negative ground systems, the bridge is assembled with the long cooling fins next to the generator end frame, and the short fins next to the transformer as is presently shown in Fig. 8–57.

On positive ground systems, the rectifier bridge is turned 180 degrees, so that the short fins are next to the end frame, and the long fins are now next to the transformer.

FIGURE 8–56 Model 30-SI/TR generator external wiring circuit. (*Courtesy of Delco-Remy Division, General Motors Corporation.*)

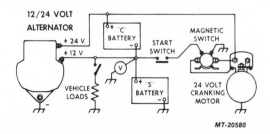

6. Refer to Fig. 8–57, and connect the ohmmeter three ways as indicated, in positions B, C and D. Each ohm-meter reading should be infinite (very high), otherwise replace the transformer.

7. Install the TR unit back onto the generator and when it is wired into place and secured by the holding screws, remove the 24-volt lead from the generator (do not allow it to touch ground).

8. Connect an ammeter between the 24 volt TR terminal and the previously disconnected lead.

9. Place a load across the 12 volt cranking battery such as one or two 12 volt headlamps, or the equivalent of 5 to 20 amperes.

10. Start and run the vehicle engine at a high enough rpm to produce maximum rated generator output.

11. The registered amperes flowing to the cranking (C) battery must be at least 5 amperes or more, otherwise the TR unit is faulty and should be replaced. If current flow to the TR unit is 5 amperes or greater, then the TR unit is operational.

LEECE-NEVILLE ALTERNATORS

Introduction

The Leece-Neville Company was founded in 1909 by Mr. B. M. Leece, who with Mr. S. M. Neville organized the company in 1910 for the purpose of manufacturing start-ing and lighting equipment. Therefore this company was one of the pioneers in the development of automotive/truck electrical equipment. Several major reorganizations have taken place within the company over the years. In 1974 Leece-Neville became a division of Sheller-Globe Corporation, which is a major OEM supplier to the auto-motive industry. In 1986 Leece-Neville became a part of Prestolite Electric Incorporated, which was founded in 1911 as the Electric Autolite Company, and which has a long reputation as being a supplier of quality electrical products to the automotive, heavy duty truck, industrial, marine, aircraft, and military markets. The incorpora-tion of Leece-Neville into the Prestolite Electric Incor-porated, Heavy Duty Products Division allows the organization to retain its identity as one of the leaders of electrical equipment for all facets of the heavy-duty truck, automotive, marine, and off-highway markets.

Leece-Neville Alternator Models

Commonly used truck alternators from Leece-Neville in-clude the 2500J family which are recognized by the ma-jority of heavy-duty truck manufacturers who offer this model line as standard equipment on many truck models. These particular model alternators can be seen through-out this section. See Figure 8–58 for a typical example. All of these alternator models include enclosed slip rings and brushes, an encapsulated adjustable solid-state vol-tage regulator, plus a simple two-wire connection design feature. The 2500J models are used on heavy-duty trucks,

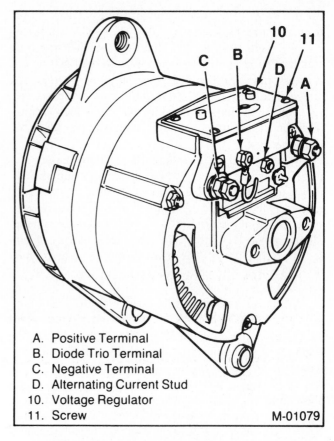

A. Positive Terminal
B. Diode Trio Terminal
C. Negative Terminal
D. Alternating Current Stud
10. Voltage Regulator
11. Screw

M-01079

FIGURE 8–58 Leece-Neville 2600JB and 2700JB alternator external features. (*Courtesy of GMC Truck Division, General Motors Corporation.*)

buses, school buses, fire trucks, industrial, and off-high-way and marine applications. This model range is avail-able in 12, 24, or 32 volt designs and includes the follow-ing models:

12 VOLT	
65 AMP	2300J
75 AMP	2360J
100 AMP	2500J
105 AMP	2600J
115 AMP	2670J
130 AMP	2700J
145 AMP	2805J
160 AMP	2800J
24 VOLT	
20 AMP	2301J*
45 AMP	2303J*
60 AMP	2509J*
65 AMP	2304J
85 AMP	2511J
32 VOLT	
60 AMP	2302

*UL listed units — UL Spec.
#1112 for marine applications

Note that the amperage output ratings shown in the chart are only produced at the maximum driven speed; at lower alternator speeds the output will be less than that shown. Alternators rated at 12 volts are generally adjusted to produce 14 volts, while 24 volt models are usually adjusted to develop approximately 28 volts while in operation on the vehicle.

The 3425J alternator models shown in Figure 8–59 are specifically designed for use on Detroit Diesel Corporation 71 and 92 series two-stroke cycle engines, since these models are a direct drive/flange mount design that are usually bolted to the engine flywheel housing where it is gear driven. This model is also available in 12, 24 or 32 volts with rated outputs ranging from 75 amps to 130 amps. These models are brush-type units featuring an encapsulated solid-state regulator equipped with plug-in connections, a built-in diode trio, and a three-step voltage adjustment. In addition, all models are equipped with a built-in load-dump feature protected voltage regulator to guard against transient voltage spikes that might cause alternator damage.

These Leece-Neville alternators are self-load limiting, and feature a fully adjustable, built-in solid state voltage regulator. The rotor shaft may be rotated in either direction without affecting the output or cooling of the unit, due to its bidirectional pulley fan arrangement. Six silicon diodes mounted in heat sinks convert alternating current from the delta-wound stator into direct current. A capacitor connected between the heat sinks assists in suppressing transient voltage spikes, which could possibly burn out or damage the diodes. The brushes and voltage regulator are located in a waterproof housing and may be removed for replacement or inspection without disassembling the alternator unit. An external relay terminal can be used for power supply to electrical accessories, or for charge-light relays.

A common feature of these alternators is that the unit has ungrounded output terminals so that it can be adapted to either a positive- or negative-ground system. The only wiring hookup required is the vehicle wiring to the correct output terminals, which eliminates the need for field relays or ignition switch connections.

The regulators used with these alternators are equipped with transient voltage protection; therefore, they can withstand instantaneous opening of the charging circuit under full-load conditions.

Basic Generator Operation

The operation of Leece-Neville generators is very similar to that used by other major manufacturers described in this chapter. Basically, the voltage regulator on Leece-Neville models is designed to relay a low current feed to the brushes and slip rings, which then passes into the rotor coil winding to increase the existing residual magnetic field around the rotor. No generator output can occur until the engine is cranked and starts, after which the spinning rotor will induce low-voltage ac in the stator. When the current created in the stator windings is forced by approximately 1 V of electrical pressure, the regulator will turn on automatically and allow full battery power to flow in the field coil. Full battery power triggers the stator output to rise to its maximum value, thereby producing

FIGURE 8–59 Model 3425JC Leece-Neville generator features. (*Courtesy of GMC Truck Division, General Motors Corporation.*)

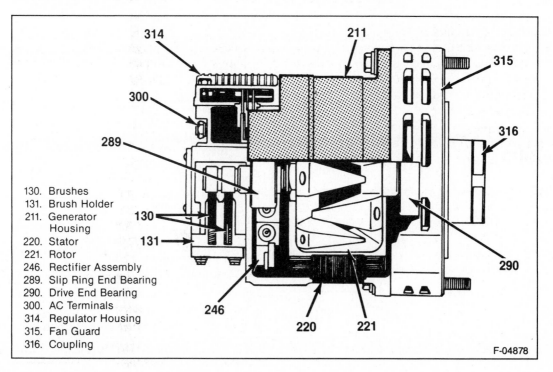

130. Brushes
131. Brush Holder
211. Generator Housing
220. Stator
221. Rotor
246. Rectifier Assembly
289. Slip Ring End Bearing
290. Drive End Bearing
300. AC Terminals
314. Regulator Housing
315. Fan Guard
316. Coupling

F-04878

its rated voltage and current (amperes). Rotor field current can range from 2.8 A on the JB2600 model, to between 5 and 6 A on the JB2700 and JB2800 models. Table 8-4 lists typical specs for these alternator models.

All current produced in the stator windings is directed to the rectifier assemblies, where it is converted from ac to dc. The alternator output terminals are connected to the rectifier assemblies and serve as junction points to the rest of the truck/bus electrical system. Connected to the rectifier assemblies are regulator sensing leads to allow the voltage regulator to monitor the output voltage. Should the voltage drop lower than or climb higher than the preset voltage limits, the regulator will initiate the necessary corrective action to maintain this preset voltage level as close as possible.

Generator Output Test Check

The sequence used for checking the output of the 2500, 2540, 2600, 2700, and 2800JB generators is the same and is discussed below. There are some minor changes to the test sequence for the 3425JC flange-type model, and these are discussed under the procedural check for this model. However, prior to proceeding with a generator output check/test, the following preservice considerations should be adhered to.

Preservice Checks. The most important checks are that the battery be in at least a 75% state of full charge, the terminals and connections must be clean and tight, the belts should be adjusted correctly, and the alternator assembly should be secure on its mounting brackets. As indicated at the start of the general troubleshooting section on alternators and charging systems, trouble in the system usually results from the state of charge of the battery being either continually low or overcharged (excess use of water on non-maintenance-free batteries).

To assist you in determining if the problem is in the alternator or the voltage regulator, connect an accurate voltmeter across the positive and negative posts of the battery with the engine stopped. Note the specific reading on the voltmeter. Start the vehicle engine and raise its speed to about 1000 rpm, at which time the voltmeter reading should increase above that noted earlier when the engine was stopped. If the voltmeter reading rises excessively, the charging system may be defective or in need of adjustment. If the voltmeter reading does not increase, proceed to the full field test. Figure 8-60 shows a typical diagnosis sequence for use with Leece-Neville generators.

Generator Rotor Residual Magnetism. Residual magnetism within the rotor assembly facilitates initial generator output, along with a small current flow from

FIGURE 8-60 Diagnostic chart for troubleshooting Leece-Neville generators. (*Courtesy of GMC Truck Division, General Motors Corporation.*)

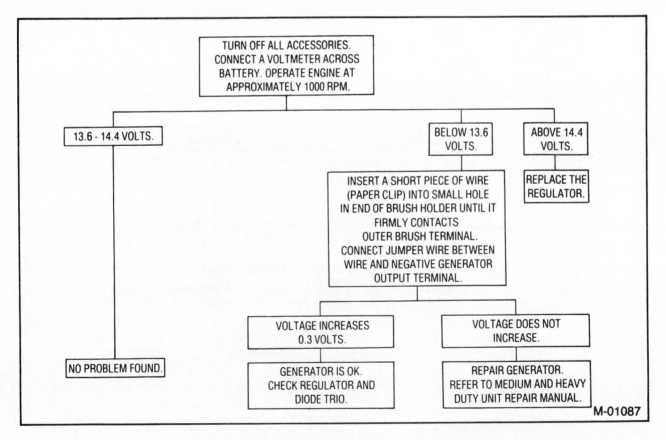

the voltage regulator. If the generator assembly has been removed for repair and disassembled, or if the battery cable connections have been removed for other service repair procedures, it is possible to weaken or lose this residual magnetism from the rotor assembly. If you are moving directly to a generator output test after receiving a charging system complaint on a truck that has been operating in service, reestablishment of rotor magnetism will normally not be required. To establish generator rotor magnetism, momentarily connect a jumper wire between the diode-trio terminal and the generator positive output terminal as shown in Fig. 8–61, with the engine off.

CAUTION: Diode trio and/or regulator failure due to improper field flashing. It has come to Prestolite/Leece-Neville's attention that subject failures are occurring for the following reasons:

1. Connection being made with engine running, causing transient voltage spikes.
2. Connecting jumper between diode-trio terminal and the negative rather than positive terminal.

To avoid these occurrences, it is Prestolite/Leece-Neville's

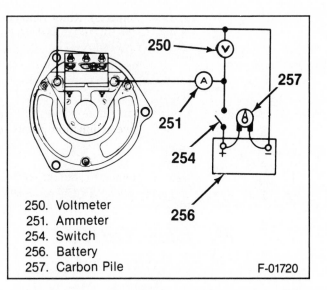

250. Voltmeter
251. Ammeter
254. Switch
256. Battery
257. Carbon Pile

F-01720

FIGURE 8–62 Test connections for a Leece-Neville generator. (*Courtesy of GMC Truck Division, General Motors Corporation.*)

FIGURE 8–61 Reestablishing magnetism with a jumper lead on a Leece-Neville generator. (*Courtesy of GMC Truck Division, General Motors Corporation.*)

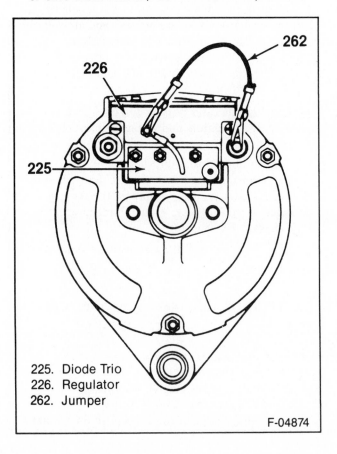

225. Diode Trio
226. Regulator
262. Jumper

F-04874

recommendation that the full field test method be used instead of field flashing to restore magnetism.

Output Test: 2500, 2540, 2600, 2700, and 2800JB Models. If your shop or maintenance facility is equipped with a commercial test block, the generator positive and negative output leads can be connected directly to the block, due to the fact that the generator contains an integral voltage regulator. If a test block is not readily available, simply proceed with the test hookup illustrated in Fig. 8–62.

Procedure

1. Mount the generator assembly into position on a suitable test stand and adjust the generator/test stand pulley drive belt correctly.
2. Make sure that the generator and battery ground polarity are the same; otherwise, generator damage can result.
3. The carbon pile shown as item 257 in Fig. 8–62 should be in the OFF position while connected to the battery at this time. If the carbon pile is on, current will flow from the battery, reducing its available power.
4. Start the test stand and increase the drive speed to spin the generator at 2500 rpm.
5. Read the voltage output of the generator; this value should be somewhere between 13.6 and 14.2 V.
6. A voltage value higher than that in step 5 means that the regulator is in need of adjustment as decribed below.

The 2500JB series units (as well as other models) are equipped with two types of regulators: fully adjustable (flat top) and three-step adjustable (dome top). Both regulator styles are removed and reinstalled in the same way.

(a)

Brush
Contact Pads

(b)

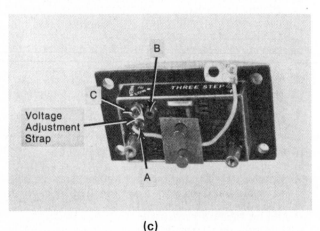

B

C

Voltage
Adjustment
Strap

A

(c)

FIGURE 8–63 (a) Adjusting the flat top type voltage regulator on a Leece-Neville generator; (b) brush pad inspection on a dome-top three-step adjustable regulator; (c) three-position voltage regulator adjustment strap. (*Courtesy of Prestolite Electric Incorporated, Heavy Duty Products Division.*)

Fully adjustable regulator (flat top)

Procedure

1. Remove the plastic screw from the regulator cover and engage a small screwdriver with the adjustment screw inside the regulator. Turn the screw clockwise to increase voltage, or counterclockwise to decrease voltage (see Fig. 8–63(a).

NOTE: Prestolite/Leece-Neville recommends that the regulator be set so that voltage at the battery terminals is as follows: 13.8 to 14.1 V for 14-V systems, 27.8 to 28.0 V for 28-V systems, 34.9 to 35.1 V for 35-V systems (15 cells of battery), and 37.4 to 37.6 V for 37.5-V systems (16 cells of battery). Consult the vehicle manufacturer's specifications because different applications may require higher or lower voltage settings.

CAUTION: Do not attempt to turn the screw past the preset stops at either end of the adjustment range, to avoid regulator damage.

2. Reinstall the plastic screw in adjustment access hole to keep out dirt, moisture, and other contaminants.

Three-step adjustable regulator

Procedure

1. Stop the engine and disconnect the battery ground cable.
2. Remove the No. 10-32 nuts and lockwasher from the regulator terminal, and disconnect the diode-trio lead (if the alternator is equipped with a diode trio).
3. Remove the four screws from the regulator cover. Lift the regulator out of the housing and move it out of the way as far as the leads will permit. Inspect the two regulator brush contact pads. If dirt or corrosion is noticed, clean the pads with No. 600 sandpaper (or finer) [see Fig. 8–63(b)].

NOTE: In some cases dirty or corroded pads can cause a low-charge condition, and voltage adjustment may not be necessary.

4. Inspect and reinstall brushes.
5. To adjust the voltage, remove and reinstall the voltage adjustment strap in any of the three positions available: A and B (low), A and C (medium), or C and B (high) [see Fig. 8–63(c)].

Each change in position of the adjustment strap will result in an increase or decrease in voltage of approximately 0.4 V.

CAUTION: Use a magnetic-tip screwdriver, to avoid loss of screws.

For example:

    a. Voltage at battery with engine at 1000 to 1200 rpm: 13.6 V
    b. Vehicle manufacturer specification for voltage setting: 14.0 ± 0.1 V
    c. Voltage adjustment strap position: A and C

1. *Necessary adjustment:* Voltage adjustment strap should be changed to C and B position to increase voltage by (approximately) 0.4 V, to 14.0 V.

CAUTION: Recommended torque for the No. 4 cross head screws used for securing the voltage adjustment strap is 4 to 5 in.-lb. Overtightening these screws may cause them to break and the regulator would become unusable.

2. Complete regulator installation.

CAUTION: On 2540JB series (dust-protected) alternators, the access hole used for pinning the brushes in place during regulator installation must be sealed with a piece of Varglass tape to avoid a short service life. The area around the access hole must be clean to ensure proper tape adhesion.

3. Reinstall the battery ground cable and repeat the "Regulator Voltage Adjustment" procedure to ensure proper voltage.

4. If the generator voltage value was low and adjustment failed to alter it, you can confirm if the problem is in the regulator, the diode trio, or the generator itself, by the test described in step 5.

5. a. Refer to Fig. 8–64 and connect a jumper wire with alligator clips between the negative generator output terminal and a short piece of wire (paper clip or small welding wire) about 3 to 4 in. (75 to 100 mm) long.

b. carefully insert the wire into the small access hole in the end of the brush holder until you feel it firmly contact the outer brush terminal. Should the voltage value increase on the face of the voltmeter, this confirms that the generator is operating correctly but that a problem exists in the voltage regulator or diode trio.

FIGURE 8–64 Testing the Leece-Neville generator by inserting a jumper lead. (*Courtesy of GMC Truck Division, General Motors Corporation.*)

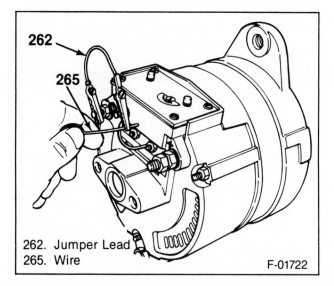

262. Jumper Lead
265. Wire

F-01722

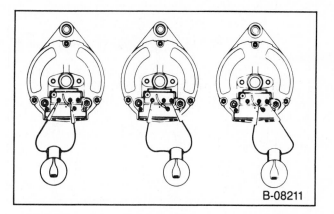

B-08211

FIGURE 8–65 Leece-Neville generator output test sequence. (*Courtesy of GMC Truck Division, General Motors Corporation.*)

6. If the voltage regulator responds to a screw adjustment and you can bring its setting to between 13.6 and 14.2 V, the generator current output can now be checked according to the specifications shown in Table 8–4 and described in step 7.

7. Run the test stand at 2500 rpm and turn the carbon pile on. Slowly adjust the carbon pile until the ammeter registers the maximum generator output as per Table 8–4. If the output value in amperes is within 10 % of the rated output, the generator is operating correctly.

8. If the generator amperage output is not within 10% of the published specs, proceed to step 9.

9. Check the generator output across each phase of the stator by connecting a test lamp as shown in Fig. 8–65. The test lamp can be manufactured from a readily available two-filament sealed beam unit (headlamp) as long as the filaments are connected in parallel.

10. With the test lamp still operating at 2500 rpm, individually connect the test lamp across each stator phase. The brightness of the test lamp will confirm if a problem exists. Less brilliance on one or two phases signifies that a problem exists in either the diode trio, stator, or power diode. Should the diode trio check out OK, the generator assembly should be removed and disassembled for further checks.

Output Test: 3425JC Generator. On the 3425JC flange-mounted and gear-driven generator assembly, the test arrangement is very similar to that described above for the 2600, 2700, and 2800JB models. The preservice checks and rotor magnetism restoration procedures are the same as described for these models. Due to the different design and voltage regulator features of the 3425JC model, Fig. 8–66 illustrates the test hookup.

Procedure

1. Mount the generator in position on the test stand and adjust the pulley drive belt correctly.

2. Make certain that all connections are as shown in Fig.

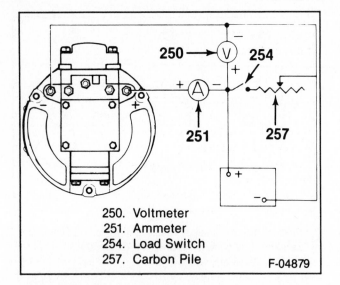

250. Voltmeter
251. Ammeter
254. Load Switch
257. Carbon Pile

F-04879

FIGURE 8–66 Leece-Neville generator connections for an output test. (*Courtesy of GMC Truck Division, General Motors Corporation.*)

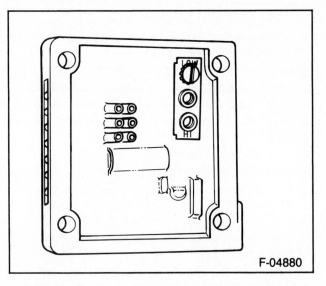

F-04880

FIGURE 8–67 Leece-Neville voltage adjustment screw in the "down" position. (*Courtesy of GMC Truck Division, General Motors Corporation.*)

8–66 and that the battery and generator ground polarity are the same.

3. Make sure that the carbon pile is turned off at this time.

4. Start at the test stand motor and increase the speed to produce 2500 generator rpm.

5. Note the voltage output value on the test stand voltmeter, which should be between 13.6 and 14.2 V on a 12-V system.

6. If the voltage output is too high or two low, the voltage regulator can be adjusted by relocating a setscrew after stopping the test stand.

    a. To reduce the voltage value if too high, refer to Fig. 8–67 and after regulator removal, take out and install the voltage setscrew in a lower-position hole setting. The lowest position is shown as being the top hole in the regulator in the diagram.

    b. To increase the voltage value if too low, refer to Fig. 8–67 and remove and reinsert the adjusting screw in a higher-setting hole. As you can see in the diagram, there are three holes: a low, an intermediate, and a high setting.

NOTE: If voltage regulator screw relocation still fails to bring the generator output value within 13.6 and 14.2 V, a new voltage regulator should be installed and the output test repeated. Check the information in step 7 first.

7. To confirm if the voltage control problem lies in the generator or the voltage regulator, the full field test described in Steps 8 through 12 can be performed. This is particularly applicable when the output test has shown that regulator adjustment still failed to lower the output voltage level to at least 14.2 V on a 12-V system.

8. Begin by measuring the voltage across the generator output terminals.

9. Carefully remove the generator brush housing cover plate; then, using a paper clip, welding rod, or small drill bit, gently insert it into the brush holder access hole, which is shown clearly in Fig. 8–68.

10. Connect an alligator clip jumper wire from the negative generator output terminal to the test clip, welding wire, or drill bit.

11. Run the test stand to 2500 rpm and note carefully the voltmeter output value.

12. Connect an ac voltmeter across each stator phase (terminals 1 and 2, 1 and 3, 2 and 3) to check the output of each. This is similar to the test that was done using a two-filament sealed beam headlight for the 2600, 2700, and 2800 JB models described in Fig. 8–65 (step 9) for these models. If the ac voltmeter readings are close to being the same, the stator windings are fairly well balanced and the stator is acceptable.

Test result interpretation

- If the voltage reading is higher in step 11 than that recorded in step 8 but the stator ac voltages appear to be balanced (similar), the generator and stator are operating correctly and voltage regulator adjustment should correct the problem.

- If the voltage reading in step 11 is higher than that recorded in step 8 but the stator ac voltages are not balanced (similar), this confirms that the generator stator is at fault.

- If the voltage reading in step 11 is lower or the same as that recorded in step 8 and the ac voltages are balanced (similar), this confirms that the stator is OK but that a fault exists inside the generator assembly.

- If the voltage reading in step 11 is lower or the same as that recorded in step 8 and the ac voltages are not balanced (similar), the stator is at fault.

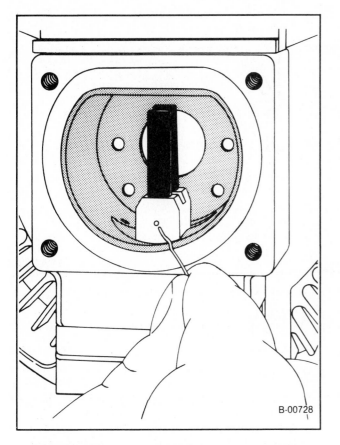

FIGURE 8-68 Inserting a wire into the brush holder access hole of a model 3425JC Leece-Neville generator. (*Courtesy of GMC Truck Division, General Motors Corporation.*)

Leece-Neville Transformer Rectifiers

These units operate in the same general manner as those used by Delco-Remy on their 30-SI/TR models, Delcotron Integral Charging System, discussed in this chapter. Two main T/R (transformer rectifier) models are available from Leece-Neville and these are the 5114T T/R and 5116T T/R units shown in Figure 8-69. The 5114T is used with the 2500J family of alternators, while the 5116T is designed for use with the flange mounted 3425J family of alternators which are widely used on Detroit Diesel Corporation Series 71/92 two-stroke cy-

cle engines. The T/R unit is designed to charge the truck starting battery in a vehicle equipped with a 12 volt electrical system and a 24 volt starter motor.

The main function of the 5114T and 5116T transformer rectifiers used by Leece-Neville is to replace the conventional Series/Parallel switch. As with any system that employs a transformer rectifier unit, they are used to provide a source of power for charging the cranking battery on 12 volt vehicles equipped with a 24 volt starter motor assembly. Figure 8-70 shows the arrangement and wiring circuit for both a negative and positive ground system that employs the transformer rectifier unit. The T/R is offered in kit-form so that it can be mounted onto an existing 2500J or 3425J alternator, and is designed to function on either a positive or negative ground system. The T/R installation does not require any modification to the existing alternator or standard 24 volt starter motor. Note in Figure 8-70 that two 12 volt batteries, a primary and a secondary battery which are wired in series, provide the 24 volts for starting. Once the engine starts, the starter solenoid disconnects the starting circuit and keeps the primary battery in use for the vehicle 12 volt loads. The 12 volt alternator charges both batteries. The primary battery is charged in the conventional manner, while the secondary battery which is only required for starting purposes, is charged through the transformer/rectifier unit.

The alternator used with the TR system is of conventional 12 volt output capacity. All vehicle accessories, therefore, are powered from a 12-volt system battery, while the system utilizes two sets of 12-volt batteries in series to provide 24 volts for cranking.

The sequence for charging the batteries with this system is rather unique in that the cranking battery is charged by the transformer rectifier unit at a rate conducive to its state of charge. For example, the maximum rate of output from the TR unit is 20 amps which is sufficiently high to charge the cranking battery, since with the engine running, no load is placed on the cranking battery. If the cranking battery is in a good state of charge, or as it rises to its full charge state, the output current from the TR unit will gradually drop to about one amp when the terminal voltage of the battery reaches 13.8 volts.

(a)   **(b)**

FIGURE 8-69 Features of a TR (transformer-rectified) unit: (a) 5114T TR unit mounted on a 2500J model alternator; (b) 5116T TR unit mounted on a gear-driven, flange-mounted 3425J model alternator. (*Courtesy of Prestolite Electric Incorporated, Heavy Duty Products Division.*)

NEGATIVE GROUND

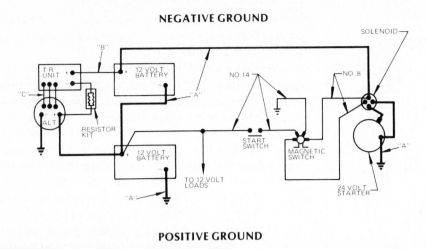

POSITIVE GROUND

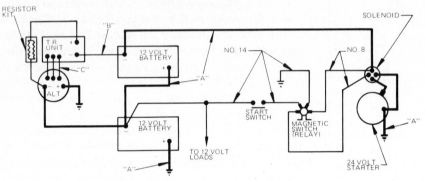

FIGURE 8–70 Transformer rectifier circuit. (*Courtesy of Prestolite Electric Incorporated, Heavy Duty Products Division.*)

It should be noted, that if an 85 ampere alternator is used on a vehicle, for example, and if the TR unit is supplying its maximum current of 20 amperes to the charging battery, then the available alternator output to the vehicle system would be reduced to 65 amperes. Once the cranking battery has reached its full-state of charge, then the full 85 amperes would be available to the vehicle accessories system. On an average vehicle application, the cranking battery will reach a full-state of charge within approximately 15 minutes. The adoption of one of these transformer rectifier units allows conversion of any existing 12 volt system into a 12/24 volt unit.

Troubleshooting the Leece-Neville TR Unit

The TR (transformer–rectifier) unit is sealed at manufacture; therefore, only a few tests can be carried out to determine its condition. Its output can be checked while on the vehicle while it is coupled to its alternator assembly, which is considered the best method of checking for any problem. However, the use of an ohmmeter will assist you in determining possible problem areas on the TR unit after it has been removed from the alternator assembly.

Transformer Primary Continuity Check. Use the ohmmeter, as shown in Fig. 8–71, to establish that continuity exists between each of the three phases of the TR unit. Due to the extremely low resistance that exists be-

tween the transformer windings, the exact level of resistance of each phase cannot be determined. If the resistance readings at each phase are high, or vary somewhat, the winding is open and the TR unit should be replaced.

Ground Test. Using an ohmmeter as shown in Fig. 8–72, an infinity reading should be obtained between any of the five terminals of the TR unit and the housing (ground). An internal ground would be indicated if any other reading but infinity (high) is obtained. Replace the TR unit if any other such reading is obtained.

Rectifier Test. Figure 8–73 shows the hookup of the ohmmeter required to test the rectifier of the TR unit.

FIGURE 8–71 Checking resistance of each phase; transformer primary circuit. (*Courtesy of Prestolite Electric Incorporated, Heavy Duty Products Division.*)

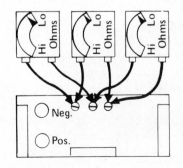

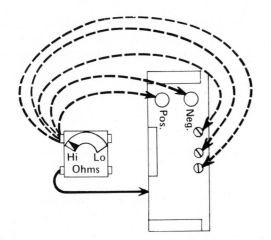

FIGURE 8-72 Ground test of the TR unit. (*Courtesy of Prestolite Electric Incorporated, Heavy Duty Products Division.*)

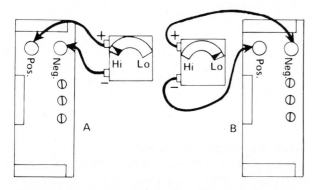

FIGURE 8-73 Transformer rectifier test hookups. (*Courtesy of Prestolite Electric Incorporated, Heavy Duty Products Division.*)

An infinity reading should be obtained when the ohmmeter leads are connected as shown at A in the figure; when the ohmmeter leads are reversed as in B, a low reading should be obtained. If no reading is obtained in either connection A or B, the rectifiers are open, while a similar reading in both directions indicates shorted rectifiers. Should either one of these conditions be noticed, replace the TR unit.

MULTI-BATTERY HOOKUP CHARGING PROBLEMS

In the diagrams shown in Figures 3-11, 3-12 and 3-13, as well as in Figure 8-44, Figure 8-56 and Figure 8-70, various combinations of battery voltages and hookups used on mid-range and heavy-duty truck electrical systems are illustrated. Hooking up batteries that contain different internal plate materials can result in poor system performance due to the different resistance values offered through the type of materials used in the battery construction. This poor system performance is most notice-

able when connecting batteries in a parallel hookup arrangement.

The problem with a multi-battery hookup problem is best explained by reference to Figure 8-74(a), which illustrates a simplified dual battery hookup. Items 1 and 2 represent two 12 volt heavy duty batteries, while item 3 is the battery charging alternator, and item 4 is a voltage regulator assembly which may or may not be part of the alternator assembly. In the system shown in Figure 8-74(a), when the system is fully charged, the pressure

FIGURE 8-74 (a) Simplified dual-battery hookup. Items 1 and 2 are 12-V batteries; item 3 is the alternator; item 4 is the voltage regulator. (b) Switch installed into wiring system above number 2 battery. (c) Two diodes (2 A 1) installed into a basic two-battery charging system. (*Courtesy of Sure Power Industries, Inc.*)

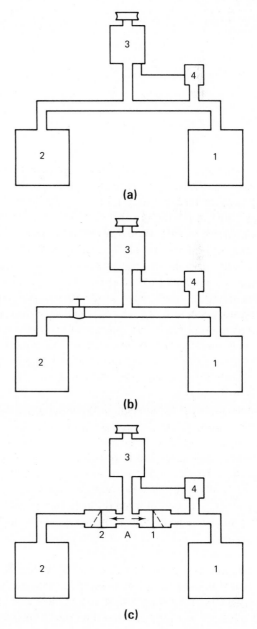

(a)

(b)

(c)

(voltage) is the same throughout the circuit. When the alternator is not operating, and current (amperes) is used from No. 2 battery, pressure (voltage) will be lowered in No. 1 battery also. To prevent this condition, we could install a switch above No. 2 battery as shown in Figure 8–74(b), so that circuit flow may be blocked from No. 1 battery anytime No. 2 battery is being used.

However, when No. 2 battery has been used and its state of charge is low, if the switch is activated above No. 2 battery, then No. 1 battery can now very rapidly dump its charge into battery No. 2 due to the large voltage difference between them. Therefore no current (amperes) control would exist under such a situation. If we assume that No. 2 battery requires 150 amps, then that amount of current can flow freely from No. 1 to No. 2 battery. The other problem that would exist with such a system, is that within seconds after reconnecting the two batteries through the switch, not only do we have uncontrolled current flow, but both batteries have nearly equalized with each other. This would result in both batteries being in a less than full state of charge.

In order to eliminate the problem shown in Figure 8–74(b), we can install two diodes to isolate the two batteries, by placing one diode in each connecting wire as shown in Figure 8–74(c). The arrangement shown in Figure 8–74(c) will allow both batteries to receive current from the alternator, and the voltage will still equalize throughout the system while the alternator is in operation. When current (amps) is used from battery No. 2, the No. 1 diode stops current flow from the No. 1 battery, since the function of a diode is to allow flow in only one direction, which in this case would be from the alternator. When the alternator is running, a controlled current flow passes to No. 2 battery, and a different amount of controlled charge will flow at the same time to battery No. 1 since each battery controls the amount of current that flows into it due to its own voltage (pressure).

The maximum current that any alternator can produce is limited by its own capacity. For example, if No. 1 battery requires 30 amps and No. 2 battery needs 50 amps, for a total system demand of 80 amps, but the alternator is only rated for 60 amps, then the alternator can not satisfy the system demands placed upon it. However with the system arrangement shown in Figure 8–74(c) using two diodes and the correctly sized alternator, a balanced charging circuit and proper battery isolation and control can be achieved thereby solving the multi-battery hookup problem. In such a system, the voltage is the same everywhere in the circuit when the alternator is operating. The voltage sensing device can be tapped into either battery No. 1 or battery No. 2. Proper voltage causes correct current to flow to each battery.

In order to ensure that a balanced battery circuit is available, there are many switches, relays, solenoids and other devices on the market that claim to be effective battery isolation devices, however invariably they do not isolate, but simply disconnect one battery from the other when OFF, and reconnect the batteries when turned ON. During the ON position, the full battery can discharge at an uncontrolled rate into the low battery such as that illustrated in the system in Figure 8–74(b).

Should the low battery be substantially lower in charge than the other, the resultant current flow can be very high and create overheating of electrical wiring, connecting plugs and receptacles, and any switch contacts thereby creating a possible serious fire danger. The other serious problem that can occur when an ineffective battery isolator system is used, is that when the engine is stopped soon after starting, the two batteries have been connected long enough to cause the cranking battery to discharge into the auxiliary within only a few seconds. This usually results in both batteries now being partially discharged, and effective cranking/starting of the engine is now not possible.

A unique and highly advanced battery isolator system now on the market that can ensure that none of the problems discussed above can occur, is the DUVAC 11 system manufactured by Sure Power Industries, Inc., in Tualatin, Oregon 97062. This company manufactures 12/24 volt or 24/12 volt voltage isolator systems for use on heavy-duty trucks and buses. Several of these component models are shown within this chapter.

Figure 8–75 illustrates the basic 12 volt charging system, while Figure 8–76 shows that for a 24 volt charging system. Various series/parallel switches and transformer rectified circuits are in wide use on heavy-duty trucks today. Both are described in this chapter. However when a heavy duty truck or bus employs 12 volt electrical accessories, but requires a 24 volt starting motor, the problem of these mixed voltages when using a 12 volt alternator can create a series of electrical problems. Typical examples of where mixed battery voltages would be required would be:

1. A 12 volt vehicle equipped with. . .
    a. a 12 volt charging system requiring 24 volts for starting only.
    b. a 12 volt charging system requiring continuous 24 volts for supporting various types of 24 volt equipment, as well as the continuing 12 volt load requirements.
2. A 24 volt vehicle equipped with a 24 volt charging system, but needing 12 volts for supporting various types of 12 volt accessories, in addition to the continuous 24 volt requirements.

Most maintenance personnel would feel that the obvious solution to this problem would be to change the charging system to the higher voltage and tap the battery bank from the appropriate point to support the lower voltage loads. This approach however wouldn't work correctly since tapping off a load will throw the entire system out of electrical balance. One battery will overcharge, one will undercharge and sulfate and in a short time period, both

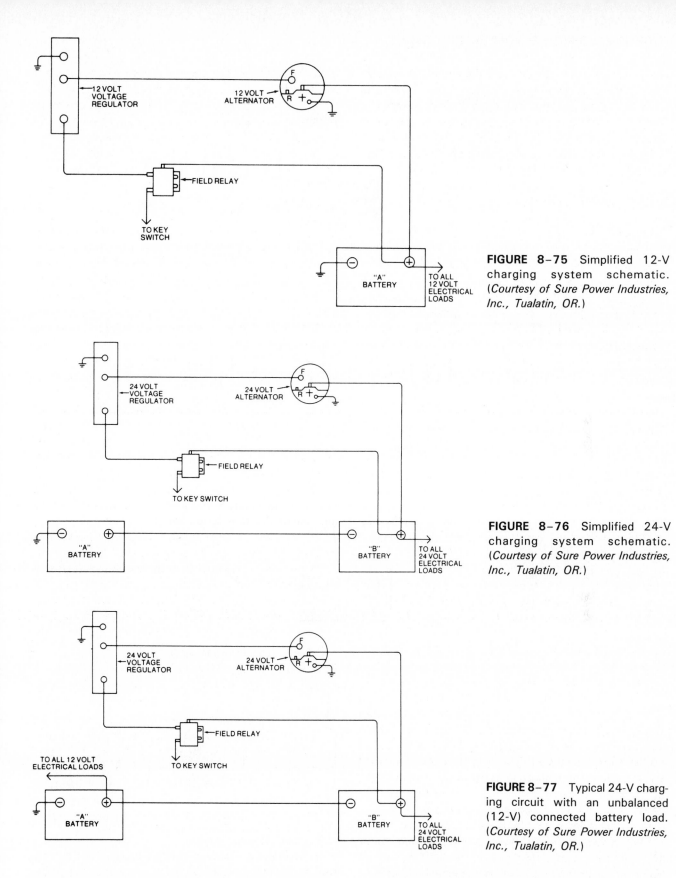

FIGURE 8–75 Simplified 12-V charging system schematic. (*Courtesy of Sure Power Industries, Inc., Tualatin, OR.*)

FIGURE 8–76 Simplified 24-V charging system schematic. (*Courtesy of Sure Power Industries, Inc., Tualatin, OR.*)

FIGURE 8–77 Typical 24-V charging circuit with an unbalanced (12-V) connected battery load. (*Courtesy of Sure Power Industries, Inc., Tualatin, OR.*)

batteries will be damaged. The reasons for this battery damage are due to the fact that both 12 volt batteries are connected in series as shown in Figure 8–77 in order to deliver 24 volts necessary to support the 24 volt loads. They are also charged in series with each battery receiving the same amount of charging current (amps). The total amount of current that battery "B" in Figure 8–77 delivers to the system is equal to the current requirements of the 24 volt load. The total amount of current that battery "A" delivers to the system is also equal to the current requirements of the 24 volt load, plus all of the current requirements of the 12 volt equipment being used.

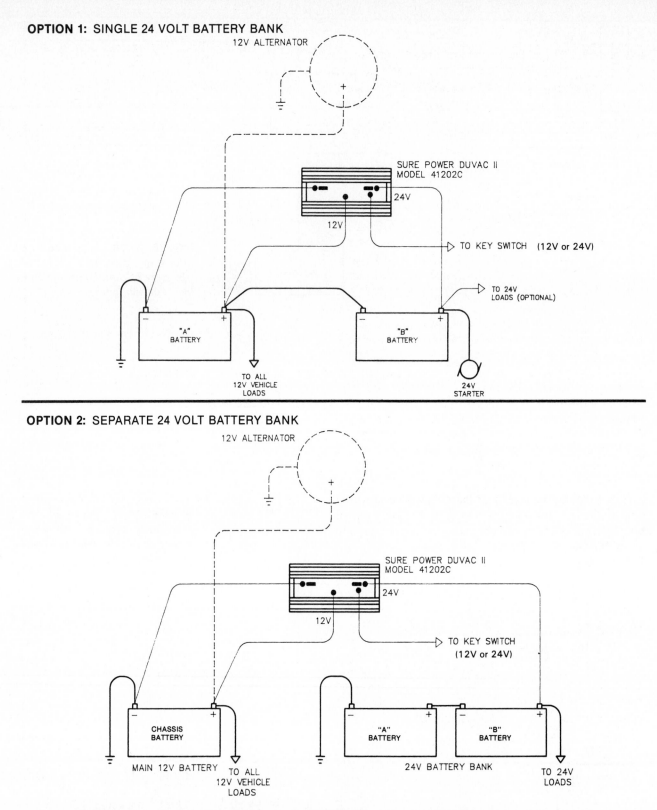

OPTION 1: SINGLE 24 VOLT BATTERY BANK

12V ALTERNATOR

SURE POWER DUVAC II
MODEL 41202C

24V

12V

TO KEY SWITCH (12V or 24V)

TO 24V
LOADS (OPTIONAL)

"A"
BATTERY

"B"
BATTERY

TO ALL
12V VEHICLE
LOADS

24V
STARTER

OPTION 2: SEPARATE 24 VOLT BATTERY BANK

12V ALTERNATOR

SURE POWER DUVAC II
MODEL 41202C

24V

12V

TO KEY SWITCH
(12V or 24V)

CHASSIS
BATTERY

"A"
BATTERY

"B"
BATTERY

MAIN 12V BATTERY

TO ALL
12V VEHICLE
LOADS

24V BATTERY BANK

TO 24V
LOADS

FIGURE 8–78 Typical wiring diagram for the DUVAC 11 multi-voltage management system showing two different options. (*Courtesy of Sure Power Industries, Inc., Tualatin, OR.*)

Consequently the "A" battery is delivering more current to the system than is the "B" battery. This necessitates that both batteries receive different charging requirements, however this can not happen since both batteries are being charged in series at an equal rate in this system. Consider that in this system if it was applied to a transit bus requiring 80 amps of connected 24 volt load, but it is found desirable to add an additional 40 amps of 12 volt load through the addition of radios, fare boxes, and lights which if they can be used in place of their 24 volt counterpart, can save the manufacturer and end user, substantial dollars on equipment purchases and maintenance. With the addition of the 40 amp, 12 volt load, "A" battery will deliver its original 80 amps of load plus the added 40 amps of 12 volt load for a 120 amp total current draw. Battery "B" is still providing only 80 amps of load. Therefore the total charging circuit current needed to maintain both batteries in a constant state of charge would be. . . . .

$$
\begin{array}{r}
80 \text{ amps (24 volt load)} \\
+ \ 40 \text{ amps (12 volt load)} \\
\hline
120 \text{ amps (total system battery load)}
\end{array}
$$

Since both 12 volt batteries are connected in a series hookup (24 volts), and the 24 volt voltage regulator is constantly monitoring system voltage for both batteries, each battery will receive an equal amount of the alternator recharge current. It is exactly at this point that the system problem occurs! Since the "B" battery only requires 80 amps to maintain a full state of charge, it will be overcharged since the voltage regulator provides the overall system voltage control. The "A" system battery needs 120 amps to maintain a full state of charge, yet it will receive less charging current than necessary due also to the voltage regulator operation. This results in the "A" battery delivering the amount of current necessary to make up the balance of the 12 volt load, with the end result that the "A" battery will be constantly undercharged leading to a sulfation problem.

The interesting thing to note in this unbalanced system is that the damage to the batteries will occur within the first hour of unbalanced operation. The only way in which this problem can be eliminated is to regulate each individual battery circuit according to its needs. This can be achieved through the use of the DUVAC system shown in Figure 8–78 which can be equipped with either a 12 or 24 volt alternator as desired.

DUVAC (Dual Voltage Alternator Control) Control System

The DUVAC control system is designed to direct the alternator to charge in either the 12 or 24 volt mode depending upon the needs of each individual battery circuit in the coupled system. The DUVAC control is normally off by the fact that a silicon controlled rectifier creates an open between terminals A and 1 of the DUVAC module. See Figure 8–78. The alternator B+ wire terminal (green wire of the Sure Power Regulator) is the power source for the alternator field coils. Its connection point is determined by the rated voltage of the alternator. For 12 volt alternators, this terminal is directly connected to the A+ terminal of the voltage regulator. For 24 volt alternators, this terminal is connected to a 24 volt point. If however the alternator is equipped with an integral voltage regulator, some modification of that regulator is required if it is not totally removed from the system. Sure Power Industries can supply details on this necessary change.

When the alternator begins to charge, the DUVAC regulator system shown in Figure 8–79 (1), directs the cur-

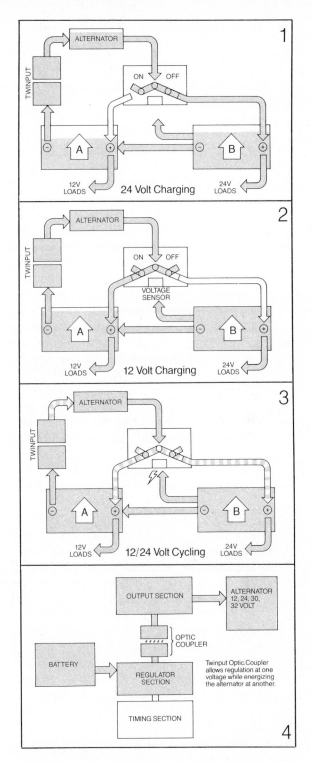

FIGURE 8–79 (1) DUVAC 11 system 24-V charging schematic; (2) DUVAC 11 12-V charging schematic; (3) DUVAC 11 12/24-V cycling schematic; (4) DUVAC 11 optic coupler system schematic. (*Courtesy of Sure Power Industries, Inc., Tualatin, OR.*)

rent through the entire battery system in series. At the same time, DUVAC monitors the voltage of the "B" half of the battery system, which is providing some of the power required for the vehicle's 24 volt loads. When the "B" battery is fully charged, a voltage sensor in the DUVAC control unit, turns the DUVAC on as shown in Figure 8–79 (2). The "B" battery is then bypassed temporarily, and the current is directed to the "A" battery which is providing the other 12 volt half needed for the 24 volt loads as well as the entire 12 volt portion for 12 volt accessories.

As long as the DUVAC control is on, the charging system will be in the 12 volt mode, and charging current will bypass the "B" battery. If this condition were to continue, the "B" battery would be run down. To avoid this undesirable situation, a "twinput regulator" with an internal timing circuit is employed. The output section of this regulator delivers power to the alternator fields through a power transistor. The alternator output voltage is regulated by turning a transistor off approximately 1500 times per second. In addition, every 55-60 seconds, the regulator timing circuit takes control and turns off the power transistor for about 2 seconds, thereby lowering (interrupting) the alternator excitation field voltage to almost zero. When this happens, the alternator stops charging and current stops flowing through the SCR (silicon controlled rectifier) in the DUVAC module, causing it to turn itself off. After 2 seconds the field voltage is restored, and the alternator once again begins to charge, but with the DUVAC module now operating in the 24 volt mode, where it monitors the "B" battery and charges it as necessary as shown in Figure 8–79 (3). It is important to note that the "twinput regulator" cycles only to insure that the DUVAC has the opportunity to change charging modes, not to cause it to change. Since the regulator timing circuit is totally separate from the DUVAC switching process, it will cycle every 55-60 seconds regardless of what charging mode the DUVAC is in. If the DUVAC, due to the state of charge of the "B" battery, stays in the 24 volt mode throughout the 55-60 second timing period, the regulator will cycle just the same. Therefore all of the batteries in the system are properly balanced, regardless of how different each load is on the individual battery. This 12 volt load on a 24 volt system is possible due to the use of an optic coupler design illustrated in diagrammatic form in Figure 8–79 (4) for the "twinput regulator" system. In summation, the DUVAC control determines whether the alternator should charge at 12 or 24 volts regardless of its specified voltage, while regulating one 12 volt "B" battery portion of the entire battery system.

For more detailed information on the DUVAC system, contact Sure Power Industries, Inc; 10189 S.W. Avery, Tualatin, OR. 97062.

NIPPONDENSO ALTERNATORS

Alternators manufactured by Nippondenso are designed to cover a broad range of cars and light-, medium-, and heavy-duty trucks. In North America, Nippondenso alternators are found on such medium-duty trucks as the GMC W4, W7, and W7 HV steel tilt cab models, the same basic models produced by Isuzu, Hino, and UD

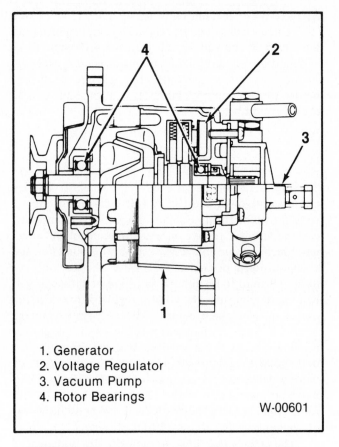

1. Generator
2. Voltage Regulator
3. Vacuum Pump
4. Rotor Bearings

W-00601

FIGURE 8–80 Basic features of a Nippondenso alternator. (*Courtesy of GMC Truck Division, General Motors Corporation.*)

Nissan. The basic design of these alternators is similiar throughout the model range, with some models employing an extension of the alternator shaft that is used for driving a vacuum pump assembly. Figure 8–80 illustrates a 94175448 12-V 3-kW model with a solid-state regulator mounted to the brush holder. The regulated voltage on this unit is 13.5 V, to produce a rated output of 70 A (67 A at 5000 rpm). The construction and arrangement of the generator component parts are very similar to those of other brush-type generators discussed and illustrated earlier in this chapter. Figure 8–81 illustrates a circuit wiring diagram for a 94175448 model where two brushes carry current through slip rings to the field coil. The stator windings are assembled on the inside of a laminated core that forms part of the generator frame. A rectifier bridge connected to the stator windings contains six diodes to change the generated ac current/voltage to dc power. Note also that this system uses a wye-wound stator rather than a delta-wound model.

Generator Output Check

The generator output check sequence follows the same procedure as that described earlier in this chapter for the Delco and Leece-Neville units; however, we will describe this quickly here since once this method has been used,

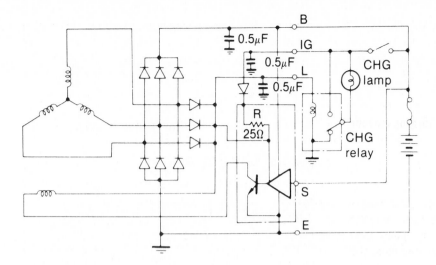

FIGURE 8-81 Nippondenso generator wiring schematic. (*Courtesy of GMC Truck Division, General Motors Corporation.*)

you can employ a special tester instrument that will confirm exactly where the generator problem is prior to disassembly and inspection.

Procedure

1. The output test can be performed on the vehicle or on a suitable commercially avilable test stand such as that described below.

2. Install the generator assembly onto the test bench and adjust the belt to the generator drive pulley.

3. Make sure that the test battery is in full state of charge; otherwise, a false output value will be obtained.

4. Make certain that the battery and generator polarity are the same.

5. Refer to Fig. 8-82 and connect the necessary test instrumentation. Do *not,* however, connect the carbon pile at this time.

6. Start the test drive motor and slowly increase the speed while carefully noting the voltage value registering on the voltmeter. Should the generator output voltage rise quickly regardless of speed control and exceed 15.5 V, replace the regulator and check the rotor winding. If the voltage remains below 15.5 V, you can connect up the carbon pile across the battery positive and negative posts as shown in Fig. 8-82.

CAUTION: Make certain that the carbon pile control knob is turned off when you connect it; otherwise, there will be a spark and an immediate surge of battery power through the open carbon pile.

7. Increase the test stand speed to 4000 rpm and slowly rotate the carbon pile control knob until you obtain the maximum current output, which should be between 55 and 70 A at 13.5 V.

8. If the rated output current is not within 10 A of the specification, check the rotor winding, the rectifier bridge, and the stator as described in the section "Alternator Disassembly and Repair" later in this chapter.

Use of a Special Generator Tester. Nippondenso offer a special generator tester as do all generator manu-

facturers. Often these special testers can be obtained from a local tool supplier. The one in question here for use with the Nippondenso generator models is manufactured by Kent-Moore Heavy Duty Division, SPX Corporation. Use of Kent-Moore tester J-33895 or the J-26290-A model is shown in Fig. 8-45 and described below.

Procedure

1. Make sure that no power is flowing to the generator during the connection stage.

FIGURE 8-82 Nippondenso generator output test hookup. (*Courtesy of GMC Truck Division, General Motors Corporation.*)

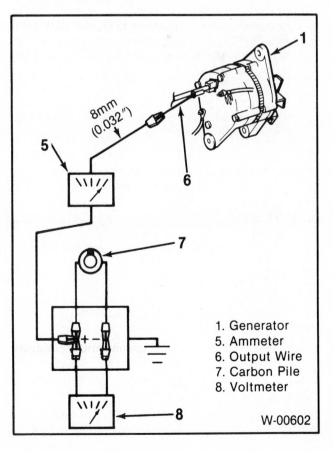

1. Generator
5. Ammeter
6. Output Wire
7. Carbon Pile
8. Voltmeter

W-00602

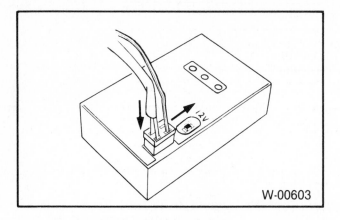

FIGURE 8–83 Connecting wiring harness to tester. (*Courtesy of GMC Truck Division, General Motors Corporation.*)

2. Turn the switch on the tester to the 24-V position.
3. Refer to Fig. 8–83 and connect the tester wiring harness connector (black, red, white/red wires) in the four-prong connector to the tester.
4. Connect the extension harness (white/red wire, single female connector) to the tester harness.
5. Connect the other end of the tester harness to the generator L-lead wire (white/blue) as shown in Fig. 8–84.
6. Refer to Fig. 8–85 and connect the black alligator clip to the negative battery terminal. Connect the red alligator clip to the positive battery terminal.
7. Interpret the generator condition as follows:
  a. Turn the ignition key to the ON position.
  b. Check to see if the instrument charge indicator light is on.
  c. Start the engine and turn the headlights to the low-beam position.

NOTE: The special tester yellow light may illuminate for up to 5 seconds after starting or stopping the engine. This is a normal condition.
  d. Accelerate the engine to 1500 rpm and hold the speed here for at least 10 seconds while observing the special tester indicator lights. Refer to Table 8–5, which illustrates the various generator test conditions.

Nippondenso 94038565 Generator

The 94038565 generator assembly shown in Fig. 8–86 is a 12-V 65-A model with the voltage regulator adjusted to provide 13.5 V at the 65-A output at 4000 rpm. This model can be found on GMC/Isuzu W7 and W7 HV medium-duty steel tilt cab models. The voltage regulator on this model is mounted on the top of the brush housing, while the heavy leads connected at the large terminals are the battery lead (B) and the ground lead (E). Take careful note that the third lead ending in a white connector has two conductors; one wire supplies reference voltage to the regulator, while the other controls the charge relay, which is used to turn on the instrument panel charge indicator lamp as well as providing a bulb check for the other warning lamps. The voltage regulator shown in Fig. 8–87 is mounted on the brush holder and is a solid-state unit totally encased in plastic; however, both the regulator and the brush holder are removable without disassembling the generator assembly. The operation of this model is the same as that for the earlier Nippondenso unit described in this section.

FORD MOTORCRAFT ALTERNATORS

Ford Motor Company manufactures a number of alternator assemblies under the tradename Motorcraft in var-

FIGURE 8–84 Connecting tester harness to generator. (*Courtesy of GMC Truck Division, General Motors Corporation.*)

FIGURE 8–85 Generator output tester connections. (*Courtesy of GMC Truck Division, General Motors Corporation.*)

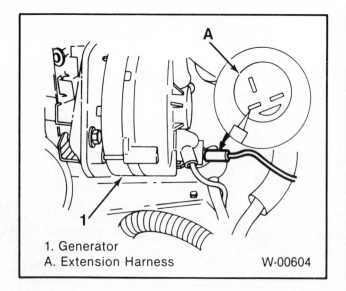

1. Generator
A. Extension Harness

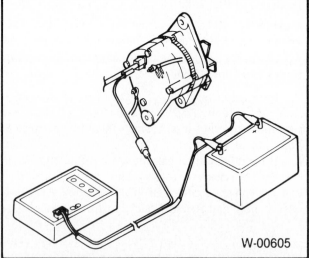

TABLE 8–5 Generator tester indicator diagnosis chart

TEST INDICATOR LIGHTS			INSTRUMENT PANEL CHARGE INDICATOR LIGHT	CONDITION
RED	YELLOW	GREEN		
OFF	OFF	ON	OFF	Normal.
ON	ON	OFF	OFF	Bad positive diode.
ON	ON	OFF	ON	Bad negative diode.
ON	ON	OFF	OFF	Bad auxiliary diode.
ON	OFF	OFF	ON	Bad rotor coil.
ON	OFF	OFF	OFF	Bad internal (IC) regulator.
ON or OFF	ON	ON	OFF	Bad stator coil.
OFF	ON	ON	OFF	Bad auxiliary diode. Bad stator coil. Bad negative diode.
ON	OFF	OFF	ON	Bad rotor coil. Bad internal (IC) regulator. Poor or no brush contact.
OFF	OFF	ON	OFF	Bad positive diode. Bad charge indicator light.

Source: GMC Truck Division, General Motors Corporation.

FIGURE 8–86 External features of a Nippondenso generator. (*Courtesy of GMC Truck Division, General Motors Corporation.*)

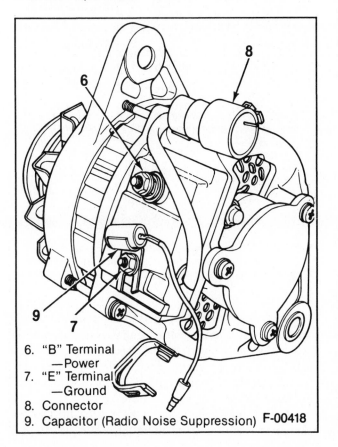

6. "B" Terminal —Power
7. "E" Terminal —Ground
8. Connector
9. Capacitor (Radio Noise Suppression)   F-00418

ious rated outputs and designs. Depending on the truck model and size, many Ford trucks can be ordered with either a Delco or a Leece-Neville (Prestolite Electric, Inc.) alternator and starter motor assemblies. Information on both Delco and Leece-Neville alternators is given in this chapter. Motorcraft generators are available in 60 A (rear terminal) and 75- and 90-A side terminal large frame alternator models with an externally mounted voltage

FIGURE 8–87 Nippondenso generator regulator component ID. (*Courtesy of GMC Truck Division, General Motors Corporation.*)

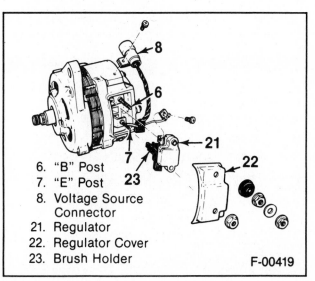

6. "B" Post
7. "E" Post
8. Voltage Source Connector
21. Regulator
22. Regulator Cover
23. Brush Holder   F-00419

regulator assembly. Motorcraft also manufactures an integral alternator/regulator (IAR) model that uses brushes and slip rings.

Basic Alternator Operation

The operation of the 60-, 75-, and 90-A generators is very similiar and parallels the description of operation for other brush-type generators described in this chapter. A typical Motorcraft alternator is illustrated in Fig. 8–88. Figures 8–89 and 8–90 illustrate the system wiring schematic for the 75- and 90-A side terminal, large frame alternator models. The 60-A rear terminal model can be considered common to this description.

Since these alternators use brushes and slip rings, battery current is supplied to the rotating field of the generator through the brushes and slip rings via the alternator/regulator system. All internally produced alternating current (ac) is rectified to direct current (dc) by the use of six diodes. The output of the alternator is controlled by the regulator, which automatically adjusts field current. When the ignition key is switched to the RUN position, the warning lamp will illuminate since it receives power from the warning lamp control circuit. There is no voltage present at terminal S at this time.

In warning lamp circuits, the regulator switching circuit receives voltage from the ignition switch through the warning lamp control circuit. If no warning lamp is used and an ammeter is installed instead, the regulator switching circuit receives ignition switch voltage through terminal S. Anytime that an input voltage is present, the switching circuit turns on the voltage control circuit, which in turn controls the output circuit. Turning the ignition key switch off will open the output circuit; therefore, no current can flow to the alternator field.

When the engine is started and the generator rotor spins, voltage will be produced and will appear at terminal S when a preset value is obtained. This causes the warning lamp on the instrument panel to go out since cur-

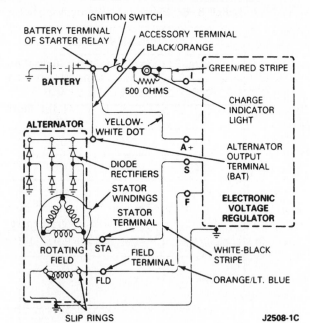

FIGURE 8–89 Wiring schematic for a Motorcraft 75-A model alternator. (*Reprinted with Ford Motor Company's permission.*)

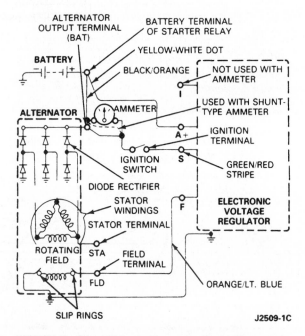

FIGURE 8–90 Wiring schematic for a Motorcraft 90-A side terminal alternator. (*Reprinted with Ford Motor Company's permission.*)

rent is no longer available. This particular procedure will of course not occur on vehicles equipped with an ammeter rather than a warning lamp. As shown in Fig. 8–89, a 500Ω $\frac{1}{4}$ -W resistor is connected across the terminals of the lamp at the instrument cluster of trucks with a warning lamp circuit.

Commonly used fusible links are installed in the charging system wiring on all Ford truck models to pro-

FIGURE 8–88 Motorcraft alternator features. (*Reprinted with Ford Motor Company's permission.*)

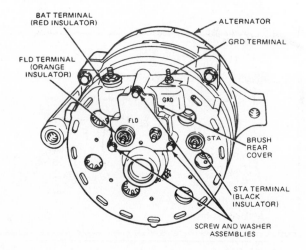

tect both the wiring harness and the alternator assembly should a booster battery be connected to the charging system with the wrong polarity or if the wiring harness should become grounded during vehicle operation. Motorcraft alternator output checks and tests are very similar to those shown in this chapter for Delco and Leece-Neville models (See pp. 263 and 274 for more information.

Remote-Mounted Electronic Regulator

On all Motorcraft alternators that do not use an integral voltage regulator assembly, a 100% solid-state electronic regulator is remote-mounted in the alternator wiring system. Figure 8–91 illustrates a typical Motorcraft charging system. The voltage regulator is designed with three basic circuits:

1. An output stage
2. A voltage stage
3. A solid-state relay and the field circuit over current protection stage

No adjustment is required or can be attempted to the electronic regulator since it is preset for use with a specific model alternator system. The regulator is available under two different part numbers with color codes. Although they look alike, they are not interchangeable with the regulator wiring harness connector plugs. However, the service part number regulator is interchangeable with either system!

The difference is that one regulator is designed for use with an ammeter-equipped charging system, while the other one is used with trucks employing an alternator warning indicator lamp.

Operation. The phases of electronic regulator operation can be understood more easily by reference to Fig. 8–89.

1. *Output stage.* Any time that the ignition switch is turned on, the output stage of the regulator relays power to the alternator field windings. Cranking and then starting the engine will cause the alternator rotor speed to increase quickly, which will generate an output from the stator winding terminal to a level that is controlled by the preset voltage regulator setting.

2. *Voltage stage.* When the engine is stopped and the ignition key is turned off, the voltage regulator solid-state relay circuit will automatically turn off the output stage. This action stops all current flow through the regulator to ensure that there is no standby current drain on the battery.

3. *Field circuit overcurrent protection stage.* Specifically, this part of the voltage regulator is designed to protect the internal circuits from damage that would occur as a result of shorts in the field circuit such as in the field wire, the alternator rotor, or the brushes. Should a short occur, the alternator charging system warning lamp will be illuminated, or the ammeter will register a discharge with no damage caused to the regulator. Once the service technician has corrected the cause of the short, the charging system will operate again with no voltage regulator service being necessary.

FIGURE 8–91 Example of the wiring circuit for a remote-mounted solid-state alternator regulator. (*Reprinted with Ford Motor Company's permission.*)

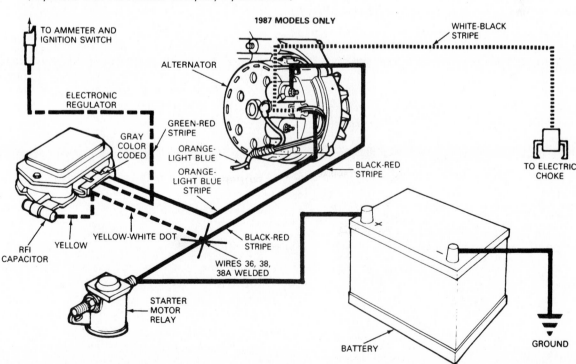

PRESTOLITE/MOTOROLA ALTERNATORS

Motorola sold its alternator manufacturing business to Prestolite Electric Incorporated as of January 29th, 1988. Motorola did however retain ownership of its voltage regulator and charging system related businesses. Consequently all alternators that were previously manufactured under the Motorola brand name are now sold to the automotive and heavy-duty truck OEM's under the trade name of the Load Handler. Load Handler is a registered trademark of Prestolite Electric Incorporated, Heavy Duty Products Division.

Prestolite manufactured Load Handler alternators are similar in appearance to former Motorola models. Figure 8–92 illustrates the general construction features of the Load Handler series of alternators. The various Load Handler models are interchangeable with Leece-Neville, Delco, Motorcraft (Ford) and Niehoff/TRW models. All models are equipped with an integral voltage regulator, which in conjunction with the alternator design, provides a self-excited charging system eliminating the need for relays or switches to initiate charging. In addition to the ground connection, only one wire needs to be connected to the alternator output terminal. Both the positive and negative output terminals are clearly marked on the alternator housing. Each alternator series can be identified from the information stamped on the alternator identification plate. The test procedure for Load Handler alternators follows closely that given for other major makes of alternators in this chapter.

Prior to performing any alternator output test, refer first of all to Fig. 8–93, Troubleshooting Logic chart which identifies some of the more common complaints and possible causes.

On-Vehicle Alternator Check. When a problem exists in the charging system, refer first to the troubleshooting logic chart Fig. 8–93. It is imperative prior to any alternator output test check that you consider the following preservice checks:

1. Make certain that the battery is in a full state of charge. If battery charging is required, it is often best to substitute the weak battery for one known to be good for the test while the regular battery is placed on charge. After checking the alternator charging system, if when the original vehicle battery is placed back into the truck, a problem occurs that was not apparent while using the good test battery, this confirms that the original battery is at fault.

CAUTION: Should you decide to charge the battery while in place in the vehicle, always disconnect the positive and negative battery cables!

2. Never disconnect the alternator or voltage regulator while the engine is running.

3. Do not ground the field winding.

4. Prior to removing or installing an alternator on the vehicle, always disconnect the battery first.

There are five basic checks/tests that can be performed on an alternator charging system with the use of an ammeter and a voltmeter.

Procedure

1. *Ignition off.* Refer to Fig. 8–94 which illustrates Load Handler alternator series wiring diagrams at the rear of the alternator housing. With a voltmeter connected between one phase of the alternator and ground and between the winding and the positive (+) terminal, if any

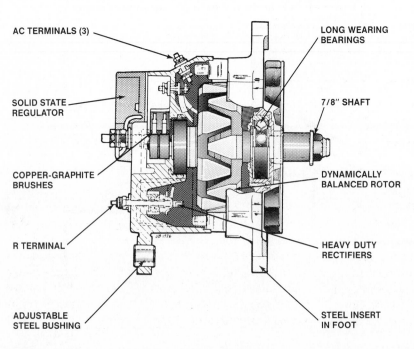

AC TERMINALS (3)

LONG WEARING BEARINGS

SOLID STATE REGULATOR

7/8" SHAFT

COPPER-GRAPHITE BRUSHES

DYNAMICALLY BALANCED ROTOR

R TERMINAL

HEAVY DUTY RECTIFIERS

ADJUSTABLE STEEL BUSHING

STEEL INSERT IN FOOT

FIGURE 8–92 General design features of a Load Handler alternator. (*Courtesy of Prestolite Electric Incorporated, Heavy Duty Products Division.*)

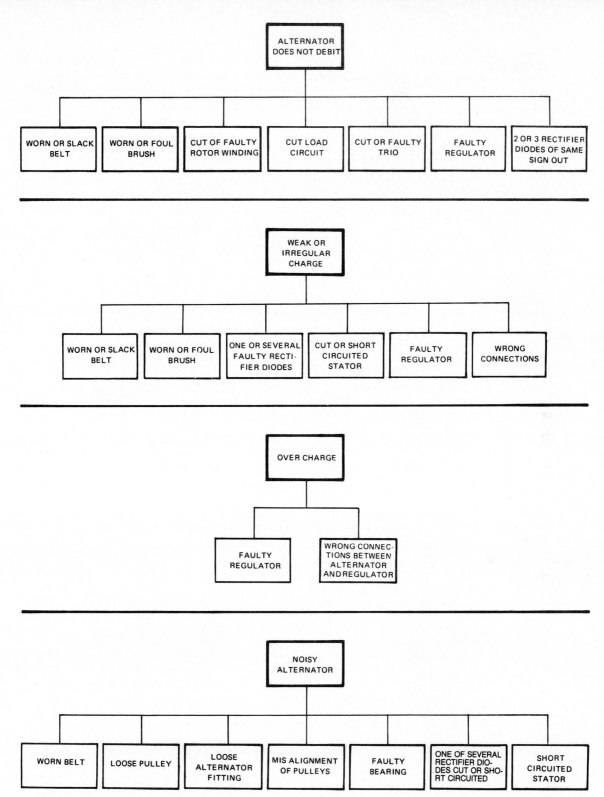

FIGURE 8–93 Troubleshooting logic chart for alternator diagnosis. (*Courtesy of Mack Trucks, Inc.*)

reading appears on the voltmeter, there is a shorted positive rectifier diode.

2. *Ignition off.* Connect a voltmeter so that the voltage value at the alternator output terminal and the positive battery terminal can be monitored. The voltage reading should be the same at both points. If the voltage reading at the alternator output terminal is lower or erratic, closely inspect the alternator for signs of broken wires, loose

or corroded terminals, or a possible burned connection. Check also that there is no corrosion at the battery post terminals. If there is any corrosion at the wires or battery terminals, clean them and repeat the test procedure.

3. *Ignition on, engine not running.* Check the voltage value at the positive alternator terminal. This voltage should register approximately 2V. If you record a voltage value between 8 and 12 V, this confirms that the alter-

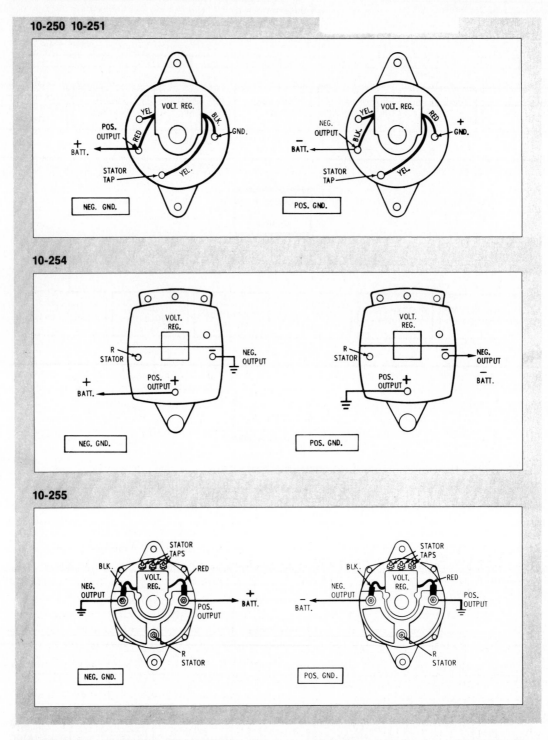

FIGURE 8-94 Typical Load Handler alternator series wiring diagrams. (*Courtesy of Prestolite Electric Incorporated, Heavy Duty Products Division.*)

nator excitation circuit is damaged. If the charging system warning lamp on the instrument panel is off, check the system fuse and the load signal lamp (bulb).

4. *Ignition on, engine running above an idle speed.* Check the voltage value at the battery, then at the alternator output terminal (B+) with the engine running at a speed between idle and 1500 rpm maximum. The voltmeter should record approximately 14 V at 25°C (77°F)

ambient temperature. If the difference between these two voltage readings exceeds 0.3 V, closely inspect the alternator wiring and terminals for signs of corrosion (high circuit resistance), or possible wire damage.

5. *Engine running.* Remove and disconnect the voltage regulator located as shown in the exploded views in Fig. 8-94. With the regulator disconnected from the alternator, reconnect terminal B+ and brush + (Ex). Start

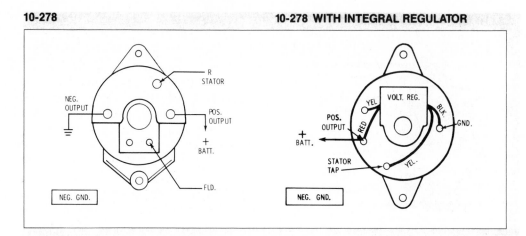

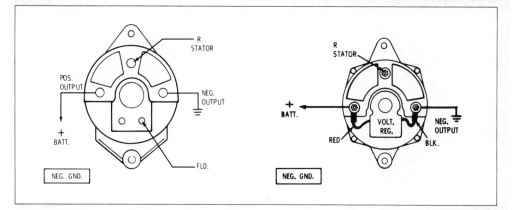

FIGURE 8-94 (*cont.*)

and run the engine at approximately 1000 rpm and check the voltage between the output terminal B+ and ground. If the voltage is higher than 14 V but was less than 14 V in step 4, the voltage regulator is damaged and requires replacement.

ALTERNATOR DISASSEMBLY AND REPAIR

Although there are many makes, styles, and designs of alternators used on cars, trucks, buses, industrial, and marine applications, the general design and disassembly procedures are basically the same. The following procedures, checks, and tests are not meant to be all-inclusive, but to deal with typical and widely used different makes of alternators. The test procedures required to establish the condition of the diodes, regulators, rectifiers, stators, rotors, and so on, are common to all units, with the use of an ohmmeter being mandatory for most of the checks.

Pulley Removal

The first thing you do after you remove a belt-driven alternator from the engine or test stand is to remove the drive pulley. Pulley removal involves the use of a puller

after the removal of a retaining nut first. An example of pulley removal can be seen in Fig. 8-95.

Figure 8-95(a) shows the use of a special cutaway socket that can accept an Allen wrench (Snap-On S-8183). This arrangement can be used to remove and to retighten the pulley nut upon reassembly. It may be necessary to place a small piece of pipe over the Allen wrench to give you more leverage when removing or installing the pulley retaining nut.

An alternative method is to use an Allen wrench and a box wrench over the pulley retaining nut. In this instance, clamp the pulley in a vise using an old oversized belt or similar material wrapped around the puley to protect it from the vise jaws. The alternator shaft can be held stationary with the Allen wrench, while loosening or tightening the retaining nut with the box-end wrench; or an air impact wrench and socket can be used as shown in 8-95(b).

Always exercise care when clamping any pulley in a vise, since any damage to the pulley groove can cause severe and irreparable damage to the pulley. Drive belts will suffer shortened lives if installed into a damaged pulley groove. Remove the woodruff key from the shaft after pulley removal.

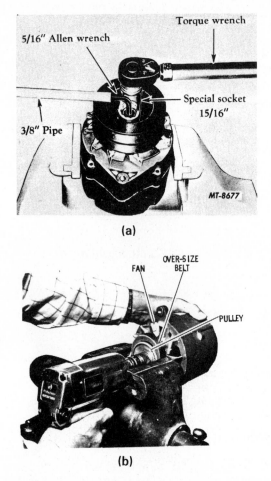

FIGURE 8-95 (a) Use of a special socket and Allen wrench to remove the alternator pulley; (b) air impact wrench and socket use to remove alternator pulley nut in a vise. (*Courtesy of Prestolite Electric Incorporated, Heavy Duty Products Division.*)

Separation of the Alternator Housing

Prior to separating the alternator housing, place a small match mark on both halves to ensure reassembly in the same position. Also, on some models of alternators, it is first necessary to remove the voltage regulator assembly from the rear end frame on direct-mounted units. This is achieved, for example, on Motorola and Leece-Neville units simply by removing the two regulator/cover mounting screws, then pulling the cover straight back to unplug the unit as shown in Fig. 8-92.

On this type of voltage regulator arrangement used by Motorola, the brush assembly should then be removed by the removal of the two brush assembly mounting screws as shown in Fig. 8-92.

On alternators without the external voltage regulator on the end frame, it may first be necessary to remove the end plate screws such as those found on the rear of Delco brushless alternators. After this, and on most other alternator models, take out the four long through bolts that pass from one half of the alternator assembly through the stator and into the other half of the alternator unit (see Fig. 8-96, item 21, and Fig. 8-98, item 28). Separate

the drive end frame and rotor as one assembly, and the stator and rear housing as another. It may be necessary to use two screwdrivers for this purpose.

The alternator housing separation will vary slightly between makes and models. For example, on Delco 25-SI and 30-SI models, the generator can be disassembled from either end. If, for example, you only want to remove and test or replace the voltage regulator components, the rectifier end only has to be disassembled (see exploded views in Figs. 8-96 through 8-99). If, on the other hand, service of the stator, the field coil, and the drive end bearing are desired, you must disassemble the drive end.

Stator and Rotor Separation

Separate the stator from the generator end frame by removing the stator wire lead attaching nuts or screws, as the case may be. To remove the drive end frame from the rotor, it is necessary on some alternators to place the rotor/housing assembly on an arbor press and push the rotor, with its front bearing, from the housing.

Other models of alternators, such as Delco-Remy automotive models, require that the rotor be placed in a soft-jaw vise to permit removal of the shaft nut. First remove the four through bolts, separate the drive end frame from the stator assembly, remove the nut, washer, pulley, fan, and collar, and separate the drive end frame from the rotor shaft. Remove any other components that require replacement or repair, taking care not to damage anything. Note and label all terminals, wires, and so on.

Stator/Rectifier Bridge Disassembly

When the stator is connected to the alternator rectifier bridge assembly, it is often necessary to unsolder the stator leads from the bridge assembly terminals on some models of alternators. On others, simply remove the stator lead terminal nuts. (See Figs. 8-96 through 8-99 for some typical examples).

Alternator Exploded Views

Since there are a great many makes and models of alternators used in light-, medium-, and heavy-duty truck applications worldwide, it is not possible or desirable to display all of them. All manufacturers provide exploded views of their various models in both the respective service manual literature and in their excellent parts books. However, since we are concerned with performing an inspection and a series of checks/tests on the more widely used alternator models, as a frame of reference for this purpose, a number of exploded views are included in this section to assist you not only in identifying the component parts, but also to allow you to see just where they are located within the alternator assembly.

Most Delco-Remy alternator models that we have discussed so far related to medium- and heavy-duty trucks are either of the brush and slip-ring type or the brushless type. The basic design of the SI (systems integral) brush-

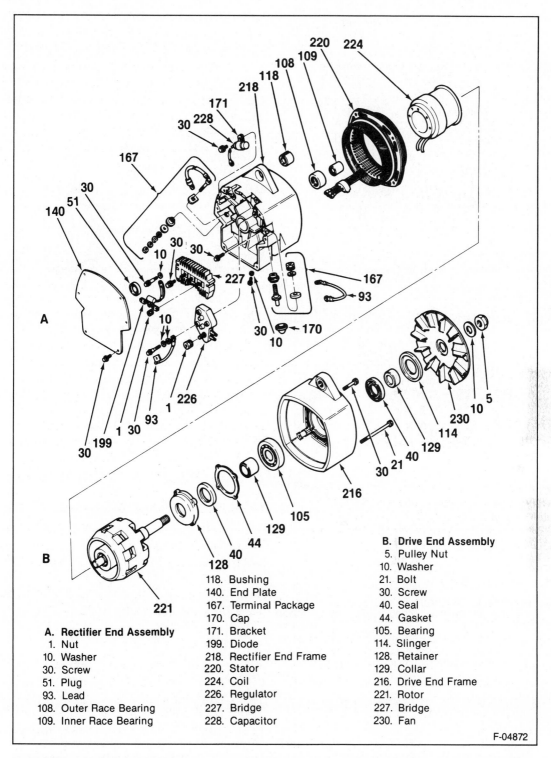

FIGURE 8–96 Model 30-SI Delco series 400 generator components. (*Courtesy of GMC Truck Division, General Motors Corporation.*)

A. Rectifier End Assembly
1. Nut
10. Washer
30. Screw
51. Plug
93. Lead
108. Outer Race Bearing
109. Inner Race Bearing

118. Bushing
140. End Plate
167. Terminal Package
170. Cap
171. Bracket
199. Diode
218. Rectifier End Frame
220. Stator
224. Coil
226. Regulator
227. Bridge
228. Capacitor

B. Drive End Assembly
5. Pulley Nut
10. Washer
21. Bolt
30. Screw
40. Seal
44. Gasket
105. Bearing
114. Slinger
128. Retainer
129. Collar
216. Drive End Frame
221. Rotor
227. Bridge
230. Fan

F-04872

type models, such as the I0-SI, 12-SI, 15-SI, 17-SI, 21-SI, and 27-SI are very similar; therefore, it is not necessary to show exploded views for all of these. Figure 8–96 illustrates an exploded view of a 30-SI series 400 brushless-type generator, which is very similar to the 20-SI and 25-SI models. Figure 8–97 illustrates an exploded view

of 10-SI and 15-SI series 100 alternators, which can be considered common for all the other brush-type SI units.

Figure 8–98 is an exploded view of the Prestolite/Leece-Neville flange-mounted 3425JC model alternator, and Fig. 8–99 shows the 2600JB, 2700JB, and 2800 units. The component parts and arrangement of

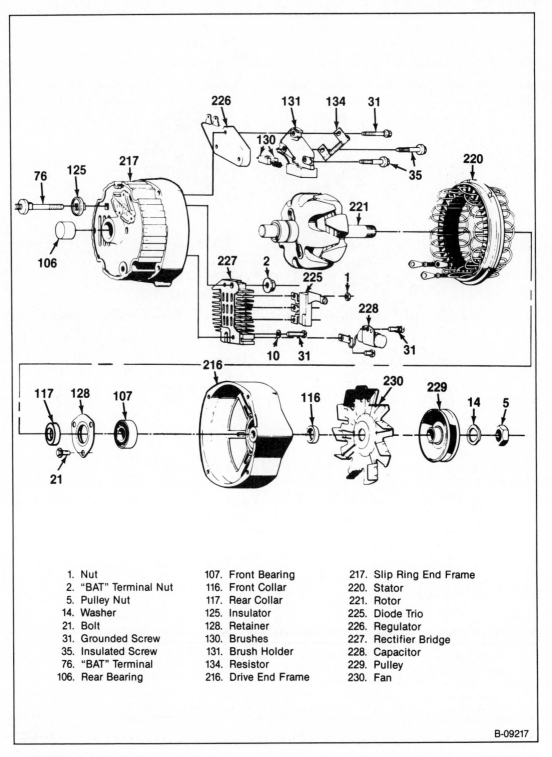

FIGURE 8-97 Model 10-SI and 15-SI series 100 generator components. (*Courtesy of GMC Truck Division, General Motors Corporation.*)

1.	Nut	107.	Front Bearing	217.	Slip Ring End Frame
2.	"BAT" Terminal Nut	116.	Front Collar	220.	Stator
5.	Pulley Nut	117.	Rear Collar	221.	Rotor
14.	Washer	125.	Insulator	225.	Diode Trio
21.	Bolt	128.	Retainer	226.	Regulator
31.	Grounded Screw	130.	Brushes	227.	Rectifier Bridge
35.	Insulated Screw	131.	Brush Holder	228.	Capacitor
76.	"BAT" Terminal	134.	Resistor	229.	Pulley
106.	Rear Bearing	216.	Drive End Frame	230.	Fan

these various alternator models can be used as a guide when servicing other well-known models of alternators.

Inspection Checks

Begin by cleaning all metal parts except the voltage regulator, rectifier bridge rotor, stator, and bearings in a com-mercially available solvent, then wipe and blow dry the parts. Neatly lay all alternator parts on a clean and well-organized bench work area in a logical format similar to how they would appear in the exploded views shown in this section. The following checks and tests are required to determine where the problem area(s) may be and what components might require replacement. These checks fall

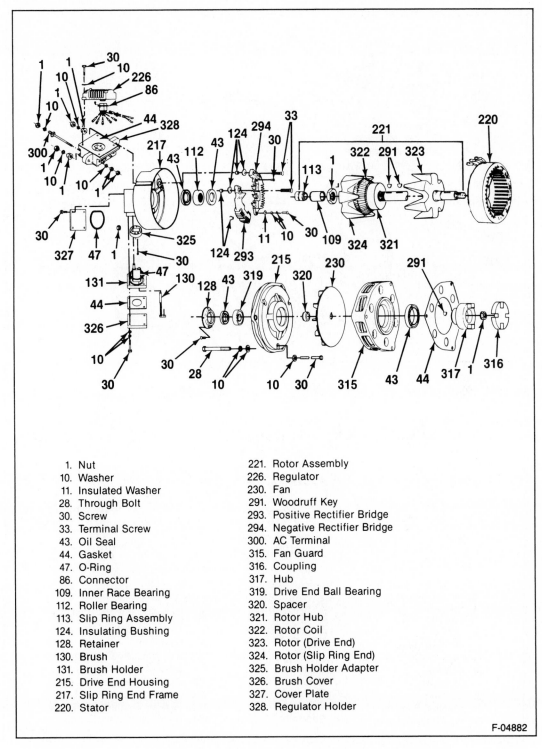

1. Nut
10. Washer
11. Insulated Washer
28. Through Bolt
30. Screw
33. Terminal Screw
43. Oil Seal
44. Gasket
47. O-Ring
86. Connector
109. Inner Race Bearing
112. Roller Bearing
113. Slip Ring Assembly
124. Insulating Bushing
128. Retainer
130. Brush
131. Brush Holder
215. Drive End Housing
217. Slip Ring End Frame
220. Stator

221. Rotor Assembly
226. Regulator
230. Fan
291. Woodruff Key
293. Positive Rectifier Bridge
294. Negative Rectifier Bridge
300. AC Terminal
315. Fan Guard
316. Coupling
317. Hub
319. Drive End Ball Bearing
320. Spacer
321. Rotor Hub
322. Rotor Coil
323. Rotor (Drive End)
324. Rotor (Slip Ring End)
325. Brush Holder Adapter
326. Brush Cover
327. Cover Plate
328. Regulator Holder

F-04882

FIGURE 8–98 Leece-Neville model 3425JC gear-driven, flange-mounted DDC 71/92 engine generator components. (*Courtesy of GMC Truck Division, General Motors Corporation.*)

into the following list of categories for all alternators. Each item in the list is described in more detail under its own subheading.

Systematic Checklist

1. Physical inspection for signs of obvious damage
2. Rotor field winding checks
3. Stator checks
4. Diode trio check
5. Rectifier bridge check
6. Capacitor check
7. Voltage regulator check
8. Generator output test

Check 1: Physical Inspection. Once the component parts have been removed, cleaned and dried, and laid out

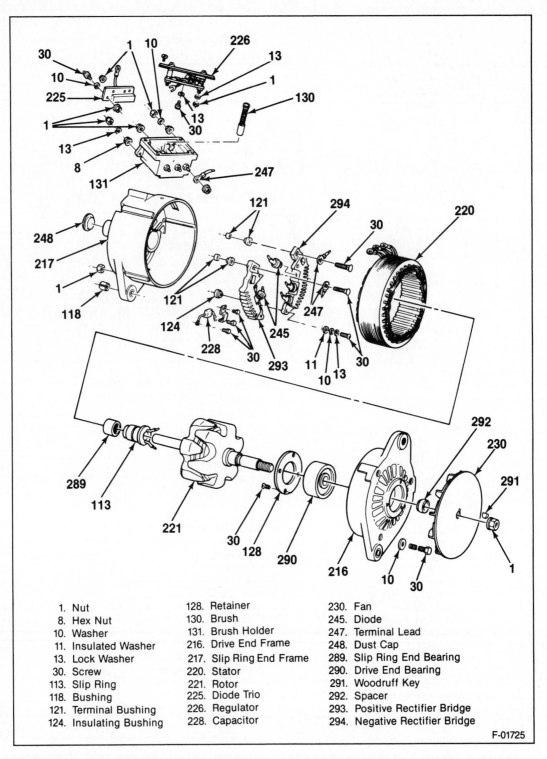

FIGURE 8–99 Leece-Neville Model 2600JB, 2700JB, and 2800JB generator components. (*Courtesy of GMC Truck Division, General Motors Corporation.*)

1. Nut	128. Retainer	230. Fan
8. Hex Nut	130. Brush	245. Diode
10. Washer	131. Brush Holder	247. Terminal Lead
11. Insulated Washer	216. Drive End Frame	248. Dust Cap
13. Lock Washer	217. Slip Ring End Frame	289. Slip Ring End Bearing
30. Screw	220. Stator	290. Drive End Bearing
113. Slip Ring	221. Rotor	291. Woodruff Key
118. Bushing	225. Diode Trio	292. Spacer
121. Terminal Bushing	226. Regulator	293. Positive Rectifier Bridge
124. Insulating Bushing	228. Capacitor	294. Negative Rectifier Bridge

neatly on a clean workbench, closely check all items for signs of wear. An example would be the brushes on brush-type models; if they are worn to one-half or less of a new brush, replace them. Check the brush leads for signs of burning, chafing, corrosion, or breaks.

The brushes used in most electronic alternators to-day are assembled into a brush holder, which is then held into position by the use of two small screws. To check the brushes for continuity, an ohmmeter with a 1.5-V test cell or a 12-V dc test lamp can be used. An example of testing both a single and a dual terminal brush arrangement is shown in Fig. 8–100.

An original brush set can be reused if it passes the tests shown in Fig. 8–100 and if the brushes are not worn

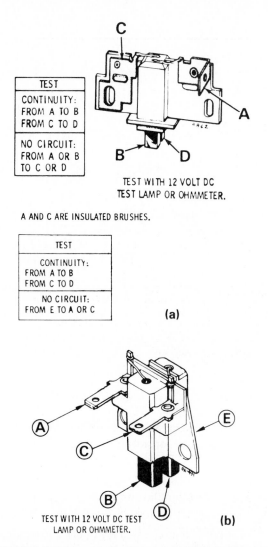

TEST
CONTINUITY: FROM A TO B FROM C TO D
NO CIRCUIT: FROM A OR B TO C OR D

TEST WITH 12 VOLT DC
TEST LAMP OR OHMMETER.

A AND C ARE INSULATED BRUSHES.

TEST
CONTINUITY: FROM A TO B FROM C TO D
NO CIRCUIT: FROM E TO A OR C

(a)

TEST WITH 12 VOLT DC TEST
LAMP OR OHMMETER.

(b)

FIGURE 8-100 (a) Single-terminal brush holder test; (b) dual-terminal brush holder test. (*Courtesy of Prestolite Electric Incorporated, Heavy Duty Products Division.*)

beyond midway, and are not oil soaked, cracked, or otherwise damaged. Check all seals and bearings/bushings; however, these two items are generally replaced automatically if a generator has been in service for any length of time and you expect it to go back into service and provide long, trouble-free life. The rotor slip rings must be checked; however, see "Check 2: Rotor" below. Similarly, the stator windings should be checked for signs of discoloration that indicate overheating (see also "Check 3: Stator" for more information). Check the generator housing for signs of cracks, warping, and physical damage to the exterior.

Check 2: Rotor. The rotor requires both a physical and an electrical check routine to determine its suitability for reuse. Although the rotor slip rings must be carefully inspected for signs of overheating or scoring, do not attempt any mechanical repair to the slip rings until you have confirmed that there are no electrical problems. More on slip-ring repair later.

If the rotor appears to be burned by traces of discoloration or insulation that appears as very dark or blackened wiring, a strong acid odor will be evident. Replace the rotor automatically without further checks. Perform the following electrical tests on the rotor using either a 110-V test lamp or an ohmmeter, as shown in Fig. 8-101. Check the rotor for opens in the winding by connecting the test lamp or ohmmeter test lead prods to each slip ring as shown in Fig. 8-101 connection B. If the test lamp fails to light or if the ohmmeter reading is high (infinite), this confirms that the winding is open. If you recollect the basic operation of the alternator (see Fig. 8-5), one slip ring brush is connected to the negative side of the battery, while the other is connected to the positive side of the battery system. Check the rotor for grounds by connecting a test lamp or ohmmeter from one slip ring to the rotor shaft according to connection A in Fig. 8-101. If the test lamp illuminates, or if the ohmmeter reading is low, the rotor winding is grounded! Check the rotor for resistance or a short circuit by one of the following two methods:

1. Connecting a battery and ammeter in series with the edge of the two slip rings. Place the test leads on the slip ring edges to avoid creating arc marks on the brush contact surfaces. The ammeter reading is then compared with the manufacturer's published specs (see Table 8-4, which lists acceptable field current values for both Delco-Remy and Leece-Neville alternator models). An ammeter reading higher than that in the specs indicates shorted rotor field windings, while a value lower than listed indicates excessive resistance.

2. Using an ohmmeter with its two leads connected to each slip ring according to connection B in Fig. 8-101. Table 8-4 lists typical field ohms resistance values for

FIGURE 8-101 Checking rotor field windings with an ohmmeter. (*Courtesy of GMC Truck Division, General Motors Corporation.*)

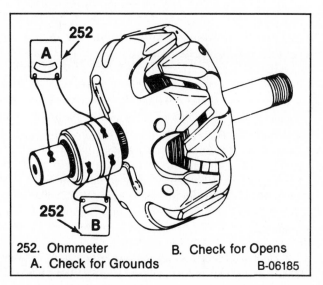

252. Ohmmeter   B. Check for Opens
A. Check for Grounds   B-06185

Delco alternator models. For example, the 17-SI series 100 Delco model has a resistance value of 1.7 to 2.1 Ω at 27 °C (80 °F), while the 15-SI series 100 has a higher resistance value of between 2.6 and 3.0 Ω. The rotor coil resistance value on Leece-Neville alternators is:

a. 2600JB: 2.3 to 4.1Ω
b. 2700JB and 2800 JB: 1.9 to 2.3 Ω
c. 3425JC: 3.0 to 3.3 Ω

If a resistance specification is not available to you, this can be determined by using the Ohm's law formula in Chapter 1, simply by dividing the voltage by the current. A higher-than-listed ohmmeter reading signifies that the rotor winding has excessive resistance. If you suspect that an open coil winding exists in a rotor, closely inspect the solder joints at the slip-ring lead area since a poor connection can cause you to interpret the test reading as an open coil winding. You may be able to resolder the connection successfully; then, if after rechecking with an ohmmeter the proper resistance value is obtained, the rotor can be reused. If the rotor passes these electrical tests, but the generator still does not put out its rated current/voltage, check the diode trio, rectifier bridge, stator, or voltage regulator.

If the rotor is electrically acceptable and the copper slip rings appear to be worn, scored, or pitted, the slip rings can be cleaned up by either using 400-grit emery cloth or by removing a small amount of copper by machining in a lathe. Even if the slip rings are only to be polished, it is suggested that you check the rotor in a lathe or a drill chuck to ensure that the slip rings will remain true to within 0.002 in. (0.05 mm). Attempting to remove material from the slip rings by hand and a piece of emery cloth can result in flat spots if you do not spin the rotor. Remove only enough copper from the slip rings to true them up.

SERVICE TIP: Should the alternator slip rings require clean-up with 400 or greater grit polishing cloth, or require machining to true them up, you should determine what the manufacturer's minimum slip-ring-diameter specification is. Determine if it is worth attempting slip-ring machining from this information! You should also consider whether it is practical from a time and cost standpoint to replace the slip rings. Some manufacturers do offer replacement slip rings through their service/parts departments. The old slip rings can be removed after unsoldering the slip-ring and rotor coil connections. You will require the use of a suitable split-bearing type of puller connected to a conventional leg puller, as illustrated in Fig. 8–102. This arrangement can be used to pull rotor bearings. The rotor halves can also be separated to get at the field coil on some models; however, never attempt to replace one half of the rotor since the two halves are balanced.

Check 3: Stator. Minor variations exist between different makes and models of stator assemblies with

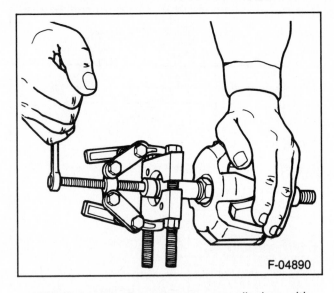

FIGURE 8–102 Removing generator slip rings with a puller. (*Courtesy of GMC Truck Division, General Motors Corporation.*)

regard to the checking procedure required to confirm that the stator is acceptable. We concentrate on Delco-Remy and Leece-Neville models here, since information relevant to them can be considered common to other makes as well.

Delco stator checks: Due to some minor variations in the stator checks on the brush-type and brushless Delco models, we discuss these in two segments, as follows:

1. The stator can be checked for opens and grounds on the 10-SI models using a wye-wound stator.
2. The stator can only be checked for grounds on the series 15-SI and 17-SI models as well as on the 27-SI series 100, 200, and 205 models. The reason for this is because the delta-wound stator arrangement exhibits a very low winding resistance.

Figure 8–103 illustrates the ohmmeter connection to the stator for checking both ground and open conditions on a 10-SI wye-wound stator. On delta-wound stators such as the 15-SI, 17-SI, and 27-SI models, the only connection required would be the A hookup for grounds. When checking for grounded windings, either a 110-V test lamp or ohmmeter can be used. If the lamp lights or the ohmmeter reading is low when connected from any stator lead to the frame (ground), this confirms that the stator windings are in fact grounded. On the 10-SI wye-wound stator, when the test light or ohmmeter is connected as per step B in Fig. 8–103 if the lamp fails to light or the resistance value is high when successively connected between each pair of stator leads, the stator windings are open.

Since delta-wound stators cannot be checked effectively for opens, if a generator passes the ground check and there is no sign of overheating or other physical damage, the stator can be reused. However, after reas-

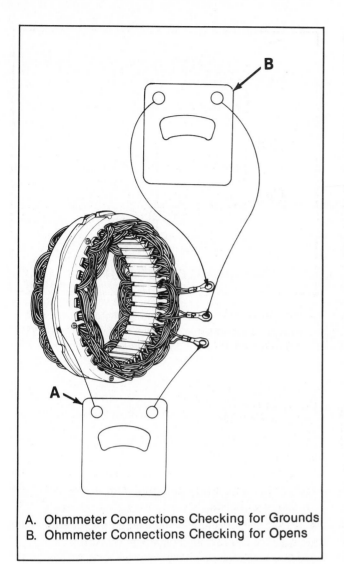

A. Ohmmeter Connections Checking for Grounds
B. Ohmmeter Connections Checking for Opens

FIGURE 8–103 Checking the stator windings. (*Courtesy of GMC Truck Division, General Motors Corporation.*)

sembly, if the generator fails to develop its rated current output, shorted stator windings or an open-delta winding is probably the problem.

The heavy-duty Delco brushless models, such as the 25-SI and 30-SI units, require a slightly different stator check to that described for the brush-type units above. The 25-SI uses a wye-wound stator that can be checked for both grounds and opens. However, the 30-SI, which uses a delta-wound stator winding, can be checked only for grounds. Figure 8–104 illustrates the electrical tests that can be performed on the 25-SI model using either an ohmmeter or a 110-V test lamp.

The windings are grounded in the 25-SI model if the lamp illuminates or the ohmmeter readings are low when connected from any stator lead to the stator frame (broken insulation). An open in the stator is confirmed if with the test equipment successively connected between each pair of stator leads, the lamp fails to light or the ohmmeter value reads high. Due to the very low resistance

of the wye-wound stator windings, a short circuit is not easy to locate with conventional test equipment, so if the generator fails to produce rated current output, you can assume that the stator windings are shorted.

Figure 8–55 shows the rectifier end plate removed from a 30-SI series 400 Delco generator, along with identification of the various components. This schematic, along with the ohmmeter lead placement illustrated in Fig. 8–105 will assist you when making the various electrical tests that should be performed on a 30-SI delta-wound stator/generator using an ohmmeter. Since the 30-SI generator employs a delta-wound stator, only a check for grounds can be made. Ohmmeter connections can be made from either lead to the frame. All readings should be infinite; otherwise, replace the stator. This check is not necessary if the problem complaint was an overcharging condition. Replace the stator if all of the other electrical components are within normal range but the

FIGURE 8–104 Electrical tests of a model 25-SI Delco generator using an ohmmeter. (*Courtesy of GMC Truck Division, General Motors Corporation.*)

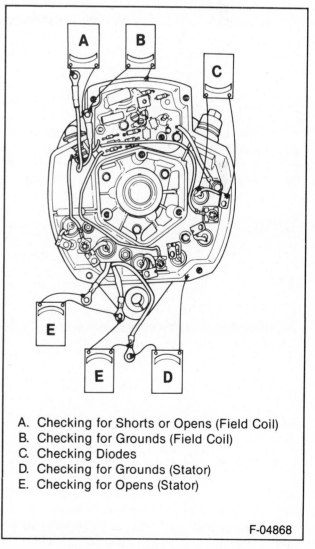

A. Checking for Shorts or Opens (Field Coil)
B. Checking for Grounds (Field Coil)
C. Checking Diodes
D. Checking for Grounds (Stator)
E. Checking for Opens (Stator)

F-04868

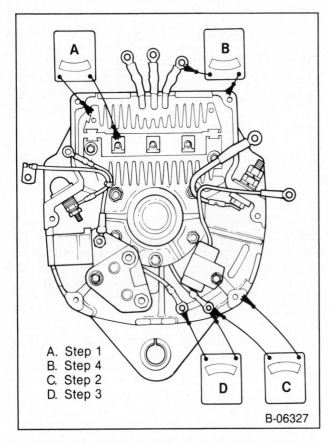

FIGURE 8–105 Electrical tests of a Delco model 30-SI generator. (*Courtesy of GMC Truck Division, General Motors Corporation.*)

A. Step 1
B. Step 4
C. Step 2
D. Step 3

B-06327

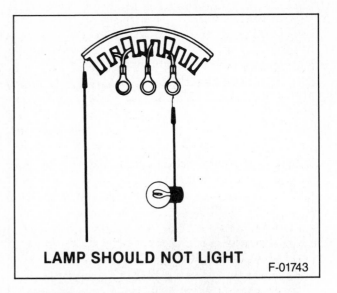

LAMP SHOULD NOT LIGHT

F-01743

FIGURE 8–106 Stator ground test light sequence for a Leece-Neville alternator. (*Courtesy of GMC Truck Division, General Motors Corporation.*)

generator assembly fails to produce its rated current output on a bench test.

Leece-Neville stator checks: The stator checks required on Leece-Neville heavy-duty 2600-2700-2800JB alternator models differ slightly from that used on Delco-Remy models. The stator exhibits a very low resistance value due to its construction design and the size and type of wire used for the windings. Consequently, a conventional ohmmeter will not be suitable for this check, and it is recommended that you use a digital ohmmeter capable of reading to 1/1000 of an ohm. On the 2600-2700 and 2800JB models, the stator can be tested for grounds and continuity between phases. Use of a 115 to 120-V test lamp is preferable to an ohmmeter, since the higher voltages applied to the stator will improve the chances of picking up on a phase winding that may be a borderline case. Note the following precaution, however, prior to using a test lamp.

CAUTION: Remove the stator from the generator frame before attempting to check each phase winding with a 115 to 120-V test lamp; otherwise, the voltage impressed through the heat sink can damage the diodes.

Figure 8–106 illustrates a test lamp or ohmmeter connection with one test lead contacting the bare metal outer

surface of the stator, while the other test lead can be connected individually to each of the three stator phase windings one at a time. The test lamp should not illuminate or the stator is grounded. When using an ohmmeter, a high resistance reading indicates that the stator is not grounded. A stator phase resistance test can be performed using either a test lamp or a digital ohmmeter. Connect the test leads to the stator terminals as shown in Fig. 8–107. If the resistance values noted on the ohmmeter are more or less the same (balanced) across the 1–2, 2–3, and 1–3 terminals, the stator is usable. If a test lamp is used, the bulb should illuminate on all three phases!

FIGURE 8–107 Stator resistance test (Leece-Neville). (*Courtesy of GMC Truck Division, General Motors Corporation.*)

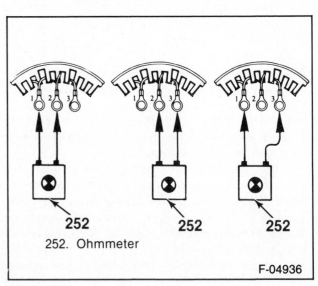

252   **252**   **252**

252. Ohmmeter

F-04936

Check 4: Diode Trio. Generator field current is supplied through a diode trio connected to the stator windings. The physical shape of the diode trio used with alternators will vary between makes; however, the purpose of the check remains the same, to establish whether each diode in the trio is in satisfactory condition. Several ways can be employed to test the diode condition: an ohmmeter with a 1.5-V cell, a commercial diode tester, or 12-V dc test lamp.

CAUTION: Do not use a 120-V ac test lamp or diode damage will result.

Diodes are tested to ensure that they pass current in only one direction. Diodes that do not pass current in either direction are open, while diodes passing current in both directions are shorted. Figures 8–108 through 8–110 show the ohmmeter lead connections required to check the condition of the diode trio.

Diode-trio checks are conducted with an ohmmeter using a 1.5-V battery cell and the ohmmeter range switched to the lowest scale. Because of minor variations between Delco-Remy and Leece-Neville generator designs, we will illustrate the test sequence connections for both types. On Delco 10, 15, 17, and 27-SI series 100 generator models, the diode trio would appear as illus-

FIGURE 8–108 Diode-trio check for models 10-15-17 and 27-SI type 100 generators. (*Courtesy of GMC Truck Division, General Motors Corporation.*)

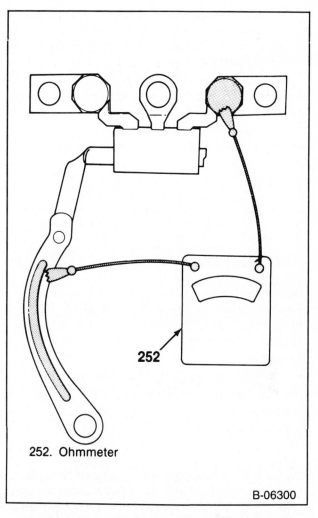

252. Ohmmeter

B-06300

FIGURE 8–109 Diode-trio check for 27-SI 200/205 models and 30-SI generator model. (*Courtesy of GMC Truck Division, General Motors Corporation.*)

FIGURE 8–110 Diode-trio test on a Leece-Neville alternator. (*Courtesy of GMC Truck Division, General Motors Corporation.*)

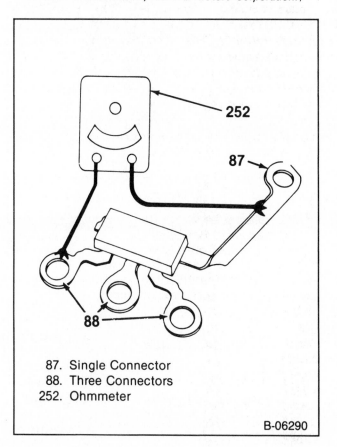

87. Single Connector
88. Three Connectors
252. Ohmmeter

B-06290

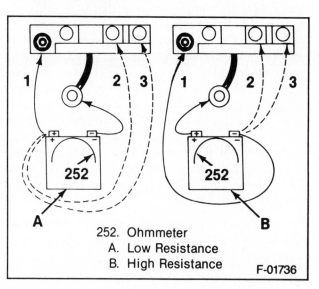

252. Ohmmeter
A. Low Resistance
B. High Resistance

F-01736

trated in Fig. 8–108. The diode-trio for the Delco 27-SI series 200/205 and the 30-SI 108 type 400 is shown in Fig. 8–109. Remove the diode trio from the end frame assembly by removing the nuts and screw. Connect the ohmmeter to the single connector and to one of the three connectors according to the diagram for the type of generator diode trio to be tested. Carefully note and record the ohmmeter reading, then reverse the leads to the same two connectors. If the readings are the same, replace the diode trio, since a good diode trio will always exhibit one high and one low reading on the ohmmeter. Repeat this test for each of the other two connectors. You should also connect the ohmmeter to each pair of the three connectors (not shown), and if any reading registers zero ohms, replace the diode trio.

NOTE: The diode trio for the Delco 25-SI brushless generator is contained in a panel board assembly that contains the voltage regulator. Each diode should read 5 to 50 ohms. If zero or substantially above 50, replace the diode being tested. Refer to Fig. 8–116 under testing of the voltage regulator (check 7) for identification of this diode trio, which is identified as item 225.

On Leece-Neville model 2600-2700 and 2800JB units, the diode trio can be tested using the 1.5-V cell ohmmeter, as shown in Fig. 8–110. A low-resistance ohm reading should be obtained and if a test lamp is used, it should light when connected as shown in step A of the figure. A high resistance or no illumination of the test light should occur when connected as shown in step B of the figure. Replace the diode trio if it does not pass all the tests. On the 3425JC flange-mounted alternator the diode trio is sealed inside the voltage regulator holder; therefore, it cannot be checked for resistance. The only way to determine the condition of the unit is to install the regulator holder into a generator that is known to be OK, then if the generator fails to produce its rated output, replace the voltage regulator assembly.

Check 5: Rectifier Bridge. Various types of heat sinks and rectifier bridges are used; thus slight differences exist in the check procedure required. Once again, for discussion purposes, we concentrate on the Delco-Remy and Leece-Neville medium- and heavy-duty truck alternator models. This check involves checking the three negative and the three positive diodes contained in the respective heat sinks. Use a special diode tester if available; otherwise, use an ohmmeter. All diodes are designed to allow current flow in only one direction; therefore, a good diode will register one high and one low ohmmeter reading. Diodes that allow current flow in both directions are shorted, while no current flow in either direction signifies an open diode.

CAUTION: Never use a 110-V test lamp or high-voltage test equipment to check diodes, because they could be permanently damaged.

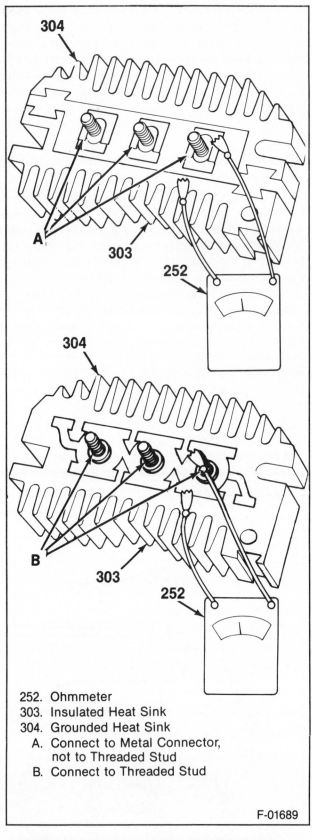

252. Ohmmeter
303. Insulated Heat Sink
304. Grounded Heat Sink
  A. Connect to Metal Connector, not to Threaded Stud
  B. Connect to Threaded Stud

F-01689

FIGURE 8–111 Generator rectifier bridge check for Delco 10-SI, 15-SI, 17-SI, and 27-SI series 100 and 27-SI series 200/205 models. (*Courtesy of GMC Truck Division, General Motors Corporation.*)

The rectifier bridge check for Delco 10-SI, 15-SI, 17-SI, and 27-SI series 100 and 27-SI series 200/205 models is the same. To check these units, refer to Fig. 8–111, which illustrates two types of rectifier bridges that can be found in these units. Identify the type in use on the rectifier bridge that you are checking first. Connect the ohmmeter, using the lowest-range scale, to:

1. The grounded heat sink and one of the three flat metal connectors, as in diagram A of Fig. 8–111
2. The grounded heat sink and one of the three threaded studs, as in diagram B of Fig. 8–111

Note and record the ohmmeter value, then reverse the lead connectors to the grounded heat sink and the same flat connector or threaded stud. A good rectifier bridge will respond similar to the check for a diode trio in that it will give one high and one low reading. Repeat this test for the other two connections, as well as between the insulated heat sink and each of the three terminals or connectors, for a total of six checks. The rectifier bridge should be replaced if any pair of readings is the same! On some models of rectifiers, the diodes can be replaced.

On the Delco 25-SI brushless generator, the six rectifier diode leads shown in Fig. 8–104 (item C) have to be removed from the stud. Connect one ohmmeter lead to the diode lead and the other to the case, then reverse the position of the leads. We are looking for one high and one low reading here. If both readings are the same, replace the diode. Repeat this procedure for each diode (a total of 12 readings). On the 30-SI Delco generator, rectifier bridge diode checks are not required if the problem was an overcharging rate. Refer to Fig. 8–105, which illustrates the end plate removed to expose the diodes.

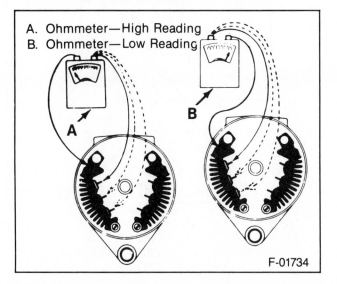

FIGURE 8–112 Leece-Neville generator positive heat sink test. (*Courtesy of GMC Truck Division, General Motors Corporation.*)

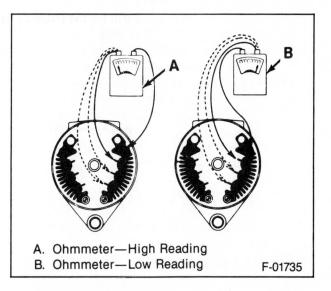

A. Ohmmeter—High Reading
B. Ohmmeter—Low Reading   F-01735

FIGURE 8–113 Leece-Neville generator negative heat sink test. (*Courtesy of GMC Truck Division, General Motors Corporation.*)

Connect one of the ohmmeter leads to the heat sink and the other to one of the flat metal clips as in step 1(A) in the diagram. Note and record the reading, then reverse the connections. A good diode will show one high and one low reading. Repeat the test between the same heat sink and the other two diodes as well as between the other heat sink and each of the three flat metal clips for a total of six checks, including two ohmmeter value readings per check on each rectifier bridge, for a total of 12 readings. On Leece-Neville generators the same diode checks are performed as for the Delco-Remy models with Figs. 8–112 and 8–113 illustrating the ohmmeter connections to both the positive and negative heat sinks of the generator. The + heat sink is the one to which the + output terminal is connected. It has a square hole in the terminal end of the + heat sink that is larger than that in the negative heat sink. If a shorted or open diode is found, replace the complete heat sink assembly. Minor variations may appear between heat sinks; however, they are all interchangeable.

Check 6: Capacitor. The capacitor or condensor that is usually mounted to the generator end frame is designed to protect the rectifier bridge and diode trio from high temporary voltage as well as acting to suppress radio noise (interference). If you review the operation of the Delco-Remy alternator circuit shown in Fig. 8–23 for the 10-15-17 SI models and in Fig. 8–26 for the 27-SI models, the capacitor C1 smooths out the voltage across resistor R3. Capacitors are best tested with a special capacitor tester, if available. The capacitor value will vary between makes and models of generators; however, it is usually in the range of 0.5 μF (microfarad) and up to 200 volts dc. Use an ohmmeter connected across the terminals as

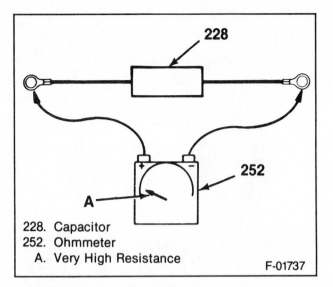

228. Capacitor
252. Ohmmeter
A. Very High Resistance

F-01737

FIGURE 8-114 Generator capacitor test hookup. *(Courtesy of GMC Truck Division, General Motors Corporation.)*

in Fig. 8–114 to check for shorts if a capacitor tester is unavailable. A low resistance value is indicative of a shorted or leaking capacitor; therefore, it should be replaced.

Check 7: Voltage Regulator. All current medium- and heavy-duty truck voltage regulators are solid-state devices that normally do not allow provision for adjustment, but some models do provide for this. Examples of generator models that we have discussed that do provide such an adjustment include the Delco-Remy 25-SI type 400 and 450, which have an internal voltage adjustment potentiometer screw mounted on the regulator, but the generator rear cover must be removed to gain access to this screw. An adjustment is also provided on Leece-Neville model 2600-2700 and 2800JB units, as well as the 3425JC flange-mounted model.

To check the condition of the voltage regulator, whether or not it has an adjustment, refer to the following information dealing with Delco-Remy 10-15-17 and 27-SI series 100 and 27-SI 200/205 generators and the 30-SI type 400 generator.

Procedure

1. Refer to Fig. 8–115 and connect a voltmeter (250) and fast-charger (258) to the system 12-V battery (256), making sure that correct battery polarity is observed.
2. Connect the regulator (226) and test lamp (264) into the test system hookup as shown in Fig. 8–115. The test lamp is hooked into the system in the same place that the rotor would be; therefore, the voltage regulator will turn off any current flow to the rotor field when the preset voltage is reached.
3. At this time the test lamp (264) should be illuminated. If not, check the system hookup and bulb. Check for voltage at the regulator outlets to the test bulb.

4. Turn on the fast charger, then slowly and carefully increase the charging rate to find out at what voltage the test light goes out (no illumination). The voltmeter will confirm when this occurs, which should be somewhere between 13.5 and 16 V. The setting on the 30-SI model is between 13 and 15 V maximum.
5. If the voltage regulator does not cut out within the correct voltage range, replace the regulator assembly.

On the Delco 25-SI model, the voltage regulator is contained in the panel board of the generator rectifier end frame. The view in Fig. 8–39 (item 226) and the end view in Fig. 8–116 illustrate this arrangement. A close-up view of the voltage rectifier panel board is shown in Fig. 8–116 without the sealing compound in order that the seven serviceable parts can be easily identified. With the regulator removed from the generator rectifier end frame, the procedure is as described below.

Procedure

1. Refer to Fig. 8–116 and remove the screw and transistor TR1 (142), then carefully/gently pry apart the heat sink and panel board with a small electric screwdriver.
2. Closely inspect the printed circuit for any signs of burning due to overheating and for poor soldered joints as well as damaged parts.

FIGURE 8-115 Testing the Delco voltage regulator assembly. *(Courtesy of GMC Truck Division, General Motors Corporation.)*

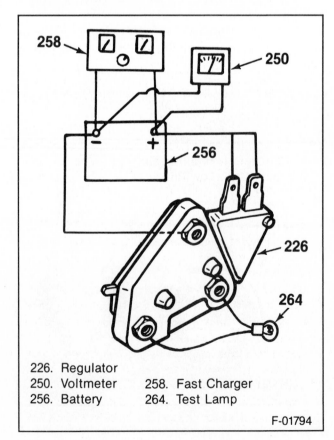

226. Regulator
250. Voltmeter   258. Fast Charger
256. Battery   264. Test Lamp

F-01794

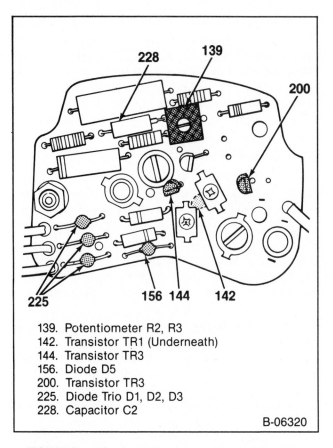

FIGURE 8–116 Delco 25-SI model generator panel board assembly. (*Courtesy of GMC Truck Division, General Motors Corporation.*)

139. Potentiometer R2, R3
142. Transistor TR1 (Underneath)
144. Transistor TR3
156. Diode D5
200. Transistor TR3
225. Diode Trio D1, D2, D3
228. Capacitor C2

B-06320

meter should read between 5 and 50 ohms. If a zero or substantially higher value than 50 Ω is obtained, replace the diode.

d. Check the diode trio (D1, D2, and D3) identified as check D in Fig. 8–117. Each diode should read between 5 and 50 Ω. If the reading is well above 50, or zero, replace the diode under test.

e. Check the capacitor C2 (identified as item E in Fig. 8–117). The ohmmeter should read high; if zero, replace the capacitor.

f. Check the potentiometer R2 (identified as item F in Fig. 8–117). Set the ohmmeter to the *X*10 or middle scale and connect it according to connection F in the diagram. Refer next to Fig. 8–116 and rotate the slotted pot screw (139); the ohmmeter needle should deflect slightly; otherwise, replace resistor R2.

g. Refer to Fig. 8–116 and identify transistor TR1 (shown as item 142 in the diagram). Rotate the ohmmeter scale to the × 1 or low scale. Perform a three-step check exactly as you did for the TR3 test in step b.

If the regulator still does not operate correctly, replace it. If you have replaced any components, you will have to reseal all components with a clear sealant such as Dow Chemical RTV (room-temperature vulcanizing)

FIGURE 8–117 Ohmmeter checks required on the Delco voltage regulator components. (*Courtesy of GMC Truck Division, General Motors Corporation.*)

3. If all components appear to be in satisfactory condition, use an ohmmeter with a 1.5-V cell set to the lowest range scale. To obtain an ohmmeter reading, you will have to carefully penetrate the transparent coating over the soldered joints with a sharp instrument to allow good contact with the ohmmeter lead prod.

4. Figure 8–117 illustrates the checks and tests that have to be performed on the regulator panel board assembly.

a. The first check is a three-part procedure. Check item A (transistor TR2 in the diagram) as in ohmmeter hookup 1. The ohmmeter should read between 5 and 50 Ω. Replace the transistor if the value is either zero or substantially above 50 Ω. In step A, hookup 2, the ohmmeter should register very high; otherwise, replace the transistor. In step A, hookup 3 is the same as hookup 1.

b. This is also a three-part check procedure. Check item B (transistor TR3 in the diagram) as in ohmmeter hookup B in Fig. 8–117. Step 1 should register a very high ohmmeter reading; otherwise, replace the transistor. In step 2, hookup B2, the ohmmeter should read between 5 and 50 Ω. If a zero or substantially higher than 50-Ω value is obtained, replace the transistor. Step 3, hookup B3, is the same as step 2.

c. Check diode D5 (item C in Fig. 8–117). The ohm-

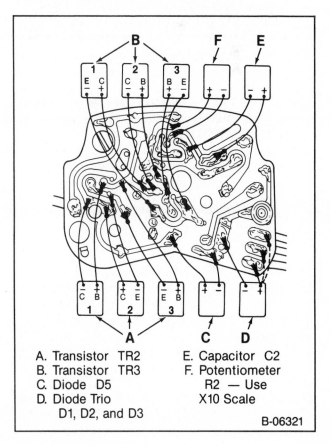

A. Transistor TR2
B. Transistor TR3
C. Diode D5
D. Diode Trio D1, D2, and D3
E. Capacitor C2
F. Potentiometer R2 — Use X10 Scale

B-06321

Silastic 732 silicone rubber seal, or equivalent commercially available sealant. Replace the regulator in the generator and perform a full generator output test for rated current (amperes) and voltage settings. On Leece-Neville alternators, the voltage regulator, although adjustable, cannot be effectively checked with an ohmmeter; therefore, install the regulator into a good generator and perform a full generator output test for rated current and voltage settings.

Check 8: Generator Output Test. After any repairs to a generator and its components, it should be reassembled carefully in the basic reverse order of disassembly. Depending on the make and model in question and whether or not you have completely disassembled the generator, the reassembly can be performed by referring to the exploded views shown in Figs. 8–96 through 8–99. A generator output test was discussed earlier in this chapter with the necessary test hookup for various models shown in Figs. 8–50, 8–51, 8–52, 8–54, 8–62, 8–65, and 8–82. Refer to the section "Generator Output Test: Bench Check" for specific information.

ALTERNATOR DRIVE BELTS

Charging system problems are often assumed to be caused by the alternator, the regulator, or the associated wiring, when in many cases the cause may be an improperly adjusted drive belt system. Drive belts used on medium- and heavy-duty trucks can be either a poly-vee design or a multirib belt design such as those illustrated in Fig. 8–118. In addition, only one drive belt may be used, although dual or triple arrangements are also commonly used on heavy-duty truck applications.

FIGURE 8–118 V-belt versus multirib belt design comparison. (*Courtesy of GMC Truck Division, General Motors Corporation.*)

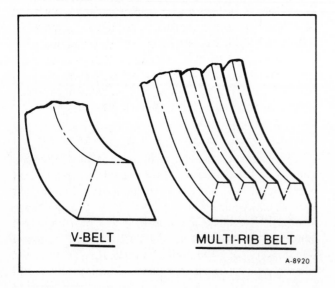

V-BELT   MULTI-RIB BELT

A-8920

A loose drive belt will slip in the pulley groove, resulting in a low rotational speed of the alternator rotor, the end result being that the current output from the generator will remain too low for the batteries to maintain a full state of charge. The vehicle electrical load will shortly drain the battery cranking power and the batteries' ability to operate all of the various electrical accessories. Many heavy-duty truck alternators employ double-groove pulleys to distribute the power requirements of the belts over a greater-cross-sectional surface area. In this way the drive belts can be made less wide as well as being cheaper. It also offers the advantage of still being able to drive the alternator should one belt break.

When it is necessary to adjust an alternator drive belt(s), a belt tension gauge should always be used to ensure the longest belt life as well as minimizing possible damage to the alternator support bearings should the belt be adjusted too tightly. Drive belts that are too loose can result in slippage, tearing, burning, grabbing and snapping as well as chirping or a high-pitched squeal particularly when the engine is accelerated under load. More drive belts fail as a direct result of being too loose than of being too tight. If the drive belt(s) are adjusted too tightly, they can cause excessive side loading, particularly on multiple-drive belt hookups. High-drive-belt tension has been shown to cause crankshaft bearing damage and in severe cases can contribute to crankshaft breakage. It will also cause excessive side thrust not only on the alternator bearings, but also to other drive accessories that share the same belt drive arrangement. Even if no direct damage is noticeable on these accessories, too much belt tension will definitely stretch and weaken the belts.

Regular inspection of drive belts and mounting bracket bolts should be a part of any vehicle maintenance check, with many fleets doing belt inspection at each engine oil change or at a specific mileage based on their operating conditions. When drive belts are worn, an adjustment will not stop them from slipping, and they can cause pulley damage if left in position. If an inspection reveals wear in any drive belt, replace it! Different engine manufacturers state that once a drive belt has made one complete revolution, it is considered to be a used belt, whereas others state that once a belt has been in operation for 10 minutes, it would be considered a used belt. Regardless of these differences, belt installation and adjustment remains the same. Most manufacturers quote a new unused belt tension as well as a used belt tension specification in their respective service literature.

Although there are a number of commercially available belt dressings in rub-on or spray-on form, most belt and engine manufacturers advise against using these since most of them contain chemicals that can soften the belt material. Note that any time that multiple-belt drives are to be replaced, all belts should be replaced as a matched set since if only one new belt is installed, it will absorb all of the tension, resulting in early failure.

Belt Life Considerations

Never attempt to clean drive belts while the engine is running since serious personal injury could result. Remove all traces of oil or grease as soon as possible since belt deterioration can occur fairly quickly due to the chemicals used in these lubricants. The belts should be cleaned using a clean rag and a nonflammable cleaner or solvent, or even detergent soap and water is acceptable.

If drive belts are removed from an engine for any reason other than replacement, such as when performing an engine repair, minimize possible damage to the belts by storing them in a safe, clean, cool, and dry environment. Simply throwing the belts onto a wet, moist, or damp floor or near excessive heat may cause shrinkage or deterioration of the belts. An area of heat that is often overlooked when laying belts aside temporarily is direct sunlight, or sunlight reflected through a glass window, which can create excessive heat on the belt fabric.

Stacking, rolling, or twisting belts to make them fit into a parts storage bin is another procedure that can cause belt distortion and should be avoided. Hanging belts on pegboard nails, particularly heavy-duty ones that can weigh a substantial amount, should also be avoided since this action can weaken or possibly distort the belt, causing problems once it has been installed. Finally, if an engine is to be placed into storage, or the truck is to lie for an extended time for any reason, the drive belt tension should be removed by slackening off the adjustment bracket. Failure to relieve belt tension can result in lumpy belts that can cause a vibration. If you know that a truck is to be mothballed or placed in storage for any length of time, it is best to remove, clean, and store the belts in a safe manner. Additional service would include coating the drive pulley grooves with a spray-on rust preventive or grease; however, if you do this, ensure that the rust preventive or grease is removed prior to belt insstallation.

Belt and Pulley Inspection

If a drive belt requires adjustment or replacement, there are a number of systematic checks that should be noted prior to performing the service repair procedure. The pulleys should always be closely inspected for signs of grooving, which can be caused by dirt/oil/grease buildup and improper belt tension. Also inspect the pulley grooves for signs of rust, corrosion, damaged sidewalls, chips, nicks, tool marks, and possible cracking. If the belt shows signs of worn sides or has exhibited squeak, squeal, or whine during operation, this could indicate that the pulley alignment is not correct. To check the belt pulley alignment refer to Fig. 8–119.

Procedure

1. To check the drive and driven pulley alignment, either place a metal straightedge or position a cord line across

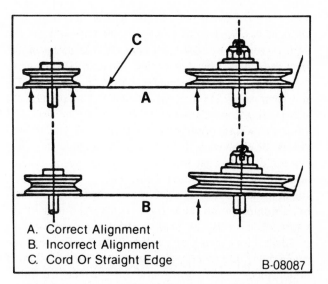

A. Correct Alignment
B. Incorrect Alignment
C. Cord Or Straight Edge

B-08087

FIGURE 8–119 Pulley alignment comparisons. (*Courtesy of GMC Truck Division, General Motors Corporation.*)

both pulleys. Check the diagram in Fig. 8–119 to compare correct versus incorrect alignment.

2. Rotate each pulley to several positions and recheck for parallel alignment. Contact should be made at all points on the pulleys. Pulley distortion is not uncommon on pressed steel pulleys, particularly if poor installation procedures are used, such as forcing a belt into position by using a screwdriver or bar. This will not only damage the pulley, but will also create belt damage.

Belt Life

Short drive-belt life can usually be attributed to one of eight causes:

1. A severe operating environment (too hot or too cold; extremely muddy or dirty/dusty conditions; operation in heavy coal dust at mines)
2. Incorrect belt installation procedures (forcing the belt into position on the grooves)
3. Incorrect belt tension procedures after installation
4. Use of an incorrect belt size (too narrow or too wide, which will result in belt and pulley groove damage)
5. Incorrect belt length (remember that dual or triple belt drives *must* be installed as matched sets)
6. A defective belt that may have been damaged by improper storage procedures (discussed earlier)
7. Misaligned pulleys
8. Damaged pulley grooves or bent pulley shafts

Typical belt problems that you will most often encounter can be traced to conditions that usually exhibit a condition that attracts immediate attention or that become noticeable due to short belt life. Examples of such a condition would be belt squeak, squeal, or whine. Both squeaks and squeals are usually most noticeable at engine idle speed or when the engine is accelerated quickly from idle when the vehicle is stationary, although both conditions can occur during certain vehicle operating conditions. Experience will confirm that both squeak and squeal seem to be most prevalent on cold damp mornings and when sheet steel pulleys are used. If the condition disappears once the engine warms up, this is usually due to moisture in the pulley grooves drying out and the belt settling down as it warms up. If the condition continues, however, both belt tension and pulley alignment should be checked as described in this section. Belt flexing can usually cause squeak/squeal, but a high-pitched whine is usually an indication of damage in a ball bearing in the alternator, fan hub, power steering pump, air-conditioning pump, and so on. Isolate and correct the cause, then adjust the belts to the correct tension.

Excessive glazing of a belt reflects itself as a baked appearance due to belt slippage due to any number of conditions, such as oil/grease on the belt or pulley grooves or pulley damage. Slip burns are a direct result of a lack of belt tension, the wrong-size belt, or slippage under load. Closely inspect the pulley grooves for wear. Belt damage such as base cracking, fabric rupture, cover tears, gouged edges, worn sides, cord damage, belt flip-over, or belt disintegration can be traced to such items as too much tension, or pulley wear, damage, or misalignment.

Drive Belt Replacement

When it is necessary to replace a drive belt(s), keep in mind that dual belt sets are sold only as matched sets. You should never use only one belt from a two- or three-belt set. On some truck installations, depending on the number of other accessories that are also belt driven, you may have to remove all of the outside belts to get to the single or dual alternator drive belt arrangement, which may be located on the inside of the drive setup. Although not common, you may also have to remove a drive accessory to get the old belt off and the new one on.

Most alternator installations adopt a slotted adjusting bracket to allow easy belt tension adjustment. Although these may differ slightly in design and location, Fig. 8–120 illustrates a typical example for a heavy-duty truck diesel engine.

FIGURE 8–120 Typical alternator and related parts location for a heavy-duty diesel engine. (*Courtesy of Detroit Diesel Corporation.*)

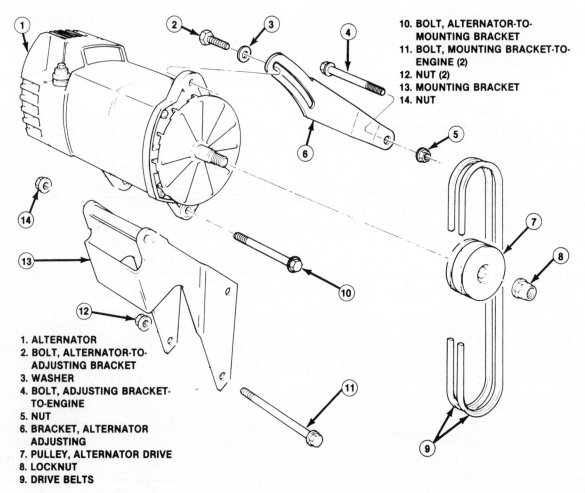

10. BOLT, ALTERNATOR-TO-
    MOUNTING BRACKET
11. BOLT, MOUNTING BRACKET-TO-
    ENGINE (2)
12. NUT (2)
13. MOUNTING BRACKET
14. NUT

1. ALTERNATOR
2. BOLT, ALTERNATOR-TO-
   ADJUSTING BRACKET
3. WASHER
4. BOLT, ADJUSTING BRACKET-
   TO-ENGINE
5. NUT
6. BRACKET, ALTERNATOR
   ADJUSTING
7. PULLEY, ALTERNATOR DRIVE
8. LOCKNUT
9. DRIVE BELTS

Procedure

1. Loosen the alternator capscrew located in the slotted adjusting bracket as well as the adjusting link capscrew or nut that passes through both the alternator and the bracket that is bolted to the engine. Loosening only the slotted bracket retaining bolt will not allow alternator movement.

2. The alternator body can be pushed toward the engine to loosen the drive belt(s), while moving the alternator body away from the engine will result in tightening of the drive belt(s).

3. If the belts are being changed, remove them, and clean and inspect the pulley grooves for signs of wear, damage, or misalignment if short belt life has been reported.

4. When installing a new belt or belts, make certain that you have moved the alternator far enough to allow the belts to slip into position. If the belts have to be forced into position, check for any more alternator movement, or double check that you have the correct belts. Forcing belts into position will result in belt and possible pulley damage.

5. With the belts properly installed in position, select a pry bar and install it between the engine block and the alternator housing so that pressure can be applied to the alternator without causing any damage.

6. Apply enough pressure on the bar to take up the slack in the belts.

7. Select a belt tensioner gauge, such as the one illustrated in Fig. 8–121 which identifies the gauge parts and shows how the gauge would be hooked around the V-belt. The gauge handle fits into the palm of your hand while your fingers are used to pull the gauge fingers and belt toward you. The tension can then be read directly from the gauge face. Belt tension gauges are readily available from most tool suppliers.

NOTE: If a dual or triple belt arrangement is used, select a gauge such as the one illustrated in Fig. 8–122 which is capable of grabbing all the belts at once.

8. Placement of the belt tension gauge is important to achieving the correct belt or engine manufacturer's specification. Belt tension is listed in the engine or truck manufacturer's service manual. The belt tension for V-belts is normally listed as being for a two- or three-pulley arrangement, such as that shown in Fig. 8–123.

9. The actual belt tension value will depend on the width and length of the belt(s) used. This cannot be stated exactly here due to the many trucks and drive belt arrangements. However, consider that this tension can range from as low as 50 to 70 lb for a single ½-in. (12.5-mm)-wide belt, while a dual ½-in. (12.5-mm) alternator belt

FIGURE 8–121 Using a V-belt tension gauge. (*Courtesy of GMC Truck Division, General Motors Corporation.*)

FIGURE 8–122 Using a multibelt tension gauge. (*Courtesy of GMC Truck Division, General Motors Corporation.*)

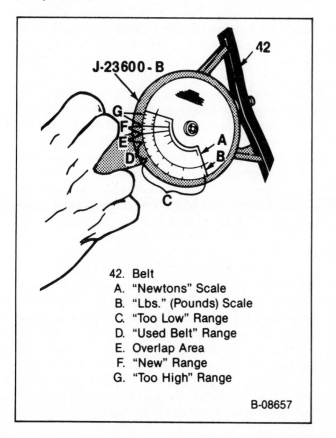

42. Belt
A. "Newtons" Scale
B. "Lbs." (Pounds) Scale
C. "Too Low" Range
D. "Used Belt" Range
E. Overlap Area
F. "New" Range
G. "Too High" Range

B-08657

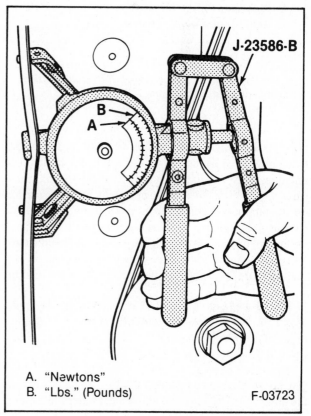

A. "Newtons"
B. "Lbs." (Pounds)

F-03723

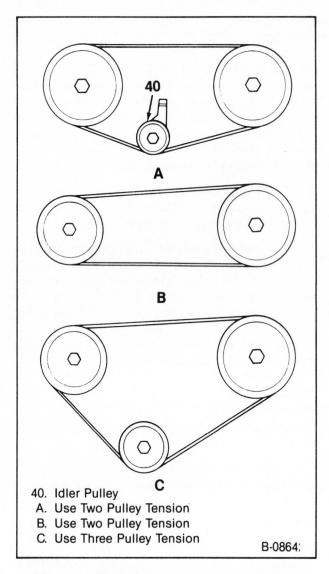

40. Idler Pulley
A. Use Two Pulley Tension
B. Use Two Pulley Tension
C. Use Three Pulley Tension

B-0864?

FIGURE 8–123 Examples of where to measure belt tension requirements. (*Courtesy of GMC Truck Division, General Motors Corporation.*)

taining pressure on the pry bar between the alternator body and engine block. Check the tension with the gauge and readjust if necessary. Once the belt tension is correct, final tighten the alternator bolts and recheck the belt tension.

11. New belts should be checked again for tension after about a half-hour or 15 miles/24 kilometers of operation and again after 8 hours or 240 miles/386 kilometers. Recheck them at succeeding intervals of 200 hours or 6000 miles/9656 kilometers, unless fleet experience has determined recheck intervals that are more suitable.

ALTERNATOR SELECTION PROCESS

Now that you have had an opportunity to study the operation, testing, troubleshooting, disassembly and repair of a heavy-duty truck alternator, you will realize that simply installing any make and model of alternator onto an engine can lead to problems of inadequate charging system rates. When it is necessary to select an alternator for installation onto a truck application, there are a number of important considerations that must be taken into account. Failure to adequately consider the various operating conditions that the vehicle will be subjected to can lead to a continual state of undercharged batteries and the associated electrical problems that emanate from such a condition.

Fleet maintenance personnel should be aware that prior to selecting any alternator, an "alternator selection guide questionnaire" such as the one illustrated in Table 8–6 should be used. The example shown in the table is produced by Electrodyne Heavy Duty Alternators, Division of Gauss Corporation, P.O. Box 660, Scarborough, ME 04074-0660, which offers a wide selection of brushless alternators for use on both midrange and heavy-duty trucks, transit buses, and emergency vehicles where heavy electrical loads are accompanied by long periods of operation at or near engine idle conditions. Table 8–7 exhibits a typical example of an Electrodyne alternator selection guide for 12-V systems. Such guides have been prepared for other popular engine options. The chart example has been prepared for a Cummins (14-L, 855-in.^{3}) model where the alternator drive pulley is mounted on the engine crankshaft. Some popular Electrodyne alternator models are listed down the left-hand side of the chart, while the maximum vehicle electrical loads from 40 to 80 A are listed horizontally along the top of the chart. Simple directions are listed 1 through 6 underneath the chart, which describes the selection process to use. Figure 8–124 illustrates an Electrodyne brushless alternator on a CAT 3408 engine in a Peterbilt truck.

Often truck maintenance personnel fail to remember that although an alternator does produce current/voltage at an engine idle speed, the rated output of the alternator does not occur until an elevated engine rpm is obtained. The engine speed at which the alternator's rated output

arrangement might be as low as 40 to 50 lb of tension, extending up to as high as 130 to 150 lb for both single and dual belts. If you do not have access to the manufacturer's specs, the tension gauge usually has information on it that shows typical recommended belt tension for various sizes. When a V-belt is used, the tension on a two-pulley drive system is usually less than that which would be recommended for a three-pulley drive system. Two- and three-pulley drive systems are shown in Fig. 8–123.

SERVICE NOTE: If a belt tension gauge is not available, adjust the belt tension so that a firm push with the thumb at a point midway between the two pulleys will depress the belt between $\frac{1}{2}$ and $\frac{3}{4}$ -in. (12.7 to 19 mm).

10. To obtain the correct belt tension, you can snug up the alternator retaining and adjustment bolts while main-

TABLE 8–6 Alternator selection guide questionnaire

1. Vehicle Manufacturer and Model Number...

2. Engine Option Manufacturer and Model Designation..

3. Crankshaft RPM At Engine Idle...

4. Crankshaft RPM At Top Engine Speed.......................................

5. Crankshaft RPM At Turnpike Driving Speeds Or At 65 MPH.......................................

6. Diameter Of Pulley On Engine Or Engine Accessory Which Drives Alternator...

7. Number of Belts...

8. Belt Size and Type (Example: 1/2" - V)..

9. Ratio -Drive Pulley RPM To Crankshaft RPM...

10. Maximum Electrical Load Which Can Be Simultaneously Connected During Night-Winter Driving

   Conditions...

11. Minimum Required Charging System Voltage After Cable Losses At:

   A. Battery Terminals...

   B. Electrical Load Accessories Or Vehicle Bus Bar...

   C. Cranking Motor...

12. Maximum Permissible Charging System Voltages After Cable Losses At:

   A. Battery Terminals...

   B. Electrical Load Accessories Or Vehicle Bus Bar...

   C. Cranking Motor...

13. Maximum Ambient Temperatures Anticipated In Engine Compartment At Alternator Location...................

14. Battery Installation:

   Number of Batteries...............BCI Group...............CCA/each..............Reserve Cap/each..............

   No. of Plates/each...............Type (Circle One)..........Maint. Free..........Lead-Antimon..........Hybrid.

15. Battery Connection Layout. *Attach Schematic of Battery Installation Wiring*

Remarks...

....

Company Name..

Your Name...Title.......................................

Mail Address or P. O. Box...

City...State or Province...Zip..................................

Country...................................Telephone No..

Form Q1000.1189 Printed in the *U.S.A.*

Source: Electrodyne Division of Gauss Corporation, Scarborough, ME.

occurs is dependent on the ratio between the alternator and engine drive pulley diameters. As an example, if we consider the output curve for an Electrodyne model E-80LC alternator as being rated for 80 A at 3000 rpm, assume the Cummins 14-L engine mentioned in our earlier discussion to be idling at 650 rpm. At this speed, with a recommended alternator pulley drive ratio of 2.85:1 as in Table 8–7, the alternator is turning at approximately 1850 rpm. At this speed the model E-80LC alternator will be producing about 67 to 68 A. This amperage is typical of the electrical system load requirements that would occur on a heavy-duty truck operating at night during winter conditions of snow and ice. With all of the vehicle lights in operation, plus the heater/defrost blowers, and a

TABLE 8–7 Alternator selection guide for a 12-V system

ENGINE OPTION: <u>CUMMINS N SERIES</u>

IDLE RPM: 650
ENGINE DRIVE PULLEY DIAM: 10.2"
MAXIMUM RPM: 2100
MAXIMUM BSFM: 5234

LOAD	40				50				60				70				80			
ALT. MODEL	RPM ALT. IDLE	BELT RATIO	*ALT. PULLEY DIAM.	RPM ALT. MAX.	RPM ALT. IDLE	BELT RATIO	*ALT. PULLEY DIAM.	RPM ALT. MAX.	RPM ALT. IDLE	BELT RATIO	*ALT. PULLEY DIAM.	RPM ALT. MAX.	RPM ALT. IDLE	BELT RATIO	*ALT. PULLEY DIAM.	RPM ALT. MAX.	RPM ALT. IDLE	BELT RATIO	*ALT. PULLEY DIAM.	RPM ALT. MAX.
E80S	1620	2.49	4.09	5234	1725	2.65	3.85	5573	1900	2.92	3.49	6138								
E90S	1620	2.49	4.09	5234	1725	2.65	3.85	5573	1900	2.92	3.49	6138								
E100S	1620	2.49	4.09	5234	1725	2.65	3.85	5573	1900	2.92	3.49	6138								
E80									1575	2.42	4.21	5088	1925	2.96	3.44	6219				
E80LC													1850	2.85	3.58	5977				
E105													1625	2.50	4.06	5250	1825	2.81	3.63	5896

DIRECTIONS:

1. SELECT SHEET CORRESPONDING TO ENGINE OPTION.

2. DETERMINE NIGHT-WINTER DRIVING CONDITION ELECTRICAL LOAD.

3. SELECT THAT LOAD FROM COLUMN HEADER WHICH IS EQUAL TO OR NEXT LARGER THAN DETERMINED NIGHT-WINTER DRIVING CONDITION LOAD.

4. FROM THE SETS OF DATA WHICH CORRESPOND TO THE DETERMINED LOAD, SELECT A SINGLE SET OF ALTERNATOR ROTATIVE SPEED, PULLEY DIAMETER AND BELT RATIO CONSISTENT WITH FLEET STANDARDS.

5. SELECT THE ALTERNATOR MODEL WHICH CORRESPONDS TO SELECTIONS MADE IN STEP #4. MORE THAN ONE ALTERNATOR SELECTION MAY BE INDICATED AS ACCEPTABLE.

6. THE ALTERNATOR SO SELECTED SHOULD BE CAPABLE OF SUPPLYING AT LEAST NIGHT-WINTER DRIVING CONDITIONS ELECTRICAL LOAD OVER THE ENTIRE OPERATING RANGE OF THE VEHICLE.

* SELECT NEAREST STANDARD DIAMETERS.

Source: Electrodyne Division of Gauss Corporation, Scarborough, ME.

80 - 350 AMPS   12V. - 64V. DC

500,000 Mile - 5,000 Hour Capability

FIGURE 8–124 Features of an Electrodyne heavy-duty brushless alternator. (*Courtesy of Electrodyne, Gauss Corporation, Scarborough, ME.*)

radio/tape deck/CD system in operation, and the truck moving slowly in traffic or at a standstill for a good portion of the driving cycle, the alternator *must* be capable of supplying the necessary output to the batteries. Also keep in mind that at lower ambient temperatures the batteries will not accept a charge as readily as they will during warmer weather operation.

Table 3–6 and Fig. 3–31 list the decrease in battery power as the ambient temperature is lowered. For example, the battery power at 32°F (0°C) is only 65% of what it is at 80°F (27°C). Under such conditions if your alternator charging system is unable to handle the electrical load requirements of the system, the batteries will be forced to supply the difference in current demand, resulting in a continuous low state of battery charge. With the vehicle operating at or near idle for extended periods, the alternator may not be capable of supplying the electrical load demands of the system. This condition becomes even worse if the selection of the alternator drive pulley is such (too large) that the drive ratio speed is too low to allow adequate alternator output. Continued low-idle operating conditions force the batteries to supply the current demands of the electrical system. As the battery voltage begins to drop under such an operating environment, few people realize that the alternator voltage will also drop off, since truck alternators usually rely upon a source voltage from the vehicle batteries for field excitation. The actual discharge rate of the battery (batteries) is proportional to the amperes which are being drawn from them. Obviously using higher rated CCA batteries, plus a multiple battery hookup, will lengthen this discharge time.

The voltage at the alternator will equal the voltage at the battery because electrically these two points are the same and therefore have the same electrical potential. Note, however, that Electrodyne offers alternators for battery-less installations whose fields are energized by methods (a) and (b) below. These models can also see excessively low voltages across the buss-bars of the system and thereby incur abuse even though their fields are energized (a) by batteries not connected to the alternator output circuit or (b) by the use of permanent magnets. When a battery is used, if its voltage supply becomes low enough, then there is a distinct danger that the solid state voltage regulator within the alternator end frame assembly will not operate correctly, since the voltage regulator requires a voltage equal to alternator full-load voltage in order to trigger the regulating mechanism. At any voltage less than full voltage, the regulator will stop switching and it will revert to a nonswitching mode even though it may be operating correctly otherwise. Since the function of the voltage regulator is to act as a high-speed switching device for the field coil circuit, low battery voltage can result in the voltage regulator failing to trigger the switching mechanism to the field coil circuit. This can result in a continuous field coil current output that will flow uninterrupted, causing a dramatic increase in the operating temperature of the various alternator internal components. The end result is that damage can occur to diodes, IC chips, power transistors, and even field windings. Keep in mind that it is not the fact that voltage regulator switching may or may not occur that damages well designed voltage regulators. The damage is caused by excessive heat generated within the windings and the rectifier diodes of the alternator which is then transferred by conduction and radiation to the body of the voltage regulator, which is mounted integrally with, and in close proximity to, the windings and rectifier diodes within the alternator housing. The transfer of this heat to the solid-state electronic components of the voltage regulator is what causes the damage. Therefore for severe service operation, a remote-mounted voltage regulator is recommended.

The use of an oscilloscope pattern which actually portrays the switching pattern of the voltage regulator is suggested, since this analysis will indicate the heating portion of the cycle during which electrical output flows in the alternator windings, and the cooling portion during which electrical output does not flow. A profile of the electrical load demand is helpful prior to selecting a suitable alternator and voltage regulator, since the duration of the heating portion of the cycle will be directly affected by the application and the operational cycle. Each particular fleet encounters specific operational cycles. Therefore the proper alternator and voltage regulator combination can then be safely selected to minimize possible equipment failure and unnecessary vehicle downtime.

Once the vehicle is on the open road, there will be

a sudden increase in the speed of rotation of the engine and alternator assembly. You may now assume that at this elevated speed the alternator is now capable of restoring the electrical charging system to a suitable state. However, the alternator must now handle not only the system electrical loads, but is also required to recharge the batteries, which are now in a low state-of-charge condition. Load demands under such a condition can force the alternator to attempt to supply almost twice the normal system loads. Since it will take some time to bring the battery voltage back up to a suitable state of charge, low voltage will continue to feed to the alternator field-coil assembly, and the voltage regulator will remain in a nonswitching mode. This means that unchecked output from the alternator as it attempts to restore the batteries to a suitable state of charge will keep the operating temperature of the internal components at an elevated point. This condition will remain as long as the batteries are in a low state of charge. The problem becomes worse as the temperature remains high, since the wiring that carries the electricity will exhibit a high resistance when it becomes hot, which adds to the problem of the alternator as it attempts to create sufficient current/voltage output to the batteries. Therefore, since all alternators are designed to supply their rated amperage output at speeds well beyond engine idle rpm, an alternator that is capable of producing electrical output adequate to meet the demands of the truck electrical system can do much to prevent undercharged batteries when the operating conditions are similar to those described above. Using an alternator selection guide such as illustrated in Table 8-7 is one example of how to properly select an alternator and fully size so as to alleviate this problem. Keep in mind also that simply installing a larger output alternator may or may not correct the problem, since all alternators are designed to produce their rated output at speeds higher than that encountered at engine idle rpm. The key is to select an alternator that will produce electrical output adequate to supply to the electrical loads experienced in your particular fleet operating environment.

QUESTIONS

8-1. The word *alternator* is derived from the fact that the electrical current produced within motor windings is ac (alternating current). *True* or *False* (see page 233)

8-2. On a separate piece of paper, write down as many advantages as you can for an alternator over a dc generator. (see page 234)

8-3. The two major components of an alternator or ac generator are:
   a. The rotor and the rectifying diodes
   b. The stator and the rotor assembly
   c. The rotor and drive pulley
   d. The stator and the diode trio
   (see page 236)

8-4. Battery current on brush-type ac generators is supplied to the field winding by:
   a. A conventional transistor
   b. A zener diode
   c. A slip ring
   d. A voltage regulator
   (see page 236)

8-5. The stator windings within a alternator are generally wired to produce:
   a. Single-phase power
   b. Two-phase power
   c. Three-phase power
   d. Quadruple-phase power
   (see pages 236, 240)

8-6. Technician A says that ac generators are said to be externally excited in order to initiate the production of electricity when the ignition key is switched on and the engine is first cranked over. Technician B disagrees, saying that the alternator is internally excited. Who is correct? (see page 236)

8-7. Technician A says that the stator frame is generally made from a solid iron core. Technician B says that a laminated iron core is used for better performance. Who is right? (see page 236)

8-8. Technician A says that the alternator rotor consists of a series of iron interlacing fingers of opposite polarity. Technician B says that the rotor is made up of one north and one south pole. Who is correct? (see page 236)

8-9. In alternating current, amperes flow in one direction and then in the other within the stator windings, to complete one cycle. *True* or *False* (see page 239)

8-10. Commonly employed stator windings use:
   a. A single winding
   b. Two windings
   c. Three windings
   d. Six windings
   (see page 240)

8-11. Alternating current within stator windings is normally rectified by the use of:
   a. Two diodes
   b. Three diodes
   c. Four diodes
   d. Six diodes
   (see page 243)

8-12. Voltage at the alternator/generator BAT output terminal is dc. *True* or *False* (see page 238)

8-13. Generator output is controlled by a voltage regulator, which actually adjusts:
   a. The field current
   b. The field voltage
   c. The field resistance
   d. The rotational speed of the alternator
   (see pages 236, 238)

8-14. The electrical flow within the stator windings is induced by:
   a. Current flow
   b. Voltage
   c. Circuit resistance
   d. Strength of the magnetic field
   (see page 236)

8-15. Technician A says that the basic difference between a dc generator and an ac generator/alternator is that the magnets are stationary in a dc generator, whereas they rotate in an ac unit. Technician B says that it is the opposite way around. Who is correct? (see page 239)

8-16. Technician A says that magnetic lines of force tend to flow from the north to the south poles. Technician B says that they flow from south to north. Who knows their basic fundamentals best? (see page 239)

8-17. A single sine wave is simply a graphical representation of one cycle of operation of generated current/voltage within an ac generator. *True* or *False* (see page 240)

8-18. Technician A says that the generator drive pulley diameter has no effect on its rated output. Technician B disagrees, saying that this can have a dramatic effect on the generators output capacity. Who is correct? (see page 240)

8-19. The generator windings are:
  a. 90° apart in phase relationship
  b. 120° apart in phase relationship
  c. 270° apart in phase relationship
  d. 360° apart in phase relationship
  (see page 240)

8-20. The actual dimension of the air gap that exists between the rotor finger magnets and the stator windings will affect generator output? *True* or *False* (see page 242)

8-21. Supply the missing words in the following statement. The two commonly used types of alternator stator windings are the _DELTA_ and the _WYE, STAR_ connection. (see page 243)

8-22. Which of the two stator windings listed in your answer to Question 8–21 is most commonly used in car and truck alternators? (see page 243) _DELTA_

8-23. Technician A says that if the battery cables are connected in a reverse polarity hookup, the alternator diodes can be damaged unless a reverse polarity diode fuse is employed. Technician B says that this will simply result in no generator output with no diode damage or no generator output due to a blown fuse. Which technician knows his basics better? (see page 244)

8-24. In a Delco generator, the letters SI stand for "systems integral." *True* or *False* (see page 245)

8-25. In a Delco generator the letters CS stand for "charging system." *True* or *False* (see page 246)

8-26. Technician A says that in a model CS Delco generator there is no need for a diode-trio since a digital regulator and passivated chips are used in place of button diodes. Technician B says that a diode trio must be used to rectify the current from ac to dc. Which technician is up to date on his knowledge? (see page 246)

8-27. Supply the missing words from the following statement. The two most widely used types of alternators are the _Slip Ring & Brush_ type and the _Brushless_ type. (see page 245)

8-28. Technician A says that numbers, such as 130, appearing after the letters CS in a Delco generator indicate the diameter of the alternator in centimeters. Technician B disagrees, saying that the number is in millimeters. Who knows his metric conversion theory better? (see page 246)

8-29. A small black triangle in a generator wiring circuit indicates:
  a. A transistor   c. A resistor
  b. A diode   d. A capacitor
  (see page 247)

8-30. Technician A says that the return circuit to the battery in a brush-type generator is normally via a slip ring and brush. Technician B says that the return circuit is via the large battery ground cable to the vehicle frame. Who is correct? (see pages 237–238)

8-31. The purpose of a capacitor or condensor mounted in the generator end frame acts to protect:
  a. The rectifier bridge   c. The radio noise

  b. The diode trio when   interference
     used   d. All of the above
     (see page 236)

8-32. The individual stator leads are connected to:
  a. One diode each   c. Three diodes each
  b. Two diodes each   d. Six diodes each
  (see page 238)

8-33. Technician A says that in a delta-wound stator, the windings are not connected in pairs but act independently, although they are producing voltage/current flow at 120° intervals. Technician B says that the stator windings operate in pairs, so that the output voltage is the total voltage between one stator winding lead and another. Which technician is correct? (see page 243)

8-34. Technician A says that the rotor field current supply on Delco model truck generators is normally between 3.6 and 7.1 A, depending on the type and model of generator being used. Technician B says that all generators require at least 5 A of field current to operate. Who is correct? (see page 248)

8-35. The major difference between a Delco type 100 and 200 generator is in:
  a. The generator output
  b. The size of the bearings used to support the rotor
  c. The fact that one is a brush type and the other is brushless
  d. One type uses a warning light and the other does not
  (see page 249)

8-36. On a Delco type 200 generator, if the number 1 and 2 terminal connector and wires are taped back on the wiring harness:
  a. The output current has been reduced
  b. The system is operating on half of normal voltage
  c. This model is self-energizing
  d. The voltage regulator is nonadjustable
  (see page 249)

8-37. Technician A says that if the taped-back wires in question 8-36 were connected to a Delco model 27SI type 200 generator by mistake, the output current would be reduced by half. Technician B says that this action would result in possible damage to the voltage regulator and subsequent battery discharge. Which technician has better knowledge of the product? (see page 250)

8-38. Delco CS model generators use a diode trio to rectify ac to dc. *True* or *False* (see page 250)

8-39. On Delco CS model generators the field current is regulated by:
  a. A diode trio
  b. A PWM (pulse-width-modulated) signal from the digital regulator
  c. Generator speed and drive ratio
  d. Battery voltage
  (see page 250)

8-40. The regulator on Delco CS generators switches the field current on and off at a rate of approximately:
  a. 90 cycles/second   c. 325 cycles/second
  b. 200 cycles/second   d. 400 cycles/second
  (see page 252)

8-41. A commonly employed method used to protect the generator system against high voltage in the stator is to use:
  a. A number of zener diodes within the rectifier bridge

b. A number of transistors within the diode trio

c. A number of resistors within the diode trio or rectifier bridge

d. A number of capacitors within the rectifier bridge
(see page 253)

8-42. Some vehicle manufacturers who use Delco generators connect their engine tachometer to the generator:

a. S terminal   c. F terminal

b. L terminal   d. P terminal
(see page 253)

8-43. Technician A says that the term *forward biased* implies that a diode will not conduct any current. Technician B says that when a diode will not conduct current it is *reverse biased*. Which technician knows basic electronics theory better? (see page 254)

8-44. Technician A says that in temperature-compensated voltage regulators, that voltage will decrease with an increase in temperature, and will increase with a decrease in temperature. Technician B disagrees, saying that it would be exactly opposite. Who is correct? (see page 255)

8-45. A brushless-type generator uses a rotor with permanent magnetism. *True* or *False* (see page 256)

8-46. A transformer-rectifier (TR) generator is generally used on trucks that require:

a. Half-system voltage rectification

b. The use of 24-V cranking and 12-V charging

c. The use of four 6-V batteries

d. The use of two 12-V batteries in parallel hookup
(see pages 256, 259)

8-47. Many current-model generators are not equipped with any means of voltage regulator adjustment since they are factory set. On those models with a means of voltage adjustment, you usually have to:

a. Remove the external voltage regulator and replace it with a new one

b. Remove the generator end plate on many current-model generators to gain access to the potentiometer screw

c. Change the diameter of the drive pulley to alter the drive ratio

d. Use a larger-rated generator assembly
(see page 257)

8-48. Technician A says that you should never disconnect the batteries while the engine and alternator are operating, since this can lead to diode damage. Technician B says that this will simply allow you to determine if the alternator is in fact producing enough current flow to keep the engine running. Who is correct? (see page 261)

8-49. Technician A says that it is not necessary to use a ground strap on an insulated starter motor. Technician B says that failure to use a ground strap correctly installed can result in faulty generator operation. Which technician is correct? (see page 261)

8-50. Grounding of the generator field circuit can result in:

a. Reduced generator output

b. Increased generator output

c. Diode burnout

d. Resistor damage
(see page 261)

8-51. Technician A says that prior to welding on a vehicle, always disconnect the battery cables and isolate the generator. Technician B says that this is not necessary

since the reverse polarity diode fuse will protect the generator components. Who is right? (see page 261)

8-52. Technician A says that you should never attempt to polarize an ac generator. Technician B says that normally this is so; however, in some instances where residual magnetism has been lost due to generator overhaul or it has been inactive for some time, polarizing the generator according to the manufacturer's procedure is acceptable. Which technician knows his systems better? (see page 261)

8-53. The letters VAT stand for:

a. Volts/amps/tester

b. Voltage and time tester

c. Variable amperage tester

d. Variable alternator tester
(see page 262)

8-54. A carbon pile tester is used to:

a. Apply a fixed load to a vehicle's batteries

b. Apply a variable load as desired to the batteries

c. Apply a fixed or variable load to the battery/generator system

d. All of the above
(see page 262)

8-55. The most important precaution prior to hooking up a carbon pile tester is to ensure that:

a. The carbon pile control knob is in the OFF position

b. The carbon pile control knob is in the ON position

c. The ignition switch is OFF

d. The ignition switch is ON
(see page 265)

8-56. Generally, if the voltage output from the generator rises quickly above 15.5 V on a 12-V system without showing signs of change during an output test, this would require you to:

a. Replace the nonadjustable type of voltage regulator

b. Adjust the voltage regulator with an adjustment screw

c. Check the generator field winding

d. All of the above
(see page 268)

8-57. Rotor field current draw on Leece-Neville heavy-duty generators should be a minimum of 5 A. *True* or *False* (see page 274)

8-58. Technician A says that when performing a generator test stand output check, you should always run the test stand to produce a generator drive speed of 3600 rpm. Technician B says that each generator must be run up to a specific speed as recommended by the manufacturer. Who is correct? (see pages 270, 275, 278, 287)

8-59. Supply the two missing words in the following statement: A generator isolation diode electronically operates a charge indicator lamp by being wired in _____ with the alternator output, so that the lamp is electrically connected across the _____ .

8-60. A strong acid odor from a disassembled alternator is usually indicative of:

a. Overheating and/or insulation damage

b. A high dust/dirt buildup within a high-mileage generator

c. The fact that the rotor support bearing lubricant has run dry

d. A slipping drive belt
(see page 301)

8-61. When checking a generator rotor for serviceability, you should conduct both:

a. A current and voltage output check
b. A resistance and short-circuit check
c. A current and resistance check
d. A voltage and short-circuit check
   (see page 301)

8-62. When performing a Delco generator output test, to ground the field, you can:
   a. Directly ground the R terminal from the generator
   b. Insert a small screwdriver into the hole at the rear of the generator and depress the small internal tab
   c. Use a ¼-Ω resistor connected to the field terminal connection and ground the wire
   d. All of the above
      (see page 268)

8-63. On a Delco generator stator test check, technician A says that the ohmmeter connections are different for a delta than for a wye-wound stator. Technician B says that they are exactly the same. Who is correct? (see page 302)

8-64. Technician A says that delta-wound stators can be checked for both opens and grounds. Technician B says that a delta-wound stator can only be checked for grounds. Who is correct? (see page 302)

8-65. Generally, when checking stators with an ohmmeter, it is recommended that you use a digital ohmmeter capable of reading to:
   a. 1/10 of an ohm   c. 1/1000 of an ohm
   b. 1/100 of an ohm   d. 1/10,000 of an ohm
      (see page 304)

8-66. Technician A says that using a 110-V test lamp can result in alternator diode damage. Technician B says that is not so, that you can safely use a 120-V test lamp on diodes. Who is right? (see page 304)

8-67. When checking a diode trio with an ohmmeter, you should ensure that the battery voltage does not exceed the manufacturer's specifications. This voltage is generally:
   a. 0.5 V   c. 1.5 V
   b. 1.0 V   d. 9 V
      (see page 305)

8-68. Technician A says that a good diode should exhibit one high and one low ohmmeter reading value as the leads are switched during testing. Technician B says that both readings should be the same to show equal continuity through the diode. Who understands the basic makeup of a diode better? (see page 306)

8-69. Technician A says that diodes that do not pass current in either direction are shorted. Technician B says that this would indicate an open. Who is correct? (see pages 305 and 306)

8-70. Technician A says that diodes that pass current in both directions are open. Technician B says that this would indicate a shorted diode condition. Who is correct? (see page 305)

8-71. Technician A says that if a shorted or open diode is found in a generator rectifier bridge heat sink, you should replace the heat sink. Technician B says that it is only necessary to replace the individual diode. Who is correct? (see page 307)

8-72. Generator capacitor values are generally in the range:
   a. 0.5 μF (microfarads) and up to 200 V
   b. 1.0 μF and up to 200 V
   c. 0.5 μF and up to 16 V
   d. 1.0 μF and up to 16 V
      (see page 307)

8-73. When checking a generator diode for resistance, the measured value for a good unit will generally register between:
   a. 5 and 10 Ω   c. 5 and 40 Ω
   b. 5 and 25 Ω   d. 5 and 50 Ω
      (see page 309)

8-74. Technician A says that when adjusting a generator drive belt(s), a belt tension gauge should always be used. Technician B says that ½ in. of free play is an acceptable industry level. Who is correct? (see page 310)

8-75. Technician A says that a high-pitched squeal from a generator drive belt is an indication of a belt adjusted too tight. Technician B says that this would indicate a belt adjusted too loosely. Who is correct? (see page 310)

8-76. Multiple drive belt sets should always be replaced as a complete set regardless of the condition of each. *True* or *False* (see page 310)

8-77. Technician A says that if a vehicle is to be placed into storage for an extended period of time, drive belt tension should be removed by slackening off the adjustment bracket; otherwise, lumpy belts can occur, leading to possible vibration when the equipment is restarted. Technician B says that this is not necessary since drive belts are designed to be placed under tension anyway. Who is right? (see page 311)

8-78. Technician A says that drive belts that show signs of worn sides indicate too tight a belt adjustment. Technician B says that it is more liable to be caused by pulley misalignment. Who is correct? (see page 311)

8-79. Technician A says that generator belt pulley bolts should always be loosened prior to installing new belts. Technician B says that the belt can simply be rolled over the pulley and into position by cranking the engine over. Who knows the correct procedure? (see page 313)

CHAPTER
9
Electric Starting Motors

OBJECTIVES

In this chapter we deal with the various types of electric starter motors commonly found on both midrange and heavy-duty trucks. Specifically, you will acquire or review the skills needed to:

1. Identify the starter motor and its location on the engine. *Flywheel*
2. Describe the function and operation of an electric starter motor assembly. *To Turn OVER fast enough for combustion*
3. Identify and describe the various types of starter motors.
4. Identify and describe the various types of starter motor pinion drives.
5. Describe the operation of and trace the starter motor switch control circuitry.
6. Describe the function and operation of a series–parallel starter motor switch circuit.
7. Describe how to perform a system check of a faulty series–parallel starter motor switch circuit.
8. Describe the function and operation of a TR

(transformer-rectifier) starter motor circuit, checks, and tests.
9. Describe how a starter motor overcrank protection device operates.
10. Perform an on-vehicle starter motor diagnostic check.
11. Perform an off-vehicle starter motor diagnostic (bench) check.
12. Determine what-size starter motor cable to use. Know how to fabricate a set of starter motor cables.
13. Disassemble, overhaul, and repair a starter motor assembly.
14. Perform troubleshooting, analysis, and repair of a typical starter motor system and electrical circuit faults.

INTRODUCTION

The function and purpose of any starter motor assembly is, of course, to crank the engine over at a high enough speed to initiate combustion within the engine cylinders so that the engine will run. This is achieved by using battery power to rotate the starter motor (armature), which in turn spins a pinion (small gear). This gear engages with the engine flywheel ring gear teeth to rotate the engine

over for starting purposes. Starter motors found on midrange and heavy-duty trucks vary in physical size and design, although their principle of operation is the same. Each model of starter motor is rated for a specific output, which is generally listed in the manufacturer's test specifications as being in either kW (kilowatt) or hp (horsepower). Higher-output starter motors are generally applied to diesel engines because of the fact that the diesel engine has a much higher compression ratio than a gasoline engine. Consequently, the diesel starter motor is physically larger and produces more output energy than that found in gasoline engines.

Gasoline engines usually require a simple 12-V battery system for operation, while midrange and heavy-duty truck diesel engines can operate on either a 12-V parallel-connected battery system, or alternatively, a 12/24-V system that requires a series–parallel switch mechanism to provide 24-V starting and 12-V charging. On special applications, some heavy-duty trucks and bus/coach installations use batteries connected in series to supply 24 V to the starter motor, along with a 24-V alternator charging system. When 24 V is used, all electrical components, such as lighting, operate on 24 V. Although not common, some off-highway diesel-powered equipment employs up to a 32-V electrical system. Two basic types of starter motors are used on trucks and buses:

1. The direct-drive starter, which does not use any gear reduction within its body to reduce the speed of rotation of the starter motor armature and pinion (small gear), which engages with the engine flywheel ring gear for rotation purposes.

2. The gear reduction type of starter motor, which uses a gear reduction within the motor body to reduce the speed of the cranking pinion when meshed with the flywheel ring gear. This speed reduction allows an increase in starting torque.

Major manufacturers of starter motors include such well-known names as:

- Delco-Remy Division of General Motors Corporation
- Robert Bosch Corporation
- Nippondenso of Japan
- Leece-Neville (Prestolite Electric, Inc.)
- Lucas Industries (CAV)
- Prestolite Electric, Inc.

The starter motor must develop a high cranking torque (twisting or turning force) for a limited period of time when the starting switch is closed. It must include a means of engaging the pinion drive with the flywheel ring gear on the engine, and of disengaging the pinion as soon as the engine starts to prevent overspeeding of the starter armature, which would cause serious damage. Various types of starter motor drive engagement systems are used with different makes of starter motors, and these are discussed in this chapter in detail. These drives are designed to allow automatic starter drive gear disengagement once the engine starts, to prevent any possibility of starter motor damage.

In addition, most starter motors found on heavy-duty diesel engines are designed so that the nose cone housing can be unbolted and rotated to different positions to allow flexibility of mounting on different models of engines. This is also shown and discussed in this chapter. The majority of starter motors used on midrange and heavy-duty truck diesel engines manufactured by Caterpillar, Cummins, Detroit Diesel Corporation, and Mack are supplied by the Delco-Remy Division of GMC. This manufacturer also supplies most of the starter motors found on gasoline-powered North American–produced trucks. With the fairly recent manufacturing agreements between various truck marques, many imported midrange diesel-powered trucks can be fitted with starter motors supplied by either Robert Bosch (Germany) or by Nippondenso in Japan. We will concentrate on the design, operation, overhaul, and testing of Delco-Remy starter motors; however, we will also discuss and show Robert Bosch, Nippondenso, Prestolite, and Leece-Neville systems.

BASIC MOTOR OPERATION

An understanding of starter motor operation involves a recall of information discussed in detail in Chapter 1 and Chapter 3. Since the starter motor relies on battery power and a magnetic field to operate, if you require further clarification of these two main principles, refer back to Chapters 1 and 3.

A typical simplified schematic of an electric starter motor system is illustrated in Fig. 9–1. The following operating description is simply to give you a quick mental picture of the general layout of the cranking system. A detailed description of operation is included in the following pages. In this diagram we can see the power source (battery), an ignition key switch to carry the small current required to activate the solenoid switch, and the switch that carries the heavy CCA (cold cranking amperes) battery current necessary to rotate the starter motor armature assembly within the motor body. Once the starter armature is rotated by an offset magnetic field, the small pinion (gear) is forced into engagement with the engine flywheel ring gear to cause engine crankshaft rotation.

NOTE: The starter can be engaged through either a key-type switch, as shown in Fig. 9–1, or it may be a separate magnetic switch that can only be energized by turning on the ignition key. On diesel systems, one or more switch

FIGURE 9–1 Simplified starter motor cranking circuit. *(Courtesy of GMC Truck Division, General Motors Corporation.)*

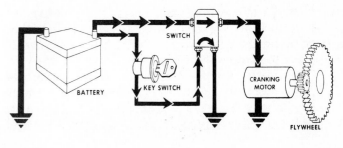

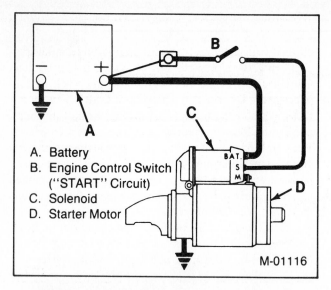

FIGURE 9–2 Cranking circuit for a gasoline engine with a manual transmission. *(Courtesy of GMC Truck Division, General Motors Corporation.)*

A. Battery
B. Engine Control Switch ("START" Circuit)
C. Solenoid
D. Starter Motor

M-01116

midrange trucks. Usually, this switch is clutch pedal–mounted on gear shift transmissions; therefore, the driver must depress the clutch pedal to complete the starter circuit. This feature ensures that the engine can only be started in the neutral position on an automatic transmission. On gear shift transmissions, the clutch depression disengages the clutch to decrease the load on the starter during cranking. Specific starter motor circuit wiring diagrams are shown in Figs. 9–2 through 9–6 for various types of systems on both gasoline and diesel engines used in both midrange and heavy-duty diesel truck applications.

Study these wiring arrangements closely so that you are familiar with the minor differences that exist between them. In each schematic you will notice that the battery power is supplied from either one battery or two; however you will recall from our earlier discussion on batteries that as many as four batteries can be used to supply the system power requirements. The most popular heavy-duty truck system is one in which four model 31, 12-V batteries are used. For recall purposes, various battery hookup systems are shown in Figs. 3–11, 3–12, 3–13, and 3–36. All of the starter motor wiring circuits shown are for systems that employ enclosed shift lever starter motors whereby the shift lever mechanism and the starter motor

relays are generally used to carry the heavy current to the starter motor solenoid and armature assembly.

Not shown in Fig. 9–1 is the use of a neutral safety switch which can be used on vehicles with automatic transmissions or on gear shift transmissions in light and

FIGURE 9–3 Cranking circuit for a gasoline engine with an automatic transmission. *(Courtesy of GMC Truck Division, General Motors Corporation.)*

FIGURE 9–4 Starter diagram, midrange diesel truck with two-battery parallel hookup system. *(Courtesy of GMC Truck Division, General Motors Corporation.)*

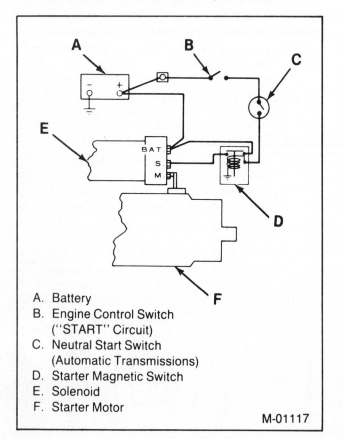

A. Battery
B. Engine Control Switch ("START" Circuit)
C. Neutral Start Switch (Automatic Transmissions)
D. Starter Magnetic Switch
E. Solenoid
F. Starter Motor

M-01117

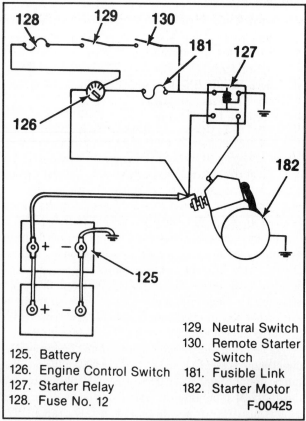

125. Battery
126. Engine Control Switch
127. Starter Relay
128. Fuse No. 12
129. Neutral Switch
130. Remote Starter Switch
181. Fusible Link
182. Starter Motor

F-00425

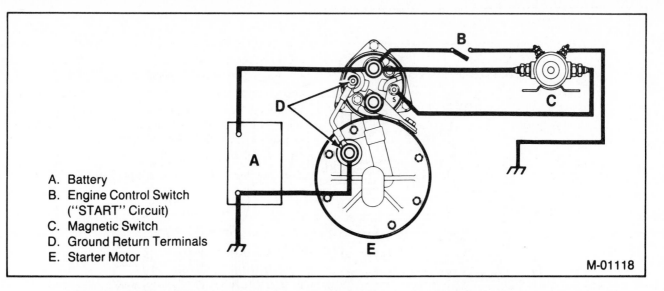

A. Battery
B. Engine Control Switch ("START" Circuit)
C. Magnetic Switch
D. Ground Return Terminals
E. Starter Motor

M-01118

FIGURE 9–5 Medium heavy-duty diesel truck 12-V starting system. *(Courtesy of GMC Truck Division; General Motors Corporation.)*

solenoid plunger are contained within the sealed drive housing, for protection against the environmental operating conditions. In these various systems the starter motor is energized when the starter switch is turned to the START position. On vehicles so equipped the neutral start switch ensures that the transmission must be in neutral on an automatic model, or the clutch pedal must

FIGURE 9–6 Heavy-duty diesel truck engine 12-V starting system wiring circuit. *(Courtesy of GMC Truck Division, General Motors Corporation.)*

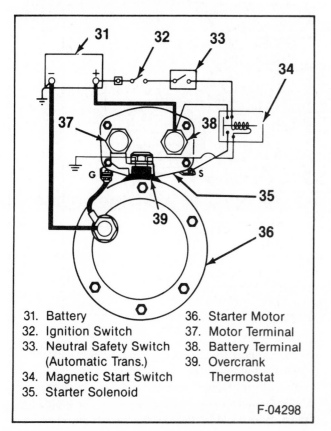

31. Battery
32. Ignition Switch
33. Neutral Safety Switch (Automatic Trans.)
34. Magnetic Start Switch
35. Starter Solenoid
36. Starter Motor
37. Motor Terminal
38. Battery Terminal
39. Overcrank Thermostat

F-04298

be held down on a gear shift model. The solenoid plunger and the attached shift lever mechanism will push the pinion into engagement with the engine flywheel ring gear, and the solenoid main contacts will remain closed to allow battery power to continue to spin the starter motor armature. Once the enginer starts, the pinion is protected from overspeed by the use of an overrunning clutch drive mechanism. When the driver of the truck releases the starter control switch (either key type or pushbutton) to the run position, an internal return spring positively allows the drive pinion (gear) to disengage with the flywheel ring gear. Obviously, it is important that the driver release the starter switch as soon as the engine starts to prevent overrun, regardless of the type of starter pinion drive mechanism in use.

STARTER DESIGNS: MAIN COMPONENTS

Prior to describing the starter motor operation in detail, it would be advantageous if we were to illustrate several typical models in wide use on mid- and heavy-duty trucks. The location of the various motor components will allow you to picture the function of each unit as we explain the individual steps involved in causing the starter to rotate the engine. The design of the starter motor follows a similar pattern regardless of the actual make. Minor variations exist between types, with the major differences being in the physical size, the type of pinion (gear) drive used, the solenoid and switch type used, and whether the starter motor is a straight-through drive or employs a gear reduction system for increased torque characteristics.

Throughout this chapter we show various types of starter motor designs; therefore, to allow you to key-in on the major components that function together to create the motor action, Figs. 9–7 and 9–8 illustrate two typical starter motors that you will be exposed to when servicing midrange, medium-heavy, and heavy-duty trucks. Figure 9–7 illustrates an external view of a typical en-

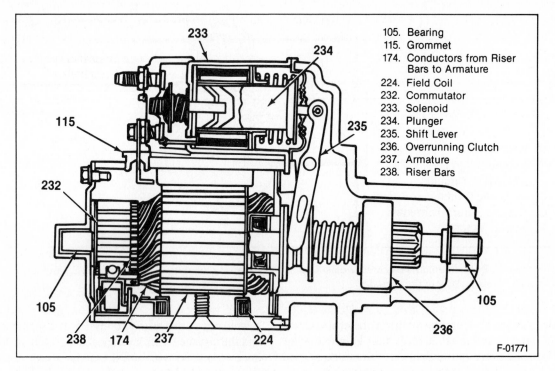

FIGURE 9–7 Cross-sectional view of the features of a Delco 10MT starting motor. *(Courtesy of GMC Truck Division, General Motors Corporation.)*

FIGURE 9–8 Cross-sectional view of a 42MT model heavy-duty starting motor assembly. *(Courtesy of GMC Truck Division, General Motors Corporation.)*

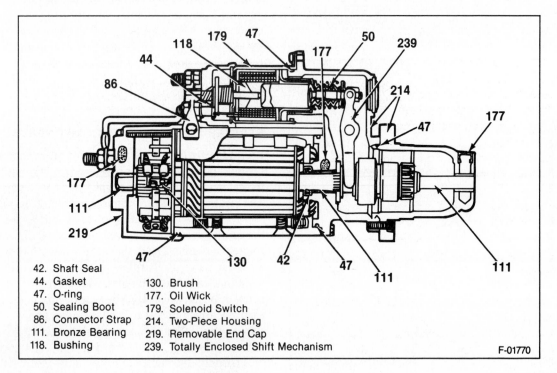

closed shift-type starter motor that would be found on gasoline engines used in medium-duty trucks. Note that the part number is normally stamped on the end frame. The diagram illustrates clearly the various components that are used within the starter motor assembly. This is an overrunning clutch type of starter design, with the actual drive end housing extended to enclose the shift lever and electric solenoid plunger assembly. Sealing compound is used between the solenoid flange and the motor field frame. Sealed and lubricated bearings are used to ensure long life between overhauls. The 10MT type 100 Delco starter shown in Fig. 9–7 is designed to rotate at a minimum no-load speed of 6500 rpm and a maximum speed of 10,700 rpm. Other Delco starter motors, including the 27MT model used with medium-duty diesel trucks (Mack Midliner) are similar in design and construction to the 10MT model shown. The major difference is that the armature and the pole shoes (magnets) are longer.

The main components of a starter motor assembly are:

- The frame and field assembly
- The armature
- The commutator end head
- The pinion housing
- The drive pinion (different types available and used)
- The intermediate housing assembly

Details on these components follow.

1. The frame or starter motor body physically supports the other component parts of the motor: the field coils, the brush holders and brushes, and the pole shoes (magnets). The field coils are wrapped around the pole shoes to provide the strong magnetic field necessary to produce torque, while the pole shoes (magnets) and frame provide the path for the magnetic field.

2. The motor armature consists of a laminated soft-iron core mounted on an armature shaft, a commutator, and the windings, which are wound in slots in the core and connected to the commutator. The commutator itself consists of a number of copper segments insulated from one another and from the armature shaft, which extends through the pinion housing and supports the pinion drive assembly.

3. The commutator end head supports a bearing in which the armature shaft rotates.

4. The pinion housing encloses the actual pinion drive mechanism and supports the other end bearing, in which the armature shaft rotates.

5. The drive pinion is shifted by an electric solenoid to engage the starter with the engine flywheel ring gear. The type of drive mechanism used with the pinion (small gear) on the end of the armature shaft, protects the pinion assembly from damage due to overspeed once the engine starts. However, the types of drive are discussed in more detail later.

6. The intermediate housing is that part of the starter motor assembly located between the main frame and the pinion housing.

It is found on heavy-duty starter motors such as shown in Fig. 9–8. This intermediate housing contains a bronze bearing that supports the center of the armature shaft, as well as containing the mechanism of the shift lever. Some intermediate housings are equipped with a solenoid access hole, providing a means for solenoid and drive timing adjustment, and solenoid removal for servicing. In addition, some units contain an oil reservoir to provide lubrication for the bronze center bearing, plus an oil seal to prevent any oil, water, or dirt from entering the motor.

Midrange, medium-heavy, and heavy-duty diesel-powered trucks can use Delco, Leece-Neville (Prestolite) Bosch, or Nippondenso starter motors in trucks sold in North America and overseas. Exploded views of the Bosch and Nippondenso starters are illustrated later in this chapter. Delco starter motors used in diesel-powered trucks can be model 37MT, 40MT, 42MT, or 50MT. The most popular unit now in use in medium-heavy and heavy-duty class 8 trucks is the 42MT model, which is illustrated in Fig. 9–8.

NOTE: In November 1986, Delco-Remy stopped producing the 40MT commercial starting motors and replaced them with 42MT motors, which provide extended service life.

The 40MT starter was used for many years and there are still a number of these units in fleet service. Figure 9–9 illustrates the difference in outward appearance between the 42MT, which has a die cast end cap to permit easier access to the brushes during servicing, whereas the 40MT starter had access holes with plugs in the side of the housing. In addition, the 42MT starter has a flange-

FIGURE 9–9 External features of a 40MT and 42MT Delco heavy-duty starting motor. (*Courtesy of Detroit Diesel Corporation.*)

FORMER 40 MT STARTING MOTOR

NEW 42 MT STARTING MOTOR

mounted solenoid with improved sealing features, while the 40MT starter used a bracket-mounted solenoid. The former 40MT and newer 42MT starter motors are completely interchangeable on an engine; however, only the 42MT unit is available for service.

There are four types of starter drive clutches used on the 37MT, 40MT, 42MT, and 50MT starting motors. These are a heavy-duty sprag overrunning clutch, a Positork drive, a seven-roll roller clutch, and an intermediate clutch which is a four-roll type. More information on starter drives can be found in the section "Starter Motor Pinion Engagement."

STARTER MOTOR OPERATION

Now that we are familiar with the major components of a starter motor assembly, let's look at the principles of its operation. This will involve some of the material from Chapter 1 dealing with basic electricity, which is reviewed in the following paragraphs.

The starter motor in its simplest form is shown in Fig. 9–1. The starting switch can be ignition key combined or may be a separate switch that can be energized only when the ignition key is turned on. Usually, one or more switch relays are also used which are required to carry the heavy current to the motor or solenoid.

From an earlier study of Figs. 9–7 and 9–8, you will have noticed that every starter motor contains pole shoes (magnets) bolted to the starter motor frame.

The armature consists of a series of copper wires wound around a soft-iron core. This assembly is then placed within the motor field frame so that it is surrounded by these field poles, or magnets. The number of magnets will vary in the various starter motor sizes and models. In addition, the physical diameter of starters becomes larger as the cranking requirements increase, in order to produce more torque. To simplify the description of the rotation of the starter motor armature and pinion, let's use a simple two-pole or two-magnet unit, consisting of one north pole and one south pole, as shown in Fig. 9–10.

From our earlier discussion of basic electrical fundamentals, you will recall that when current flows through a wire, a magnetic field is created around that wire proportional to the current flowing in the wire, as shown in Fig. 9–10(a). Similarly, if we pass a wire through a magnetic field, current is induced in the wire. The stronger the magnetic field, the greater the current induced in the wire. Also, the faster that the wire cuts these magnetic lines of force, the greater the inducement. If we bend a length of copper wire into a coil and wrap it around a soft-iron core, the magnetic field becomes more concentrated, due to the fact that iron is a better conductor of magnetism or electricity than is the surrounding air.

The iron frame and pole shoes (magnets) of the starter motor plus the iron laminations and copper wind-

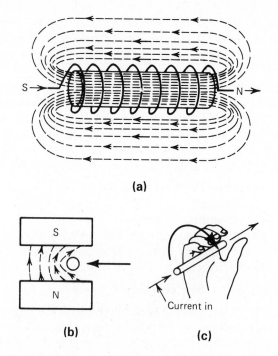

(a)

(b) **(c)**

FIGURE 9–10 Basic theory of starter motor operation: (a) magnetic field with current flowing through a wire coil; (b) weak and strong magnetic field; (c) right-hand-rule theory. *(Courtesy of Delco Remy Division, General Motors Corporation.)*

ings of the armature represent an area in which the strength of the magnetic field can be concentrated.

Figure 9–10(a) shows that the magnetic lines of force always emanate from the north to the south pole. Figure 9–10(b) shows that the path of current flow through the wire is established by the flow path of the magnetic lines of force, plus the direction of movement of the conductor (wire) in relation to the magnetic field. The wire in Fig. 9–10(b) is moving to its left to effectively cut the magnetic lines of force. This left side therefore becomes the leading side of the wire. Figure 9–10(c) shows the method used to establish the direction of current flow by grasping the wire as shown with the right hand.

When we place a conductor (wire) or series of wires around a soft-iron core and pass current through these wires (armature), a magnetic field is created around the wires. At the same time as this is happening, we have the armature surrounded by pole shoes (magnets), which are also creating a magnetic field. We therefore have not one, but two, magnetic fields within the assembly. This is shown in simplified form in Fig. 9–11.

From earlier discussions we know that magnetic lines of force emanate from the north to the south pole, and from the right-hand rule we know that current flowing through the wire will produce a magnetic field that encircles the wire in a clockwise direction [see Fig. 9–11(a)].

This arrangement produces a magnetic field around the wire or wires (armature assembly) whereby the field

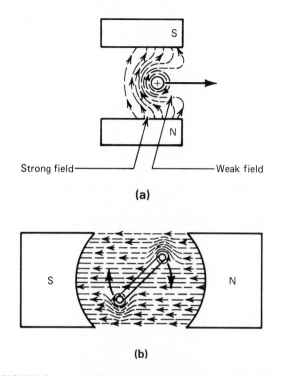

(a)

Strong field ————————— Weak field

(b)

FIGURE 9–11 (a) Field strength stronger on the left-hand side than on the right-hand side; (b) strong and weak magnetic field reaction on armature wires. *(Courtesy of Delco Remy Division, General Motors Corporation.)*

strength is stronger on the left-hand side of the wires than on the right-hand side.

This condition, shown in Fig. 9–11(b), will tend to make the conductor (wires) want to move from the strong (left-hand side) field to the weak (right-hand side) magnetic field. This is the basic principle of a starter motor and the means by which it causes starter motor armature rotation.

Now that we have set forth the basic theory behind the motor's rotation, let's take it a stage further and look at how the battery is connected into the basic circuit as shown in Fig. 9–12. For simplicity, we have shown only

FIGURE 9–12 Battery flow through a basic starter. *(Courtesy of Delco Remy Division, General Motors Corporation.)*

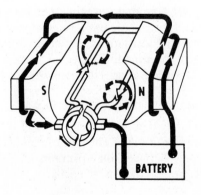

one loop of wire and one set of pole shoes (one north and one south).

In Fig. 9–12, battery current can flow to and through both the loop of wire (armature winding) and around the wire wrapped over each pole piece (N and S). This current is carried through two carbon or bronze brushes to a commutator bar after passing through both pole pieces. The current therefore flows from the battery, around the north pole piece, through the wire to the south pole piece, into the brush and commutator segment, through the loop of wire to the other commutator segment, out the other brush, and back to the battery, to complete the circuit.

The magnetic fields created in both magnets or pole pieces, plus that in the wire loop, result in the condition described in Fig. 9–11. Both strong and weak magnetic fields are created which cause the loop of wire to rotate toward the weak side of the magnetic field, resulting in the rotation of the starter motor armature.

As shown in these illustrations, the use of one wire loop would, in theory, produce a turning force; however, there would never be enough torque produced in this one wire loop to rotate an engine. To produce a starter motor with enough power to rotate an engine, we must add a large number of these wire loops, individually wrapped around a soft-iron core such as an armature. Also, starter motors today employ more than one set of pole shoes or magnets, with four and six magnets being commonly used in order to increase the magnetic field and increase the torque produced by the motor. An example of a two-pole motor with only one set of wires or conductors is shown in Fig. 9–13(a), and Fig. 9–13(b) shows a typically used motor that employs four poles with 12 pairs of conductors.

The individual loops of wire are assembled into the armature in individual slots. In addition, the armature is made up of a series of individual sheet steel laminations which are insulated from one another, then pressed together on the armature shaft to form the completed armature core. Once the commutator is mounted to the armature shaft, we have a completed unit. Figure 9–14 shows the armature laminations, the actual armature core made from the laminations, and the complete armature assembly.

Starter Motor Counter-Electromotive Force

Maximum torque produced by a starter motor must occur at initial engagement in order to cause engine rotation. In other words, the breakaway torque has to be high enough to initiate rotation to overcome the resistance of friction, engine compression, oil drag, and so on. Without going into a detailed explanation of torque, let's just say that the slower the rotation, the greater the torque. As speed increases, torque decreases, and vice versa. Once the armature starts rotating, the initial breakaway torque will decrease. However, the starter motor must still have adequate torque to rotate the engine until it starts. This brings us to a point that requires further explanation.

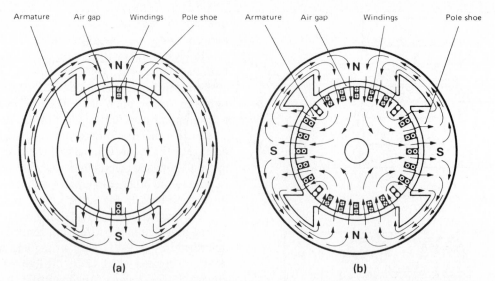

FIGURE 9–13 (a) Two-pole motor with only one set of wires; (b) four-pole motor with 12 pairs of conductors. *(Courtesy of Robert Bosch Corporation.)*

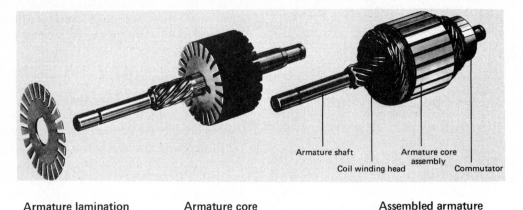

Armature lamination   **Armature core**   **Assembled armature**

FIGURE 9–14 Typical armature assembly of a starter motor. *(Courtesy of Robert Bosch Corporation.)*

As the current and voltage flow through the wire loops of the armature and the pole pieces, the net effect of the induced voltage, called the *counter-electromotive force* (CEMF), will oppose the battery voltage and therefore reduce the current supplied by the battery. This action occurs because the voltage induced in the wires is directly proportional to the speed at which the wire or conductor cuts across the magnetic lines of force. Similarly, the value of the CEMF is proportional to the speed at which the wire is rotating. Therefore, as the speed of the armature increases, the CEMF will increase, and the battery current flowing through the motor windings will decrease. This CEMF, however, will never reach the battery voltage level, but there is a decrease in starter motor torque with an increase in speed.

Starter Motor Field Coils

In the basic description of operation of the starter shown in Fig. 9–12, we illustrated a starter using one set of poles,

or a north and a south pole magnet. As you will recall from Chapter 1, when a copper wire is wound around a conducting metal object, the strength of the magnetic field will increase with a rise in current flow through the wire. To increase the field strength of the motor magnets, typical midrange and heavy-duty starters use either four or six pole pieces (magnets). An example of the typical arrangements used in these types of starters is shown in Fig. 9–15, which shows an end-on view of the starter motor assembly so that the actual number of poles can be seen. Each pole piece has a heavy-duty wire harness wound around it to control the strength of the magnetic field created. To provide the greatest breakaway torque, these windings are arranged in a series format.

Starter Motor Pinion Engagement

There are many sizes and types of starter motors in use around the world today. The type of pinion clutch drive used will vary between manufacturers and will depend, to some degree, on the type of engine to which the starter

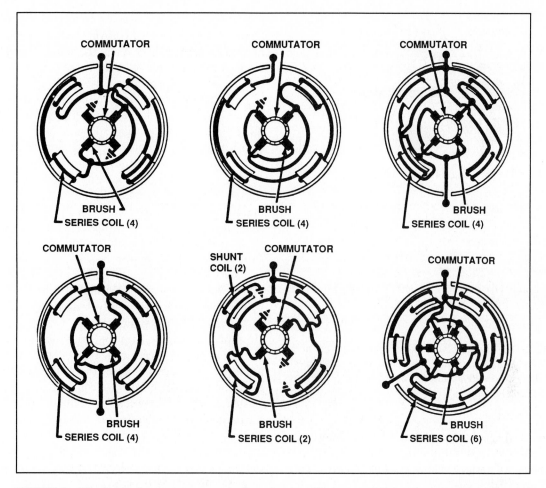

FIGURE 9–15 Typical starter motor winding circuits. *(Courtesy of Delco Remy Division, General Motors Corporation.)*

motor is fitted. Over the years there have been a number of starter motor pinion clutch drives designed to protect the pinion gear from damage once the engine starts. These have ranged from the early Dyer-type drive up to the most widely used system today, which is an overrunning sprag clutch drive mechanism. Illustrated in this section are a number of starter drive pinion mechanisms, along with a description of operation of each. Basically, these drives can be classified as:

1. A heavy-duty sprag drive
2. A Positork drive
3. A Bendix drive
4. A seven-roll clutch drive
5. A four-roll (intermediate-duty) clutch drive

All drive types are moved into engagement or mesh with the engine flywheel ring gear by the action of the solenoid. The pinion remains engaged with the ring gear until the engine starts and the solenoid circuit is disengaged by the driver releasing the switch. When the heavy-duty sprag or Positork clutch drive is used, should the starter drive pinion gear fail to engage the ring gear (butt engagement), the starter will not be energized, since the solenoid windings are constructed so that full battery

power cannot flow through the system. This safety feature ensures that both the flywheel ring gear and drive pinion gear teeth are not chewed up.

CAUTION: The starter motor should never be operated for longer than 30 seconds at one time since overheating and serious damage can occur. If an engine fails to start within this time frame, allow the starter to cool for at least 2 minutes before attempting to restart.

Some heavy-duty starter motors are equipped with an overcrank protection device which employs a built-in thermostat that will open as the starter motor operating temperature rises. This action will inhibit the cranking cycle until the motor has cooled off, which can be as long as 1 to 6 minutes, after which time the thermostat will close and allow a cranking cycle again. For more information on this type of protection feature, refer to the section "Overcrank Protection Devices" later in the chapter.

Roller Clutch Drive. Figure 9–16 shows the concept employed with a roller clutch driver. As noted in Fig. 9–16, a shell and sleeve assembly is splined internally to match either a straight or spiral splined armature shaft. The pinion (gear) sits inside the shell, where it is held by

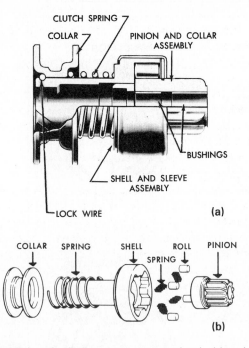

FIGURE 9-16 Roller starter motor clutch drive: (a) cutaway view; (b) exploded view. *(Courtesy of Delco Remy Division, General Motors Corporation.)*

the action of spring-loaded rollers bearing against the round area immediately behind the pinion. The spring-loaded rollers are wedged against the pinion and a taper cut inside the shell.

The number of rollers used can vary between makes; however, four is fairly common. Also, variations in the types of roller springs exist, with some manufacturers employing helical and others, accordion style. To com-

plete this arrangement, a collar connected to a shift lever, along with a spring located over the sleeve, provides the necessary components. When the starter switch is energized, the collar is moved horizontally along the shaft to compress the coil spring on the sleeve.

The action of the compressed spring will force the pinion into mesh with the flywheel ring gear. However, if the pinion does not engage properly with the ring gear (tooth abutment), the spring continues to be compressed as the shift lever continues to move, which will allow closure of the solenoid or relay switch used with the starter. This completes battery power to the starter armature and it begins to rotate. This causes the pinion to snap into engagement with the flywheel ring gear, due to the compressive force on the coil spring between the shift collar and the pinion.

Rotation of the armature cranks the engine, with the drive torque being carried through the shell to the pinion by the rollers, which are tightly wedged between the taper of the shell and the pinion area.

Once the engine fires and runs, the pinion is now turning at engine speed, which is faster than that of the armature. This action causes the rollers to move away from the taper of the shell, freeing up the contact that existed previously between the shell and pinion, so that the pinion is free to overrun or turn faster than the shell. This action minimizes the possibility of the engine driving the armature of the starter motor. However, when the engine starts, immediately release the starting switch to avoid prolonged overrun.

Once the solenoid or switch is deenergized, the solenoid return spring (or in some units, manual action) causes the shift lever and collar to move the pinion out of mesh, which in effect terminates the cranking cycle.

FIGURE 9-17 (a) Sprag clutch assembly; (b) disassembled view of heavy-duty sprag clutch drive assembly. *(Courtesy of Delco Remy Division, General Motors Corporation.)*

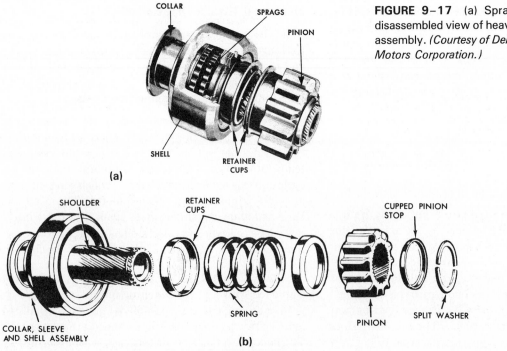

Sprag Clutch Drive. The operation of the sprag clutch is similar to that of the roller clutch described above. However, the sprag unit employs a series of sprags rather than rollers between the shell and sleeve assembly. The number of sprags can vary between manufacturers, but 30 is a usual number. Figure 9–17 shows a cutaway and exploded view of this drive and the action of the sprags, which are similar in operation to those found in certain automatic car transmissions.

The sprags are held in position against the shell and sleeve surfaces by a garter spring, with the shell and collar being splined to the starter motor armature shaft. The pinion is in turn splined to the sleeve, which is cut with a spiral spline and a stop collar.

Solenoid engagement causes the complete clutch assembly to move along the splined shaft, and the pinion attempts to engage with the ring gear of the flywheel. If tooth contact exists, continued movement of the shell and spiral splined sleeve causes rotation of the pinion. It will snap into engagement with the ring gear via the action of the compressed meshing spring.

However, if insufficient rotational movement is not obtained, the operator may have to attempt starter engagement again, since this may prevent pinion engagement with the ring gear. This safety feature is controlled by two retainer cups, which will stop shift collar and lever movement to prevent closure of the switch contacts; otherwise, with the pinion not engaged, the pinion and ring gear could be chewed up.

Once the pinion does engage through normal means, the motor switch contacts will close, allowing full battery power to the windings, and cranking will take place. Figure 9–18 shows the sequence of events above. Rotational torque is carried through the shell, sleeve, and pinion by the sprags, which tilt and wedge tightly between the shell and sleeve.

Once the engine fires and runs, the ring gear begins turning faster than the motor pinion and sleeve, which

FIGURE 9–18 Example of the stages of a preengaged starter motor action. *(Courtesy of Robert Bosch Corporation.)*

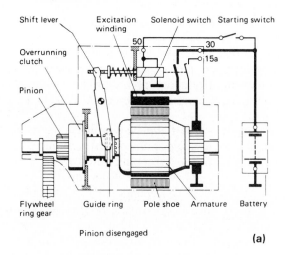

Pinion disengaged

(a)

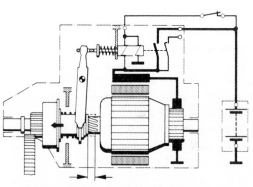

Shift lever shifts the driver forward (axial movement)

(c)

(d)

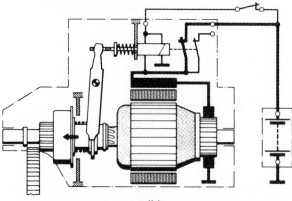

Shift lever in end position / meshing spring compressed / pull-in winding not energized / main current flows / armature turns / pinion teeth wait for spaces between ring gear teeth and then mesh completely / vehicle engine is cranked.

(b)

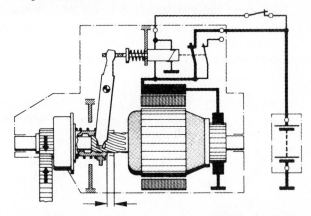

Shift lever in end position / pull-in winding not energized / main current flows, pinion meshes completely / engine is cranked

Driver shifted forward by armature rotation (helical movement)

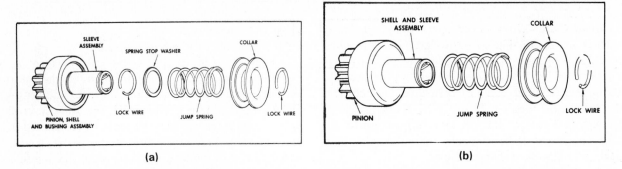

FIGURE 9-19 Disassembled view of an intermediate-duty sprag clutch drive assembly: (a) early type; (b) late type. *(Courtesy of Peterbilt Motors Company, Division of PACCAR, Newark, CA.)*

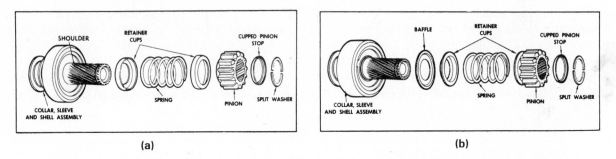

FIGURE 9-20 Disassembled view of a heavy-duty sprag clutch drive assembly: (a) early type; (b) late type. *(Courtesy of Peterbilt Motors Company, Division of PACCAR, Newark, CA.)*

can result in overspeeding of the starter armature. To prevent this condition, the motion transfer to the pinion and sleeve will cause the sprags to tilt in the opposite direction, thereby freeing the pinion and sleeve from the shell and armature. This results in an overrun condition (freewheeling) of the pinion; however, to prevent prolonged overrun (as with the roller clutch drive), the operator should disengage the power flow to the motor switch or solenoid just as soon as the engine starts.

Depending on the vintage and model of the starter motor, it can be equipped with an intermediate- or heavy-duty sprag clutch drive. Figure 9-19 illustrates both an early and a later type of intermediate sprag clutch drive mechanism. Figure 9-20(a) shows a disassembled view of an earlier-model heavy-duty sprag clutch drive assembly; Fig. 9-20(b) is an exploded view of a later-design heavy-duty sprag system. The sprag drive mechanism used on Delco-Remy 50MT starter motors featured in Fig. 9-8 in assembled schematic form is referred to as a DR250 drive mechanism. This drive is shown in its disassembled

FIGURE 9-21 Disassembled view of a Delco model DR-250 starter motor drive. *(Courtesy of Peterbilt Motors Company, Division of PACCAR, Newark, CA.)*

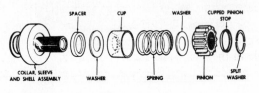

state in Fig. 9-21. A comparison of an intermediate- and heavy-duty drive mechanism can be seen in Fig. 9-22 along with information regarding the part number and month and year of manufacture of a Delco drive unit.

Bendix Drive. The Bendix drive, used for many years, is not used much anymore due to introduction of the roll and sprag overrunning clutch drives. Several improvements were made to the Bendix drive over the years; however, the basic concept has remained the same. Figure 9-23 shows the Bendix drive arrangement. The Bendix principle of engagement is one of inertia to cause the pinion to engage with the flywheel ring gear. From the views shown in Fig. 9-23, operation of the Bendix drive is as follows.

Type A: This system incorporates a pinion and sleeve assembly, a drive spring, and a drive head. The pinion and sleeve assembly fits loosely over the armature shaft, but is connected through the drive spring to the drive head, which is keyed to the shaft. Closing the starter switch causes the armature to rotate, as well as the drive head and drive spring to the sleeve. The drive pinion is usually unbalanced by a counterweight on one side, and it has screw threads or spiral splines cut on its inner bore to match those on the outer surface of the Bendix sleeve. Type A is shown in Fig. 9-23(a).

When the armature rotates, the spiral splined sleeve rotates within the pinion, which moves along the shaft to engage the flywheel ring gear. Cranking occurs when the pinion reaches its stop on the sleeve, with the spring

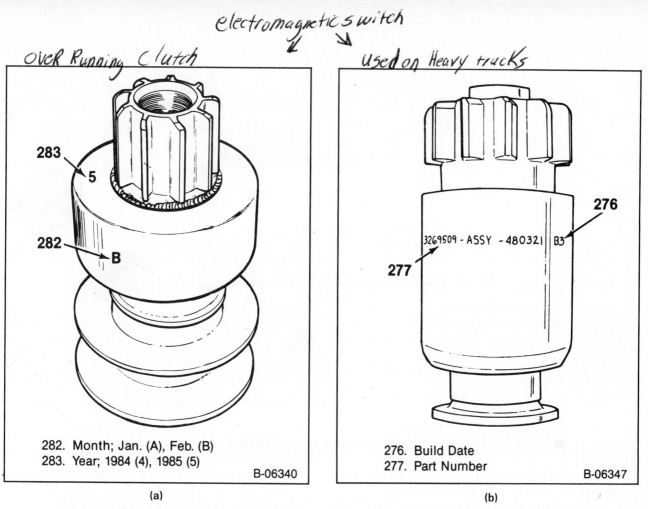

[handwritten: electromagnetic switch]

[handwritten: over Running Clutch]   *[handwritten: used on Heavy trucks]*

283
5

282
B

282. Month; Jan. (A), Feb. (B)
283. Year; 1984 (4), 1985 (5)

B-06340

(a)

276

3269509 - ASSY - 480321 B3

277

276. Build Date
277. Part Number

B-06347

(b)

FIGURE 9–22 (a) Intermediate-duty drive clutch ID; (b) heavy-duty drive clutch ID. *(Courtesy of GMC Truck Division, General Motors Corporation.)*

FIGURE 9–23 Bendix-type starter motor drive gear; (a) typical inertia drive; (b) Folo-Thru drive. *(Courtesy of Delco Remy Division, General Motors Corporation.)*

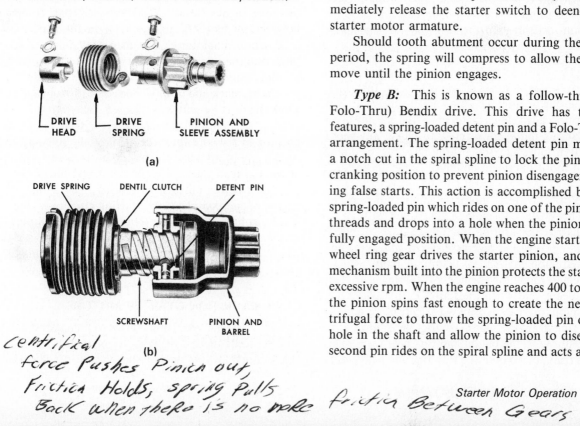

DRIVE HEAD   DRIVE SPRING   PINION AND SLEEVE ASSEMBLY

(a)

DRIVE SPRING   DENTIL CLUTCH   DETENT PIN

SCREWSHAFT   PINION AND BARREL

(b)

[handwritten: Centrifical force Pushes Pinion out, Friction Holds, spring Pulls Back when there is no more friction Between Gears]

taking up any shock loading. Once the engine fires and runs, the faster-turning ring gear will drive the pinion back out of mesh. The operator should, however, immediately release the starter switch to deenergize the starter motor armature.

Should tooth abutment occur during the cranking period, the spring will compress to allow the sleeve to move until the pinion engages.

Type B: This is known as a follow-through (or Folo-Thru) Bendix drive. This drive has two extra features, a spring-loaded detent pin and a Folo-Thru drive arrangement. The spring-loaded detent pin moves into a notch cut in the spiral spline to lock the pinion in the cranking position to prevent pinion disengagement during false starts. This action is accomplished by using a spring-loaded pin which rides on one of the pinion screw threads and drops into a hole when the pinion is in the fully engaged position. When the engine starts, the flywheel ring gear drives the starter pinion, and a clutch mechanism built into the pinion protects the starter from excessive rpm. When the engine reaches 400 to 500 rpm, the pinion spins fast enough to create the needed centrifugal force to throw the spring-loaded pin out of the hole in the shaft and allow the pinion to disengage. A second pin rides on the spiral spline and acts as an anti-

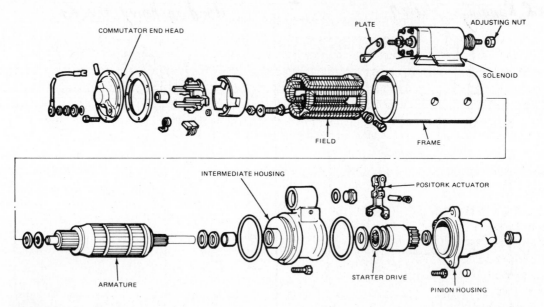

FIGURE 9–24 Prestolite Positork starter assembly. *(Courtesy of Prestolite Electric Incorporated, Heavy Duty Division.)*

drift device during engine operation. Type B is shown in Fig. 9–23(b).

The second feature, the Folo-Thru drive, is actually a sleeve or screwshaft (two-piece) connected by a dentil clutch arrangement which consists of ratcheting teeth to prevent armature overspeed, yet allows the pinion and its sleeve to overrun the ratchet teeth until the detent pin has disengaged the notch.

Type C: This system includes a small rubber cushion located inside the cup to take up the shock of initial cranking. It also includes a small spring located over the screwshaft inside the pinion barrel to stop the pinion from drifting into the ring gear during engine operation.

Type D: This system includes a friction-clutch used on some of the larger diesel cranking motors. Instead of the drive spring or rubber cushion arrangement, a series of flat spring-loaded clutch plates inside the housing allow slippage during initial engagement to relieve any shock loading. It includes a meshing spring to allow the pinion to clear a tooth abutment condition, plus an antidrift spring located over the spiral splined sleeve.

The Positork starter motor assembly shown in Fig. 9–24 is a heavy-duty solenoid-actuated unit with an armature shaft center bearing and a drive assembly which is an indexing type of engagement system to assure complete drive pinion engagement before the motor will actually begin to rotate the engine flywheel ring gear. This features means that when the starter is first energized, should pinion tooth abutment occur between it and the flywheel ring gear, the motor will not be energized, to prevent damage to the pinion and ring gear teeth. This feature is common to both the Positork and heavy-duty

sprag clutch drive mechanisms. The disadvantage of the Positork drive is that the complete drive assembly must be replaced should a problem or service be required.

COAXIAL STARTER MOTORS

These types of starter motors include a solenoid winding installed within the pinion housing to eliminate the piggyback mounting of the solenoid and the shifting linkage. Less room is required for the installation of the unit on the engine. This enclosed design prevents dirt, mud, slush, and snow from entering the unit. This also offers the advantages of positive shift engagement, compactness, and extremely flexible terminal mounting positions.

In the coaxial starter, the solenoid winding, the contacts, and the solenoid core are assembled in the pinion housing. The solenoid core has a spring-loaded sleeve that provides a quick and positive release of the solenoid core when the starting switch is released, which in turn provides a fast break of the solenoid contacts. The second purpose of the core spring is to allow the solenoid core to move forward when the pinion butts against the flywheel ring gear. The core is allowed to continue forward, which further compresses the spring, closes the switch contacts, and completes the starting circuit. As the armature rotates it spins the pinion, and the compressed spring in the solenoid core snaps the pinion into the flywheel ring gear. An overrunning clutch is commonly used with these starter motors.

GEAR REDUCTION STARTER MOTORS

The use of a gear reduction starter to increase torque is used on some models of light- to medium-duty trucks. One example of this type of starter motor is illustrated in Fig. 9–25, which shows the unit in exploded-view form. This starter is a Nippondenso 12-V model with a rated output of 3 kW that is used on both GMC and Isuzu W7 medium-duty steel tilt cab truck models equipped with the Isuzu model 6BD1-T or 6SA1-T diesel engine. The armature drive gear (176) meshes with an intermediate gear (151) to transfer the drive torque to the pinion gear (149). Robert Bosch manufactures similar gear reduction starter motors for use in heavy-duty 24-V diesel starting systems. In addition, many Chrysler car and light truck products employ gear reduction starter motors.

HEAVY-DUTY TRUCK STARTER MOTOR RELAYS: SWITCHES AND SOLENOIDS

The high current demands of the starter motor for cranking purposes in heavy-duty trucks requires that a magnetic relay switch be used to conduct the battery power (amperage) to the starter motor directly, or to the heavy-duty starter mounted solenoid switch. The ignition and pushbutton starter motor switches are there to handle the small current required to trigger or switch on the relay, which is also referred to as a magnetic switch. The term *mag switch* is used since the small current flow from the ignition key switch or starter pushbutton switch flows through the mag switch/relay coil to form an electromagnet which opens or closes the relay contacts. Figure 9–26 illustrates a typical system schematic of two common types of relays found in heavy-duty truck applications regardless of the type/make of diesel engine used. The terms *NO (normally open)* and *NC (normally closed)* are often used when describing these types of mag switches (relays). NO and NC describe the state of the switch contacts without battery power being applied to the mag switch/relay coil.

Switches and solenoids used with starter motors can be direct or remote mounted from the starter. Several ar-

FIGURE 9–25 Nippondenso gear reduction type of starter motor. *(Courtesy of GMC Truck Division, General Motors Corporation.)*

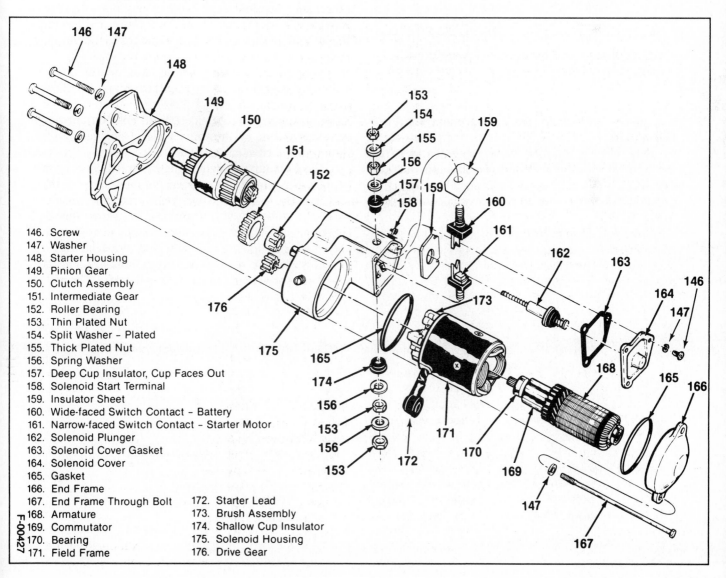

146. Screw
147. Washer
148. Starter Housing
149. Pinion Gear
150. Clutch Assembly
151. Intermediate Gear
152. Roller Bearing
153. Thin Plated Nut
154. Split Washer – Plated
155. Thick Plated Nut
156. Spring Washer
157. Deep Cup Insulator, Cup Faces Out
158. Solenoid Start Terminal
159. Insulator Sheet
160. Wide-faced Switch Contact – Battery
161. Narrow-faced Switch Contact – Starter Motor
162. Solenoid Plunger
163. Solenoid Cover Gasket
164. Solenoid Cover
165. Gasket
166. End Frame
167. End Frame Through Bolt
168. Armature
169. Commutator
170. Bearing
171. Field Frame
172. Starter Lead
173. Brush Assembly
174. Shallow Cup Insulator
175. Solenoid Housing
176. Drive Gear

F-00427

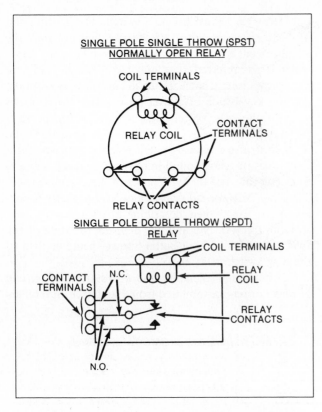

FIGURE 9-26 Schematics of two types of starter motor relays. *(Reproduced courtesy of Caterpillar, Inc.)*

motor current can range from several hundred amperes up to over a thousand amperes on heavy-duty truck diesel starting motors, these switches and solenoids play an important part in activation of the starter motor.

The basic difference between a straight magnetic switch and a solenoid is that the magnetic switch simply opens and closes the circuit from the battery to the starter motor, while the solenoid not only opens and closes the circuit between the battery and starter, but also has a plunger that shifts the motor drive mechanism into mesh with the flywheel ring gear.

Figure 9-27 shows a simple magnetic switch and solenoid which basically contains a winding mounted around a hollow cylinder, within which is a movable hollow core or plunger. Connected to one end of the plunger is a contact disk. When electricity is passed through the switch winding, a magnetic field draws the plunger and its contact disk tightly against two main switch terminals which are connected to the main battery power flow. In this manner, the starter motor can be energized. The switch itself is energized by a small current fed through a key switch hookup or similar arrangement. Figure 9-28(a) shows a pushbutton switch capable of carrying the current to the starter solenoid. Figure 9-28(b) shows a key switch that relays the current through a magnetic switch to the starter solenoid.

Once the engine starts and the starter button or key switch is returned to the normal off or run position, the magnetic switch is deenergized. An internal return spring forces the plunger back to its released position, thereby effectively breaking the contact disk from the starter motor switch terminals.

The solenoid is usually mounted directly to the top of the starter motor so that it can not only complete the circuit to the starter, but also control the shift linkage, as shown in Fig. 9-29(a). Figure 9-29(b) shows the actual terminal arrangement of the solenoid, and Fig. 9-30 shows a Delco 10MT starter solenoid disassembled.

The solenoid contains two sets of windings, known as the pull-in winding and the hold-in winding. The pull-

rangements can be used. Some applications use a key switch to carry the small current required to activate a switch or solenoid; however, the high current draw to the armature of the starter motor would burn out key switches; a heavy-duty switch or solenoid is necessary to avoid this condition. Several styles of switches are shown in Fig. 9-27.

Switches and solenoids used in starting circuits are electromagnetic, in that they are energized electrically (contacts closed) and released (contacts opened) by spring pressure when the electrical circuit is broken. Since starter

FIGURE 9-27 Magnetic starter motor switch: (a) light-duty type and (b) heavy-duty type. *(Courtesy of Delco Remy Division, General Motors Corporation.)*

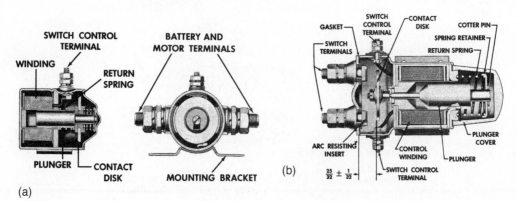

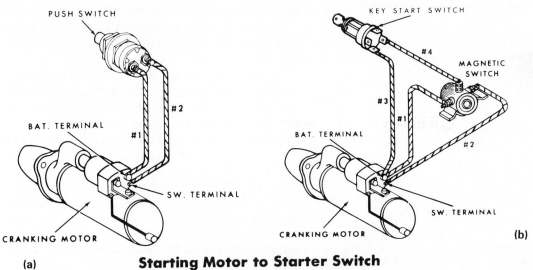

PUSH SWITCH

BAT. TERMINAL

#2

#1

SW. TERMINAL

CRANKING MOTOR

(a)

KEY START SWITCH

#4

MAGNETIC SWITCH

#3

#1

BAT. TERMINAL

#2

SW. TERMINAL

CRANKING MOTOR

(b)

Starting Motor to Starter Switch
or Starter Relay Circuit Chart

(c)

Wire Size	TOTAL LENGTH OF A + B—FEET*	
	12 Volt	24 & 32 Volt
12	8	16
10	11	22
8	17	34
6	27	54
4	42	84
2	64	132

*Resistance of Starter Switch Circuit should not exceed .0114 ohm total.

FIGURE 9–28 (a) Typical circuit employing a push-type switch; (b) wiring circuit employing a key and magnetic switch; (c) starting motor to starter switch or starter relay circuit chart. *(Courtesy of Detroit Diesel Corporation.)*

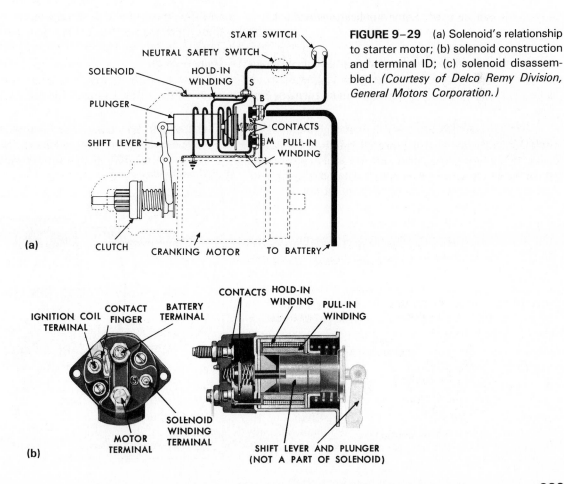

FIGURE 9–29 (a) Solenoid's relationship to starter motor; (b) solenoid construction and terminal ID; (c) solenoid disassembled. *(Courtesy of Delco Remy Division, General Motors Corporation.)*

START SWITCH

NEUTRAL SAFETY SWITCH

SOLENOID

HOLD-IN WINDING

S

PLUNGER

B

SHIFT LEVER

CONTACTS

M

PULL-IN WINDING

(a)

CLUTCH

CRANKING MOTOR

TO BATTERY

IGNITION COIL TERMINAL

CONTACT FINGER

BATTERY TERMINAL

CONTACTS

HOLD-IN WINDING

PULL-IN WINDING

MOTOR TERMINAL

SOLENOID WINDING TERMINAL

SHIFT LEVER AND PLUNGER (NOT A PART OF SOLENOID)

(b)

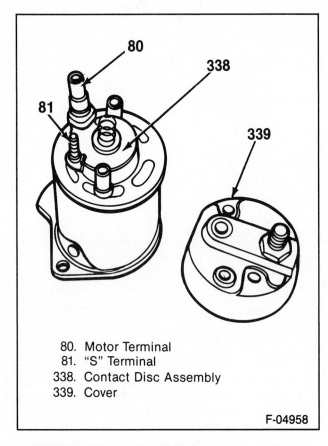

80. Motor Terminal
81. "S" Terminal
338. Contact Disc Assembly
339. Cover

F-04958

FIGURE 9–30 Model 10MT Delco starter solenoid with cover removed to expose components. *(Courtesy of GMC Truck Division, General Motors Corporation.)*

in winding contains the same number of turns as the hold-in winding, but the pull-in unit contains a larger-diameter wire. The hold-in winding contains many turns of fine wire.

From an earlier chapter, you may recollect that magnetism is created when current is passed through a wire. When the operator turns the key switch to the start position, current will flow from the battery to the S or switch terminal of the solenoid, through the hold-in winding to ground, and back to the battery to complete the circuit. Current will also flow through the pull-in winding to the M terminal of the solenoid and through the starter motor windings to ground. The magnetism created in both sets of windings is strong enough to pull the plunger of the solenoid into the core, which shifts the drive pinion into mesh with the flywheel ring gear, as well as moving the contact disk to close the circuit between the solenoid B (battery) terminal and the starter motor (M) terminal. This completed circuit allows the armature of the starter motor to rotate.

Once the plunger of the solenoid has been pulled into the engagement position, less magnetism is required to hold it there, so once the contact disk comes into actual contact with the solenoid B and M terminals, the pull-in winding is shorted and no current flows through it

anymore. This is an important feature because this action will not only reduce battery current draw, but does much to reduce heat buildup within the solenoid assembly.

Once the engine starts and the operator releases the switch for the starter, current flow will pass through the contact disk to the solenoid M terminal, through the pull-in winding in a reverse direction to the solenoid or S terminal, through the hold-in winding, and back to the battery. This action, as brief as it is, causes opposing magnetic fields in the pull-in and hold-in windings to cancel each other out. The internal return spring will positively return the shift mechanism to the nonengaged position.

Heavy-Duty Starter Motor Switch Wiring

Current diesel-engine-powered class 8 trucks generally employ a 12-V high-output torque starter motor in which the current draw is considerably higher than in a similar series–parallel (24-V starting/12-V charging) system. To carry the higher current safely, one of two types of switches must be used:

1. A push-type switch of adequate current-carrying capacity, or
2. A key-type switch, or any other with low current-carrying capacity in conjunction with a magnetic switch.

A typical circuit employing a push-type switch is shown in Fig. 9–28(a). To determine what size of stranded wire should be used between the push-switch and starter motor terminals, measure the total length of wires 1 and 2 in Fig. 9–28(a), and select the proper size from the table [Fig. 9–28(c)].

In Fig. 9–28(a), wire 1 may be connected from the push switch to an ammeter instead of to the BAT ter-

FIGURE 9–31 Delco heavy-duty 50MT starter solenoid with cover removed to expose components. *(Courtesy of GMC Truck Division, General Motors Corporation.)*

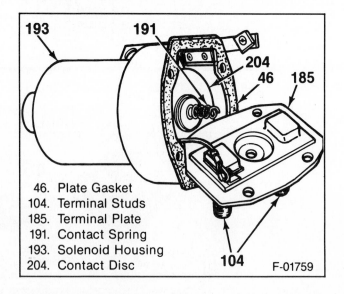

46. Plate Gasket
104. Terminal Studs
185. Terminal Plate
191. Contact Spring
193. Solenoid Housing
204. Contact Disc

F-01759

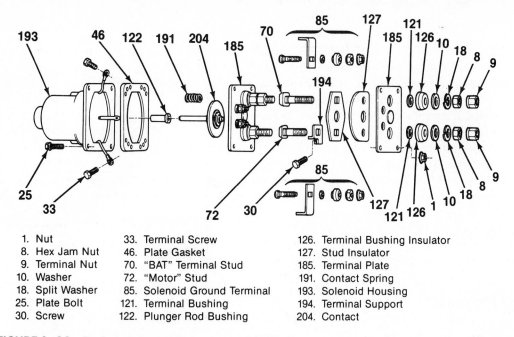

FIGURE 9–32 Exploded view of Delco model 50MT starter motor solenoid components. *(Courtesy of GMC Truck Division, General Motors Corporation.)*

1. Nut	33. Terminal Screw	126. Terminal Bushing Insulator
8. Hex Jam Nut	46. Plate Gasket	127. Stud Insulator
9. Terminal Nut	70. "BAT" Terminal Stud	185. Terminal Plate
10. Washer	72. "Motor" Stud	191. Contact Spring
18. Split Washer	85. Solenoid Ground Terminal	193. Solenoid Housing
25. Plate Bolt	121. Terminal Bushing	194. Terminal Support
30. Screw	122. Plunger Rod Bushing	204. Contact

minal of the starter motor solenoid. In this case, measure the length of wire 1 from the switch to the ammeter. For example, No. 10 wire should be used for both wires 1 and 2 if wire 1 is 45 in. long and wire 2 is 50 in. long, for a total length of 95 in. or 7.9 ft.

Figure 9–28(b) illustrates a wiring circuit employing a key-type switch and a magnetic switch. To determine the size of stranded wire to be used in this system, measure the length of wires 1 and 2 and select the proper size from the table. For example, the length of wire 1 is 25 in. and the length of wire 2 is 30 in., for a total length of 55 in. or 4.6 ft. Therefore, from Fig. 9–28(c) No. 12 stranded wire should be employed for wires 1 and 2. The

stranded wire size for wires 3 and 4 should be No. 16 minimum, or a larger wire can be used. The starter motor–mounted solenoid switch used on heavy-duty diesel truck applications can be identified by part number, voltage, year, month, and day of manufacture, which are stamped onto the support bracket. A typical heavy-duty solenoid is shown in Fig. 9–31 with its front cover removed to expose the major components. For further clarification, this heavy-duty solenoid is shown in an exploded view (Fig. 9–32) from a Delco 50MT starter assembly showing all the components and how they are assembled. The solenoid assembly for the very widely used and popular Delco 42MT starter found on most heavy-duty

FIGURE 9–33 Exploded view of Delco starter motor model 42MT solenoid components. *(Courtesy of GMC Truck Division, General Motors Corporation.)*

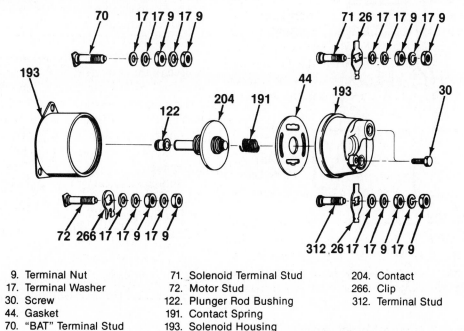

9. Terminal Nut	71. Solenoid Terminal Stud	204. Contact
17. Terminal Washer	72. Motor Stud	266. Clip
30. Screw	122. Plunger Rod Bushing	312. Terminal Stud
44. Gasket	191. Contact Spring	
70. "BAT" Terminal Stud	193. Solenoid Housing	

341

class 8 highway trucks is shown in exploded-view form in Fig. 9–33 to allow you to see the differences that exist between these solenoid arrangements. A basic solenoid pull-in and hold-in winding circuit for a Delco model 40MT and 50MT starter motor model is shown in Fig. 9–34, while Fig. 9–35 shows the wiring circuit used with a heavy duty 12-V starter that uses a pushbutton or key switch, a motor-mounted solenoid, and a relay switch. Figure 9–36 shows the complete circuit for a typical 12-V heavy-duty starter and alternator charging system. Figure 9–37 illustrates a 24-V starting system arrangement. In Fig. 9–35, when the starter switch is closed (START position), battery current will flow through the relay winding to ground, thereby completing the electrical circuit and allowing the relay to close. This now connects the starter motor solenoid S terminal directly to the battery or batteries, depending on how many are used in the system. The solenoid windings are energized, which draws the plunger into the solenoid housing, and the shift lever movement causes the drive pinion (gear) to engage with the engine flywheel ring gear. This engagement allows the main contacts inside the solenoid to close, and engine cranking will occur. As soon as the engine fires and runs, the pinion overrunning clutch protects the starter motor armature from excessive speed (the engine is driving the pinion now) until the driver releases the start switch (opens it). This of course should be done the instant the

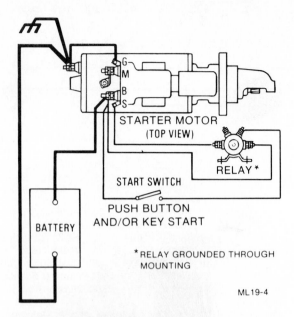

FIGURE 9–35 Typical medium/heavy-duty truck starter motor wiring circuit. *(Courtesy of Mack Trucks, Inc.)*

engine fires. When this happens, the return spring will cause the drive pinion to disengage with the flywheel ring gear.

SERIES–PARALLEL STARTER CIRCUITS

Many diesel engines in trucks and heavy-duty equipment employ a 24-V starter motor with a 12-V charging and accessory system. Two types of series–parallel circuits are readily available and used in the industry.

1. A series–parallel switch arrangement
2. A transformer rectifier assembly built-in to the charging system alternator assembly

We will deal here briefly with the second type, since it was discussed in some depth earlier in Chapter 8 dealing with alternators wherein both the Delco-Remy and Leece-Neville units were shown.

The transformer rectifier is now the more commonly used of the two types; however, many pieces of equipment still employ the former type that uses a separate series–parallel switch. The reason for using the series–parallel circuit whether it is the older or newer type is, of course, to allow the use of a 24-V starter motor which is often necessary and desirable on diesel-powered equipment.

Either four heavy-duty 6-V batteries can be used, or two heavy-duty 12-V units as shown in Fig. 9–38. For starting purposes, the batteries are connected in series through the series–parallel switch arrangement to provide 24 V for cranking. Once the engine starts, the charging system automatically is switched back to a 12-V setup so that all accessories can be operated on the conventional 12-V circuitry. However, some diesel-powered equipment

FIGURE 9–34 Basic heavy-duty starter motor solenoid circuit. *(Courtesy of GMC Truck Division, General Motors Corporation.)*

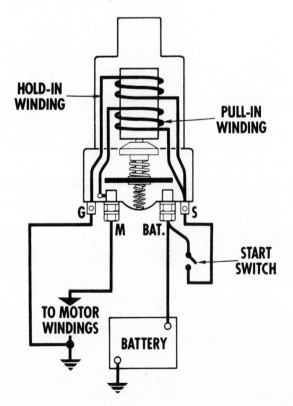

12 Volt Starting System

NOTE: Numbers on wires show wire size.

RECOMMENDATION OF BATTERY CABLE SIZE FOR LENGTH	
CABLE SIZE	DIRECT ELECTRIC STARTING
	12 VOLT
0	1.22 m (4.0 ft.)
00	1.54 m (5.0 ft.)
000	1.83 m (6.0 ft.)
0000	2.28 m (7.5 ft.)

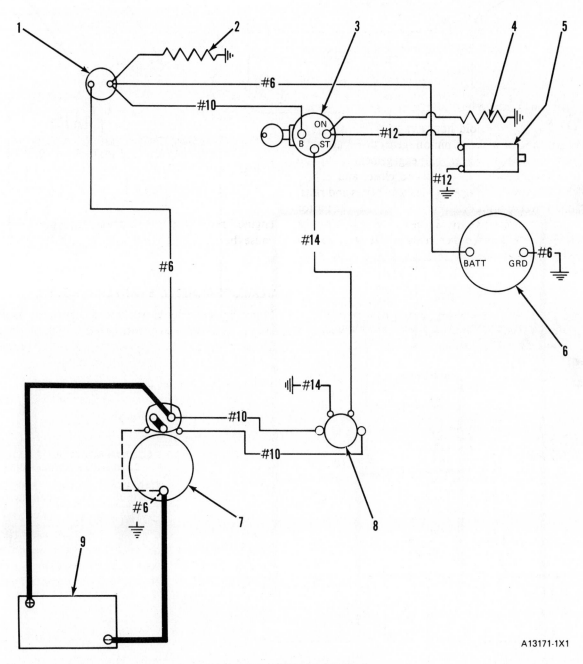

A13171-1X1

12 VOLT STARTING SYSTEM

1. Ammeter. 2. Lights. 3. Key Switch. 4. Gauges. 5. Shut-off solenoid (energized to run). 6. Alternator. 7. Starter motor. 8. Switch. 9. Battery (12 volt).

FIGURE 9–36 Wiring diagram showing all of the 12-V starter motor wiring and component hookup. *(Reproduced courtesy of Caterpillar, Inc.)*

24 Volt Starting System

System has two 12 volt batteries and a series-parallel switch.

NOTE: Numbers on wires show wire size.

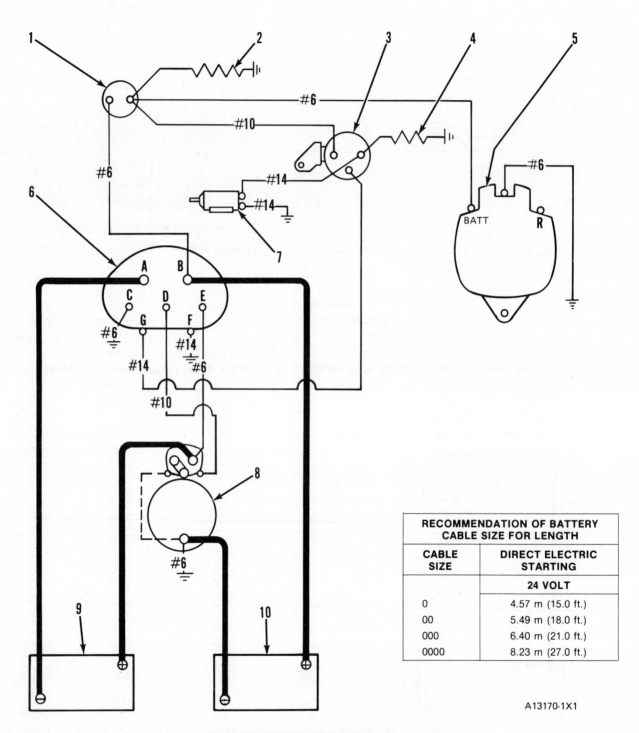

24 VOLT STARTING SYSTEM

1. Ammeter. 2. Lights. 3. Key switch. 4. Gauges. 5. Alternator. 6. Series-parallel switch. 7. Shut-off solenoid. 8. Start motor (24 volt). 9. Battery (12 volt). 10. Battery (12 volt).

FIGURE 9–37   24-V starting motor wiring and component hookup. (*Reproduced courtesy of Caterpillar, Inc.*)

344

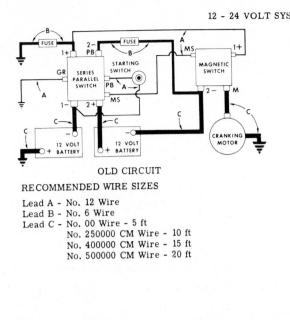

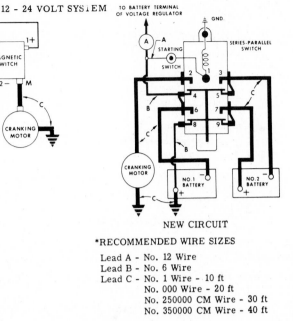

OLD CIRCUIT

RECOMMENDED WIRE SIZES

Lead A - No. 12 Wire
Lead B - No. 6 Wire
Lead C - No. 00 Wire - 5 ft
              No. 250000 CM Wire - 10 ft
              No. 400000 CM Wire - 15 ft
              No. 500000 CM Wire - 20 ft

NEW CIRCUIT

*RECOMMENDED WIRE SIZES

Lead A - No. 12 Wire
Lead B - No. 6 Wire
Lead C - No. 1 Wire - 10 ft
              No. 000 Wire - 20 ft
              No. 250000 CM Wire - 30 ft
              No. 350000 CM Wire - 40 ft

*Sizes based on five percent drop at 1000 amps.

FIGURE 9–38 Series–parallel system wiring diagram. *(Courtesy of Prestolite Electric, Incorporated, Heavy Duty Products Division.)*

can operate on both 24-V starting and 24-V charging systems. An example of a typical series–parallel switch wiring circuit is shown in Fig. 9–37, item 6.

The two most commonly used series–parallel circuit arrangements are those manufactured by both Delco-Remy and Leece-Neville. Therefore, we shall concentrate on these two types.

The current model of Leece-Neville series–parallel switch arrangement uses a solenoid that operates eight sets of contacts as shown in Fig. 9–38.

As can readily be seen in Fig. 9–38, two batteries are connected into the circuit along with a starting switch, series–parallel or (SP switch), an alternator, plus the necessary wiring to the starter motor.

Contact sets 2, 3, 6, and 7, when closed, connect the batteries in series for cranking. Contact sets 4, 5, 8, and 9, which are smaller, connect the batteries in parallel for charging purposes. The solenoid is activated when the starter switch is closed; therefore, the action is as follows:

1. When the solenoid is energized it will:
   a. Open the charging contacts
   b. Close cranking contacts 2, 3, 6, and 7, which connect the two 12-V batteries in series
2. Once the engine starts, the series–parallel switch will:
   a. Open cranking contacts 2, 3, 6, and 7
   b. Reconnect the batteries in parallel by closing charging contacts 4, 5, 8, and 9, and connect the generator/alternator to both batteries

Troubleshooting the Leece-Neville S/P Circuit

If the S/P switch in Fig. 9–38 should fail to operate correctly, remove it from the vehicle circuit and test.

Procedure

1. With a test lamp, check terminals 2 through 9 for possible short circuits (grounds) to the switch base. Ensure that a circuit does exist, however, between terminals 4-5 and 8-9. There should be no circuit between terminals 2-3 and 6-7, which are the cranking terminals.
2. To establish if the solenoid plunger is actually moving when it is energized, apply rated battery voltage to the operating coil terminal 1 and to the switch base.
3. If the two tests indicate that the switch is operational, proceed to check out the other areas of the cranking and charging circuit, prior to attempting to condemn or disassemble the S/P switch.

NOTE: When it becomes necessary to check the S/P switch assembly, avoid using jumper cables to bridge cranking circuit contacts 2, 3, 6 or 7 because burning of the contacts can occur. Using a jumper switch across terminals 2 and 3, for example, will result in the starter motor attempting to crank the engine on only one battery. The contacts will weld or burn out. The same condition will result at terminals 6 and 7 if a jumper wire is used.

Alternate S/P System

Now that you have a basic understanding of how the S/P (series–parallel) switch system operates, let's look at how this system might appear on a heavy-duty class 8 truck/tractor. Figure 9–39 illustrates an example of the system used on Peterbilt 379 conventional truck models. The engine harness is routed the same as the Peterbilt model 359 with some minor changes. Notice that this S/P switch only has seven sets of contacts versus the eight shown

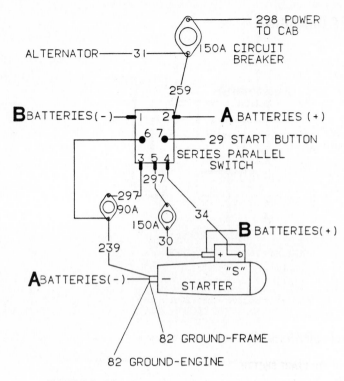

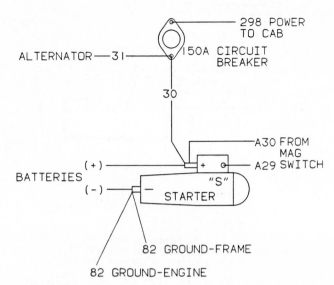

FIGURE 9–39 Typical series–parallel wiring arrangement in a heavy-duty class 8 truck. *(Courtesy of Peterbilt Motors Company, Division of PACCAR, Newark, CA.)*

FIGURE 9–40 Simplified wiring diagram showing hookup to the starter motor for a 12-V charging circuit. *(Courtesy of Peterbilt Motors Company, Division of PACCAR, Newark, CA.)*

earlier in Fig. 9–38. This is simply a newer design that operates in a similar fashion to the S/P switch already described. For ease of clarity, compare this S/P 12/24-V circuit arrangement shown in Fig. 9–39 with a typical 12-V starting/charging circuit on the same type of truck and shown in Fig. 9–40. The 12-V starter system is now standard with a magnetic switch; however, a magnetic switch is not required on all starters since many starter motors are designed with an integral mag switch or a series–parallel system. The numbers shown in both the 12- and 24-V Peterbilt starting systems refer to the wiring number that would appear on each wire for tracing

and troubleshooting purposes. These wire numbers and their wire size function are shown in Table 9–1.

Delco-Remy Series–Parallel Circuits

Delco supplies S/P switches to a variety of heavy-duty truck manufacturers, who wire the circuit in one of three acceptable ways:

1. An A circuit as shown in Fig. 9–41. The A or vehicle accessory battery is connected to switch terminal 1. If more than one wire lead is connected to this terminal, an A circuit is confirmed.

2. Figure 9–42 shows a B circuit in which terminal 2 contains more than one lead.

3. A combined series–parallel and magnetic switch is identified by four large terminals, as shown in Fig. 9–43.

In all types of circuits, it makes no difference whether the leads at terminals 6 and 7 are reversed. The circuit will still operate.

TABLE 9–1

Wire Number	Wire Size	Circuit Name	Description
29	14 and up	Starter button	Button to S/P switch or solenoid and auxiliary starter switch
30	8 and up	A battery line	Circuit breaker to S/P switch or solenoid
31	8 and up	Regulator armature line	Generator to voltage regulator junction block
34	14 and up	Transfer line	S/P switch to starter solenoid
82	8 and up	Starter ground	Terminal to ground
239	16 and up	Ground	Miscellaneous grounds
259	4	Charging-24-V start	CB to S/P switch
297	8	B battery charge	S/P switch terminal 5 to CB
298	10 and up	Power	Accessory relay to CB

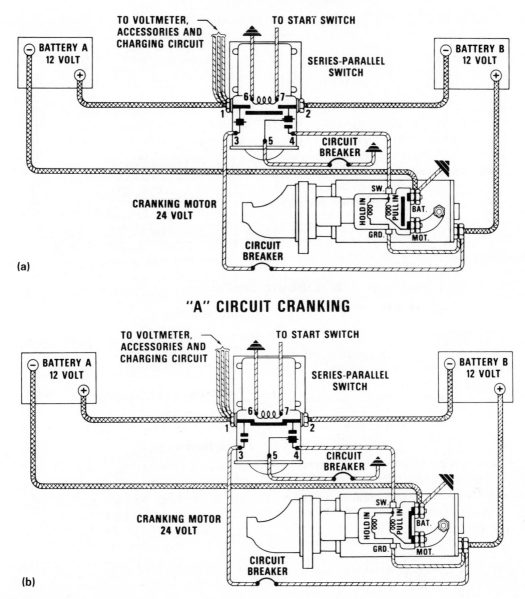

"A" CIRCUIT CHARGING

(a)

"A" CIRCUIT CRANKING

(b)

FIGURE 9–41 (a) A-circuit charging; (b) A-circuit cranking. *(Courtesy of Delco Remy Division, General Motors Corporation.)*

Circuit Operation

A circuit: charging and combined S/P and magnetic switch models: Current flows from the alternator to terminal 1 of the S/P switch when the S/P switch is in the charging or disengaged position and the engine is running. Current divides to both circuit batteries via half passing through the A or accessory battery to ground, while the other half passes through contact points between terminals 1 and 3, the B battery (cranking only), and the contact points between terminals 2 and 5 to ground [see Fig. 9–41(a)].

A circuit: cranking: Closing the switch to coil terminal 7 energizes the S/P switch assembly, allowing the

plunger to be pulled into the core by the magnetic field produced in the coil winding [see Fig. 9–41(b)]. This action happens very quickly, and in fact takes three distinct forms:

1. Step 1 involves opening of the normally closed (NC) points between terminals 1, 3, 2, and 5 by the plunger as it moves.

2. The plunger, as it continues to move, causes the large contact disk to close terminals 1 and 2.

3. The normally open (NO) points between terminals 4 and 5 are also closed by the movement of the plunger.

Movement of the large contact disk ties terminals 1 and 2 together, which effectively places both the A

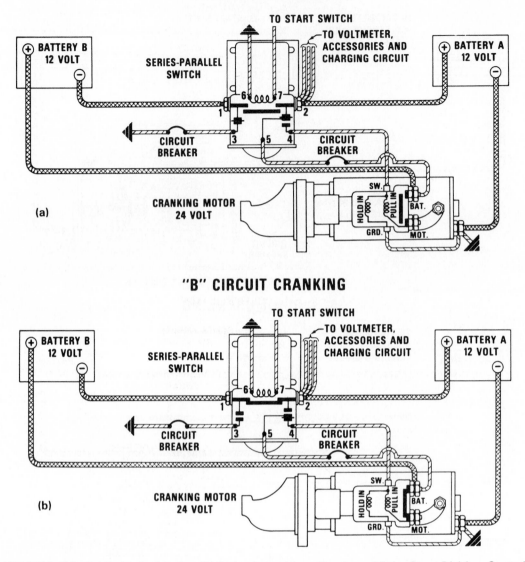

FIGURE 9–42 (a) B-circuit charging; (b) B-circuit cranking. *(Courtesy of Delco Remy Division, General Motors Corporation.)*

(system battery), and B (cranking battery) in series for 24 V starting or cranking. Both batteries supply current to the starter end terminal, frame area, and MOT terminal of the solenoid, pull-in coil, and over to the SW terminal of the solenoid. The rest of the circuit allows the remaining current flow to travel from the end terminal of the starter motor to the GRD terminal of the solenoid, through the hold-in coil and to the SW terminal of the solenoid. Total circuit current flows through terminals 4 and 5 to ground. The starter drive pinion is pulled into mesh with the engine flywheel ring gear to close the terminals between the BAT and MOT of the solenoid, which allows full battery voltage in series (24 V) to the cranking motor. Once the engine starts, the S/P switch returns by spring force to its disengaged position.

Cranking: combined S/P and magnetic switch circuit: Closing the circuit to the switch coil 7 pulls the solenoid plunger into the core. Normally, closed terminals at 1, 3, 2, and 5 are opened by plunger movement, and the two large contact disks between 1, 2, 3, and 4 come into contact with these terminals to tie both batteries into series for 24-V starting. Current flows to the BAT terminal of the solenoid and to the SW terminal, where part of the current passes through the pull-in winding to the MOT solenoid terminal and cranking motor circuit to the motor end terminal and back to the A or system battery. The rest of the circuit current flows through the hold-in winding, out the GRD terminal to the motor end terminal, and back to the A or system battery. Engagement of the pinion with the flywheel ring gear closes the cir-

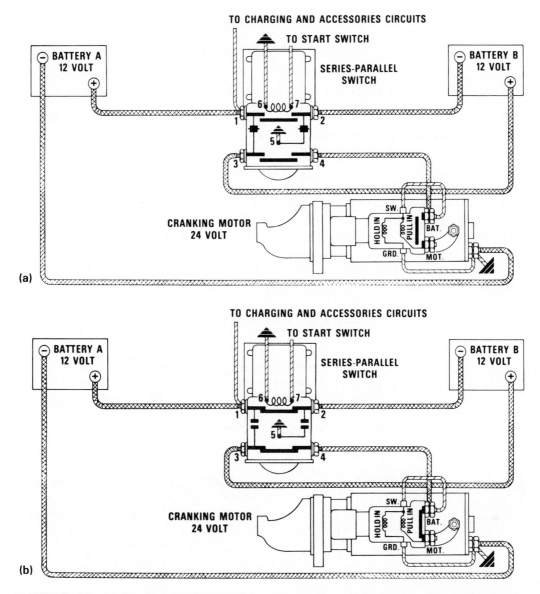

FIGURE 9-43 (a) Combined series–parallel and magnetic switch charging; (b) combined series–parallel and magnetic switch cranking. *(Courtesy of Delco Remy Division, General Motors Corporation.)*

cuit from the BAT and MOT solenoid terminals to give full battery voltage to the starter. When the engine starts and the switch is opened, the S/P switch is opened by internal spring pressure as the solenoid is deenergized [see Fig. 9–43(b)].

B circuit: charging: Current flows to S/P switch terminals when the engine is running. This current splits, with half going to the A or system battery to ground, while the other half passes through the points of terminals 2 and 5 through the B or cranking battery to the contacts between terminals 1 and 3 to ground [see Fig. 9–42(a)].

B circuit: cranking: Initial solenoid action is the same as that described for the A circuit cranking above.

With terminals 1 and 2 bridged by the large contact disk of the solenoid, current flows to the BAT terminal of the solenoid, where it travels through contact points at terminals 4 and 5 to the SW terminal on the cranking motor [see Fig. 9–42(b)].

Current flows through the hold-in and pull-in coils and to the GRD terminal and the frame terminal of the motor and on to both the A and B batteries. The pinion engages the flywheel ring gear and the circuit between the BAT and MOT terminals of the solenoid to provide full voltage to the starter motor (24 V). When the engine starts, the switch contacts are opened by the operator and the S/P switch returns to its charging position. Typical problems encountered with S/P switches are given in Table 9–2.

TABLE 9-2 Series–parallel (S/P) switch troubleshooting chart

Problem Symptom	Problem Cause	Remedy
Corrosion in switch	Water	Check switch gaskets
Blown fuse or circuit breaker	(a) Under capacity fuse or breaker	Install correct breaker
	(b) Pinion and ring gear abutment	Replace pinion or ring gear
	(c) Grounded motor	Repair motor
	(d) Faulty wiring	Repair wiring
Oscillating solenoids and burned contacts	Low batteries	Check batteries
	Wiring resistance	Check for cause
	Defective solenoid	Replace solenoid
Both A and B batteries under-charged	Low regulator setting	Adjust regulator
	Faulty alternator	Repair alternator
	Faulty wiring	Repair wiring
	Faulty regulator	Repair regulator
	Undercapacity Alternator	Replace with larger output alternator
Battery B Undercharged	High circuit resistance through B	Remove resistance
Burned or melted circuits in switch	No circuit breakers in #3 or #5 circuit	Install breakers
	Circuit breaker rating too high	Install proper units
	Improperly wired circuit breakers	Rewire circuit breakers to proper circuit

TRANSFORMER-RECTIFIER CIRCUITS

Both Leece-Neville and Delco-Remy alternators with a built-in TR (transformer-rectifier) system does away with the need for a series–parallel switch arrangement and simplifies the wiring needed to provide 24 V for starting along with a 12-V charging system. Figure 8–56 shows a typical wiring circuit for a Delco-Remy model 30SI-TR system. A typical Leece-Neville TR system is shown in Fig. 8–69 and Fig. 9–44, where only one additional wire is required over a straight 12-V system. This wire is a feed wire to charge the cranking batteries. Therefore, by eliminating the S/P switch, the cranking system is simplified and reliability is improved. Correct ground is determined by connection of an external jumper wire supplied as part of the alternator.

In the diagram shown in Fig. 9–44, four 6-V batteries permanently connected in series (24 V) are shown. All four batteries are therefore used for engine cranking purposes. When the engine is cranked over and then starts, one pair of batteries is electrically isolated from the other pair by the TR unit to ensure that only 12 V is fed to the truck chassis electrical system. This means that only two of the four 6-V batteries are used to supply power when the engine is running. The two batteries that supply chassis electrical power are charged by the alternator in the normal manner, while the two cranking batteries are charged by the TR (transformer-rectifier) unit, which is mounted on and is an integral part of the alternator assembly. The TR unit provides an isolated 12-V power source to charge the cranking batteries with no need for

a separate voltage regulator unit since the voltage output is controlled by the alternator regulator system. This means that when the engine is operating, that voltage at the cranking batteries is totally independent of the chassis electrical system voltage. TR alternators are physically interchangeable with those used on a standard 12-V charging system.

FIGURE 9-44 Typical 12/24-V electrical system wiring diagram. *(Courtesy of Mack Trucks, Inc.)*

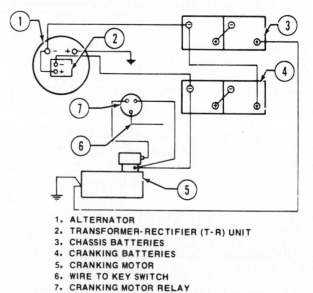

1. ALTERNATOR
2. TRANSFORMER-RECTIFIER (T-R) UNIT
3. CHASSIS BATTERIES
4. CRANKING BATTERIES
5. CRANKING MOTOR
6. WIRE TO KEY SWITCH
7. CRANKING MOTOR RELAY

Troubleshooting the Leece-Neville TR System

An example of how to troubleshoot a Leece-Neville 2500 JB alternator with a TR system follows. Note that Fig. 9–45 shows a positive grounded system, while Fig. 9–46 illustrates a negative grounded system.

Procedure

1. Check all batteries for an OCV (open-circuit voltage) value on all maintenance-free models, and/or specific gravity on conventional cell-top batteries.

2. Closely inspect vehicle wiring for loose connections, corroded terminals, and wire damage.

3. Disconnect the T-R to the battery charge lead (wire connection).

4. Refer to Fig. 3–29 or 8–46 and connect a VAT carbon pile (must be in the OFF position) and ammeter unit similar to that shown across the T-R (+) and (−) terminals (item 7 in Fig. 9–46).

5. Start and run the engine at 1500 rpm.

6. Turn on various vehicle electrical accessories until the ammeter registers a load of approximately 30 A.

7. Check the alternator voltage across the alternator (+) to (−) terminals. The recorded voltage should read between 13.5 and 14.0 V.

8. If the voltage noted in step 7 is not recorded, check the alternator output.

9. Change the voltmeter leads to TR (+) and (−) terminals and adjust the carbon pile load to read 15 A. The voltage of the T-R unit must be 11.8 to 12.4 V.

10. Replace the TR unit if the correct voltage is not achieved.

NOTE: Additional information on both the Delco and Leece Neville TR (transformer-rectifier) alternators is described in detail in Chapter 8. See page 258 for more information on Delco 30SI-TR models and page 279 for Leece-Neville models.

FIGURE 9–45 TR (transformer-rectifier) unit in positive-ground system. *(Courtesy of Mack Trucks, Inc.)*

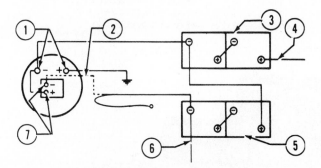

1. ALTERNATOR TERMINALS
2. CHARGING LEAD (SHOWN DISCONNECTED)
3. CHASSIS BATTERIES
4. TO CRANKING MOTOR
5. CRANKING BATTERIES
6. TO CRANKING MOTOR SOLENOID
7. TRANSFORMER-RECTIFIER (T-R) TERMINALS

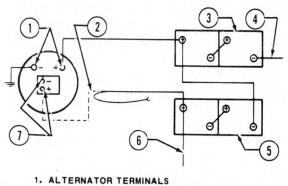

1. ALTERNATOR TERMINALS
2. CHARGING LEAD (SHOWN DISCONNECTED)
3. CHASSIS BATTERIES
4. TO CRANKING MOTOR
5. CRANKING BATTERIES
6. TO CRANKING MOTOR SOLENOID
7. TRANSFORMER-RECTIFIER (T-R) TERMINALS

FIGURE 9–46 TR (transformer-rectifier) unit in a negative-ground system. *(Courtesy of Mack Trucks, Inc.)*

MULTIVOLTAGE MANAGEMENT SYSTEM

Many heavy-duty truck/tractors may employ a 24-V starter motor but use a 12-V alternator charging system to supply the electrical components with 12 V for normal operation. This is achieved in most cases by the use of the series–parallel battery switch arrangement shown and discussed in Figs. 9–37 and 9–43 and in Chapter 3 (Figs. 3–12 and 3–13). An alternative arrangement to using a series–parallel switch is to employ a T/R (transformer-rectifier) system such as that shown in Figs. 9–44 through 9–46.

Advanced technology now allows a further option by which a 12/24-V, or alternatively, a 24/12-V electrical system, can be used on heavy-duty trucks and buses. On many heavy-duty truck/tractors it is often desirable to have a system that can provide a fully regulated 24 V from a 12-V chassis for auxiliary components. Prime applications for such a system are when 24 V starting is required, 12-V run and 24-V engine/transmission/brake controls, or 24 V for an on-board computer system. In addition, 12-V vehicles can be equipped with a 24-V battery bank for boost starting of heavy-duty engines. In other cases there may be a requirement for a 24- to 12-V converter to provide a fully regulated 12 V for auxiliary components such as electronic controls, radios, and on-board computer systems.

Figure 8–78 illustrates the 12- to 24-V Duvac II system, and Fig. 8–79 shows the 24- to 12-V Duvac II system. Both of these components are protected against reverse polarity, loss of ground, short circuits, overcurrent, overvoltage, and low-voltage conditions.

OVERCRANK PROTECTION DEVICES

Although the use of the sprag overrunning clutch and roller clutch drives has done much to improve the life of starter motors, damage can still result as a consequence of not releasing the switch quickly enough after the engine starts, or attempting to start an engine before it has actually stalled out. Shortened life can also be caused by accidental starter motor engagement while the engine is running.

One of the principal factors in shortened starter motor life is that of continued attempts to start a faulty engine, or long periods of starter motor engagement during either cold or hot weather in an attempt to start the engine. Few people ever allow the starter to cool for several minutes after continued cranking, even when they know that continued cranking is damaging to the starter motor and windings. Starter motor manufacturers recommend that no starter motor should ever be cranked longer than 30 seconds without allowing it to cool down.

Several optional devices are available to prevent both accidental starter motor engagement while the engine is running, rapid deenergizing of the motor on startup, and protection against cranking beyond the 30-second time period. An example of such a device to prevent cranking

the engine beyond the 30-second time period is shown in Fig. 9–47.

In the starter motor circuit shown in Fig. 9–47(b), the built-in thermostat located inside the motor and permanently attached to the field coils ensures that the starter motor cannot be continually cranked beyond the 30-second interval or at least against continued cranking for excessively long periods of time.

With the circuit shown in Fig. 9–47(b), battery current can flow to the magnetic switch winding, and the thermostatic control to ground when the switch is closed by the operator, an action that connects the motor solenoid to the battery via the S terminal. The pinion will engage the flywheel ring gear once the solenoid plunger is activated through the shift lever movement.

Once the pinion is engaged with the flywheel ring gear the main contacts of the solenoid close, and full battery power can crank the armature assembly of the motor. The action of the pinion drive mechanism will allow pinion overrun once the engine starts, as explained earlier, to protect the armature from excessive overspeed until

FIGURE 9–47 (a) Typical thermostat; (b) thermostatic wiring circuit; (c) starter motor showing thermostat connector. *(Courtesy of Delco Remy Division, General Motors Corporation.)*

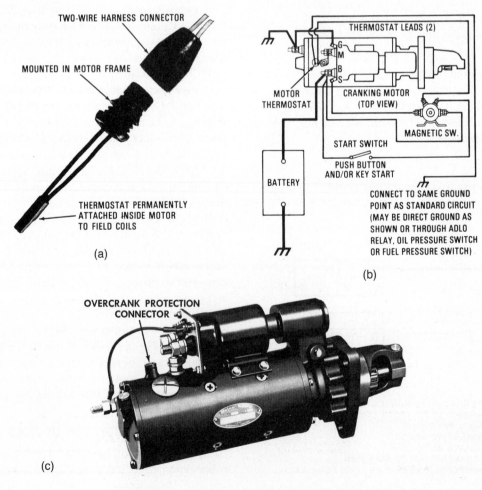

the starter switch is opened by the operator. If the switch is not opened quickly by the operator, armature damage can result.

If cranking time is ever allowed to continue for excessive periods of time, the temperature rise within the armature and field windings will cause the thermostatically controlled switch to open the circuit, and the engine cannot be cranked again for anywhere from 1 to 6 minutes, depending on the surrounding ambient temperature and the rate of cooling. Figure 9–47(c) shows the location of the overcrank protection connector.

Thermostat or Overcrank Protection Check

Procedure

1. Be sure the motor is cool, when the circuit should be closed.
2. Connect an ohmmeter to the two thermostat terminals on the motor.
3. The ohmmeter should read zero. If not, the thermostat is open-circuited. Replace the thermostat and field coil.

ADLO Circuits

Another type of protective circuit is the ADLO or automatic disengagement and lockout action, which can be used on starter motors with solenoid electrical systems, and which is also fitted with Delco-Remy Delcotron alternators, although other companies offer similar features. Figure 9–48 shows the wiring circuit that would be used with the ADLO feature.

The circuit shown in Fig. 9–48(a) is known as a frequency-sensing relay. When the operator pushes the starter button or moves the key switch to the START position, battery current can flow through the magnetic circuit to ground through the normally closed (NC) frequency-sensing relay contacts. The solenoid on the

starter is energized from the closed contacts of the magnetic switch. As soon as the engine starts, voltage from the alternator R or ac terminal energizes the frequency-sensing relay winding through the capacitor C1, which causes the relay contacts to open.

This action will automatically break the circuit through the magnetic switch, and the battery current can no longer flow to the starter. Opening of the relay switch contacts causes an induced voltage within the magnetic switch winding, thereby causing current flow through resistor R1, diode D2, and the relay winding to cause rapid opening of the contacts, which will reduce contact arcing. These induced voltages in the relay winding flow through ground and diode D1 back to the winding. Regardless of the operator keeping the starter switch closed (engaged), the motor would be disconnected the instant the engine starts.

In Fig. 9–48(b) the relay winding is connected directly to the generator R or the ac terminal. To ensure that the proper amount of R or ac terminal voltage with the start switch closed is maintained, resistor R1 connected between the switch and field winding of the generator assures rapid opening of the relay contacts immediately as the engine starts.

STARTER MOTOR TROUBLESHOOTING: ON VEHICLE

Starter motor troubles are often a direct result of poor maintenance practices caused by such simple items as a low-battery-charge condition, corroded terminals, and loose or corroded battery cables or connections at either the starter or solenoid. Many time a starter has been diagnosed as being the culprit, when in fact a simple connection or low-battery condition was the remedy required to correct the fault. Problems associated with batteries are described in Chapter 3, where both conventional and

FIGURE 9–48 (a) ADLO circuit with frequency-sensing relay; (b) ADLO circuit with voltage-sensing relay. *(Courtesy of Delco Remy Division, General Motors Corporation.)*

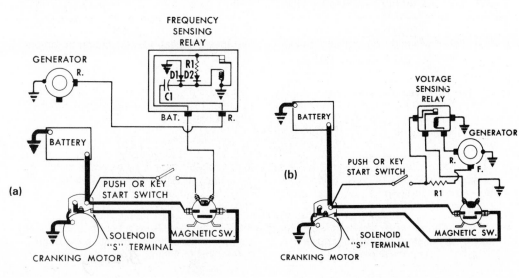

maintenance-free batteries are discussed. Next to low batteries, more cranking problems are caused by defective cables and connections than by any other reason. When cables are bolted to the vehicle frame to complete the ground circuit, it is suggested that the area around the bolt hole be cleaned of dirt, paint undercoating, and so on, and the area thoroughly tinned with solder to ensure a low-resistance connection.

If the cranking motor solenoid or magnetic switch does not operate properly, check the control circuit elements, such as the key switch, starter button, and relay. If voltage is low at the solenoid due to high circuit resistance, for example, it can prevent proper indexing of the drive if tooth abutment occurs. A common condition and symptom caused by this condition is chattering, which will destroy the cranking contacts quickly. Shift solenoids can draw from 45 to 90 A; therefore, it is imperative that switches, push buttons, relays, and wiring be of sufficient capacity to carry the solenoid current.

On vehicles so equipped, particularly automatic transmission trucks, check the neutral-start switch since a fault here can prevent starter operation. On heavy-duty starters check the overcrank thermostat for an open condition (see the discussion of Fig. 9-47).

One of the main causes of starter motor damage is a low state of battery charge. Repeated attempts to crank the engine over with low battery cranking voltage can cause failure due to:

1. Sluggish cranking
2. No cranking, but possibly clicking of the solenoid
3. The starter may chatter or pulse the drive in and out of the flywheel ring gear at a rapid rate, causing both pinion gear and flywheel ring gear damage. One or more but not all starter pinion gear drive teeth will show signs of case-hardening crushing, along with badly chipped or broken engine flywheel ring gear teeth.
4. Repeated attempts to try and start the engine can cause the solenoid to overheat, and in some cases the disk

will weld itself to the studs; the starter circuit is now continually connected to the batteries, resulting in steady motoring of the starter with or without cranking the engine. This condition can play havoc with any starter motor, and it usually results in the starter having to be removed and disassembled. Typical conditions exhibited after disassembly include:

    a. Blue, badly worn, or broken starter drive gear and worn bearings
    b. Discoloration of the armature shaft, particularly in the area of the drive pinion, accompanied by excessive wear of the support bearing
    c. Possible locking up of the armature shaft so that it cannot be rotated
    d. Discoloration or melting of the paint at the brush end of the starter motor and possible commutator and brush damage

5. The inability of the batteries to spin the engine over fast enough can result in compression kickback or engine rockback, which can result in a bent armature shaft.

Both starter motor and battery life can be lengthened by following the procedures listed below.

1. Never crank the engine longer than 30 seconds
2. Always wait at least 2 minutes before attempting to restart the engine.
3. If the engine fails to start, particularly in cold ambient operating conditions, steps 1 and 2 can be repeated for a total of seven 30-second cranking cycles if the batteries have enough power to attempt this many starts. You may have to recharge the batteries!
4. Wait for 30 minutes before attempting to recrank the engine. You may also have to either boost charge or change the batteries out if after this time period insufficient cranking power is available.
5. Repeat steps 1 and 2 once again.
6. Repeat steps 3 and 4 three more times for a total of four 30-second cranking cycles.

TABLE 9-3 Starter motor noise diagnosis

PROBLEM	CAUSE
1. High pitched whine during cranking (before engine fires) <u>but engine cranks and fires okay.</u>	Distance too great between starter pinion and flywheel.
2. High pitched whine after engine fires. As key is being released engine cranks and fires okay; this intermittent complaint is often diagnosed as "starter hang in" or "solenoid weak."	Distance too <u>small</u> between starter pinion and flywheel. Flywheel runout contributes to the intermittent nature.
3. Loud "whoop" after the engine fires but while the starter is still held engaged. Sounds like a siren if the engine is revved while starter is engaged.	Most probable cause is a defective clutch. A new clutch will often correct this problem.
4. "Rumble", "growl" or (in severe cases) a "knock" as the starter is coasting down to a stop after starting the engine.	Most probable cause is a bent or unbalanced starter armature. A new armature will often correct this problem. *Bearing*

7. Wait for another 30 minutes.

8. Repeat steps 5 through 7 as needed.

Although a starter may start the engine, if in the process, loud whining, growling, or a loud whoop occur, this can tip you off that there are indications of problems in the starter motor. Most starter motor noises can be traced to problems such as those listed in Table 9-3. Starter motor misalignment is usually not a problem on midrange and heavy-duty trucks since the starter nose cone is manufactured with a machined flange that ensures that it will fit snugly into the bore of the engine flywheel housing. However, on some light-duty gasoline and diesel pickup trucks, and certainly in many automotive applications, the starter does not have this self-alignment feature. Consequently, misalignment can occur, which requires the installation of shims between the flat surface of the starter mounting flange and engine block. In some cases centering of the starter drive pinion can be checked by removing the clutch inspection or lower engine flywheel cover. The starter pinion gear can be manually moved into engagement with the flywheel ring gear after disconnecting the battery power, and the clearance of the pinion teeth to the ring gear can be checked. A small wire gauge bent into a hook can be used to check the clearance between the pinion and ring gear as well as noting if there is equal clearance all around. Figure 9-49 illustrates how to perform this check. This dimensional clearance is usually around 5 mm (0.200 in.); otherwise, the starter must be shimmed away from the flywheel. Should the clearance exceed 6.5 mm (0.260 in.), shimming of the starter motor outboard mounting pad only is required (see Fig. 9-50).

When a problem exists in either the cranking motor circuit or the motor itself, it should never be removed from the engine before making a few general checks and tests. This action can save you unnecessary labor and expense, for often the problem can be traced to a minor

FIGURE 9-50 Starter motor shim placement (light-duty truck). *(Courtesy of GMC Truck Division, General Motors Corporation.)*

condition such as those discussed above. To assist you when a starter motor problem occurs, refer to Figs. 9-51 and 9-52, which systematically list typical problem areas that might result from a no-cranking condition or one where the starter cranks slowly or the solenoid clicks or chatters. Once the troubleshooting charts have been referred to, proceed to follow the recommended correction procedure. A number of procedures, checks, and tests are listed below in detail to assist you when attempting to pinpoint a starter motor problem.

Cable Sizes and Cranking Power

Prior to performing the various recommended tests and checks on a nonoperating starter motor and electrical circuit, let's quickly recall that for the starter motor to operate, it must have a battery or batteries that are close to, or at, a full state of charge, in order to spin the engine fast enough to initiate combustion. In Chapter 3 we discussed the terms *CCA* (cold cranking amperes) and *reserve capacity,* which both play an important part in the efficiency of starter motor operation. Examples of CCA ratings for various widely used midheavy and heavy-duty truck diesel engines were listed in Table 3-3. Failure to select a battery or batteries that have a sufficient CCA rating will lead to cranking problems, particularly when operating in low ambient temperatures (winter operation). In addition to the correct CCA rating, the heavy-duty cables that run from the battery to the starter motor and ground connections must be of the correct size and offer minimum resistance of flow.

SPECIAL NOTE: Table 3-4 lists the correct size of cable that must be used for a given length from the battery to the starter motor. The table also lists the maximum allowable starter circuit voltage drop per 100 A of battery power for both 12- and 24-V circuits. Refer to Table 3-4 when either new battery/starter cables are to be fabricated or when it has been confirmed by a resistance test that there is too much voltage drop between the battery and starter motor circuit.

Figure 9-53 illustrates a typical multiple-battery hookup to a heavy-duty starter motor on a class 8 highway truck/tractor. Note that two positive and two negative cables are used in this 12-V parallel circuit. The positive cables are connected to the solenoid, while the negative cables are connected to the starter stud. Many heavy-duty

FIGURE 9-49 Starter motor pinion and ring gear engagement. *(Courtesy of GMC Truck Division, General Motors Corporation.)*

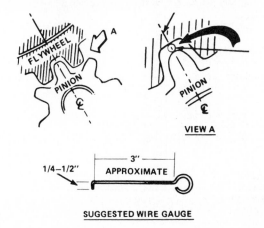

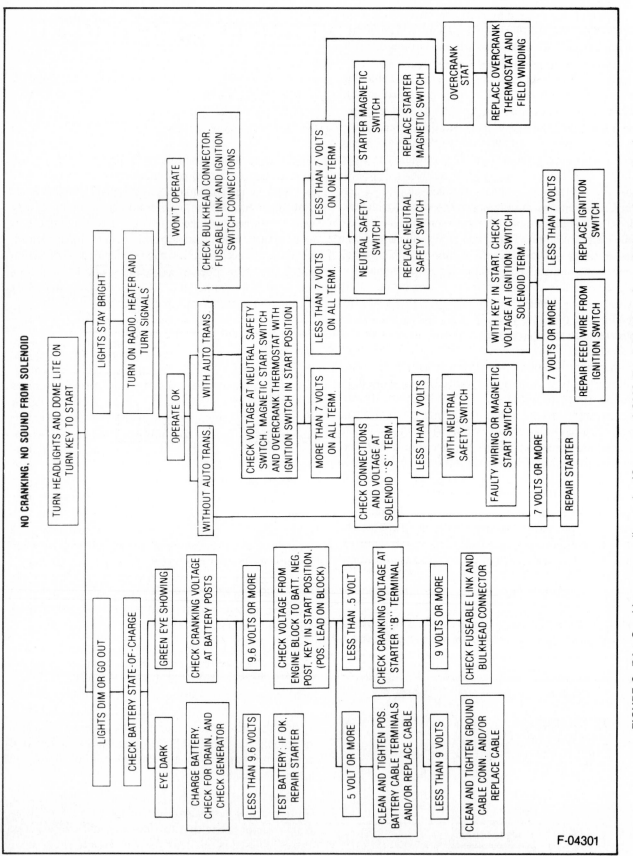

FIGURE 9-51 Cranking system diagnosis. *(Courtesy of GMC Truck Division, General Motors Corporation.)*

F-04301

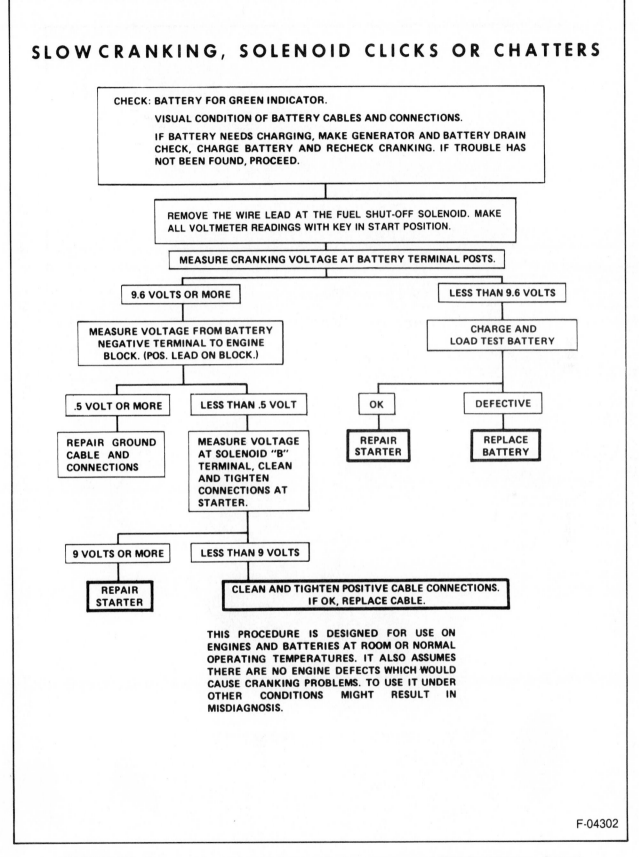

FIGURE 9–52 Slow cranking, solenoid clicks, or chatters. *(Courtesy of GMC Truck Division, General Motors Corporation.)*

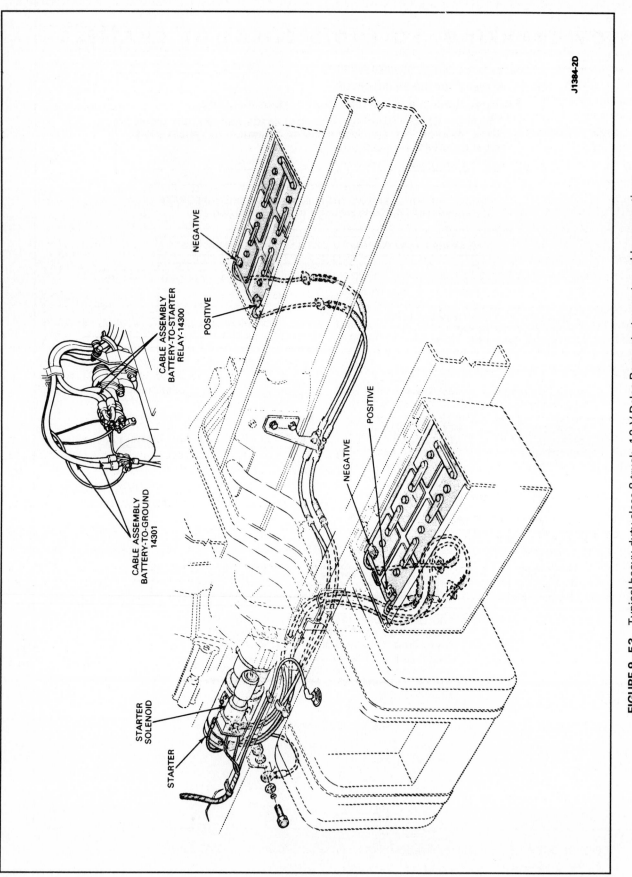

FIGURE 9–53 Typical heavy-duty class 8 truck, 12-V Delco Remy starter motor cable connections. *(Reprinted with Ford Motor Company's permission.)*

CABLE ASSEMBLY BATTERY-TO-STARTER RELAY-14300

CABLE ASSEMBLY BATTERY-TO-GROUND 14301

STARTER SOLENOID

STARTER

NEGATIVE

POSITIVE

NEGATIVE

POSITIVE

J1384-2D

class 7, and particularly class 8 truck manufacturers, prefer to use a high-output 12-V starting motor with an overrunning clutch drive on large-displacement high-horsepower diesel engines that require the equivalent of 24 V for cranking, but use 12-V lighting and accessory circuits. The same total battery capacity that would normally be used on a 24-V system must be retained and connected in parallel for the high-output 12-V starter motor. The battery cable sizes and lengths required for proper cranking circuit resistance for the 12-V high-output starter are shown in Table 3-4, which also lists the wire size, length, and resistance values necessary to ensure correct starter engagement through the switch leads.

Refer to Table 3-4 to determine the correct battery cable size for the heavy-duty starter motor circuit shown in Fig. 9-53, which illustrates the connections from the battery to the starter motor for a circuit using separate cables to and from the starter for each set of batteries, as well as for a circuit using one cable to and from the starter motor. Table 9-4 lists industry-acceptable standards for wire size (AWG) and length for 12-V standard starter motors, 12-V high-output models, and 24/32-V models, with typical resistance values given for both 12- and 24-V systems. The actual wiring connections to the starter motor from the batteries will vary on different makes of trucks, depending on the actual starter model used and the type of starter drive gear employed. Typical examples of two commonly employed wiring arrangements used on heavy-duty on-highway trucks can be seen in Figs. 9-36 and 9-37 for 12- and 24-V systems.

Making and Installing Starter Motor Cables

Due to the high current flow to the starter motor assembly, especially on heavy-duty diesel starters, for maximum protection, cables should be shrouded with sleeving to avoid abrasion damage from vibration. The cables should also be supported at intervals to prevent sagging.

Although there is a variety of cable terminal styles

TABLE 9-4 Acceptable industry standards for starter circuit resistance, plus recommended battery cable sizes

Type of starter motor	Maximum starting circuit resistance
12 V starter	0.00075 ohms
24 V starter	0.00200 ohms

Battery Cable Sizes American Wire Gauge	Maximum Length in Cranking Motor Circuit
12 V	
No. 00	3.7 m (12 ft)
No. 000	4.9 m (16 ft)
No. 0000 or two no. 0*	6.1 m (10 ft)
Two no. 00	7.6 m (25 ft)
12 V high output	
No. 00	2.1 m (7 ft)
No. 000	2.7 m (9 ft)
No. 0000 or two no. 0*	3.7 m (12 ft)
Two no. 00	4.3 m (14 ft)
24-32 V	
No. 00	6.1 m (20 ft)
No. 000	8.2 m (27 ft)
No. 0000 or two no. 0*	10.7 m (35 ft)
Two no. 00	13.7 m (45 ft)

Source: Cummins Engine Company, Inc.
*Two strands of No. 0 cable may be used in place of one no. 0000 cable providing all connections are carefully made to ensure equal current flow in each parallel cable.

readily available and used throughout the industry, it is recommended that the ends of starter motor cables be tinned and soldered to their respective terminal fittings to reduce the possibility of voltage drop and to ensure a good electrical connection under all operating conditions.

When grounding any wires or cables to the vehicle frame, wire-brush the area to remove any rust and paint so that bare metal is exposed to ensure a good connection.

Figure 9-54 illustrates the method for attaching a new starter cable terminal and filling it with solder.

FIGURE 9–54 Forming a starter motor fitting onto a cable by crimping, followed by soldering.

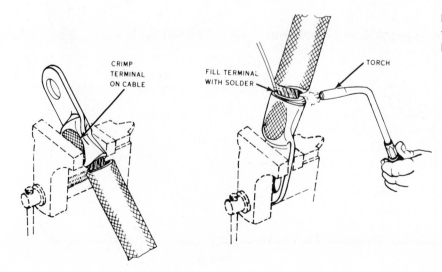

CRIMP TERMINAL ON CABLE

FILL TERMINAL WITH SOLDER

TORCH

SYSTEMATIC STARTER MOTOR CHECKS: ON VEHICLE

Experience with large truck fleet operation has shown that a problem with the starter cranking circuit can often be traced directly to poor wiring connections caused by corrosion. In the preceding section we discussed the importance of using the correct size of battery-to-starter motor cable and how to fabricate suitable cable fittings. Figures 9-51 and 9-52 are sequential starter motor troubleshooting charts that can be referred to as a means of pinpointing the possible problem area for poor starter motor operation. Although these charts can be used as a starting point, they do not list the actual methods and procedures required to confirm where the specific problem may be.

Basically, four main areas/circuits must be checked when a starter motor cranking problem exists. Since the starter motor relies heavily on adequately charged batteries, we must include a quick check of the charging system when slow- or no-cranking problems exist, so that we can isolate and or confirm that this circuit is performing as it should. The circuits that require checking are:

1. The cranking motor circuit
2. The starter solenoid circuit
3. The control circuit (key, pushbutton, and magnetic switch)
4. The charging circuit

SPECIAL NOTE: A typical heavy-duty truck starter/charging circuit procedural check recommended by the TMC/ATA (The Maintenance Council, American Trucking Associations), which appears in their *Recommended Maintenance Practices Manual* under Advisory Number AV1-6, is available as a wall chart. This chart is ideal for fleet maintenance service shop use.

Failure of the starter to crank the engine fast enough can be caused by low battery voltage, poor connections, switch problems, and so on. If the batteries have been checked and confirmed serviceable by a load test and a visual check of the cranking circuit fails to reveal a specific reason for the problem, you can quickly isolate the cause to the magnetic switch or the starter solenoid, as follows. If a magnetic switch in addition to a solenoid is used with the starter motor, shown in Fig. 9-55, and the starter motor sounds as though it is failing to remain in engagement, this could be due to low voltage releasing the electrical connection of the magnetic switch. Determine if the problem is in the magnetic switch using the following procedure.

Procedure

1. To prevent the engine from starting during the voltage test, you can disconnect the electric fuel solenoid connection, or tie the start/run lever in the stop position. On gasoline-powered trucks, disconnect the ignition and tachometer harness from the distributor.

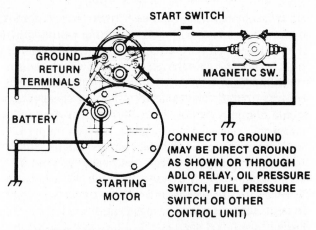

FIGURE 9-55 Layout of a typical heavy-duty starter motor cranking circuit using both a magnetic switch and a starter motor solenoid. *(Courtesy of Detroit Diesel Corporation.)*

2. Clamp a heavy battery jumper cable between the two large studs of the magnetic switch while cranking. Since the mag switch studs are at battery voltage, if the engine cranks normally during this test, the problem is in the magnetic switch since we are bypassing the switch with the use of the jumper cable.

3. If the engine still cranks slowly, and the batteries, switches, and wiring have been checked, proceed to check for available voltage at the cranking motor solenoid while cranking (see step 4).

4. A starter motor voltage drop check can quickly confirm whether or not the starter should be removed for service. Figure 9-56 illustrates a typical quick check that

FIGURE 9-56 Voltmeter connections at the starter motor to determine the available cranking voltage. *(Courtesy of Detroit Diesel Corporation.)*

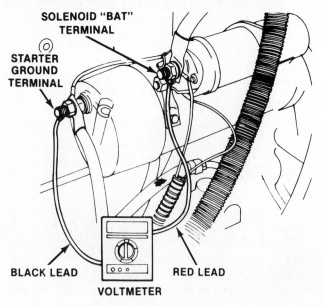

can be performed with the starter motor in position on the engine.

5. Place the positive (red) lead of a voltmeter against the solenoid BAT terminal and the negative (black) voltmeter lead against the starter motor ground terminal.

6. Close the starter switch (key or button) to crank the engine while noting the voltage reading on the face of the meter.

7. If the voltage is 9 V or less on a 12-V starter system while cranking at normal room temperature of 60 to 70 °F (15 to 21 °C), check the resistance and voltage loss between the interconnecting cables of the batteries. This can be done by moving to step 4.

8. While cranking the engine, touch the voltmeter leads to the positive and negative posts or stud nut of each battery. There should not be more than 0.5 V difference between any two battery readings; otherwise, there is high resistance level between connections. A starting circuit resistance check procedure is listed below.

Typical starter circuit voltage drops are established by the use of a voltmeter connected across sections of the circuit in parallel, then isolating the problem area. Examples of voltage drops for a standard 12-V system are generally as follows:

1. Starter motor-to-battery cable length under 1 m (3 ft), a maximum of 0.1 V.

2. Same as (1) above, but a cable length of 1 to 2 m (3 to 6.5 ft), a maximum of 0.2 V.

3. A mechanical switch, a maximum of 0.1 V.

4. Starter solenoid switch, a maximum of 0.2 V.

5. Starter magnetic switch, preferably within 0.3 V, although some manufacturers quote up to 0.5 V.

6. There should be as little voltage drop as possible at all connections. When voltage drop tests are performed correctly, poor connections or corroded or undersized cables can be detected quickly. When connecting the voltmeter, attach the lead to the terminal stud rather than to the terminal so that the drop across the connection will be made. The various starter circuit resistance checks are generally completed in the following order:

1. Starting circuit resistance check
   a. Power supply check (voltage drop)
   b. Solenoid and magnetic switch check
   c. Ground check
   d. Magnetic switch-to-solenoid check
2. Overcrank thermostat check

Starting Circuit Resistance Test

The series of checks required here will confirm specifically where the actual problem may lie. This procedure involves the subchecks listed above as 1a through 1d. Refer to Fig. 9-57 which illustrates the starter motor circuit along with the necessary volt-ohmmeter connections required to check the resistance through the circuit of a Delco starter motor. The same basic checks and tests illustrated and

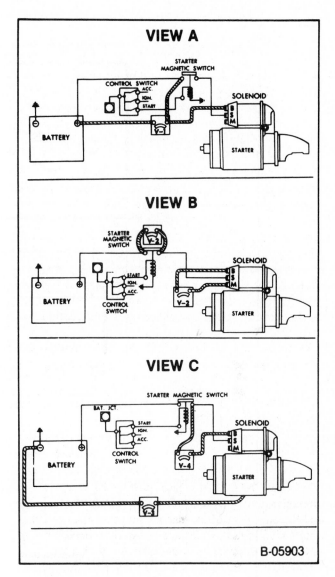

FIGURE 9-57 Volt/ohmmeter connections for checking starter motor circuit resistance. *(Courtesy of GMC Truck Division, General Motors Corporation.)*

described below for Delco starter motors apply equally to other major makes. Fig. 9-58 illustrates typical voltmeter connections for voltage drop tests for diesel engines equipped with Leece-Neville heavy-duty starter assemblies. Note that the lower diagram in this schematic represents a system with a series-parallel switch. Refer to the section in this chapter dealing with series parallel switches for more information on this type of system.

NOTE: To prevent the engine from starting while performing the circuit resistance check, you should disconnect the ignition and tachometer harness from the distributor on gasoline engines, and on diesel engines you should disconnect the wire lead at the fuel shutoff solenoid. If the engine is not equipped with an electric fuel shutoff solenoid, tie the fuel injection pump governor stop lever in the NO FUEL/STOP position. Connect a

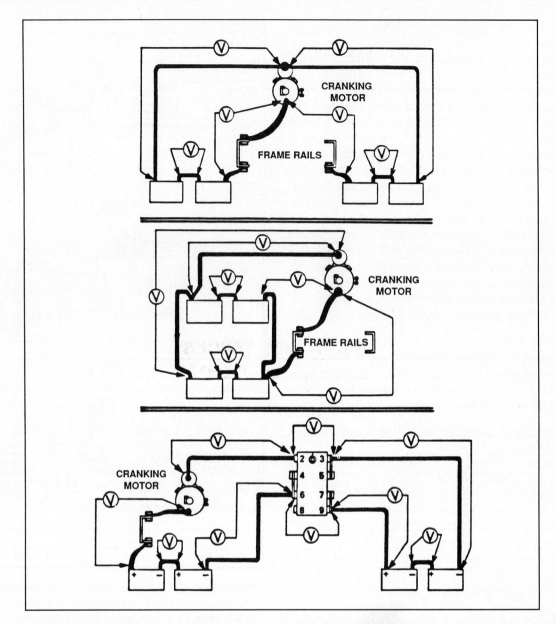

FIGURE 9-58 Typical voltmeter connections to determine the voltage drop at various locations on a series–parallel starter motor circuit. *(Courtesy of Peterbilt Motors Company, Division of PAC-CAR, Newark, CA.)*

remote starter button/switch to allow you to crank the engine over for test purposes. Also keep in mind that the starter motor cannot be checked against specifications while on the vehicle (e.g., a no-load test); however, a check can be made for excessive resistance in the circuit.

CAUTION: Do *not* operate the starter motor for longer than 15 seconds during these tests. Allow approximately 2 minutes for cooling purposes between cranking tests if the 15-second time period is reached.

Procedure

1. *Power supply check.* Connect the voltmeter as shown in Fig. 9-57, view A; this is between the battery positive post (red lead) and the battery terminal (black lead) on the starter solenoid. If the starter has a solenoid and a magnetic switch, connect the voltmeter leads to the battery positive post first, then the battery terminal on the starter solenoid, and read the voltage value. Now switch one voltmeter lead from the solenoid to the battery terminal on the magnetic switch and repeat the resistance check. If the voltmeter registers in excess of 0.5 V for a 12-V system in either test while the engine is being cranked, at more than 1 V for a 24-V system, excessive resistance is apparent. This resistance could be caused by loose, corroded, or dirty connections or possibly by frayed cables.

TABLE 9-5   Typical Delco starter motor test specs

MEDIUM DUTY TRUCKS

Starter Motor	Series	Type	Volts	No Load Test				Spec. No.
				AMPS		RPM		
				Min.	Max.	Min.	Max.	
1998473[b]	10MT	100	10	60	90	6500	10500	3592
1998474[b]	10MT	100	10	60	90	6500	10500	3592
1998499[b]	10MT	100	10	70	110	6500	10700	3563
1998500[b]	10MT	100	10	70	110	6500	10700	3563
1998501[b]	10MT	100	10	70	110	6500	10700	3563
1993759[c]	37MT	300	10	140	175	6600	8200	7104
1990304[a]	40MT	400	10	140	215	4000	7000	3501
1990369[a]	42MT	400	10	100	170	5500	7800	7113

Pinion Clearance:
  a. 8.3 to 9.9 mm (0.33 to 0.39 inch)
  b. 0.25 to 4.06 mm (0.01 to 0.16 inch)
  c. 0.25 to 1.78 mm (0.01 to 0.07 inch)

HEAVY DUTY TRUCKS

Starter Motor	Series	Type	Volts	No Load Test				Spec. No.
				AMPS		RPM		
				Min.	Max.	Min.	Max.	
1990261[a]	50MT	400	11	210	270	5500	7400	3599
1990354[a]	42MT	400	10	100	170	5500	7800	7113
1990369[a]	42MT	400	10	100	170	5500	7800	7113
1990391[a]	42MT	450	10	100	170	5500	7800	7113
1990431[a]	42MT	450	10	100	170	5500	7800	7113
1990449[a]	42MT	450	10	100	170	5500	7800	7113
1990450[a]	42MT	400	10	100	170	5500	7800	7113
1990451[a]	42MT	450	10	100	170	5500	7800	7113

Pinion Clearance:
  a. 8.3 to 9.9 mm (0.33 to 0.39 inch)

SOLENOID SWITCH SPECIFICATIONS

Starter	Solenoid	Volts	Pull-In		Hold-In	
			AMPS	Volts	AMPS	Volts
All 10MT	1114489	12	11-18	5	13-18	10
1993759	1115609	12	24-29	5	16-20	10
1990304	1115561	12	28-35.7	5	13-15.4	10
1990369	1115598	12	34-46	5	16.5-20	10
1990354	1115593	12	34-46	5	16.5-20	10
1990431	1115593	12	34-46	5	16.5-20	10
1990450	1115598	12	34-46	5	16.5-20	10
1990261	1115556	12	28-35.7	5	13-15.4	10
1990391	1115593	12	34-46	5	16.5-20	10
1990449	1115593	12	34-46	5	16.5-20	10
1990451	1115598	12	34-46	5	16.5-20	10

Source: GMC Truck Division, General Motors Corporation.

2. *Solenoid and magnetic switch check.* Connect the voltmeter as shown in Fig. 9-57, view B; this is between the battery terminal and the motor terminal on the solenoid. If both a solenoid and a magnetic switch are used, connect the voltmeter leads to the battery terminal and the motor terminal on the magnetic switch. Crank the engine over on the starter motor and note the voltage value recorded on the meter. Again, if this value exceeds 0.5 V on a 12-V system (1 V on a 24-V system), excessive resistance is apparent in the circuit. Check for the same causes as those listed in check 1.

3. *Starter ground check.* Connect the voltmeter leads as shown in Fig. 9-57 view C; this is with the leads connected to the battery negative post and to the ground on the starter motor field frame. The maximum allowable value is 0.5 V on a 12-V system or 1 V on a 24-V system. Both hard starting and charging system problems can occur if poor connections or high circuit resistance is encountered on the battery ground circuit.

With the voltmeter leads connected across the starter motor and battery ground post, the allowable voltage drop is usually in the region of 0.2 V. More than 0.2 V indicates a poor ground, a loose motor mounting bolt, or a bad battery ground to the engine or frame.

4. *Magnetic switch to solenoid check.* Connect the voltmeter leads as shown in Fig. 9-57 view C; this is with the leads connected between the solenoid and the magnetic switch (leads connected to the motor terminal on the magnetic switch and the battery terminal on the starter solenoid). Crank the engine and note the voltage, which should not exceed 0.5-V on a 12-V system (1 V on a 24-V system); otherwise, excessive resistance is apparent.

NOTE: The maximum resistance values of 0.5 V given above for the tests are considered acceptable for a heavy-duty 12-V circuit; however, always refer to the truck manufacturer's specifications since these values may be lower. Some examples of starter motor off-vehicle test specifications are given in Table 9-5 (see p. 363). Voltage readings across the solenoid coil terminals of heavy-duty starter motors should be at least 11 V for a 12-V system and 22 V for a 24-V system. Note that on some systems the starter will still operate with a reading as low as 10 V on a 12-V system, or as low as 20 V on a 24-V system. Depending on the starter motor voltage, the shift solenoid can draw from 45 to 90 A during operation.

Overcrank Thermostat Check

The overcrank thermostat system is used on heavy-duty cranking motors to prevent excessive cranking time. It operates by using a thermostat located in the starter motor as shown in Fig. 9-47. On starter motors so equipped, if the driver continues to crank a nonstarting engine, the temperature will rise steadily, due to the high amperage flow from the batteries. Once a preset temperature is reached, the overcrank protective feature will cause a no-crank condition, in order to protect the starter.

Procedure

1. For the circuit to be closed, the motor must be cool. If a check is made when the motor is hot, the circuit will be "open" and no reading can be obtained on the ohmmeter.

2. Connect an ohmmeter to the two thermostat terminals on the motor as shown in Fig. 9-47(b).

3. There should be a zero value reading on the ohmmeter at this time; otherwise, the thermostat is open-circuited. If so, replace the thermostat and field coil.

STARTER MOTOR CHECKS: OFF VEHICLE

After performing the resistance tests above and correcting any loose, corroded, or frayed connections, if the starter motor still fails to perform satisfactorily, remove the motor from the engine and perform the off-vehicle tests described in this section.

FIGURE 9-59 Delco Model 10MT starter motor attachment connections. *(Courtesy of GMC Truck Division, General Motors Corporation.)*

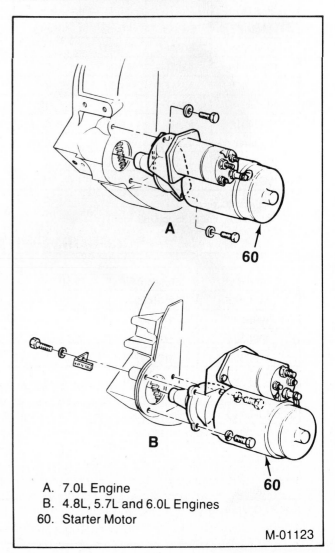

A. 7.0L Engine
B. 4.8L, 5.7L and 6.0L Engines
60. Starter Motor

M-01123

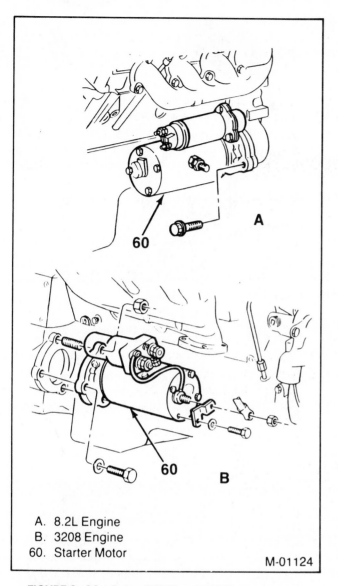

A. 8.2L Engine
B. 3208 Engine
60. Starter Motor

M-01124

FIGURE 9-60 Delco 37MT and 42MT starter motor attachment arrangement to the engine. *(Courtesy of GMC Truck Division, General Motors Corporation.)*

Starter Motor Removal

Procedure

1. Disconnect the batteries to prevent any possibility of the starter being energized during the removal process.
2. Refer to Figs. 9–59 and 9–60 which illustrate examples of Delco 10MT and 37/42 MT starter motor attachment to midrange and heavy-duty engines. Minor variations exist between starter-to-engine attachments; however, this removal procedure can be considered common for all engines. In some applications a heat shield may be bolted to the starter motor when an exhaust pipe is routed in close proximity to it.
3. Disconnect the wiring from both the starter solenoid and the battery cable connections.
4. Do not remove all of the starter retaining bolts prior to ensuring that you will be able to support the weight

of the starter itself. Many heavy-duty diesel engine starter motors can weigh up to 50 to 70 lb (23 to 32 kg).
5. Once you have ensured that the starter motor can be handled safely, remove the remaining retaining bolts and pull the motor away from the engine mounting pad.

Starter Diagnosis Prior to Disassembly

When a starter motor exhibits cranking problems, and both the battery and charging circuits have been checked using the respective procedural tests in this chapter, perform the following checks on the starter motor after it has been removed from the engine and prior to conducting a no-load test:

CAUTION: Do not connect any battery power to the starter at this time.

1. Attempt to rotate the starter motor pinion (drive gear) manually on its splined shaft. If it does not rotate freely, proceed to step 2.
2. Attempt to pry the pinion gear over with a screwdriver. If the pinion still refuses to rotate or is tight, it is probably due to tight shaft bearings/bushings, a possible bent armature shaft, or even a loose pole shoe screw.

NOTE: If the pinion and armature cannot be rotated freely manually, the starter should be disassembled. Do *not* attempt to rotate it by connecting battery power to it since serious damage can result. However, if the pinion/armature shaft can be rotated freely, perform a no-load test as described in this section under the relevant heading. If the starter is equipped with a thermostat or overcrank protection device, ensure that it is operational according to the check procedure stated earlier.

No-Load Test

This test actually confirms whether or not the starter motor assembly is receiving the correct voltage, drawing the right amperage, and rotating at the recommended speed. To conduct the test effectively, you must refer to the starter motor manufacturer's specifications. An example of typical test specs for a number of Delco starter assemblies is given in Table 9–5. Automotive/truck electrical rebuild shops are generally equipped with all of the necessary special test equipment to service/repair starters and alternators. If a starter test bench is available, use it; if not, the no-load test can be performed by clamping the starter motor securely in a vise.

The necessary test hookup connections to the starter motor will vary slightly depending on the make of the starter and the model; however, Fig. 9–61 illustrates a typical test hookup for a light/medium-duty starter motor assembly, and Fig. 9–62 shows the difference in the no-load test hookup for a heavy-duty starter with ground terminals.

Procedure

1. Connect the necessary test instrumentation as shown in Fig. 9–61 or 9–62.

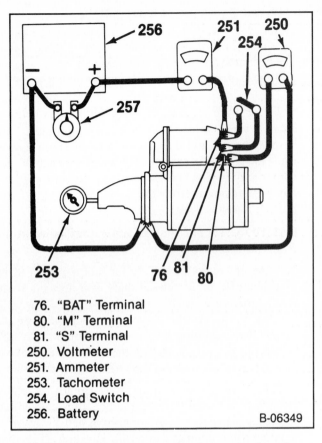

76. "BAT" Terminal
80. "M" Terminal
81. "S" Terminal
250. Voltmeter
251. Ammeter
253. Tachometer
254. Load Switch
256. Battery

B-06349

FIGURE 9–61 Typical no-load test hookup for light/medium-duty starter motors. *(Courtesy of GMC Truck Division, General Motors Corporation.)*

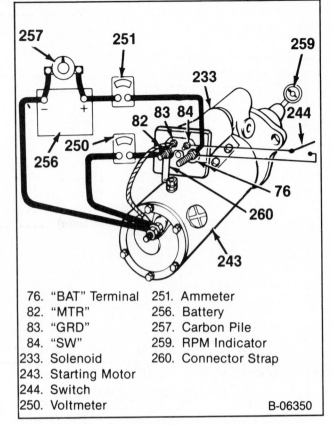

76. "BAT" Terminal	251. Ammeter
82. "MTR"	256. Battery
83. "GRD"	257. Carbon Pile
84. "SW"	259. RPM Indicator
233. Solenoid	260. Connector Strap
243. Starting Motor	
244. Switch	
250. Voltmeter	

B-06350

FIGURE 9–62 No-load test hookup on heavy-duty starter motors with ground terminals. *(Courtesy of GMC Truck Division, General Motors Corporation.)*

2. Make sure that the voltmeter is connected between the motor terminal and the motor frame on light/medium-duty starter models. On heavy-duty starting motors with ground terminals, always connect the voltmeter to it rather than to the starter frame.

CAUTION: Although some maintenance personnel connect/bolt the positive battery cable to the solenoid, then simply touch the negative battery cable directly to the starter motor frame or vise in order to motor the starter pinion, this is a dangerous practice, since heavy amperage is being transformed through the negative connection. This can result in sparks flying and possible personal injury. Always ensure that a switch control mechanism, as shown in Figs. 9–61 and 9–62 is connected into the test circuit to avoid these dangerous possibilities.

3. Prior to connecting the negative battery terminal, make certain that the control switch is in the OFF position; otherwise, the starter will motor as soon as the connection is made.

4. With all instrumentation—the voltmeter, ammeter, and tachometer—in position, close the control switch and note the voltage value, amperage draw, and rotative speed of the pinion shaft on the tach. Examples of starter motor no-load test specifications appear in Table 9–5.

SPECIAL NOTE: Table 9–5 lists the test specifications for a number of 12-V Delco midrange and heavy-duty truck starters. If a truck is equipped with a Delco 24-V starter model, typical test specs would call for between 350 and 450 A of current draw under normal load. The maximum load in amperes should not exceed 900 A, while the current draw on a no-load test hookup should be 123 A at 23.3 V. If special equipment is available to check the starter motor stall torque, the minimum stall torque for 12-V Delco models should be 21 N·m (15 ft-lb) at 1.5 V and 700 A. The 24-V starters should have a minimum stall torque of 21 N·m (15 ft-lb) at 1.5 V and 350 A. Clamp the starter motor securely in a vise with an adapter that would lock the starter pinion drive gear from rotating during the stall test. Consequently, with an ammeter, a voltmeter, and a torque gauge meter connected into position, all of these features can be monitored and recorded and compared to the manufacturer's test specifications.

Tables 9–6 and 9–7 list starter test specs for a Nippondenso unit used on GMC/Isuzu medium-duty trucks. The voltages given in the example test specs are minimum values. Higher voltage readings may be obtained with a fully charged battery or batteries. Keep in mind, however, that if the voltage is higher than the minimum level,

TABLE 9-6 Nippondenso starter motor specifications, GMC/Isuzu model W4 medium-duty steel tilt cab

Part No	94039465
Rated Voltage	12
Rated Output (kw)	3
Terminal Voltage (No Load)	11
Maximum Current (Amperes) (No Load)	220
Minimum rpm (No Load)	4200
Maximum Voltage (Load)	7
Maximum Current (No Load)	890
Minimum rpm (Load)	940
Maximum Solenoid Voltage	3
Maximum Solenoid Current	1800
Maximum Cranking Time	30 sec.
Number of Pinion Gear Teeth	11
Pinion Gear Rotation (View From Pinion Side)	Clockwise
Brush Length	
Standard	20.5 mm (0.81″)
Limit	13 mm (0.51″)
Commutator Diameter	
Standard	43 mm (1.693″)
Limit	42 mm (1.653″)
Mica Segment Undercut	
Standard	0.5–0.8 mm (0.020–0.031″)
Limit	0.2 mm (0.0079″)
Brush Spring Tension	
Limit	3.3 kg (7.3 lbs.)
Starter Motor Weight	10.5 kg (23 lbs.)

Source: GMC Truck Divison, General Motors Corporation.

TABLE 9-7 Nippondenso starter motor specifications, GMC/Isuzu model W7 and W7HV medium-duty steel tilt cab

Part Number	94039465
Manufacturer	Nippon Denso
Rated Voltage	12
Rated Output (kW)	3
Terminal Voltage (No Load)	11
Maximum Current (Amperes) (No Load)	220
Minimum RPM (No Load)	4200
Continuous Operator Limit (Seconds)	30
Solenoid Switch	
Series Coil Resistance—Ohm at 20°C (63°F)	0.20-0.24
Shunt Coil Resistance—Ohm at 20°C (63°F)	0.61-0.71
Brush Length	
Standard	20 mm, 0.79-inch
Limit	10 mm, 0.39-inch
Commutator Diameter	
Standard	43 mm, 1.69-inch
Limit	42 mm, 1.65-inch
Mica Undercut	
Standard	0.5-0.8 mm, 0.02-0.03-inch
Limit	0.2 mm, 0.008-inch

Source: GMC Truck Division, General Motors Corporation.

starter motor speed will also be higher, while the amperage draw will remain basically unchanged. Note in Fig. 9–62 a carbon pile, shown as item 257. This pile can be used if it is desired to control the voltage value to that shown in the manufacturer's test specifications. Also note that if the specified current draw does not include the solenoid, subtract from the ammeter reading the specified current draw of the solenoid hold-in winding.

The no-load test specs can be compared to the manufacturer's specifications to determine the condition of the starter motor assembly. The test specs obtained would indicate the following situations:

1. The starter motor is operating correctly if at the minimum voltage value, both the amperage draw and the no-load speed registered on the tachometer are as in the published test specs.

2. If the current draw exceeds the test specs and the no-load speed is low, the starter motor would require disassembly to confirm the following possible problem areas:

a. A grounded armature or field coil

b. Excessive friction due to worn or tight bearings, loose pole shoes, or a bent armature shaft, which would cause the armature to drag

c. Possible short circuits in the armature windings (check with the use of a growler as in Fig. 9–70)

3. If the ammeter registers a high current draw but the starter fails to rotate, check for a direct ground circuit in either the field windings or the terminal connection. This could also be caused by frozen bearings, which you should have noticed during the visual/manual inspection test earlier when the pinion gear was rotated by hand.

4. If there is no current draw on the ammeter (starter inoperative), check for:

a. Broken brush springs or worn brushes, which can be inspected on some starter motors by removing the band clamp around the starter body opposite the drive end.

b. High insulation between the armature commutator bar segments, which would prevent good contact between the brushes and commutator.

c. Opens in the armature coil windings, which can usually be confirmed by signs of burning on the commutator bar segments.

d. Open field circuit, which can be checked and confirmed only after the starter motor has been disassembled by inspecting the internal connections and tracing the circuit with a suitable test lamp.

5. A low rotative speed accompanied by a low current draw is generally indicative of high internal circuit resistance, which can be caused by loose or poor connections, defective leads, glazed/dirty commutator bars, plus some of the problems associated with item 4.

6. A high current draw accompanied by high rotative speed can normally be traced to shorted field coils, although it is also possible that the armature is shorted.

Check the field coils and the armature on a growler. If shorted field coils are suspected, replace the field coil assembly and recheck the starter motor test conditions.

STARTER MOTOR OVERHAUL

Should the starter motor fail to pass the various checks and tests described above, it should be disassembled with care and a series of close inspections, tests, and replacement parts installed to bring it back to 100% operational condition. Although there are many types and styles of starter motors in use on midrange and heavy-duty class 8 trucks, the disassembly, inspection, test, and reassembly can be considered common for most starters, with minor exceptions.

Although many service personnel disassemble the starter motor only as far as is necessary to effect the necessary repair, if there are a lot of service hours/miles on a starter, it is generally wise to do a complete teardown and inspection to ensure that the unit will continue to operate trouble-free for many more hours/miles of service.

Such an example would include inspection and replacement of the motor brushes without checking the condition of the commutator bar segments. Failure to clean up the commutator can result in short life of the new brushes and slow-cranking or no-cranking problems, particularly if there are any signs of discoloration or burning around the commutator bar segments. Prior to disassembling the starter motor, refer to the various sectional and exploded views of various model starters in this chapter to give yourself a mental image of just how and where the component parts are located in relation to one another. Use these diagrammatic views to assist you when disassembling, inspecting, or reassembling the starter motor assembly.

Recommended repair operations that should be conducted on a starter motor at overhaul include the following:

1. Brush replacement

2. Check of brush spring tension and possible replacement

3. Check or replacement of all bearings or bushings

4. Inspection check and possible replacement of the starter drive gear and clutch assembly

5. Field coil checks for shorts or opens

6. Armature winding check for shorts or opens

7. Possible remachining of the armature commutator

8. Inspection and possible undercutting of the commutator bar segments' insulation depth

9. Check and adjustment of all end plays and torque values

10. Solenoid assembly inspection and repair

11. Bench test of reassembled starter motor (see no-load testing as shown in Fig. 9–62).

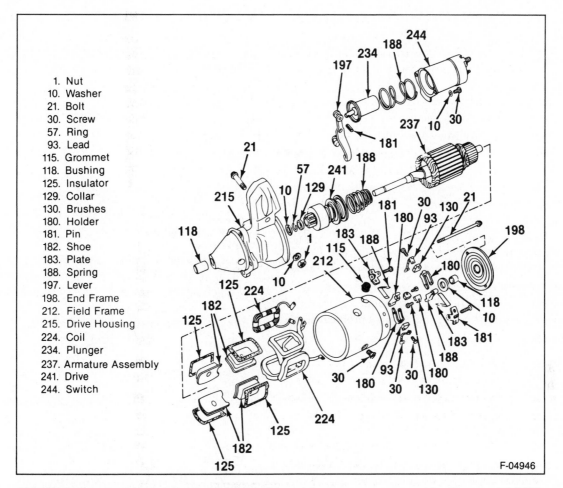

Parts list:

1. Nut
10. Washer
21. Bolt
30. Screw
57. Ring
93. Lead
115. Grommet
118. Bushing
125. Insulator
129. Collar
130. Brushes
180. Holder
181. Pin
182. Shoe
183. Plate
188. Spring
197. Lever
198. End Frame
212. Field Frame
215. Drive Housing
224. Coil
234. Plunger
237. Armature Assembly
241. Drive
244. Switch

F-04946

FIGURE 9–63 Exploded view of a Delco 10MT model starter motor assembly. *(Courtesy of GMC Truck Division, General Motors Corporation.)*

Disassembly of the Starter Motor

To assist you with regard to starter motor disassembly, refer to Fig. 9–63, which illustrates a Delco model 10MT starter, and to Fig. 9–64, which shows an exploded view of a heavy-duty truck Delco model 42MT starter motor assembly. These two views illustrate a light/medium-duty starter as well as the most widely used heavy-duty starter in North America. Notice the similarities in design between the two models. Information relative to these two models can be used when performing checks and tests on other makes of starters.

SAFETY NOTE: Always wear safety glasses when performing starter overhaul procedures.

Teardown Procedure. With the starter motor removed from the engine, clean the exterior surfaces with solvent or a mineral degreaser and a stiff brush. Take care not to submerge the starter assembly in solvent or a degreasing tank since the windings will be saturated and you will have problems upon reassembly of the rebuilt starter. Refer to Fig. 9–64 which shows a Delco model 42MT heavy-duty starter in exploded form; we shall use this unit as our example for teardown, inspection, and overhaul purposes. An assembled sectional view of the 42MT starter was shown in Fig. 9–8. In addition, since there are still many thousands of 40MT model starters in use on heavy-duty trucks, Fig. 9–65 illustrates an exploded view of this unit. It is very similar in appearance to the 42MT, which superseded the 40MT model. The overhaul information described for the 42MT model can be applied equally to the Delco model 37MT, 40MT, and 50MT starter assemblies, with much of this also being applicable to the Delco lighter-duty 10MT and 27MT models used on gasoline and light-duty diesel models.

Procedure

1. Since most starter motors are designed for use on more than one model of engine, both the solenoid and nose cone should be match marked as to their respective location to the starter body to ensure replacement in the same position. Also match mark the field frame and end frame to the main starter body housing. Often, service personnel will omit this step and find that after starter

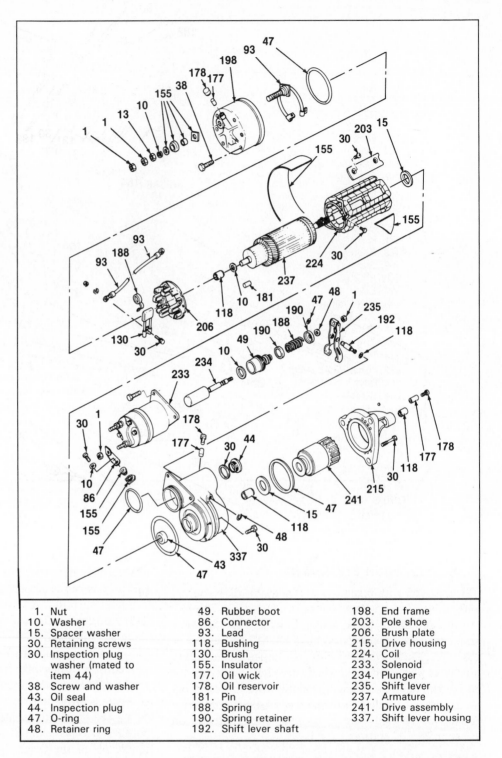

FIGURE 9-64 Exploded view of a Delco heavy-duty model 42MT starter motor assembly. *(Courtesy of GMC Truck Division, General Motors Corporation.)*

1. Nut	49. Rubber boot	198. End frame
10. Washer	86. Connector	203. Pole shoe
15. Spacer washer	93. Lead	206. Brush plate
30. Retaining screws	118. Bushing	215. Drive housing
30. Inspection plug	130. Brush	224. Coil
washer (mated to	155. Insulator	233. Solenoid
item 44)	177. Oil wick	234. Plunger
38. Screw and washer	178. Oil reservoir	235. Shift lever
43. Oil seal	181. Pin	237. Armature
44. Inspection plug	188. Spring	241. Drive assembly
47. O-ring	190. Spring retainer	337. Shift lever housing
48. Retainer ring	192. Shift lever shaft	

reassembly, either the solenoid or nose cone are in the wrong position, making it impossible to bolt the assembly back onto the engine.

NOTE: Unless otherwise stated, all reference items in the following descriptive text relate to the exploded view of the 42MT starter model shown in Fig. 9-64. Please take careful note that a number of items shown in these exploded views have the same identification number. A good example of this would be item 30, which appears in seven different places in Figs. 9-64 and 9-65 for the

40MT and 42MT starter motor. Therefore, when a reference is made to remove item 30, check the exploded view closely to determine the specific retaining screw that should be removed to free-up a component.

2. Refer to Fig. 9-64 and remove the large threaded plug (44) and its gasket (30) from the shift lever housing. These same items are shown as 51 and 45 for the 40MT starter in Fig. 9-65.

3. Remove the six bolts (38) that hold the brush end frame housing (198) to the main starter housing, which

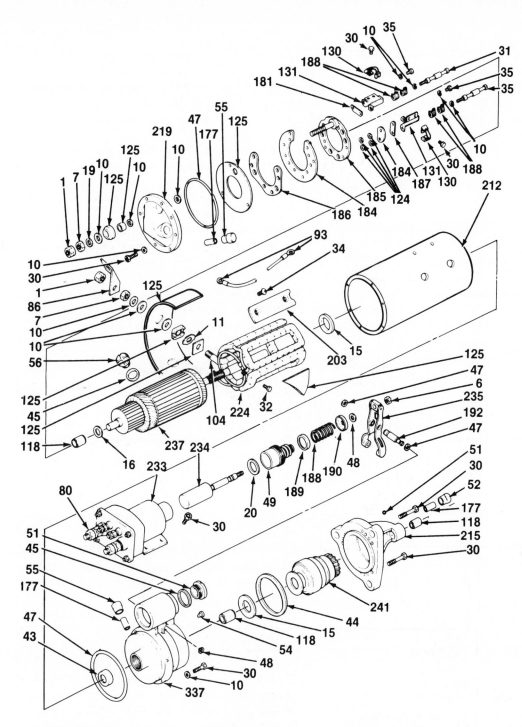

1. Nut	48. Retainer Ring	185. Terminal Plate
6. Adjusting Nut	49. Boot	186. Support Plate
7. Jam Nut	51. Plug	187. Spacing Plate
10. Washer	52. Oil Reservoir Plug	188. Spring
11. Insulation Washer	54. Mount Hole Plug	189. Inner Spring Retainer
15. Spacer Washer	55. Oil Wick Plug	190. Spring Retainer
16. Thrust Washer	56. Inspection Plug	192. Shift Lever Shaft
19. Internal Tooth Washer	80. "MTR" Terminal	203. Pole Shoe
20. Spring Retaining Washer	86. Connector	212. Field Frame
30. Screw	93. Lead	215. Drive Housing
31. Ground Screw	104. Terminal Stud	219. End Frame
32. Lead Screw	118. Bushing	224. Field Coil
34. Pole Shoe Screw	124. Insulating Bushing	233. Solenoid
35. Insulating Screw	125. Insulation	234. Plunger
43. Oil Seal	130. Brush	235. Shift Lever
44. Gasket	131. Brush Holder	237. Armature
45. Plug Gasket	177. Oil Wick	241. Drive
47. O-Ring	184. Insulating Plate	337. Lever Housing

FIGURE 9–65 Exploded view of a Delco heavy-duty model 40MT starter motor assembly. *(Courtesy of GMC Truck Division, General Motors Corporation.)*

is shown as item 212 in Fig. 9–65 for the 40MT model. The starter main housing is not shown in the exploded view in Fig. 9–64 for the 42MT model.

4. Remove the ground stud nuts and terminal and insulating washers from item 93 on the 42MT model.

5. On the 42MT starter you can now remove the brush end housing (198). Note that if only the starter motor brushes are to be replaced, this can be performed without any further starter motor disassembly. Note that for Delco model 40MT and 50MT starters, brush inspection plugs are shown as item 56 in Fig. 9–65 for the 40MT model; these plugs are screwed into the starter field frame (212). On the 40MT and 50MT models, the field leads can be disconnected from the brush holders by removing the lead screws (item 30 in Fig. 9–65), which are accessible after plug removal. These screws are threaded into the brush holders (131). Once the screws are removed, it allows the end frame (219) to be removed. A close-up of brushscrew removal for the 40MT and 50MT models can be seen in Fig. 9–66.

6. Remove the connector strap (86) on both the 40MT and 42MT models.

7. Remove the screws (30) that hold the starter drive end housing (215), then withdraw the end housing.

8. Remove the bolts (30) that secure the solenoid shift

FIGURE 9–66 Removing or installing brush lead and field lead attaching screws. *(Courtesy of GMC Truck Division, General Motors Corporation.)*

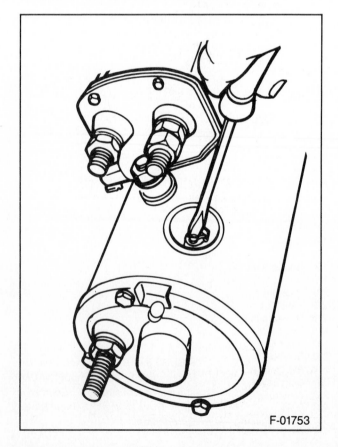

F-01753

lever housing (337) from the main starter motor housing. This main housing is not shown for the 42MT starter, but can be seen as item 212 in Fig. 9–65 for the 40MT model. Note that during this disassembly procedure, the solenoid and drive assembly will come off with the housing.

9. Remove the armature (237) from the starter frame housing. This main housing is shown in Fig. 9–65 for the 40MT model as item 212.

10. Remove the solenoid assembly by taking off the connector strap (86) and ground wire.

11. Remove the three screws that attach the solenoid (233) to the actual lever housing (337). Withdraw the solenoid from the lever housing.

Although the procedural steps above will allow you to break the starter assembly down into its individual components, the following information relates to further disassembly and testing of these subcomponents.

Shift Lever Housing Disassembly

The shift lever housing contains the linkage between the solenoid and the starter drive pinion gear. Following is the procedure used to fully disassemble this component, identified as item 337 in the exploded views of Figs. 9–64 and 9–65 for the 40MT and 42MT models.

Procedure

1. Disconnect the starter drive pinion gear/clutch assembly (241) from the shift lever fingers (235) and set the drive assembly (241) to the side.

2. If not done earlier during starter motor disassembly, remove the solenoid adjustment access plug (item 44 for the 42MT model and item 51 for the 40MT model) from the shift lever housing (337).

3. Refer to Fig. 9–67 and clamp the solenoid plunger (234) into a soft-jawed vise.

4. Remove the solenoid plunger shaft adjusting nut (item 1 in Fig. 9–64 for the 42MT model; item 6 in Fig. 9–65 for the 40MT model starter motor assembly). This is best done by using a socket, short extension, and a ratchet drive, as shown in Fig. 9–67.

5. Once the nut has been removed, unscrew the vise to allow removal of the solenoid plunger.

6. Remove the snap-ring retainer (48) on item 337 in Fig. 9–64 from the shift lever shaft (192). Do not confuse the snap ring (48) for the shaft with the snap ring (48) located on the end of the solenoid plunger (234).

7. Drive the retainer pin/shaft from the shift lever (235) and the shift lever housing (337).

8. Remove the shift lever (235).

Pole Shoe Removal

The starter motor housing (item 212 in Fig. 9–65) contains the field coils (224) and the magnetic pole shoes (203). Generally, these items should be cleaned with a cloth, but do not submerge this housing into a solvent

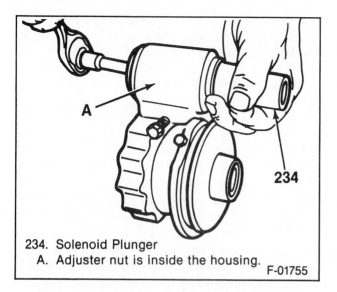

234. Solenoid Plunger
A. Adjuster nut is inside the housing.

F-01755

FIGURE 9-67 Removing or installing the starter motor solenoid adjuster nut. *(Courtesy of GMC Truck Division, General Motors Corporation.)*

or degreasing bath since the field coil insulation will be soaked and is almost impossible to dry. A small amount of mineral spirits and a hard bristle brush can be used to clean especially dirty surface buildup. When finished, use a clean, lint-free rag to dry the cleaned area.

To check the condition of the field windings, you can use a 12-V test light or the test light leads connected to all growler testers. To check for shorts in the field windings to the housing or pole shoes, connect one test light lead/probe to the starter housing and the other lead/probe tip individually, in turn, to each of the field coil brush leads. If the test or growler light illuminates any time the test lead is connected to a field coil connection, a short circuit has been confirmed. One example of how to check the starter motor for opens and grounds on light- and medium-duty trucks using Delco model 10MT, 25MT, and 27MT units is illustrated in Fig. 9-68. If a short, open, or ground is confirmed, this will require field coil removal and replacement with a new one. Should it be necessary to remove a field pole shoe, refer to Fig.

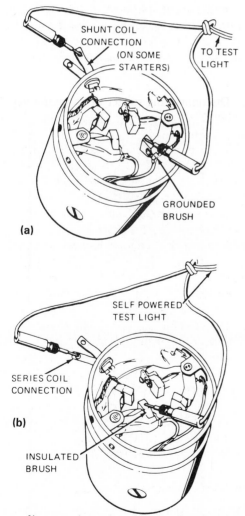

(a)

(b)

Using a test lamp, place one lead on the series coil terminal and the other lead on the insulated brush. If the lamp fails to light, the series coil is open and will require repair or replacement. This test should be made from each insulated brush to check brush and lead continuity.

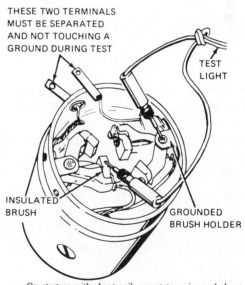

(c)

On starters with shunt coil, separtate series and shunt coil strap terminals during this test. Do not let strap terminals touch case or other ground. Using a test lamp place one lead on the grounded brush holder and the other lead on either insulated brush. If the lamp lights, a grounded series coil is indicated and must be repaired or replaced.

FIGURE 9-68 (a) Testing the shunt coil for an open condition; (b) testing the series coil for an open condition; (c) testing the series coil for a ground condition. *(Courtesy of GMC Truck Division, General Motors Corporation.)*

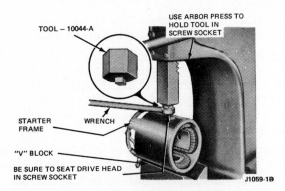

FIGURE 9-69 Starter motor pole shoe retaining screws removal. *(Reprinted with Ford Motor Company's permission.)*

9-69, which illustrates a special tool that is required to loosen the pole shoe retaining screws. This is done in conjunction with the starter housing in an arbor press to hold the tool in the retaining screw socket; a special wrench is needed to actually loosen the retaining screw. In some cases an impact drive screwdriver or socket attachment might be successful in removing the pole shoe screw retainer. Take note when re-installing new pole shoes that they are replaced in the same position since some pole shoes have a longer lip on one side, and it is imperative

that the long lip be installed in the direction of rotation of the armature assembly. Also ensure that the pole shoe retaining screws are torqued to specifications.

Armature Inspection

The armature must be closely inspected for signs of overheating, which can be confirmed by signs of discoloration. Shiny spots on the armature laminations (outside diameter) generally indicate worn bushings that have allowed the armature to come into contact with the field coils and pole shoes. This would have been further confirmed earlier when attempting to manually rotate the armature and pinion gear drive mechanism.

Check the armature further for broken or burned insulation and for signs of unsoldered connections. Closely inspect the commutator surface for wear, such as grooving or scoring, and with a micrometer for possible out-of-round. Acceptable readings for out-of-round should not exceed 0.002 in. (0.0508 mm); otherwise, the commutator will require machining to true it up. However, prior to performing any corrective repairs to the armature, it should be checked out thoroughly by placing it on a growler, where it can be checked for short circuits, opens, or grounds. Fig. 9-70 illustrates an armature placed in the growler between the two electrically (wall socket plug-in) energized magnets.

VISUAL INDICATION OF
OPEN CIRCUIT IN ARMATURE

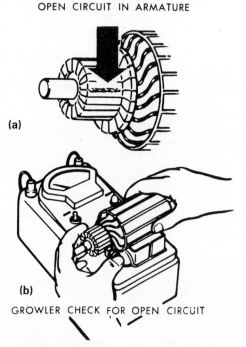

(a)

(b)

GROWLER CHECK FOR OPEN CIRCUIT

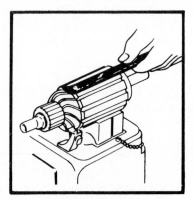

(c) GROWLER CHECK FOR SHORT CIRCUIT

(d) TEST LAMP CHECK FOR GROUND CIRCUIT

FIGURE 9-70 (a) Visual check of armature commutator; (b) growler check of armature for an open circuit and a short circuit; (c) short-circuit check; (d) test lamp check of armature for a grounded circuit. *(Courtesy of Delco Remy Division, General Motors Corporation.)*

NOTE: The name *growler* comes from the fact that when the armature is placed between the growler magnets, a strong magnetic field that emanates between them will offer strong resistance to manual rotation of the armature accompanied by a growling sound. This rotation must be done manually by the service technician to check the complete armature assembly for shorts, opens, or grounds.

Short circuits in the armature are established as shown in Fig. 9–70(c) by placing the flat steel strip that comes with the growler tester lengthwise across the armature core. The armature must be manually rotated during this test to confirm any short circuits. If at any time the flat steel strip vibrates, a short circuit exists at that point. If the growler steel strip has been lost, use a hacksaw blade in its place to perform the same test routine. Shorts between the commutator bars can be caused by normal wear of the brushes, which produces copper dust. Grounds in the armature can be found as shown in Fig. 9–70(d) by placing each prod of the growler test lamp so that one test prod is in contact with one commutator bar segment, while the other test prod is placed against the armature metal core or support shaft. Should the growler test lamp illuminate, the armature is grounded. Manual rotation of the armature within the growler magnets is required to confirm that there is no ground between a commutator segment and the armature assembly.

Opens within the armature/commutator assembly can be located by visually inspecting the condition of the commutator bars. Loose or bad connections between the brushes will cause arcing and burning of the commutator bar segments. Look for loose connections where the conductors join the commutator bars. If the bars are not badly burned, the leads can be resoldered. If the commutator is considered serviceable, the commutator can be turned down (machined) in a metal lathe to provide a clean new surface for the brushes to ride on. Most manufacturers publish specifications that state the minimum acceptable diameter of the commutator after machining. *Always* check the starter motor manufacturer's service information manual to determine whether commutator machining is acceptable. In some cases machining is not recommended, but the use of 240-grit emery cloth is acceptable to true the commutator. In addition, some manufacturers recommend that the commutator bar segment insulation be undercut any time the commutator has been turned true or been cleaned up with the use of emery cloth. Your guide should always be the manufacturer's service manual or service information literature.

By way of example, Delco opposes any undercutting of the 10MT starter motor commutator, while recommending that an undercut of the insulation between the commutator bar segments be done to a depth of $\frac{1}{32}$ in. (0.8 mm) as well as to the same width on their heavy-duty truck models. They recommend further that the commutator be deburred by sanding lightly with No. 00 sandpaper. Use compressed air to lightly blow any cop-

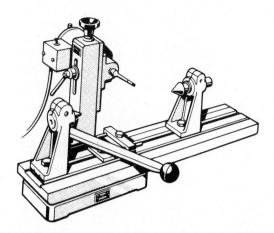

FIGURE 9–71 Starter motor commutator undercutting machine. *(Courtesy of Robert Bosch Corporation.)*

per dust or dirt from between the commutator bar segments. Specifically, Delco recommends that heavy-duty starter motor assemblies with specification numbers 2412, 2415, 3501, 3564, 3574, 3599, 7104, or 7113 *not* be undercut.

When it is necessary to undercut the insulation between the commutator bar segments, many service technicians carefully use an old hand hacksaw blade that has been broken in half and lightly sharpened to allow it to be used like a small knife. However, if possible, the use of a commutator undercutting machine such as the one illustrated in Fig. 9-71 should be used, since it can be adjusted for depth and width of cut, thereby ensuring that the manufacturer's specifications are strictly adhered to.

Brush Replacement

The brushes carry the high current necessary to cause rotation of the armature assembly. Since they come into direct contact with the commutator bar segments, they must be spring loaded to ensure a minimum of arcing when battery power flows through them. The brush springs and brush holders should be checked for signs of discoloration due to overheating, especially the brush springs, since they may have lost their tension. The brushes should be between 60 and 70% of the length of a new brush, which is best done by comparing the used ones with new ones. Delco 12- and 24-V truck starter brushes are normally 19 mm (0.75 or $\frac{3}{4}$ in.) long when new. They should be replaced when they have worn to a length of 6.35 mm (0.25 or $\frac{1}{4}$ in.).

The make and model of starter will determine the procedure required to replace the brushes. This can often be done by removing either the access plugs or the band clamp around the starter body, which exposes the individual brushes. On other starter motors you may have to remove the starter end plate located opposite the drive pinion gear. The locations of brushes and springs for the 42MT and 40MT starter models is shown in Figs. 9-64 and 9-65. To remove the brush from its holder, special tools are available or you can fabricate a small piece of bent wire into a hook so that you can grasp the brush spring, which must be pulled back to allow the brush to be removed from its holder. In cases where brush leads are insulated, take care that you do not break this insulation, or that it has not already been damaged due to wear or burning from starter overheating. Brushes must contact the commutator over at least 60% of the brush contact area; otherwise, rapid brush wear will occur due to the high current flow. New brushes are generally manufactured so that they have a slight curvature on one side to match that of the commutator; ensure that you always install these correctly. Even so, if they do not fit the commutator correctly, they can be fitted to the commutator curvature by using fine sandpaper (not emery; it is metallic) until the desired seating pattern is achieved. This usually does not require much effort. When finished fitting a new brush, clean it and the commutator with compressed air so that no abrasive particles are left embedded in the contact area between the brushes and commutator. Brush spring tension can be checked by the use of a small spring-type scale hooked under the brush spring lip. Replace any brush springs that have less than the minimum amount of tension. Typical Delco 12/24-V truck

starter motors should have a minimum spring tension of 1.276 kg (45 oz, or 2 lb 13 oz).

The number of brushes used in a particular starter motor depends on its voltage rating and the power requirements of the starter motor assembly. Generally, four to six brushes are standard on 12-V units. Such an example can be seen by referring to Fig. 9-15. On most midrange and heavy-duty truck starters manufactured by Delco, the four brushes can be removed from their holders simply by removing the individual screws. On Delco 24-V starters, this requires the removal of 10 screws, which hold 12 brushes in their holders. Examples of the end plate and brush assembly can be seen in Figs. 9-64 and 9-65 for the 40MT and 42MT starter models, and Fig. 9-72 illustrates the starter end plate and brush assembly for a Delco 50MT model unit.

Drive Pinion Replacement

Inspect the drive pinion gear teeth for excessive wear or damage, which can be the result of many hours or miles of operation. In addition, damage to a new drive pinion gear teeth can be caused by a badly chewed flywheel ring gear, which should be checked and replaced if it shows

FIGURE 9-72 Delco model 50MT heavy-duty starter motor end plate and brush assembly. *(Courtesy of GMC Truck Division, General Motors Corporation.)*

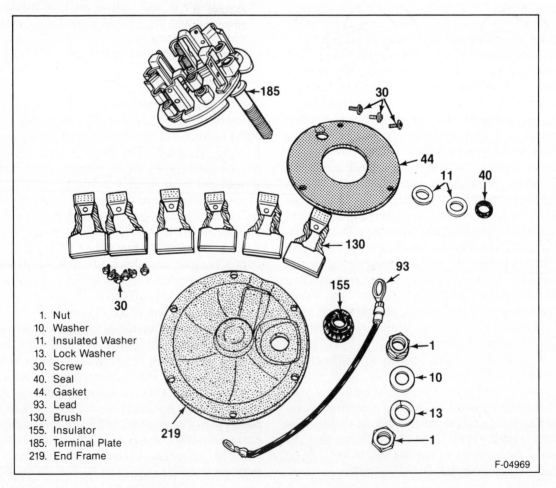

1. Nut
10. Washer
11. Insulated Washer
13. Lock Washer
30. Screw
40. Seal
44. Gasket
93. Lead
130. Brush
155. Insulator
185. Terminal Plate
219. End Frame

F-04969

signs of wear and damaged teeth. If the ring gear is not replaced when damaged, the starter pinion drive gear can hang-up, even though the key or pushbutton switch is released as soon as the engine starts. Accidental starter motor engagement once the engine starts can also contribute to rapid and severe wear of the flywheel ring gear and starter drive pinion assembly. Another source of pinion and ring gear damage can be attributed to attempting to crank the engine over with a low battery (batteries) voltage, which will result in sluggish cranking or possibly no cranking, accompanied by a solenoid click, or the starter may chatter or pulse the drive pinion in and out of the ring gear at a rapid rate.

Repeated attempts to crank the engine over under low-voltage conditions will cause one or more (but not all) starter pinion drive gear teeth to exhibit signs of case crushing of the normally hardened tooth surfaces as well as badly chipped or broken engine ring gear teeth. In addition, a bent armature shaft at the drive end can be caused by the engine "rocking back," due to compression forces. Premature wear of the pinion/ring gear teeth can also be caused by starter motor misalignment due to improper installation procedures. For example, on light/medium-duty engines the starter motor often has to be shimmed to effect proper alignment. This procedure is more common to cars and light-duty trucks. On any starter motor, wear of the armature shaft support bushings can cause early pinion wear. Figure 9-73 illustrates typical starter pinion ring gear tooth wear.

Removal of the drive pinion and clutch assembly from the armature shaft often requires that a snap-ring retainer be popped off carefully. An example of this would involve the drive mechanism on a Delco 37MT model starter. Fig. 9-74 illustrates how best to do this. Slide either a piece of $\frac{1}{2}$-in. black pipe coupling or similar metal cylinder such as an old pinion over the end of the armature shaft so that the end of the coupling butts against the edge of the retainer ring (item 48). Strike the end of the pipe coupling with a hammer to drive it down enough to expose the snap ring. Remove the snap ring

FIGURE 9–73 Typical starter motor pinion ring gear tooth wear. *(Reprinted with Ford Motor Company's permission.)*

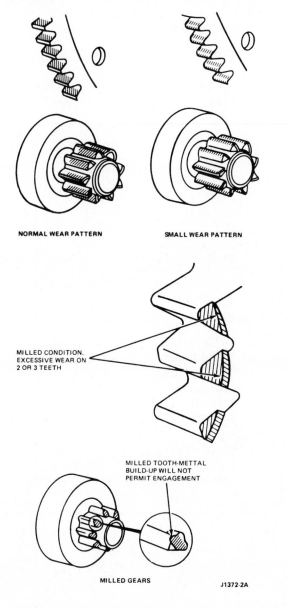

FIGURE 9–74 Removing the starter motor drive pinion retaining ring. *(Courtesy of GMC Truck Division, General Motors Corporation.)*

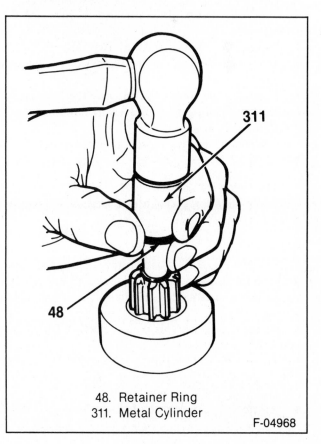

48. Retainer Ring
311. Metal Cylinder

F-04968

from the armature shaft using a pair of pliers. Generally, it is wise to use a new snap ring during reassembly since the old one will stretch or distort during the removal process.

Depending on the type of drive pinion and clutch mechanism in use, you may be able to disassemble it and replace the worn and damaged components; however, the parts and labor charges often make this too costly; therefore, a new replacement unit is used instead. Intermediate starter drive mechanisms usually require lubrication of the internal sprags of the drive clutch if they have been disassembled, while sprags on the heavy-duty starters require no lubrication. Always consult the starter motor manufacturer's service literature regarding lubrication procedures. Figures 9-16 through 9-23 show assembled and exploded views of typical starter pinion drive mechanisms.

Starter Clutch Drive Service

Should a starter drive repair be attempted rather than a new one being fitted, refer first to Figs. 9-19 through 9-21, which illustrates all of the various drive pinion and clutch mechanisms in exploded-view form. The following disassembly information is relative to an intermediate-duty sprag clutch drive disassembly shown in Fig. 9-19(b).

Procedure

1. Refer to Fig. 9-19(b) and remove the lock wire, collar, and jump spring from the sleeve assembly.
2. Remove the spring stop washer and second lock wire from the early-model drive mechanism only [see Fig. 9-19(a)].
3. Remove the retainer ring and large washer, but do not remove the sleeve assembly or sprags from the shell assembly.
4. Lubricate the sprags and saturate the internal felt washer with 5W-20 engine oil. Heavier oil can cause the sprags to hang up.
5. Reassemble the components in the reverse order of teardown.

The following disassembly procedure is relevant to the heavy-duty sprag clutch and Delco DR-250 drive mechanism.

Procedure

1. Refer to Fig. 9-20(b) and remove the cupped pinion stop and split washer. Generally, the cupped pinion stop will suffer some damage upon removal; if it does, replace it with a new one during reassembly.
2. Remove the remaining pinion/clutch drive parts as required.
3. Do not lubricate the sprags of heavy-duty clutches. These sprags are lubricated for life with a special oil at the time of original manufacture.
4. Assembly is the reverse of disassembly.

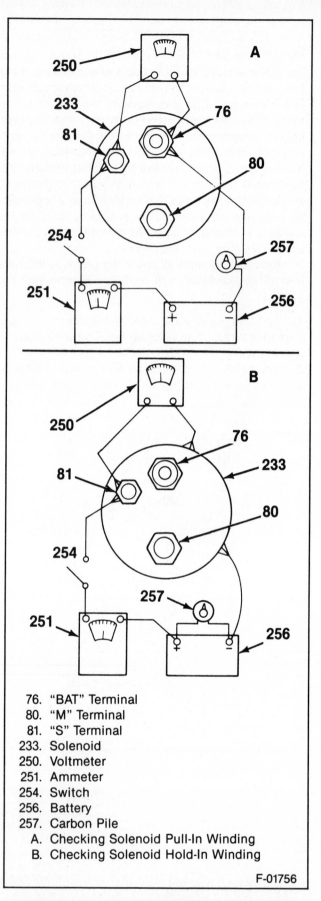

76. "BAT" Terminal
80. "M" Terminal
81. "S" Terminal
233. Solenoid
250. Voltmeter
251. Ammeter
254. Switch
256. Battery
257. Carbon Pile
A. Checking Solenoid Pull-In Winding
B. Checking Solenoid Hold-In Winding

F-01756

FIGURE 9–75 Light/medium-duty starter motor solenoid test connections. *(Courtesy of GMC Truck Division, General Motors Corporation.)*

Solenoid Disassembly and Repair

The solenoid is the trigger switch between the starter key or pushbutton switch. Its relationship to the starter motor operation was discussed earlier and shown in Figs. 9-26 through 9-37. These individual diagrams show the solenoid in both assembled and disassembled views. The solenoid can be tested for internal shorts or open circuits using an ohmmeter or 110-V test lamp connected across the windings. Two examples of how to perform a solenoid check are shown in Figs. 9-75 and 9-76 for both Delco light/medium 10MT, 25MT, and 27MT starter models as well as for the heavy-duty Delco 37MT, 40MT, 42MT, and 50MT models. The following test procedure can also be applied to the solenoids illustrated in Figs. 9-75 and 9-76.

Procedure

1. To check the solenoid for grounds, connect a 110-V test lamp between the solenoid case and each terminal one at a time.

2. There should be no test light illumination if the solenoid is operating correctly. However, if the test light does illuminate, the terminal is grounded and the solenoid should be replaced.

3. To check the solenoid hold-in and pull-in windings, disconnect all of the wire leads from the solenoid and make the test connections as shown in Figs. 9-75 and 9-76.

SPECIAL PRECAUTION: Serious damage to the solenoid pull-in winding can occur if during this test you allow current to flow for longer than 15 seconds. The carbon pile (item 257 in the diagrams) must be used to limit the voltage to that specified in the manufacturer's printed data. Note also that the current draw to the winding will decrease as the winding temperature increases.

4. Turn the load switch (254) on and adjust the carbon pile to lower the battery voltage to the value shown in Table 9-5 for Delco solenoid switch specifications.

5. Carefully note the amperage reading; a higher reading than specified is indicative of a shorted or grounded winding, a low-amperage reading indicates excessive resistance.

6. The winding resistance value can be read directly by using a digital ohmmeter capable of measuring in tenths

FIGURE 9–76 Heavy-duty Delco starter motor solenoid test connections. *(Courtesy of GMC Truck Division, General Motors Corporation.)*

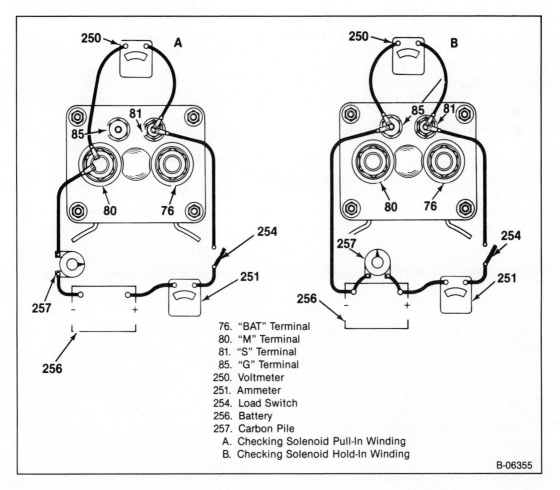

76. "BAT" Terminal
80. "M" Terminal
81. "S" Terminal
85. "G" Terminal
250. Voltmeter
251. Ammeter
254. Load Switch
256. Battery
257. Carbon Pile
A. Checking Solenoid Pull-In Winding
B. Checking Solenoid Hold-In Winding

B-06355

of an ohm, since most values for the pull-in winding will be between 0.14 and 0.16 Ω. Values for the hold-in winding on heavy-duty Delco starters is usually between 0.65 and 0.70 Ω. A low resistance value reading usually indicates that there is an internal short circuit, while no reading indicates an open circuit. If a coil resistance value is not available, you can determine this by using Ohm's law (see Chapter 1); divide the voltage by the current (ampere) value shown in the Table 9-5 test specifications.

If the solenoid fails any of the tests above, disassemble it and inspect all components for signs of over-heating, burning, and damage to the internal contacts such as the disk plate.

Cranking with a low-battery condition will cause the solenoid to overheat, resulting in possible welding (closing) of the contacts, which will result in the starter circuit being continuously energized and the engine attempting to crank steadily. Alternatively, the pinion may not engage with the ring gear, but the starter will continue to motor without cranking the engine. Disassembly of the solenoid is straightforward, usually requiring only the removal of the cover screws and attachments to expose the internal components. An example of a disas-

FIGURE 9–77 (a) Normal wear pattern on a heavy-duty starter motor solenoid contact disk; (b) damage to contact disk due to low battery condition; (c) damaged contact disk also because of a low battery condition; (d) damage to solenoid contacts due to low battery condition. *(Reproduced courtesy of Caterpillar, Inc.)*

(a)

(c)

(b)

(d)

sembled solenoid for a midrange (10MT model Delco model) starter is shown in Fig. 9-30, and Fig. 9-31 illustrates the cover plate removed from the solenoid used with a heavy-duty Delco starter motor. An exploded view of the solenoid components for the Delco model 42MT starter is shown in Fig. 9-33, and Fig. 9-32 shows the solenoid parts for the Delco model 50MT unit.

Generally, the part that requires the most attention is the circular solenoid contact disk, identified as item 204 in Figs. 9-31, 9-32, and 9-33. This circular disk comes into contact with the terminal stud that is connected to the battery power when energized. If the contact disk and terminals are not badly burned, the disk and terminals can be cleaned up. The disk can be turned over and the terminals rotated 180° to provide an unworn surface. First you have to remove the contact disk.

Procedure

1. Remove the small spring from the end of the disk, then carefully compress the contact cushion spring.
2. Remove the small roll pin from the plunger pin.
3. Remove the spring retainer, spring, and plunger pin from the disk.
4. Replace or turn the disk over to expose a new clean surface, and reinsert the small pin.
5. Install the spring, retainer, small roll pin, and spring in front of the disk.

Fig. 9-77(a) illustrates normal wear that might appear on a solenoid circular contact disk, and Fig. 9-77(b) shows typical damage to the disk due to attempting to crank the engine over with batteries that are in a state of low charge. Fig. 9-77(c) illustrates serious damage to the solenoid contact disk as a result of repeated attempts to start the engine with low battery power. In addition to the disk contact, Fig. 9-77(d) illustrates typical damage that can occur to the solenoid contact studs due to low battery power.

It is therefore extremely important that batteries be kept in a good state of charge at all times, particularly during operation in cold ambient temperatures, where the battery cranking capacity will drop substantially. Refer to Chapter 3 for more information on battery maintenance.

STARTER MOTOR REASSEMBLY

Although basically a reverse of the disassembly procedure, reassembly of the starter motor will require some slightly different assembly procedures based on the make and model of starter unit. However, most of the major assembly has already been discussed within the section ''Starter Motor Overhaul.'' For example if the field coils and pole shoes were in need of service/repair, Fig. 9-68 illustrates how to check the individual field coils for shorts, opens, and grounds, and Fig. 9-69 shows how to remove the pole shoes from the field frame or main starter motor housing, which is shown as item 212 in Fig. 9-65.

Since the disassembly procedure concentrated on Delco midrange and heavy-duty starter motor models, we shall continue with these models as our example starters for the reassembly procedures. The following headings cover the general procedures necessary to reassemble the starter motor.

Armature Bearings

The starter armature, which is the heaviest component part of the starter motor assembly, is supported by three bushings. This is best illustrated by viewing Fig. 9-64, which shows an exploded view of the very popular and widely used heavy-duty Delco model 42MT starter assembly. If you identify item 118 in this diagram (shown at the bottom center and just right of bottom center, as well as at the upper center of the figure), you will note that there are three bushings used to support the armature within the starter housing. These bushings are often referred to as bearings, but as you can see, there are no balls or rollers used; therefore, they are, in fact, solid bushings. One of these bushings is located in the end cap housing, which supports the brush plate; another is located in the middle; and the third one is located within the drive housing (item 215).

If new bushings are to be installed, the old ones can be tapped out or removed with a suitable puller. Note that new bushings are supplied to size; do *not* attempt to ream, drill, or machine sintered bushings since the inside diameter will end up being too large as well as creating a condition whereby the open grain structure of the bushing material pores will be sealed over by such action. Also be aware that the center bushing is a support unit to prevent armature deflection during engine cranking. Consequently, the clearance between the center bushing and the armature shaft is greater than that experienced with the end support bushings. This will therefore make it appear that the center bushing has too much clearance when assembled since it will be a loose fit, but this is normal. Also be aware that it is not necessary to cross-drill a sintered bushing when it is used with a tangent oil wick. Due to the open or porous grain structure, oil from the wick that comes into contact with the outside of the bearing will seep through and lubricate the armature shaft. Sintered bronze bushings will appear dull in finish compared to earlier type machined cast bronze bushings, which had a shiny finish. Bushings, wicks, and oil reservoirs used with midrange and heavy-duty truck starter motors can be saturated with SAE 20 engine oil, while the washer located on the shaft between the armature and solenoid shift lever housing can be lightly coated with Delco-Remy lubricant 1960954 or equivalent as long as it is a grade 1 molydisulfide-filled multipurpose grease.

NOTE: Although the armature can be slid into the bore of the field frame (item 212 in Fig. 9-65 for 40MT model), it cannot at this time be pushed into the end frame that supports the brushes. With the brushes in place in their

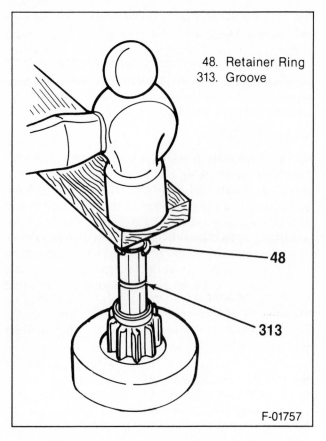

48. Retainer Ring
313. Groove

48

313

F-01757

FIGURE 9-78 Forcing the starter motor pinion gear retainer onto the shaft. *(Courtesy of GMC Truck Division, General Motors Corporation.)*

FIGURE 9-79 Using a washer to facilitate retainer installation over the pinion shaft snap ring. *(Courtesy of GMC Truck Division, General Motors Corporation.)*

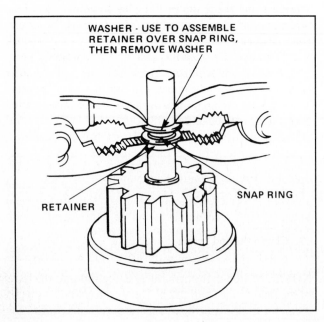

WASHER - USE TO ASSEMBLE
RETAINER OVER SNAP RING,
THEN REMOVE WASHER

RETAINER

SNAP RING

holders, the spring pressure would force them down too far to allow the commutator to move past the brushes (refer to the section "Brush End Frame").

Starter Drive

On starter motor models that use a snap ring and retainer on the armature shaft as a pinion stop, there is a recommended sequence of steps in assembly of the ring and its retainer.

Procedure

1. Refer to Fig. 9-78 and place the retainer over the end of the armature shaft making sure that the cupped surface is facing up toward the end of the shaft. If the cupped surface is installed facing down, it will be very difficult to engage the snap ring. In addition, the snap ring could be distorted and pop loose.

2. Slide the cupped retainer ring over the shaft, and using a piece of hardwood, strike it with a light hammer blow, then slide the ring down into the groove.

3. To force the retainer over the snap ring, place a suitable washer over the shaft and squeeze with a pair of pliers as shown in Fig. 9-79; then remove the washer.

Shift Lever Housing

The following information can be considered to apply to Delco 37MT, 40MT, 42MT, and 50MT heavy-duty starter models. The shift lever, which is solenoid controlled, is located inside the shift lever housing, which can be identified as item 337 in Figs. 9-64 , 9-65, and 9-80. The next step is to assemble the shift lever into the housing.

Procedure

1. Place the shift lever (235) into the housing (337).

2. Insert the support pivot pin (192) in Fig. 9-64, through the hole in the shift lever housing (337) so that it passes through the mating holes of the actual shift lever assembly.

3. When the pivot pin is in position, secure it in place with the small O-ring and snap ring (47).

4. Refer to Fig. 9-64, and slide the solenoid plunger shaft (234) through the shift lever trunnion hole and secure it in position by use of the adjusting nut (item 1 in Fig. 9-64. Thread the nut onto the plunger shaft to approximately the same position that it had prior to disassembly. This nut has to be adjusted anyway once the starter has been completely assembled, and the method is discussed in the section "Pinion Clearance Check" below.

5. If necessary, install new seals, which are identified as items 43 and 47 in Fig. 9-64 at the bottom left of the diagram.

6. On those starters that use spacer 15 (see Fig. 9-64 and 9-80) install it into the shift lever housing (337). Secure this spacer in position by the use of rubber cement, RTV (room-temperature vulcanizing), or hot glue.

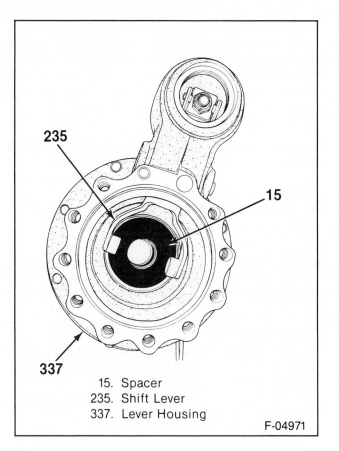

235

15

337

15. Spacer
235. Shift Lever
337. Lever Housing

F-04971

FIGURE 9–80 Close-up of the internal components of a heavy-duty starter motor shift lever housing. *(Courtesy of GMC Truck Division, General Motors Corporation.)*

7. The shift lever housing (337) can now be attached to the starter motor field frame (item 212 in Fig. 9-65) with the bolts (30) and washers if used. Tighten these bolts to 20 N·m (15 ft-lb) on Delco starters.

8. Place/install the starter drive assembly collar (item 241 in Fig. 9-64) into the housing (337) so that it sits between the shift lever fingers. Note that you will have to compress the solenoid return spring manually to lower the shift lever to facilitate collar engagement.

9. Refer to Fig. 9-64 and attach the drive housing (215) and its O-ring gasket (47) into position on the shift lever housing (337) and secure it in place with the use of the bolts (30). Tighten the retaining screws to 20 N·m (15 ft-lb).

Brush End Frame

The end frame, or end plate as it is sometimes referred to, varies in design relative to the size, make, and model of starter motor. Refer to Fig. 9-63, item 198, for the 10MT Delco starter and to Fig. 9-64, item 198, for the Delco 42MT starter model and compare the differences between the two. Now compare these two end frames to the one (item 219) in use with the Delco model 40MT

starter illustrated in Fig. 9-65. As you can readily see, each starter model has a different design end frame; however, each is designed to support the armature end bushing as well as the brush plate. In addition to the exploded views described, there are a number of other cross-sectional diagrams throughout this chapter that show alternative views of these starter motors and their component part layout.

For assembly purposes slight variations are required for the installation of the respective starter end frame. Fig. 9-72 shows all the parts that make up the end frame for a Delco heavy-duty model 50MT starter motor. If the end frame shown in Fig. 9-72 for a Delco 50MT model heavy-duty starter was previously disassembled for purposes of installing new component parts, reassemble it now.

Procedure

1. Place the large outer O-ring seal (not shown) onto the outer circumference of the end plate/frame (219).

2. Place the large circular gasket (44) with its mating hole over the terminal plate stud (185).

3. Slide the two insulated washers (11) and the O-ring seal (40) over the terminal plate stud (185).

4. Assemble the end plate (219) to the terminal plate (185) with the small retaining screws (30).

5. Install an insulator (155) and wire lead (93) over the terminal plate stud (185).

6. Install item 1, the nut, the flat plain washer (10), the spring lock washer (13), and the locknut (1) onto the terminal plate stud (185).

This completes the reassembly of the end plate components for this particular model; however, this sequence would be similar for many other starter motor end plates. For example, on heavy-duty drive starters such as the 37MT, 40MT, 42MT, and 50MT Delco units, to reassemble the end frame onto the field frame, you can pull the armature out of the starter field frame (item 212 in Fig. 9-65) just far enough to allow the brushes to be placed over the commutator. You can then push the commutator end frame and the armature back against the field frame.

However, another acceptable method, which also allows you to install the brushes into their holders and then to place the brush end frame onto the main starter body, is as described next.

Procedure

1. Refer to Fig. 9-65 and install the thrust washer (16) onto the armature shaft at the commutator end.

2. Refer to Fig. 9-65 and place the end frame (219) onto the armature shaft with the commutator under the brush holders.

3. Clamp the end frame into a vise as shown in Fig. 9-81 and install the brushes into the brush holders. A tip here is to use a thin-bladed screwdriver or a pair of needle nose pliers such as those shown in Fig. 9-81 to rock the brush tension spring back to facilitate ease of brush installa-

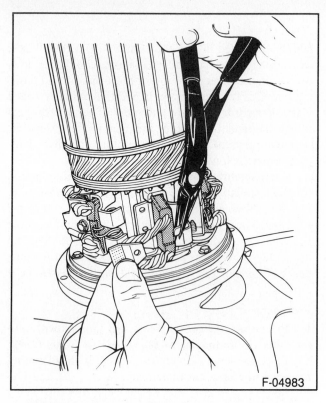

FIGURE 9-81 Installing the brushes into their holders. *(Courtesy of GMC Truck Division, General Motors Corporation.)*

tion. On intermediate-duty drive clutch motors, make sure that you assemble the brushes into their holders so that the long side of the brush faces toward the riser bars.

4. Attach the brush lead retaining screws to secure the assembly.

5. The end frame and armature assembly can now be placed into the field frame (item 212 in Fig. 9-65). It may be necessary to rotate the drive assembly manually with a screwdriver to allow the armature splines to engage.

6. Install the end frame bolts with the lock washers and tighten them to 27 N·m (20 ft-lb).

7. On Delco 40MT starter models install the field winding lead screw shown as item 32 in Fig. 9-65.

8. Attach the brush lead to the insulated brush holder.

9. On Delco 40MT and 50MT starters (Fig. 9-65) install the brush inspection plugs (56) and their plug gasket (45) into the housing.

10. Secure the solenoid assembly to the top of the starter field frame with the necessary attaching screws.

11. Connect the strap from the solenoid motor terminal to the field coil stud with the respective nuts.

12. Place the washer and nut on the solenoid motor terminal and tighten securely in place.

13. Place the solenoid ground lead onto the starter end frame terminal and tighten the nut securely.

Pinion Clearance Check

Once the starter has been completely reassembled, it is necessary to check and adjust the solenoid plunger and

shift lever movement so that the pinion drive mechanism will shift the gear drive into proper engagement with the flywheel ring gear once the starter switch has been closed. All heavy-duty starter solenoids have an adjustment for linkage stroke; however read the following special note, which refers to the actual pinion clearance check and adjustment.

SPECIAL NOTE: Heavy-duty starter motor drives have a provision to adjust the pinion clearance if it is incorrect; however, there are no provisions for adjusting the pinion clearance on starter motors using an intermediate-duty clutch. These types of starter drives were shown in Figs. 9-19 through 9-21.

To check and adjust the solenoid plunger and shift lever movement requires that connections be made to the starter circuit as shown in Fig. 9-82. Mount the starter motor into a test bench or clamp the starter field frame into a vise.

Procedure

1. To check the pinion clearance, disconnect the motor field coil connector from the solenoid motor terminal (item 80 in Fig. 9-82).

2. Connect the necessary battery voltage to match the solenoid rating (either 12 or 24 V) from the solenoid

FIGURE 9-82 Starter motor pinion clearance check circuit hookup. *(Courtesy of GMC Truck Division, General Motors Corporation.)*

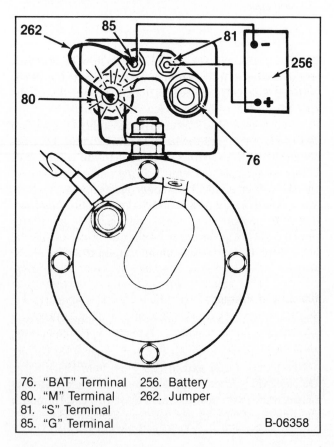

76. "BAT" Terminal	256. Battery
80. "M" Terminal	262. Jumper
81. "S" Terminal	
85. "G" Terminal	B-06358

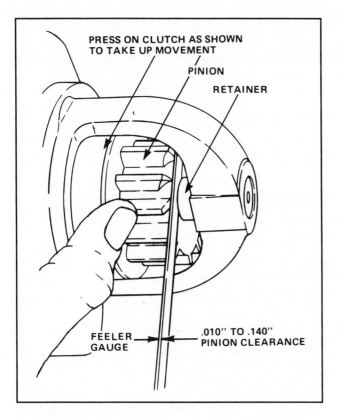

FIGURE 9-83 Using a feeler gauge to check the starter motor pinion clearance check on a Positork type drive system. *(Courtesy of GMC Truck Division, General Motors Corporation.)*

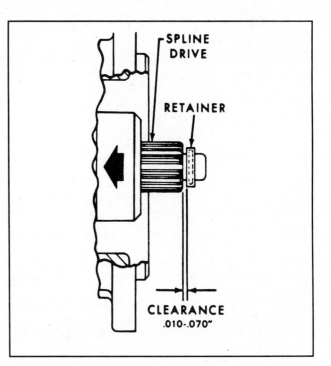

FIGURE 9-84 Starter motor pinion clearance check on a spline drive type starter. *(Courtesy of GMC Truck Division, General Motors Corporation.)*

FIGURE 9-85 Measuring pinion clearance on a heavy-duty Delco starter motor. Also note adjustment nut location. *(Courtesy of GMC Truck Division, General Motors Corporation.)*

switch terminal (item 81 in Fig. 9-82) to the solenoid frame or ground terminal.

3. Prepare to conduct the next step as quickly as possible to minimize power flow through the solenoid. Momentarily flash a jumper lead shown as item 262 in Fig. 9-82 from the solenoid motor terminal (80) to the solenoid frame or ground terminal (85). This will immediately energize the solenoid and shift the pinion gear and clutch drive into the cranking position, where it will remain as long as the jumper wire is held in place.

4. Refer to Fig. 9-83 and manually push the pinion or drive back toward the commutator end to eliminate all free play.

5. Using a feeler gauge, measure the distance between the drive gear pinion and the nose cone retainer. Note that the clearance limits for different starter drive types will vary. The clearance limits shown are for minimum and maximum limits, with the high end spec being the clearance that you might encounter on used starters or starters that have been rebuilt, but with only some new parts having been installed. The clearance shown in Fig. 9-83 is that used on Positork drive units, and Fig. 9-84 shows the clearance for a spline drive starter model. Although these specs can be used as a general guide for many truck starters, it is best to refer to the manufacturer's own published specifications. Specs for Delco

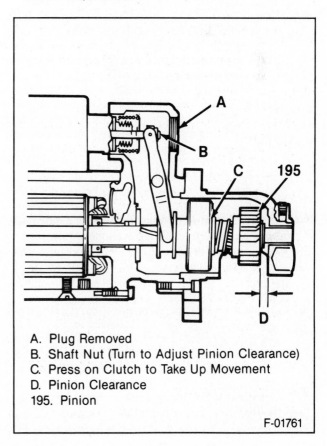

A. Plug Removed
B. Shaft Nut (Turn to Adjust Pinion Clearance)
C. Press on Clutch to Take Up Movement
D. Pinion Clearance
195. Pinion

F-01761

medium- and heavy-duty truck starter models are given in Table 9-5.

6. After any starter rebuild, solenoid lever adjustment is invariably required; therefore, disconnect the battery power temporarily if you have not already removed the shift lever housing access plug, shown as item A in Fig. 9-85 (see page 385).

7. To adjust the pinion clearance to within the published limits, use a socket, short extension, and ratchet drive similar to that shown in Fig. 9-67 which was used to remove the solenoid plunger adjustment nut during disassembly.

8. Using the jumper wire again, energize the starter pinion drive and with hand pressure against the pinion as shown in Fig. 9-83 recheck the pinion-to-nose cone clearance. Rotate the shaft adjusting nut (item B in Fig. 9-85 clockwise or counterclockwise until an acceptable clearance value is obtained.

9. Always recheck the clearance at least once more to confirm that there is sufficient free play between the pinion gear and nose cone.

10. Reinstall the access plug from the shift lever housing and tighten it securely.

SPECIAL NOTE: Always perform a no-load test on the starter after assembly and after completing the pinion clearance check. Details of this test were discussed and shown earlier in this chapter.

QUESTIONS

9-1. Higher-output starter motors are generally required on diesel engines, due to their higher compression ratio than that for equivalent-sized gasoline engines. *True* or *False* (see page 322)

9-2. Technician A says that many heavy-duty high-speed diesel truck engines employ a 24-V starting motor, with a 12-V charging system. Technician B disagrees, saying that you can have either a 12-V system or a 24-V system, but not two different voltages. Who is correct? (see page 323)

9-3. Technician A says that a direct-drive starter operates with no gear reduction between the armature and the drive pinion. Technician B says that this simply means that the starter is engaged without the aid of a solenoid or magnetic switch. Who is correct? (see page 323)

9-4. Technician A says that heavy-duty truck diesel starter motors can only be mounted in one position. Technician B says that the starter nose cone can be rotated to allow flexibility of mounting for use on different model engines. Who is right? (see page 323)

9-5. Technician A says that the only function of the ignition key switch on a heavy-duty diesel truck starter motor is to carry the small current required to activate the solenoid switch, which in turn carries the heavy current necessary to activate the starter motor. Technician B says that the key switch carries the heavy current for starting, and that the solenoid switch simply acts as a hold-in winding to keep the starter motor engaged. Who knows this system better? (see page 323)

9-6. A neutral start safety switch for a starter motor system on a gear shift transmission is normally located on:
a. The brake pedal
b. The clutch pedal
c. The accelerator pedal
d. The top of the gear shift lever

(see page 324)

9-7. Technician A says that current heavy-duty line-haul trucks tend to use four 12-V model 31 batteries for cranking and charging purposes. Technician B says that the better choice is four 6-V model batteries. Which technician is conversant with current industry preference? (see page 324)

9-8. The starter motor drive pinion is engaged with the engine flywheel ring gear by the action of:

a. The solenoid plunger and attached shift-lever mechanism
b. The rotative speed of the armature
c. The pinion centrifugal force
d. The gear reduction mechanism

(see page 325)

9-9. Typical starter motor armature rotative speeds for the light-duty trucks such as a Delco model 10MT type 100 would be in the region of:
a. 3500 rpm minimum to 6000 rpm maximum
b. 4500 rpm minimum to 7200 rpm maximum
c. 6500 rpm minimum to 10,700 rpm maximum
d. 8300 rpm minimum to 12,500 rpm maximum

(see page 327)

9-10. Technician A says that the starter motor field coils are generally wrapped around the armature. Technician B says that the field coils are wrapped around the pole shoes. Who is correct? (see page 327)

9-11. Technician A says that the starter motor armature consists of a laminated iron core mounted on an armature shaft. Technician B says that a solid armature core is used to provide increased magnetism for high torque output. Who is right? (see page 327)

9-12. The most popular Delco starter motor model now in use in heavy-duty high-speed truck diesel engines is:
a. The 10MT
b. The 37MT
c. The 40MT
d. The 42MT

(see page 327)

9-13. Technician A says that the Delco 42MT model starter motor and the 40MT starters are completely interchangeable on an engine. Technician B says that this is not so and that you need to change the starter motor nose cone assembly. Who is up to date on his product knowledge? (see page 328)

9-14. Technician A says that three different types of starter drive clutches can be used on Delco heavy-duty starters. Technician B says that four are available. Who is correct? (see page 328)

9-15. The starter motor armature consists of a series of copper wires wound around a soft-iron core. *True* or *False* (see page 328)

9-16. Technician A says that all starter motors contain the same number of pole shoes or magnets and that only the field strength varies. Technician B says that the physical size and the number of magnets will vary between various models of starter motors. Who is correct? (see page 328)

9-17. Magnetic lines of force within the starter motor always emanate from the south pole to the north pole. *True* or *False* (see page 328)

9-18. Technician A says that the principle behind causing a starter motor armature to rotate is based on creating a stronger magnetic field on one side and a weaker magnetic field on the opposite side. Technician B says that rotation is caused by creating a strong magnetic field and then suddenly collapsing it. Who better understands the concept of starter operation? (see page 329)

9-19. Maximum starter motor torque occurs at:
   a. Initial engagement
   b. 4000 rpm
   c. Maximum speed
   (see page 329)

9-20. The term CEMF (counter electromotive force) is the force that:
   a. Opposes battery voltage to reduce the current supplied by the battery
   b. Is created within the armature to assist rotation
   c. Pushes the battery current through the starter solenoid
   d. Rotates the starter pinion into engagement with the flywheel
   (see page 330)

9-21. The strength of a magnetic field will decrease with a rise in current flow through the wire due to an increase in resistance. *True* or *False* (see page 330)

9-22. Technician A says that in order to create the greatest starter motor breakaway torque, the field pole windings are arranged in a series hookup. Technician B says that a parallel hookup would be better. Who knows his/her theory better? (see page 330)

9-23. The most commonly used type of starter motor drive is:
   a. The Dyer drive
   b. The sprag overrunning clutch
   c. The Bendix drive
   d. The Positork drive
   (see page 331)

9-24. Technician A says that if a heavy-duty sprag clutch drive on a starter motor fails to engage completely with the engine flywheel ring gear, starter rotation can still occur. Technician B says that if this occurs, the starter motor will not be energized since the solenoid windings are constructed so that full battery power cannot flow through the system. Who is right? (see page 331)

9-25. A starter motor should never be operated for longer than:
   a. 15 seconds   c. 1 minute
   b. 30 seconds   d. 2 minutes
   (see page 331)

9-26. Failure of the engine to start after cranking for the specified time in Question 9-25 would necessitate allowing a cool-down period of approximately:
   a. 30 seconds   c. 1.5 minutes
   b. 1 minute   d. 2 minutes
   (see page 331)

9-27. Continued use of a heavy-duty starter motor may result in the starter motor circuit being automatically opened by a built-in thermostat within the starter housing to prevent continued use until it cools down sufficiently. *True* or *False* (see page 331)

9-28. An overrunning clutch type starter pinion drive design will ensure that the armature assembly cannot be oversped by allowing automatic disengagement when:
   a. The engine rotates at a speed of 350 rpm
   b. The transmitted torque drops to half the value required to crank the engine
   c. The engine fires and runs
   d. The engine governor reduces the starting fuel to the engine
   (see page 332)

9-29. Technician A says that all overrunning clutch starter motor drives employ either roller or sprag drive sytems. Technician B says that only sprag drives are now in use. Who is correct? (see pages 332-333)

9-30. A Folo-Thru starter motor drive system is common to:
   a. Bendix drives
   b. Overrunning clutch drives
   c. Dyer drives
   d. Positork drives
   (see page 335)

9-31. The purpose of using a gear reduction starter motor drive is to:
   a. Increase the speed of drive pinion engagement to provide a higher-horsepower starter
   b. Decrease the speed of drive pinion engagement to increase the pinion engagement torque
   (see page 336)

9-32. Write down the meaning of the terms NO and NC. (see page 337)

9-33. Technician A says that a magnetic switch for a starter motor circuit is used to open and close the circuit from the battery to the starter motor, while a solenoid does the same function and also shifts the drive pinion into engagement with the engine flywheel. Technician B says that the mag switch and the solenoid perform the same duties. Who is correct? (see pages 337-338)

9-34. Technician A says that a solenoid contains one set of windings to operate the shift control mechanism of the starter. Technician B disagrees, saying that there are two sets of windings within the solenoid. Who is correct? (see page 338)

9-35. Write down the meaning of the letters, B, M, and S, which are used on many starter motor solenoid housings to assist you in connecting the wiring correctly. (see page 340)

9-36. Technician A says that a series–parallel starter motor circuit allows for 24-V cranking and 12-V charging. Technician B disagrees, saying that a 12-V starter can be used, with all accessories being 24 V, such as on a bus application. Who is right? (see page 340)

9-37. Many heavy-duty trucks and buses that previously used a series–parallel circuit now employ the newer TR (transformer-rectifier) system. In this system, four 6-V batteries can provide 24-V cranking only when connected in parallel. *True* or *False* (see page 342)

9-38. Technician A says that in a TR circuit using four 6-V batteries, once the engine is running, usually only two of the 6-V batteries are used to supply power to the vehicle electrical accessories. Technician B says that all four 6-V batteries would be used to do this. Who is correct? (see pages 342, 350, 59)

9-39. Technician A says that you cannot interchange TR alternators with those used on a standard 12-V electrical system. Technician B says that this is not true and that you can physically interchange these components. Who is correct? (see page 350)

9-40. One of the principal factors affecting starter motor life is:
  a. Continued attempts to start the engine without allowing adequate cool-down time
  b. High starter motor voltage
  c. Low starter motor voltage
  d. High circuit resistance
  (see page 352)

9-41. An automatic starter disengagement circuit on a diesel engine often uses a sensor switch that relies on:
  a. Engine oil pressure
  b. Oil temperature
  c. Fuel pressure
  d. Coolant temperature
  (self-research)

9-42. Technician A says that the type of switch used in the answer to Question 9-41 usually employs a break-type unit. Technician B says that it employs a make-type unit. Who is correct? (self-research)

9-43. Technician A says that next to low battery voltage, more cranking problems are caused by defective cables and connections than for any other reason. Technician B believes that next to low battery voltage, solenoid problems are more common. Who do you think is right? (see page 354)

9-44. Technician A says that low voltage at the starter motor solenoid will simply result in a no-crank condition. Technician B believes that low voltage at the starter solenoid can result in chattering, which can destroy the solenoid contacts fairly quickly. Who understands the symptom better? (see page 354)

9-45. Generally speaking, truck starter motor shift solenoids can draw between:
  a. 15 and 20 A   c. 45 and 90 A
  b. 25 and 50 A   d. 150 and 200 A
  (see page 354)

9-46. One of the main causes of starter motor damage can be traced directly to a low state of battery charge. Write down as many causes as you can for failure resulting from repeated attempts to crank the engine over with low cranking voltage. (see page 354)

9-47. In cold ambient temperatures, when the truck batteries have failed to start the engine after a total of seven 30-second maximum attempts and no boost charger is available, prior to attempting to recrank the engine, you should wait at least:
  a. 2 minutes   c. 15 minutes
  b. 5 minutes   d. 30 minutes
  (see page 354)

9-48. Technician A says that a loud "whoop" from a starter motor after the engine fires, but while the starter is still engaged, is probably likely caused by a defective drive clutch. Technician B disagrees saying that misalignment is the more probable cause. Who is correct? (see Table 9-3 on page 354)

9-49. Technician A says that a rumble or growl from a starter motor as the starter motor is coasting to a stop after starting the engine is probably due to misalignment. Technician B believes that the most probable cause is a bent or unbalanced armature. Whose diagnosis do you think is correct? (see Table 9-3 on page 354)

9-50. Technician A says that a loud whine during starter motor cranking and before the engine cranks and fires can be traced to too small a distance between the starter pinion and flywheel ring gear. Technician B thinks the more probable cause is too great a distance between the starter pinion and flywheel. Who do you think is right? (see Table 9-3 on page 354)

9-51. Technician A says that starter motor misalignment is generally not a problem on midrange and heavy-duty trucks, since the starter motor nose cone is manufactured with a machined flange to facilitate proper alignment in the flywheel housing mounting bore. Technician B says that both automotive light- and heavy-trucks experience the same problems of starter motor misalignment. Who do you think is right? (see page 355)

9-52. Technician A says that 12-V batteries should be connected in parallel when employing a high-output 12-V starter on a heavy-duty truck. Technician B says that the batteries should be wired in series. Who knows the difference between a parallel and a series hookup? (see page 359)

9-53. Write down the four main circuits that should be checked out when a starting motor problem exists. (see page 360)

9-54. Voltage readings across the solenoid coil terminals of 12-V heavy-duty starter motors should be at least
  a. 9 V   c. 10.5 V
  b. 10 V   d. 11 V
  (see page 364)

9-55. Voltage readings across the solenoid coil terminals of a 24-V heavy-duty starter motor should be at least:
  a. 20 V   c. 22 V
  b. 21 V   d. 23 V
  (see page 364)

9-56. Technician A says that care should be taken when removing heavy-duty starter motors since they can weigh between 25 and 35 lb (11.3 to 15.8 kg). Technician B says that they generally weigh closer to 50 to 70 lb (23 to 32 kg). Who has a better feel for the weight of heavy-duty starter motors? (see page 365)

9-57. Once a heavy-duty starter motor has been removed from an engine if you cannot manually rotate the pinion armature by hand, it is acceptable to connect a 24-V battery supply to it to see if you can determine the reason why it will not turn. *True* or *False* (see page 365)

9-58. A no-load test of the starter motor confirms whether the starter is:
  a. Receiving the correct voltage
  b. Drawing the right amperage
  c. Rotating at the recommended speed
  d. All of the above
  (see page 365)

9-59. Typical current draw for a heavy-duty 24-V starter motor under normal load would generally fall within:
  a. 150 to 250 A   c. 350 to 450 A
  b. 250 to 350 A   d. 450 to 550 A
  (see page 366)

9-60. The maximum load in amperes that a typical heavy-duty 24-V starter motor should draw should not exceed:

a. 650 A   c. 825 A
b. 750 A   d. 900 A
(see page 366)

9-61. Technician A says that if an ammeter registers a high-current draw but the starter fails to rotate, you should check for a broken brush spring. Technician B says that you should check for a direct ground circuit in either the field windings or the terminal connection. Who do you think is correct? (see page 368)

9-62. Technician A says that no current draw on an ammeter with an inoperative starter motor could be caused by high insulation between the armature commutator bar segments. Technician B says that this could also be caused by worn brushes or broken brush springs. Are both technicians correct in their statements? (see page 368)

9-63. When checking a starter motor that exhibits a low rotative speed accompanied with a low current draw, technician A says that this is more than likely due to shorted field coils. Technician B feels that it would be due to high internal circuit resistance. Who is correct? (see page 368)

9-64. Technician A feels that a high current draw when checking a starter motor, accompanied by a high rotative speed, can normally be traced to shorted field coils as well as a possible shorted armature. Technician B thinks that it is due to an open field circuit in the solenoid. Who do you think is right? (see page 368)

9-65. Technician A says that when cleaning the starter motor field coils housing at overhaul, you can safely submerge the assembly in clean solvent and use a soft bristle brush. Technician B says that this can create problems with drying of the field coil insulation; therefore, you should use a small amount of mineral spirits and a hard bristle brush. Which technicians procedure would you use? (see page 369)

9-66. Technician A says that if a short, open, or ground exists in a starter motor field coil, they should be removed and replaced with a new one. Technician B says that you can splice a new wire into place without coil removal as long as you solder it correctly? Which technician would you believe? (see page 373)

9-67. Technician A says that if the starter commutator bars show out-of-round readings of more than 0.002 in. (0.0508 mm), you should remachine the commutator to true it up. Technician B says that you would only remachine the commutator if the out-of-round condition exceeded 0.010 in. (0.245 mm). Which technician is correct? (see page 374)

9-68. Technician A says that shiny spots on the starter armature laminations generally indicate excessive current draw. Technician B says that it is indicative of worn bushings, allowing the armature to come into contact with the field coils/pole shoes. Who do you think is right? (see page 374)

9-69. A starter motor armature is generally checked for shorts, opens, and grounds by using:
a. A growler tester   c. A voltmeter
b. An ohmmeter   d. An ammeter
(see page 374)

9-70. Technician A says that when using a flat steel strip placed length-wise along an armature, it should vibrate. This confirms that a short circuit exists at that point. Technician B says that this would confirm that a ground condi-

tion exists. Which technician is correct? (see page 375)

9-71. Placing one test prod of the growler test lamp against a commutator bar segment and the other prod against the armature metal core or support shaft is done to check for:
a. A short condition
b. An open condition
c. A ground condition
d. All of the above
(see page 375)

9-72. All starter motor manufacturers recommend machining of the commutator assembly to true it up when worn? *True* or *False* (see page 375)

9-73. Technician A says that undercutting the insulation between the starter motor commutator bars be done to a depth of $\frac{1}{16}$ in. (1.58 mm). Technician B says that undercutting should be limited to a maximum depth of $\frac{1}{32}$ in. (0.79 mm). Who do you think is correct? (see page 375)

9-74. Starter motor brushes are designed to:
a. Carry the current necessary to cause rotation of the armature
b. Pick up the current that flows through the armature and then the commutator
c. Keep the commutator bar segments clean and shiny
d. Complete the circuit to and through the solenoid
(see page 375)

9-75. Starter motor brushes should be replaced when they have worn to one-third the length of a new one. *True* or *False* (see page 375)

9-76. To prevent rapid brush wear on a starter motor, the brushes must contact the commutator over at least:
a. 40% of the brush contact area
b. 50% of the brush contact area
c. 60% of the brush contact area
d. 70% of the brush contact area (see page 376)

9-77. Technician A says that new starter motor brushes are generally manufactured so that they have a slight curvature on one side to match that of the commutator. Technician B disagrees, saying that all brushes are flat and that they must be profiled to fit the commutator with the use of fine sandpaper in all instances. Who is correct? (see page 376)

9-78. A bent armature shaft can be caused by:
a. Accidentally engaging the starter while the engine is running
b. An engine "rocking back" due to compression forces while attempting to crank the engine with a low-battery-voltage condition
c. Pinion-to-ring gear hangup
d. Using 24 V to crank a 12-V starter
(see page 377)

9-79. Technician A says that testing of the solenoid can be done for internal shorts or open circuits using an ohmmeter or 110-V test lamp connected across the windings. Technician B says that you would have to use a growler to determine this. Which technician is correct? (see page 379)

9-80. The solenoid winding resistance value for a hold-in winding on a Delco heavy-duty starter would generally fall between:
a. 0.65 and 0.70Ω   c. 650 and 700 Ω
b. 65 and 70 Ω   d. 6500 and 7000 Ω
(see page 380)

9-81. Technician A says that continued cranking with a low battery voltage condition can result in ignition key switch damage. Technician B says that this would result in possible welding (closing) of the contacts in the solenoid, leading to the starter circuit being continually energized. Which technician do you think is right? (see page 380)

9-82. Technician A says that new sintered bushings that support the starter motor armature shaft should never be reamed, drilled, or machined in an attempt to make them fit, since this action can lead to too large an inside diameter as well as closing up of the normally open grain structure of the bushing. Technician B says that all new bushings generally require honing, reaming, or drilling to make them fit properly. Who is right? (see page 381)

9-83. Technician A says that once a starter motor has been overhauled and reassembled, you should perform a no-load test first. Technician B says that you should always check and adjust the pinion clearance first. Which technician is correct? (see page 386)

CHAPTER

10

Truck Electrical Accessories

OBJECTIVES

In this chapter you will gain information that will allow you to describe the function and operation of the various electrical accessories found on midrange and heavy-duty trucks. Specifically, you will acquire or review the skills needed to:

1. Trace and repair the horn circuit.
2. Trace the windshield wiper motor circuit and perform necessary adjustments and repairs.
3. Describe the operation of a Jacobs engine brake. Perform the necessary engine slave cylinder adjustments. Trace and perform the various Jake brake switch adjustments and solenoid wiring repair.
4. Describe the operation and necessary electrical repairs to the Caterpillar Brakesaver unit.
5. Describe how to access and repair a power window switch.
6. Identify and describe what adjustments are required

7. Describe the operation of a thermatic engine fan. Trace and repair the electrical control circuit.
8. Describe how to remove and install a radio receiver. Trace and repair the wiring circuitry. Perform an AM radio antenna trimmer adjustment.
9. Trace and repair the electric controls to the cab heater and air-conditioning systems.
10. Describe the basic operation of an electronic ABS (anti-brake-skid) system.
11. Describe the operation and troubleshoot the control system for a two-speed-axle electric shift system.

INTRODUCTION

There are a number of electric accessories on medium- and heavy-duty trucks that we address in this chapter. Some of these are considered to be standard equipment; others are optional order items that may or may not appear on all vehicles.

ELECTRIC HORN

Most-medium-duty trucks, particularly those equipped with hydraulic brakes, and some heavy-duty models employ an electric horn(s), although most heavy-duty truck/tractors are equipped with air horns, which rely upon compressed air from the vehicle reservoir to operate. The location of the horn will vary between different models of trucks; however, the horn or horns (duals) are generally mounted close to the front of the vehicle to allow radiation of the warning noise forward. Figure 10-1 is an example of an electric horn found on a heavy-duty truck along with its relay.

Figure 10-2 shows a typical operating wiring schematic for an electric horn circuit. Basically, the horn

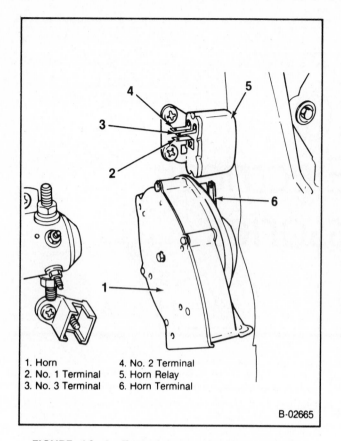

FIGURE 10-1 Typical horn relay and mounting features. (*Courtesy of GMC Truck Division, General Motors Corporation.*)

1. Horn
2. No. 1 Terminal
3. No. 3 Terminal
4. No. 2 Terminal
5. Horn Relay
6. Horn Terminal

B-02665

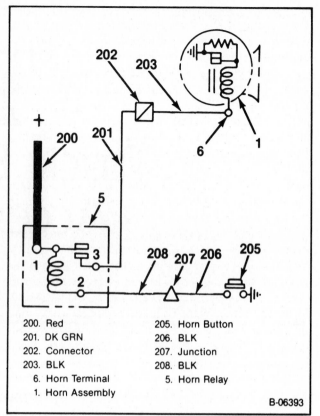

200. Red
201. DK GRN
202. Connector
203. BLK
  6. Horn Terminal
  1. Horn Assembly

205. Horn Button
206. BLK
207. Junction
208. BLK
  5. Horn Relay

B-06393

FIGURE 10-2 Basic electrical schematic for the horn circuit. (*Courtesy of GMC Truck Division, General Motors Corporation.*)

control button mounted in the center of the steering wheel is connected in series with the horn relay operating coil at relay terminal 2 in the wiring schematic. When the truck driver depresses the horn button, this completes the circuit through the relay operating coil, and a small amount of current flows from the battery through the coil winding. This causes the armature to be attracted to the core, resulting in a set of contact breaker points closing. Battery current can then flow through terminal 1 and the relay contacts, then out terminal 3 to cause the horn to emanate a tone sound. The relay assembly thus provides a higher voltage at the horn by avoiding a voltage drop through the long wire circuit from the horn button. The relay is a nonadjustable item and must be replaced if it becomes inoperative. The horn circuit is protected by either a fuse or circuit breaker located in the main fuse/circuit breaker panel. Blade-type terminal connections are used to connect the components. All wiring is identified by both an insulated wire color and by numbers.

Horn Operation

The electric horn consists of the components shown in Fig. 10-3. In order to obtain a sound (note) from the horn assembly, a steel armature is made to vibrate at high fre-

quency. The control circuit to the horn is maintained through the horn contact button at the steering wheel, or by a small button lever arrangement on the steering column.

Note that the horn assembly shown in Fig. 10-3 contains a set of contact breaker points similar to a conventional ignition system. However, they are not opened and closed by the distributor shaft breaker cam as in the ignition system. These points in the horn are normally

FIGURE 10-3 Typical vibrating electric horn. (*Courtesy of Delco Remy Division, General Motors Corporation.*)

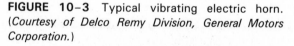

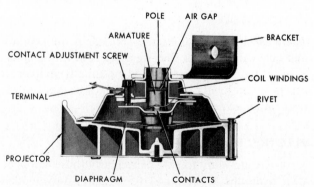

closed (in contact), until the driver pushes the steering wheel contact button. When the horn button is depressed, current flows to and through the field coil and the contact points.

You may remember from our discussion of basic electricity that when a current is passed through a wire, a magnetic field is created. You can then appreciate that such a magnetic field will exist in the horn field coil when current flows through it. This magnetic field causes the iron/steel armature above it to be pulled down toward the field coil core, which also separates the points and opens the circuit. The collapsing magnetic field allows the armature to return to its previous position, where the points will again close and complete the circuit.

The rapid opening and closing of the points cycle the magnetic fields in the coil off and on so that in reality the armature movement causes a rapid flexing of the armature within the horn. The horn sound emanates from this vibrating diaphragm. The faster this vibration, the higher the horn's pitch. To prevent burning at the points through arcing, the horn contains a condensor or resistor across the points similar to the ignition condensor.

Horn Tone

The horn shown in Fig. 10-3 is commonly referred to as an air-tone model. Different types of air-tone horns are used on cars and trucks in order to produce a more blended sound when activated. To arrive at this, some vehicles are equipped with two air-tone horns. One horn is constructed to produce a slightly lower sound than the other one, effecting a blended sound. As an example, some vehicles use two horns with mixed sounds of E flat and G, which produce 313 and 390 vibrations per second, while other vehicles use the notes of F and A, with 360 and 447 vibrations per second to produce their blended sound. Some vehicles can be fitted with as many as four horns, to produce a chord effect rather than a blended sound arrangement.

Horn Contact Buttons

The horn control is normally located in the center hub or in the spokes of the steering wheel. Figure 10-4 shows a typical horn and relay common to light and medium/heavy truck applications, with the horn button removed. The horn button cap is simply pryed up to remove it.

Horn Adjustment

The horn can be adjusted through correct setting of the air gap, and then by adjustment of the screw shown in Fig. 10-5. This adjustment simply alters the current draw of the field coil and therefore the tone of the horn. Some horns can be adjusted by an external adjustment screw on the rear of the body (behind the trumpet).

When it becomes necessary to test or troubleshoot the electric horn, this can be done using either a voltmeter

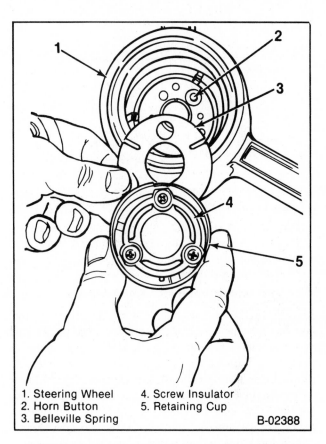

1. Steering Wheel   4. Screw Insulator
2. Horn Button   5. Retaining Cup
3. Belleville Spring   B-02388

FIGURE 10–4 Example of a heavy-duty truck horn contact button arrangement showing removal of the retaining cup and belleville washer. (*Courtesy of GMC Truck Division, General Motors Corporation.*)

and an ammeter, or simply with a jumper wire arrangement as shown in Fig. 10-6. Should the horn fail to operate, check any circuit fuses first, then inspect the condition of the wiring for corrosion, loose connections, and so on. If no problems exist in the wiring, and the horn still fails to operate, proceed with the tests described below.

FIGURE 10–5 Horn test using a voltmeter and ammeter. (*Reprinted with Ford Motor Company's permission.*)

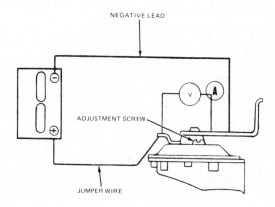

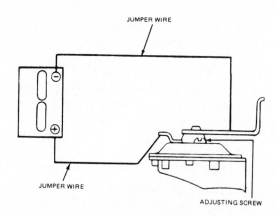

FIGURE 10-6 Horn test without a voltmeter and ammeter. (*Reprinted with Ford Motor Company's permission.*)

Horn Test with a Voltmeter and Ammeter

Refer to Fig. 10-5 and connect both the voltmeter and ammeter into the horn circuit as shown. In addition, connect a jumper wire from the positive battery terminal to the horn as indicated in Fig. 10-5. Should the current at the ammeter be zero, this indicates an open circuit; therefore, turn the adjusting screw on the rear of the horn assembly CCW until between 5.0 and 5.5 A registers on the face of the ammeter. However, if the current is greater than 5.5 A, turn the adjusting screw CW until the ammeter registers 5.5 A.

If repeated attempts to adjust the horn to these limits fail to correct the condition, the problem is internal, and the horn assembly should be replaced. Some horns are repairable; however, labor charges must be considered in relation to a replacement unit.

Horn Test without a Voltmeter and Ammeter

Should no voltmeter or ammeter be available, simply connect two jumper wires as shown in Fig. 10-6. If the horn produces no noise but there is evidence of a spark at the battery terminal, turn the adjusting screw at the rear of the horn CCW from one-quarter to three-eighths of a turn. Should the horn still fail to produce any sound after this adjustment, when the wire is again connected to the positive battery terminal, replace the horn assembly.

ELECTRIC WINDSHIELD WIPERS

Electric windshield wipers are used on both medium- and heavy-duty trucks, although many heavy-duty vehicles do use air-operated wipers. Minor differences exist between the arrangement used to power the electric wipers; therefore, we will discuss a typical system used on a medium-duty truck as well as that for a heavy-duty truck. The wiper motor system is protected by a fuse or circuit breaker where the power flows from an accessory bus bar, through the motor, the armature, and the controlling switch at the instrument panel, to ground. Most windshield wiper motors also contain a washer pump assem-

bly within the housing to allow the truck driver to spray windshield washer fluid onto the window glass for cleaning purposes. Before we study the electric circuitry for the windshield wiper and washer system, you should be familiar with just how the rotation of the electric motor is transferred to the actual wiper blades. Fig. 10-7 illustrates the motor and linkage necessary to operate the windshield wipers on a medium-duty truck. This linkage and its pivot shaft are located in the cowl under the ventilator grille. The electric motor armature shaft rotates in a circular path, but due to the offset linkage/cam arrangement used, the wipers are pushed/pulled back and forth across the expanse of windshield glass. Fig. 10-8 shows more clearly how the windshield wiper arm (24) is connected to the transmission point of the linkage.

FIGURE 10-7 Windshield wiper linkage and blade. (*Courtesy of GMC Truck Division, General Motors Corporation.*)

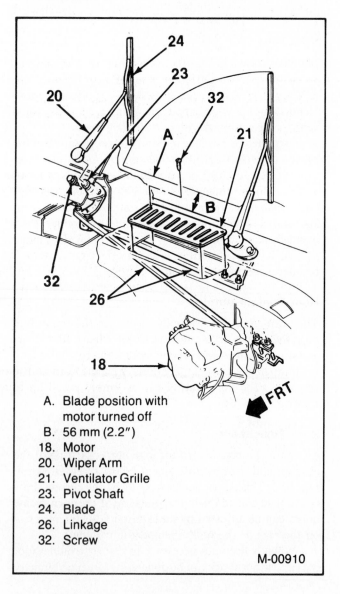

A. Blade position with motor turned off
B. 56 mm (2.2″)
18. Motor
20. Wiper Arm
21. Ventilator Grille
23. Pivot Shaft
24. Blade
26. Linkage
32. Screw

M-00910

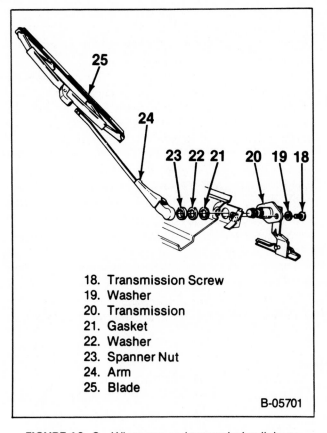

18. Transmission Screw
19. Washer
20. Transmission
21. Gasket
22. Washer
23. Spanner Nut
24. Arm
25. Blade

B-05701

FIGURE 10–8 Wiper arm and transmission linkage. (*Courtesy of GMC Truck Division, General Motors Corporation.*)

The actual wiper motor mounting will vary between makes and models of trucks; however, it is generally mounted on the cowl of the cab at the rear of the engine, as shown in Fig. 10-9 (conventional cab), it may be arranged as illustrated in Fig. 10-10 for a COE model, where the motor crank arm (19) is connected through a ball joint to the linkage bracket (item 17 in Fig. 10-9). This linkage is shown more clearly in Fig. 10-7 as item 26.

Medium-Duty Truck Wiper Motor Operation

Figure 10-11 illustrates a typical permanent-magnet two-speed wiper motor wiring diagram used in a medium-duty truck application. This particular wiper motor is protected by an automatic reset circuit breaker on the motor brush holder assembly (see item 20 in the diagram). This automatic reset breaker is in addition to the fuse found in the fuse block that protects the wiper and washer circuit wiring. Wiper motor operation is controlled by a sliding lever control switch on the vehicle instrument panel, and the wipers will operate any time that the ignition key is ON or in the, ACC position.

In Fig. 10-11 three motor brushes are used: item 23, the low-speed brush; item 22, a high-speed brush, and item 21, a common brush. The windshield wiper switch is shown as item 25, and the ignition key switch is shown as item 14. Placing the ignition key switch in either the ON or ACC position will allow battery power to flow to the common brush (21) by way of the inboard terminal (19), which is part of the three-terminal wiper motor con-

FIGURE 10–9 Windshield wiper motor arrangement on a conventional model truck. (*Courtesy of GMC Truck Division, General Motors Corporation.*)

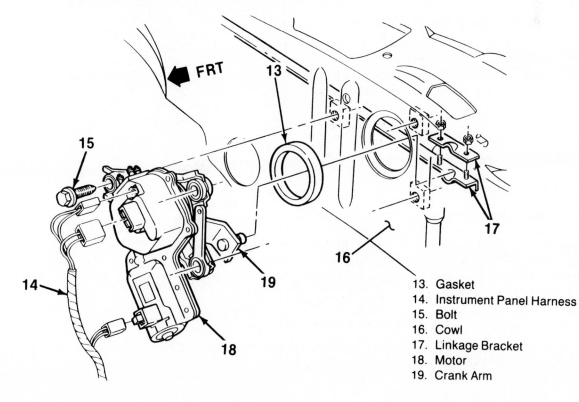

13. Gasket
14. Instrument Panel Harness
15. Bolt
16. Cowl
17. Linkage Bracket
18. Motor
19. Crank Arm

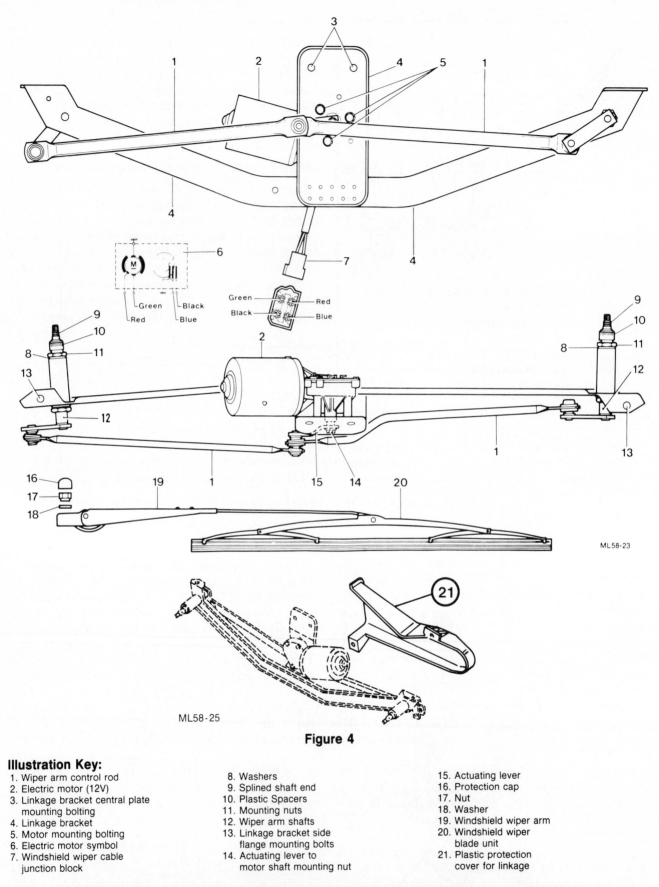

ML58-23

ML58-25

Figure 4

Illustration Key:

1. Wiper arm control rod
2. Electric motor (12V)
3. Linkage bracket central plate mounting bolting
4. Linkage bracket
5. Motor mounting bolting
6. Electric motor symbol
7. Windshield wiper cable junction block
8. Washers
9. Splined shaft end
10. Plastic Spacers
11. Mounting nuts
12. Wiper arm shafts
13. Linkage bracket side flange mounting bolts
14. Actuating lever to motor shaft mounting nut
15. Actuating lever
16. Protection cap
17. Nut
18. Washer
19. Windshield wiper arm
20. Windshield wiper blade unit
21. Plastic protection cover for linkage

FIGURE 10–10 Windshield wiper components for a Mack Mid-Liner COE (cab over engine) model. *(Courtesy of Mack Trucks, Inc.)*

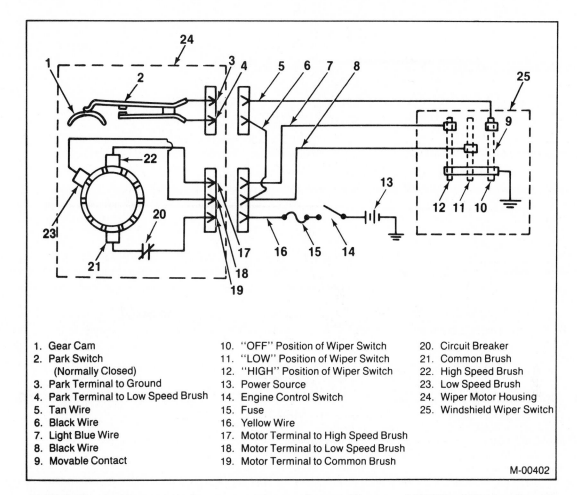

FIGURE 10-11 Two-speed wiper motor and pump diagram. (*Courtesy of GMC Truck Division, General Motors Corporation.*)

1. Gear Cam
2. Park Switch
   (Normally Closed)
3. Park Terminal to Ground
4. Park Terminal to Low Speed Brush
5. Tan Wire
6. Black Wire
7. Light Blue Wire
8. Black Wire
9. Movable Contact
10. "OFF" Position of Wiper Switch
11. "LOW" Position of Wiper Switch
12. "HIGH" Position of Wiper Switch
13. Power Source
14. Engine Control Switch
15. Fuse
16. Yellow Wire
17. Motor Terminal to High Speed Brush
18. Motor Terminal to Low Speed Brush
19. Motor Terminal to Common Brush
20. Circuit Breaker
21. Common Brush
22. High Speed Brush
23. Low Speed Brush
24. Wiper Motor Housing
25. Windshield Wiper Switch

M-00402

nector. For the wiper motor to operate, its circuit must be grounded through the wiper motor control switch (25). If the switch is in the OFF position (10), the circuit cannot be grounded and no wiper action will occur. Therefore, placing the wiper control switch (25) in either its LOW position (11) or its HIGH position (12) will complete either the low-speed brush (23) circuit or the high-speed brush (22) circuit to ground at the switch as shown in the diagram, and the wipers will run at the preselected speed.

Movement of the wiper control switch (25) to the OFF position (10) while the motor is running will result in the low-speed brush (23) circuit being completed to ground at the switch (25) via the park switch (2) contained in the wiper motor housing (24). The park switch contacts (2) are NC (normally closed) when the motor is running; however, when the wiper blades reach their park position, a cam (1) on the motor drive gear opens the NC park switch contacts to shut off the wiper motor.

The windshield washer pump system used on this medium-duty truck is contained within the motor housing. To spray washer fluid onto the windshield, a reservoir of fluid is required, which is normally located in the engine compartment in a plastic container. Some trucks employ a separate foot pump, which must be actuated to draw fluid from the reservoir through a hose. The pump then sprays washer fluid onto the windshield. On some systems fluid can be sprayed automatically onto the windshield by momentarily pressing in on the control lever of the windshield wiper switch. This action completes the electric current for the washer pump to ground while moving the wiper motor switch to the low-speed position so that the wipers will move as the washer fluid is squirted onto the windshield. Generally, 10 squirts at full system pressure will occur, after which time the wash cycle stops, but the wipers will continue to operate until the driver turns them off. Windshield washer spray nozzles generally consist of small-bore metal tubes pushed into rubber hoses which carry the washer fluid from the washer pump to the windshield. Spray nozzles should be carefully bent so that the washer fluid is directed against the desired area of the windshield.

One type of windshield washer pump is shown in schematic form in Fig. 10-12. The pump employs the spring-loaded piston shown as item 42 in the diagram, which rides in the bore of a plastic cylinder. Piston movement is controlled by a slotted actuator (44) which moves

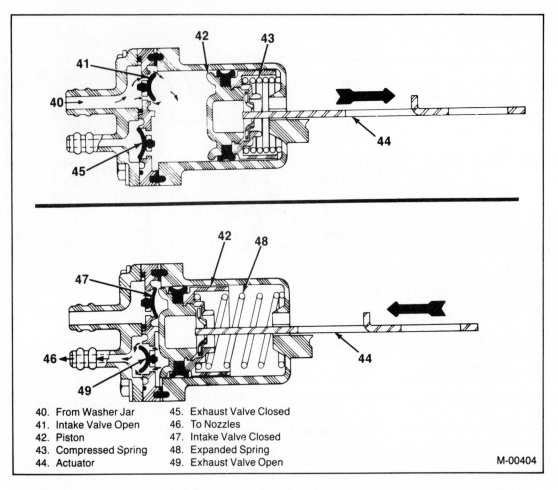

40. From Washer Jar
41. Intake Valve Open
42. Piston
43. Compressed Spring
44. Actuator
45. Exhaust Valve Closed
46. To Nozzles
47. Intake Valve Closed
48. Expanded Spring
49. Exhaust Valve Open

M-00404

FIGURE 10-12 Windshield washer pump assembly schematic. (*Courtesy of GMC Truck Division, General Motors Corporation.*)

back and forward through the motor linkage necessary to move this actuator back and forth. The wiper motor gear is designed with a cam that is in contact with a cam follower and pin; the pin actually fits into a slot in the washer pump piston actuator (see item 44 in Fig. 10-12). No movement of the washer pump actuator lever will occur when the control switch for the washer pump is in the OFF position; this is accomplished by the fact that a lock-out tang will keep the actuator (44) extended against the force of the compressed piston spring (item 43 in Fig. 10-12). When the truck driver depresses the windshield wiper washer control switch, the electric circuit is completed to the relay at the pump. A relay armature will now disengage a stop on a ratchet gear to allow it to rotate in response to the pressure exerted by a lock-out tang against a ramp located on the ratchet gear. Movement of this ramp allows a cam follower and pin to stroke the washer pump actuator (item 44 in Fig. 10-12) back and forward in a manner similar to the action of a piston connecting rod. After one full revolution, the armature will again come into contact with a stop and ratchet gear to stop the pump's operation until the control switch is again

depressed momentarily. During washer pump operation, the actuator (item 44 in Fig. 10-12) pulls the piston (42) back against the force of the return spring (43) on the intake stroke shown in the upper part of the diagram. Washer fluid flow both into and out of the piston cylinder is controlled by one intake and two exhaust check valves (only one exhaust check valve is shown in the simplified diagram of Fig. 10-12, for reasons of clarity).

Heavy-Duty Truck Wiper Motor Operation

Figure 10-13 illustrates a wiring diagram for a windshield wiper washer system. In this two-speed system the depressed motor and gear train are constructed so that the windshield wiper blades park approximately 2 in. (50 mm) above the windshield during the OFF position. The motor is a rectangular 12-V compound wound unit coupled to a gear train that consists of a helical drive gear at the end of the motor armature shaft. The motor also contains an intermediate gear and pinion assembly as well as an output gear and shaft assembly that attaches to the wiper linkage crank arm. The motor is activated by two switches that consist of a control switch on the instrument panel

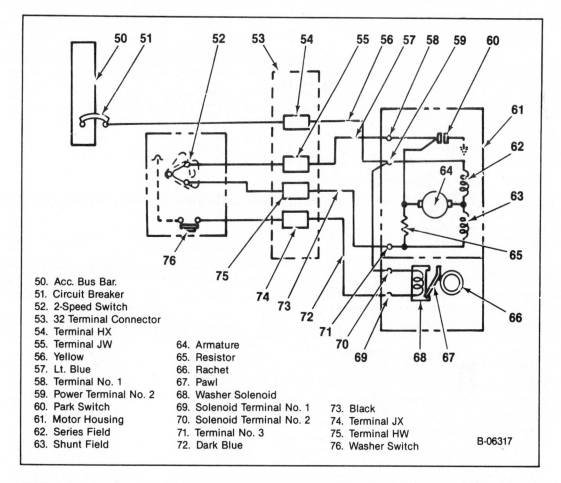

50. Acc. Bus Bar.
51. Circuit Breaker
52. 2-Speed Switch
53. 32 Terminal Connector
54. Terminal HX
55. Terminal JW
56. Yellow
57. Lt. Blue
58. Terminal No. 1
59. Power Terminal No. 2
60. Park Switch
61. Motor Housing
62. Series Field
63. Shunt Field

64. Armature
65. Resistor
66. Rachet
67. Pawl
68. Washer Solenoid
69. Solenoid Terminal No. 1
70. Solenoid Terminal No. 2
71. Terminal No. 3
72. Dark Blue

73. Black
74. Terminal JX
75. Terminal HW
76. Washer Switch

B-06317

FIGURE 10–13 Wiper motor and washer wiring diagram. (*Courtesy of GMC Truck Division, General Motors Corporation.*)

and a parking switch within the motor. To allow the wiper arms/blades always to stop at a park position that is approximately 2 in. (50 mm) above the windshield base, the actual parking switch contacts are connected across the control switch at the instrument panel so that they can act as a set of holding contacts any time that the main wiper switch is turned off. This will ensure that the wiper circuit will stay closed to ensure that the wipers will continue to operate until the regular stop/park position of the blades is reached. If you refer to Fig. 10-13, battery voltage will be present at terminal 2 (59) any time that the wiper control switch is turned on. Placing the wiper control switch (52) to the low-speed position will allow terminals (58) and 3 (71) to be completed to ground at the instrument panel. Current will now flow from the battery terminal 2 (59) through the series field winding and divide as follows; some current will flow through the shunt field to ground by wiper terminal 3 (71) to the dash switch to ground, while the remainder of the current flow will pass through the armature to ground by the wiper terminals 1 (58) to the dash switch to ground. In the high-speed wiper position, the shunt field coil circuit is opened

to ground at the control switch but keeps the motor armature circuit closed to ground. This action means that the shunt field coil current must flow through the 20-Ω resistor (65), which is located on the wiper terminal board across terminals 3 (71) and 1 (58). The shunt field current then flows through terminal 1 (58) and then through the same lead, which connects the armature circuit to ground through the control switch.

When the wipers are turned off, current flows through the control switch to the wiper PARK switch and ground. Should the wiper arms be in any position other than the normal 2 in. (50 mm) above the bottom of the windshield, the wiper motor circuits are completed to ground by the wiper motor PARK switch as follows.

1.   The series field motor armature circuit is completed to ground through the parking switch to the wiper housing and chassis through terminal No. 1 (58).
2.   The shunt field coil circuit is completed to ground through wiper motor terminal 3 (71) through the wiring harness to the wiper control switch and back through the

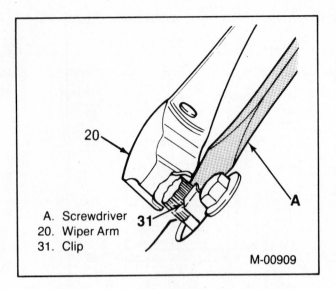

FIGURE 10–14 Wiper arm retention clip location. (*Courtesy of GMC Truck Division, General Motors Corporation.*)

Wiper Arm and Blade Replacement

Although not a direct part of the electric system, you should be familiar with how to remove a wiper arm and blade assembly. Fig. 10-14 illustrates one method to use when removing the wiper arm from the serrated shaft, which is a part of the wiper linkage. Any time that a wiper arm is removed, it must be reinstalled in the same position to ensure that the correct arc of travel across the windshield is achieved. On some serrated shafts, a master spline is used to ensure that this will occur. However, if no master spline is used, take careful note of the position of the wiper arm when removing it so that you can install it or a new one in the proper position; otherwise, you may have to remove it to reposition it. Fig. 10-15 illustrates another type of wiper arm and blade retention system used on Ford heavy-duty L series trucks. Fig. 10-16 shows you how to remove one wiper blade from the arm by using a small screwdriver to release the tab.

Troubleshooting Wipers

Table 10-1 lists various problems that you might encounter with electric windshield wipers, the possible causes, and suggested correction procedures.

harness to wiper terminal 1 (58) and through the parking switch to ground.

The windshield wiper washer circuit employs a pump within a cylinder similar to that described and shown in Fig. 10-12 for the medium-duty truck system.

FIGURE 10–15 Wiper arm and blade assembly installation. (*Reprinted with Ford Motor Company's permission.*)

FIGURE 10–16 Removing the wiper blade. (*Courtesy of GMC Truck Division, General Motors Corporation.*)

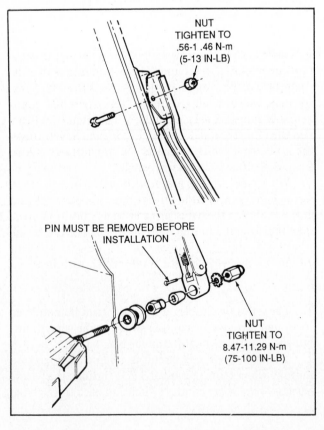

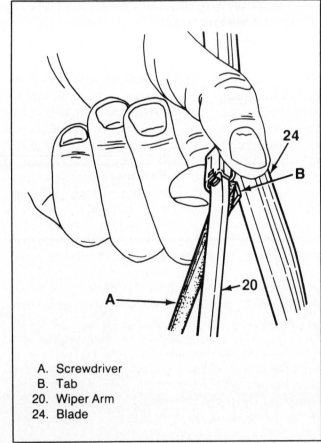

A. Screwdriver
B. Tab
20. Wiper Arm
24. Blade

TABLE 10–1 Diagnosis chart for windshield washer and windshield washer problems

DIAGNOSIS OF WINDSHIELD WIPER ON-VEHICLE

PROBLEM	POSSIBLE CAUSE	CORRECTION
Wiper Not Working or Intermittent	1. Blown fuse. 2. Overload. 3. Open circuit in feed wire (center terminal on the wiper motor). 4. Loose mounting of wiper switch. 5. Faulty wiper switch. 6. Open circuit in wire to wiper switch (inboard terminal on wiper motor).	1. Locate short circuit and repair it. Replace fuse. 2. Remove heavy snow, ice, etc., that causes motor to overheat and trip circuit breaker. 3. Locate broken wire and repair it. 4. Tighten switch mounting. 5. Replace switch. 6. Locate broken wire and repair it.
Wiper Will Not Shut Off. Wiper Has Both "LOW" and "HIGH" speeds	Grounded wire (inboard terminal on wiper motor) to wiper switch.	Locate short circuit and repair it.
Wiper Will Not Shut Off. Wiper Has Only "LOW" Speed.	1. Faulty wiper switch. 2. Grounded wire (outboard terminal on wiper motor) to wiper switch.	1. Replace wire switch. 2. Locate and repair short circuit.
Wiper Will Not Shut Off. Wiper Has Only "HIGH" Speed.	1. Faulty wiper switch. 2. Open circuit in wire (outboard terminal on wiper motor) to the wiper switch.	1. Replace the wiper switch. 2. Locate and repair the broken wire.
Wiper Has Only "HIGH" Speed	Open circuit in wire (outboard terminal on wiper motor) to the wiper switch.	Locate and repair the broken wire.
Wiper Has Only "LOW" Speed	1. Grounded wire (outboard terminal on wiper motor) to wiper switch. 2. Faulty wiper switch.	1. Locate and repair the short circuit. 2. Replace the wiper switch.
Blades Do Not Return to Full Park Position	Loose wiper ground strap connection.	Tighten strap connection.

DIAGNOSIS OF WINDSHIELD WIPER OFF-VEHICLE

PROBLEM	POSSIBLE CAUSE	CORRECTION
Wiper Not Working or Intermittent	1. Broken or damaged gear train (only if not working). 2. Poor solder connections at terminal board. 3. Loose splice joints at brush plate. 4. Brushes binding in brush holder. 5. Open circuit in the armature.	1. Replace the gears as required. 2. Resolder the wires at terminals. 3. Recrimp or solder the splice joints. 4. Clean holder or replace the brush, spring or brush plate assembly. 5. Replace the armature.
Wiper Will Not Shut-Off. Wiper Has Normal "HIGH" and "LOW" Speeds	1. Faulty park switch. 2. Grounded red lead wire.	1. Replace the terminal board assembly. 2. Repair the short circuit in red wire.
Wiper Will Not Shut Off. Wiper Has Only "LOW" Speed	1. Grounded shunt field coil. 2. Grounded black wire.	1. Replace the frame and field assembly. 2. Repair the short circuit in black wire.
Wiper Will Not Shut Off. Wiper Has Only "HIGH" Speed	1. Open circuit in shunt field coil. 2. Open circuit in black wire.	1. Replace the frame and field assembly. 2. Repair the broken wire or poor solder connection.

TABLE 10-1 (con't)

PROBLEM	POSSIBLE CAUSE	CORRECTION
Wiper Shuts Off—But Not in Park Position	Faulty park switch or dirty contacts.	Replace the terminal board assembly or clean contacts.
"HIGH" Speed Too Fast	Faulty resistor.	Replace the terminal board assembly.

DIAGNOSIS OF WINDSHIELD WASHER

PROBLEM	POSSIBLE CAUSE	CORRECTION
Washer Fluid Does Not Spray on the Windshield	1. No fluid. 2. Clogged jets. 3. Clogged filter in the reservoir.	1. Check the fluid reservoir. Fill if necessary. 2. Using a fine pin, carefully clear the jets. 3. Remove the filter and back flush it. Also clean the reservoir.
Washers Inoperative	1. Not enough fluid. 2. Hoses damaged or loose. 3. Plugged screen at end of jar cover hose. 4. Loose electrical connection to washer pump or wiper switch. 5. Open circuit in feed wire to ratchet relay coil. 6. Wiper switch faulty. 7. Ratchet relay coil faulty. 8. Washer nozzles plugged. 9. Ratchet wheel tooth missing. 10. Ratchet pawl spring missing. 11. Faulty pump valve assembly.	1. Add fluid. 2. Cut a short length off the end of the hose to insure a air tight connection or replace the hose. 3. Clean the screen. 4. Check electrical connections and repair if necessary. 5. Locate the open circuit and repair it. 6. Replace the wiper switch. 7. Replace the ratchet relay. 8. Clean the washer nozzles. 9. Replace the ratchet wheel. 10. Replace the ratchet pawl spring. 11. Replace the pump valve assembly.
Washer Pumps Continuously When Wipers are Operating	1. Grounded wire from the ratchet relay to the switch. 2. Wiper switch faulty. 3. Ratchet gear tooth missing. 4. Ratchet gear dog broken or not contacting ratchet gear teeth. 5. Lock-out tang broken or bent on actuator.	1. Locate the grounded wire and repair it. 2. Replace the wiper switch. 3. Replace the ratchet gear. 4. Replace or repair the ratchet gear dog. 5. Replace the actuator.

Source: Courtesy of GMC Truck Division, General Motors Corporation.

JACOBS ENGINE BRAKE

A detailed description of the Jacobs (Jake) brake will not be given here, since much of its operation is mechanical, as are a number of adjustments. For a complete description of the operation, maintenance, adjustment, and troubleshooting of the Jacobs engine brake, refer to the book by Robert N. Brady, *Heavy Duty Truck Fuel Systems: Operation, Service, and Maintenance,* (Englewood Cliffs, N.J.: Prentice-Hall, 1991) Chapter 13.

The Jacobs engine brake is a hydramechanical device that converts a power-producing diesel engine into an air compressor. Through an electrical control circuit a number of solenoids are activated that trap pressurized engine oil within the Jake brake housings. The cylinder exhaust or injector rocker arm pushrod is then used to increase this oil pressure against a slave piston. The slave piston then forces the exhaust valve bridge down just before the engine cylinder piston reaches TDC on its compression

stroke. At the same time, fuel is cut off, resulting in a release or blowdown of the high-pressure air within the engine cylinder. This results in a net loss of energy since no power is returned to the engine cylinders after the piston has compressed the air charge. Different models of Jake brakes are used on Caterpillar, Cummins, Mack, and Detroit Diesel Corporation engines; however, the basic principle of operation remains the same.

From an electrical operational standpoint, the technician must understand how the various switches and solenoids operate. A simplified diagram of a Jacobs engine brake, where all six engine cylinders brake once the series circuit has been completed through the main dash switch, the throttle pedal switch, and the clutch switch, is shown on the left-hand side of Fig. 10-17; the right-hand side of this figure illustrates the addition of a three-position selector switch that allows the driver to select either two-, four-, or six-cylinder braking.

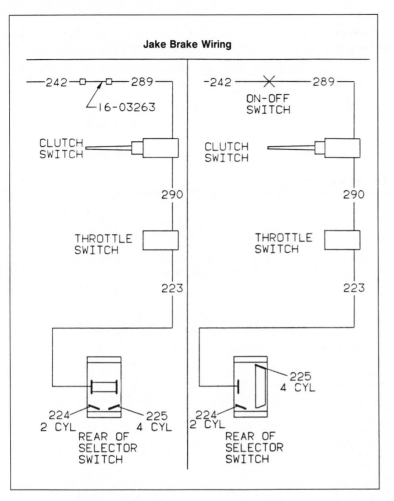

Jake Brake Wiring

FIGURE 10–17 Simplified Jake brake wiring schematic for a heavy-duty class 8 truck. (*Courtesy of Peterbilt Motors Company, Division of PACCAR, Newark, CA.*)

A typical example of how the Jake brake wiring circuit might appear on a heavy-duty truck is shown in Fig. 10-17. The clutch and throttle microswitches are fed from the engine main wire harness. The simplified wiring arrangement shows the optional two-, four-, or six-cylinder brake selection switch for a Cummins NTC-14L engine in a Peterbilt model 379 conventional cab heavy-duty class 8 truck/tractor. The wire numbers on the diagram indicate the circuits shown in Table 10-2.

The mechanical and electrical components used with the Jacobs engine brake can be seen in schematic form in Fig. 10-18 for a two-stroke cycle Detroit Diesel Corporation 92 series engine with and without the DDEC (DD Electronic Controls) system. The various electrical controls required for operation of the Jake brake system, as well as a description of the basic mechanical operation, are described below.

Figure 10-19 illustrates the Jacobs brake model 760 used on the DDC series 60 (12.7 L) engine, which is only available with the DDEC (Detroit Diesel Electronic Controls) electronically controlled unit injector fuel system. The actual hardware, such as the master piston for the Jake brake system, is actuated from the unit injector roller follower, while the slave piston is located above the exhaust valve bridge mechanism similar to that found on both Caterpillar 3406 and Cummins 14-L six-cylinder engines. The slave piston clearance on the series 60 DDC engine is 0.020 in. (0.50 mm).

TABLE 10–2

Wire Number	Circuit Description
223	14-gauge wire; engine brake—Jacobs selective; fuel pump switch to select switch.
224	14-gauge wire; engine brake—Jacobs selective; two cylinders Cummins.
225	14-gauge wire; engine brake—Jacobs selective; four cylinders Cummins.
242	14-gauge wire and up; miscellaneous accessory power feed. This wire is a switched power fuse from the main cab harness to the engine feed-through, to the chassis feed-through, to buzzer, to A panel, to tach panel, to light bar, to speedo panel, to C panel, to engine brake, to engine fan switch, to electric windshield pump washer, and press switch 2.
289	14-gauge wire; Jacobs brake; dash switch to clutch switch.
290	14-gauge wire; Jacobs brake; clutch switch to engine

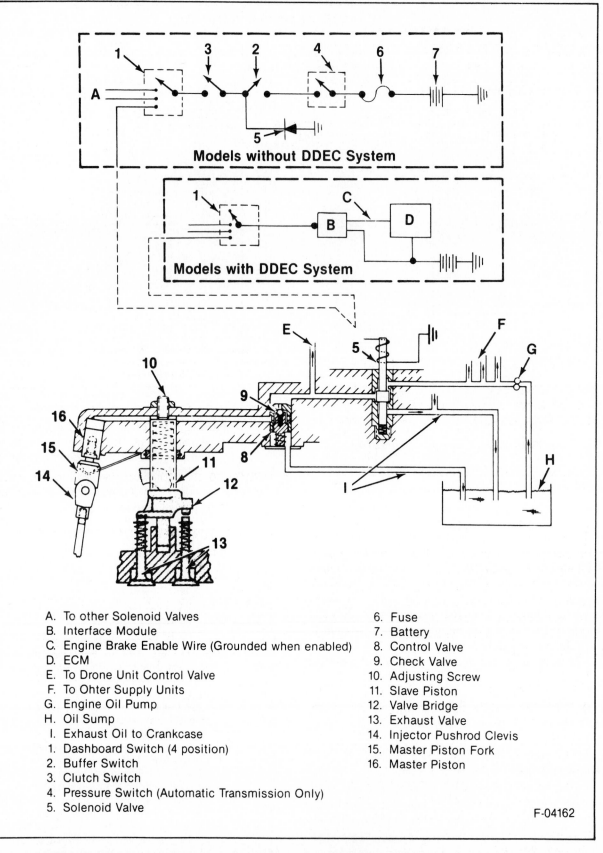

Models without DDEC System

Models with DDEC System

A. To other Solenoid Valves
B. Interface Module
C. Engine Brake Enable Wire (Grounded when enabled)
D. ECM
E. To Drone Unit Control Valve
F. To Ohter Supply Units
G. Engine Oil Pump
H. Oil Sump
I. Exhaust Oil to Crankcase
1. Dashboard Switch (4 position)
2. Buffer Switch
3. Clutch Switch
4. Pressure Switch (Automatic Transmission Only)
5. Solenoid Valve

6. Fuse
7. Battery
8. Control Valve
9. Check Valve
10. Adjusting Screw
11. Slave Piston
12. Valve Bridge
13. Exhaust Valve
14. Injector Pushrod Clevis
15. Master Piston Fork
16. Master Piston

F-04162

FIGURE 10–18   Jacobs engine brake schematic for a two-stroke-cycle Detroit Diesel Corporation 92 series engine. (*Courtesy of GMC Truck Division, General Motors Corporation.*)

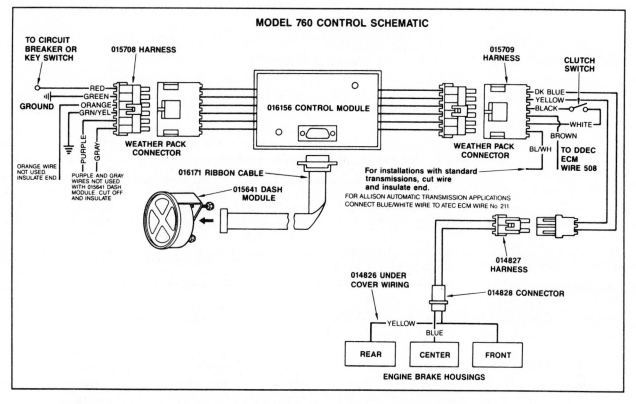

FIGURE 10–19 Detroit Diesel 12.7-L series 60 four-stroke engine Jake brake schematic. (*Courtesy of the Jacobs Vehicle Equipment Division, Chicago Pneumatic Tool Company.*)

Controls

The brake controls are electrically activated by the use of a series of switches as shown in Fig. 10-17 and in Fig. 10-18 for Detroit Diesel two-cycle engine models. The system used on Cummins 14-L (855 in.³) NT six-cylinder truck engines would be the same as that shown in Fig. 10-18. On CAT3406B and Mack engines, the master piston is actuated by the exhaust pushrod rather than by the injector pushrod since these engines do not use pushrod-activated fuel injectors similar to those used on DDC and Cummins engines.

1. Dash-mounted control switch, on or off.

2. Clutch microswitch actuated by the movement of the pedal. With your foot off the pedal, the contacts in the microswitch are closed, completing the circuit through it. When the pedal is pushed down, the contacts open, breaking the electrical circuit. Figure 10-20 illustrates an example of the clutch micro-switch location.

3. Fuel injection pump, governor mounted; micro- or buffer switch, which is closed and completes the circuit when the throttle is in the idle position, and is opened, thereby deenergizing the circuit, when the throttle is in any position but idle.

4. On some engines, an optional selector switch labeled 1, 2, or 3 varies the degree of braking by activating either two, four, or six engine cylinders. On both six-cylinder Caterpillar and Mack engines, a progressive switch pro-

FIGURE 10–20 Jacobs engine brake clutch micro-switch location example. (*Courtesy of GMC Truck Division, General Motors Corporation.*)

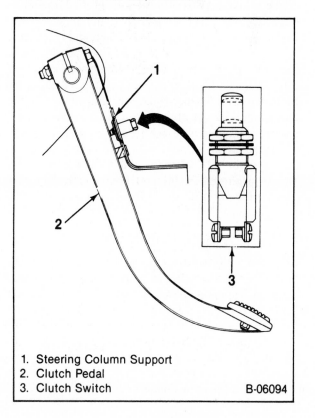

1. Steering Column Support
2. Clutch Pedal
3. Clutch Switch

B-06094

vides either three- or six-cylinder engine brake operation. On Detroit Diesel Corporation two-stroke-cycle engines, a progressive switch provides one-half or full engine brake operation. On DDC series 60 four-stroke-cycle engines, an electronic control system provides two-, four-, or six-cylinder engine brake operation. This is achieved with a dash-mounted control switch that has low, medium, and high positions, corresponding to the degree of braking required.

5. *Optional control systems.* Jacobs offers three different systems for engine brake control. Besides the standard semiautomatic system, the customer now has the choice of two added options: fully automatic control with a low-speed shutoff, or fully manual control with a foot switch.

a. The *foot switch* is installed on the cab floor within easy reach of the operator's left foot. After installation, light pressure on the top plate is all that is needed to operate the Jake brake. The throttle switch remains in the system to ensure that fueling and engine braking do not occur at the same time.

b. The *engine brake low-speed shutoff switch* is a fully automatic engine brake control system that senses engine speed (rpm) and electrically deactivates the engine brake at engine speeds below approximately 900 rpm.

The low-speed shutoff switch kit provides added driver convenience in frequent stop/start operations to both experienced and less experienced drivers. Additionally, the low-speed shutoff switch kit is useful for slip seat operations where a variety of drivers use one vehicle.

The kit consists of a speed-sensing module and an environmentally sealed, solid-state switch module. Also included are wires, connectors, and adapters required to join the two modules and connect the system to the engine brake. The speed-sensing module mounts on either the engine tachometer drive adapter or the dash-mounted tachometer head, if a mechanical tachometer is used. The switch module can be mounted on the firewall or under the dash.

The maximum amount of braking at the engine flywheel is about 75% of the engine's rated power on a naturally aspirated engine and about 90% on turbocharged engines. Once the brake is activated, it comes on in $\frac{1}{4}$ second; for all intents and purposes, it is instantaneous.

The rule of thumb for best use of the brake is that the driver should select the same gear range to go down a hill as he would use to come up the hill. If he selects a higher gear, braking power will be reduced and he may have to slow the vehicle speed with the service brakes. On the other hand, if he selects too low a gear, braking effort will increase, and he may have to use the throttle occasionally to maintain a suitable road speed. Remember that because of the series wiring, the instant that he moves the throttle from an idle position, the brake is de-

activated. If the vehicle is used with an automatic transmission, no clutch switch is required.

Operation

With reference to Fig. 10-18 on engines such as Detroit Diesel and Cummins, that employ an injector pushrod actuated from the engine camshaft, a master piston located in the individual Jake brake housing is moved as the injector pushrod is lifted by the engine cam. This motion is then transferred hydraulically to the exhaust valve of the respective cylinder. This is accomplished only when the three-way electric solenoid valve is activated, which allows engine oil under pump pressure to flow along the low-pressure passage to the base of the control valve, where the oil pressure forces the ball check valve off its seat against the action of the light return spring. The oil then forces the master piston into contact with the injector push tube or pushrod. When oil pressures on both sides of the ball check valve are equal, the light return spring will seat the ball.

As the master piston is raised by the upward moving pushrod, the trapped oil between the ball check valve and piston increases in pressure until it forces the slave piston down against the valve crosshead (Cummins) or valve bridge (Detroit Diesel), thereby opening the exhaust valves just before top dead center.

When the three-way solenoid valve is deenergized, oil pressure is released from below the control valve, which then exhausts the oil trapped in the master/slave piston-circuit, allowing the master piston to return to the nonoperating position by means of its return spring.

On engines that do not use an injector pushrod but deliver fuel to the injectors through high-pressure fuel lines from the injection pump, it becomes necessary to employ an exhaust cam and pushrod from another cylinder to provide the required master and slave piston actuation. A good example of this necessity is on Caterpillar and Mack diesel engines, as well as those European engines presently using the Jake brake.

The location of both the master and slave pistons for a Mack or Caterpillar engine, for example, with a 1-5-3-6-2-4 firing order on a clockwise-rotating engine, is shown in Table 10-3.

TABLE 10-3 Location of master and slave piston assemblies for a six-cylinder in-line engine

Location of Master Piston	Location of Slave Piston
No. 1 Pushrod	No. 3 Exhaust Valve
No. 5 Pushrod	No. 6 Exhaust Valve
No. 3 Pushrod	No. 2 Exhaust Valve
No. 6 Pushrod	No. 4 Exhaust Valve
No. 2 Pushrod	No. 1 Exhaust Valve
No. 4 Pushrod	No. 5 Exhaust Valve

The Jake brake can also be used very effectively when upshifting a standard transmission through the driver employing a double-clutch principle on those engines that have an inherently slow deceleration rate. As the driver removes his foot from both the clutch and throttle (gear lever in neutral), the Jake brake is immediately energized, which decelerates the engine rapidly to allow a shift into the next higher gear while maintaining a fairly constant road speed.

The wiring harness for the Jake brake solenoids under the engine rocker cover originates from the engine wiring harness. One good example of how the solenoid control wires enter the rocker cover area is shown in Fig. 10-21, where the feed wire actually passes through a nylon insulator nut, shown as item 30 in the diagram. This nylon nut threads into the side of the cylinder head after removing a small pipe plug. The solenoid wire (25) is then connected by a spade terminal to the actual side of the solenoid, the location of which can be seen in Fig. 10-24 for a 14-L Cummins six-cylinder NTC engine.

Adjustments

Adjustments to the Jacob's engine brake are only required when a problem is suspected. Electrical problems such as loose, broken, or corroded circuit terminals at any of the brake control switches can also cause the brake to be inoperative.

In addition, the clutch and throttle control microswitches must be adjusted so that you can actually hear them click. Both switches can be checked for successful operation by using a test light connected to the respective terminals. The throttle switch should be energized (test light on) when the pedal is in the normal idling position, while it should be deenergized (test light off) when the pedal is pushed down. The clutch switch should be energized (test light on) when the pedal is in the relaxed or pedal-up position (clutch engaged). The test light at the clutch pedal should go off when the pedal is depressed (pushed down), thereby disengaging the clutch. Fig. 10-20 shows a typical clutch microswitch location.

The throttle microswitch is usually not found underneath the throttle pedal, but is located on the fuel injection pump and supported on a bracket. On four-stroke cycle engines such as Caterpillar, Cummins, and Mack models, the throttle switch mounting has to be positioned by adjustment so that you can hear a distinct click within the switch as the throttle linkage is allowed to return to its normal low-idle speed position. Remember that this switch must be closed to complete the series circuit to the Jake brake when it is in the idle position. As soon as the throttle linkage is moved from low idle, the electrical circuit should be opened to prevent any possibility of the Jake brake coming into operation. On Detroit Diesel two-stroke-cycle 71 and 92 series engines without DDEC (DD Electronic Controls), the throttle switch is actually mounted on a bracket that is bolted to the mechanical governor assembly. The governor is bolted to the front of the gear-driven blower at the front of the engine. Adjust the throttle switch, which is located against the governor buffer screw, so that you can hear a distinct click

FIGURE 10–21 Engine brake wiring replacement. (*Courtesy of GMC Truck Division, General Motors Corporation.*)

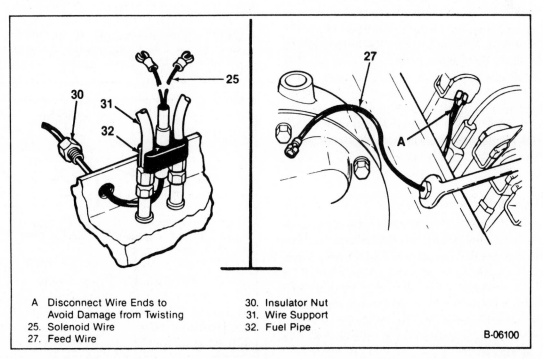

A	Disconnect Wire Ends to Avoid Damage from Twisting	30.	Insulator Nut
25.	Solenoid Wire	31.	Wire Support
27.	Feed Wire	32.	Fuel Pipe

B-06100

to indicate that the switch has in fact closed the electrical circuit when the throttle linkage is in its normal idle position and will open the circuit the instant the throttle linkage is moved from idle toward an increased fuel setting position. In all cases, a non-powered test light can be used to confirm when the throttle switch actually opens and closes.

The clutch switch is normally located so that when the clutch pedal linkage is moved (pedal down), the Jake brake electric circuit is opened to disengage the brake; the circuit is closed when the pedal is in the up position, which is in the clutch-engaged position. Some clutch microswitches may employ a remote-mounted switch that is activated by a small mechanical arm that is bolted to the side of the switch and is activated when the clutch pedal linkage is moved. You can also use a small test light to confirm when the clutch switch opens and closes the circuit to the Jake brake. Effective troubleshooting can be accomplished by the use of a test light to confirm that power does in fact flow through the circuit to the individual electric solenoids located underneath the engine rocker covers. If there is power flowing when the main, clutch, and throttle switches are closed, but the Jake brake still does not operate, remove the solenoids and inspect the condition of the O-rings. Also, check the solenoid oil screen filters for signs of plugging. In addition, the slave piston may have to be adjusted to set the correct clearance between its linkage (feet) and the exhaust valve bridge (crosshead) mechanism. Each slave piston is adjusted to a specific clearance value for the model of brake being used. This is achieved by making sure that the exhaust valves are fully closed when this adjustment is made. Table 10-3 lists the location of the slave and master pistons for Caterpillar and Mack engines. The Cummins adjusting screw is shown as item 206 in Fig. 10-22. The slave piston can easily be adjusted on a Cummins engine by rotating the engine over to the respective valve set positions. The Cummins slave clearance for the NTC-14L engine is 0.018 in. (0.457 mm); for a Caterpillar 3406B engine it is 0.070 in. (1.778 mm); for a DDC 92 engine it is 0.059 in. (1.498 mm), and for the DDC series 60 engine it is 0.020 in. (0.50 mm). Special Jake brake gauges are available for this purpose. Figure 10-22 shows where the slave piston adjustment clearance would be taken for a Cummins 14-L engine.

Solenoid Valve Replacement

Replacement of the individual solenoid valves or their O-ring seals may be required after a certain mileage has been accumulated or due to solenoid valve malfunction. When a problem with the solenoid valves is suspected, the valve(s) can be replaced after the electrical wire has been disconnected, with the aid of Jacobs special tool socket 011494, which is illustrated in Fig. 10-23. The solenoid can be unscrewed. Seal replacement of the solenoid valve is shown in Fig. 10-24.

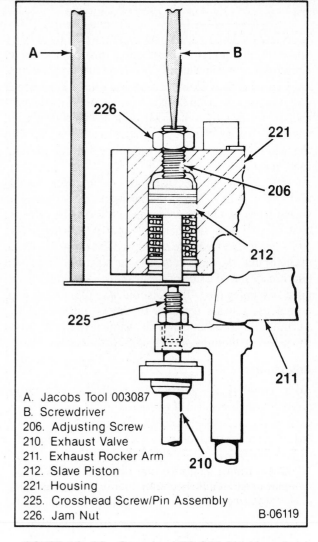

A. Jacobs Tool 003087
B. Screwdriver
206. Adjusting Screw
210. Exhaust Valve
211. Exhaust Rocker Arm
212. Slave Piston
221. Housing
225. Crosshead Screw/Pin Assembly
226. Jam Nut

B-06119

FIGURE 10–22 Cummins NTC-855 (14-L) engine brake slave piston adjustment. (*Courtesy of GMC Truck Division, General Motors Corporation.*)

FIGURE 10–23 Removing engine brake solenoid valve with a special Jacobs brake socket 011494. (*Courtesy of GMC Truck Division, General Motors Corporation.*)

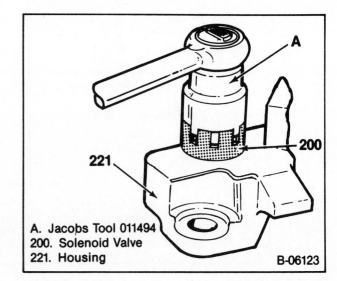

A. Jacobs Tool 011494
200. Solenoid Valve
221. Housing

B-06123

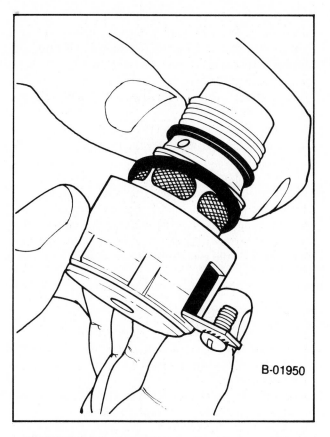

FIGURE 10–24 Engine brake solenoid valve seal ring replacement. (*Courtesy of GMC Truck Division, General Motors Corporation.*)

CATERPILLAR BRAKESAVER

The Caterpillar Brakesaver is a hydraulic retarder device located at the rear of the engine between the crankshaft and the flywheel. It uses engine oil as its medium of operation and is fed pressurized engine oil from a gear oil pump with two sets of gears. One gear set supplies the Brakesaver requirements, while the other pump gear set handles the normal engine lubrication requirements. The Brakesaver system employs an accelerator pedal microswitch, a clutch microswitch, and an electric solenoid valve to control the oil flow, although an optional manual control valve is available. Fig. 10-25 illustrates a simplified electrical wiring diagram for the Brakesaver system used on a Caterpillar 3406B six-cylinder heavy-duty truck engine used in a Peterbilt model 379 heavy-duty conventional cab truck/tractor. The numbers in the diagram are allocated to the various wires used with the system and are as listed in Table 10-4.

The Brakesaver system operates similar to a Jake brake system in that both the throttle and clutch switches have to be in the released position (throttle at low idle; clutch pedal up) to complete the electrical system to the control solenoid valve. The degree of braking from the Brakesaver depends on the rotative speed of the engine during any braking action, since the oil pressure from the supply pump is dependent on engine speed. The hand control valve can be used to supply air pressure from the vehicle air reservoirs when manual control of the Brakesaver is required. Failure of the Brakesaver to operate can be confirmed by a lack of sound at the control valve (no clunk) when the system is activated. This problem may be in the electrical system; check the fused power supply first, then using an unpowered test-light check for continuity through the switches. Continuity should exist only when the throttle and clutch pedals are in their released positions (the test lamp should illuminate); no test light illumination through the lamp should occur when the clutch or throttle pedals are depressed since the circuit is opened. For a detailed description of operation of the Caterpillar Brakesaver, refer to the publication by Robert N. Brady, *Heavy-Duty Truck Power Trains: Transmissions, Drive Lines, and Axles* (Englewood Cliffs, N.J.: Prentice-Hall, 1989).

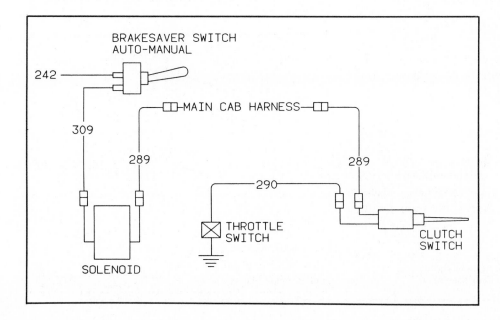

FIGURE 10–25 Example of the wiring circuit used on a heavy-duty truck equipped with a Caterpillar Brakesaver. (*Courtesy of Peterbilt Motors Company, Division of PACCAR, Newark, CA.*)

TABLE 10-4 Cat Brakesaver wire number and circuit index for Fig. 10-25

Wire Number	Circuit
242	Wire gauge size 14 and up; miscellaneous accessory power feed
289	Wire gauge size 14; dash switch to clutch switch
290	Wire gauge size 14; clutch switch to engine throttle switch
309	Wire gauge size 14; Brakesaver switch to solenoid valve

POWER WINDOWS

Many heavy duty-trucks employ power windows, which can either be air operated from the vehicle air reservoir, or operated electrically by a single permanent-magnet motor for each door. Fig. 10-26 illustrates a typical power window switch control mechanism, with the driver's door panel having two switches, one for each door window, while the passenger door only has one control switch.

The individual power window motors have a self-resetting circuit breaker built in to them so that should the window jam or the motor be overloaded and stall, the motor is protected. In addition, the feed to the power windows would be protected from the main fuse/circuit breaker panel. Table 10-5 lists typical problems that you might encounter with electric power windows, the possible causes, and suggested correction procedures. Should

it become necessary to replace a power window switch, always disconnect the battery ground cable first, then remove the door trim panel, the inner handle housing, the harness connector, and then the switch, which can be removed simply by pressing in the spring clips that hold it in position. Installation is basically the reverse procedure of removal.

Should it become necessary to replace the power window motor, always raise the window to its full-up position first. If the motor will not allow this, attempt to pull the window up manually. Disconnect the battery ground cable first, then remove the door trim panel if you have to push the window all the way up. If an armrest bracket is used, remove it also. Disconnect the motor wiring harness and remove the electric motor and window regulator. Reverse the procedure for installation of the new motor.

ELECTRONIC CRUISE CONTROL

A cruise control feature may be air operated on older-model trucks, or on newer models, built into the engine ECM (electronic control module) such as you would find on Detroit Diesel Electronic Controls (DDEC) and Caterpillar's PEEC (Programmable Electronic Engine Control) systems. Both the DDEC and PEEC systems are described in detail in Chapter 11. The cruise control system on trucks equipped with DDEC or PEEC utilizes the zero-droop feature to control vehicle speed. This means that the ECM has been programmed to operate with no speed change between the maximum no-load rpm (high idle)

FIGURE 10-26 Typical location of a heavy-duty truck power window switch. (*Courtesy of GMC Truck Division, General Motors Corporation.*)

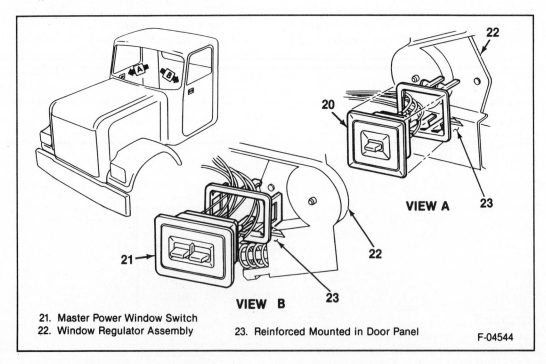

21. Master Power Window Switch
22. Window Regulator Assembly
23. Reinforced Mounted in Door Panel

F-04544

TABLE 10-5 Diagnosis chart for power window problems

PROBLEM	POSSIBLE CAUSE	CORRECTION
Passenger Window Will Not Work, Using Either Passenger Switch Or Driver Switch	1. No power at the passenger switch. 2. Passenger switch is not working. 3. Motor has an internal open.	1. Engine Control switch at RUN or ACC. Check for voltage at the passenger switch. If there is no voltage, find the open between the switch and the fuse block. 2. With the voltage on the PNK wire at the switch, move the switch to "UP." There should be voltage at the DK BLU WHT STR wire. If there is no voltage, replace the switch. 3. With the window switch moved to the "UP" position, check for voltage on the DK BLU wire at the motor. If there is no voltage, find the open between the switch and the motor. If there is voltage on the DK BLU wire, back-probe a jumper ground at the BRN wire at the motor. If the motor does not run, replace the motor. If the motor does run, find the open in the ground circuit. Note: The ground circuit does run back through the passenger window "DN" contacts and the driver window switch "DN" contacts before reaching ground.
Passenger Window Will Not Work Using The Passenger Switch. The Window Will Work Using The Driver Switch.	1. No power at the passenger switch. 2. Switch has internal open.	1. Check for voltage on the PNK wire at the passenger switch. If voltage is not present, find the open in the circuit between the switch and the instrument panel harness connector. 2. If voltage is present, replace the switch.
Passenger Window Won't Work Using The Driver Switch	1. No power. 2. Open in driver switch. 3. Open in harness.	1. Check driver window action. If the driver window works, power is at the switch. 2. With the driver switch moved to "UP," check for voltage on the DK BLU wire at the driver switch. If voltage is not present, replace the switch. 3. With voltage present on the DK BLU wire at the driver switch, find the open between the driver switch and the passenger switch.
Driver Window Won't Work. Passenger Window Works	1. Switch won't work. 2. Motor has internal open. 3. Motor ground circuit is open.	1. Switch moved to "UP." Check for voltage at the DK BLU wire at the switch. If voltage is not present, replace the switch. 2. Switch moved to "UP." Check for voltage on the DK BLU wire at the motor. If voltage is present, backprobe a jumper ground at the BRN wire at the motor. If the motor won't run, replace the motor. 3. Backprobe a jumper ground at the BRN wire at the motor. Move the driver switch to "UP." If the motor runs, find the open in the ground circuit.

Source: Courtesy of GMC Truck Division, General Motors Corporation.

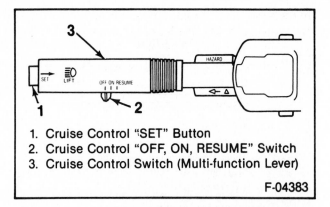

1. Cruise Control "SET" Button
2. Cruise Control "OFF, ON, RESUME" Switch
3. Cruise Control Switch (Multi-function Lever)

F-04383

FIGURE 10–27 Component ID of a multifunction steering column–mounted stalk lever showing the cruise controls. (*Courtesy of GMC Truck Division, General Motors Corporation.*)

and the full-load (rated) speeds. EEPROM (electronically erasable programmable read-only memory) calibration data, which define vehicle axle ratio, tire size, top gear ratio, and desired road speed, are required inputs to the computer. The vehicle speed sensor is used as a cruise control input in conjunction with the road speed governing feature and/or Allison automatic transmission ATEC (Allison Transmission Electronic Controls), which interface with the engine ECM. The cruise control switch illustrated in Fig. 10-27 is a multifunction lever (part of the turn-signal lever), which allows the driver to select a steady-state speed without having to touch the accelerator pedal. The system can hold a preset road speed until the engine speed drops below 100 rpm. The system is designed to resume a preset speed after:

1. Braking
2. Clutching with a manual transmission, without using the accelerator pedal
3. Accelerating from a given set speed to a higher speed

The cruise control system also allows the driver to "tap up" and increase speed, or "tap down" to decrease vehicle speed in increments of about 1 mph (1.6 km/hr), as desired. Since the cruise control feature is programmed into the engine ECM, always refer to the particular DDEC or PEEC service literature when a problem is encountered with this system. For example, if a Code 31, 54, or 58 is logged in ECM memory on a DDEC system, a fault has been confirmed in the cruise control circuitry. These codes can be accessed using a DDR, shown in Chapter 11 for both DDC and Cat systems. A description of the DDEC codes is also given in Chapter 11. Fig. 10-28 shows one example of where the cruise control clutch switch is located for a vehicle equipped with a DDEC system. If it is suspected that the problem lies in the multifunction switch, remove the trim housing from the steering column as shown in Fig. 10-29 to access the multifunction switch assembly.

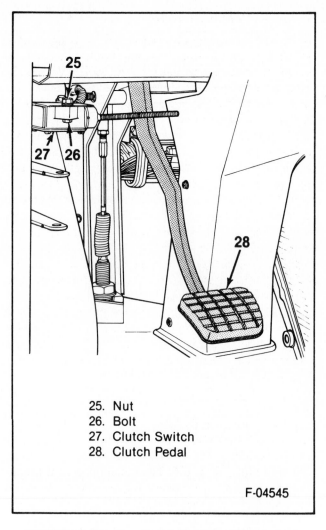

25. Nut
26. Bolt
27. Clutch Switch
28. Clutch Pedal

F-04545

FIGURE 10–28 Location of the cruise control circuit clutch control switch. (*Courtesy of GMC Truck Division, General Motors Corporation.*)

FIGURE 10–29 Components ID of the parts related to removal of the steering column–mounted multifunction lever.

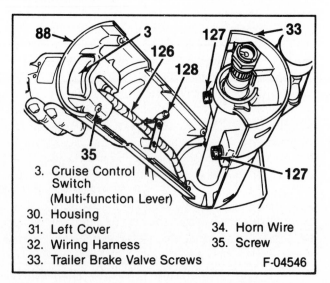

3. Cruise Control Switch (Multi-function Lever)
30. Housing
31. Left Cover
32. Wiring Harness
33. Trailer Brake Valve Screws
34. Horn Wire
35. Screw

F-04546

THERMATIC ENGINE FANS

Many heavy-duty highway trucks employ a thermatic fan, which is engaged when the engine attains a preset operating temperature. Since a fan is only required approximately 10 percent of the time during engine operation for cooling purposes, disengaging the fan assembly for 90% of the engine's operating time results in a substantial fuel saving, since very little horsepower is required to turn the fan hub by itself. The thermatic fan employs a fan hub that is driven via a multiple-drive belt set from the crankshaft pulley. The fan blades, which are bolted to the fan hub, will rotate only when the internal clutches of the hub are engaged. These internal clutches can be engaged by either spring pressure or by air pressure. The Bendix thermatic fan uses spring pressure to apply the fan clutches, and compressed air to release them. The Horton type fan clutch uses air pressure to apply the fan clutches, and spring pressure to release them. In both types of fans, an engine coolant mounted electrical sensor assembly controls the flow of compressed air to the fan hub through an electrically actuated air-supply/exhaust-valve solenoid. The following information describes the operation of the Horton thermatic fan. Figure 10–30 illustrates a schematic diagram of the system.

Two main options are available with the Horton fan clutch illustrated in Fig. 10–30. One is an indicator light which provides the driver with a visual check that the fan clutch is either on or off. The second option is the installation of a manual by-pass feature that is wired into the system between the fan clutch switch and the battery power source. In addition, the Horton fan clutch system is available as either an NC (normally closed) or an NO (normally open) electrical control system. The difference between the two systems is shown in Fig. 10–30.

Operation

Refer to Fig. 10–30, which illustrates the Horton fan clutch electric control system. The ignition key supplies battery power to the optional manual toggle control switch and to the engine-coolant-mounted thermal time switch. When the engine coolant temperature is high enough, the thermal time switch completes the electrical circuit to the NO or NC solenoid fan clutch valve. This valve opens and allows vehicle reservoir compressed air to flow to and through the tee fitting and optional air pressure switch. The air pressure switch will complete the electrical circuit to the dash-mounted indicator light to inform the operator that the fan is engaged. Air flows through the tee fitting and into the fan clutch hub, where it overcomes the force of the return spring in order to apply the clutch hub to the rotating belt driven pulley. When the engine coolant temperature drops, the NO or NC thermal time switch will break or open the electrical circuit to deenergize the fan clutch hub. This is achieved by exhausting the compressed air from the fan clutch hub

to the atmosphere through an exhaust port in the NO or NC solenoid valve. The dash-mounted indicator light would also go out once the air has been exhausted from the clutch system.

Troubleshooting

Problems with the fan clutch system can be due to either a lack of compressed air from the vehicle system, or by a loss of air from the fan clutch hub due to leakage. Table 10–6 lists typical electrical causes and solutions for a Horton fan clutch, while the following information describes how to systematically check the clutch, air and electric controls.

Procedure

1. Inspect all electrical connections and wires. Tighten if loose, replace if damaged.
2. Verify clutch engagement.
    a. Normally closed (series) electrical system (see Fig. 10–30)
        (1) With the engine temperature below the thermal switch setting, turn the ignition on and build up air pressure.
        (2) Disconnect the (+) thermal switch terminal. This will engage the fan clutch.
        (3) Reconnect the (+) terminal of the thermal switch. This will exhaust air and disengage the fan clutch.
    b. Normally open (parallel) electrical system (see Fig. 10–30)
        (1) With the engine temperature below the thermal switch setting, turn the ignition on and build up air pressure.
        (2) Install a jumper wire between the terminals of the thermal switch. This will engage fan clutch.
        (3) Remove the jumper wire to exhaust air and disengage the fan clutch.
3. Check all air connections for air leaks.
4. Drain the air filter. Clean the bowl and filter if necessary.
5. Check the fan hub friction facing for wear. Replace when worn to $\frac{1}{16}$ in. thick.
6. Check for air leaks in the fan clutch hub.
    a. Normally closed electrical system
        (1) To determine if air is leaking from the clutch, turn the engine off. This will engage the clutch.
        (2) Lightly brush a bubble solution on the bleed hole on the fan pilot between the air chamber and the piston friction disk and around the come-home holes on the piston disk. If this is impractical, listen or feel for air leaks.
    b. Normally open electrical system
        (1) To determine if air is leaking from the clutch, turn the key to the ON position (*do not start the*

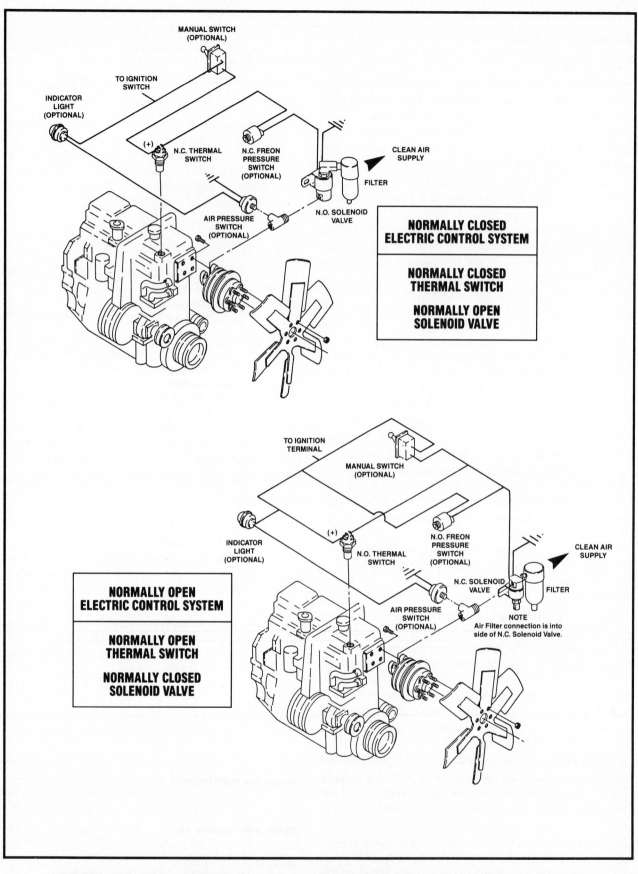

FIGURE 10–30 Horton Dieseltemp fan clutch equipped with an optional indicator light and optional manual bypass toggle switch. (*Courtesy of Horton Industries Inc.*)

TABLE 10–6 Horton fan clutch electrical troubleshooting guide

Problem	Probable Cause	Solution
Fan clutch fails to engage	Electrical problem 1. Broken current (normally open system). 2. Improperly wired. 3. Thermal switch incorrect (for application) or defective. 4. Bad solenoid valve.	1. Check electrical connections. 2. Check wiring according to diagram. 3. Check thermal switch (NO or NC) application. Replace if wrong or defective. 4. Check resistance of solenoid valve. 18 ohms is normal for a 12 volt system. Replace if bad.
Fan clutch fails to disengage	Electrical problem 1. Broken current (normally closed system). 2. Improperly wired. 3. Thermal switch incorrect (for application) or defective.	1. Check electrical connections. 2. Check wiring according to diagram. 3. Check thermal switch (NO or NC) application. Replace if wrong or defective.
Fan clutch cycles frequently	Electrical problem 1. Poor ground or wire connection. 2. Improper temperature control settings. 3. A/C pressure switch setting too low. 4. Restriction in front of radiator blocking air flow. 5. Faulty thermal switch.	1. Check electrical connections. 2. Check temperature settings of all controls. The thermal switch setting should engage the clutch 10° higher than the shutter sensor. 3. Check A/C pressure switch. Use higher switch. 4. Check for proper shutter operation, winter fronts, or other restrictions in or in front of the radiator. 5. Replace thermal switch.

Source: Courtesy of Horton Industries, Inc.

engine). Install a jumper wire to the thermal switch terminals. This will engage the clutch.

(2) Lightly brush a bubble solution on the bleed hole on the fan pilot between the air chamber and the piston friction disk and around the come-home holes on the piston disk. If this is impractical, listen or feel for air leaks. *If an air leak is detected, install a Minor Repair Seal Kit.*

7. Check for bearing wear in the fan clutch.
   a. Normally closed electrical system
      (1) Turn the key to the ON position (*do not start the engine*); this will disengage the clutch.
      (2) Rotate the fan to check for front bearing roughness.
      (3) If the belts are removed, rotate the sheave to check for pulley bearing roughness. *If bearing wear is detected, install a Bearing/Seal Kit.*

Emergency Operation

Horton Dieseltemp S and HT/S fan clutches are designed to permit continued operation in the event of a fan clutch or control malfunction. In the event of a fan clutch or control malfunction:

1. Disconnect and plug the air line to the fan clutch.
2. Align two holes in the piston/friction disk with two holes in the sheave.
3. Install two 5/16-18 NC × 1 in. grade 8 socket head cap screws (Horton 994201) and tighten to 25 ft-lb torque.

NOTE: Clamping of plates, not bolts, provides turning force. The procedure above is only a temporary solution; the problem must be corrected as soon as possible.

Optional Thermatic Fans

In addition to the Horton air fan illustrated in Fig. 10–30 both Rockford and Bendix manufacture similar types of fans. Both employ a coolant temperature sensor similar to that of the Horton unit; however, the Rockford model is an oil-cooled, spring-loaded multiplate clutch that adjusts the fan to the precise speed needed to maintain a specific coolant temperature. When the engine is cold, air pressure is fed into the fan clutch hub to overcome spring pressure and disengage it. As the coolant temperature of the engine rises, the coolant sensor smoothly reduces the air pressure at the fan clutch to zero. At zero pressure, the fan clutch is completely locked by spring force in order to drive the fan at input speed (belt driven from the crankshaft or auxiliary drive on the engine).

The Bendix fan clutch is an air operated, thermostatically controlled dry cone clutch that engages as required for maintenance of coolant temperature within a specific range. This clutch uses a sensor similar to both the Horton and Rockford models; however, the fan clutch hub receives air pressure as soon as the engine is started, in order to disengage the fan; when the coolant probe sensor is triggered at 195 °F, the air in the fan clutch hub is exhausted to the atmosphere, allowing the spring-loaded clutch to engage the fan at full input speed.

Therefore, if you are called on to troubleshoot one

of these fans, remember the two different types of operation; one exhausts air, while the other supplies it at a given temperature.

RADIO

The radio location and type (AM, AM/FM) will differ between makes and models of medium- and heavy-duty trucks. In addition, some trucks may be equipped with stereo cassette players or CD (compact disc) decks. The truck mechanic/technician is generally not expected to remove, disassemble, and repair any of these components, since this type of a repair is best left to an electronic component specialist technician at a factory or OEM authorized distributor/dealer location. In many cases, these components are not even repaired here, but are forwarded to the factory for determination of the cause of failure, where the unit can be either repaired or exchanged. The truck mechanic/technician should, however, be able to trace basic power supply faults and make minor repairs to these components. Often this simply involves replacement of a fuse or circuit breaker assembly, or the installation of a new antenna or wiring repair. In some cases the truck technician may have to perform an antenna trimmer adjustment to the radio system. Figure 10–31 shows a troubleshooting chart that lists how to diagnose radio noises systematically, and Fig. 10–32 shows how to diagnose typical problems that you might face when analyzing a radio unit.

CAUTION: When troubleshooting a radio system, never operate the radio with the speakers disconnected, or unplug the speakers with the radio in operation, since internal damage to the radio chassis can occur as a result of this action.

FIGURE 10–31 Diagnosis chart of radio noise problems. (*Courtesy of GMC Truck Division, General Motors Corporation.*)

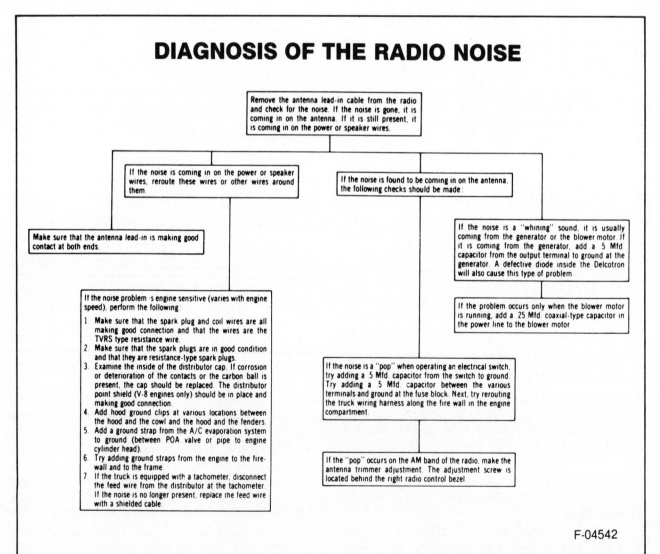

DIAGNOSIS OF THE RADIO

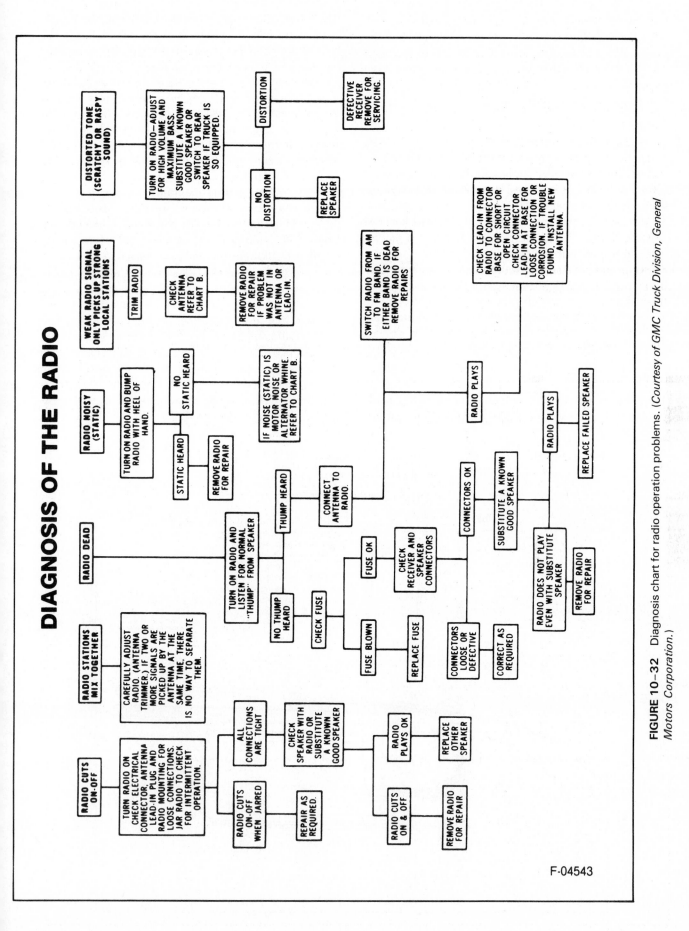

FIGURE 10–32 Diagnosis chart for radio operation problems. (*Courtesy of GMC Truck Division, General Motors Corporation.*)

F-04543

Radio Tuning

Most truck radios offer both an AM (amplitude modulation) and an FM (frequency modulation) selector system. To tune a radio to a desired pushbutton station, manually rotate the manual tuning control knob for the best reception to set up the pushbuttons.

Procedure

1. Manually tune to the desired station.
2. Select the pushbutton you wish to use to key in this station. Pull the selector button straight out, then push it back in firmly until it stops. Repeat this procedure for each of the radio buttons.
3. If the radio is equipped with both an AM and FM selector button, you may choose an AM station and an FM station for each pushbutton.
4. If the radio is equipped with a selector bar, it operates by sliding it to the right or left, and setting each button for AM stations, then sliding the selector bar the opposite way and doing the same procedure for FM stations. Do *not* slide the radio selector bar if any pushbutton is pulled out or the radio could be damaged.

Radio Harness

The radio power harness is battery powered from the vehicle and takes its supply power from a fused or cir-cuit breaker–protected accessory panel. The wire harness is usually connected to the back or side of the receiver, with outlet harnesses or cables being routed to the roof or fender-mounted antenna as well as to the cab speakers. The antenna wire harness usually employs a single pin connector mounted to the shielded wire. The location of the radio will vary between truck makes; however, one example of a roof-mounted antenna with the radio installed into the cab headliner is shown in Fig. 10–33. The wire harness connections for this system are shown in Fig. 10–34.

A simplified wiring diagram of a standard radio system as well as that for a CB (citizens' band) radio is illustrated in Fig. 10–35. The individual numbers in the diagram refer to the actual numbers that will appear on the wires to allow the mechanic/technician to identify and trace the source of the wire when troubleshooting or when referring to a cab and chassis wiring diagram. The circuit number is repeated continually along the length of the wire. Figure 10–36 further illustrates an example of the cab radio and its speaker system wiring, showing two speakers in the cab and two in the truck sleeper, with their respective wire numbers also shown for a Peterbilt Model 379 conventional model truck. Note that the cab speakers and radio are fed from the cab roof harness by three hard-shell connectors. One connector provides the switched

FIGURE 10–33 Heavy-duty truck internal cab-roof mounted radio installation. (*Courtesy of GMC Truck Division, General Motors Corporation.*)

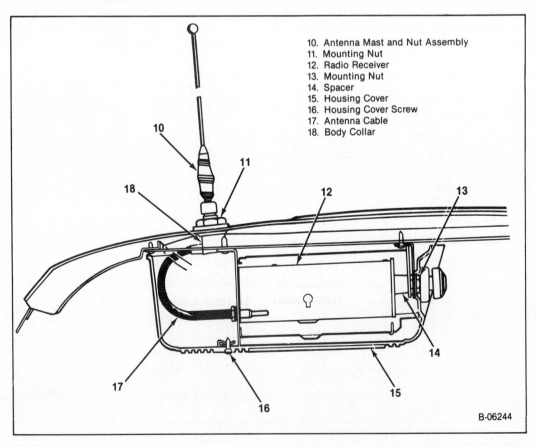

10. Antenna Mast and Nut Assembly
11. Mounting Nut
12. Radio Receiver
13. Mounting Nut
14. Spacer
15. Housing Cover
16. Housing Cover Screw
17. Antenna Cable
18. Body Collar

B-06244

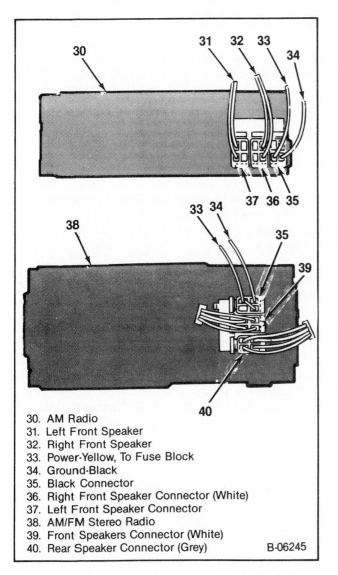

30. AM Radio
31. Left Front Speaker
32. Right Front Speaker
33. Power-Yellow, To Fuse Block
34. Ground-Black
35. Black Connector
36. Right Front Speaker Connector (White)
37. Left Front Speaker Connector
38. AM/FM Stereo Radio
39. Front Speakers Connector (White)
40. Rear Speaker Connector (Grey)   B-06245

FIGURE 10-34 Radio harness connections. (*Courtesy of GMC Truck Division, General Motors Corporation.*)

and constant power requirements, while the other two contain circuits for the forward and rear speakers. Another connector in the same area provides switched and constant power for the CB. It has different circuits from the main radio and also has an identification label. All speaker power and ground wires are connected to the radio. The Peterbilt CB radio is wired into the standard radio speaker system and utilizes the left-front speaker. The radio power supply in the Peterbilt 379 conventional cab truck originates at the vehicle main distribution panel at the top left of the diagram, which is shown as circuit 252, alongside the word "radio." This wiring circuit can be seen by referring to Fig. 6-13.

Radio Removal

Removal of the radio will vary between vehicles; however, the radio is normally mounted in a support frame. Begin

by disconnecting the vehicle ground cable from the battery (batteries). Remove the headliner-mounted radio shown in the example in Fig. 10-33.

Procedure

1. Pull off the left- and right-hand control knobs (volume and tuning knobs) on the front of the radio. Generally, these are a push-on design, although on some radios you may find that a small Allen head screw retains each knob on its shaft.
2. Remove the mounting nuts (13).
3. Remove the radio receiver housing cover mounting screws (16) from the bottom of the housing.
4. Remove the housing cover (15).
5. Tilt the forward end of the housing down.
6. Remove the speaker connectors.
7. Slide the housing over the radio control shafts until it is free.
8. Remove the antenna cable (17).
9. Remove the radio harness connectors.
10. Remove the ground wire from the mounting brackets.
11. Remove the mounting nut from the stud at the rear of the radio receiver.
12. To remove the receiver (12), pull the unit toward the rear of the cab until the stud is free from the mounting bracket.
13. Pull the rear end of the receiver downward until it clears the mounting bracket.
14. Move the receiver toward the windshield to release the radio control shafts from the brackets.

Some radios are mounted in the dash in a mounting sleeve that locks on both sides of the radio. To remove the radio, pry off the bezel, then insert the radio removal keys provided by the truck or radio manufacturer. Keys are marked "left" and "right" on some models, such as the Sony radios used in both Peterbilt and Kenworth trucks. Insert the keys and pull on them evenly to remove the radio from its sleeve. Other Kenworth/Peterbilt radios, such as the Panasonic, employ a mounting bracket with a spring clip on both sides. To remove the radio, use a slotted screwdriver and push in on the spring clip while pulling on the control knobs. Once the radio moves, apply even pulling pressure on both control knobs to remove the radio assembly, as shown in Fig. 10-37.

Radio Light Replacement

To replace the light behind the radio tuner bar usually requires that you first disconnect the battery ground cable. Remove the control knobs from the front of the unit along with the mounting nuts and cover housing. Remove the bezel as shown in Fig. 10-38 by pushing downward on it. Pull the upper edge of the bezel outward. Pull the light bracket forward to release the clip from the radio chassis, then slide the bracket and light out. Remove the light bulb from its holder and replace.

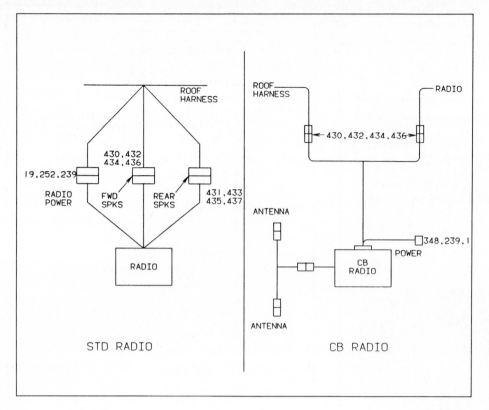

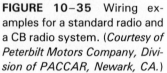

FIGURE 10–35 Wiring examples for a standard radio and a CB radio system. (*Courtesy of Peterbilt Motors Company, Division of PACCAR, Newark, CA.*)

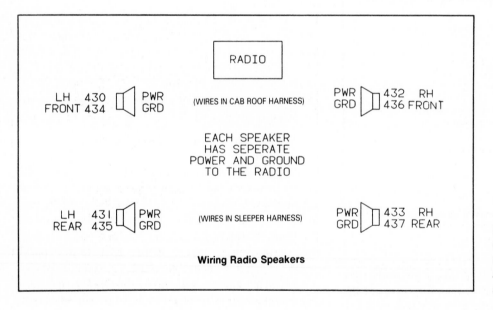

Wiring Radio Speakers

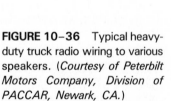

FIGURE 10–36 Typical heavy-duty truck radio wiring to various speakers. (*Courtesy of Peterbilt Motors Company, Division of PACCAR, Newark, CA.*)

Antenna Trimmer Adjustment

The mechanic/technician may have to perform an adjustment to the AM antenna trimmer adjustment screw provided for matching the antenna coil receiver to the vehicle antenna. This adjustment is normally required any time that a radio receiver has been installed, or the antenna has been removed and replaced, or a service repair has been made to the radio. In addition, when a truck moves from one geographical area of the country to another, you may have to perform this adjustment when a complaint of unsatisfactory AM radio reception is reported. This adjustment only applies to AM radios or to the AM portion of an AM/FM receiver. The FM antenna trim-

mer is internal to the radio and is therefore independent of the antenna being used.

Procedure

1. Turn the ignition key to the ACC (accessory) position.

2. Turn the radio volume control to the maximum position.

3. Tune the radio to a weak station somewhere around 1400 KC on the AM band scale.

4. Remove the tuner control knob, the wave washer, and the bezel.

5. Adjust the antenna trimmer screw until the maximum volume is obtained.

6. Figure 10–39, item 80, illustrates the location of one

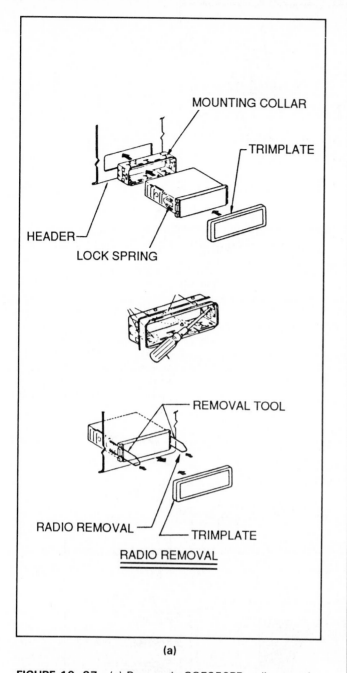

(a)

FIGURE 10-37 (a) Panasonic CQE352PB radio retention and removal system; (b) Sony XR-747R radio mounting hardware. (*Courtesy of Peterbilt Motors Company, Division of PAC-CAR, Newark, CA.*)

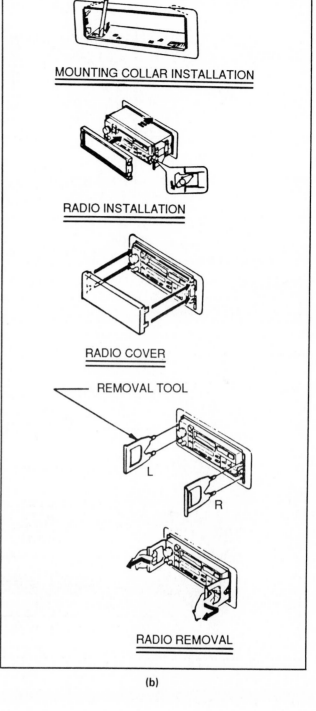

(b)

possible position for the antenna trimmer adjustment screw. Note that if the trimmer adjustment screw is located on the radio chassis adjacent to the tuning shaft (see Fig. 10–40), it may be necessary to loosen the mounting nut on the tuning shaft and reposition the spacer to allow access to the trimmer condensor.

7. Using a small screwdriver, turn the adjustment screw back and forward until maximum volume is achieved. Generally, this will require no more than one-half turn of the screw in either direction.

8. Turn the radio volume off and replace the tuner con-

trol bezel, the wave washer (if used), and the knob. Turn the engine ignition switch off.

In addition to the antenna trimmer adjustment, if it is necessary to remove and replace the antenna assembly, refer to Fig. 10–41, which illustrates a typical roof-mounted antenna and its retaining components.

Speaker Access

The location and number of speakers used with a radio, cassette, or CD set will vary between vehicles. The ac-

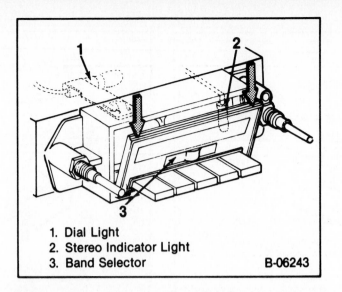

1. Dial Light
2. Stereo Indicator Light
3. Band Selector

B-06243

FIGURE 10-38 How to access and replace the radio light.
(*Courtesy of GMC Truck Division, General Motors Corporation.*)

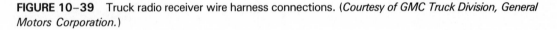

FIGURE 10-39 Truck radio receiver wire harness connections. (*Courtesy of GMC Truck Division, General Motors Corporation.*)

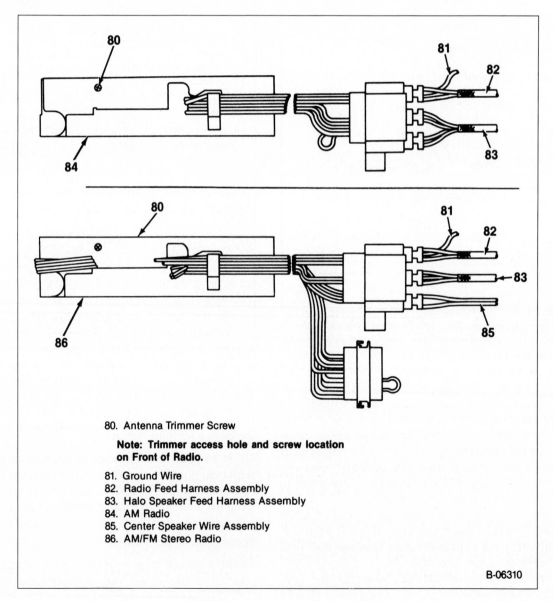

80. Antenna Trimmer Screw

   **Note: Trimmer access hole and screw location
   on Front of Radio.**

81. Ground Wire
82. Radio Feed Harness Assembly
83. Halo Speaker Feed Harness Assembly
84. AM Radio
85. Center Speaker Wire Assembly
86. AM/FM Stereo Radio

B-06310

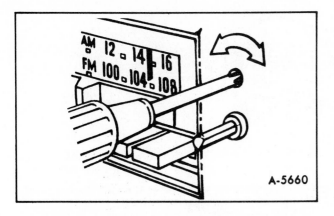

FIGURE 10-40 Radio antenna trimmer adjustment screw location. (*Courtesy of GMC Truck Division, General Motors Corporation.*)

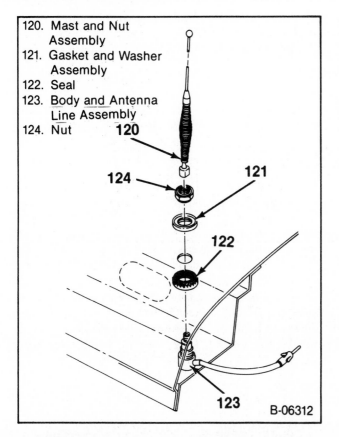

120. Mast and Nut Assembly
121. Gasket and Washer Assembly
122. Seal
123. Body and Antenna Line Assembly
124. Nut

B-06312

FIGURE 10-41 Radio antenna components and installation. (*Courtesy of GMC Truck Division, General Motors Corporation.*)

tual accessibility of the speaker will also vary between vehicle models. Figure 10-42 illustrates one example of a stereo radio speaker location and its various components. The speakers may be located in the dash, the side panels, or the cab roof headliner. Speaker access is usually provided simply by removing a chrome surround that is held in position by small screws, or it may simply be a push and snap-in retainer surround. If the speaker

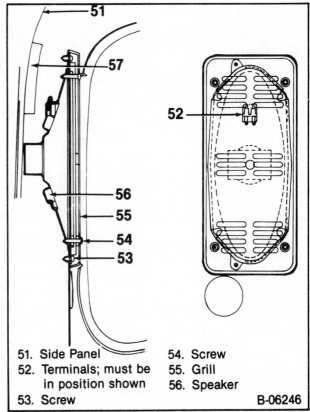

51. Side Panel
52. Terminals; must be in position shown
53. Screw
54. Screw
55. Grill
56. Speaker

B-06246

FIGURE 10-42 Location and identification of radio speaker components. (*Courtesy of GMC Truck Division, General Motors Corporation.*)

is located in the door panels, you usually have to remove the inside door panel to get at the speaker.

BASIC CAB HEATER SYSTEM

The basic cab heater system obtains its heat from the temperature of the circulated engine coolant. Fresh-air makeup is controlled through the use of a cable-controlled supply door that is activated from the vehicle instrument or accessory dash panel by a sliding lever assembly. Cold air from outside and inside the truck is drawn through the heater core by the electrically driven blower motor fans, and then distributed through ducting to the cab. The temperature of the air leaving the ducting is controlled by the water valve, which controls the flow of engine coolant through the heater core, and a blend door, which is used to vary the mixture of warm and cool air. Since the heater system relies on engine coolant for its operation, in this book we are not concerned with a detailed description of operation of a nonelectrical system. We must, however, be aware that the blower motor used to circulate the warm air throughout the vehicle cab and to the defroster system is an electrically operated assembly.

The heater blower motor location will vary with the make and model of truck. Figure 10-43 illustrates a

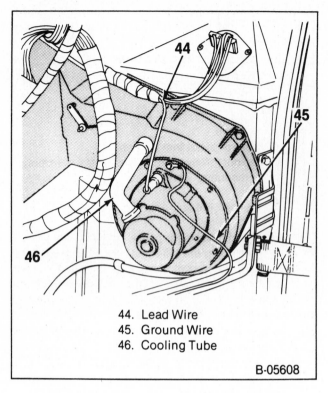

44. Lead Wire
45. Ground Wire
46. Cooling Tube

B-05608

FIGURE 10–43 Cab heater blower motor and housing wiring. (*Courtesy of GMC Truck Division, General Motors Corporation.*)

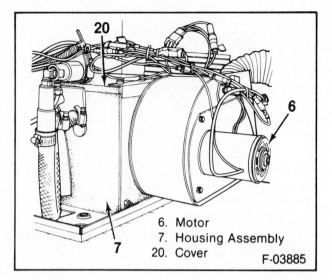

6. Motor
7. Housing Assembly
20. Cover

F-03885

FIGURE 10–44 Sleeper cab heater installation and component I.D. (*Courtesy of GMC Truck Division, General Motors Corporation.*)

typical blower motor and housing that is located underneath the right-hand dash panel of a conventional body truck, and Fig. 10–44 illustrates the blower motor for the sleeper cab heating system, located in the sleeper storage compartment behind the driver seat. Both of these heaters use engine-circulated coolant for operation; however, the blower motor fan is an electrically driven unit.

Both heater blower motors are protected by either a fuse or a circuit breaker, which can be found in the vehicle electrical accessory fuse block panel or combination fuse block/circuit breaker panel. This panel is normally found underneath the vehicle dash or behind a side cover kick panel on either the driver or passenger side.

BASIC AIR-CONDITIONING SYSTEM

The air-conditioning (A/C) system, although not electrically operated per se, does employ a number of electrical accessories for successful operation. The A/C compressor, which is either gear or belt driven from the engine, employs an electromagnetic in/out (on/off) clutch that allows the engine drive to be transferred through the clutch assembly to the A/C compressor shaft. When the electromagnetic clutch is on, the compressor operates to pump Freon (R-12 vapor) through the A/C system. When the clutch is off or deenergized, the compressor simply enters a freewheeling state, since the compressor is not actually pumping under such a condition.

FIGURE 10–45 Schematic of the refrigerant flow within an air-conditioning system. (*Courtesy of GMC Truck Division, General Motors Corporation.*)

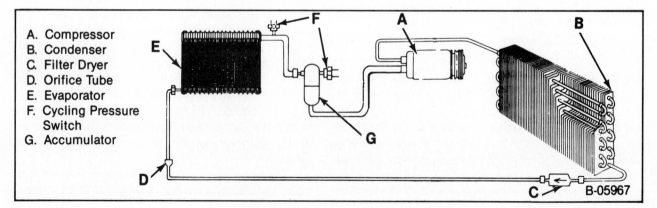

A. Compressor
B. Condenser
C. Filter Dryer
D. Orifice Tube
E. Evaporator
F. Cycling Pressure Switch
G. Accumulator

B-05967

A simplified diagram of an A/C system is shown in Fig. 10–45, where the A/C compressor is shown as item A, and its cycling pressure switch is shown as item F. Figure 10–46 describes briefly in the schematic how the A/C system operates. The function of the cycling pressure switch in the system is to sense refrigerant pressure on the low side of the circuit and to cycle the compressor on/off as necessary. Refrigerant pressure and temperature have a close relationship; the switch is located on a Schrader-type valve on the evaporator inlet tube. During moderate ambient temperatures of between 60 and 80 °F (16 to 26 °C), the equalized pressures within the charged A/C system will close the electrical contacts of the cycling pressure switch. When the driver selects the A/C mode, electrical current is supplied to the compressor electromagnetic clutch coil to transfer engine belt or gear-driven power to the compressor assembly. With the compressor now operating, the A/C system evaporator pressure is lowered to approximately 24 psi (175 kPa), at which point the cycling pressure switch will open and turn the compressor clutch coil off. As the A/C system equalizes, the cycling pressure switch contacts will close at approximately 45 psi (310 kPa) and reengage the compressor clutch coil. This continuous cycling action will continue and maintain system evaporator air temperature at approximately 33 °F (1 °C).

The cycling pressure switch is designed to control the evaporator temperature by cycling the compressor clutch off when the evaporator pressure (temperature) gets too low. It cycles the compressor back on when the evaporator pressure (temperature) has increased. This switch also acts as an ambient temperature switch since at freezing temperatures, it will not allow the compressor to be engaged. Additional compressor protection is assured from the low side due to the operating characteristics of the low-side pressure cycling system. If, for example, a massive discharge occurs, or the orifice tube becomes plugged, low-side pressures would be incapable of closing the contacts of the pressure switch. If a low-charge condition exists, poor cooling accompanied by rapid compressor clutch cycling action will be noticed at high ambient temperatures. Should replacement of the pressure cycling switch be required, it is not necessary to remove the refrigerant charge since a Schrader valve is located in the fitting on the accumulator.

A current surge diode is used and located in the A/C

FIGURE 10–46 Identification of the major components in an air conditioning system. (*Courtesy of GMC Truck Division, General Motors Corporation.*)

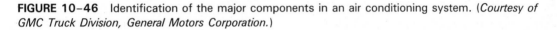
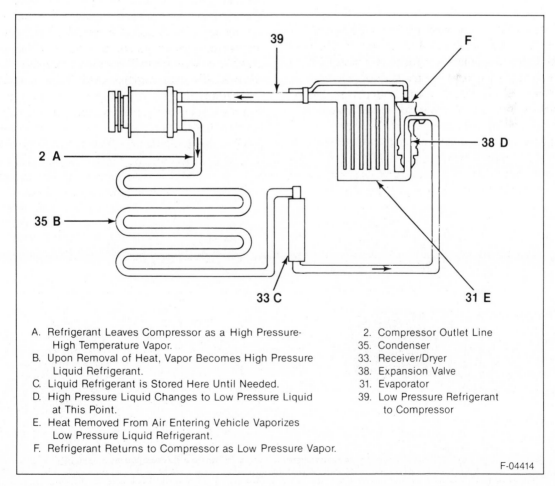

A. Refrigerant Leaves Compressor as a High Pressure-High Temperature Vapor.
B. Upon Removal of Heat, Vapor Becomes High Pressure Liquid Refrigerant.
C. Liquid Refrigerant is Stored Here Until Needed.
D. High Pressure Liquid Changes to Low Pressure Liquid at This Point.
E. Heat Removed From Air Entering Vehicle Vaporizes Low Pressure Liquid Refrigerant.
F. Refrigerant Returns to Compressor as Low Pressure Vapor.

2. Compressor Outlet Line
35. Condenser
33. Receiver/Dryer
38. Expansion Valve
31. Evaporator
39. Low Pressure Refrigerant to Compressor

F-04414

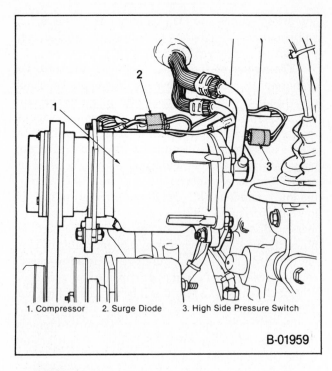

1. Compressor   2. Surge Diode   3. High Side Pressure Switch

B-01959

FIGURE 10–47 A/C compressor surge diode location. (*Courtesy of GMC Truck Division, General Motors Corporation.*)

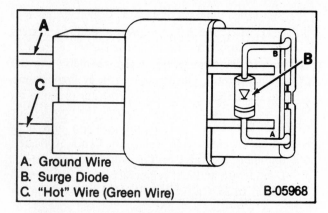

A. Ground Wire
B. Surge Diode
C. "Hot" Wire (Green Wire)

B-05968

FIGURE 10–48 Identification of the surge diode wiring. (*Courtesy of GMC Truck Division, General Motors Corporation.*)

system wiring harness at the compressor as shown in Fig. 10–47. The purpose of this diode is to prevent electrical current surge spikes from damaging the cycling pressure switch when the compressor cycles on and off. A close-up view of the surge diode is shown in Fig. 10–48.

Air Compressor Diagnosis

Figure 10–49 illustrates an exploded view of a typial A/C compressor and its drive mechanism. Note particularly items 7 and 8, the clutch coil ring and the coil, re-

spectively. If the A/C compressor fails to operate or does not engage, check to see if there is voltage present at the compressor coil. If necessary, retrace the electrical circuit back to the source of the power loss. Keep in mind, however, that the circuit is protected by either a fuse or a circuit breaker. Therefore, when no power is evident at the compressor when using a voltmeter, begin by checking the fuse or circuit breaker. If there is correct voltage at the compressor coil, yet it still fails to operate, check for a proper ground circuit and that there is good clean electrical contact at the terminals. If the coil is still inoperable, replace the coil assembly. If the compressor engages but is not operational, check the clutch for slipping. You may have to check the air gap. Obtain the correct spec from the compressor or truck manufacturer's service literature and adjust as necessary. If the air gap adjustment does not correct the problem, replace or repair the compressor. Also check that the compressor belt drive is not slipping. Adjust the belt, if necessary. Any other

FIGURE 10–49 Exploded view of the A/C compressor clutch plate, pulley, and electromagnetic coil assembly. (*Courtesy of GMC Truck Division, General Motors Corporation.*)

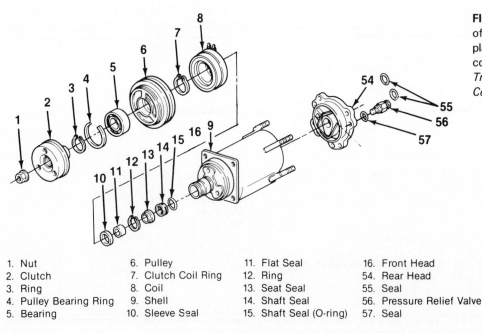

1. Nut	6. Pulley	11. Flat Seal	16. Front Head
2. Clutch	7. Clutch Coil Ring	12. Ring	54. Rear Head
3. Ring	8. Coil	13. Seat Seal	55. Seal
4. Pulley Bearing Ring	9. Shell	14. Shaft Seal	56. Pressure Relief Valve
5. Bearing	10. Sleeve Seal	15. Shaft Seal (O-ring)	57. Seal

problems can be traced to a lack of refrigerant in the system if the compressor operates but no cooling occurs.

Cycling Pressure Switch Diagnosis

When the cycling pressure switch malfunctions, it may remain in either the open or closed position. To test the switch for continuity, connect an ohmmeter across the switch terminals with the electrical harness connector disconnected. The ohmmeter should read zero, indicating continuity. If the switch requires bench checking, you will require a suitable A/C gauge set so that a hydraulic source can be applied to the pressure switch. You will require a minimum pressure between 425 and 450 psi (2800 and 3200 kPa). Connect a 12-V test light in series to the pressure switch. This light should illuminate. Then apply hydraulic pressure through a pressure gauge, taking careful note of when the light goes off. Gradually decrease the pressure and note when the light comes on. As an example, the light may go out at a pressure of 400 ± 10 psi (2760 ± 70 kPa), and come on at a pressure of 300 ± 10 psi (2070 ± 70 kPa). The actual compressor cutout range will vary between makes of trucks depending on the make and model of air compressor used. Generally, the compressor will cut out at a pressure range of 21 to 27 psi (145 to 186 kPa), and it will cut in between 43 and 49 psi (296 to 338 kPa).

A/C Fluid or Viscous Fan Control

Many trucks that are equipped with A/C and a fluid fan or viscous fan require an air-conditioning pressure-sensing system. An electrical high-pressure limit switch is used to disengage the compressor clutch if pressure reaches 400 psi (2760 kPa). The compressor will be turned back on when the pressure has dropped back to 300 psi (2070 kPa). In addition, a mechanical pressure relief valve located at the rear of the compressor will open if system pressure exceeds 400 psi (2760 kPa). Figure 10–50 illustrates the wiring circuit that might be found on a truck using either a viscous or fluid fan system.

Electronic Temperature Control

Some heavy-duty trucks employ electronic temperature control systems in which the A/C system is automatically activated in the defrost mode when ambient temperatures are above freezing. One such system, that is used in Peterbilt heavy-duty class 8 trucks, is shown in Fig. 10–51. This system, known as the CTC II (constant temperature control), is designed to maintain a preselected temperature by pulsing the flow of hot water through the heater core when the control selector is in the heating mode; the A/C compressor will also be cycled on/off in the A/C mode. The system is controlled by an electronic control module that is designed to sense the output temperature, then react accordingly to maintain a preset temperature within the truck cab.

The electronic control module, located on the heater A/C unit, supplies electrical power to the control panel resistor and water valve solenoid shown in Fig. 10–51. The water valve solenoid is an NC (normally closed) switch in the A/C clutch circuit and is electrically located between the A/C thermostat and the trinary switch. The control module monitors and controls the output air

FIGURE 10–50 Wiring arrangement for a viscous or fluid fan system. (*Courtesy of GMC Truck Division, General Motors Corporation.*)

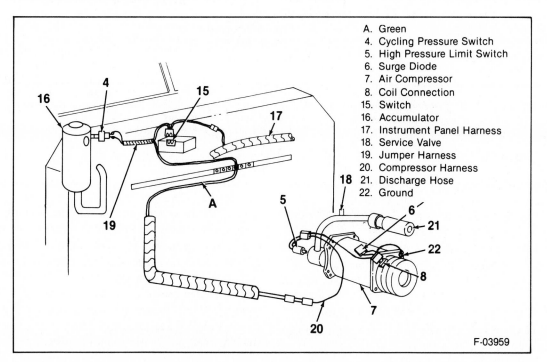

A. Green
4. Cycling Pressure Switch
5. High Pressure Limit Switch
6. Surge Diode
7. Air Compressor
8. Coil Connection
15. Switch
16. Accumulator
17. Instrument Panel Harness
18. Service Valve
19. Jumper Harness
20. Compressor Harness
21. Discharge Hose
22. Ground

F-03959

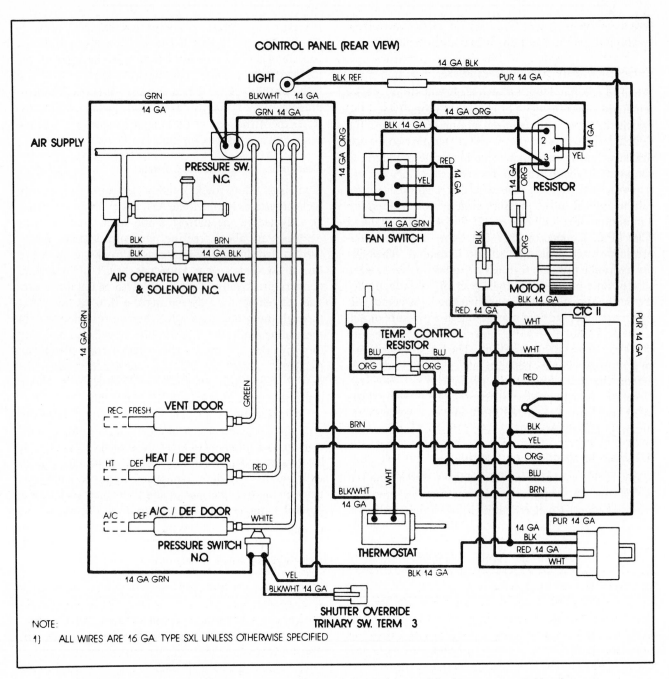

FIGURE 10–51 Schematic diagram of an automatic heater/air conditioning system used in a heavy-duty truck. (*Courtesy of Peterbilt Motors, Division of PACCAR, Newark, CA.*)

temperature. The trinary switch operates similar to the cycling pressure switch described above. The trinary switch performs three functions to monitor and control pressure within the A/C system:

1. It prevents the A/C compressor from operating if the system charge is lost or the ambient temperature is too cold. This low-pressure switch will close (power on) at 40 psig (psi gauge or 276 kPa) maximum with a rising pressure. The switch will open and turn the power off between 30 to 15 psig (207 to 103 kPa) with a falling-pressure condition.

2. The trinary also has a midrange pressure function to turn on the engine fan clutch or activate the radiator shutters. When the system pressure approaches midrange, the switch will engage the fan clutch and/or open the shutters. This action will act to stabilize or lower the A/C system operating pressure by increasing flow across the A/C system condensor. This function is cycled to maintain operating pressures. The midrange switch will close (power on) at pressures between 200 and 230 psig (1379 to 1586 kPa) rising pressure. The switch opens to turn the electrical power off when the pressure drops to be-

tween 140 and 195 psig (965 to 1345 kPa), which is 30 to 60 psig (207 to 414 kPa) below closing pressure.

3. The trinary switch also functions at high pressure to turn the A/C compressor off should the system pressure exceed a safe operating value. The switch closes (power on) when the system is 80 to 120 psig (552 to 827 kPa) below opening pressure. The switch will open, turning the electrical power off when the rising pressure is between 270 and 330 psig (1862 to 2275 kPa).

The trinary switch pressures are automatically reset when the proper system pressure is achieved, although the actual A/C compressor head pressure values will be approximately 10 to 20 psi (69 to 138 kPa) higher than those listed because of pressure loss through the compressor itself. The trinary switch harness on the Peterbilt 379 conventional model truck comes off the engine wire harness to feed the A/C system. The trinary switch is mounted to the moisture indicator on the Freon dryer. The wire harness is equipped with a relay to carry the heavy electrical load required by the compressor electromagnetic clutch. The Dill Blox fuse and circuit breaker panel, which is located inside the cab at the left-hand forward corner, is covered with a door in the kick panel. Inside the door is a list of the spare electrical circuits. Opening the door turns on a light on the Dill Blox to illuminate the circuit panel. The main cab harness begins at the feed-through connectors and feeds to the Dill Blox, where the harness then passes up behind the steering column support and across to the right-hand side of the cab to the roof harness and feed-through grommet. This wire bundle not only feeds the air conditioner CTC wires, but also carries power to the main cab power on early model 379 trucks, as well as to the electric speedometer wires, the electric washer pump wires, and the engine exhaust temperature (pyrometer) wires.

The trinary switch circuit shown in Fig. 10–52 is designed with two independent electrical circuits, with the actual terminal numbers being molded into the top of the switch assembly. Terminals 1 and 2 operate the high- and low-pressure functions to control the A/C compressor clutch circuit. Should the A/C system pressure be too high or too low, the switch will open, thereby breaking the electrical circuit and turning off the A/C compressor electromagnetic clutch. Terminals 3 and 4 control the midrange pressure function to operate the fan or shutter override circuit. When the system pressure is at midrange, the switch closes, energizing the electrical circuit to the fan clutch or to the radiator shutters, which will open. The trinary switch, with its high/low-pressure arrangement, will thereby act as a circuit breaker for the A/C system. When a problem exists in the A/C system, the cause is usually in an area other than the trinary switch itself. Keep in mind, however, that the high/low function of the trinary switch does act to interrupt current flow when an abnormal system pressure condition exists. When a problem exists in the A/C system, always check

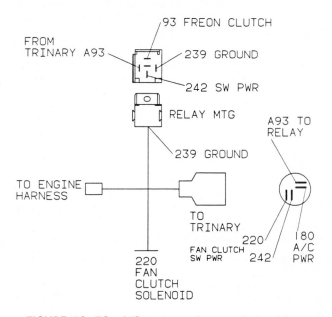

FIGURE 10–52 A/C system trinary switch wiring system. (*Courtesy of Peterbilt Motors Company, Division of PACCAR, Newark, CA.*)

that system fuses or circuit breakers are operational. Use a voltmeter and an ohmmeter to systematically trace the wiring to the various components, which may be causing the system to be inoperative. Checking procedures for the A/C compressor circuit were given earlier in the chapter.

ANTI-BRAKE-SKID SYSTEMS

In this section we deal only briefly with ABS (anti-brake-skid) systems. A separate book would be required to do justice to this increasingly popular system which is making inroads into medium- and heavy-duty truck design. The concept of the antilock braking device is not new; the first official record of ABS development was in 1932 in Great Britain. A number of well-known companies have expended much time and effort since then to perfect such a system for medium- and heavy-duty trucks and buses. In 1970 in the United States, the NHTSA (National Highway Traffic Safety Administration) initiated rules for a FMVSS (Federal Motor Vehicle Safety Standard) for air brake systems, which proposed stringent stopping requirements calling for trucks capable of stopping within 216 ft (66 m) at 60 mph (96 km/hr) on dry pavement without more than a momentary wheel-lock condition. In early 1971 the NHTSA issued FMVSS 121, dealing with antilock air brake systems for trucks and buses. This new law required trucks to stop at 60 mph within 245 ft (75 m). By the 1975 model year seven manufacturers were producing all-electrical antilock systems: the AC Spark-plug Division of General Motors Corporation, Berg,

Eaton, Goodrich, Kelsey-Hayes, Rockwell, and Wagner. All of these systems were axle-by-axle control systems on both steer and dead drive axles. Tandem-axle-drive control systems were not introduced until the 1977 model year. In the previous year (1976) the FMVSS 121 had been further relaxed to a stopping distance of 293 ft (89 m). There were a variety of problems with these early antilock brake systems for trucks, and in 1978, the Ninth Circuit U.S. Court of Appeals in California, in response to a petition lodged in 1975 by a major truck manufacturer, invalidated all of the stopping requirements in the 121 Standard for trucks and trailers. Since that time manufacturers have tentatively resumed development of truck/ trailer antilock braking systems. In 1986 in Europe, the Common Market countries amended their regulations on brakes to allow motor vehicles with antilock systems. Further, the EEC amended this earlier regulation to ensure that all new-model trucks and buses of the types listed in their mandate be equipped with antilock devices.

In the United States, Freightliner was the first major truck manufacturer to offer the new-generation antilock systems on their 1987 model trucks as an optional item. No doubt their move was initiated by the fact that they are owned by their parent West German organization, Mercedes-Benz, which felt that the Wabco (Westinghouse Air Brake Company) system was satisfactory for use on heavy-duty class 8 trucks and trailers. The Freightliner system for two-axle vehicles is similar to that used in Europe. However, in Europe, the three-axle vehicle arrangement uses a four-channel braking system in which only one wheel on each side of the tandem is sensed and a single brake modulation valve controls both wheels on the same side. The three-axle Freightliner antilock system uses a six-channel system relying on individual control for each wheel. By 1988 in the United States there were five manufacturers offering antilock brake systems for heavy-duty trucks. These were Wabco, Robert Bosch Corporation, Midland, Bendix, and Rockwell. In addition, both Eaton and Dana Corporations began a two-year test of a 200-tractor fleet using in-axle speed-sensing systems, which are being evaluated by the NHTSA. Basically, the current antilock systems employ electronics, whereby the early mechanical wheel speed sensors have been replaced with an electronic wheel speed sensor and an ECM (electronic control module) to control the braking system response and prevent wheel lockup, which would create a truck/trailer jacknife reaction. Wheel speed sensors constantly monitor wheel speed, although some systems utilize a design whereby the wheel speed sensor is located on the top of the axle differential housing. This design allows the sensor to be totally enclosed within the housing, which offers superior protection to that of an external wheel speed sensor. The sensor picks up its speed reference from the differential ring gear rotational speed.

The wheel speed sensors constantly send an electrical signal to the ABS ECM or ECU (electronic control unit).

The ECM or ECU can then determine the rotational speed of the wheel based on this input signal and determine both an acceleration and deceleration condition. The antilock system interprets the wheel speed sensor signals and compares them to a preprogrammed wheel slip condition. The ECU can then send out corrective signals to the brake modulator valve to increase or decrease the brake application pressure, thereby avoiding wheel lockup. In addition, the ABS ECU continually tracks the information from all of the vehicle's wheel speed sensors with the brakes on or off, and by interpretation of this information the ECU can compute a vehicle reference speed, which it is continually upgrading based on the frequency of the wheel speed sensor signals. The major components used with any antilock brake system include:

1. The wheel speed sensors
2. The ECU or ECUs (electronic control units)
3. Brake modulators
4. Various failure warning devices
5. Electrical cables and wiring
6. Diagnostic equipment

Two basic types of sensors are used in truck ABS systems: the active and passive designs. The active design requires an electrical input to the sensor in order to operate, whereas the passive sensor requires no electrical source to activate it. The passive design relies upon a magnetic field for its operation. Figure 10–53 illustrates the passive wheel sensor concept whereby a toothed wheel that rotates at vehicle wheel speed is used to make and break the strength of the existing magnetic field between the magnet and the toothed wheel. This changing magnetic flux condition will induce a small alternating voltage in the sensor coil windings, resulting in a small pulsed current output to the ECU. Regardless of the type of sensor used, the ECU must receive a wheel speed sensor signal in order to control air brake system application/ release pressure to avoid a wheel lockup that could induce a skid or jacknife.

FIGURE 10–53 Variable-reluctance wheel speed sensor. (*Reprinted with permission, © 1989, Society of Automotive Engineers, Inc., Warrendale, PA.*)

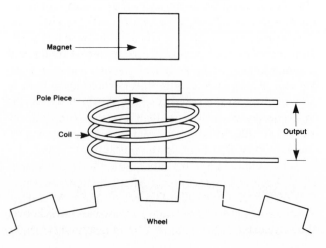

Many ABS manufacturers now place the wheel speed sensors inboard on the wheel hub cap or within the differential housing. These areas provide sensor protection from the elements. The ECU is designed so that it can self-monitor system operation and conditions. Should any part of the ABS system not operate correctly, the ECU can place the system into a fail-safe mode, which simply means that the brakes will still operate; however, there will be no antilock skid protection during this time. The ECU will then store information in memory, which can be accessed using diagnostic equipment similar to that shown in Chapter 11 and illustrated in Fig. 11–74, where a stored trouble code keys the mechanic/technician into a specific area where a series of checks and tests will confirm where the specific problem may be. When an ABS system malfunction occurs, the driver is alerted to the condition by the illumination of a flashing dash-mounted warning light, a series of LEDs (light-emitting diodes) on the ECU, or by trouble code numbers which are displayed on the diagnostic readout tool. Depending on the specific ABS system being used, the truck may be equipped with only one ECU, or it may have a separate ECU for each axle or tandem axle arrangement. With the one ECU system, this unit can generally be found inside the truck cab, where it is in a protected environment, while multiple ECU systems generally mount the ECUs along the inside of the chassis frame rails. The ECU system is usually protected by a fused circuit or by a circuit breaker arrangement, which can be located in the vehicle cab close to the main power supply system.

The Bosch truck ABS system is similar in mechanical design to that produced by Wabco (Westinghouse Air Brake Company) for trucks and trailers except for the new Wabco trailer systems. The sensors and modulators for these two makes of ABS systems are interchangeable, with the Bosch ECU being able to operate with the Wabco modulators and wheel speed sensors. However, in the Wabco antilock system the ABS warning lamp will illuminate and remain on until the vehicle has achieved a speed of approximately 3 to 4 mph (5 to 6.5 km), after which time the ECU runs through a quick check of the wheel sensors. If all sensors are operational, the warning light goes off. In the Bosch ABS system, the warning light is illuminated and then goes out after the ECU has performed its self-check, even without the vehicle moving. Once the truck does move and attains a road speed of 3 to 4 mph (5 to 6.5 km), the ECU monitors the wheel speed sensors and will cause the warning light to flash if the system is operating correctly. Any problem in the ABS system during vehicle operation will initiate the warning light, and a trouble code is stored in memory for withdrawal later by the mechanic/technician.

COMMERCIAL VEHICLE ABS SYSTEMS

In this section we look at two widely used and well-known ABS systems now offered for use in heavy-duty truck/

tractors and trailers. Robert Bosch Corporation and Rockwell International Corporation, Automotive Operations, have joined forces with Wabco to release ABS systems, which are basically joint ventures between these individual companies. The Bosch/Wabco and Rockwell/Wabco ABS systems are very similar in design and operation, with only minor variations between them. Because of this fact, the following information can be considered common to both systems since they both employ Wabco air brake system components. The Bosch/Wabco system is available for use on trucks using either hydraulic or air brake systems.

These new-generation ABS systems are so highly regarded in many European countries that a number of vehicle insurance corporations offer reduced premiums to trucking companies that employ ABS on their fleets of trucks and buses. Whether the ABS system is used on a hydraulic or air-brake-equipped vehicle, the following major components, illustrated in Fig. 10–54, are required for use with the ABS (anti-brake-skid) system:

1. A series of individual wheel speed sensors with their mating toothed wheel
2. An ECU (electronic control unit)
3. A brake modulator valve assembly

In addition to the three major components listed above, the Rockwell/Wabco system employs a clamping bushing to retain the wheel speed sensor at a close, constant distance from the rotating toothed wheel; therefore, there is no need for a periodic adjustment to maintain the air gap between the sensor and the rotating toothed wheel. Figure 10–54 illustrates the rigid-mounted sensor concept used on the Rockwell/Wabco system of a heavy-duty truck. The final component required to complete the ABS system is a complete wiring harness that is fully encased

FIGURE 10–54 Major component parts of a Rockwell-WABCO antiskid system for heavy-duty trucks. (*Courtesy of Rockwell International.*)

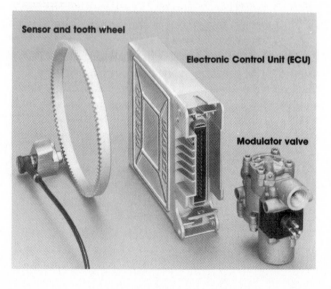

in a flexible, protective conduit to simplify installation and provide trouble-free operation during the life of the ABS system. All of the various components used with the ABS system would be installed on a truck or truck/tractor as shown in Fig. 10-55, which illustrates the four-sensor, four-modulator-valve system used on a tandem-axle vehicle.

Concept of Operation

Although the general purpose and design of the commercial vehicle ABS is similar to that for the passenger car, due to the physical size and various combinations of trucks, truck/tractors, and semitrailers, the potential for loss of vehicle steering and accident damage through wheel lockup is more severe on these applications. Even when a vehicle is equipped with an ABS system, with wet road conditions, or if ice or snow is present, the tendency of a commercial vehicle, particularly a tractor/trailer combination, when the brakes are applied is to attempt to rotate about its own vertical axis. This tendency is compounded if one side of the vehicle has a better grip between the tire and road surface than the other one does, since the deceleration rate of the wheels due to a different coefficient of friction will not be the same. The result is that the tractor or trailer wants to pull to one side, or to rotate about its vertical axis. The driver, sensing this condition, immediately attempts to pull the steering wheel to an opposite lock condition to maintain directional control of the vehicle in a straight line. With an ABS system employed on the vehicle, however, the wheel speed sensors are able to advise the ECU of the deceleration characteristics of each wheel/tire, and the ECU would automatically apply and release the brakes on the wheel/tire with a better grip at a faster rate than it would on the wheel/tire with the poorer traction. This reaction of applying and releasing the brakes of each wheel, anywhere between 4 and 15 times per second, allows independent control at each wheel, which results in the driver

having to apply up to 2.5 times less effort to try and compensate for loss of steering control. The vehicle stopping distance would, however, increase by about 10%, due to the rapid application and release of the brakes by ECU action.

ECU Function. Within the ECU are a series of microcomputers designed to evaluate the voltage signals that are constantly relayed to the ECU from the individual wheel speed sensors. During braking, if a wheel begins to lock, the ECU transmits intermittent electrical impulses to the individual axle modulator valves, which can rapidly apply, release, or hold the air pressure in the air brake chamber. This rapid modulation of air pressure at rates of up to five times per second on the Rockwell/Wabco ABS system prevents wheel lockup and allows the driver to maintain, control, and complete a quick, safe stop under all types of road conditions and speeds.

Wheel Speed Sensors. The major purpose of each individual wheel speed sensor is to monitor the actual rotational wheel speed and relay this information continuously by sending a voltage signal back to the microcomputers within the ECU for processing. For example, the wheel speed sensor may employ 100 teeth on its rotating toothed wheel or hub assembly; therefore, when the vehicle is moving, the inductive speed sensor, which is mounted to provide a small air gap between its tip and the rotating toothed wheel, will output a sinusoidal or wavelength voltage, with a frequency or output proportional to the wheel's rpm. Depending on the type of wheel speed sensor mounting, the air gap may vary slightly once it has been installed, due to such things as the small play in the supporting wheel bearings, as well as the small deflection of the axle housing during normal vehicle operation. If, however, the air gap were to become excessive at any time, the ECU would log a trouble code into memory. In addition, due to the excessive air gap, an irregular or no-signal condition from the wheel speed

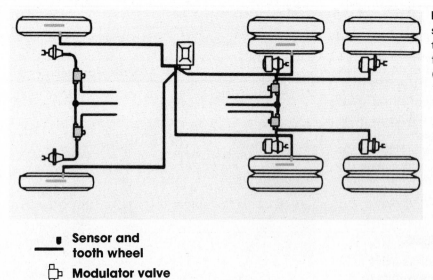

FIGURE 10-55 ABS four-channel system for a 6 × 4 truck, or truck/tractor showing four wheel speed sensors and four brake pressure modulation valves. (*Courtesy of Rockwell International.*)

▪ **Sensor and tooth wheel**

⌐⊏ **Modulator valve**

sensor would cause the ECU to switch off the ABS control, or only that component it considers defective. On the Rockwell/Wabco system, should a malfunction occur during any stage of the ABS operation, a fail-safe circuit activates a warning lamp, notifying the driver that a fault has been detected, and the ECU will switch off the faulty half of the system to normal braking to ensure that the vehicle can still be driven, but without full ABS control.

Pressure Modulation Valve. The number of air pressure modulation valves used on the ABS system depend on the actual system in use, but the example illustrated in Figure 10–55 shows a four-sensor, four-modulator system for use on a tandem-axle truck or truck/tractor. The modulation valves receive electrical signals from the ECU based on the wheel speed sensor signals that have been processed within the ECU. The modulation valves also receive air pressure from the air brake pedal controlled by the truck driver. If during a brake application, the wheel speed sensors inform the ECU of a difference in rotational speed between individual wheels, or individual axles, the ECU signal to the air brake modulation valve will cycle it on and off up to five times per second to prevent wheel lockup. The modulation valve therefore adjusts brake pressure quickly for controlled braking. A unique ''pressure hold'' mode ensures smooth braking and minimizes the total air consumption of the system.

Dual Diagonal Circuit Design

The Rockwell/Wabco ABS system is designed with what is known as a redundant dual diagonal circuit system. This system offers ABS system benefits even with partial system failure. Figure 10–56 shows the concept of the dual diagonal circuit, where diagonally opposite wheels on the truck are completely independent. Should a failure

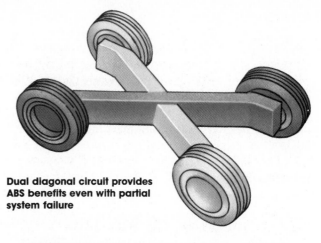

Dual diagonal circuit provides ABS benefits even with partial system failure

FIGURE 10–56 Concept of a dual-diagonal ABS circuit. (*Courtesy of Rockwell International.*)

occur in one of the diagonally opposite ABS circuits, the failed circuit will automatically revert to a normal (non-ABS control) braking condition. Even though only one of the diagonally opposite systems might be functioning under ABS control, the vehicle is still able to maintain stability and steering control, resulting in shorter stopping distances.

Brake Channel Configuration

The number of wheel speed sensors and air brake modulation valves used on any truck, truck/tractor, or semitrailer will vary between makes of vehicles. For example, the system shown in Fig. 10–55 is known as a four-channel design, since it includes four-wheel speed sensors and four modulator valves. This is a widely used and ideal arrangement for many 4 × 2, 6 × 2, and 6 × 4 tractor, truck, and bus applications. On three-axle applications, the steering axle and one of the two remaining tandem axles (the axle most likely to lock first) are provided with individual wheel-by-wheel monitoring. Note, however, that in this type of system, all six wheels of the

FIGURE 10–57 Popular semitrailer ABS installations. (*Courtesy of Rockwell International.*)

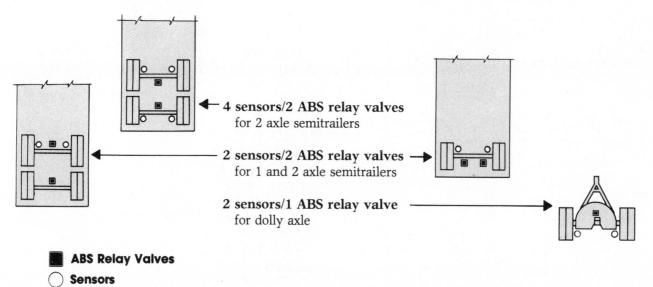

4 sensors/2 ABS relay valves for 2 axle semitrailers

2 sensors/2 ABS relay valves for 1 and 2 axle semitrailers

2 sensors/1 ABS relay valve for dolly axle

■ **ABS Relay Valves**
○ **Sensors**

vehicle are controlled by the four air pressure modulation valves. On a six-channel configuration system, each wheel of a three-axle vehicle is constantly monitored to regulate the applied brake pressure from the operator-controlled brake pedal. Tests have confirmed that wheel lockup on the drive axle is the primary cause of jackknifing in tractor/trailer applications; therefore, ABS control on the drive axle eliminates the tendency for vehicle instability during any brake application. Popular installations now offered for semitrailers are shown in Fig. 10-57, which indicates various available combinations of wheel speed sensors and relay valves. On tractor/trailer systems, the truck/tractor would have its own ECU, and the trailer would have its own ECU mounted on the trailer chassis. Another unique feature of the Rockwell/Wabco system on trailers is that in applications with a liftable axle, the ECU automatically detects axle lift and controls only the load-bearing axles. Both the tractor or trailer ECU can be accessed to provide a "blink code" or flashing light when unerasable codes are stored in ECU memory. An ABS diagnostic tester, which is similar in function to the DDR (diagnostic data reader) used on electronically controlled diesel fuel injection systems shown in Fig. 11-74, can be connected into the ABS ECU system to withdraw stored trouble codes and direct the technician quickly to the suspected cause of the problem. The digital diagnostic data reader display flashes coded information indicating the nature and position of the malfunction. In addition to the Rockwell/Wabco ABS system, technological advancements offer an optional ATC (automatic traction control) system to increase the ease of acceleration under poor traction conditions automatically.

BOSCH/WABCO ABS SYSTEM

The features of the Bosch/Wabco ABS system are very similar to those described for the Rockwell/Wabco system. The function and operation of the various wheel

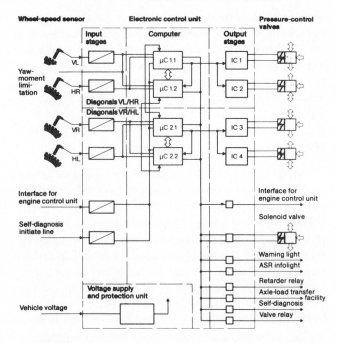

FIGURE 10-58 Schematic of the Bosch antilock brake system. (*Reprinted with permission, © 1989, Society of Automotive Engineers, Inc., Warrendale, PA.*)

speed sensors, air brake modulation valves, and the ECU can be considered to be similar for general discussion purposes. Figure 10-58 is a schematic of a typical wiring circuit for the Bosch antilock system used on heavy-duty commercial vehicles. Individual wheel speed sensor signals are input to the ECU, which analyzes and computes an output signal to the individual pressure control (modulation) valves. These output signals are commonly referred to as pulse-width-modulated signals, since during any brake application, the rotational speed of each wheel will cause the ECU electrical signal to the brake modulation valves to cycle the applied air or hydraulic brake pressure on and off at a rate of up to five times

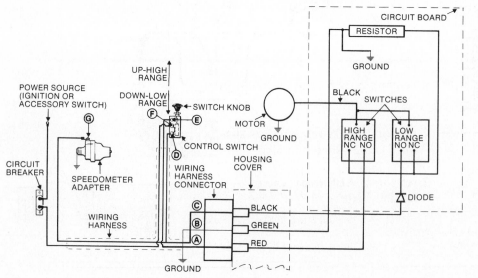

FIGURE 10-59 Electrical wiring schematic for a two-speed-axle shift system with late-style shift unit. (*Courtesy of Eaton Corporation, Axle & Brake Division, Kalamazoo, MI.*)

per second. Also shown in the schematic is the vehicle voltage supply to the ECU, as well as various other connection ports for such items as the self-diagnostic plug-in line. This is where the diagnostic data reader would be plugged in to withdraw stored trouble codes from ECU memory. Other output ports are shown on the right-hand side of the ECU diagram.

TWO-SPEED-AXLE ELECTRIC SHIFT SYSTEM

When a truck is equipped with a two-speed axle, the shift mechanism can be operated either by air pressure or by electrical means. In the electric shift system illustrated in Fig. 10–59, the control system consists of:

1. A control switch
2. A speedometer adapter
3. A shift unit
4. Interconnecting wire harness

Operation

The electric two-speed-axle system receives power from a circuit breaker–protected point on the vehicle, which is normally in the vicinity of the fuse/CB panel inside the truck cab. The engine ignition switch must be on for the axle shift system to operate. The actual control switch for the two-speed axle shift system is located on the transmission shift lever and simply consists of a button that can be moved back and forward, or it may employ a small lever that can be pulled up for high axle range and pushed down for the low axle range. Any movement of this shift button will complete the circuit to one field

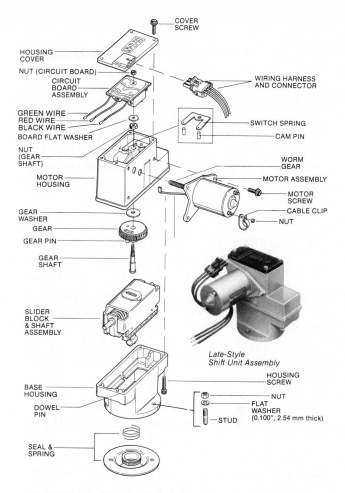

FIGURE 10–60 Exploded view of current-style-axle electric shift system. (*Courtesy of Eaton Corporation, Axle & Brake Division, Kalamazoo, MI.*)

FIGURE 10–61 Schematic diagram of the complete control circuit for a two-speed-axle electric shift system. (*Courtesy of GMC Truck Division, General Motors Corporation.*)

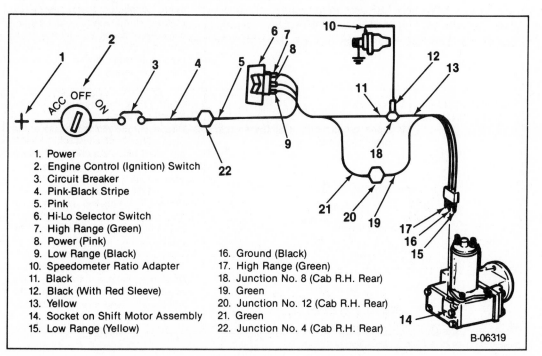

1. Power
2. Engine Control (Ignition) Switch
3. Circuit Breaker
4. Pink-Black Stripe
5. Pink
6. Hi-Lo Selector Switch
7. High Range (Green)
8. Power (Pink)
9. Low Range (Black)
10. Speedometer Ratio Adapter
11. Black
12. Black (With Red Sleeve)
13. Yellow
14. Socket on Shift Motor Assembly
15. Low Range (Yellow)
16. Ground (Black)
17. High Range (Green)
18. Junction No. 8 (Cab R.H. Rear)
19. Green
20. Junction No. 12 (Cab R.H. Rear)
21. Green
22. Junction No. 4 (Cab R.H. Rear)

B-06319

of the axle-mounted shift unit motor when in HIGH range, and to the opposite field when the selector is in the LOW range.

The actual axle shift unit mechanism is externally mounted on and bolted to the differential carrier assembly. The axle-mounted shift unit assembly consists of an internal reversible electric motor, automatic switch, drive screw, and torsion spring drive. It is mechanically connected to the axle assembly by a shift fork similar to that for an air shifted unit. An exploded view of the electric shift mechanism is shown in Fig. 10–60 (see page 435). With the gear lever selector switch in the HIGH axle range, current is fed to one field of the unit motor, and the internal armature and drive screw rotate in a clockwise direction, moving the nut downward on its screw thread to wind up the torsion spring. When the nut has traveled down its screw thread, a contact bumper on the nut breaks an electrical connection on the automatic switch and stops the motor. A small ball screw detent spring holds the nut at the end of its travel on the screw

TABLE 10–7 Diagnosis of an electric axle shift system

PROBLEM	POSSIBLE CAUSE	CORRECTION
Axle Will Not Shift Into LOW Range	1. Engine control switch is not in the "ON" position. 2. Short in the low range circuit. 3. Open in the "LO" range circuit. 4. Axle shift motor won't run.	1. Put the engine control switch in the "ON" position. 2. Find the short and repair. 3. Check for voltage at Junction No. 8 (18). If voltage is present, check for voltage on the shift motor connector, pin (15). If voltage is present, replace the shift motor assembly. If voltage is not present at Junction 8 (18), look for the open in the cab harness. If voltage was not present at the switch motor connector, pin (15), look for the open in the chassis harness. 4. Check axle shift motor connector for voltage on pin (15). If voltage is present, replace the motor assembly.
Axle Will Not Shift Into HIGH Range	1. Open in the circuit. 2. Short in the circuit.	1. Check for voltage at the axle shift motor connector-pin (17). If voltage is present, replace the shift motor assembly. If voltage is not present, look for an open in the harness. 2. Check the circuit breaker. If it is open, turn off the circuit. Disconnect the motor connector. Reset the circuit breaker. Turn the circuit on. If the circuit breaker opens, look for a short or ground in the harness. If the circuit breaker remains closed, replace the shift motor assembly.
Axle Won't Shift Into LOW Or HIGH Range.	1. No power. 2. Open ground circuit at the switch motor connector. 3. No power.	1. Check to see that the Engine Control Switch is in the "ON" position. 2. Disconnect the motor harness at the motor. Check with a test light between the HIGH range pin (17) or LO range pin (15) and a known good ground. This will verify that voltage is present on pin (17) or pin (15). Then check with the test light between pin (17) or pin (15) and pin (16). If the test light does not light, check for an open in the ground circuit. 3. Check for voltage at junction No. 4 (22). If there is no voltage check at the circuit breaker for voltage. If there is voltage at the junction, check for voltage at the switch. If voltage is present, replace the switch.

Source: GMC Truck Division, General Motors Corporation.

thread to prevent any possibility of the nut backing up due to normal vibration. With the torsion created in the spring by this action, the axle shift mechanism will be snapped into the high-speed differential ratio as soon as the truck driver relieves the load on the axle gears by momentarily releasing the throttle pedal. The actual torsion spring within the shift mechanism is assembled so that it is under a load of 50 to 90 lb (222 to 400 N), depending on the size of the axle. When the spring winding lever is wound down, this raises the force of the spring to 90 to 140 lb (400 to 619 N), again depending on the axle size. Once a shift has been completed by the high force of the spring through the axle shift mechanism, the spring will return to its lower preload force of 50 to 90 lb (222 to 400 N) to hold the axle in the HIGH gear range. Placing the selector into the LOW gear range allows the electric motor to reverse its direction of drive and the drive screw will rotate the nut in the opposite direction. The shift into the LOW range is achieved in the same manner as that described for the high range.

The purpose of the electric speedometer adapter is that when the axle control shift button is placed into the LOW range position, an electromagnet shifts the adapter mechanism into a position to compensate for the difference in gear reduction between the HIGH and LOW gear ranges. Shifting the axle into the HIGH range position releases current from the electromagnet, and a spring holds the adapter mechanism in the HIGH position. The voltage of the speedometer adapter can be either 12 or 24 V for trucks, with the voltage being stamped on the housing below the wire terminals.

Troubleshooting

To troubleshoot the two-speed-axle electric shift system, refer to Figs. 10–59 and 10–60, which show the system arrangement. An example of how this system might appear on a truck is shown in the diagram for Fig. 10–61 (see p. 461). Refer to this circuit diagram and the diagnosis charts shown in Table 10–7 to pinpoint a problem.

QUESTIONS

10-1. Technician A says that the horn button is usually connected in series with the horn relay. Technician B says that it would have to be connected in parallel. Which technician is correct? (see page 392)

10-2. Technician A says that when the horn relay coil is activated and battery current flows through it, the armature is pulled away from the core, resulting in a set of contact points opening. Technician B disagrees, saying that the armature is attracted to the iron core, resulting in a set of contact breaker points closing. Who is right? (see page 392)

10-3. The purpose of a horn relay assembly is to:
   a. Avoid a voltage drop through an otherwise long wire circuit
   b. Decrease the battery current to the actual horn
   c. Provide the horn button with overvoltage protection
   d. Provide a parallel hookup circuit
   (see page 392)

10-4. Technician A says that the horn relay can be adjusted to provide a different horn tone quality, as desired. Technician B says the horn relay is nonadjustable. Which technician do you think is correct? (see page 392)

10-5. Technician A says that the horn circuit is protected by either a fuse or a circuit breaker. Technician B says that the horn circuit does not require protection since the horn relay contains a thermoelectric bimetallic strip that will open to protect the circuit as required. Which technician is right? (see page 392)

10-6. Sound is obtained from an electric horn by:
   a. Passing alternating current through a resistor at a varying value
   b. Causing a steel armature to vibrate at high frequency
   c. Ensuring that a magnetic field around a thermoelectric bimetallic strip is made to collapse at regular intervals
   d. Operating an electric solenoid to allow a compressed

air valve to open and direct air through a venturi (see page 392)

10-7. Technician A says that the horn sound/tone can be altered by an adjustment screw that varies the current draw of the field coil. Technician B says that the sound is altered by setting the air gap between the horn button and the armature. Who is correct? (see page 393)

10-8. Technician A says that horns can be toned for a mixed or blended sound of E and G flat, which produces between 813 and 890 vibrations per second. Technician B says that an F and G flat would require a vibration frequency of between 313 and 390 per second. Who is correct? (see page 393)

10-9. Technician A says that when testing an electric horn, should the current on the test ammeter register zero, this indicates an open-circuit condition. Technician B says that it would indicate a grounded condition. Which technician is correct? (see page 394)

10-10. Electric windshield wipers are pulled back and forth across the windshield by:
   a. Offset linkage and a cam arrangement
   b. A reciprocating (back-and-forth) piston
   c. A solenoid that is energized and deenergized repeatedly
   d. An electric motor driving a hydraulic swash plate pump
   (see page 394)

10-11. Many permanent/magnet electric wiper motors are protected by:
   a. A fusible link
   b. A miniature blade fuse
   c. A glass tube fuse
   d. An automatic reset circuit breaker
   (see page 395)

10-12. Technician A says that wiper motors will operate only when the ignition key is in the ON position. Technician

B says that they will operate in either the ignition ON or ACC position. Who is right here? (see page 395)

10-13. For the electric wiper motor to operate, its circuit must be grounded through
  a. The common brush
  b. The wiper motor control switch
  c. The ignition key switch
  d. The high-speed brush
  (see page 397)

10-14. Technician A says that movement of the wiper control switch to the OFF position while the motor is running will result in the low-speed brush circuit being completed to ground at the switch, via the park switch contained in the wiper motor housing. Technician B says that this is correct but it is done through the high-speed brush circuit. Which technician is correct? (see page 397)

10-15. Technician A says that when an operator momentarily presses in on the windshield wiper control lever switch to initiate fluid spray onto the windshield, the washer pump circuit is completed to ground and the wipers move in the low-speed position. Technician B says that the wipers are already grounded; therefore, they are activated and move to the high-speed position. Who is correct? (see page 397)

10-16. When a windshield wiper washer system is activated by pressing in on the control switch/button, the following number of full squirts will occur at full system pressure:
  a. Five   c. Fifteen
  b. Ten   d. Twenty
  (see page 397)

10-17. Technician A says that windshield washer fluid flow into and out of the piston cylinder is generally controlled by two intake and one exhaust check valves. Technician B says that there are usually only one intake and two exhaust check valves. Who is correct? (see page 398)

10-18. Technician A says that in order to allow the wiper/arm blades always to stop at a PARK position above the windshield base, the actual parking switch contacts are connected across the control switch at the instrument panel so that they act as a set of "holding contacts" when the wiper switch is tuned off. Technician B says that the parking switch acts as a "pull-in" winding similar to a starter motor solenoid. Which technician is correct? (see page 399)

10-19. Technician A says that when a two-speed wiper motor will not shut off, it is probably due to a broken wire. Technician B says that he/she would check for a grounded wire to the wiper switch and therefore look for a short circuit. Who do you think is on the right track? (see Table 10-1 on pages 401–402)

10-20. Technician A says that if a two-speed wiper motor will operate only in the high-speed position, a broken wire may be the cause, and she would look for an open circuit. Technician B says that he would look for a grounded wire, short circuit, or faulty wiper switch. Who do you think is correct? (see Table 10-1A on page 401)

10-21. Technician A says that a Jacobs engine brake converts the diesel engine into an air compressor by opening the exhaust valves just BTDC on the compression stroke. Technician B says that the exhaust valves are opened earlier than normal during the exhaust stroke. Which

technician better understands the theory of operation? (see page 402)

10-22. Technician A says that both a throttle switch and a master control switch are required for operation of a Jacobs engine brake. Technician B says that in addition to both of these switches, a clutch pedal/linkage switch is required on a standard gear shift transmission. Which technician is correct? (see page 402)

10-23. Technician A says that the switches in question 10–22 are wired in parallel. Technician B says that they must be wired in series. Who is right? (see page 402)

10-24. Technician A says that the throttle pedal must be in the idle position in order to complete the electrical circuit through its microswitch on the Jake brake system. Technician B says that the throttle pedal must be in any position but idle. Who is correct? (see page 405)

10-25. Technician A says that in a Jake brake system, the exhaust valves are opened by the action of the master piston. Technician B says that they are opened by the slave piston. Which technician better understands the system? see page 402)

10-26. Technician A says that when the Jake brake is activated, no fuel is injected into the cylinders. Technician B says that idle fuel must be injected; otherwise, the engine would stall. Which technician is correct? (see page 402)

10-27. Technician A says that the degree of braking from the engine when using a Jake brake can be varied by use of a selector switch to allow all-cylinder braking, or only some cylinders braking. Technician B says that the same amount of braking is supplied at all times. Which technician knows the correct system operation? (see page 402)

10-28. When using a Jake brake, the accepted rule-of-thumb for best braking is to:
  a. Select the same gear range to go down a hill that you would use to climb the hill
  b. Select as low a gear as possible
  c. Select as high a gear as possible
  d. Answer b, plus liberal use of the service brakes
  (see page 406)

10-29. Technician A says that the use of the optional low-speed shutoff switch with the Jake brake is to deactivate the engine brake at engine speeds below approximately 600 rpm. Technician B says that the brake would be activated at engine speeds below approximately 900 rpm. Who do you think is right? (see page 406)

10-30. Technician A says that the master piston is usually activated by employing either an injector or exhaust valve pushrod depending on the specific make of engine. Technician B says that the master piston is activated by engine oil pressure. Which technician best understands Jake brake operation? (see page 405)

10-31. Technician A says that when a Jake brake is activated, a solenoid valve above the braking cylinder is activated in order to exhaust engine oil from the actuating circuit. Technician B says that when the solenoid valve is energized, it opens to allow engine oil under pressure to flow into the actuating circuit. Who is correct? (see page 406)

10-32. Technician A says that the slave piston is generally adjusted to ensure that the Jake brake will operate (exhaust valves open) at the correct time. Technician B says that it is the master piston that must be adjusted with a special feeler gauge for this same reason. Which technician is correct? (see page 408)

10-33. To determine if the Jake brake control switches are operating correctly, you would normally use
a. A VAT tester
b. An ohmmeter
c. A 12-V test light
d. A digital diagnostic data reader
(see page 407)

10-34. Technician A says that the Caterpillar Brakesaver is an engine compression brake similar to the Jake brake system. Technician B says that it uses engine oil on a rotor located behind the flywheel and housing to brake the engine crankshaft. Who knows the product better? (see page 409)

10-35. Technician A says that the electrical circuit for the Cat Brakesaver is similar in many respects to that for the Jake brake in that both a throttle and clutch switch are employed. *True* or *False* (see page 409)

10-36. Technician A says that either manual or automatic control of the Cat Brakesaver is possible. Technician B says that only automatic control, similar to a Jake brake, is possible. Who is right? (see page 409)

10-37. When checking the Cat Brakesaver electrical system for continuity through the switches, technician A says that you should use a self-powered test light. Technician B disagrees, saying that only a nonpowered test light should be used. Which technician do you think is right? (see page 409)

10-38. Technician A says that "continuity" should only exist in the electrical system of the Cat Brakesaver when the throttle and clutch pedals are in their released positions (pedals up). Technician B says that test lamp illumination should occur when both pedals are depressed (pushed down). Which technician is correct? (see page 409)

10-39. Most power-operated electric windows are constructed with a self-resetting circuit breaker built in for protection of the motor. *True* or *False* (see page 410)

10-40. Technician A says that in order to replace a power window motor, the window must be in the full-down position. Technician B says that the window should be raised to its full-up position by manual means, if necessary, in order to replace the motor. Who is right? (see page 410)

10-41. Technician A says that the electronic cruise control feature used on heavy-duty trucks is designed to operate with an engine zero-droop capability. Technician B says that normally a 150-rpm droop is employed for better response. Who is correct? (see page 410)

10-42. The function of a dash-mounted pyrometer gauge on a heavy-duty diesel truck is usually to monitor:
a. Engine oil pressure
b. Fuel pressure
c. Oil temperature
d. Exhaust temperature
(self-research)

10-43. Thermatic engine fans are generally activated by a signal from an engine oil temperature sensor. *True* or *False* (see page 413)

10-44. Technician A says that when troubleshooting a radio system, it does not matter whether the speakers are connected or disconnected. Technician B says that if the speakers are disconnected, or are unplugged while the radio is in operation, damage to the radio chassis can result. Which technician is correct? (see page 416)

10-45. Technician A says that CB radios are generally wired into the standard radio speaker system. Technician B says that CB radios always employ their own speaker system. Who is right? (see page 419)

10-46. Technician A says that the radio power harness is usually connected to a fusible link in the wiring harness. Technician B says that in heavy-duty trucks, it is more common to employ either a fuse or a circuit breaker. Who is right? (see page 418)

10-47. Technician A says that adjustment to the AM radio antenna trimmer is required to ensure that the antenna coil receiver is matched to the vehicle antenna, and is required any time that a radio receiver has been installed, or the antenna has been removed and replaced, or a service repair has been made. Technician B says that this adjustment is required only once, and that it is done on a new truck once it has been delivered to the end user. Who is right? (see page 420)

10-48. Technician A says that the level of cab heating is controlled by manipulation of a thermostat-type control valve. Technician B says that a water control valve controls the flow of coolant through the heater core, and that a blend door is used to vary the mixture of warm and cool air. Who is right? (see page 423)

10-49. Technician A says that the air-conditioning compressor pulley is always belt driven during engine operation; therefore, the A/C system is always on unless switched off by the operator. Technician B says that although it is true that the pulley is usually belt driven, no compressor operation results unless the electromagnetic pulley clutch is energized. Which technician is correct? (see page 424)

10-50. Technician A says that the function of the cycling pressure switch in the A/C system is to sense the refrigerant pressure on the low side of the circuit and to cycle the compressor on/off as necessary. Technician B says that it senses the refrigerant pressure on the high side of the circuit and shuts the compressor off. Who is right? (see page 425)

10-51. Technician A says that the A/C cycling pressure switch is generally located on a Schrader-type valve on the evaporator outlet tube. Technician B says that it is located on the evaporator inlet tube. Which technician knows A/C systems better? (see page 425)

10-52. During moderate ambient temperatures, technician A says that the A/C cycling pressure switch contacts would be closed. Technician B says that they would be open. Who is right? (see page 425)

10-53. Technician A says that if a low-charge condition exists in an A/C system, excessive cooling accompanied by a permanently engaged compressor will result. Technician B says that poor cooling accompanied by rapid compressor clutch cycling action will be noticeable at high ambient temperatures. Which technician is correct? (see page 425)

10-54. Technician A says that the purpose of a current surge diode in the A/C system wiring harness at the compressor is to prevent electrical surges from damaging the cycling pressure switch. Technician B says that it is to protect the electromagnetic compressor clutch from a voltage overload with rapid on/off cycling conditions. Which technician do you think is correct? (see page 425)

10-55. Technician A says that if an A/C compressor fails to operate/engage, the first thing to check for is voltage at the compressor coil. Technician B says that you would check for a blown fuse or circuit breaker. Are both technicians right here, or is only one correct? (see page 426)

10-56. Technician A says that if voltage is observed at the A/C compressor coil, yet it fails to operate, he would then check for a proper ground circuit. Technician B says that voltage at the compressor coil with no operation would confirm a burned-out coil. Who is correct? (see page 426)

10-57. Technician A says that if the A/C compressor clutch engages but the compressor fails to operate, you should replace it. Technician B says that she would check for a slipping clutch first and also check the air gap. Who do you think is correct? (see page 426)

10-58. Technician A says that if the A/C compressor operates but no cooling occurs, the condition can probably be traced to a lack of refrigerant in the system. Technician B says that a slipping drive belt could cause no cooling. Which technician do you believe? (see page 427)

10-59. Technician A says that when an A/C system cycling pressure switch malfunctions, it may remain in either the open or the closed position. Technician B says that they always fail in the closed position. Who is right? (see page 427)

10-60. Although the A/C system compressor cut-in and cut-out pressure ranges will vary between systems, generally this will occur at the following pressures:
   a. Cut out at 10 to 12 psi (69 to 83 kPa), cut in at 20 to 24 psi (138 to 165 kPa)
   b. Cut out at 15 to 17 psi (103 to 117 kPa), cut in at 32 to 35 psi (221 to 241 kPa)
   c. Cut out at 21 to 27 psi (145 to 186 kPa), cut in at 43 to 49 psi (296 to 338 kPa)
   d. Cut out at 35 to 40 psi (241 to 280 kPa), cut in at 79 to 82 psi (545 to 565 kPa)
   (see page 427)

10-61. Technician A says that some A/C pressure sensing systems are equipped with an electrical high-pressure limit switch that is used to disengage the compressor clutch should pressure reach a value of about 200 psi (1379 kPa). Technician B says that the high-pressure limit switch would disengage the compressor at a value closer to 400 psi (2760 kPa). Which technician is correct? (see page 427)

10-62. What is the purpose and function of the "trinary switch" used with some electronic temperature control systems whereby the A/C system is automatically activated? (see page 428)

10-63. Technician A says that a trinary switch such as that used on a Peterbilt model 379 conventional truck is usually mounted onto the moisture indicator on the Freon dryer. Technician B says it is normally located on the A/C compressor. Who is correct? (see page 429)

10-64. Technician A says that the three-axle anti-brake-skid system found on Freightliner trucks uses a six-channel system that relies on individual control for each wheel. Technician B says the ABS system used relies on axle-by-axle operation rather than individual wheel control. Who is correct? (see page 430)

10-65. Current ABS electronic wheel speed sensors constantly send an electrical signal to the ABS ECM so that it can determine the rotational speed of the wheel. The ECM or ECU then sends out corrective signals to the brake modulator valves to either increase or decrease the brake application pressures to avoid wheel lockup. *True* or *False* (see page 430)

10-66. Technician A says that should any part of an ABS system not operate correctly, the brakes will fail to operate. Technician B says that the ECM or ECU would place the system into a "fail-safe mode," allowing the brakes to operate normally but without ABS protection. Which technician is correct? (see page 431)

10-67. Failure of an ABS system generally results in a dash-mounted warning light illuminating or flashing to warn the operator of the condition. *True* or *False* (see page 431)

10-68. Technician A says that current Eaton two-speed-axle electric shift control systems consist of an internal reversible electric motor. Technician B says that a two-position toggle switch energizes a solenoid to direct air pressure to one side or the other of a piston assembly. Who is correct? (see page 435)

CHAPTER

11

Engine/Vehicle Sensors and Computers

OBJECTIVES

The purpose of this chapter is to introduce you to the concepts of operation of the on-board computer system as it applies to the control of both gasoline and diesel fuel injection systems. When you have completed this chapter, you will have gained new knowledge that will allow you to use these skills successfully when faced with performing a diagnostic procedural check of an ECM (electronic control module)-equipped truck. Specifically, you will acquire or review the skills needed to:

1. Describe the major reasons behind the adoption of on-board computer systems for heavy-duty trucks.
2. Identify and describe the function and operation of the various subsystems within the computer as well as the major advantages of using an on-board computer system.
3. Identify the various sensors and their function/purpose and how they interact with the vehicle computer system.
4. Identify the major servicing precautions required when working with and around computer systems.
5. Identify typical special diagnostic tools and in-

strumentation that can be used to isolate a problem with a computer-controlled system.
6. Describe the basic concept and function of operation of a DDEC (Detroit Diesel Electronic Controls), a PEEC (Programmable Electronic Engine Controls), manufactured by Caterpillar, and a Cummins CELECT system.
7. Systematically describe how to troubleshoot both a DDEC and a PEEC system with the aid of the various special manufacturers' tools available from both companies.

INTRODUCTION

The introduction of vehicle exhaust emissions mandated by the EPA (Environmental Protection Agency) in the United States, along with the legislated CAFE (Corporate Average Fuel Economy) standards for passenger cars throughout the 1980s, was the catalyst needed to direct the major automobile manufacturers to adopt electronic controls for their various engine and drive train re-

quirements. The experiences and successes gained with electronic controls for a number of vehicle systems, such as electronic fuel injection, ignition, instrumentation, heating/ventilation and air conditioning, cruise control, transmissions, and suspension systems created demands from the medium- and heavy-duty trucking industries for similar adoptions.

Figure 11–1 illustrates some of the areas on a heavy-

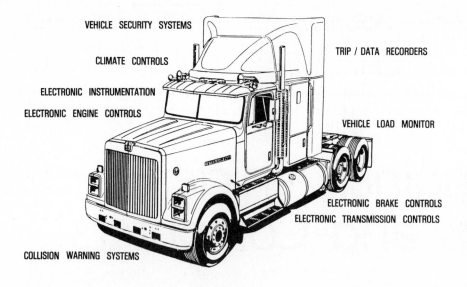

VEHICLE SECURITY SYSTEMS

CLIMATE CONTROLS

ELECTRONIC INSTRUMENTATION

ELECTRONIC ENGINE CONTROLS

TRIP / DATA RECORDERS

VEHICLE LOAD MONITOR

ELECTRONIC BRAKE CONTROLS

ELECTRONIC TRANSMISSION CONTROLS

COLLISION WARNING SYSTEMS

FIGURE 11-1 Future electronic applications to a heavy-duty class 8 truck/tractor. (*Reproduced with permission,* © *1990, Society of Automotive Engineers, Inc., Warrendale, PA.*)

duty truck that now employ electronic controls. Contained within this chapter is basic information on a number of systems now being used on heavy-duty trucks that owe their success to the adoption of electronics. The dominant electronic system since 1985 on diesel-powered heavy-duty trucks has been its adaption to the diesel fuel injection system. A typical layout for such a system is shown in Fig. 11-2. Two other areas that are now employing electronic controls are the fully automatic transmission and the semiautomatic gear shift transmission, both of which are illustrated in Figs. 11-3 and 11-4. The automatic transmission system can interface (exchange information) with the diesel fuel systems ECM (electronic control module). In the semiautomatic transmission, some models will require use of the clutch only during stopping of the vehicle and when starting from a stationary position. From there on the transmission is fully automatic, with gear selection and clutch engagement depending on the vehicle and engine load (grade). Other models of semiautomatic transmissions would simply require manual gear lever movement for gear selection, with the clutch operation being fully automatic. The use of

electronic engine and transmission control systems provides optimum fuel economy.

Other areas where electronics will be used include power steering systems, such as that shown in Fig. 11-5. These systems employ variable electronic control of the power steering pump flow rate, which will be inversely proportional to vehicle road speed. This system will provide a degree of power assist required for low-speed vehicle maneuverability, yet still provide much-improved steering feel at highway speeds. Future systems will look at using microprocessors to control electric motors and drives to power the steering system in place of the conventional hydraulic pumps and gears in use on today's trucks.

Adaptive air suspension systems, which are increasingly popular on many heavy-duty trucks, will provide a relatively low and variable spring rate. Working in conjunction with tandem-axle height control valves and variable-rate shock absorbers, we can anticipate semiactive or adaptive suspension systems. Figure 11-6 illustrates one concept that might be employed on an adaptive air suspension and shock absorber system for a heavy-duty truck sometime in the 1990s. Braking systems

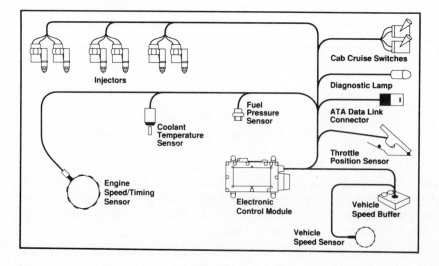

Injectors

Coolant Temperature Sensor

Fuel Pressure Sensor

Engine Speed/Timing Sensor

Electronic Control Module

Cab Cruise Switches

Diagnostic Lamp

ATA Data Link Connector

Throttle Position Sensor

Vehicle Speed Buffer

Vehicle Speed Sensor

FIGURE 11-2 Electronic control system used on an electronically controlled diesel fuel injection system. (*Reproduced with permission,* © *1990, Society of Automotive Engineers, Inc., Warrendale, PA.*)

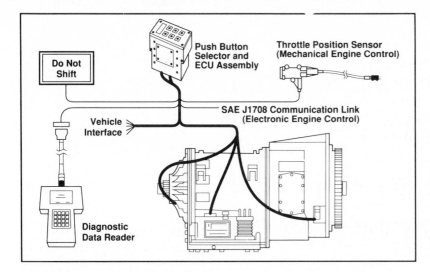

FIGURE 11–3 Concept of an electronic control system used with a fully automatic heavy-duty truck/bus transmission. Typical OEMs using this type of system include, Allison, Voith, and ZF. (*Reproduced with permission, © 1990, Society of Automotive Engineers, Inc., Warrendale, PA.*)

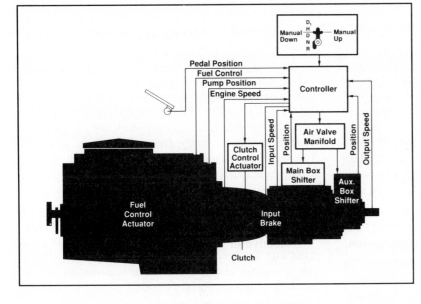

FIGURE 11–4 Electronic control system for a semiautomatic transmission. (*Reproduced with permission, © 1990, Society of Automotive Engineers, Inc., Warrendale, PA.*)

FIGURE 11–5 Concept for an electronically enhanced power steering system. (*Reproduced with permission, © 1990, Society of Automotive Engineers, Inc., Warrendale, PA.*)

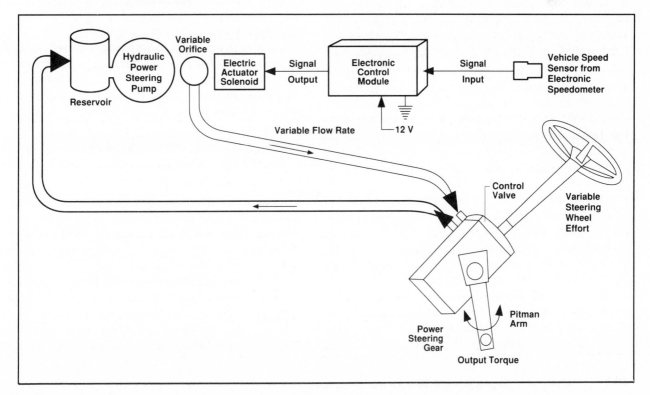

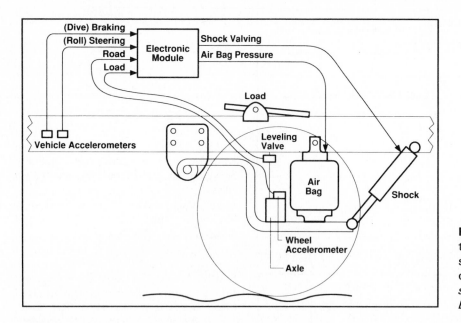

FIGURE 11–6 Electronically controlled adaptive air suspension and shock absorber system for a heavy-duty truck. (*Reproduced with permission, © 1990, Society of Automotive Engineers, Inc., Warrendale, PA.*)

are one other area in which electronic controls are again being used. Several major OEMs (original equipment manufacturers) are now offering ABS (anti-brake skid) as well as future traction and antislip systems. Traction control systems will operate electronically with the ABS system and the engine throttle to prevent drive wheel spinout. These are just some of the major advancements that are now in use or will probably appear in the near future on midrange and heavy-duty trucks.

COMPUTER CONSIDERATIONS

No attempt will be made in this chapter to describe the mechanical function, operation, service, maintenance, and troubleshooting of the gasoline or diesel computer-controlled fuel injection system since they fall into a separate category entirely from electricity and electronics, for which this book was intended. The intent of this chapter is to describe the basic design, function, and operation of the electronics components that together form the on-board ECM (electronic control module) or computer system: how they operate, control, and self-diagnose the various sensor inputs. Although computer controlled, the fuel injection and ignition systems on gasoline engines are best covered under the topic of automotive engine tuneup and diagnosis. A number of excellent books are available dealing with these subjects.

For a detailed description and excellent coverage of automotive computers, as well as an overview of gasoline fuel injection and ignition systems, cruise control, and other electronic accessories and components, refer to the book by Robert N. Brady, *Automotive Computers and Digital Instrumentation* (Englewood Cliffs, N.J.: Prentice-Hall, Inc., 1988). Similarly, the mechanical operation, tune-up, troubleshooting, and diagnosis of electronic diesel fuel injection controls are best covered in a book addressing this topic. For detailed information

on the function, operation, service, maintenance, repair, and troubleshooting of Detroit Diesel Corporation (DDEC), Caterpillar (PEEC), and Cummins and Mack electronic systems used in heavy-duty trucks, refer to the book by Robert N. Brady, *Heavy-Duty Truck Diesel Fuel Systems: Operation, Maintenance, and Tune-up* (Englewood Cliffs, N.J.: Prentice-Hall, Inc., 1991). Due to the importance of computer-controlled systems on medium- and heavy-duty trucks in such areas as engine fuel injection, engine and road speed governing, antiskid braking systems, HVAC automatic control, trip-recording devices, satellite navigation, trailer refrigeration automatic temperature control, cruise control, and automatic transmission electronic controls such as ATEC (Allison Transmission Electronic Controls) and Voith and ZF automatics in buses and trucks, the commercial transport mechanic/technician today must have a solid foundation in the basics of both electricity and electronics as preparation for an understanding of the major role that the on-board computer plays in successful operation of most systems on trucks. This chapter expands on the knowledge that you gained in Chapters 1, 2, and 4.

DIESEL ENGINE ELECTRONIC FUEL INJECTION CONTROLS

The adoption of electronics to light- and heavy-duty diesel engines is a fairly recent phenomenon. It has lagged behind the use of this technology in gasoline-powered passenger cars, which began with the 1980 model year. This was due in part to the fact that there are fewer heavy-duty trucks than passenger cars, which makes for a much higher per unit cost. In addition, the EPA (Environmental Protection Agency) regulations in the United States were not as severe for diesel engines as for passenger cars. However, the long-term plans are for diesel exhaust emission regulations to become more stringent; therefore, the move to electronic fuel injection controls was a necessity, just as it was with the gasoline engine.

The electronic fuel injection system controls employed on heavy-duty truck diesel engines has basically been an outgrowth of the systems that are in use in gasoline-powered passenger cars. Although the mechanic/technician employed in automotive, diesel, heavy-duty equipment maintenance, commercial transport, locomotive, and marine applications is not expected to repair ECMs (electronic control modules), it is imperative that you have a working knowledge of the general electronic control system so that you can effectively and efficiently connect test instruments to the system in order to access the stored trouble codes retained in computer memory. The writer assumes that the reader has a general understanding of the basic laws of electricity as well as a concept of the operation of solid-state devices prior to proceeding into a description of the operation of a typical ECM (electronic control module), which is the heart of both a gasoline and diesel fuel injection control system. See Figs. 11–7 and 11–8, which illustrate an ECM for a gasoline- and diesel-powered truck, respectively.

In 1984, approximately 60% of all passenger cars powered by gasoline engines were fitted with electronically controlled fuel injection systems of either TBI (throttle body injection) or MPFI (multiport fuel injection) design. By 1988, almost all cars built in North America were equipped with electronic gasoline fuel injection systems. Even those vehicles that continue to use feedback carburetors, employ a number of engine/vehicle sensors that continually feed a voltage signal back to an on-board computer for control of exhaust emissions. The success

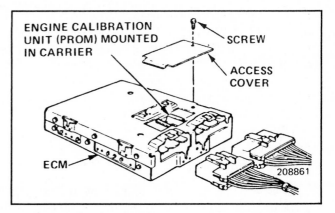

FIGURE 11–7 ECM (electronic control module) for a gasoline engine. (*Courtesy of GMC Truck Division, General Motors Corporation.*)

of gasoline fuel injection systems has carried over to diesel-powered vehicles and engines, where a number of major engine manufacturers are now employing electronic devices and sensors to control the diesel fuel injection system. Several of these electronically controlled diesel fuel injection systems are described in this book, with the Detroit Diesel Corporation DDEC (Detroit Diesel Electronic Controls) system, Caterpillar's 3406B engine PEEC (Programmable Electronic Engine Control) and 3176 electronic unit injector engine, and Cummins ECI (electronically controlled injection) systems being the three major ones on the market at this time.

All of these systems use an ECM that is similar in both function and operation. A detailed description of

FIGURE 11–8 ECM (electronic control module) for a diesel engine. (*Courtesy of Detroit Diesel Corporation.*)

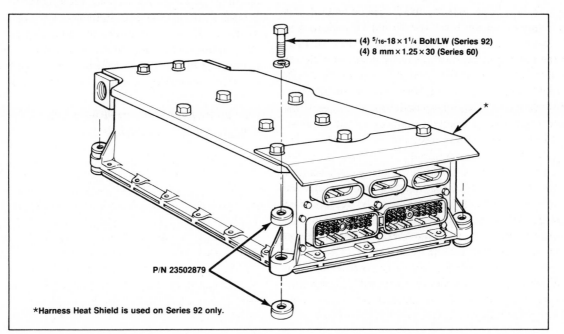

how an ECM (electronic control module) and its system operate is provided in this chapter. Most readers who are involved with gasoline and diesel engine maintenance will readily appreciate that both types of engines operate in a similar fashion other than for the fact that there is no electrical ignition system on a diesel engine, and that the gasoline and diesel injection systems do have specific differences regarding the operating pressures and fuel distribution. However, the function and operation of the ECM are basically the same for both engines, and that is to control the timing and injection of the fuel to the combustion chamber in order to meet the stringent U.S. EPA exhaust emissions and improve the overall fuel economy and performance of the engine/vehicle.

ENGINE CONTROL COMPUTERS

The following information will highlight and describe the basic arrangement, general service access procedures, and safety requirements when working around and with on-board computers on both gasoline- and diesel-powered trucks. Engine and vehicle control on-board computers are more commonly referred to as an ECM (electronic control module), an ECU (electronic control unit), or an EEC (electronic engine control) module. These terms vary between vehicle manufacturers, but the purpose of all of them is the same—to monitor engine and vehicle operating conditions continually through the use of a series of sensors located on the engine and transmission. Each sensor is fed a source voltage, usually in the 5-V dc range. Once the engine is started, each sensor monitors the system for which it was designed; for example, oil pressure, oil temperature, coolant level, coolant temperature, turbocharger boost pressure, air temperature, fuel pressure, throttle pedal position, and vehicle road speed are just some of the major systems with their own individual sensors.

The technology for truck system computers grew out of the highly successful passenger car market, where they appeared in the late 1970s on some European upscale fuel-injected model cars. This was followed in North America in the 1980 model year, with the first computers being used with FBC (feedback carburetor controls). Subsequently, computer technology was expanded and very few passenger cars manufactured today employ mechanical carburetors. The recent adoption (1989–1990) of fuel injection for the GMC medium-duty 6-L and 7-L gasoline-powered truck lineup is further testimony to the fact that the on-board computer is gaining increased worldwide use. Carburetors have largely been displaced by either TBI (throttle body injection), which employs either one or two fuel injectors located in a throttle body in place of the long used and conventional carburetor. On MPFI (multiport fuel injected) engines, an individual gasoline fuel injector is located in the intake manifold and strategically located very close to the intake valve port-

ing. In this way, fuel can be sprayed directly into the opening intake valve for better performance and fuel economy.

On light-duty pickup trucks and the larger medium-duty gasoline-powered trucks such as those offered by the GMC Truck Division of General Motors Corporation, the adoption of fuel injection not only improves engine performance, but also reduces overall maintenance. In the heavy-duty truck end, Detroit Diesel Corporation was the first major diesel engine manufacturer to adopt electronic engine controls to their line of two-stroke-cycle 92 series engines in September 1985, followed shortly thereafter by the series 60 four-stroke-cycle engine. The DDC system is known as DDEC (DD Electronic Controls), which was updated by new computer technology in September 1987 to what is known as the DDEC II system, which has expanded capabilities and diagnostics.

Also in 1987, Caterpillar released their PEEC (Programmable Electronic Engine Controls) on their 3406B model engine, followed in 1989 by its adoption to their 3176 engine models. Both the DDC and Cat 3176 engines employ electronic unit injectors, while the 3406B Cat uses a conventional multiple-plunger in-line scroll-type fuel injection pump. Cummins initially offered a system known as PACE, which is basically an electronic cruise control feature for their line of heavy-duty truck diesel engines. They also have a Compuchek engine diagnostic option to monitor and assist the mechanic/technician in diagnosing engine performance complaints. Cummins now uses an ECI (electronically controlled injector) CELECT system that employs computer control and self-diagnostics features similar to those of both DDC and Caterpillar. Mack also employs computer-controlled fuel injection on their in-line six-cylinder E7 diesel engine.

The ECMs (electronic control modules) in use on gasoline- and diesel-powered trucks are very similar in design, construction, and function. They differ only in the fact that each is designed to control specific engine, transmission, and vehicle control functions unique to the gasoline or diesel engine. However, many of these functions are so similar that the ECM can be constructed as a "base unit" with specific performance characteristics for a given make and type of truck being hardwired into a replaceable PROM (programmable read-only memory) solid-state integrated circuit chip or an EEPROM (electrically erasable programmable read-only memory) on later models. Consider, for example, that major truck OEMs (original equipment manufacturers) such as General Motors, Ford, Freightliner, Kenworth, Peterbilt, Volvo/GMC, and Western Star, with their different truck models and available engines, transmissions, axle ratios, and tire sizes, would not want to use a different ECM for each vehicle. Therefore, what they actually do is use one model of ECM in many different trucks. Specific operational parameters for a given vehicle are contained in the PROM unit, which is located inside the ECM, and it contains information on the vehicle weight, engine, transmission, axle ratio, and so on. This means that one part number can be used for the ECM across many truck lines. It is very important that the correct PROM chip be used in an ECM that has been designed with the operating conditions for that specific vehicle.

The same considerations hold true for ECMs used in both gasoline- and diesel-powered trucks. Depending on the type and make of vehicle in which the ECM is installed, the physical location of the ECM will vary. It may be found under the instrument panel, a side kick panel in the cab, or under a passenger seat. The ECM illustrated in Fig. 11–8, which is used on heavy-duty diesel engines, is required to handle a much larger operating current than is the one used on gasoline engines. This current increase is due to the fact that the electronic unit injector on the diesel engine is physically larger and therefore requires a stronger coil than that for a smaller gasoline injector. For this reason, the ECM is usually physically larger on the diesel unit. In addition, since a much higher current is required on the diesel ECM, more heat is generated within the ECM housing. To keep the ECM solid-state circuitry cool, some diesel engine ECMs often route diesel fuel from the fuel transfer pump through the ECM housing cold plate on a continuous basis. In addition, sometimes a heat shield is used around the diesel ECM to deflect and carry away any heat buildup.

Generally, the ECM is packaged in a die-cast aluminum housing with sealed connectors (Weather-Pack type) to prevent the possible entrance of moisture, water, or dirt into the ECM housing. The ECM is usually mounted on a bracket on the side of the engine block, as shown in Fig. 11-9. The ECM receives battery power at 12 V, then usually supplies 5 V to the various engine/vehicle sensors for operation, although some vehicles require 12 V from the ECM to operate certain switches. The reduction in battery voltage is achieved through the use of resistances inside the ECM which are so high in value that a normal 12-V test light will not illuminate when connected into the circuit. In many cases an analog voltmeter (swinging needle type) will not provide an accurate reading because its resistance is too low. Therefore, in most cases when checking an ECM for a voltage value or a resistance value, you must use a digital voltmeter with a 10-MΩ input impedance to assure an accurate voltage or resistance reading. Such a voltmeter can be seen in Fig. 4-8. All ECMs receive input voltages from the various sensors which continually monitor the engine and vehicle operating parameters. The ECM then controls the various systems to suit the operating conditions. In addition, the ECM is designed to recognize engine/vehicle operating problems and take corrective action to prevent engine damage should a system fall outside the predesigned value limits. Such a condition might involve high oil temperature, low oil pressure, coolant

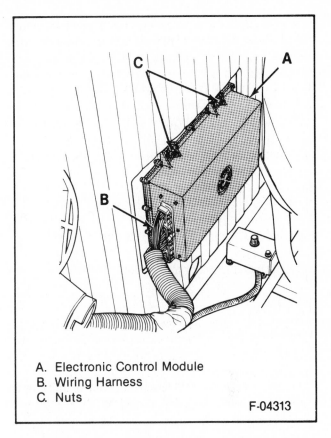

A. Electronic Control Module
B. Wiring Harness
C. Nuts

F-04313

FIGURE 11–9 Typical Electronic Control Module mounting on a heavy-duty truck diesel engine. (*Courtesy of Detroit Diesel Corporation.*)

overheating, and so on. In cases where the condition is not considered serious enough to cause engine shutdown, the ECM will illuminate a dash-mounted warning lamp along with an audible buzzer on heavy-duty truck applications. When the "service engine soon" or CEL (check engine light) is illuminated, the engine power and speed are generally reduced to provide "limp home" capability. In serious cases, the ECM will illuminate a SEL (stop engine light), which normally gives the truck operator only 30 seconds in which to pull the vehicle over to the side of the road, park it, and stop the engine. An optional SEL override button can be used to extend this shutdown time slightly to ensure that the vehicle can be brought to a safe stop.

When a problem occurs in a sensor or monitored engine/vehicle system, the ECM will log into its memory a stored trouble code that can be withdrawn at a later date by the service technician. This code can be cross-referenced in the engine/truck service manual, where a systematic test/check procedure will lead you to the system and the possible problem area or item. Components sensed and controlled by the ECM will vary between different makes of trucks and the type of engine used—gasoline versus diesel—as well as options such as cruise control, road speed governing, and automatic transmission electronic controls that interface with the ECM.

BASIC HISTORY AND TERMINOLOGY OF MINICOMPUTERS

The adoption of "on-board" minicomputers not only to passenger cars (1980) but also to heavy-duty diesel-powered highway trucks since the 1985 model year in North America came about as a direct result of the necessity to comply with the U.S. EPA (Environmental Protection Agency) exhaust-emissions legislation and to meet the similarly legislated EPA CAFE (Corporate Average Fuel Economy) standards, which have become more stringent over the years. Other countries have enacted similar legislation, with both the EEC (European Economic Community) and the Australian government following a similar stance against exhaust emissions and in favor of improved fuel economy in passenger cars, heavy-duty trucks, and buses.

The only way that these standards could have been met was through the application of electronics as a substitute for mechanical components. The carburetor, as we have known it, is to all intents and purposes a part of history, since both throttle body injection (TBI) and multiport fuel injection (MPFI) systems have shown that they are not only technically superior to the carburetor but also absolutely necessary if the ever-stringent exhaust emissions are to be met. The brains behind the success of these fuel injection systems is the solid-state minicomputer or "on-board" black box.

Various vehicle manufacturers refer to this on-board computer as:

1. An ECU: electronic control unit.
2. An ECM: electronic control module.
3. A CPU: central processing unit, although the CPU is actually an operational part of the on-board computer. When the CPU is combined into an integrated circuit, it is commonly referred to as a microprocessor, because it is in this device that all of the arithmetic and logical decisions are carried out. The CPU is, in effect, the part of the computer that performs the necessary calculations.

Regardless of the terminology used by various manufacturers, the major purpose of this electronic control unit is to monitor all of the various engine and vehicle parameters through a number of sensor systems, to control the various systems, such as the ignition and fuel control systems (gasoline and diesel), and to ensure that the exhaust emission and fuel economy standards are maintained. In addition, the on-board computer system ensures that vehicle driveability and satisfactory performance are maintained under all operating conditions.

The automotive computer is, of course, a direct result of development of computer applications that have been widely adapted for use in business and industry. There have been several main events that have led to the cur-

rent technology now in use in our everyday dealings with on-board vehicle minicomputers, and these chief points are:

1. The development of first-generation computers, which made use of a large number of vacuum tubes to operate. This development occurred during the years 1951–1958.
2. The second-generation units, which took advantage of the discovery of solid-state devices, such as the transistor, not only to downsize the computer but also to increase its speed of operation. This phase took place between 1959 and 1964.
3. The third-generation models, which adopted the technology of integrated circuit design. This happened in the years of 1965 to 1970.
4. The fourth-generation systems were downsized even more by advancements in technology, such as miniaturized integrated circuits. This application began in 1971.
5. The adoption of multiple miniaturized circuits and a further reduction of system size as well as an improvement in the materials used to produce silicon wafer chips in the late 1970s and throughout the 1980s.
6. The integration of both gasoline fuel injection and ignition systems into a computer-controlled arrangement by Robert Bosch in the early 1980s. This concept was subsequently adopted by every major passenger car manufacturer worldwide.
7. The introduction of distributorless ignition systems into passenger cars in the mid-1980s by the Buick Motor Car Division of GMC, which was followed shortly thereafter by other GMC car divisions and other major passenger car manufacturers.
8. The adoption of both an ECM to control the engine/transmission operation, plus a BCM (body computer module) in the mid/late-1980s to handle and control the vehicle HVAC (heating/ventilation/air conditioning), ride height, suspension harshness, and various other electronic comfort features to passenger cars.
9. The release in 1985 of the first fully computer-controlled diesel unit injector and governor system by Detroit Diesel Corporation for use on heavy-duty truck/bus applications. Much of the technology for these on-board computers was a direct result of the research and development done by General Motors passenger car divisions.
10. The release by Diesel Kiki and Robert Bosch of in-line multiple-plunger diesel fuel injection pumps (automotive and truck) in the mid-1980s.
11. The release in 1988 by Caterpillar of an electronic diesel fuel injection and governing system for their line of heavy-duty truck diesel engines.
12. Cummins' adoption of the PT PACER cruise control and CELECT/ECI (electronically controlled injection), along with an optional Compucheck diagnostic system for their line of heavy-duty truck diesel engines.
13. Mack's adoption of VMAC electronic diesel fuel injection controls for their model E7 engine in 1990.

14. The integration of on-board truck recording computer devices in the mid-1980s to replace the long-used electromechanical tachographs to record vehicle operating hours, fuel economy, and driver operating habits.

15. The implementation of satellite navigation tracking devices to the trucking industry in the late 1980s to allow home base tracking and message transfer between vehicles throughout the country.

The next generation of computers, due in the 1990s, may be capable of artificial intelligence (AI). These machines hopefully will be able to deduce, infer, and learn on their own.

ANALOG- VERSUS DIGITAL-TYPE COMPUTERS

Integrated circuits are classified as being of either analog or digital type. The analog-type IC is one that handles or processes a wave-like analog electrical signal, such as that produced by the human voice, and is also similar to that shown on an ignition oscilloscope. An analog signal changes continuously and smoothly with time as shown in Fig. 11–10. Its output signal is proportionate to its input signal.

Digital signals, on the other hand, show a more rectangular wavelength, as shown in Fig. 11–11. This is because these signals change intermittently with time, which means that, simply put, they are either on or off. This, of course, is quite different from the analog operating mode. The general characteristic of operation of the digital circuit can best be explained by considering that when the input voltage signal rises to a predetermined level, the output signal is then triggered into ac-

FIGURE 11–12 Digital voltage signal in an on/off mode; 5-V reference or trigger value.

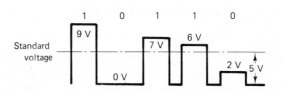

FIGURE 11–13 Digital wave signal when the voltage values are either above or below the standard voltage reference.

tion. For example, assume that a sensor is feeding a varying 5-V maximum reference signal to a source such as a diode. In this condition, the output signal remains at zero until the actual input signal has climbed to its maximum of 5 V.

This is why digital signals are classified as being either on or off. ON means that a signal is being sent, and OFF, that a signal is not being sent. For convenience sake, in electronics terminology, when a voltage signal is being sent (ON), the numeral 1 is used. When no voltage signal is being sent (OFF), it is indicated by the numeral 0. These numerals are used so that the computer can distinguish between an ON and an OFF voltage signal.

Figures 11–12 and 11–13 show how this numerical system operates. Since most sensors in use today in automotive applications are designed to operate on a 5-V reference signal, anything above this level is considered as being in an ON or numeral 1 condition, while any voltage below this value is considered as an OFF or 0 numeral, since the voltage signal is too low to trigger a diode response. Digital systems consist of many numbers of identical "logic gates" and "flip-flops," to perform the necessary computations.

There are few home appliances, entertainment devices, children's toys, cars, trucks, and industrial machines that do not use solid-state devices to perform one or more functions. When these solid-state devices are combined to operate in a system, they are generally referred to as *integrated circuits*, with each one doing a specific job in the overall successful performance of the designed unit, whether it be a microwave oven, a car or home stereo system, a wristwatch, an on-board vehicle computer, or a child's fancy toy.

Many later model cars and trucks now on the market are leaving the factory with digital-type instrument clusters rather than the long-used and conventional analog system that was used for decades. Many of the electronic circuits in vehicles now interact with one another and provide feedback to engine control functions

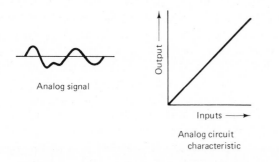

FIGURE 11–10 Analog-wave signal shape.

FIGURE 11–11 Digital-wave signal shape.

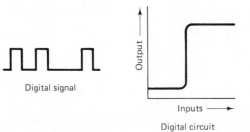

or to other systems based on signals received from other operating sensors.

There are two basic types of computers in use today, with the choice being dependent on the type of job that has to be done. One of these is the analog computer, and the other, the digital computer. Analog computers are designed to accept continually varying signals, with the computer consisting of signal adders, multipliers, and other circuitry designed specifically for analog interpretation. The digital computer, on the other hand, is designed for use with digital circuitry, comprised of logic gates, binary adders, multipliers, data latches, memory circuits, and so on. The major advantage of the digital system over the analog type is that it overcomes the inherent problems of temperature drift and noise disturbance that affect the analog systems.

An analog computer is designed to measure quantities, such as the amount of fuel pumped into your truck fuel tank. Another example is the VSS (vehicle speed sensor), which employs an analog signal to measure drive shaft rotation. This signal is then converted into a speedometer reading. This signal is used on heavy-duty trucks for purposes of road speed governing and cruise control.

A digital computer, on the other hand, is designed to count rather than measure. On a gasoline-powered fuel injected truck, for example, various counters are used by the digital system functioning in the computer. The exhaust gas oxygen sensor feeds information to the CPU many times a second to inform the computer how often the oxygen content in the engine exhaust system changes. In other words, the sensor counts the number of times that this air/fuel ratio changes in a given time period. This is known as a discrete phenomenon, since this action is specific to the exhaust oxygen sensor circuit. Other sensors and systems that are monitored also feed information to the on-board computer system on a continuous basis.

The main problem with analog circuits and analog computers, however, is that their performance changes with an increase or decrease in temperature, supply voltage, signal levels, and noise levels. These problems can be eliminated when a digital circuit is used.

Digital computers used in automotive and truck applications are fed analog signals from a variety of engine and vehicle sensors, and these signals are then sent through a signal processor, commonly known as an analog-to-digital converter (ADC) so that the CPU (central processing unit) within the ECM can process this information. The computer processes information very quickly, with some computers capable of performing this operation in milliseconds (thousandths of a second), while some can do it in microseconds (millionths of a second). In the latest industrial computers used in business and industry, a cycle of informational computation can be done in a nanosecond, which is a billionth of a second. As an example, there is now a computer that can compute a cycle of in-

formation in 12.5 nanoseconds. Simply put, this means that it can complete 80 million cycles every second.

COMPUTER LAYOUT AND ARRANGEMENT

The on-board computer used today in passenger cars and trucks is normally classified as a minicomputer because of its relatively small physical size. It does not perform as many and as varied a number of calculations as that of the large mainframe computer that you might find in a large business organization or factory.

An example of a minicomputer in its basic arrangement is that of a wristwatch with a built-in calculator. Figure 11–14 compares the well-known mechanical type of wristwatch with two electronic models. In the description included with the figure, note the "function" and basic details of the three timepieces.

Unlike a mainframe computer, which would contain literally thousands of microchips, the digital wristwatch

FIGURE 11–14 Comparison of mechanical and solid-state digital readout watches.

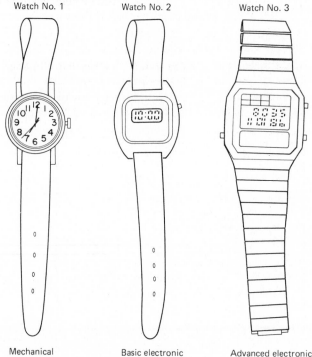

Watch No. 1   Watch No. 2   Watch No. 3

Mechanical   Basic electronic   Advanced electronic

Mechanical watch

Function is to tell time only. To operate, it employs all mechanical components that include a small and large hand, a gearing mechanism, an internal spring, and a small winding knob.

Solid-state electronic watch

Can function not only to tell time and date, but also the actual day of the week; acts as a wakeup alarm or reminder buzzer/beep, and a stop watch; used to enter coded messages; and also functions as a calculator. Small mercury batteries are required to power the IC's, which display their information in LCD (Liquid Crystal Display) mode.

shown in Fig. 11–14 would contain all of the necessary solid-state componentry in a few tiny silicon chips, depending on the various options required in the watch other than simply to tell time.

Minicomputers now in use in passenger cars and heavy-duty trucks would still have only a small number of chips containing the necessary circuits, and not the hundreds or thousands necessary for a mainframe computer to operate successfully.

Even though the minicomputer is smaller than its larger mainframe computer, it is designed to perform substantially the same tasks of receiving, computing, and sending out corrective controlling voltage signals that effectively maintain successful operation of all of the sensed "on-vehicle options," such as the ignition system, the gasoline or diesel fuel injection system, ride quality, automatic interior temperature control, antiskid monitoring, and trip computing. Typical engine operating conditions sensed and fed into the computer or electronic control module and the resultant systems controlled by this action are illustrated in Fig. 11–15 for a gasoline engine, while Fig. 11–16 shows those for a heavy-duty diesel truck. Prior to studying the various data-processing actions within the computer, it would be helpful for you to refer to Fig. 11–16, which illustrates the three major operating sections of an on-board minicomputer. These three sections are as follows:

1. The *input section*, which consists of the various sensors used to constantly monitor numerous functions on the engine or vehicle.

2. The *control section*, which incorporates the actual minicomputer and its componentry. Input signals are logically converted within the computer by a series of logic gates into digital signals from analog signals. These digital signals are stored as strings of Os (OFF) and 1s (ON). The computer then compares these sensor signals to preprogrammed levels, makes the necessary decisions of acceptance, and a corrected signal is then sent out of the computer to control each on-board electronic system.

3. The *output section*, which is generally made up of "actuators" such as the fuel injectors on a gasoline or diesel engine. These components receive a pulsed-voltage signal, the duration of which determines how much fuel will be delivered to the individual cylinders. In this case the electrical signal is converted into mechanical energy through a small solenoid that acts to open or close the fuel injector valve. The longer the pulse-width signal, the longer the fuel injection duration and therefore the speed

FIGURE 11–15 ECM (electronic control module) operating conditions sensed and systems controlled. (*Courtesy of GMC Truck Division, General Motors Corporation.*)

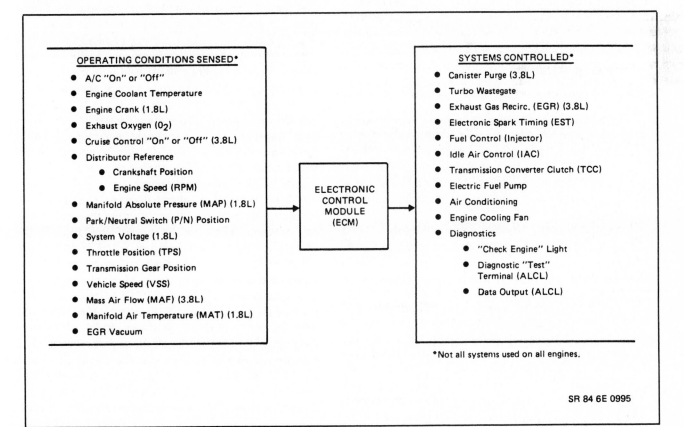

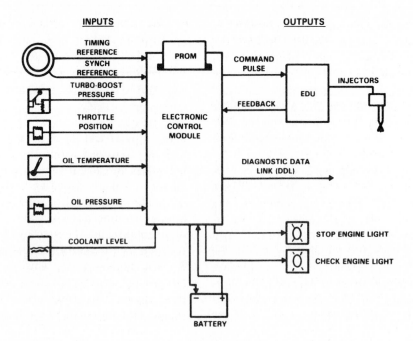

FIGURE 11–16 Basic operational schematic of the DDEC system. The Electronic Control Module (ECM) is a microprocessor. It is the control center of the DDEC system. (*Courtesy of Detroit Diesel Corporation.*)

and horsepower developed by the engine for a given throttle position. A shorter pulse-width signal will result in less fuel delivery and therefore a lower engine speed and horsepower setting. The ignition or fuel injection system would also have the timing advanced or retarded as necessary, which would be based on the decision made by the computer from the sensor-input data that it has received.

COMPUTER MEMORY

Three types of *memory* are used in a microcomputer:

1. ROM (read-only memory) allows the computer to read a predetermined pattern of zeros and ones (binary notation). This predetermined information is permanently stored in ROM at the time of manufacture. A ROM is similar to a dictionary in that a certain address that is accessed in ROM will result in a predetermined output of information.

The ROM is hardwired or soldered into the printed circuit boards at the time of manufacture and therefore cannot be changed. This programmed information can be read only by the ECM. Therefore, the ROM contains the overall fuel injection system (gasoline/diesel) control algorithms. Since the ROM is hardwired into the system at the time of manufacture, the ROM will be retained if the battery voltage is disconnected. Therefore, the ROM unit is said to be *nonvolatile*. Some systems may employ an EEROM (electrical erasable read-only memory), in which the memory can be erased and new information programmed into the device.

2. The PROM system (programmable read-only memory) also consists of stored programs and data that

have been hardwired. This means that a circuit board has been constructed and arranged so that specific information is retained and generally cannot be erased or changed even when the battery is disconnected.

In some systems the PROM is an electronic memory that may be permanent (nonvolatile) or semipermanent (erasable electronically or with ultraviolet light) and therefore can be programmed one or more times. This type of PROM is generally referred to as EEPROM (electrically erasable programmable read-only memory) and is commonly used in heavy-duty truck applications.

PROM chips are designed for use in particular vehicles and include information on engine calibration data, transmission, vehicle weight, and rear-axle ratio. Therefore, the PROM should never be intermixed between computers in different vehicles, even though they may be of the same manufacture.

Some PROM ICs (integrated circuits) can be removed if faulty and replaced with a new unit of the same design and program. There will be more on this topic in the troubleshooting and service section. The PROM is a nonvolatile memory (does not need battery power to be retained) that is read only by the ECM. Some vehicles have been manufactured using two PROMs. However, most use only one. The ECM is able to tell what specific PROM unit has been installed in the system, and it will indicate the actual PROM either by model or part number when the mechanic/technician accesses the diagnostic system of the ECM with a diagnostic data reader during a troubleshooting sequence. However, if the wrong PROM is installed in an ECM, the PROM may become unreadable to the ECM. Should this ever happen, the ECM is programmed to run the engine on a *backup fuel mode* that is retained in ROM. When this occurs, however, a trouble code will be set in memory, and the *Check Engine, Service Engine Soon,* or *Service Engine Now* light will illuminate on the vehicle instrument panel to warn the driver of a problem.

3. RAM or random access memory comprises data that can be erased or changed after they have been read. RAM is sometimes called primary memory. The stored information in RAM is available immediately when addressed, regardless of the previous memory address location. Since the memory words can be selected in any other, there is equal access time to all. This unit is the decision-making center for the central processing unit (CPU). It, in effect, becomes the microprocessor's *scratch pad*, and the processor can write new updated operational information into or read from this memory as needed. This memory is *volatile*, meaning that it requires a constant battery voltage in order to be retained. Therefore, a loss of voltage quite simply means a loss of stored memory in the system.

The volatile memory in RAM contains the following information:

a. Block learn and fuel integrator values (pulse counts).

b. Malfunction codes—pending flags.

c. Ignition counter—counts the number of on/off cycles of the ignition switch since a trouble code was stored, usually 50 cycles, after which time the system will reset to 0 and the trouble code will be erased from memory.

d. FDP (fuel data panel) information if used and OAT (outside air temperature).

e. Check sums.

Unlike the PROM unit, however, the information stored in the RAM unit can be lost if the battery power is disconnected from the system. The major function of the RAM unit is simply to store informational data that is to be erased or changed. Data delivered by the sensors are stored in the RAM unit until summoned by the microprocessor or superseded by more recent input data. Informational data are erased when the ignition system is switched off. Therefore, it must be updated continuously during engine operation. Intermediate storage of calculated values for subsequent processing also occurs in this unit.

This backup mode is a rough gasoline fuel-spark calibration system built into ROM. Therefore, the ECM will operate in backup when the PROM is not readable for any reason. Diesel trucks have a similar limp-home feature.

When the vehicle is in the backup mode, it is characterized by the following symptoms:

- Poor driveability and performance.
- Erratic or no ECM serial data.
- *Check Engine, Service Engine Soon, or Service Engine Now* warning light is on.

- ISC (idle speed control) motor is inoperative on gasoline engines.
- ECM diagnostics may not be accessible.
- FDP (fuel data panel) and OAT (outside air temperature) read zero or become blank.

These three types of memory should not be confused with the various registers also used within the computer. These registers store information data temporarily for immediate use only. For this reason the memory circuit is often referred to as *main memory* to distinguish it from the other computer registers or accumulators. Informational data that are to be read from or written into a specific memory location or filing drawer cabinet are identified via an address bus. Since large amounts of data are constantly being entered (written) into and removed (read) from computer memory, all of the various locations for information storage must be identified by their own address. Therefore, each location has a number assigned to it in digital form, within the computer.

INPUT/OUTPUT INTERFACE SYSTEM

The ECM contains power supplies, input/output (I/O) devices, memory, and the processing unit, with the power supplies regulating the battery's 12-V input to 5 V for the various sensors, and with certain switches, and so on, being regulated to 8 V. The I/O devices include analog-to-digital converters, signal buffers, counters, and special drivers to handle larger loads, such as the fuel injectors and solenoids.

Sensors used in automobiles and trucks because of their design relay an analog type of voltage signal to the computer. For the computer to make sense out of these input analog signals, they must be converted into digital signals before being sent to the CPU (central processing unit). The actual process for converting analog signals into digital signals is performed within the computer by an analog-to-digital converter. The input/output (I/O) interface is the device that allows data to be transferred between input and output devices, CPU, and memory. Output voltage signals are amplified in order to operate electrical loads, such as the fuel injector solenoids. Figure 11–17 illustrates in simplified form the sequence of events between an input/output interface.

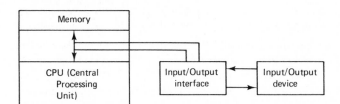

FIGURE 11–17 Computer input/output interface allows sensor input data to be understood by the CPU and storable by memory. In addition, the I/O interface reconverts output data into a language that the output device can understand and comprehend.

This schematic and the operational principles described here apply to microcomputers and microprocessors in general. Differences lie mainly in the memory capacities of the ICs used, the necessary programs and the data quantities to be processed.

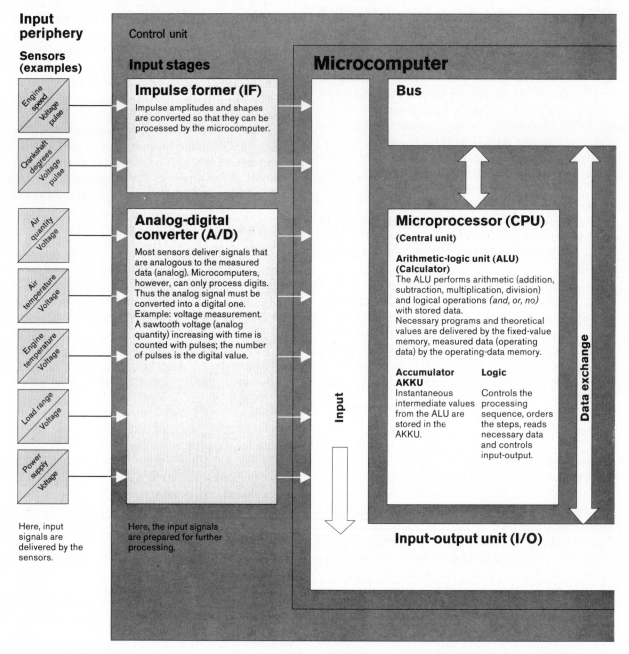

Input periphery

Sensors (examples)

- Engine speed / Voltage pulse
- Crankshaft degrees / Voltage pulse
- Air quantity / Voltage
- Air temperature / Voltage
- Engine temperature / Voltage
- Load range / Voltage
- Power supply / Voltage

Here, input signals are delivered by the sensors.

Control unit

Input stages

Impulse former (IF)

Impulse amplitudes and shapes are converted so that they can be processed by the microcomputer.

Analog-digital converter (A/D)

Most sensors deliver signals that are analogous to the measured data (analog). Microcomputers, however, can only process digits. Thus the analog signal must be converted into a digital one. Example: voltage measurement. A sawtooth voltage (analog quantity) increasing with time is counted with pulses; the number of pulses is the digital value.

Here, the input signals are prepared for further processing.

Microcomputer

Bus

Microprocessor (CPU)

(Central unit)

Arithmetic-logic unit (ALU) (Calculator)
The ALU performs arithmetic (addition, subtraction, multiplication, division) and logical operations *(and, or, no)* with stored data. Necessary programs and theoretical values are delivered by the fixed-value memory, measured data (operating data) by the operating-data memory.

Accumulator AKKU
Instantaneous intermediate values from the ALU are stored in the AKKU.

Logic
Controls the processing sequence, orders the steps, reads necessary data and controls input-output.

Input

Data exchange

Input-output unit (I/O)

FIGURE 11–19   Data-processing path within the vehicle computer. (*Courtesy of Robert Bosch Corporation.*)

Although the heart of the on-board computer system is the electronic control unit (ECU) or electronic/engine control module (ECM), depending on the term used by the particular vehicle manufacturer, these solid-state computer devices are connected to the vehicle electric system by a conventional wiring harness fitted with a multipin Weather-Pack terminal adapter.

Most sensors are similar to simple sending units, such as an oil pressure switch or a fuel level gauge. Therefore, they are usually in an ON or an OFF condition. While the

IF: Impulse former
A/D: Analog-digital converter
CPU: Central processor unit
ALU: Arithmetic-logic unit
I/O: Input-output
ROM: Read-only memory
RAM: Random-access memory

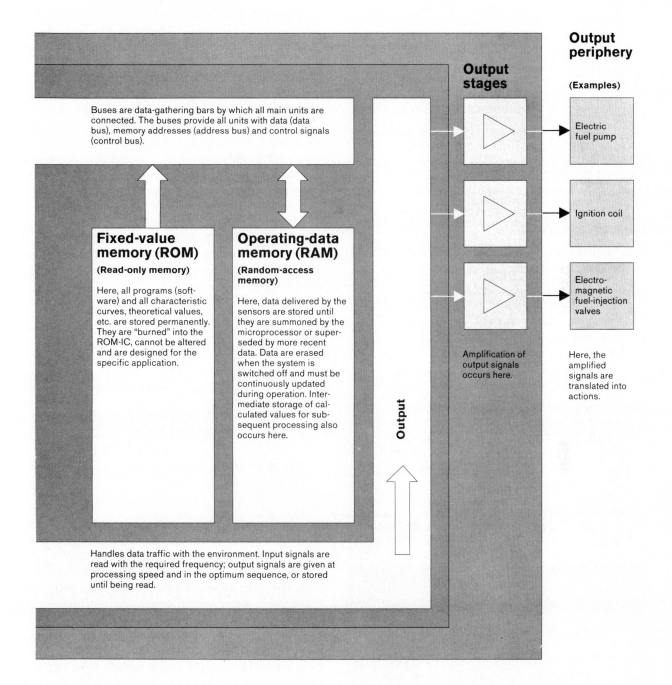

Output periphery

Output stages

(Examples)

Buses are data-gathering bars by which all main units are connected. The buses provide all units with data (data bus), memory addresses (address bus) and control signals (control bus).

Fixed-value memory (ROM)

(Read-only memory)

Here, all programs (software) and all characteristic curves, theoretical values, etc. are stored permanently. They are "burned" into the ROM-IC, cannot be altered and are designed for the specific application.

Operating-data memory (RAM)

(Random-access memory)

Here, data delivered by the sensors are stored until they are summoned by the microprocessor or superseded by more recent data. Data are erased when the system is switched off and must be continuously updated during operation. Intermediate storage of calculated values for subsequent processing also occurs here.

Output

Amplification of output signals occurs here.

Here, the amplified signals are translated into actions.

Electric fuel pump

Ignition coil

Electro-magnetic fuel-injection valves

Handles data traffic with the environment. Input signals are read with the required frequency; output signals are given at processing speed and in the optimum sequence, or stored until being read.

engine is running at normal operating temperature and the vehicle is moving, however, the sensors are continuously feeding voltage signals back to the ECM to alter the operating parameters of the vehicle constantly for optimum efficiency. Each sensor is designed to operate either on a changing temperature or pressure condition which causes its internal resistance to change with a resultant variation in its output voltage signal.

The ECM (electronic control module) generally applies and monitors a 5-V reference signal to the sensor at all times, although some sensors may operate on a voltage signal as high as 8 V. As each sensor is subjected to either a changing temperature or pressure condition, the ECM checks each sensor input continuously and makes a decision based on preprogrammed inputs to alter one or more operating conditions on either the engine or vehicle systems.

Once the ECM receives these sensor voltage signals, computer commands are carried out by various solenoids, small motors, and other control devices. For example, solenoids are used to control the fuel injectors (gasoline and diesel) and therefore also control the fuel flow, air bleed valves, vacuum controls, EGR, and so on.

If, for example, a detonation sensor on a gasoline engine interprets a "knocking" condition, the computer will retard ignition timing either directly or, on some systems, the ECM will activate a solenoid to cut off distributor vacuum advance if so used. Various methods are in use on different makes of vehicles. However, the end result is the same.

COMPUTER DEVICES

The on-board vehicle computer contains the following major operating devices:

1. A CPU (central processing unit)
2. Temporary storage units
3. Arithmetic–logic unit (ALU) or section
4. Control unit
5. Backup storage units
6. Input devices or sensors
7. Output devices or actuators

Figure 11–18 illustrates a typical electronic control unit or minicomputer that is typical of that now in use in many heavy-duty trucks. The function and operation of the computer components shown in Fig. 11–18 can best be understood by referring to the simplified operational diagram shown in Fig. 11–19 (see pages 454–455), which illustrates the actual data-processing function within the computer unit.

COMPUTER PROGRAMMING

Although each computer contains the same major basic components for successful operation, the system must be programmed with a set of instructions that, in effect, tell the computer what it must do.

With its diodes, transistors, and resistors, the computer cannot accept a program that has been written in the normal everyday form of letters and numbers. Therefore, one function of a computer program is to transform data into a recognizable computer language so that the computer's solid-state devices can react to various commands. This requires that the input analog-voltage signals from the various sensor devices be converted into "digital" form (1's for ON and 0's for OFF).

Figure 11–20 illustrates, in simplified form, the wave sine for an analog signal and the rectangular box shape of the digital sine wave. The operation of both of these sine waves was discussed earlier and was shown in Fig. 11–10 and 11–11.

Analog data on this plate

Spooning in digital food from plate

FIGURE 11–20 Computer accepts (eats) only digital signals in order to operate.

Although we could take the regular digital numbers of 1 and 0 and program the computer, it would be very difficult to understand and use strings of 1's and 0's, particularly when we would need to use thousands of numbers. Therefore, to simplify this bulky system into a more manageable state, special programming language has been developed.

Minicomputers in use in automobiles and trucks perform a limited number of calculations when compared to that of a large mainframe computer in an office or factory. Therefore, their programs are fairly simple to construct. A fixed program is built directly into the computer at the factory and is commonly referred to as handwiring, because it is burned into the PROM (programmable read-only memory) or ROM (read-only memory) unit integrated chip by a laser beam in the latest systems. The PROM unit cannot be altered unless it is removed and replaced with another memory chip. EPROM (electrical PROM) or EEPROMs (electrically erasable PROMs) can be altered.

FIGURE 11–18 View of a heavy-duty high-speed diesel engine DDEC II electronic control module. (*Courtesy of Detroit Diesel Corporation.*)

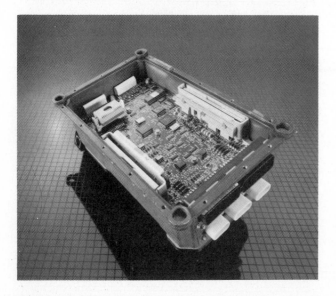

Binary Notation

Since the computer is constructed to understand only "digital" voltage signals, which are either in the ON (1) or OFF (0) mode, the many combinations of these numbers are represented in what is called *binary form*. What this means is that only the numerals 1 or 0 are used rather than the numbers from 0 through 9, which would represent 10 possible numbers.

To convert the decimal numbers into binary notation or form, a device within the minicomputer known as an *encoder* is required. In addition, in order to convert digital data (i.e., binary numbers) into decimal form at any time, the computer also contains a *decoder*. Table 11–1 illustrates the system of numbers used with the binary system of notation. This is the system of numbers used to tell the computer what is going on at any time.

The binary system of numbers used with a computer is commonly called a *base 2 system*, while the conventional decimal system using 10 digits is known as a *base 10 system*. The word *decimal* is derived from the Latin word for *ten*.

The computer can interpret numbers only in the base 2 system. Since only zeros or ones (0's = OFF and 1's = ON) are continually produced by the various input sensors (analog-to-digital conversion done through an analog-to-digital converter within the computer unit), some form of equitable conversion system must be employed. Table 11–1 illustrates a comparison between a base 2 and a base 10 system. Note, for example, that the binary number 0011 is read and interpreted as the number "zero-zero-one-one," not as the number eleven.

Your initial reaction to viewing Table 11–1 is probably the same as that for most people when they are initially confronted with such a comparison. It just does not make any sense, does it? Therefore, let's see if we can simplify this concept, so that you will have a solid foundation on which to base your interpretation of just how the computer is able to understand all these strings of 1's and 0's and make sense out of them.

The position of each individual digit in the decimal system, when read from right to left, represents the base number to the power 10. For example, the number 1, which would be the first number on the right, would simply be represented by 10 to the power zero, or 10^0. Note the small zero above and to the right of 10.

The second position from the right would be representative of 10 to the power 1, or 10^1, with a small 1 above it. Therefore, 10 times 1×10! The third position from the right would represent 10 to the power 2 or 100, commonly stated as 10^2, with a small 2 above the 10. Therefore, 10 times 10 = 100!

The fourth position from the right would represent 10 to the power 3, or 1000, which is calculated simply by multiplying 10 times 10 times 10. Therefore, the 10 would be commonly represented by the number 10^3, with a small 3 above it! Each successive digit to the right would increase the number ten's power by another number up the line—namely, to the power 4, 5, 6, and so on.

In the binary system of numbers used within the computer, the numbers are also grouped from right to left, with each additional digit increasing the power of the number from 0 to 1, 2, 3, 4, and so on.

As with the decimal system, in the binary system the first digit on the right is in the one's place. Therefore, it is represented by 2 to the power zero, or 2^0 with a small "0" above it. Since the computer is programmed to accept only 0's and 1's, this second digit must be the two's place, with 2^1 being raised now to the power "1." Moving left, the third digit would represent the four's place or 2 to the power $2—2^2$, with a small 2 above it.

Moving left, the fourth digit would represent the eight's position or place, or 2 to the power three (2^3, with a small 3 above it). Each successive digit to the left would represent another power added to the base figure of 2. If you compare this system of decimal and binary notation, which is shown in Table 11–2, the above-listed information may be easier to understand.

From the information presented, we can now readily understand that a number such as 6524 in the decimal system can be presented by the following notational system:

$$6 \times 10^3 \text{ (to the power 3) plus}$$
$$5 \times 10^2 \text{ (to the power 2) plus}$$
$$2 \times 10^1 \text{ (to the power 1) plus}$$
$$4 \times 10^0 \text{ (to the power 0)}$$

TABLE 11–1 Minicomputer binary notation (base 2) system of numbering versus decimal (base 10) system

Decimal Base 10 System	Binary Base 2 System
0	0 0 0 0
1	0 0 0 1
2	0 0 1 0
3	0 0 1 1
4	0 1 0 0
5	0 1 0 1
6	0 1 1 0
7	0 1 1 1
8	1 0 0 0
9	1 0 0 1
10	1 0 1 0
11	1 0 1 1
12	1 1 0 0
13	1 1 0 1
14	1 1 1 0
15	1 1 1 1
16	1 0 0 0 0
255	1 1 1 1 1 1 1 1
256	1 0 0 0 0 0 0 0 0

The number 6524 can also be shown as follows:

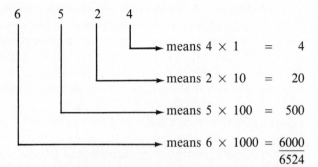

10^3	10^2	10^1	10^0	Ten taken to different
(1000)	(100)	(10)	(1)	powers

6	5	2	4	

means $4 \times 1 \quad = \quad 4$

means $2 \times 10 \quad = \quad 20$

means $5 \times 100 \quad = \quad 500$

means $6 \times 1000 = \underline{6000}$
$\qquad\qquad\qquad\qquad\quad 6524$

To convert from decimal to binary, let's use the number 49 as an example, and transpose it into its equivalent binary number. What we have to do here is to consider that we are going from a base 10 system to a base 2 system.

Therefore, we have to start by determining the largest number that is a power of 2 (divisor) and which will actually divide into the decimal number (49 in this case), with a 1 as a quotient. The largest number that is a power of 2 and which will divide into 49, with a quotient of 1, is 32 (2 to the power 5). This conversion is calculated at the top of the next column.

$(2^5)\ \dfrac{49}{32} = 1 \qquad 49 - 32 = 17$

$(2^4)\ \dfrac{17}{16} = 1 \qquad 17 - 16 = 1$

$(2^3)\ \dfrac{1}{8} = 0$

$(2^2)\ \dfrac{1}{4} = 0$

$(2^1)\ \dfrac{1}{2} = 0$

$(2^0)\ \dfrac{1}{1} = 1 \qquad 1 - 1 = 0$

Therefore, the decimal number 49 in binary form appears as 110001, and is known as "one-one-zero-zero-zero-one" and not as one hundred and ten thousand and one. Conversely, we could take a known binary number, such as 110001 for 49, and find its decimal equivalent, remembering, of course, that the binary system operates on a base 2 rather than a base 10 system.

We start with the decimal number to the power of 5 on the left-hand side of the power number shown below. If we multiply each binary number (1 or 0) by its power base of 2, we get the results shown below:

Power number	5	4	3	2	1	0
Binary number	1	1	0	0	0	1
Multiplied	1×2^5 +	1×2^4 +	0×2^3 +	0×2^2 +	0×2^1 +	1×2^0
Result	32 +	16 +	0 +	0 +	0 +	$1 = 49$

Therefore, we have proved that the decimal number 49 is shown in its binary equivalent number as 110001! Another way to show this and perhaps easier for you to see is to present the data in tabular form:

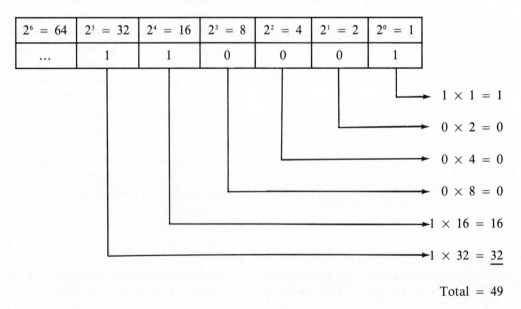

$2^6 = 64$	$2^5 = 32$	$2^4 = 16$	$2^3 = 8$	$2^2 = 4$	$2^1 = 2$	$2^0 = 1$
...	1	1	0	0	0	1

$1 \times 1 = 1$

$0 \times 2 = 0$

$0 \times 4 = 0$

$0 \times 8 = 0$

$1 \times 16 = 16$

$1 \times 32 = \underline{32}$

Total $= 49$

TABLE 11-2 Comparison of decimal (base 10) and computer (base 2) binary systems

	Decimal—Base 10				Binary—Base 2				
Place	4	3	2	1	5	4	3	2	1
Value	1000	100	10	1	16	8	4	2	1
Power of base	3	2	1	0	4	2	2	1	0

Base 8, or Octal System

Although we have discussed the decimal system (base 10) and compared it to that of the binary system (base 2), any base to power number can be used. Computers often employ a "base 8" system, which is referred to as an *octal* system since it uses the number 0 through 7. Instead of using numbers 0 through 9 as in the decimal system (base 10 system), each digit 0–1–2–3–4–5–6–7 represents the base number 8 raised to an exponent related or based on that position.

Since digital signals are either on or off and are represented by a 1 or 0, the binary system is based on a base 2 system, with the position of each digit representing the number 2, which is the base number raised to an exponent based on that particular position. One other numbering system used with computers is the *hexadecimal* or what is more commonly known as a *base 16* system.

Earlier we considered how to convert the decimal number 49 into binary form, and vice versa. However, as decimal numbers increase in relative size, for example into the thousands, the equivalent binary length of 1's and 0's also increases and can, in effect, become quite cumbersome. In addition, true binary numbers can only represent numeric data, such as the counting of digital pulses that have been produced in analog form from a sensor and then converted through an analog/digital converter within the computer. True binary representation cannot, however, handle items or bits of data such as letters of the alphabet, or special characters such as periods, commas, exclamation marks, question marks, + signs, dollar signs, and various other special symbols that we often use.

Because of the change in length of the binary number when a decimal number such as 49 versus 6524 is represented, the computer would have some trouble when receiving or transmitting data in pure binary form, since it would not quite know when one string of bits ended and the other began. Therefore, fixed-length codes allow the computer to determine when one character ends and another begins.

EBCDIC and ASCII Codes

The two most widely used codes that are employed to allow the computer to determine between decimal num-bers, letters of the alphabet, and special lettering are known as:

1. EBCDIC: Extended Binary-Coded Decimal Interchange Code
2. ASCII: American Standard Code for Information Interchange

The EBCDIC system was developed by IBM (International Business Machines) and is used extensively in their line of computers, while the ASCII system is widely used on other makes of CPUs (central processing units). The EBCDIC system uses 8 bits (a bit is a unit of information, either a 0 or a 1) to represent a character, and since the binary system is known as a base 2 system, a group of 8 bits has 256 (2 to the power 8) different combinations that can represent 256 characters. This number of 256 is sufficient to allow for all the letters of the alphabet (both upper and lower case), the 10 decimal digits, and for a number of special characters as well.

ASCII, on the other hand, was developed as a 7-bit code and can represent only 128 characters (2 to the power 7 obtained from the base 2 system of 1's and 0's). Whether a 7-bit or 8-bit code system of word length is used to represent information characters, each is referred to as a *byte*. Table 11–3 illustrates the sequence of characters and its equivalent EBCDIC and ASCII binary bit number.

Bits and Bytes

The digital signals created and interpreted in the computer are, as we now know, identified by binary numbers of 1 or 0, with 1 being an ON signal and with 0 representing an OFF signal. These 1's and 0's are commonly referred to as *bits*, which is a word combination form contrived from the two words *binary digits*. A bit is the term used to indicate one unit of data or information and is indicated to the computer by the numeral 1 or 0. Each one of these digital numbers contains a very small unit of information. Therefore, to handle large amounts of usable information, the computer is designed to combine and handle these separate bits into words of different lengths. Various computers are designed to handle information data in word lengths of 4, 8, 16, 32, or 64 bits.

The term *kilobyte* or the letter "K" indicates that the memory storage unit of the CPU can hold 1000 bytes

TABLE 11-3 EBCDIC and ASCII character and bit number representation

Character	EBCDIC Bit Representation	ASCII Bit Representation	Character	EBCDIC Bit Representation	ASCII Bit Representation
0	1 1 1 1 0 0 0 0	0 1 1 0 0 0 0	I	1 1 0 0 1 0 0 1	1 0 0 1 0 0 1
1	1 1 1 1 0 0 0 1	0 1 1 0 0 0 1	J	1 1 0 1 0 0 0 1	1 0 0 1 0 1 0
2	1 1 1 1 0 0 1 0	0 1 1 0 0 1 0	K	1 1 0 1 0 0 1 0	1 0 0 1 0 1 1
3	1 1 1 1 0 0 1 1	0 1 1 0 0 1 1	L	1 1 0 1 0 0 1 1	1 0 0 1 1 0 0
4	1 1 1 1 0 1 0 0	0 1 1 0 1 0 0	M	1 1 0 1 0 1 0 0	1 0 0 1 1 0 1
5	1 1 1 1 0 1 0 1	0 1 1 0 1 0 1	N	1 1 0 1 0 1 0 1	1 0 0 1 1 1 0
6	1 1 1 1 0 1 1 0	0 1 1 0 1 1 0	O	1 1 0 1 0 1 1 0	1 0 0 1 1 1 1
7	1 1 1 1 0 1 1 1	0 1 1 0 1 1 1	P	1 1 0 1 0 1 1 1	1 0 1 0 0 0 0
8	1 1 1 1 1 0 0 0	0 1 1 1 0 0 0	Q	1 1 0 1 1 0 0 0	1 0 1 0 0 0 1
9	1 1 1 1 1 0 0 1	0 1 1 1 0 0 1	R	1 1 0 1 1 0 0 1	1 0 1 0 0 1 0
A	1 1 0 0 0 0 0 1	1 0 0 0 0 0 1	S	1 1 1 0 0 0 1 0	1 0 1 0 0 1 1
B	1 1 0 0 0 0 1 0	1 0 0 0 0 1 0	T	1 1 1 0 0 0 1 1	1 0 1 0 1 0 0
C	1 1 0 0 0 0 1 1	1 0 0 0 0 1 1	U	1 1 1 0 0 1 0 0	1 0 1 0 1 0 1
D	1 1 0 0 0 1 0 0	1 0 0 0 1 0 0	V	1 1 1 0 0 1 0 1	1 0 1 0 1 1 0
E	1 1 0 0 0 1 0 1	1 0 0 0 1 0 1	W	1 1 1 0 0 1 1 0	1 0 1 0 1 1 1
F	1 1 0 0 0 1 1 0	1 0 0 0 1 1 0	X	1 1 1 0 0 1 1 1	1 0 1 1 0 0 0
G	1 1 0 0 0 1 1 1	1 0 0 0 1 1 1	Y	1 1 1 0 1 0 0 0	1 0 1 1 0 0 1
H	1 1 0 0 1 0 0 0	1 0 0 1 0 0 0	Z	1 1 1 0 1 0 0 1	1 0 1 1 0 1 0

(1 byte being equal to a word length of 8 bits, for example). Actually, 1K represents 1024 bytes, which is arrived at by taking the digital "base 2" system and elevating it to the power of 10—namely, 2 to the power 10. (The base 2 system was discussed under binary notation.) A greater unit of measurement is a megabyte (MB), which represents 1 million bytes.

In order for the computer to handle as much information as possible in as small a space as possible, it is advantageous to use longer words rather than shorter ones, since this will allow a greater amount of data to be handled at any given time, and by doing so, the computer will have greater information-processing capability. The word size that the computer can handle is indicated by its capacity number such as 8 bit, 16 bit, 32 bit, 64 bit.

Most home computers and main frames can handle substantially greater information than that used in a truck microprocessor. The information and computations that the microprocessor is required to handle can normally be accommodated by using an 8-bit word length system, although some of the newer models are now up to a 16-bit system to accommodate the greater number of systems that are now electronically controlled.

By using an 8-word bit system, 2 to the power 8, or 256 combinations are possible, while a 16-bit system can handle 512 combinations for a total of 65,536 memory locations (2 to the power 16). Therefore, the greater the word bit capacity of the computer, the larger its memory capacity as well as its speed of computation will be. Typically, on a 16-bit machine, the first 16 bits are reserved for instructions, which permits 2 to the power 2^6 or 64 different instructions.

Since we have discussed that more than single bits of information are required in a on-board truck microprocessor system, consider that if we were to use a simple three (binary digit)-bit binary number as our base, we would have a system that would be represented as shown in Fig. 11–21, where the left-hand square represents the MSB (most significant bit), while the right-hand square represents the LSB (least significant bit) of information. With this three-bit system we can represent eight unique binary codes, as shown in Fig. 11–22. This system is equal to 2^N, where N = number of bits in the binary code

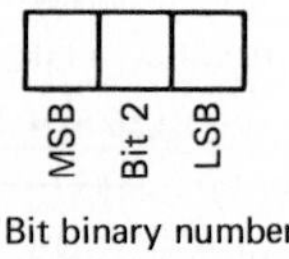

3 Bit binary number

FIGURE 11-21 Example of a 3-bit binary number system.

FIGURE 11-22 Three-bit system can represent eight unique binary codes.

Code

1	0	0	0
2	0	0	1
3	0	1	0
4	0	1	1
5	1	0	0
6	1	0	1
7	1	1	0
8	1	1	1

Binary codes

number, which in this case is $2^8 = 8$. The system shown in Figure 11–22 has eight discrete binary codes, depending on the combination of ON–OFF states for each bit. As mentioned earlier, an eight-bit device has 2^8 or $2 \times 2 \times 2 \times 2 \times 2 \times 2 \times 2 \times 2 = 256$ discrete codes, while a 16-bit system would have 65,536 codes. A common method used in microprocessors to represent the system above is to assign a decimal number weight to each bit and then use the binary codes to represent decimal numbers. In this (BCD) binary-coded decimal technique, which provides for handling decimal-numbered information in a digital system, the BCD 8-bit register would appear as follows:

128	64	32	16	8	4	2	1

LOGIC CIRCUITS

In Chapter 2 we discussed briefly the makeup of an integrated circuit or IC. Several examples of the use of diodes, transistors, and resistors were discussed and how they would function in the typical alternator used in a car or truck. The overall purpose of each solid-state device, and its importance to the successful operation and control of the charging system discussed in Chapter 8, provide one example of an electronic circuit. Let's build on that knowledge now, and move one step further toward understanding the function and operation of the on-board minicomputer now in use on many passenger cars and trucks.

We also talked earlier about the difference between analog and digital voltage signals. You may recollect that analog signals resemble the sound made by the human voice in that the voltage signal is undulating or wavy, whereas the digital signal is either on or off and is reflected by rectangular box shapes rather than by a wavy sine line. If you wish, refer to Figs. 11–10 and 11–11 to refresh your memory before proceeding.

Since microprocessors operate on digital signals, any analog signal must be converted to a digital signal so that the feedback information from any sensor can be readily understood and acted upon. Components within the computer are designed and programmed to recognize voltage signals by a number assigned to a specific input signal. Because of the many functions that the computer is asked to do, the various input signals are converted to a specific binary digit number through the use of logic gates, which are discussed below. Figure 11–16 illustrates typical operating conditions that are sensed by specific sensors attached to the engine/vehicle. These voltage signals are then fed into the on-board electronic control module (minicomputer), where the various solid-state devices, assisted by the different logic gates, are able to interpret these input data's binary digit (bit) representation of the analog sensor's amplitude. The electronic control module then outputs a voltage signal to the gas or diesel fuel injectors, for example, to control how long they operate. In this way the amount of fuel delivered to the engine cylinders becomes proportional to the throttle position. Similarly, an output voltage signal from the computer controls the injection and ignition timing and any other sensed components.

Paramount to the importance of ICs is the operation of the transistors. The converted digital voltage signals or circuits are known as *logic circuits*, and they consist of a series or combinations of varying types of systems and numbers, and interconnection patterns that are commonly referred to as *gates*. These gates are designed to accept voltage signals and logically make sense of them. In effect, they process two or more voltage signals. This is why they are called *logic gates*. They have the ability to make some sense out of all the various voltage feedback signals that are fed to the computer from the numerous sensors on the vehicle.

There are five basic types of logic gates in use on microprocessor-equipped vehicles:

1. AND gates
2. OR gates
3. NOT or INVERT gates
4. NAND gates
5. NOR gates

Each logic gate listed above is designed to perform a specific function within the computer.

AND Gate Circuit

The logic symbol that is commonly used to identify an AND gate in a schematic diagram of an electronic circuit is shown in Fig. 11–23. The logic symbol for an AND gate actually contains two diodes, three transistors, three variable resistors, and four fixed resistors as shown in Figs. 11–23 and 11–24. In these schematics, A and B represent the two voltage input terminals, and C represents the output. You may find that the letter X is also often used to signify the output terminal.

Compare Fig. 11–24 with Fig. 11–25 and consider the parallels that exist between a typical mechanical-switch electrical circuit and that of a solid-state circuit (Fig. 11–24). The mechanical switches A and B function the same as the voltage input terminals A and B in the solid-state AND gate circuit, while the small light bulb in the mechanical circuit is the same as the output terminal C in the AND gate system. The term *AND gate* is used in this context because power can flow to the light bulb only

FIGURE 11–23 Typical logic symbol for an AND gate system.

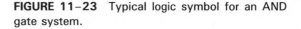

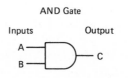

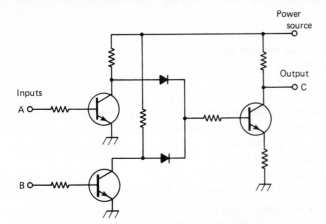

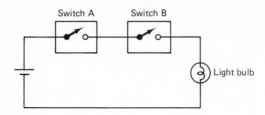

FIGURE 11-24 Equivalent electronic circuit arrangement for an AND gate logic circuit.

FIGURE 11-25 Equivalent mechanical circuit for an AND gate logic circuit.

when switches *A* and *B* are both closed or both inputs are high (1). Should one or both switches be open (low or zero), then obviously the light bulb would not come on, because the output would also be low or zero (0). If we therefore compare this arrangement of the mechanical circuit with that of the solid-state AND gate system, the same thing holds true. Voltage at the output terminal *C* exists only if a voltage is evident at terminals *A* and *B*.

Earlier when we discussed the fact that the computer requires analog voltage signals to be converted to a digital format so that the computer can make sense out of data, the numeral 1 was used to signify an ON condition with a voltage present, while the numeral 0 was defined as an OFF condition, with no voltage signal present. Since various combinations of these numbers can occur at any time, it is industry practice to display such combinations in what is known as a *truth table* (see Fig. 11-26).

FIGURE 11-26 Truth table for *A* and *B* inputs, with a *C* output for an AND gate logic circuit.

AND Gate

| Inputs | | Output |
A	B	C
0	0	0
0	1	0
1	0	0
1	1	1

OR Gate Circuit

Illustrated in Figs. 11-27, 11-28, and 11-29 are the logic symbol, the solid-state element arrangement, and the equivalent mechanical circuit for an OR gate system. Solid-state components used in the OR gate circuit are made up of two transistors, two diodes, three fixed, and three variable resistors. The OR gate circuit differs from the AND circuit in that the light bulb will be illuminated

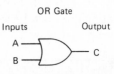

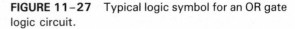

FIGURE 11-27 Typical logic symbol for an OR gate logic circuit.

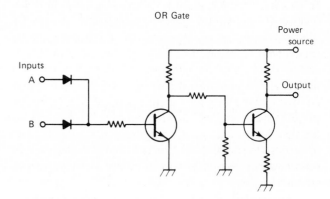

FIGURE 11-28 Equivalent OR gate system electronic circuit.

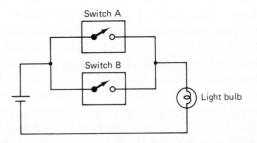

FIGURE 11-29 Equivalent mechanical OR circuit.

whenever one or both inputs are high (1). For the bulb to have been illuminated in the AND gate circuit, both switches had to be closed. (Both inputs have to be high or 1.) In Fig. 11-27 a voltage signal at either *A* or *B* or both reflects an output voltage signal at *C*. Possible combinations for this OR circuit are shown in the truth table in Fig. 11-30.

OR Gate

Inputs A	B	Output C
0	0	0
0	1	1
1	0	1
1	1	1

FIGURE 11–30 Truth table for *A* and *B* (voltage at both input terminals, or voltage at only one) and the resultant output for an OR gate logic circuit.

NOT Gate Circuit

The logic symbol for a NOT gate circuit is similar to that for a diode, and it is illustrated in Fig. 11–31. The actual solid-state arrangement and equivalent mechanical circuits are shown in Figs. 11–32 and 11–33. The NOT gate system has one transistor, no diodes, two fixed resistors, as well as one variable resistor.

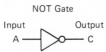

NOT Gate

FIGURE 11–31 Typical logic symbol for a NOT gate circuit.

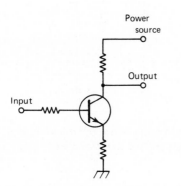

FIGURE 11–32 Equivalent NOT gate logic system electronic circuit layout.

FIGURE 11–33 Typical equivalent mechanical system for a NOT gate logic circuit.

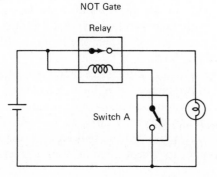

NOT Gate

In the OR gate circuit, the light bulb is illuminated when either one or both switches are closed. [Inputs are high (1).] However, in the NOT gate circuit, when the switch *A* is closed (input is high or 1), the relay shown in Fig. 11–33 is opened. There is no power flow to the bulb, and it will *not* light. When switch *A* is opened (input is low or zero), the relay will close, and the light bulb will illuminate.

Therefore, in the solid-state circuit shown in Fig. 11–32, a voltage signal at the input terminal *a* will result in no output signal *c*, and vice versa. In other words, the output signal is always the opposite of the input signal, or inverted. The truth table in Fig. 11–34 illustrates the various combinations in numeric form, with 1 representing an ON condition, and with 0 signifying an OFF condition.

NOT Gate

Input A	Output C
1	0
0	1

FIGURE 11–34 Truth table for a NOT gate logic circuit (output is always opposite the input).

NAND Gate Circuit

The term NAND gate is a combination of both the AND and NOT gate circuits discussed earlier (NAND = NOT AND for the reduced term NAND). The logic symbol for a NAND gate circuit is illustrated in Fig. 11–35, while its truth table depicting the various input/output combinations possible from such an arrangement is shown in Fig. 11–36.

Because of the combination of an AND and NOT gate in this system, zero voltage will appear at the output terminal *C* only if a voltage signal 1 is apparent at both input terminals *A* and *B*. Conversely, if there is a 0 or no input voltage signal at either input terminal *A* or *B*, an output voltage signal 1 will appear at terminal *C*.

FIGURE 11–35 Typical logic gate symbol for a NAND circuit.

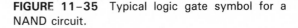

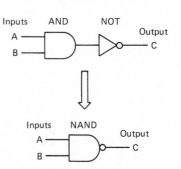

NAND Gate

NAND Gate

Inputs A	B	Output C
0	0	1
0	1	1
1	0	1
1	1	0

FIGURE 11-36 Truth table for a NAND gate logic circuit composed of a combination NOT and an AND gate system.

NOR Gate Circuit

The last type of logic circuit that we will look at is known as the NOR gate circuit. Its symbol is shown in Fig. 11-37, and its truth table is illustrated in Fig. 11-38. This particular circuit consists of a combination OR gate and NOT gate arrangement (NOR = NOT OR); hence the term NOR. In this circuit, when a 0 or no input voltage is apparent at terminals A and B, an output voltage 1 will appear at the terminal C. If on the other hand, there is a 1 (voltage signal) at either input terminal A or B, or both, the output terminal C will be 0.

Application of Logic Gates to a Computer System

For an on-board minicomputer to receive an assortment of voltage signals, analyze their meaning, and send out a controlling or corrected signal to the ignition or fuel injection system, for example, it is necessary that all of

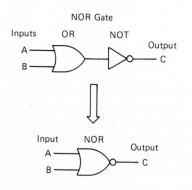

FIGURE 11-37 Typical logic symbol for a NOR gate circuit.

FIGURE 11-38 Truth table for a NOR gate logic system composed of a combination OR and NOT gate circuit.

NOR Gate

Inputs A	B	Output C
0	0	1
0	1	0
1	0	0
1	1	0

the logic circuits discussed above be used within the electronic control system. Some logic circuits will supply the required function under certain conditions, while others alone or in combination with another must perform the necessary output information that engine systems need to operate under all types of conditions. Consequently, both NAND and NOR gates, which are combinations of the single-circuit AND, OR, and NOT gates, are used extensively within the computer circuitry.

A circuit designed to output a voltage 1, when both inputs (A and B) have the same value, is not yet available from a single logic circuit alone. Therefore, a combination of several of the logic circuits illustrated above must be used to operate in such a mode. Such a circuit is illustrated in Fig. 11-39, while Fig. 11-40 shows the truth table that proves the facts of such a system.

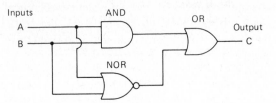

FIGURE 11-39 Typical combination AND, NOR, and OR gate logic circuit arrangement.

Logic Circuit

Inputs A	B	Output C
0	0	1
0	1	0
1	0	0
1	1	1

FIGURE 11-40 Truth table for a combination logic circuit for an OR, AND, and NOR gate system.

XOR Adder Circuits

Another logic gate that is commonly used for comparison of two binary numbers (used to add binary numbers) is the XOR gate. If both inputs are the same (1 + 1), the output is zero. A 1, now called a *carry*, is placed in the next place value to be added with any bits in that place value. Figure 11-41 illustrates an XOR gate schematic symbol, truth table, and logic symbol. In the XOR gate, the output is high only when one input or the other is high, but not both.

A typical digital automotive circuit that performs the addition of two binary bits is illustrated in Fig. 11-42 and is commonly known as a *half-adder*, because it produces the sum and any necessary carry, as shown in the accompanying truth table. Since a half-adder is not provided with an input to accept a carry from a previous place

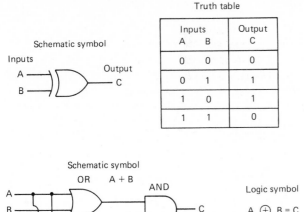

Truth table

| Inputs | | Output |
A	B	C
0	0	0
0	1	1
1	0	1
1	1	0

Schematic symbol

Inputs

A

B

Output

C

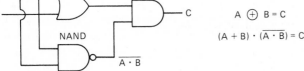

Schematic symbol

OR   A + B

AND

NAND

A

B

C

$\overline{A \cdot B}$

Logic symbol

$A \oplus B = C$

$(A + B) \cdot (\overline{A \cdot B}) = C$

FIGURE 11–41 An XOR gate schematic symbol, truth table, and logic symbol.

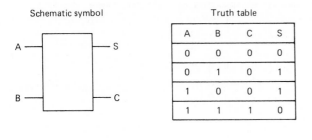

Schematic symbol

A

B

S

C

Truth table

A	B	C	S
0	0	0	0
0	1	0	1
1	0	0	1
1	1	1	0

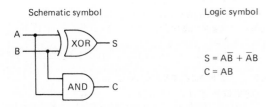

Schematic symbol

A

B

XOR   S

AND   C

Logic symbol

$S = A\overline{B} + \overline{A}B$

$C = AB$

FIGURE 11–42 Half-adder circuit schematic symbol and truth table.

value, a circuit known as a *full-adder* is used when required (Fig. 11–43). Coupling a number of full-adder circuits together in series allows the addition of binary numbers with as many digits as necessary to handle the information being generated.

A good example of where full-adder circuits are used is in a typical hand-held calculator. It performs all of the arithmetic operations, together with several other logic circuits. This configuration is required because for computations to be made, subtraction is changed to addition, multiplication becomes repeated addition, and division becomes repeated subtraction.

Sequential Memory Logic Circuits

The various combinations of logic circuits discussed so far have mainly involved the use of AND, OR, and NOT gates, with the output of each system being controlled

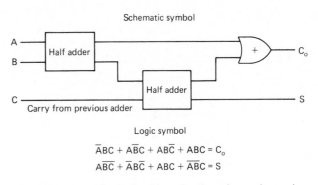

Schematic symbol

A

B

Half adder

Half adder

C

Carry from previous adder

+

C_o

S

Logic symbol

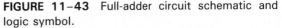

$$\overline{A}BC + A\overline{B}C + AB\overline{C} + ABC = C_o$$
$$A\overline{B}\,\overline{C} + \overline{A}\,\overline{B}C + ABC + \overline{A}B\overline{C} = S$$

FIGURE 11–43 Full-adder circuit schematic and logic symbol.

by the actual input signals. Consequently, these circuits are known as combinational logic circuits. The basis of semiconductor computer memories rely on these sequential logic circuits, since they hold or retain information even after the input signal has been removed.

It is desirable in certain circumstances to employ a logic circuit that is capable of retaining previous input signals or past logic states. This circuit is called a *sequential logic system*, because the actual sequence of past input signals/values and logic state at the time determines the present output state or mode. Such a circuit can be put together by interconnecting two NAND gates, as shown in Fig. 11–44. This type of sequential logic circuit is commonly referred to as an *R-S (reset-set) flip-flop*, since it describes the action of the logic-level changes.

For example, in Fig. 11–44 note that when S is high (a 1 signal) and R is low (a 0 signal), the output Q is set to a high (1), where it will stay regardless of whether S is high (1) or low (0). In other words, the high (1) state of S is latched into the state of Q, and the only way Q can become unlatched (to a 0 signal) is to allow R to go high (1) and S to go low (a 0 signal). This action will reset the latch. Also notice from the truth table that R and S must not be high (1) at the same time; otherwise, the two gates would be opposing or bucking one another, and this action would create an output in a flip-flop condition or an uncertain state.

This uncertain state could be solved by using what is known as a *J-K flip-flop*, which is illustrated in Fig. 11–45. This arrangement can be obtained from the use of an *R-S* flip-flop arrangement (a synchronized one) with an additional logic gate, as shown in the figure. When the input signal of both J and K are high (1), the flip-flop will change to a different state at a particular time that is determined by a timing pulse called a "clock applied," which is shown in the circuit illustration at the terminal by a triangle symbol. The small circle at the clock terminal indicates that the circuit responds only when the clock switches from a high (1) level to a low level (0). If no circle were present in a clock circuit diagram, the circuit would respond only when the clock switched from a low (0) level to a high (1) level.

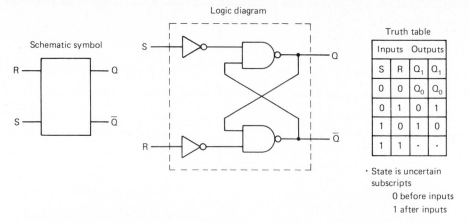

FIGURE 11–44 Sequential memory *R-S* (reset-set) flip-flop logic circuit.

Schematic symbol

Logic diagram

Truth table

Inputs		Outputs	
S	R	Q_1	$\bar{Q}_1$
0	0	Q_0	$\bar{Q}_0$
0	1	0	1
1	0	1	0
1	1	·	·

· State is uncertain
subscripts
    0 before inputs
    1 after inputs

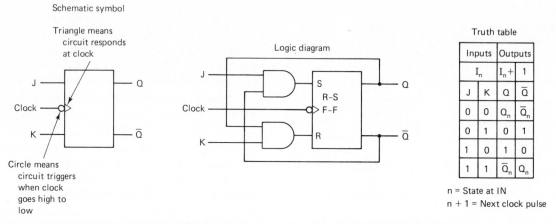

Schematic symbol

Triangle means
circuit responds
at clock

Circle means
circuit triggers
when clock
goes high to
low

Logic diagram

Truth table

Inputs		Outputs	
I_n		$I_n + 1$	
J	K	Q	$\bar{Q}$
0	0	Q_n	$\bar{Q}_n$
0	1	0	1
1	0	1	0
1	1	$\bar{Q}_n$	Q_n

n = State at IN
n + 1 = Next clock pulse

FIGURE 11–45 Sequential memory *J-K* (uncertain state) flip-flop logic circuit.

SYNCHRONOUS CLOCK COUNTER

Synchronous counters are the basis of digital clocks and are employed extensively in circuits that convert binary values (base 2 system) to decimal numbers (base 10 system), as discussed earlier in this chapter. These synchronous counters are made up from a succession of *J-K* flip-flops. Figure 11–46 illustrates a four-stage synchronous counter, so named because all stages are triggered at the same time by the same clock pulse signal. Since the clock has a four-stage unit, it counts 2 (2 to the power 4), which equals 16 clock pulses, before it returns to a starting position. Since the system is digital in nature (ON = 1 or OFF = 0), these waveforms are also shown in Fig. 11–46 as they would appear at each *Q* output.

Because of this waveform, it becomes an easy matter to employ this type of circuitry for any circuit that requires a count to be monitored in order to activate/deactivate a signal. It could also be used for generating other timing pulses and is particularly helpful for establishing any engine timing sequence or other circuit requiring timed responses. Various engine-monitored systems can be accessed during troubleshooting by withdrawing stored trouble codes from the computer memory system. See each manufacturer's ECM system descrip-

tion for the correct procedure. Typical systems that employ "counters" for their monitoring system are such items as:

NOTE: Items 1 to 6 pertain to gasoline fuel-injected engines such as the 6-L and 7-L models used in the GMC 1990 Topkick and Kodiak midheavy trucks.

1. Detonation sensor, with the counter increasing from 0 to 255 and repeating.

2. Oxygen sensor counter, which also ranges from 0 to 255 before it is automatically reset.

3. Fuel integrator (makes temporary changes in the amount of fuel delivered to the engine during closed-loop operation); the counter operates with a nominal value of 128, which varies slightly based on a rich or lean condition. This value can vary between engine manufacturers and from engine to engine.

4. Block-learn memory, which operates similar to the fuel integrator during closed-loop operation, with 128 being the nominal value.

5. Idle air-control motor, which is used to control engine rpm during closed throttle conditions to prevent stalling when loads are applied at idle. Counter operates from 0 to 255 counts.

6. Engine load counter, which is based on the amount of air entering each cylinder in grams per second. Arrived

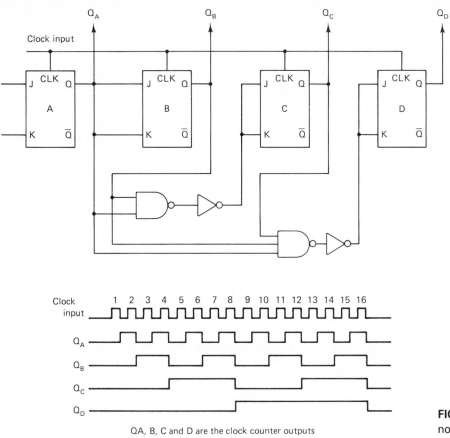

FIGURE 11–46 Four-stage synchronous counter with clock input circuit.

QA, B, C and D are the clock counter outputs

at by taking the intake airflow divided by the engine rpm. Counter operates between 0 and 255 counts.

7. The ignition cycle counter counts the number of ON/CRANK/OFF cycles of the ignition switch since a trouble code was stored. Operates on a 0- to 50-cycle display, then resets to zero, and erases from memory the stored trouble code.

On heavy-duty truck electronically controlled diesel fuel systems, such items as the coolant level sensor are monitored every 10 seconds with the digital counts ranging between 0 and 255 counts. The same would apply to the oil-level sensor system and also to the PTO set speed. Employing a series of clock stages allows storing the digits of a binary number. If the storage is temporary, the combination of the various clock stages is known as a *register*, while if the storage is permanent, it is referred to as *memory*.

NOTE: All of the logic gates discussed herein are so small that literally hundreds of them can actually be placed in the area of a . (dot). The number of gates that can actually be placed on a single integrated chip has mushroomed over the years with the advancement in technology of producing silicon chips. For example, consider the following advancements:

- 1960: (SSI = small-scale integration), 10 to 12 gates per chip
- 1969: (MSI = medium-scale integration), 1000 gates per chip

- Early 1970s: (LSI = large-scale integration) to VLSI (very-large-scale integration), 50,000 + gates per chip

ANALOG-TO-DIGITAL CONVERTER

So far we have discussed the basic operation of the various logic gates used within the CPU (central processing unit) to perform a number of different tasks related to its successful operation. You may recollect that the engine and vehicle sensors that are employed to monitor the various systems (see Figs. 11–10 and 11–11) produce an analog voltage signal, while the computer is designed to operate only on *digital* signals.

Therefore, in order to supply a continuous input to the computer of the constantly changing conditions of both the engine and vehicle in digital form, we must employ what is commonly called an ADC (analog-to-digital converter). The type of computer and bit size employed determines just how fast this ADC must operate. This can be as quick as a few millionths of a second to as long as a second.

The analog signals from the sensors produce an output sine much like a wave (Fig. 11–10), while the computer requires an input signal which is digital (either ON or OFF), (Fig. 11–11), with ON represented by a binary number 1 and with OFF by 0. Figure 11–47 illustrates in line diagram form one method that is employed to produce this conversion.

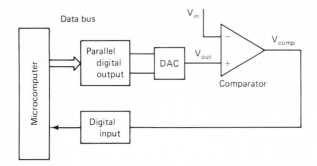

FIGURE 11-47 ADC (analog-to-digital converter) system circuitry.

In Fig. 11-47, a DAC (digital-to-analog) converter and a voltage comparator are used, with the input signal to the DAC being in binary form. This signal is generated at the parallel output of the computer, beginning with a minimum value and increasing to its maximum. The output from the DAC or V_{out} is only one of the inputs fed to the comparator, while the other input signal originates at V_{in}, which is the actual sensor analog input voltage. If the analog voltage value at V_{in} is greater than V_{out} from the DAC, the voltage output signal from the comparator V_{comp} would be a low logic level. On the other hand, if the V_{in} analog signal is lower than the V_{out} signal from the DAC, the output voltage signal from the comparator would be a high logic level.

The voltage output signal (binary number of 1) from the computer immediately causes the DAC output to be higher than the analog V_{in} signal. This will cause the comparator output to be high, which will halt the computer and prevent it from altering the binary number input any further. Since the computer can only recognize a binary number, it is this number that indicates to the computer the value of the analog input voltage signal V_{in}. Continuous sampling of the analog input voltage signal is carried out by the computer so that it can determine when to reset and start the binary number generation all over again. In this way, a binary number that is equivalent to the changing analog input voltage signal is being output from the computer on a continuing basis. The output voltage signal from the comparator is always fed back to the computer through its digital input.

Figure 11-47 illustrates the ADC (analog-to-digital converter) system in its simplified form. Let's look now at just what actually transpires within the CPU to switch this analog input signal to an actual digital signal that it can interpret. To consider an application, let's look at how the coolant, lube oil, and fuel temperature sensor used on the engine transfers its changing analog signal and converts it into a digital signal for various temperature readings. All of these sensors are similar in operation.

The coolant and oil temperature sensors are mounted on the engine, while the fuel sensor is mounted on the fuel filter. Each sensor relays temperature information to the ECM (electronic control module). The ECM monitors a 5-V reference signal, which it applied to the sensor signal circuit through a resistor in the ECM. Note that these sensors are in reality a thermistor, which means that they change their internal resistance as the temperature changes. Specifically, when the sensor is cold, such as when starting up an engine which has been sitting for some time, the sensor resistance is high, and the ECM monitors a high signal voltage. As the engine warms up, however, the internal resistance of the sensor will decrease and cause a similar decrease in the reference voltage signal. Therefore, the ECM will then interpret this reduced voltage signal as signifying a warm engine. The coolant and oil temperature sensors range will vary between various engine/vehicle manufacturers, but normally this is between −10 and 300°F. At the low temperature end of the scale, the resistance of the sensor tends to be about 100,000 Ω, while at the high range its internal resistance would have dropped to only 70 Ω. Figure 11-48 illustrates how a temperature of 150°F (65.5°C), which is an analog signal, is converted from analog to digital within the A/D converter. In Fig. 11-48 we see a typical upward-moving sine wave which is representative of the changing voltage output signal from the oil or coolant sensor as the engine temperature increases because of the decreasing resistance value of the sensor. At a temperature of 150°F, the sensor analog output voltage is sampled by the A/D converter, which converts values into a *binary number value* or code.

The A/D controller uses the binary code and refers to a *look-up* table that is stored within the computer memory to determine the equivalent temperature in °F

FIGURE 11-48 Coolant temperature versus analog output voltage signal.

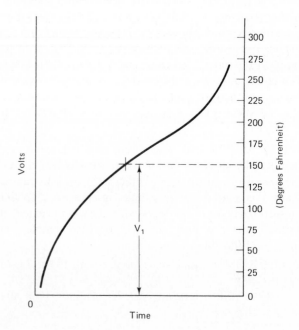

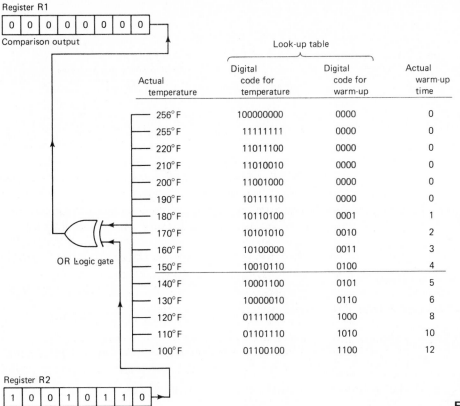

Register R1

| 0 | 0 | 0 | 0 | 0 | 0 | 0 | 0 |

Comparison output

Look-up table

Actual temperature	Digital code for temperature	Digital code for warm-up	Actual warm-up time
256°F	100000000	0000	0
255°F	11111111	0000	0
220°F	11011100	0000	0
210°F	11010010	0000	0
200°F	11001000	0000	0
190°F	10111110	0000	0
180°F	10110100	0001	1
170°F	10101010	0010	2
160°F	10100000	0011	3
150°F	10010110	0100	4
140°F	10001100	0101	5
130°F	10000010	0110	6
120°F	01111000	1000	8
110°F	01101110	1010	10
100°F	01100100	1100	12

OR Logic gate

Register R2

| 1 | 0 | 0 | 1 | 0 | 1 | 1 | 0 |

MSB — LSB

Input from sensor

FIGURE 11–49 Temperature look-up table, OR logic gate, and registers.

or °C from this series of binary numbers. The 150°F voltage reading from the sensor is placed in a temporary storage register such as R2 (see Fig. 11–49). The CPU controller then goes through a comparison check of the stored binary code numbers equivalent to 150°F on a bit-by-bit basis using an OR logic gate (see the section "Logic Circuits" in this chapter) and then stores the comparisons in another register—R1 in this example. Basically, an OR logic gate has the capability to output a binary number of 1 if either of the inputs to the OR gate is 1. If, however, both inputs are 1 or 0, the output will be the binary number 0! When the binary codes are the same, each comparison, bit by bit, will produce an output code from the OR gate that has a 0 in each bit position in register R1.

When this occurs, the controller is alerted that the correct temperature code has been located in the stored *look-up* table. Once matched, the controller uses the warm-up time code in the look-up table that corresponds to the 150°F code. For 150°F, the digital code is 10010110, which in this example represents a warm-up time of 4 minutes.

Since the oil or engine coolant temperature sensor is used to calculate the control parameters for most of the other ECM-controlled systems, this digital produced number through the A/D converter becomes critical to successful operation of the engine. In Fig. 11–49 we have only shown temperature changes of 10°F. In reality, the computer look-up table would be constructed in multiples of 1°F changes, so that very close control of the engine fuel and ignition systems can be maintained under all conditions of operation. Figure 11–50 illustrates just how the analog-to-digital (A/D) converter would output the temperature reading based on the analog signal, which has been converted to binary number codes that are

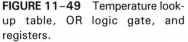

	Bit no.	Logic level	Decimal value	Decimal temperature
Analog/digital converter	7	1	128	128°F
	6	0	64	0
	5	0	32	0
	4	1	16	16
	3	0	8	0
	2	1	4	4
	1	1	2	2
	0	0	1	0
				150°F

FIGURE 11–50 Analog-to-digital converter binary-to-decimal number 8-bit temperature scale.

equivalent to the 150 °F oil or coolant temperature. This example is similar to the way that many of the other sensor signals would be received and converted to a digital signal for control of the engine systems.

DIGITAL-TO-ANALOG CONVERTER

It is often necessary to employ a DAC (digital-to-analog converter) in the computer system to convert binary signals (numbers) from the computer into analog output voltages that are proportional to the binary number that has been encoded in the actual input signals. DACs are available in a wide variety of versions. However, one of the most widely used type of DAC has 8 bit inputs and a 0- to 5-V output range to match the sensors used on the engine and vehicle. The 0 output represents an OFF signal, and the 5 represents an ON signal.

Figure 11–51 illustrates a typical DAC using a parallel input interface to examine and control an 8-bit DAC, together with two operational amplifiers, which are also discussed in this chapter. The 8 bits are written into the parallel interface and stored in what are commonly called data latches. The digital output from each latch is always zero if the bit is low and 5 V if the bit is high (1).

The first op amp in this simplified system is known as a summing amp with a gain (output) of $-R_f/R_i$. The second op-amp is designed for a gain of -1, which indicates that it is, in fact, only an inverter. The net result of using these two op-amps is to scale each individual bit of the parallel interface by a predetermined factor, and then to add the resultant voltages together. The easiest way to understand this DAC is to give an actual example and calculate it to its conclusion.

Familiarize yourself first with the diagram shown in Fig. 11–51. Then consider the following situation. Suppose that for instructional purposes we assume that only bit 0 is high, and the other 7 bits are low. Then what kind of analog output might we have at the V_{out} terminal?

EXAMPLE 11–1

Bit 0 is high, and all others are low. Therefore,

$$V_{out} = 5 \text{ V} \left[1\left(\frac{1}{256}\right) + 0\left(\frac{1}{128}\right) + 0\left(\frac{1}{64}\right) + \cdots + 0\left(\frac{1}{2}\right) \right]$$

Therefore, V_{out} now equals (5/256) carried to $V_{out} = 0.0195$ V.

EXAMPLE 11–2

Bits 0 and 7 are high, all others are low. Therefore,

$$V_{out} = 5 \text{ V} \left[1\left(\frac{1}{256}\right) + 0\left(\frac{1}{128}\right) + 0\left(\frac{1}{64}\right) + \cdots + 1\left(\frac{1}{2}\right) \right]$$

carried to $V_{out} = (645/256)$. Therefore, $V_{out} = 2.5195$ V.

Although you would expect the output voltage from the DAC system to be in analog form (wavy sine), because the voltage levels would be output at constantly changing discrete signals of the high and low values (ON and OFF) reaction within the DAC, the actual output would still be a digital signal, similar to that shown in Fig. 11–52. This results from the binary number at the input increas-

FIGURE 11–51 DAC (digital-to-analog converter) system.

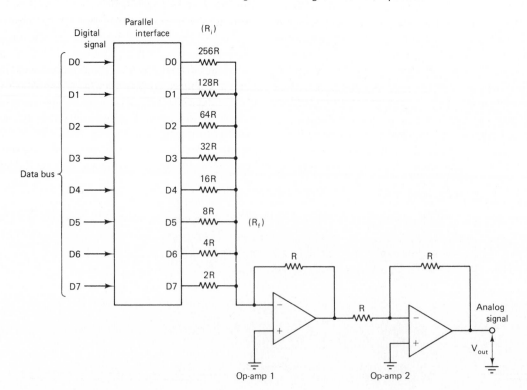

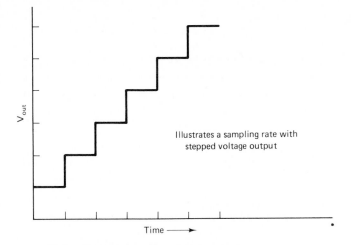

FIGURE 11-52 Typical stepped output voltage from a DAC (digital-to-analog converter) system to form a nearly analog voltage signal.

ing in graduations of one bit at a time from its minimum to its maximum value so that it provides a total possible combination of 256 different voltage levels. With this many levels and although the output appears in step form, if we were to draw an average value line through all of these stepped signals, the result would closely resemble an "analog voltage signal output." If the sampling rate were less than 256 different levels, the analog voltage output would not be as smooth as that shown in Fig. 11–52.

DATA AND ADDRESS BUSES

Figure 11–19 represented the computer unit in its simplest form, namely that of a block diagram representing the input and output devices, the computer memory, the CPU (central processing unit), and the input/output in-

terface. Within the various sections of the computer, these devices are all interconnected by signal wires or lines commonly known either as *address buses* or *data buses* and which are similar to the copper wires used in a typical automotive electrical system. The difference is that the buses are etched or burned onto a chip by the use of laser technology and assembled into a circuit board to form a complete system.

These buses can be as thin as 1.5 microns (0.00006 in.) in size. Figure 11–53 illustrates both the address and data buses in a typical microcomputer and shows how they interconnect the CPU with the memory and input/output interface components. The bus transmits information in the form of 0 V dc or 5 V dc signals.

When the CPU requests information from memory, it does so by calling up these data from their allocated memory address. This information is drawn from either the PROM or ROM unit, which are both hardwired (memory is nonchangeable), or from the RAM memory, which is updated continually during computer operation as the various sensors relay changing data to the system.

PROM, ROM, and RAM are described in greater detail later in this section. PROM means (programmable read-only memory), ROM, (read-only memory), and RAM (random access memory). Each address in ROM and PROM memory stores fixed data, while accessing an address in RAM results in the latest up-to-date information being received from the various sensor systems while the engine/vehicle is running. The address of each location in memory never changes, but can be likened to that of a mailbox.

Keep in mind, however that although the address may not change, the contents will change when retained data (picking up mail) are removed and when new data (new mail) is inserted. Each address with its character bits of

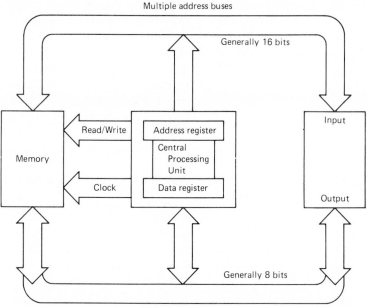

FIGURE 11-53 Data and address buses within a typical on-board ECM (electronic control module) circuit.

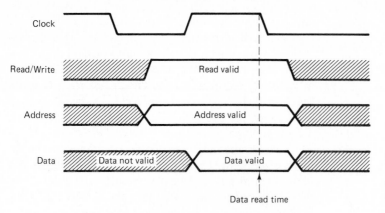

FIGURE 11–54 Typical timing diagram for CPU (central processing unit) memory read and write functions. The clock provides the synchronization for the system.

information is stored in the CPU as a binary number in a temporary data latch type memory called a *register*. The size of the register depends on the computer design, but it can be either an 8-, 16-, 32-, or 64-bit system. For example, if the address register contains a 16-bit system, the CPU has direct access, when required, to 65,536 memory locations or addresses, a total arrived at by taking the binary base 2 system to a power of 16.

Informational data are sent *to* the CPU via the various data buses, while information signals on the address buses come *from* the CPU and are sent to the various devices attached to the bus. Therefore, information signals on the data bus can be sent or received at the CPU by the data register, which in effect makes the data bus capable of two-way information flow. The address bus is only capable of single direction flow. The data bus carries information to the microprocessor for processing and sends out processed signals and information to other devices in the system. The number of bus wires used relates to the width of the data word. Microprocessors are defined in terms of their data bus: for example, 4-bit, 8-bit, 16-bit, 32-bit, and so on.

Keep in mind, however, that although the data bus is capable of transmitting information signals in both directions, it can only do this in one direction at a time. For the memory storage system to know in what direction the information data signals are flowing, the CPU is designed to provide a control signal that indicates whether the information is to be read from or written into memory.

This control signal goes through a timing system that appears as shown in Fig. 11–54. Any time that the read/write signal is high (1), the CPU is requesting or reading information from a specifically accessed memory location. If, on the other hand, the read/write signal is low (0), the CPU is trying to insert (write) information into a particular memory address location. The action illustrated in Fig. 11–54 can be listed as follows:

1. The computer is commanded to fetch (read) data from a specific memory address: for example, location 9.
2. The CPU activates the read/write signal to the high (1) level to alert the memory for a read rather than a write

cycle of operation, as shown in the second line in the figure.
3. The specific address, for example, location 9 (binary number 1001), is placed on the address bus or on the third line down in the figure.
4. When memory location 9 recognizes that its address has been signaled, it then places a copy of its mail (data or instruction) on the data bus as shown on the bottom line.
5. Although this information is extracted very quickly, to ensure that the information/data does have time to receive and relay this signal, the CPU will momentarily delay its action. Then the CPU will open the necessary logic gate circuitry between the data bus and the CPU data register to lock address 9 data into the CPU. The CPU clock (timing signal) tells the memory when it can take and release control of the data bus. This read cycle is terminated when the clock signal switches from high (1) to low (0) within the time frame that the read signal is valid.

MICROCOMPUTER CONTROL

Voltage signals generated by the system control section allows the computer to perform its designed task related to the CPU (central processing unit) and memory and input/output (I/O) interface (Fig. 11–53). The control section therefore becomes the coordinating device within the system. It does this by generating a signal through its *clock signal generating circuitry* shown in Fig. 11–55, which synchronizes all of the ongoing computer devices to ensure that they output their voltage signals in an order and sequence that will not interfere with one another.

FIGURE 11–55 Microcomputer clock signal generator circuitry.

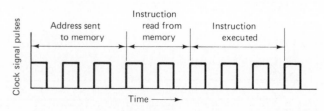

System Layout. Figure 11–56 illustrates a typical system layout for a minicomputer in line form, while Fig. 11–57 shows the same components but in an acceptable block form, similar to how it would appear inside an assembled minicomputer on a vehicle.

CPU (CENTRAL PROCESSING UNIT)

The brain or heart of the minicomputer is the CPU, which contains the following devices:

1. Control section
2. Arithmetic–logic section
3. Register section

Figure 11–58 shows how these devices are interconnected within the CPU.

Control Section

Within the control section (Fig. 11–59) of the CPU are the control signal generating circuitry and a command decoder. Program instructions from the computer memory are accessed by the control system as needed and are temporarily stored in the command register, where they are then decoded by the operation decoder. From here, signals are sent via the buses to the relevant parts of the microcomputer to carry out the necessary action. These signals are timed by the control circuit generator,

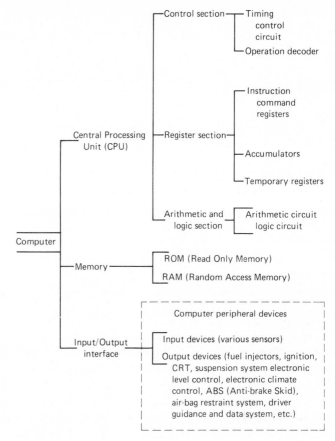

FIGURE 11–56 General arrangement of the on-board electronic control unit system.

FIGURE 11–57 Typical layout and arrangement of operating components within the on-board computer system.

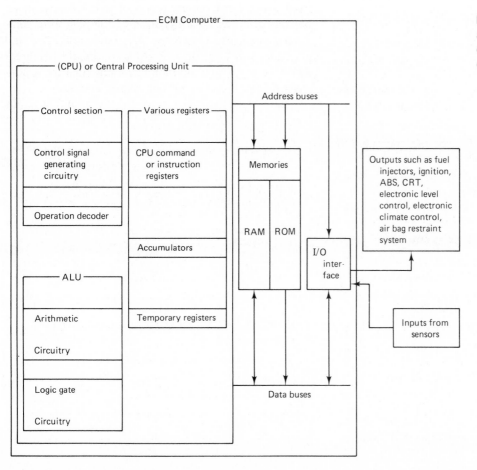

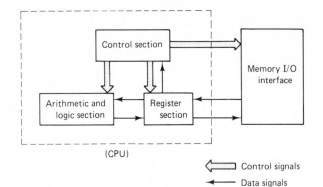

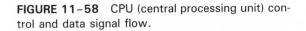

FIGURE 11–58 CPU (central processing unit) control and data signal flow.

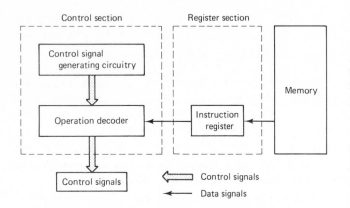

FIGURE 11–59 On-board computer control section data and control signal flow arrangement.

with the control signals performing the following operations:

1. Arithmetic calculations
2. Relaying data from one area of the computer to another
3. If necessary, jumping to (accessing) another instruction during running of a program
4. Inputting or outputting data to or from the microcomputer
5. Stopping computer operations at any time

In summation, the control section or unit of the CPU is designed to direct the flow of information between the memory and the arithmetic–logic unit, as well as between the CPU and the input/output devices. Therefore, we can safely say that it coordinates the computer operation.

Arithmetic–Logic Section

This section of the computer actually carries out the processing of informational data under the guidance of the control section, as was discussed above. Within the solid-state devices of the arithmetic and logic section are the various logic gates such as the AND, OR, NOT, NAND,

and NOR systems. All of the addition, multiplication, square root extraction, and any other necessary calculations are performed here.

The sequence of events involved in doing these calculations is that the information from the memory or input/output interface is temporarily stored within the register section. When this information is required, the logic section withdraws the data from these temporary registers or accumulators, where it then sends the data to either the arithmetic or logic circuitry. Any additional calculations are then carried out, and the results of these are sent to the relevant accumulators: to the memory (RAM) or to the input/output interfaces.

Logical operations involve the comparison of two items of data to determine whether or not they are equal. If not, the computer (CPU) determines which is larger. This action is shown in schematic form in Fig. 11–60.

Computer memory consists of stacks of registers or rows of circuits, each having one output that can either be ON or OFF (+ 5 or 0 V). A register therefore can hold any number that has first been converted into a row of ON/OFFs, that is, a row of bits. The majority of microcomputer operations are simply transfers of data from one register to another, or sometimes between registers of slightly different kinds. Consequently, computer memory (groups of registers) can be made up of stacks of registers known as RAMs (random access memory) which store data only as long as they are supplied with electric battery power. The RAM system can be considered as the scratchpad of the operating computer since it can be written into, read, rewritten, and erased by rewriting. Since RAM is continually being updated during engine operation, its information is consistently up to date regarding sensor operation.

Latest technology offers SRAM (staticram), whereby bits of data are held in memory as a state in a flip-flop

FIGURE 11–60 On-board computer data signal flow paths within the arithmetic–logic sections of the CPU.

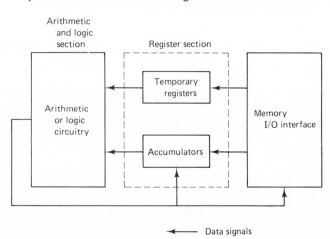

circuitry (see Fig. 11–44). DRAM or dynamic random access memory is a circuit where bits of data are held as charges in capacitors. Consequently, DRAM must be continually updated or the data will be lost. ROMs (read-only memory) is a hardwired nonchangeable series of registers that are filled with data at the factory level and cannot be changed. PROMs or programmable read-only memory can be programmed by the user. However, the most recent versions are called EPROM (electrically erasable read-only memory) or EEPROM (electrically erasable programmable read-only memory). Obviously, being able to change the register data has given the computer expanded capabilities to suit changing operating conditions.

Register Section

The register section is designed to store data or programs temporarily until they are required for use by the arithmetic or logic sections or by the control section (Fig. 11–61). Several basic types of registers are used, which are the *instruction registers*, address register, storage register, and *temporary registers* (accumulators), which store data.

Before the CPU can process a command, it must first break the command information into two distinct parts. First, it must advise the system to add, multiply, or compare within the instruction register, and then it must give the address of the data to be accessed to the address register.

The storage register temporarily stores data that has been taken from memory immediately prior to processing. The accumulation of temporary registers also temporarily store the results of ongoing arithmetic calculations. Therefore, when each operation or addition, subtraction, and so on, are completed, the answers are accumulated into this particular register.

The three main parts of the computer—the memory, the arithmetic–logic section, and the registers—all work together to process a desired request of information data effectively.

DATA/INSTRUCTION PROCESSING

When the computer is asked for information, the control unit initiates the necessary activity within the computer. This is often referred to as a *machine cycle*, and it involves two major operations.

1. An *I* or instruction cycle
   a. Withdrawn or pulled from memory by the control unit is the next instruction to be performed.
   b. Decoding of this instruction/data by the control unit.
   c. Directing and inserting the necessary action into the instruction register by the control unit.
   d. Inserting the necessary instruction into the address register to indicate where the desired data are located by the control unit.
2. An *E* or execution cycle
   e. Information stored in the address register is used by the control unit to retrieve data from main memory and insert them into the storage register within the arithmetic–logic unit (ALU).
   f. The control unit directs the ALU to perform the required operation based on the information withdrawn from the instruction register.
   g. The ALU carries out the desired command.
   h. The result of this action computed within the ALU is then transferred to the accumulator by the control unit.

Figure 11–62 illustrates graphically just what the sequence of events is in the two main steps of the machine cycle, explained in steps 1 and 2 above (a through h). Note that the upper half of the circle represents the *I* (instruction) part of the process of steps a through d, while the lower half represents the *E* (execution) part of the cycle, steps e through h.

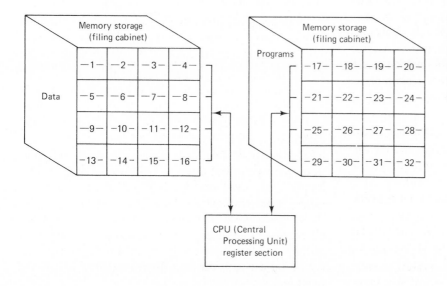

FIGURE 11–61 The CPU (central processing unit) register section can access memory (filing cabinet), and data can be read from or written into a specific memory location by calling up a specific address (drawer number).

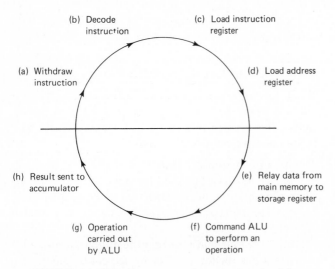

FIGURE 11-62 Sequence of events involved in a computer machine cycle.

(a) Withdraw instruction
(b) Decode instruction
(c) Load instruction register
(d) Load address register
(e) Relay data from main memory to storage register
(f) Command ALU to perform an operation
(g) Operation carried out by ALU
(h) Result sent to accumulator

SENSORS

Basic Sensor Arrangement

All sensors used on cars and medium- and heavy-duty trucks are devices that are designed to convert energy from one medium to another. Sensors are activated either through heat being applied to them or by heat being reduced, while others are designed to respond to a change in pressure. Current vehicle sensors are designed to operate on an input voltage signal from the 12-V battery system. However, because of each sensor's individual operating characteristics, a sensor's output voltage signal is designed to operate in a range of from 0 to 5 V.

Some of the more common signals that need to be monitored on gasoline- or diesel-powered trucks are such items as throttle position, exhaust oxygen content (air/fuel ratio), air inlet temperature, air inlet pressure (turbocharger boost), coolant temperature, oil temperature, oil pressure, and so on. Sensors convert a portion of these various energies into a form that can be used by a signal processor. Because of changing engine/vehicle operating conditions and the corresponding changing output of the sensor, a signal processor is required to monitor this change on a continuous basis. The ideal is for a stoichiometric air/fuel ratio of 14.7:1 to be maintained on all gasoline engines under all operating conditions of closed-loop control.

NOTE: Closed-loop control is the condition that exists when the engine is at operating temperature and the on-board computer is controlling the air/fuel ratio as close to stoichiometric as possible, based on the various feedback signals that it receives from the different sensors.

Figure 11-63 illustrates a simplified diagram of the basic sensor measurement system, where the sensor itself absorbs either a heat or pressure signal from a monitored engine condition. The sensor then converts this signal into an electrical output and relays it to the signal processor.

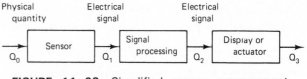

FIGURE 11-63 Simplified sensor measurement operational system.

Within the signal processor, the sensor signal is amplified so that it can be sent to an analog or digital display, or alternatively, it may be used to activate a specific actuator on the engine or vehicle.

Signal processing can be accomplished with either analog devices or digital devices, both of which were discussed earlier (see Figs. 11-10 and 11-11). Analog signals resemble the human voice and have a continuous waveform signal, while a digital signal forms a series of boxes to indicate either an ON or OFF voltage condition.

Analog signal processing employs the use of amplifiers, filters, adders, multipliers, and other components, while digital signal processing employs the use of logic gates. In addition, digital processing requires the use of counters, binary adders, and microcomputers.

A simplified example of an analog signal is that generated from a speedometer sensor that changes continuously as the vehicle speed increases or decreases. An example of an applied digital signal that is either ON or OFF can be related to the opening and closing of a car door. When open, the interior light comes on; therefore, the signal is at its maximum of 12 V. If, on the other hand, the door is closed, the signal is at zero volts.

Types of Sensors

Various engine/vehicle sensors are described within this chapter. However, the physical operating characteristics of each unit depends on the following design types:

1. Two-wire design
2. Three-wire design
3. Pulse-counter design

Each of these operating types is illustrated and explained below so that an understanding of just how various sensors operate can be more clearly understood.

1. *Two-wire design.* Figure 11-64 illustrates the two-wire design type of sensor, which is basically a variable resistor in series with a known-fixed resistor contained within the ECM. Sensors that use the two-wire type of design are the CTS (coolant temperature sensor), OTS, FTS, MAT (manifold air temperature), and OAT (outside air temperature) units. All of these sensors operate on a varying resistance, since their resistance varies inversely with temperature (thermistor principle).

Since most sensors in use in automotive applications use a base voltage input of 5 V (some use 8 V), the value of the variable resistor can be determined from the base voltage along with the known voltage drop across the fixed resistor.

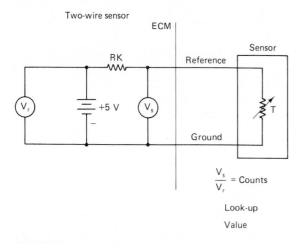

FIGURE 11–64 Basic arrangement of a two-wire design sensor unit.

$$\frac{V_s}{V_r} = \text{Counts}$$

Look-up Value

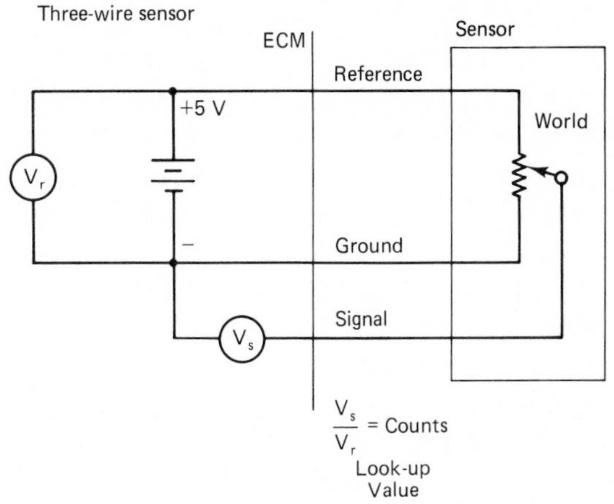

FIGURE 11–65 Basic arrangement of a three-wire design sensor unit.

$$\frac{V_s}{V_r} = \text{Counts}$$

Look-up Value

2. *Three-wire design.* Figure 11–65 illustrates the three-wire design type of sensor arrangement, which is commonly in use in TPS (throttle position sensors), MAP (manifold absolute pressure), and BARO (barometric pressure sensors). These types of sensors have a reference voltage, a ground, and a variable wiper, with the lead coming off the wiper being the actual signal feed to the ECM. A change in the wiper's position will automatically change the signal voltage being sent back to the ECM.

3. *Pulse counters.* Figure 11–66 illustrates the basic operation of a pulse counter. Sensors relying on this type of counting system are typically the VSS (vehicle speed sensor), the rpm or engine speed sensor, which could be a crankshaft or camshaft-sensed Hall-effect type on various makes of vehicles, and also the distributor reference sensor on vehicles employing this style of ignition system.

Consider, for example, that many gasoline-powered cars and light-duty trucks today employ a distributorless ignition system. These systems rely on a crankshaft- or camshaft-mounted sensor, or both, to pick up a gear position, usually through the use of a raised tooth on the gear wheel. The resultant voltage signal produced is relayed by the sensor to the ECM, which then determines when to trigger the ignition pulse signal to the respective spark plug. On heavy-duty truck engines such as those employing the Detroit Diesel Corporation series 60 four-stroke-cycle DDEC engines, an electronic TRS (timing reference sensor) extends through an opening in the engine gear case and is positioned to provide a small air gap between it and the teeth of the crankshaft timing gear. The TRS sends a voltage signal to the ECM, which uses it to determine fuel injector solenoid operation/timing. This same engine employs a SRS (synchronous reference sensor) that is mounted to the rear of the engine gear case, where it is positioned to provide a small air gap between it and the rear of a bull gear driven from the crankshaft gear. The SRS sends a voltage signal to the ECM, which uses this information to determine engine speed.

The speed at which sensor signals are transmitted and

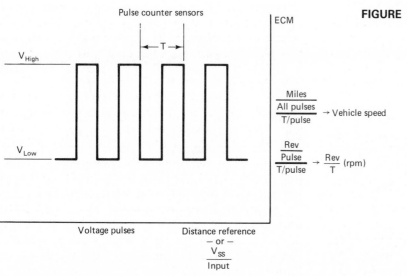

FIGURE 11–66 Pulse counter mode of operation.

$$\frac{\text{Miles}}{\text{All pulses}} \cdot \frac{}{\text{T/pulse}} \rightarrow \text{Vehicle speed}$$

$$\frac{\text{Rev}}{\text{Pulse}} \cdot \frac{}{\text{T/pulse}} \rightarrow \frac{\text{Rev}}{\text{T}} \text{ (rpm)}$$

monitored by the ECM microprocessor are usually updated a given amount of times in a second. Update rates for the following typical heavy-duty truck sensor inputs would be as follows:

1. Road speed limit status = once per second.
2. Road speed = 10 times per second. Diagnostic counts range from 0 to 255.
3. Cruise control switch status = 10 times per second.
4. Cruise control set speed = once every 10 seconds.
5. Cruise control high set limit = on request only.
6. Cruise control low set limit = on request only.
7. Percentage of throttle depression = 10 times per second. This value is the percent of opening of the throttle as determined from the throttle position sensor. Range is 0 to 100%.
8. Percent of engine load = 10 times per second, which is calculated from engine rpm and torque.
9. Engine oil pressure = once per second.
10. Turbo boost pressure gauge = once per second.
11. Barometric pressure = once per second.
12. Coolant temperature = once per second.
13. Coolant level = once every 10 seconds. This is an indication of coolant level in digital counts. Range is 0 to 255 counts.
14. Engine governor droop = on request only.
15. Engine horsepower rating = on request only.
16. Battery voltage = once per second.
17. Fuel temperature = once per second.
18. Engine oil temperature = once per second.
19. Fuel rate = five times per second.
20. PTO (power take off) set speed = once every 10 seconds. PTO counts is a digital representation of the PTO sensor voltage. Range 0 to 255 counts.
21. Idle set speed = on request only.
22. Rated engine speed = on request only.
23. Engine speed = 10 times per second.
24. Total fuel used = on request only.
25. Oil level is displayed as a percentage. Range 0% (empty) to 100% (full).

For those on request sensor values, the nominal response time in current ECMs used in heavy-duty trucks is 100 milliseconds.

Oil Pressure Sensor Operation

For purposes of understanding just how a typical sensor operates in a heavy-duty electronically controlled diesel truck engine, let's consider the oil pressure sensor as one example. The sensor outputs an analog signal, with the sensor resistance changing as a result of engine oil pressure changes. This oil pressure and sensor resistance change, in turn, creates changes in the sensor–resistor–battery circuit current flow. Any current increase will similarly create an increase in the voltage value across the resistor. Consequently, during engine operation, any oil pressure change is reflected by a sensor voltage output

that the analog-to-digital subsystem will process accordingly.

Consider that the oil pressure sensor used on the Detroit Diesel Electronic Control system has a sensor range between 0 and 65 psi (0 to 448 kPa) with a sensor output update rate of once per second and a resolution of 0.5 psi/bit. During engine operation, if the sensor failed, the check engine light would illuminate on the dash, while if low oil pressure at the current engine speed is sensed, the check engine light will illuminate and the ECM would power-down the engine. Unsafe oil pressure would result in the SEL (stop engine light) illuminating, followed 30 seconds later by an ECM-actuated engine shutdown procedure. If the engine is equipped with an SEO (stop engine override), the shutdown sequence can be delayed by holding the SEO button in for a couple more times only, after which time the ECM shuts the engine off.

For ease of instruction, let's assume that the voltage across the oil pressure sensor is converted from an analog to a digital signal by an A/D converter in the form of a VCO (voltage-controlled oscillator), where the sensor voltage varies from 0 to 10 V. As you know from earlier information, the digital system is a square-wave signal typical of that shown in Figure 11–66. The amplitude (voltage strength) changes of the digital signals would have very fast ON/OFF reactions, varying from 0 to 5 V, with 0 V representing a logic number 0 and the 5-V amplitude representing a logic number 1.

Figure 11–67 illustrates a simplified system that represents this oil pressure sensor function. If a scale is selected to represent a change of engine oil pressure of from 0 to 65 psi (0 to 448 kPa), a change in voltage from 0 to 10 V can be used to duplicate/scale this change in oil pressure. If we assume that the VCO's output oscillates back and forth between 0 and 10 V based on changing engine oil pressure, the frequency of the voltage signal (how often it happens) in our scaled example would vary between 400 and 1000 Hz (400 to 1000 times a second) based on the 0- to 10-V input signal to the VCO. A change in voltage from 0 to 10 V would cause a change in frequency of 600 (= 1000 − 400) Hz in our example. The voltage output of the VCO is connected to one input of an AND logic gate. See Figs. 11–23 through 11–26 for a description of an AND gate and its truth table combinations.

Due to the operation of the AND logic gate shown to the immediate right of the VCO in Fig. 11–67, the output of the VCO is connected to one input of the AND gate, while the other input is held to a logic level 1. This results in the output of the AND gate being a reproduction of the VCO's output. But when the second input from the VCO is at logic 0, the output of the AND gate would be a steady logic 0. Therefore, by actively controlling the logic levels on the second input, the VCO's output pulse can be gated through for a given amount of

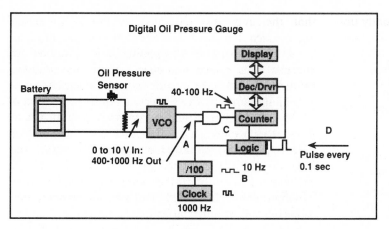

FIGURE 11–67 Simplified electronic oil pressure sensor system. (*Reproduced with permission,* © *1990, Society of Automotive Engineers, Inc., Warrendale, PA.*)

time, then blocked, then gated through again, with the process being repeated over and over.

For scaling purposes, let's consider that when a zero engine oil pressure exists, we will also have zero volts across the oil pressure sensor resistor. At 0 lb oil pressure we will equate this to a frequency of 400 Hz. With the engine running and the oil pump creating 65 psi (448 kPa) of pressure, the voltage value is 10 V and the frequency is equivalent to a VCO output of 1000 Hz. If we also assume that the engine oil pressure rises linearly (gradual straight line increase), there is a direct relationship created between the oil pressure, the voltage, and the frequency. Since our scale runs between 400 and 1000 Hz to represent 0 to 65 psi (0 to 448 kPa), this means that over the 600-Hz range between these two numbers, we can scale the VCO's output frequency to represent any given oil pressure. For example, based on our graduated scale, a 32.5-psi (224-kPa) oil pressure would correspond to a signal of 5 V and a frequency halfway between 400 and 1000, which would be 700 Hz. Therefore, as you can see, it is quite easy to convert a given oil pressure at the sensor into a voltage input at the VCO, along with a frequency output from the VCO. The engine oil pressure sensor used on the DDEC system on DDC's 71, 92, and series 60 heavy-duty truck diesel engines have an update rate of once per second; therefore, when the oil pressure is 65 psi (448 kPa), the VCO will be outputting a signal every second that is representative of this pressure. In our descriptive example, this would be equivalent to the VCO outputting 1000 square-wave pulses (digitally shaped) per second. For better resolution or monitoring of the changing oil pressure system, we could choose to set the logic gate up so that it is open for 0.1 second. This can be achieved by directing a signal to the second AND gate input, which has a logic 1 period equal to 0.1 second. We can ensure this operating condition by employing a square-wave oscillating clock with a fixed frequency of 1000 Hz. The output can then be directed through a series of logic ICs (integrated circuits) that effectively divide the input count by 10, then by a further 10. Reference to Fig. 11–67 indicates this clock system identified as /100 above

the 1000-Hz clock. This means that the 1000-Hz signal is divided by 100 to produce a square output wave with a 10-Hz frequency. Consequently, the signal would have a time period of 1/10 or 0.1 second.

If the logic gate pulses open for 0.1 second, it is closed, then opened once again on a continuing basis; then every time the logic gate is opened, 100 square waves will pass through as long as the oil pressure remains at 65 psi (448 kPa). If the engine speed is reduced, or the oil pressure were to drop to 32.5 psi (224 kPa), the VCO frequency would be reduced from 1000 Hz to 700 Hz. This means that in a 0.1-second period, only 70 square-wave pulses will pass through the logic gate. When the 10-Hz signal is a logic 1 input, the VCO's output will pass through the AND gate. When the 10-Hz signal is logic 0, the AND gate's output is logic 0. Therefore, when the oil pressure is 65 psi (448 kPa), the internal digital clock counter will count 100 pulses in 0.1 second. At a pressure of 32.5 psi (224 kPa), it will count 70 pulses every 0.1 second. With zero oil pressure, the counter will register 40 pulses every 0.1 second. The clock counter's output is then input to a decoder/driver IC to drive a digital display that allows the truck driver to visually determine the engine oil pressure condition at a glance. Generally, the output of the decoder/driver is a latched output. What this means is that the output value changes only when a latch pulse, shown as item D in Fig. 11–67, is input to a latch input.

Electronic Foot Pedal Assembly

A unique feature of the DDEC system is that the foot throttle pedal assembly consists of a small potentiometer (variable resistor) rather than direct mechanical linkage as is found on the non-DDEC system. This throttle arrangement is often referred to as a "drive by wire" system, since there is no mechanical linkage, only electrical wires to transmit the position of the throttle to the ECM (electronic control module). The potentiometer is electrically connected to the ECM (electronic control module). Figure 11–68 illustrates the EFPA (electronic foot pedal assembly), which is easy to install and requires

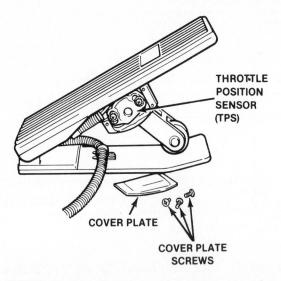

THROTTLE
POSITION
SENSOR
(TPS)

COVER PLATE

COVER PLATE
SCREWS

FIGURE 11-68 Throttle position sensor cover plate removal on the DDEC system. (*Courtesy of Detroit Diesel Corporation.*)

no throttle linkage adjustment because of the electrical connection to the ECM. The output voltage from the potentiometer at the foot pedal is proportional to the travel of the pedal; mechanical stops calibrated by the EFPA manufacturer limit the open and closed throttle positions and thereby the voltage signal from the potentiometer. No adjustment is required with this assembly unless the potentiometer requires replacement.

The throttle position sensor shown in Fig. 11-68 contains a potentiometer (variable resistor) that is designed to output a voltage in direct response to the depression of the pedal. This sensor is designed to receive a 5-V input reference signal from the ECM. The output voltage, however, is totally dependent on how far down the pedal is pushed for any given condition. When the throttle pedal is at its normal idle position, its voltage output is low; therefore, the signal sent to the ECM advises the system of its relative position, and the solenoid on each fuel injector is activated for a short pulse-width time. This results in a small delivery of fuel to each cylinder and therefore a low idle speed. As the operator pushes the throttle pedal down, the voltage signal from the sensor will increase, and when the ECM recognizes this voltage change, it will send out a signal to activate the solenoid on each fuel injector for a longer pulse-width period. This results in a greater amount of fuel being delivered to the cylinders and therefore a higher speed. The actual quantity of fuel delivered, and therefore the horsepower produced by the engine, also depend on the engine coolant temperature, the turbocharger boost pressure, and both the oil pressure and temperature sensor readings. Each of these sensors is continually relaying a voltage signal back to the ECM, which then computes the injector pulse-width signal.

Electronic Foot Pedal Adjustment. Should it become necessary to remove a faulty or damaged EFPA

(electronic foot pedal assembly), extreme caution should be exercised to ensure that the routing and clamping locations of the wire before disassembly is carefully noted and marked. Most DDEC-equipped highway vehicles use a Williams Controls electronic foot pedal assembly, which is manufactured by the Precision Controls Division of Dana Corporation located in Portland, Oregon. Should it become necessary to replace the EFPA potentiometer, refer to Figures 11-68 and 11-69, which illustrate the location of the potentiometer assembly within the EFP assembly. Ensure that the ignition switch is OFF before attempting to replace the throttle position sensor/potentiometer and its wire harness.

Procedure

1. Loosen and remove the wire harness cable clamp screw.
2. Loosen and remove the three cover plate screws shown in Fig. 11-68.
3. Remove the two screws that hold the sensor/potentiometer in place, which are shown in Fig. 11-69.
4. With the damaged sensor/potentiometer and its wire harness removed from the EFP assembly, position the new sensor/potentiometer with its flat side up or toward the sensor cover. Carefully press the potentiometer onto its support shaft, matching the cutouts in the shaft with the drive tangs on the actual potentiometer.
5. Apply hand pressure only until the potentiometer is bottomed in the housing and install the new retaining screws and washers hand-tight to hold the unit in position.
6. Manually grasp and rotate the potentiometer CCW (counterclockwise) as far as possible, then tighten the screws to 10 to 20 in.-lb of torque.
7. Install a new rubber grommet ahead of the wire cable clamp, which will ensure that dirt, water, and so on, cannot enter the EFP assembly.
8. Replace the sensor/potentiometer cover and three

FIGURE 11-69 DDEC throttle position sensor adjustment. (*Courtesy of Detroit Diesel Corporation.*)

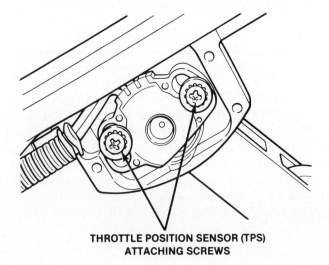

THROTTLE POSITION SENSOR (TPS)
ATTACHING SCREWS

screws, which are shown in Fig. 11–68. Tighten these screws to between 10 and 20 in.-lb of torque.

9. Install new cable clamps and screws and take care that the wire harness is routed exactly the same as the original one was. Tighten the retaining screws to 34 to 45 in.-lb of torque.

10. Carefully install the EFP assembly wiring harness to the vehicle wiring harness. It will now be necessary to recalibrate the potentiometer.

11. Using either the DDEC I DDL (diagnostic data line) or DDEC I or DDEC II DDR (diagnostic data reader shown in Fig. 11–74), connect the reader to the vehicle diagnostic data link.

12. Turn the ignition on.

13. Select the necessary throttle counts position on the diagnostic data reader. Check and record the throttle counts with the EFP assembly in its normal idle position (engine off). Push the throttle pedal manually to its full-throttle position (engine off) and record the number of counts on the DDR reader face.

SERVICE TIP: The proper pedal potentiometer setting should indicate a count reading on the DDR of between 20 and 30 at the idle position. The full throttle position should record a reading of between 200 and 235 counts.

14. If adjustment of the sensor/potentiometer is required, loosen the potentiometer cover (Fig. 11–68), then loosen the retaining screws just enough to allow manual rotation of the potentiometer in a clockwise direction to increase the counts, or in a CCW direction to decrease the counts.

15. Once the proper range number of counts has been recorded on the DDR with the ignition on but the engine stopped, retighten the retaining screws. Recheck the number of counts before installing the EFP cover.

16. Retorque the cover to between 10 and 20 in.-lb of torque.

17. Install the pedal assembly into position in the vehicle, taking special care that the wire harness is not pinched or stretched so that damage could occur during operation.

Coolant Temperature Sensor

The coolant temperature sensor is located on the engine and screwed into one of the top coolant passages to sense the actual operating temperature of the engine. Its exact location will vary between different sizes of engines and also with the make of the vehicle.

The on-board ECU or ECM supplies a 5-V reference voltage signal to the coolant sensor at all times through a resistor located in the ECM. The ECM monitors the voltage signal generated from the coolant temperature sensor, which is, in effect, a thermistor unit. This means that the voltage from the sensor will be high when the engine is cold, and low when the engine is hot. A thermistor is a device that is made of oxidized nickel, cobalt, manganese, iron, and copper that have been fused together. This combination of metals causes the electrical

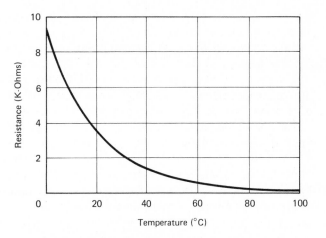

FIGURE 11–70 Negative-temperature thermistor characteristic curve.

resistance of the sensor to vary with a change in temperature. Two types of thermistors are in common use:

1. The negative temperature coefficient type, in which the resistance decreases as the temperature increases. This type is most commonly used in cars and trucks.

2. The positive temperature coefficient type, in which the resistance increases with a temperature rise.

Figure 11–70 illustrates the temperature characteristic of a negative type of thermistor.

Low-coolant temperature will generally produce a high circuit resistance, in the range of 100,000 Ω at coolant temperatures of $-40\,°C/40\,°F$, while high coolant temperatures of $130\,°C/266\,°F$ will exhibit very low circuit resistance, in the region of about 70 Ω. Information from the coolant temperature sensor can be used to advance/retard the ignition timing and alter the injector PWM (pulse width modulation) and timing. Failure of a coolant temperature sensor or circuit will result in a trouble code being set in the memory bank of the on-board computer, as well as illumination of the CEL.

Oil Temperature Sensor

In heavy-duty diesel engine applications that employ electronic control of both fuel injection and governing, an OTS (oil temperature sensor) is used in place of the water temperature sensor. The OTS is usually screwed into the engine main oil gallery along the side of the engine block. The signal received at the ECM from the OTS is used to increase engine idle speed after a cold weather start and faster engine warm-up. The ECM system is designed so that when it receives an oil temperature reading that exceeds preprogrammed specs for 2 seconds or longer, the ECM will initiate a reduction in engine speed and power while illuminating the CEL (check engine light). If the oil temperature exceeds safe levels, the ECM will energize the SEL (stop engine light) and audible warning buzzer. The engine will begin to power down and the operator usually only has 30 seconds to bring the vehicle to a safe stop unless the vehicle is equipped with a temporary manual override button to allow enough time to pull the truck/bus to a safe parking position.

The reason for this is that the oil temperature more truly reflects the actual internal operating conditions of the engine much more closely than the coolant. The oil is used not only for lubrication purposes but acts specifically as a cooling medium. One excellent example of this is the pressurized lube oil that is directed up through a rifle-drilled connecting rod to the underside of the piston crown, or alternatively, the use of oil cooling jets for the same purpose. Detroit Diesel Corporation employ an oil temperature sensor to tell the ECM (computer) the operating temperature of the engine in their DDEC system. The oil temperature sensor operates in the same manner as described for the coolant temperature sensor, in that low oil temperature will create a high resistance value through the sensor, while a warm/hot operating condition will cause the sensor resistance value to decrease. The actual resistance values of both the coolant and oil temperature sensors are almost identical.

Coolant Level Sensor

Detroit Diesel Corporation employs a coolant-level sensor located in the radiator to monitor engine coolant level. Should a low coolant level exist, the sensor signal to the ECM will cause a reduction in engine power and speed (decreases the unit injector solenoid pulse width time). In addition, the ECM will cause the CEL (check engine light) to illuminate; it will cause the SEL (stop engine light) to illuminate and a warning buzzer to sound if the low coolant level is serious enough, such as a ruptured radiator hose. An example of the placement of the coolant level sensor is illustrated in Fig. 11–71 for a radiator used in a heavy-duty class 8 truck.

Fuel Temperature Sensor

A fuel temperature sensor screwed into the fuel filter is used on some heavy-duty diesel engine electronically controlled fuel injection systems. One such example is the fuel temperature sensor found on the DDEC II (Detroit Diesel Electronic Controls second generation) system. This sensor is used to develop a more accurate fuel consumption number. The ECM sends engine fuel consumption information out on a data link for instant recall by the truck driver, or it can also be used for recall later if an on-board recording device is used. The fuel temperature sensor is also a negative temperature thermister type similar to that used with the coolant and oil temperature sensors, in that it will exhibit a high circuit resistance value in ohms when the fuel temperature is low, while it will show a low resistance value when the fuel temperature is warm. It can be checked with a digital ohmmeter in the same way as the coolant and oil temperature units.

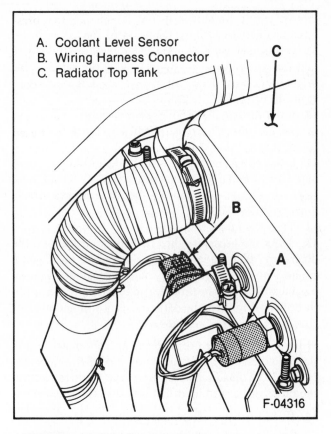

A. Coolant Level Sensor
B. Wiring Harness Connector
C. Radiator Top Tank

F-04316

FIGURE 11–71 Coolant level sensor location. (*Courtesy of Detroit Diesel Corporation.*)

Manifold Air Temperature Sensor

The MAT sensor or ACT (air charge temperature) is very similar in design to the coolant temperature sensor, since it monitors and reacts to the air temperature within the engine intake manifold or air cleaner assembly. It exhibits the same basic resistance values as those stated for the coolant temperature sensor. This sensor also receives a 5-V reference voltage signal from the ECM.

Manifold Absolute Pressure Sensor

The MAP (manifold absolute pressure) sensor measures intake manifold pressure and under certain conditions will also measure barometric conditions. However, many vehicles are equipped with both a MAP and BARO sensor. Its voltage signal, along with that from the MAT sensor, is relayed to the ECU or ECM to determine how long the fuel injector(s) will be energized (held open). The ECU or ECM also uses the MAP sensor signal on gasoline engines to establish both the fuel delivery and ignition timing characteristics. The MAP sensor for a gasoline-injected truck is connected electrically to the ECM. If not threaded directly into the intake manifold, it may have a hose running from the throttle body, which provides a pressure signal to the sensor.

With an opening throttle, the intake manifold pressure will increase. Consequently, more fuel is required. Along with the TPS, the MAP sensor sends a voltage signal to the ECM to increase the fuel injector pulse width in order to deliver more fuel. With a closing throttle condition, the exact opposite happens, and the injector pulse width is shortened to decrease fuel delivery.

Figure 11–72 illustrates the basic design concept used in the MAP sensor, which is constructed using a silicon wafer diaphragm. The majority of passenger cars and light/medium trucks use this type of design, with others using an alumina ceramic capacitor design. The silicon wafer diaphragm type is often referred to as a *silicon capacitor absolute pressure sensor*, or SCAP. Very simply, within the assembled MAP sensor housing, one side of the silicon wafer diaphragm is exposed to intake manifold pressure, while the other side is acted upon by a vacuum. Consequently, a changing throttle position will create a deflection of the silicon wafer diaphragm, and therefore a change in the resistance value of the chip based on this deformation. Within the sensor is a small IC (integrated circuit) that converts this resistance value into a voltage. This signal is relayed to the on-board computer, which uses this signal and others to help determine both the air/fuel ratio (injector pulse width) and ignition advance characteristics for the engine.

Should either a MAP or BARO pressure sensor be suspected of being faulty, a quick check can be made by using a simple hand-operated vacuum pump along with a DVOM (digital volt/ohm meter). By supplying a 5-V reference voltage to the MAP or BARO unit inlet port, the voltage signal can easily be plotted for any given position. Since these sensors are designed to have a linear voltage-pressure curve between 20 and 110 kPa (2.9 and 16 psi), failure to have such a progressive voltage reading indicates a faulty sensor.

FIGURE 11–73 Turbo boost sensor for a DDEC system. (*Courtesy of Detroit Diesel Corporation.*)

Turbocharger Boost Sensor

Medium- and heavy-duty turbocharged diesel truck engines use a TBS (turbocharger boost sensor) located on the intake manifold, which, of course, is on the pressure side of the T/C. Externally, this sensor is very similar in appearance to a MAP (manifold absolute pressure) sensor used on gasoline fuel-injected engines. The device is a pressure sensor that sends an electrical signal to the ECM. The ECM then uses this information to compute the quantity of air entering the engine so that the fuel injector PWM (pulse-width-modulated) time can be lengthened or shortened. In this way exhaust smoke emissions are limited and engine fuel economy and performance are enhanced. Figure 11–73 illustrates a TBS sensor. Both the gasoline MAP sensor and the diesel engine TBS are nonserviceable with no adjustment possible. Therefore, when it is suspected that a problem exists in this sensor as a result of a specific computer-stored trouble code, it can be checked out with a vacuum pump and digital ohmmeter. Obtain the engine manufacturer's specification for acceptable resistance values, or compare the used one with a new TBS.

DIESEL TRUCK COMPUTER SYSTEMS

Both a gasoline and diesel engine electronic fuel injection system depend on three major subsystems for their effective operation. These three subsystems are illustrated in Figs. 11–15 and 11–16:

1. An input section consisting of various engine and vehicle sensors. These sensors receive a reduced voltage from the vehicle electrical system through the ECM and operate on a 5-V reference signal. Each sensor outputs a voltage back to the ECM based on the engine operating condition. The ECM, through its CPU, then determines the start and duration of the fuel injection period. Each sensor monitors its respective system as often as several hundred times a second in some cases.

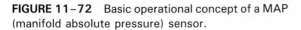

FIGURE 11–72 Basic operational concept of a MAP (manifold absolute pressure) sensor.

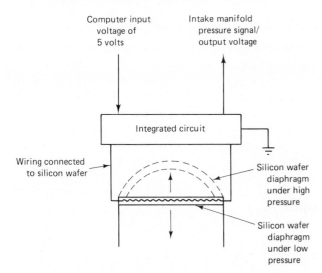

Computer input voltage of 5 volts

Intake manifold pressure signal/output voltage

Integrated circuit

Wiring connected to silicon wafer

Silicon wafer diaphragm under high pressure

Silicon wafer diaphragm under low pressure

Typical sensors used with the DDC/DDEC, Cummins CELECT/ECI, and Caterpillar PEEC systems are:

a. TPS or throttle position sensor (variable resistor).

b. TBS or turbocharger boost sensor (discharge air pressure from the compressor side of the turbo).

c. Coolant level sensor (low coolant in the radiator) or a coolant temperature sensor.

d. Oil temperature sensor (OTS), which is used to determine initial idle speed at engine startup. This provides a faster idle when cold and will reduce idle rpm as the engine warms up. It will also systematically reduce the duration of fuel injection (power reduction) when oil temperature rises beyond a predetermined level, shutting the engine down when a maximum allowable temperature is obtained.

e. Oil pressure sensor (OPS), which will also reduce engine fuel in order to reduce power, should a low oil pressure condition occur. It will also shut the engine down if the oil pressure drops to a predetermined minimum safe operating level.

f. SRS or synchronous reference sensor, which is used to determine when piston 1 approaches TDC.

g. TRS or timing reference sensor, which establishes where each piston is on its respective compression stroke.

Other than the TPS, which operates on a changing resistance value in relation to how far the throttle is opened, the other sensors are designed so that their voltage signal will change based on either a temperature or pressure increase/decrease brought about by a resistance change in the sensor element. Therefore, the sensors are devices that convert nonelectrical parameters or conditions such as temperature, pressure, light, position, rpm, and so on, into electrical signals, which are then sent to the computer or ECM.

2. A controlling device known as a CPU (central processing unit), which is contained within the ECM. The CPU consists of a memory and an input/output interface. The CPU processes information that it receives from the individual sensors and determines just how much fuel is required by the engine at any given time related to throttle position, and so on. In other words, the computer stores the data from the sensors in RAM (random access memory), makes decisions, and drives the actuators such as the fuel injector solenoids so that fuel injection can take place. The ECM sends a signal to the EDU (electronic distributor unit) on the DDC/DDEC system, for example, to handle the high current necessary to activate the individual unit injectors.

3. A series of output devices or actuators, which in the DDC/DDEC system for example, consists of the EDU (electronic distributor unit) and the individual fuel injectors as well as the governor controls, cruise control, engine brake (Jake), tachometer, and so on. In reality, the actuators convert the electrical signals from the computer or ECM into mechanical energy and bring these devices into operation by means of pressure or electric/hydraulic power utilization.

The average ECM current draw for various Detroit Diesel Corporation truck engine models is listed in Table 11-4.

TABLE 11-4. Current draw (average DC amps)

Engine	Condition	Current
All	Ignition off	10 mA
All	Ignition on and Engine stopped	300 mA (nom.) 500 mA (max.)
4-Cycle		
Series 60	Idle	1.0 A
Series 60	1800 RPM, F.L.	3.2 A
Series 60	2100 RPM, F.L.	3.5 A
2-Cycle		
6-Cylinder	Idle	2.0 A
6-Cylinder	1800 RPM, F.L.	6.0 A
6-Cylinder	2100 RPM, F.L.	6.5 A
8-Cylinder	Idle	2.7 A
8-Cylinder	1800 RPM, F.L.	8.0 A
8-Cylinder	2100 RPM, F.L.	8.5 A

ELECTRONICS INTERFACE

The introduction of on-board computer systems to heavy-duty trucks such as the DDC-DDEC system and the Caterpillar PEEC system to control the diesel engine fuel injection and governing systems has also been expanded to trip-recording computers as well as to satellite navigation systems. To coordinate these various on-board computer systems and make it easier for a truck fleet, for example, to off-load stored information into a company data bus and electronic individual vehicle files, various standards have been established through the auspices of the Society of Automotive Engineers (SAE) and the American Trucking Associations (ATA). The information in these standards can be obtained from SAE at 400 Commonwealth Drive, Warrendale, PA 15096-0001. These standards are:

1. J1843, which deals with a standardized accelerator pedal position sensor.

2. J1922, which deals with a powertrain interface for electronic controls used in medium- and heavy-duty diesel vehicle applications.

3. J1708, which deals with data bus methodology additions, allowing future users an additional message identifier.

4. J1939 (high-speed data bus) which has been standardized on the Robert Bosch system with certain modifications.

5. J1587, which deals with a data format standard request originally submitted by Freightliner/Mercedes-Benz

FIGURE 11–74 DDEC DDR (diagnostic data reader) model J38500 Pro-Link 9000. (*Courtesy of Kent-Moore Heavy Duty Division, SPX Corporation.*)

COMPUTER ACCESS AND TROUBLESHOOTING

When a sensed engine operating condition falls outside the normal parameters, the ECM (electronic control module) will log into computer memory a trouble code that is labeled for a specific sensor or system problem condition. These codes can be extracted by initiating a test sequence by use of a dash-mounted control switch/button arrangement, or use a jumper wire across terminals A to M of the DDEC diagnostic data connector. However, all existing ECM systems are best accessed by using a hand-held DDR (diagnostic data reader) similar to the one shown in Fig. 11–74. The DDR is plugged into its mating DDR plug in the vehicle access wiring harness, and all stored trouble codes can be withdrawn. The service technician can then refer to the vehicle or engine manufacturers service literature to pinpoint the cause of a specific trouble code. This often requires the use of a digital volt/ohmmeter in order to verify either a resistance value or a voltage value at a sensor or wire connection. The DDR can also be used to short out electronically controlled injectors individually along with a wide variety of other tests. A sensor tester illustrated in Fig. 11–75 is also available to check and confirm quickly the operating condition of the individual sensors on the engine.

For detailed information on Detroit Diesel Corporations DDEC (DD Electronic Controls) system, Caterpillar's PEEC (Programmable Electronic Engine Controls) and 3176 electronic unit injector engine, and Cummins CELECT ECI (Electronically Controlled Injector) systems, each manufacturer produces a series of booklets and service literature which will lead you systematically through a series of analytical checks and tests for their individual systems. These booklets can be obtained from any local sales/service outlet for each of these major diesel engine manufacturers.

SPECIAL NOTE: In addition to the individual manufacturers' service literature, the operation, maintenance, and

tune-up of these electronically controlled engine systems can also be found in the publication by Robert N. Brady, *Heavy-Duty Truck Fuel Systems: Operation, Service,* and *Maintenance* (Englewood Cliffs, N.J.: Prentice-Hall, 1991). This book and the one you are now reading are both part of the Reston Diesel Mechanics Series. Other books in this series by the same author include *Heavy-Duty Truck Suspension, Steering, and Braking Systems* (1989) and *Heavy-Duty Truck Power Trains: Transmissions, Drive Lines, and Axles* (1989).

ECM Pre-service Checks and Precautions

COMPUTER PRECAUTIONS: Care must be exercised at all times when working around computers, since damage frequently attributable to poor work habits can cause serious and expensive harm to these components. The computer system is designed to withstand normal current draws such as those that normally occur during vehicle operation. Overloading a circuit can result in damage.

When you are testing for opens or shorts in a circuit, *never* ground or apply voltage to any of the circuits unless the service manual or diagnostic procedure specifically calls for such action. When testing computer cir-

FIGURE 11–75 DDEC sensor tester J37264. (*Courtesy of Kent-Moore Heavy Duty Division, SPX Corporation.*)

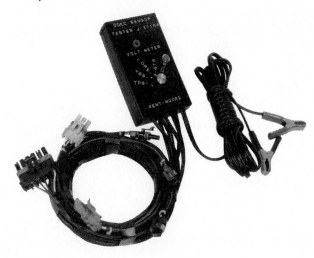

cuits, voltage readings are normally very small; therefore, these circuits should only be tested using a high-impedance multimeter, such as those shown in Figs. 4–8 and 4–9, if they remain connected to either one of the on-board computers.

CAUTION: Before removing/connecting battery cables, fuses, or harness wire connectors, *always* turn the ignition key to the LOCK position. Power should never be applied or removed to any one of the on-board computers when the ignition key is in the ON position.

The following items *must* be adhered to at all times when testing/analyzing ECM systems:

1. The engine and ignition should always be off before the harness connectors are disconnected or reconnected.
2. When disconnecting harness connectors, be sure that the pulling force is always applied to the connectors, not to the wires that extend from them.

IMPORTANT SERVICING PRECAUTION: Prior to performing any type of service on electronic systems or ICs (integrated circuits), you *must* discharge yourself of static electricity or ESD (electrostatic discharge) by touching a good vehicle ground, such as the door post or vehicle shift lever. Failure to do so can result in damage to voltage-sensitive electronic components. If, for any reason, you leave the vehicle during servicing, after reentering to continue work, you *must* again ground yourself of ESD in order to drain any static electrical charge. Also, if you are performing control head/radio checks on a new vehicle, remove the plastic seat covers, since they increase the possibility of creating a static charge.

Electrostatic Discharge

Since the mass introduction of on-board vehicle computer systems in the 1980–1981 model year in North America, many mechanic/technicians have felt that these *black boxes*, as they were referred to initially, were not robust enough to stand up to the rigors of automotive service. In some cases, computers and their associated circuitry failed, and this failure was blamed on the inadequacies of the black box. Further analysis, however, led to attributing many of these failures and difficulties not to the design characteristics of the microprocessor (computer) itself, but often to the improper installation of these black boxes into the vehicle, either at the factory or OEM (original equipment manufacturer) dealer level.

Many hours of research at Delco Electronics have disclosed that *electrostatic discharge* (ESD) has been directly responsible for the damage to electronic components, either at the production stage or when service is carried out by a mechanic/technician at a dealership. Both ESD and a related problem known as EOS (electrical overstress) account for 40% of the failures in on-board computers, and 44% of the failures in car and truck

radio systems. ESD failures can result in a radio switching from AM to FM without the driver or passenger touching the control panel, and with the radio drifting from station to station and unable to hold the selected station. Sometimes the radio becomes totally inoperative.

ESD can not be seen, heard, or felt, but it can destroy any electronic component made. ESD is the same electrical phenomenon that causes socks to cling to shirts in the dryer, and a spark to jump from your hand to a door knob when you walk on carpets in your home or office.

ESD in much larger doses is like a lightning bolt that can shatter a tree! The human body can detect ESD only when it reaches approximately 3500 V, which by then is too late, since ICs (integrated circuits) can be damaged by voltages of as little as 100 V. Approximately 40% of ICs used in automotive applications are capable of withstanding 2000 V, which is still well below the level at which a human being can perceive this ESD.

This static electricity has been measured on the skin of employees working in plants that produce ICs, with values as high as 12,000 V. Tests by Delco Electronics engineers found that employees carried a charge that averaged nearly 6000 V under low-humidity conditions, while high-humidity conditions lowered this value to about 1500 V. Both values are still well in excess of the 100 V required to kill many electronic components.

Investigators have found that under high-humidity conditions, foam-padded chairs can give off 2000 V of ESD, fiberglass tote pans and conveyor belts up to 1500 V, radio faceplates up to 1200 V, and plastic-foam coffee cups up to 1000 V. The value charge of static electricity depends on four main elements:

1. Material involved
2. Closeness of their contact
3. Speed of separation
4. Moisture in the air

Synthetic materials, mainly plastics, generate static charges easily. Therefore, to protect ICs from the possibly devastating ESD voltages, the following basic rules can help to control this invisible problem:

1. Sensitive parts and assemblies *must* be handled at an ESD-protected work station.
2. Parts *must* be transported and stored in conductive containers or static-shielded bags.
3. Where frequent movement of parts and assemblies is necessary and it is not practical for operators to wear wrist straps, conductive floors must be installed and maintained properly, and operators *must* wear heel straps.

ECM Connector Checkout

Once a code has been withdrawn from ECM memory, the technician can systematically follow the code checkout procedure in the engine or vehicle troubleshooting guide, if available. If this booklet is not available to you, you must determine if the problem exists within the various ECM connectors, the wiring or harness, the sensors, switches, or ECM. Is the problem in the connector, the wiring, the individual unit injector solenoid connection or solenoid itself, the ECM control channel, or the EDU (electronic distributor unit) channel within the ECM housing that controls that cylinder? It is always wise to begin by:

1. Stopping the engine and turning the ignition off after having used a DDR or jumper wire to determine what codes are in ECM memory.

2. Refer to the system wiring diagram and zero-in on the colored and numbered wiring that feeds the circuit and sensors.

3. Carefully disconnect the wiring harness connector that is associated with the suspected defective component. Be sure that the pulling force is always applied to the connectors and not to the wires that extend from them.

Check for poor mating at the connector halves or for signs of terminals not seated in the connector body, such as backed-out terminals. Are there any poorly formed or damaged terminals? If so, all connector terminals should be carefully re-formed to contact tension. Check for bent, broken, or dirty terminals or mating tabs and clean, straighten, or replace as necessary.

SERVICE TIP: Often when diagnosing the electrical system of an ECM unit, a high circuit resistance can be attributed to dirty connections at the pins and sockets. If the pins and sockets become dirty, they should be cleaned with a good-quality Freon-based cleaning solvent. A solvent containing at least 90% Freon as its active ingredient should be used since Freon has two qualities that make it the recommended connector cleaner. It will not conduct electricity, therefore will not cause shorting between connector pins and sockets. In addition, it evaporates almost instantly, thereby eliminating the possibility of condensation within the connectors. Always blow or shake any excess Freon from the connector prior to assembling it to its mating connector; Freon trapped in the connector can affect the seal between mating units.

All engine/vehicle sensors are designed to receive a 5-V reference signal from the ECM; then, depending on the engine operating conditions and temperature, each sensor will output 0 to 5 V back to the ECM to advise it of its system condition. Some of the sensor and wire connectors can be checked, with some specifications calling for an ohms reading, while others may require a voltage value. Since most system signals are low voltage, any corrosion between connectors or terminals can make them inoperative. Do not pierce or puncture the back of any connector to check for a resistance or voltage value since this action will expose the otherwise weatherproof connections to the elements. Serious problems will occur once this damage has been done such as intermittent

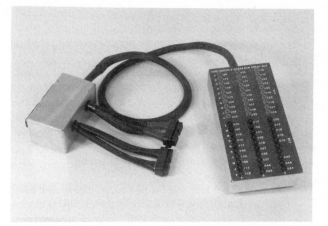

What's A Break-Out Box?
It's a hand held device which allows the technician to ''Break-Out'' or access electronic circuits so they can be checked for proper voltage, resistance, and continuity.

Why Use The Break-Out Box?
• The Break-Out Box allows complete interrogation of any DDEC circuit (engine or vehicle) from one convenient device at a comfortable position away from the engine compartment.
• No need to probe the back of the harness connectors or pierce wire insulation to pick-readings.
• All testing is done after ''one'' initial hook-up of the Break-Out Box. No Individual jumper wires to install in male and female connectors. No chance of error in locating the proper circuit.

How Is The Break-Out Box Used?
• Simply disconnect the vehicle and engine harness at the Electronic Control Module (ECM) and connect to the Break-Out Junction Box. The vehicle and engine connectors from the junction box are then connected to the ECM.
• The probes from a Volt/Ohm Meter (such as Kent-Moore J 34039-A) are then inserted into the proper sockets to take readings with ignition on and with or without engine running.

Specifications
• Uses same connectors as found in DDEC.
• Six foot cable between junction box and probe panel.
• Sixty socket probe panel with connector cavities marked to correspond with vehicle and engine connectors (DDEC II) and J1A and J1B (DDEC I).
• Includes handy reference card to identify connector cavities.

FIGURE 11–76 ECM breakout box J35634 for use on the DDEC system. (*Courtesy of Kent-Moore Heavy Duty Division, SPX Corporation.*)

faults or system failures, and will affect the ECM warranty on the vehicle. Use only a digital volt-ohmmeter when checking for a resistance or voltage value.

You should also check for electrical system interference, which might be due to a defective relay, an ECM-driven solenoid, or a switch causing an electrical surge. You may also be wise in checking the alternator charging system for problems since an ECM problem may occur only when the faulty component is in operation. Once a problem has been found, reconnect all connectors only after ensuring that the ignition is off. Recheck the system with the DDR or the jumper wire after having cleared the ECM codes. It is wise to use a *breakout box*, which has special connector adapters to couple up to the ECM connectors when you need to probe any ECM pins or connector harness. This avoids shorting between pin connectors, and bending or possible pin damage. Figure 11–76 illustrates a breakout box.

QUESTIONS

11-1. ECM stands for *electronic control module*. *True* or *False* (see page 441)

11-2. Technician A says that most engine/vehicle sensors employed on computer-controlled electronic systems are designed to operate on 12-V battery voltage. Technician B says that they operate on a reduced voltage signal of approximately 5 V from the ECM. Which technician is correct? (see page 446)

11-3. Write down the meaning of DDEC and PEEC. (see page 441)

11-4. Technician A says that the first major high-speed diesel engine manufacturer to adopt electronic fuel injection controls was Caterpillar in 1983, followed by Cummins in 1984. Technician B says that Detroit Diesel Corporation was first with the release of their DDEC I system in September 1985. Who is correct? (see page 446)

11-5. Technician A says that the Cummins PACE system is an electronic cruise control feature. Technician B says that it is an electronically controlled injector system. Who knows the systems better? (see page 446)

11-6. The letters PROM mean:
   a. Projected readout of memory
   b. Programmable read-only memory
   c. Pneumatic regulation of motor operation
   (see page 446)

11-7. Technician A says that the letters EEPROM mean that the PROM unit is electrically erasable. Technician B says that it means that the PROM unit is electronically encoded. Who is correct? (see page 446)

11-8. Technician A says that some diesel engine ECMs route diesel fuel through a cold plate on the rear of the ECM to prevent possible overheating of the solid-state components. Technician B says that this action could lead to corrosion of the ECM and damage to the internal circuitry and is therefore avoided. Who is right? (see page 447)

11-9. Technician A says that when checking an ECM for a voltage value, a self-powered test light should always be used due to the high resistance values used with the ECM. Technician B says that you should always use a digital voltmeter with a 10-MΩ resistance value. Which technician is correct? (see page 447)

11-10. What do the letters CEL and SEL mean in relation to an electronically controlled diesel fuel injection system? (see page 447)

11-11. Technician A says that when an ECM causes the CEL to illuminate, the operator can continue to operate the engine but should have the condition checked out as soon as possible. Technician B says that when the CEL illuminates, the ECM will automatically shut the engine down within 30 seconds. Which technician is correct? (see page 447)

11-12. What does the term DDR mean? (see page 485)

11-13. What is "limp home" capability in reference to an ECM fuel injection system? (see page 447)

11-14. Technician A says that the CPU (central processing unit) is that part of the computer that contains the truck cruise control and road speed governing components. Technician B says that the CPU is that part of the computer that performs all of the arithmetic and logical

decisions. Which technician understands the system best? (see page 448)

11-15. Technician A says that an "analog signal" is similar to that produced by the human voice on a magnetic tape or to that shown in a sine-wave fashion on an ignition oscilloscope. Technician B disagrees, saying that an analog signal, if projected onto an oscilloscope screen, would represent an ON/OFF series of rectangular diagrams. Which technician is correct? (see page 449)

11-16. Technician A says that any problem occurring in an ECM must be traced systematically by the technician by using a VAT tester. Technician B says that all problems will be stored in ECM memory. These problems will initiate a stored trouble code to be logged into ECM memory, which can be withdrawn at a later date by a technician using a DDR. Which technician knows the system better? (see page 447).

11-17. Technician A says that digital signals are classified as being either ON or OFF. An ON condition means that the voltage value must be above a minimum designed value; anything less than the minimum value means that the signal is OFF. Technician B says that they continually fluctuate between a high and low voltage value, therefore they are never in the OFF position. Who is correct here? (see page 449)

11-18. Technician A says that digital systems are comprised of combinations of logic gates and flip-flop devices. Technician B says that they are comprised of diodes and transistors only. Which technician knows the basics of computers better? (see page 449)

11-19. Technician A says that digital computers are used more than analog systems because they are cheaper to manufacture. Technician B says that digital systems are used since their major advantage over an analog system is that the digital system overcomes the inherent problems of temperature drift and noise disturbance which tends to affect analog systems. Who is correct? (see page 450)

11-20. Technician A says that an analog computer is designed to measure quantities, while technician B says that a digital computer is designed to count rather than to measure. Are both technicians statements correct, or just one? (see page 450)

11-21. Technician A says that many sensors used on automotive and truck applications generate an analog signal which is then converted into a digital signal through an analog-to-digital converter within the ECM. Technician B says that only digital sensors can be used with digital ECMs. Which technician is correct? (see page 450)

11-22. List the three operating sections of an on-board computer system. (see page 451)

11-23. Technician A says that the letters RAM mean *register accessibility modem*. Technician B says that it means *random access memory*. Which technician is correct? (see page 453)

11-24. Technician A says that RAM is basically the ECM scratchpad used continually to inform the CPU of changing operating conditions. Technician B says that it contains the cruise control information for a specific truck. Who is right? (see page 453)

11-25. Technician A says that *volatile memory* means that the stored information in the ECM, such as RAM, is lost when the ignition key is turned off or when the battery voltage is disconnected. Technician B says it means that the computer memory and solid-state devices can be damaged if a cold plate such as that described in Question 11-8 is faulty. Who is right? (see page 453)

11-26. Technician A says that ECM output signals are used directly to operate/control various actuators on the engine. Technician B says that the output voltage signals are generally amplified within the ECM to ensure that there is sufficient current to activate its particular electric device. Who is right? (see page 453)

11-27. Technician A says that the term *hardwiring* implies that a program or feature such as the PROM information has been burned into the computer memory and cannot be altered. Technician B says that all computers can have their memory altered. Who is correct? (see page 456)

11-28. Technician A says that a decimal system of measurement is used to keep track of all sensor inputs to the ECM. Technician B says that a binary system of numerals known as a base^2 system is used in all automotive/truck computers to keep track of the various sensor signals. Which technician is correct? (see page 457)

11-29. Technician A says that a series of numerals, specifically zeros and ones are used to indicate to the computer that a sensor signal is either off or on. Technician B says that a numeral 1 generally indicates an OFF condition and a numeral 0 indicates an ON condition. Who is correct? (see page 457)

11-30. In addition to the base 2 system mentioned above, some computers are designed to operate on a base 8 or octal system. *True* or *False* (see page 459)

11-31. The two most widely used codes that are used to allow the computer to determine between decimal numbers and letters of the alphabet are:
a. EBCDIC (Extended Binary-Coded Decimal Interchange Code)
b. ASC11 (American Standard Code for Information Interchange)
c. SCNLIS (Standard Computer Numbers/Letters Information System)
d. DINS (Digital Information Numbers System)
(see page 459)

11-32. Technician A says that the computer word *bits* is derived from the combined words *binary digits*. Technician B on the other hand, says that it is derived from the term *bite-sized digits*. Who is right? (see page 459)

11-33. The word *bit* is the term used to indicate:
a. One unit of data or information and is indicated to the computer by the numeral 1 or 0
b. A four-digit word length
c. An eight-digit word length
d. A 16-digit word length
(see page 459)

11-34. Technician A says that the word *byte* means that the memory storage unit of the CPU can hold 100 bytes. Technician B says that the word byte means that one byte is equal to a word length of 8 bits as one example, with the word length being based on the actual ECM design. Which technician is correct? (see page 460)

11-35. Technician A says that when interpreting a TPS (throttle position sensor) count with the use of a DDR, the maximum number of 256 counts is an indication that the computer being used is an 8-bit computer, since 2 to the power 8 equals 256. Technician B says that this has nothing to do with it at all. Which technician understands the operational aspects of the computer better? (see pages 460 and 481)

11-36. The term 1K or *kilobyte* infers a value of:
a. 100 bytes
b. 1000 bytes
c. 10,000 bytes
d. 100,000 bytes
(see page 459)

11-37 Technician A says that a logic gate is a solid-state device that converts either a numeral 1 or a 0 into a voltage signal. Technician B says that a logic gate is designed to accept and process two or more voltage signals. Who is correct? (see page 461)

11-38. List the five basic types of logic gate circuits used in a microprocessor system. (see page 461)

11-39. Technician A says that voltage at the output terminal of an AND gate logic circuit can exist only if a voltage is present in both the input terminals. Technician B says that it is the other way around; voltage must be present at the single AND gate input terminal in order to generate an output at both output terminals. Which technician understands the AND gate logic circuit? (see page 462)

11-40. Technician A says that a logic-gate truth table illustrates the various combinations of operation of any circuit. *True* or *False* (see page 462)

11-41. Technician A says that combinations of logic gates are used to make sense out of various signals being input to the computer system. Technician B says that only one logic gate is selected at any time to illicit an output signal from the computer. Which technician is correct? (see page 464)

11-42. Technician A says that a commonly used logic gate used for comparison of two binary numbers (to add binary numbers) is the OR gate. Technician B says that the XOR adder circuit is more commonly used for this purpose. Which technician is correct? (see page 464)

11-43. Technician A says that the type of sequential logic circuit that is commonly referred to as an *R-S* (reset-set) flip-flop consists of interconnecting two NAND gates. Technician B says that an *R-S* logic gate consists of an analog-to-digital converter. Which technician is correct? (see page 465)

11-44. Technician A says that the purpose of a synchronous clock counter is to convert an analog signal to a digital signal within a 1-second period. Technician B says that its function is to monitor or count a specific sensor signal in order to activate/deactivate the signal as desired. Which technician is correct? (see page 466)

11-45. Technician A says that employing a series of clock stages within the computer allows storing the digits of a binary number. *True* or *False* (see page 467)

11-46. Technician A says that if a series of clock stages are used and storage is temporary, the combination of the various clock stages is known as a *register*. Technician B says that if storage is permanent, it is referred to as *memory*. Are both technicians correct in their statements, or just one? If one, which one? (see page 467)

11-47. Technician A says that a coolant temperature, oil temperature, or diesel fuel temperature sensor all operate on the same basis. Technician B says that this is impossible since they all monitor liquids of different viscosities. Which technician is correct? (see page 468)

11-48. Technician A says that in reality a temperature sensor is in fact a *thermistor* meaning that its thermal conductivity will alter its resistance value as the fluid temperature increases and decreases. Technician B says that it has one cold value and one hot value, with nothing in between. In this way a digital signal can be created; meaning that the signal is either on or off. Which technician is correct? (see page 468)

11-49. Technician A says that a typical coolant temperature sensor would exhibit a high resistance value when cold, generally in the range of about 1,000,000 Ω, dropping off to a low resistance value of approximately 100,000 Ω as the coolant temperature increases. Technician B says that the cold value would be closer to 100,000 ohms, dropping off to about 70 Ω when hot. Which technician is correct? (see page 468)

11-50. Technician A says that the resistance value from the coolant temperature sensor is converted to a digital value by the A/D converter within the computer. The A/D controller uses the binary code and refers to a look-up table stored within computer memory to determine the equivalent temperature in degrees from this series of binary numbers. Technician B says that a flip-flop is used to do this, not an A/D controller. Which technician is correct? (see page 468)

11-51. Technician A says that information can be continually written into or read from the PROM chip during engine operation. Technician B says that information can only be written into or read from the RAM chip during engine operation. Which technician is correct? (see page 471)

11-52. Technician A says that informational data are sent to the CPU via the address buses, while information signals come from the CPU via the data buses. Technician B says that the data buses carry the informational data to the CPU, while the address buses bring information signals from the CPU. Which technician is correct? (see page 472)

11-53. Technician A says that the address bus is capable of only single direction information flow, whereas the data bus is capable of two-way informational flow. Technician B says that both buses are single-direction information carriers. Which technician is right? (see page 472)

11-54. The CPU (central processing unit) contains what three sections? (see page 473)

11-55. Technician A says that there are basically two-types of sensors used on cars and trucks. Technician B says that there are three types of sensors. Who is correct? (see page 476)

11-56. Technician A says that a TRS (timing reference sensor) such as that used on DD's DDEC system is used to monitor engine speed. Technician B says that it is the SRS (synchronous reference sensor) that is used to determine engine speed and that the TRS is used to deter-

mine fuel injector solenoid operating times. Which technician is right? (see page 477)

11-57. To what do the letters EFPA refer to? (see page 479)

11-58. Technician A says that the throttle assembly used on diesel engine electronic fuel injection control systems is simply a variable resistor in its simplest form. Technician B says that it is a potentiometer. Are both technicians correct in their statements, or only one? (see page 479)

11-59. Technician A says that with the throttle pedal in its normal idle position on DDEC system, the voltage output is low and the ECM outputs a short injector solenoid pulse-width signal. Technician B agrees that the injector pulse-width time is short but believes that the throttle pedal output is high with a closed throttle. Which technician do you think is right? (see page 480)

11-60. Technician A says that the TPS sensor alone determines the pulse-width-modulated time for the injector on the DDEC system. Technician B says that in addition to the TPS, the turbocharger boost, engine oil temperature, and pressure sensors also allow the ECM to determine just how much fuel should be injected. Which technician is correct? (see page 480)

11-61. Technician A says that the EFPA TPS cannot be adjusted since it is factory preset. Technician B says that you can adjust the EFPA TPS. Which technician is correct? (see page 480)

11-62. Technician A says that to adjust a new EFPA TPS, you have to use a DDR (diagnostic data reader) to determine the number of counts at both an idle and wide-open throttle position. Technician B says that to adjust the EFPA TPS a 12-V test light is all that is required. Which technician is correct? (see page 481)

11-63. Technician A says that the DDEC system relies on an oil temperature sensor to advise the ECM of the engine operating temperature. Technician B says that a coolant temperature sensor is used for this purpose. Which technician is correct? (see page 481)

11-64. During engine operation, technician A says that a low coolant level will trigger the warning light/buzzer on the vehicle dash of a DDEC-equipped truck and actually initiate a power reduction that can cause the engine to shut down within a 30-second period. Technician B says that a loss of coolant will simply activate the CEL (check engine light). Which technician is correct? (see page 482)

11-65. Technician A says that a fast-idle on a DDC DDEC-equipped engine is determined by the temperature of the engine oil surrounding the oil temperature sensor. Technician B says that the coolant temperature sensor determines this speed. Which technician is correct? (see page 481)

11-66. Technician A says that both the oil pressure and engine coolant sensors can cause the ECM to reduce engine power and speed on a DDEC engine if they exceed preset maximum values. Technician B says that either the oil pressure or oil temperature sensors can cause this reduction in speed and power output if they exceed their normal operating parameters. Which technician is correct? (see page 484)

11-67. Technician A says that the DDEC system still requires the use of a rocker arm to actuate the electronic unit injector and create the high pressures necessary for injection. Technician B says that a rocker arm is not required since a solenoid controls the amount of fuel delivered. Which technician understands the DDEC system? (self-research)

11-68. Technician A says that on the DDEC system, pulse width or injector solenoid ON time is determined by converting the requested crank angle degrees sensor signal to an equivalent time period plus the solenoid response time. Technician B says that the position of the EFPA sensor alone determines the injector pulse-width-modulated time. Which technician is correct? (see page 480)

11-69. Technician A says that on the DDEC system a STEO button can be used to extend the automatic engine shutdown procedure. Technician B says that once the ECM has determined an engine shutdown procedure, the operator has 30 seconds to pull the truck over prior to engine shutdown. Which technician is correct?

11-70. Technician A says that the DDEC system an be equipped with a 3 to 100-minute idle shutdown timer. Technician B says that the idle shutdown timer is generally set for either 3 or 5 minutes. Which technician do you think is right?

11-71. The ignition switch should always be in the OFF position prior to disconnecting or connecting batteries to an ECM-equipped vehicle. *True* or *False*. (see page 486)

11-72. Technician A says that ESD (electrostatic discharge) from your body can actually damage voltage-sensitive equipment on ECM systems. Technician B says that ESD from your body is not nearly strong enough to do damage to an ECM. Which technician do you think is right? (see page 486)

11-73. Technician A says that the only way in which you can determine the stored trouble codes in DDEC ECM memory is to use the DDR special digital diagnostic tool. Technician B says that a jumper wire can be used to initiate the CEL on the dash. The flashing light can then be used to determine the stored trouble code. Are both technicians correct? (see page 485)

11-74. Technician A says that "active" trouble codes in DDEC ECM memory will continue to illuminate the CEL and can only be read by using the DDR. Technician B says that only historical codes will activate the CEL. Which technician is correct?

11-75. Technician A says that the DDR can be interfaced with a PC computer to provide expanded diagnostic capability such as providing a graphical representation on the screen of the PC when shorting out the DDEC electronic unit injectors. Technician B says that only the DDR or the PC can be used at one time on a specially equipped DDEC engine ECM. Which technician is correct?

11-76. Technician A says that to activate the CEL with a jumper wire, pins B to N would be bridged on the DDEC 12-pin diagnostic communication link connector. Technician B says that you have to bridge the wire across terminals A to M. Which technician knows the system better? (see page 485)

11-77. Technician A says that to clean the pins and sockets of the ECM and connectors, diesel fuel should be lightly wiped across each connection and then blown dry with shop air. Technician B says that a good-quality Freon-based cleaning solvent is best. Which technician knows the correct procedure?

11-78. Technician A says that DDEC II codes can only be cleared by the use of the DDR. Technician B says that disconnecting the batteries will do the same thing. Who is right?

11-79. Technician A says the 3406B PEEC and 3176 Cat engine electronic systems contain an EEPROM within the ECM. Technician B says that only the 3176 ECM has an EEPROM. Who is right?

11-80. Technician A says that the 3406B Cat PEEC system features limp-home capability at 10% power should engine oil pressure be reduced at any time. Technician B says that he agrees, but that the power is far higher than 10%. Which technician is correct?

11-81. Technician A says that the purpose of the vehicle speed buffer on the Cat 3406B PEEC engine is to increase the magnetic field of the sensor. Technician B says that the buffer is required in order to amplify as well as wave-shape the voltage signal of the vehicle magnetic speed sensor. Who is right?

11-82. The Cat 3406B PEEC and 3176 engines can be monitored by the use of a DDT (digital diagnostic tool) similar to the DDR used on DDC DDEC engines. *True* or *False*

11-83. Technician A says that the Cummins ECI system still uses the PT fuel pump to operate. Technician B says that a simple gear pump is all that is required with this system. Who is right?

11-84. Technician A says that an idle speed adjust switch on the truck instrument panel can be used to increase the engine speed up or down in increments of 25 rpm between 550 and 800 rpm. Technician B says that you can bring the engine speed from idle to maximum with this switch. Who is right?

11-85. Cummins ECI system contains both a yellow warning and a red stop engine light on the dash panel. Stored trouble codes can be flashed out on these lights similar to that for the DDEC and PEEC systems. *True* or *False*

Information for questions 11-67, 11-69, 11-70, 11-74, 11-75, and 11-77 through 11-85 can be found in *Heavy-Duty Truck Fuel Systems: Operation, Service, and Maintenance,* by Robert N. Brady, and published by Prentice-Hall (1991), 113 Sylvan Avenue, Route 9W, Englewood Cliffs, N.J. 07632.

Glossary
of Automotive and Truck
═══ Electronic Terms ═══

Access motion time　The time taken between the initial request for information when reading or writing data, and the instant that this information is available.

Accumulator　The arithmetic and logic operations are commonly stored in the accumulator, which is the basic work register of a computer, and the result of the operation becomes the new data.

Active display　A display capable of emitting light, such as incandescent and gas discharge.

Active element　A component of an IC unit such as a transistor, tunnel diode, or a thyristor capable of producing power gain.

Active filter　A device which employs passive network elements and amplifiers used to transmit or reject signals in certain frequency ranges, or alternately for controlling the relative output of various signals in certain frequency ranges. In addition, the device can control the relative output of signals as a direct function of frequency.

Active transducer　A unit whose output signal waves are dependent upon power sources separate from those supplied by any of the actuating waves, whose power is controlled by one or more of the waves.

Actuator　A transducer whose output is a force or torque involving motion in response to an electrical signal.

ADC　Analog to digital converter that produces a number proportional to the analog voltage level input.

Adder　A switching circuit that combines binary bits to generate the "sum and carry" of these bits.

Address　A numerical expression which designates a specific location in a storage or memory device of the computer system.

Address format　This can best be explained in two ways, which are: (a) The layout and arrangement of the address component parts relative to a specific instruction. For example, an expression of "plus-one" is often used to imply that one particular address specifies the location of the next instruction that is to be executed, which might be "one-plus-one," or "two-plus-two," possibly "three-plus-one," and so on; (b) In a single specific address, the information or parts must be arranged in such a way that they can be readily identified as to particular information required.

Address register　A specific register that contains the memory location of a particular instruction that is to be executed from that address.

Algorithm　A systematic sequence of defined processes and operations required to ensure the solution of a problem.

Alphanumeric code　A code whose set of information is made up of letters, numbers, digits, or all three combinations.

Alphanumeric display　A visual display which presents stored information within the computer, such as trouble code letters and numbers used in automotive on-board computer systems to indicate to the mechanic/technician what system has logged-in a problem complaint. Only visible once the system memory has been activated in most cases, although a warning light can be made to flash automatically on the instrument panel to warn the driver of a problem situation.

ALU　Shortened version for "Arithmetic Logic Unit," which is the part of the computer containing the necessary designed circuitry to carry out the computational information requirements such as addition, subtraction, multiplication, division, and compairing of operations of a digital system.

American wire gauge (AWG)　Accepted standard system of assigned numerical designations for electrical wire size related to its circular mil area. The system starts with the number 4/0 (0000) as the largest size, reducing to 3/0 (000), 2/0 (00), 1/0 (0), 1, 2, 3, and on up to 40 and beyond for the smaller sizes.

Ampere　The accepted standard unit of measuring the quantity/volume of strength of an electric current. Technically referred to as the actual rate of flow of the charge quantity in a conductor, such as in a wire for example, or similar conducting medium of one coulomb per second.

Amplifier　A unit, device, system, or circuit that is designed to increase the output signal of its input.

Amplitude modulation　System designed to regulate or tone down the amplitude of a wave to a desired characteristic.

Analog　A device or circuit whereby the output varies as a continuous function of its input. The representation does not have discrete values, but is continuously variable. Similar to the sound of the human voice, which fluctuates up and down. Is represented as a wavy line.

Analog circuits　Electronic circuits designed to actually amplify, reduce, or change a voltage signal of the analog type.

Analog computer　A computer that is designed to receive electrical and physical input variables and measure them, such as conditions of speed and height; then it manipulates these variables, usually converting them into numbers, in order to accomplish solutions to mathematical problems.

Analog output　Continuous transducer output which may be modified by the resolution of the transducer.

Analog transmission　The ability to transmit informational data as a continuous wave pattern.

AND gate　A combination logic element whereby its output signal channel is in one state, only if each input signal channel is also in one state. In other words, there are two input points, but only one output point.

Angstrom   Unit of length for light wavelength measurements equal to 10 to the power minus 10 meter. Nanometer is the more preferred and widely accepted SI unit of measurement.

Annunciator   A device used to sound an alarm to indicate what particular monitored circuit has developed a specific problem.

Anode   The positive pole of a battery, galvanic cell, or plating device, or the positive lead of a diode in an electronic solid-state circuit.

Array logic   A configuration of logic circuits forming a rectangular network shape of intersections of its input/output leads, and which has some elements connected at some of these intersections. This arrangement, or network system, is generally designed to function/operate either as an "encoder" or a "decoder."

Artificial intelligence   The ability of a computer to respond systematically to information fed to it by reacting in a human manner to such things as reasoning and the ability to learn.

ASCII   A shortened version that stands for "American Standard Code for Information Interchange." It is a 7-bit code that is widely used to represent informational data for processing and communications.

Assembly language   Accepted language that people use to program computers, normally by taking information and converting it into "binary form" or "notation."

Asynchronous device transmission   A device in which the speed of operation is unrelated to any frequency in the system through which it is connected. Data can be transmitted over a line one character at a time, with each character being preceded by a "start bit," and then followed by a "stop bit."

Avalanche breakdown   In IC circuits employing semiconductor diodes, for example, this is the nondestructive breakdown point that is created when the cumulative multiplication of carriers is subjected to field-induced impact ionization.

Avalanche diode   A term which is sometimes referred to also as a "silicon breakdown diode" that has a high ratio of reverse-to-forward resistance up to a certain level, after which, avalanche breakdown occurs and the voltage drop across the actual diode itself is basically constant, but is dependent upon the current flow. Such diodes are found in systems where either regulation or voltage limiting is desired. At one time, this type of diode was often referred to as a "zener diode," until it was discovered that this zener effect played no major role in the actual operation of these particular types of diodes.

Base   The region when referring to a transistor that actually lies between the "emitter" and the "collector," and into which minority carriers are injected.

Battery backed   A means of using battery power to maintain essential information data when the normal power source has been interrupted or disconnected.

Bias   The condition existing that influences or disposes to one direction, for example with applied direct voltage or with a spring. It can also be described as the persistent positive or negative deviation of the method average from an accepted reference value.

Bidirectional diode thyristor   A thyristor with two terminals that have basically an equal switching behavior in both their first and third quadrants of the principal voltage/current characteristic.

Binary coding number system   In digital computers which employ solid state electrical devices, these components can operate in either an *ON* or an *OFF* state, meaning that current is available or is not available. This is sometimes referred to as clockwise or counterclockwise. The on state is usually attributed a numeral of "one" (1), while an off state is issued a number zero (0). Generally, the binary numbering system for coding decimal numbers is in groups of 4 bits, with the actual binary value of these 4 bit groups ranging from 0000 to 1001, with the decimal digits running from 0 to 9. Therefore, to count up to a value of 9 requires 4 bits; up to 99 requires two groups of 4 bits; up to 999 requires three groups of 4 bits and so on as the value required is increased.

Bipolar   This is a term used to describe a specific type of IC construction whereby both the majority and minority carriers are present. The two most widely used IC constructions involve both bipolar and MOS types.

Bit   Refers to the smallest element of information in binary language that the computer can manipulate, such as a number 0 or 1, with the 0 representing an off condition, and the 1 an on condition. Computer word length and its memory capacity, for example, can be expressed in the number of bits of its information capability. Bits are most often assembled into "bytes" and words when they are placed in a storage address.

Bleeder resistor   Once an IC has been de-energized, this resistor is used to discharge a filter capacitor. In other words, it is a resistor that can be used to draw or absorb a fixed current value.

Blocking   A collection of continuous records combining two or more records in order to conserve storage space and to increase computer processing efficiency. Blocks per se are generally separated by what is known as "block gaps."

Borrow   Describes the action of an arithmetically negative carry during a CPU action.

Branching   While a particular program is in progress, the next operation to be executed is already being selected, based upon the incoming and stored results.

Break point   A condition during computer operation whereby an interruption or a stop command can be issued upon request.

Breakdown voltage (rating)   During operation, the point or value at which a disruptive voltage discharge occurs, either through or over the surface of the insulation. Therefore, the breakdown voltage level is kept below this point in order to prevent arcing or conduction above a specified current value across the insulated portions of a transducer.

Buffer   Within the computer itself, buffers are employed to store physical records so that logical analysis may be processed faster when transmitting information from one device to another. A buffer can also be an isolating circuit employed to avoid a reaction of a driven circuit on its corresponding driver circuit. When used as a temporary storage area, it operates to balance the speeds of the two devices.

Bug   An error or fault in a computer program or system.

Bus   A path or paths over which computer information can be transmitted.

Byte   A technical term developed by IBM that indicates a specific number of consecutive "bits" that are grouped to form a single entity. A byte normally consists of either 7 or 8 bits that are used to represent a single character of information, or alternately two numerals.

Capacitance   In an electronic or electrical system, it refers to that property which allows the storage of electrically separated charges when potential differences exist between the system conductors. Generally, its actual value is expressed as the ratio of a quantity of electrical charge to a potential difference.

Capacitor   Sometimes referred to as a condenser, since it is a device that is constructed of two electrodes which are physically separated by a dielectric or insulator that may be simply in the form of an air gap to introduce capacitance into the electrical circuit.

Carrier   An a.c. (alternating current) voltage with a suitably high frequency that can be modulated by electrical signals.

Carry   When an arithmetic operation is initiated within the CPU portion of the computer, one or more digits may be forwarded (carried forward) to another digit place for processing there.

Carry look-ahead   Within the computer CPU, this is a type of "adder" whereby the actual input signals to more than one stage can be examined; then the correct number of carries can be produced simultaneously, instead of initiating the outcome through a series of operations.

Cascade   When two or more similar circuits or amplifying stages are arranged so that an output signal or value from one becomes the input for the next.

Cathode ray tube (CRT)   A cathode is a negative electrode; therefore, a CRT consists of an electronbeam tube where a luminescent display can be projected, such as your home television screen. The beam is focused onto the screen where it can be varied in position and intensity to produce a desired display.

Character   Basically a symbol that is used to describe a specific bit of information. In microcomputers, such as those used in automotive applications, the numerals 0 through 9 are used singularly or in combination to address a piece of information contained and stored within the computer. In addition, the letters of the alphabet can also be used, as well as any other desired symbols, to allow identification of stored pieces of information.

Check bit   To check on and validate data within the computer memory system, a parity bit or binary check digit is employed.

Chip   The actual unit on which all the desired active and passive elements of a specific electronics circuit have been manufactured. Generally, in automotive applications, chips used within the computer have terminals extending from them that are then attached to the desired control system and operating components. In some hybrid circuits, however, such as IAR and TFI, this is not necessary. Similarly, items such as a resistor or capacitor that are to be surface-mounted onto a printed circuit board or film hybrid substrates can be leadless and simply soldered into the system.

Clock   Within the computer system, this unit is used to generate periodic signals that are used for purposes of synchronization of various stages. The clock times the changing state of a circuit response, for example, from a high to a low level. Such timed waveforms can be used for counting, for generating other timing pulses, and for determining timed sequences.

Closed loop   The situation that exists when an engine is running, and the exhaust gas oxygen sensor is sending a voltage signal to the computer, which accepts this signal (rich/lean) and uses it along with other sensor inputs to maintain both the ignition timing and the stoichiometric air/fuel ratio. (See open-loop description for the exact opposite condition.)

Collector   That part of a transistor through which the primary flow of the charge carriers leaves the base.

Collector amplifier   Sometimes referred to as the emitter-follower of a transistor, or a grounded-collector amplifier. Basically, the collector element is common to both the input and the output circuits.

Combinational logic   Digital system logic circuits that do not utilize memory elements, but whose outputs depend strictly on the existing logic input signals.

Comparator (analog)   The electronic device that compares the voltage applied to an input.

Compensation   A supplemental device used to modify and improve the performance of sources of systematic error in a circuit or system.

Computation   The actions that are conducted within the CPU of the computer system that involve addition, subtraction, multiplication, division, and so forth.

Computer   The computer is the electronic device that performs all the necessary computations of input data and provides desired output information to control various system operations.

   Often referred to as the ECM (electronic control module), the ECU (electronic control unit), the CPU (central processing unit), etc., by various car and truck manufacturers. True computer systems must contain a provision for input data, a control unit, a storage or memory capability, an arithmetic logic section, and an output system.

Concentrator   Concentrators are communication devices combining the features of both controllers and multiplexers. They also have the capability to store and forward information from several low-speed devices prior to sending this information forward at high-speed to another device.

Conditional branch   Any instruction that might cause the computer to actually execute an instruction other than the one that would normally follow the designed program.

Controller   A digital device that is responsible for supervising and implementing communications traffic and how the system is to function, thereby relieving the computer of an otherwise heavy processing burden.

Control structure   The pattern or design of the computer system that allows a systematic flow of logic to ensure an order of priority to more than one control system, particularly when coming from more than one source. Basically, this follows three control structures, which are sequence, selection, and looping.

Counter   Somewhere similar to a "clock" in that within the digital circuit it counts the number of input pulses, and when a predetermined number have been received, it allows an output pulse to flow.

CPU (central processing unit)   Often referred to as the computer itself in general discussion, since it is the actual component part of the computer system that is delegated to interpret and execute the arithmetic functions through the logic and control circuits. The CPU communicates with the input, output, and storage devices at all times. The CPU may contain the memory unit, as well as an operator's console.

Cutoff   The condition or operating mode of a transistor whereby very little current flows between the collector and emitter.

Cycle   A series or set of events conducted in a set time period. A good example is the sequence of events performed in an alternator when the voltage flows first to its maximum value (positive), then reverses itself in the opposite direction (negative) during which time one cycle of events is performed. Illustrated by the use of a sine wave when shown graphically.

DAC (digital analog converter)   Digital to analog converter is an electronic device capable of producing a voltage that is proportional to the digit input number or magnitude.

Darlington amplifier   A circuit consisting of two transistors where the collectors are tied together, and the emitter of the first transistor is coupled directly to the base of the second transistor. This produces a condition whereby the emitter current of transistor one is equal to the base current of transistor two. Such a connection between two transistors is regarded as a compound unit with three terminals.

Data   Unorganized informational facts that are collected from the various engine and vehicle sensor devices, but which have not yet been processed into logical information.

Data access   The ability of the computer to read or write data onto a device in either a sequential or direct format.

Database   A collection of integrated informational data which is stored within the computer on a direct-access storage device.

Databus   The path along which the transfer of data to and from the CPU, storage, and peripheral devices flows.

Deadband   A fairly narrow range through which a measured signal can be varied without actually initiating a response from a component.

Decibel   Scale of noise (sound) used to indicate loudness. Also in electronic systems, it is a measure of the amount of power, with the number of decibels denoting the ratio of the amounts (two) of power.

Decoder   A component in the system which allows acceptance of digital input signal information, such as in the case of a memory address decoder or a binary address information system. The decoder selects and activates one line of a large number of output lines in order to act as a conversion circuit.

Demux   Shortened version of a demultiplexer which is a type of electronic switch that is used to select one of several output lines.

Diagnostic sensor   A unit or component that is employed to sense specific operating conditions and then transmit this information to the computer system.

Dielectric   A component or medium in which it is actually possible to maintain an electric field with little or no energy supply from an outside source.

Digit   Generally, a decimal or alphabetical notation that represents a specific character of information, although other identifying notations can be employed.

Digital computer   A computer system that is designed to operate and recognize input information that is usually in numerical form, such as number of people or dollars for example. These digital computers normally employ and use binary or decimal notation and process this information by repeated high-speed use through an arithmetic logic process that includes addition, subtraction, multiplication, and division. Constructed to recognize an "on" signal as a number 1, and an "off" signal as a zero.

Digital circuits   Electronic circuits whose output signals can change only at specific instances and between a limited number of varying voltages.

Diode   A semiconductor device that acts like a current (ampere) check valve. Sometimes referred to in its simplest form

as a two-electrode electron tube which contains both an anode and a cathode. As a semiconductor, it also has two terminals and exhibits an operating characteristic of nonlinear voltage-current. If the diode is used in a restricted mode, it will exhibit an asymmetrical voltage-current characteristic exemplified by a single p-n junction.

Diode transistor logic (DTL)   Used in typical computer logic circuits to obtain the desired output signals and values required to operate the system successfully. It consists of diodes at the input which are employed to perform the desired electronic logic function required to activate the circuit transistor output. When used in a monolithic circuit, the DTL diodes operate as a positive level logic/function, or alternately as a negative level or function. Therefore, the output transistor acts as an inverter which causes the circuit to become either a positive NAND (combination NOT/AND gate), or alternately a negative NOR (combination OR/NOT gate) operating system.

Dip   Shortened wording for a single "dual in-line package."

EBDIC   Means Extended Binary Coded Decimal Interchange. EBDIC actually employs an 8-bit byte and is used to represent up to 256 characters.

E-cycle   The sequence of the computer cycle whereby data is located, an instruction is executed, and the results are stored in memory.

Eddy currents   Currents that exist as a direct result of inducing voltages in the body of a conducting mass through a variation of magnetic flux.

EEPROM   Electrically Erasable Programmable Read Only Memory. A computer using an EEPROM module over a straight PROM unit can have its contents altered while plugged into a peripheral device. Computers using straight PROM's must physically be changed out for another in order to change the operating characteristics of the computer.

EEROM   Electrically Erasable Read Only Memory. Can have the contents of memory electrically altered similar to that described for an EEPROM (above). The EEROM is sometimes referred to as EAROM or, simply, electrically alterable ROM. EEROM cannot be erased by users or programmers.

Electromotive force (EMF)   The electrical force that can cause current to flow any time that a difference in potential exists between two points.

Electron   The basic negative electrical charge which is one of the natural constituents of matter.

Emitter   That part of a transistor from which current is conducted and flows to the collector in an npn transistor only when the base and collector are positive with respect to the emitter. In a pnp type transistor, the emitter current will flow to the computer only when the base and collector are negative with respect to the emitter.

Error   The discrepancy that exits in a system between the computed or observed and measured quantity, with the true and specified theoretically correct value.

Execute   The operation that is conducted during the normal computer cycle, in which a selected control word or instruction is actually carried out or completed.

Exponent   The mathematical power to which the base number is raised in a floating point representation.

Feedback   The ability of a closed-loop system circuit to recycle some percentage of the output signal back to the input side.

This feedback signal may pass through an amplifier first in order to modify the performance of the amplifier.

Fiber optics Consists of cables composed of thousands of hair-thin transparent fibers along which informational data can be passed from lasers as light intensive waves.

Field effect transistor (FET) When a voltage is applied to a logic gate terminal, a field is produced to create a resistance between the source and the drain terminals of this semiconductor device.

Filter In digital instrumentation systems, a filter can be employed to improve the visual characteristics of the display, while in other electronic circuits, it can include resistors, inductors, capacitors, or active filter elements that offer minor opposition to certain frequencies. Can also be used to direct current flow, while at the same time blocking or attenuating undesirable additional frequencies.

Fixed-length word approach Each computer address is designed to hold/store a word composed of a certain number of characters.

Fixed binary point number Each binary number is represented by a sign bit and one or more numbered bits, with a binary point placed somewhere between two neighboring bits.

Flip-flop The capability of a storage element consisting of two stable states that has the capability of changing from one state to another when a control signal is applied to it. It will remain in this state after signal removal.

Flux The total amount of all of the actual lines of magnetic force crossing a unit area in given or unit time period.

Font The term used to describe a set of symbols which a typical CRT (cathode ray tube) display can present.

FORTRAN Means Formula Translating System, and it indicates a programming language that is used primarily to express computer programs by arithmetic formulas.

Frequency and assorted terms The term natural frequency signifies basically how many times an action occurs (angular speed or flow rate) within a given time period. Can also be expressed as the number (frequency) of free oscillations (without force) of a sensing element in a fully assembled transducer.

The resonant frequency refers to the measured frequency at which a transducer will respond with maximum output signal amplitude. Therefore when one states a frequency response, it is a statement of measure of the gain or loss of a circuit device/system based upon the frequencies applied to it.

Full-adder A logic-circuit that incorporates the provision for a carry-in from a preceding arithmetic calculation addition.

Full-duplex transmission The ability of the computer to send informational data/messages in two directions simultaneously along a bus or communications path.

Gain Very simply put, gain is the ratio of a system's output magnitude to its input magnitude. An example of gain can be found in a transistor which provides an increase in power when a signal is transmitted from one point to another. The gain is then expressed in decibels.

Gate The term used to describe a device or element used in solid-state system circuits to either allow or alternately prevent the flow of a signal, depending upon one or more specified inputs. Typically used GATES in electronic logic circuits are the AND, NOR, OR, and NOT gate types.

GCS Simply an abbreviation for a Gate Controlled Switch.

Half-adder Compare with the "Full Adder" described earlier. However, the half-adder is a logic gate circuit device that is capable of adding two binary numbers, but it does not have the capability for a carry-in from a preceding computer arithmetic function such as a preceding addition.

Hall-effect A magnetic element employed in both solid-state ignition systems and various engine sensors achieved through the development of a transverse electric potential gradient in any current carrying semiconductor or conductor when a magnetic field is applied to it.

Heat sink A heat conducting or radiating device that is employed extensively in most solid-state semiconducting systems to prevent overheating and the resultant damage that would occur. The heat sink is usually made of a metallic compound and is finned/ribbed to increase its heat radiating efficiency.

Hertz The technical term used to describe the unit of frequency, which is accepted as one cycle per second. For example, the electrical frequency of the electrical components used in your home in North America is 60 cycles per second, while in other countries it is often only 50 cycles per second. This frequency is obtained by employing a number of windings and magnetic poles in power generators and spinning them at a fixed speed to maintain the designed frequency.

Hexadecimal In certain types of computers, it is the term used to identify the number system encompassing sixteen possible states, namely that of 0,1,2,3,4,5,6,7,8,9, and A, B, C, D, E, and F.

Hybrid circuit A system with circuits employing either "thin" or "thick-film" semiconductor technology, with the passive components made with thin-film, and the active components by the semiconductor technique.

Hysteresis The response difference that exists in a circuit whereby the hysteretical reaction is characterized by its inability to perform exactly as it did on the previous swing regarding its input/output signal conditions.

I-cycle The sequence reaction within the computer whereby the CPU control unit fetches an instruction from main memory and subsequently prepares it for processing.

Inductor A component or device that is magnetic and therefore capable of storing energy within the magnetic field produced by current flowing within it.

Impedance This is the total opposition expressed in ohms (resistance) presented by any component or circuit in response to the flow of an alternating or varying current source. Impedance generally infers that it is an a.c. circuit which is opposite to the accepted resistance value of a.d.c. circuit. The impedance value can be calculated from the formula $Z = E/I$, where E is the applied a.c. voltage, and I is the resulting a.c. current flowing in the circuit.

Indexed address A reaction that occurs prior to or during computer operation when an execution is being performed to modify an address through the content of an index register. Simply a method of address modification.

Indexed register During or prior to the computer carrying out an instruction, this register's content can be added or subtracted from the operand address.

Indirect address The computer program is set up so that the initial address is designated as the information storage location of a certain word that itself contains another address. Once this second address is identified, it is then used to obtain the stored data that is to be acted upon.

Inductance In an electric circuit when a varying current is passed through it, it creates a varying magnetic field which itself then induces a voltage in the same circuit or in a nearby circuit. Measured in a term known as henrys.

Inductor Any device with one or more windings that may or may not contain a magnetic core.

Infrared The term used to describe the fact that a portion of a light spectrum has a wavelength greater than the naked eye can visibly see.

Instruction counter A counter device within the computer, whose job it is to indicate the location of the next computer instruction that should be interpreted.

Instruction register That device within the computer that stores an instruction and prepares it for execution. Basically, it tells the computer what to do next.

Insulator A device made from a material that will not allow electron flow (offers high resistance to flow); therefore it is employed in electrical and electronic circuits to separate conductors (allow electron flow) to prevent any flow of current between them or to any other circuits.

Integrated circuit A solid-state (semiconductor) device that actually contains numerous circuit functions etched on a single silicon chip. The IC can contain diodes, transistors, logic gates, etc.

Interface A computer hardware device that links two components, or alternately it can be a portion of storage or registers accessed by two or more computer programs.

Interrupter A method whereby the computer's attention can be quickly drawn to a specific external event.

Inverse voltage During the half-cycle when current does not flow in an a.c. circuit, it is the effective voltage across the rectifier.

Joule The unit of energy in the SI system of measurement. For example Joule's Equivalent states that 1 BTU will produce 778 foot pounds of energy.

Keep-alive memory Computer memory system that must have continuous power in order to retain memory information. If power is lost, then the stored memory information is also lost; therefore, in this type of system, battery back-up power can be used when main power is lost.

Kilobyte Represents 1024 bytes in a computer. The primary memory on smaller computer systems is generally measured by its kilobyte capability.

LSI (large scale integration) A term used to describe the fact that an integrated circuit has a high density of chips in it. Compare to "SCI" or small scale integration.

Latch In a symmetrical digital electronic circuit employing, for example, a "flip-flop," the latch acts as a feedback loop to ensure retention of a given state. Locks in a state in other words.

LCD Means liquid crystal display, which is a passive display whereby the light transmission or polarization is changed by the influence of an electric field.

LED Means light emitting diode, which is an active display with the degree of light emitted based upon the current flow in a semiconductor circuit. LED's consist of a pn junction that will emit light when it is biased in the forward direction.

Limit cycle An action of the control system operation whereby the controlled variable actually cycles between extreme limits, with the average being near the predetermined desired value.

Linear region The mode of operation of the transistor when the collector current is proportional to the base current.

Logic element An element within the IC that is used to ensure/provide circuit functions inside the computer, such as an AND, OR, NOT, and NAND gate. These devices employ a mathematical approach in order to solve complex situations through the use of symbols that define these basic concepts. The logic gates allow addition, subtraction, division, and multiplication to be carried out.

Look-up table A table that is contained in computer memory, and which is employed to convert an input value from a sensor, for example, into a related value in order to execute that technique.

Loop A repeated sequence of instructions that is executed until a terminal condition exists. Compare with the terms "open loop" and "closed loop."

Luminosity The term used to indicate the brightness or intensity of an electronic display.

Magnetic bubble storage Computer memory that uses magnetic bubbles to indicate both the 0 or off, and 1 or on bit states.

Magnetic particle display This is a passive display that operates on the basic principle of orienting permanently magnetized particles under the influence of an applied magnetic field.

Magneto resistive effect The application of a magnetic field to a conductor or semiconductor will alter its resistance value.

Mainframe It implies that within the computer the processing portion (CPU) contains storage capability, as well as the arithmetic logic unit, and a group of registers.

Majority carrier In n-type semiconductors, there are a greater number of electrons than holes; therefore, the electrons become the majority carrier. In a p-type semiconductor, however, there are more holes than electrons; therefore, the holes become the majority carrier in this case.

Mask A mask can act as a type of filter to control the retention or elimination of portions of another pattern of characters within the computer information system.

Mass storage unit Simply a computer storage device that is capable of storing literally billions of bytes of on-line informational data.

Matrix In computer systems, this refers to the logic network in the form of array or input and output leads with logic elements connected at some of these intersections.

Measureand The term used to describe either a physical quantity, property, or a condition that is being measured.

Megabyte Consists of about one million bytes of information and is generally used to express the secondary storage capacity of many computers.

Microcomputer Describes the smallest type and usually the cheapest style of computer system available.

Micron A term used to describe the physical size of a particle, with one micron being equal to one, one-millionth of a meter. This is shown as 0.00003937″ as a decimal, or simply 10 to the power minus 6.

Microprocessor The digital CPU (central processing unit) on a chip that is allotted the task of performing both the arithmetic and control logic functions.

Microsecond   Denotes time as being one millionth of a second.

Microwave   An electromagnetic wave that occurs only in a high-frequency range, such as that employed in a home microwave oven.

Millisecond   Denotes time as being one thousandth of a second.

Minicomputer   A computer that is a step up from a microcomputer, but not as advanced as a mainframe computer.

Minority carrier   Compare to the term, "majority carrier," described earlier.

Mnemonic symbol   Simply a chosen symbol to assist the human memory by using an abbreviation (such as "MPY" for multiply or multiplication) that can easily be remembered.

Monitor   A device that can warn either visually or by sound by monitoring and comparing a measured value against a set standard. In effect, it is the supervising program within an operating system.

MNOS   An abbreviation for metal-nitride-oxide semiconductor unit.

MOS   An abbreviation for a metal-oxide semiconductor unit.

Multiplexing   Advances in electronics are aimed at reducing the number and bulk of wires and harnesses used in automotive applications. By multiplexing, several measurements can be transmitted over the same signal wire path or bus, either through a time-sharing process or simultaneously. However, multiplexing uses either a time division (sharing) method, or a frequency division process, with the time sharing employing the principle of actual sharing amongst measurement channels, while the frequency process utilizes the sharing process amongst information channels whereby the informational data from each channel is used to modulate sinusoidal signals known as subcarriers. This results in a signal which represents each channel and contains only those frequencies within a narrow range.

NAND and NOR logic gates   In the CPU section of the computer, when an AND gate is followed by an inverter, it is referred to as a NOT AND or NAND gate. In this arrangement, should all the inputs have a value of 1 (on), the output will be 0 or off. If any of the inputs have a value of 0 (off), then the output will be 1 (on). Used extensively in binary circuit functions.

Nanosecond   A time expression that is measured in one billionth of a second.

Negative logic   The situation whereby the logic is the more negative voltage signal, and it therefore represents the 1 or on state, with the less negative voltage representing the 0 or off state.

NMOS   Simply, MOS devices constructed on a p-type silicon chip, with the active carriers being electrons flowing between n-type sources and drain contacts.

NVM (nonvolatile memory)   Computer memory that is not lost when the main power supply is disconnected or interrupted.

NOR logic gate   In the CPU system of the computer, it is an OR logic gate that is followed by an inverter in order to form a binary circuit whereby the output is logic 0 (off), as long as either of the input signals is 1 (on) and vice versa.

npn transistor   A type of transistor using a p-type base and an n-type collector and emitter.

n-type material   A crystal of pure semiconductor material, such as silicon, which has been doped by adding an impurity to pro-

duce electrons that serve as the majority charge carriers.

Ohm   The unit of resistance whereby one ohm is created when one volt will maintain a current of one ampere.

Operand   The term used to describe a device that is operated upon, and is normally identified by an address part of an instruction.

OR logic gate   Within the CPU section of the computer, the OR logic gate consists of a multiple input circuit whose output is energized any time that one or more of the input signals is in a predetermined state.

Oscillator   An electronic device employed to generate a.c. (alternating current) power at a frequency determined by the value of certain predetermined constants designed into the circuits.

Output   Processed informational data within the computer from the various input signals output after processing as usable information.

Parallel operation   The simultaneous computation of instructions by a computer having multiple arithmetic logic functions, or the transmission of data whereby each bit in a byte has its own path.

Parity bit   A check or extra bit that is added to an array of binary digits or to the byte representation of a character to ensure that all of the binary digits including the check bit will always be either an odd or an even number of 1 bits transmitted with each and every character.

Passive display   Both liquid crystal and electrochromic systems are passive displays whereby the transmission or reflection of external light is modulated.

Peripheral equipment   The secondary storage units, as well as the input and output devices, within a computer system.

Photocell   A solid-state device that exhibits photovoltaic or photoconductive effects.

Piezo-electric   The ability of certain crystals either to produce a voltage when subjected to a mechanical stress or alternately to undergo mechanical stress when subjected to a voltage.

PMOS   Abbreviation for a p-type MOS which is manufactured on an n-type silicon chip for example, with the active carriers being holes flowing between p-type sources and drain controls.

pnp transistor   A transistor that is made up of two p-type elements separated by an n-type element or region.

pnpn diode   A semiconductor regarded as a two-transistor structure that has two separate emitters feeding to a common collector.

Polarizer   Material that is employed to generate polarized light from a nonpolarized source or supply.

Potential   The difference in voltage that exists between two points in any circuit.

PROM   Abbreviation for Programmable Read Only Memory, which is the software in the hardware module that is capable of being programmed. However, once the PROM has been programmed, it cannot be altered or erased. When a permanent PROM is used in a system, it is called nonvolatile since it is not erasable when the power supply is disconnected or temporarily lost. The PROM module basically contains specific informational data that applies, for example, to a specific model of car or truck related to its engine size and power, the transmission and axle ratios, tire size, etc. Therefore, such a PROM cannot be interchanged and placed into another vehicle having different characteristics; otherwise, serious performance complaints would result. Refer to the abbreviation EEPROM for a PROM that can be erased electronically.

p-type material   Doped semiconductor material that produces free holes from an excess of acceptor impurity atoms.

RFI (radio frequency interference)   The interference that exists in electronic equipment as a direct result of frequency energy emitted from a ratio signal.

RAM (random access memory)   This type of memory is continually being updated as the computer is operating, based on information it receives from changing sensor signals. It is, in effect, the working scratch-pad of the computer unit. Temporarily stored information is always immediately available, regardless of the previous memory address location. Since memory information can be accessed in any order, equal access is assured to all bits of data.

Rectifier   A device to convert alternating current into unidirectional current.

Register   A temporary storage device for digital informational data.

Relay   A device designed to respond to specific input signals and information. Sometimes, more than one unit is assembled into a relay to provide a wider scope of operation whereby these unit combinations together will provide a predetermmined output.

Resistivity   When electric current is applied through or on the surface of a material (conductor), this is a measurement of that resistance.

Resistor   A device that is inserted into an electrical or electronic circuit to slow down, by resistance, the flow of current in that circuit.

RCTL (resistor-capacitor-transistor logic)   Within the design of a particular logic circuit, the use of a resistor and a speed-up capacitor that are in parallel for each input signal of the logic gate. A transistor is also employed with its base connected to one end of the RC arrangement. When a positive voltage is applied to the RC input, this energizes the transistor unit, turning it on to provide almost a zero output voltage signal. Such a circuit design is commonly known as a positive NOR gate, or negative NAND when ever npn type transistors are employed in the actual circuit design.

RTL (resistor-transistor logic)   Another type of logic gate circuit design that employs a resistor as the input signal unit that is also attached to the base of an npn transistor. The transistor acts as an inverting element as it does in the RCTL circuit design to produce a positive NOR gate, or alternately, a negative NAND gate logic functioning system.

Response time   The actual time required for a computer actually to respond to a specific input command.

ROM (read only memory)   Part of the software in the actual hardware module that can, in fact, be read, but cannot be written upon, such as the RAM can. The ROM allows reading of a predetermined pattern of zeros (off) and ones (on). The memory in ROM is hardwired at the time of manufacture and cannot be altered. ROM memory is not lost when power is disconnected, such as in the case of RAM.

Sample-and-hold circuit   The system is capable of looking at a voltage level, then storing that reading for a much longer time period.

Saturation voltage   The condition that exists in a circuit when a self-limiting feature comes into being. In other words, the circuit is unable to respond to excitation in a proportional manner.

Schottky barrier   A metal to semiconductor interface that exhibits a nonlinear impedance.

Self-generating   A component such as a piezo-electric, electromagnetic, or thermoelectric transducer that is capable of providing an output signal without applied excitation.

Semiconductor   Semi implies that it is a component capable of conducting some electrical qualities, but also of offering some insulating effect. Therefore, it is an electronic conductor wherein the electric-charge-carrier concentration will increase with a rise in temperature over a specified tolerance range. It is possible, depending upon the type of semiconductor material used, to produce a unit that has two types of carriers, namely that of negative electrons and positive holes.

Sensitivity   How fast a device or electronic element can react or respond to a change at its input.

Sensor   A device that is designed to respond to the value of a measured quantity, such as a throttle position sensor, oil pressure sensor, vehicle speed sensor, etc.

Sequencing   The method of structure of control that is designed into a computer system to ensure that the various informational operations will occur in a predetermined order.

Sequential logic systems   The operating mode in a digital computer system that relies on a number of different design memory elements, such as the various logic type gates described in this glossary.

Serial-parallel   The decimal digits are handled in serial fashion, whereas the actual bits that form the digit are handled in parallel.

Serial transmission   A system wherein the informational data transmission in which each and every bit in a byte has to travel down the same path one after the other.

Shift register   Consisting of a logic gate network whereby a series of memory cells and therefore the binary code can shift into the register by serial input to the first cell, or where the stored data can be moved either right or left.

Signal generator   Used for example in a vehicle speed sensor. It consists of a shielded source of power with the output level and frequency being calibrated for a predetermined range of operation.

Silo memory   A system of stored data that is read on the basis of first-in/first-out.

Solid-state circuit or device   Any circuit or component that employs nonmoving parts made up of semiconductors.

Steady-state   The operating condition whereby the circuit values remain reasonably constant.

Storage register   The area where informational data from primary memory is stored immediately prior to processing.

Strain gauge   The ability of a measurement system to convert a strain level into a resistance value.

Substrate   The foundation material upon which an electronic circuit is actually fabricated.

Synchronous circuit   Any circuit that has been designed to ensure that all of its computed informational offerings are sent out through equally spaced signals controlled from a master clock unit.

Synchronous transmission   The transmitting of informational data over or across a line by a block of characters at a time.

Temporary storage register Memory storage locations that have been reserved for intermediate results.

Thermistor Used as a sensor in automotive applications as an oil, fuel, coolant, and air temperature sensor, where a temperature rise causes a decrease in its resistance value (negative characteristic value), versus one with a positive temperature characteristic which would exhibit a resistance value increase as temperature rises. The negative type is more common to automotive applications.

Thermocouple Simply a device for measuring temperature change whereby two dissimilar conductors are joined at two points to cause production of an electromotive force.

Thick-film A design of film pattern achieved by applying conductive and insulating materials to a ceramic substrate in order to form conductors, resistors, and capacitors.

Thin-film A conductive film of insulating material formed in a pattern to produce electronic components and conductors on a substrate, or alternately it can be used as an insulation between successive layers of a component.

Threshold The minimum driving signal level at which a perceptible change will take place.

Thyristor A semiconductor device consisting of three or more junctions that can be switched from either off state to the on state, or vice versa; therefore, often known as a bistable device.

Track A path on an input/output medium on which informational data is recorded.

Transducer A device that is capable of transferring energy (flow) from more than one system or media to more than one other system.

Transformer A device that can be wired in such a way that voltage can be stepped up or, alternately, stepped down to meet a known system demand rating. An ignition coil is a good example of a transformer, since it takes the 12 volt battery supply and steps it up through the primary winding first to a voltage that is proportional to the number of windings in the coil. This voltage is then increased further in the coil secondary winding to about 25,000 volts in a conventional contact breaker point system, while in a solid-state ignition system, the voltage can be as high as 40,000 volts. The ignition coil contains a metal core to enhance this magnetic field buildup, thereby assisting the voltage increase in the coil windings. However, some transformers may not contain a magnetic core for introducing mutual coupling between electric circuits.

Transients The term transient usually implies that there is a temporary increase or decrease of the voltage or current signal. These transients take the form of what is commonly called "spikes" or "surges," since they occur for a very short time period. Discharge control of such spikes or surges is handled through the insertion of capacitors, resistors, or inductors into the circuit, which suppresses these transients that are caused by a switching action within a circuit (on to off and vice versa).

Transistor This is what is known as an "active" semiconductor device, since it is capable of providing "gain" in a circuit. It generally contains three or more terminals. Gain simply means that current can be amplified and switched on and off through the action of the transistor. The word transistor is a combination of the words "transfer" and "resist." Since a transistor is used at junction points in the electronic system, it is often referred to as a "junction transistor." Therefore, the transistor is designed to operate similar to a current check valve.

The three main parts of the transistor are the base, the emitter, and the collector. Automotive-type transistors employ either a signal-type unit which operates with an input voltage up to 10 millivolts, or a power transistor that functions with an input voltage greater than 10 millivolts.

True binary representation A commonly employed method in computer construction that represents numerical values as a string of binary bits.

Triac Within a logic gate circuit, it is often desirable to be able to control a switching action for either polarity of voltage being applied, and to be able to control this action in either polarity from a single gate electrode. Therefore, a five-layer npnpn device, equivalent in action to two SCR's (rectifiers) connected in an antiparallel design with a common gate system, is employed to achieve this action.

Truth table In a semiconductor circuit, various combinations of logic gates are employed to control effectively the output values based upon such input signals as those coming from the numerous engine/vehicle sensors on a continuous basis to the ECM (electronic control module) or computer. A truth table is a chart that is something like a look-up table, in that this chart tabulates and summarizes all of the possible combinations or states of the inputs and outputs for a given circuit. Such truth tables are discussed and illustrated in Chapter 11.

TTL or T2L (transistor-transistor logic) This is a logic gate circuit which has some similarities to a DTL or diode transistor logic system, except that the diode inputs are replaced with a multiple emitter transistor.

Twisted wire This type of wiring simply consists of pairs of wires twisted together, then bound into a cable. A good example of this is the telephone system cabling used to connect your handset to the main system.

UART Abbreviation for Universal Asynchronous Receiver Transmitter system used in many automotive computer systems.

Ultraviolet That portion of a light spectrum with wavelengths shorter than are visible to the naked eye, which wavelengths are less than 3900 angstroms.

Unconditional branch A computer instruction which causes execution of a specific statement other than the one that would normally immediately follow the set sequence of operation.

Unijunction transistor A type of transistor that contains three terminals and which will exhibit a stable open-circuit with negative resisting characteristics.

VFD (vaccum fluorescent display) An active display system that operates upon the emission of light provided by a phosphor that is excited by electrons emitted from a filament in vacuum.

VAR (volt ampere reactive) A unit of reactive-power as opposed to real-power in watts (amps × volts), with one VAR being equal to one reactive volt-ampere.

Variable length word approach The storage design whereby a single character of informational data occupies a single address. Compare this to the "fixed-word-length system."

Varistor Consists of a two-electrode semiconductor device having a voltage dependent, nonlinear resistance that falls off or drops significantly as the voltage being applied to the circuit is increased.

Visible Contrast with ultraviolet light, which is not visible to the naked eye. We can see any portion of light between 390 to 770 nm.

Volatile memory   The word "volatile" implies that should the normal power supply be lost or interrupted, then the electronic memory such as RAM, which acts as the computer scratch-pad during operation, will lose that information/memory any time that the ignition switch is turned off.

Volatile storage   Simply means that any stored data is lost as soon as the ignition key is turned off or the power supply is interrupted.

Volt   The term used to describe electrical pressure existing between two points of a conductor, such as a wire that is carrying a constant current in amperes, when the power dissipated between these points is one watt (amps × volts).

Watt   The term used to describe amps × volts, with 1000 watts being equal to 1KW (kilowatt). Therefore, it is the power required to produce work at an accepted rate of one joule per second, or when one amp of direct current flows through a conductor having one ohm of resistance.

Word   Includes either a group of bits or characters that the computer treats as an entity, and which can be stored in a single memory location.

Write enable   Within the computer, it is the control signal sent to a storage element or a memory location that will activate the write mode for the computer system. Any time that the write mode of operation is inactive, then the read mode of the computer can be accessed.

Zener diode   A special type of diode that, when forward-biased, becomes a ordinary rectifier; however, when reverse-biased, it exhibits a sharp break in its actual current/voltage characteristics. In this state, the voltage remains reasonably constant with any further increase of reverse current on up to the diodes dissipation rating. The accepted norm for a zener diode is a breakdown voltage slightly less than 6 volts; therefore, this type of diode can act as a voltage regulator, overvoltage protection unit, voltage reference unit, or as a voltage level shifter (trigger).

Index